PHILIP'S

CW00429574

# STREET ATLAS

# Lancashire

## Blackburn, Blackpool, Burnley, Lancaster, Preston, Southport

**www.philips-maps.co.uk**

First published in 1997 by

Philip's, a division of
Octopus Publishing Group Ltd
www.octopusbooks.co.uk
2-4 Heron Quays, London E14 4JP
An Hachette Livre UK Company

Fourth colour edition 2008
First impression 2008
LANDA

ISBN-13 978-0-540-09193-5 (spiral)

© Philip's 2008

Ordnance Survey®

This product includes mapping data licensed from Ordnance Survey® with the permission of the Controller of Her Majesty's Stationery Office. © Crown copyright 2008. All rights reserved. Licence number 100011710.

No part of this publication may be reproduced, stored in a retrieval system or transmitted in any form or by any means, electronic, mechanical, photocopying, recording or otherwise, without the permission of the Publishers and the copyright owner.

To the best of the Publishers' knowledge, the information in this atlas was correct at the time of going to press. No responsibility can be accepted for any errors or their consequences.

The representation in this atlas of a road, track or path is no evidence of the existence of a right of way.

Data for the speed cameras provided by PocketGPSWorld.com Ltd.

Ordnance Survey and the OS Symbol are registered trademarks of Ordnance Survey, the national mapping agency of Great Britain.

Printed by Toppan, China

## Contents

II **List of mobile speed cameras**

III **Key to map symbols**

IV **Key to map pages**

VI **Route planning**

X **Administrative and Postcode boundaries**

1 **Street maps** at 3½ inches to 1 mile

226 **Street maps** at 1¾ inches to 1 mile

244 **Index** of towns, villages, streets, hospitals, industrial estates, railway stations, schools, shopping centres, universities and places of interest

## Digital Data

The exceptionally high-quality mapping found in this atlas is available as digital data in TIFF format, which is easily convertible to other bitmapped (raster) image formats.

The index is also available in digital form as a standard database table. It contains all the details found in the printed index together with the National Grid reference for the map square in which each entry is named.

For further information and to discuss your requirements, please contact james.mann@philips-maps.co.uk

# Mobile speed cameras

The vast majority of speed cameras used on Britain's roads are operated by safety camera partnerships. These comprise local authorities, the police, Her Majesty's Court Service (HMCS) and the Highways Agency.

This table lists the sites where each safety camera partnership may enforce speed limits through the use of mobile cameras or detectors. These are usually set up on the roadside or a bridge spanning the road and operated by a police or civilian enforcement officer. The speed limit at each site (if available) is shown in red type, followed by the approximate location in black type.

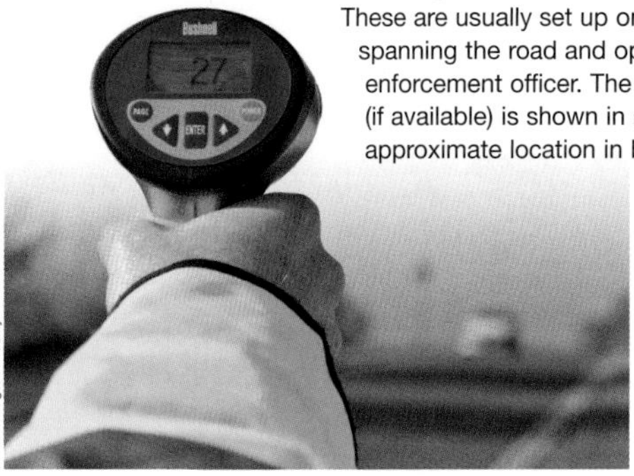

Mike Harrington / Alamy

**A6**
- 40 Broughton, Garstang Rd (north of M55)
- 30, 40 Chorley, Bolton Rd
- 30 Fulwood, Garstang Rd (south of M55)
- 30 Fulwood, Garstang Rd, north of Blackpool Rd
- 30 Lancaster, Greaves Rd
- 50 Lancaster, Scotforth Rd nr Burrow Lane Bailrigg
- 30 Preston, North Rd
- 30 Preston, Ringway

**A56**
- 30 Colne, Albert Rd
- 30 Colne, Burnley Rd
- 30 Nelson, Leeds Rd

**A59**
- 60 Gisburn, Gisburn Rd
- 50 Hutton, Liverpool Rd
- 30 Preston, New Hall Lane

**A65**
- 40, 60 Lancaster, Cowan Bridge

**A570**
- 40 Scarisbrick, Southport Rd, Brook House Farm

**A581**
- 40 Ulnes Walton, Southport Rd

**A583+A5073**
- 30 Blackpool, Whitegate Drive/Waterloo Rd

**A583+B5266**
- 30 Blackpool, Church St/Newton Drive

**A584**
- 30 Blackpool, Promenade
- 30 Lytham, West/Central Beach
- 30, 50 Warton, Lytham Rd

**A584+A587**
- 30 Blackpool, Promenade/ Fleetwood Rd

**A587**
- 30 Blackpool, East/North Park Drive
- 30 Cleveleys, Rossall Rd/Crescent East

**A588**
- 60 Pilling, Head Dyke Lane
- 60 Wyre, Lancaster Rd, Cockerham at Gulf Lane

**A666**
- 30, 50 Darwen, Blackburn Rd
- 30 Darwen, Bolton Rd nr Cross St
- 30 Darwen, Duckworth St

**A671**
- 30 Read, Whalley Rd

**A674**
- 30 Cherry Tree, Preston Old Rd

**A675**
- 50 Belmont, Belmont Rd (south of village)
- 50 Darwen, Belmont Rd, north of Belmont Village
- 30, 60 Withnell, Bolton Rd (Dole Lane to Calf Hey Bridge)

**A680**
- 40, 60 Edenfield, Rochdale Rd

**A682**
- 60 Barrowford, Gisburn Rd nr Moorcock Inn
- 30 Brierfield, Colne Rd
- 40 Crawshawbooth, Burnley Rd
- 60 Gisburn, Gisburn Rd
- 60 Gisburn, Long Preston Rd

**A683**
- 30 Lancaster, Morecambe Rd

**A5073**
- 30 Blackpool, Waterloo Rd

**A5085**
- 30 Lane Ends, Blackpool Rd

**A5209**
- 30 Newburgh, Course Lane/Ash Brow

**A6062**
- 30 Blackburn, Livesey Branch Rd

**A6068**
- 50 Barrowford, Barrowford Rd

**A6114**
- 30 Burnley, Casterton Avenue

**A6177**
- 50 Haslingden, Grane Rd West of Holcombe Rd
- 40, 50 Hyndburn, Haslingden Rd/Elton Rd

**B5192**
- 30 Kirkham, Preston St

**B5251**
- 30 Chorley, Pall Mall

**B5242**
- 30 Scarisbrick, Bescar Brow Lane

**B5254**
- 30 Lostock Hall, Leyland Rd/Watkin Lane
- 30 South Ribble, Leyland Rd

**B5256**
- 30 Leyland, Turpin Green Lane

**B5269**
- 40 Goosnargh, Whittingham Lane

**B6231**
- 30 Oswaldtwistle, Union Rd

**B6243**
- 50 Longridge, Preston Rd

**UNCLASSIFIED**
- 60 Belmont, Egerton Rd
- 30 Blackburn, East Park Rd
- 30 Blackburn, Revidge Rd nr Pleckgate
- 30 Blackburn, Whalley Old Rd, west of Railway Bridge
- 30 Blackpool, Dickson Rd, Queens St to Pleasant St
- 30 Briercliffe, Burnley Rd
- 30 Darwen, Lower Eccleshill Rd
- 60 Galgate, Bay Horse Rd
- 30 Nelson, Netherfield Rd
- 30 Preston, Lytham Rd
- 30 Preston, St Georges Rd
- 30 St Anne's, Church Rd to Albany Rd, nr High School

# Key to map symbols

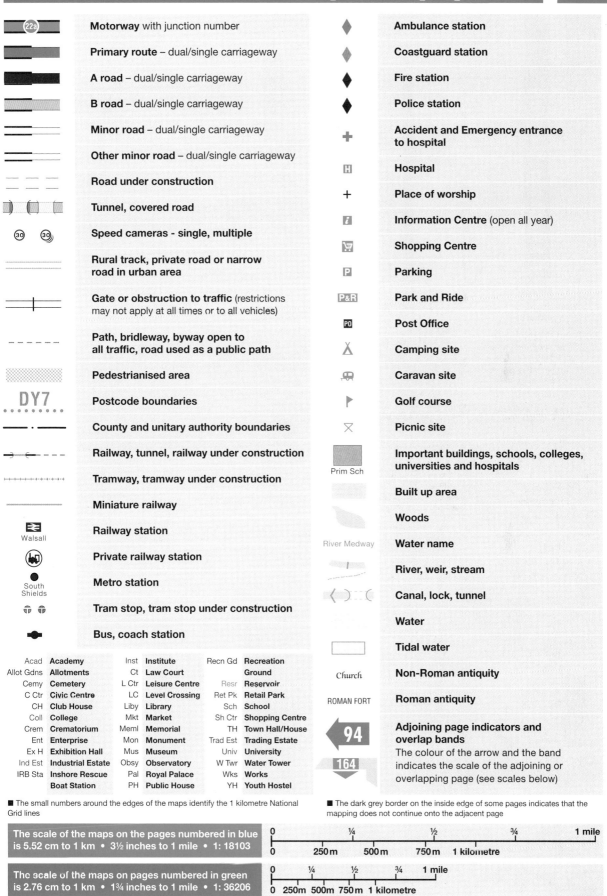

**Motorway** with junction number

**Primary route** – dual/single carriageway

**A road** – dual/single carriageway

**B road** – dual/single carriageway

**Minor road** – dual/single carriageway

**Other minor road** – dual/single carriageway

**Road under construction**

**Tunnel, covered road**

**Speed cameras - single, multiple**

**Rural track, private road or narrow road in urban area**

**Gate or obstruction to traffic** (restrictions may not apply at all times or to all vehicles)

**Path, bridleway, byway open to all traffic, road used as a public path**

**Pedestrianised area**

DY7 **Postcode boundaries**

**County and unitary authority boundaries**

**Railway, tunnel, railway under construction**

**Tramway, tramway under construction**

**Miniature railway**

Walsall **Railway station**

**Private railway station**

South Shields **Metro station**

**Tram stop, tram stop under construction**

**Bus, coach station**

**Ambulance station**

**Coastguard station**

**Fire station**

**Police station**

**Accident and Emergency entrance to hospital**

**Hospital**

**Place of worship**

**Information Centre** (open all year)

**Shopping Centre**

**Parking**

**Park and Ride**

**Post Office**

**Camping site**

**Caravan site**

**Golf course**

**Picnic site**

Prim Sch **Important buildings, schools, colleges, universities and hospitals**

**Built up area**

**Woods**

River Medway **Water name**

**River, weir, stream**

**Canal, lock, tunnel**

**Water**

**Tidal water**

Church **Non-Roman antiquity**

ROMAN FORT **Roman antiquity**

94 164 **Adjoining page indicators and overlap bands**
The colour of the arrow and the band indicates the scale of the adjoining or overlapping page (see scales below)

| | | | | | |
|---|---|---|---|---|---|
| Acad | Academy | Inst | Institute | Recn Gd | Recreation Ground |
| Allot Gdns | Allotments | Ct | Law Court | Resr | Reservoir |
| Cemy | Cemetery | L Ctr | Leisure Centre | Ret Pk | Retail Park |
| C Ctr | Civic Centre | LC | Level Crossing | Sch | School |
| CH | Club House | Liby | Library | Sh Ctr | Shopping Centre |
| Coll | College | Mkt | Market | TH | Town Hall/House |
| Crem | Crematorium | Meml | Memorial | Trad Est | Trading Estate |
| Ent | Enterprise | Mon | Monument | Univ | University |
| Ex H | Exhibition Hall | Mus | Museum | W Twr | Water Tower |
| Ind Est | Industrial Estate | Obsy | Observatory | Wks | Works |
| IRB Sta | Inshore Rescue Boat Station | Pal | Royal Palace | YH | Youth Hostel |
| | | PH | Public House | | |

■ The small numbers around the edges of the maps identify the 1 kilometre National Grid lines

■ The dark grey border on the inside edge of some pages indicates that the mapping does not continue onto the adjacent page

The scale of the maps on the pages numbered in blue is 5.52 cm to 1 km • 3½ inches to 1 mile • 1: 18103

0 ¼ ½ ¾ 1 mile
0 250 m 500 m 750 m 1 kilometre

The scale of the maps on pages numbered in green is 2.76 cm to 1 km • 1¾ inches to 1 mile • 1: 36206

0 ¼ ½ ¾ 1 mile
0 250m 500m 750m 1 kilometre

# Key to map pages

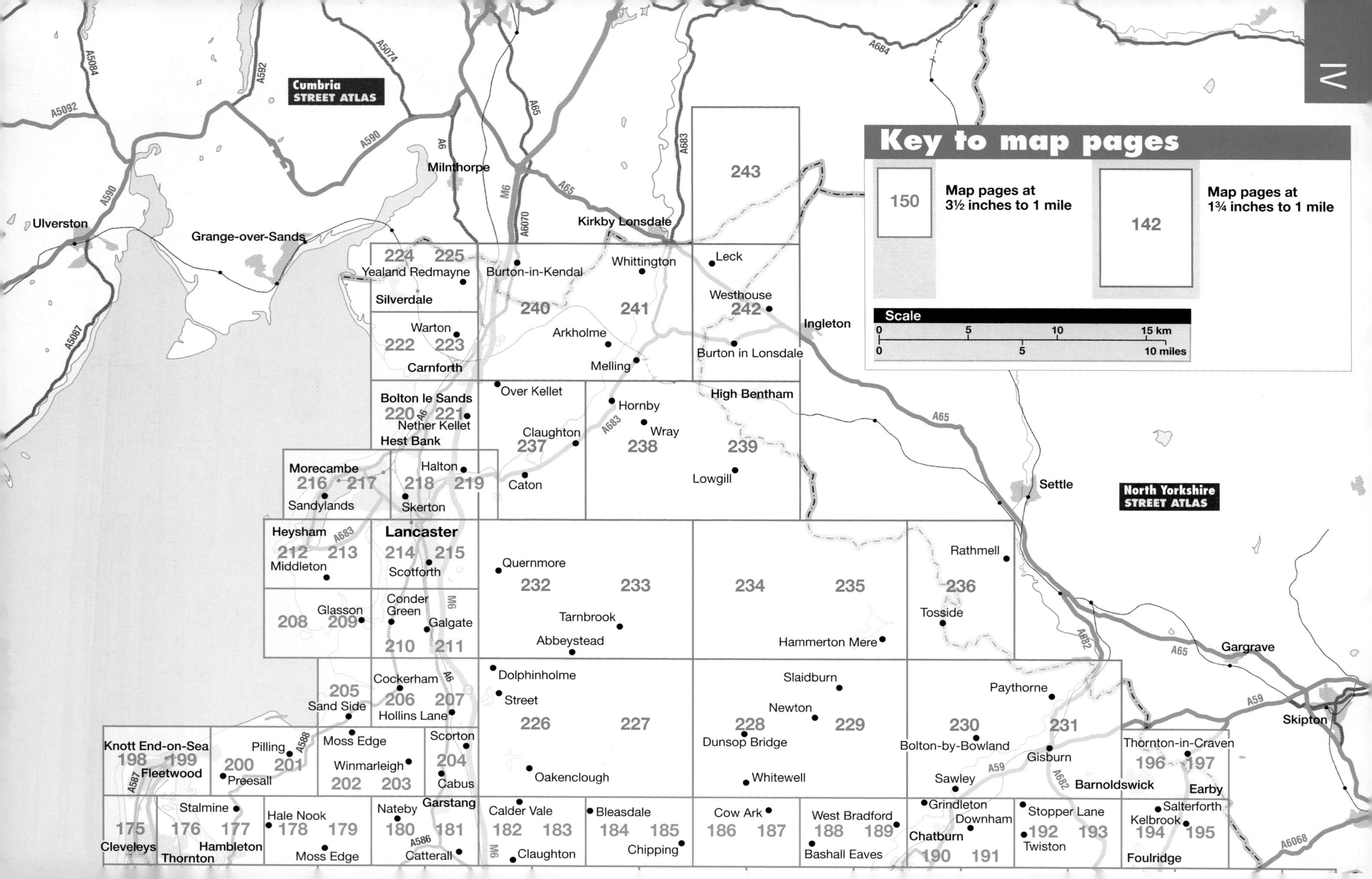
150
Map pages at
3½ inches to 1 mile
142
Map pages at
1¾ inches to 1 mile
Scale
0 5 10 15 km
0 5 10 miles
Cumbria STREET ATLAS
North Yorkshire STREET ATLAS
Ulverston
Grange-over-Sands
Milnthorpe
Kirkby Lonsdale
Ingleton
Settle
Gargrave
Skipton
A5084
A5092
A5087
A592
A5074
A590
A6
A65
A6070
M6
A683
A684
A682
A59
A6068
A586
A587
A588
243
224 225
Yealand Redmayne
Silverdale
Burton-in-Kendal
Whittington
240
241
Arkholme
Melling
Leck
Westhouse
242
Burton in Lonsdale
Warton
222 223
Carnforth
Bolton le Sands
220 221
Nether Kellet
Hest Bank
Over Kellet
Claughton
237
Caton
Hornby
Wray
238
High Bentham
239
Lowgill
Morecambe
216 217
Sandylands
Halton
218 219
Skerton
Heysham
212 213
Middleton
Lancaster
214 215
Scotforth
Quernmore
232
233
Tarnbrook
Abbeystead
234
235
Hammerton Mere
Rathmell
236
Tosside
208
Glasson
209
Conder Green
Galgate
210 211
205
Sand Side
Cockerham
206 207
Hollins Lane
Dolphinholme
Street
226
227
Oakenclough
Slaidburn
Newton
228
229
Dunsop Bridge
Whitewell
Paythorne
230
231
Bolton-by-Bowland
Gisburn
Sawley
Barnoldswick
Thornton-in-Craven
196 197
Earby
Knott End-on-Sea
198 199
Fleetwood
Pilling
200 201
Preesall
Moss Edge
Winmarleigh
202 203
Scorton
204
Cabus
Garstang
Stalmine
175
176 177
Cleveleys
Hambleton
Thornton
Hale Nook
178 179
Moss Edge
Nateby
180 181
Catterall
Calder Vale
182 183
Claughton
Bleasdale
184 185
Chipping
Cow Ark
186 187
West Bradford
188 189
Bashall Eaves
Grindleton
Downham
Chatburn
190 191
Stopper Lane
192 193
Twiston
Salterforth
Kelbrook
194 195
Foulridge

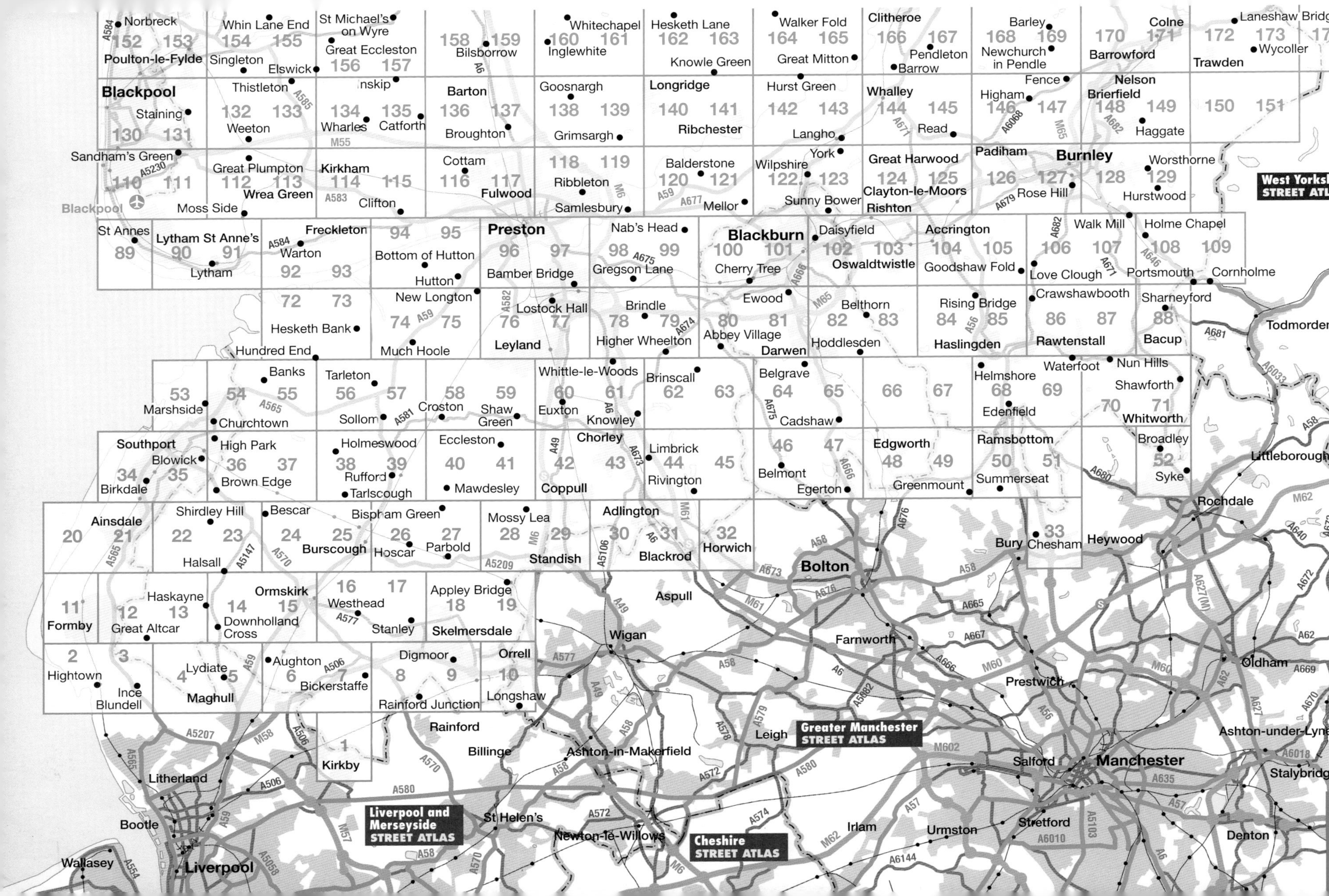
West Yorkshire STREET ATLAS
Greater Manchester STREET ATLAS
Liverpool and Merseyside STREET ATLAS
Cheshire STREET ATLAS
Norbreck
Poulton-le-Fylde
Whin Lane End
Singleton
Elswick
St Michael's on Wyre
Great Eccleston
Bilsborrow
Whitechapel
Inglewhite
Hesketh Lane
Knowle Green
Walker Fold
Great Mitton
Clitheroe
Pendleton
Barrow
Barley
Newchurch in Pendle
Colne
Barrowford
Laneshaw Bridge
Wycoller
Trawden
Blackpool
Staining
Thistleton
Weeton
Wharles
Catforth
Barton
Broughton
Goosnargh
Grimsargh
Longridge
Ribchester
Hurst Green
Langho
Whalley
Read
Higham
Fence
Nelson
Brierfield
Haggate
Sandham's Green
Great Plumpton
Wrea Green
Moss Side
Kirkham
Clifton
Cottam
Fulwood
Ribbleton
Samlesbury
Balderstone
Mellor
Wilpshire
York
Sunny Bower
Great Harwood
Clayton-le-Moors
Rishton
Padiham
Burnley
Rose Hill
Worsthorne
Hurstwood
St Annes
Lytham St Anne's
Lytham
Freckleton
Warton
Bottom of Hutton
Hutton
Preston
Bamber Bridge
Nab's Head
Gregson Lane
Blackburn
Cherry Tree
Daisyfield
Oswaldtwistle
Accrington
Goodshaw Fold
Walk Mill
Love Clough
Holme Chapel
Portsmouth
Cornholme
Hesketh Bank
Hundred End
New Longton
Much Hoole
Lostock Hall
Leyland
Brindle
Higher Wheelton
Ewood
Abbey Village
Darwen
Belthorn
Hoddlesden
Rising Bridge
Haslingden
Crawshawbooth
Rawtenstall
Sharneyford
Bacup
Todmorden
Marshside
Banks
Churchtown
Tarleton
Sollom
Croston
Shaw Green
Whittle-le-Woods
Euxton
Knowley
Brinscall
Belgrave
Cadshaw
Helmshore
Edenfield
Waterfoot
Nun Hills
Shawforth
Whitworth
Southport
Blowick
Birkdale
High Park
Brown Edge
Holmeswood
Rufford
Tarlscough
Eccleston
Mawdesley
Chorley
Coppull
Limbrick
Rivington
Belmont
Egerton
Edgworth
Greenmount
Ramsbottom
Summerseat
Broadley
Syke
Littleborough
Ainsdale
Shirdley Hill
Halsall
Bescar
Burscough
Bispham Green
Hoscar
Parbold
Mossy Lea
Standish
Adlington
Blackrod
Horwich
Bury
Chesham
Heywood
Rochdale
Formby
Haskayne
Great Altcar
Ormskirk
Downholland Cross
Westhead
Stanley
Appley Bridge
Skelmersdale
Hightown
Ince Blundell
Lydiate
Maghull
Aughton
Bickerstaffe
Digmoor
Rainford Junction
Orrell
Longshaw
Bolton
Aspull
Wigan
Farnworth
Prestwich
Oldham
Rainford
Billinge
Kirkby
Ashton-in-Makerfield
Leigh
Salford
Manchester
Ashton-under-Lyne
Stalybridge
Litherland
Bootle
Wallasey
Liverpool
St Helen's
Newton-le-Willows
Irlam
Urmston
Stretford
Denton

# Route Planning

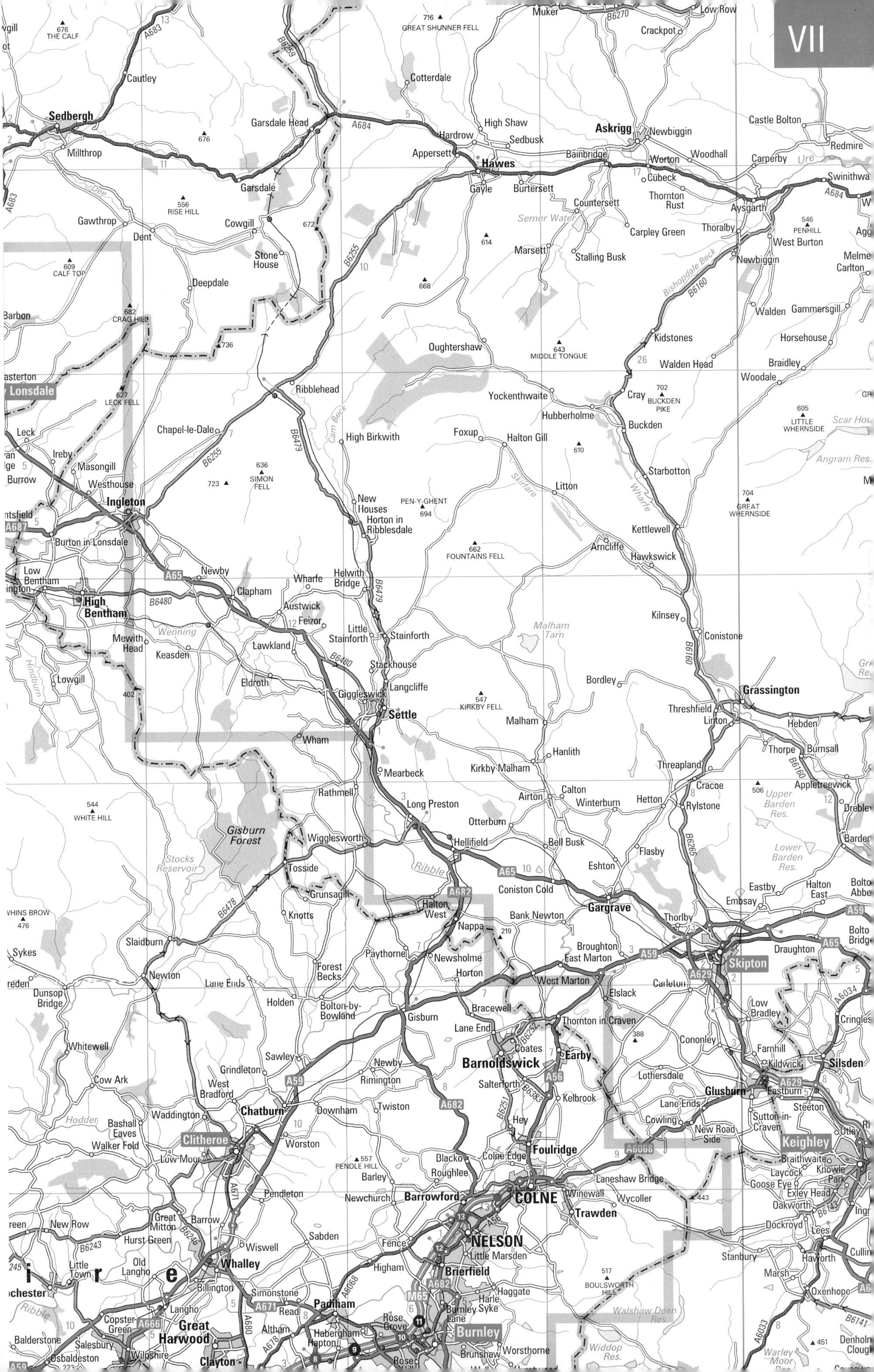
Sedbergh
Cautley
676 THE CALF
Millthrop
Garsdale Head
Garsdale
716 GREAT SHUNNER FELL
Muker
Low Row
Crackpot
Cotterdale
Hardrow
High Shaw
Sedbusk
Appersett
Hawes
Gayle
Burtersett
Askrigg
Newbiggin
Bainbridge
Worton
Woodhall
Cubeck
Thornton Rust
Castle Bolton
Redmire
Carperby
Swinithwaite
Aysgarth
Countersett
Semer Water
Carpley Green
Thoralby
546 PENHILL
West Burton
Marsett
Stalling Busk
Newbiggin
Bishopdale Beck
Walden
Gammersgill
Melmerby
Carlton
556 RISE HILL
Gawthrop
Dent
Cowgill
672
Stone House
609 CALF TOP
Deepdale
614
668
Barbon
682 CRAG HILL
736
Kidstones
Horsehouse
Oughtershaw
643 MIDDLE TONGUE
Walden Head
Braidley
Woodale
Casterton
Lonsdale
627 LECK FELL
Ribblehead
Yockenthwaite
Cray
702 BUCKDEN PIKE
Hubberholme
Buckden
605 LITTLE WHERNSIDE
Scar House
Angram Res.
Leck
Chapel-le-Dale
Cam Beck
High Birkwith
Foxup
Halton Gill
610
Ireby
Masongill
Burrow
Westhouse
723
636 SIMON FELL
Starbotton
Litton
Skirfare
Wharfe
Ingleton
New Houses
Horton in Ribblesdale
PEN-Y-GHENT 694
704 GREAT WHERNSIDE
Kettlewell
Burton in Lonsdale
662 FOUNTAINS FELL
Arncliffe
Hawkswick
Low Bentham
High Bentham
Newby
Clapham
Wharfe
Helwith Bridge
Austwick
Feizor
Little Stainforth
Stainforth
Malham Tarn
Kilnsey
Conistone
Wenning
Mewith Head
Keasden
Lawkland
Stackhouse
Langcliffe
Bordley
Grassington
Hindburn
Lowgill
402
Eldroth
Giggleswick
Settle
547 KIRKBY FELL
Malham
Threshfield
Linton
Hebden
Wham
Hanlith
Thorpe
Burnsall
Mearbeck
Kirkby Malham
Threapland
Cracoe
506
Appletreewick
Upper Barden Res.
Rathmell
Airton
Calton
Winterburn
Hetton
Rylstone
544 WHITE HILL
Long Preston
Otterburn
Gisburn Forest
Wigglesworth
Hellifield
Bell Busk
Flasby
Lower Barden Res.
Stocks Reservoir
Tosside
Ribble
Eshton
Coniston Cold
Gargrave
Embsay
Halton East
Bolton Abbey
Grunsagill
Halton West
WHINS BROW 476
Knotts
Nappa
Bank Newton
Thorlby
219
Broughton
Draughton
Slaidburn
Paythorne
Newsholme
East Marton
Skipton
Sykes
Newton
Forest Becks
Horton
Lane Ends
West Marton
Carleton
Dunsop Bridge
Holden
Bolton-by-Bowland
Elslack
Low Bradley
Bracewell
Gisburn
Lane End
Thornton in Craven
388
Cononley
Cringles
Farnhill
Kildwick
Silsden
Whitewell
Coates
Earby
Barnoldswick
Sawley
Newby
Lothersdale
Glusburn
Eastburn
Cow Ark
Grindleton
Rimington
Salterforth
Kelbrook
West Bradford
Steeton
Hodder
Bashall Eaves
Waddington
Chatburn
Downham
Twiston
Hey
Lane Ends
Cowling
New Road Side
Sutton-in-Craven
Utley
Walker Fold
Clitheroe
Worston
Foulridge
Keighley
Low Moor
557 PENDLE HILL
Blacko
Colne Edge
Laneshaw Bridge
Braithwaite
Barley
Roughlee
Laycock
Knowle Park
Goose Eye
Pendleton
Newchurch
Barrowford
COLNE
Winewall
Wycoller
Exley Head
443
Trawden
Oakworth
Green
New Row
Great Mitton
Barrow
Hurst Green
Wiswell
Sabden
Fence
NELSON
Dockroyd
Lees
Little Marsden
Stanbury
Haworth
Cullingworth
Little Town
Old Langho
Whalley
Higham
Brierfield
Marsh
Billington
517 BOULSWORTH HILL
Oxenhope
Ribchester
Simonstone
Padiham
Haggate
Harle Syke
Langho
Read
Burnley Lane
Walshaw Dean Res.
Copster Green
Great Harwood
Altham
Rose Grove
Habergham
Hapton
Burnley
Balderstone
Salesbury
Wilpshire
Brunshaw
Worsthorne
Widdop Res.
Denholme Clough
Osbaldeston
Clayton-
Rose
Warley Moor
451
A683
A684
B6259
B6255
B6479
B6270
B6160
A65
A687
B6480
B6478
A682
A59
A629
A6034
A56
B6252
B6383
B6251
A6068
A671
A680
A678
A666
B6245
B6243
M65
B6265
B6143
B6141
A6033
A6068

Blackpool
Blackpool
Anchorsholme
Norbreck
Bispham
Warbreck
North Shore
Queenstown
Thornton
Hambleton
Poulton-le-Fylde
Carleton
Skippool
Little Singleton
Singleton
Layton
Staining
Great Marton
South Shore
Hawes Side
Mereside
Common Edge
Squires Gate
Little Plumpton
Great Plumpton
Weeton
Westby
Moss Side
Wrea Green
Higher Ballam
Ansdell
Lytham
St Annes
Lytham St Anne's
Fairhaven
Warton
Freckleton
Kirkham
Wesham
Treales
Dowbridge
Newton
Scales
Clifton
Lea Town
Cottam
Ingol
Fulwood
Ribbleton
Cadley
Preston
Broughton
Woodplumpton
Catforth
Wharles
Corner Row
Esprick
Thistleton
Roseacre
Inskip
Elswick
Great Eccleston
Crossmoor
Myerscough
Cuddy Hill
Barton
St Michael's on Wyre
Out Rawcliffe
Little Eccleston
Moss Edge
Ratten Row
Catterall
Bilsborrow
Claughton
Whitechapel
Inglewhite
Hesketh Lane
Longridge
Goosnargh
Haighton Green
Grimsargh
Sharoe Green
Samlesbury
Lancashire
Ribble
Bottom of Hutton
Higher Penwortham
Walton-le-Dale
Middleforth Green
Bamber Bridge
Higher Walton
Coup Green
Gregson Lane
Hoghton
Hutton
Longton
New Longton
Lostock Hall
Farington
Walmer Bridge
Much Hoole
Midge Hall
Leyland
Broadfield
Clayton Green
Clayton-le-Woods
Whittle-le-Woods
Higher Wheelton
Brindle
Wheelton
Hesketh Bank
Becconsall
Hundred End
Tarleton
Banks
Bretherton
Sollom
Croston
Ulnes Walton
Shaw Green
Euxton
Chorley
Crossens
Marshside
Churchtown
Mere Brow
Southport
Holmeswood
Rufford
Tarlscough
Eccleston
Mawdesley
Heskin Green
Charnock Richard
Coppull
Adlington
Blowick
Birkdale
Brown Edge
Snape Green
Bescar
Scarisbrick
Shirdley Hill
Hillside
Ainsdale-on-Sea
Ainsdale
Woodvale
New Lane
Burscough
Burscough Bridge
Parbold
Pinfold
Halsall
Bispham Green
Wrightington Bar
Hill Dale
Mossy Lea
Dangerous Corner
Shevington Moor
Standish
Blackrod
Newburgh
Appley Bridge
Shevington Vale
Boars Head
Shevington
Red Rock
Haigh
Beech Hill
Marylebone
Barton
Haskayne
Ormskirk
Westhead
Stanley
Dalton
Roby Mill
Gathurst
Freshfield
Formby
Little Altcar
Great Altcar
Downholland Cross
Aughton Park
Blaguegate
Skelmersdale
Digmoor
Up Holland
Orrell
Wigan
Pemberton
Stanley Gate
Aughton
Royal Oak
Bickerstaffe
Rainford Junction
Higher End
Goose Green
Ince in Makerfield
Hightown
Ince Blundell
Lydiate
Maghull
Lunt
Little Crosby
Barrow Nook
Melling Mount
Crawford
Longshaw
Rainford
Billinge
Bryn
Bryn Gates
Abram
Crank Wood
Thornton
Netherton
Sefton
Melling
Kirkby
Southdene
Crank
Moss Bank
Garswood
Chadwick Green
Ashton-in-Makerfield
Golborne
Great Crosby
Aintree
Litherland
Waterloo
Seaforth
Orrell
Fazakerley
Knowsley
Denton's Green
St Helens
Eccleston
Blackbrook
Broad Oak
Haydock
Bootle
Gillar's Green
Peasley Cross
Collins Green
Newton-le-Willows
New Brighton
Walton
Norris Green
Kirkdale
Merseyside
Anfield
West Derby
Longview
Prescot
Thatto Heath
Eccleston Park
Rainhill
Sutton
Sutton Leach
Burtonwood
Winwick
Liscard
Egremont
Wallasey
Everton
Liverpool
Knotty Ash
Whiston
Sutton Manor
Clock Face
Leasowe
Moreton
Meols
Hoylake
Poulton
Seacombe
Bidston
Roby
Huyton
Rainhill Stoops
Bold Heath
Dallam
Houghton Green
Edge Hill
Wavertree
Childwall
Warrington
Great Sankey
Claughton
Upton
Greasby
Grange
Woodchurch
Frankby
Birkenhead
Tranmere
Rock Ferry
Toxteth
Dingle
Mossley Hill
Netherley
Tarbock Green
Cronton
Farnworth
Barrow's Green
Appleton
Penketh
Doe Green
Gateacre
Woolton
Hough Green
Ditton
Widnes
West Kirby
Caldy
Prenton
New Ferry
Aigburth
Grassendale
Allerton
Halewood
Hunt's Cross
Hale Bank
Higher Walton
Moore
Thurstaston
Irby
Thingwall
Bebington
Storeton
Port Sunlight
Barnston
Brimstage
Pensby
Garston
Speke
Hale
Runcorn
Halton
Keckwick
Daresbury
Heswall
Thornton Hough
Bromborough
Eastham Ferry
Liverpool John Lennon
Liverpool Airport
Mersey
Norton
Preston Brook
Preston on the Hill
Dutton
Gayton
Raby
Eastham
Weston
Parkgate
Hinderton
Willaston
Hooton
Childer Thornton
Ellesmere Port
Sutton Weaver
Aston
Newtown
Frodsham
Neston
Walwen
Little
Overpool
Dones Green
BELFAST 8:00
DOUGLAS 4:00 (Winter only)
DUBLIN 7:45
DOUGLAS 2:30
Crosby Channel
Lancaster Canal
TOLL
M6
M55
M58
M57
M62
M53
M56
M61
M65
A565
A570
A59
A580
A5058
A562
A561
A5300
A557
A56
A533
A49
A58
A577
A57
A552
A41
A583
A585
A582
A584
B5269
B5266
B5260

Clitheroe
Foulridge
COLNE
NELSON
Brierfield
Burnley
Whalley
Padiham
Great Harwood
Clayton-le-Moors
Rishton
Blackburn
ACCRINGTON
Oswaldtwistle
Haslingden
RAWTENSTALL
Bacup
Todmorden
Hebden Bridge
Mytholmroyd
DARWEN
Blackburn with Darwen
Ramsbottom
Edgworth
Littleborough
Wardle
Whitworth
Rochdale
Milnrow
HEYWOOD
Bury
Tottington
Horwich
Bolton
Radcliffe
Whitefield
Middleton
ROYTON
Shaw
FARNWORTH
Kearsley
ATHERTON
Tyldesley
Leigh
Worsley
Swinton
Pendlebury
PRESTWICH
Chadderton
Oldham
Failsworth
Ashton-under-Lyne
STALYBRIDGE
Mossley
MANCHESTER
SALFORD
Eccles
Droylsden
Dukinfield
Hyde
Denton
GLOSSOP
Trafford Park
URMSTON
Stretford
Irlam
Cadishead
Partington
SALE
Altrincham
Hale
GATLEY
Cheadle
Stockport
Bredbury
Romiley
Marple
HAZEL GROVE
Bramhall
Poynton
Lymm
Bowdon
Manchester Airport
WILMSLOW
Alderley Edge
Knutsford
Prestbury
Bollington
Whaley Bridge
New Mills
Low Leighton
Greater Manchester
Scale
0 5 10 km
0 1 2 3 4 5 6 miles

# Major administrative and Postcode boundaries

County and unitary authority boundaries
District boundaries
Postcode boundaries
Area covered by this atlas
Scale
0 5 10 15 km
0 5 10 miles
Cumbria
North Yorkshire
Lancashire
Lancaster
Wyre
Ribble Valley
Pendle
Blackpool
Fylde
Preston
South Ribble
Hyndburn
Burnley
Blackburn with Darwen
Rossendale
Chorley
West Lancashire
Calderdale
Bradford
Rochdale
Bolton
Bury
Oldham
Wigan
Salford
Sefton
St Helens
Manchester
Tameside
Liverpool
Knowsley
Warrington
Trafford
Stockport
SD
SJ
LA10
LA7
LA5
LA6
LA4
LA1
LA2
LA3
BD24
BD23
BD22
BB7
BB18
BB9
BB8
HX7
BB12
BB6
BB10
BB1
BB11
BB2
BB5
BB4
BB3
OL13
OL14
OL12
OL10
BL10
BL7
BL8
BL9
BL6
FY7
FY6
FY5
FY2
FY3
FY1
FY4
FY8
PR3
PR2
PR1
PR4
PR5
PR25
PR26
PR6
PR7
PR9
PR8
L40
L37
L39
L38
L31
L29
L33
WN1
WN6
WN2
WN8
WN5
WA11
Burton-in-Kendal
Silverdale
Burton in Lonsdale
Carnforth
High Bentham
Hornby
Caton
Morecambe
Lancaster
Heysham
Overton
Glasson
Galgate
Dolphinholme
Tosside
Slaidburn
Dunsop Bridge
Gisburn
Barnoldswick
Earby
Fleetwood
Pilling
Scorton
Garstang
Hambleton
Cleveleys
Chipping
Clitheroe
Great Eccleston
Bilsborrow
Colne
Trawden
Poulton-le-Fylde
Nelson
Blackpool
Longridge
Whalley
Padiham
Great Harwood
Burnley
Kirkham
Fulwood
Mellor
Preston
Blackburn
Holme Chapel
Warton
Lytham St Anne's
Accrington
Bamber Bridge
Walmer Bridge
Haslingden
Bacup
Leyland
Darwen
Brinscall
Banks
Tarleton
Croston
Eccleston
Chorley
Whitworth
Southport
Belmont
Ramsbottom
Adlington
Burscough
Ainsdale
Parbold
Standish
Horwich
Bury
Haskayne
Ormskirk
Formby
Aughton
Skelmersdale
Orrell
Hightown
Maghull
30
40
50
60
70
80
90
400

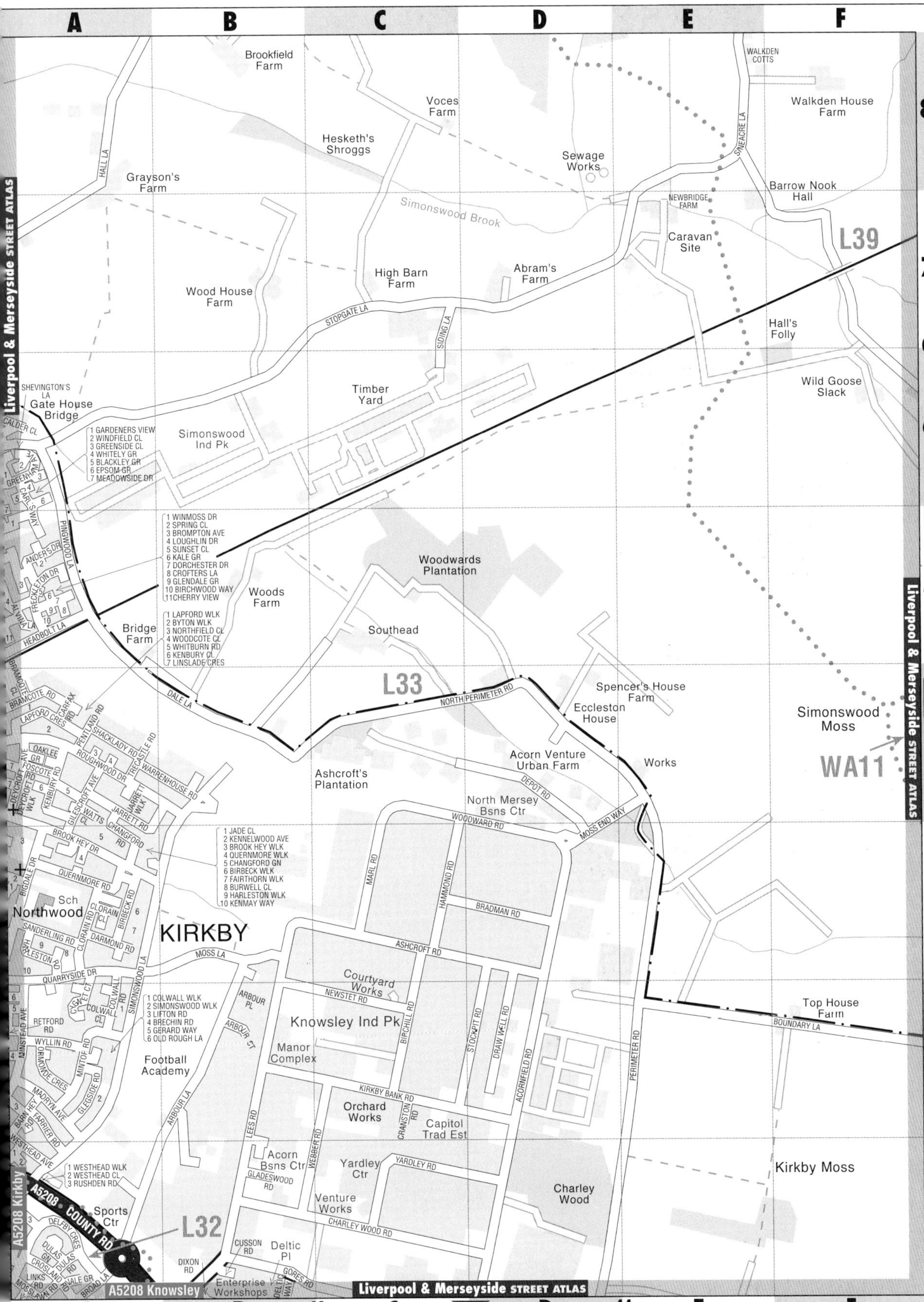
A B C D E F
8
7
01
6
5
00
4
3
99
2
1
98
42 A B 43 C D 44 E F
Brookfield Farm
Voces Farm
Hesketh's Shroggs
Grayson's Farm
Sewage Works
Walkden Cotts
Walkden House Farm
Barrow Nook Hall
Newbridge Farm
Simonswood Brook
Caravan Site
L39
High Barn Farm
Abram's Farm
Wood House Farm
Stopgate La
Siding La
Hall's Folly
Wild Goose Slack
Timber Yard
Simonswood Ind Pk
Shevington's La
Gate House Bridge
Hall La
Sineacre La
1 GARDENERS VIEW
2 WINDFIELD CL
3 GREENSIDE CL
4 WHITELY GR
5 BLACKLEY GR
6 EPSOM GR
7 MEADOWSIDE DR
1 WINMOSS DR
2 SPRING CL
3 BROMPTON AVE
4 LOUGHLIN DR
5 SUNSET CL
6 KALE GR
7 DORCHESTER DR
8 CROFTERS LA
9 GLENDALE GR
10 BIRCHWOOD WAY
11 CHERRY VIEW
Woodwards Plantation
Woods Farm
Bridge Farm
1 LAPFORD WLK
2 BYTON WLK
3 NORTHFIELD CL
4 WOODCOTE CL
5 WHITBURN RD
6 KENBURY CL
7 LINSLADE CRES
Southead
L33
North Perimeter Rd
Dale La
Spencer's House Farm
Eccleston House
Simonswood Moss
WA11
Acorn Venture Urban Farm
Works
Ashcroft's Plantation
Depot Rd
North Mersey Bsns Ctr
Woodward Rd
Moss End Way
1 JADE CL
2 KENNELWOOD AVE
3 BROOK HEY WLK
4 QUERNMORE WLK
5 CHANGFORD GN
6 BIRBECK WLK
7 FAIRTHORN WLK
8 BURWELL CL
9 HARLESTON WLK
10 KENMAY WAY
Marl Rd
Hammond Rd
Bradman Rd
Ashcroft Rd
KIRKBY
Northwood
Sch
Moss La
Courtyard Works
Newstet Rd
Knowsley Ind Pk
Birchill Rd
Stockpit Rd
Draw Well Rd
Acornfield Rd
Perimeter Rd
Top House Farm
Boundary La
Manor Complex
1 COLWALL WLK
2 SIMONSWOOD WLK
3 LIFTON RD
4 BRECHIN RD
5 GERARD WAY
6 OLD ROUGH LA
Football Academy
Arbour Pl
Arbour Ct
Arbour La
Kirkby Bank Rd
Orchard Works
Granston Rd
Capitol Trad Est
Lees Rd
Webber Rd
Acorn Bsns Ctr
Yardley Ctr
Yardley Rd
Gladeswood Rd
Venture Works
Charley Wood Rd
Charley Wood
Kirkby Moss
1 WESTHEAD WLK
2 WESTHEAD CL
3 RUSHDEN RD
Sports Ctr
L32
A5208 Kirkby
A5208 County Rd
A5208 Knowsley
Cusson Rd
Deltic Pl
Dixon Rd
Enterprise Workshops
Gores Rd
Deltic Way
Calder Cl
Greenhill
Carl's Way
Pingwood La
Anders Dr
Freckleton Dr
Headbolt La
Bramcote Rd
Lapford Cres
Carfax Rd
Pentland Rd
Shacklady Rd
Trecastle Rd
Warrenhouse Rd
Oaklee Gr
Foscote Rd
Kenbury Rd
Roughwood Dr
Gilescroft Ave
Watts Cl
Jarrett Wlk
Jarrett Rd
Changford Rd
Brook Hey Dr
Quernmore Rd
Clorain Rd
Birbeck Rd
Darmond Rd
Sanderling Rd
Quarryside Dr
Simonswood La
Colwall Rd
Retford Rd
Wyllin Rd
Mintor Rd
Ormonde Cres
Glegside Rd
Madryn Ave
Farrier Rd
Westhead Ave
Delfby Cres
Dulas Gn
Dulas Rd
Crosland Rd
Links
Broad La
Bigdale Dr
Minstead Ave
Deycroft Ave
Hall La
Headbolt La

11

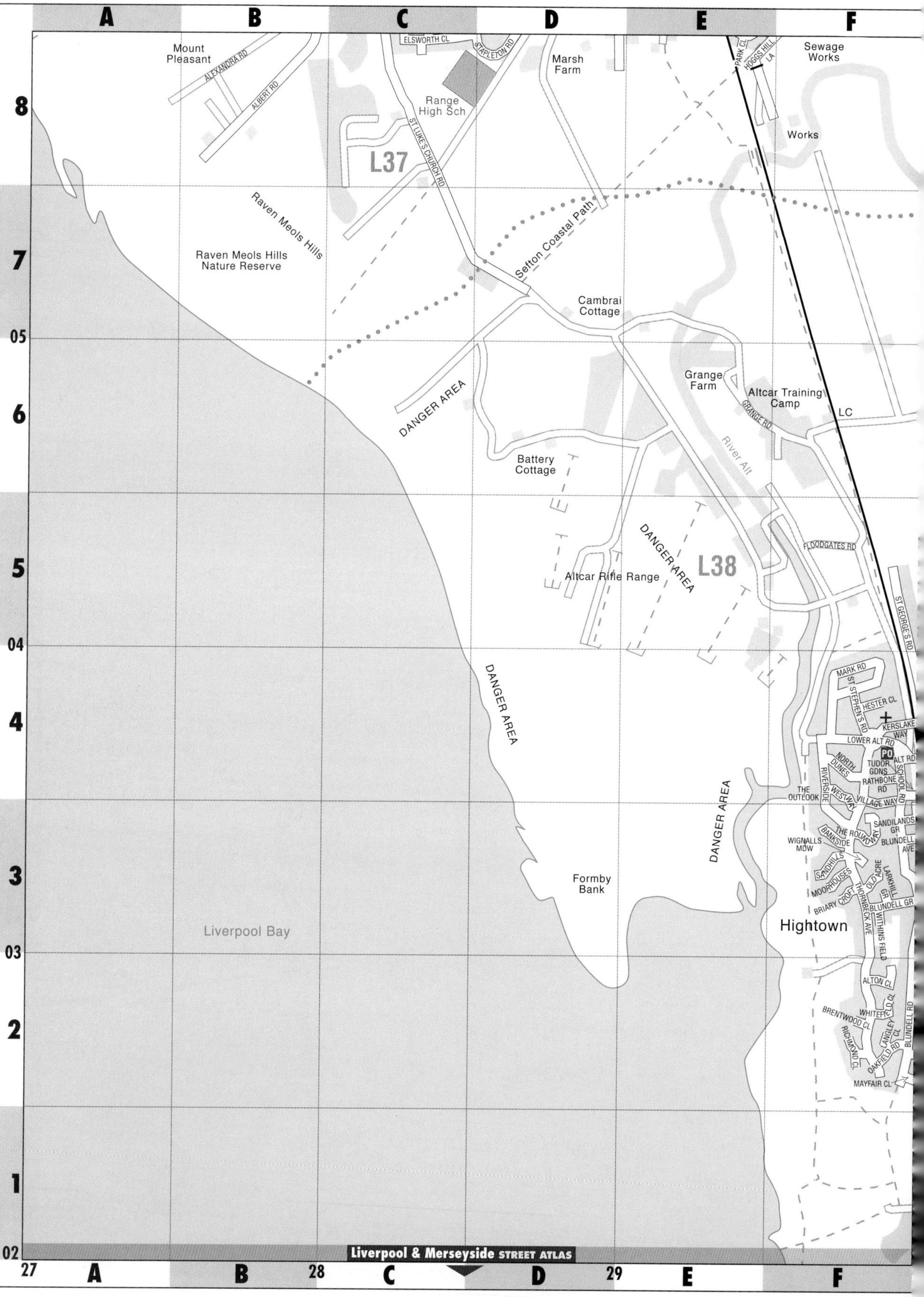
A
B
C
D
E
F
8
7
05
6
5
04
4
3
03
2
1
02
27
28
29
Mount Pleasant
ALEXANDRA RD
ALBERT RD
ELSWORTH CL
STAPLETON RD
Range High Sch
Marsh Farm
PARK CL
HOGGS HILL LA
Sewage Works
Works
L37
ST LUKE'S CHURCH RD
Raven Meols Hills
Raven Meols Hills Nature Reserve
Sefton Coastal Path
Cambrai Cottage
DANGER AREA
Grange Farm
Altcar Training Camp
GRANGE RD
LC
River Alt
Battery Cottage
DANGER AREA
L38
FLOODGATES RD
Altcar Rifle Range
ST GEORGE'S RD
DANGER AREA
MARK RD
ST STEPHEN'S RD
HESTER CL
KERSLAKE WAY
LOWER ALT RD
PO
NORTH DUNES
TUDOR GDNS
ALT RD
SCHOOL RD
RATHBONE RD
THE OUTLOOK
RIVERSIDE
WESTWAY
VILLAGE WAY
SANDILANDS GR
THE ROUNDWAY
BLUNDELL AVE
WIGNALLS MDW
BANKSIDE
SANDHILLS
MOORHOUSES
OLD ACRE
LARKHILL GR
BRIARY CROFT
THORNBECK AVE
BLUNDELL GR
WITHINS FIELD
DANGER AREA
Formby Bank
Hightown
Liverpool Bay
ALTON CL
BRENTWOOD CL
WHITEFIELD CL
LANGLEY CL
BLUNDELL RD
RICHMOND CL
OAKFIELD RD
MAYFAIR CL

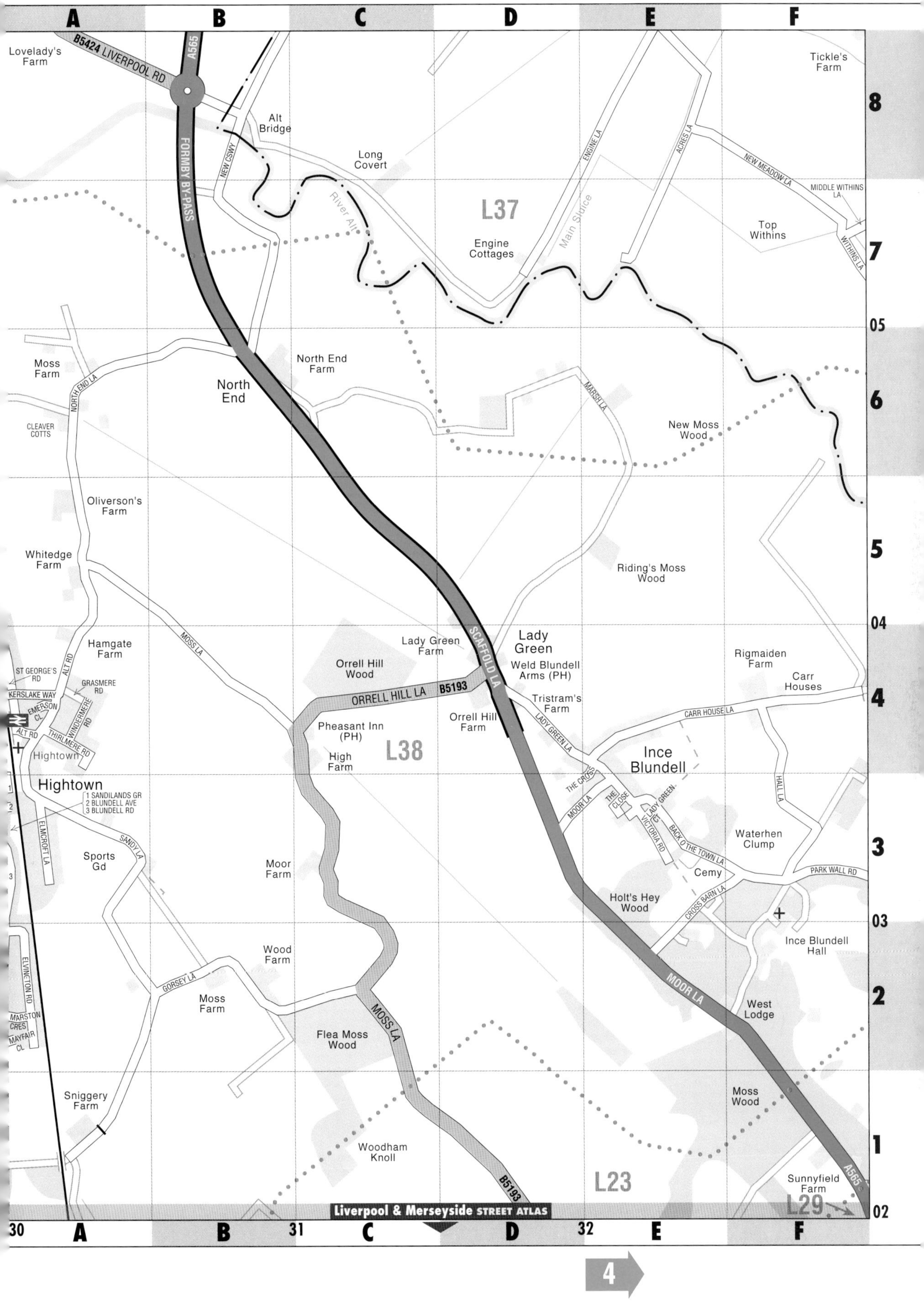
12
4
A
B
C
D
E
F
Lovelady's Farm
B5424 LIVERPOOL RD
A565
Alt Bridge
NEW CSWY
FORMBY BY-PASS
Long Covert
River Alt
L37
ENGINE LA
Main Sluice
ACRES LA
NEW MEADOW LA
MIDDLE WITHINS LA
Tickle's Farm
Top Withins
WITHINS LA
Engine Cottages
8
7
05
6
5
04
4
3
03
2
1
02
Moss Farm
NORTH END LA
North End
North End Farm
MARSH LA
New Moss Wood
CLEAVER COTTS
Oliverson's Farm
Whitedge Farm
Riding's Moss Wood
Hamgate Farm
MOSS LA
Lady Green Farm
Lady Green
SCAFFOLD LA
Weld Blundell Arms (PH)
Rigmaiden Farm
Carr Houses
ST GEORGE'S RD
ALT RD
GRASMERE RD
KERSLAKE WAY
EMERSON CL
WINDERMERE RD
THIRLMERE RD
Orrell Hill Wood
ORRELL HILL LA
B5193
Tristram's Farm
CARR HOUSE LA
Pheasant Inn (PH)
Orrell Hill Farm
LADY GREEN LA
L38
High Farm
Ince Blundell
Hightown
1 SANDILANDS GR
2 BLUNDELL AVE
3 BLUNDELL RD
THE CROSS
MOOR LA
THE CLOSE
LADY GREEN CT
VICTORIA RD
BACK O'THE TOWN LA
HALL LA
Waterhen Clump
ELMCROFT LA
SANDY LA
Sports Gd
Moor Farm
Cemy
PARK WALL RD
Holt's Hey Wood
CROSS BARN LA
Ince Blundell Hall
ELVINGTON RD
Wood Farm
GORSEY LA
Moss Farm
MOSS LA
MOOR LA
West Lodge
MARSTON CRES
MAYFAIR CL
Flea Moss Wood
Sniggery Farm
Moss Wood
Woodham Knoll
B5193
L23
Sunnyfield Farm
A565
L29
30
31
32
4

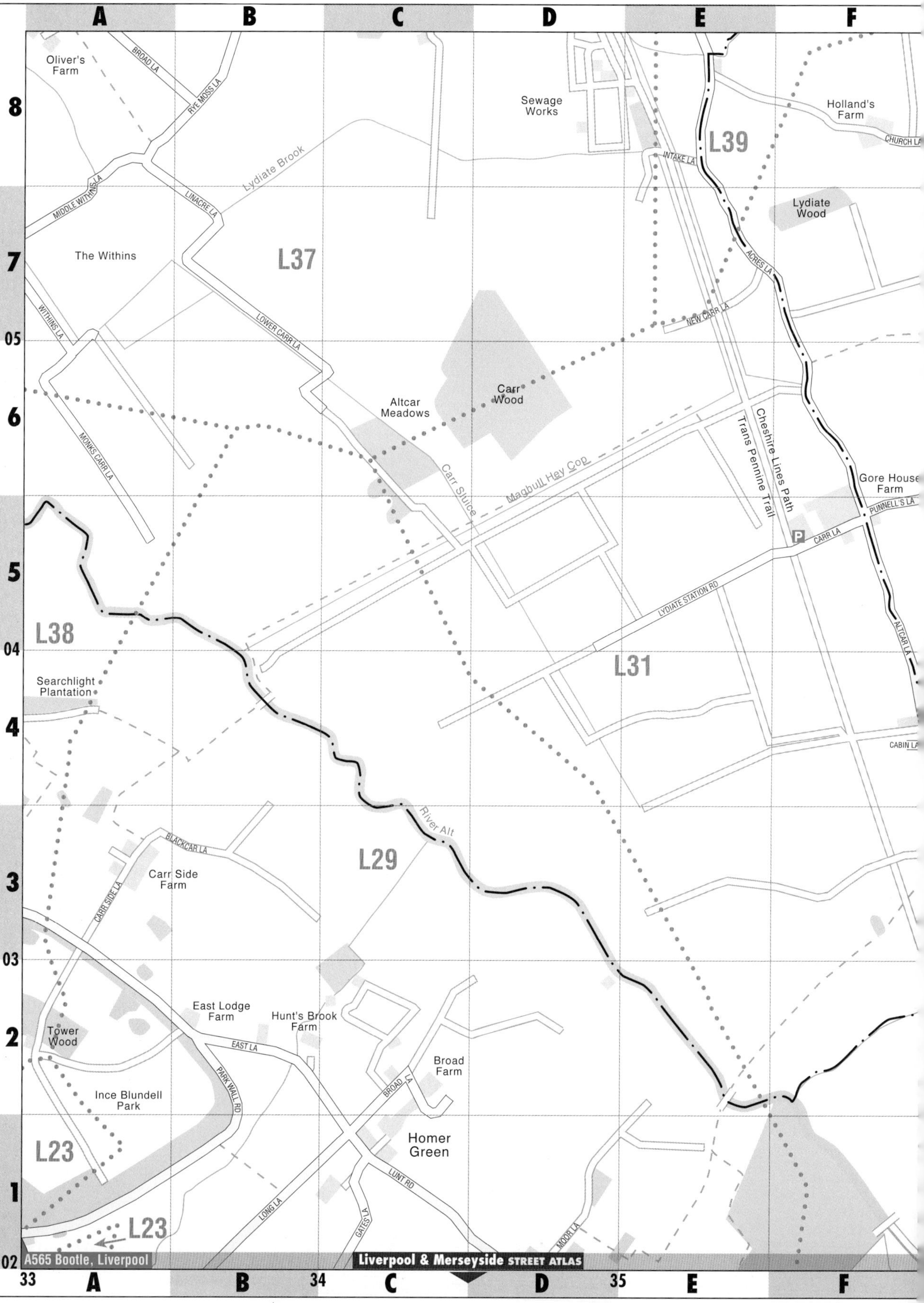
A
B
C
D
E
F
8
7
05
6
5
04
4
3
03
2
1
02
33
34
35
Oliver's Farm
BROAD LA
RYE MOSS LA
MIDDLE WITHINS LA
LINACRE LA
Lydiate Brook
The Withins
L37
WITHINS LA
LOWER CARR LA
MONKS CARR LA
Altcar Meadows
Carr Wood
Carr Sluice
Magbull Hey Cop
Sewage Works
INTAKE LA
L39
Holland's Farm
CHURCH LA
Lydiate Wood
ACRES LA
NEW CARR LA
Cheshire Lines Path
Trans Pennine Trail
Gore House Farm
PUNNELL'S LA
P
CARR LA
LYDIATE STATION RD
ALTCAR LA
L31
CABIN LA
L38
Searchlight Plantation
BLACKCAR LA
River Alt
L29
Carr Side Farm
CARR SIDE LA
East Lodge Farm
Hunt's Brook Farm
Tower Wood
EAST LA
PARK WALL RD
Ince Blundell Park
Broad Farm
BROAD LA
Homer Green
L23
LUNT RD
LONG LA
GATES LA
MOOR LA
L23
A565 Bootle, Liverpool

14
6

A
B
C
D
E
F
L39
A5147
MAIRSCOUGH LA
Lydiate Brook
Rimmer's Bridge
GREEN'S LA
Hotel
8
CHURCH LA
Church View Farm
EAGER LA
Hollin House Green Farm
A59
HALL LA
7
Bridgefoot Farm
Hollin House Farm
Lydiate Hall Farm
CANAL BANK PYGONS HILL
CANAL BANK COTTS
Jackson's Bridge Farm
SUDELL LA
PYE'S COTTS
Beaconsfield Farm
ST MICHAEL RD
05
SMITHY LA
Hill Top Farm Kennels
SWAN LA
BACK LA
PH
6
STATION RD
PYGON'S HILL LA
Rose Hill Farm
SPRINGFIELD RD
PUNNELL'S LA
Cherry Tree Farm
SOUTHPORT RD
SANDHURST WAY
SANDY LA
Sudell Brook
BIRCHFIELD WAY
SILVER BIRCH WAY
Rosemount Nurseries
CHARLESWORTH CL
MANION AVE
MANION CL
PO
Northway Nurseries
NELL'S LA
5
MOSS LA
AVELON CL
PILLING LA
L31
ROBBIN'S BRIDGE
BUTCHERS LA
B5407
04
St Gregory's RC Prim Sch
OLD LA
Windmill
Leeds & Liverpool Canal
Lydiate
LAMBSHEAR LA
Mill House Farm
Crisp's Farm
Gore Houses
Lydiate Prim Sch
4
KINGFISHER CT 1
AYLESBURY HO 2
HERONS CT
MALLARD HO
SEAFORE CL
LIVERPOOL RD
St Thomas CE Prim Sch
NORTHWAY
KNUTSFORD WLK
ALTCAR LA
COPPULL RD
HAVEN WLK
THE ELMS
ALEXANDER DR
BELL'S LA
VIRGINIA AVE
MARLBOROUGH AVE
KENYONS LA
MERCER CT
REDWOOD AVE
NEDENS LA
Maghull Brook
1 CROXTETH CL
2 GARSWOOD CL
KENYONS LODGE
3
THE CLEVES
MILLBANK LA
Maghull Smallholdings Est
STONEBARN DR
Northway Prim Sch
Cheshire Lines Path
CRAWFORD AVE
SCARISBRICK CL
PARK LA
03
WENSLEYDALE CL
LOWTHER AVE
BROOK AVE
UPTON BARN
DODD'S LA
St John Bosco RC Prim Sch
Green Park Prim Sch
GREEN LA
LIVERPOOL RD N
TRENT AVE
2
C2
1 HINDLEY BEECH
2 ROCKFIELD GDNS
SUDELL AVE
MOSS LA
Peel Farm
MERSEY AVE
CORN MILL LODGE
WINDERMERE DR
B5422 WESTWAY
A5147
30
Trans Pennine Trail
MILTON WAY
CANNOCK GN
DEYES LA
MAGHULL
Deyes High Sch
Red Lion Sh Ctr
Liby
St Andrew's Maghull CE Prim Sch
1
B5422 GREEN LA
BALMORAL RD 1
ALEXANDER WHARF 2
The Maghull Homes
STANSFIELD AVE
1 EAST RD
2 HOWARD CL
3 LANCASTER CL
4 LABURNUM GR
5 BEECHWOOD CT
6 ORCHARD CT
LIVERPOOL RD S
BUCKINGHAM RD
A59 Liverpool
HOLLIERS CL
TWYFORD CL
02
36
37
38



6

5
15

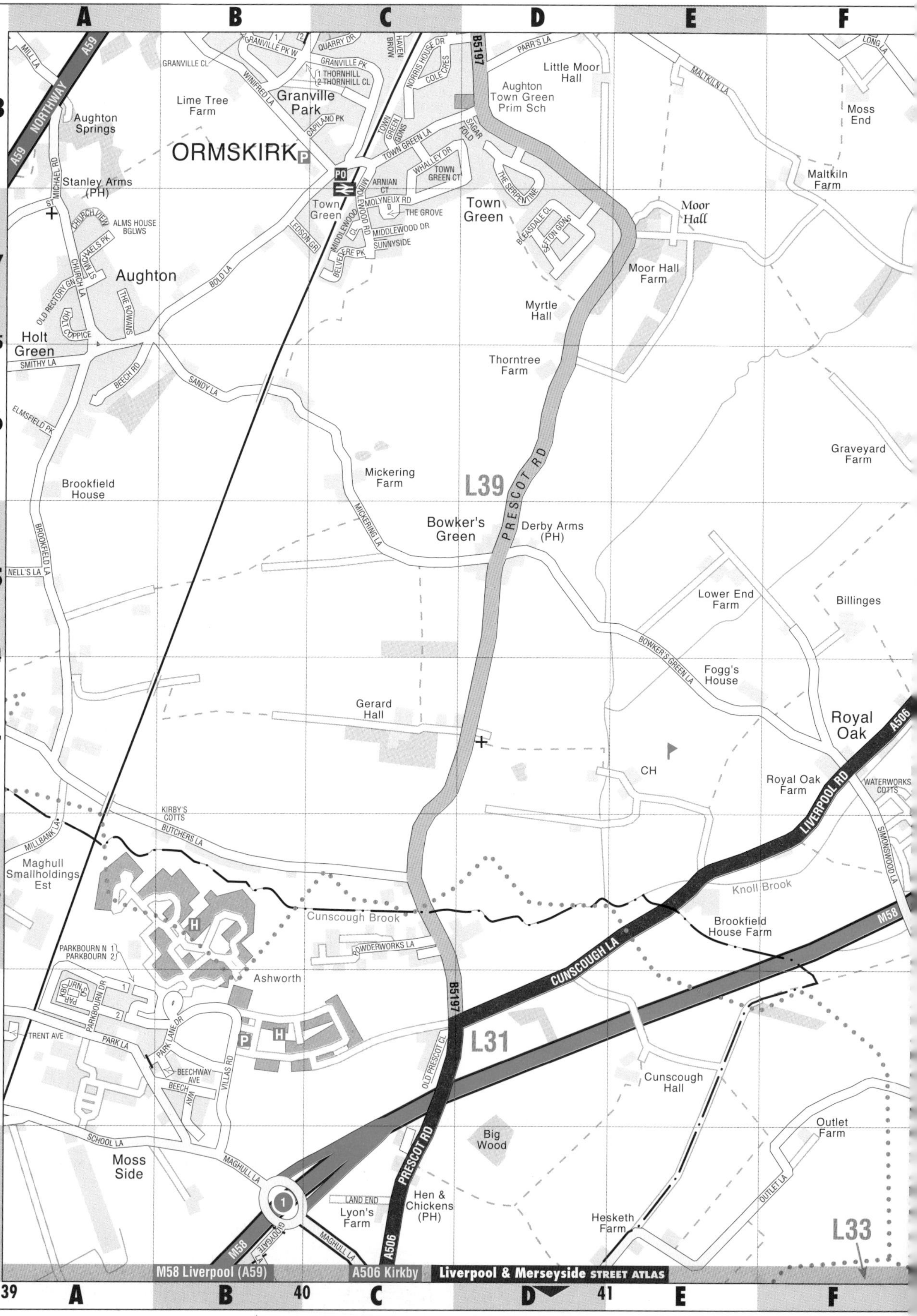
A
B
C
D
E
F
8
7
05
6
5
04
4
3
03
2
1
02
39
40
41
A59
NORTHWAY
MILL LA
GRANVILLE CL
GRANVILLE PK W
QUARRY DR
HAVEN BROW
NORRIS HOUSE DR
COLE CRES
B5197
PARR'S LA
LONG LA
GRANVILLE PK
1 THORNHILL
2 THORNHILL CL
WINIFRED LA
Granville Park
CAPILANO PK
Lime Tree Farm
Aughton Springs
ORMSKIRK
Little Moor Hall
Aughton Town Green Prim Sch
MALTKILN LA
Moss End
TOWN GREEN GDNS
TOWN GREEN LA
SAGAR FOLD
WHALLEY DR
TOWN GREEN CT
Maltkiln Farm
PO
ARNIAN CT
MOLYNEUX RD
MIDDLEWOOD RD
THE GROVE
THE SERPENTINE
BLEASDALE CL
SEFTON GDNS
MICHAEL RD
Stanley Arms (PH)
Town Green
Moor Hall
CHURCH VIEW
ALMS HOUSE BGLWS
HAELS PK
LEDSON GR
MIDDLEWOOD CL
MIDDLEWOOD DR
SUNNYSIDE
BELVEDERE PK
CHURCH LA
Aughton
BOLD LA
Moor Hall Farm
OLD RECTORY GN
HOLT COPPICE
THE ROWANS
Myrtle Hall
Holt Green
SMITHY LA
BEECH RD
SANDY LA
Thorntree Farm
ELMSFIELD PK
Mickering Farm
Graveyard Farm
Brookfield House
L39
PRESCOT RD
MICKERING LA
Bowker's Green
Derby Arms (PH)
BROOKFIELD LA
NELL'S LA
Lower End Farm
Billinges
BOWKER'S GREEN LA
Fogg's House
Gerard Hall
Royal Oak
A506
CH
Royal Oak Farm
LIVERPOOL RD
WATERWORKS COTTS
KIRBY'S COTTS
BUTCHERS LA
MILLBANK LA
SIMONSWOOD LA
Maghull Smallholdings Est
Knoll Brook
Cunscough Brook
Brookfield House Farm
M58
H
POWDERWORKS LA
PARKBOURN N 1
PARKBOURN 2
Ashworth
CUNSCOUGH LA
PARKBOURN DR
PARKBOURN SQ
TRENT AVE
PARK LA
PARK LANE DR
P
L31
OLD PRESCOT CL
BEECHWAY AVE
BEECH WAY
VILLAS RD
Cunscough Hall
SCHOOL LA
Big Wood
Outlet Farm
Moss Side
MAGHULL LA
Hen & Chickens (PH)
LAND END
Lyon's Farm
GIDDYGATE LA
Hesketh Farm
OUTLET LA
L33
M58 Liverpool (A59)
A506 Kirkby
Liverpool & Merseyside STREET ATLAS

5

16
8

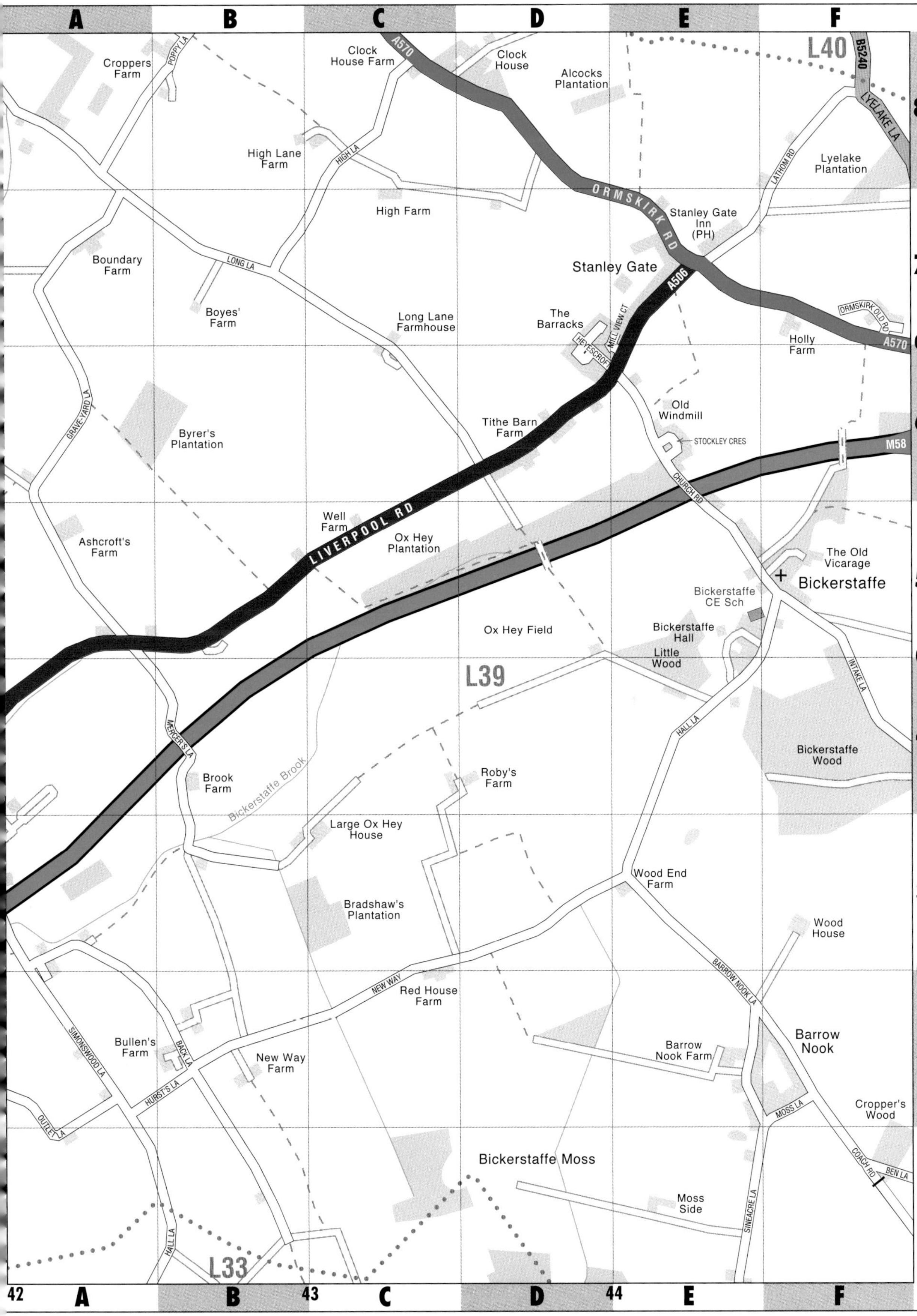
A B C D E F
8 7 05 6 5 04 4 3 03 2 1 02
42 43 44
L40
L39
L33
B5240
A570
A506
M58
LYELAKE LA
Croppers Farm
POPPY LA
Clock House Farm
Clock House
Alcocks Plantation
High Lane Farm
HIGH LA
High Farm
ORMSKIRK RD
Lyelake Plantation
LATHOM RD
Stanley Gate Inn (PH)
Boundary Farm
LONG LA
Stanley Gate
Boyes' Farm
Long Lane Farmhouse
The Barracks
MILL VIEW CT
HEYESCROFT
ORMSKIRK OLD RD
Holly Farm
GRAVEYARD LA
Byrer's Plantation
Tithe Barn Farm
Old Windmill
STOCKLEY CRES
CHURCH RD
Well Farm
LIVERPOOL RD
Ox Hey Plantation
Ashcroft's Farm
The Old Vicarage
Bickerstaffe
Bickerstaffe CE Sch
Ox Hey Field
Bickerstaffe Hall
Little Wood
INTAKE LA
HALL LA
MERCER'S LA
Bickerstaffe Wood
Brook Farm
Bickerstaffe Brook
Roby's Farm
Large Ox Hey House
Wood End Farm
Bradshaw's Plantation
Wood House
BARROW NOOK LA
NEW WAY
Red House Farm
Barrow Nook
SIMONSWOOD LA
Bullen's Farm
BACK LA
New Way Farm
Barrow Nook Farm
HURST'S LA
MOSS LA
Cropper's Wood
OUTLET LA
Bickerstaffe Moss
COACH RD
BEN LA
Moss Side
SINEACRE LA
HALL LA

1
8

7
17

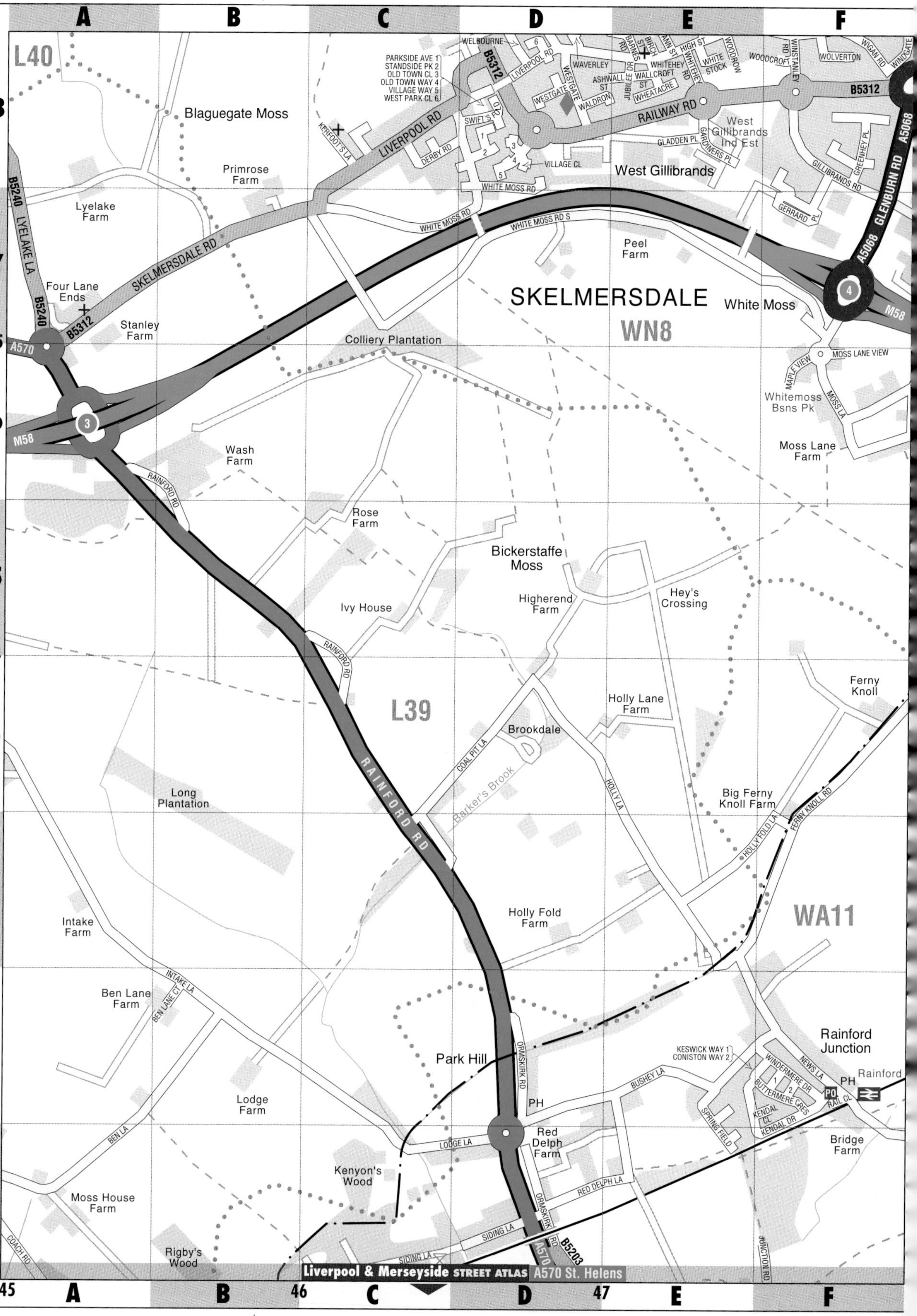
A
B
C
D
E
F
L40
Blaguegate Moss
Primrose Farm
Lyelake Farm
B5240
LYELAKE LA
SKELMERSDALE RD
Four Lane Ends
B5312
Stanley Farm
A570
M58
3
PARKSIDE AVE 1
STANDSIDE PK 2
OLD TOWN CL 3
OLD TOWN WAY 4
VILLAGE WAY 5
WEST PARK CL 6
WELBOURNE
LIVERPOOL RD
KERFOOT'S LA
DERBY RD
SWIFT'S FOLD
WESTGATE
WALDRON
ASHWALL ST
WAVERLEY
JUBILEE DR
BARNES RD
BIRCH ST
ANN ST
WHITEHEY RD
WALLCROFT ST
WHEATACRE
HIGH ST
WHITE STOCK
WOODROW
WOODCROFT
WINSTANLEY RD
WOLVERTON
WIGAN RD
WINDGATE
RAILWAY RD
B5312
VILLAGE CL
WHITE MOSS RD
GLADDEN PL
GARDINERS PL
West Gillibrands Ind Est
West Gillibrands
GILLIBRANDS RD
GREENHEY PL
GERRARD PL
A5068
GLENBURN RD
WHITE MOSS RD
WHITE MOSS RD S
Peel Farm
SKELMERSDALE
WN8
White Moss
4
M58
Colliery Plantation
MAPLE VIEW
MOSS LANE VIEW
Whitemoss Bsns Pk
MOSS LA
Moss Lane Farm
Wash Farm
RAINFORD RD
Rose Farm
Bickerstaffe Moss
Higherend Farm
Hey's Crossing
Ivy House
RAINFORD RD
L39
Holly Lane Farm
Brookdale
Ferny Knoll
COAL PIT LA
Barker's Brook
HOLLY LA
Long Plantation
RAINFORD RD
Big Ferny Knoll Farm
FERNY KNOLL RD
HOLLYFOLD LA
Intake Farm
Holly Fold Farm
WA11
INTAKE LA
Ben Lane Farm
BEN LANE CT
Park Hill
ORMSKIRK RD
KESWICK WAY 1
CONISTON WAY 2
BUSHEY LA
NEWS LA
WINDERMERE DR
BUTTERMERE CRES
KENDAL CL
KENDAL DR
SPRING FIELD
Rainford Junction
Rainford
PH
PO
RAIL CL
Lodge Farm
PH
BEN LA
LODGE LA
Red Delph Farm
Bridge Farm
Kenyon's Wood
Moss House Farm
RED DELPH LA
ORMSKIRK RD
COACH RD
SIDING LA
Rigby's Wood
A570
B5203
JUNCTION RD
8
7
05
6
5
04
4
3
03
2
1
02
45
46
47



7

18
10

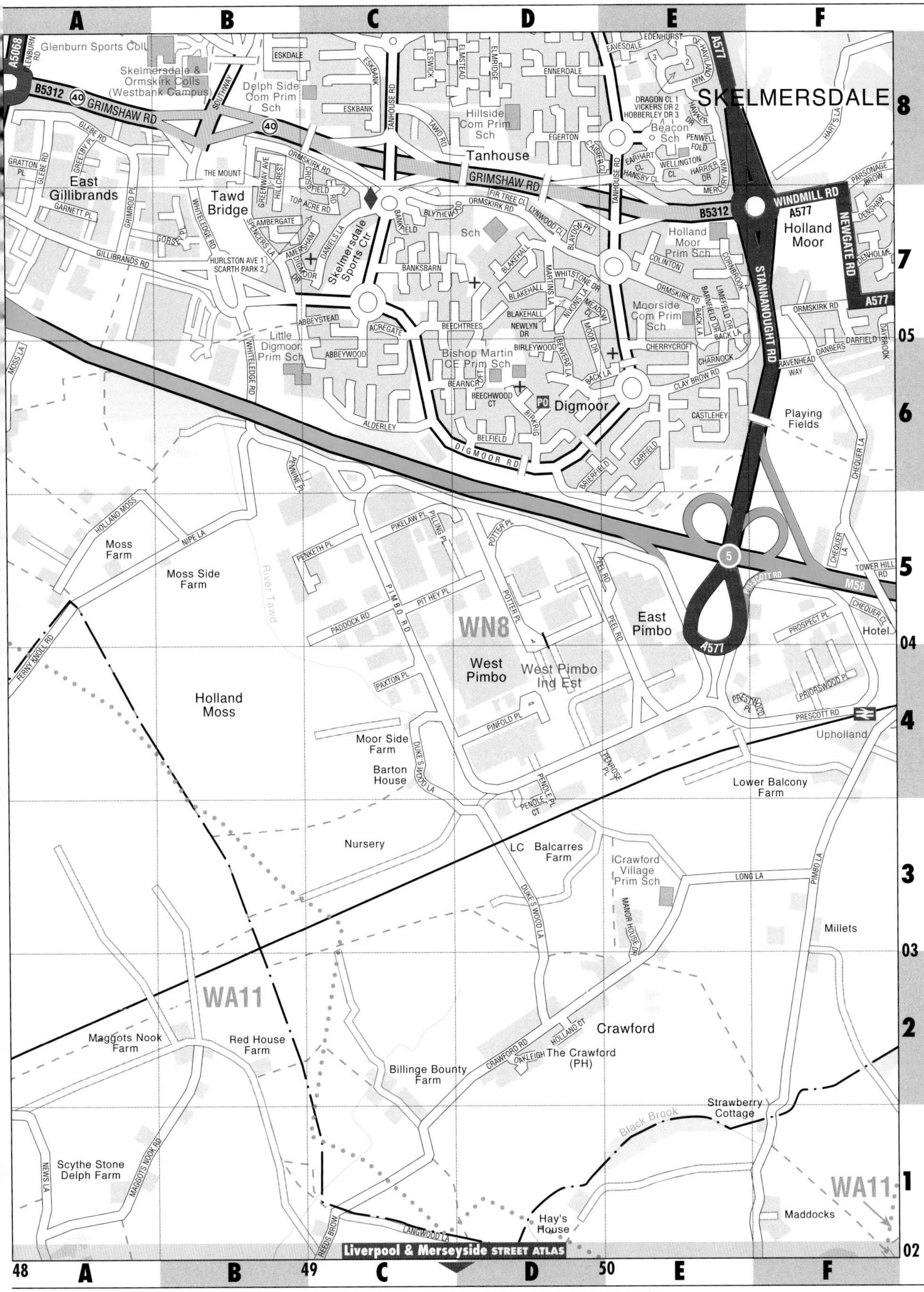
A
B
C
D
E
F
8
7
05
6
5
04
4
3
03
2
1
02
48
49
50
SKELMERSDALE
Glenburn Sports Coll
Skelmersdale &
Ormskirk Colls
(Westbank Campus)
Delph Side
Com Prim
Sch
Hillside
Com Prim
Sch
Tanhouse
Beacon
Sch
East
Gillibrands
Tawd
Bridge
Skelmersdale
Sports Ctr
Sch
Holland
Moor
Prim Sch
Holland
Moor
Moorside
Com Prim
Sch
Little
Digmoor
Prim Sch
Bishop Martin
CE Prim Sch
Digmoor
Playing
Fields
Moss
Farm
Moss Side
Farm
River Tawd
WN8
West
Pimbo
West Pimbo
Ind Est
East
Pimbo
Hotel
Holland
Moss
Moor Side
Farm
Barton
House
Upholland
Lower Balcony
Farm
Nursery
LC
Balcarres
Farm
Crawford
Village
Prim Sch
Millets
WA11
Maggots Nook
Farm
Red House
Farm
Crawford
The Crawford
(PH)
Billinge Bounty
Farm
Strawberry
Cottage
Black Brook
Scythe Stone
Delph Farm
Hay's
House
Maddocks
WA11
A5068
B5312
GRIMSHAW RD
A577
M58
WINDMILL RD
NEWGATE RD
STANNANOUGHT RD
ORMSKIRK RD
DIGMOOR RD
GILLIBRANDS RD
WHITELEDGE RD
PIMBO RD
PRESCOTT RD
DUKE'S WOOD LA
CRAWFORD RD
PIMBO LA
LONG LA
MAGGOTS NOOK RD
NEWS LA
MOSS LA
FERNY KNOLL RD
HOLLAND MOSS
NIPE LA
CHEQUER LA
TOWER HILL RD
LANGWOOD LA
REEDS BROW
PEEL RD
POTTER PL
PIT HEY PL
PADDOCK RD
PAXTON PL
PINFOLD PL
PENKETH PL
PIKELAW PL
PILLING PL
PENNINE PL
PENDLE PL
PENDLE CT
PENROSE PL
MANOR HOUSE DR
HOLLAND CT
OAKLEIGH
PRIORSWOOD PL
PRESTWOOD PL
PROSPECT PL
CHEQUER CL
RAVENHEAD WAY
DANBERS
DARFIELD
DAYBROOK
ALDERLEY
ABBEYWOOD
ABBEYSTEAD
ACREGATE
BEECHTREES
BANKSBARN
BLAKEHALL
NEWLYN DR
BIRLEYWOOD
BEARNCROFT
BEECHWOOD CT
BELFIELD
BIRKRIG
BRIERFIELD
CARFIELD
CASTLEHEY
CHARNOCK
CLAY BROW RD
CHERRYCROFT
BACK LA
COLINTON
CORNBROOK
WHITSTONE DR
MARTINS LA
NIXONS LA
MEADOW
MOOR DR
BEAVERS LA
ESKDALE
ESKBANK
TANHOUSE RD
ELSWICK
ELMSTEAD
ELMRIDGE
ENNERDALE
EGERTON
EDENHURST
EAVESDALE
DE HAVILAND WAY
DRAGON CL 1
VICKERS DR 2
HOBBERLEY DR 3
PENWELL FOLD
WELLINGTON CL
HARRIER DR
MERCURY WAY
EARHART CL
HANSBY CL
CAISER CL
FIR TREE CL
LYNWOOD CL
BLAYDON PK
BLYTHEWOOD
BANKFIELD
TOP ACRE RD
CROSSFIELD
DANIELS LA
AMERSHAM
AMBERGATE
SPENCERS LA
GREENWAY AVE
HILLCREST
THE MOUNT
SOUTHWAY
HURLSTON AVE 1
SCARTH PARK 2
GORSEY
GRIMROD PL
GARNETT PL
GLEBE RD
GREETBY PL
GRATTON PL
GLENBURN RD
HART'S LA
PARSONAGE BROW
DENSHAW
DENHOLME

A7
1 DENHOLME
2 FIELDVIEW
3 MEADOWFIELD

9
19

E5
1 COSGATE CL
2 MIDDLECOT CL
3 THE ORCHARDS

F7
1 THIRLMERE AVE
2 LATIMER CL
3 BYRON CL
4 WINCHESTER CL

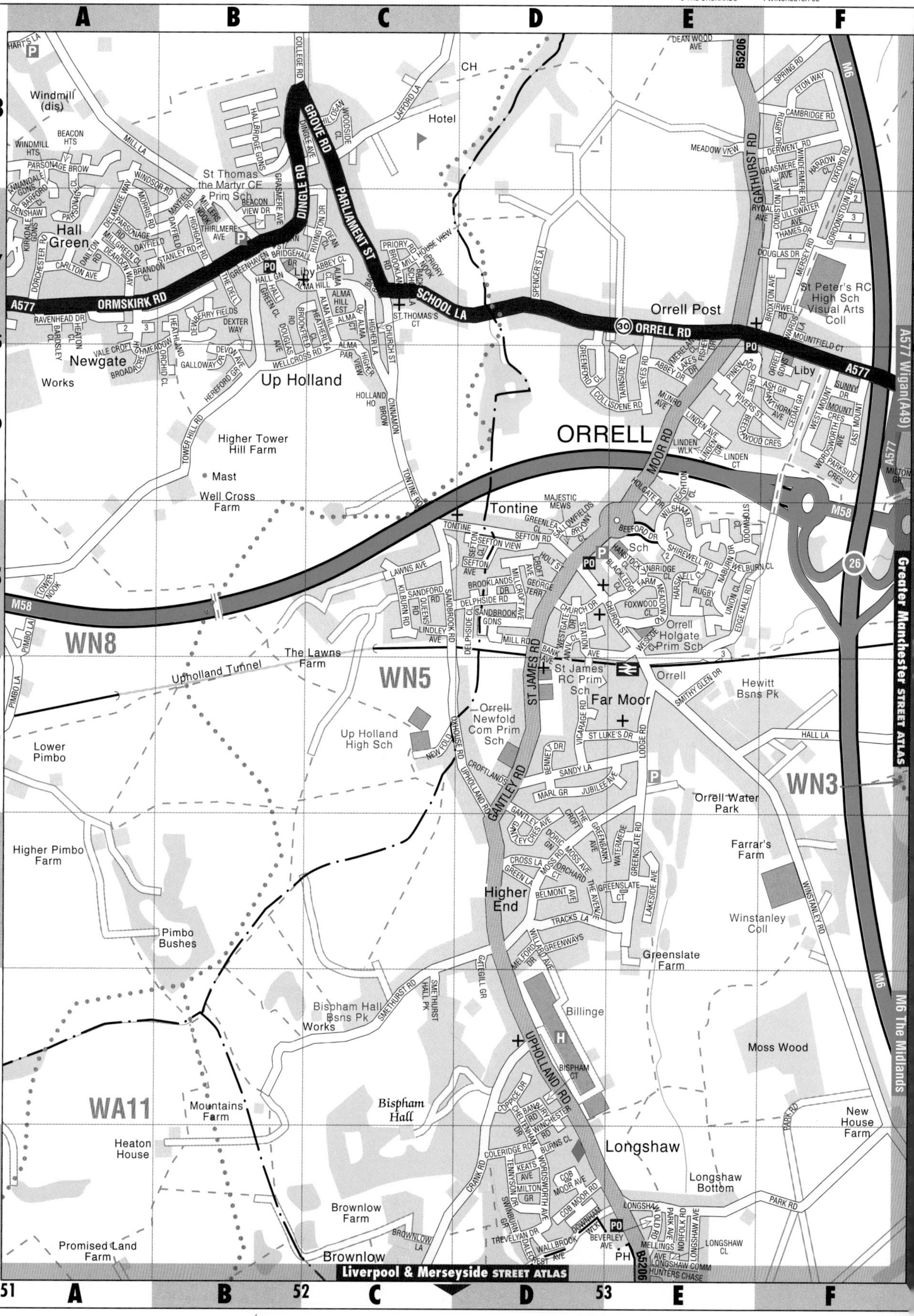




9

20
12

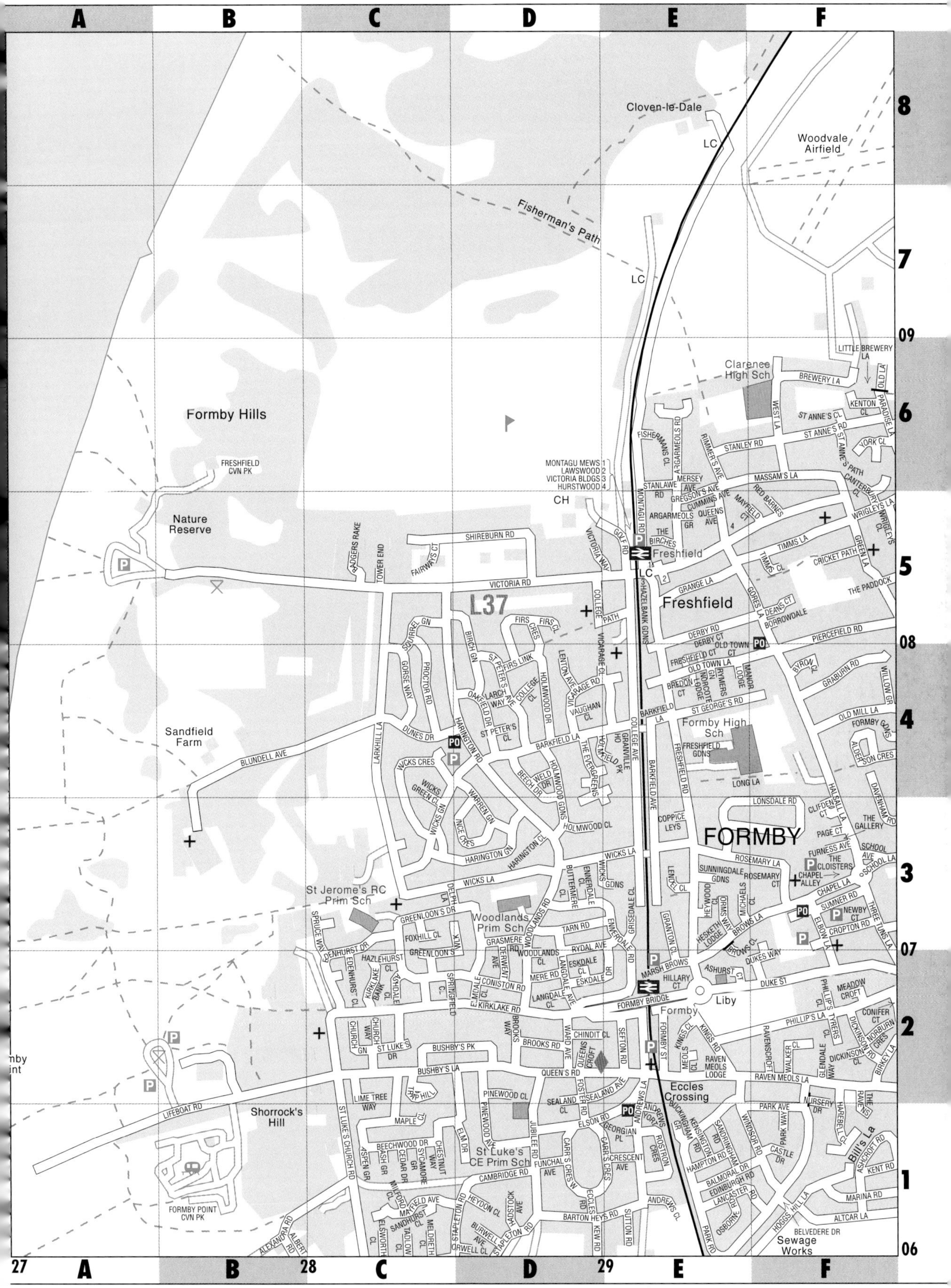
A
B
C
D
E
F
8
7
09
6
5
08
4
3
07
2
1
06
27
28
29
Cloven-le-Dale
LC
Woodvale Airfield
Fisherman's Path
LC
LITTLE BREWERY LA
OLD LA
Clarence High Sch
BREWERY LA
KENTON CL
PARADISE LA
WEST LA
ST ANNE'S CL
ST ANNE'S RD
ST ANNE'S PATH
YORK CL
Formby Hills
FISHERMANS CL
ARGARMEOLS RD
RIMMER'S AVE
STANLEY RD
CANTERBURY CL
MASSAM'S LA
FRESHFIELD CVN PK
MONTAGU MEWS 1
LAWSWOOD 2
VICTORIA BLDGS 3
HURSTWOOD 4
STANLAWE RD
MERSEY AVE
GREGSON'S AVE
CUMMINS AVE
RED BARNES
MAYFIELD CT
WRIGLEYS LA
WRIGLEYS CL
CH
MONTAGU RD
ARGARMEOLS GR
QUEENS AVE
Nature Reserve
SHIREBURN RD
BADGERS RAKE
TOWER END
FAIRWAYS CT
VICTORIA WAY
GOLF RD
THE BIRCHES
Freshfield
TIMMS LA
TIMMS CL
CRICKET PATH
GREEN LA
LC
VICTORIA RD
COLLEGE PATH
HAZELBANK GDNS
GRANGE LA
GORES LA
THE PADDOCK
L37
Freshfield
DEANS CT
BORROWDALE
SQUIRREL GN
FIRS CRES
FIRS CL
DERBY RD
DERBY CT
OLD TOWN CT
PIERCEFIELD RD
GORSE WAY
PROCTOR RD
BIRCH GN
ST PETER'S AVE
FIRS LINK
COLLEGE CL
HOLMWOOD DR
LENTON AVE
VICARAGE CL
VICARAGE RD
FRESHFIELD CT
OLD TOWN LA
MANOR LODGE
BYRON CL
GRABURN RD
WILLOW GR
LARCH WAY
OAKFIELD DR
VAUGHAN CL
BREDON CT
NORCOTE LODGE
RYMERS GN
ST GEORGE'S RD
BARKFIELD LA
DUNES DR
ST PETER'S CL
Formby High Sch
OLD MILL LA
FORMBY GDNS
Sandfield Farm
LARKHILL LA
HARINGTON RD
BARKFIELD LA
THE EVERGREENS
HOLMFIELD PK
GRANVILLE HO
COLLEGE AVE
FRESHFIELD RD
FRESHFIELD GDNS
ALDERSON CRES
BLUNDELL AVE
WICKS CRES
WICKS GREEN CL
WICKS GN
WARREN GN
BEECH DR
WELD DR
HOLMWOOD GDNS
BARKFIELD AVE
LONG LA
HALSALL LA
DAVENHAM RD
LONSDALE RD
CLIFDEN CT
INCE CRES
HOLMWOOD CL
COPPICE LEYS
FORMBY
THE GALLERY
PAGE CT
HARINGTON GN
HARINGTON CL
WICKS LA
WICKS GDNS
ENNERDALE CL
GRISEDALE CL
LENDAL CL
ROSEMARY LA
FURNESS AVE
THE CLOISTERS
SCHOOL AVE
SCHOOL LA
WICKS LA
SUNNINGDALE GDNS
ROSEMARY CT
CHAPEL ALLEY
St Jerome's RC Prim Sch
DELPH LA
BUTTERMERE CL
GRANTON CL
HEYWOOD CL
ORMS WAY
MICHAELS CL
CHAPEL LA
SUMNER RD
NEWBY CT
THREE TUNS LA
Woodlands Prim Sch
GREENLOON'S DR
WOODLANDS RD
TARN RD
ENNERDALE RD
HESKETH LODGE
BROWS LA
CROPTON RD
ELBOW LA
SPRUCE WAY
FOXHILL CL
VICK
GRASMERE RD
RYDAL AVE
BROWS CL
DUKES WAY
DENHURST DR
HAZLEHURST CL
GREENLOON'S
DERWENT AVE
WOODLANDS CL
ESKDALE CL
LANGDALE AVE
MARSH BROWS
ASHURST CT
EDENHURST CL
KIRKLAKE BANK
RYDALE CL
SPRINGFIELD
ELMDALE CL
CONISTON RD
MERE RD
ESKDALE DR
HILLARY CT
DUKE ST
PHILLIPS CL
MEADOW CROFT
LANGDALE CL
FORMBY BRIDGE
Formby
Liby
KIRKLAKE RD
CONIFER CT
CHURCH RD
CHURCH WAY
BROOKS WAY
WARD AVE
CHINDIT CL
SEFTON RD
FORMBY ST
KINGS CL
KINGS RD
PHILLIP'S LA
TYRERS CL
DICKINSON CL
NORBURN CRES
ST LUKE'S DR
BUSHBY'S PK
BROOKS RD
QUEENS CROFT
MEOLS CL
RAVEN MEOLS LODGE
RAVENSCROFT
WALKER CL
GLENDALE WAY
DICKINSON RD
BIRKEY LA
BUSHBY'S LA
QUEEN'S RD
RAVEN MEOLS LA
Eccles Crossing
LIME TREE WAY
TRAP HILL
PINEWOOD CL
SEALAND AVE
SEALAND CL
FOSTER RD
ANDREWS LA
PARK AVE
NURSERY DR
THE RAVENS
Shorrock's Hill
LIFEBOAT RD
MAPLE CL
PINEWOOD AVE
ELSON RD
GEORGIAN PL
YORK RD
ROSTRON CRES
BUCKINGHAM GR
KENSINGTON RD
SANDRINGHAM RD
WINDSOR RD
PARK WAY
HAREBELL CL
ST LUKE'S CHURCH RD
BEECHWOOD DR
ASPEN GR
ASH GR
CEDAR DR
SYCAMORE GR
CHESTNUT WAY
ELM DR
St Luke's CE Prim Sch
JUBILEE RD
CARR'S CRES W
CARR'S CRES
CRESCENT AVE
HAMPTON RD
CASTLE DR
Bill's La
ASHCROFT RD
KENT RD
FUNCHAL AVE
CAMBRIDGE RD
BALMORAL DR
EDINBURGH RD
MARINA RD
MILFORD CL
MAYFIELD AVE
HEYDON CL
HADSTOCK AVE
ECCLES RD
LANCASTER RD
OSBORNE RD
HOGGS HILL LA
ALTCAR LA
FORMBY POINT CVN PK
SANDHURST CL
STAPLETON RD
BURWELL AVE
STAPLETON RD
BARTON HEYS RD
SUTTON RD
ANDREWS CL
PARK RD
BELVEDERE DR
Sewage Works
ALEXANDRA RD
ALBERT RD
ELSWORTH CL
TADLOW CL
MELDRETH CL
ORWELL CL
KEW RD
nby
int

2
12

11
21

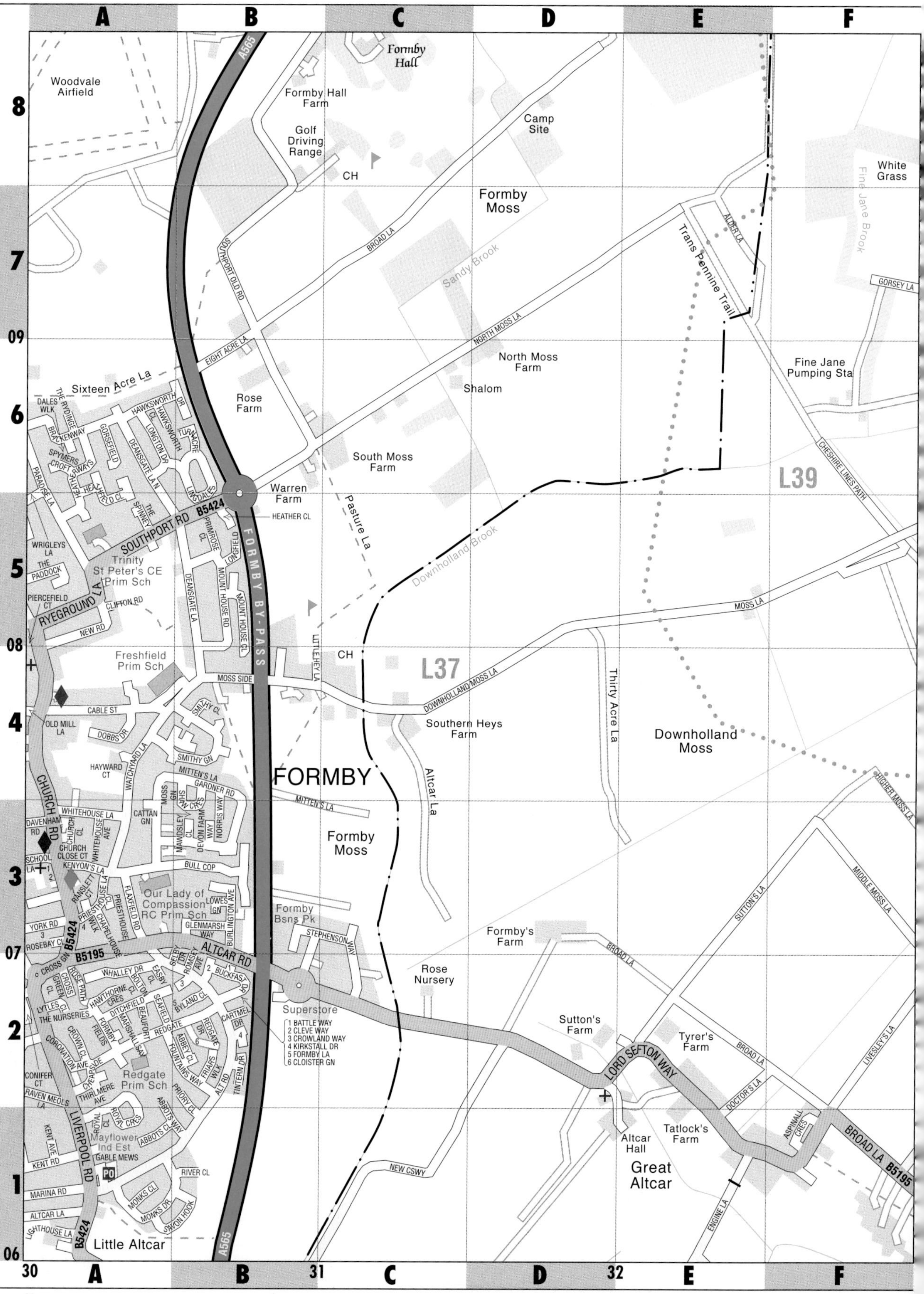
A
B
C
D
E
F
8
7
09
6
5
08
4
3
07
2
1
06
30
31
32
Woodvale Airfield
Formby Hall
Formby Hall Farm
Golf Driving Range
CH
Camp Site
Formby Moss
White Grass
Fine Jane Brook
A565
SOUTHPORT OLD RD
BROAD LA
Sandy Brook
ALDER LA
Trans Pennine Trail
GORSEY LA
EIGHT ACRE LA
NORTH MOSS LA
North Moss Farm
Shalom
Fine Jane Pumping Sta
Sixteen Acre La
DALES WLK
THE RYDINGS
HAWKSWORTH DR
HAWKSWORTH CL
LONGTON DR
TURNACRE
BRACKENWAY
GORSEFIELD
DEANSGATE LA N
SPYMERS CROFT
SWAYS
HEATHWAY
PARADISE LA
LINSDALES
THE SPINNEY
Rose Farm
South Moss Farm
Warren Farm
HEATHER CL
Pasture La
CHESHIRE LINES PATH
L39
SOUTHPORT RD
B5424
WRIGLEYS LA
THE PADDOCK
Trinity St Peter's CE Prim Sch
PRIMROSE CL
LONGFIELD
FORMBY BY-PASS
Downholland Brook
PIERCEFIELD CT
RYEGROUND LA
CLIFTON RD
NEW RD
DEANSGATE LA
MOUNT HOUSE RD
MOUNT HOUSE CL
LITTLE HEY LA
MOSS LA
Freshfield Prim Sch
MOSS SIDE
L37
DOWNHOLLAND MOSS LA
Thirty Acre La
CABLE ST
SMITHY CL
OLD MILL LA
DOBBS DR
Southern Heys Farm
Downholland Moss
SMITHY GN
HAYWARD CT
WATCHYARD LA
MITTEN'S LA
GARDNER RD
FORMBY
HIGHER MOSS LA
CHURCH RD
MOSS GN
SHAW CRES
NORRIS WAY
WHITEHOUSE LA
CATTAN GN
MAWDSLEY CL
DEVON FARM WAY
Altcar La
DAVENHAM RD
CHURCH CL
WHITEHOUSE AVE
Formby Moss
CHURCH CLOSE CT
SCHOOL LA
KENYON'S LA
BULL COP
MIDDLE MOSS LA
RANSLETT CT
PRIESTHOUSE LA
PRIESTHOUSE CL
FLAXFIELD RD
Our Lady of Compassion RC Prim Sch
LOWES GN
BURLINGTON AVE
SUTTON'S LA
Formby Bsns Pk
YORK RD
PRIESTS WLK
CHAPEL HOUSE
GLENMARSH WAY
STEPHENSON WAY
Formby's Farm
ROSEBAY CL
ALTCAR RD
B5195
CROSS GN
CROSS GREEN CL
ROSE PATH
WHALLEY DR
BOLTON AVE
EASBY CL
SELBY DR
ROMSEY AVE
BUCKFAST DR
Rose Nursery
BROAD LA
LYTLES CL
THE NURSERIES
HAWTHORNE CRES
DITCHFIELD
SEAFIELD
BYLAND CL
Superstore
1 BATTLE WAY
2 CLEVE WAY
3 CROWLAND WAY
4 KIRKSTALL DR
5 FORMBY LA
6 CLOISTER GN
Sutton's Farm
CARTMEL DR
CROWN CL
FORMBY FIELDS
MARSHALLS CL
BEAUFORT RD
REDGATE
ABBEY CL
REDGATE DR
LORD SEFTON WAY
Tyrer's Farm
LIVESLEY'S LA
CORONATION AVE
FOUNTAINS WAY
FRIARS WLK
ALT RD
TINTERN DR
Redgate Prim Sch
CONIFER CT
THIRLMERE AVE
RAVEN MEOLS LA
PRIORY CL
DOCTOR'S LA
ASPINALL CRES
Altcar Hall
Tatlock's Farm
ROYAL CL
ROYAL CRES
ABBOTS CL
ABBOTS WAY
BROAD LA
B5195
KENT AVE
Mayflower Ind Est
GABLE MEWS
LIVERPOOL RD
KENT RD
PO
RIVER CL
NEW CSWY
Great Altcar
MARINA RD
MONKS CL
MONKS DR
SWAN HOOK
ENGINE LA
ALTCAR LA
LIGHTHOUSE LA
Little Altcar

A3
1 KENSINGTON CT
2 SPRINGFIELD HO
3 THE HAWTHORNS
4 THE GOWERY

11
3

22
14

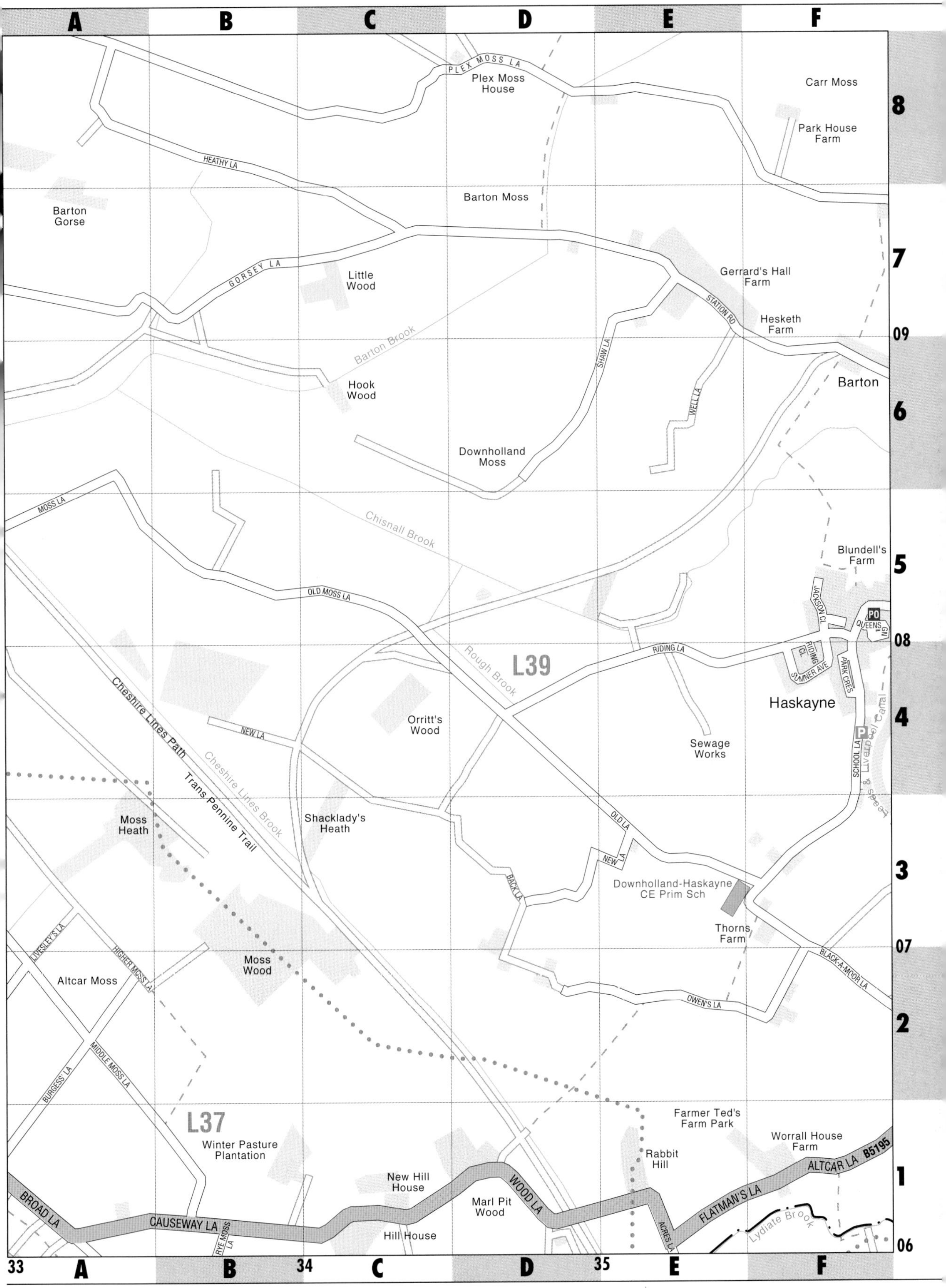
A
B
C
D
E
F
8
7
09
6
5
08
4
3
07
2
1
06
33
34
35
PLEX MOSS LA
Plex Moss House
Carr Moss
Park House Farm
HEATHY LA
Barton Moss
Barton Gorse
GORSEY LA
Little Wood
Gerrard's Hall Farm
STATION RD
Hesketh Farm
Barton Brook
SHAW LA
Hook Wood
Barton
WELL LA
Downholland Moss
MOSS LA
Chisnall Brook
Blundell's Farm
OLD MOSS LA
JACKSON CL
PO
QUEENS GN
RIDING LA
RIDING CL
SUMNER AVE
PARK CRES
Rough Brook
L39
Haskayne
Orritt's Wood
NEW LA
Cheshire Lines Path
Sewage Works
P
SCHOOL LA
Leeds & Liverpool Canal
Cheshire Lines Brook
Trans Pennine Trail
Moss Heath
Shacklady's Heath
OLD LA
NEW LA
BACK LA
Downholland-Haskayne CE Prim Sch
Thorns Farm
LIVESLEY'S LA
HIGHER MOSS LA
Altcar Moss
Moss Wood
BLACK-A-MOOR LA
OWEN'S LA
MIDDLE MOSS LA
BURGESS' LA
L37
Winter Pasture Plantation
Farmer Ted's Farm Park
Worrall House Farm
Rabbit Hill
B5195
ALTCAR LA
New Hill House
WOOD LA
Marl Pit Wood
FLATMAN'S LA
BROAD LA
CAUSEWAY LA
RYE MOSS LA
Hill House
ACRES LA
Lydiate Brook

4
14

13
23

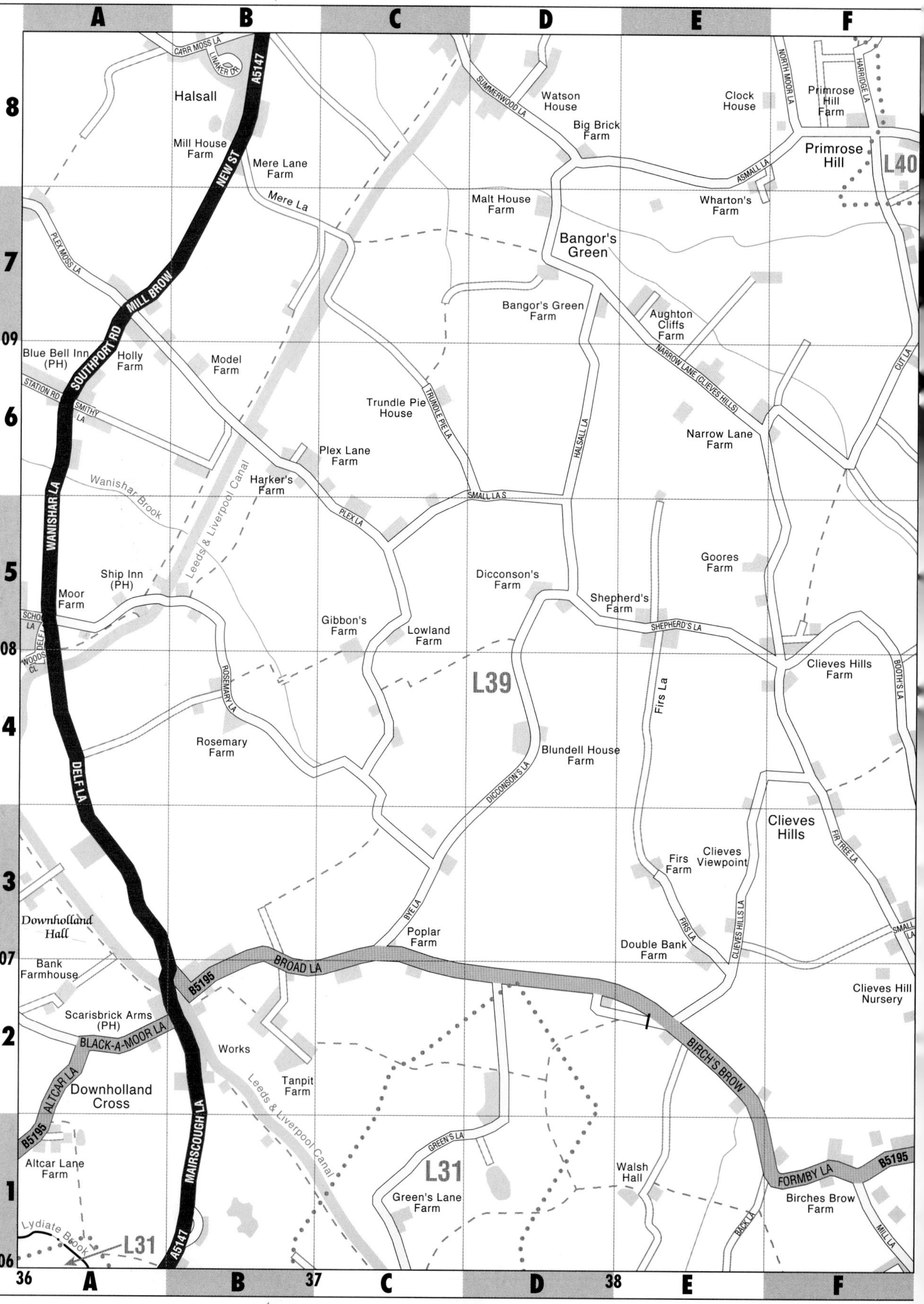
A
B
C
D
E
F
8
7
09
6
5
08
4
3
07
2
1
06
36
37
38
CARR MOSS LA
LINAKER DR
A5147
Halsall
Mill House Farm
NEW ST
Mere Lane Farm
Mere La
PLEX MOSS LA
MILL BROW
SOUTHPORT RD
Blue Bell Inn (PH)
Holly Farm
Model Farm
STATION RD
SMITHY LA
Wanishar Brook
WANISHAR LA
Leeds & Liverpool Canal
Harker's Farm
Plex Lane Farm
PLEX LA
Ship Inn (PH)
Moor Farm
SCHOOL LA
DELF LA
WOODS CL
ROSEMARY LA
Rosemary Farm
Gibbon's Farm
Lowland Farm
Trundle Pie House
TRUNDLE PIE LA
SUMMERWOOD LA
Watson House
Big Brick Farm
Malt House Farm
Bangor's Green
Bangor's Green Farm
SMALL LA S
HALSALL LA
Dicconson's Farm
L39
DICCONSON'S LA
Blundell House Farm
DELF LA
BYE LA
Poplar Farm
Downholland Hall
Bank Farmhouse
B5195
BROAD LA
Scarisbrick Arms (PH)
BLACK-A-MOOR LA
Works
Tanpit Farm
ALTCAR LA
Downholland Cross
B5195
MAIRSCOUGH LA
Altcar Lane Farm
Lydiate Brook
L31
A5147
Leeds & Liverpool Canal
GREEN'S LA
L31
Green's Lane Farm
Clock House
NORTH MOOR LA
Primrose Hill Farm
HARRIDGE LA
Primrose Hill
L40
ASMALL LA
Wharton's Farm
Aughton Cliffs Farm
NARROW LANE (CLIEVES HILLS)
CUT LA
Narrow Lane Farm
Goores Farm
Shepherd's Farm
SHEPHERD'S LA
Clieves Hills Farm
BOOTH'S LA
Firs La
Clieves Hills
FIR TREE LA
Firs Farm
Clieves Viewpoint
FIRS LA
CLIEVES HILLS LA
Double Bank Farm
SMALL LA
Clieves Hill Nursery
BIRCH'S BROW
Walsh Hall
FORMBY LA
B5195
Birches Brow Farm
BACK LA
MILL LA

13
5

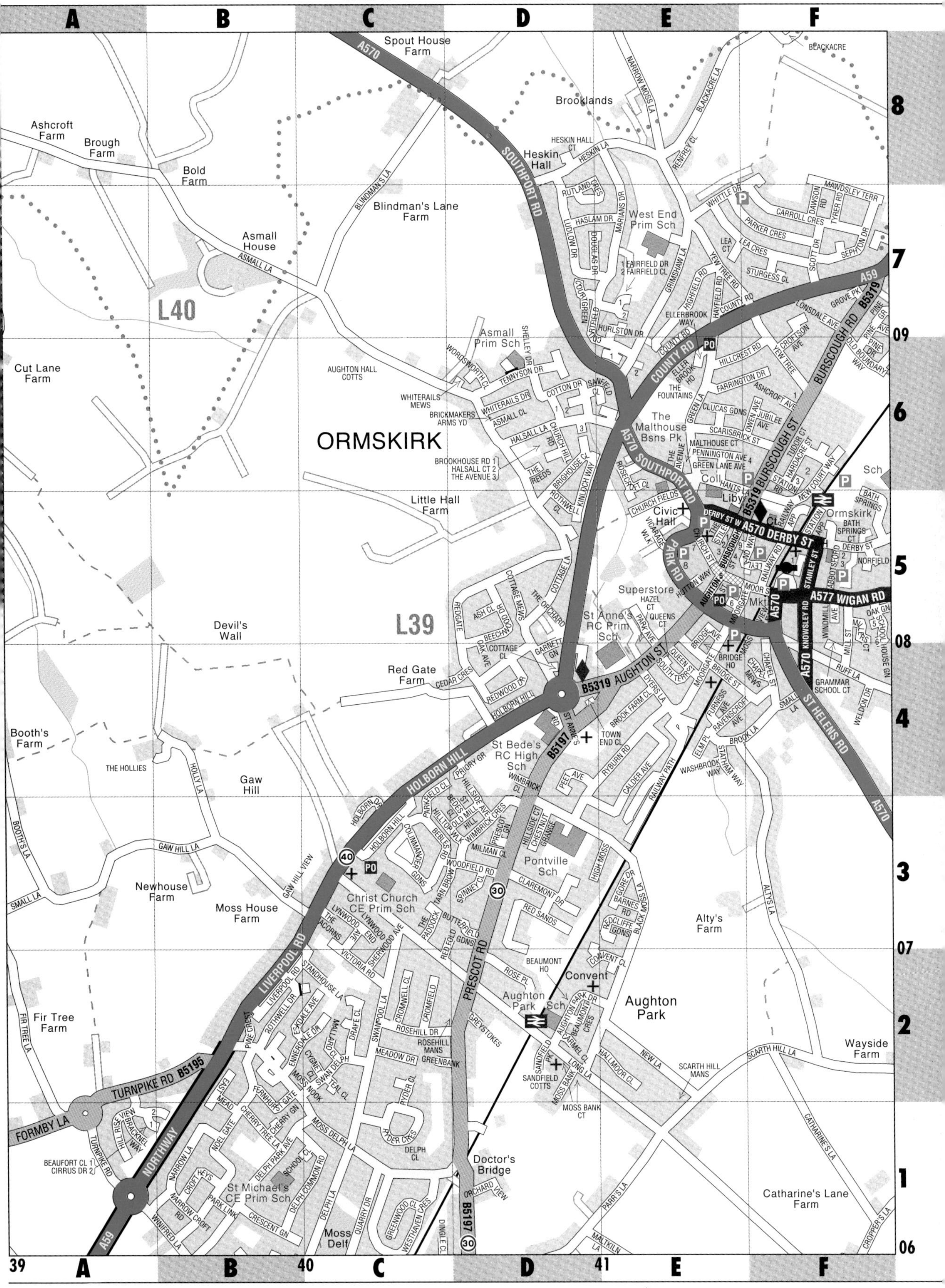

A
B
C
D
E
F
8
7
09
6
5
08
4
3
07
2
1
06
39
40
41
ORMSKIRK
L40
L39
Spout House Farm
Ashcroft Farm
Brough Farm
Bold Farm
Brooklands
Heskin Hall
Blindman's Lane Farm
West End Prim Sch
Asmall House
Cut Lane Farm
Asmall Prim Sch
AUGHTON HALL COTTS
The Malthouse Bsns Pk
Little Hall Farm
Civic Hall
Coll
Liby
Ormskirk
Sch
Superstore
St Anne's RC Prim Sch
Devil's Wall
Red Gate Farm
Booth's Farm
THE HOLLIES
Gaw Hill
St Bede's RC High Sch
Bridge HO
Newhouse Farm
Moss House Farm
Christ Church CE Prim Sch
Pontville Sch
Alty's Farm
Fir Tree Farm
Aughton Park
Convent
BEAUMONT HO
Wayside Farm
SCARTH HILL MANS
SANDFIELD COTTS
MOSS BANK CT
Doctor's Bridge
St Michael's CE Prim Sch
Moss Delf
Catharine's Lane Farm
A570
SOUTHPORT RD
A59
B5319
COUNTY RD
BURSCOUGH ST
A570 DERBY ST
DERBY ST W
A577 WIGAN RD
PARK RD
AUGHTON ST
ST HELENS RD
KNOWSLEY RD
STANLEY ST
HOLBORN HILL
B5197
PRESCOT RD
LIVERPOOL RD
NORTHWAY
TURNPIKE RD
B5195
FORMBY LA
ASMALL LA
BLINDMAN'S LA
NARROW MOSS LA
BLACKACRE LA
BLACKACRE
HESKIN HALL CT
HESKIN LA
RENFREY CL
MAWDSLEY TERR
WHITTLE DR
CARROLL CRES
PARKER CRES
DAWSON RD
TYRER RD
SCOTT DR
SEPHTON DR
LEA CT
LEA CRES
STURGESS CL
RUTLAND CRES
HASLAM DR
LUDLOW DR
DOUGLAS DR
MARIANS DR
GRIMSHAW LA
YEW TREE RD
HAYFIELD RD
HIGHFIELD RD
1 FAIRFIELD DR
2 FAIRFIELD CL
COURTGREEN
HURLSTON DR
ELLERBROOK WAY
COUNTY RD
LONSDALE AVE
GROVE PK
PINE CL
PINE GR
OLD BOUNDARY WAY
CROFTSON AVE
HILLCREST RD
FARRINGTON DR
ASHCROFT AVE
CLUCAS GDNS
JUBILEE AVE
OWEN AVE
SCARISBRICK ST
TUDOR CT
HARDACRE ST
NEW COURT WAY
STATION RD
MALTHOUSE CT
PENNINGTON AVE
GREEN LANE AVE
HANTS LA
THE AVENUE
GREEN LA
ELLER BROOK HO
THE FOUNTAINS
WORDSWORTH CL
SHELLEY DR
TENNYSON DR
COTTON DR
SANFIELD CL
WHITERAILS MEWS
WHITERAILS DR
BRICKMAKERS ARMS YD
ASMALL CL
HALSALL LA
CHURCH HILL RD
BROOKHOUSE RD 1
HALSALL CT 2
THE AVENUE 3
THE REEDS
BRIGHOUSE CL
KINLOCH WAY
ROTHWELL CL
ROSECROFT CL
CHURCH FIELDS
VICARAGE WLK
BATH SPRINGS
BATH SPRINGS CT
STATION APP
RAILWAY RD
MOOR ST
MOORGATE
CHAPEL ST
BRIDGE ST
HUTTON WAY
AUGHTON ST
DERBY ST
NORFIELD
ABBOTSFORD
OAK GN
SCHOOL HOUSE GN
MILL ST
WINDMILL AVE
RUFF LA
GRAMMAR SCHOOL CT
WELDON DR
COTTAGE LA
COTTAGE MEWS
THE ORCHARD
REDGATE
ASH CL
HOLLY CL
BEECH
OAK AVE
COTTAGE CL
GARNETT GN
HAZEL CT
QUEENS CT
PARK AVE
CEDAR CRES
REDWOOD DR
HOLBORN HILL
ST ANNE'S RD
TOWN END CL
BROOK FARM CL
DYERS LA
QUEEN ST
SOUTH TERR
FURNESS AVE
RAVENSCROFT AVE
BROOK LA
SMALL LA
ELM PL
STATHAM WAY
WASHBROOK WAY
RAILWAY PATH
CALDER AVE
RYBURN RD
PEET AVE
WIMBRICK CL
PRIORY GR
PARKFIELD CL
HILLSIDE AVE
HILLTOP WLK
OLD MILL HILL
WIMBRICK CRES
HILLSIDE CT
CHESTNUT GRANGE
PRESCOT GN
MILMAN CL
COLLIMANDER GDNS
BEBLES RD
WOODFIELD RD
TARN BROW
SPINNEY CL
CLAREMONT DR
RED SANDS
HIGH MOSS
GORE DR
BARNES RD
REDCLIFFE GDNS
BLACK MOSS LA
CONVENT CL
ALTYS LA
HOLLY LA
BOOTH'S LA
GAW HILL LA
GAW HILL VIEW
SMALL LA
LYNWOOD AVE
LYNWOOD END
THE ACORNS
SHERWOOD AVE
VICTORIA RD
THE PADDOCK
BUTTERFIELD GDNS
RED FOLD
ROSE PL
STANDHOUSE LA
PINE CREST
ROTHWELL DR
ESKDALE AVE
ENNERDALE DR
MALLARD CL
DRAKE CL
SWAN DELPH
CYGNET CL
TEAL CL
MOSS NOOK
SWANPOOL LA
CROMWELL CL
CROMFIELD
ROSEHILL DR
ROSEHILL MANS
MEADOW DR
GREENBANK
GREYSTOKES
AUGHTON PARK DR
BEAUMONT CRES
CARMEL CL
SANDFIELD PK
LONG LA
MOSS BANK
HALLMOOR CL
NEW LA
SCARTH HILL LA
CATHARINE'S LA
RYDER CL
RYDER CRES
DELPH CL
FERNHURST GATE
CHERRY TREE LA
CHERRY GN
EAST MEAD
NOEL GATE
SCHOOL CL
DELPH PARK AVE
DELPH COMMON RD
MOSS DELPH LA
NARROW LA
CROFT HEYS
PARK LINK
NARROW CROFT RD
CRESCENT GN
DELPH LA
QUARRY DR
GREENWOOD CL
WESTHAVEN CRES
DINGLE CL
ORCHARD VIEW
PARR'S LA
MALTKILN LA
CROPPER'S LA
FIR TREE LA
HILL RISE VIEW
BRACKNEL WAY
TURNPIKE RD
BEAUFORT CL 1
CIRRUS DR 2
WINIFRED LA
HOLBORN HILL
PO
P
40
30

15
25

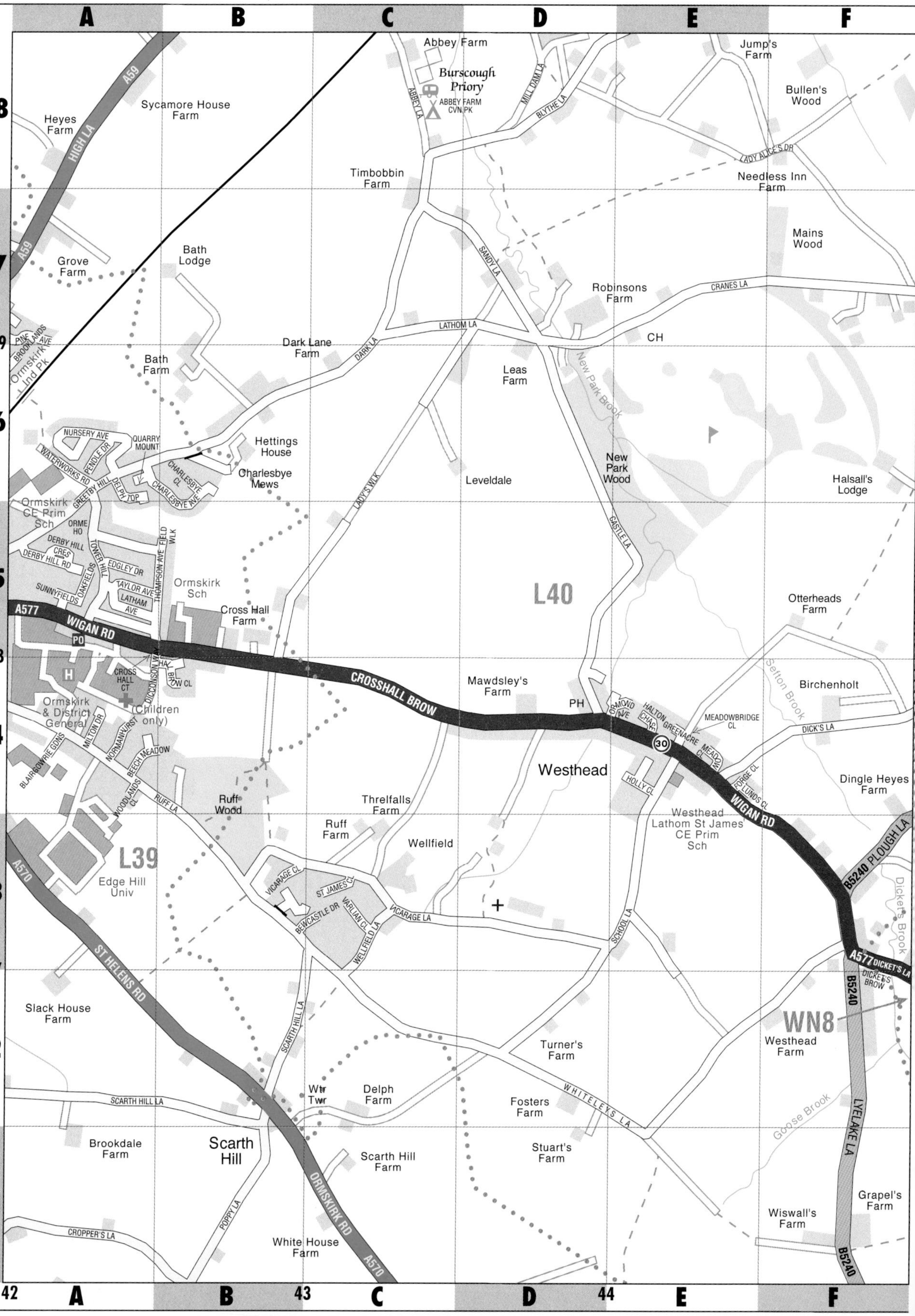
A
B
C
D
E
F
8
7
09
6
5
08
4
3
07
2
1
06
42
43
44
Abbey Farm
Burscough Priory
ABBEY LA
ABBEY FARM CVN PK
MILL DAM LA
BLYTHE LA
Jump's Farm
Bullen's Wood
LADY ALICE'S DR
Needless Inn Farm
Mains Wood
Heyes Farm
HIGH LA
A59
Sycamore House Farm
Timbobbin Farm
Grove Farm
Bath Lodge
SANDY LA
Robinsons Farm
CRANES LA
LATHOM LA
CH
Dark Lane Farm
DARK LA
BROOKLANDS AVE
Ormskirk Ind PK
Bath Farm
Leas Farm
New Park Brook
NURSERY AVE
QUARRY MOUNT
PENDLE DR
WATERWORKS RD
Hettings House
Charlesbye Mews
CHARLESBYE CL
CHARLESBYE AVE
GREETBY HILL
DELPH
Leveldale
New Park Wood
Halsall's Lodge
Ormskirk CE Prim Sch
ORME HO
DERBY HILL CRES
DERBY HILL RD
TOWER HILL
OAKFIELDS
EDGLEY DR
THOMPSON AVE
FIELD WLK
LADY'S WLK
CASTLE LA
SUNNYFIELDS
TAYLOR AVE
LATHAM AVE
Ormskirk Sch
L40
Otterheads Farm
A577
WIGAN RD
PO
Cross Hall Farm
H
CROSS HALL CT
DICCONSON WAY
CROSSHALL BROW
Mawdsley's Farm
Birchenholt
Ormskirk & District General
(Children only)
MILTON DR
NORMANHURST
BLAIRGOWRIE GDNS
BEECH MEADOW
PH
ORMOND AVE
HALTON CHAC
GREENACRE CL
MEADOWBRIDGE CL
DICK'S LA
30
Westhead
HOLLY CL
FORGE CL
LUNDS CL
Dingle Heyes Farm
WOODLANDS CL
RUFF LA
Ruff Wood
Threlfalls Farm
Ruff Farm
Wellfield
Westhead Lathom St James CE Prim Sch
L39
Edge Hill Univ
A570
VICARAGE CL
ST JAMES CL
BEWCASTLE DR
VARLIAN CL
WELLFIELD LA
VICARAGE LA
SCHOOL LA
B5240 PLOUGH LA
Dickets Brook
A577 DICKET'S LA
DICKET'S BROW
B5240
ST HELENS RD
Slack House Farm
SCARTH HILL LA
WN8
Westhead Farm
Turner's Farm
WHITELEYS LA
Wtr Twr
Delph Farm
Fosters Farm
Goose Brook
LYELAKE LA
Brookdale Farm
Scarth Hill
Scarth Hill Farm
Stuart's Farm
ORMSKIRK RD
Grapel's Farm
Wiswall's Farm
POPPY LA
CROPPER'S LA
White House Farm

15
7

26 18

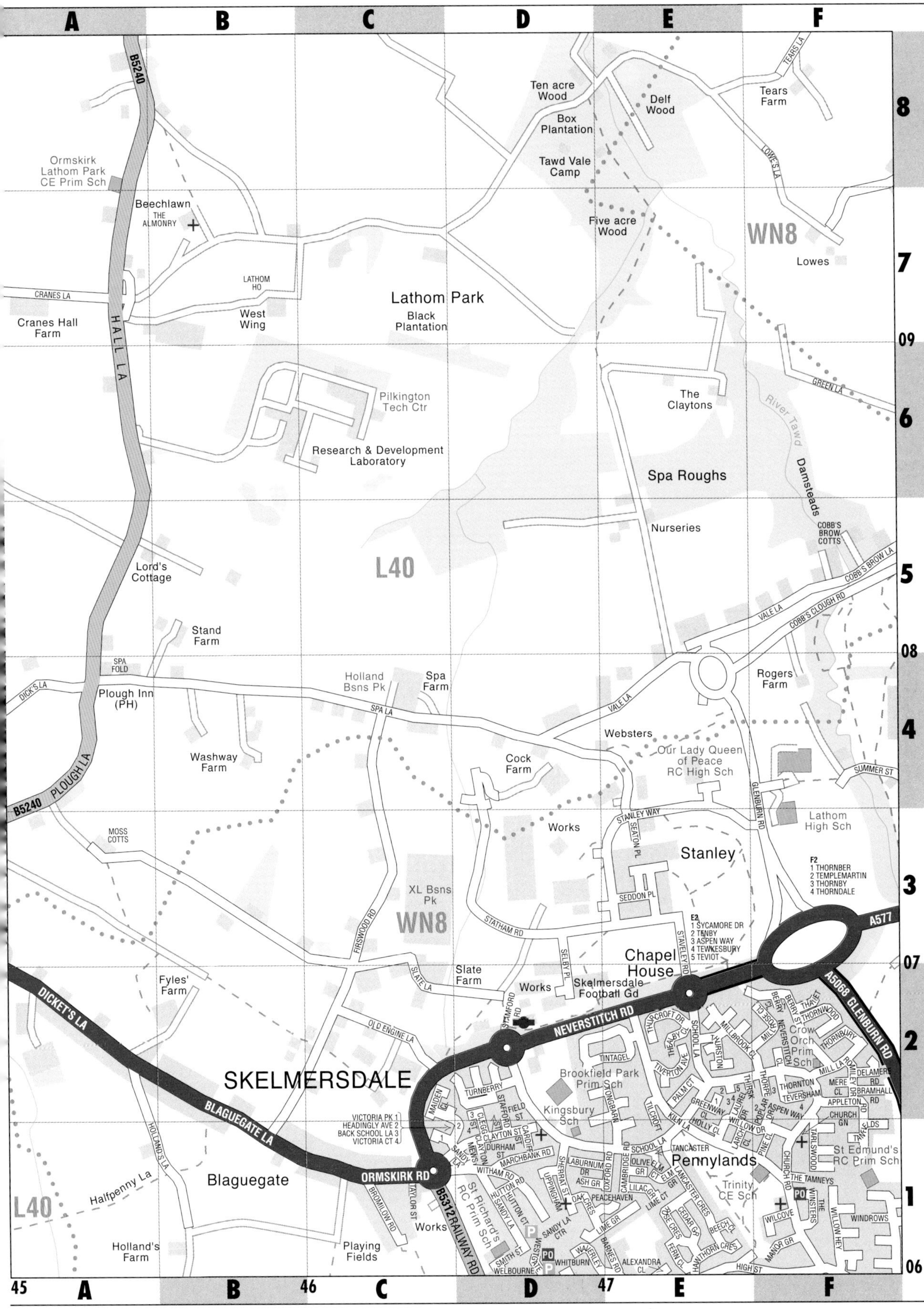
A B C D E F
8
7
09
6
5
08
4
3
07
2
1
06
45 46 47
B5240
HALL LA
PLOUGH LA
Ormskirk Lathom Park CE Prim Sch
Beechlawn
THE ALMONRY
LATHOM HO
West Wing
CRANES LA
Cranes Hall Farm
Ten acre Wood
Box Plantation
Tawd Vale Camp
Delf Wood
Five acre Wood
TEARS LA
Tears Farm
LOWE'S LA
WN8
Lowes
Lathom Park
Black Plantation
GREEN LA
The Claytons
River Tawd
Pilkington Tech Ctr
Research & Development Laboratory
Spa Roughs
Damsteads
Nurseries
COBB'S BROW COTTS
COBB'S BROW LA
L40
Lord's Cottage
VALE LA
COBB'S CLOUGH RD
Stand Farm
SPA FOLD
DICK'S LA
Plough Inn (PH)
Holland Bsns Pk
Spa Farm
SPA LA
Rogers Farm
Websters
Our Lady Queen of Peace RC High Sch
Washway Farm
Cock Farm
SUMMER ST
GLENBURN RD
Lathom High Sch
MOSS COTTS
Works
STANLEY WAY
SEATON PL
Stanley
F2
1 THORNBER
2 TEMPLEMARTIN
3 THORNBY
4 THORNDALE
XL Bsns Pk
WN8
SEDDON PL
STATHAM RD
FIRSWOOD RD
E2
1 SYCAMORE DR
2 TENBY
3 ASPEN WAY
4 TEWKESBURY
5 TEVIOT
A577
STAVELEY RD
SELBY PL
Chapel House
Slate Farm
SLATE LA
Works
Skelmersdale Football Gd
A5068 GLENBURN RD
Fyles' Farm
DICKET'S LA
STAMFORD RD
NEVERSTITCH RD
OLD ENGINE LA
SKELMERSDALE
Brookfield Park Prim Sch
Crow Orch Prim Sch
Kingsbury Sch
BLAGUEGATE LA
VICTORIA PK 1
HEADINGLY AVE 2
BACK SCHOOL LA 3
VICTORIA CT 4
HOLLAND'S LA
Blaguegate
ORMSKIRK RD
Pennylands
Trinity CE Sch
St Edmund's RC Prim Sch
Halfpenny La
L40
BROMILOW RD
TAYLOR ST
B5312 RAILWAY RD
St Richard's RC Prim Sch
Works
Holland's Farm
Playing Fields
TURNBERRY
MAIDEN CL
STAFFORD ST
FIELD ST
CLAYTON ST
DURHAM ST
MARCHBANK RD
WITHAM RD
HUTTON RD
SANDY LA
UPPINGHAM
SHERRAT ST
LABURNUM DR
ASH GR
OXFORD RD
CAMBRIDGE RD
SCHOOL LA
OLIVE GR
LILAC GR
LIME CT
TANCASTER
LANCASTER CRES
CEDAR GR
BEECH CL
HAWTHORN CRES
FERN CL
ALEXANDRA CL
HIGH ST
PEACEHAVEN
LIME GR
WAVERLEY
BARNES RD
WHITBURN
WELBOURNE
SMITH ST
WESTGATE
SANDY LA CTR
TINTAGEL
THURCROFT DR
TIVERTON AVE
TONGBARN
TILCROFT
KILN LA
PALM CT
GREENWAY
HOLLY CL
LARCH CL
WILLOW DR
PINE CL
ASPEN WAY
CHURCH RD
THORNTON
TEVERSHAM
MERE CL
DELAMERE RD
BRAMHALL RD
APPLETON RD
CHURCH GN
MILL LA
THORNBURY
THORNWOOD
BERRY ST
NEVERSTITCH CL
THIRSK
POPLAR DR
LAUREL DR
MILLBROOK CL
SCHOOL LA
ISLINGTON
YARLSWOOD
THE TAMNEYS
WINSTERS
THE WILLOW HEY
WINDROWS
WILCOVE
MANOR GR
PO
P

8 18

17 27

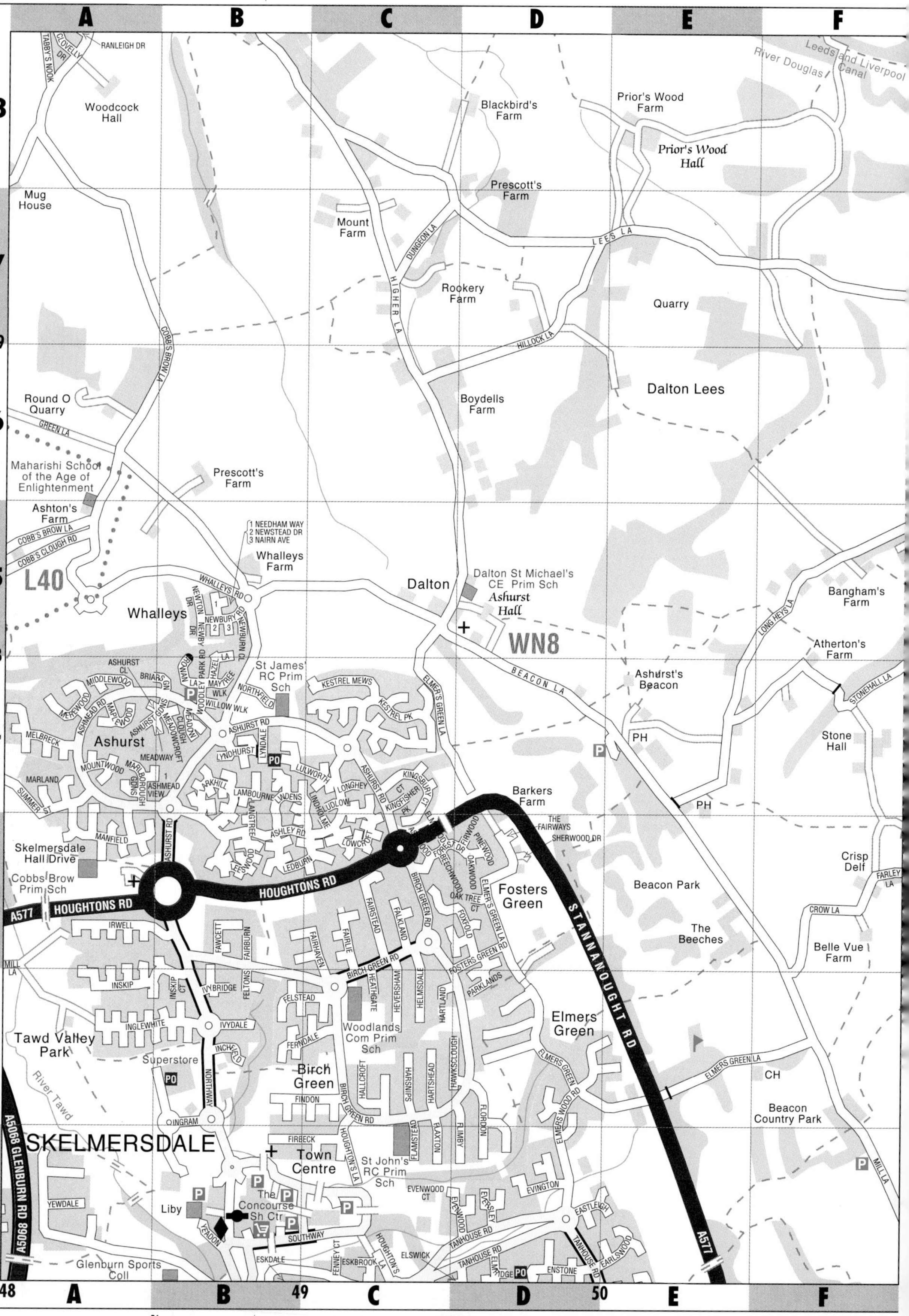


B4
1 MARLBOROUGH CT

17 9

28

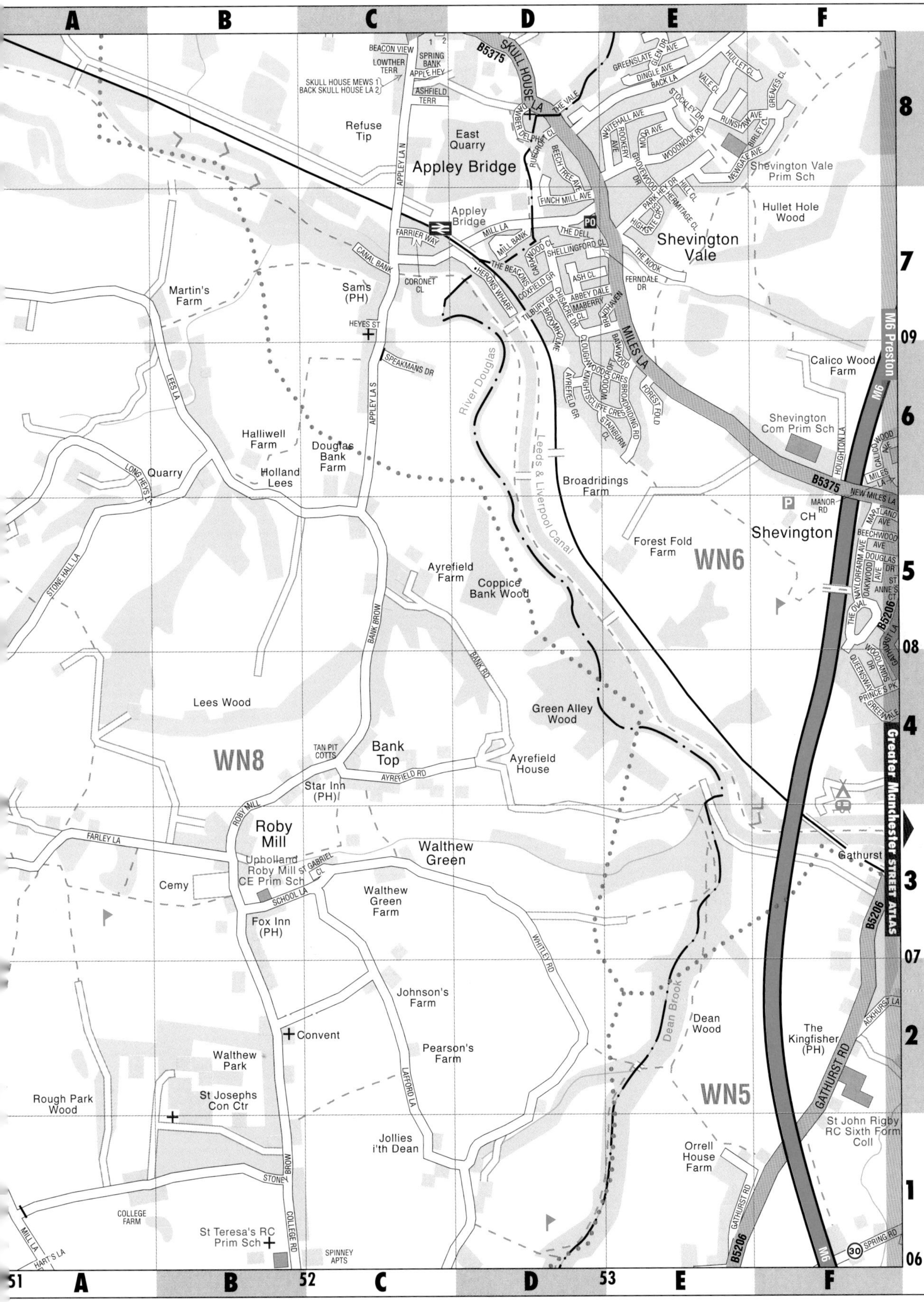
A
B
C
D
E
F
8
7
09
6
5
08
4
3
07
2
1
06
51
52
53
Appley Bridge
East Quarry
Refuse Tip
Shevington Vale
Shevington Vale Prim Sch
Hullet Hole Wood
Martin's Farm
Sams (PH)
Halliwell Farm
Douglas Bank Farm
Holland Lees
Quarry
Calico Wood Farm
Shevington Com Prim Sch
Broadridings Farm
Forest Fold Farm
Shevington
WN6
Ayrefield Farm
Coppice Bank Wood
Lees Wood
WN8
Green Alley Wood
Bank Top
Ayrefield House
Star Inn (PH)
Roby Mill
Walthew Green
Upholland Roby Mill CE Prim Sch
Cemy
Walthew Green Farm
Fox Inn (PH)
Gathurst
Johnson's Farm
Convent
Pearson's Farm
Dean Wood
The Kingfisher (PH)
Walthew Park
St Josephs Con Ctr
Rough Park Wood
WN5
St John Rigby RC Sixth Form Coll
Jollies i'th Dean
Orrell House Farm
College Farm
St Teresa's RC Prim Sch
Spinney Apts
River Douglas
Leeds & Liverpool Canal
Dean Brook
B5375
B5206
M6
M6 Preston
Greater Manchester STREET ATLAS
SKULL HOUSE LA
MILES LA
APPLEY LA N
APPLEY LA S
BANK BROW
BANK RD
AYREFIELD RD
ROBY MILL
FARLEY LA
SCHOOL LA
ST GABRIEL CL
WHITLEY RD
LAFFORD LA
COLLEGE RD
STONE
MILL LA
HART'S LA
LEES LA
LONG HEYS LA
STONE HALL LA
CANAL BANK
HEYES ST
SPEAKMANS DR
CORONET CL
FARRIER WAY
MILL LA
MILL BANK
THE BEACONS
HERONS WHARF
BEACON VIEW
LOWTHER TERR
SPRING BANK
APPLE HEY
ASHFIELD TERR
SKULL HOUSE MEWS 1
BACK SKULL HOUSE LA 2
FINCH MILL AVE
BEECH TREE AVE
RUECROFT CL
THE VALE
THE DELL
SHELLINGFORD CL
CARRWOOD CL
COXFIELD GR
TILBURY GR
ASH CL
ABBEY DALE
MABERRY CL
BROOMHOLME
CHISACRE DR
BRADHAVEN
AYREFIELD GR
KNIGHTSCLIFFE CRES
CLOUGHWOOD CRES
WOODCROFT
BANKWOOD
BROADRIDING RD
STAINBURN CL
FOREST FOLD
FERNDALE DR
THE NOOK
HIGHGATE CRES
PARK HEY DR
HERMITAGE CL
HILL CL
GROVEWOOD DR
MOOR AVE
WOODNOOK RD
ROOKERY AVE
WHITEHALL AVE
STOCKLEY DR
VALE CL
RUNSHAW AVE
BIRLEY CL
NEWGATE AVE
GREAVES CL
HULLET CL
BACK LA
DINGLE AVE
GREENSLATE CT
GLEN DR
AVE
HOUGHTON LA
CALICO WOOD AVE
MILES LA
NEW MILES LA
MANOR RD
CH
MARTLAND AVE
BEECHWOOD AVE
DOUGLAS DR
MAYLORFARM AVE
OAKWOOD AVE
ST ANNE'S CT
THE OVAL
QUEENSWAY
WOODLANDS DR
PRINCE'S PK
GREENVALE
GATHURST RD
ACKHURST LA
SPRING RD
30
TAN PIT COTTS
PO
P

10

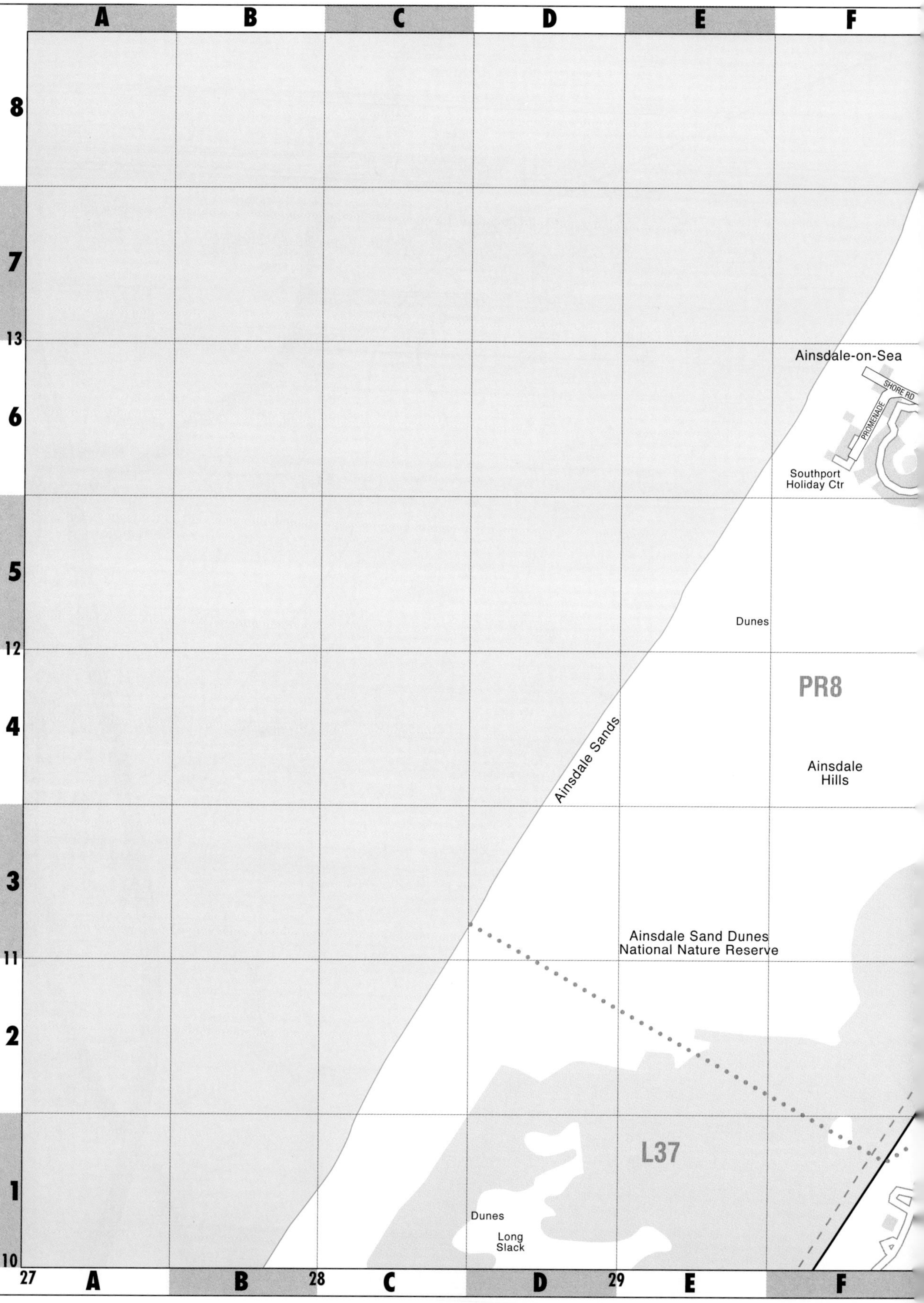
A
B
C
D
E
F
8
7
13
6
5
12
4
3
11
2
1
10
27
28
29
Ainsdale-on-Sea
SHORE RD
PROMENADE
Southport
Holiday Ctr
Dunes
PR8
Ainsdale Sands
Ainsdale
Hills
Ainsdale Sand Dunes
National Nature Reserve
L37
Dunes
Long
Slack

11

34
22

A
B
C
D
E
F
8
7
6
5
4
3
2
1
13
12
11
10
30
31
32
Recn Gd
Birkdale Hills
Dunes
Ainsdale and Birkdale Sandhills Nature Reserve
Howes House
COASTAL RD
Birkdale High Sch
Cemy
PR8
SOUTHPORT
CH
Recn Gd
Railway Cottages
PH
Anderson's Farm
Ainsdale
Halsall Moss
Liby
Allot Gdns
Trans Pennine Trail
Shoreside Prim Sch
Merefield Sch
Ainsdale St John's CE Prim Sch
White Otter Farm
Dunes
Hill House Farm
Big Ball's Hill
Sewage Works
Plex Moss
Kings Meadow Prim Sch
Mast
West End Lodge
Segar's Farm
St John Stone RC Prim Sch
Woodvale
Cheshire Lines Path
WILLOWBANK HOLIDAY HOME & TOURING PK
Headbolt Farm
L39
Caravan Park
Motel
Woodvale Airfield
Formby Wood
L37
Gettern Farm
Trans Pennine Trail
A565 WATERLOO RD
A5267 LIVERPOOL RD
LIVERPOOL RD
LIVERPOOL AVE
A565 FORMBY BY-PASS
SOUTHPORT OLD RD
CROWN BLDGS
Sch
CENTRAL AVE
WINDY HARBOUR RD
CARR LA
RANELAGH DR
NIXON'S LA
HEATHFIELD RD
PHILIP DR
ELIZABETH AVE
MARY AVE
GEORGE DR
OAKWOOD AVE
ELM PARK DR
SEGAR'S LA
CHATSWORTH RD
KNOWLE AVE
HAREWOOD AVE
UPTON AVE
CHILTERN RD
MICKLETON DR
STRATFORD CL
BARFORD CL
ARDEN CL
GRAFTON DR
DANEWAY
SHORE RD
BELVEDERE RD
SANDRINGHAM RD
MOUNTWOOD LODGE
LONGTON CT
SHERWOOD HO
STATION RD
QUEEN CHARLOTTE VILLAS
BURNLEY RD
FAIRFIELD RD
FAULKNER GDNS
FAULKNER CL
BERWICK AVE
MILLHOUSE LODGE
BRADSHAW'S LA
REGAL CT
MILL RD
LIMONT RD
GREEN WLK
UNIT RD
SALFORD RD
SALFORD CT
HILLSVIEW RD
CHESTERFIELD RD
CHESTERFIELD CL
KENILWORTH RD
BLUNDELL LINKS CT
LONGCLIFFE DR
THE PADDOCK
SUNBURY DR
STAVELEY RD
ORCHARD LA
THE ORCHARDS
SANDBROOK RD
CONISTON CT
KESWICK CL
BOWNESS AVE
WINDERMERE CRES
PENRITH AVE
GLENEAGLES DR
ULDALE CL
WATERFOOT AVE
WOODSIDE AVE
FURNESS CL
THIRLMERE DR
PINFOLD LA
SANDBROOK WAY
THE BROOKDALE
MEADOW LA
HEATHER CL
CHERRY RD
LILAC AVE
ROSE CRES
SOMERSET DR
DORSET AVE
CORNWALL WAY
DUNLOP AVE
VALE CRES
MOOR LA
MOOR CL
WOODVALE RD
PLEX MOSS LA
SIXPENNY LA
ARUNDEL RD
HALSALL RD
DUNSTER RD
LYNTON RD
CLOVELLY DR
DUNBAR CRES
RYDER CRES
FARNBOROUGH RD
WELWYN AVE
ALSTON CT
30

12
22

21
35

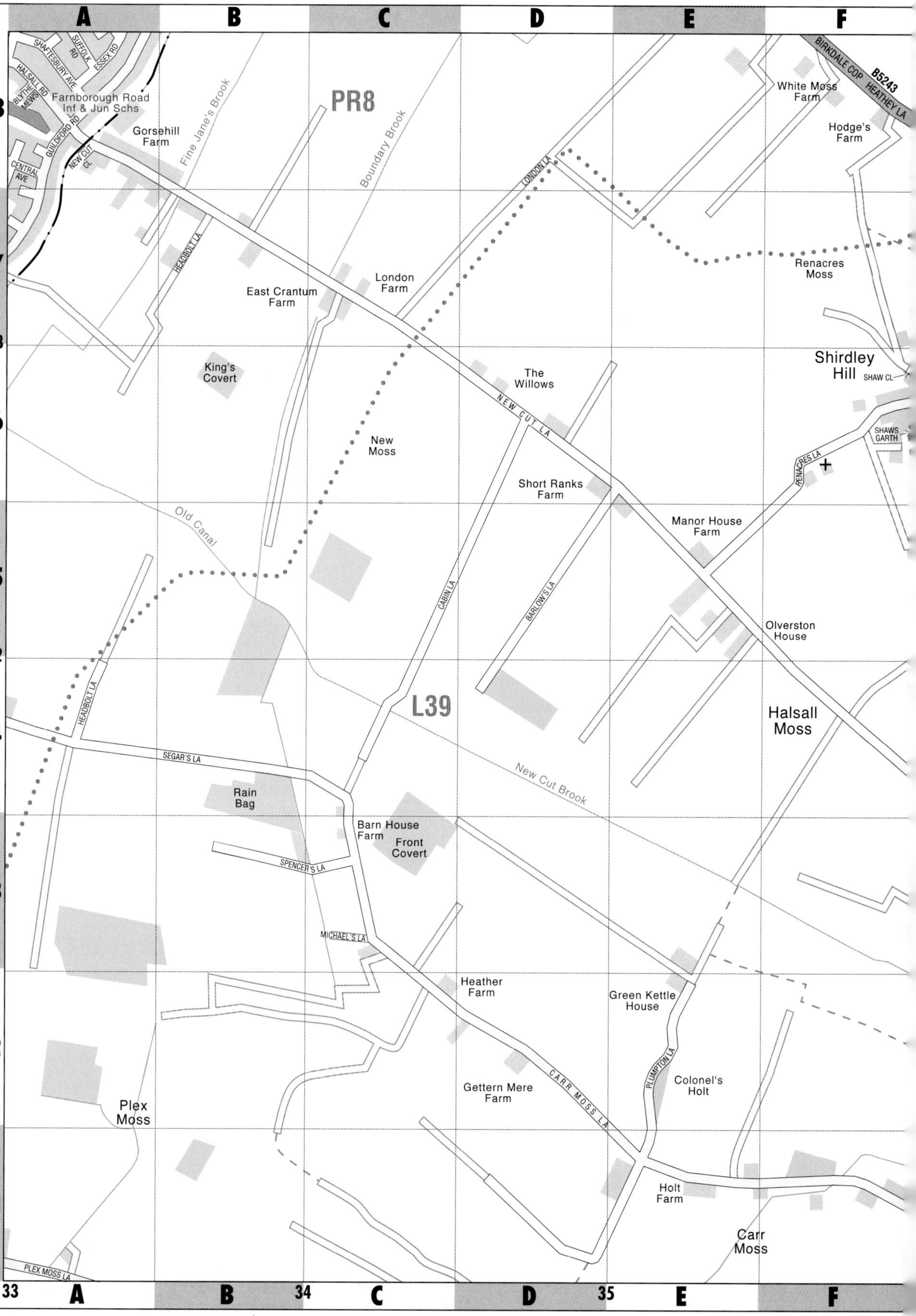
A
B
C
D
E
F
PR8
L39
SHAFTESBURY AVE
SUFFOLK RD
ESSEX RD
HALSALL RD
BLYTHE MEWS
Farnborough Road Inf & Jun Schs
GUILDFORD RD
NEW CUT CL
CENTRAL AVE
Gorsehill Farm
Fine Jane's Brook
Boundary Brook
HEADBOLT LA
East Crantum Farm
London Farm
LONDON LA
White Moss Farm
BIRKDALE COP
B5243
HEATHEY LA
Hodge's Farm
Renacres Moss
Shirdley Hill
SHAW CL
SHAWS GARTH
RENACRES LA
King's Covert
The Willows
NEW CUT LA
New Moss
Short Ranks Farm
Manor House Farm
Old Canal
CABIN LA
BARLOW'S LA
Olverston House
Halsall Moss
SEGAR'S LA
Rain Bag
New Cut Brook
Barn House Farm
Front Covert
SPENCER'S LA
MICHAEL'S LA
Heather Farm
Green Kettle House
PLUMPTON LA
Colonel's Holt
Gettern Mere Farm
CARR MOSS LA
Plex Moss
Holt Farm
Carr Moss
PLEX MOSS LA
8
7
13
6
5
12
4
3
11
2
1
10
33
34
35

21
13

36 24

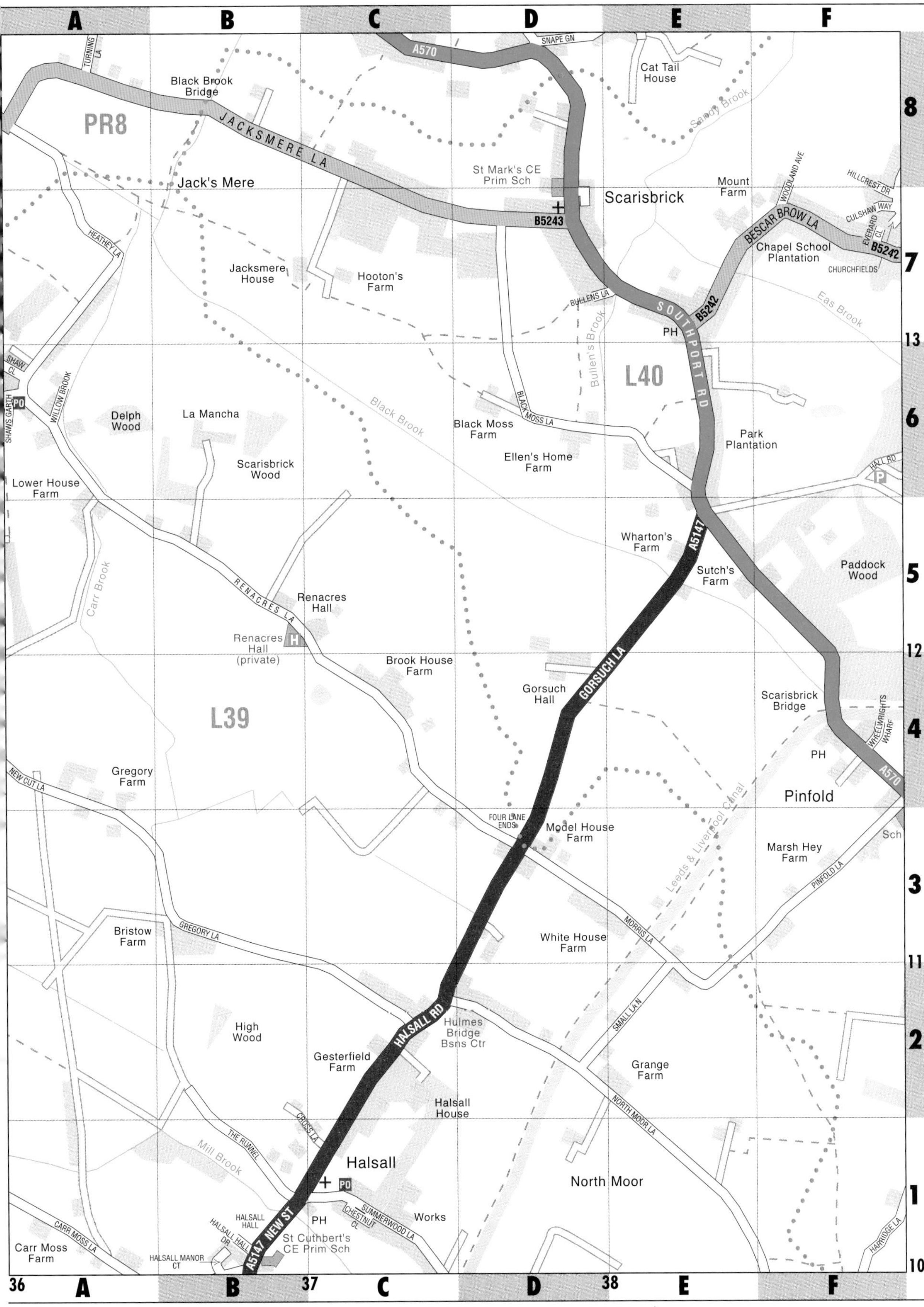
A B C D E F
A570
SNAPE GN
Cat Tail House
Black Brook Bridge
TURNING LA
PR8
JACKSMERE LA
Sandy Brook
Jack's Mere
St Mark's CE Prim Sch
Scarisbrick
Mount Farm
WOODLAND AVE
HILLCREST DR
BESCAR BROW LA
CULSHAW WAY
EVERARD CL
B5243
B5242
Chapel School Plantation
CHURCHFIELDS
HEATHEY LA
Jacksmere House
Hooton's Farm
BULLENS LA
SOUTHPORT RD
Eas Brook
PH
SHAW CL
WILLOW BROOK
Bullen's Brook
L40
PO
SHAWS GARTH
Delph Wood
La Mancha
Black Brook
Black Moss Farm
BLACK MOSS LA
Park Plantation
Ellen's Home Farm
HALL RD
Lower House Farm
Scarisbrick Wood
P
Wharton's Farm
A5147
Sutch's Farm
Paddock Wood
Carr Brook
RENACRES LA
Renacres Hall
Renacres Hall (private)
H
Brook House Farm
GORSUCH LA
Gorsuch Hall
Scarisbrick Bridge
WHEELWRIGHTS WHARF
L39
PH
Gregory Farm
NEW CUT LA
Pinfold
A570
FOUR LANE ENDS
Model House Farm
Leeds & Liverpool Canal
Marsh Hey Farm
Sch
PINFOLD LA
Bristow Farm
GREGORY LA
MORRIS LA
White House Farm
SMALL LA N
High Wood
HALSALL RD
Hulmes Bridge Bsns Ctr
Gesterfield Farm
Grange Farm
Halsall House
NORTH MOOR LA
CROSS LA
THE RUNNEL
Mill Brook
Halsall
PO
North Moor
HALSALL HALL
HALSALL HALL DR
PH
CHESTNUT CL
SUMMERWOOD LA
Works
CARR MOSS LA
Carr Moss Farm
A5147 NEW ST
St Cuthbert's CE Prim Sch
HALSALL MANOR CT
HARRIDGE LA
8 7 13 6 5 12 4 3 11 2 1 10
36 A B 37 C D 38 E F

14 24

23
37

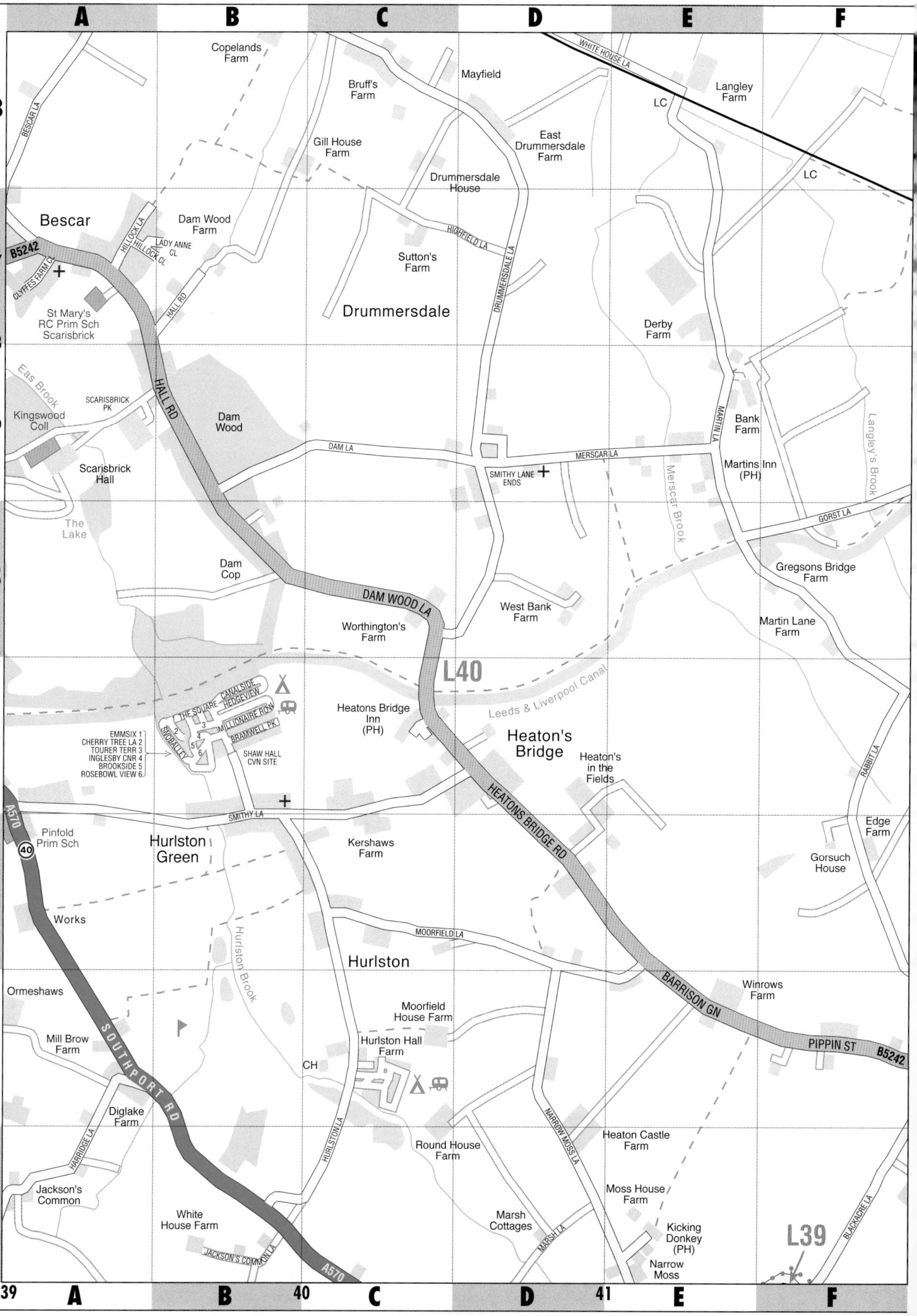
A
B
C
D
E
F
8
7
13
6
5
12
4
3
11
2
1
10
39
40
41
Copelands Farm
Bruff's Farm
Mayfield
WHITE HOUSE LA
Langley Farm
LC
BESCAR LA
Gill House Farm
East Drummersdale Farm
Drummersdale House
LC
Bescar
Dam Wood Farm
HILLOCK LA
LADY ANNE CL
HILLOCK CL
HIGHFIELD LA
B5242
CLYFFES FARM CL
Sutton's Farm
HALL RD
DRUMMERSDALE LA
Drummersdale
St Mary's RC Prim Sch Scarisbrick
Derby Farm
Eas Brook
SCARISBRICK PK
Kingswood Coll
HALL RD
Dam Wood
MARTIN LA
Bank Farm
Langley's Brook
DAM LA
MERSCAR LA
Scarisbrick Hall
SMITHY LANE ENDS
Martins Inn (PH)
Mercar Brook
The Lake
GORST LA
Dam Cop
Gregsons Bridge Farm
DAM WOOD LA
West Bank Farm
Worthington's Farm
Martin Lane Farm
L40
CANALSIDE
HEDGEVIEW
THE SQUARE
MILLIONAIRE ROW
BRAMWELL PK
Heatons Bridge Inn (PH)
Leeds & Liverpool Canal
Heaton's Bridge
SNOBALLEY
EMMSIX 1
CHERRY TREE LA 2
TOURER TERR 3
INGLESBY CNR 4
BROOKSIDE 5
ROSEBOWL VIEW 6
SHAW HALL CVN SITE
Heaton's in the Fields
RABBIT LA
HEATONS BRIDGE RD
SMITHY LA
A570
Pinfold Prim Sch
40
Hurlston Green
Kershaws Farm
Edge Farm
Gorsuch House
Works
MOORFIELD LA
Hurlston Brook
Hurlston
Ormeshaws
BARRISON GN
Winrows Farm
Moorfield House Farm
Mill Brow Farm
SOUTHPORT RD
Hurlston Hall Farm
PIPPIN ST
B5242
CH
Diglake Farm
HARRIDGE LA
HURLSTON LA
NARROW MOSS LA
Round House Farm
Heaton Castle Farm
Jackson's Common
Moss House Farm
White House Farm
Marsh Cottages
Kicking Donkey (PH)
L39
BLACKACRE LA
MARSH LA
JACKSON'S COMMON LA
A570
Narrow Moss
A
B
C
D
E
F

23
15

38
26

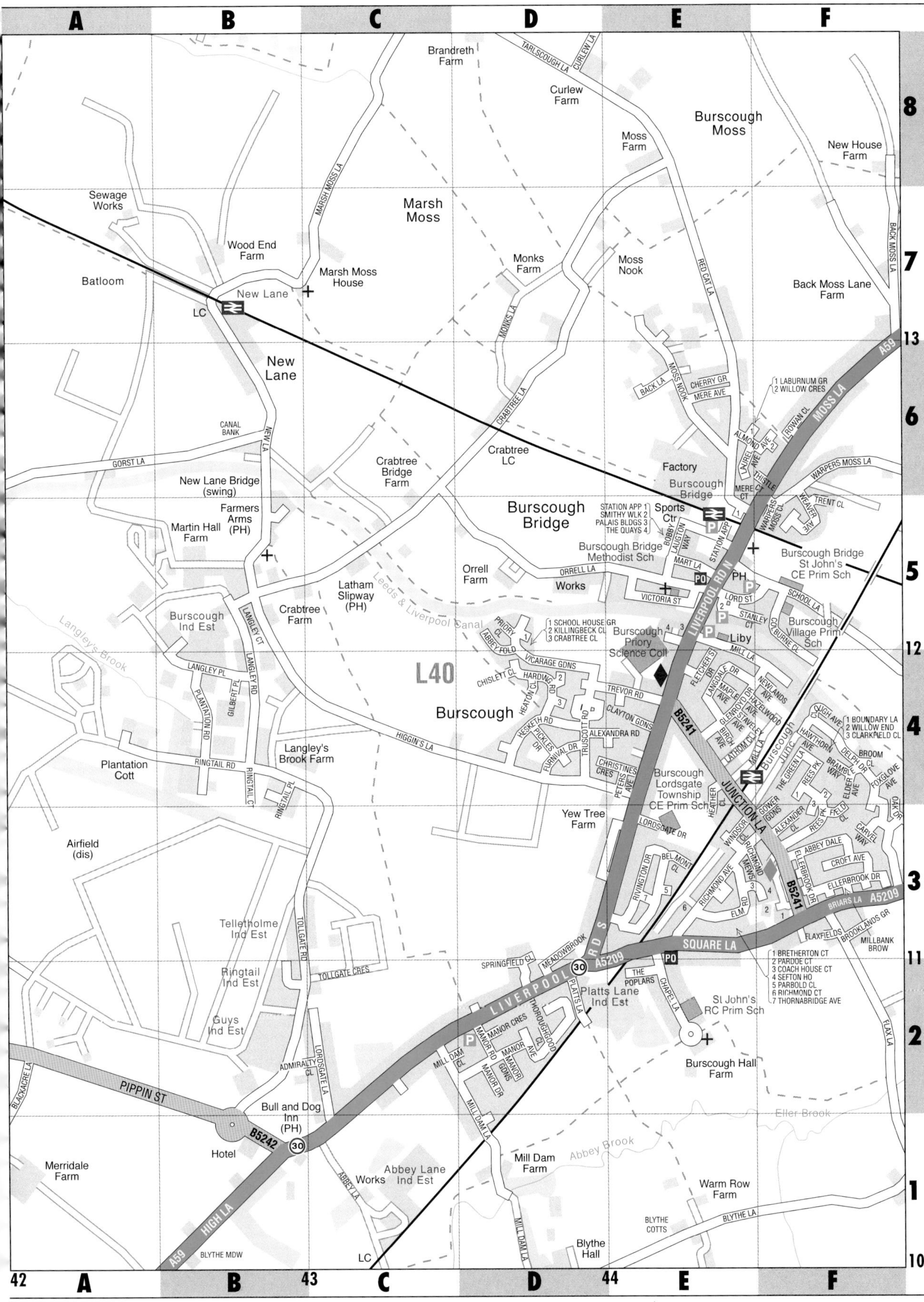
A
B
C
D
E
F
8
7
13
6
5
12
4
3
11
2
1
10
42
43
44
Brandreth Farm
Curlew Farm
TARLSCOUGH LA
CURLEW LA
Burscough Moss
Moss Farm
New House Farm
Sewage Works
Marsh Moss
MARSH MOSS LA
Wood End Farm
Marsh Moss House
Monks Farm
Moss Nook
Batloom
New Lane
LC
RED CAT LA
BACK MOSS LA
Back Moss Lane Farm
MONKS LA
A59
New Lane
BACK LA
MOSS NOOK
CHERRY GR
MERE AVE
1 LABURNUM GR
2 WILLOW CRES
MOSS LA
ROWAN CL
ALMOND AVE
LAUREL AVE
THISTLE
MERE CT
CANAL BANK
NEW LA
CRABTREE LA
Crabtree LC
Factory
GORST LA
Crabtree Bridge Farm
Burscough Bridge
WARPERS MOSS LA
WEAVER AVE
TRENT CL
New Lane Bridge (swing)
Farmers Arms (PH)
Martin Hall Farm
Burscough Bridge
STATION APP 1
SMITHY WLK 2
PALAIS BLDGS 3
THE QUAYS 4
Sports Ctr
BOBBY LANGTON WAY
STATION APP
Burscough Bridge Methodist Sch
MART LA
Burscough Bridge St John's CE Prim Sch
Orrell Farm
ORRELL LA
Works
PO
PH
LIVERPOOL RD N
Latham Slipway (PH)
Leeds & Liverpool Canal
VICTORIA ST
LORD ST
SCHOOL LA
Langley's Brook
Burscough Ind Est
Crabtree Farm
LANGLEY CT
PRIORY CL
ABBEY FOLD
1 SCHOOL HOUSE GR
2 KILLINGBECK CL
3 CRABTREE CL
Burscough Priory Science Coll
STANLEY CT
COLBURNE CL
Burscough Village Prim Sch
Liby
MILL LA
VICARAGE GDNS
LANGLEY PL
LANGLEY RD
L40
CHISLETT CL
HARDING RD
HEATON CL
FLETCHER'S DR
LANGDALE DR
NEWLANDS AVE
PLANTATION RD
GILBERT PL
TREVOR RD
MAPLE AVE
HAZELWOOD
Burscough
CLAYTON GDNS
B5241
GLENROYD DR
STAVELEY AVE
CLOUGH AVE
1 BOUNDARY LA
2 WILLOW END
3 CLARKFIELD CL
HESKETH RD
TRUSCOTT RD
ALEXANDRA RD
BIRCH AVE
Burscough Junc
HAWTHORN AVE
Plantation Cott
Langley's Brook Farm
HIGGIN'S LA
PICKLES DR
FURNIVAL DR
LATHOM CL
DELPH DR
BROOM CL
RINGTAIL RD
RINGTAIL CT
CHRISTINES CRES
Burscough Lordsgate Township CE Prim Sch
THE GREEN LA
BRAMBLE WAY
FOXGLOVE AVE
RINGTAIL PL
PETERS AVE
JUNCTION LA
REES PK
ELDER AVE
Yew Tree Farm
HEATHER CL
GOWER GDNS
ALEXANDER CL
FIELD CL
OAK DR
Airfield (dis)
LORDSGATE DR
WINDSOR CL
REES PK
CARVEL WAY
ABBEY DALE
BELMONT CL
RICHMOND MEWS
CROFT AVE
RIVINGTON DR
RICHMOND AVE
ELLERBROOK DR
ELLERBROOK DR
ELM RD
BRIARS LA
A5209
Telletholme Ind Est
TOLLGATE RD
FLAXFIELDS
BROOKLANDS GR
MILLBANK BROW
SQUARE LA
TOLLGATE CRES
SPRINGFIELD CL
MEADOWBROOK
A5209
30
PO
1 BRETHERTON CT
2 PARDOE CT
3 COACH HOUSE CT
4 SEFTON HO
5 PARBOLD CL
6 RICHMOND CT
7 THORNABRIDGE AVE
Ringtail Ind Est
THE POPLARS
PLATTS LA
Platts Lane Ind Est
CHAPEL LA
LIVERPOOL RD S
St John's RC Prim Sch
Guys Ind Est
MANOR CRES
THOROUGHGOOD CL
MANOR AVE
FLAX LA
MANOR RD
MANOR GDNS
MANOR DR
MILL DAM CL
ADMIRALTY CL
LORDSGATE LA
Burscough Hall Farm
PIPPIN ST
BLACKACRE LA
Bull and Dog Inn (PH)
Ellers Brook
B5242
MILL DAM LA
30
Hotel
Abbey Brook
Mill Dam Farm
Merridale Farm
Abbey Lane Ind Est
Works
ABBEY LA
Warm Row Farm
HIGH LA
A59
BLYTHE COTTS
BLYTHE LA
MILL DAM LA
Blythe Hall
BLYTHE MDW
LC

16
26

25
39

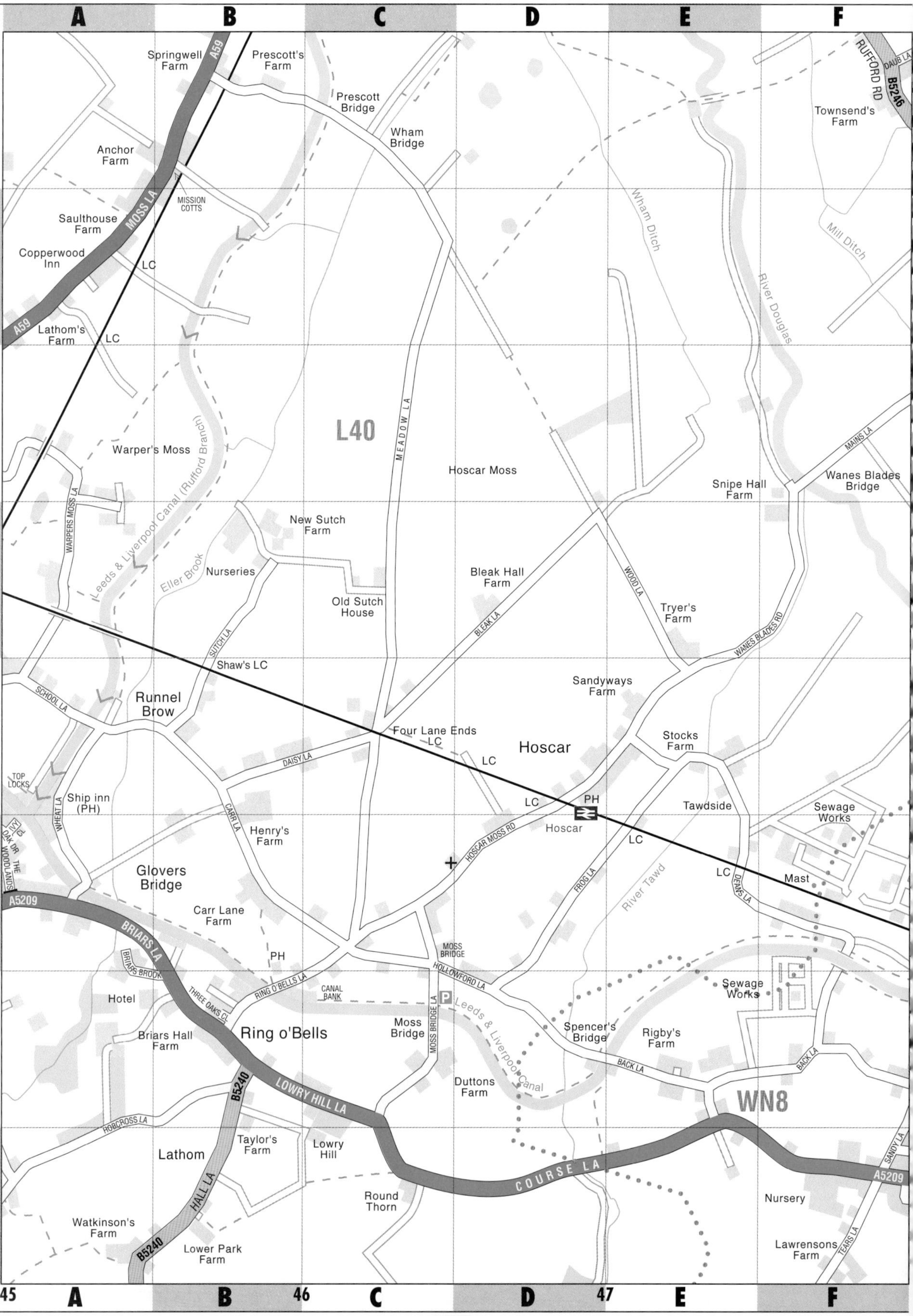
A B C D E F
8 7 6 5 4 3 2 1
13 12 11 10
45 46 47
Springwell Farm
Prescott's Farm
Prescott Bridge
Wham Bridge
Anchor Farm
Saulthouse Farm
Copperwood Inn
MISSION COTTS
MOSS LA
A59
LC
Lathom's Farm
RUFFORD RD
B5246
DAUB LA
Townsend's Farm
Wham Ditch
Mill Ditch
River Douglas
L40
MEADOW LA
Hoscar Moss
Warper's Moss
Leeds & Liverpool Canal (Rufford Branch)
WARPERS MOSS LA
New Sutch Farm
Nurseries
Eller Brook
Old Sutch House
Bleak Hall Farm
BLEAK LA
WOOD LA
Tryer's Farm
Snipe Hall Farm
MAINS LA
Wanes Blades Bridge
WANES BLADES RD
SUTCH LA
Shaw's LC
Sandyways Farm
SCHOOL LA
Runnel Brow
Four Lane Ends LC
Hoscar
Stocks Farm
DAISY LA
TOP LOCKS
Ship inn (PH)
WHEAT LA
IVY CL
OAK DR
THE WOODLANDS
CARR LA
Henry's Farm
PH
Tawdside
Sewage Works
HOSCAR MOSS RD
Glovers Bridge
FROG LA
River Tawd
DEANS LA
Mast
A5209
BRIARS LA
Carr Lane Farm
BRIARS BROOK
MOSS BRIDGE
HOLLOWFORD LA
THREE OAKS CL
RING O' BELLS LA
CANAL BANK
Hotel
Leeds & Liverpool Canal
Ring o'Bells
Moss Bridge
MOSS BRIDGE LA
Spencer's Bridge
Rigby's Farm
Briars Hall Farm
BACK LA
B5240
LOWRY HILL LA
Duttons Farm
WN8
HOBCROSS LA
Taylor's Farm
Lowry Hill
Lathom
SANDY LA
COURSE LA
HALL LA
Round Thorn
Nursery
Watkinson's Farm
Lower Park Farm
Lawrensons Farm
TEARS LA

25
17

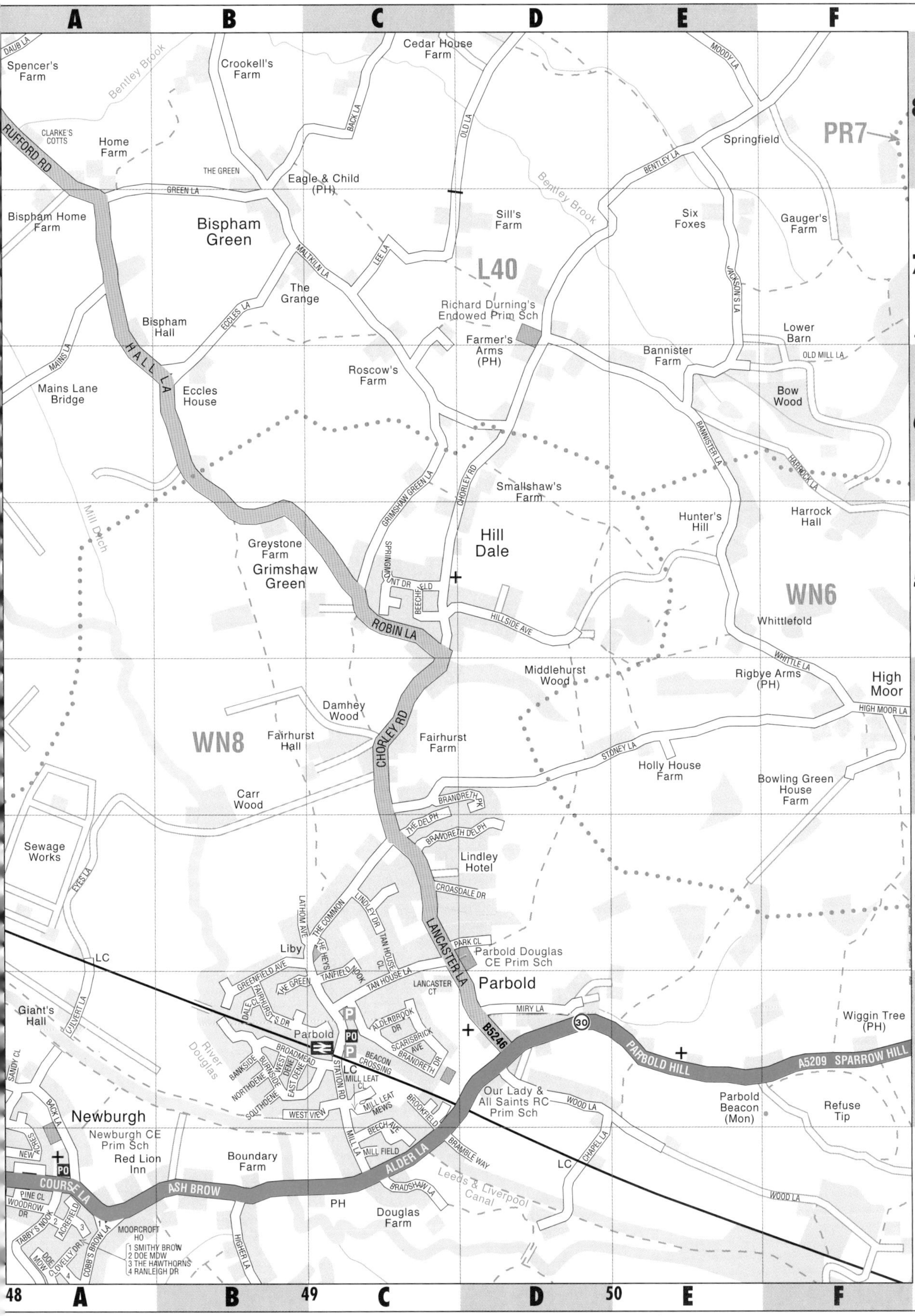
A B C D E F
8 7 6 5 4 3 2 1
13 12 11 10
48 49 50
Spencer's Farm
Crookell's Farm
Cedar House Farm
Bentley Brook
Rufford Rd
Clarke's Cotts
Home Farm
The Green
Green La
Back La
Old La
Moody La
Springfield
PR7
Eagle & Child (PH)
Bentley La
Bispham Home Farm
Bispham Green
Sill's Farm
Six Foxes
Gauger's Farm
Maltkiln La
Lee La
L40
Jackson's La
The Grange
Richard Durning's Endowed Prim Sch
Bispham Hall
Eccles La
Farmer's Arms (PH)
Lower Barn
Bannister Farm
Old Mill La
Hall La
Mains La
Mains Lane Bridge
Eccles House
Roscow's Farm
Bow Wood
Bannister La
Harrock La
Mill Ditch
Grimshaw Green La
Chorley Rd
Smallshaw's Farm
Hunter's Hill
Harrock Hall
Greystone Farm
Grimshaw Green
Hill Dale
Springmount Dr
Beechfield
WN6
Robin La
Hillside Ave
Whittlefold
Whittle La
Middlehurst Wood
Rigbye Arms (PH)
High Moor
High Moor La
Damhey Wood
WN8
Fairhurst Hall
Fairhurst Farm
Stoney La
Holly House Farm
Bowling Green House Farm
Carr Wood
Brandreth Pk
The Delph
Brandreth Delph
Sewage Works
Lindley Hotel
Eyes La
Croasdale Dr
Lathom Ave
The Common
Lindley Dr
Tan House Cl
Lancaster La
Park Cl
Parbold Douglas CE Prim Sch
Liby
LC
The Heys
Tanfield Nook
Tan House La
Greenfield Ave
The Green
Fairhurst's Dr
Dale Cl
Lancaster Ct
Parbold
Giant's Hall
Culvert La
Miry La
Wiggin Tree (PH)
Alderbrook Dr
Parbold
Scarisbrick Ave
B5246
30
Parbold Hill
A5209 Sparrow Hill
Sandy Cl
River Douglas
Bankside
Broadmead
Burnside
Dene
East Dene
Beacon Crossing
Brandreth Dr
Station Rd
Northdene
Southdene
Mill Leat Cl
Mill Leat Mews
Our Lady & All Saints RC Prim Sch
Wood La
Parbold Beacon (Mon)
Refuse Tip
Back La
West View
Brookfield
Newburgh
Acres
Newburgh CE Prim Sch
Beech Ave
Mill La
Mill Field
Bramble Way
Chapel La
New
Red Lion Inn
Boundary Farm
Alder La
Leeds & Liverpool Canal
PO
Course La
Ash Brow
Bradshaw La
Wood La
Pine Cl
Woodrow Dr
Acrefield
PH
Douglas Farm
Tabby's Nook
Doe Mdw
Clovelly Dr
Cobb's Brow La
Moorcroft Ho
1 Smithy Brow
2 Doe Mdw
3 The Hawthorns
4 Ranleigh Dr
Higher La

27
41

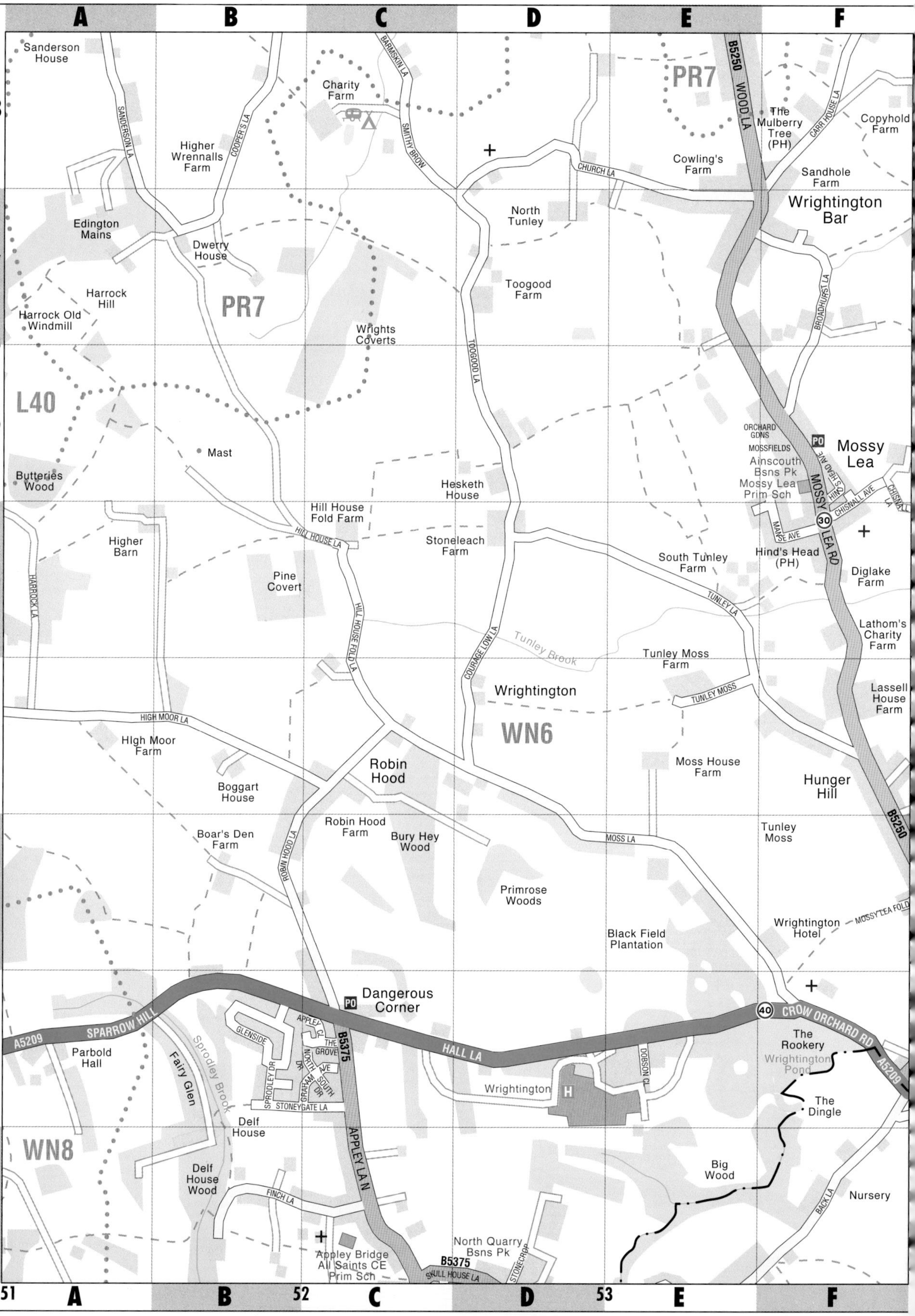
A
B
C
D
E
F
8
7
13
6
5
12
4
3
11
2
1
10
51
52
53
Sanderson House
SANDERSON LA
COOPER'S LA
BARMSKIN LA
Charity Farm
SMITHY BROW
PR7
B5250
WOOD LA
The Mulberry Tree (PH)
CARR HOUSE LA
Copyhold Farm
Higher Wrennalls Farm
CHURCH LA
Cowling's Farm
Sandhole Farm
Wrightington Bar
Edington Mains
North Tunley
Dwerry House
Toogood Farm
Harrock Hill
Harrock Old Windmill
PR7
Wrights Coverts
BROADHURST LA
TOOGOOD LA
L40
ORCHARD GDNS
MOSSFIELDS
Ainscouth Bsns Pk
Mossy Lea Prim Sch
Mossy Lea
MOSSY LEA RD
CHISNALL AVE
CHISNALL LA
Mast
Butteries Wood
Hesketh House
Hill House Fold Farm
HILL HOUSE LA
Higher Barn
Stoneleach Farm
South Tunley Farm
MANSE AVE
Hind's Head (PH)
Diglake Farm
Pine Covert
HARROCK LA
HILL HOUSE FOLD LA
COURAGE LOW LA
Tunley Brook
TUNLEY LA
Lathom's Charity Farm
Tunley Moss Farm
Wrightington
TUNLEY MOSS
Lassell House Farm
HIGH MOOR LA
High Moor Farm
WN6
Boggart House
Robin Hood
Moss House Farm
Hunger Hill
B5250
Robin Hood Farm
Bury Hey Wood
Boar's Den Farm
ROBIN HOOD LA
MOSS LA
Tunley Moss
Primrose Woods
Black Field Plantation
Wrightington Hotel
MOSSY LEA FOLD
Dangerous Corner
A5209
SPARROW HILL
GLENSIDE
APPLEY CL
THE GROVE
B5375
HALL LA
40
CROW ORCHARD RD
Parbold Hall
Fairy Glen
Sprodley Brook
SPRODLEY DR
GRAHAM DR
NORTH AVE
SOUTH DR
STONEYGATE LA
DOBSON CL
Wrightington
H
The Rookery
Wrightington Pond
The Dingle
A5209
Delf House
WN8
Delf House Wood
APPLEY LA N
FINCH LA
Big Wood
BACK LA
Nursery
Appley Bridge All Saints CE Prim Sch
North Quarry Bsns Pk
B5375
SKULL HOUSE LA
STONECROP

27
19

42
30

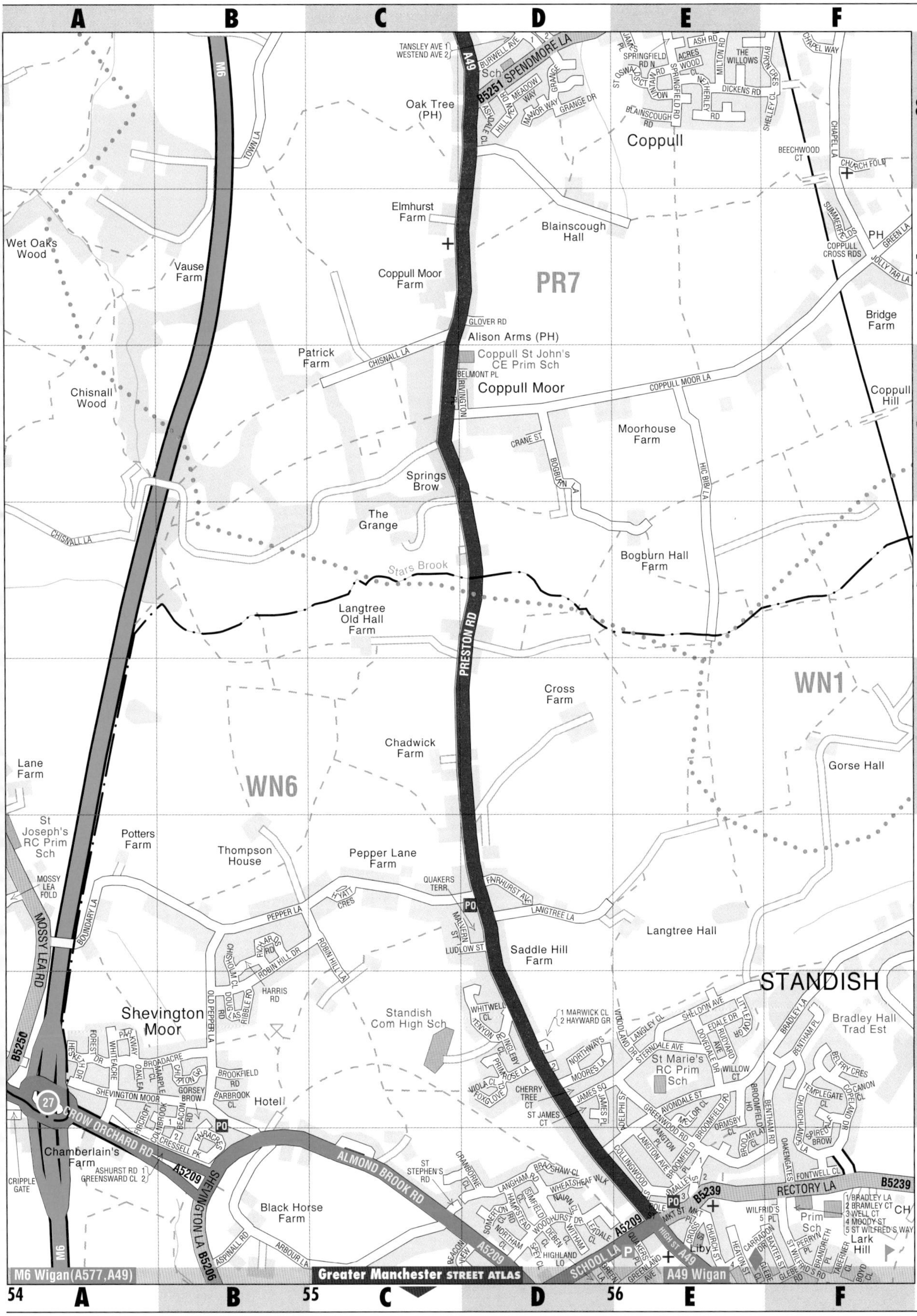
A
B
C
D
E
F
8
7
13
6
5
12
4
3
11
2
1
10
54
55
56
M6
A49
B5251 SPENDMORE LA
TANSLEY AVE 1
WESTEND AVE 2
BURWELL AVE
Sch
Oak Tree (PH)
TOWN LA
MEADOW WAY
MANOR WAY
GRANGE DR
SPRINGFIELD RD N
ASH RD
ACRES WOOD
MILTON RD
THE WILLOWS
BYRON CRES
CHAPEL WAY
DICKENS RD
BLAINSCOUGH RD
SPRINGFIELD RD
SHELLEY CL
Coppull
BEECHWOOD CT
CHAPEL LA
CHURCH FOLD
Elmhurst Farm
Blainscough Hall
Wet Oaks Wood
Vause Farm
Coppull Moor Farm
PR7
PH
GREEN LA
COPPULL CROSS RDS
JOLLY TAR LA
Bridge Farm
GLOVER RD
Alison Arms (PH)
Patrick Farm
CHISNALL LA
Coppull St John's CE Prim Sch
BELMONT PL
RIVINGTON PL
Coppull Moor
COPPULL MOOR LA
Coppull Hill
Chisnall Wood
Moorhouse Farm
CRANE ST
BOGBURN LA
HIC BIB LA
Springs Brow
The Grange
CHISNALL LA
Bogburn Hall Farm
Stars Brook
Langtree Old Hall Farm
PRESTON RD
Cross Farm
WN1
Chadwick Farm
Lane Farm
WN6
Gorse Hall
St Joseph's RC Prim Sch
Potters Farm
Thompson House
Pepper Lane Farm
MOSSY LEA FOLD
QUAKERS TERR
FAIRHURST AVE
PO
LANGTREE LA
PEPPER LA
YATE CRES
MALVERN ST
Langtree Hall
MOSSY LEA RD
BOUNDARY LA
ROBIN HILL LA
LUDLOW ST
Saddle Hill Farm
STANDISH
CHISHOLM CL
RICHARDS RD
ROBIN HILL DR
HARRIS RD
Standish Com High Sch
1 MARWICK CL
2 HAYWARD GR
WHITWELL CL
KENYON RD
INGLEBY CL
WOODLAND DR
LANGLEY CL
STERNDALE AVE
SHELDON AVE
EDALE DR
LITTLETON GR
BRADLEY LA
BENTHAM PL
Bradley Hall Trad Est
Shevington Moor
OLD PEPPER LA
DOUGLAS RD
RIBBLE RD
B5250
FOREST DR
WHITEACRE
PARKWAY
OAKLEA
BROADACRE
MARPLE CL
CHILTON GR
BROOKFIELD RD
PRIMROSE LA
NORTHWAYS
MOORES LA
St Marie's RC Prim Sch
DOVEDALE DR
RUDYARD AVE
WILLOW CT
BELFRY CRES
CANON CL
TEMPLEGATE CL
COPELAND DR
27
SHEVINGTON MOOR
GORSEY BROW
BARBROOK CL
Hotel
VIOLA CL
FOXGLOVE
CHERRY TREE CT
JAMES SQ
JAMES PL
AVONDALE ST
MELLOR CL
BROOMFIELD RD
ORMSBY CL
BROOMFIELD CL
BENTHAM RD
SPIRE BROW
CROW ORCHARD RD
FIRCROFT
COLNBROOK
BEACON RD
CRESSELL PK
FARACRES
ST JAMES CT
GREENWOOD RD
LANGTON PL
Chamberlain's Farm
ASHURST RD 1
GREENSWARD CL 2
A5209
SHEVINGTON LA
ALMOND BROOK RD
ST STEPHEN'S RD
CRANBORNE CL
BRADSHAW CL
WHEATSHEAF WLK
LANGHAM RD
COLLINGWOOD
OAKENGATES
FONTWELL CL
B5239
RECTORY LA
CRIPPLE GATE
Black Horse Farm
MKT ST
MKT PL
CROSS ST
CHURCH ST
WILFRID'S PL
Prim Sch
1 BRADLEY LA
2 BRAMLEY CT
3 WELL CT
4 MOODY ST
5 ST WILFRED'S WAY
CH
Lark Hill
ASPINALL RD
ARBOUR LA
HAMPSTEAD
SOMERTON
NORTHAM CL
WOODHURST DR
DEBEN CL
WITHAM
2 HIGHLAND LO
SCHOOL LA
P
A49 Wigan
Liby
HEATON ST
CARRADON
GLEBE
BAXTER ST
PERRYN PL
BRANDRETH
ST WILFRID'S RD
TABERNER CL
BOYD CL
B5206
M6 Wigan (A577, A49)
Greater Manchester STREET ATLAS

30

29
43

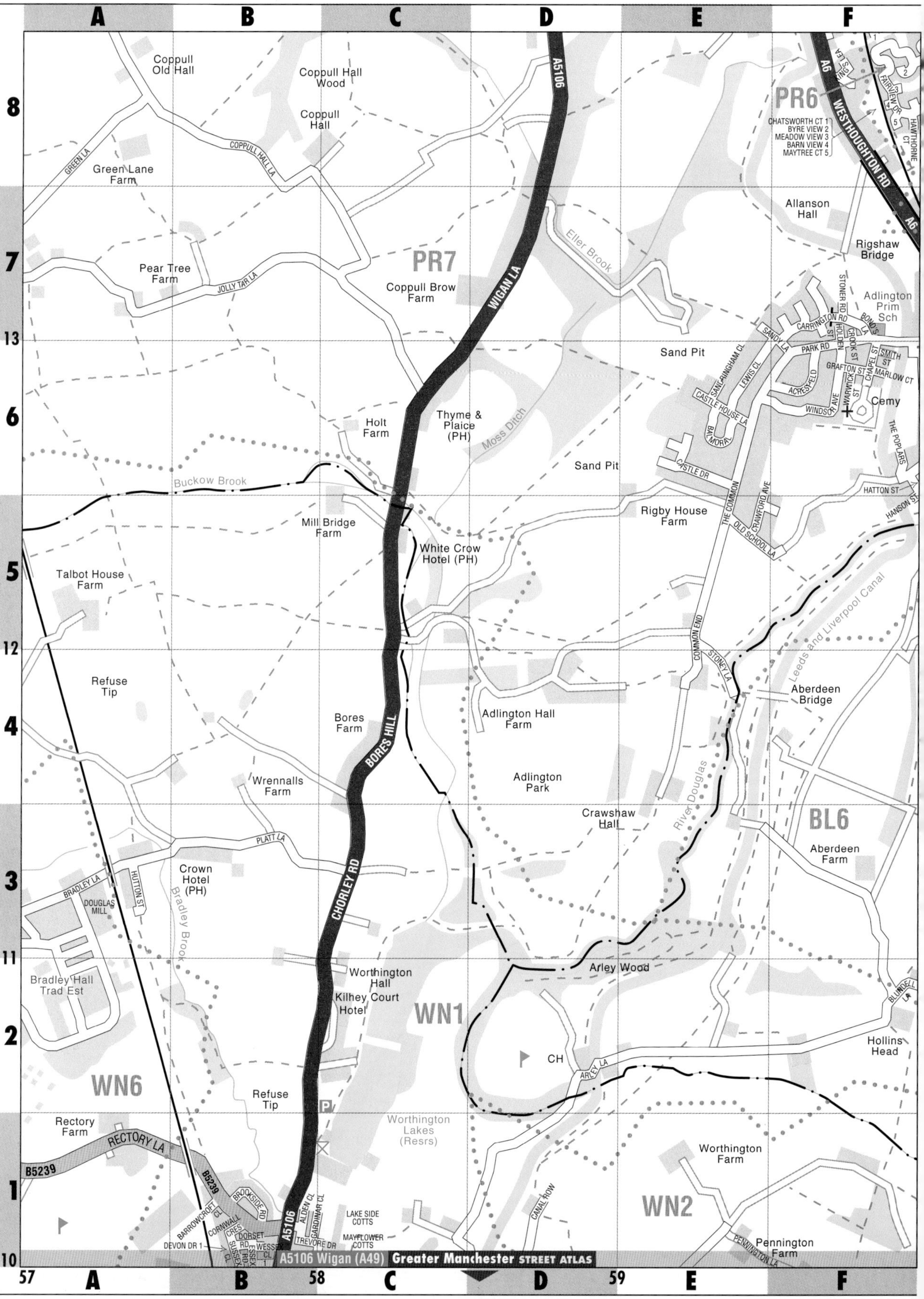
A
B
C
D
E
F
8
7
13
6
5
12
4
3
11
2
1
10
57
58
59
Coppull Old Hall
Coppull Hall Wood
Coppull Hall
COPPULL HALL LA
GREEN LA
Green Lane Farm
Pear Tree Farm
JOLLY TAR LA
PR7
Coppull Brow Farm
WIGAN LA
A5106
Eller Brook
PR6
A6
WESTHOUGHTON RD
CHATSWORTH CT 1
BYRE VIEW 2
MEADOW VIEW 3
BARN VIEW 4
MAYTREE CT 5
FAIRVIEW DR
HAWTHORNE CT
Allanson Hall
Rigshaw Bridge
Adlington Prim Sch
STONER RD
CARRINGTON RD
BOND S
SANDY LA
PARK RD
HOLDEN ST
CROOK ST
SMITH ST
MARLOW CT
GRAFTON ST
CHAPEL ST
SANDRINGHAM CL
LEWIS CL
ACRESFIELD
WARWICK AVE
WINDSOR
Cemy
CASTLE HOUSE LA
BALMORAL
Sand Pit
Holt Farm
Thyme & Plaice (PH)
Moss Ditch
Sand Pit
CASTLE DR
THE POPLARS
HATTON ST
HANSON ST
Buckow Brook
Mill Bridge Farm
White Crow Hotel (PH)
Rigby House Farm
THE COMMON
CRAWFORD AVE
OLD SCHOOL LA
Talbot House Farm
Leeds and Liverpool Canal
COMMON END
STONEY LA
Refuse Tip
Aberdeen Bridge
Adlington Hall Farm
Bores Farm
BORES HILL
Adlington Park
Wrennalls Farm
River Douglas
Crawshaw Hall
BL6
PLATT LA
Aberdeen Farm
Crown Hotel (PH)
BRADLEY LA
HUTTON ST
DOUGLAS MILL
Bradley Brook
CHORLEY RD
Worthington Hall
Arley Wood
Bradley Hall Trad Est
Kilhey Court Hotel
WN1
BLUNDELL LA
Hollins Head
CH
ARLEY LA
WN6
Refuse Tip
Rectory Farm
RECTORY LA
Worthington Lakes (Resrs)
Worthington Farm
B5239
B5239
BROOKSIDE RD
CANAL ROW
WN2
BARROWCROFT CL
CORNWALL CRES
DORSET RD
WESSEX CL
ALDEN CL
GARDINAR CL
LAKE SIDE COTTS
MAYFLOWER COTTS
TREVORE DR
DEVON DR 1
SUSSEX CL
ESSEX RD
Pennington Farm
PENNINGTON LA


29

44
32

A8
1 OLLERTON ST
2 NIGHTINGALE ST
3 CARLISLE PL
4 BROAD OAK CL
5 ADELAIDE ST
6 THE ROWANS

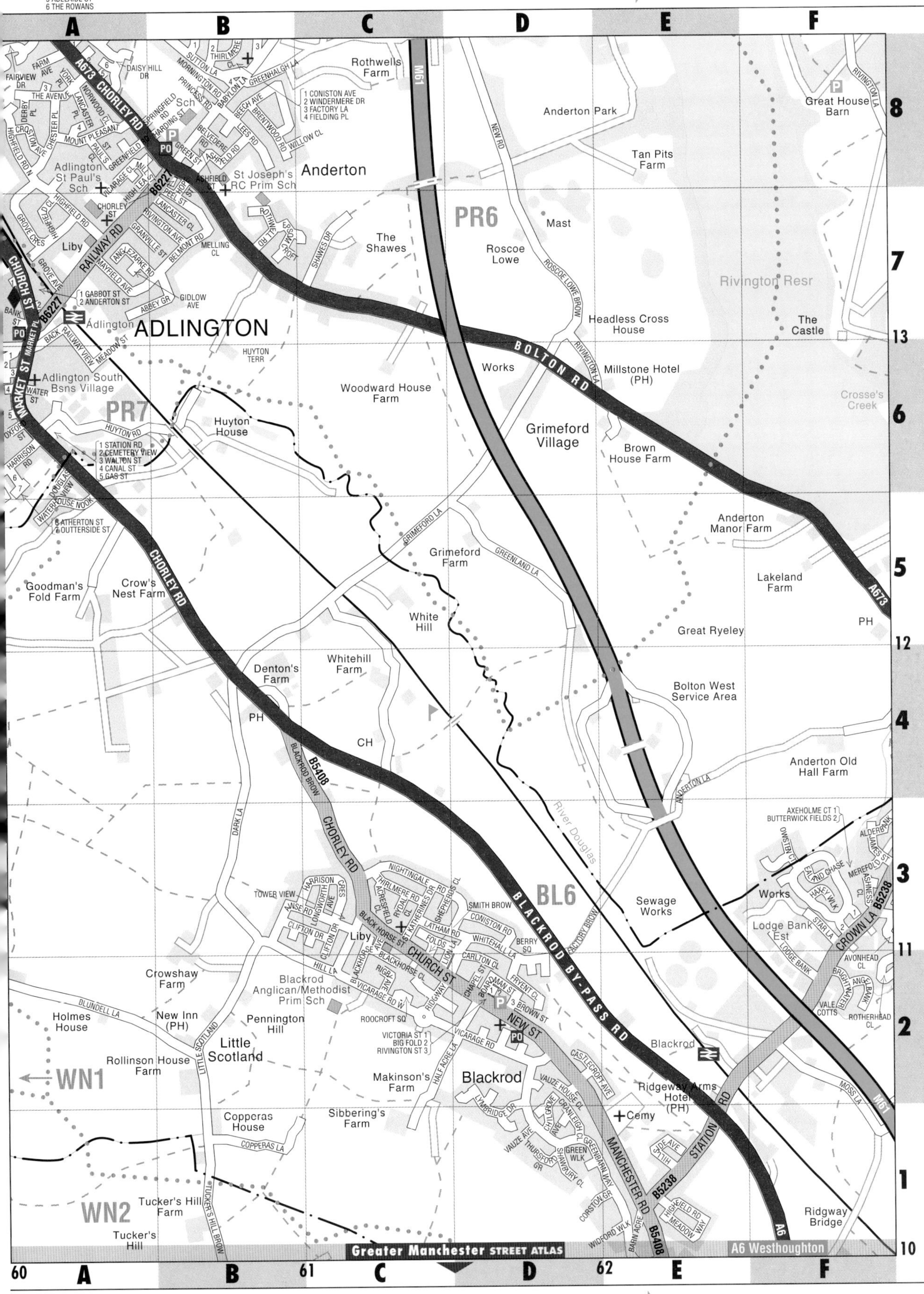

31
45

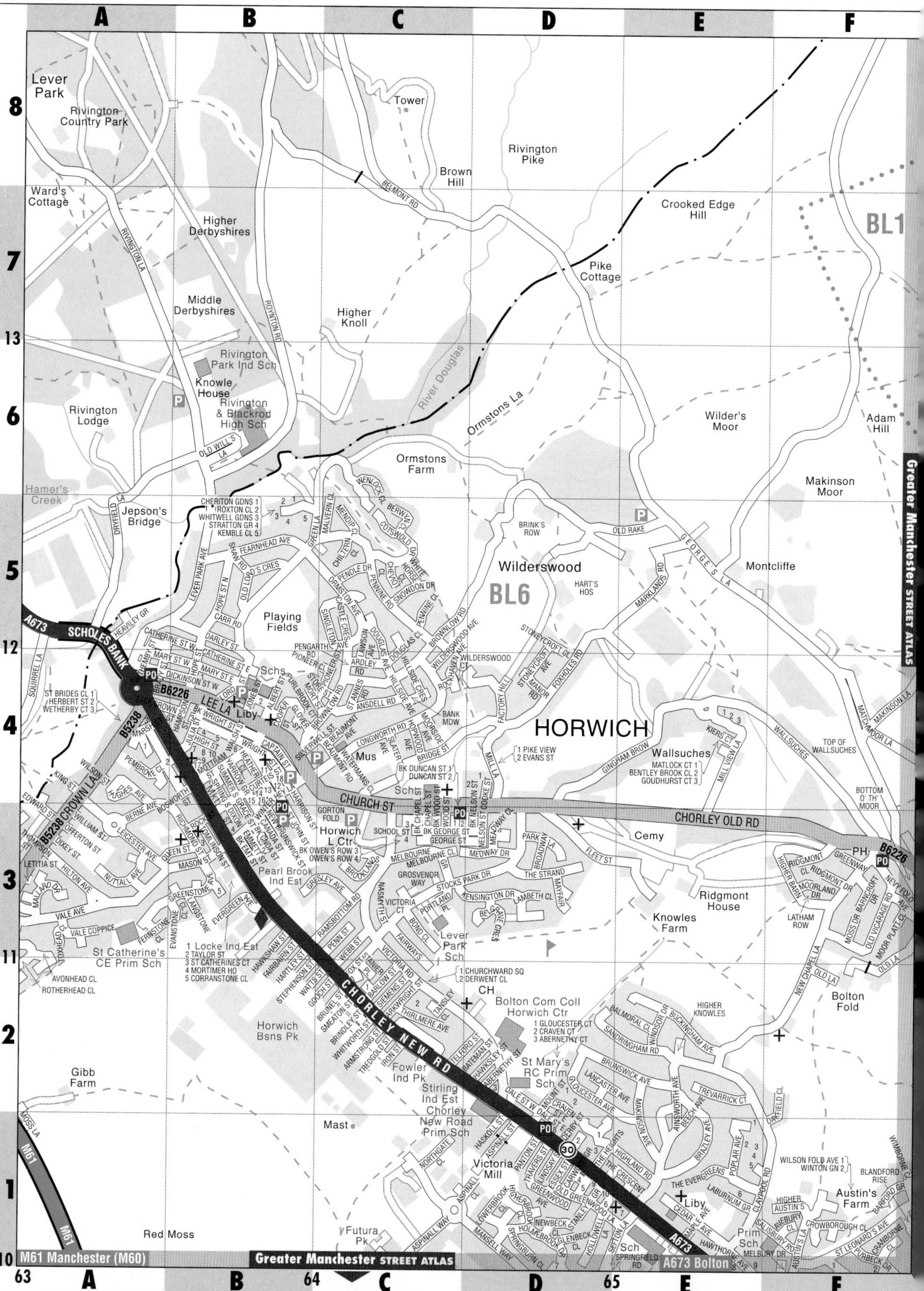
A B C D E F
8
7
13
6
5
12
4
3
11
2
1
10
63 64 65
Lever Park
Rivington Country Park
Tower
Rivington Pike
Brown Hill
Ward's Cottage
Higher Derbyshires
Crooked Edge Hill
BL1
Pike Cottage
Middle Derbyshires
Higher Knoll
Rivington Park Ind Sch
Knowle House
Rivington & Blackrod High Sch
Rivington Lodge
River Douglas
Ormstons La
Wilder's Moor
Adam Hill
Ormstons Farm
Hamer's Creek
Jepson's Bridge
Makinson Moor
Wilderswood
BL6
Montcliffe
Playing Fields
HORWICH
Wallsuches
TOP OF WALLSUCHES
BOTTOM O' TH' MOOR
CHORLEY OLD RD
CHURCH ST
Cemy
SCHOLES BANK
A673
B6226
LEE LA
B5238
CROWN LA
Mus
Horwich L Ctr
Pearl Brook Ind Est
Ridgmont House
Knowles Farm
Lever Park Sch
St Catherine's CE Prim Sch
CHORLEY NEW RD
Bolton Com Coll Horwich Ctr
HIGHER KNOWLES
Bolton Fold
Horwich Bsns Pk
Gibb Farm
Fowler Ind Pk
St Mary's RC Prim Sch
Stirling Ind Est
Chorley New Road Prim Sch
Mast
Victoria Mill
Austin's Farm
Red Moss
Futura Pk
M61
M61 Manchester (M60)
Greater Manchester STREET ATLAS
A673 Bolton
Greater Manchester STREET ATLAS

B4
1 DICKINSON CT
2 PETER MARTIN ST
3 WRIGHT ST W
4 JULIA MEWS
5 WHITTON MEWS
6 MOTTRAM MEWS
7 FLOCKTON CT
8 CROXTON WLK
9 BEATRICE MEWS

31

B4
10 HARCOURT MEWS
11 ABRAHAM ST
12 SPRING GDNS
13 RAWLINSON ST
14 ABBOTT ST
15 ROBINSON ST
16 BACK RAWLINSON ST
17 BEATRICE ST
18 JAMESTON RISE

D1
1 LOWER MAKINSON FOLD
2 MOUNT PLEASANT ST
3 GREENBANK
4 KILLINGWORTH MEWS
5 KNOWSLEY GR
6 CARLTON GR
7 ASHBURN CL
8 MULBERRY CT
9 DAISYFIELD
10 FERNLEIGH

E1
1 SYCAMORE WLK
2 ROWAN AVE
3 FIR TREE WAY
4 BIRCH TREE WAY
5 CHERRY TREE WAY
6 ELM GR
7 ARROWSMITH CT
8 ASH GR
9 OAK AVE

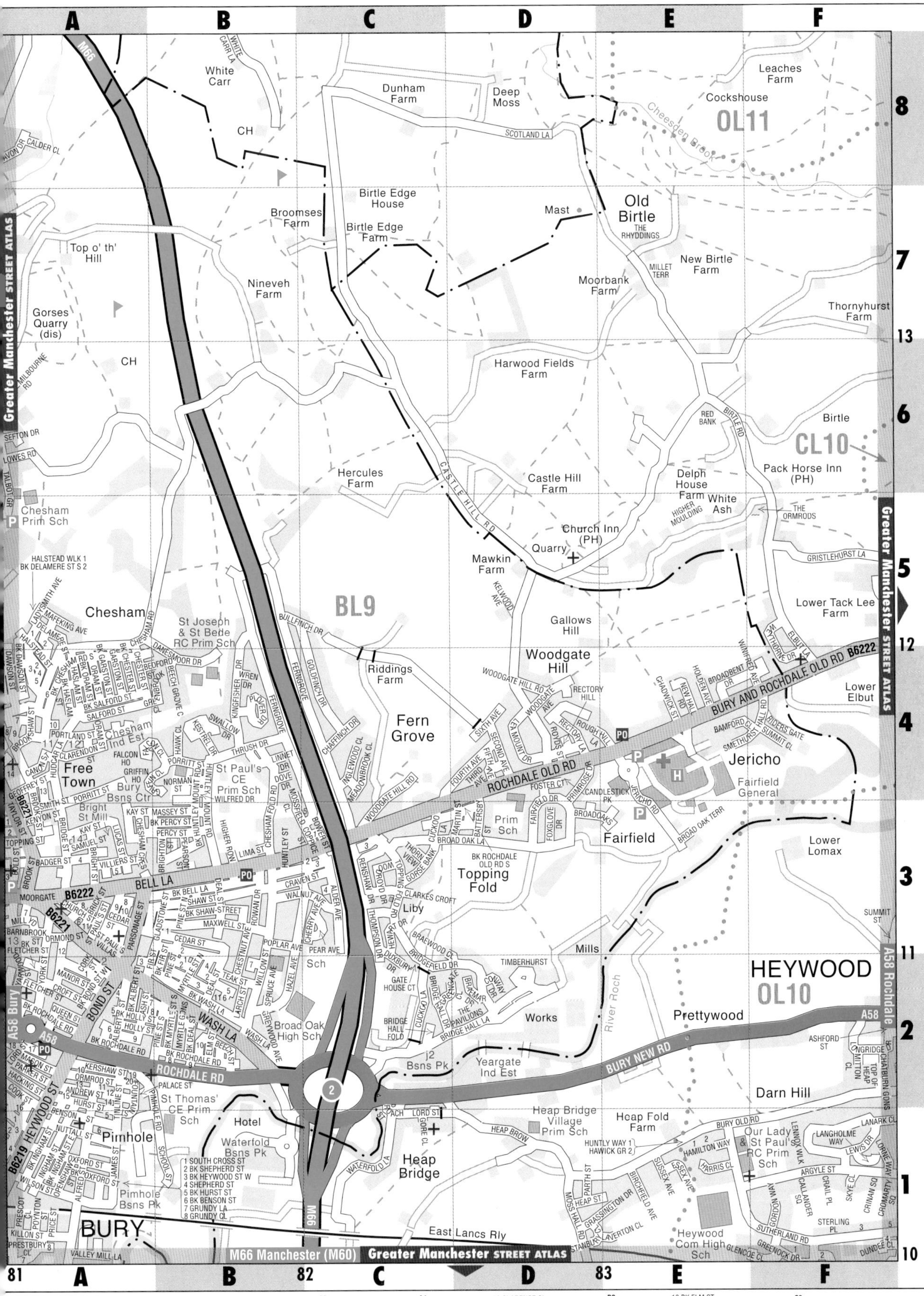


| | | | | | | | | |
|---|---|---|---|---|---|---|---|---|
| **A2** | 10 BK KERSHAW ST | **A2** | **A3** | **A4** | 10 CLARENCE CL | **B2** | 10 BK ELM ST | **C3** |
| 1 BK MANOR ST | 11 BK ORMROD ST | 20 ORMROD CT | 8 BK BELL LA | 1 BK HAMILTON ST | 11 Freetown Bsns Pk | 1 BK PINE ST | 11 EASTWOOD CT | 5 RACHEL HO |
| 2 Brenton Bsns Complex | 12 BK TINLINE ST | **A3** | 9 SANDERSON ST | 2 BK HALSTEAD ST | 12 Portland Ind Est | 2 BK LAUREL ST | **B3** | **F1** |
| 3 PARSONAGE CL | 13 BK ANDREW ST N | 1 BK RICHARD BURCH ST | 10 BK PARSONAGE ST | 3 DUCKWORTH ST | 13 BK BROOK ST N | 3 LAUREL ST | 1 BK CEDAR ST N | 1 GIRVAN WLK |
| 4 ST THOMAS CT | 14 BK ANDREW ST | 2 RICHARD BURCH ST | 11 HUGHES CL | 4 BK DUCKWORTH ST | 14 SCHOLARS WAY | 4 BK MYRTLE ST | 2 BK CEDAR ST | 2 GALLOWAY CL |
| 5 AUDLUM CT | 15 BK HEYWOOD ST E | 3 BK PETER ST | 12 FOUNTAIN ST N | 5 BK CHESHAM RD N | | 5 BK TEAK ST | **C3** | 3 STROMNESS GR |
| 6 BARRETT CT | 16 BK SOUTH CROSS ST E | 4 COBDEN ST | 13 Moorgate Ret Pk | 6 GREENBROOK ST | | 6 EASTWOOD CL | 1 BK ROCHDALE OLD RD N | 4 DOUGLAS SQ |
| 7 BK WASH LA S | 17 BK MASON ST | 5 POTTER ST | 14 Britannia Mill | 7 BK CHESHAM RD S | | 7 MAPLE AVE | 2 YEW ST | 5 STRATHAVEN PL |
| 8 BK ASH ST | 18 BK ROCHDALE RD S | 6 CHURCH CT | | 8 LATHOM ST | | 8 MYRTLE ST S | 3 BK ROCHDALE OLD RD S | |
| 9 BK HOLLY ST S | 19 HOLLY CT | 7 LOMAX ST | | 9 BK LATHOM ST | | 9 DEAL ST | 4 ALMOND AVE | |

21

F4
1 CARNEGHIE CT
2 WELD PAR
3 HOMECHASE HO
4 VICTORIA CT
5 WELDALE HO
6 OXFORD CT

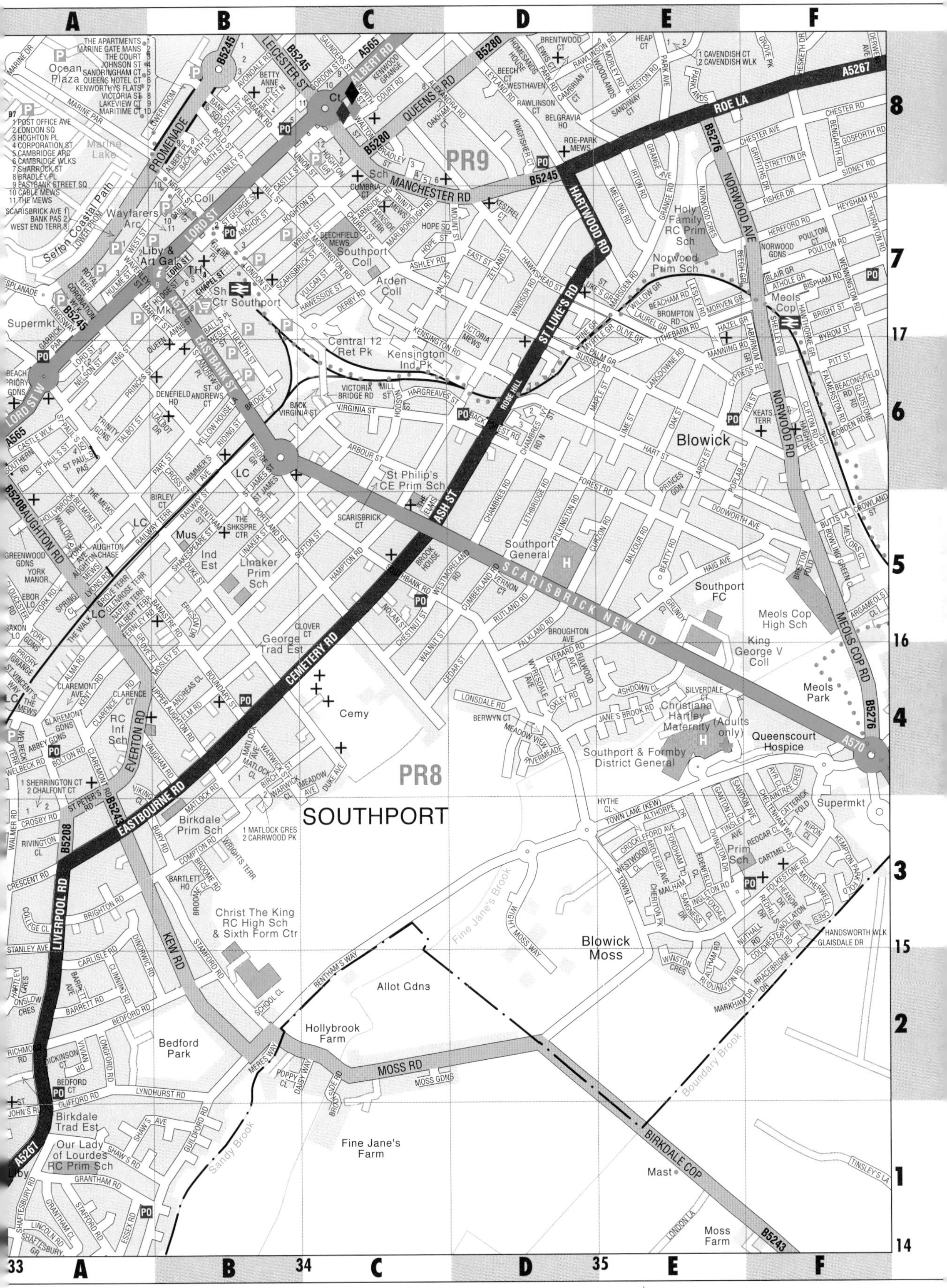

A B C D E F
8 7 17 6 5 16 4 3 15 2 1 14
33 34 35
THE APARTMENTS 1
MARINE GATE MANS 2
THE COURT 3
JOHNSON ST 4
SANDRINGHAM CT 5
QUEENS HOTEL CT 6
KENWORTHYS FLATS 7
VICTORIA ST 8
LAKEVIEW CT 9
MARITIME CT 10
B7
1 POST OFFICE AVE
2 LONDON SQ
3 HOGHTON PL
4 CORPORATION ST
5 CAMBRIDGE ARC
6 CAMBRIDGE WLKS
7 SHARROCK ST
8 BRADLEY PL
9 EASTBANK STREET SQ
10 CABLE MEWS
11 THE MEWS
SCARISBRICK AVE 1
BANK PAS 2
WEST END TERR 3
Ocean Plaza
Marine Lake
Sefton Coastal Path
Wayfarers Arc
Liby & Art Gal
TH
Sh Ctr Southport
Mkt
Supermkt
Coll
Sch
Southport Coll
Arden Coll
Central 12 Ret Pk
Kensington Ind Pk
Holy Family RC Prim Sch
Norwood Prim Sch
Meols Cop
Blowick
St Philip's CE Prim Sch
Southport General
Southport FC
Meols Cop High Sch
King George V Coll
Meols Park
Christiana Hartley Maternity (Adults only)
Queenscourt Hospice
Southport & Formby District General
Supermkt
Prim Sch
Blowick Moss
Mus
Ind Est
Linaker Prim Sch
George Trad Est
Cemy
RC Inf Sch
Birkdale Prim Sch
SOUTHPORT
PR8
PR9
Christ The King RC High Sch & Sixth Form Ctr
Bedford Park
Allot Gdns
Hollybrook Farm
Fine Jane's Farm
Birkdale Trad Est
Our Lady of Lourdes RC Prim Sch
Liby
Mast
Moss Farm
1 MATLOCK CRES
2 CARRWOOD PK
1 SHERRINGTON CT
2 CHALFONT CT
ROE LA
A5267
B5245
B5280
A565
A570
B5276
B5208
B5243
MANCHESTER RD
HARTWOOD RD
NORWOOD AVE
NORWOOD RD
ST LUKE'S RD
ASH ST
SCARISBRICK NEW RD
CEMETERY RD
EASTBOURNE RD
LIVERPOOL RD
KEW RD
MOSS RD
BIRKDALE COP
MEOLS COP RD
LORD ST
EASTBANK ST
PROMENADE
QUEENS RD
ALBERT RD
LEICESTER ST
AUGHTON RD
EVERTON RD
ROSE HILL
Fine Jane's Brook
Boundary Brook
Sandy Brook
HANDSWORTH WLK
GLAISDALE DR
TINSLEY'S LA

35
54

A
B
C
D
E
F
8
7
17
6
5
16
4
3
15
2
1
14
36
37
38
ROE LA A5267
BAMBER GDNS
HIGH PARK PL
CHURCH CL
CHESTER RD
VERNON RD
SIDNEY RD
HEYSHAM RD
POULTON RD
BISPHAM RD
NEWTON ST
MILTON ST
RUSSELL AVE
SALISBURY ST
CANNING RD
COBDEN RD
WENNINGTON RD
OLD PARK LA
HIGH PARK RD
WARREN RD
FARM CL
TARLETON RD
DEVONSHIRE RD
BRADSHAW CT
LAWSON ST
CHURCH MEWS
SCOTT ST
TEDDER AVE
VICTORY AVE
WAVELL AVE
BROOKE CL
WAVELL CL
MONTGOMERY AVE
RUSSELL RD
CROWLAND CL
CROWLAND ST
CH
OLD LINKS CL
FINE JANE'S WAY
FOSTERS CL
PITTS HOUSE LA
High Park
SOUTHPORT
Bishop David Sheppard CE Prim Sch
A K Bsns Pk
Southport Ent Ctr
Recn Gd
Wks
Blowick Bsns Pk
Blowick Ind Pk
Old Hall Farm Bsns Pk
P&R
Hodge's Farm
FOUL LA
Meols Cop Ret Pk
NEW FOUL LA
Kew Ret Pk
SCARISBRICK NEW RD
A570
40
MEOLS VIEW CL
Pool Hey
Nursery
POOL HEY LA
PR8
High Brows Covert
Crem
COVERTSIDE RD
COVERT CL
KEW HOUSE DR
FIELDLANDS
ALDERLEE PK CVN SITE
BROWN EDGE CL
Brown Edge
SOUTHPORT RD
TURNING LA
Boundary Farm
TINSLEY'S LA
Black Brook
NEW HALL DR
PINEWOOD CL
GREENFIELD RD
HARES LA
Carr Cross
RIMMER GN
SNAPE GN
CAT TAIL LA
Snape Green
Sandy Brook Farm
WYKE COP RD
Wyke Road Farm
Sandy Brook
WOODMOSS LA
L40
Drummersdale Drain
Wyke Cop Crossing
Shaw's Farm
Scarisbrick Moss
Perch Pool Covert
Pool Hey Crossing
New House Farm
Sandy Brook
Sheepfold Farm
Wyke Thorn Farm
Heath Covert
PERCH POOL LA
Twist's Covert
Big Wood
THE AVENUE
WYKE LA
The Old Pool
PR9
Brook Farm Bridge
Three Pools Waterway
Pitts House Covert
Wyke House Farm
WYKE WOOD LA
Middle Drain
Hooton's Cottages
Wyke Hey Farm
Peet's Farm
LONG MEANYGATE
DOLLY'S LA
MOSS LA
Pool House Farm

35
23

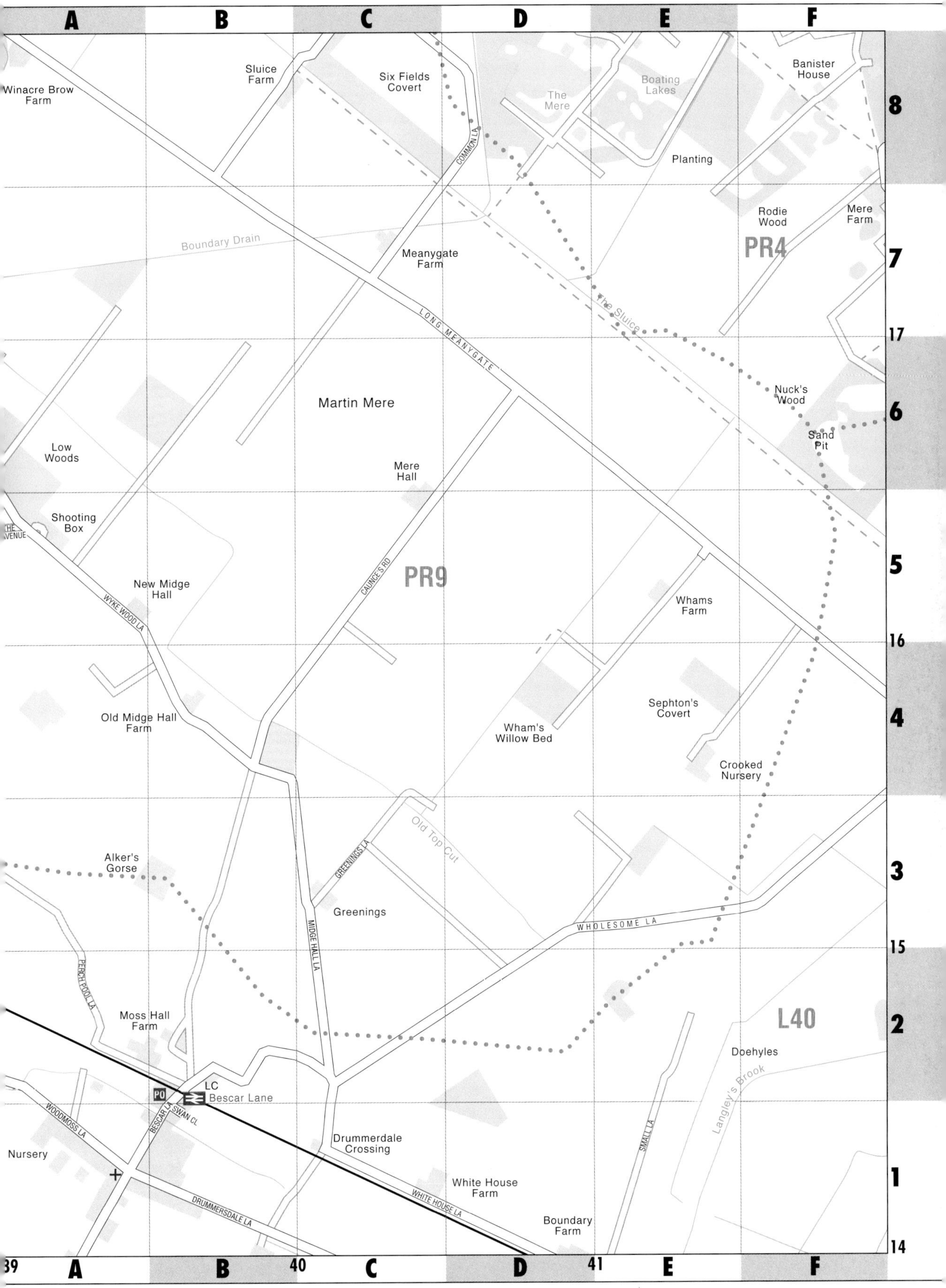
A
B
C
D
E
F
Winacre Brow Farm
Sluice Farm
Six Fields Covert
The Mere
Boating Lakes
Banister House
COMMON LA
Planting
Rodie Wood
Mere Farm
PR4
Boundary Drain
Meanygate Farm
The Sluice
LONG MEANYGATE
Nuck's Wood
Martin Mere
Sand Pit
Low Woods
Mere Hall
Shooting Box
THE AVENUE
PR9
CAUNCE'S RD
New Midge Hall
WYKE WOOD LA
Whams Farm
Sephton's Covert
Old Midge Hall Farm
Wham's Willow Bed
Crooked Nursery
Old Top Cut
Alker's Gorse
GREENINGS LA
Greenings
WHOLESOME LA
MIDGE HALL LA
PERCH POOL LA
L40
Moss Hall Farm
Doehyles
Langley's Brook
PO
LC
Bescar Lane
WOODMOSS LA
BESCAR LA
SWAN CL
Drummerdale Crossing
SMALL LA
Nursery
White House Farm
DRUMMERSDALE LA
WHITE HOUSE LA
Boundary Farm
8
7
17
6
5
16
4
3
15
2
1
14
39
40
41

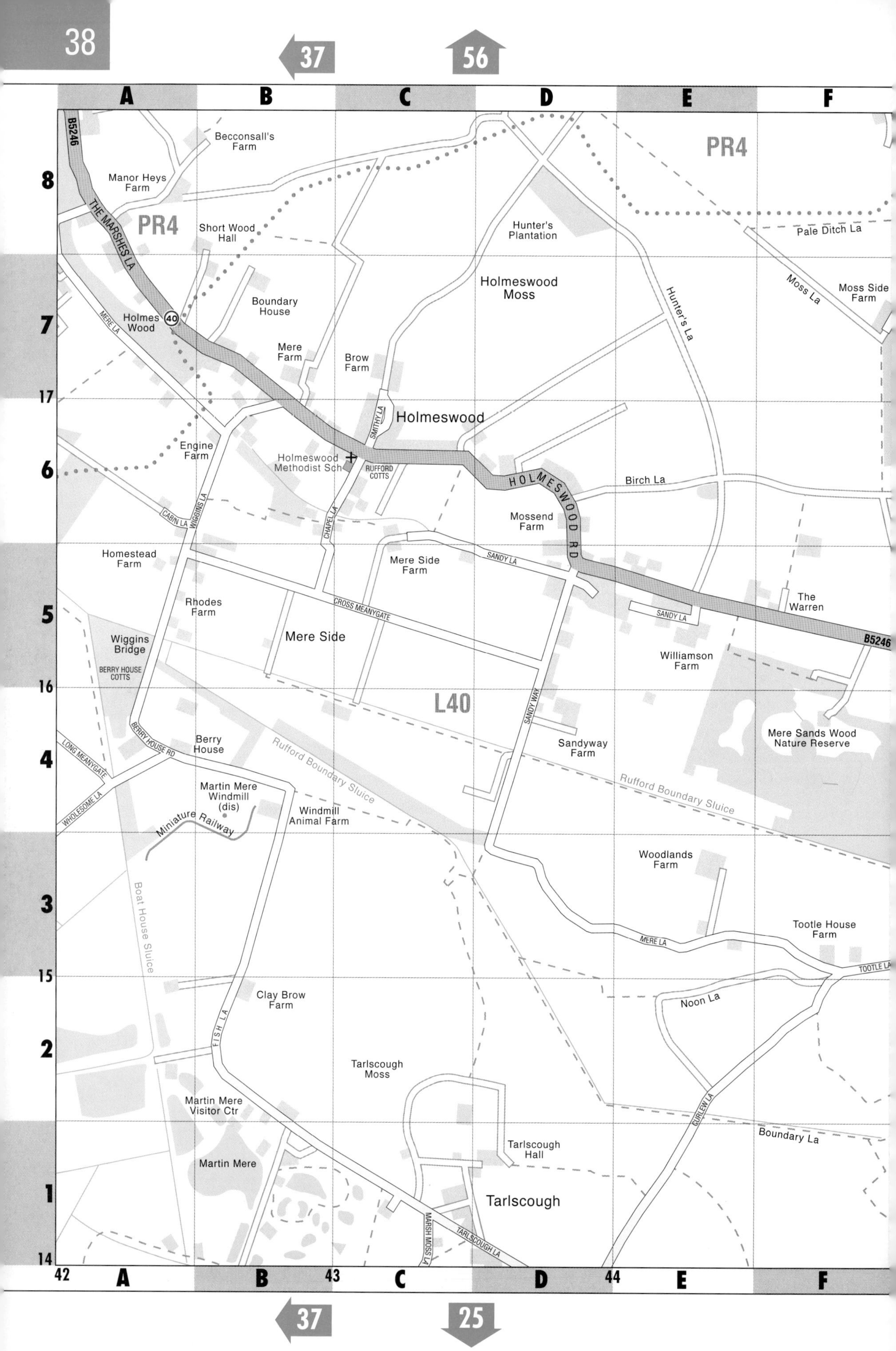
37
56
A B C D E F
8
7
17
6
5
16
4
3
15
2
1
14
42
43
44
B5246
Becconsall's Farm
Manor Heys Farm
PR4
THE MARSHES LA
Short Wood Hall
Hunter's Plantation
Pale Ditch La
Moss La
Moss Side Farm
Holmeswood Moss
Boundary House
Holmes Wood
40
MERE LA
Mere Farm
Brow Farm
Hunter's La
SMITHY LA
Holmeswood
Engine Farm
Holmeswood Methodist Sch
RUFFORD COTTS
HOLMESWOOD RD
Birch La
CABIN LA
WIGGINS LA
CHAPEL LA
Mossend Farm
Homestead Farm
Mere Side Farm
SANDY LA
Rhodes Farm
CROSS MEANYGATE
The Warren
SANDY LA
Wiggins Bridge
Mere Side
BERRY HOUSE COTTS
Williamson Farm
L40
SANDY WAY
BERRY HOUSE RD
Berry House
Sandyway Farm
Mere Sands Wood Nature Reserve
LONG MEANYGATE
Rufford Boundary Sluice
Martin Mere Windmill (dis)
WHOLESOME LA
Miniature Railway
Windmill Animal Farm
Woodlands Farm
Boat House Sluice
Tootle House Farm
MERE LA
TOOTLE LA
Clay Brow Farm
Noon La
FISH LA
Tarlscough Moss
Martin Mere Visitor Ctr
CURLEW LA
Boundary La
Tarlscough Hall
Martin Mere
Tarlscough
MARSH MOSS LA
TARLSCOUGH LA
A B 43 C D 44 E F
37
25

57
40
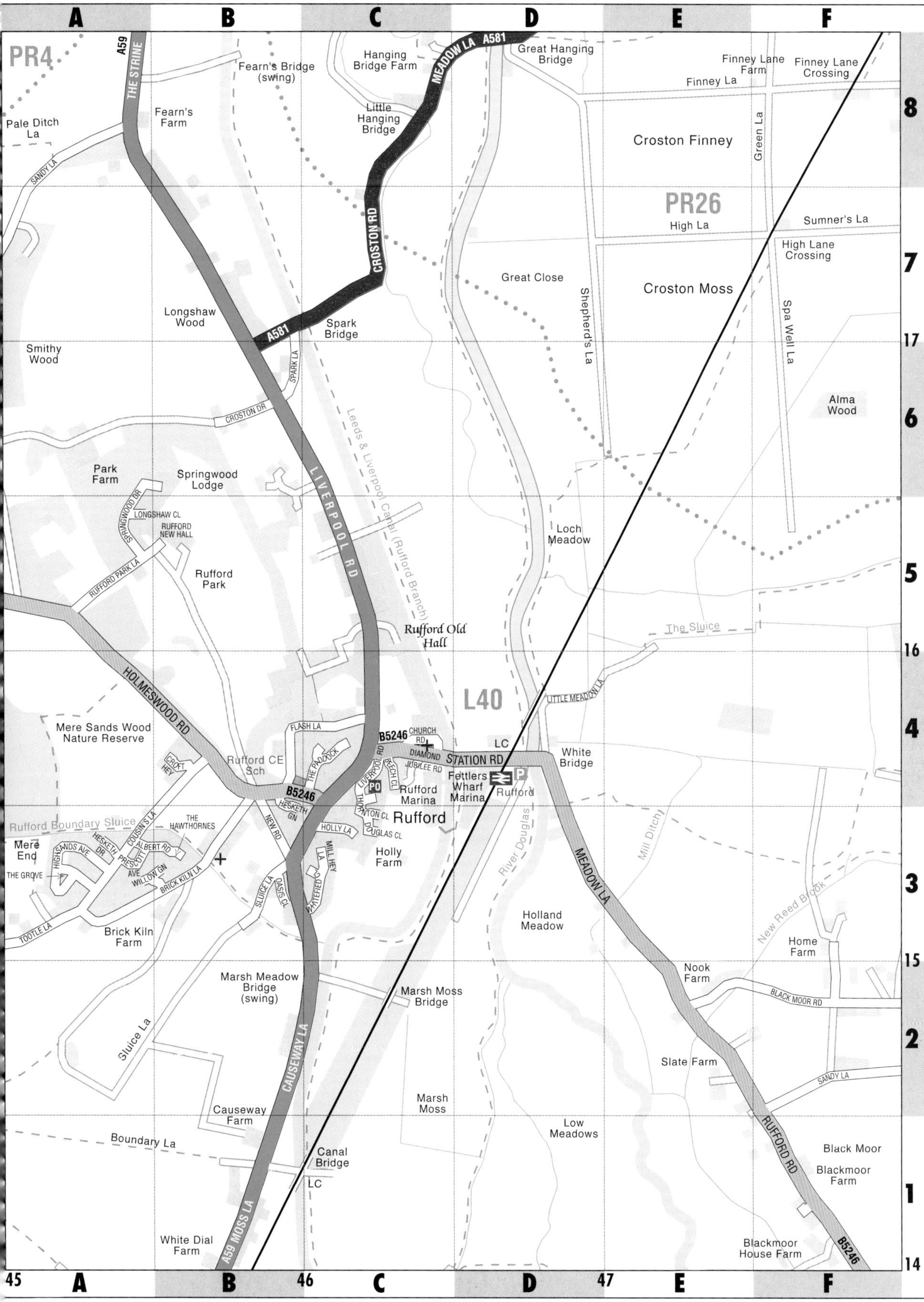
A
B
C
D
E
F
PR4
A59
THE STRINE
Fearn's Bridge (swing)
Hanging Bridge Farm
MEADOW LA
A581
Great Hanging Bridge
Finney Lane Farm
Finney Lane Crossing
Finney La
Pale Ditch La
Fearn's Farm
Little Hanging Bridge
Croston Finney
Green La
SANDY LA
PR26
High La
Sumner's La
High Lane Crossing
CROSTON RD
Great Close
Croston Moss
Shepherd's La
Spa Well La
Longshaw Wood
Spark Bridge
Smithy Wood
SPARK LA
CROSTON DR
Alma Wood
Leeds & Liverpool Canal (Rufford Branch)
Park Farm
Springwood Lodge
LIVERPOOL RD
SPRINGWOOD DR
LONGSHAW CL
RUFFORD NEW HALL
Loch Meadow
Rufford Park
RUFFORD PARK LA
The Sluice
Rufford Old Hall
HOLMESWOOD RD
L40
LITTLE MEADOW LA
Mere Sands Wood Nature Reserve
FLASH LA
B5246
CHURCH RD
LC
THE PADDOCK
DIAMOND
STATION RD
White Bridge
CROFT HEY
Rufford CE Sch
JUBILEE RD
BEECH CL
LIVERPOOL RD
Fettlers Wharf Marina
PO
Rufford Marina
Rufford
HESKETH GN
THORNTON CL
Rufford Boundary Sluice
THE HAWTHORNES
NEW RD
HOLLY LA
DOUGLAS CL
River Douglas
Mill Ditch
Mere End
HESKETH DR
COUSIN'S LA
ALBERT RD
HIGHLANDS AVE
PRESCOTT AVE
MILL HEY LA
Holly Farm
MEADOW LA
THE GROVE
WILLOW GN
BRICK KILN LA
SLUICE LA
OASIS CL
WHITEFIELD CL
New Reed Brook
Holland Meadow
TOOTLE LA
Brick Kiln Farm
Home Farm
Nook Farm
Marsh Meadow Bridge (swing)
Marsh Moss Bridge
BLACK MOOR RD
Sluice La
CAUSEWAY LA
Slate Farm
SANDY LA
Causeway Farm
Marsh Moss
Low Meadows
Boundary La
Canal Bridge
RUFFORD RD
Black Moor
Blackmoor Farm
LC
A59 MOSS LA
White Dial Farm
Blackmoor House Farm
B5246
8
7
17
6
5
16
4
3
15
2
1
14
45
46
47
26
40

39
58

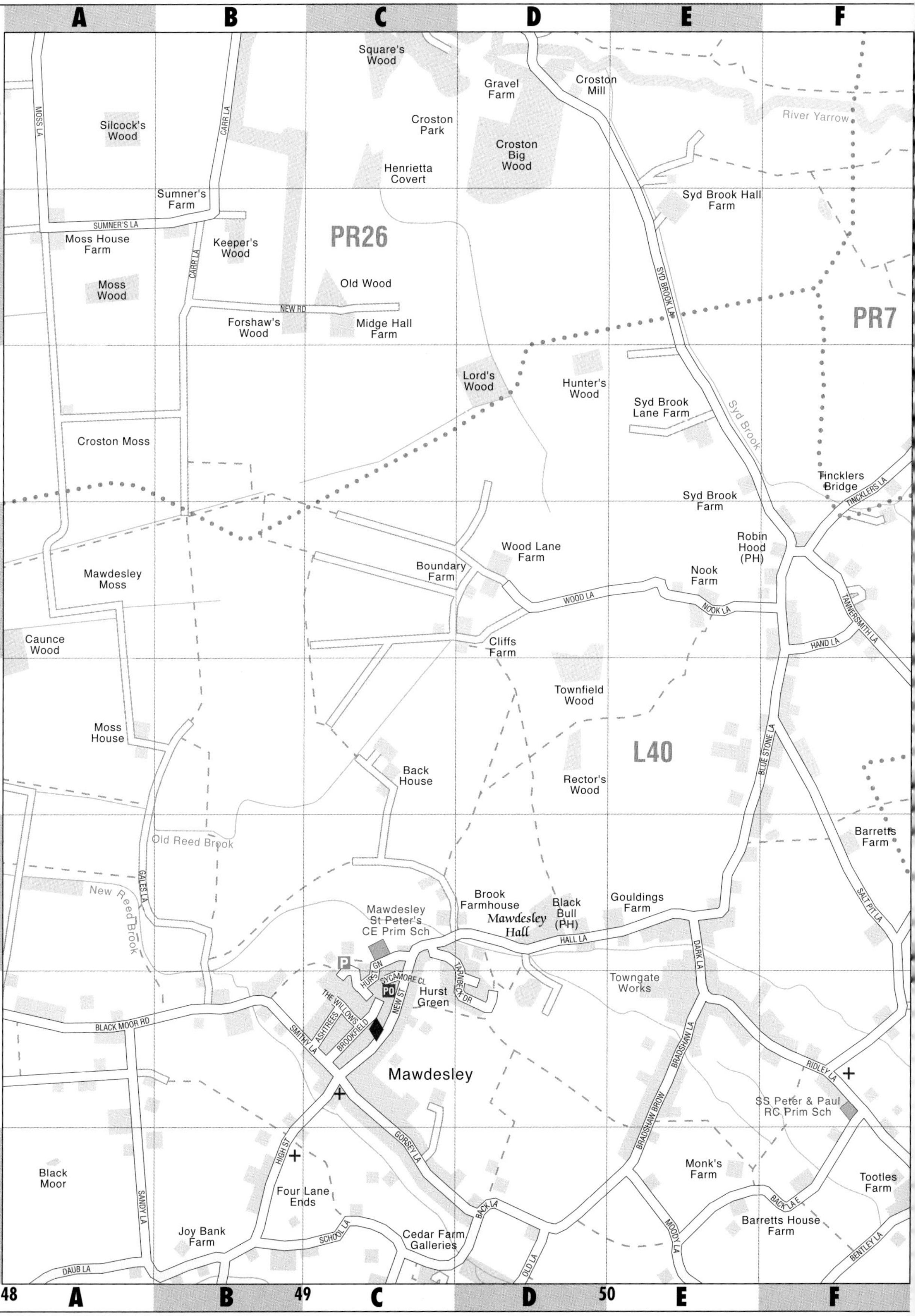
A
B
C
D
E
F
8
7
17
6
5
16
4
3
15
2
1
14
48
49
50
Square's Wood
Gravel Farm
Croston Mill
River Yarrow
Silcock's Wood
MOSS LA
CARR LA
Croston Park
Croston Big Wood
Henrietta Covert
Sumner's Farm
SUMNER'S LA
Syd Brook Hall Farm
Moss House Farm
Keeper's Wood
PR26
Moss Wood
Old Wood
SYD BROOK LA
PR7
NEW RD
Forshaw's Wood
Midge Hall Farm
Lord's Wood
Hunter's Wood
Syd Brook Lane Farm
Syd Brook
Croston Moss
Tincklers Bridge
TINCKLERS LA
Syd Brook Farm
Robin Hood (PH)
Wood Lane Farm
Boundary Farm
Nook Farm
Mawdesley Moss
WOOD LA
NOOK LA
TANNERSMITH LA
Caunce Wood
Cliffs Farm
HAND LA
Townfield Wood
Moss House
BLUE STONE LA
L40
Back House
Rector's Wood
Barretts Farm
Old Reed Brook
New Reed Brook
GALES LA
Brook Farmhouse
Black Bull (PH)
Gouldings Farm
Mawdesley St Peter's CE Prim Sch
Mawdesley Hall
HALL LA
SALT PIT LA
DARK LA
HURST GN
SYCAMORE CL
TARNBECK DR
Towngate Works
THE WILLOWS
NEW ST
Hurst Green
ASHTREES
BROOKFIELD
BLACK MOOR RD
SMITHY LA
BRADSHAW LA
Mawdesley
RIDLEY LA
BRADSHAW BROW
SS Peter & Paul RC Prim Sch
GORSEY LA
HIGH ST
Black Moor
Monk's Farm
Tootles Farm
Four Lane Ends
SANDY LA
BACK LA
BACK LA E
Joy Bank Farm
MOODY LA
Barretts House Farm
Cedar Farm Galleries
SCHOOL LA
OLD LA
DAUB LA
BENTLEY LA

39
27

59
42

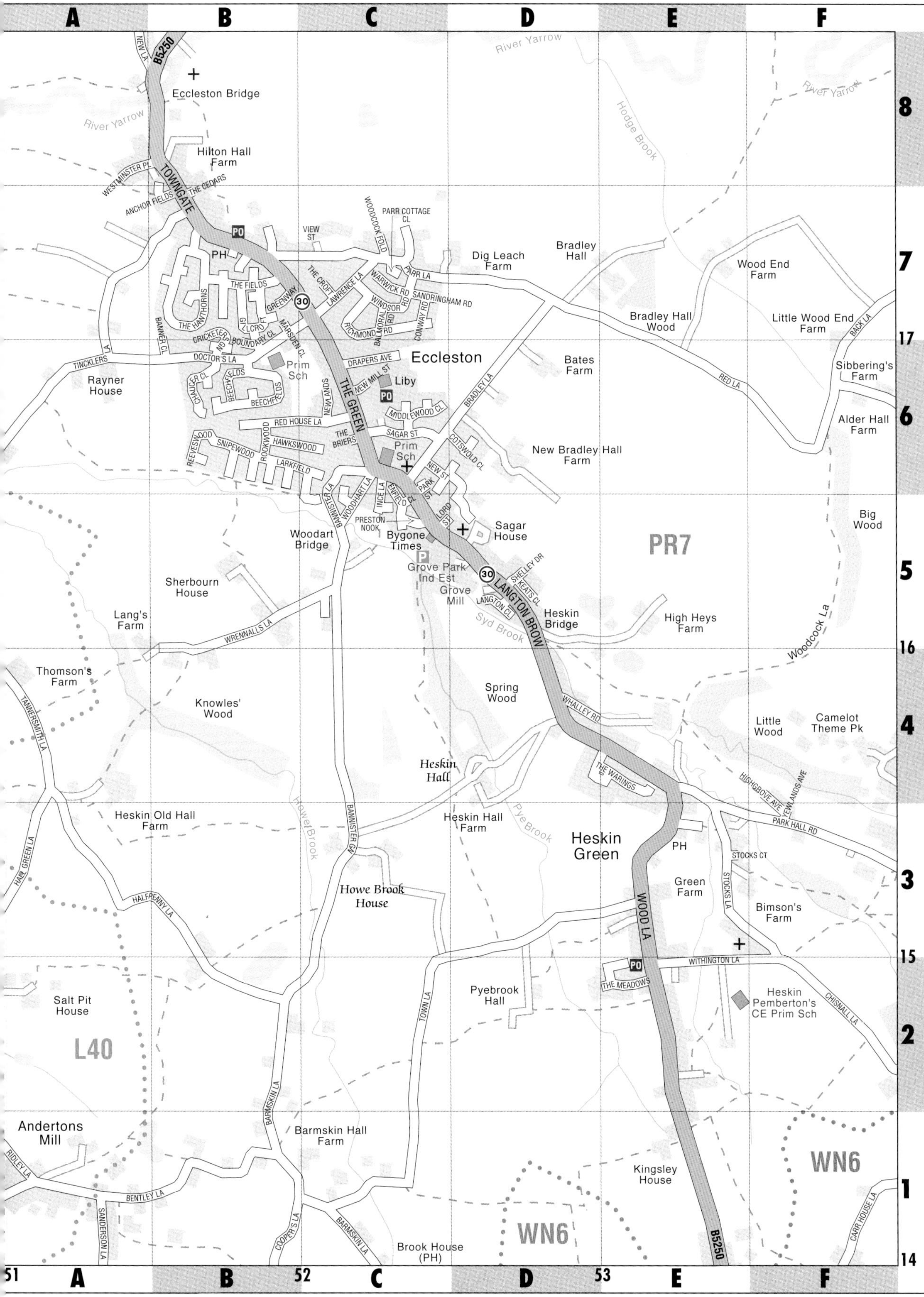
A
B
C
D
E
F
8
7
17
6
5
16
4
3
15
2
1
14
51
52
53
B5250
NEW LA
Eccleston Bridge
River Yarrow
Hilton Hall Farm
WESTMINSTER PL
TOWNGATE
THE CEDARS
ANCHOR FIELDS
PO
PH
VIEW ST
WOODCOCK FOLD
PARR COTTAGE CL
Dig Leach Farm
Bradley Hall
Wood End Farm
Hodge Brook
THE FIELDS
THE HAWTHORNS
GREENWAY
THE CROFT
LAWRENCE LA
WARWICK RD
PARR LA
SANDRINGHAM RD
WINDSOR RD
BALMORAL RD
RICHMOND RD
CONWAY RD
30
BANNER CL
CRICKETERS
BOUNDARY CL
MARSDEN CL
Bradley Hall Wood
Little Wood End Farm
BACK LA
TINCKLERS LA
DOCTOR'S LA
DRAPERS AVE
Eccleston
Bates Farm
Sibbering's Farm
Rayner House
CHAUCER CL
BEECHFIELDS
Prim Sch
NEW MILL ST
Liby
NEW LANDS
THE GREEN
BRADLEY LA
RED LA
Alder Hall Farm
MIDDLEWOOD CL
RED HOUSE LA
SAGAR ST
THE BRIERS
REEVESWOOD
SNIPEWOOD
ROOKWOOD
HAWKSWOOD
LARKFIELD
COTSWOLD CL
New Bradley Hall Farm
NEW ST
PARK
BANNISTER LA
WOODHART LA
INCE LA
ENFIELD CL
LORD ST
PRESTON NOOK
Bygone Times
Sagar House
Woodart Bridge
Big Wood
PR7
SHELLEY DR
KEATS CL
Grove Park Ind Est
Grove Mill
Sherbourn House
LANGTON CL
LANGTON BROW
Heskin Bridge
High Heys Farm
Lang's Farm
WRENNALLS LA
Syd Brook
Woodcock La
Thomson's Farm
Spring Wood
Knowles' Wood
TANNERSMITH LA
WHALLEY RD
Little Wood
Camelot Theme Pk
Heskin Hall
THE WARINGS
HIGHGROVE AVE
YEWLANDS AVE
Heskin Old Hall Farm
Howe Brook
BANNISTER GR
Heskin Hall Farm
Pye Brook
Heskin Green
PARK HALL RD
HALL GREEN LA
STOCKS CT
STOCKS LA
Green Farm
HALFPENNY LA
Howe Brook House
WOOD LA
Bimson's Farm
WITHINGTON LA
THE MEADOWS
Salt Pit House
Pyebrook Hall
TOWN LA
Heskin Pemberton's CE Prim Sch
CHISNALL LA
L40
BARMSKIN LA
Andertons Mill
Barmskin Hall Farm
WN6
RIDLEY LA
BENTLEY LA
Kingsley House
CARR HOUSE LA
SANDERSON LA
COOPER'S LA
Brook House (PH)

28
42

41
60

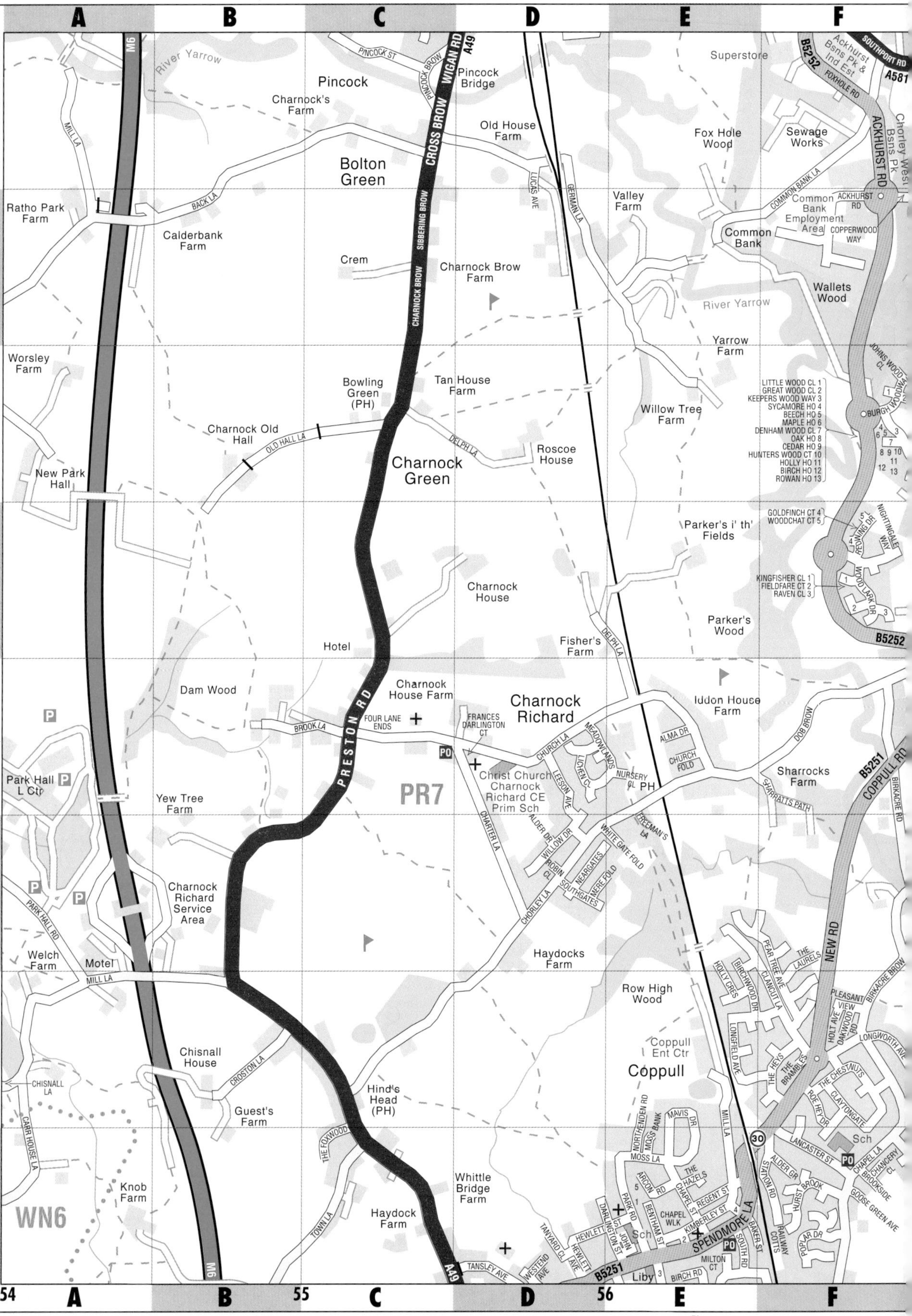


E1
1 GERMAN LA
2 CLEVELAND ST
3 SPRINGFIELD RD N
4 MILL ST
5 ARCON HO

41
29

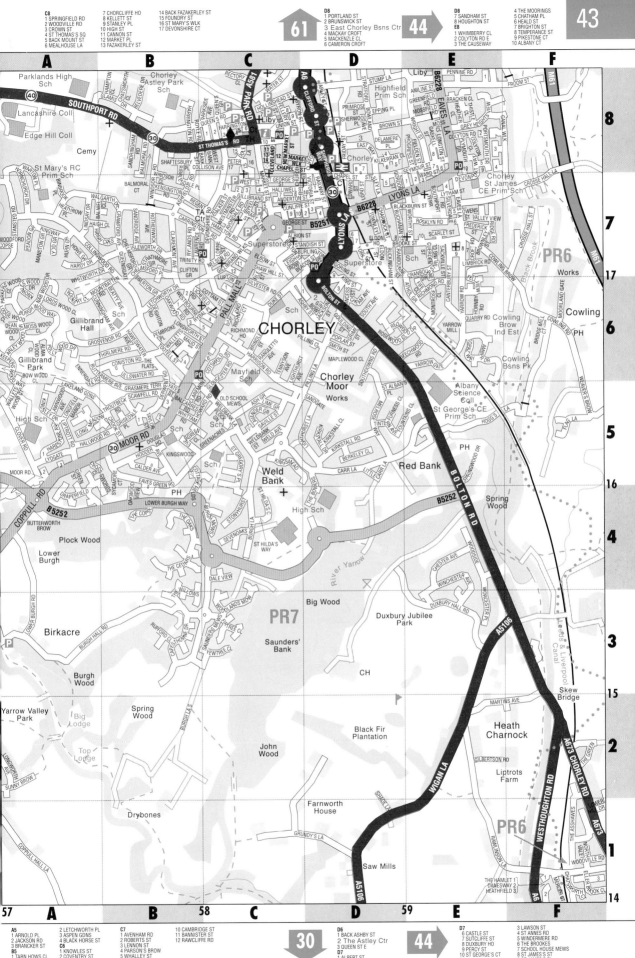

C8
1 SPRINGFIELD RD
2 WOODVILLE RD
3 CROWN ST
4 ST THOMAS'S SQ
5 BACK MOUNT ST
6 MEALHOUSE LA
7 CHORCLIFFE HO
8 KELLETT ST
9 STANLEY PL
10 HIGH ST
11 CANNON ST
12 MARKET PL
13 FAZAKERLEY ST
14 BACK FAZAKERLEY ST
15 FOUNDRY ST
16 ST MARY'S WLK
17 DEVONSHIRE CT

61

D8
1 PORTLAND ST
2 BRUNSWICK ST
3 East Chorley Bsns Ctr
4 MACKAY CROFT
5 MACKENZLE CL
6 CAMERON CROFT

44

D8
7 SANDHAM ST
8 HOUGHTON ST
E8
1 WHIMBERRY CL
2 COLYTON RD E
3 THE CAUSEWAY
4 THE MOORINGS
5 CHATHAM PL
6 HEALD ST
7 BRIGHTON ST
8 TEMPERANCE ST
9 PIKESTONE CT
10 ALBANY CT

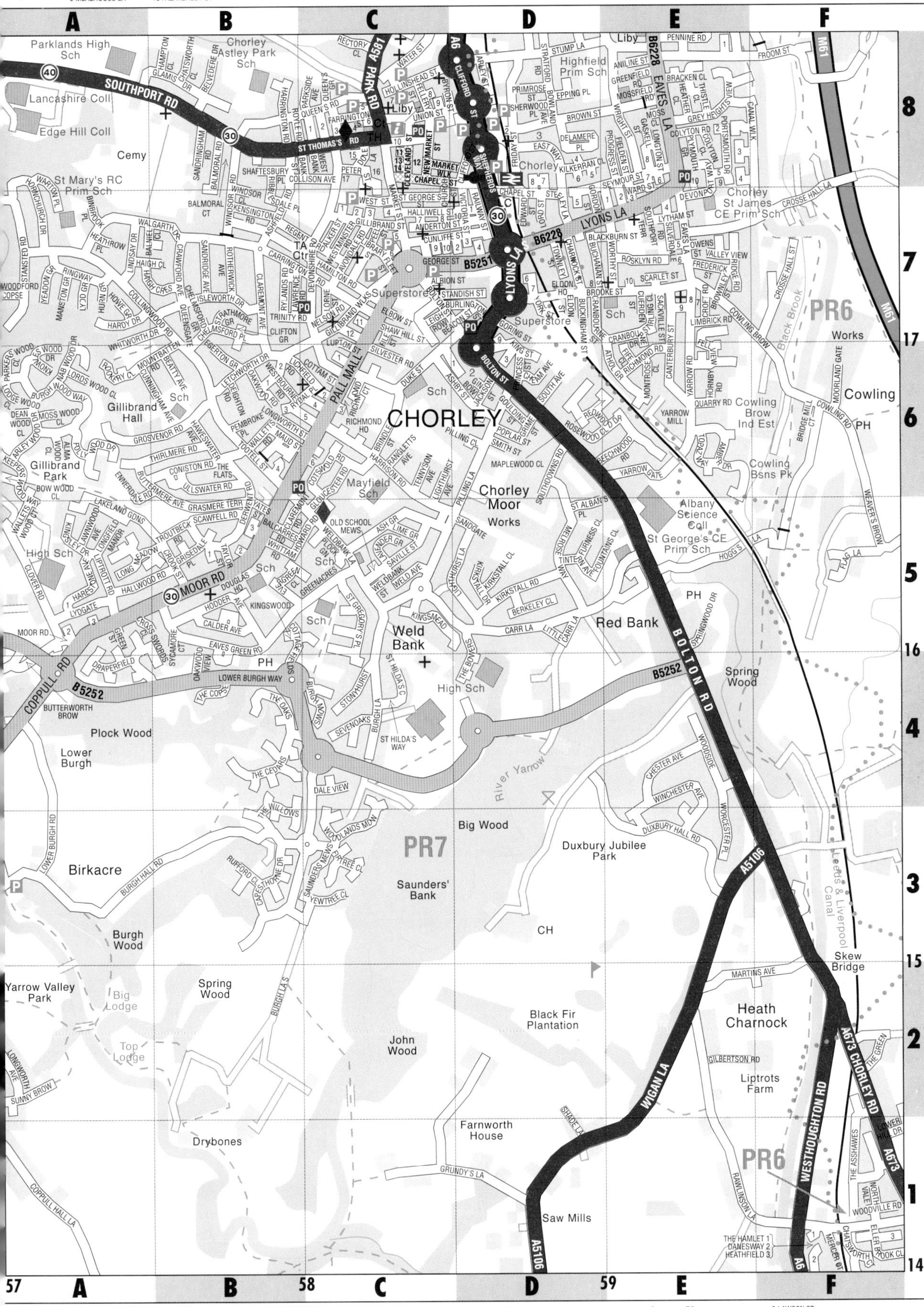

A B C D E F
8 7 6 5 4 3 2 1
17 16 15 14
57 58 59
Parklands High Sch
Chorley Astley Park Sch
Lancashire Coll
Edge Hill Coll
Cemy
St Mary's RC Prim Sch
SOUTHPORT RD
ST THOMAS'S RD
PARK RD
Liby
Highfield Prim Sch
EAVES LA
LYONS LA
Chorley St James CE Prim Sch
TA Ctr
Superstore
Gillibrand Hall
Gillibrand Park
CHORLEY
PALL MALL
BOLTON ST
BOLTON RD
Chorley Moor Works
Mayfield Sch
Yarrow Mill
Cowling Brow Ind Est
Cowling Bsns Pk
Cowling
Works
PR6
M61
Albany Science Coll
St George's CE Prim Sch
High Sch
MOOR RD
Weld Bank
Red Bank
High Sch
COPPULL RD
LOWER BURGH WAY
Plock Wood
Lower Burgh
Spring Wood
River Yarrow
Big Wood
PR7
Duxbury Jubilee Park
Birkacre
Saunders' Bank
Leeds & Liverpool Canal
CH
Burgh Wood
Skew Bridge
Yarrow Valley Park
Big Lodge
Spring Wood
Black Fir Plantation
Heath Charnock
Top Lodge
John Wood
Liptrots Farm
WIGAN LA
WESTHOUGHTON RD
CHORLEY RD
Farnworth House
Drybones
GRUNDY'S LA
Saw Mills
RAWLINSON LA
COPPULL HALL LA


A5
1 ARNOLD PL
2 JACKSON RD
3 BRANCKER ST
B5
1 TARN HOWS CL
2 BAMBER ST
3 GRAFTON CT
B6
1 VENTNOR RD
2 LETCHWORTH PL
3 ASPEN GDNS
4 BLACK HORSE ST
C6
1 KNOWLES ST
2 COVENTRY ST
3 NORRIS ST
4 GILBERT ST
5 HINDLEY ST
6 CATHERINE ST
C7
1 AVENHAM RD
2 ROBERTS ST
3 LENNON ST
4 PARSON'S BROW
5 WHALLEY ST
6 CHEAPSIDE
7 HALLIWELL CT
8 HALLIWELL PL
9 OXFORD ST
10 CAMBRIDGE ST
11 BANNISTER ST
12 RAWCLIFFE RD

30

D6
1 BACK ASHBY ST
2 The Astley Ctr
3 QUEEN ST E
D7
1 ALBERT ST
2 NORTHUMBERLAND ST
3 SALISBURY ST
4 CLARENCE ST
5 SHERBOURNE ST

44

D7
6 CASTLE ST
7 SUTCLIFFE ST
8 DUXBURY HO
9 PERCY ST
10 ST GEORGE'S CT
E7
1 CAVENDISH ST
2 STEPHENSON ST
3 LAWSON ST
4 ST ANNES RD
5 WINDERMERE RD
6 THE BROOKES
7 SCHOOL HOUSE MEWS
8 ST JAMES'S ST
9 ST JAMES'S PL
10 CLARENDON ST

43
62

A
B
C
D
E
F
8
7
17
6
5
16
4
3
15
2
1
14
60
61
62
Grey Heights
Grey Heights Wood
Hurst Hill
Siddow Fold
White House
CROSSE HALL LA
Works
Spen Cob
Manor House
HEAPEY FOLD LA
MOOR RD
Johnson's Farm Bungalow
High Bullough Resr
Jepson's Gate
Bibbys Farm
M61
Anglezarke Woodland Trail
Fish Barn Farm
Jepson's Farm
Kays Farm
Limbrick
Ainsworths Farm
Stone's House
PH
P
Brindles Farm
Anglezarke Resr
BACK LA
Waring's Farm
Parson's Bullough
PARSON'S BULLOUGH RD
HODGE BROW
PR6
Alance Bridge
Hallsworth Fold Farm
OLDE STONEHEATH CT
Holland Fold
Nab's Farm
Yarrow Resr
LANE ENDS
KNOWSLEY LA
LONG LA
HUT LA
BROAD OAK COTTS
Yew Tree Inn (PH)
River Yarrow
THE STREET
NICK HILTON'S LA
NICK HILTON'S BROW
Dill Hall Brow
CH
Dean Wood House
PR7
Nick Hilton's Bridge
Blindhurst
Hall o' th' Hill Farm
Upper Rivington Resr
BL6
Broad Oak Farm
NICKLETON BROW
SLACK'S LA
NICKLETON
SLACK'S LA
Slack's Farm
Rivington
SHEEP HOUSE LA
Cunliffe Farm
Bay Horse Hotel (PH)
MILL HILL COTTS
Shaw Place
Lonsdale Farm
Fairview
Mast
MAJOR BOTTOMS
LOWER HILL DR
BABYLON LA
NEW RD
New House
Rivington Prim Sch
Croft Bridge
WATERFORD CL
1 BROOKDALE
2 FAIRVIEW DR
RIVINGTON LA
HORROBIN LA
A673 CHORLEY RD
STONEACRE DR
MILLBROOK ROW
STONEGATE FOLD
Springfield Cottages
CONISTON AVE
BROOK ST
OLLERTON ST
DAISY HILL DR
SUTTON LA
SUTTON FOLD
WINDERMERE DR
THIRLMERE CL
HORROBIN LA

43
31

63
46

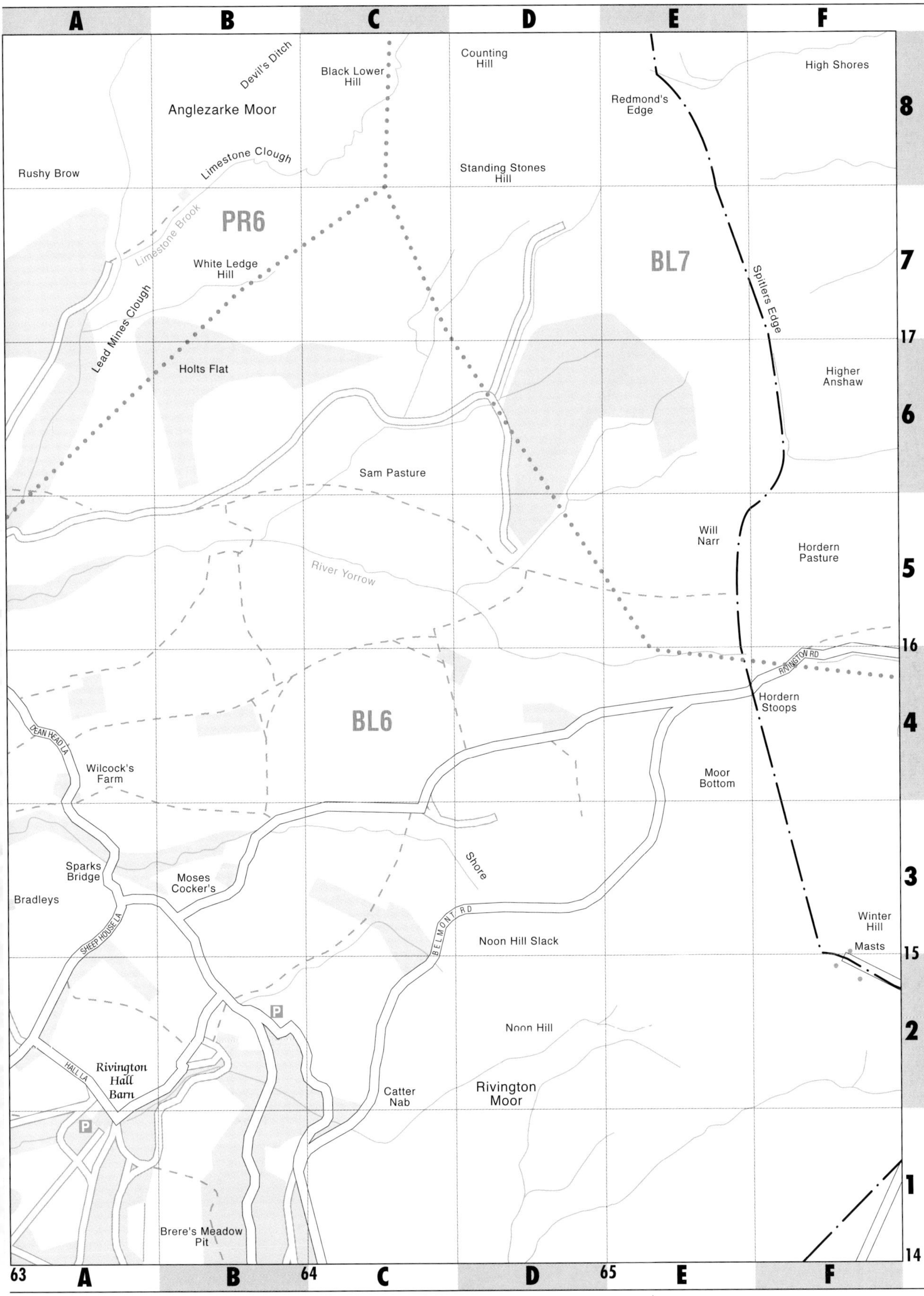
A
B
C
D
E
F
8
7
17
6
5
16
4
3
15
2
1
14
63
64
65
Devil's Ditch
Anglezarke Moor
Black Lower Hill
Counting Hill
Redmond's Edge
High Shores
Limestone Clough
Rushy Brow
Standing Stones Hill
PR6
Limestone Brook
White Ledge Hill
BL7
Spitlers Edge
Lead Mines Clough
Holts Flat
Higher Anshaw
Sam Pasture
Will Narr
Hordern Pasture
River Yorrow
RIVINGTON RD
Hordern Stoops
BL6
DEAN HEAD LA
Wilcock's Farm
Moor Bottom
Shore
Sparks Bridge
Moses Cocker's
Bradleys
SHEEP HOUSE LA
BELMONT RD
Noon Hill Slack
Winter Hill
Masts
P
Noon Hill
HALL LA
Rivington Hall Barn
Catter Nab
Rivington Moor
Brere's Meadow Pit

32
46

45
64

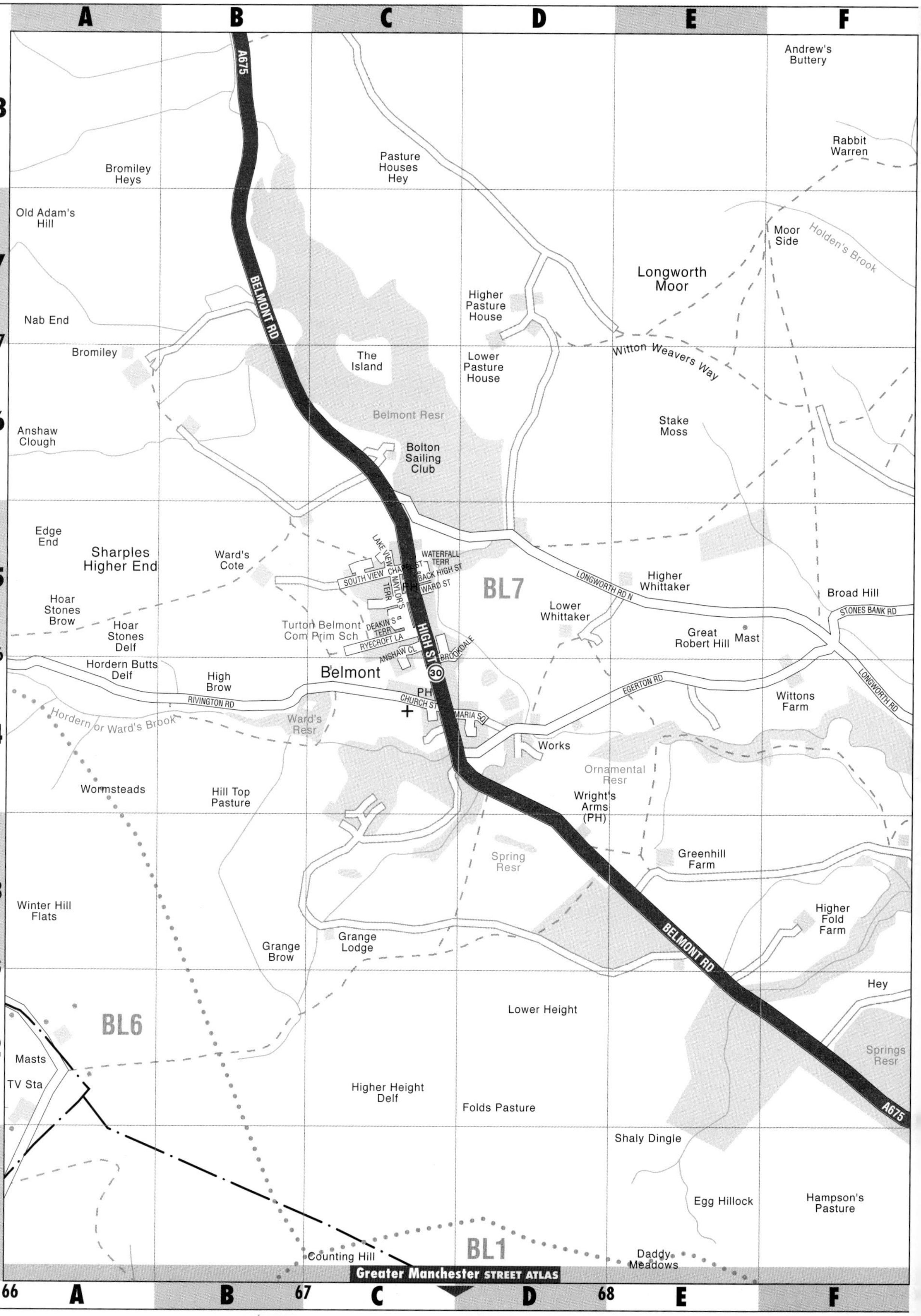
A
B
C
D
E
F
8
7
17
6
5
16
4
3
15
2
1
14
66
67
68
A675
Andrew's Buttery
Bromiley Heys
Pasture Houses Hey
Rabbit Warren
Old Adam's Hill
Moor Side
Holden's Brook
Longworth Moor
BELMONT RD
Higher Pasture House
Nab End
Bromiley
The Island
Lower Pasture House
Witton Weavers Way
Belmont Resr
Anshaw Clough
Stake Moss
Bolton Sailing Club
Edge End
Sharples Higher End
Ward's Cote
LAKE VIEW
CHAPEL ST
WATERFALL TERR
SOUTH VIEW
NAYLOR'S TERR
BACK HIGH ST
WARD ST
PH
BL7
LONGWORTH RD N
Higher Whittaker
Broad Hill
Hoar Stones Brow
Lower Whittaker
STONES BANK RD
Hoar Stones Delf
Turton Belmont Com Prim Sch
DEAKIN'S TERR
RYECROFT LA
HIGH ST
Great Robert Hill
Mast
ANSHAW CL
BROOKDALE
Hordern Butts Delf
30
High Brow
Belmont
EGERTON RD
LONGWORTH RD
RIVINGTON RD
PH
CHURCH ST
Wittons Farm
Hordern or Ward's Brook
Ward's Resr
MARIA SQ
Works
Ornamental Resr
Wormsteads
Hill Top Pasture
Wright's Arms (PH)
Spring Resr
Greenhill Farm
Winter Hill Flats
Higher Fold Farm
BELMONT RD
Grange Brow
Grange Lodge
Hey
BL6
Lower Height
Masts
Springs Resr
TV Sta
Higher Height Delf
Folds Pasture
A675
Shaly Dingle
Egg Hillock
Hampson's Pasture
BL1
Counting Hill
Daddy Meadows



45

65
48

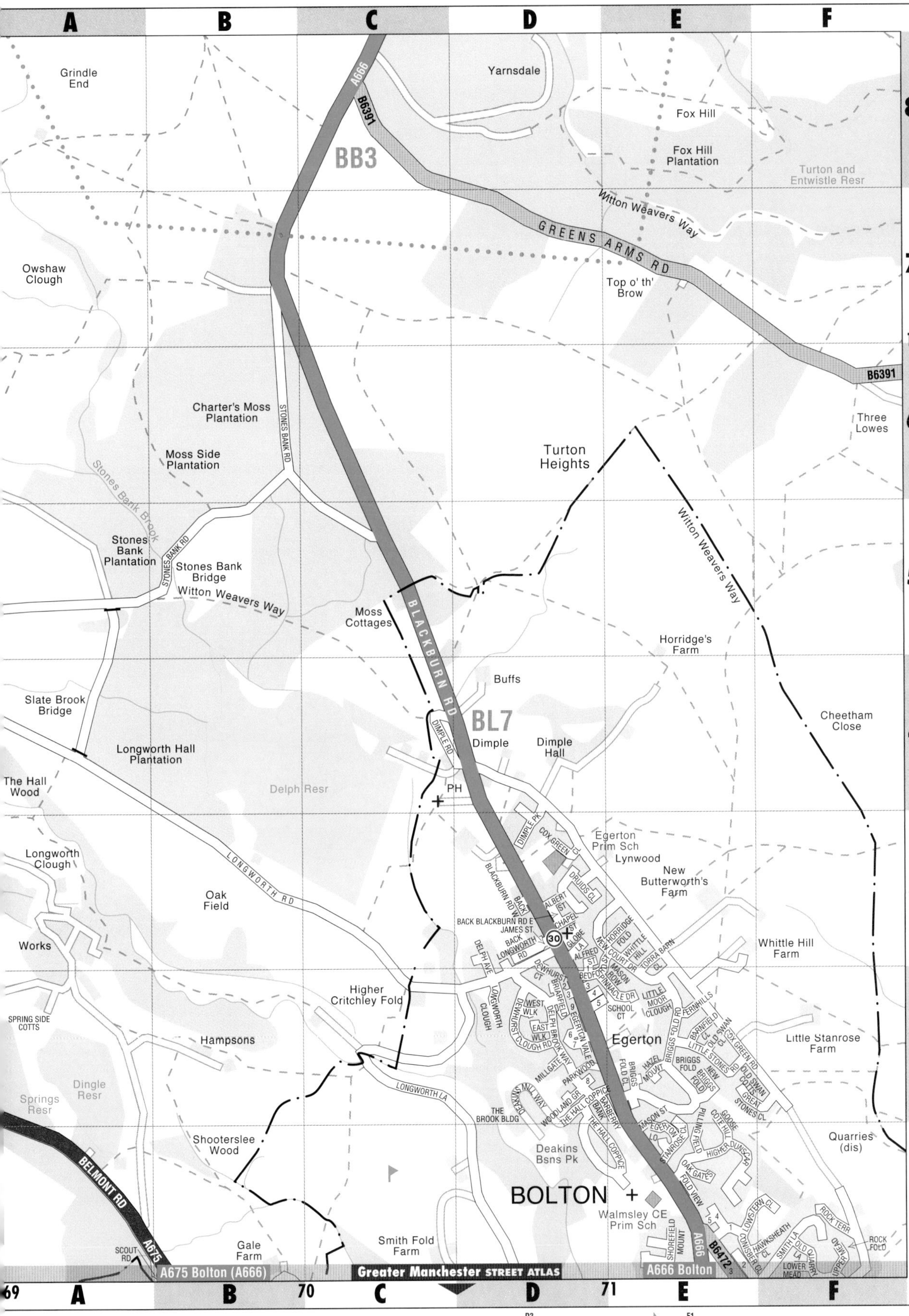
A
B
C
D
E
F
8
7
17
6
5
16
4
3
15
2
1
14
69
70
71
Grindle End
Yarnsdale
Fox Hill
Fox Hill Plantation
Turton and Entwistle Resr
BB3
A666
B6391
GREENS ARMS RD
Witton Weavers Way
Owshaw Clough
Top o' th' Brow
Charter's Moss Plantation
Moss Side Plantation
STONES BANK RD
Stones Bank Brook
Three Lowes
Turton Heights
Stones Bank Plantation
Stones Bank Bridge
Moss Cottages
BLACKBURN RD
Horridge's Farm
Buffs
Slate Brook Bridge
BL7
Cheetham Close
Longworth Hall Plantation
Dimple
Dimple Hall
DIMPLE RD
The Hall Wood
Delph Resr
PH
Longworth Clough
LONGWORTH RD
Egerton Prim Sch
Lynwood
New Butterworth's Farm
Oak Field
Works
Whittle Hill Farm
Higher Critchley Fold
SPRING SIDE COTTS
Hampsons
Egerton
Little Stanrose Farm
Dingle Resr
Springs Resr
LONGWORTH LA
THE BROOK BLDG
Shooterslee Wood
Deakins Bsns Pk
Quarries (dis)
BELMONT RD
A675
BOLTON
Walmsley CE Prim Sch
Gale Farm
Smith Fold Farm
SCOUT RD
A675 Bolton (A666)
Greater Manchester STREET ATLAS
A666 Bolton
B6472

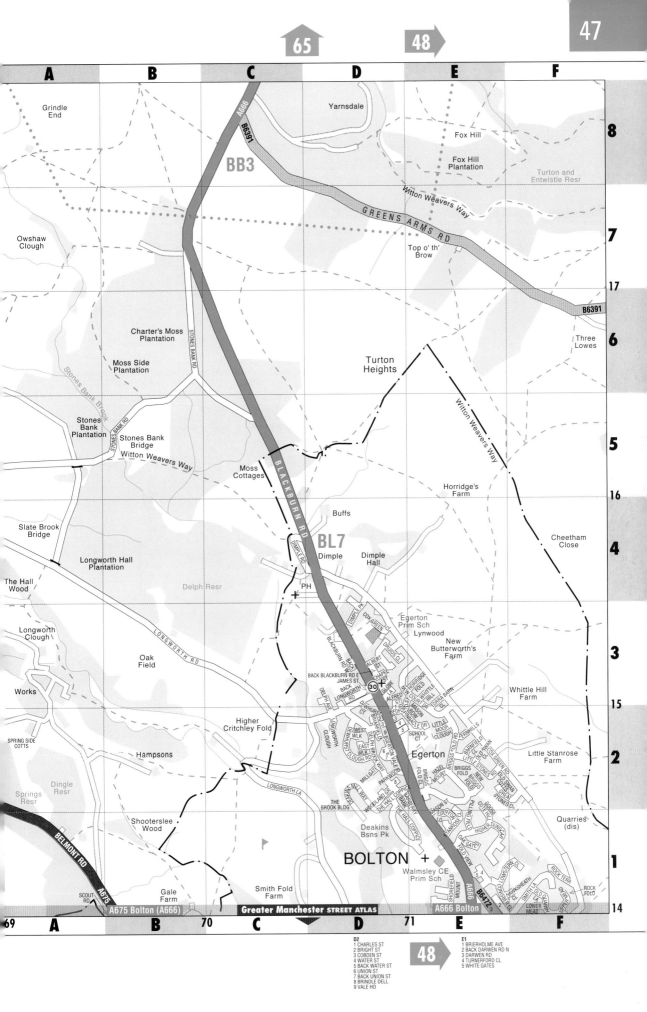

48

D2
1 CHARLES ST
2 BRIGHT ST
3 COBDEN ST
4 WATER ST
5 BACK WATER ST
6 UNION ST
7 BACK UNION ST
8 BRINDLE DELL
9 VALE HO

E1
1 BRIERHOLME AVE
2 BACK DARWEN RD N
3 DARWEN RD
4 TURNERFORD CL
5 WHITE GATES

47
66

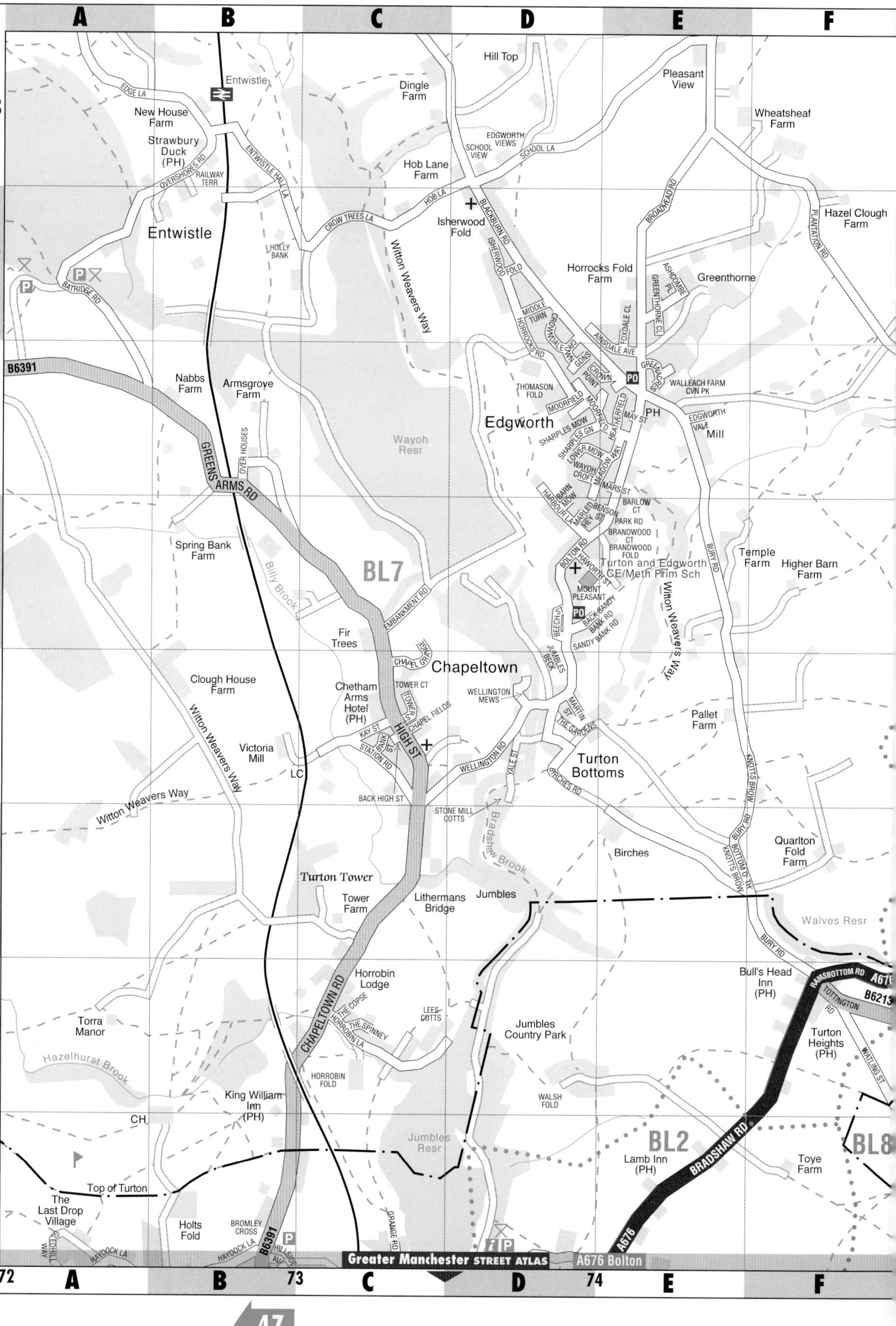
Entwistle
New House Farm
Strawbury Duck (PH)
Entwistle
Hill Top
Dingle Farm
Pleasant View
Wheatsheaf Farm
Hob Lane Farm
Isherwood Fold
Hazel Clough Farm
Horrocks Fold Farm
Greenthorne
Witton Weavers Way
Nabbs Farm
Armsgrove Farm
Edgworth
Wayoh Resr
Mill
Spring Bank Farm
BL7
Billy Brook
Turton and Edgworth CE/Meth Prim Sch
Temple Farm
Higher Barn Farm
Fir Trees
Chapeltown
Clough House Farm
Chetham Arms Hotel (PH)
Victoria Mill
Pallet Farm
Turton Bottoms
Birches
Quarlton Fold Farm
Turton Tower
Tower Farm
Lithermans Bridge
Jumbles
Walves Resr
Horrobin Lodge
Bull's Head Inn (PH)
Torra Manor
Jumbles Country Park
Turton Heights (PH)
Hazelhurst Brook
King William Inn (PH)
Jumbles Resr
BL2
BL8
Lamb Inn (PH)
Toye Farm
Top of Turton
The Last Drop Village
Holts Fold
B6391
A676
B6213
Greater Manchester STREET ATLAS
A676 Bolton

67
50

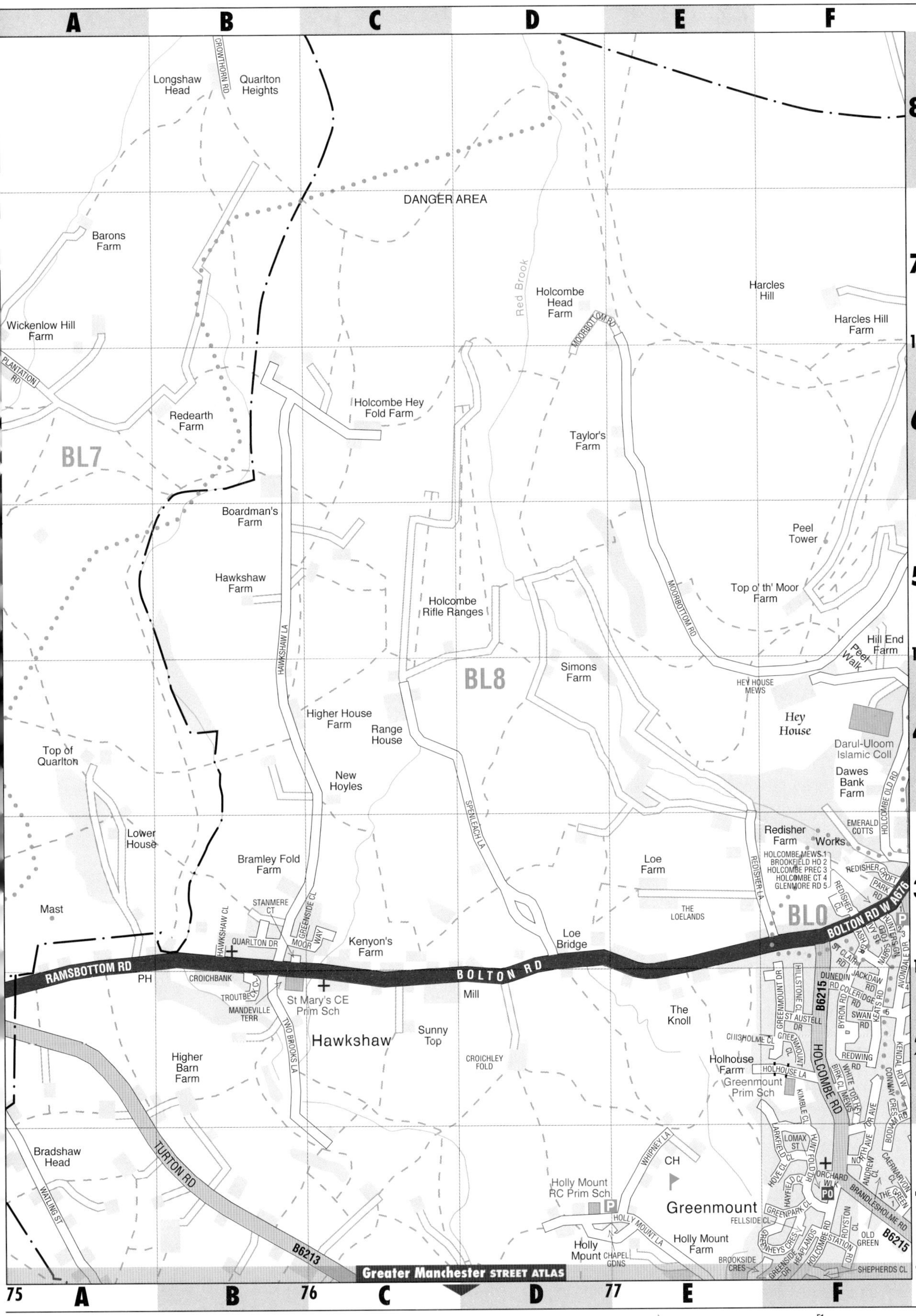
A
B
C
D
E
F
8
7
17
6
5
16
4
3
15
2
1
14
75
76
77
Longshaw Head
CROWTHORN RD
Quarlton Heights
DANGER AREA
Barons Farm
Wickenlow Hill Farm
PLANTATION RD
Redearth Farm
BL7
Boardman's Farm
Hawkshaw Farm
Holcombe Hey Fold Farm
Red Brook
Holcombe Head Farm
MOORBOTTOM RD
Harcles Hill
Harcles Hill Farm
Taylor's Farm
Peel Tower
Top o' th' Moor Farm
Hill End Farm
Peel Walk
HEY HOUSE MEWS
Hey House
Darul-Uloom Islamic Coll
Dawes Bank Farm
HOLCOMBE OLD RD
Holcombe Rifle Ranges
HAWKSHAW LA
BL8
Simons Farm
Higher House Farm
Range House
Top of Quarlton
New Hoyles
SPENLEACH LA
Lower House
Bramley Fold Farm
Loe Farm
Redisher Farm
Works
EMERALD COTTS
REDISHER LA
HOLCOMBE MEWS 1
BROOKFIELD HO 2
HOLCOMBE PREC 3
HOLCOMBE CT 4
GLENMORE RD 5
REDISHER CROFT
PARK
REDISHER CL
THE LOELANDS
BLO
BOLTON RD W A676
Mast
HAWKSHAW CL
STANMERE CT
GREENSIDE CL
MOOR WAY
QUARLTON DR
Kenyon's Farm
Loe Bridge
RAMSBOTTOM RD
PH
CROICHBANK
BOLTON RD
TROUTBECK CL
MANDEVILLE TERR
St Mary's CE Prim Sch
Mill
TWO BROOKS LA
Hawkshaw
Sunny Top
The Knoll
CROICHLEY FOLD
Higher Barn Farm
GREENMOUNT DR
HILLSTONE CL
B6215
DUNEDIN RD
JACKDAW RD
COLERIDGE RD
KEATS RD
BYRON RD
SWAN RD
ST AUSTELL DR
REDWING RD
HOLCOMBE RD
Holhouse Farm
HOLHOUSE LA
Greenmount Prim Sch
WHITE TOR RD
KIMBLE CL
KENDAL RD W
CONWAY CRES
BODIAM RD
AVONDALE DR
Bradshaw Head
TURTON RD
WATLING ST
B6213
WHIPNEY LA
CH
LOMAX ST
LARKFIELD CL
HUNT FOLD DR
HOVE CL
HAYFIELD CL
ORCHARD WLK
PO
ANDREW CL
CAERNARVON CL
THE GREEN
BRANDLESHOLME RD
Holly Mount RC Prim Sch
P
Greenmount
GREENPARK CL
FELLSIDE CL
HOLLY MOUNT LA
Holly Mount
CHAPEL GDNS
Holly Mount Farm
BROOKSIDE CRES
GREENSIDE DR
HOLCOMBE RD
STATION RD
ROYSTON CL
OLD GREEN
B6215
SHEPHERDS CL



F1
1 NAILERS GREEN

50

B5
1 GLENEAGLES WAY
2 BROWN ST
3 AJAX ST
4 CHARLOTTE ST
5 KERENHAPPUCH ST
6 WELL ST W
7 WEST ST
8 WATER ST
9 COLLING ST
10 ALFRED ST
11 BK ALFRED ST
12 FREDERICK ST
13 DOROTHY ST

49

B5
14 PILKINGTON ST
15 OX ST
16 EDGAR ST
17 EDGAR ST W
18 TIB ST
19 ELLIS ST

68

B5
20 SILVERMERE CL
21 MAYBURY CL
B6
1 COULTHURST ST
2 TAPE ST
3 KATE ST
4 RAKE
5 TANNERS CROFT
6 VESTA ST
7 BUCHANAN ST
8 CALTHA ST
9 CALLENDER CT

C6
1 KILLER ST
2 BK BRIDGE ST
3 ROOK ST
4 ST PAUL'S ST
5 CHURCH ST
6 MARKLAND ST
7 SMITHY ST
8 OLD GROUND ST
9 STRANG ST
10 PALATINE ST
11 SCOTLAND PL
12 THE OLD ENGINE HO
13 THE CORNERHOUSE
14 BARWOOD LEA MILL
15 VERNA ST
16 LEVER ST
17 ST JOHNS CT
18 PRINCES CT

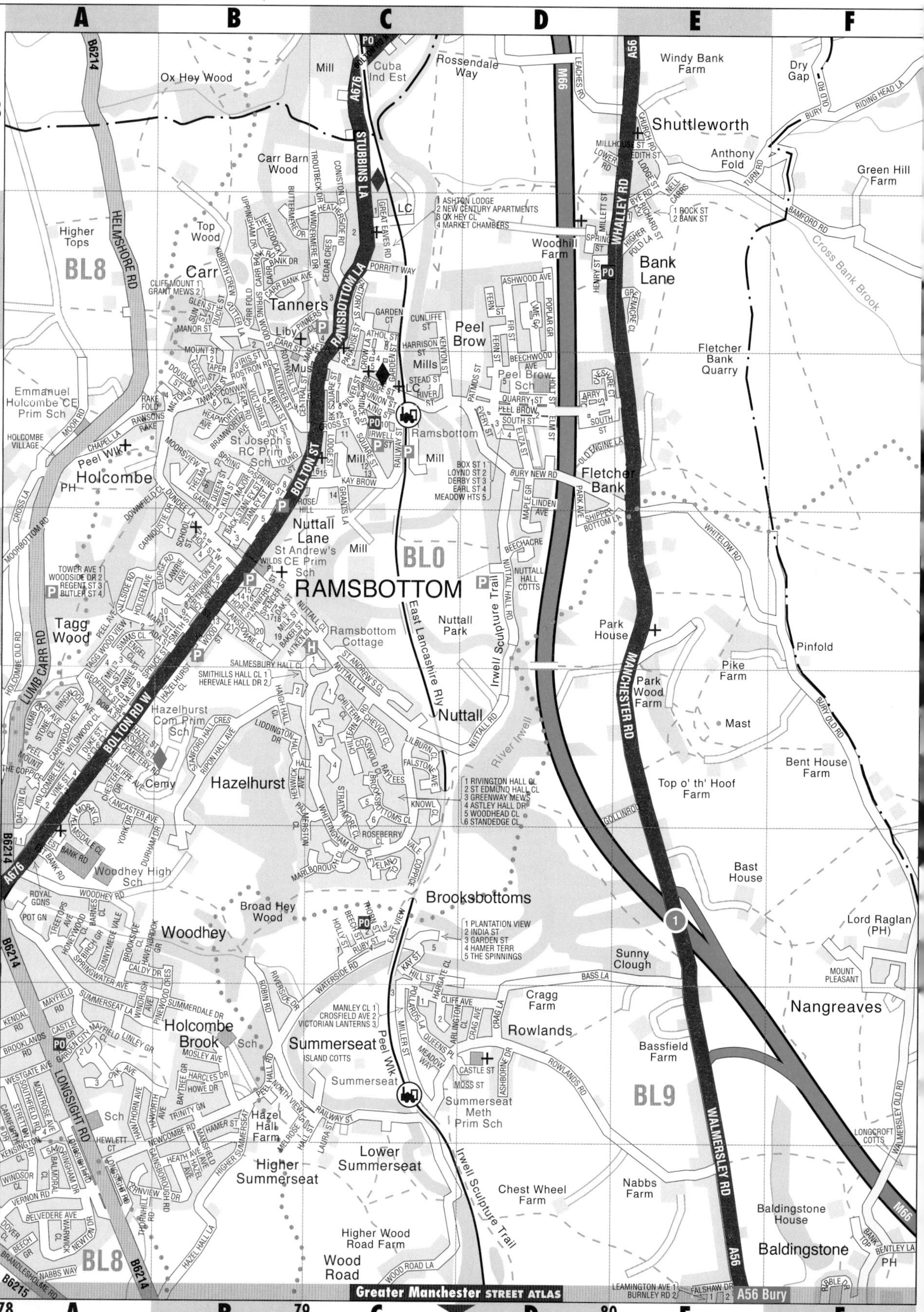




A2
1 KINROSS CL
2 AVIEMORE CL
3 BEAULY CL
4 SPRINGFIELD RD
A3
1 CROFTLANDS
A4
1 HILL RISE
2 ADELAIDE ST
3 BLOOM ST
4 CATO ST
5 ISA ST
6 CANNON ST
7 GRIME ST
8 FLAX ST
9 ZAMA ST
10 ELSIE ST

49

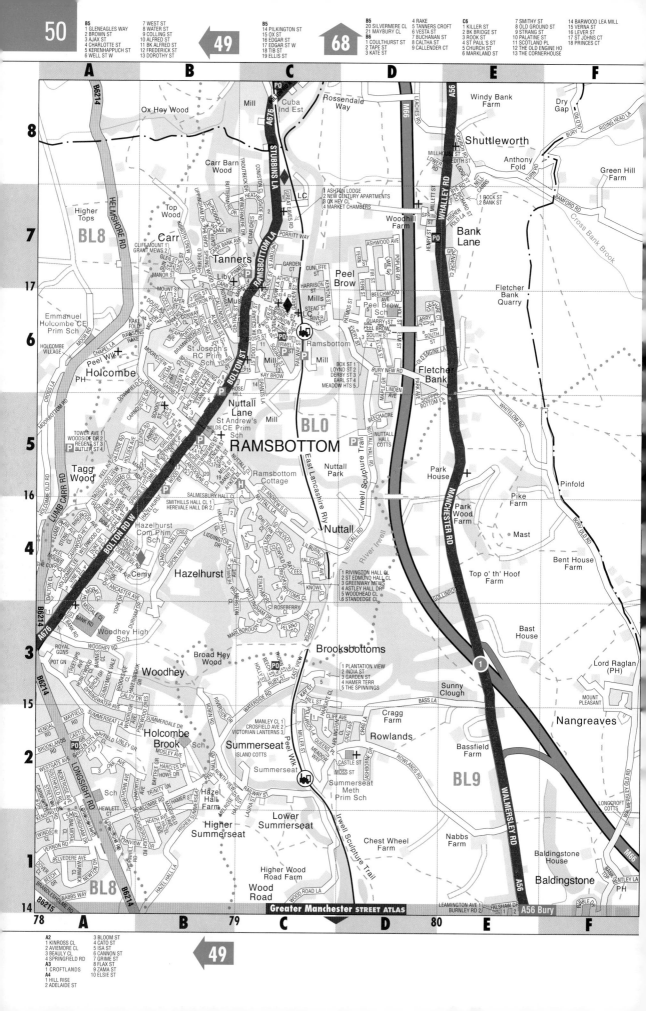

69

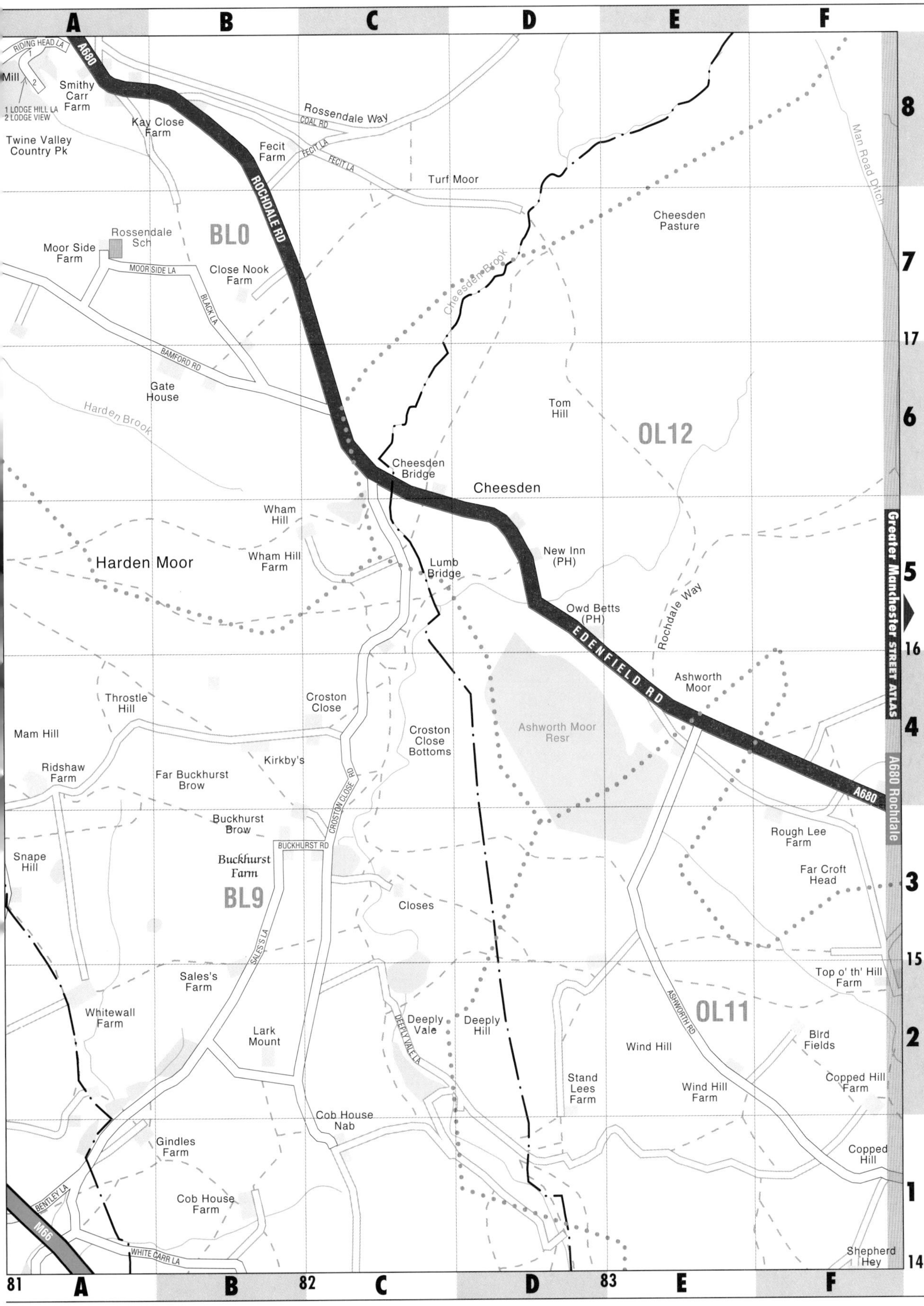
A
B
C
D
E
F
RIDING HEAD LA
A680
Mill
Smithy Carr Farm
1 LODGE HILL LA
2 LODGE VIEW
Kay Close Farm
Twine Valley Country Pk
Rossendale Way
COAL RD
FECIT LA
Fecit Farm
Turf Moor
Man Road Ditch
8
ROCHDALE RD
Rossendale Sch
BL0
Moor Side Farm
MOOR SIDE LA
Close Nook Farm
BLACK LA
Cheesden Brook
Cheesden Pasture
7
17
BAMFORD RD
Gate House
Harden Brook
Tom Hill
OL12
6
Cheesden Bridge
Cheesden
Wham Hill
Harden Moor
Wham Hill Farm
Lumb Bridge
New Inn (PH)
Owd Betts (PH)
Rochdale Way
5
Greater Manchester STREET ATLAS
16
EDENFIELD RD
Ashworth Moor
Throstle Hill
Croston Close
Mam Hill
Croston Close Bottoms
Ashworth Moor Resr
4
Ridshaw Farm
Far Buckhurst Brow
Kirkby's
CROSTON CLOSE RD
A680
A680 Rochdale
Buckhurst Brow
BUCKHURST RD
Rough Lee Farm
Snape Hill
Buckhurst Farm
BL9
Far Croft Head
3
Closes
15
Sales's Farm
SALES'S LA
Top o' th' Hill Farm
Whitewall Farm
Lark Mount
Deeply Vale
DEEPLY VALE LA
Deeply Hill
ASHWORTH RD
OL11
Bird Fields
2
Wind Hill
Stand Lees Farm
Wind Hill Farm
Copped Hill Farm
Cob House Nab
Gindles Farm
Copped Hill
1
BENTLEY LA
Cob House Farm
M66
WHITE CARR LA
Shepherd Hey
14
81
82
83

33

71

F2
1 CROSBY ST
2 PAVILION CL
3 JOY PL
4 WINDERMERE ST
5 JACOB BRIGHT MEWS

F3
1 NOOK TERR
2 BACK NOOK TERR

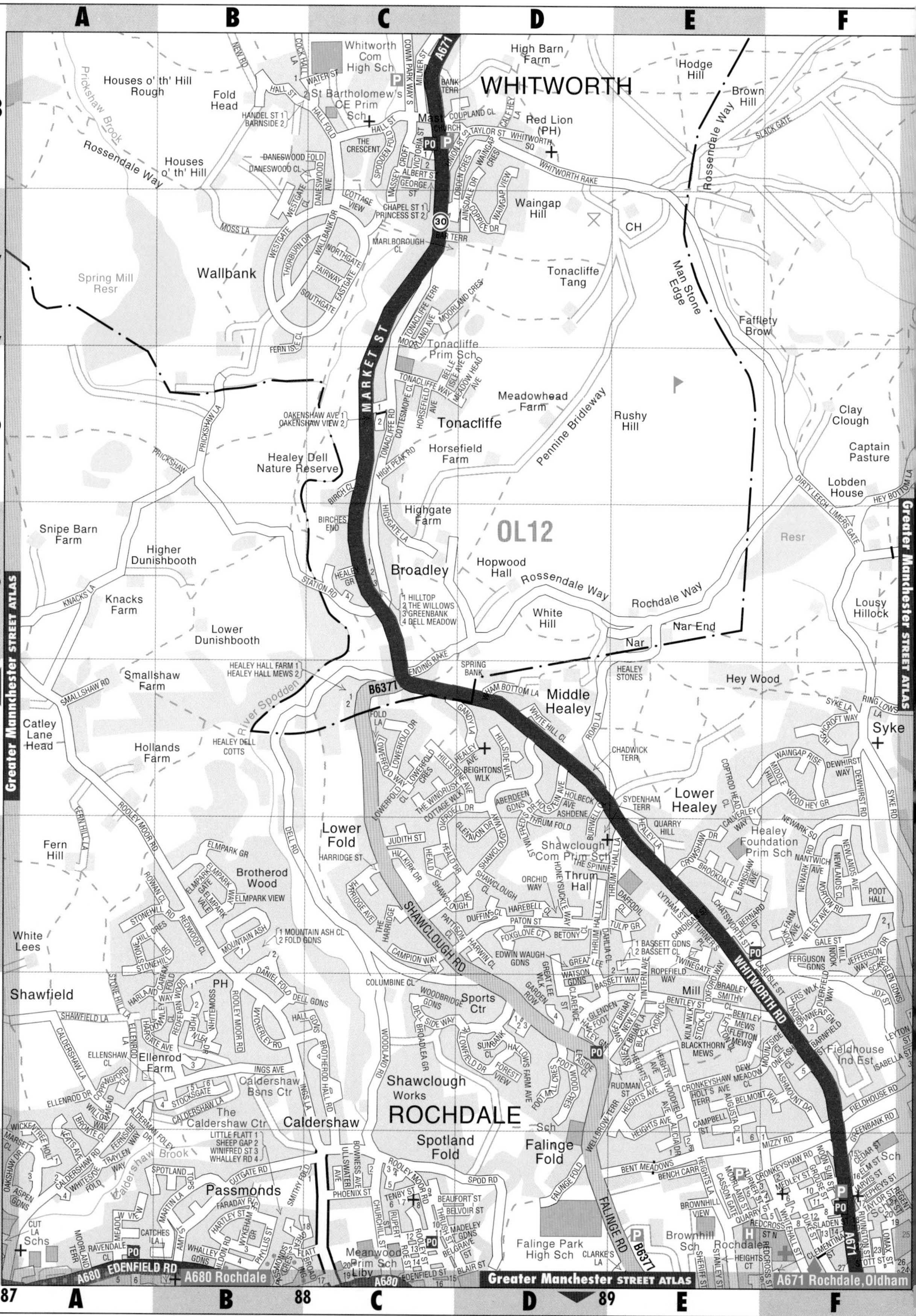

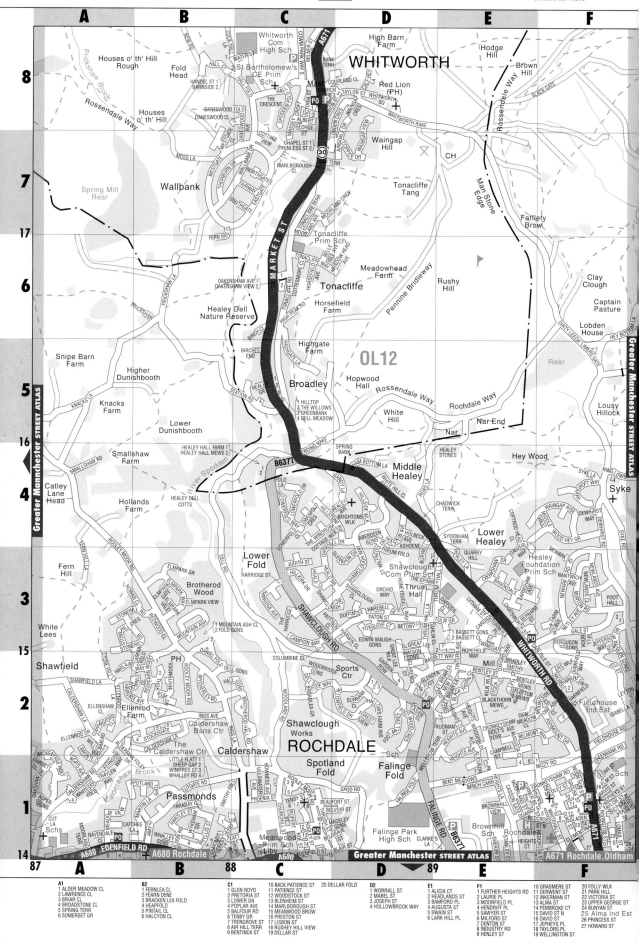

A1
1 ALDER MEADOW CL
2 LAWRENCE CL
3 BRIAR CL
4 BROADSTONE CL
5 SPRING TERR
6 SOMERSET GR

B2
1 FERNLEA CL
2 FEARN DENE
3 BRACKEN LEA FOLD
4 HEAPFOLD
5 PINTAIL CL
6 HALCYON CL

C1
1 GLEN ROYD
2 PRETORIA ST
3 LOWER GN
4 POPLAR AVE
5 BALFOUR RD
6 TENBY GR
7 TRENGROVE ST
8 AIR HILL TERR
9 BENTINCK ST
10 BACK PATIENCE ST
11 PATIENCE ST
12 WOODSTOCK ST
13 BLENHEIM ST
14 MARLBOROUGH ST
15 MEANWOOD BROW
16 PRESTON ST
17 LISBON ST
18 RUSHEY HILL VIEW
19 DELLAR ST
20 DELLAR FOLD

D2
1 WORRALL ST
2 MABEL ST
3 JOSEPH ST
4 HOLLOWBROOK WAY

E1
1 ALICIA CT
2 HEADLANDS ST
3 BAMFORD PL
4 AUGUSTA ST
5 SWAIN ST
6 LARK HILL PL

F1
1 FURTHER HEIGHTS RD
2 LAURIE PL
3 MOORFIELD PL
4 HENDRIFF PL
5 SAWYER ST
6 MILFORD ST
7 DENTON ST
8 INDUSTRY RD
9 HENLEY ST
10 GRASMERE ST
11 DERWENT ST
12 INKERMAN ST
13 ALMA ST
14 PEMBROKE CT
15 DAVID ST N
16 DAVID ST
17 JEPHEYS PL
18 TAYLORS PL
19 WELLINGTON ST
20 FOLLY WLK
21 PARK HILL
22 VICTORIA ST
23 UPPER GEORGE ST
24 BUNYAN ST
25 Alma Ind Est
26 PRINCESS ST
27 HOWARD ST

54

A
B
C
D
E
F
8
7
21
6
5
20
4
3
19
2
1
18
33
34
35
Marshside Sands
Wks
Hide
Marshside Nature Reserve
Marshside Marsh
PR9
Stanley High Sch Sports Coll
Sefton Coastal Path
Marshside
Southport Sands
MARINE DR
SOUTHPORT
HESKETH RD
CH
P&R
FAIRWAY
PR8
Marine Lake
Sefton Coastal Path
PROMENADE
BELGRAVIA APARTMENTS
LEICESTER ST
B5245
Hesketh Park
1 HAYMARKET LODGE
2 PARKSIDE CT
3 FLEETWOOD CT
PARK CRES
B5280
A565
ALBERT RD
CAMBRIDGE RD
Tower Dene Sch
FLEETWOOD RD
MARSHSIDE RD
PREESALL CL
SALWICK CL
PILLING CL
ELSWICK RD
GARSTANG RD
RECKLETON RD
CATON CL
FYLDE RD
ST ANNES RD
LYTHAM RD
TREETOP VILLAS
WILLOWHEY
ST MICHAEL'S CL
GRANBY CL
PAUL'S LA
BANK NOOK
KNOB HALL LA
COTTYS BROW
CROSTON'S BROW
KNOB HALL GDNS
RADNOR DR
LONGACRE
CLENGERS BROW
BAKER'S LA
WINDMILL HO
THRELFALL'S LA
EMMANUEL RD
CAMBRIDGE GDNS
CAMBRIDGE AVE
MAPLEWOOD
GRIFFON HO
BERESFORD GDNS
CHASE HEYS
KINGS HEY DR
BERESFORD DR
MONTROSE DR
CARISBROOKE DR
CHURCHGATE
DERWENT AVE
HESKETH LINKS CT
COCKLE DICK'S LA
CAMBRIDGE CT
THE LAWNS
BROCKLEBANK RD
DARWIN CT
WESTDENE
ARGYLE CT
ARGYLE RD
STUDLEY CT
CLIFF RD
HOWARD CT
ALBERT CT
GRANVILLE CT
WEST PARK
ETON CT
REGENCY GDNS
PARK RD W
PARK RD
POPLAR BANK
PO
BRENTWOOD CT
MORLEY RD
PARK AVE
AARON CT
ALLERTON RD
RAWLINSON RD
ENNISMORE GDNS
PRESTON RD
HENLEY CT
HENLEY DR
ROOKERY RD
HILBRE DR
HESKETH DR
SANDHEYS DR
COUDRAY RD
SILVERTHORNE DR
LEYLAND RD
AVONDALE RD N
GORDON ST
ALEXANDRA RD
GORDON AVE
BENNISON CT
AVONDALE RD
SUNNYSIDE CT
KNOWSLEY RD
WESTHOLME CT
LATHOM RD
ALBANY RD
SAUNDERS ST
IRVING ST


35

54

53

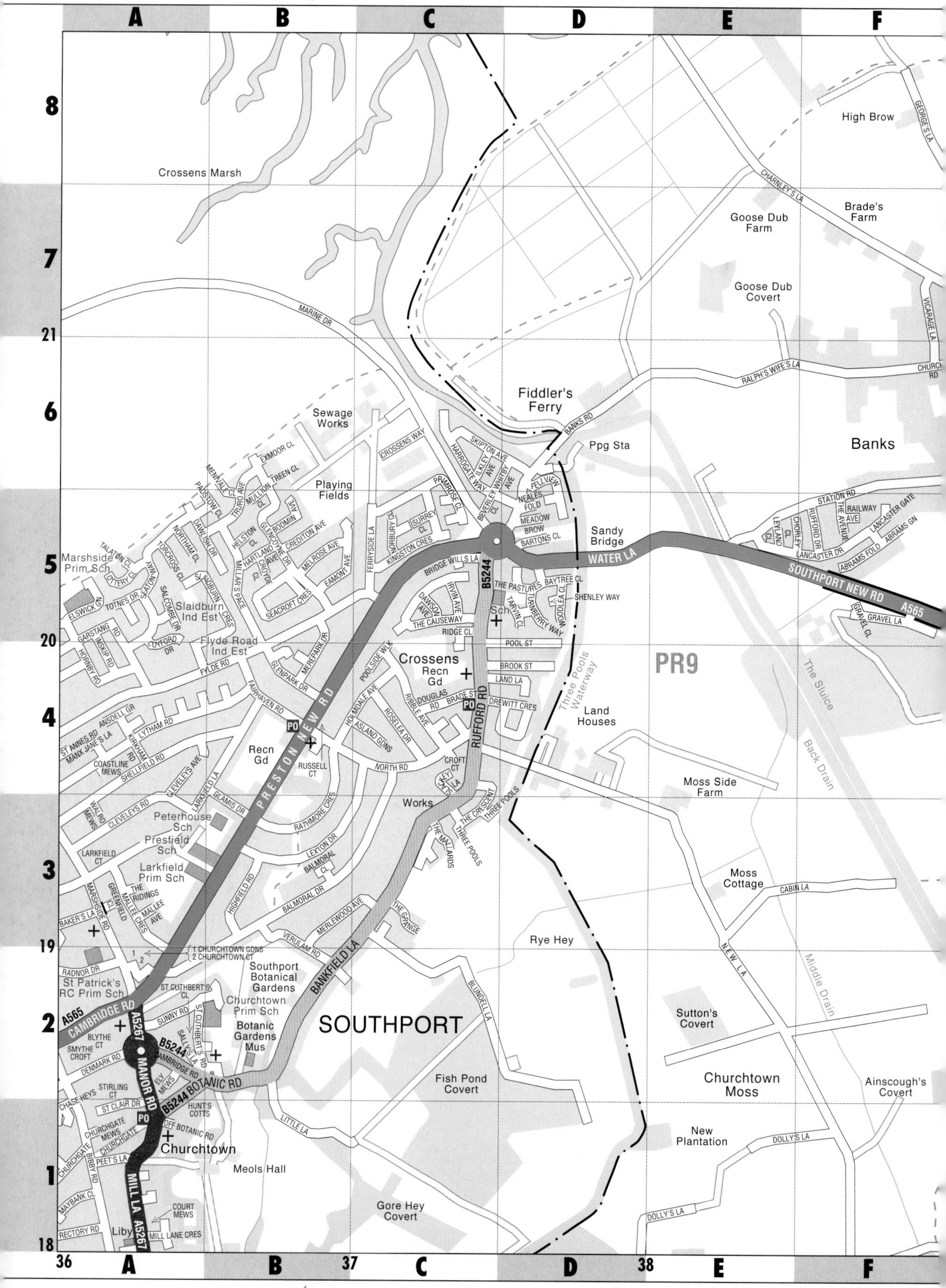

A
B
C
D
E
F
8
7
21
6
5
20
4
3
19
2
1
18
36
37
38
Crossens Marsh
High Brow
GEORGE'S LA
CHARNLEY'S LA
Goose Dub
Farm
Brade's
Farm
Goose Dub
Covert
VICARAGE LA
MARINE DR
RALPH'S WIFE'S LA
CHURCH
RD
Fiddler's
Ferry
Sewage
Works
BANKS RD
Ppg Sta
Banks
CROSSENS WAY
SKIPTON AVE
HARROGATE WAY
ILKLEY AVE
WHITBY AVE
BEVERLEY CL
FELLVIEW
NEALES FOLD
MEADOW BROW
BARTONS CL
PRIMROSE CL
Playing
Fields
EXMOOR CL
TREEN CL
MENIVALE CL
MULLION CL
PADSTOW CL
TRURO AVE
DAWLISH DR
NORTHAM CL
HELSTON CL
BODMIN AVE
GLENCOYNE DR
CREDITON AVE
HARTLAND AVE
CROYDE CL
MELROSE AVE
SURREY CL
NORBURY CL
KINGSTON CRES
FERRYSIDE LA
EAMONT AVE
SEACROFT CRES
MILLAR'S PACE
TORCROSS CL
TALATON CL
OTTERY CL
SEATON WAY
SALCOMBE DR
SLADBURN CRES
Marshside
Prim Sch
Slaidburn
Ind Est
ELSWICK GN
TOTNES DR
GARSTANG RD
INSKIP RD
HORNBY RD
OXFORD DR
Flyde Road
Ind Est
FYLDE RD
GLENPARK DR
MEREPARK DR
FAIRHAVEN RD
Sandy
Bridge
WATER LA
STATION RD
RAILWAY AVE
THE AVENUE
RUFFORD DR
CHORLEY CL
LEYLAND CL
LANCASTER GATE
ABRAMS GN
LANCASTER DR
ABRAMS FOLD
SOUTHPORT NEW RD
A565
GRAVEL CL
GRAVEL LA
BRIDGE WILLS LA
B5244
THE PASTURES
BAYTREE CL
SHENLEY WAY
TURNBERRY WAY
WOODLEA CL
TARVIN CL
IRVIN AVE
DAWSON AVE
THE CAUSEWAY
RIDGE CL
Sch
POOL ST
BROOK ST
LAND LA
DREWITT CRES
Crossens
Recn
Gd
POOLSIDE WLK
DOUGLAS RD
BRADE ST
PO
RUFFORD RD
PR9
The Sluice
Three Pools
Waterway
Land
Houses
PRESTON NEW RD
ANSDELL GR
ST ANNES RD
MANX JANE'S LA
LYTHAM RD
KIRKHAM RD
COASTLINE MEWS
SHELLFIELD RD
CLEVELEYS AVE
Recn
Gd
RUSSELL CT
HOLMDALE AVE
RIBBLE AVE
ROSELEA DR
ASLAND GDNS
NORTH RD
CROFT CT
THE CRESCENT
THREE POOLS
Works
Moss Side
Farm
Back Drain
LARKFIELD LA
GLAMIS DR
WALRO MEWS
CLEVELEYS RD
Peterhouse
Sch
Presfield
Sch
LARKFIELD CT
Larkfield
Prim Sch
RATHMORE CRES
LEXTON DR
BALMORAL CL
THE MALLARDS
THREE POOLS
Moss
Cottage
CABIN LA
MARSHSIDE RD
GREENFIELD CL
THE RIDINGS
MALLEE CRES
MALLEE AVE
HIGHFIELD RD
BALMORAL DR
MERLEWOOD AVE
THE GRANGE
BAKER'S LA
VERULAM RD
1 CHURCHTOWN GDNS
2 CHURCHTOWN CT
Rye Hey
RADNOR DR
St Patrick's
RC Prim Sch
Southport
Botanical
Gardens
BANKFIELD LA
NEW LA
Middle Drain
ST CUTHBERT'S CL
Churchtown
Prim Sch
A565
CAMBRIDGE RD
A5267
SUNNY RD
ST CUTHBERT'S RD
SALLY'S LA
Botanic
Gardens
Mus
SOUTHPORT
BLINDELL LA
Sutton's
Covert
BLYTHE CT
SMYTHE CROFT
DENMARK RD
B5244
CAMBRIDGE RD
MANOR RD
ELY MEWS
BOTANIC RD
Fish Pond
Covert
Churchtown
Moss
Ainscough's
Covert
CHASE HEYS
STIRLING CT
ST CLAIR DR
HUNT'S COTTS
CHURCHGATE MEWS
CHURCHGATE
OFF BOTANIC RD
Churchtown
LITTLE LA
New
Plantation
DOLLY'S LA
PEET'S LA
BIBBY RD
Meols Hall
MILL LA
A5267
MAYBANK CL
COURT MEWS
Gore Hey
Covert
DOLLY'S LA
RECTORY RD
Liby
MILL LANE CRES


53
36

72
56

A B C D E F
8
7
21
6
5
20
4
3
19
2
1
18
39 40 41
Tinsley's Farm
Far Banks
Gore Hall Farm
Boundary Farm
Heath Farm
TAYLOR'S MEANYGATE
MARSH RD
NEW LANE PACE
RYDING'S LA
Brookfield's Farm
New House Farm
GEORGE'S LA
LITTLE LA
GORSEY LA
New House Farm
BOUNDARY MEANYGATE
Bank View Farm
CHARNLEY'S LA
BOND'S LA
CHAPEL LA
SQUARE HOUSE LA
GLEBE LA
CHURCH RD
PO
Banks Meth Sch
MOSS LA
FLEETWOOD DR
FLEETWOOD CRES
LONG LA
Moss Edge Farm
Nursery
Nursery
BOUNDARY LA
Wright's Plantation
TODD'S LA
HESKETH AVE
SCHWARTZMAN DR
HOOLE LA
MEOLS CT
CHIPPING MANOR
AVELING DR
STATION RD
Sugar Stubbs Coverts
Holmes Moss
1 GREAVES CL
2 EVESHAM MANOR
3 ASTON MANOR
4 LITTLETON MANOR
5 GUINEA HALL MEWS
6 GUINEA HALL CL
BOLTON'S COP
Brand Heald
EVESHAM CL
LEVENS CL
ABINGTON DR
FAREHAM DR
LONMORE
WOODVALE CT
GUINEA HALL LA
BRIGHSTONE CL
Banks St Stephens' CE Sch
L Ctr
PR9
WESTERDALE DR
GRAVEL LA
GREAVES HALL AVE
AVENHAM CL
THE CLOSE
OAKFORD CL
MAES BROOK CL
Little Runner
Moss Side Farm
Gravel Farm
GREEN LA
Sugar Stubbs
Jump's Farm
Hollywood Farm
Woodend Farm
SUGAR STUBBS LA
BROOKLYN CVN PK
GRAVEL LA
MOSS SIDE LA
Wright's Farm
SOUTHPORT NEW RD
Dalweb Ind Pk
Tarleton Runner
Runner Plantations
GRAVEL LA
Long Ditch Bridge
Riverside L Ctr
BOBBINERS LA
GRAVEL LA
RIVERSIDE CVN SITE
PR4
Gravel Farm
Legh House Farm
A565
MERE LA
LONGFOLD
SPRING MDW
CINDER LA
PO
B5246
THE GRAVEL
B5246
Ring Ditch
Tarleton Mere Brow CE Prim Sch
Mere Brow
TABBY NOOK
Back Drain
The Sluice
Mere Meanygate
COMMON LA
LEISURE LAKES CVN PK

37
56

55
73

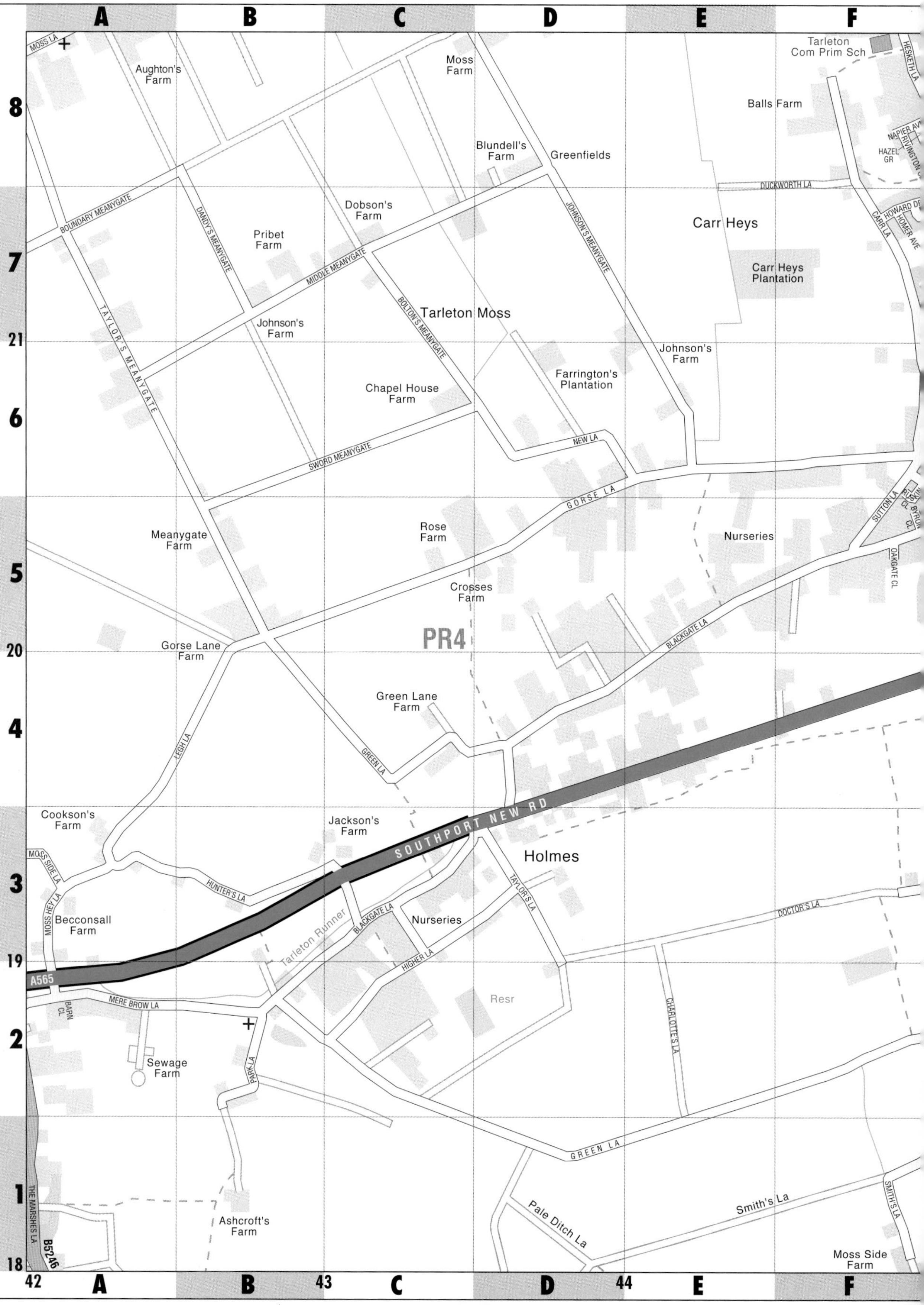
A
B
C
D
E
F
8
7
21
6
5
20
4
3
19
2
1
18
42
43
44
MOSS LA
Aughton's Farm
Moss Farm
Tarleton Com Prim Sch
HESKETH LA
Balls Farm
NAPIER AV
RIVINGTON
HAZEL GR
Blundell's Farm
Greenfields
DUCKWORTH LA
BOUNDARY MEANYGATE
DANDY'S MEANYGATE
Dobson's Farm
JOHNSON'S MEANYGATE
Carr Heys
HOWARD DR
CARR LA
HOMER AVE
Pribet Farm
MIDDLE MEANYGATE
Carr Heys Plantation
TAYLOR'S MEANYGATE
BOLTON'S MEANYGATE
Tarleton Moss
Johnson's Farm
Johnson's Farm
Farrington's Plantation
Chapel House Farm
NEW LA
SWORD MEANYGATE
GORSE LA
SUTTON LA
BYRON CL
Meanygate Farm
Rose Farm
Nurseries
OAKGATE CL
Crosses Farm
PR4
BLACKGATE LA
Gorse Lane Farm
Green Lane Farm
LEGH LA
GREEN LA
Cookson's Farm
Jackson's Farm
SOUTHPORT NEW RD
MOSS SIDE LA
Holmes
HUNTER'S LA
TAYLOR'S LA
DOCTOR'S LA
MOSS HEY LA
Becconsall Farm
Tarleton Runner
BLACKGATE LA
Nurseries
HIGHER LA
A565
Resr
MERE BROW LA
BARN CL
CHARLOTTE'S LA
Sewage Farm
PARK LA
GREEN LA
THE MARSHES LA
Pale Ditch La
Smith's La
SMITH'S LA
Ashcroft's Farm
B5246
Moss Side Farm

55
38

A
B
C
D
E
F
8
7
21
6
5
20
4
3
19
2
1
18
45
46
47
Mill Hill
HAUNDERS LA
LIVERPOOL OLD RD
Mill Hill
Farm
A59
Marsdens
Farm
Carrs
SPENCERS DR
RIVER VIEW
AVONDALE
DR
SUTTON AVE
MERLECREST
DR
HILLCREST DR
CRESTWAY
HOLLY
WILSON
CL
HESKETH LA
HAIG AVE
1 HILLCREST CL
2 MOSS LEA
Carr House
Bridge
Carr
House
B5247
Tarleton
High Sch
Tarleton
THE BEECHES
MEOLSGATE AVE
FIRBANK AVE
OAKLANDS AVE
THE
SPINNEY
LIVERPOOL RD
Long Fold
THORNFIELD
CARR HOUSE LA
KEARSLEY AVE
SANDRINGHAM CL
HUNTER AVE
LATHAM CRES
FLETCHER
AVE
MAYO
DR
HILLSIDE
1 MARK SQ
2 BANNISTRE MEWS
3 GORSE CL
4 WAVERLEY DR
Plocks
Farm
The
Windmill
Brook House
Farm
CANAL
LEACH
B5248
NORTH RD
B5248
Finches
Farm
Liby
PLOX BROW
MEADOW PK
GORSE LA
PRIORY CL
THE CLOISTERS
BAKERS MEWS
CHURCH WLK
River Asland or Douglas
NORSE
COTTS
POMPIAN BROW
Bretherton
Bretherton
Endowed CE
Prim Sch
Tarleton
Holy Trinity
CE Prim Sch
CHURCH RD
TRINITY WLKS
CHURCH
VIEW
THE CHIMES
GLEBELANDS
COE LA
MEADOWAY
LILFORD
CL
POND CL
1 BARRONWOOD CT
2 CHAPEL MDWS
3 HERITAGE WAY
4 HIGHFIELD CL
5 PARSONAGE GDNS
6 RECTORY CL
7 WINGATE FOLD
Ashcroft's
Farm
SOUTH RD
B5247
BAMFORDS
FOLD
ST HELENS
WELL
JANE'S MDW
EDWARD
CL
Canal
Bridge
Tarleton
Bridge
BANK BRIDGE
WINDGATE
A59
Hudsons
Farm
SOUTHPORT NEW RD
A565
A59
Bank
Hall
SOUTH
VIEW
SARAH LA
BACK LA
PR26
Glynwood
PR4
Cuerden
Farm
ASCROFT
LODGE
Back Lane
Leeds and Liverpool Canal
Rufford Branch
River Douglas
BROAD MEADOW LA
Odd
House
MOUNT
PLEASANT
Bretherton Eyes
LIVERPOOL RD
EYES LA
DOCTOR'S LA
River Lostock
Nursery
Bank's
Farm
White Dial
Farm
Red Bridge
Farm
GREEN LA
OLD RD
LOCK LA
Rod
Bridge
Green Lane
Farm
Moor
Farm
LIVERPOOL
SOLLOM LA
River Yarrow
A581
Sollom
Isle of Man
Farm
MEADOW LA
SMITH'S LA
Manor
Farm
Sollom Lane
THE STRINE
Cottage Lane
Strine Brook
Green
Lane
L40
A59
A581

57
75

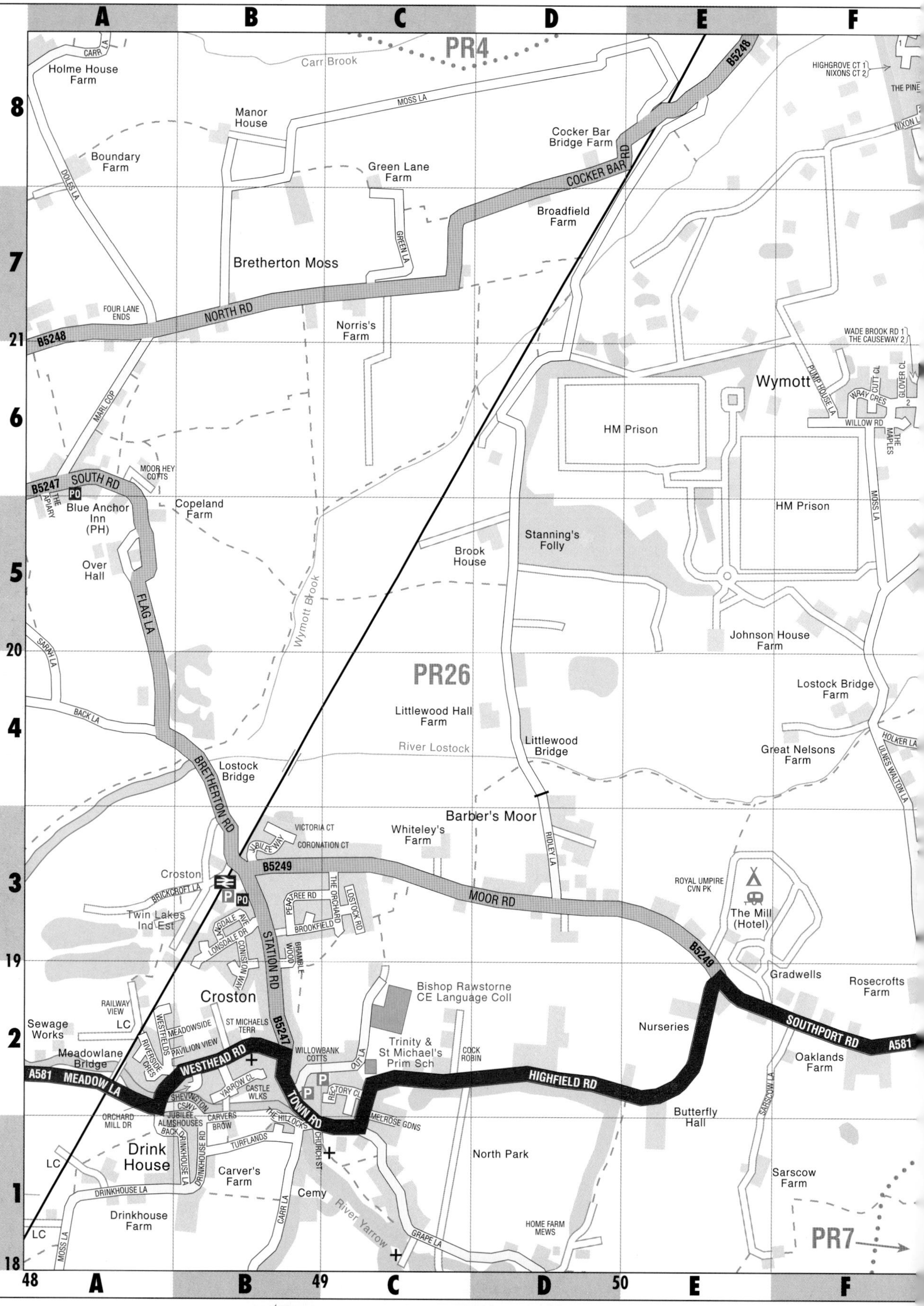
A
B
C
D
E
F
8
7
21
6
5
20
4
3
19
2
1
18
48
49
50
PR4
Carr Brook
CARR LA
Holme House Farm
Manor House
MOSS LA
B5248
HIGHGROVE CT 1
NIXONS CT 2
THE PINE
NIXON LA
Boundary Farm
DOLES LA
Green Lane Farm
Cocker Bar Bridge Farm
COCKER BAR RD
Broadfield Farm
GREEN LA
Bretherton Moss
FOUR LANE ENDS
NORTH RD
B5248
Norris's Farm
WADE BROOK RD 1
THE CAUSEWAY 2
Wymott
PUMP HOUSE LA
CUTT CL
GLOVER CL
WRAY CRES
WILLOW RD
THE MAPLES
MARL COP
HM Prison
MOOR HEY COTTS
B5247
SOUTH RD
PO
THE APIARY
Blue Anchor Inn (PH)
Copeland Farm
HM Prison
MOSS LA
Stanning's Folly
Brook House
Over Hall
FLAG LA
Wymott Brook
Johnson House Farm
SARAH LA
PR26
Lostock Bridge Farm
BACK LA
Littlewood Hall Farm
Littlewood Bridge
River Lostock
Great Nelsons Farm
HOLKER LA
ULNES WALTON LA
Lostock Bridge
BRETHERTON RD
Barber's Moor
VICTORIA CT
JUBILEE WAY
CORONATION CT
Whiteley's Farm
RIDLEY LA
B5249
Croston
BRICKCROFT LA
MOOR RD
ROYAL UMPIRE CVN PK
The Mill (Hotel)
P
PO
PEAR TREE RD
THE ORCHARD
LOSTOCK RD
Twin Lakes Ind Est
BROOKFIELD
STATION RD
B5249
LONSDALE DR
AVE
CONISTON WAY
BRAMBLE WOOD
Gradwells
Rosecrofts Farm
Croston
Bishop Rawstorne CE Language Coll
RAILWAY VIEW
LC
ST MICHAELS TERR
B5247
Sewage Works
WESTFIELDS
MEADOWSIDE
PAVILION VIEW
Nurseries
SOUTHPORT RD
A581
Meadowlane Bridge
RIVERSIDE CRES
WESTHEAD RD
WILLOWBANK COTTS
OUT LA
Trinity & St Michael's Prim Sch
COCK ROBIN
Oaklands Farm
A581
MEADOW LA
YARROW CL
CASTLE WLKS
P
HIGHFIELD RD
SARSCOW LA
SHEVINGTON CSWY
RECTORY CL
TOWN RD
ORCHARD MILL DR
JUBILEE ALMSHOUSES
CARVERS BROW
THE HILLOCKS
MELROSE GDNS
Butterfly Hall
BACK DRINKHOUSE LA
TURFLANDS
CHURCH ST
Drink House
DRINKHOUSE RD
North Park
LC
Carver's Farm
Sarscow Farm
DRINKHOUSE LA
Cemy
Drinkhouse Farm
CARR LA
River Yarrow
HOME FARM MEWS
LC
MOSS LA
GRAPE LA
PR7

57
40

76
60

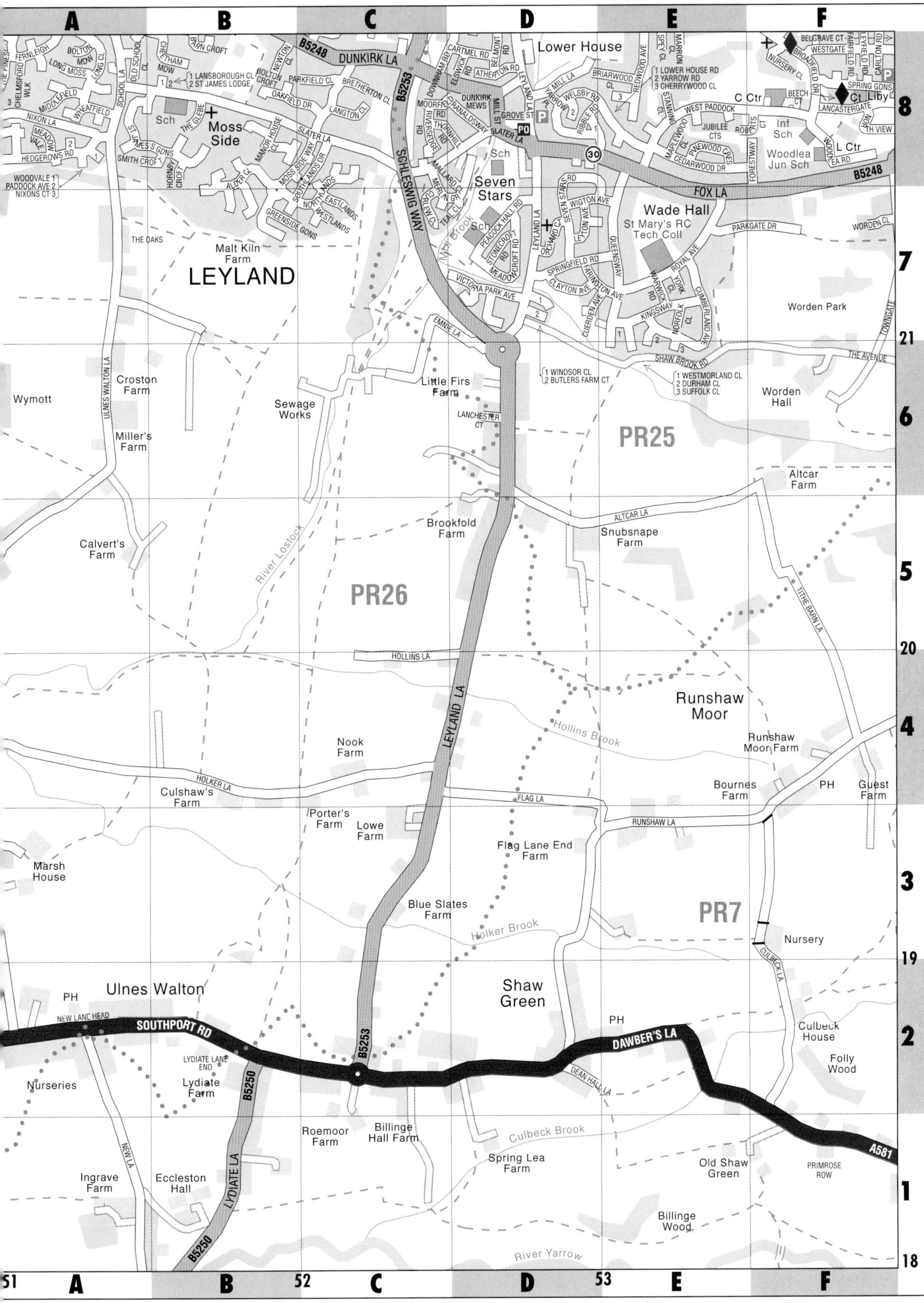
A
B
C
D
E
F
LEYLAND
Lower House
Moss Side
Seven Stars
Wade Hall
St Mary's RC Tech Coll
Malt Kiln Farm
THE OAKS
Worden Park
Worden Hall
Wymott
Croston Farm
Miller's Farm
Calvert's Farm
Sewage Works
Little Firs Farm
LANCHESTER CT
PR25
PR26
PR7
Altcar Farm
Brookfold Farm
Snubsnape Farm
River Lostock
HOLLINS LA
ALTCAR LA
TITHE BARN LA
Runshaw Moor
Runshaw Moor Farm
Hollins Brook
Nook Farm
LEYLAND LA
HOLKER LA
Culshaw's Farm
FLAG LA
Porter's Farm
Lowe Farm
Flag Lane End Farm
RUNSHAW LA
Bournes Farm
PH
Guest Farm
Marsh House
Blue Slates Farm
Holker Brook
Nursery
CULBECK LA
Ulnes Walton
Shaw Green
NEW LANE HEAD
SOUTHPORT RD
B5253
DAWBER'S LA
DEAN HALL LA
Culbeck House
Folly Wood
LYDIATE LANE END
Lydiate Farm
Nurseries
B5250
Roemoor Farm
Billinge Hall Farm
Culbeck Brook
Spring Lea Farm
Old Shaw Green
PRIMROSE ROW
A581
NEW LA
Ingrave Farm
Eccleston Hall
LYDIATE LA
Billinge Wood
River Yarrow
ULNES WALTON LA
SCHLESWIG WAY
B5248
DUNKIRK LA
FOX LA
PARKGATE DR
WORDEN CL
TOWNGATE
THE AVENUE
SHAW BROOK RD
1 WESTMORLAND CL
2 DURHAM CL
3 SUFFOLK CL
1 WINDSOR CL
2 BUTLERS FARM CT
EMNIE LA
VICTORIA PARK AVE
CLAYTON AVE
SPRINGFIELD RD
FARINGTON AVE
QUEENSWAY
KINGSWAY
CUERDEN AVE
WARWICK RD
YORK CL
NORFOLK CL
CUMBERLAND AVE
ROYAL AVE
WIGTON AVE
SEVEN STARS RD
FYLTON AVE
PEACOCK HALL RD
STONECROFT RD
MEADOWCROFT RD
Mill Brook
MALLARD CL
MERLIN GR
TEAL CL
CURLEW CL
GROVE ST
SLATER LA
MILL ST
LEYLAND LA
DUNKIRK MEWS
DRANALDSWAY
THORNHILL RD
RIVERSEDGE RD
MOORFIELD
DOWNHAM RD
ELSWICK RD
CARTMEL RD
ATHERTON RD
BELMONT RD
MILL LA
YARROW PL
WELSBY RD
RIBBLE RD
BRIARWOOD CL
REDWOOD AVE
SPEY CL
MARRON CL
1 LOWER HOUSE RD
2 YARROW RD
3 CHERRYWOOD CL
STANNING CL
MAPLEWOOD CL
WEST PADDOCK
JUBILEE CTS
PINEWOOD CRES
CEDARWOOD DR
FORESTWAY
ROBERTS CT
Inf Sch
Woodlea Jun Sch
C Ctr
L Ctr
Ct
Liby
BELGRAVE CT
WESTGATE
NURSERY CL
BROADFIELD DR
BEECH CT
FAIRFIELD RD
LEYFIELD RD
CARLTON RD
SPRING GDNS
LANCASTERGATE
TH VIEW
EA RD
Sch
PO
DUNKIRK LA
PARKFIELD CL
BRETHERTON CL
OAKFIELD DR
LANGTON CL
BOLTON CROFT
NEWTON CL
BARN CROFT
CHEETHAM MDW
1 LANSBOROUGH CL
2 ST JAMES LODGE
OLD SCHOOL CL
SCHOOL LA
LONG CL
BOLTON MDW
LONG MOSS
FERNLEIGH
CHELMSFORD WLK
MIDDLEFIELD
WHEATFIELD
NIXON LA
MEADOW VALE
HEDGEROWS RD
WOODVALE 1
PADDOCK AVE 2
NIXONS CT 3
ST JAMES'S GDNS
SMITH CROFT
HORNBY CROFT
THE GLEBE
MANOR HOUSE CL
MOSS SIDE WAY
SOUTHLANDS DR
NORTHLANDS
EASTLANDS
WESTLANDS
GREENSIDE GDNS
ALDER CL
8
7
6
5
4
3
2
1
21
20
19
18
51
52
53

41
60

A8
1 SOUTH VIEW TERR
2 EDWARD ST
3 BROAD ST
4 LIEGE RD
5 VICTORIA TERR
6 DEIGHTON AVE
7 SANDY PL
8 BROAD SQ

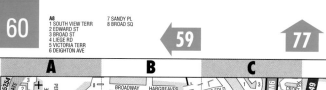

59
77

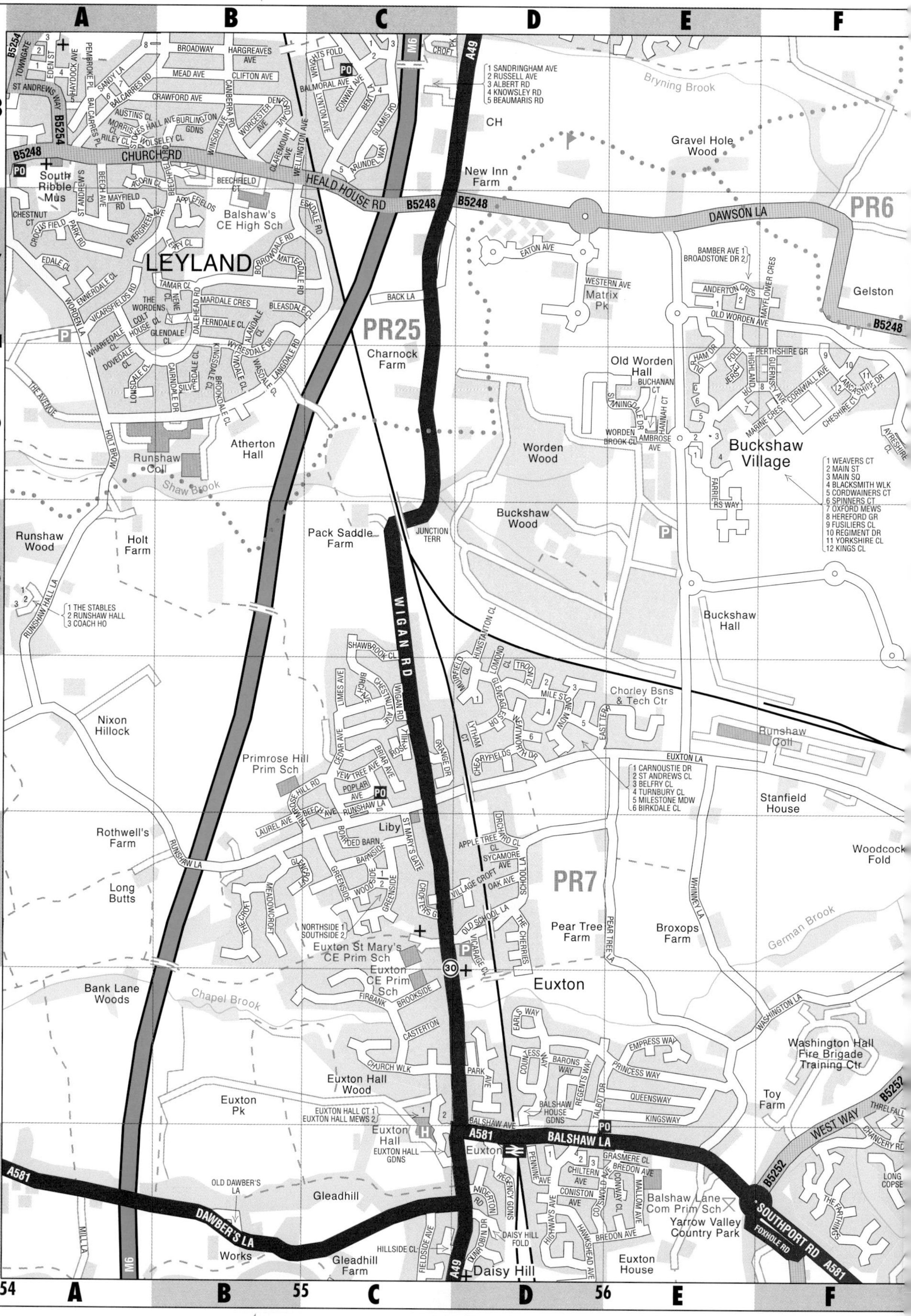


59
42

D1
1 DALE AVE
2 TALBOT ROW
3 AMBLESIDE AVE

78
62

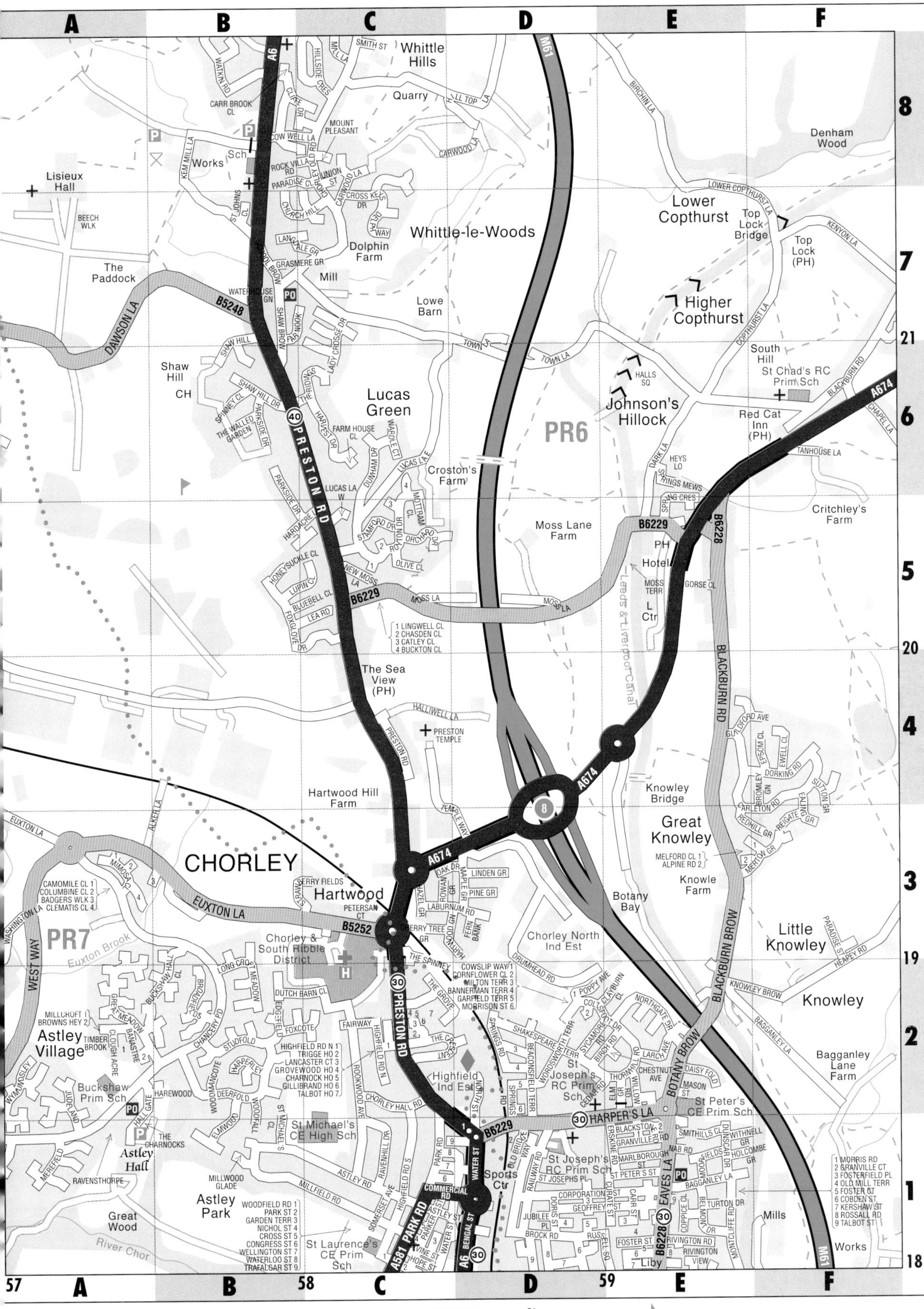
A B C D E F
8 7 6 5 4 3 2 1
21 20 19 18
57 58 59
Whittle Hills
Quarry
Denham Wood
Lisieux Hall
Works
Lower Copthurst
Top Lock Bridge
Top Lock (PH)
Whittle-le-Woods
Dolphin Farm
Mill
The Paddock
Lowe Barn
Higher Copthurst
South Hill
St Chad's RC Prim Sch
Shaw Hill
CH
Lucas Green
Johnson's Hillock
Red Cat Inn (PH)
PR6
Croston's Farm
Critchley's Farm
Moss Lane Farm
Hotel
The Sea View (PH)
PRESTON TEMPLE
Knowley Bridge
Hartwood Hill Farm
Great Knowley
CHORLEY
Hartwood
Knowle Farm
Botany Bay
Little Knowley
PR7
Chorley & South Ribble District
Chorley North Ind Est
Knowley
Astley Village
Buckshaw Prim Sch
Highfield Ind Est
St Joseph's RC Prim Sch
St Peter's CE Prim Sch
Bagganley Lane Farm
St Michael's CE High Sch
St Joseph's RC Prim Sch
Sports Ctr
Astley Hall
Astley Park
Great Wood
River Chor
St Laurence's CE Prim Sch
Mills
Works
A6
M61
A674
B5248
B6229
B6228
B5252
A581
PRESTON RD
BLACKBURN RD
BLACKBURN BROW
EUXTON LA
DAWSON LA
HARPER'S LA
EAVES LA
PARK RD
Leeds & Liverpool Canal
1 LINGWELL CL
2 CHASDEN CL
3 CATLEY CL
4 BUCKTON CL
CAMOMILE CL 1
COLUMBINE CL 2
BADGERS WLK 3
CLEMATIS CL 4
MELFORD CL 1
ALPINE RD 2
COWSLIP WAY 1
CORNFLOWER CL 2
MILTON TERR 3
BANNERMAN TERR 4
GARFIELD TERR 5
MORRISON ST 6
HIGHFIELD RD N 1
TRIGGE HO 2
LANCASTER CT 3
GROVEWOOD HO 4
CHARNOCK HO 5
GILLIBRAND HO 6
TALBOT HO 7
WOODFIELD RD 1
PARK ST 2
GARDEN TERR 3
NICHOL ST 4
CROSS ST 5
CONGRESS ST 6
WELLINGTON ST 7
WATERLOO ST 8
TRAFALGAR ST 9
1 MORRIS RD
2 GRANVILLE CT
3 FOSTERFIELD PL
4 OLD MILL TERR
5 FOSTER CT
6 COBDEN ST
7 KERSHAW ST
8 ROSSALL RD
9 TALBOT ST

D1
1 PRESTON ST
2 VICTORIA TERR
3 VICARAGE ST
4 WESTWELL RD
5 INGLE CL
6 RUSSELL SQ W
7 WHINFIELD AVE
8 MAYFIELD RD
9 BRIERCLIFFE RD

43
62

61
79

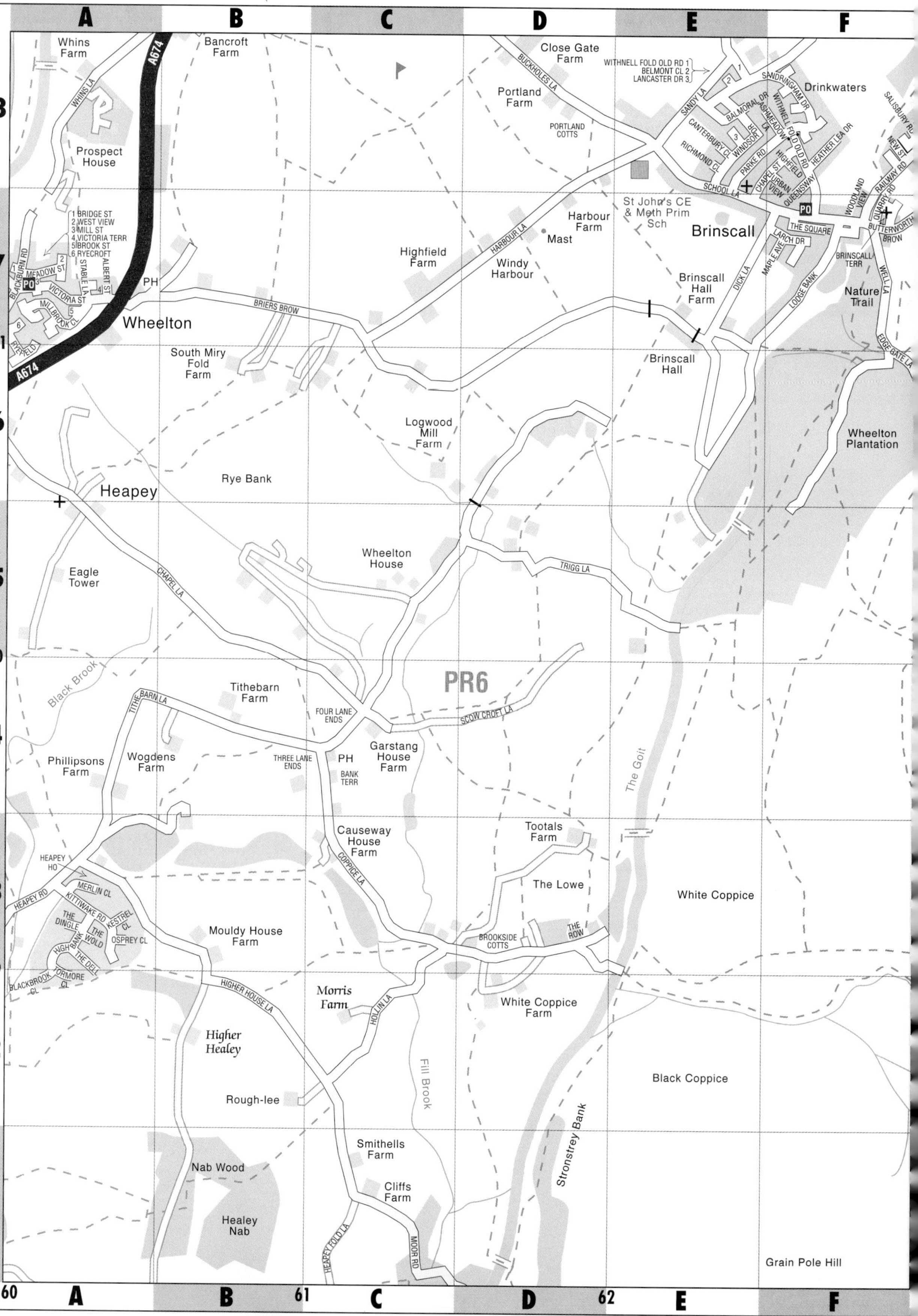
A
B
C
D
E
F
8
7
21
6
5
20
4
3
19
2
1
18
60
61
62
Whins Farm
Bancroft Farm
A674
Close Gate Farm
WITHNELL FOLD OLD RD 1
BELMONT CL 2
LANCASTER DR 3
Drinkwaters
Portland Farm
PORTLAND COTTS
BUCKHOLES LA
WHINS LA
Prospect House
1 BRIDGE ST
2 WEST VIEW
3 MILL ST
4 VICTORIA TERR
5 BROOK ST
6 RYECROFT
MEADOW ST
VICTORIA ST
MILLBROOK CL
BLACKBURN RD
STABLE LA
ALBERT ST
PO
PH
Wheelton
BRIERS BROW
Highfield Farm
HARBOUR LA
Windy Harbour
Harbour Farm
Mast
St John's CE & Meth Prim Sch
Brinscall
SANDY LA
SCHOOL LA
THE SQUARE
LARCH DR
MAPLE AVE
DICK LA
LODGE BANK
BRINSCALL TERR
WOODLAND VIEW
QUARRY RD
BUTTERWORTH BROW
RAILWAY RD
NEW ST
SALISBURY RD
HEATHER LEA DR
QUEENSWAY
SANDRINGHAM DR
Brinscall Hall Farm
Brinscall Hall
Nature Trail
WELL LA
EDGE GATE LA
South Miry Fold Farm
Logwood Mill Farm
Wheelton Plantation
Rye Bank
Heapey
Wheelton House
TRIGG LA
Eagle Tower
CHAPEL LA
Black Brook
PR6
Tithebarn Farm
TITHE BARN LA
FOUR LANE ENDS
SCOW CROFT LA
Phillipsons Farm
Wogdens Farm
THREE LANE ENDS
PH
BANK TERR
Garstang House Farm
The Goit
Causeway House Farm
Tootals Farm
HEAPEY HO
HEAPEY RD
MERLIN CL
KITTIWAKE RD
THE DINGLE
THE WOLD
KESTREL CL
OSPREY CL
HIGH BANK
THE DELL
BLACKBROOK CL
FORMORE CL
COPPICE LA
The Lowe
White Coppice
Mouldy House Farm
BROOKSIDE COTTS
THE ROW
HIGHER HOUSE LA
Morris Farm
HOLLIN LA
White Coppice Farm
Higher Healey
Fill Brook
Black Coppice
Rough-lee
Stronstrey Bank
Smithells Farm
Nab Wood
Cliffs Farm
Healey Nab
HEAPEY FOLD LA
MOOR RD
Grain Pole Hill

61
44

80
64

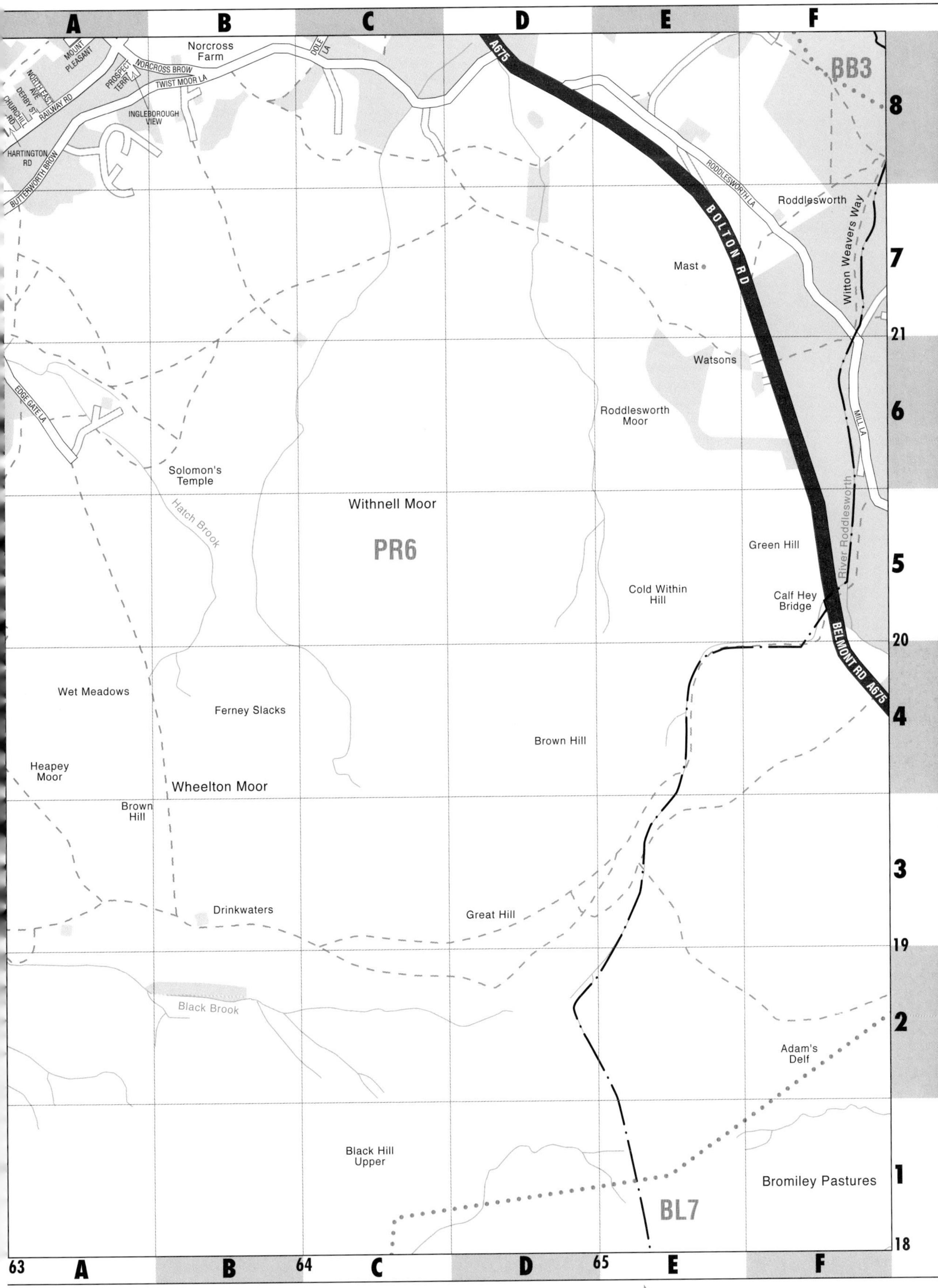
A
B
C
D
E
F
Norcross Farm
MOUNT PLEASANT
NORTH EAST AVE
DERBY ST
CHURCHILL RD
RAILWAY RD
PROSPECT TERR
NORCROSS BROW
TWIST MOOR LA
INGLEBOROUGH VIEW
HARTINGTON RD
BUTTERWORTH BROW
DOLE LA
A675
BB3
8
RODDLESWORTH LA
Roddlesworth
BOLTON RD
Witton Weavers Way
Mast
7
21
Watsons
EDGE GATE LA
6
Roddlesworth Moor
MILL LA
Solomon's Temple
Hatch Brook
Withnell Moor
PR6
River Roddlesworth
Green Hill
5
Cold Within Hill
Calf Hey Bridge
20
BELMONT RD A675
Wet Meadows
Ferney Slacks
4
Brown Hill
Heapey Moor
Wheelton Moor
Brown Hill
3
Drinkwaters
Great Hill
19
Black Brook
2
Adam's Delf
Black Hill Upper
1
Bromiley Pastures
BL7
18
63
64
65

45
64

63
81

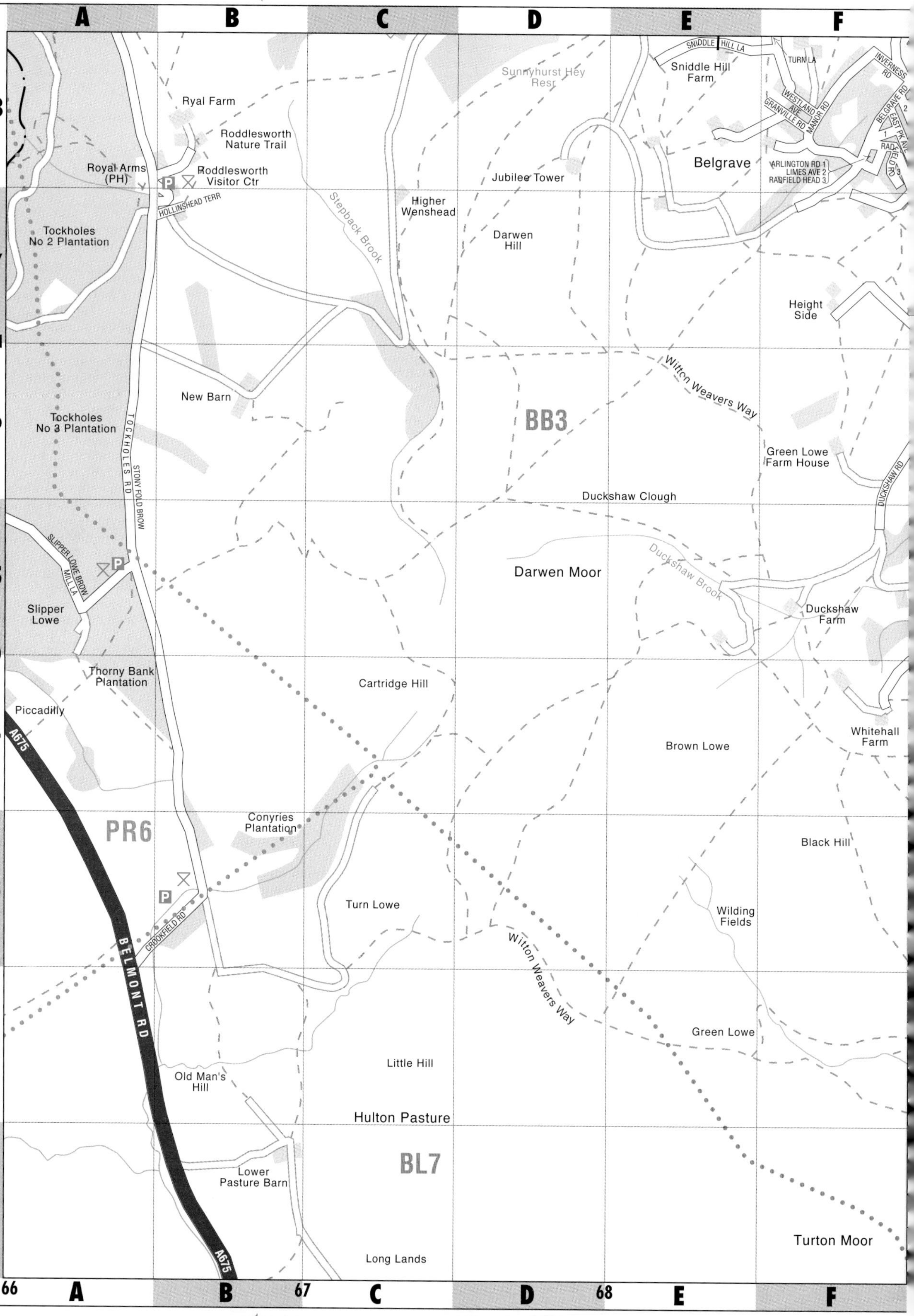
A
B
C
D
E
F
8
7
21
6
5
20
4
3
19
2
1
18
66
67
68
SNIDDLE HILL LA
TURN LA
INVERNESS RD
Sniddle Hill Farm
Sunnyhurst Hey Resr
Ryal Farm
Roddlesworth Nature Trail
WESTLAND AVE
GRANVILLE RD
MANOR RD
BELGRAVE RD
EAST PK AVE
RADFIELD RD
Belgrave
ARLINGTON RD 1
LIMES AVE 2
RADFIELD HEAD 3
Royal Arms (PH)
Roddlesworth Visitor Ctr
Jubilee Tower
HOLLINSHEAD TERR
Higher Wenshead
Stepback Brook
Tockholes No 2 Plantation
Darwen Hill
Height Side
New Barn
Witton Weavers Way
Tockholes No 3 Plantation
TOCKHOLES RD
STONY FOLD BROW
BB3
Green Lowe Farm House
DUCKSHAW RD
Duckshaw Clough
SLIPPER LOWE BROW
MILL LA
Darwen Moor
Duckshaw Brook
Slipper Lowe
Duckshaw Farm
Thorny Bank Plantation
Cartridge Hill
Piccadilly
A675
Brown Lowe
Whitehall Farm
PR6
Conyries Plantation
Black Hill
CROOKFIELD RD
Turn Lowe
Wilding Fields
BELMONT RD
Witton Weavers Way
Green Lowe
Little Hill
Old Man's Hill
Hulton Pasture
BL7
Lower Pasture Barn
Turton Moor
Long Lands
A675

63
46

**A8**
1 HESSE ST
2 GREENTHORNE TERR
3 BUFF ST
4 CLEMENT ST
5 AINSWORTH CL
6 BECKETT ST
7 STANSFIELD ST
8 SPRINGFIELD FLATS
9 ALICE ST
10 JEPSON ST
11 COBDEN ST
12 SPRING GDNS
13 RADFORD BANK GDNS
14 RADFORD BANK HO
15 NOBLE ST
16 THE OLD SAWMILL
17 RADFORD AVE
18 HILLSIDE AVE
19 HILL HOS
20 MILL GAP ST
21 HAMER ST

**B6**
1 RAWLINSON ST
2 ST BARNABAS ST
3 BLACKPOOL ST
4 MARTON WLK
5 SPRINGTHORPE ST
6 WESTCOTE ST

82

**B6**
7 MELBOURNE ST

**B8**
1 PRIMROSE TERR
2 GADFIELD ST
3 RAILWAY VIEW
4 HIGHFIELD ST

66

**B8**
5 CROSS BARN WLK
6 MELITA ST
7 ROSE HILL TERR
8 ASHTON RD

**C7**
1 THE MEWS
2 CAUSEWAY ST
3 PICKUP FOLD
4 CRANBERRY CHASE
5 TUNNEL ST

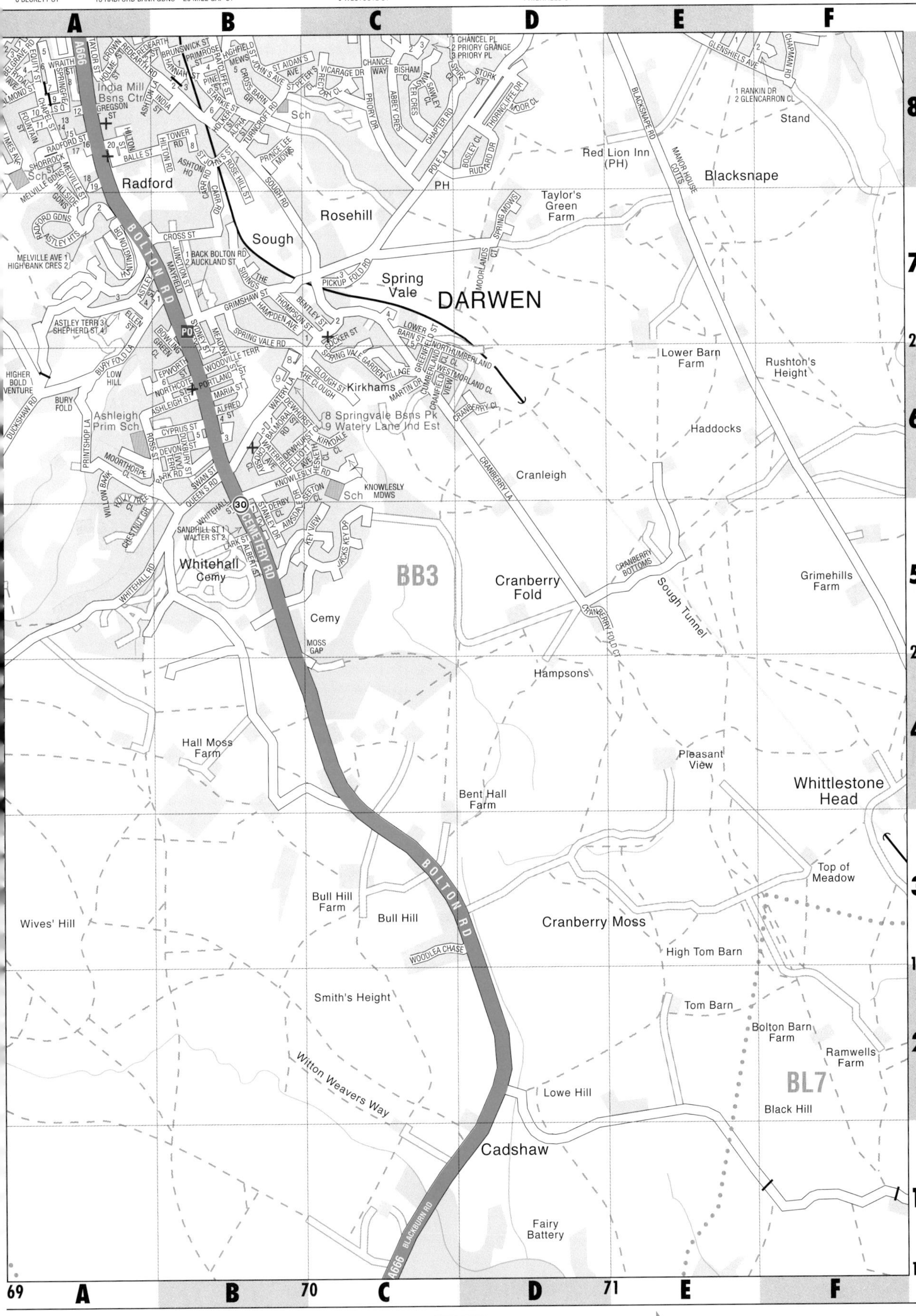


47
66

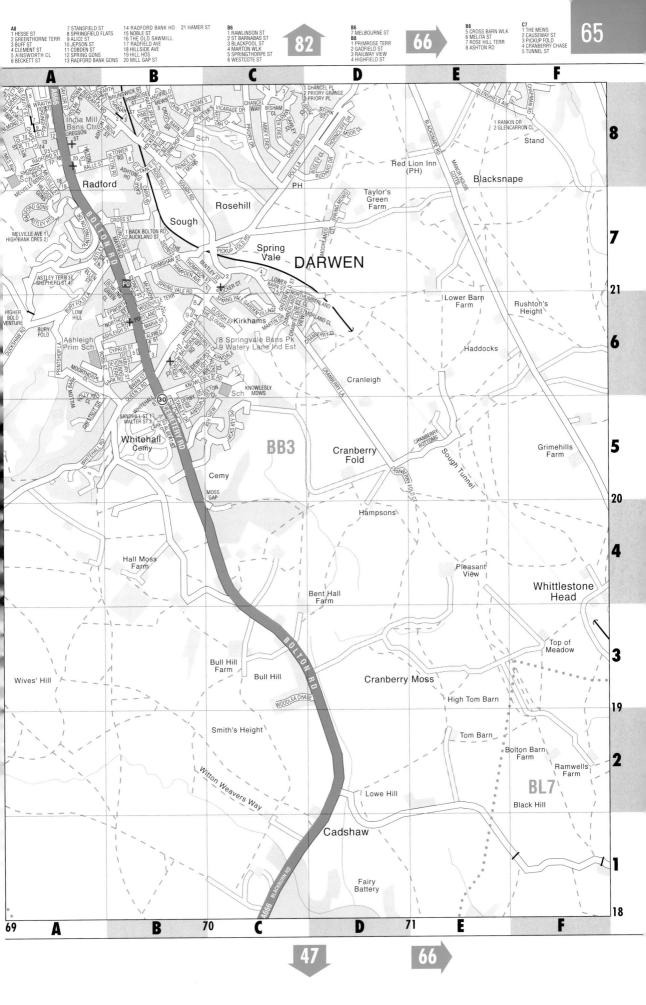

65
83

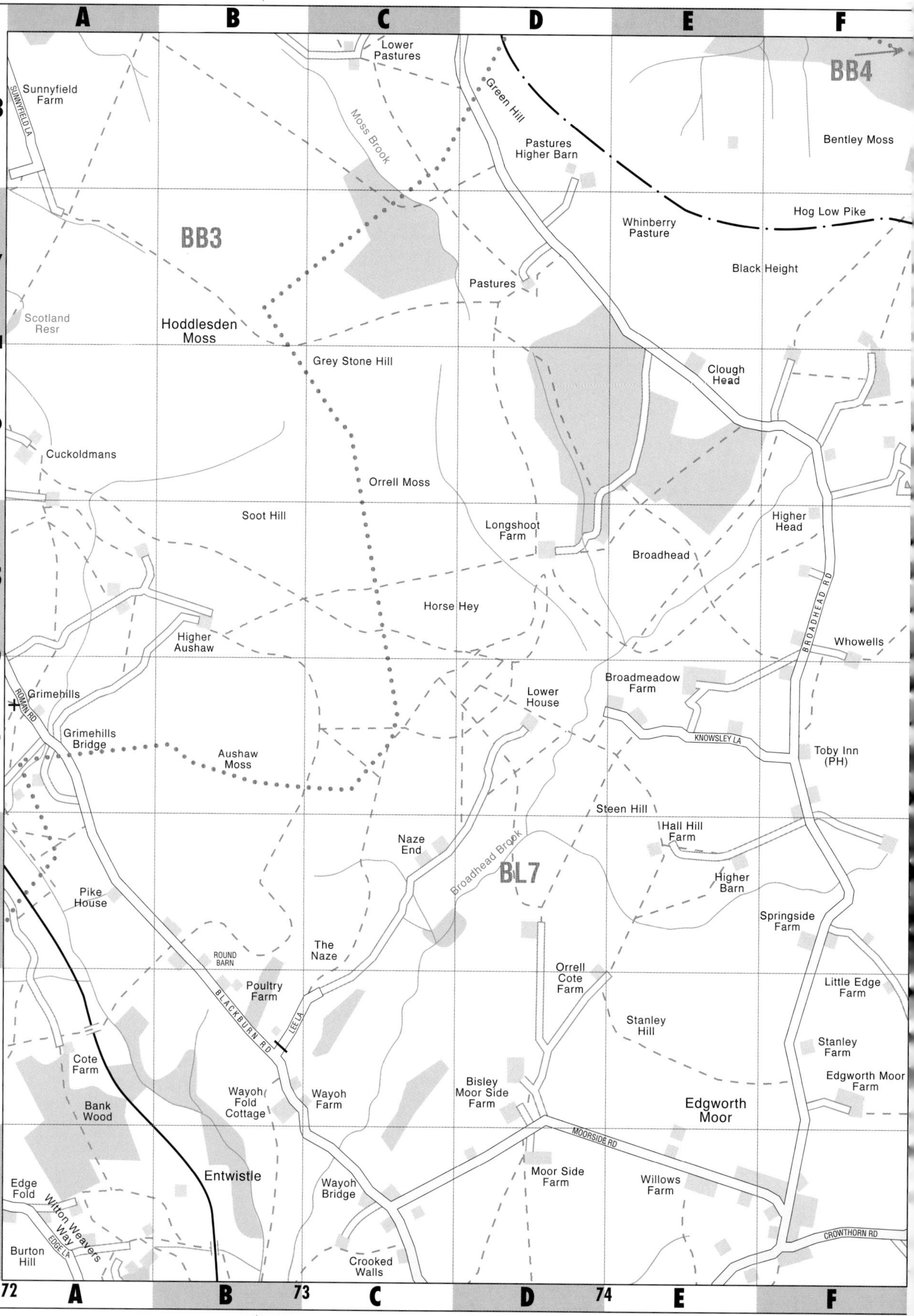
A
B
C
D
E
F
8
7
21
6
5
20
4
3
19
2
1
18
72
73
74
Lower Pastures
Sunnyfield Farm
SUNNYFIELD LA
Moss Brook
Green Hill
BB4
Bentley Moss
Pastures Higher Barn
Hog Low Pike
Whinberry Pasture
BB3
Black Height
Pastures
Scotland Resr
Hoddlesden Moss
Grey Stone Hill
Clough Head
Cuckoldmans
Orrell Moss
Soot Hill
Longshoot Farm
Higher Head
Broadhead
BROADHEAD RD
Horse Hey
Higher Aushaw
Whowells
Grimehills
ROMAN RD
Broadmeadow Farm
Lower House
Grimehills Bridge
KNOWSLEY LA
Toby Inn (PH)
Aushaw Moss
Steen Hill
Hall Hill Farm
Naze End
Broadhead Brook
BL7
Higher Barn
Pike House
Springside Farm
The Naze
ROUND BARN
Orrell Cote Farm
Little Edge Farm
Poultry Farm
BLACKBURN RD
LEE LA
Stanley Hill
Stanley Farm
Cote Farm
Edgworth Moor Farm
Bisley Moor Side Farm
Bank Wood
Wayoh Fold Cottage
Wayoh Farm
Edgworth Moor
MOORSIDE RD
Entwistle
Moor Side Farm
Willows Farm
Edge Fold
Witton Weavers Way
Wayoh Bridge
EDGE LA
CROWTHORN RD
Burton Hill
Crooked Walls

65
48

84
68

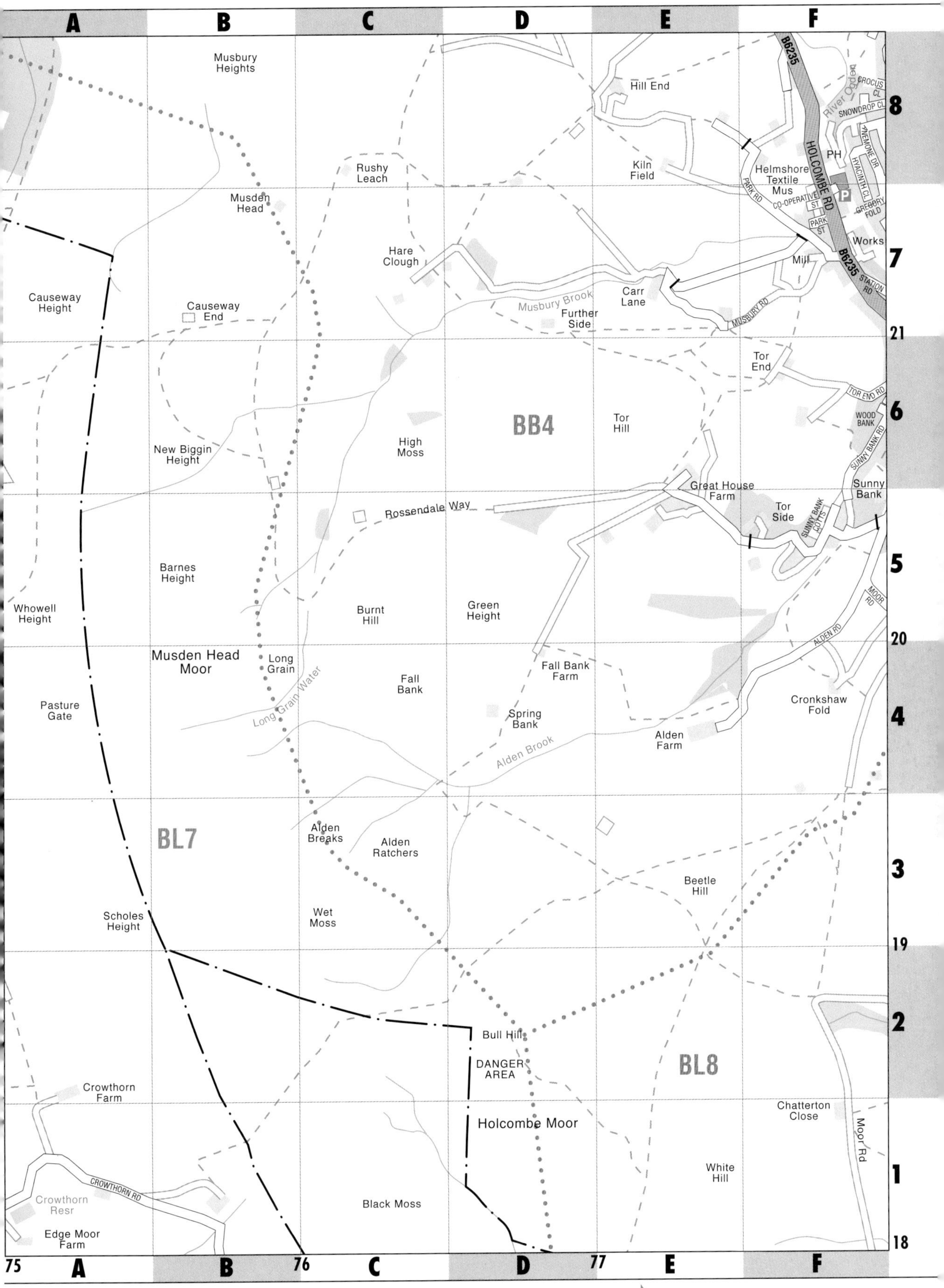
A
B
C
D
E
F
8
7
21
6
5
20
4
3
19
2
1
18
75
76
77
Musbury Heights
Rushy Leach
Hill End
Kiln Field
Helmshore Textile Mus
PH
P
Works
Mill
B6235
HOLCOMBE RD
River Ogden
CROCUS CL
SNOWDROP CL
ANEMONE DR
HYACINTH CL
GREGORY FOLD
PARK RD
CO-OPERATIVE ST
PARK ST
STATION RD
Musden Head
Hare Clough
Causeway Height
Causeway End
Carr Lane
Musbury Brook
Further Side
MUSBURY RD
Tor End
TOR END RD
WOOD BANK
SUNNY BANK RD
Tor Hill
BB4
High Moss
New Biggin Height
Great House Farm
Tor Side
Sunny Bank
SUNNY BANK COTTS
Rossendale Way
Barnes Height
Whowell Height
Burnt Hill
Green Height
MOOR RD
ALDEN RD
Musden Head Moor
Long Grain
Long Grain Water
Fall Bank
Fall Bank Farm
Pasture Gate
Spring Bank
Alden Farm
Cronkshaw Fold
Alden Brook
Alden Breaks
Alden Ratchers
BL7
Beetle Hill
Scholes Height
Wet Moss
Bull Hill
DANGER AREA
BL8
Crowthorn Farm
Holcombe Moor
Chatterton Close
Moor Rd
White Hill
CROWTHORN RD
Crowthorn Resr
Black Moss
Edge Moor Farm

49
68

67
85

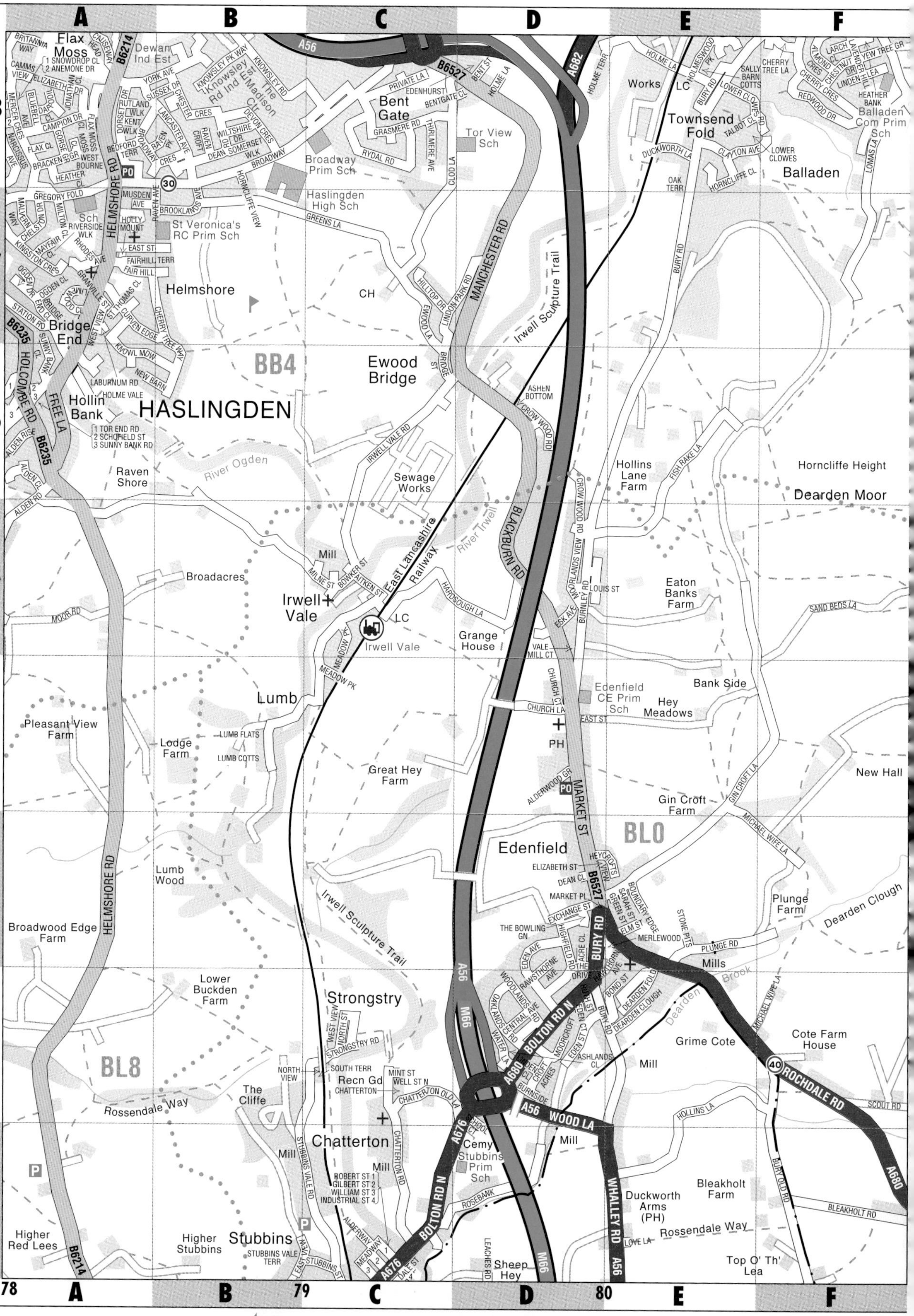
A
B
C
D
E
F
8
7
21
6
5
20
4
3
19
2
1
18
78
79
80
Flax Moss
1 SNOWDROP CL
2 ANEMONE DR
Dewan Ind Est
Knowsley Rd Ind Est
The Madison Ctr
A56
B6527
B6214
A682
Bent Gate
Tor View Sch
Broadway Prim Sch
Haslingden High Sch
St Veronica's RC Prim Sch
Sch
Helmshore
Bridge End
B6235
HOLCOMBE RD
FREE LA
Hollin Bank
HASLINGDEN
BB4
1 TOR END RD
2 SCHOFIELD ST
3 SUNNY BANK RD
Raven Shore
River Ogden
CH
Ewood Bridge
MANCHESTER RD
Irwell Sculpture Trail
ASHEN BOTTOM
Sewage Works
East Lancashire Railway
River Irwell
BLACKBURN RD
Mill
Irwell Vale
LC
Grange House
Broadacres
MOOR RD
Lumb
LUMB FLATS
LUMB COTTS
Pleasant View Farm
Lodge Farm
Great Hey Farm
HELMSHORE RD
Lumb Wood
Broadwood Edge Farm
Lower Buckden Farm
Strongstry
BL8
Rossendale Way
The Cliffe
Chatterton
Recn Gd
Mill
Stubbins
Higher Stubbins
Higher Red Lees
STUBBINS VALE TERR
Works
Townsend Fold
Balladen
Balladen Com Prim Sch
HEATHER BANK
OAK TERR
DUCKWORTH LA
BURY RD
Hollins Lane Farm
FISH RAKE LA
Horncliffe Height
Dearden Moor
Eaton Banks Farm
SAND BEDS LA
Edenfield CE Prim Sch
Bank Side
Hey Meadows
PH
PO
MARKET ST
Gin Croft Farm
GIN CROFT LA
New Hall
BL0
Edenfield
MICHAEL WIFE LA
Plunge Farm
Dearden Clough
PLUNGE RD
Mills
Dearden Brook
Grime Cote
Cote Farm House
ROCHDALE RD
A680
40
A56
M66
BOLTON RD N
A676
WOOD LA
Mill
Cemy
Stubbins Prim Sch
WHALLEY RD
Duckworth Arms (PH)
Bleakholt Farm
BLEAKHOLT RD
Rossendale Way
Top O' Th' Lea
Sheep Hey
SCOUT RD
HOLLINS LA
BURY OLD RD

67
50

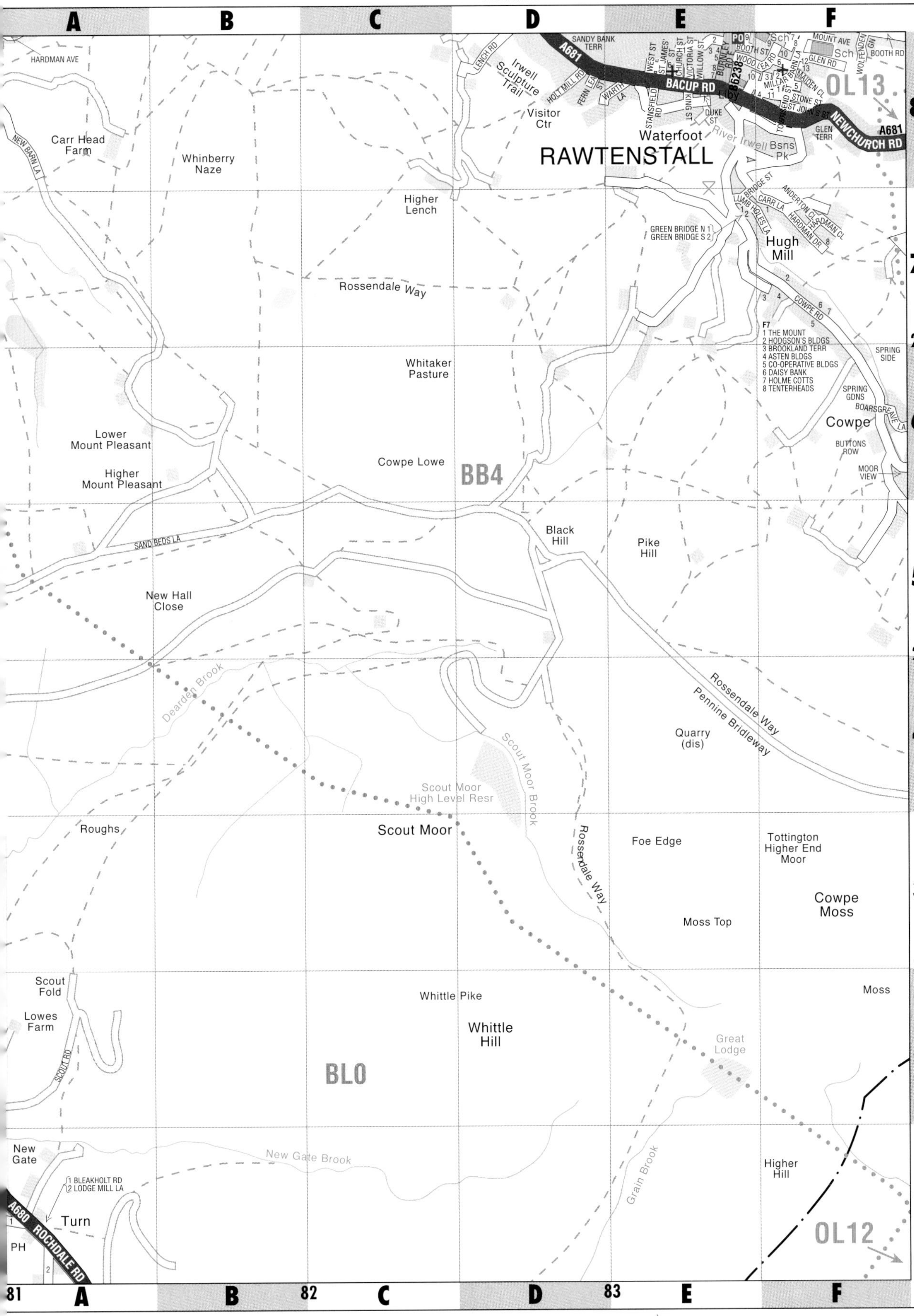
A
B
C
D
E
F
HARDMAN AVE
NEW BARN LA
Carr Head Farm
Whinberry Naze
Irwell Sculpture Trail
Visitor Ctr
SANDY BANK TERR
A681
BACUP RD
B6238
RAWTENSTALL
Waterfoot
River Irwell
Bsns Pk
OL13
NEWCHURCH RD
GLEN TERR
Higher Lench
Rossendale Way
GREEN BRIDGE N 1
GREEN BRIDGE S 2
Hugh Mill
COWPE RD
F7
1 THE MOUNT
2 HODGSON'S BLDGS
3 BROOKLAND TERR
4 ASTEN BLDGS
5 CO-OPERATIVE BLDGS
6 DAISY BANK
7 HOLME COTTS
8 TENTERHEADS
SPRING SIDE
SPRING GDNS
Cowpe
BUTTONS ROW
MOOR VIEW
Whitaker Pasture
Lower Mount Pleasant
Higher Mount Pleasant
Cowpe Lowe
BB4
Black Hill
Pike Hill
SAND BEDS LA
New Hall Close
Dearden Brook
Rossendale Way
Pennine Bridleway
Quarry (dis)
Scout Moor Brook
Scout Moor High Level Resr
Roughs
Scout Moor
Foe Edge
Tottington Higher End Moor
Cowpe Moss
Moss Top
Scout Fold
Lowes Farm
SCOUT RD
Whittle Pike
Whittle Hill
BLO
Great Lodge
Moss
New Gate
New Gate Brook
Grain Brook
1 BLEAKHOLT RD
2 LODGE MILL LA
Turn
PH
A680 ROCHDALE RD
Higher Hill
OL12
8
7
21
6
5
20
4
3
19
2
1
18
81
82
83

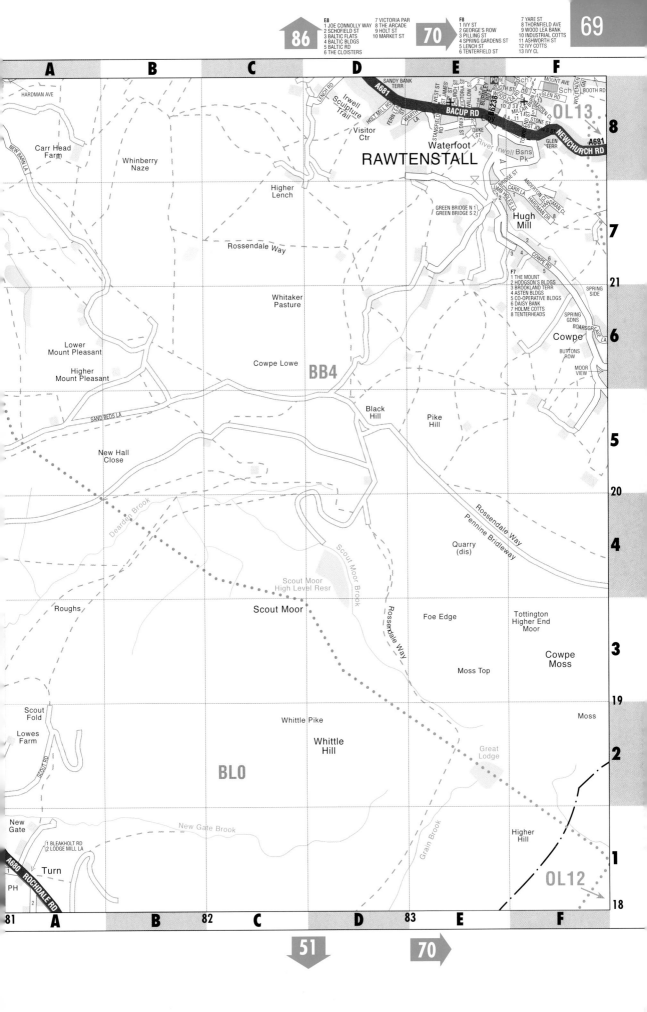

69
87

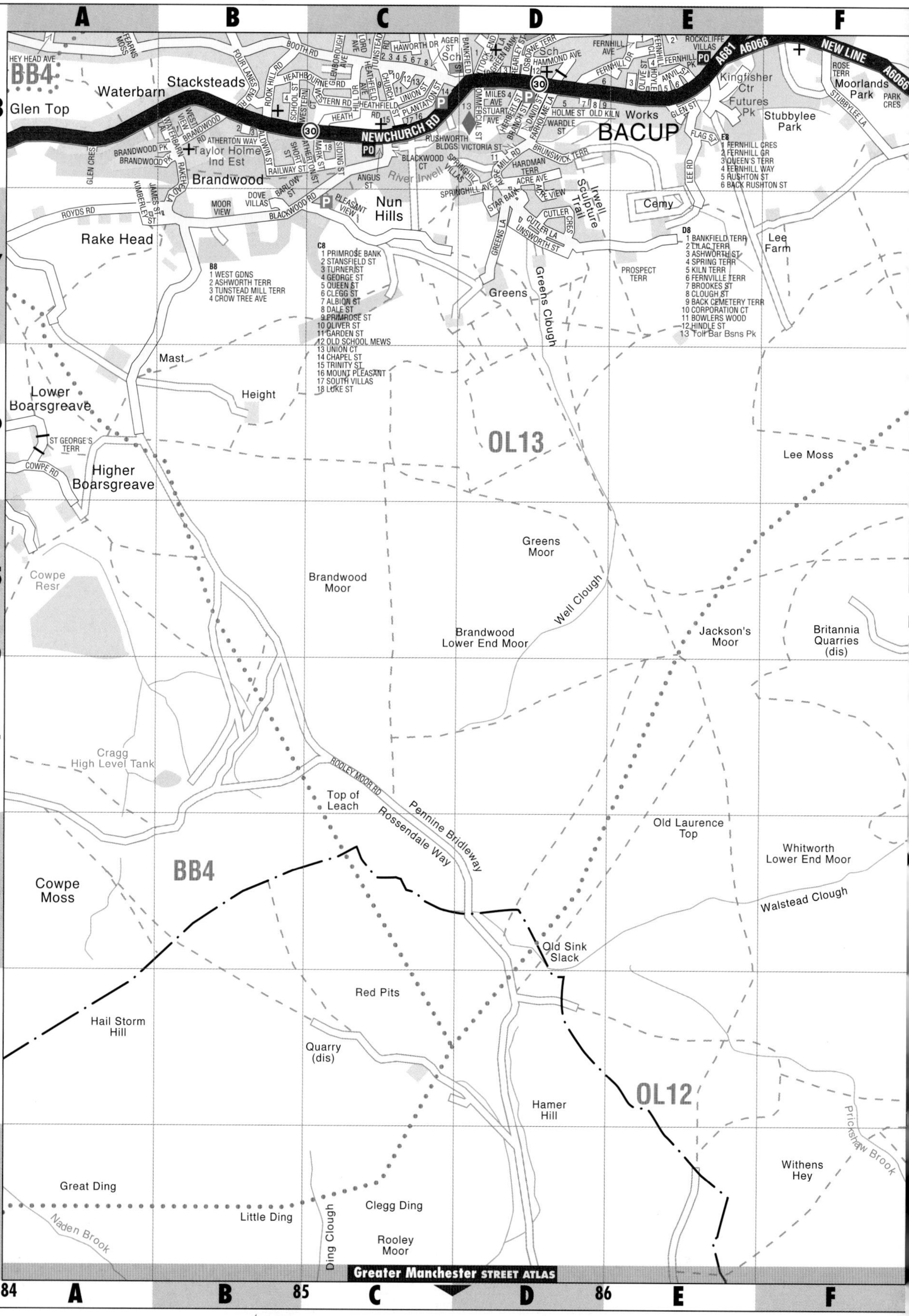
A
B
C
D
E
F
8
7
21
6
5
20
4
3
19
2
1
18
84
85
86
BB4
Glen Top
Waterbarn
Stacksteads
HEY HEAD AVE
FEARNS MOSS
BOOTH RD
FOUR LANES END RD
ROOK HILL RD
HEATHBOURNE RD
HAWORTH DR
AGER ST
Sch
BANKFIELD ST
Sch
HAMMOND AVE
FERNHILL AVE
ROCKCLIFFE VILLAS
PO
A681
A6066
NEW LINE
A6066
Kingfisher Ctr
Futures Pk
ROSE TERR
Moorlands Park
PARK CRES
STUBBYLEE LA
Stubbylee Park
NEWCHURCH RD
30
30
P
P
PO
WEST VIEW
BRANDWOOD RD
ATHERTON WAY
Taylor Holme Ind Est
BRANDWOOD PK
GLEN CRES
WATERBARN LA
RAKEFOOT
Brandwood
RAILWAY ST
River Irwell
BLACKWOOD CT
RUSHWORTH BLDGS
VICTORIA ST
MILES AVE
STUART AVE
HARDMAN TERR
ACRE AVE
WARDLE ST
HOLME ST
OLD KILN
Works
BACUP
BRUNSWICK TERR
FLAG S
GLEN ST
LEE RD
JAMES ST
KIMBERLEY ST
ROYDS RD
MOOR VIEW
DOVE VILLAS
BLACKWOOD RD
PLEASANT VIEW
ANGUS ST
Nun Hills
SPRINGHILL AVE
STAR BANK
ACRE VIEW
CUTLER CRES
CUTLER LA
UNSWORTH ST
GREENS LA
Irwell Sculpture Trail
Cemy
Rake Head
B8
1 WEST GDNS
2 ASHWORTH TERR
3 TUNSTEAD MILL TERR
4 CROW TREE AVE
C8
1 PRIMROSE BANK
2 STANSFIELD ST
3 TURNER ST
4 GEORGE ST
5 QUEEN ST
6 CLEGG ST
7 ALBION ST
8 DALE ST
9 PRIMROSE ST
10 OLIVER ST
11 GARDEN ST
12 OLD SCHOOL MEWS
13 UNION CT
14 CHAPEL ST
15 TRINITY ST
16 MOUNT PLEASANT
17 SOUTH VILLAS
18 LUKE ST
D8
1 BANKFIELD TERR
2 LILAC TERR
3 ASHWORTH ST
4 SPRING TERR
5 KILN TERR
6 FERNVILLE TERR
7 BROOKES ST
8 CLOUGH ST
9 BACK CEMETERY TERR
10 CORPORATION CT
11 BOWLERS WOOD
12 HINDLE ST
13 Toll Bar Bsns Pk
E8
1 FERNHILL CRES
2 FERNHILL GR
3 QUEEN'S TERR
4 FERNHILL WAY
5 RUSHTON ST
6 BACK RUSHTON ST
PROSPECT TERR
Lee Farm
Greens
Greens Clough
Mast
Lower Boarsgreave
Height
ST GEORGE'S TERR
COWPE RD
Higher Boarsgreave
OL13
Lee Moss
Greens Moor
Cowpe Resr
Brandwood Moor
Well Clough
Brandwood Lower End Moor
Jackson's Moor
Britannia Quarries (dis)
Cragg High Level Tank
ROOLEY MOOR RD
Top of Leach
Pennine Bridleway
Rossendale Way
Old Laurence Top
Whitworth Lower End Moor
Cowpe Moss
BB4
Walstead Clough
Old Sink Slack
Red Pits
Hail Storm Hill
Quarry (dis)
OL12
Hamer Hill
Prickshaw Brook
Withens Hey
Great Ding
Clegg Ding
Little Ding
Naden Brook
Ding Clough
Rooley Moor

88

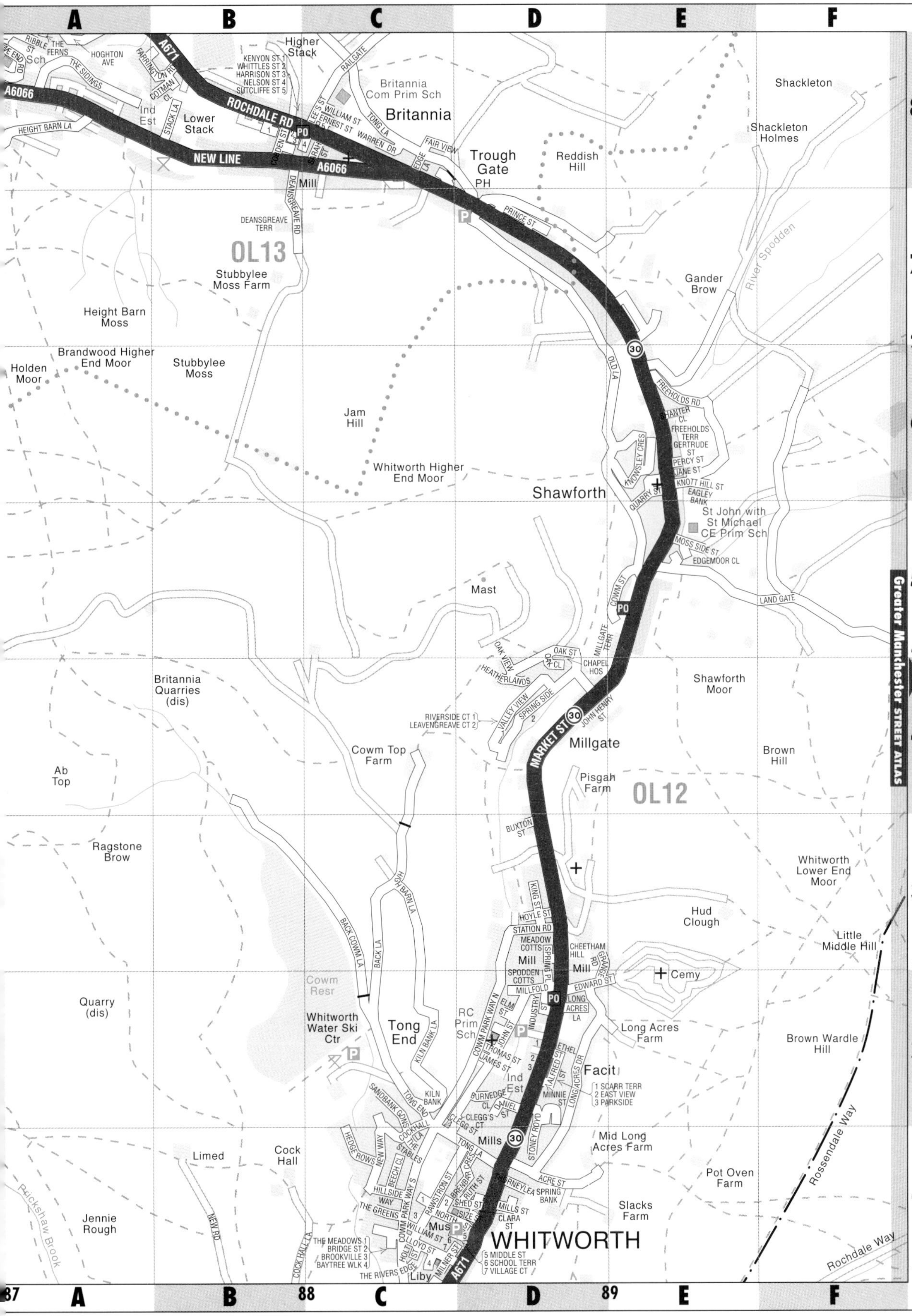

A
B
C
D
E
F
8
7
21
6
5
20
4
3
19
2
1
18
87
88
89
RIBBLE ST
THE FERNS
HOGHTON AVE
THE SIDINGS
Sch
A6066
A671
KENYON ST 1
WHITTLES ST 2
HARRISON ST 3
NELSON ST 4
SUTCLIFFE ST 5
FARRINGTON RD
COTMAN CL
STACK LA
Ind Est
Lower Stack
Higher Stack
RAILGATE
Britannia Com Prim Sch
Britannia
ROCHDALE RD
PO
LEE'S ST
WILLIAM ST
ERNEST ST
TONG LA
WARREN DR
FAIR VIEW
EDGE LA
Trough Gate
PH
Reddish Hill
Shackleton
Shackleton Holmes
HEIGHT BARN LA
NEW LINE
COBDEN ST
SARAH ST
Mill
DEANSGREAVE TERR
DEANSGREAVE RD
PRINCE ST
OL13
Stubbylee Moss Farm
Gander Brow
River Spodden
Height Barn Moss
Brandwood Higher End Moor
Holden Moor
Stubbylee Moss
OLD LA
FREEHOLDS RD
SHANTER CL
FREEHOLDS TERR
GERTRUDE ST
PERCY ST
JANE ST
KNOTT HILL ST
EAGLEY BANK
KNOWSLEY CRES
QUARRY ST
Jam Hill
Whitworth Higher End Moor
Shawforth
St John with St Michael CE Prim Sch
MOSS SIDE ST
EDGEMOOR CL
Mast
COWM ST
LAND GATE
Greater Manchester STREET ATLAS
OAK VIEW
OAK ST
OAK CL
MILLGATE TERR
CHAPEL HOS
HEATHERLANDS
Britannia Quarries (dis)
Shawforth Moor
RIVERSIDE CT 1
LEAVENGREAVE CT 2
VALLEY VIEW
SPRING SIDE
MARKET ST
JOHN HENRY ST
Millgate
Cowm Top Farm
Brown Hill
Ab Top
Pisgah Farm
OL12
BUXTON ST
Ragstone Brow
Whitworth Lower End Moor
HIGH BARN LA
BACK COWM LA
BACK LA
KING ST
HOYLE ST
STATION RD
Hud Clough
Little Middle Hill
MEADOW COTTS
SPRING PL
CHEETHAM HILL
GRANGE RD
Mill
SPODDEN COTTS
Cemy
Cowm Resr
Quarry (dis)
MILLFOLD
EDWARD ST
PO
LONG ACRES LA
Whitworth Water Ski Ctr
Tong End
KILN BANK LA
RC Prim Sch
COWM PARK WAY N
ELM ST
INDUSTRY ST
Long Acres Farm
Brown Wardle Hill
THOMAS ST
JAMES ST
BETHEL ST
ALFRED ST
LONG ACRES DR
Facit
Ind Est
SANDBANK GDNS
TONG END
KILN BANK
BURNEDGE CL
DANIEL ST
MINNIE ST
1 SCARR TERR
2 EAST VIEW
3 PARKSIDE
HEDGE ROWS
NEW WAY
COCKHALL LA
THE STABLES
CLEGG'S CT
CLEGG ST
Mills
STONEY ROYD
Mid Long Acres Farm
Rossendale Way
Limed
Cock Hall
BEECH CL
TONG LA
HILLSIDE WAY
COWM PARK WAY S
RAWSTRON ST
BREWERY ST
RUTH ST
THORNEYLEA
SPRING BANK
ACRE ST
Pot Oven Farm
Prickshaw Brook
Jennie Rough
NEW RD
THE GREENS
NORTH ST
SHED ST
MILLS ST
CLARA ST
Slacks Farm
WILLIAM ST
Mus
THE MEADOWS 1
BRIDGE ST 2
BROOKVILLE 3
BAYTREE WLK 4
COCK HALL LA
HOLT ST
LLOYD ST
THE RIVERS EDGE
Liby
MILNER ST
WHITWORTH
5 MIDDLE ST
6 SCHOOL TERR
7 VILLAGE CT
Rochdale Way


52

92

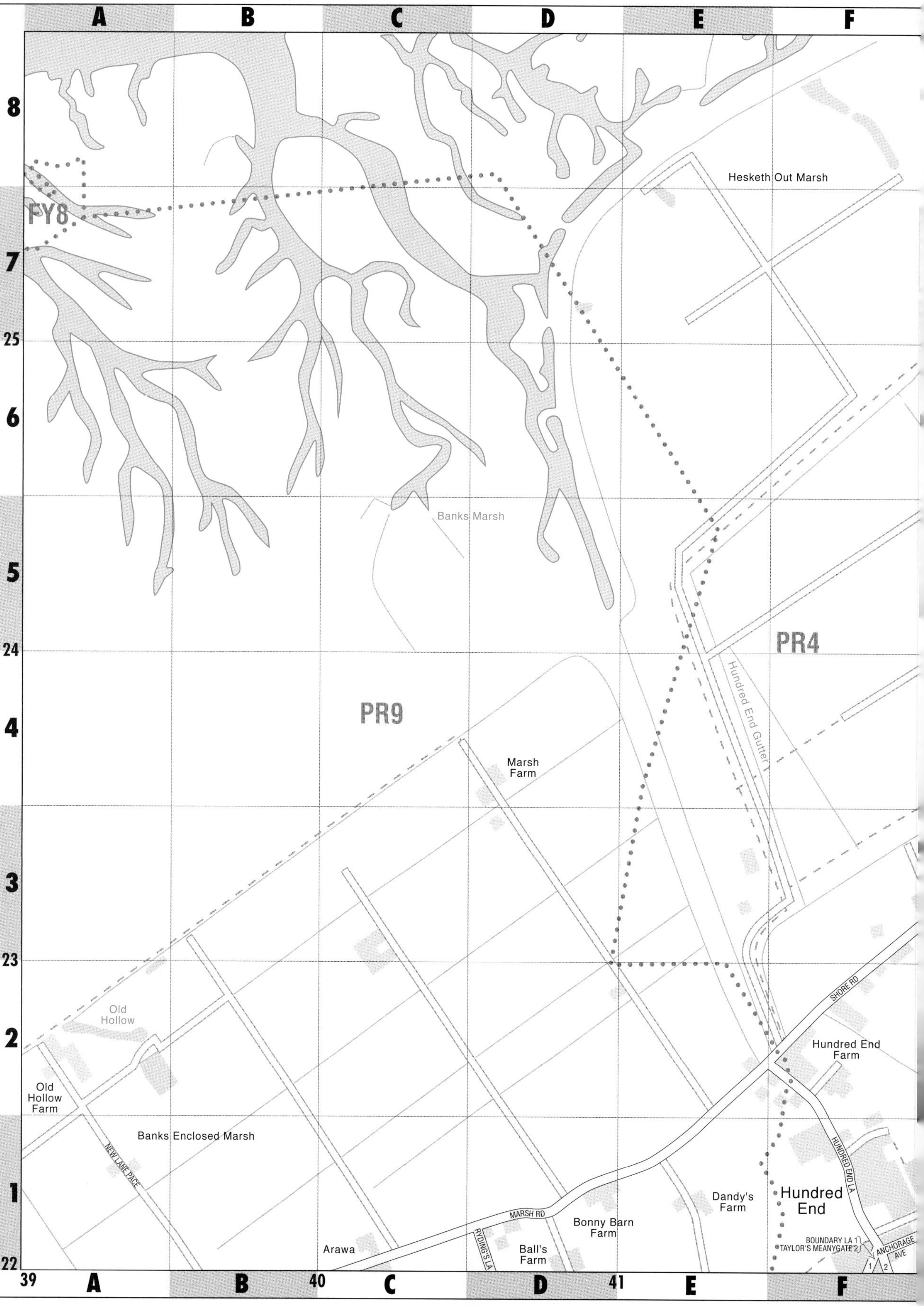
A
B
C
D
E
F
8
7
25
6
5
24
4
3
23
2
1
22
39
40
41
FY8
Hesketh Out Marsh
Banks Marsh
PR4
PR9
Hundred End Gutter
Marsh Farm
Old Hollow
SHORE RD
Hundred End Farm
Old Hollow Farm
Banks Enclosed Marsh
NEW LANE PACE
HUNDRED END LA
Dandy's Farm
Hundred End
MARSH RD
Bonny Barn Farm
RYDING'S LA
Ball's Farm
Arawa
BOUNDARY LA 1
TAYLOR'S MEANYGATE 2
ANCHORAGE AVE
1
2

55

93
74

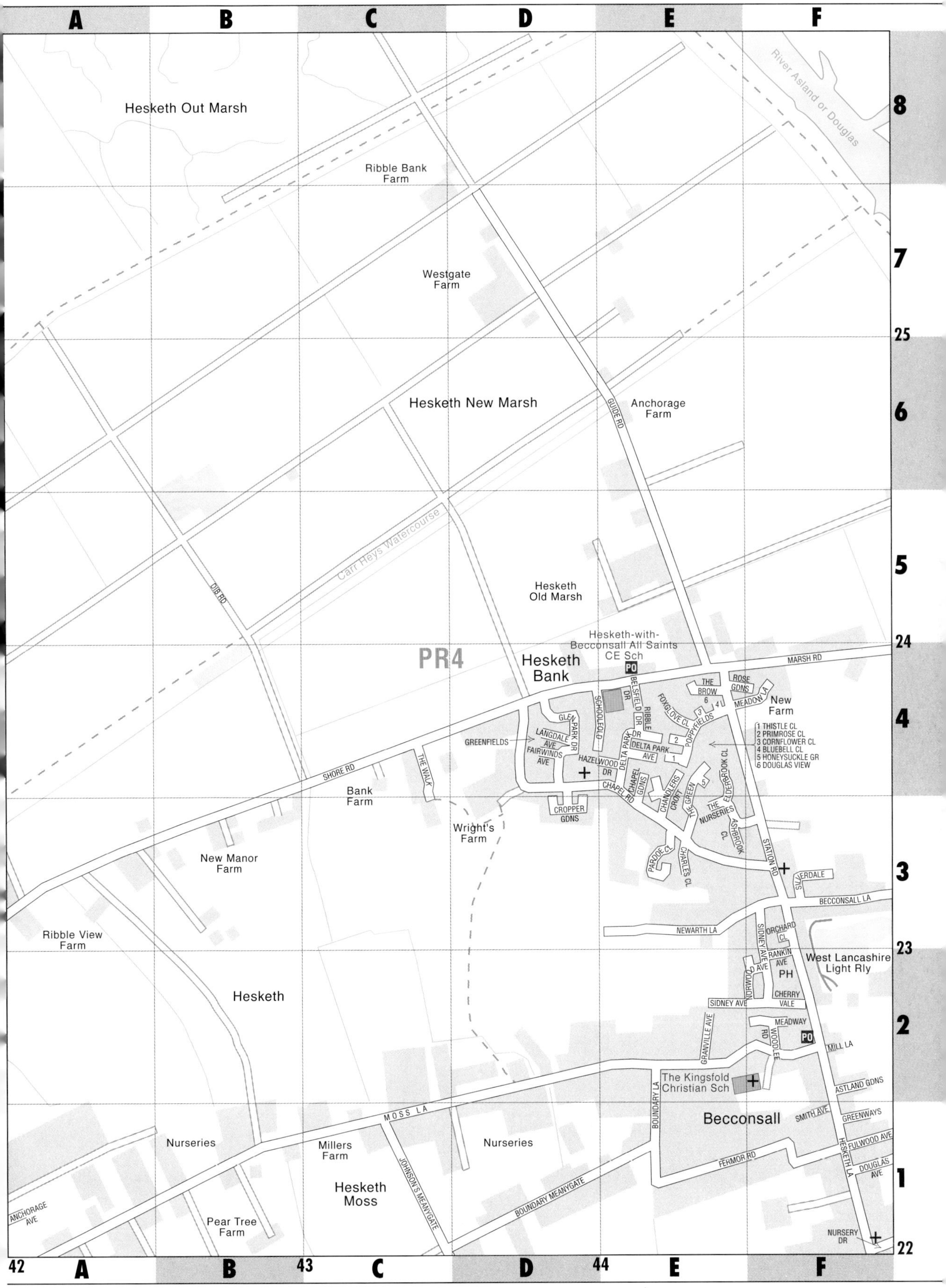
A
B
C
D
E
F
8
7
25
6
5
24
4
3
23
2
1
22
42
43
44
Hesketh Out Marsh
River Asland or Douglas
Ribble Bank Farm
Westgate Farm
Hesketh New Marsh
Anchorage Farm
GUIDE RD
Carr Heys Watercourse
DIB RD
Hesketh Old Marsh
PR4
Hesketh-with-Becconsall All Saints CE Sch
PO
Hesketh Bank
MARSH RD
ROSE GDNS
THE BROW
MEADOW LA
New Farm
1 THISTLE CL
2 PRIMROSE CL
3 CORNFLOWER CL
4 BLUEBELL CL
5 HONEYSUCKLE GR
6 DOUGLAS VIEW
FOXGLOVE CL
POPPYFIELDS
SCHOOLFOLD
BELSFIELD DR
RIBBLE DR
GLEN PARK DR
GREENFIELDS
LANGDALE AVE
FAIRWINDS AVE
HAZELWOOD DR
DELTA PARK DR
DELTA PARK AVE
CHAPEL RD
CHAPEL GDNS
CHANDLERS CROFT
THE GREEN
THE NURSERIES
ELDERBROOK CL
ASHBROOK CL
PARDOE CL
CHARLES CL
CROPPER GDNS
SHORE RD
THE WALK
Bank Farm
Wright's Farm
New Manor Farm
STATION RD
SILVERDALE
BECCONSALL LA
NEWARTH LA
SIDNEY AVE
ORCHARD CL
RANKIN AVE
NORWOOD AVE
PH
CHERRY VALE
West Lancashire Light Rly
MEADWAY
RD
WOODLEE
GRANVILLE AVE
PO
MILL LA
The Kingsfold Christian Sch
ASTLAND GDNS
BOUNDARY LA
Becconsall
SMITH AVE
GREENWAYS
FULWOOD AVE
HESKETH LA
DOUGLAS AVE
FERMOR RD
NURSERY DR
Ribble View Farm
Hesketh
MOSS LA
Nurseries
Millers Farm
Nurseries
Hesketh Moss
JOHNSON'S MEANYGATE
BOUNDARY MEANYGATE
ANCHORAGE AVE
Pear Tree Farm

56
74

73
94

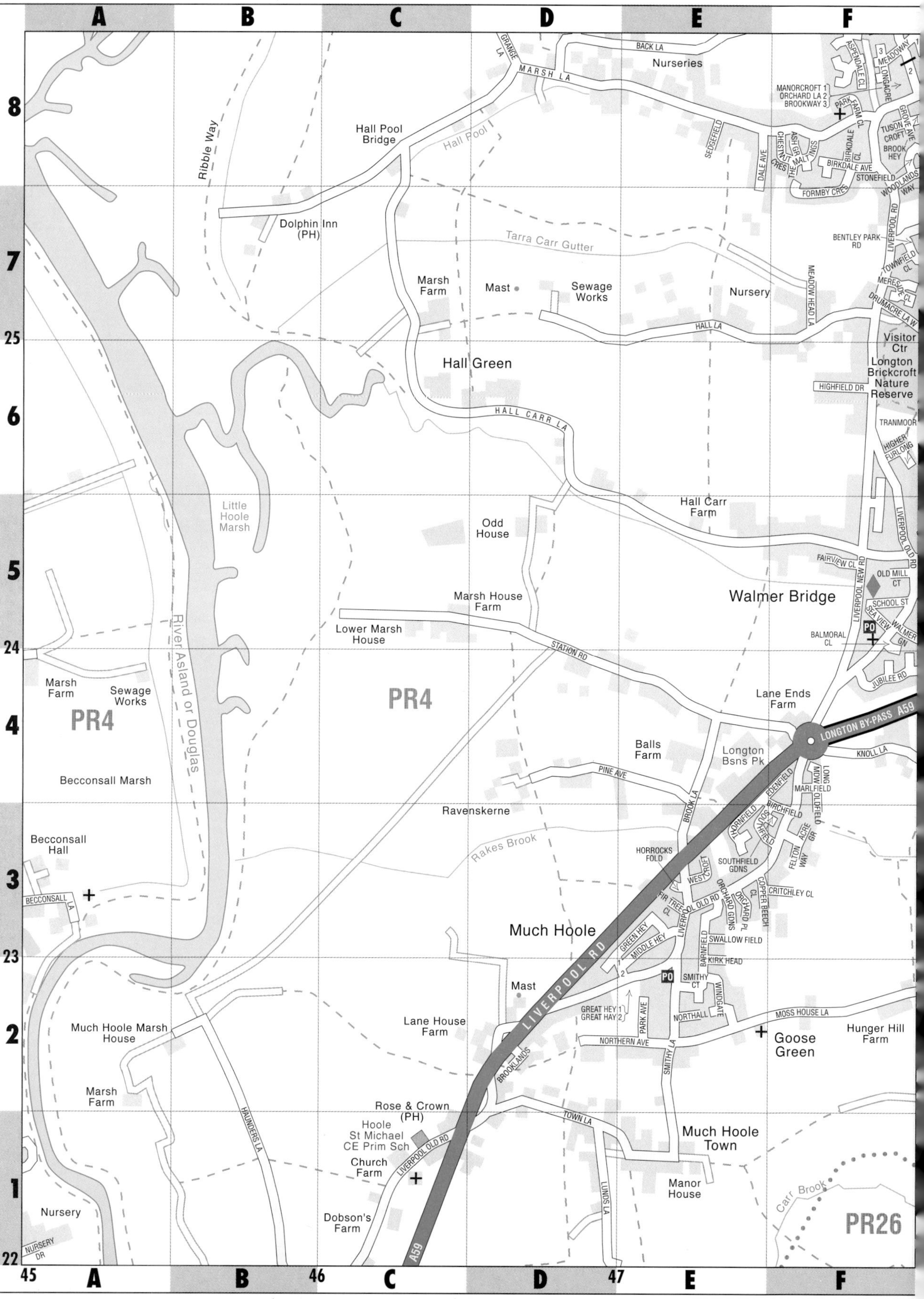
A
B
C
D
E
F
8
7
25
6
5
24
4
3
23
2
1
22
45
46
47
GRANGE LA
BACK LA
Nurseries
MARSH LA
MANORCROFT 1
ORCHARD LA 2
BROOKWAY 3
PARK FARM CL
ASPENDALE CL
MEADOWAY
LONGACRE
GROVE AVE
TUSON CROFT
BROOK HEY
WOODLANDS WAY
STONEFIELD
BIRKDALE AVE
BIRKDALE CL
FORMBY CRES
CHESTNUT CRES
ASH GR
THE MALTINGS
SEDGEFIELD
DALE AVE
Hall Pool Bridge
Hall Pool
Ribble Way
Dolphin Inn (PH)
Tarra Carr Gutter
BENTLEY PARK RD
LIVERPOOL RD
TOWNFIELD CL
MERESIDE CL
DRUMACRE LA W
Marsh Farm
Mast
Sewage Works
Nursery
MEADOW HEAD LA
HALL LA
Visitor Ctr
Longton Brickcroft Nature Reserve
Hall Green
HIGHFIELD DR
TRANMOOR
HIGHER FURLONG
HALL CARR LA
Little Hoole Marsh
Hall Carr Farm
Odd House
LIVERPOOL OLD RD
FAIRVIEW CL
LIVERPOOL NEW RD
OLD MILL CT
SCHOOL ST
SEA VIEW
WALMER GN
BALMORAL CL
JUBILEE RD
Walmer Bridge
Marsh House Farm
Lower Marsh House
STATION RD
River Asland or Douglas
Marsh Farm
Sewage Works
PR4
PR4
Lane Ends Farm
LONGTON BY-PASS A59
KNOLL LA
Balls Farm
Longton Bsns Pk
PINE AVE
Becconsall Marsh
LONG MDW
MARLFIELD
OLDFIELD
EDENFIELD
BIRCHFIELD
HORNFIELD
SOUTHFIELD
ACRE GR
FELTON WAY
BROOK LA
Ravenskerne
Becconsall Hall
Rakes Brook
HORROCKS FOLD
WESTCROFT
SOUTHFIELD GDNS
CRITCHLEY CL
BECCONSALL LA
FIR TREE CL
LIVERPOOL OLD RD
ORCHARD GDNS
ORCHARD PL
COPPER BEECH CL
Much Hoole
GREEN HEY
MIDDLE HEY
BARNFIELD
SWALLOW FIELD
KIRK HEAD
LIVERPOOL RD
SMITHY CT
WINDGATE
Mast
GREAT HEY 1
GREAT HAY 2
PARK AVE
NORTHALL
MOSS HOUSE LA
Much Hoole Marsh House
Lane House Farm
NORTHERN AVE
Goose Green
Hunger Hill Farm
SMITHY LA
BROOKLANDS
Marsh Farm
Rose & Crown (PH)
HAUNDERS LA
TOWN LA
Much Hoole Town
Hoole St Michael CE Prim Sch
LIVERPOOL OLD RD
Church Farm
LUNDS LA
Manor House
Carr Brook
Nursery
Dobson's Farm
PR26
NURSERY DR
A59

73
57

95
76

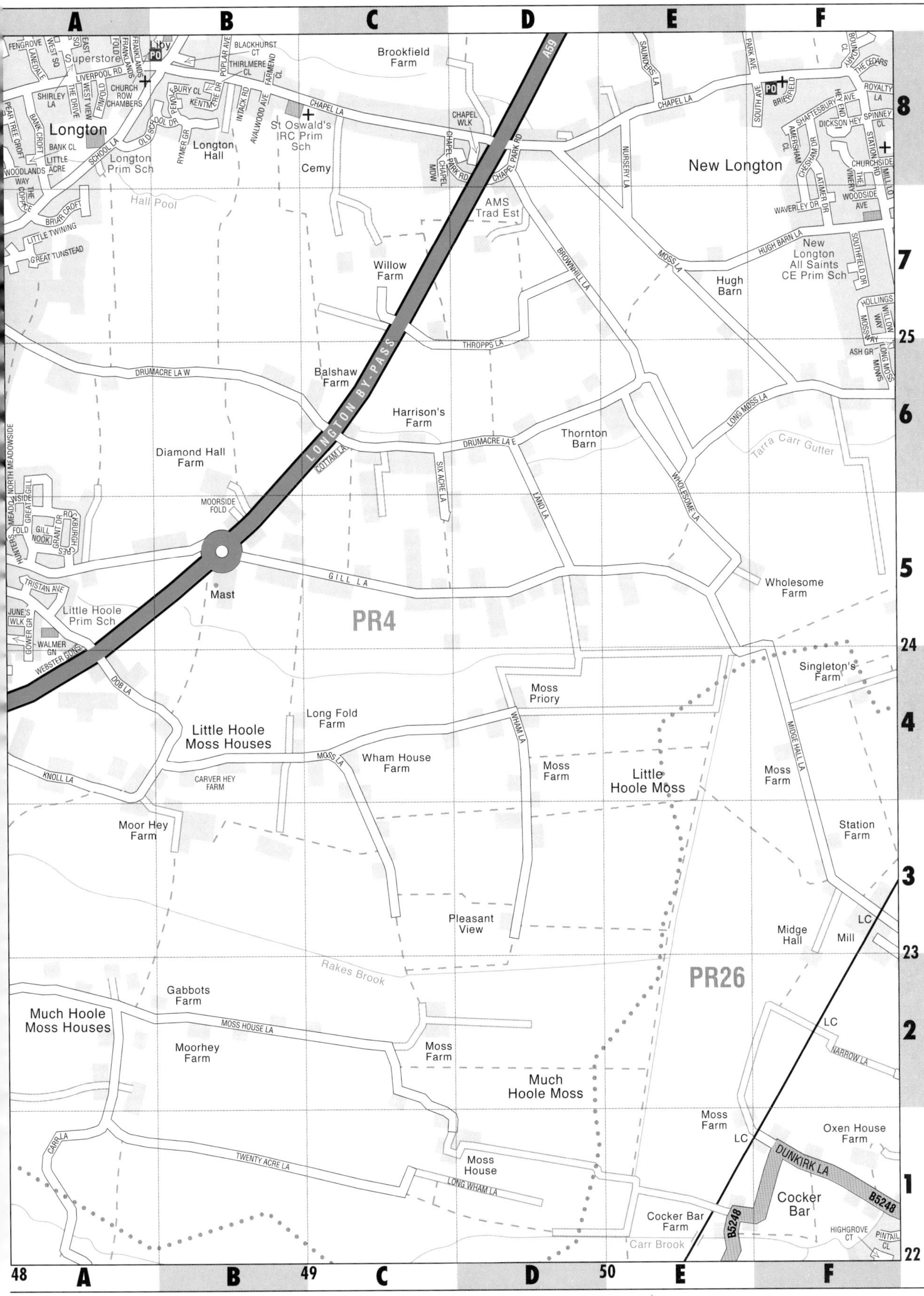
A
B
C
D
E
F
Longton
Superstore
Liby
PO
FENGROVE
LANEDALE
WEST SQ
EAST SQ
FOLD
FRANKLANDS
BLACKHURST CT
THIRLMERE CL
POPLAR AVE
FARMEND CL
LIVERPOOL RD
SHIRLEY LA
THE DRIVE
WEST VIEW
PINFOLD
CHURCH ROW CHAMBERS
BURY CL
KENTMERE DR
INTACK RD
AVALWOOD AVE
CHAPEL LA
PEAR TREE CROFT
BANK CROFT
BANK CL
LITTLE ACRE
SCHOOL LA
OLD SCHOOL DR
PENDLE
RYMER GR
Longton Hall
St Oswald's RC Prim Sch
Cemy
Longton Prim Sch
WOODLANDS WAY
THE COPPICE
Hall Pool
BRIAR CROFT
LITTLE TWINING
GREAT TUNSTEAD
Brookfield Farm
A59
CHAPEL WLK
CHAPEL MDW
CHAPEL PARK RD
AMS Trad Est
Willow Farm
THROPPS LA
SAUNDERS LA
PARK AVE
SOUTH AVE
BRIERFIELD
BOUNDARY CL
THE CEDARS
ROYALTY LA
HEY END
SHAFTESBURY AVE
SPINNEY CL
DICKSON HEY
AMERSHAM CL
CHESHAM DR
STATION RD
CHURCHSIDE
MILL LA
THE VINERY
WOODSIDE AVE
LATIMER DR
WAVERLEY DR
NURSERY LA
New Longton
MOSS LA
HUGH BARN LA
New Longton All Saints CE Prim Sch
SOUTHFIELD DR
Hugh Barn
BROWNHILL LA
HOLLINGS
WILLOW WAY
MOSSWAY
ASH GR
LONG MOSS MDWS
DRUMACRE LA W
Balshaw Farm
LONGTON BY-PASS
Harrison's Farm
DRUMACRE LA E
Thornton Barn
LONG MOSS LA
Tarra Carr Gutter
COTTAM LA
SIX ACRE LA
Diamond Hall Farm
NORTH MEADOWSIDE
MEADOWSIDE
GREAT GILL
HUNTERS FOLD
GILL NOOK
GRANT DR
ROXBURGH CRES
MOORSIDE FOLD
LAND LA
WHOLESOME LA
GILL LA
Wholesome Farm
TRISTAN AVE
Mast
JUNE'S WLK
GOWER GR
Little Hoole Prim Sch
WALMER GN
WEBSTER GDNS
PR4
DOB LA
Singleton's Farm
Moss Priory
Long Fold Farm
Little Hoole Moss Houses
WHAM LA
MOSS LA
Wham House Farm
Moss Farm
Little Hoole Moss
MIDGE HALL LA
Moss Farm
KNOLL LA
CARVER HEY FARM
Moor Hey Farm
Station Farm
Pleasant View
Midge Hall
LC
Mill
Rakes Brook
PR26
Gabbots Farm
Much Hoole Moss Houses
MOSS HOUSE LA
Moorhey Farm
Moss Farm
Much Hoole Moss
LC
NARROW LA
Moss Farm
LC
Oxen House Farm
CARR LA
TWENTY ACRE LA
Moss House
LONG WHAM LA
DUNKIRK LA
B5248
Cocker Bar
Cocker Bar Farm
Carr Brook
HIGHGROVE CT
PINTAIL CL
8
7
25
6
5
24
4
3
23
2
1
22
48
49
50

58
76

75
96

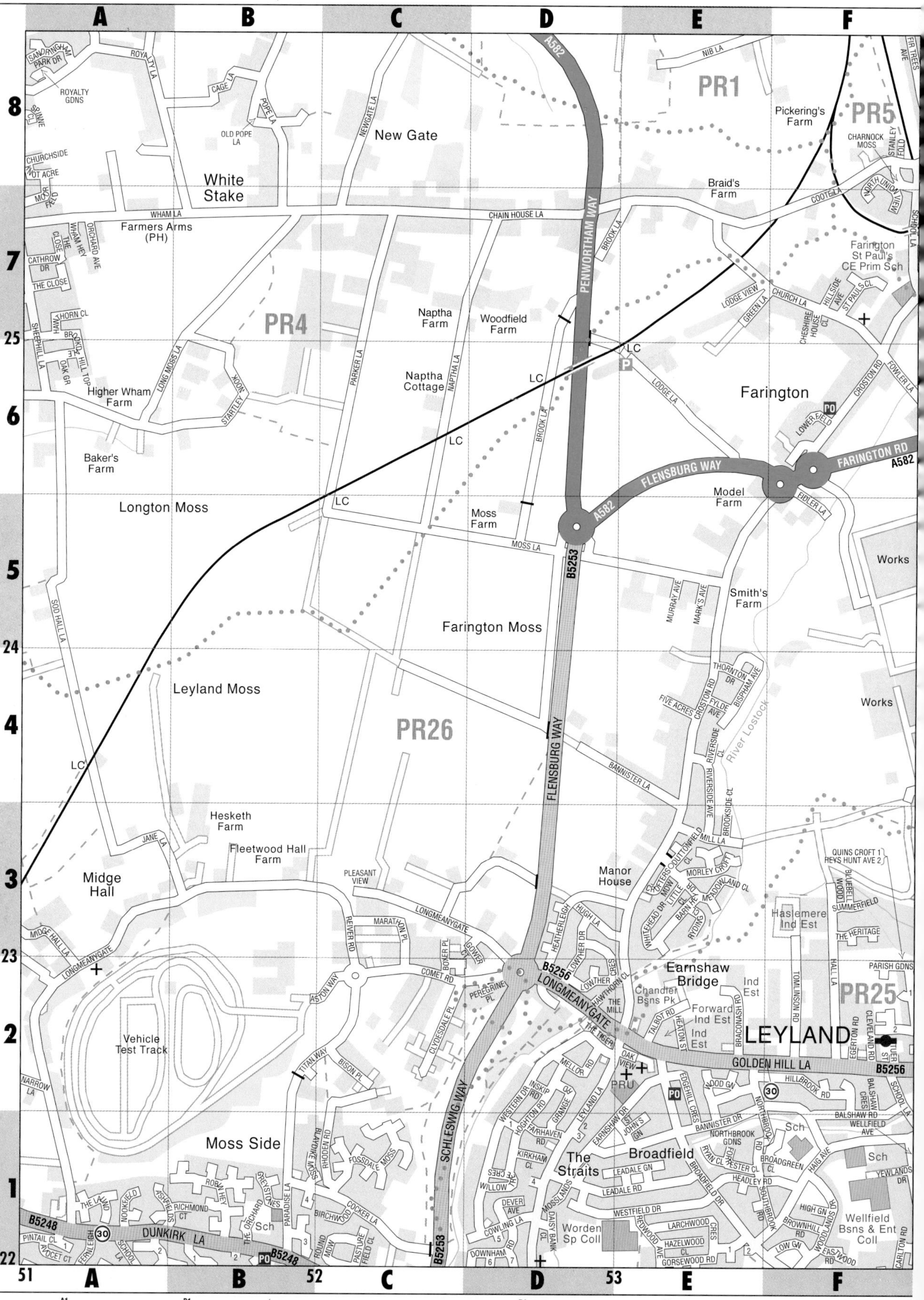


A1
1 CALDERBANK CL
2 CHEETHAM MDW

B1
1 BARN CROFT
2 THE MEADOWS
3 HOLMES MDW
4 ROSTREVOR CL

D1
1 JACKSON RD
2 MICKLEFIELD CT
3 ORRELL CL
4 HOMESTEAD CL
5 FIELDEN ST
6 LANGHOLM CL
7 BELMONT RD

E1
1 ELMWOOD AVE
2 BLEACHERS DR

75
59

**A8**
1 FIR TREES CRES
2 ORCHARD CROFT
3 BRIDGE CT
4 SCHOOL HILLOCKS COTTS
5 LONSDALE MEWS
6 BARNFIELD
7 SEPHTON ST
8 HOGHTON ST
9 JUBILEE RD
10 HOPE TERR
11 WILLIAM ST
12 VICTORIA TERR

**B8**
1 ST JAMES CT
2 FERN CL
3 MAUREEN AVE
4 MARILYN AVE
5 CEDAR AVE

**C8**
1 NORTH GR
2 THE PICKERINGS
3 BRIDGE RD
4 NEW PASTURES
5 CHARTWELL RISE
6 STONEBRIDGE CL
7 FELLWAY CL
8 WOODSTOCK CL

**E8**
1 CO-OPERATIVE ST
2 SMITHY ST
3 NELSON ST
4 HOPWOOD ST

97

**E8**
5 CHADWICK CT
6 BRIDGE MEWS
7 CRANBOURNE ST
8 REGENTSWAY
9 GARFORTH CRES

78

**F8**
1 CAM CL
2 BLEASDALE CL
3 DUNSOP CL
4 HAREDEN CL
5 FELL CL
6 HODDER CL
7 MONTGOMERY ST
8 JACKSON ST
9 CAMBRIDGE RD
10 PRINCESS ST
11 SERGEANT ST
12 GROVE ST
13 SMITH ST

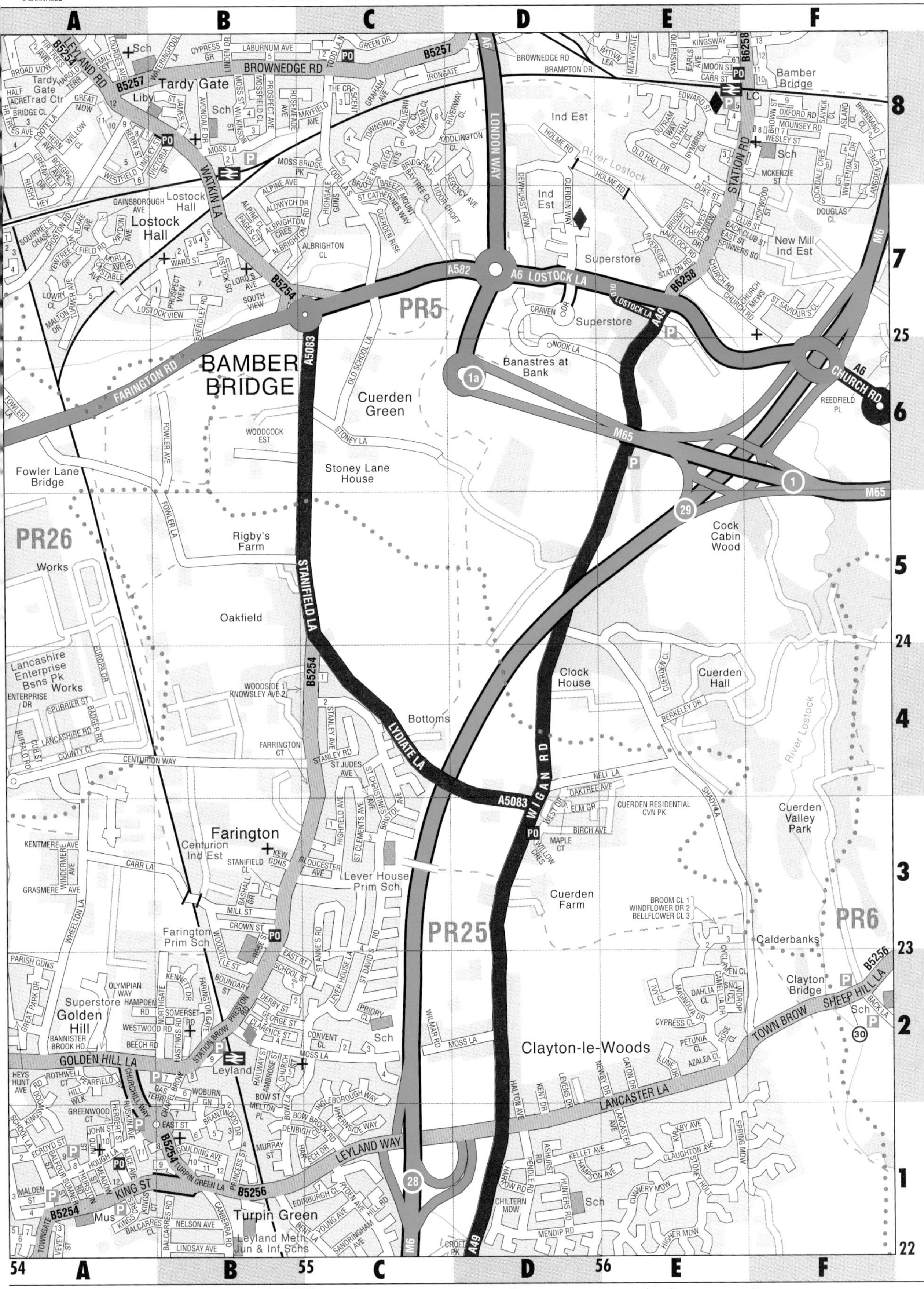


**A1**
1 CHATSWORTH RD
2 YEWLANDS DR
3 YEWLANDS AVE
4 MOSLEY ST
5 BELGRAVE RD
6 REGENT RD
7 ARGYLE RD
8 NORTHCOTE ST
9 BALFOUR CT
10 NEWSOME ST
11 DOROTHY AVE
12 KING'S CT
13 FORGE ST

**A7**
1 CHADWICK GDNS
2 SOUTH VIEW
3 EAST VIEW
4 KELLET ACRE
5 BRACKENBURY CL

**B1**
1 ORCHARD ST
2 HELMSLEY GN
3 WILTON PL
4 BURGHLEY CT
5 STRATFIELD PL
6 SPRING ST
7 CEDAR CT
8 CHARNOCK ST
9 BRETHERTON TERR
10 STANLEY ST
11 SANDFIELD ST
12 STARKIE ST

**B2**
1 THE SQUARE
2 BELVEDERE RD
3 CROSS ST
4 BAKER ST
5 ST AMBROSE TERR
6 FLEETWOOD ST
7 GRUNDY ST
8 HEWITT ST
9 GOLDEN HILL

60

**B7**
1 GARDEN ST
2 PRINCESS ST
3 BIRTWISTLE ST
4 QUEEN ST
5 FAIRFIELD ST
6 KING ST
7 CUERDEN GREEN MILLS

78

**C1**
1 STIRLING CL

**C2**
1 ST MARGARET'S RD
2 THE CLOISTERS
3 THE CHASE
4 ST CATHERINES CL

**C3**
1 SPRINGCROFT
2 STEVENSON AVE
3 ST MARLOW AVE
4 ST MICHAEL'S RD

77
98

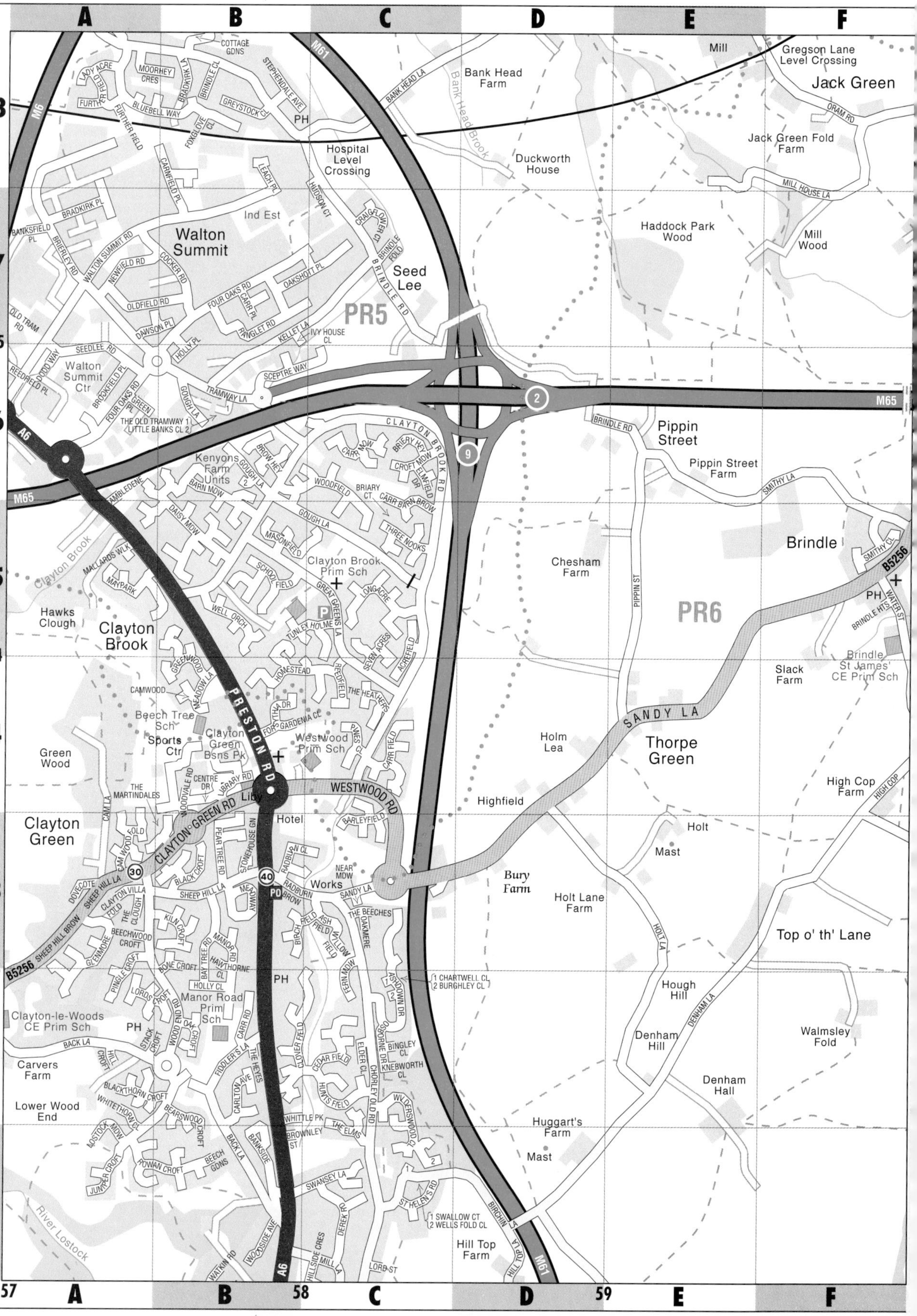
A
B
C
D
E
F
8
7
25
6
5
24
4
3
23
2
1
22
57
58
59
Walton Summit
Ind Est
Hospital Level Crossing
Seed Lee
PR5
Walton Summit Ctr
Bank Head Farm
Duckworth House
Mill
Gregson Lane Level Crossing
Jack Green
Jack Green Fold Farm
Haddock Park Wood
Mill Wood
M6
M61
M65
A6
B5256
Pippin Street
Pippin Street Farm
Brindle
PR6
Chesham Farm
Kenyons Farm Units
Clayton Brook Prim Sch
Hawks Clough
Clayton Brook
Beech Tree Sch
Sports Ctr
Clayton Green Bsns Pk
Westwood Prim Sch
Green Wood
Clayton Green
Hotel
Liby
Works
PO
PH
Holm Lea
Thorpe Green
Highfield
Slack Farm
Brindle St James' CE Prim Sch
High Cop Farm
Holt
Mast
Bury Farm
Holt Lane Farm
Top o' th' Lane
Hough Hill
Denham Hill
Walmsley Fold
Denham Hall
Huggart's Farm
Hill Top Farm
Manor Road Prim Sch
Clayton-le-Woods CE Prim Sch
Carvers Farm
Lower Wood End
River Lostock
Clayton Brook
PRESTON RD
CLAYTON GREEN RD
WESTWOOD RD
SANDY LA
CLAYTON BROOK RD
WALTON SUMMIT RD
BRINDLE RD
PIPPIN ST
HOLT LA
DENHAM LA
SMITHY LA
MILL HOUSE LA
ORAM RD
BANK HEAD LA
SHEEP HILL LA
BACK LA
CHORLEY OLD RD
1 CHARTWELL CL
2 BURGHLEY CL
1 SWALLOW CT
2 WELLS FOLD CL
THE OLD TRAMWAY 1
LITTLE BANKS CL 2

77
61

99
80
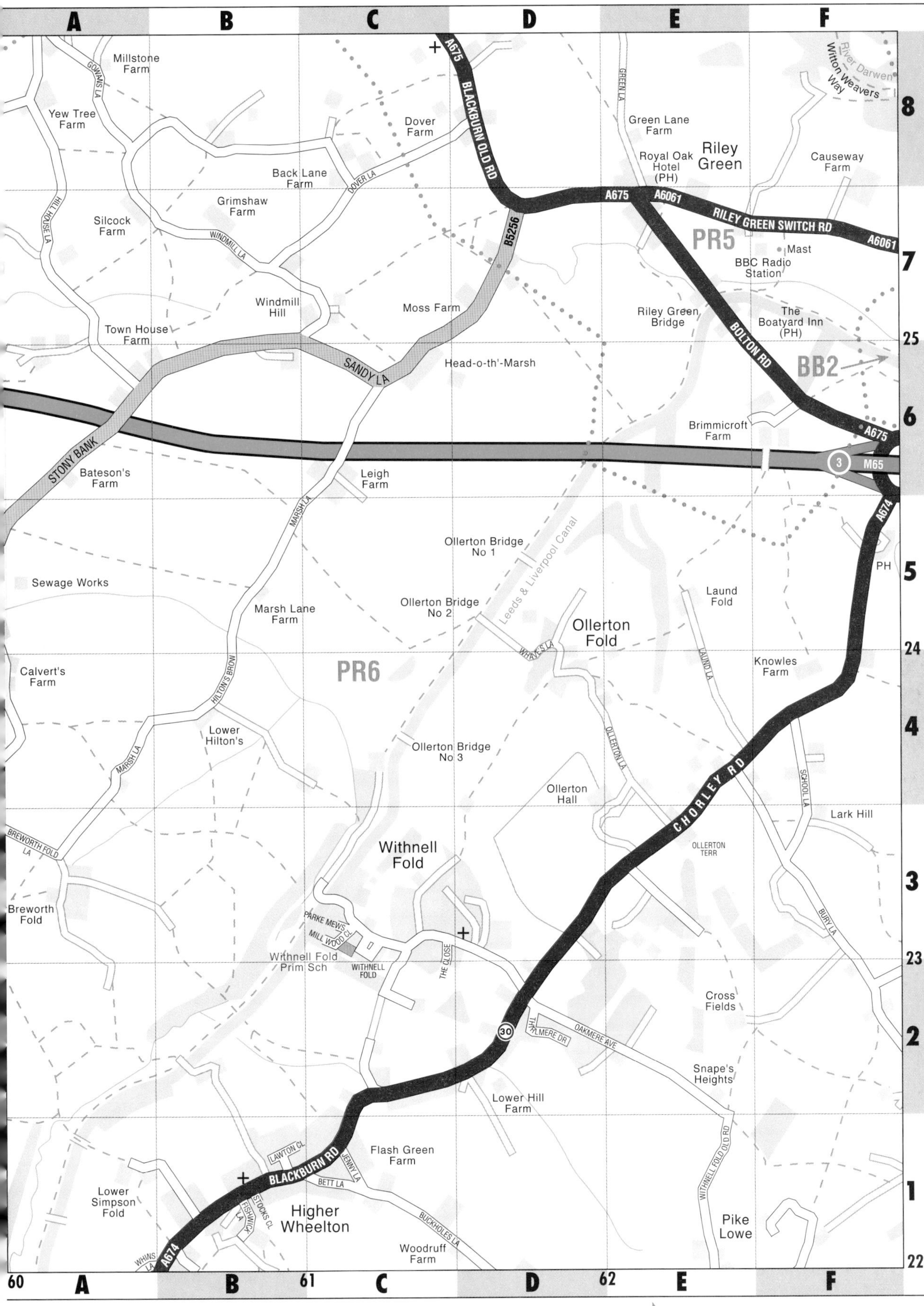
A
B
C
D
E
F
Millstone Farm
GOWANS LA
Yew Tree Farm
Dover Farm
A675
BLACKBURN OLD RD
GREEN LA
Green Lane Farm
Riley Green
Royal Oak Hotel (PH)
River Darwen
Witton Weavers Way
Causeway Farm
Back Lane Farm
DOVER LA
Grimshaw Farm
HILL HOUSE LA
Silcock Farm
WINDMILL LA
B5256
A6061
RILEY GREEN SWITCH RD
PR5
Mast
BBC Radio Station
Windmill Hill
Moss Farm
Riley Green Bridge
The Boatyard Inn (PH)
BOLTON RD
Town House Farm
SANDY LA
Head-o-th'-Marsh
BB2
STONY BANK
Brimmicroft Farm
Bateson's Farm
Leigh Farm
M65
3
A674
MARSH LA
Ollerton Bridge No 1
PH
Sewage Works
Leeds & Liverpool Canal
Laund Fold
Marsh Lane Farm
Ollerton Bridge No 2
Ollerton Fold
WHAVES LA
LAUND LA
Knowles Farm
Calvert's Farm
PR6
HILTON'S BROW
Lower Hilton's
Ollerton Bridge No 3
OLLERTON LA
SCHOOL LA
Ollerton Hall
CHORLEY RD
Lark Hill
BREWORTH FOLD LA
Withnell Fold
OLLERTON TERR
Breworth Fold
PARKE MEWS
MILL WOOD CL
BURY LA
Withnell Fold Prim Sch
WITHNELL FOLD
THE CLOSE
Cross Fields
30
THIRLMERE DR
OAKMERE AVE
Snape's Heights
Lower Hill Farm
WITHNELL FOLD OLD RD
LAWTON CL
BLACKBURN RD
JENNY LA
Flash Green Farm
BETT LA
Lower Simpson Fold
STOCKS CL
FISHWICK LA
Higher Wheelton
BUCKHOLES LA
Pike Lowe
WHINS LA
Woodruff Farm
8
7
25
6
5
24
4
3
23
2
1
22
60
61
62
62
80

79
100

E8
1 SUNNYSIDE AVE
2 VICTORIA AVE
3 CHERRY TREE LA
4 WOODLANDS AVE
5 NEWLANDS CL
6 TETBURY CL

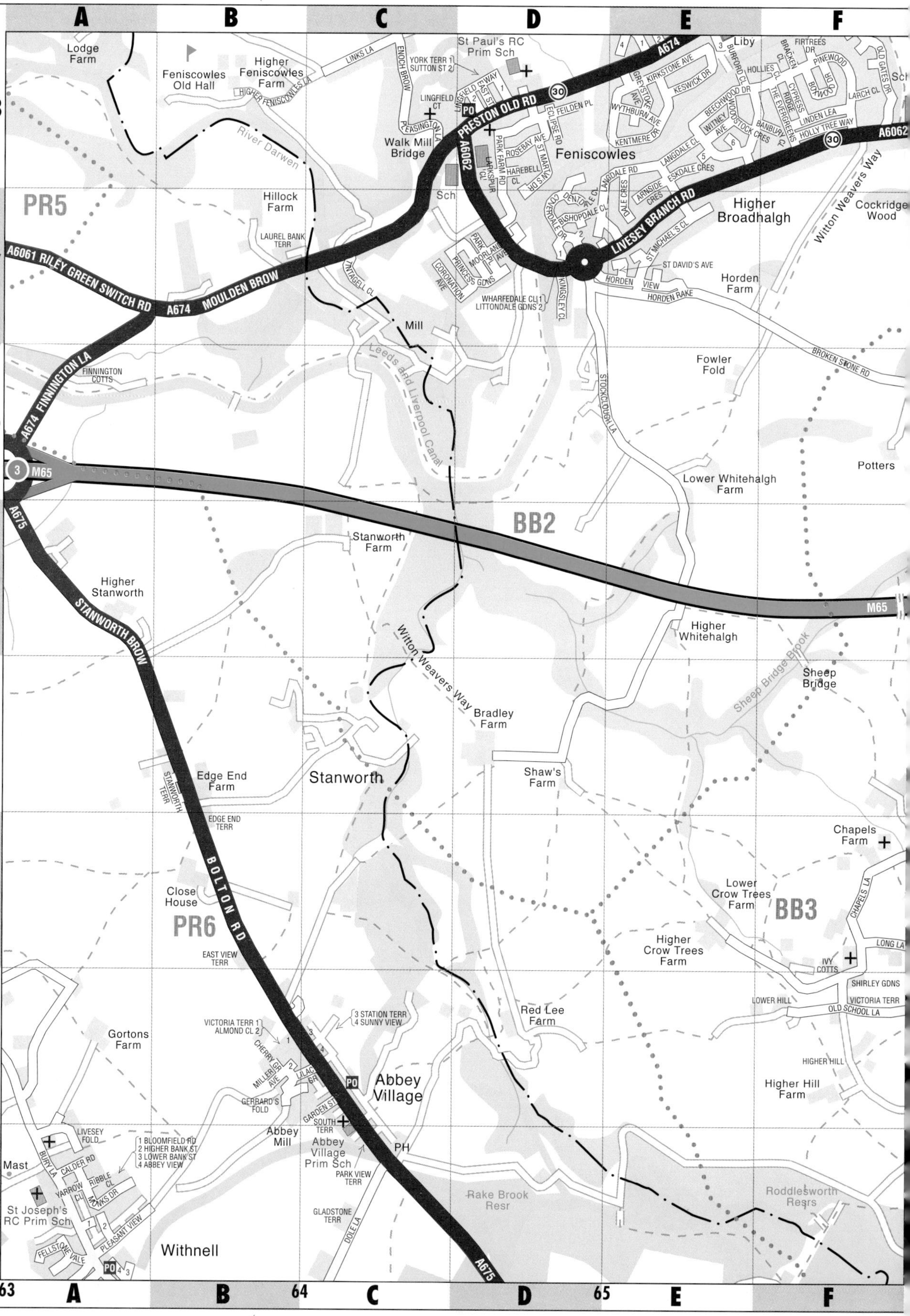


79
63

C8
1 DOROTHY ST
2 MOORGATE ST
3 CATTERALL ST
4 CARRINGTON AVE
5 DAWLISH CL
6 REWE CL

101
82

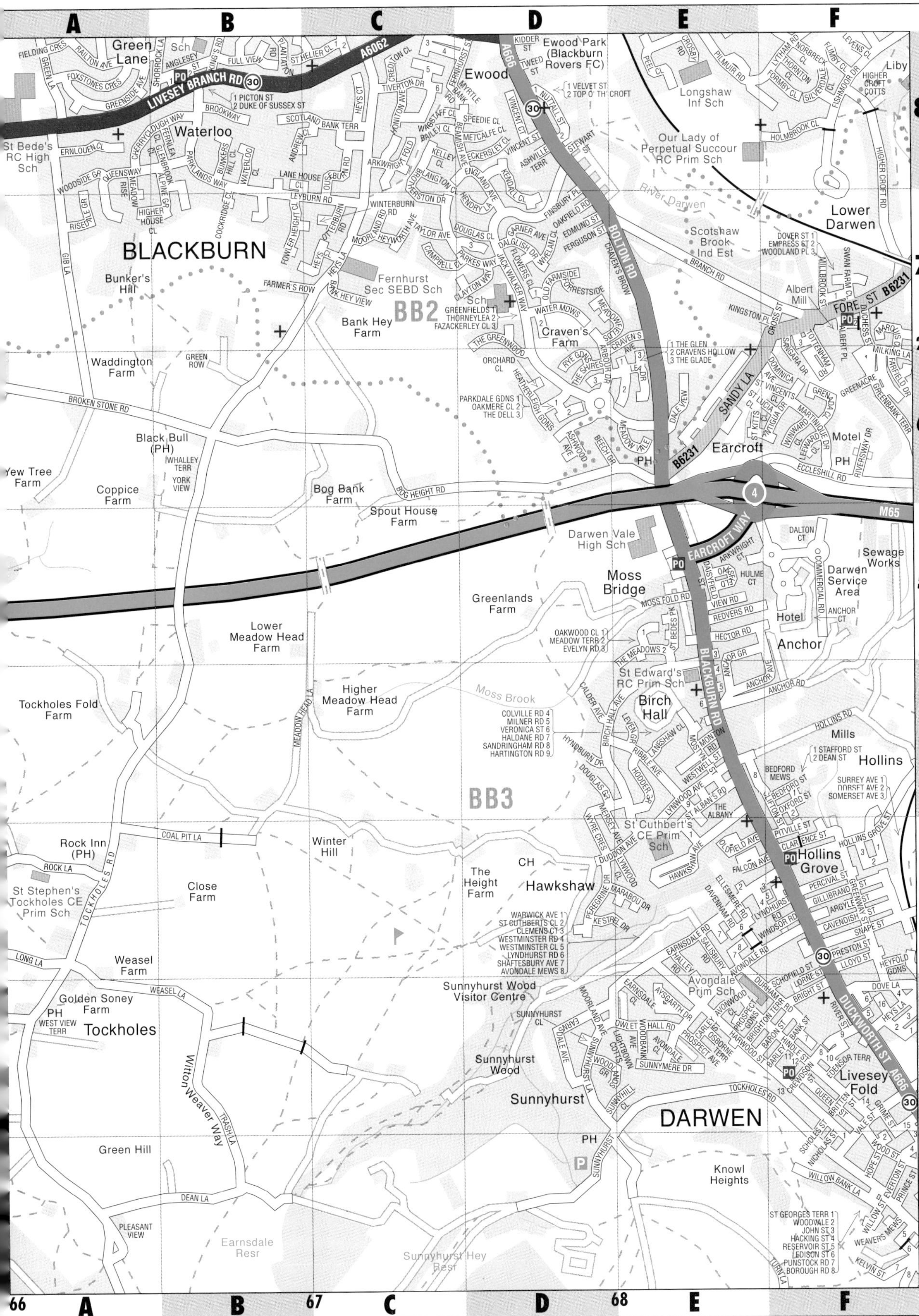


64
82

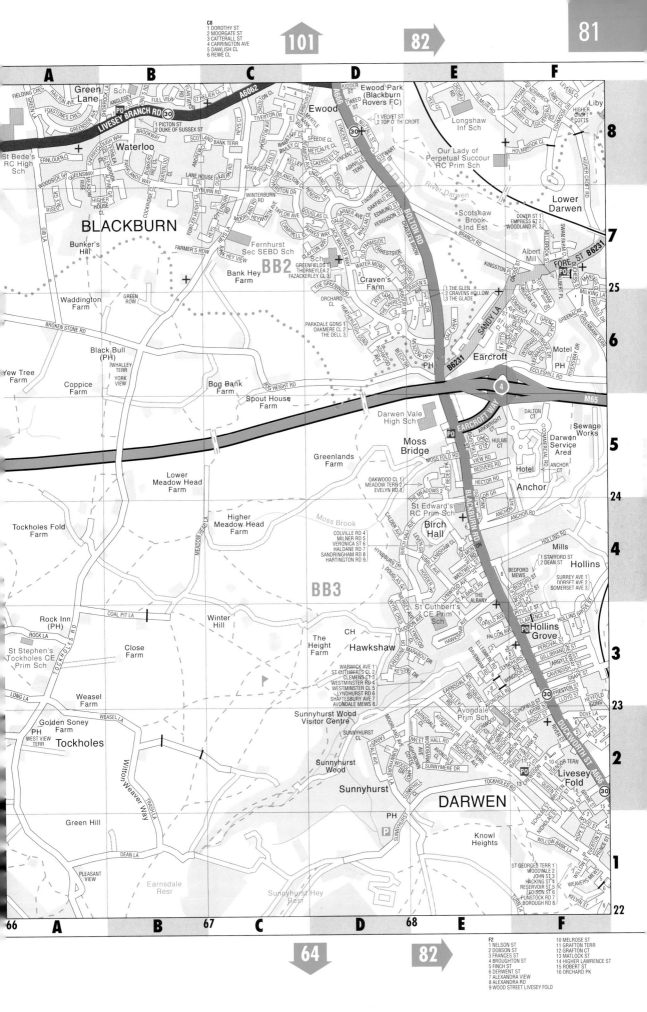

F2
1 NELSON ST
2 DOBSON ST
3 FRANCES ST
4 BROUGHTON ST
5 FINCH ST
6 DERWENT ST
7 ALEXANDRA VIEW
8 ALEXANDRA RD
9 WOOD STREET LIVESEY FOLD
10 MELROSE ST
11 GRAFTON TERR
12 GRAFTON CT
13 MATLOCK ST
14 HIGHER LAWRENCE ST
15 ROBERT ST
16 ORCHARD PK

81
102

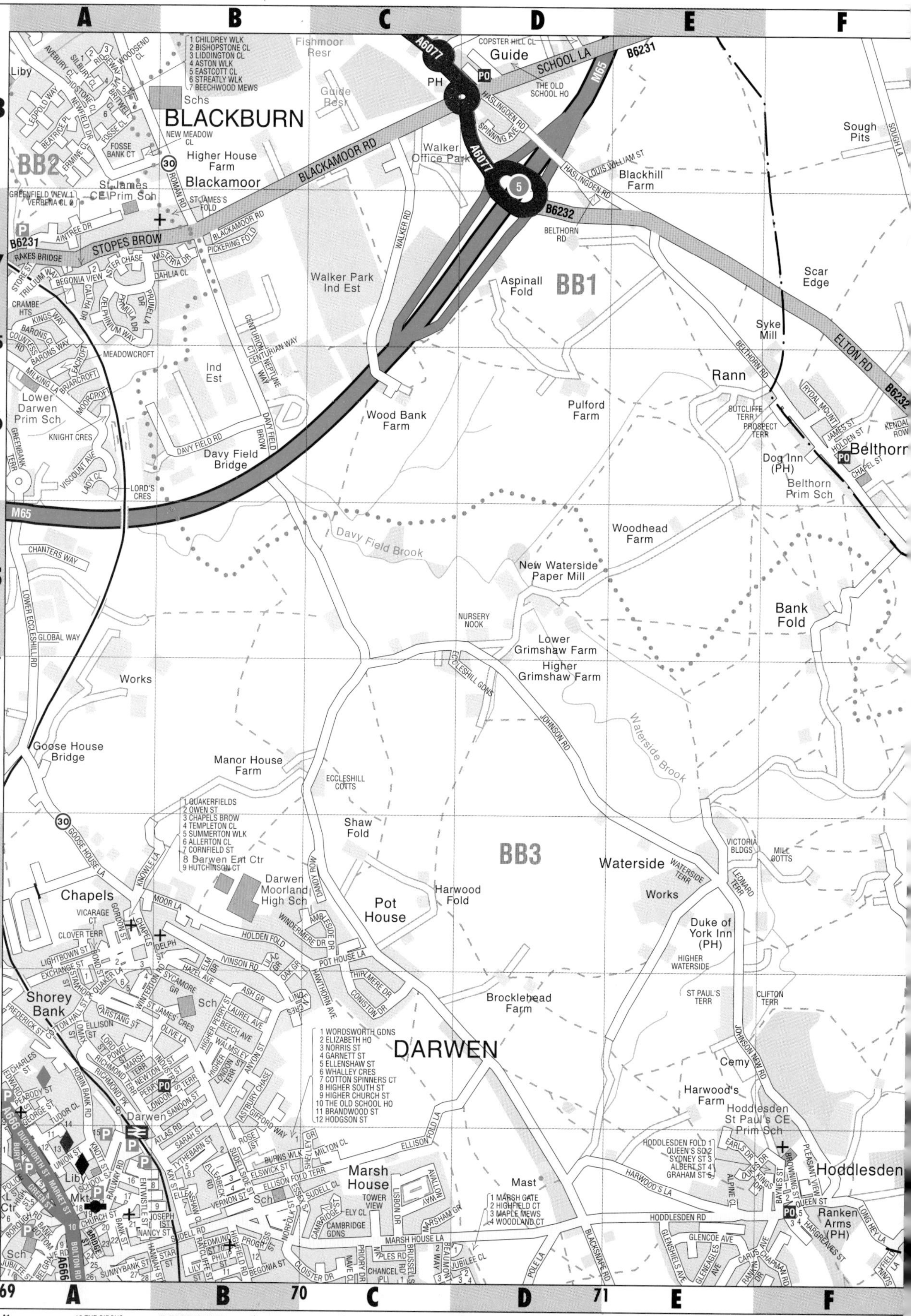


A1
1 JAMES ST
2 VARLEY ST
3 WELLINGTON FOLD
4 ARCH ST
5 THE GREEN
6 JAMES ST W
7 ASHWORTH TERR
8 HESSE ST
9 BELGRAVE SQ
10 THE CIRCUS
11 WILLIAM ST
12 BK DUCKWORTH ST
13 PEMBROKE CT
14 STUART CL
15 MIDVILLE PL
16 SOUTH ST
17 GREEN ST E
18 CROFT ST
19 PARLIAMENT ST
20 CHURCH BANK ST
21 CHURCH TERR
22 VICTORIA ST
23 BATH ST
24 FOUNDRY ST
25 HARDMAN WAY
26 COCHRAN ST
27 LOWER CROSS ST
28 FRANKLIN ST

C1
1 ABBEY PL
2 WELL SPRINGS
3 DERWENT CL

81
65

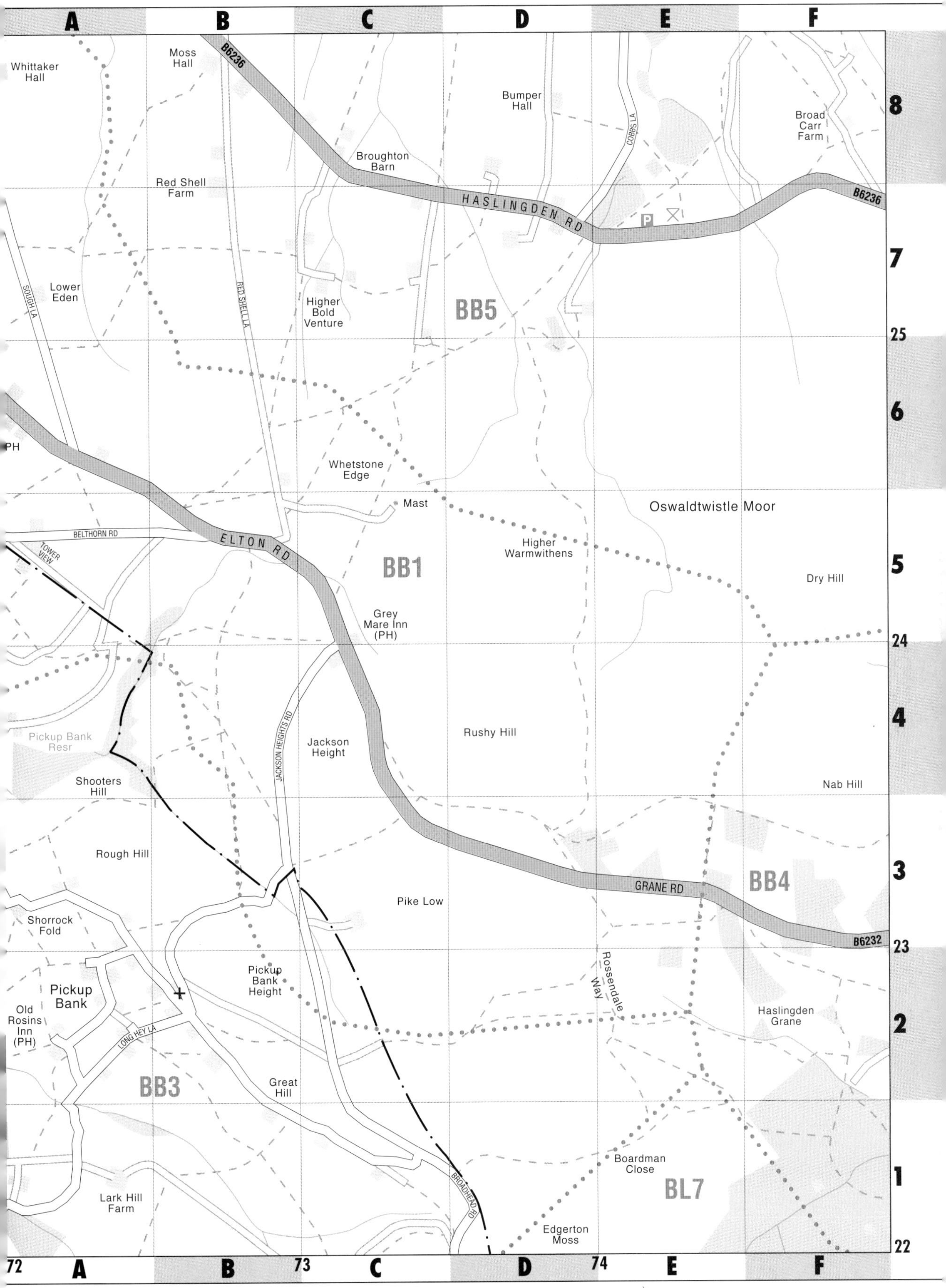
A
B
C
D
E
F
Whittaker Hall
Moss Hall
B6236
Bumper Hall
Broad Carr Farm
COBBS LA
Broughton Barn
Red Shell Farm
HASLINGDEN RD
B6236
Lower Eden
SOUGH LA
RED SHELL LA
Higher Bold Venture
BB5
PH
Whetstone Edge
Mast
Oswaldtwistle Moor
BELTHORN RD
TOWER VIEW
ELTON RD
Higher Warmwithens
BB1
Dry Hill
Grey Mare Inn (PH)
JACKSON HEIGHTS RD
Jackson Height
Rushy Hill
Pickup Bank Resr
Shooters Hill
Nab Hill
Rough Hill
BB4
GRANE RD
Pike Low
Shorrock Fold
B6232
Rossendale Way
Pickup Bank Height
Pickup Bank
Old Rosins Inn (PH)
LONG HEY LA
Haslingden Grane
BB3
Great Hill
Boardman Close
BL7
BROADHEAD RD
Lark Hill Farm
Edgerton Moss
8
7
25
6
5
24
4
3
23
2
1
22
72
73
74

83
104

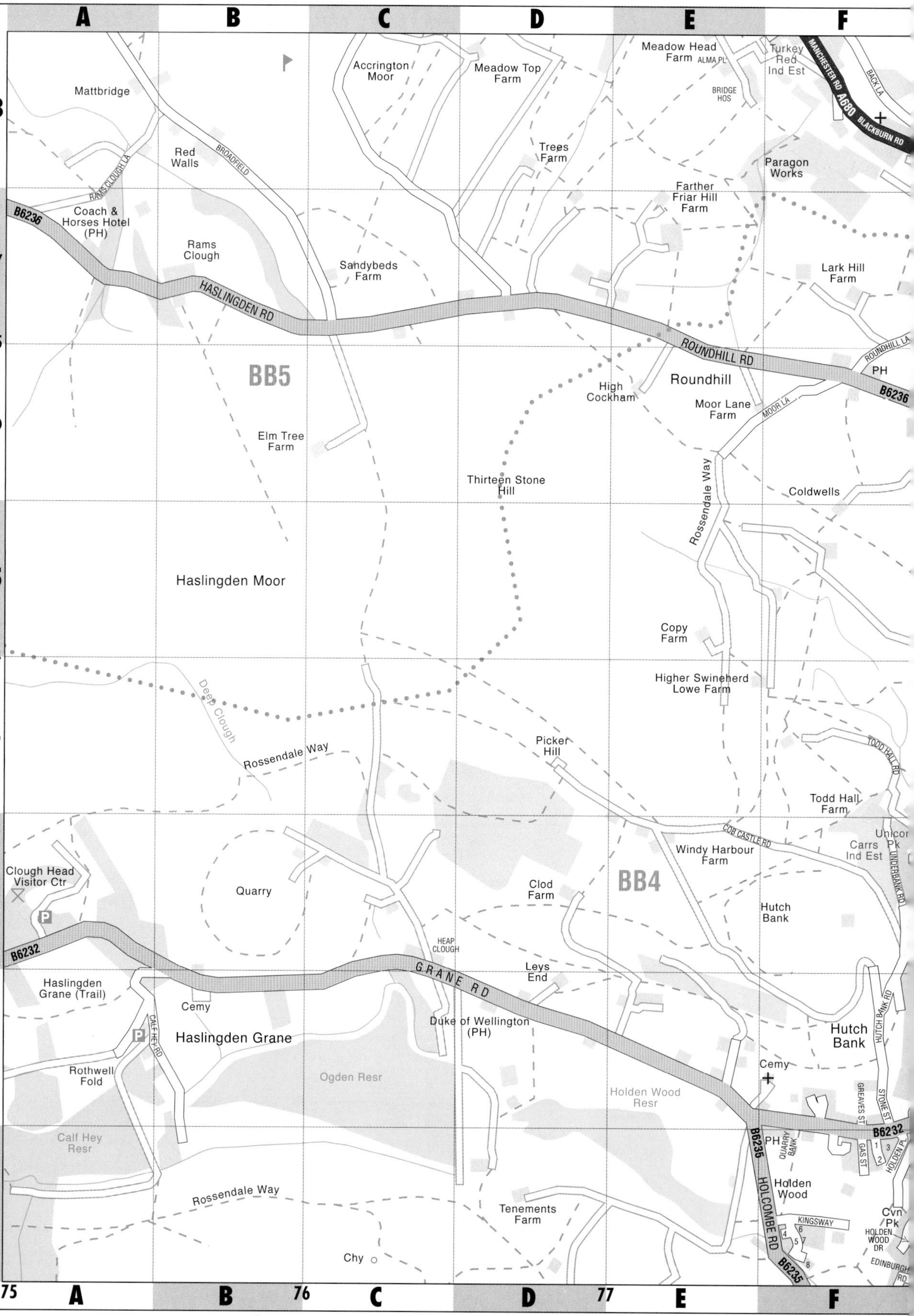


83
67

F1
1 WARBURTON ST
2 MUSBURY VIEW
3 WARBURTON BLDGS
4 MUSBURY MEWS
5 GRANGE PARK WAY
6 MILLERS VALE
7 GRANGE HTS
8 WILLOW HEY

105
86

| | | | | | | |
|---|---|---|---|---|---|---|
| **A1**<br>1 JUBILEE CT<br>2 SANDRINGHAM GR<br>3 HOLDEN WOOD DR<br>4 CLARENCE AVE<br>5 HELMCROFT<br>**A3**<br>1 TAYLOR CT<br>2 UNDERBANK WAY<br>3 LINCOLN ST<br>4 QUEEN ANNE ST | 5 HEYS AVE<br>6 MARSDEN ST<br>7 THOMAS ST<br>8 SUNNYBANK ST<br>**B1**<br>1 HELMCROFT CT<br>2 BEAUMARIS CL<br>3 CRICCIETH CL<br>**B2**<br>1 GREENFIELD GDNS | 2 HAZELDENE AVE<br>3 BANK MILL ST<br>4 NORTHCOTE ST<br>5 LANESIDE HO<br>6 SIZE HOUSE VILLAGE<br>7 ST PETER'S PL<br>8 WHITECROFT AVE<br>**B3**<br>1 BACK REGENT ST<br>2 HARTLEY ST<br>3 ST JAMES CL | **B3**<br>4 DAVITT CL<br>5 RATCLIFFE FOLD<br>6 BURGESS ST<br>7 CENTRAL SQ<br>8 OLD SCHOOL MEWS<br>9 SMITHY ST<br>10 RATCLIFFE ST<br>11 DEARDENGATE CROFT<br>12 COAL HEY<br>13 COAL HEY ST | **B3**<br>14 NEW ST<br>15 SALISBURY ST<br>16 BEACONSFIELD ST<br>17 STORE ST<br>18 ROCK ST<br>19 LACEY CT<br>20 SOUTH VIEW | **C2**<br>1 EDALE AVE<br>2 COWES AVE<br>3 LANGWOOD AVE<br>4 LANGWOOD CL<br>5 LANGWOOD GDNS<br>6 LANGWOOD CT | **E2**<br>1 OSBORNE TERR<br>2 AMBLESIDE AVE<br>3 EGYPT TERR<br>4 OLD ROW<br>5 SPRING TERR S<br>6 PARKWOOD CT<br>7 GORNALL'S BLDGS<br>8 WHITAKER GN<br>9 FIELDING'S BLDGS |

| |
|---|
| **F1**<br>1 SYCAMORE CRES<br>2 HILL VIEW<br>3 HARDMAN AVE<br>4 SHAWFIELD<br>5 BARLOWS BLDGS<br>6 DALE VIEW<br>7 CARR MOUNT |

68
86

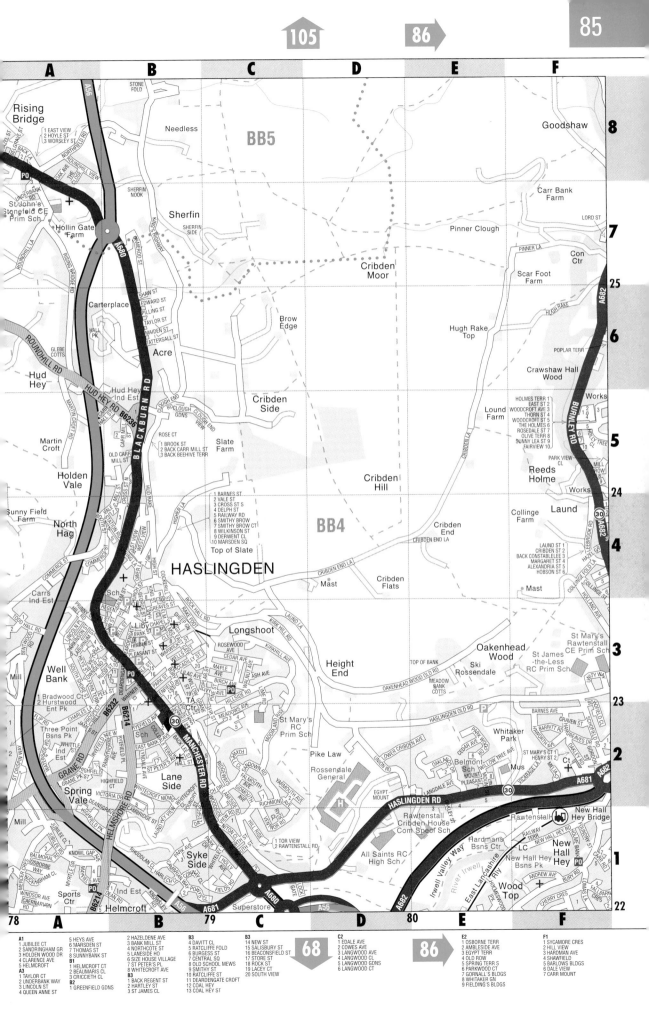

85
106

A2
1 RABY ST
2 GRANGE ST
3 WORSWICK CRES
4 The Valley Ctr
5 ANNIE ST
6 ST MARY'S TERR
7 QUEEN'S SQ
8 PARRAMATTA ST
9 LONGHOLME RD

A3
1 ST JAMES ST
2 IVY GR
3 ASH GR
4 PROSPECT HILL
5 ROCKCLIFFE ST
6 TAYLOR ST
7 ROBERTS ST
8 CURTIS ST
9 PROSPECT VIEW
10 Kingfisher Ctr
11 BARLOW ST
12 HALL ST
13 BRIGHT ST
14 BALDWIN'S BLDGS
15 MILL GATE
16 SOUTH ST
17 EAST PAR
18 MILLGATE RD
19 GRANGE TERR

85

A3
20 ALDER BANK
21 WHITEHEAD ST
22 CRANKSHAW ST

69

E1
1 BACK CHURCH ST
2 COBHAM CT
3 HALMOT CT
4 NAZE CT
5 BOLTON ST
6 BRANDWOOD

F2
1 CO-OPERATION ST
2 PARADISE ST
3 CLARKE HOLME ST
4 NAZE VIEW AVE
5 NEWBIGGING AVE
6 Waterfoot Bsns Ctr
7 Globe Mill
8 Albion Mill

F1
1 THE HAWTHORNS
2 MELBOURNE ST
3 GAGHILLS TERR
4 WEST VIEW
5 CLOUGH ST
6 BRIDGE CL

107
88

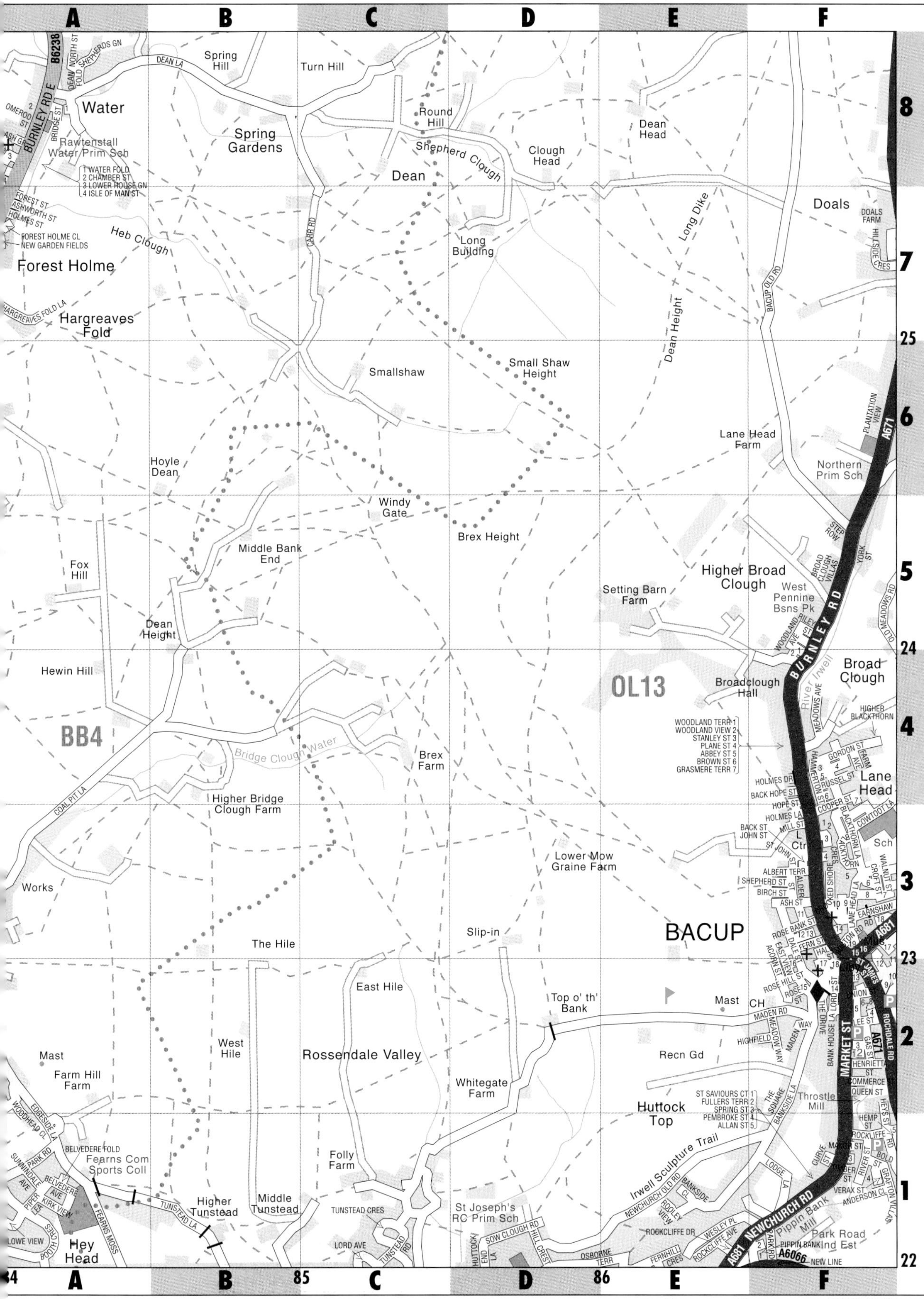


70
88

F2
1 FOUNDRY ST
2 Henrietta Street Ind Est
3 FORGE ST
4 INDUSTRIAL PL
5 KING ST
6 AUSTIN ST
7 IRWELL ST
8 KERSHAW ST
9 LUMB SCAR

F2
10 BOOTH ST
11 PICKUP ST
12 IRWELL TERR
13 TOWER ST
14 BANK ST
15 THISTLE ST
16 LILY ST
17 PRINCESS ST
18 MAITLAND ST

F3
1 UNDERBANK HO
2 MOWGRAIN VIEW
3 UNDERBANK CL
4 LAUREL ST
5 ST JOHN'S CT
6 STANLEY MOUNT
7 BENTLEY ST
8 HIGHER CROSS ROW
9 MYRTLE BANK RD

10 WATERSIDE TERR
11 DAISY BANK
12 BAKER ST
13 GOOSE HILL ST
14 HARCOURT ST
15 ST JAMES SQ
16 YORKSHIRE ST
17 HAMMERTON GN
18 EARNSHAW ROW
19 KING GEORGE CT

A7
1 WESLEY TERR
2 FIELD TOP
3 ROCHESTER CL
4 CAPTAIN ST
5 HALLEY ST
6 DEER ST
7 RICHARD ST
8 COMET ST
9 WRIGHT ST
10 HILLSIDE CRES
11 MELROSE TERR

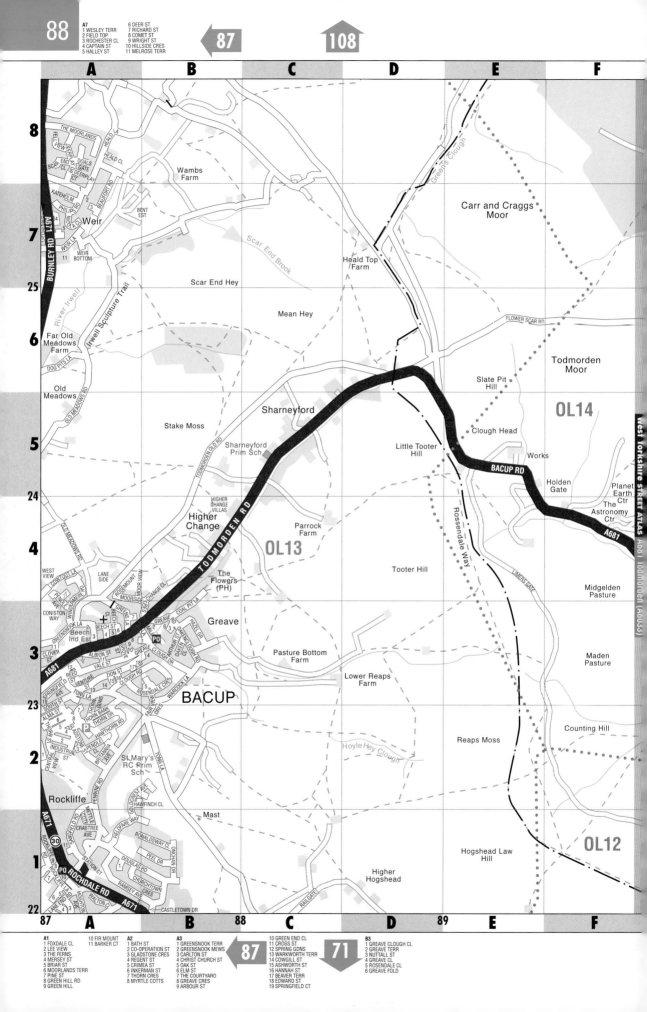

87
108

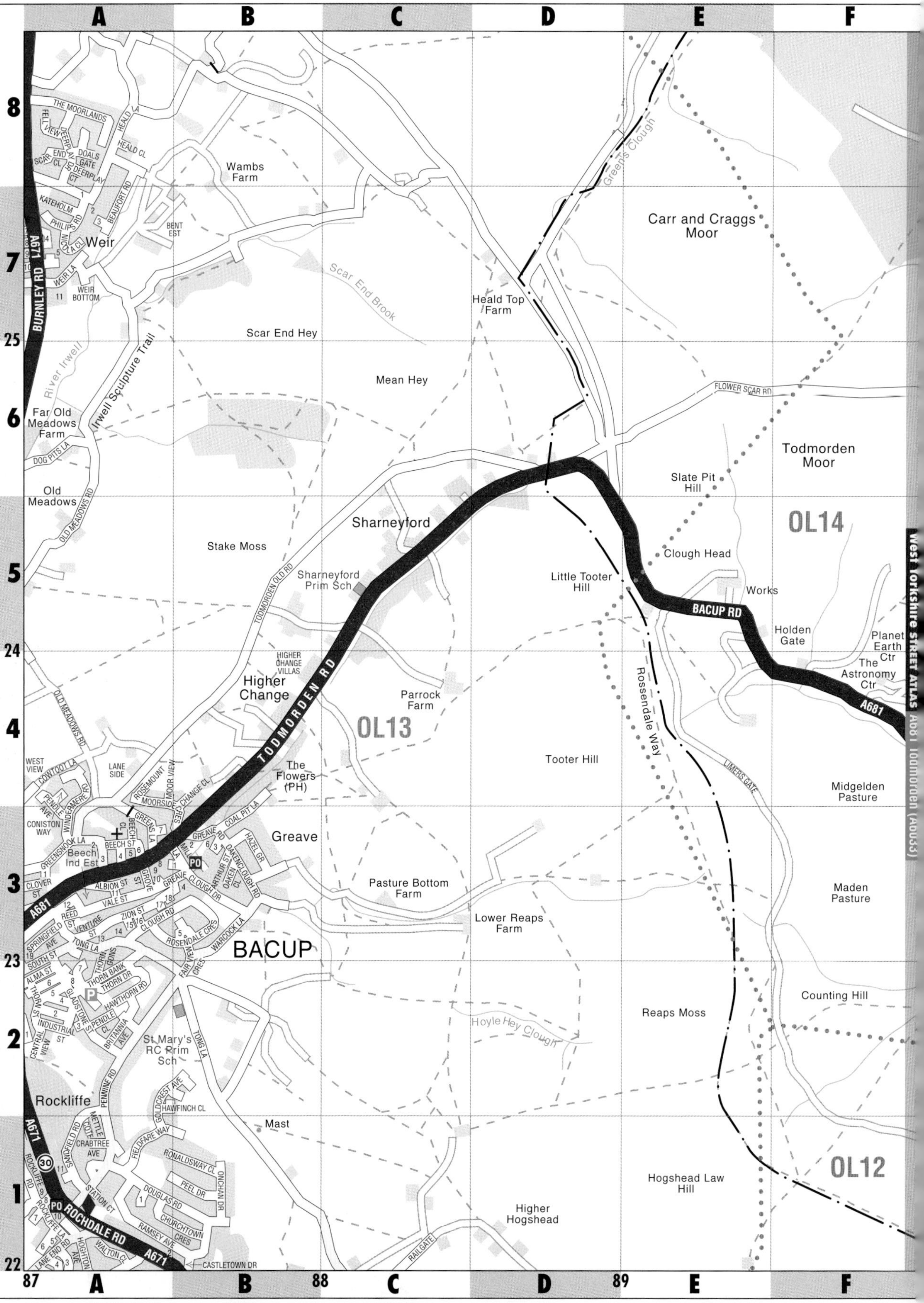


A1
1 FOXDALE CL
2 LEE VIEW
3 THE FERNS
4 MERSEY ST
5 BRIAR ST
6 MOORLANDS TERR
7 PINE ST
8 GREEN HILL RD
9 GREEN HILL
10 FIR MOUNT
11 BARKER CT

A2
1 BATH ST
2 CO-OPERATION ST
3 GLADSTONE CRES
4 REGENT ST
5 CRIMEA ST
6 INKERMAN ST
7 THORN CRES
8 MYRTLE COTTS

A3
1 GREENSNOOK TERR
2 GREENSNOOK MEWS
3 CARLTON ST
4 CHRIST CHURCH ST
5 OAK ST
6 ELM ST
7 THE COURTYARD
8 GREAVE CRES
9 ARBOUR ST
10 GREEN END CL
11 CROSS ST
12 SPRING GDNS
13 WARKWORTH TERR
14 COWGILL ST
15 HANNAH ST
16 ASHWORTH ST
17 BEAVER TERR
18 EDWARD ST
19 SPRINGFIELD CT

87
71

B3
1 GREAVE CLOUGH CL
2 GREAVE TERR
3 NUTTALL ST
4 GREAVE CL
5 ROSENDALE CL
6 GREAVE FOLD

E6
1 HARDAKER CT
2 CLIFTON CT
3 WHITEHALL CT
4 CONWAY CT
5 TWEED ST

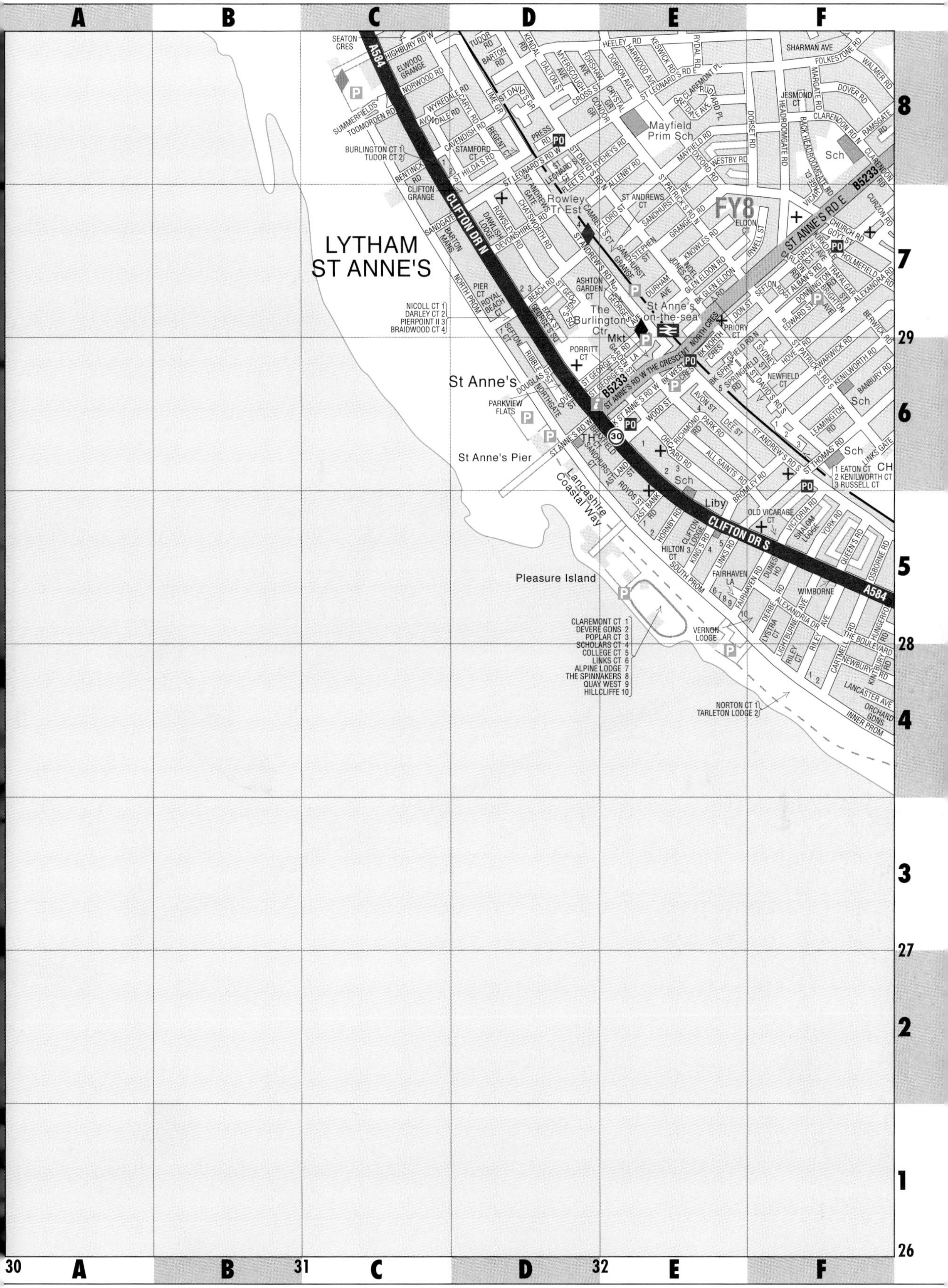
A
B
C
D
E
F
8
7
29
6
5
28
4
3
27
2
1
26
30
31
32
LYTHAM
ST ANNE'S
FY8
A584
CLIFTON DR N
CLIFTON DR S
B5233
ST ANNE'S RD E
ST ANNE'S RD W
Mayfield Prim Sch
Rowley Tr Est
St Anne's on-the-sea
The Burlington Ctr
Mkt
St Anne's
St Anne's Pier
Lancashire Coastal Way
Pleasure Island
PARKVIEW FLATS
Liby
Sch
SEATON CRES
HIGHBURY RD W
ELWOOD GRANGE
NORWOOD RD
SUMMERFIELDS
TODMORDEN RD
WYREDALE RD
BURLINGTON CT 1
TUDOR CT 2
BENTINCK RD
CLIFTON GRANGE
SANDGATE
BARTON MANS
NORTH PROM
PIER CT
ROYAL BEACH CT
NICOLL CT 1
DARLEY CT 2
PIERPOINT II 3
BRAIDWOOD CT 4
HEELEY RD
HARWOOD AVE
KESWICK RD
RYDAL RD
SHARMAN AVE
FOLKESTONE RD
WALMER RD
DOVER RD
JESMOND CT
MARGATE RD
CLARENDON RD N
RAMSGATE RD
DORSET RD
HEADROOMGATE RD
WESTBY RD
OXFORD RD
MAYFIELD RD
ST ANDREWS CT
ELDON CT
IRWELL ST
CHURCH RD
HOLMEFIELD RD
ALEXANDRA RD
BERWICK RD
KENILWORTH RD
BANBURY RD
LEAMINGTON RD
ST THOMAS' RD
LINKS GATE
1 EATON CT
2 KENILWORTH CT
3 RUSSELL CT
ORCHARD RD
RICHMOND RD
ALL SAINTS' RD
BROMLEY RD
OLD VICARAGE CT
VICTORIA RD
YORK RD
QUEEN'S RD
OSBORNE RD
WIMBORNE
HORNBY RD
HILTON CT
SOUTH PROM
FAIRHAVEN LA
FAIRHAVEN RD
DUNES RD
DERBE RD
ALEXANDRIA DR
LYSTRA CT
LIGHTBURNE AVE
RILEY AVE
RILEY CT
CARTMELL RD
THE BOULEVARD
NEWBURY RD
KINTBURY RD
LANCASTER AVE
ORCHARD GDNS
INNER PROM
VERNON LODGE
CLAREMONT CT 1
DEVERE GDNS 2
POPLAR CT 3
SCHOLARS CT 4
COLLEGE CT 5
LINKS CT 6
ALPINE LODGE 7
THE SPINNAKERS 8
QUAY WEST 9
HILLCLIFFE 10
NORTON CT 1
TARLETON LODGE 2
PORRITT CT
ASHTON GARDEN CT
DOUGLAS ST
NORTHGATE
RIBBLE ST
SEFTON CT
PRIORY CT
NEWFIELD CT
SPRINGFIELD RD
ST ANDREW'S RD S
EAST BANK
ROYDS ST
TH

A8
1 BANNISTRE CL
2 BEVERLEY CT
3 TALBOT CT
4 SILVERBURN
5 FELLBOROUGH LODGE
6 GROSVENOR CT

89

111

D6
1 TUXFORD CT
2 KNIGHTSBRIDGE CL
3 BELGRAVE CL
4 TWICKENHAM PL

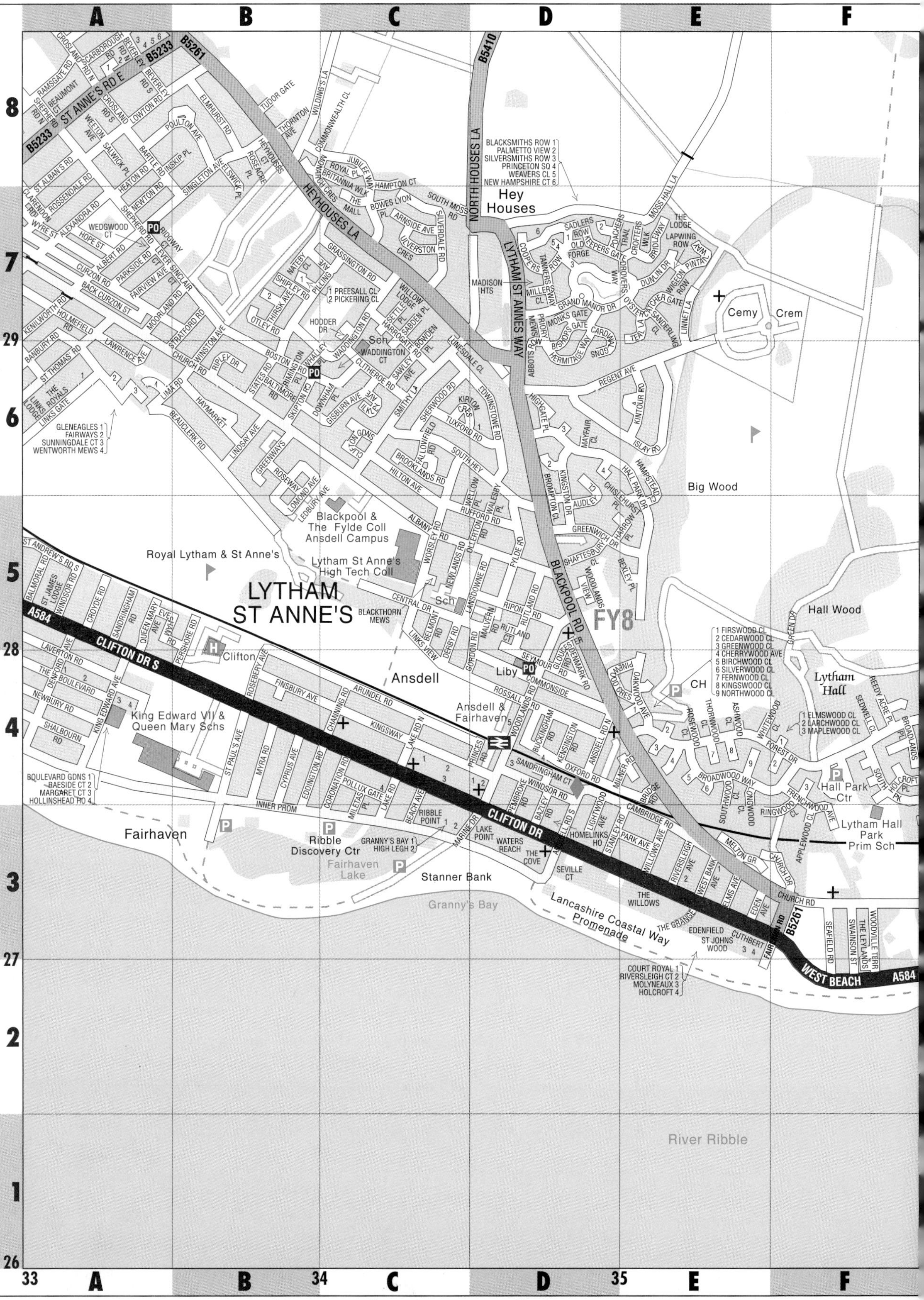


89

C4
1 WORDSWORTH CT
2 KINGSWAY CT
3 CRYSTAL LODGE
4 ST PAUL'S WLK

D4
1 BELVEDERE CT
2 FAIR HAVEN CT
3 WINDSOR LODGE
4 OXFORD CT
5 WOODLANDS CT

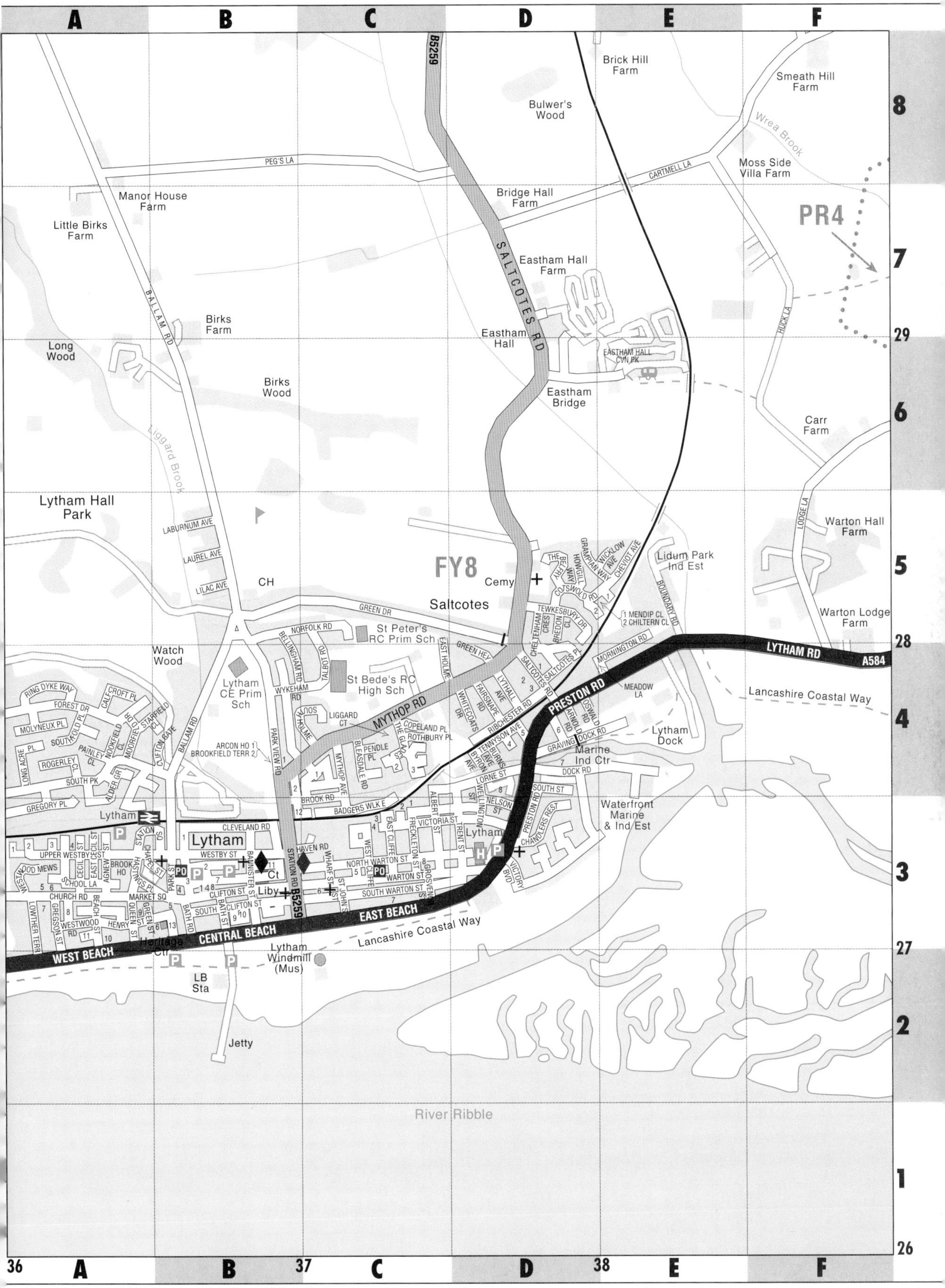


A3
1 ST CUTHBERT'S CL
2 HORSFALL AVE
3 THE SERPENTINE
4 CECIL CT
5 LOWTHER CT
6 ST CUTHBERT'S CT
7 LOWOOD LODGE
8 ASHTON ST
9 THE HOMESTEAD
10 RIBBLE LODGE
11 LIVESEY ST

B3
1 TALBOT TERR
2 SOUTH WESTBY ST
3 PLEASANT ST
4 CLIFTON PAR
5 CLIFTON SQ
6 THOMAS ST
7 NORTH CLIFTON ST
8 CLIFTON WLK
9 SHEPHERD ST
10 SQUIRES CT
11 GEORGE ST
12 BADGERS WLK W
13 DICCONSON TERR
14 Clifton Wlk Sh Ctr

C3
1 MILLBROOK MEWS
2 FRECKLETON CT
3 CLIFTON CT
4 ELIM CT
5 BIRCH ST
6 ST JOHN'S CT
7 GLENGARRY
8 PATTERSON CT

C4
1 MYTHOP CL
2 GILDERDALE CT
3 KIELDER CT

D4
1 LIONS CT
2 BRIDGE CT
3 BRIDGE HO
4 BROWNING AVE
5 WORDSWORTH AVE
6 BEDFORD RD
7 HARBOUR HO
8 HAMILTON CL

91
113

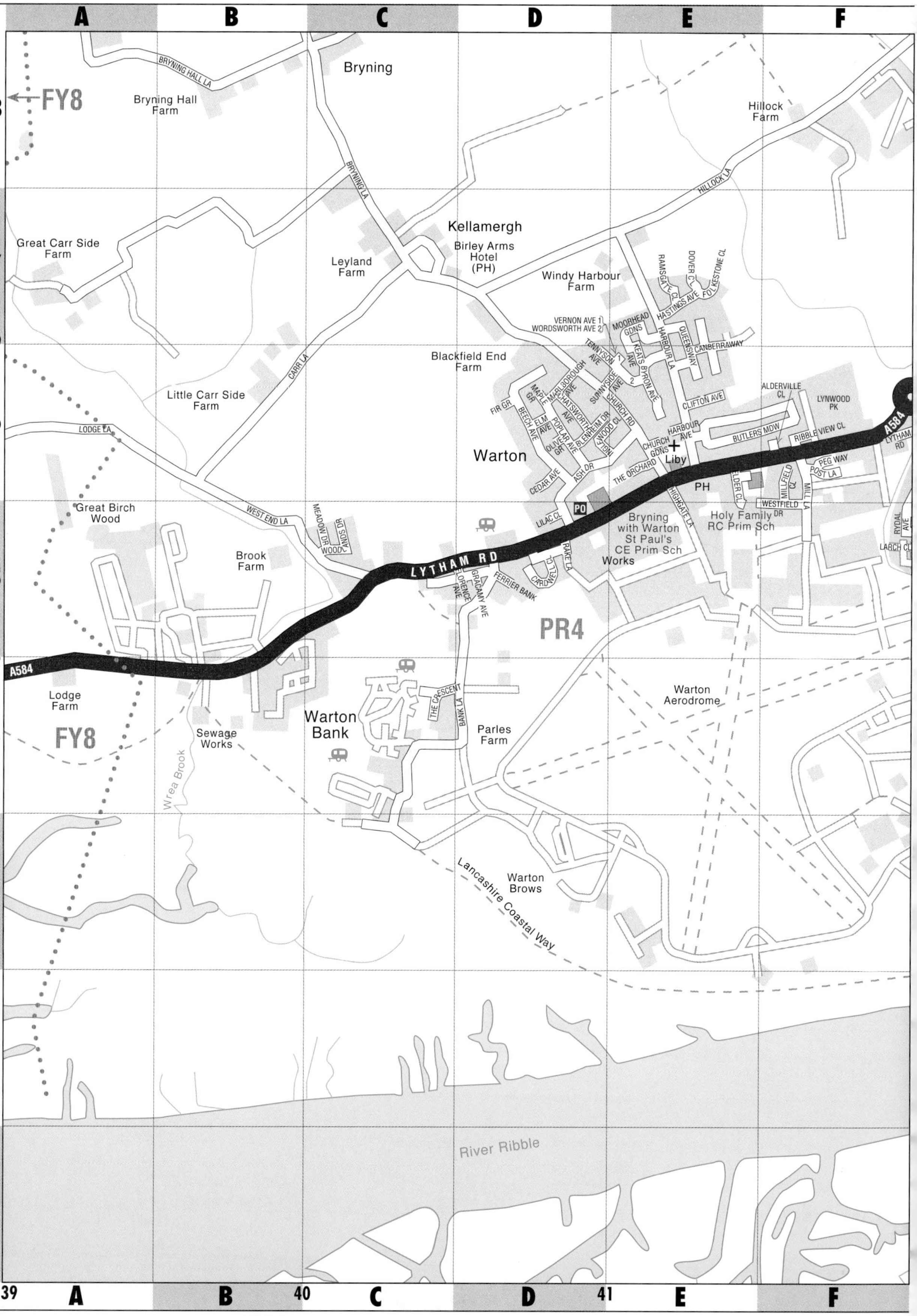
A
B
C
D
E
F
8
7
29
6
5
28
4
3
27
2
1
26
39
40
41
FY8
Bryning Hall Farm
BRYNING HALL LA
Bryning
Hillock Farm
HILLOCK LA
BRYNING LA
Kellamergh
Birley Arms Hotel (PH)
Great Carr Side Farm
Leyland Farm
Windy Harbour Farm
RAMSGATE CL
DOVER CL
FOLKESTONE CL
HASTINGS AVE
VERNON AVE 1
WORDSWORTH AVE 2
MOORHEAD GDNS
HARBOUR LA
QUEENSWAY
CANBERRAWAY
TENNYSON AVE
KEATS AVE
BYRON AVE
CARR LA
Blackfield End Farm
Little Carr Side Farm
MAPLE GR
MARLBOROUGH AVE
SUNNYSIDE AVE
CHURCH RD
ALDERVILLE CL
LYNWOOD PK
FIR GR
BEECH AVE
ELM AVE
CHATSWORTH AVE
POPLAR AVE
BLENHEIM DR
WOOD CL
CLIFTON AVE
HARBOUR AVE
BUTLERS MDW
RIBBLE VIEW CL
A584
LYTHAM RD
LODGE LA
OLIVE GR
Warton
CHURCH GDNS
Liby
ASH DR
THE ORCHARD
PEG WAY
POST LA
CEDAR AVE
PH
ELDER CL
MILLFIELD CL
MILL LA
WESTFIELD DR
Great Birch Wood
WEST END LA
MEADOW DR
LANDS DR
WOOD
PO
LILAC CL
HIGHGATE LA
Bryning with Warton St Paul's CE Prim Sch
Holy Family RC Prim Sch
RYDAL AVE
LARCH CL
Brook Farm
LYTHAM RD
RAKE LA
Works
FLORENCE AVE
GRADAMY AVE
FERRIER BANK
CARDWELL CL
PR4
28
A584
Lodge Farm
FY8
Sewage Works
THE CRESCENT
BANK LA
Warton Bank
Parles Farm
Warton Aerodrome
Wrea Brook
Lancashire Coastal Way
Warton Brows
River Ribble

91
72

114
94

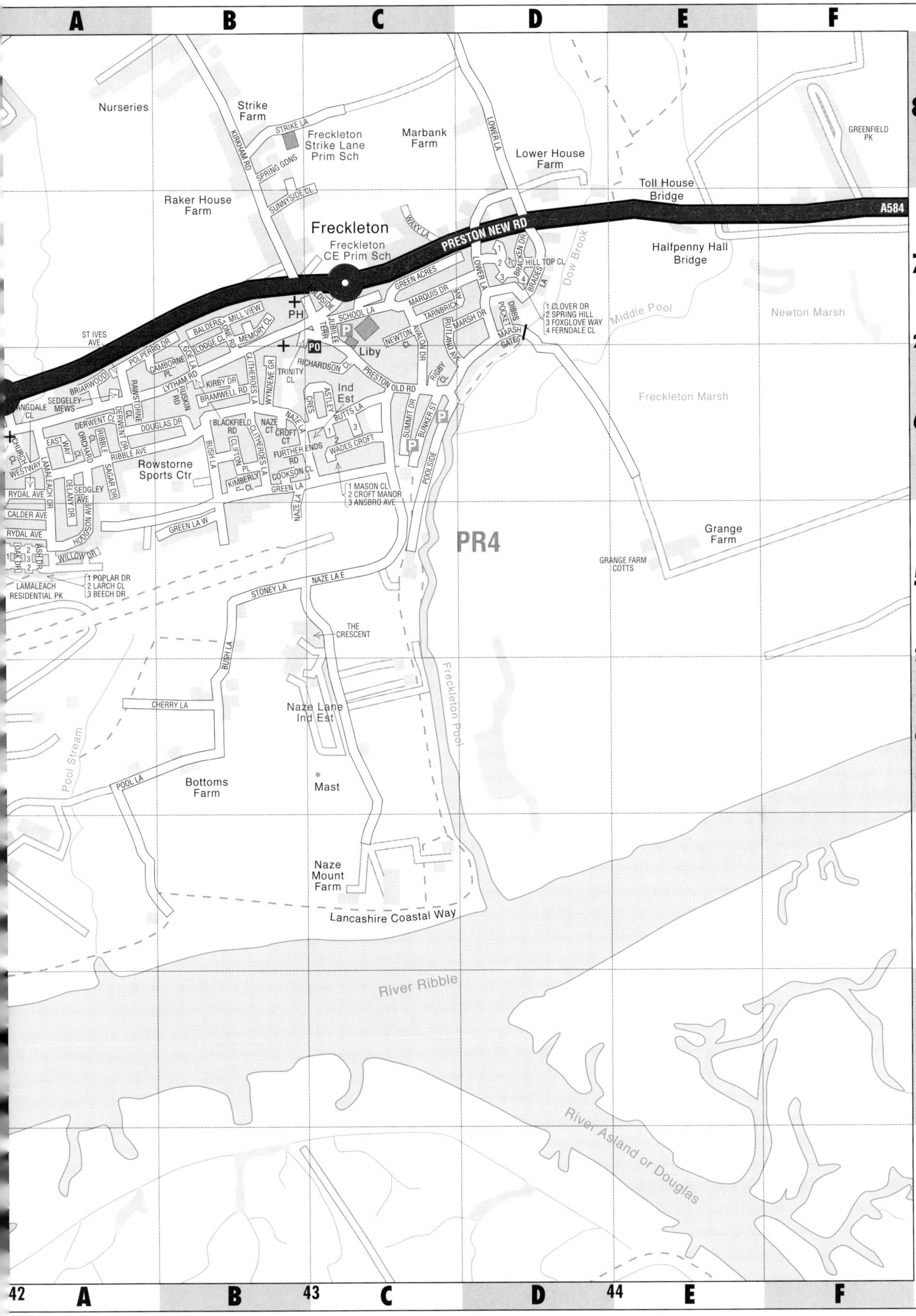
A
B
C
D
E
F
8
7
29
6
5
28
4
3
27
2
1
26
42
43
44
Nurseries
Strike Farm
Freckleton Strike Lane Prim Sch
Marbank Farm
Lower House Farm
Toll House Bridge
GREENFIELD PK
A584
Raker House Farm
Freckleton
Freckleton CE Prim Sch
PRESTON NEW RD
Halfpenny Hall Bridge
Dow Brook
Middle Pool
Newton Marsh
1 CLOVER DR
2 SPRING HILL
3 FOXGLOVE WAY
4 FERNDALE CL
PH
Liby
Ind Est
Freckleton Marsh
Rowstorne Sports Ctr
1 MASON CL
2 CROFT MANOR
3 ANSBRO AVE
PR4
Grange Farm
GRANGE FARM COTTS
1 POPLAR DR
2 LARCH CL
3 BEECH DR
LAMALEACH RESIDENTIAL PK
THE CRESCENT
Freckleton Pool
Naze Lane Ind Est
Pool Stream
Bottoms Farm
Mast
Naze Mount Farm
Lancashire Coastal Way
River Ribble
River Asland or Douglas
KIRKHAM RD
STRIKE LA
SPRING GDNS
SUNNYSIDE CL
LOWER LA
WAXY LA
GREEN ACRES
MARQUIS DR
TARNBRICK
SCHOOL LA
JUBILEE TERR
OLDSIDE
NEWTON CL
AVALON DR
RUTLAND AVE
MARSH DR
POCKET
DIBBS
MARSH GATES
BRACKEN DR
HILL TOP CL
BRADES LA
RICHARDSON CL
PRESTON OLD RD
RIGBY CL
SUMMIT DR
BUNKER ST
POOLSIDE
ASTLEY CRES
BUTTS LA
WADES CROFT
FURTHER ENDS RD
COOKSON CL
GREEN LA
NAZE LA
NAZE LA E
STONEY LA
BUSH LA
CHERRY LA
POOL LA
GREEN LA W
WILLOW DR
HODGSON AVE
DELANY DR
SEDGLEY AVE
SAGAR DR
RIBBLE AVE
DOUGLAS DR
BLACKFIELD RD
CLIFTON PL
CLITHEROES LA
KIMBERLY CL
NAZE CT
CROFT CT
TRINITY CL
WYNDENE GR
CLITHEROES LA
BRAMWELL RD
KIRBY DR
LYTHAM RD
RUSKIN RD
CAMBORNE PL
RAWSTORNE
POLPERRO DR
LODGE CL
BALDERS LA
MILL VIEW
MEMORY CL
LONE RD
ST IVES AVE
BRIARWOOD
SEDGELEY MEWS
LANGDALE CL
DERWENT CL
DERWENT DR
ORCHARD CL
RIBBLE CL
EAST WAY
CHURCH CL
WESTWAY
LAMALEACH DR
RYDAL AVE
CALDER AVE
OAK DR
ASH DR

93
115

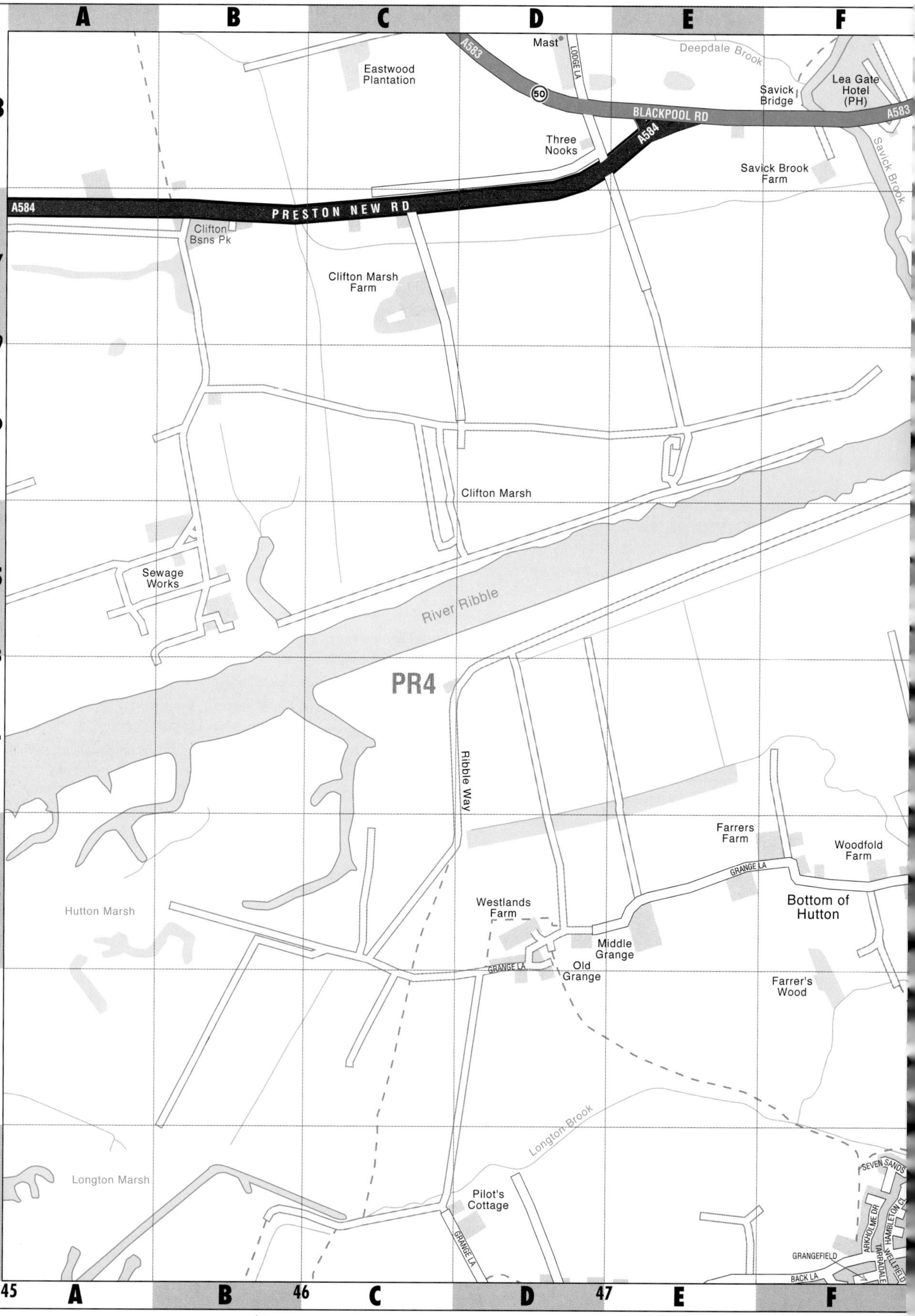
A
B
C
D
E
F
8
7
29
6
5
28
4
3
27
2
1
26
45
46
47
Mast
LODGE LA
Deepdale Brook
A583
Eastwood Plantation
50
Savick Bridge
Lea Gate Hotel (PH)
BLACKPOOL RD
A583
A584
Three Nooks
Savick Brook Farm
Savick Brook
A584
PRESTON NEW RD
Clifton Bsns Pk
Clifton Marsh Farm
Clifton Marsh
Sewage Works
River Ribble
PR4
Ribble Way
Farrers Farm
Woodfold Farm
GRANGE LA
Bottom of Hutton
Hutton Marsh
Westlands Farm
Middle Grange
Old Grange
GRANGE LA
Farrer's Wood
Longton Brook
Longton Marsh
Pilot's Cottage
GRANGE LA
SEVEN SANDS
ARKHOLME DR
HAMBLETON CL
GRANGEFIELD
TARRADALE
WELLFIELD
BACK LA

93
74

116
96

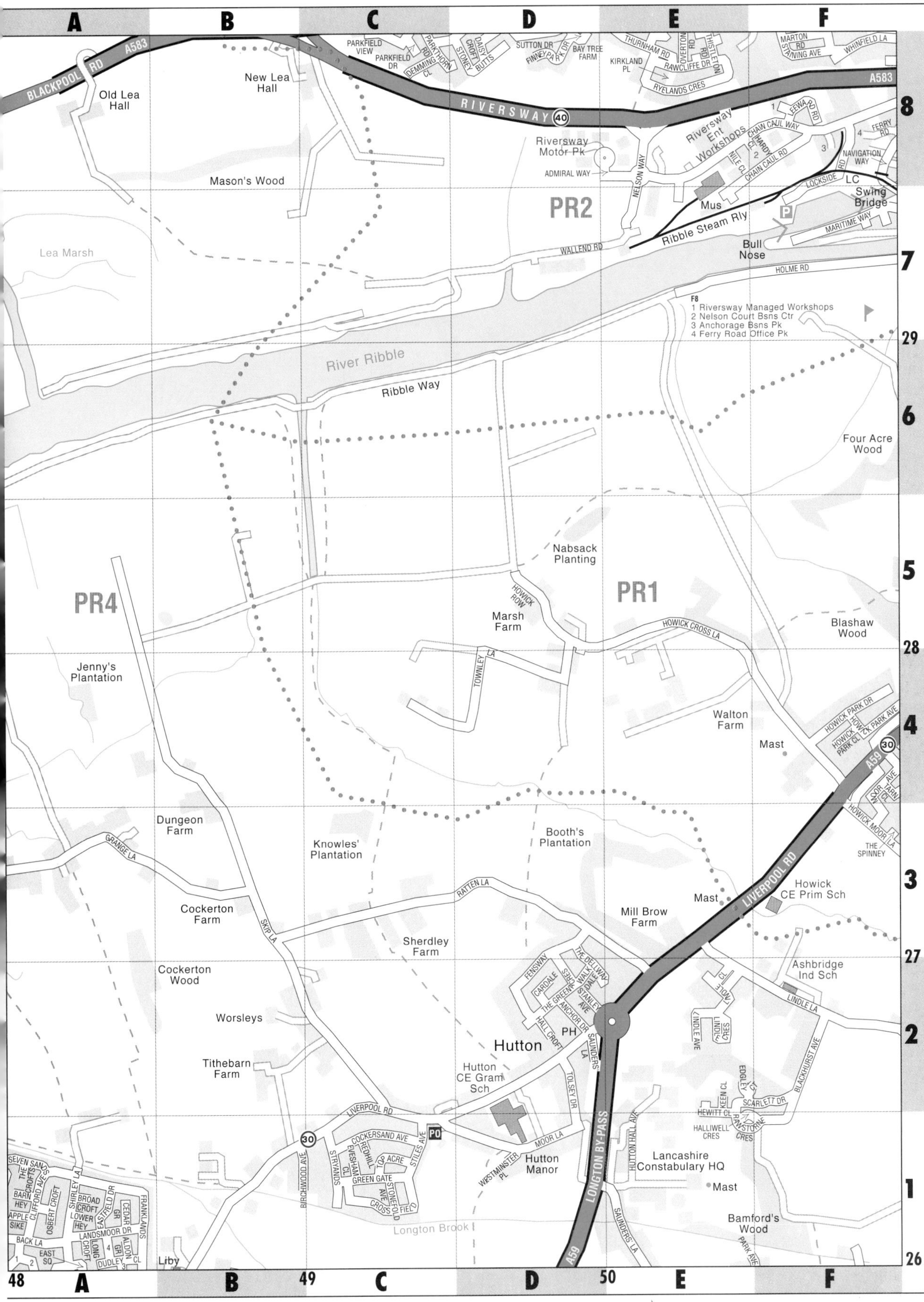
A
B
C
D
E
F
BLACKPOOL RD
A583
Old Lea
Hall
New Lea
Hall
PARKFIELD
VIEW
PARKFIELD
DR
DEMMING
CL
PARKTHORN
RD
STONEY
CROFT
DAISY
BUTTS
SUTTON DR
FINNEY PARK DR
BAY TREE
FARM
KIRKLAND
PL
THURNHAM RD
OVERTON RD
RAWCLIFFE DR
THISTLETON RD
RYELANDS CRES
MARTON
RD
STAINING AVE
WHINFIELD LA
A583
8
RIVERSWAY
40
Riversway
Motor Pk
ADMIRAL WAY
NELSON WAY
Riversway
Ent
Workshops
CHAIN CAUL WAY
NILE CL
HARDY CL
CHAIN CAUL RD
SEEWA RD
FERRY RD
NAVIGATION
WAY
LOCKSIDE RD
LC
Swing
Bridge
Mus
Mason's Wood
PR2
Ribble Steam Rly
P
MARITIME WAY
Bull
Nose
Lea Marsh
WALLEND RD
7
HOLME RD
F8
1 Riversway Managed Workshops
2 Nelson Court Bsns Ctr
3 Anchorage Bsns Pk
4 Ferry Road Office Pk
29
River Ribble
Ribble Way
6
Four Acre
Wood
Nabsack
Planting
5
PR4
PR1
HOWICK
ROW
Marsh
Farm
HOWICK CROSS LA
Blashaw
Wood
28
Jenny's
Plantation
TOWNLEY LA
Walton
Farm
HOWICK PARK DR
HOWICK PARK AVE
HOWICK PARK CL
4
Mast
30
A59
MOOR AVE
ARNOLD CL
HOWICK MOOR LA
THE
SPINNEY
Dungeon
Farm
Knowles'
Plantation
Booth's
Plantation
GRANGE LA
3
Howick
CE Prim Sch
Mast
Cockerton
Farm
RATTEN LA
LIVERPOOL RD
Mill Brow
Farm
SKIP LA
Sherdley
Farm
27
Cockerton
Wood
FENSWAY
CARDALE
THE DELLWAY
WALK
DALE
STANLEY
AVE
ANCHOR DR
THE GREEN
HALL CROFT
Ashbridge
Ind Sch
LINDLE CL
LINDLE LA
LINDLE AVE
LINDLE CRES
Worsleys
PH
SAUNDERS LA
2
Hutton
BLACKHURST AVE
Tithebarn
Farm
Hutton
CE Gram
Sch
TOLSEY DR
EDGLEY CT
KEEN CL
HEWITT CL
SCARLETT DR
RAWSTORNE CRES
HALLIWELL
CRES
LIVERPOOL RD
PO
30
COCKERSAND AVE
REDHILL
EVESHAM CL
TOP ACRE
STILES AVE
MOOR LA
HUTTON HALL AVE
LONGTON BY-PASS
Lancashire
Constabulary HQ
SEVEN SANDS
THE CROFTS
CLIFFORD AVE
BARN HEY
APPLE SIKE
OSBERT CROFT
SHIRLEY LA
BROAD CROFT
LOWER HEY
EASTFIELD DR
CEDAR GR
FRANKLANDS
STRYANDS
GREEN GATE
STONEFOLD AVE
CROSSFIELD
WESTMINSTER PL
Hutton
Manor
BIRCHWOOD AVE
Mast
1
BACK LA
LANDSMOOR DR
LONG CROFT
ALDON GR
DUDLEY CL
EAST SQ
Longton Brook
SAUNDERS LA
Bamford's
Wood
PARK AVE
A59
Liby
26
48
49
50

A1
1 MEADOWAY
2 LANEDALE
3 GORSE GR
4 ARUNDEL RD

75
96

D8
1 WEST VIEW TERR
2 MADDY ST
3 SPA ST
4 ST MARK'S PL W
5 ST MARK'S PL E
6 THE CLOISTERS
7 ASHTON ST
8 ST WALBURGES GDNS
9 WESTON ST
10 CROFT ST
11 STEWART ST
12 ATHOLL ST
13 COOKWOOD HO

95

E8
1 GILDOW ST
2 GRADWELL ST
3 BHAILOK ST
4 COLD BATH ST
5 RADNOR ST
6 POLLARD ST

117

E8
7 STOCKS ST
8 ST PETER'S SQ
9 Old Brewery Trad Est

F8
1 ST PETER'S ST
2 ADELPHI PL
3 RODNEY ST
4 HOPE ST
5 MARSH LA
6 CHANDLER ST
7 MOUNT PLEASANT
8 BACK SEED ST
9 SIMPSON ST
10 UNION ST
11 CLAYTON'S GATE
12 FORESTERS HALL
13 CRAGG'S ROW
14 SINGLETON ROW
15 ATKINSON CL
16 BECKETT CT
17 MELLING ST
18 GARDNER ST
19 MELBOURNE ST
20 TRINITY FOLD
21 BISPHAM ST
22 SIZEHOUSE ST
23 TENTERFIELD ST
24 TRINITY PL
25 LOWTHIAN ST
26 ORCHARD ST
27 BIRLEY ST

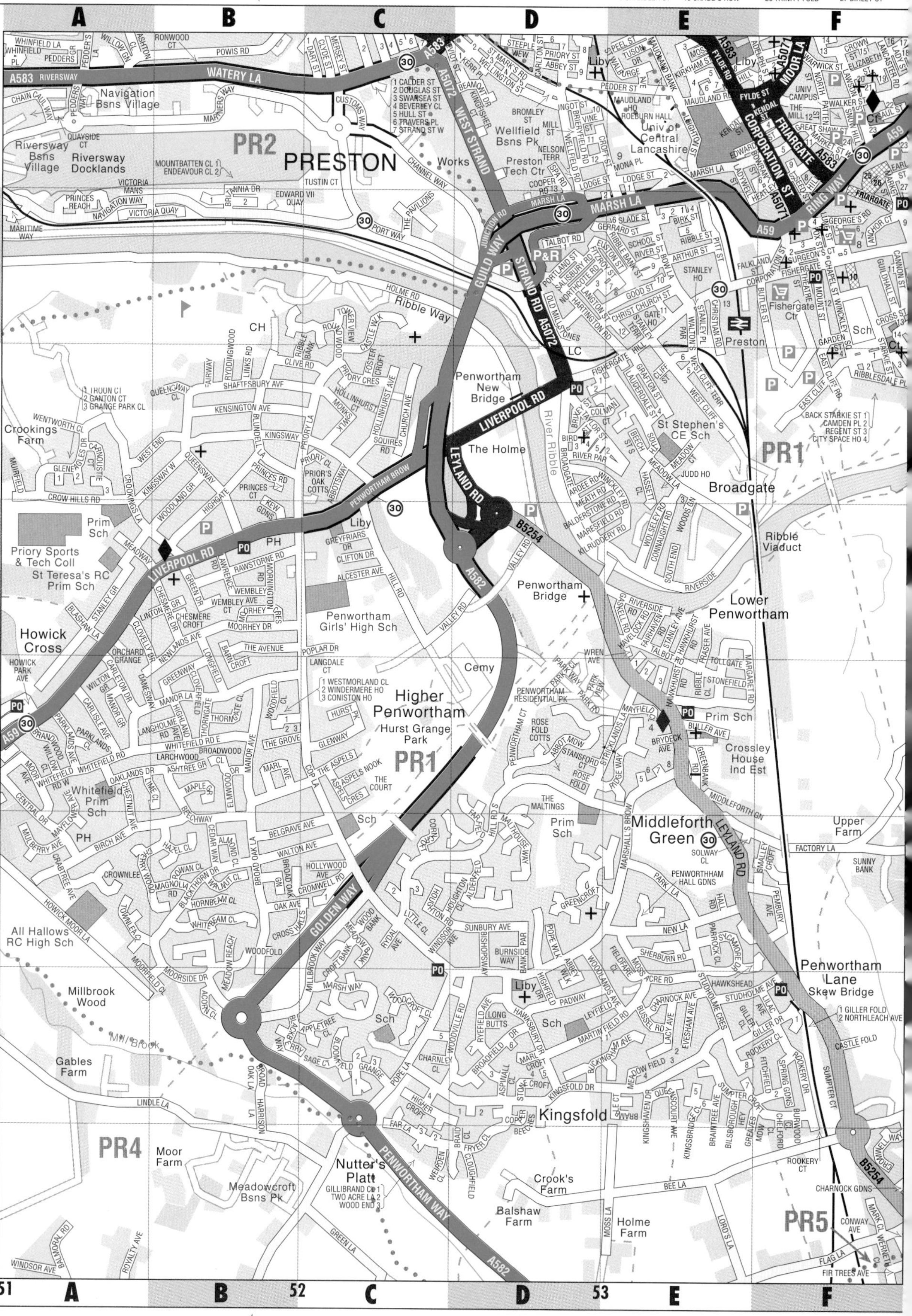




C2
1 ROSEMARY CT
2 SORREL CT
3 CINNAMON CT
4 BANNISTER'S BIT
5 WOODVILLE RD W
C3
1 CROMWELL AVE
2 WINGATES
3 BERRY FIELD

D2
1 LOWER CROFT
2 HIGHER CROFT
3 FORSHAW RD
4 CROFTERS WLK
5 OLD HEY CROFT
6 FAIRHAM AVE
7 OLDFIELD

D6
1 BEECH ST
2 RIBBLE CT
3 TAY ST
4 TYNE ST
5 CLIFTON ST
D7
1 PALEY RD
2 HUNT ST
3 CARNARVON RD

95

E2
1 PETERFIELD RD
2 TUSON HO
3 DICKENSONS FIELD
4 THE PADDOCK
5 STURMINSTER CL
6 HAMBLEDON DR
7 WINSLOW CL
8 STUDHOLME CL

76

E4
1 SWALLOW AVE
2 DOVE AVE
3 LARK AVE
4 Middleforth Ind Est
5 MARSHALL'S CL
6 FINCH'S COTTS
7 PROSPECT PL
8 CHURCH BROOK HO

E6
1 BEECH TERR
2 WARTON ST
3 RIBBLE CL
4 HIND ST
5 SOUTH CLIFF ST
6 NORTH CLIFF ST

E7
1 KAY ST
2 NUTTER RD
3 MARKLAND ST
4 SAVOY ST
5 RED CROSS ST
6 KINGSWOOD ST
7 BURLEIGH RD
8 OLD SCHOOL SQ
9 MAPLE CRES
10 LADYMAN ST
11 SPRING BANK
12 OSBOURNE ST
13 FISHERGATE CT

F7
1 VICTORIA BLDGS
2 CHARNLEY ST
3 ST WILFRED ST
4 FLEET ST
5 CHAPEL WLKS
6 FRIARGATE WLK
7 FISHERGATE WLK
8 St George's Sh Ctr
9 CHEAPSIDE
10 WINCKLEY ST
11 TEMPLE CT
12 WINCKLEY CT
13 CHADDOCK ST
14 BAIRSTOW ST

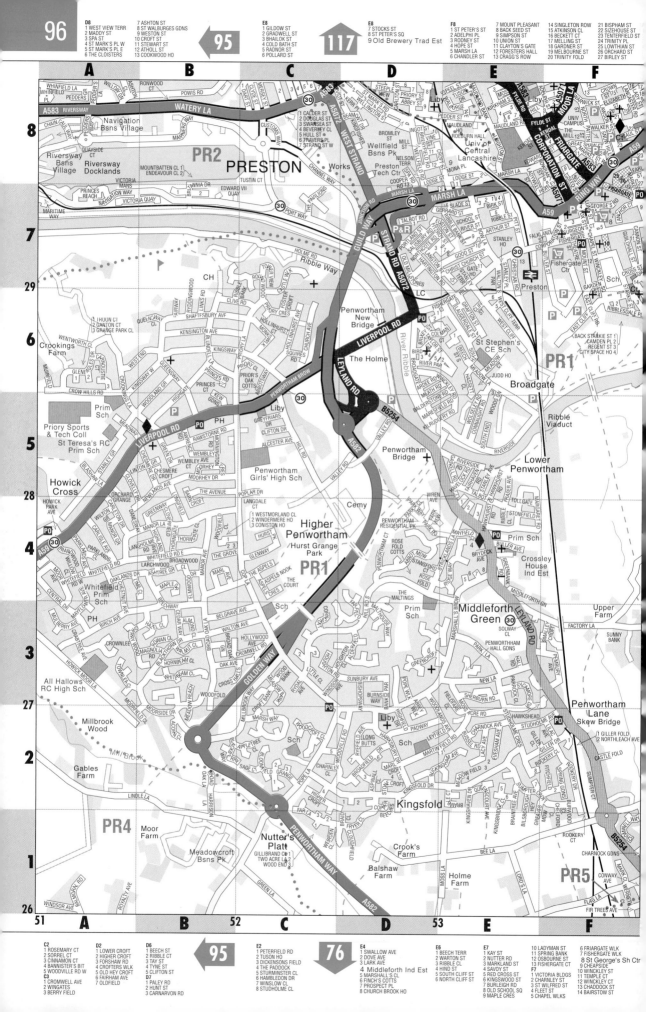

A8
1 MARGARET ST
2 LUND ST
3 PENNY ST
4 HARDWICKE ST
5 ST IGNATIUS' SQ
6 ST IGNATIUS' PL
7 MEADOW HO
8 CONSTABLE ST
9 DANEWERKE ST
10 ST PAUL'S CT
11 CUNLIFFE ST
12 AGNES ST
13 EAST ST
14 HIGH ST
15 BISHOPGATE
16 OLD VICARAGE
17 LANCASTER WAY
18 St John's Sh Ctr
19 CROOKED LA
20 HAMMOND'S ROW
21 MOLYNEUX CT
22 CHADDERTON CT
23 CROMPTON CT
24 LYCHGATE

B8
1 DRISCOLL ST
2 NEWTON ST
3 EDMUND ST
4 MILLBANK
5 CATHERINE ST
6 RIBBLETON PL

118

B8
7 ST MARY'S ST N
8 RIBBLETON ST
9 Guild Trad Est
10 Ribbleton Trad Est

98

C8
1 STEFANO RD
2 OWTRAM ST
3 WILBRAHAM ST
4 MAITLAND ST
5 MAITLAND CL
6 WILLIAM HENRY ST
7 JOHN WILLIAM ST
8 ST MARYS CL
9 CROMFORD WLK
10 CRANBORNE ST
11 MILLER ST

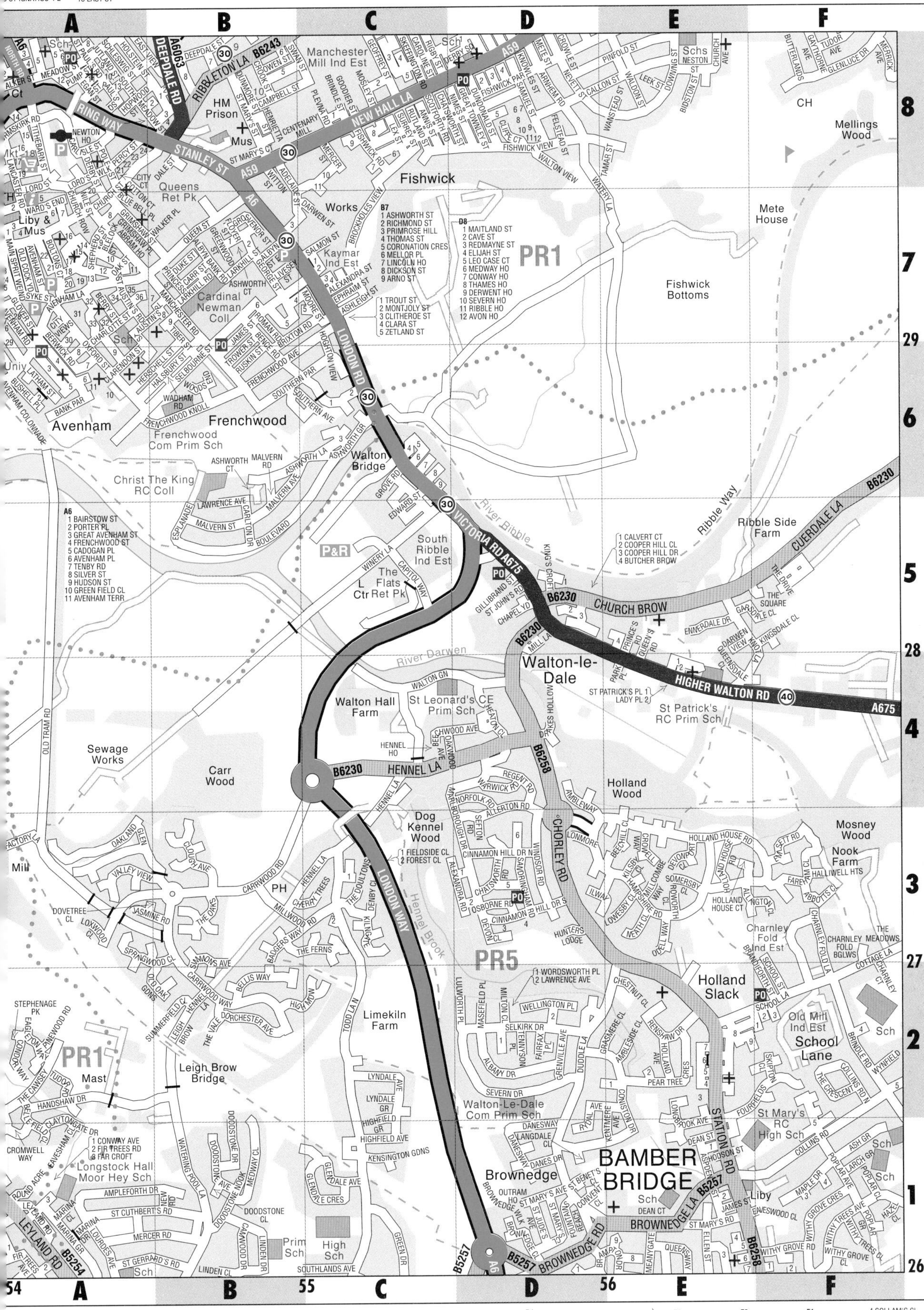


A7
1 BIRLEY ST
2 HARRIS ST
3 JACSON ST
4 MILLER HO
5 GUILD HALL ARC
6 TITHEBARN ST
7 GUILD ROW
8 BACK GRIMSHAW ST
9 GREAVES ST
10 LAUREL ST
11 RICHMOND HO
12 OAKHAM CT
13 SYKE HILL
14 ROSE ST
15 LIBRARY ST
16 ST JOHN'S PL
17 STONEYGATE
18 LENNOX ST
19 AVENHAM CT
20 WOLSELEY PL
21 BOSTOCK ST
22 TURKS HEAD YD
23 GLOVER'S CT
24 PARK PL
25 NEW COCK YD
26 SIMPSON CT
27 GOLDTHREAD WORKS
28 AVENHAM MILLS
29 CHADDOCK ST
30 GUILDFORD RD
31 SANDOWN CT
32 KNOWSLEY ST
33 CHARLOTTE PL
34 NORWICH PL
35 CARLISLE HO
36 ARUNDEL PL

C6
1 SWILL BROOK LA
2 HILLSIDE RD
3 MELLINGS FOLD
4 BRIDGE BANK
5 RIBBLE CRES
6 BRIDGE TERR
7 NORTH RIBBLE ST
8 SOUTH RIBBLE ST
9 EAST VIEW

77

D1
1 FIRBANK

D3
1 RUTLAND AVE
2 KENT AVE
3 DORSET AVE
4 YORK CL
5 BALMORAL RD
6 CAVENDISH PL

98

E1
1 GREENWOOD ST
2 JOHN ST
3 COUNTESSWAY
4 OAKLAND ST
5 TEVEN ST
6 CLAYTON ST
7 BALDWIN ST
8 WELBECK CL
9 BAXENDALE GR

E2
1 BUTTERMERE CL
2 PEAR TREE CL
3 CHARLESTON CT
4 BALSHAW ST
5 LONGWORTH ST
6 HAYDOCK ST
7 PEAR TREE ST
8 ST AIDAN'S RD
9 ST AIDANS PK

F1
1 TYNE ST
2 LODGE CL
3 ELM DR
4 YEWLANDS AVE
5 WHITEFIELD MDW

F2
1 WATER ST
2 WHALLEY ST
3 ASHWORTH ST
4 SOLLAM'S CL
5 BROWN LA

97
119

A B C D E F
8 7 6 5 4 3 2 1
29 28 27 26
57 58 59
Eyes Wood
PR2
PR1
PR5
PR6
Ribble Way
River Ribble
PRESTON NEW RD
A59
M6
31
30
M61
B6230
Works
Cowell's Farm
VICARAGE LA
Cuerdale Hall
Walmsley Fold Farm
New Hall Tavern (PH)
Roacher Hall
New Hall Farm
Cuerdale Wood
CUERDALE LA
Roach Bridge
ROACH BRIDGE COTTS
Mill
ROACH RD
GREEN LA
Woodhouse Farm
Smithy House
Roach Bridge
Silverholme
Swaines Fold
Potter Lane Farm
POTTER LA
Darwen Side Farm
Fleetwood Hall
Sallom House
Cottage Farm
Osbaldeston House Wood
River Darwen
Beeston Wood
Higher Walton
Bannister Hall
Carver Fold
Carr Wood
Jolly Fold
Coupe Green
1 ROSSALL CL
2 WINSTER CL
3 SILVERDALE CL
4 METHUEN CL
5 MANSFIELD DR
Beeston Brook
A675
HIGHER WALTON RD
BARNFLATT CL
BANNISTER CL
BANNISTER HALL LA
BANNISTER HALL DR
BANNISTER HALL CRES
DARWEN ST
SHOP LA
CANN BRIDGE ST
PO
ALBERT TERR
Works
Rass Wood
Coupe Green Prim Sch
Cuerdale Hey Farm
Higher Walton Mill
Swan Inn (PH)
Higher Walton CE Prim Sch
LARK HILL
BRIDGE ST
BROOK ST
CHURCH ST
CHURCH TERR
THE OLD SCHOOL HO
BLACKBURN RD
ROSEWOOD DR
ROSEWOOD CT
ROSEWOOD AVE
HAWTHORNE AVE
HOGHTON LA
COUPE GN
LOWICK CL
GRANGE DR
RUSLAND DR
WOODHALL CRES
POULTON CRES
THORNTON DR
CLEVELEYS RD
CARTMEL DR
ARNSIDE CL
FOX LA
HOLKER CL
METHUEN AVE
MANBY CL
METHUEN DR
MANOR CL
KITTLINGBORNE BROW
Old Oak Inn (PH)
Olive Farm
Mast
Prospect Hill
COTTAGE LA
OLD BROWN LA
ASHTREE CT
CHARLES CRES
GREGSON LA
DAUB HALL LA
BELLS LA
Cooper House Farm
CONWAY CL
CENTRAL AVE
LYDRIC AVE
RHODESWAY
SQUIRES CL
FOUR LANE ENDS
Tottering Temple Farm
Gregson Lane
BROOKHOUSE CL
BROOKHOUSE DR
KNOWSLEY DR
KNOWSLEY CL
ARROWSMITH DR
ARROWSMITH CL
MINTHOLME AVE
FRITHS AVE
HEWNGATE
SYLVAN GR
WOODLANDS AVE
BROWN LA
GOLDCREST DR
WOODCOCK CL
KINGFISHER WAY
Mast
1 BRINDLE CL
2 SANDPIPER CRES
SHUTTLING FIELDS LA
Drum Head Brook
Middle Shuttling Fields
LARCH GATE
ALMA ROW
MANY BROOKS HO
ALDERSLEIGH CRES
Black Horse (PH)
Hewn Gate Farm
Sch
HAZEL AVE
HAZEL GR
WITHY TREES AVE
BRINDLE RD
Fowler Brook
ALDER DR
BIRCH CL
HAYFIELD
MEADOWSIDE
WILLOW DR
APPLEBY CL
HAYFIELD AVE
HILLPARK AVE
WESTFIELD DR
BANK HEAD LA
OAK BANK
GREGSON LA
Brindle Gregson Lane Prim Sch
FRITH'S CT
Frith's Farm
L Ctr
COTTAGE GDNS
Livesey Green Farm
BOURNESFIELD
BOURNE'S ROW
BK BOURNE'S ROW
St Joseph's RC Prim Sch
LC

97
78

120 100

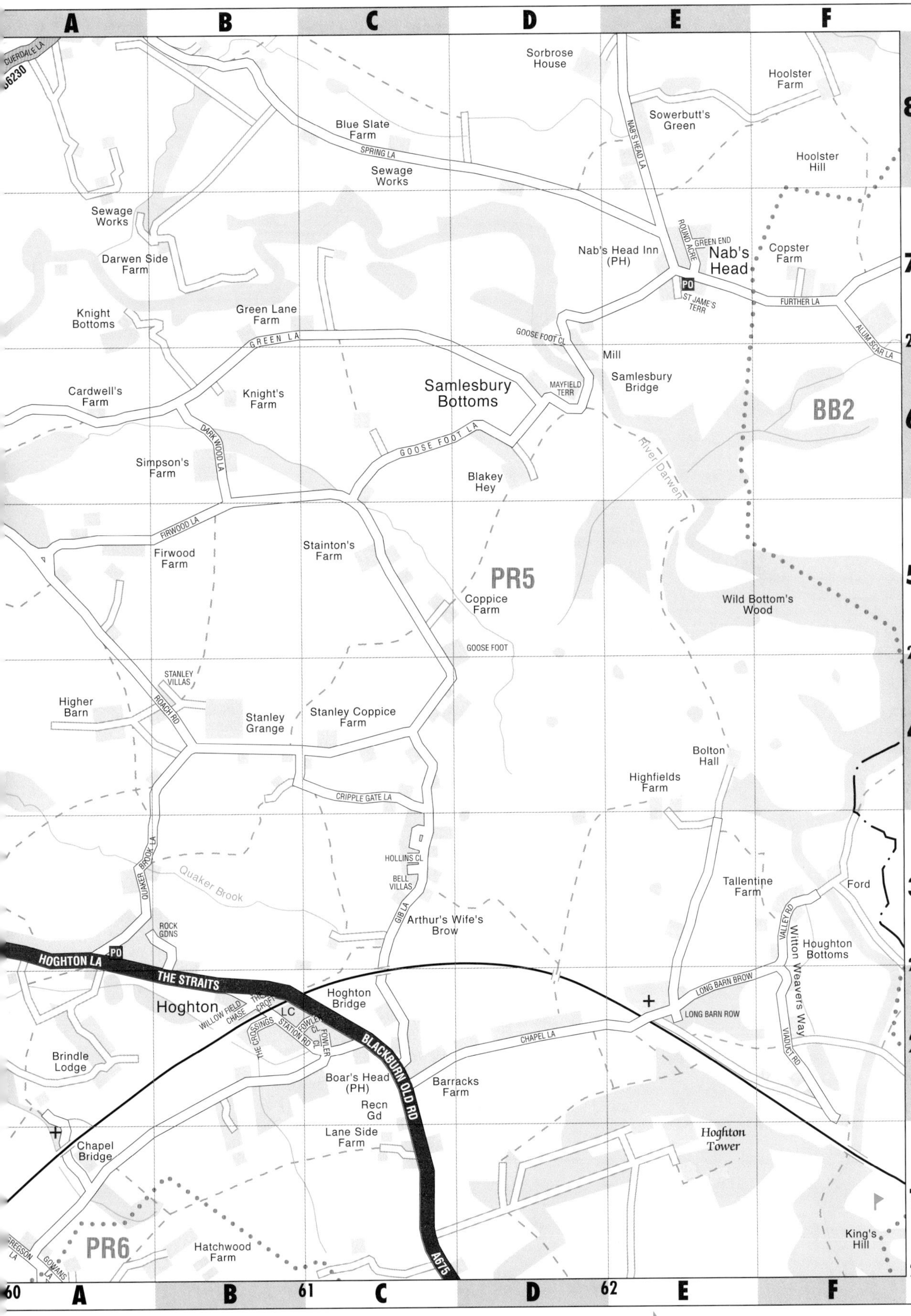


79 100

99
121

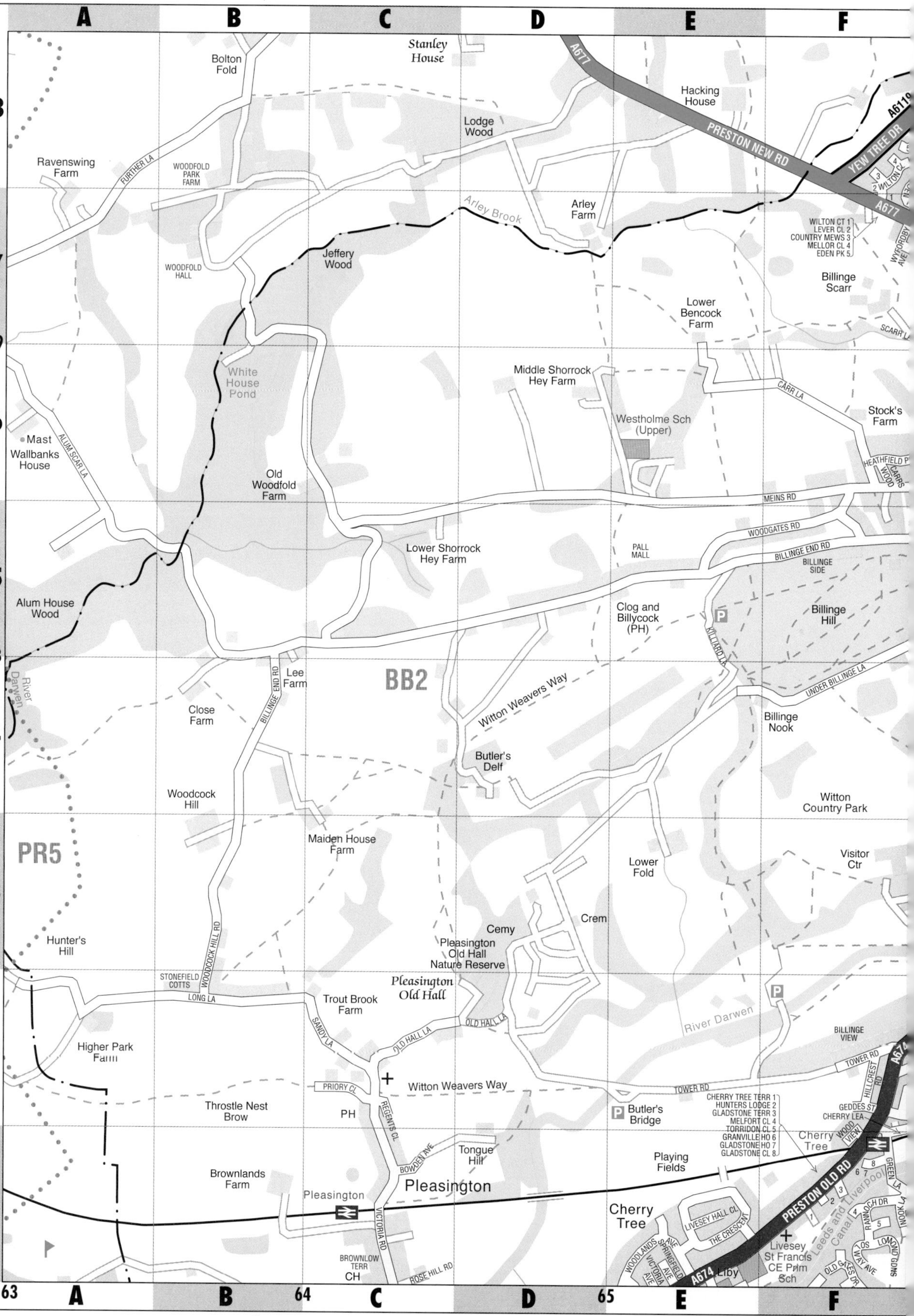
A
B
C
D
E
F
8
7
29
6
5
28
4
3
27
2
1
26
63
64
65
Stanley House
Bolton Fold
Hacking House
Lodge Wood
A677
PRESTON NEW RD
A6119
YEW TREE DR
WILTON CL
Ravenswing Farm
FURTHER LA
WOODFOLD PARK FARM
Arley Brook
Arley Farm
WILTON CT 1
LEVER CL 2
COUNTRY MEWS 3
MELLOR CL 4
EDEN PK 5
WOODFOLD HALL
Jeffery Wood
Lower Bencock Farm
Billinge Scarr
SCARR LA
White House Pond
Middle Shorrock Hey Farm
CARR LA
Stock's Farm
Mast
Wallbanks House
ALUM SCAR LA
Westholme Sch (Upper)
Old Woodfold Farm
HEATHFIELD PL
CARRS WOOD
MEINS RD
WOODGATES RD
Lower Shorrock Hey Farm
PALL MALL
BILLINGE END RD
BILLINGE SIDE
Alum House Wood
Clog and Billycock (PH)
Billinge Hill
KILLIARD LA
Lee Farm
BB2
River Darwen
Close Farm
BILLINGE END RD
Witton Weavers Way
UNDER BILLINGE LA
Billinge Nook
Butler's Delf
Woodcock Hill
Witton Country Park
PR5
Maiden House Farm
Lower Fold
Visitor Ctr
Crem
Hunter's Hill
Cemy
Pleasington Old Hall Nature Reserve
STONEFIELD COTTS
WOODCOCK HILL RD
Pleasington Old Hall
LONG LA
Trout Brook Farm
River Darwen
SANDY LA
OLD HALL LA
BILLINGE VIEW
Higher Park Farm
TOWER RD
A674
HILLCREST RD
Witton Weavers Way
PRIORY CL
TOWER RD
CHERRY TREE TERR 1
HUNTERS LODGE 2
GLADSTONE TERR 3
MELFORT CL 4
TORRIDON CL 5
GRANVILLE HO 6
GLADSTONE HO 7
GLADSTONE CL 8
GEDDES ST
CHERRY LEA
Throstle Nest Brow
PH
REGENTS CL
Butler's Bridge
Cherry Tree
WOOD VIEW
Tongue Hill
Playing Fields
BOWDEN AVE
Brownlands Farm
Pleasington
Pleasington
PRESTON OLD RD
GREEN LA
Leeds and Liverpool Canal
RANNOCH DR
Cherry Tree
LIVESEY HALL CL
THE CRESCENT
NOOK LA
VICTORIA RD
WOODLANDS AVE
SPRINGFIELD AVE
VICTORIA AVE
Livesey St Francis CE Prim Sch
LOMOND GDNS
BROWNLOW TERR
CH
ROSE HILL RD
A674
Liby
OLD GATES DR

99
80

**E5**
1 CALENDAR ST
2 MARKET AVE
3 AINSWORTH MALL
4 COBDEN CT
5 GROSVENOR WAY
6 SPRING HILL
7 VICTORIA CT
8 MARKET WAY
9 STONYBUTTS
10 LORD STREET MALL
11 CORPORATION ST
12 LORD ST W
13 LOWER COCKCROFT
14 HIGHER COCKCROFT
15 NEW MARKET ST
16 TOWN HALL ST
17 RICHMOND TERR
18 EXCHANGE ST
19 MUSEUM ST
20 SUDELL CROSS
21 LIMBRICK
22 MORTON ST
23 RICHMOND HILL
24 BOLTON'S CT
25 VICTORIA ST

**E6**
1 HODDER ST
2 BROOKFIELD ST
3 HARTLEY ST
4 VICTORIA CROSS
5 WATFORD ST
6 WILLOUGHBY ST

122

**E6**
7 WIMBERLEY GDNS
8 WIMBERLEY PL

**F6**
1 ST MICHAEL'S CT
2 ST ALBAN'S CT
3 TRINITY CT

102

**F6**
4 WINDERMERE CL
5 BUTTERMERE CL
6 THIRLMERE CL
7 BOWLAND HO
8 SANDPIPER CL
9 ORIOLE CL
10 Brookhouse Bsns Ctr
11 WHITEWELL PL
12 BROOKHOUSE GDNS
13 WILLIAM HERBERT ST
14 Whalley Range Bsns Pk

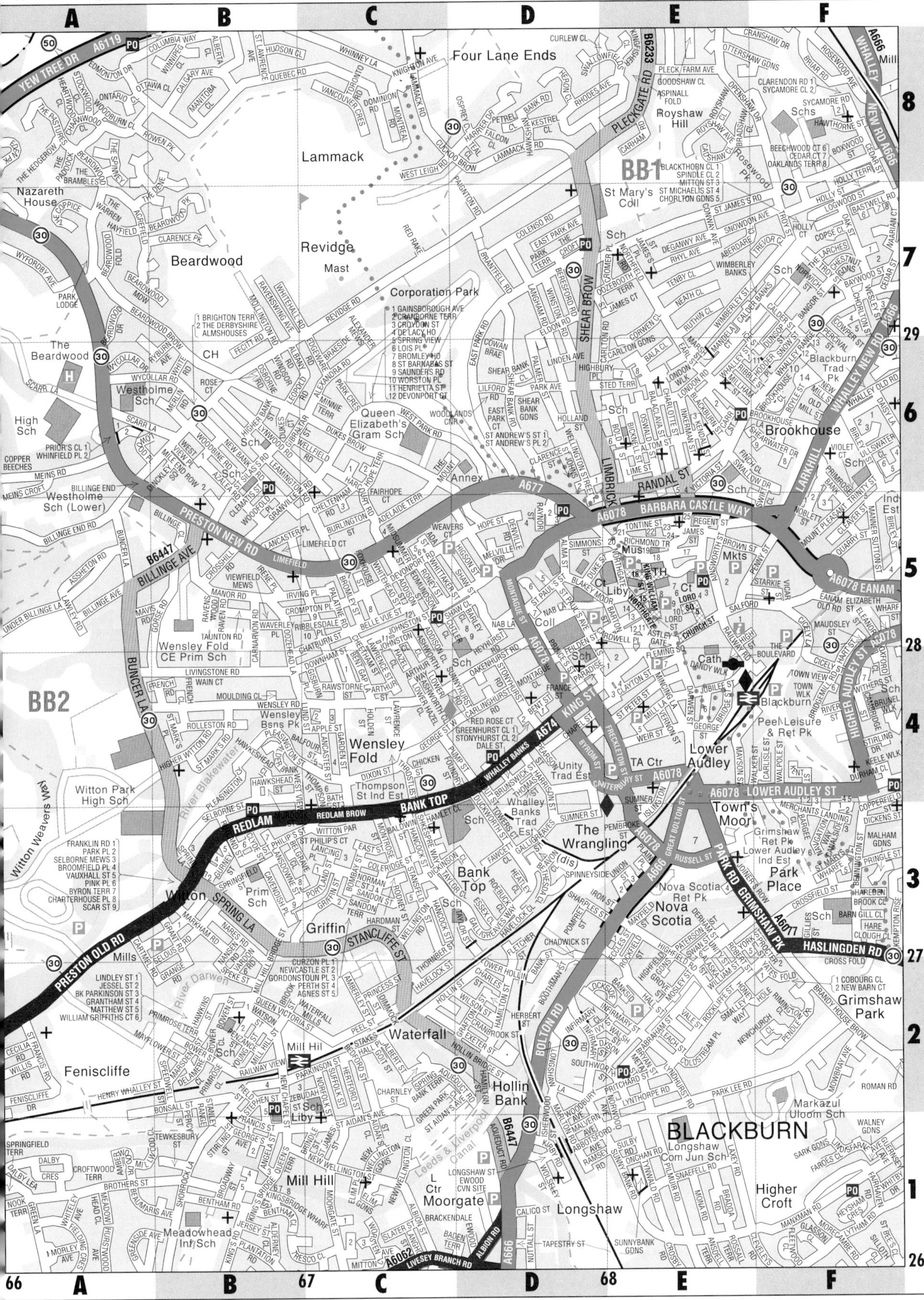




**B1**
1 CAVE ST
2 HERSCHELL ST
3 CANAL ST
4 KING'S BRIDGE CL
5 BEVERLEY ST
6 KINGSBRIDGE CT
7 BRIDGE HO
8 WHARF HO

**C1**
1 FARRINGTON CL
2 MOORGATE GDNS
3 SOULBY CL

**C4**
1 GRINDLETON RD
2 APPLE CL
3 APPLE CT
4 HORNBY CT
5 BALFOUR HO
6 BRIDGEWATER CT

**D5**
1 STRAWBERRY BANK
2 NEW PARK ST
3 BATHURST ST
4 SUMMERVILLE WLK
5 DENVILLE ST
6 BREWERY ST
7 GREGSON LA
8 COWELL WAY
9 BARLEY WAY

**E3**
1 NEW GARDEN ST
2 HARGREAVES LA
3 LISTER ST
4 ST ANN'S ST
5 FREDERICK ST
6 ROSE ST
7 Townsmoor Ret Pk

81

**E4**
1 PARADISE LA
2 PARADISE TERR
3 HEATON ST
4 OLD BANK ST
5 TATTERSALL ST
6 PILKINGTON ST
7 MARKET STREET LA

102

**F3**
1 MERCHANTS QUAY
2 WATERFRONT
3 PIER HO
4 ST FRANCES CL
5 ST ANNES CL
6 NAVIGATION HO

**F4**
1 ANCHOR HO
2 CLIPPERS QUAY
3 WATERS EDGE
4 MERCHANTS HO
5 QUAYSIDE
6 CICELY CT
7 CAMBRIDGE CL

**F5**
1 PRIMROSE CT
2 PRIMROSE DR
3 MOUNT TRINITY
4 BANCROFT ST
5 BOWMAN CT

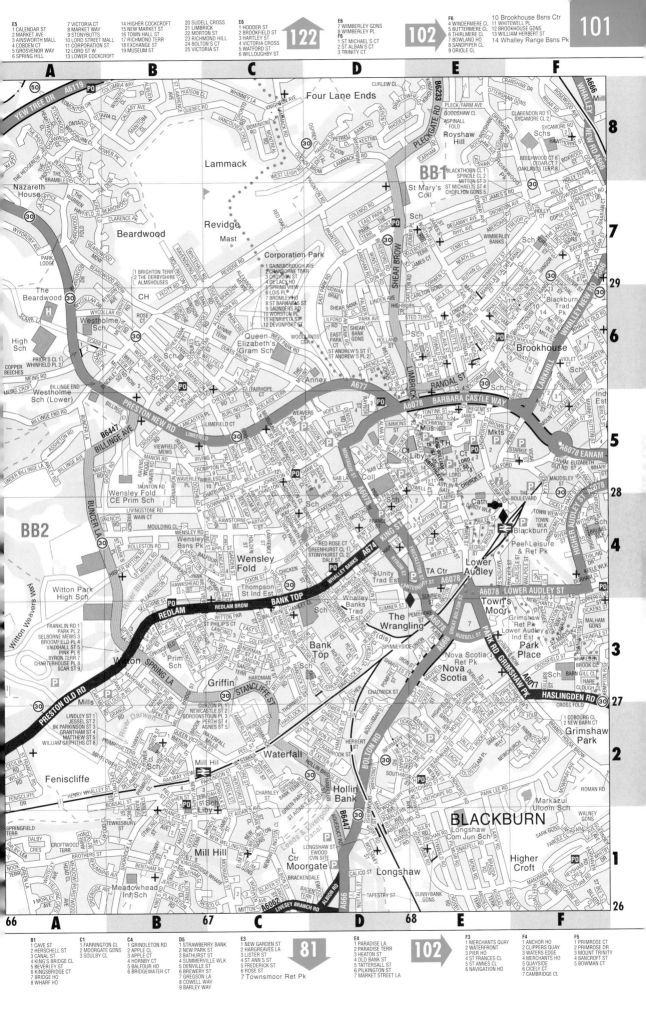

A6
1 FLORENCE PL
2 EASTWOOD ST
3 PELHAM ST
4 FERNDALE
5 CLOVERFIELDS
6 MOSSDALE
7 MOSSBANK

A7
1 SAHARA FOLD
2 POPLAR ST
3 WALNUT ST
4 ALDER ST
5 RAILWAY GR
6 JUNIPER ST
7 PLANE TREE RD

101

A7
8 ST STEPHEN'S AVE
9 ST STEPHEN'S RD
10 YEW ST
11 EBONY ST
12 BEECHWOOD RD
13 GOLDHEY ST
14 HARWOOD ST

123

A4
1 DARTFORD CL
2 CRANWELL CL
3 BRIAR HILL CL
4 BRUNEL WLK
5 AVIEMORE CL
6 SELKIRK CL
7 KINROSS WLK
8 WILLIAM HOPWOOD ST
9 BRISTOL CL
10 SUSSEX WLK
11 SHAKESHAFT ST
12 CUMBERLAND ST
13 KEELE WLK
14 READING CL
15 LEEDS CL
16 JUNE ST
17 JULY ST
18 COPPERFIELD ST
19 DORRITT ST
20 CROMWELL ST
21 RANDOLPH ST

A5
1 MILTON ST
2 HIGHER BARN ST
3 CULSHAW ST

B4
1 BIRCH WLK
2 TEMPLE CL
3 ST CLEMENTS CL

101

B5
1 ST MARGARET'S CT
2 CHERRY CL
3 MULBERRY WLK
4 ACACIA WLK
5 CHESTNUT WLK
6 CROSTON CL

82

C5
1 FERRIER CL
2 BURGESS ST
3 WINMARLEIGH ST

124
104

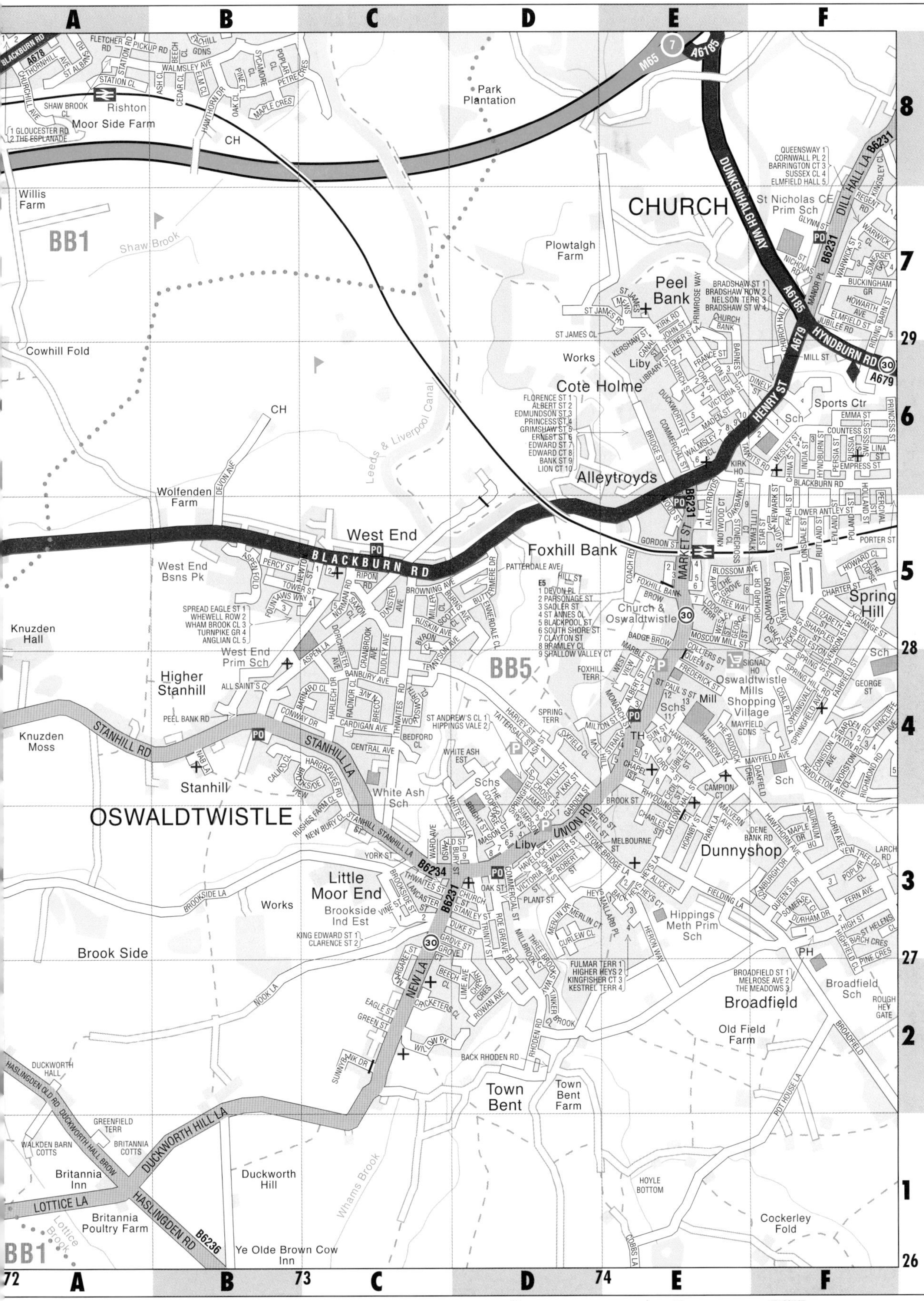


D3
1 ST ANDREW'S CT
2 SPRINGFIELD MEWS
3 KAY ST
4 BENT ST
5 COOPERS CL
6 PEEL ST
7 THOMAS ST
8 HIGHER PEEL ST
9 SMITHY BRIDGE ST

E4
1 BACKHOUSE ST
2 HARTLEY ST
3 HODGSON ST
4 DALE ST
5 SPRING ST
6 MOUNT PLEASANT ST
7 OFF MOUNT PLEASANT ST
8 WATSON ST
9 PADDOCK ST
10 LOCK ST
11 MEADOW CT
12 ST PAUL'S CT
13 WORSLEY CT

F4
1 GAYLE WAY
2 BURNSALL RD
3 REETH WAY
4 BUCKDEN RD
5 MALHAM AVE

83
104

A7
1 LINCOLN CT
2 LINDSEY HO
3 BANBURY CL
4 WORCESTER AVE
5 EVESHAM CL
6 MALVERN CL
7 STRATFORD WAY

C5
1 CHRIST CHURCH SQ
2 CHRIST CHURCH ST
3 NUTTALL ST MEWS
4 PRIESTLEY NOOK
5 EDMUND ST

103

6 NAPIER ST
7 WELLINGTON CT
8 SPRING GDNS
9 HARGREAVES ST
10 CHAPEL ST
11 ST LEGER CT

125

12 MIDLAND ST
13 QUARRY ST

C6
1 MANOR BROOK
2 ARNOLD ST
3 BRADSHAW ST E
4 HOOD ST
5 RAILWAY VIEW
6 KENYON ST
7 MASON ST
8 BURNLEY RD
9 WATER ST
10 BACK WATER ST
11 INFANT ST
12 QUEEN ST
13 TASKER ST
14 BRIDGE ST
15 DUTTON ST

E8
1 SPRUCE CT
2 ELDER CT
3 JUNIPER CT
4 FIR CT
5 CALDEW CT
6 FOXWOOD CHASE
7 NEWBY RD

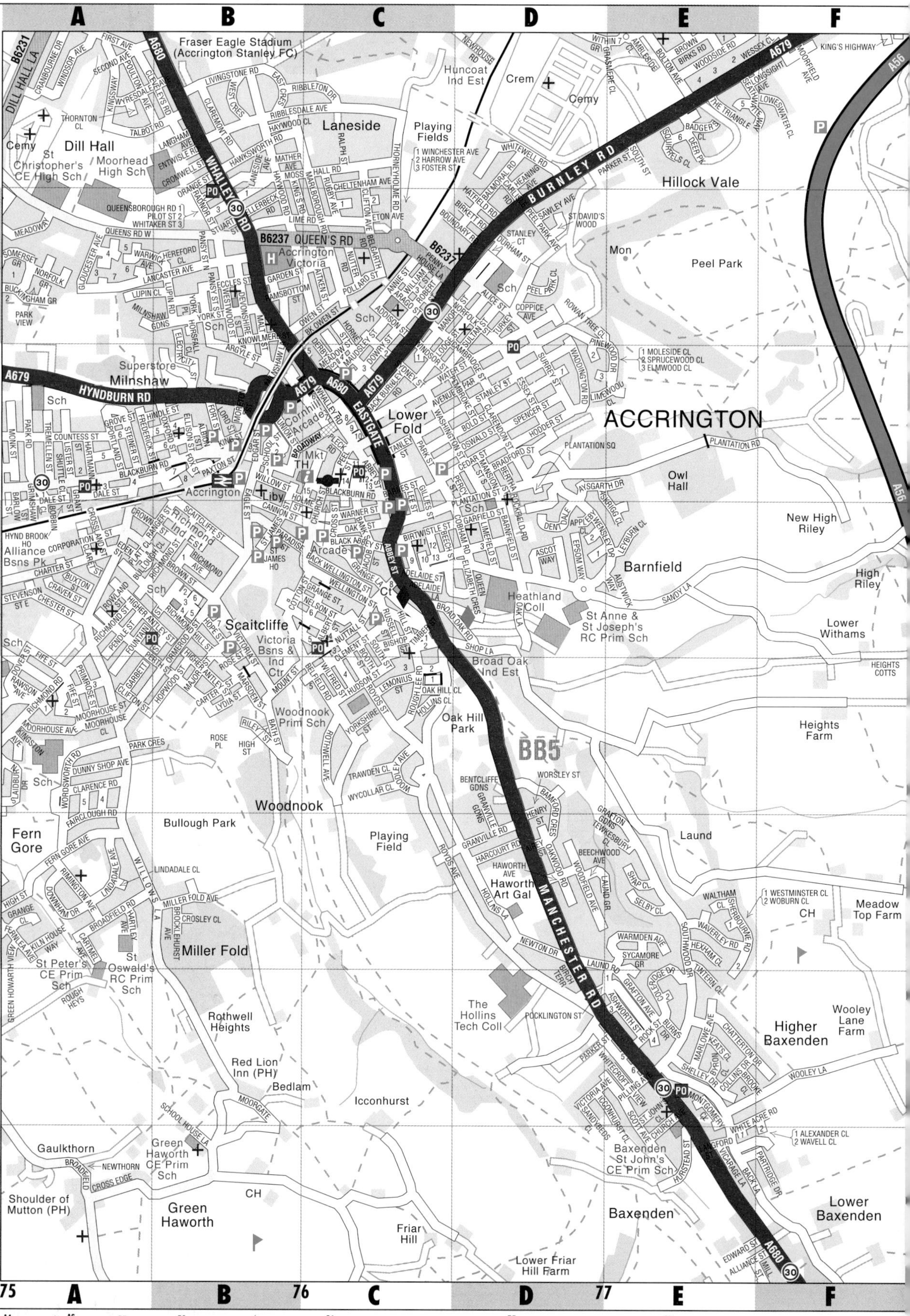




A4
1 WALKER AVE
2 GORDON AVE
3 FRASER ST
4 CHESTNUT GR
5 BEECH GR

A6
1 WHEAT ST
2 COLLEGE CT
3 LANG ST
4 LITTLE ST
5 COLLEGE ST
6 VINE ST

B5
1 FOUNTAIN PL
2 JANNAT CL
3 HANNAH ST
4 HOLDEN ST
5 MEDINA CL
6 GLEBE CL
7 ABRAHAM ST

B6
1 BIRCH ST
2 CRAWSHAW ST
3 EMPIRE HO
4 TAYLOR ST W
5 WALTER ST
6 BLAKE ST
7 BRUNSWICK TERR
8 WILLOW BROOK

103

C4
1 HOLLY BANK
2 MOUNTAIN LA
3 CHRIST CHURCH HALL
4 AUGUSTA ST
5 SPINDLE BERRY CT

84

D5
1 INGLETON CL
2 SEDBURGH CL
3 BEACONSFIELD ST

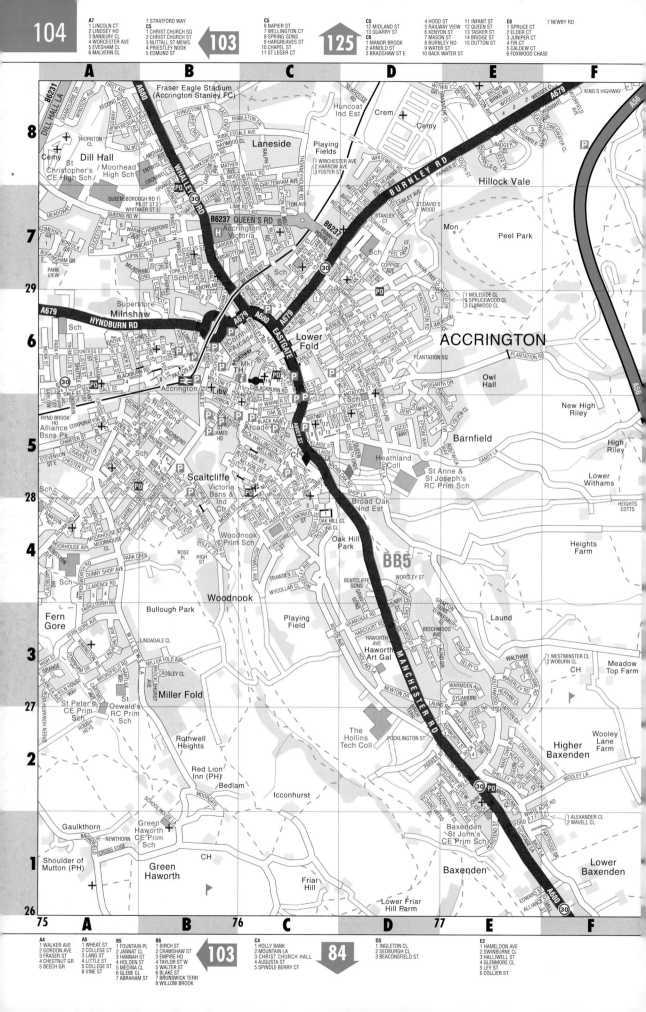

E2
1 HAMELDON AVE
2 SWINBURNE CL
3 HALLIWELL ST
4 GLENMORE CL
5 LEY ST
6 COLLIER ST

126
106

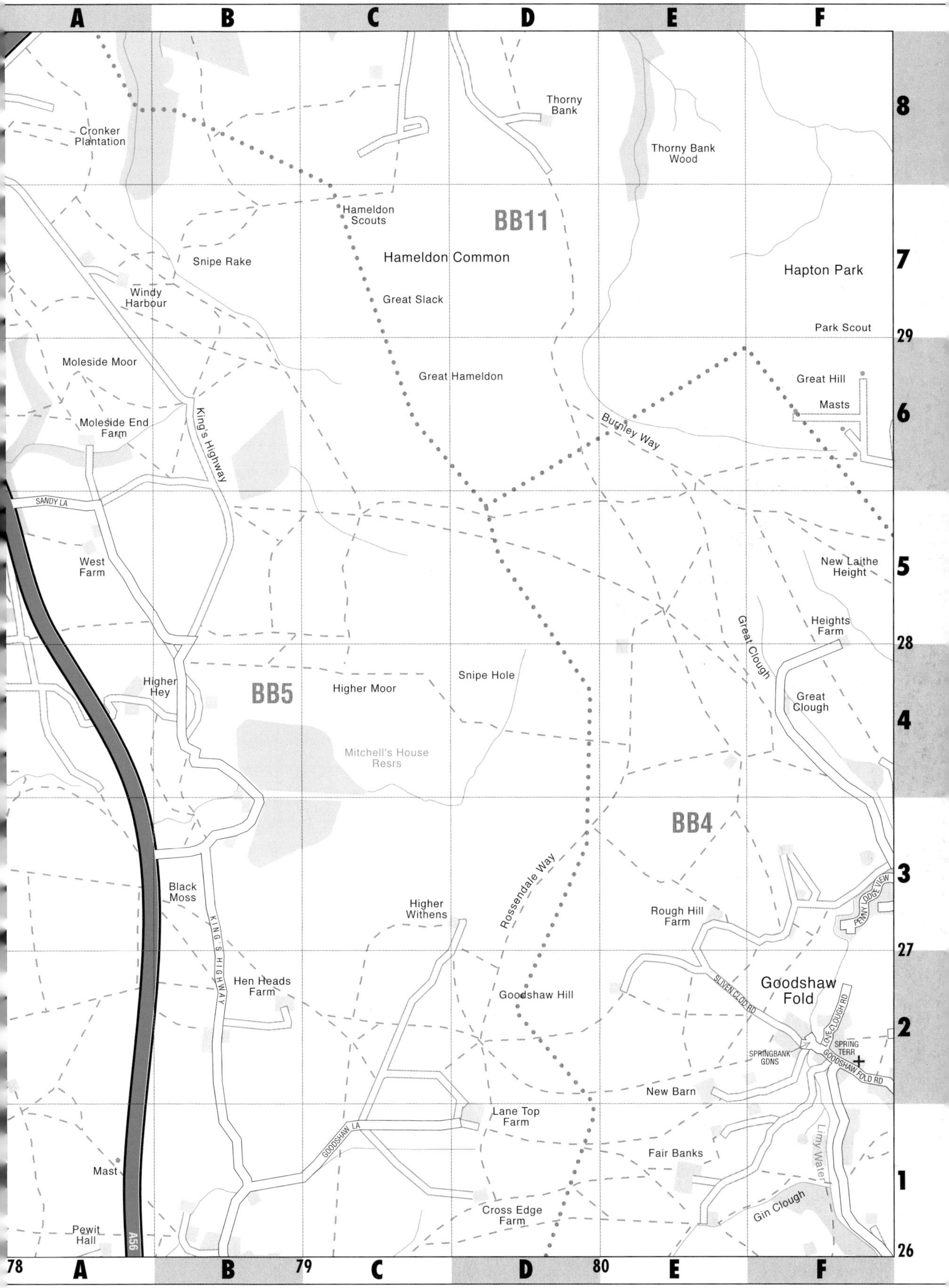
A B C D E F
8 7 29 6 5 28 4 3 27 2 1 26
78 79 80
Cronker Plantation
Thorny Bank
Thorny Bank Wood
Hameldon Scouts
BB11
Hameldon Common
Snipe Rake
Windy Harbour
Great Slack
Hapton Park
Park Scout
Moleside Moor
Great Hameldon
Great Hill
Masts
Moleside End Farm
King's Highway
Burnley Way
SANDY LA
West Farm
New Laithe Height
Heights Farm
Great Clough
Higher Hey
BB5
Higher Moor
Snipe Hole
Great Clough
Mitchell's House Resrs
BB4
Rossendale Way
Black Moss
Higher Withens
Rough Hill Farm
PENNY LODGE VIEW
KING'S HIGHWAY
Hen Heads Farm
Goodshaw Hill
SLIVEN CLOD RD
Goodshaw Fold
LOVECLOUGH RD
SPRING TERR
SPRINGBANK GDNS
GOODSHAW FOLD RD
New Barn
Lane Top Farm
GOODSHAW LA
Fair Banks
Limy Water
Mast
Cross Edge Farm
Gin Clough
Pewit Hall
A56

85
106

105
127

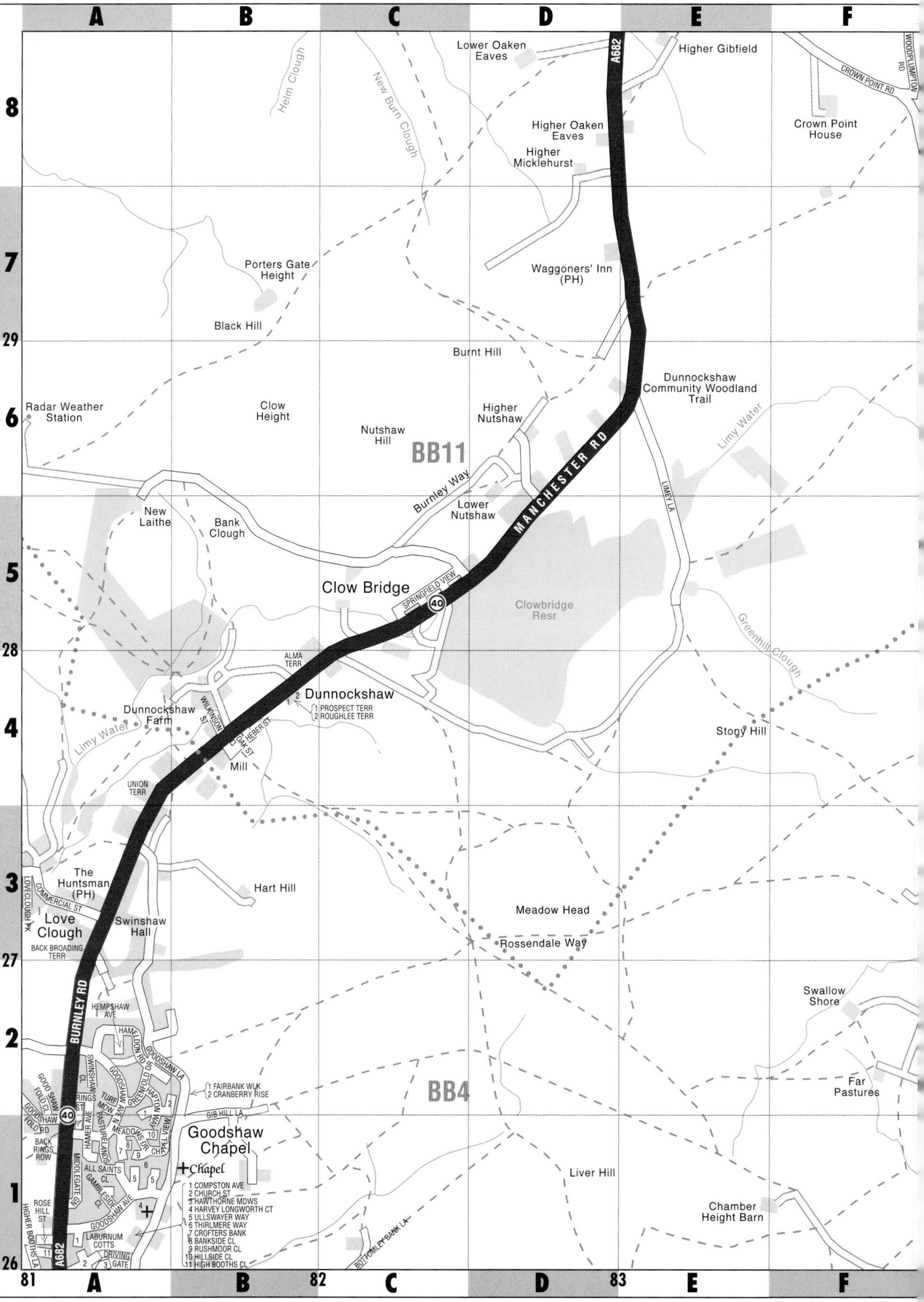


105
86

128
108

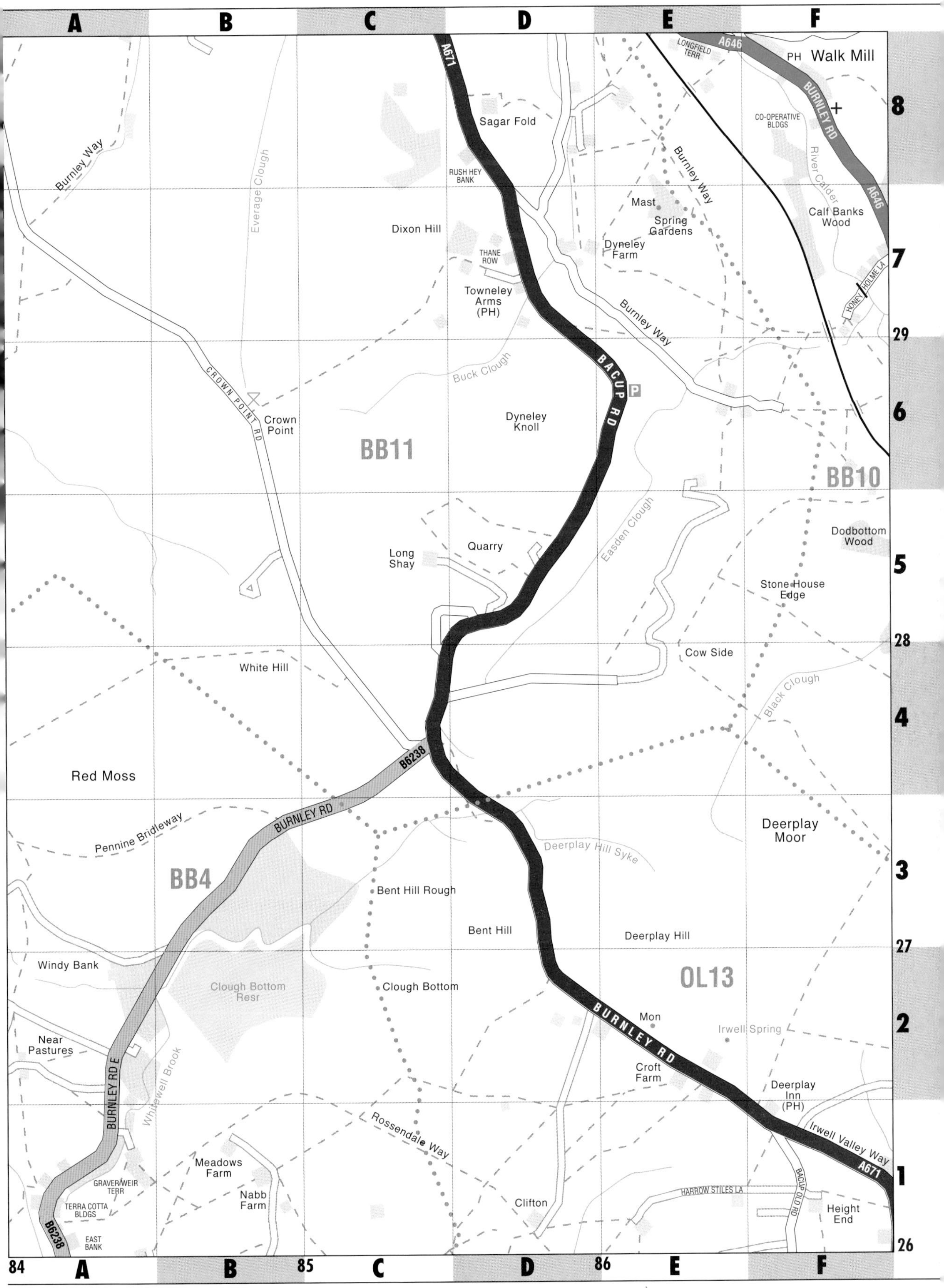


87
108

107
129

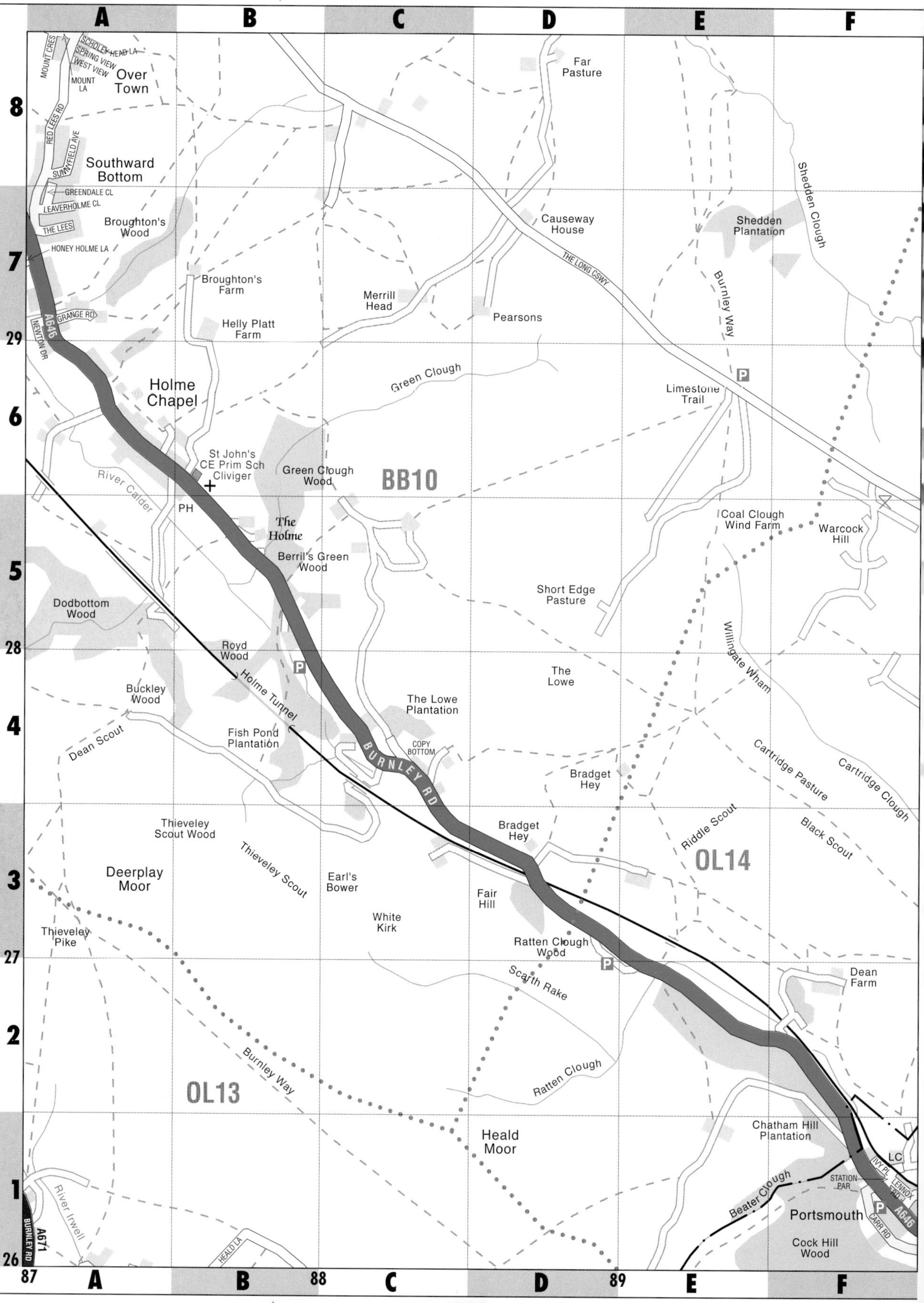
A
B
C
D
E
F
8
7
29
6
5
28
4
3
27
2
1
26
87
88
89
SCHOLEY HEAD LA
SPRING VIEW
WEST VIEW
MOUNT CRES
MOUNT LA
Over Town
RED LEES RD
SUNNYFIELD AVE
Southward Bottom
GREENDALE CL
LEAVERHOLME CL
THE LEES
Broughton's Wood
HONEY HOLME LA
GRANGE RD
A646
NEWTON DR
Broughton's Farm
Helly Platt Farm
Holme Chapel
St John's CE Prim Sch Cliviger
River Calder
PH
Green Clough Wood
The Holme
Berril's Green Wood
Dodbottom Wood
Royd Wood
Buckley Wood
Holme Tunnel
Dean Scout
Fish Pond Plantation
Far Pasture
Merrill Head
Causeway House
THE LONG CSWY
Pearsons
Green Clough
BB10
Shedden Plantation
Shedden Clough
Burnley Way
P
Limestone Trail
Coal Clough Wind Farm
Warcock Hill
Short Edge Pasture
Willingate Wham
The Lowe
The Lowe Plantation
COPY BOTTOM
BURNLEY RD
Bradgett Hey
Cartridge Pasture
Cartridge Clough
Riddle Scout
Black Scout
OL14
Bradget Hey
Thieveley Scout Wood
Thieveley Scout
Deerplay Moor
Earl's Bower
Fair Hill
White Kirk
Thieveley Pike
Ratten Clough Wood
Scarth Rake
Dean Farm
Burnley Way
OL13
Ratten Clough
Heald Moor
Chatham Hill Plantation
LC
IVY PL
LENNOX RD
STATION PAR
Beater Clough
Portsmouth
CARR RD
Cock Hill Wood
River Irwell
A671
BURNLEY RD
HEALD LA

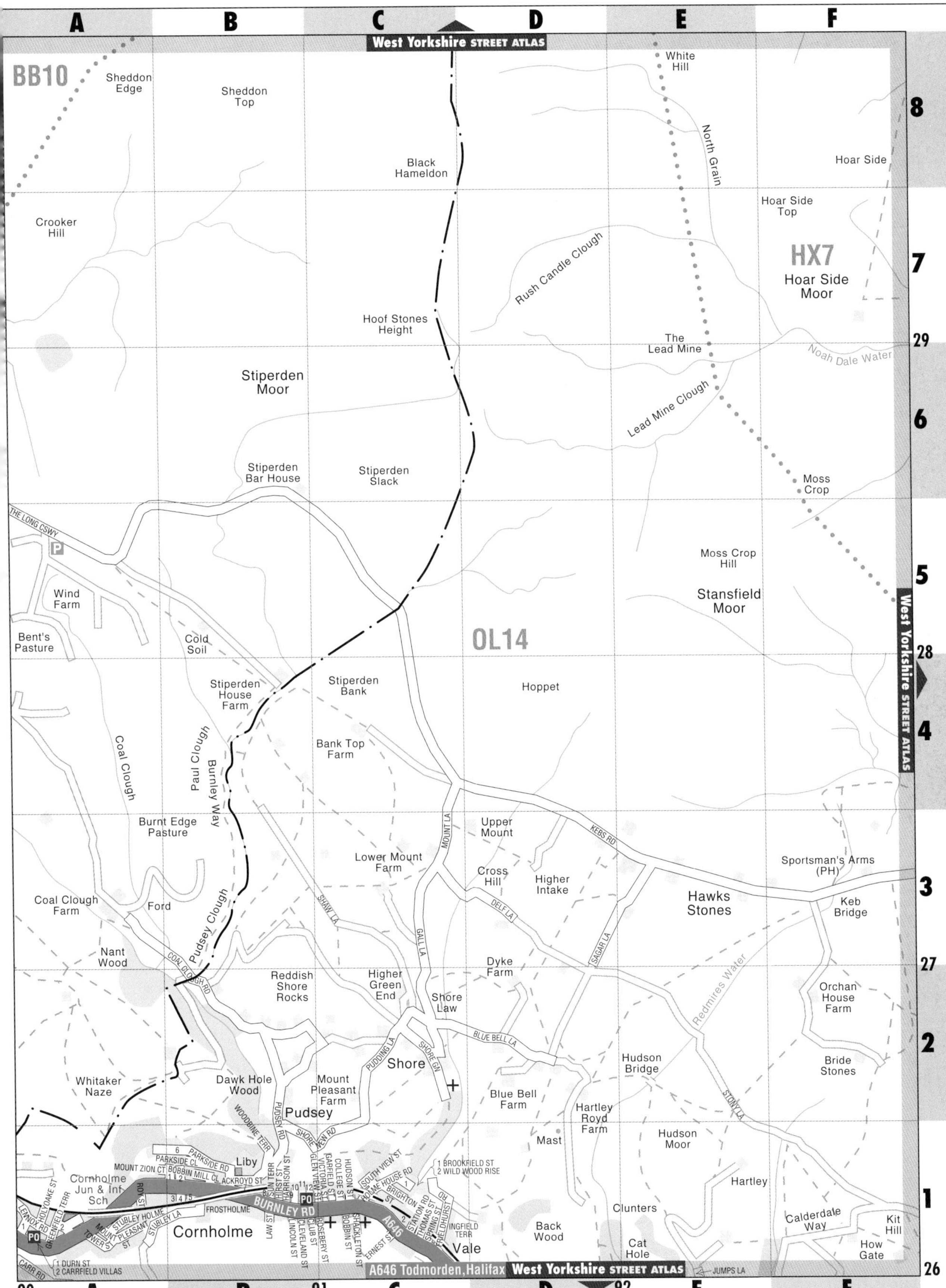
West Yorkshire STREET ATLAS
BB10
Sheddon Edge
Sheddon Top
Black Hameldon
White Hill
North Grain
Hoar Side
Hoar Side Top
HX7
Hoar Side Moor
Crooker Hill
Rush Candle Clough
Hoof Stones Height
The Lead Mine
Noah Dale Water
Stiperden Moor
Lead Mine Clough
Stiperden Bar House
Stiperden Slack
Moss Crop
THE LONG CSWY
Moss Crop Hill
Stansfield Moor
Wind Farm
OL14
Bent's Pasture
Cold Soil
Stiperden House Farm
Stiperden Bank
Hoppet
Coal Clough
Paul Clough
Burnley Way
Bank Top Farm
Burnt Edge Pasture
MOUNT LA
Upper Mount
KEBS RD
Lower Mount Farm
Cross Hill
Higher Intake
Sportsman's Arms (PH)
Coal Clough Farm
Ford
SHAW LA
DELF LA
Hawks Stones
Keb Bridge
Pudsey Clough
GALL LA
SAGAR LA
Nant Wood
COAL CLOUGH RD
Dyke Farm
Redmires Water
Orchan House Farm
Reddish Shore Rocks
Higher Green End
Shore Law
BLUE BELL LA
Whitaker Naze
Dawk Hole Wood
Mount Pleasant Farm
PUDDING LA
Shore
SHORE GN
Hudson Bridge
Bride Stones
Blue Bell Farm
STONY LA
Pudsey
WOODBINE TERR
PUDSEY RD
SHORE NEW RD
Hartley Royd Farm
Hudson Moor
Mast
PARKSIDE RD
PARKSIDE CL
Liby
MOUNT ZION CT
BOBBIN MILL CL
ACKROYD ST
Cornholme Jun & Inf Sch
1 BROOKFIELD ST
2 WILD WOOD RISE
Hartley
SOUTH VIEW ST
HOLME HOUSE RD
BRIGHTON RD
HARRISON ST
HIRST ST
VICTORIA ST
COLLEGE ST
HUDSON ST
GARFIELD ST
GLEN VIEW ST
Clunters
Calderdale Way
Kit Hill
BURNLEY RD
A646
FROSTHOLME
STUBLEY HOLME
STUBLEY LA
MOUNT PLEASANT ST
TOWER ST
Cornholme
LAW ST
LINCOLN ST
CLEVELAND ST
CLUB ST
ROSEBERY ST
BOBBIN ST
SHACKLETON ST
ERNEST ST
STATION RD
THOMAS ST
SPRING ST
FIELDHURST RD
INGFIELD TERR
Vale
Back Wood
Cat Hole
How Gate
PO
GREENFIELD TERR
HOLYOAKE ST
LENNOX RD
CARR RD
1 DURN ST
2 CARRFIELD VILLAS
A646 Todmorden,Halifax
JUMPS LA
A B C D E F
8 7 29 6 5 28 4 3 27 2 1 26
90 91 92

B1
1 BROWN BIRKS ST
2 DAISY BANK ST
3 PEAR PL
4 PEAR ST
5 SPRING VILLAS
6 STANSFIELD TERR
7 CORNHOLME TERR
8 OAKLEIGH TERR
9 GEM APARTMENTS
10 PALMA ST
11 SUNNY BANK TERR
12 GLADSTONE ST

C5
1 COLVILLE AVE
2 STONYCROFT PL
3 ROSEBANK AVE
4 WHITWELL AVE
5 THE SANCTUARY
6 CAIRN CT
7 SQUIRES CT

C6
1 ST LUKE'S CT
2 PARK VIEW CT
3 LAURIER AVE
4 SUMMERVILLE

130

D6
1 SUNNYHURST PK
2 SKERRYVORE RES PK

D8
1 SILVERWOOD CT
2 FREDRICK ST
3 NEWBURY AVE
4 CLAUGHTON MANS
5 WALVERDEN AVEW
6 HOUGHTON AVE
7 SWINDON AVE

E7
1 TEENADORE AVE
2 ANNASIDE CL
3 REANEY AVE

E8
1 TROUGHTON CRES
2 TERANCE RD

F6
1 WINDMILL HO
2 MILLDYKE CL
3 WINDMILL PL
4 RONA AVE
5 ISLAY CL
6 LISMORE AVE

F7
1 AYSGARTH CT
2 MOORVIEW C
3 MOSS WAY
4 GREEN WAY
5 GREGSON CL

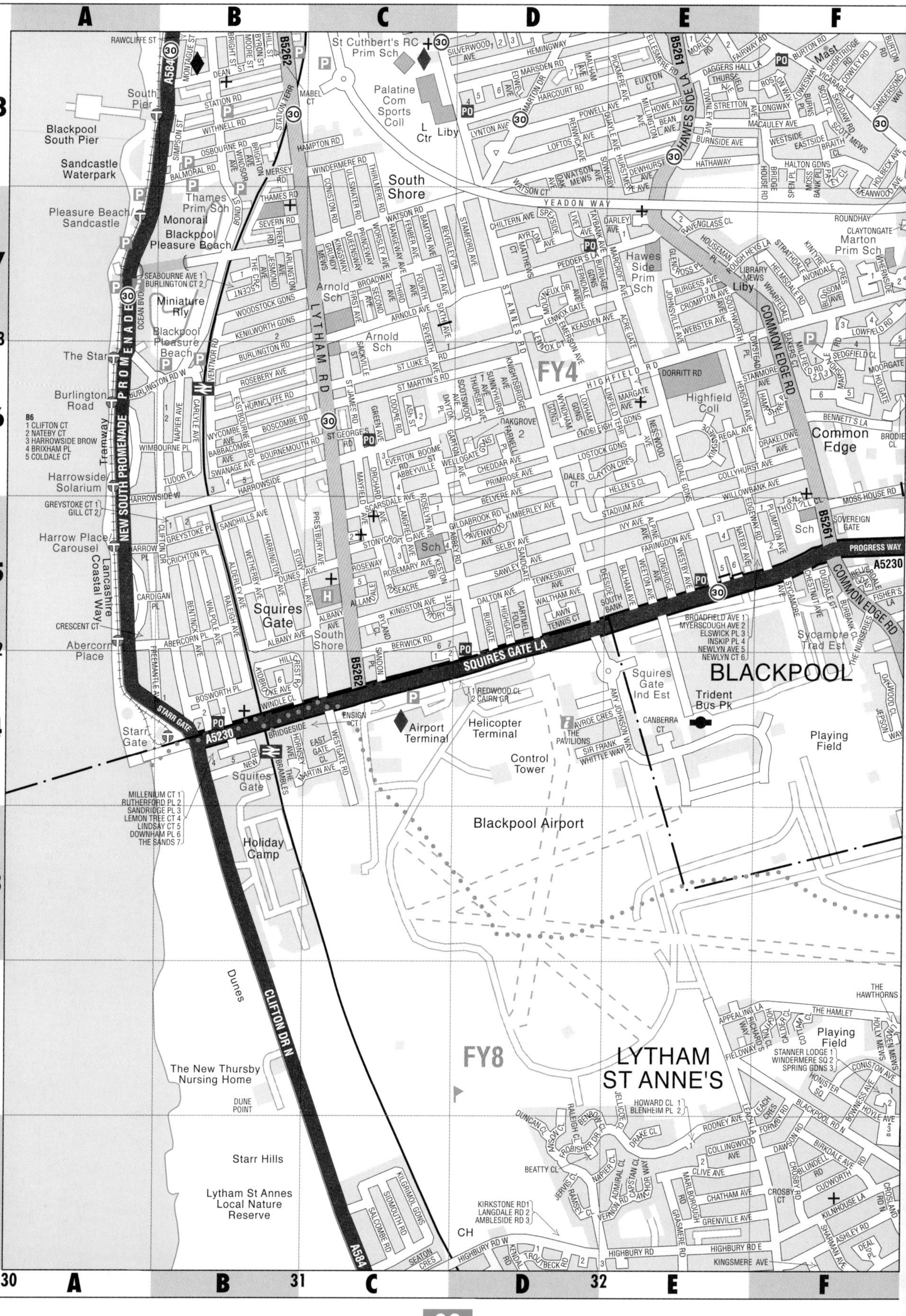


30
A
B
31
C
D
32
E
F

131
112

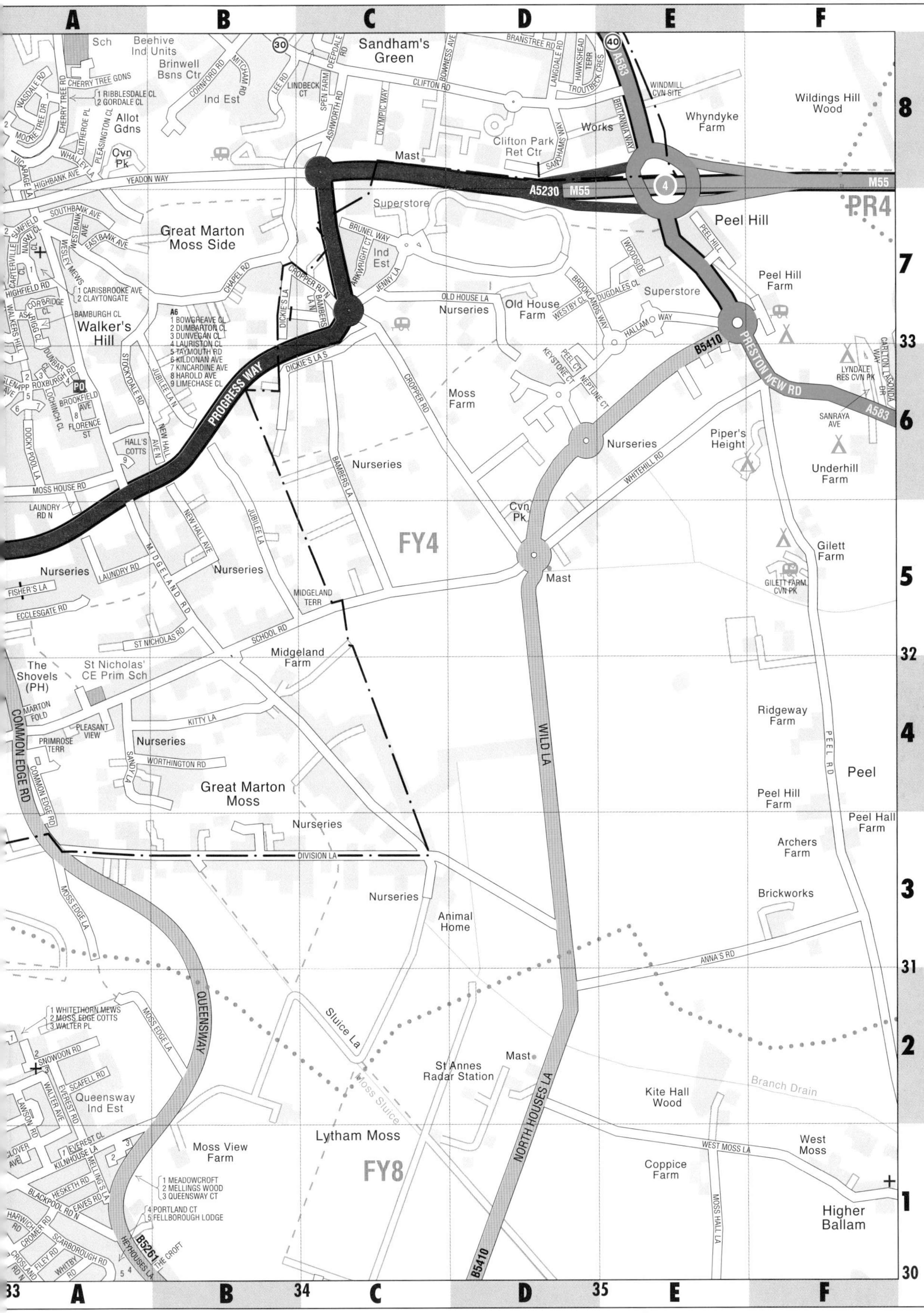


90
112

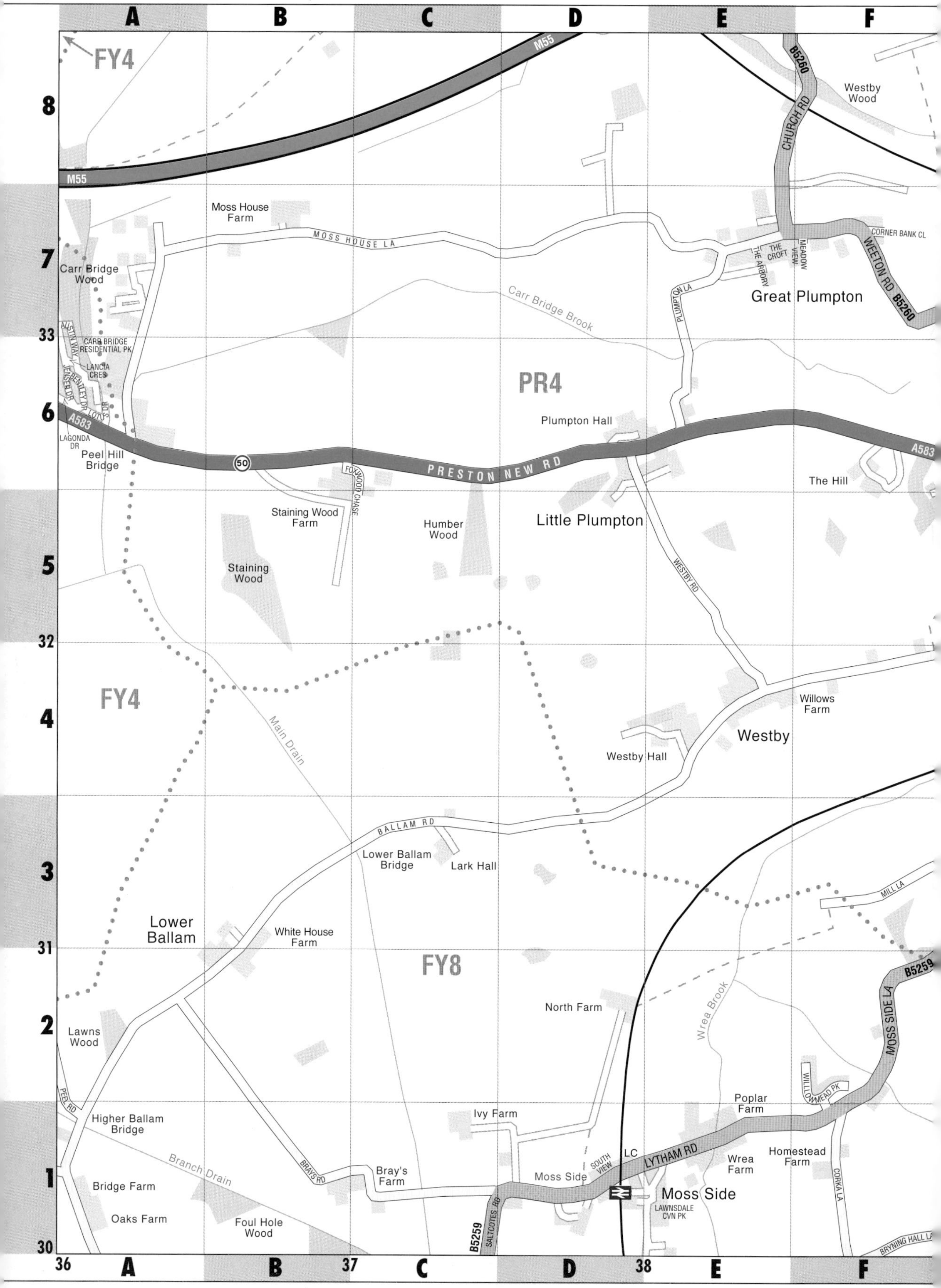
A B C D E F
8 7 33 6 5 32 4 3 31 2 1 30
36 37 38
FY4
M55
B5260
CHURCH RD
Westby Wood
Moss House Farm
MOSS HOUSE LA
CORNER BANK CL
WEETON RD
THE ARBORY
THE CROFT
MEADOW VIEW
Carr Bridge Wood
PLUMPTON LA
Great Plumpton
Carr Bridge Brook
CARR BRIDGE RESIDENTIAL PK
LANCIA CRES
BENTLEY DR
JENSEN DR
PR4
A583
LAGONDA DR
Plumpton Hall
Peel Hill Bridge
PRESTON NEW RD
50
FOXWOOD CHASE
The Hill
Staining Wood Farm
Humber Wood
Little Plumpton
Staining Wood
WESTBY RD
Main Drain
Willows Farm
Westby
Westby Hall
BALLAM RD
Lower Ballam Bridge
Lark Hall
MILL LA
Lower Ballam
White House Farm
FY8
B5259
North Farm
Wrea Brook
Lawns Wood
MOSS SIDE LA
WILLOWMEAD PK
PEEL RD
Higher Ballam Bridge
Ivy Farm
Poplar Farm
Branch Drain
BRAYS RD
Bray's Farm
SOUTH VIEW
LC
LYTHAM RD
Wrea Farm
Homestead Farm
Moss Side
CORKA LA
Bridge Farm
LAWNSDALE CVN PK
Oaks Farm
Foul Hole Wood
SALTCOTES RD
BRYNING HALL LA

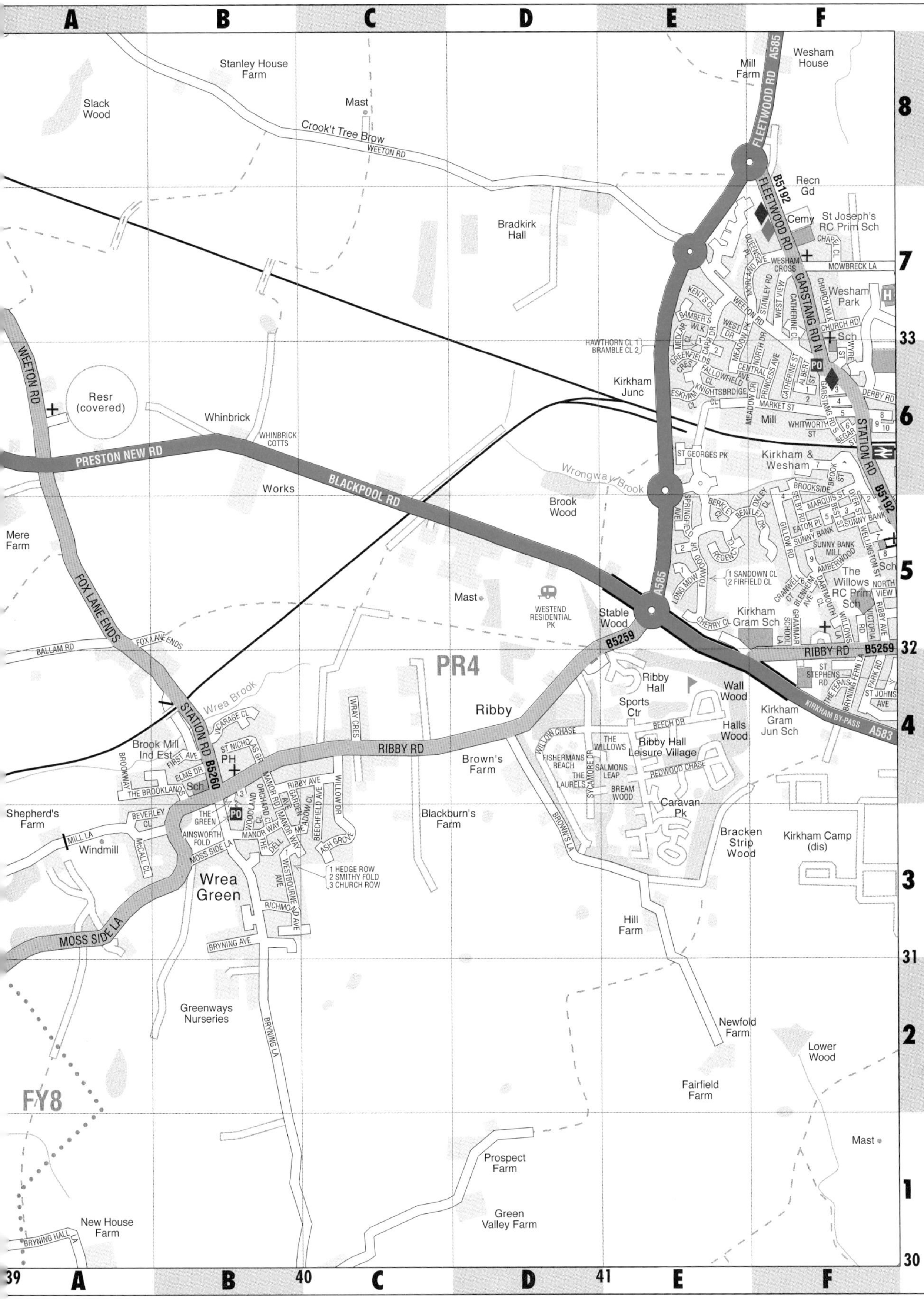
A
B
C
D
E
F
8
7
33
6
5
32
4
3
31
2
1
30
39
40
41
Stanley House Farm
Slack Wood
Mast
Crook't Tree Brow
WEETON RD
Mill Farm
Wesham House
A585
FLEETWOOD RD
Recn Gd
B5192
Cemy
St Joseph's RC Prim Sch
CHAPEL CL
Bradkirk Hall
WESHAM CROSS
MOWBRECK LA
Wesham Park
CHURCH WLK
CHURCH RD
GARSTANG RD N
Sch
HAWTHORN CL 1
BRAMBLE CL 2
WEETON RD
Resr (covered)
Whinbrick
WHINBRICK COTTS
PRESTON NEW RD
Kirkham Junc
MARKET ST
Mill
WHITWORTH ST
DERBY RD
STATION RD
ST GEORGES PK
Kirkham & Wesham
Works
BLACKPOOL RD
Wrongway Brook
Brook Wood
Mere Farm
FOX LANE ENDS
Mast
WESTEND RESIDENTIAL PK
Stable Wood
1 SANDOWN CL
2 FIRFIELD CL
The Willows RC Prim Sch
Kirkham Gram Sch
BALLAM RD
FOX LANE ENDS
B5259
RIBBY RD
PR4
Ribby Hall
Wall Wood
Sports Ctr
Kirkham Gram Jun Sch
KIRKHAM BY-PASS
A583
Wrea Brook
STATION RD
Ribby
Halls Wood
Brook Mill Ind Est
B5260
PH
Sch
RIBBY RD
Brown's Farm
Ribby Hall Leisure Village
WILLOW CHASE
BEECH DR
REDWOOD CHASE
Caravan Pk
Shepherd's Farm
MILL LA
Windmill
PO
Blackburn's Farm
BROWN'S LA
Bracken Strip Wood
Kirkham Camp (dis)
1 HEDGE ROW
2 SMITHY FOLD
3 CHURCH ROW
Wrea Green
MOSS SIDE LA
BRYNING AVE
Hill Farm
Greenways Nurseries
BRYNING LA
Newfold Farm
Lower Wood
Fairfield Farm
FY8
Mast
Prospect Farm
New House Farm
BRYNING HALL LA
Green Valley Farm

A5
1 GREENMOUNT AVE
2 LUNESDALE RD
3 CROWN MEWS
4 DEAN TERR
5 MAYFIELD AVE
6 UNION PAS

B5
1 CENTURION HO
2 ST THERESAS CT
3 THE FLATS
4 MARKET SQ
5 MULBERRY MEWS

113
134

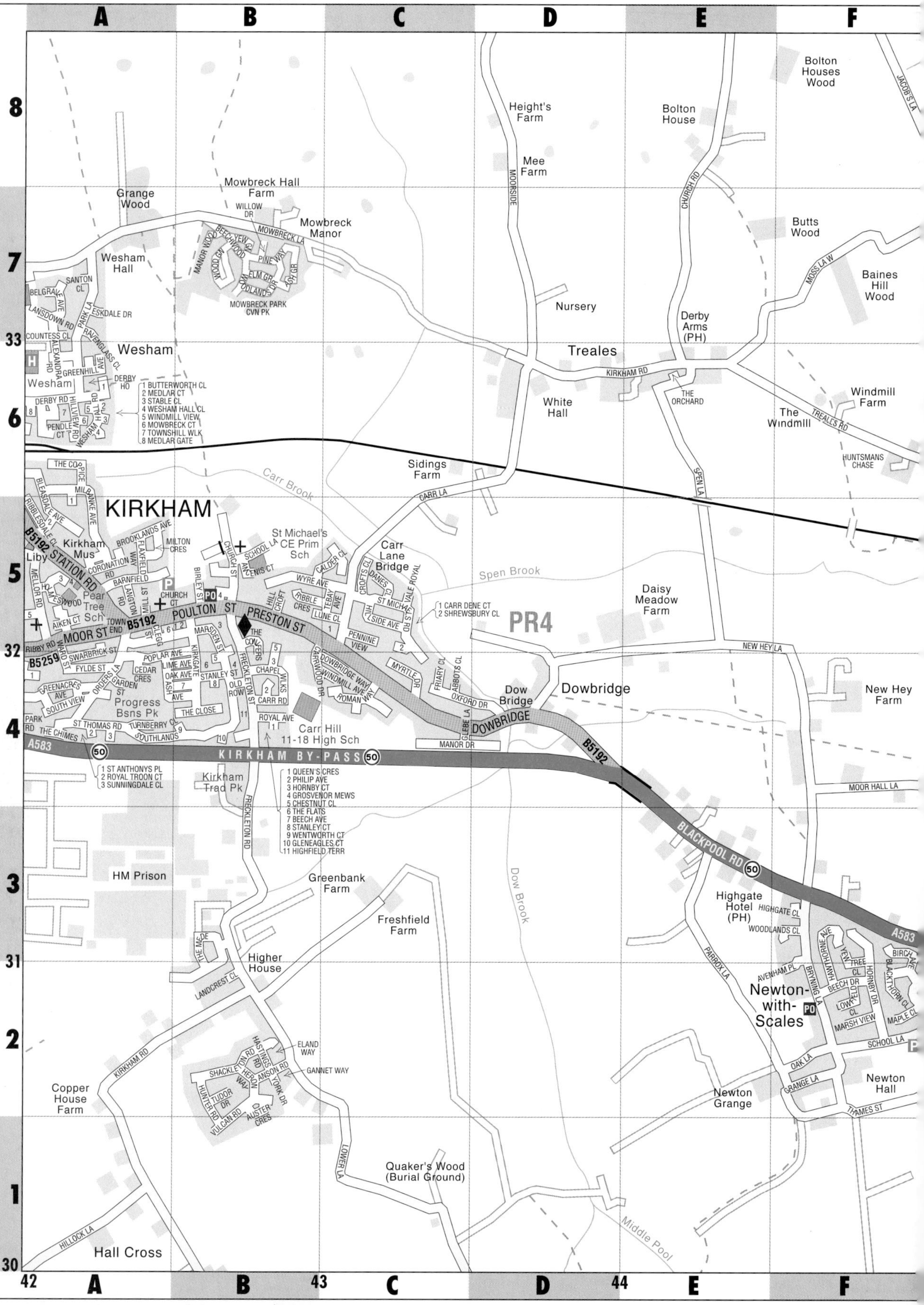
A
B
C
D
E
F
8
7
33
6
5
32
4
3
31
2
1
30
42
43
44
Bolton Houses Wood
Height's Farm
Bolton House
Mee Farm
MOORSIDE
CHURCH RD
JACOB'S LA
Grange Wood
Mowbreck Hall Farm
WILLOW DR
Mowbreck Manor
MOWBRECK LA
Butts Wood
Baines Hill Wood
MOSS LA W
Wesham Hall
MANOR WOOD
BEECHWOOD
YEW GR
PINE WAY
ELM GR
WOODLANDS DR
ASH GR
WOOD GN
MOWBRECK PARK CVN PK
SANTON CL
BELGRAVE AVE
LANSDOWN RD
PARK LA
ESKDALE DR
RAVENGLASS CL
COUNTESS CL
ALEXANDRA RD
Wesham
GREENHILL
DERBY HO
Nursery
Derby Arms (PH)
Treales
KIRKHAM RD
THE ORCHARD
White Hall
Windmill Farm
The Windmill
TREALES RD
HUNTSMANS CHASE
DERBY RD
HILLVIEW RD
PENDLE CT
WESHAM
1 BUTTERWORTH CL
2 MEDLAR CT
3 STABLE CL
4 WESHAM HALL CL
5 WINDMILL VIEW
6 MOWBRECK CT
7 TOWNSHILL WLK
8 MEDLAR GATE
THE COPPICE
MILBANKE AVE
BLEASDALE AVE
RIBBLESDALE CL
KIRKHAM
Carr Brook
Sidings Farm
CARR LA
SPEN LA
B5192
STATION RD
Kirkham Mus
Liby
BROOKLANDS AVE
MILTON CRES
FLAXFIELD WAY
CORONATION RD
BARNFIELD
LANGTON RD
MILL ST
CHURCH CT
BIRLEY ST
CHURCH ST
SCHOOL LA
ST MICHAEL'S CL
St Michael's CE Prim Sch
Carr Lane Bridge
Spen Brook
Daisy Meadow Farm
PR4
MELLOR RD
Pear Tree Sch
AIKEN CT
TOWN END
MOOR ST
POULTON ST
PRESTON ST
WYRE AVE
CALDER CL
CROFTS CL
DANES CL
VALE ROYAL
HILLSIDE AVE
ST MICHAELS RD
RIBBLE CRES
TEBAY AVE
LUNE CL
PENNINE VIEW
1 CARR DENE CT
2 SHREWSBURY CL
HILL CROFT
RIBBY RD
B5259
SWARBRICK ST
FYLDE ST
WARD ST
POPLAR AVE
LIME AVE
OAK AVE
CEDAR CRES
GARDEN ST
KIRKGATE
MARSDEN ST
STANLEY ST
CLEGG ST
THE CONIFERS
FRECKLETON ST
CHAPEL WLKS
CARR RD
OLD ROW
CARRWOOD DR
DOWBRIDGE WAY
WINDMILL AVE
ROMAN WAY
MYRTLE DR
FRIARY CL
ABBOTS CL
OXFORD DR
NEW HEY LA
New Hey Farm
GREENACRES AVE
SOUTH VIEW
ORDERS LA
Progress Bsns Pk
THE CLOSE
ROYAL AVE
Carr Hill 11-18 High Sch
GLEBE LA
MANOR DR
DOWBRIDGE
Dow Bridge
Dowbridge
PARK RD
THE CHIMES
ST THOMAS RD
TURNBERRY CL
SOUTHLANDS
A583
KIRKHAM BY-PASS
50
1 ST ANTHONYS PL
2 ROYAL TROON CT
3 SUNNINGDALE CL
Kirkham Trad Pk
1 QUEEN'S CRES
2 PHILIP AVE
3 HORNBY CT
4 GROSVENOR MEWS
5 CHESTNUT CL
6 THE FLATS
7 BEECH AVE
8 STANLEY CT
9 WENTWORTH CT
10 GLENEAGLES CT
11 HIGHFIELD TERR
FRECKLETON RD
MOOR HALL LA
BLACKPOOL RD
HM Prison
Greenbank Farm
Freshfield Farm
Dow Brook
Highgate Hotel (PH)
HIGHGATE CL
WOODLANDS CL
HAWTHORNE AVE
YEW TREE CL
BIRCH AVE
BLACKTHORN CL
THE MEADE
Higher House
LANDCREST CL
AVENHAM PL
PARROX LA
BRYNING LA
BEECH DR
HORNBY DR
LOWOOD CL
Newton-with-Scales
MAPLE CL
MARSH VIEW
SCHOOL LA
HASTINGS RD
HERON WAY
ELAND WAY
ANSON RD
YORK DR
GANNET WAY
SHACKLETON RD
HUNTER RD
TUDOR DR
AUSTER CRES
VULCAN RD
KIRKHAM RD
Copper House Farm
Newton Grange
OAK LA
GRANGE LA
Newton Hall
THAMES ST
LOWER LA
Quaker's Wood (Burial Ground)
Middle Pool
HILLOCK LA
Hall Cross

113
93

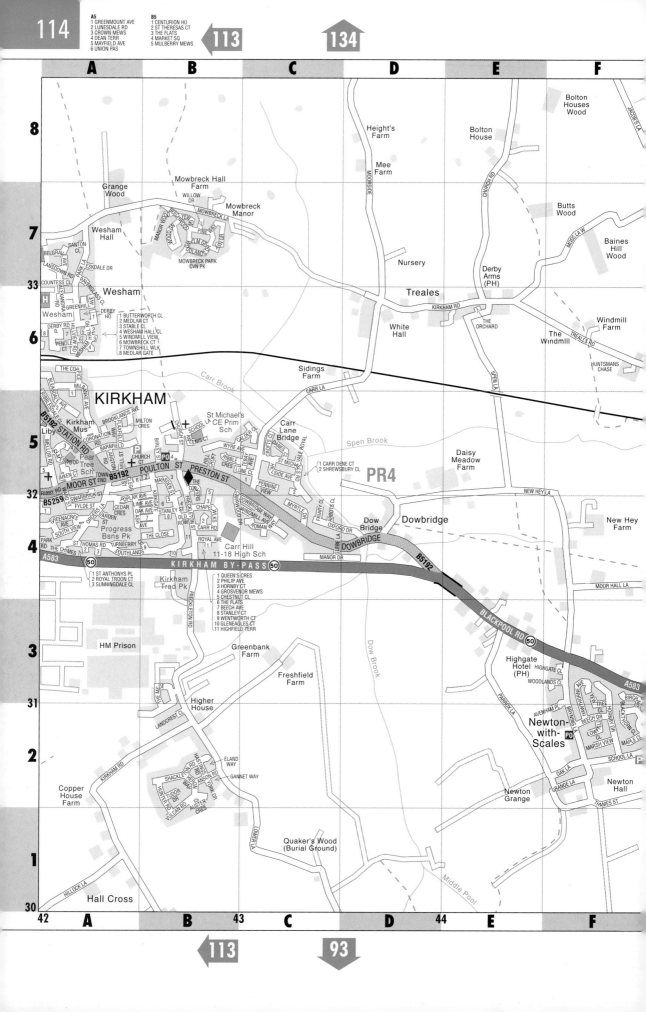

135
116

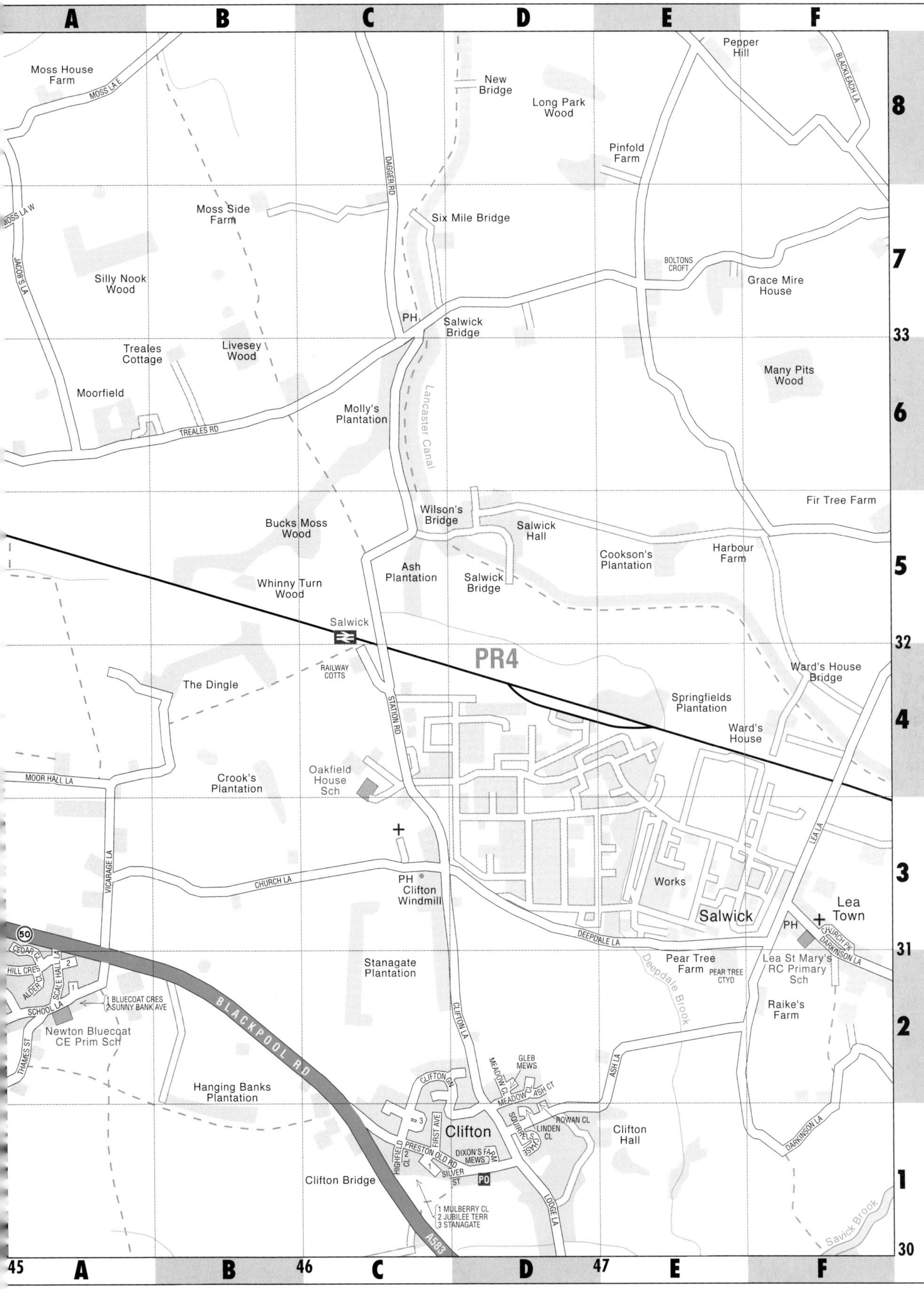


94
116

115
136

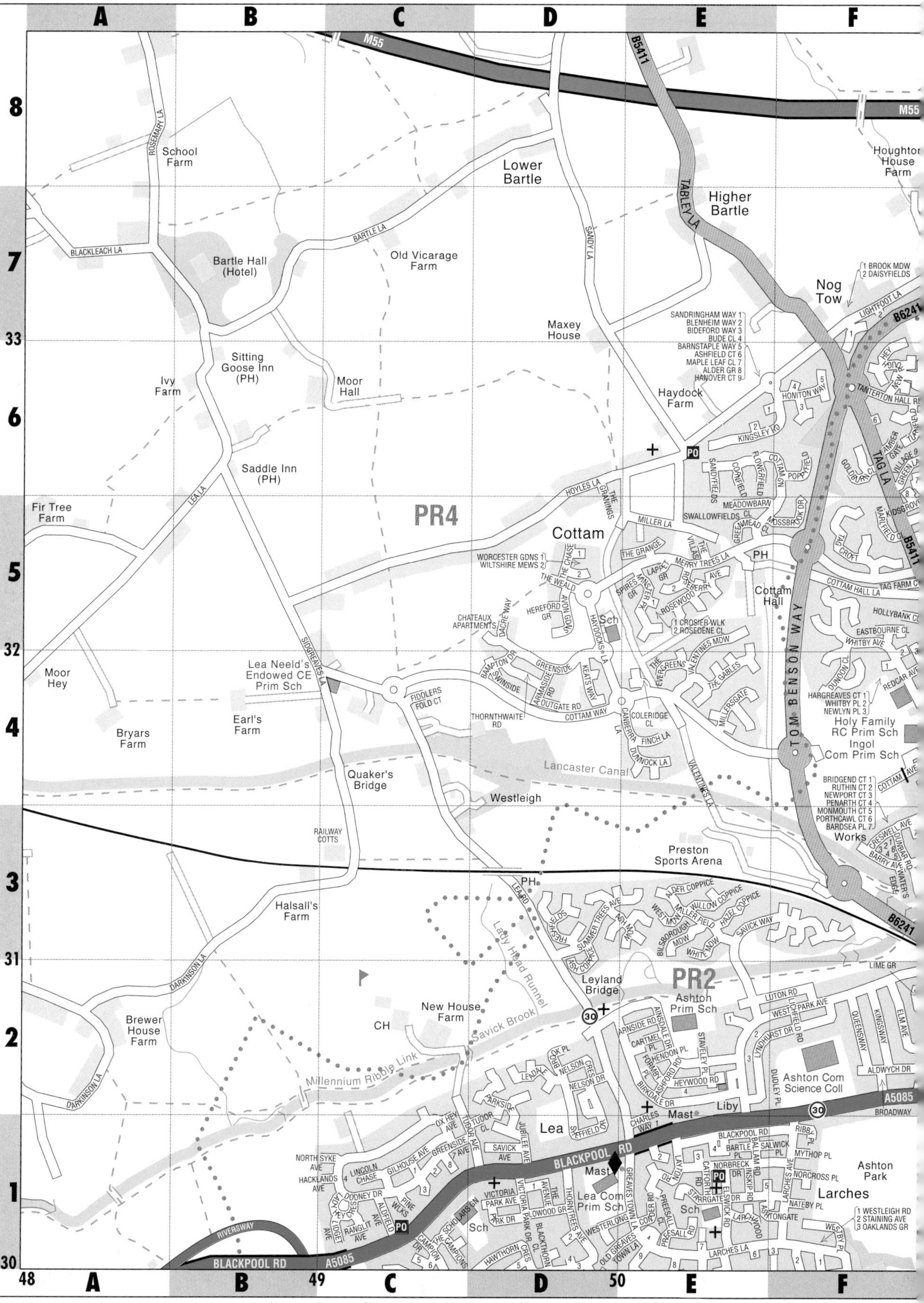
A
B
C
D
E
F
8
7
33
6
5
32
4
3
31
2
1
30
48
49
50
M55
B5411
School Farm
ROSEMARY LA
Lower Bartle
Higher Bartle
TABLEY LA
Houghton House Farm
BLACKLEACH LA
Bartle Hall (Hotel)
BARTLE LA
Old Vicarage Farm
SANDY LA
1 BROOK MDW
2 DAISYFIELDS
Nog Tow
LIGHTFOOT LA
B6241
Maxey House
Ivy Farm
Sitting Goose Inn (PH)
Moor Hall
SANDRINGHAM WAY 1
BLENHEIM WAY 2
BIDEFORD WAY 3
BUDE CL 4
BARNSTAPLE WAY 5
ASHFIELD CT 6
MAPLE LEAF CL 7
ALDER GR 8
HANOVER CT 9
Haydock Farm
HONITON WAY
KINGSLEY RD
TANTERTON HALL RD
TAG LA
Saddle Inn (PH)
PO
HOYLES LA
THE GRANINGS
SANDYFIELDS
CORNFIELD
FLOWERFIELD
COTTAM GN
POPPYFIELD
MEADOWBARN CL
SWALLOWFIELDS
GREENMEAD
MOSSBROOK DR
Fir Tree Farm
LEA LA
PR4
Cottam
MILLER LA
WORCESTER GDNS 1
WILTSHIRE MEWS 2
THE CHASE
THE GRANGE
THE VILLAS
MERRY TREES LA
PH
Cottam Hall
COTTAM HALL LA
TAG FARM CT
HOLLYBANK CL
EASTBOURNE CL
WHITBY AVE
THE WEALD
AVON GDNS
HEREFORD GR
CHATEAUX APARTMENTS
DACRE WAY
HAYDOCKS LA
Sch
ROSEWOOD AVE
1 CROSIER WLK
2 ROSEDENE CL
VALENTINES MDW
THE EVERGREENS
THE GABLES
MILLERSGATE
TOM BENSON WAY
Moor Hey
Lea Neeld's Endowed CE Prim Sch
SIDGREAVES LA
FIDDLERS FOLD CT
BAMPTON DR
SWINSIDE
GREENSIDE
ARMASIDE RD
KEATS WAY
OUTGATE RD
THORNTHWAITE RD
COTTAM WAY
COLERIDGE CL
CANBERRA LA
FINCH LA
DUNNOCK LA
HARGREAVES CT 1
WHITBY PL 2
NEWLYN PL 3
Holy Family RC Prim Sch
Ingol Com Prim Sch
REDCAR AVE
DUNOON CL
Bryars Farm
Earl's Farm
Quaker's Bridge
Lancaster Canal
Westleigh
VALENTINES LA
BRIDGEND CT 1
RUTHIN CT 2
NEWPORT CT 3
PENARTH CT 4
MONMOUTH CT 5
PORTHCAWL CT 6
BARDSEA PL 7
Works
COTTAM AVE
CRESWELL AVE
DUNBAR RD
BARRY AVE
RAILWAY COTTS
Preston Sports Arena
Halsall's Farm
PH
LEA RD
FRESHFIELDS
SUMMER TREES AVE
ASH MDW
ALDER COPPICE
WILLOW COPPICE
HAZEL COPPICE
MILLER FIELD
BILSBOROUGH MDW
WHITE MDW
SAVICK WAY
ASH COPPICE
B6241
Lady Head Runnel
DARKINSON LA
Leyland Bridge
PR2
Ashton Prim Sch
LIME GR
LUTON RD
WEST PARK AVE
LICHFIELD RD
QUEENSWAY
KINGSWAY
ELM AVE
Brewer House Farm
New House Farm
CH
Savick Brook
ARNSIDE RD
CARTMEL PL
AINSDALE DR
HENDON PL
FORMBY PL
STAVELEY PL
LYNDHURST DR
HEYWOOD RD
BIRKDALE DR
ASHFORD RD
DUDLEY PL
Ashton Com Science Coll
ALDWYCH DR
Millennium Ribble Link
NELSON CRES
NELSON DR
PARKSIDE
Lea
CHARLES WAY
Mast
Liby
A5085
BROADWAY
30
OX HEY AVE
TUDOR AVE
TUDOR CL
JUBILEE AVE
SAVICK AVE
GREENSIDE AVE
GILHOUSE AVE
LINCOLN CHASE
NORTH SYKE AVE
HACKLANDS AVE
DODNEY DR
BLACKPOOL RD
SAXFIELD DR
BLACKPOOL RD
BARTLE PL
BALLAM RD
SALWICK PL
RIBBY PL
MYTHOP PL
Ashton Park
Mast
VICTORIA PARK AVE
PARK DR
AVENUE THE
THORNPARK DR
LOWOOD GR
NORBRECK RD
INSKIP RD
CATFORTH RD
Lea Com Prim Sch
STARRGATE DR
NORCROSS PL
Larches
LARCHES AVE
NATEBY PL
Sch
ELSWICK RD
LARCHWOOD
ASHTONGATE
WESTBY PL
1 WESTLEIGH RD
2 STAINING AVE
3 OAKLANDS GR
RIVERSWAY
BLACKPOOL RD
A5085
PINE WLKS
ALDFIELD AVE
RANGLIT AVE
CAMPION DR
THE CAMPIONS
THE SCHOLARS GN
VICTORIA PARK DR
BLACKTHORN CL
HAWTHORN CRES
WESTERLONG
GREAVES TOWN LA
OLD GREAVES TOWN LA
CONDER RD
PREESALL CL
PREESALL RD
LAYTON RD
LARCHES LA
PO

C1
1 FULFORD AVE
2 ROSEBANK
3 MAPLEBANK
4 WHITELENS AVE
5 PARKFIELD CL
6 PARKFIELD CRES
7 HARDWEN AVE
8 WALNEY CL

D1
1 THE CRESCENT
2 HOLMFIELD CRES
3 THORNPARK DR
4 WHITETHORN SQ
5 DAISY CROFT

E1
1 CHARLESWAY CT
2 THE PLOUGHLANDS
3 WHITEHOLME PL
4 WEETON PL
5 ROSEACRE PL
6 THE WOODLANDS
7 ALDCLIFFE RD
8 FORTON RD
9 THURNHAM RD

E2
1 GREENDALE MEWS
2 EXETER PL
3 DOWNHAM PL
4 NEWARK PL

115
95

D3
1 ST CUTHBERT'S CL
2 DOUGLAS CT
3 LAWRENCE ST
4 FOWLER ST

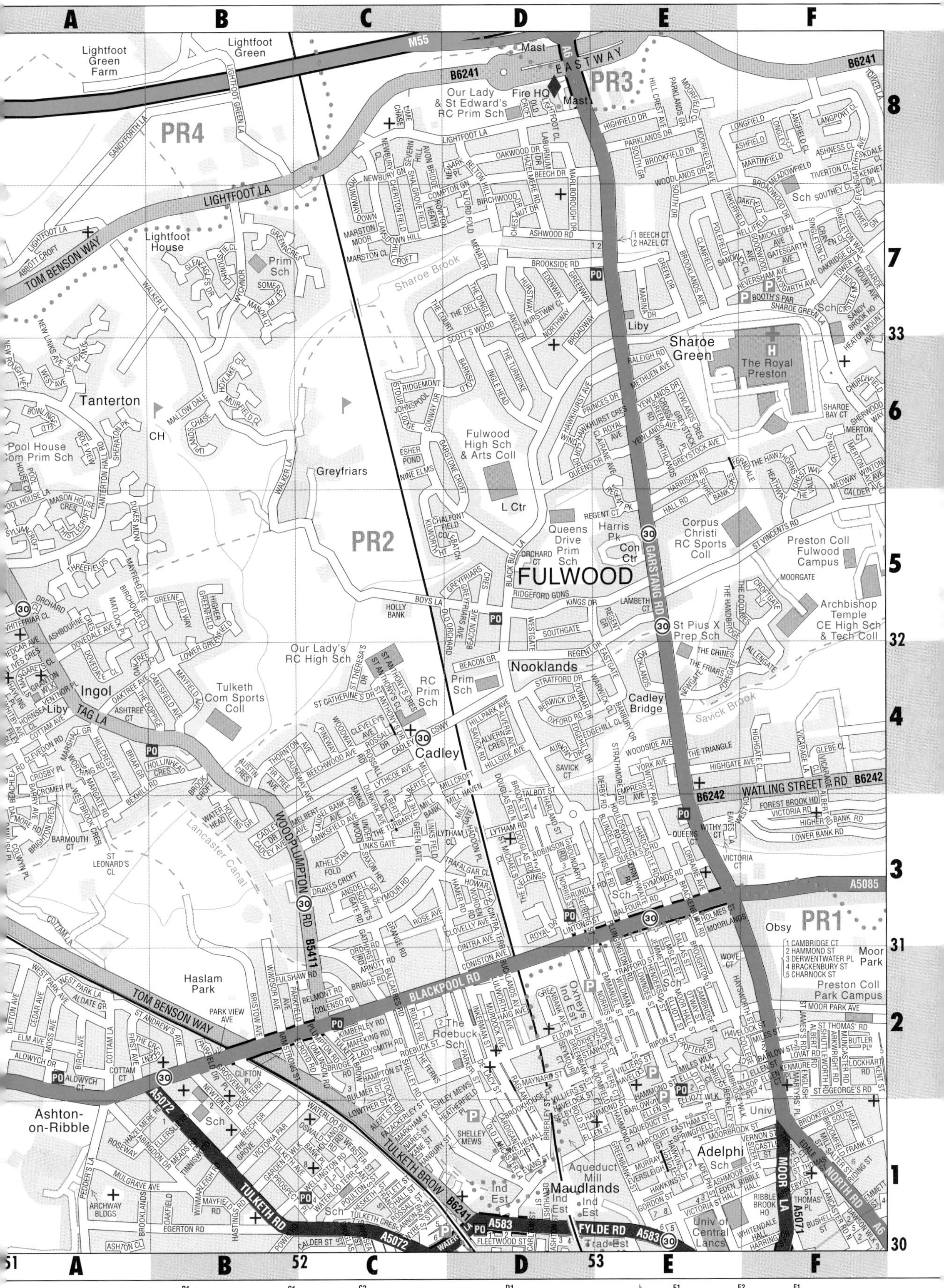


B1
1 WHINNY CLOUGH CT
2 NEWTON CT

C1
1 THRELFALL ST
2 BRAMPTON ST
3 ELTON ST
4 BRUNSWICK PL
5 PECHELL ST
6 BLANCHE ST
7 HIGHBANK HOTEL
8 GARDEN CT

C2
1 DORMAN CL
2 ATHERTON CL
3 HUNNIBALL CT



D1
1 NEWSHAM ST
2 BATH ST
3 MALTHOUSE CT
4 THE MALTHOUSE



E1
1 ADELPHI HO
2 HEYSHAM ST
3 DERWENT HALL
4 DOUGLAS HALL
5 TOWN BROOK HO
6 GREENBANK PL
7 THE WAREHOUSE
8 FOUNDRY CT
9 Springfield Ind Est

E2
1 OXHEYS CT
2 ALMELO HO

F1
1 SHELDON CT
2 AUGHTON WLK
3 BECKETT CT
4 HANOVER ST
5 FISH ST
6 Preston Ent Ctr

117
138

117
97

**A1**
1 MEADOW BROOK HO
2 SHAW ST
3 TURNER ST
4 CROMWELL ST
5 ALICE SQ
6 ALEXANDRA PAVILIONS
7 ROYAL BROOK HO
8 ELIZABETH SQ
9 ALBERT TERR
10 EDWARD SQ
11 STAFFORD RD

**B1**
1 ISHERWOOD ST
2 STRUTT ST
3 BULLFINCH ST
4 GRAHAM ST
5 DEEPDALE HO

**C1**
1 ST JOSEPH'S TERR
2 HERMON ST
3 ANSDELL ST
4 POYNTER ST
5 HOLMAN ST
6 GILLETT ST
7 CURWEN ST
8 WIGNALL ST
9 ST LUKE'S PL
10 ALEXANDRA HO

**D1**
1 ASHELDON ST
2 BRADDON ST
3 BEENLAND ST
4 TUNBRIDGE ST
5 SALISBURY ST
6 CALVERLEY ST
7 TUNBRIDGE PL
8 TRURO PL
9 WELLS ST
10 GRIMSARGH ST
11 CANTERBURY RD
12 LEVENS ST

**E1**
1 HAWARDEN RD
2 CAVENDISH RD
3 IDDESLEIGH RD
4 MANNING RD

**F3**
1 AINSCOUGH BROOK HO
2 RIBBLETON HALL CRES

**F4**
1 LAUDERDALE CRES
2 EDLESTON LODGE
3 LEICESTER LODGE
4 HOLLAND LODGE
5 ROTHWELL LODGE
6 BIRCHALL LODGE
7 ELSTON LODGE
8 TRAVERS LODGE
9 SHERBORNE LODGE
10 BEACON LODGE
11 SADDLE LODGE
12 HAZELHURST LODGE
13 GEOFFREY LODGE
14 LONGRIDGE LODGE
15 HOLMEHOUSE LODGE

139
120

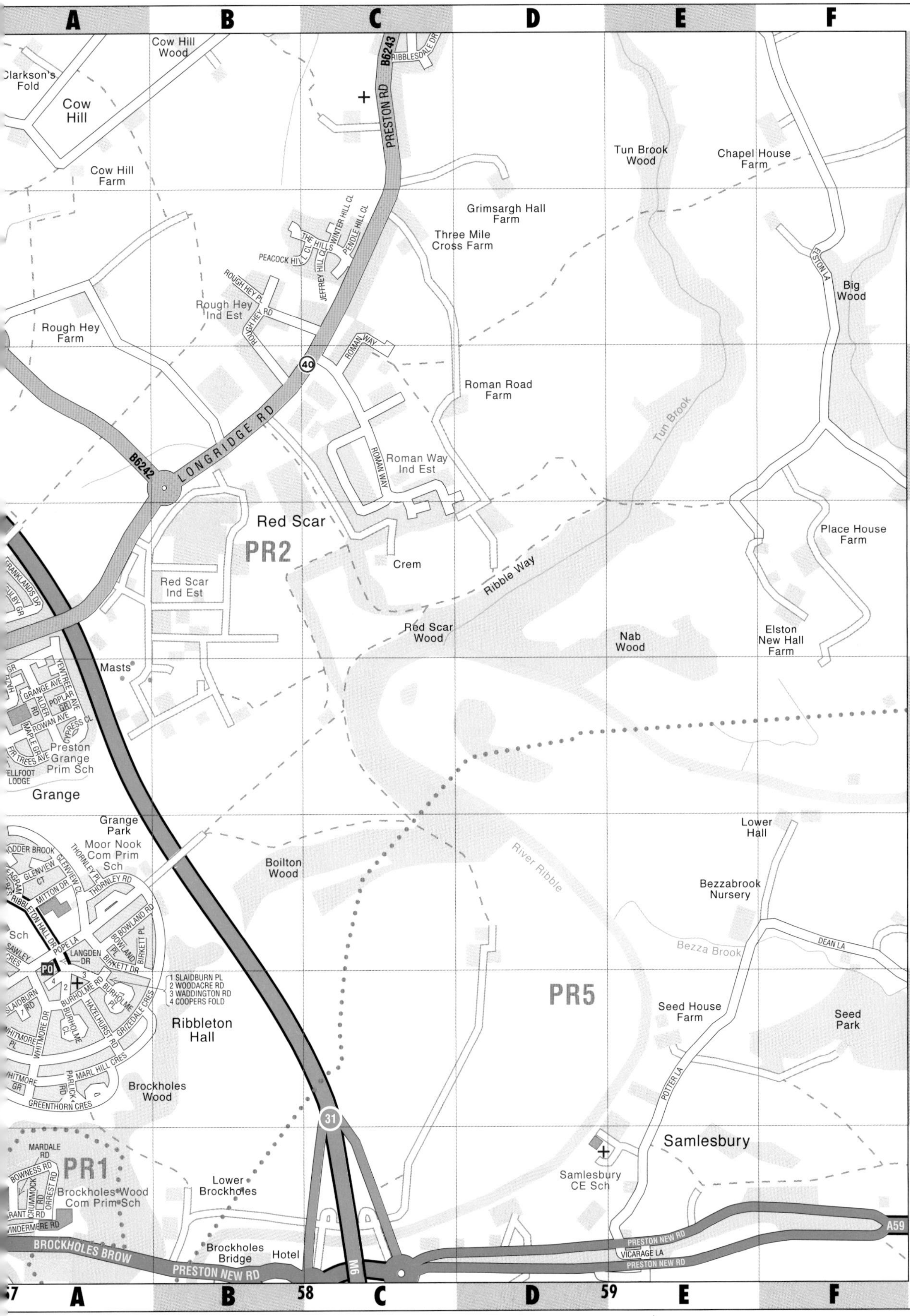


98
120

119 140

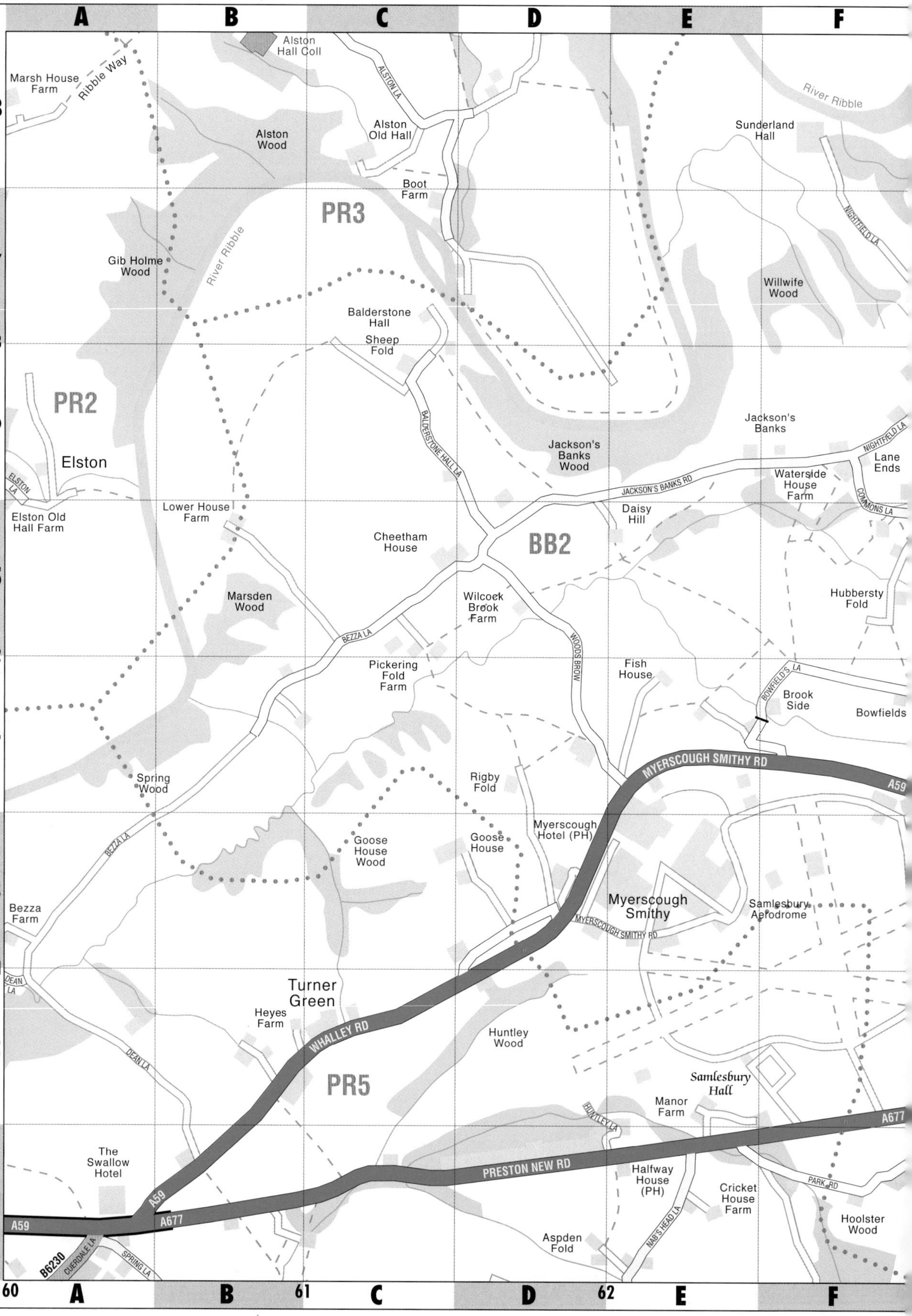
A
B
C
D
E
F
8
7
33
6
5
32
4
3
31
2
1
30
60
61
62
Alston Hall Coll
Marsh House Farm
Ribble Way
ALSTON LA
River Ribble
Sunderland Hall
Alston Wood
Alston Old Hall
Boot Farm
PR3
NIGHTFIELD LA
Gib Holme Wood
River Ribble
Willwife Wood
Balderstone Hall
Sheep Fold
PR2
Elston
BALDERSTONE HALL LA
Jackson's Banks
Jackson's Banks Wood
NIGHTFIELD LA
Lane Ends
ELSTON LA
Waterside House Farm
JACKSON'S BANKS RD
COMMONS LA
Elston Old Hall Farm
Lower House Farm
Daisy Hill
Cheetham House
BB2
Marsden Wood
Wilcock Brook Farm
Hubbersty Fold
BEZZA LA
WOODS BROW
Pickering Fold Farm
Fish House
BOWFIELD'S LA
Brook Side
Bowfields
MYERSCOUGH SMITHY RD
A59
Spring Wood
Rigby Fold
Goose House Wood
Goose House
Myerscough Hotel (PH)
BEZZA LA
Myerscough Smithy
Samlesbury Aerodrome
Bezza Farm
MYERSCOUGH SMITHY RD
DEAN LA
Turner Green
Heyes Farm
WHALLEY RD
Huntley Wood
DEAN LA
Samlesbury Hall
PR5
Manor Farm
HUNTLEY LA
A677
The Swallow Hotel
PRESTON NEW RD
Halfway House (PH)
Cricket House Farm
PARK RD
A59
A59
A677
NAB'S HEAD LA
Hoolster Wood
Aspden Fold
B6230
CUERDALE LA
SPRING LA

119 99

141
122

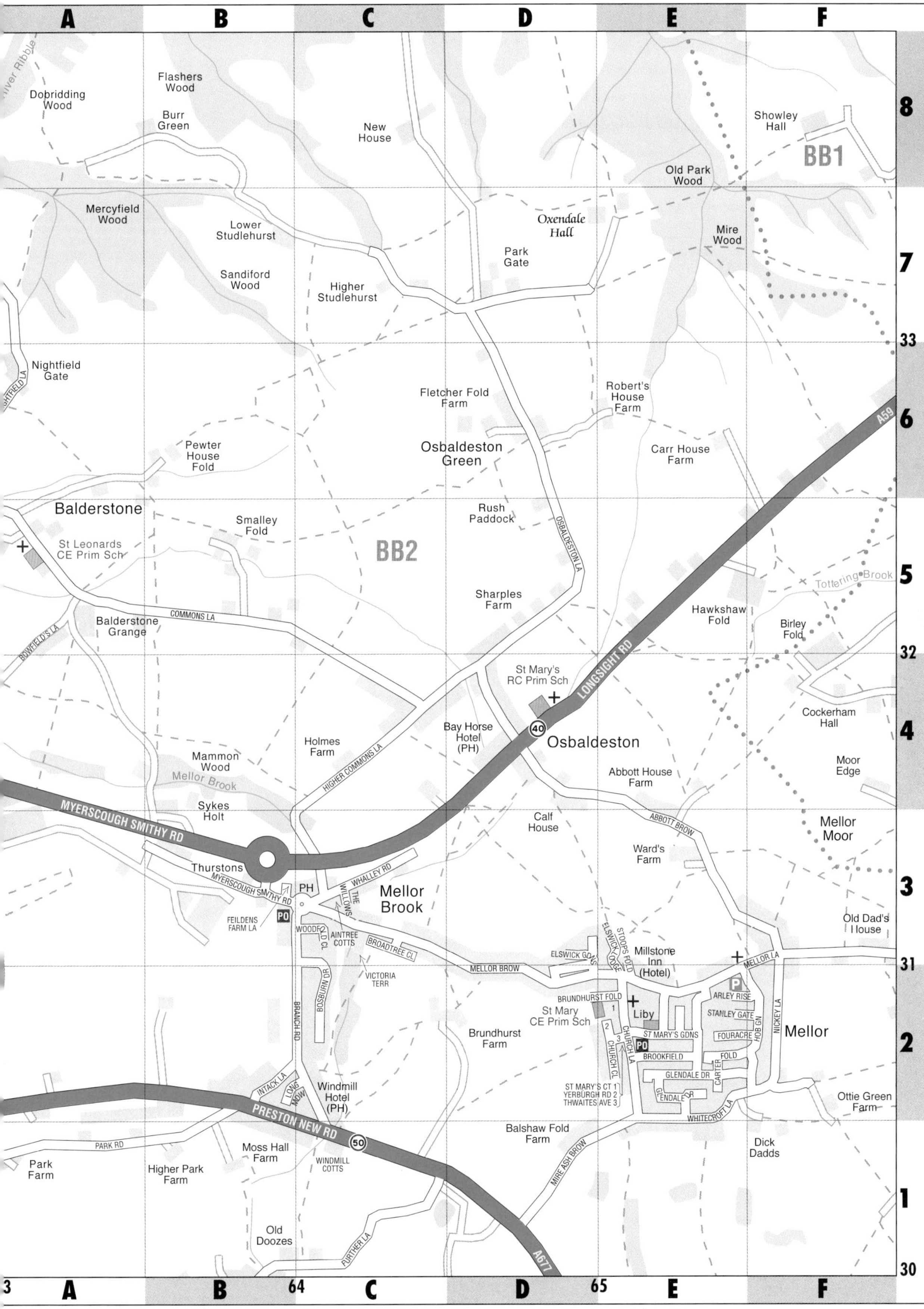


100
122

121
142

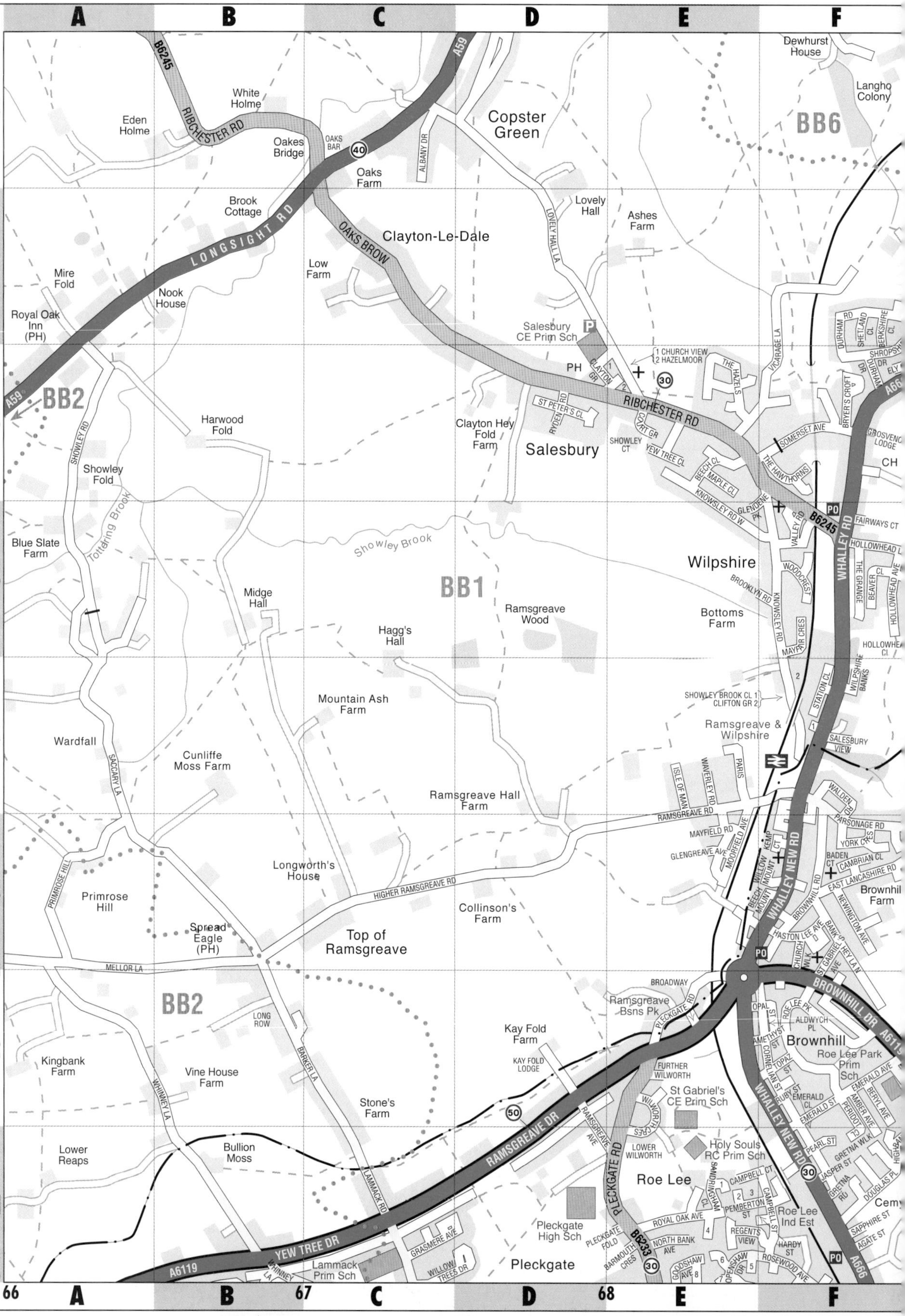


121
101

E1
1 BLENHEIM CL
2 OUTRAM LA
3 HAYDOCK ST
4 CHATSWORTH CL
5 THORNWOOD CL
6 PENSHAW CL
7 HILL VIEW
8 GOODSHAW CL

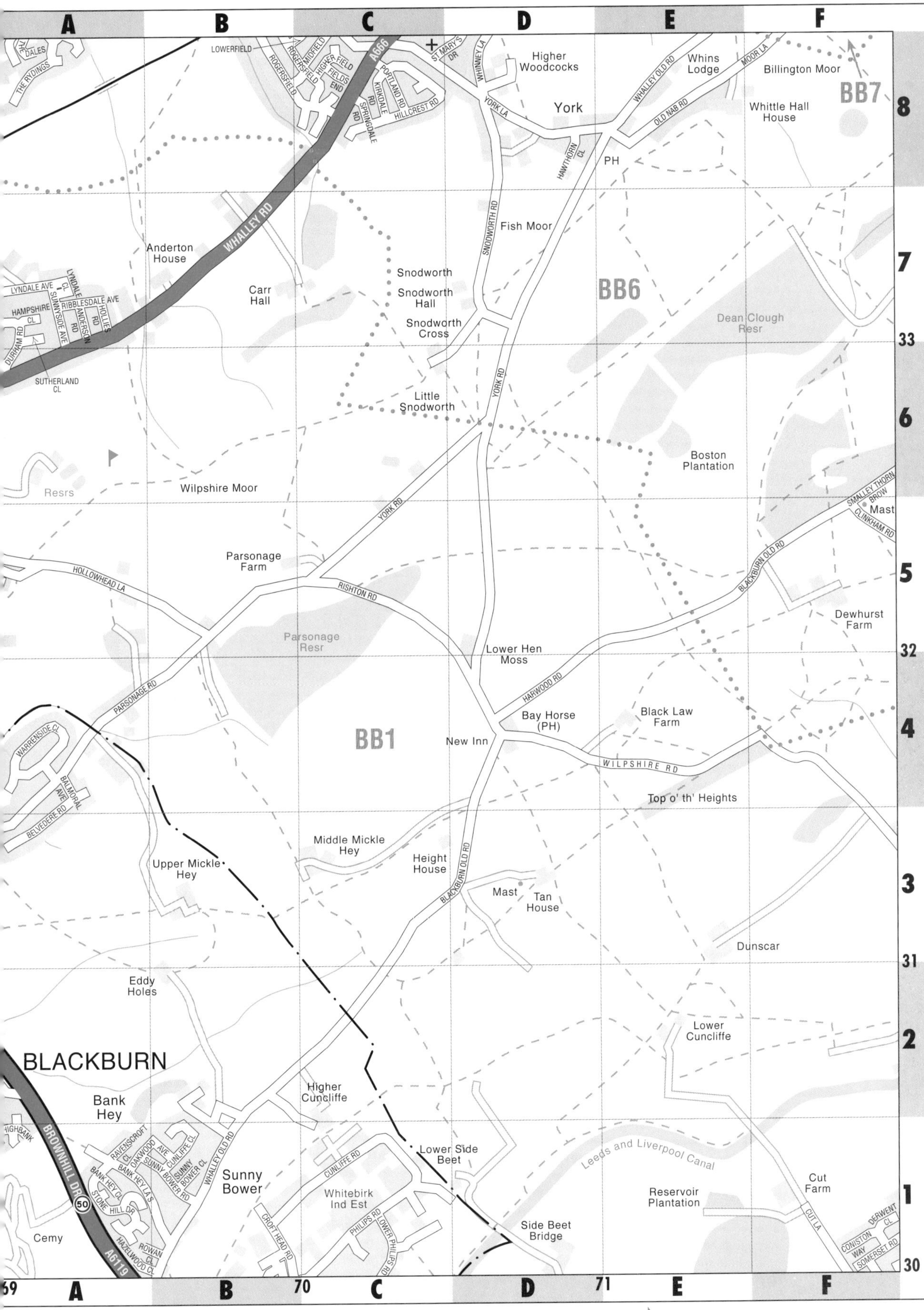
A
B
C
D
E
F
8
7
6
5
4
3
2
1
33
32
31
30
69
70
71
BB7
BB6
BB1
BLACKBURN
York
Higher Woodcocks
Whins Lodge
Billington Moor
Whittle Hall House
PH
Fish Moor
Anderton House
Carr Hall
Snodworth
Snodworth Hall
Snodworth Cross
Little Snodworth
Dean Clough Resr
Boston Plantation
Resrs
Wilpshire Moor
Parsonage Farm
Parsonage Resr
Mast
Dewhurst Farm
Lower Hen Moss
Bay Horse (PH)
Black Law Farm
New Inn
Top o' th' Heights
Middle Mickle Hey
Upper Mickle Hey
Height House
Tan House
Dunscar
Eddy Holes
Lower Cuncliffe
Higher Cuncliffe
Bank Hey
Sunny Bower
Lower Side Beet
Whitebirk Ind Est
Reservoir Plantation
Cut Farm
Side Beet Bridge
Cemy
Leeds and Liverpool Canal
WHALLEY RD
A666
YORK LA
YORK RD
SNODWORTH RD
RISHTON RD
HOLLOWHEAD LA
PARSONAGE RD
HARWOOD RD
WILPSHIRE RD
BLACKBURN OLD RD
WHALLEY OLD RD
OLD NAB RD
MOOR LA
BROWNHILL DR
A6119
CUT LA
CUNLIFFE RD
CROFT HEAD RD
PHILIPS RD
LOWER PHILIPS RD
SMALLEY THORN BROW
CLINKHAM RD
CONISTON WAY
SOMERSET RD
DERWENT CL
LOWERFIELD
ROGERSFIELD
MIDFIELD
HIGHER FIELD
FIELDS END
PORTLAND RD
KIRKDALE RD
SPRINGDALE RD
HILLCREST RD
ST MARY'S DR
WHINNEY LA
HAWTHORN CL
THE DALES
THE RYDINGS
LYNDALE AVE
LYNDALE CL
HAMPSHIRE CL
SUNNYSIDE AVE
RIBBLESDALE AVE
ANDERSON RD
HOLLIES RD
DURHAM RD
SUTHERLAND CL
WARRENSIDE CL
BALMORAL AVE
BELVEDERE RD
RAVENSCROFT CL
OAKWOOD AVE
CUNLIFFE CL
SUNNY BOWER RD
SUNNY BOWER CL
BANK HEY CL
BANK HEY LA S
STONE HILL DR
ROWAN CL
HAZELWOOD CL
HIGHBANK
50

123
144

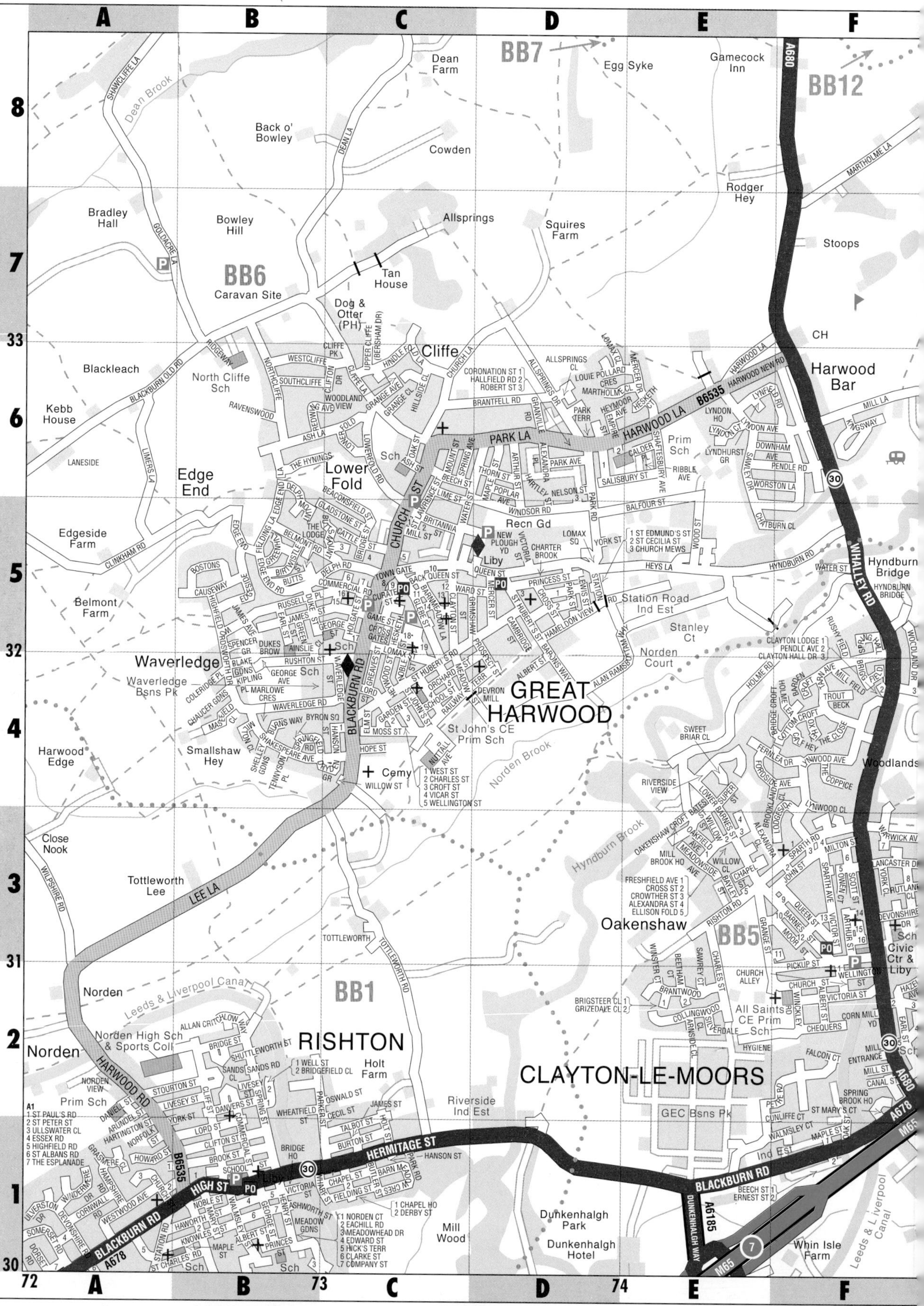
A
B
C
D
E
F
8
7
33
6
5
32
4
3
31
2
1
30
72
73
74
BB7
BB12
BB6
BB1
BB5
Dean Farm
Egg Syke
Gamecock Inn
Back o' Bowley
Cowden
Rodger Hey
Bradley Hall
Bowley Hill
Allsprings
Squires Farm
Stoops
Tan House
Caravan Site
Dog & Otter (PH)
Cliffe
Harwood Bar
Blackleach
North Cliffe Sch
Kebb House
Edge End
Lower Fold
Edgeside Farm
Recn Gd
Liby
Hyndburn Bridge
Belmont Farm
Station Road Ind Est
Stanley Ct
Norden Court
Waverledge
Waverledge Bsns Pk
GREAT HARWOOD
St John's CE Prim Sch
Harwood Edge
Smallshaw Hey
Cemy
Woodlands
Close Nook
Tottleworth Lee
Oakenshaw
Civic Ctr & Liby
Norden
Norden High Sch & Sports Coll
RISHTON
Holt Farm
All Saints CE Prim Sch
CLAYTON-LE-MOORS
Riverside Ind Est
GEC Bsns Pk
Mill Wood
Dunkenhalgh Park
Dunkenhalgh Hotel
Whin Isle Farm
Leeds & Liverpool Canal
Hyndburn Brook
Norden Brook
Dean Brook
PARK LA
HARWOOD LA
B6535
WHALLEY RD
A680
LEE LA
HARWOOD RD
HERMITAGE ST
BLACKBURN RD
A678
HIGH ST
M65
A6185
DUNKENHALGH WAY
CHURCH ST
BLACKBURN OLD RD
A1
1 ST PAUL'S RD
2 ST PETER ST
3 ULLSWATER CL
4 ESSEX RD
5 HIGHFIELD RD
6 ST ALBANS RD
7 THE ESPLANADE

C5
1 HAYDOCK SQ
2 FRANKLIN AINSWORTH HO
3 DELPH CT
4 SOUTH VIEW
5 BACK CHURCH ST
6 BRIDGE ST
7 EDWARD ST
8 TOWN HALL SQ
9 TOWN HALL ST
10 JOINERS ALLEY
11 LOYND ST
12 COMMERCIAL ST
13 NETHERTON HO
14 WESTWELL ST
15 KING ST
16 WESLEY CT
17 NOWELL ST
18 WALMSLEY ST
19 SEGAR ST

123
103

F2
1 BARNES SQ
2 GRIMSHAW ST
3 HAZEL GR
4 TALBOT AVE
5 KING ST
6 BURNLEY RD

F3
1 STOPFORD CT
2 BRANCH RD
3 FRANCIS ST
4 ANN ST
5 JACKSON ST
6 DRYDEN ST
7 NORFOLK CL
8 GLOUCESTER AVE
9 ALMA ST
10 DANIEL ST
11 FORT ST
12 JAMES ST
13 GEORGE ST
14 NEW CHURCH CL
15 BACK ARTHUR ST
16 MERCER ST

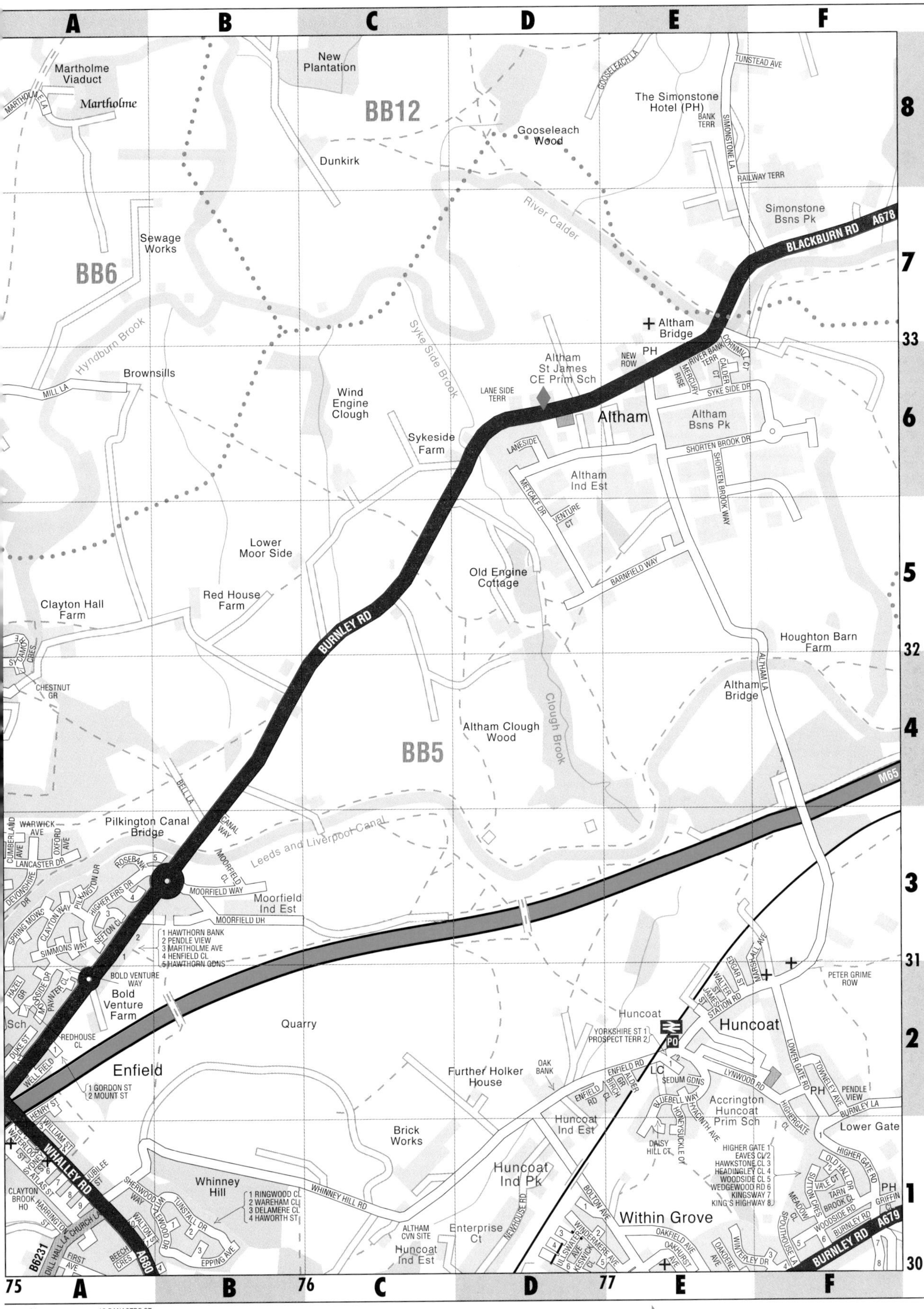
Martholme Viaduct
Martholme
MARTHOLME LA
New Plantation
BB12
Dunkirk
Gooseleach Wood
GOOSELEACH LA
The Simonstone Hotel (PH)
BANK TERR
SIMONSTONE LA
TUNSTEAD AVE
RAILWAY TERR
Simonstone Bsns Pk
BLACKBURN RD
A678
River Calder
Sewage Works
BB6
Hyndburn Brook
Brownsills
MILL LA
Syke Side Brook
Wind Engine Clough
Sykeside Farm
Altham Bridge
NEW ROW
PH
LANE SIDE TERR
Altham St James CE Prim Sch
Altham
Altham Bsns Pk
SYKE SIDE DR
SHORTEN BROOK DR
SHORTEN BROOK WAY
LANESIDE
Altham Ind Est
METCALF DR
VENTURE CT
BARNFIELD WAY
Lower Moor Side
Red House Farm
Old Engine Cottage
Clayton Hall Farm
BURNLEY RD
Houghton Barn Farm
CHESTNUT GR
Altham Bridge
ALTHAM LA
Altham Clough Wood
Clough Brook
BB5
BELL LA
M65
WARWICK AVE
Pilkington Canal Bridge
CANAL WAY
Leeds and Liverpool Canal
LANCASTER DR
ROSEBANK
MOORFIELD WAY
MOORFIELD CL
Moorfield Ind Est
MOORFIELD DR
1 HAWTHORN BANK
2 PENDLE VIEW
3 MARTHOLME AVE
4 HENFIELD CL
5 HAWTHORN GDNS
SIMMONS WAY
BOLD VENTURE WAY
Bold Venture Farm
Quarry
Huncoat
YORKSHIRE ST 1
PROSPECT TERR 2
PO
Huncoat
PETER GRIME ROW
REDHOUSE CL
Enfield
1 GORDON ST
2 MOUNT ST
Further Holker House
OAK BANK
ENFIELD RD
LC
SEDUM GDNS
LYNWOOD RD
Accrington Huncoat Prim Sch
PH
PENDLE VIEW
BURNLEY LA
Lower Gate
WHALLEY RD
Brick Works
Huncoat Ind Est
DAISY HILL CT
HIGHER GATE 1
EAVES CL 2
HAWKSTONE CL 3
HEADINGLEY CL 4
WOODSIDE CL 5
WEDGEWOOD RD 6
KINGSWAY 7
KING'S HIGHWAY 8
Whinney Hill
1 RINGWOOD CL
2 WAREHAM CL
3 DELAMERE CL
4 HAWORTH ST
WHINNEY HILL RD
Huncoat Ind Pk
Within Grove
PH
ALTHAM CVN SITE
Enterprise Ct
Huncoat Ind Est
BURNLEY RD
A679
EPPING AVE
B6231
A680
75
76
77
A
B
C
D
E
F
8
7
33
6
5
32
4
3
31
2
1
30

A1
1 CLAYTON ST
2 READ ST
3 HILL ST
4 FRANK ST
5 MERCER HO
6 MELBOURNE ST
7 ADELAIDE ST
8 BRISBANE ST
9 WHINFIELD ST
10 BANASTRE ST
11 HALLAM ST



D1
1 HAWESWATER RD
2 THIRLMERE CL
3 LANGDALE CL
4 BORROWDALE CL
5 RYDAL CL
6 WITHIN GR

B8
1 DOUBLE ROW
2 NEW ST
3 HOLLAND ST
4 ARBORIES AVE
5 VICARAGE AVE

125

C8
1 ECCLESHILL ST
2 DARWEN ST
3 CLITHEROE ST
4 SOWERBY ST
5 HANSON BLDGS
6 SHUTTLEWORTH ST

146

C8
7 BACK SHUTTLEWORTH ST
8 DRAGON ST
9 INKERMAN ST
10 BACK ALBERT ST
11 PARISH ST
12 DAME FOLD

D8
1 MORLEY ST
2 TATTERSALL ST
3 WADDINGTON ST
4 ST JAMES PL
5 BACK ALTHAM ST
6 ALTHAM ST
7 HAPTON ST
8 WESLEY ST
9 CROSS BANK
10 HAMBLEDON ST
11 PITT ST
12 HOPE ST

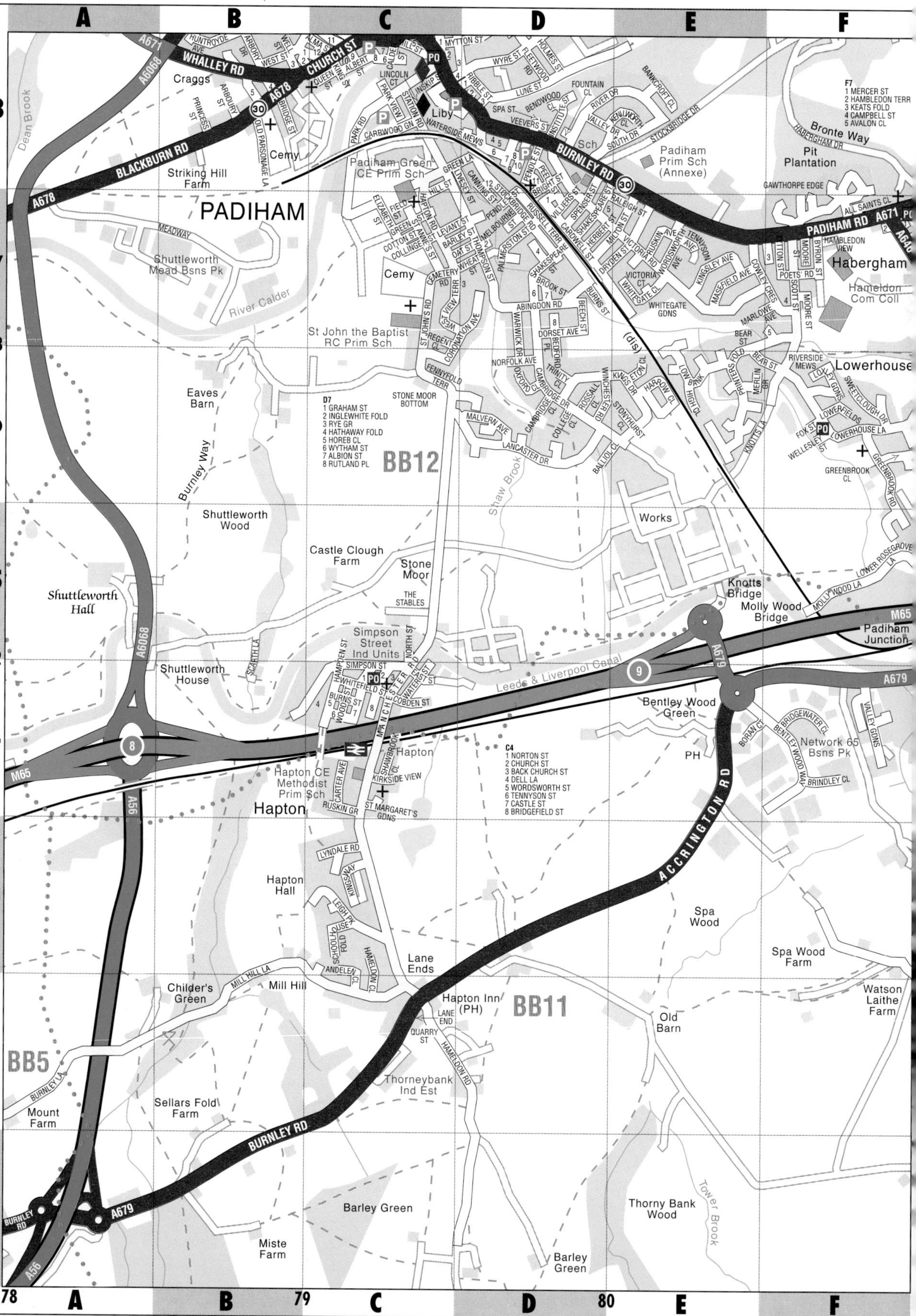

A
B
C
D
E
F
8
7
6
5
4
3
2
1
33
32
31
30
78
79
80
PADIHAM
WHALLEY RD
CHURCH ST
BLACKBURN RD
BURNLEY RD
PADIHAM RD
Craggs
Cemy
Striking Hill Farm
Shuttleworth Mead Bsns Pk
River Calder
Dean Brook
Padiham Green CE Prim Sch
St John the Baptist RC Prim Sch
Liby
Sch
Padiham Prim Sch (Annexe)
Bronte Way
Pit Plantation
Habergham
Hameldon Com Coll
Lowerhouse
F7
1 MERCER ST
2 HAMBLEDON TERR
3 KEATS FOLD
4 CAMPBELL ST
5 AVALON CL
D7
1 GRAHAM ST
2 INGLEWHITE FOLD
3 RYE GR
4 HATHAWAY FOLD
5 HOREB CL
6 WYTHAM ST
7 ALBION ST
8 RUTLAND PL
BB12
Eaves Barn
Burnley Way
Shuttleworth Wood
Castle Clough Farm
Stone Moor
THE STABLES
Shuttleworth Hall
Works
Knotts Bridge
Molly Wood Bridge
Padiham Junction
M65
A679
A6068
A56
A678
A671
Simpson Street Ind Units
Shuttleworth House
Leeds & Liverpool Canal
Bentley Wood Green
Network 65 Bsns Pk
Hapton
Hapton CE Methodist Prim Sch
C4
1 NORTON ST
2 CHURCH ST
3 BACK CHURCH ST
4 DELL LA
5 WORDSWORTH ST
6 TENNYSON ST
7 CASTLE ST
8 BRIDGEFIELD ST
ACCRINGTON RD
Hapton Hall
Spa Wood
Spa Wood Farm
Lane Ends
Childer's Green
Mill Hill
Hapton Inn (PH)
BB11
Old Barn
Watson Laithe Farm
BB5
Thorneybank Ind Est
Mount Farm
Sellars Fold Farm
BURNLEY RD
Barley Green
Thorny Bank Wood
Tower Brook
Miste Farm


125
105

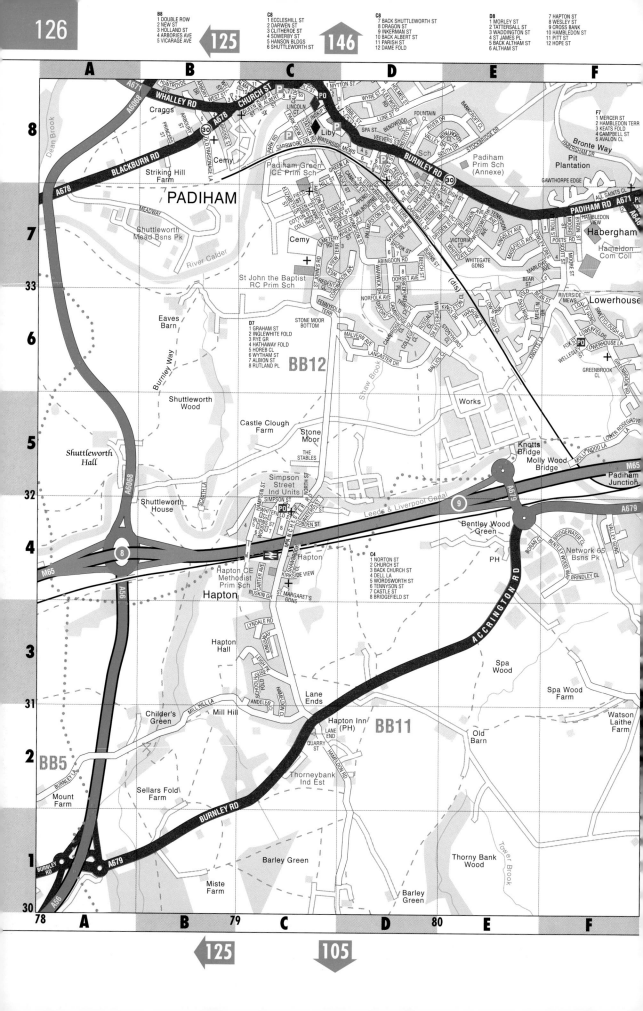

C6
1 IVORY ST
2 FRANKLIN ST
3 AINSLIE ST
4 WHITE BULL ST
5 ST JOHN'S RD
6 ST JOHN'S CT
7 COULTATE ST
8 CONISTON ST
9 BIRCHFIELD MEWS

C7
1 IGHTENHILL PK MEWS
2 ROMFORD ST
3 QUARRY BANK ST
4 LARK ST

D6
1 BROUGHTON ST
2 PLOVER VIEW
3 PADIHAM RD
4 BREAD ST
5 MONMOUTH ST
6 PENISTONE ST
7 HORACE ST

D7
1 EDGELEY CT
2 HUNTROYDE CL
3 WHEATLEY CL
4 COVERDALE WAY
5 WESLEY GR
6 GREENGATE CL
7 ARUNDE CL

E6
1 WAVERLEY ST
2 SOUTHEY ST
3 DUCKETT ST
4 Burnham Trad Pk
5 CRANMER ST
6 TRINITY TWRS
7 HOPWOOD ST

147

F6
1 SYDNEY ST
2 Westgate Trad Ctr
3 FOUNDRY ST
4 ROYLE RD
5 BLACKBURN ST

128

F6
6 ORCHARD BRIDGE
7 VEEVERS ST
8 GAS ST
9 BRICK ST
10 CURZON ST
11 PARADISE ST
12 COAL ST
13 ST JAMES'S ROW
14 HARGREAVES ST
15 TANNER ST
16 FREE TRADE ST
17 MEADOW ST
18 SUTCLIFFE ST
19 CANAL ST

B6
1 SNOWDEN ST
2 WHITE ST
3 OLD SCHOOL ROW
4 THE GROVE
5 ALLENDALE St
6 ALLENDALE CT

C5
1 HOMER ST
2 HARTLEY ST
3 WOODPECKER HILL
4 NIGHTINGALE CRES
5 SANDPIPER SQ
6 SWALLOW PK

D5
1 WOODTOP
2 HARCOURT ST
3 CAMBRIDGE ST
4 GROVE ST
5 PALM ST

106

E5
1 ELLIS ST
2 PICCADILLY SQ
3 SEFTON TERR
4 SEFTON AVE
5 AUSTIN ST
6 WILLIS ST
7 WHITEHAVEN ST
8 ALWIN ST
9 ST MATTHEW'S CT

128

E5
10 ABBEYFIELD HO
11 PRINCE ST

F5
1 VICTORIA ST
2 YORKE ST
3 MOUNT PLEASANT ST
4 PLEASANT PL
5 ST PAUL'S CT
6 STANLEY ST
7 THORNEY BANK ST
8 DENT ROW
9 ESCAR ST
10 SACKVILLE ST
11 ALBION TERR

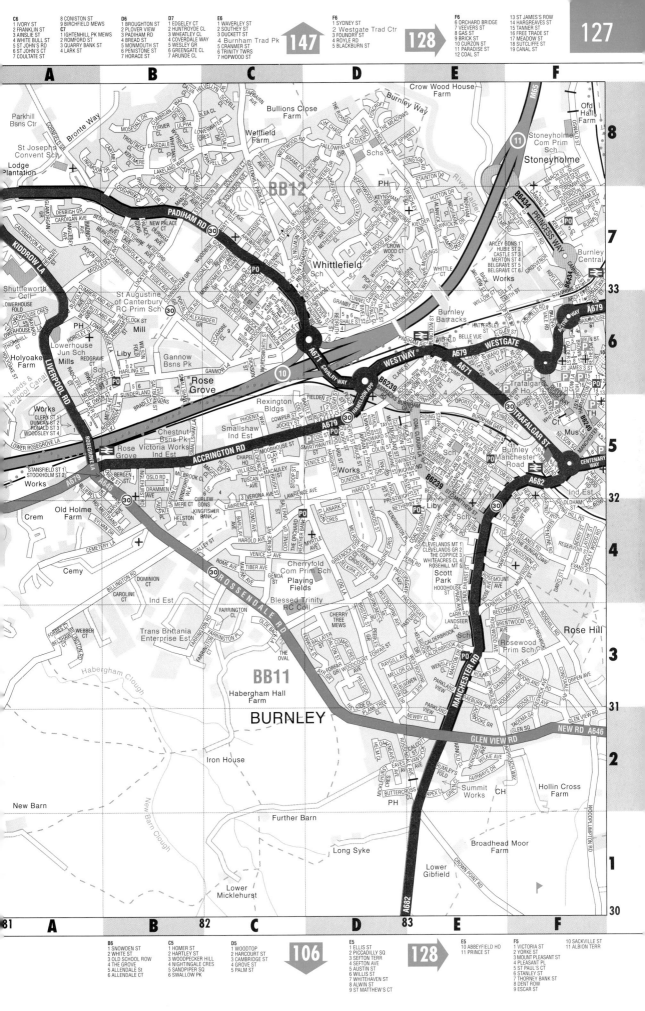

A6
1 Anchor Ret Pk
2 THE STACKHOUSES
3 CHANCERY WLK
4 HOWE WLK
5 MARKET PROM
6 FLEET WLK
7 ST JAMES LA
8 St Peter's Ctr
9 BROWN SQ

A8
1 NICHOLL ST
2 ALTHAM ST
3 LEE GREEN ST

127

A8
4 BOOTH CT
5 BARRETT ST
6 JACKSON ST
7 BUTLER ST
8 TROUT ST
9 CLEGG ST E

148

A8
10 BELLS ARC
11 ESCOTT GDNS
12 HEBREW SQ
13 BOND ST
14 GRANVILLE ST

B5
1 TOWNFIELDS
2 ANNE ST
3 WELLINGTON CT
4 CHAPELSIDE
5 MARY ST
6 ANNE CL
7 HOLMES SQ
8 HOLLY HO
9 OXFORD PL

127
107

149

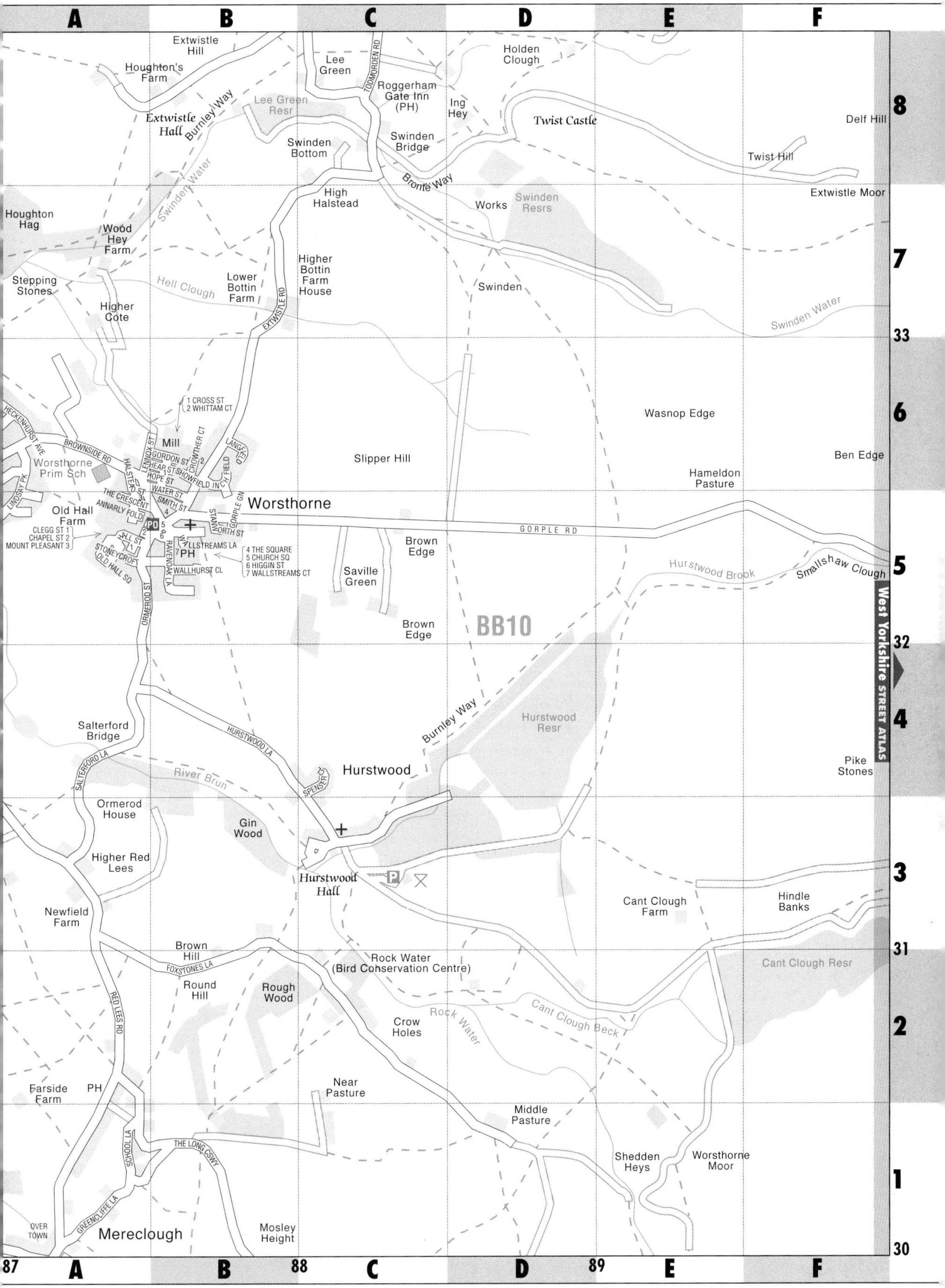

A
B
C
D
E
F
Extwistle Hill
Houghton's Farm
Lee Green
TODMORDEN RD
Holden Clough
Roggerham Gate Inn (PH)
Ing Hey
Lee Green Resr
Extwistle Hall
Burnley Way
Twist Castle
Delf Hill
8
Swinden Bottom
Swinden Bridge
Twist Hill
Swinden Water
Bronte Way
High Halstead
Extwistle Moor
Houghton Hag
Works
Swinden Resrs
Wood Hey Farm
7
Higher Bottin Farm House
Stepping Stones
Lower Bottin Farm
Hell Clough
Swinden
Higher Cote
EXTWISTLE RD
Swinden Water
33
1 CROSS ST
2 WHITTAM CT
HECKENHURST AVE
Wasnop Edge
6
Mill
BROWNSIDE RD
LENNOX ST
GORDON ST
CROWTHER CT
LANGFIELD
Worsthorne Prim Sch
Slipper Hill
Ben Edge
HALSTEAD ST
HEAP ST
SHOWFIELD
HOPE ST
FINCH FIELD
Hameldon Pasture
LINDSAY PK
THE CRESCENT
WATER ST
SMITH ST
GORPLE GN
Worsthorne
Old Hall Farm
ANNARLY FOLD
PO
STANWORTH ST
GORPLE RD
CLEGG ST 1
CHAPEL ST 2
MOUNT PLEASANT 3
STONEYCROFT
WALLSTREAMS LA
4 THE SQUARE
5 CHURCH SQ
6 HIGGIN ST
7 WALLSTREAMS CT
Brown Edge
OLD HALL SQ
PH
RAVENOAK LA
WALLHURST CL
Saville Green
Hurstwood Brook
Smallshaw Clough
5
ORMEROD ST
Brown Edge
BB10
West Yorkshire STREET ATLAS
32
Burnley Way
4
Salterford Bridge
HURSTWOOD LA
Hurstwood Resr
SALTERFORD LA
River Brun
SPENSER CT
Hurstwood
Pike Stones
Ormerod House
Gin Wood
Higher Red Lees
Hurstwood Hall
P
3
Cant Clough Farm
Hindle Banks
Newfield Farm
Brown Hill
31
FOXSTONES LA
Rock Water (Bird Conservation Centre)
Cant Clough Resr
Round Hill
Rough Wood
RED LEES RD
Crow Holes
Rock Water
Cant Clough Beck
2
Near Pasture
Farside Farm
PH
Middle Pasture
SCHOOL LA
THE LONG CSWY
Shedden Heys
Worsthorne Moor
1
GREENCLIFFE LA
OVER TOWN
Mereclough
Mosley Height
30
87
88
89


108

C6
1 HENTHORNE ST
2 GREENHILL PL
3 HARDMAN ST
4 HANDLEY RD
5 EDELSTON RD
6 IDDON CT
7 WHITESIDE ST
8 BEAUMOUNT CT
9 EDEN ST
10 AINLEY CT
11 SWAINSON ST
12 BK COOKSON ST

C7
1 STANHOPE RD
2 SUTHERLAND VIEW
3 HAMPSTEAD MEWS
4 HANDSWORTH CT
5 GRANTHAM RD
6 ALTHORP CL
7 ST ANTHONY'S PL
8 BERESFORD ST
9 SMITHY MEWS
10 GARDENERS MEWS
11 MANOR CT
12 CROFTERS MEWS
13 GRANGE CT
14 BACK ASHBURTON RD

D7
1 KYSTON CL
2 EMPIRE GR
3 WILDMAN ST
4 CHARLES CT
5 ASHWORTH CT

152

D7
6 LABURNUM ST
7 CYPRESS GR
8 STIRLING CT
9 DEVONSHIRE CT

D8
1 WYNNWOOD AVE
2 NEWMAN RD
3 DANSON GDNS
4 PENHILL CL

E7
1 CALEDONIAN AVE
2 CAMPBELL AVE
3 WILLIAM ST
4 HUNTLEY AVE
5 CROYDON RD

E8
1 ST MARK'S PL
2 HUMBER AVE
3 PELHAM AVE
4 FORREST CT

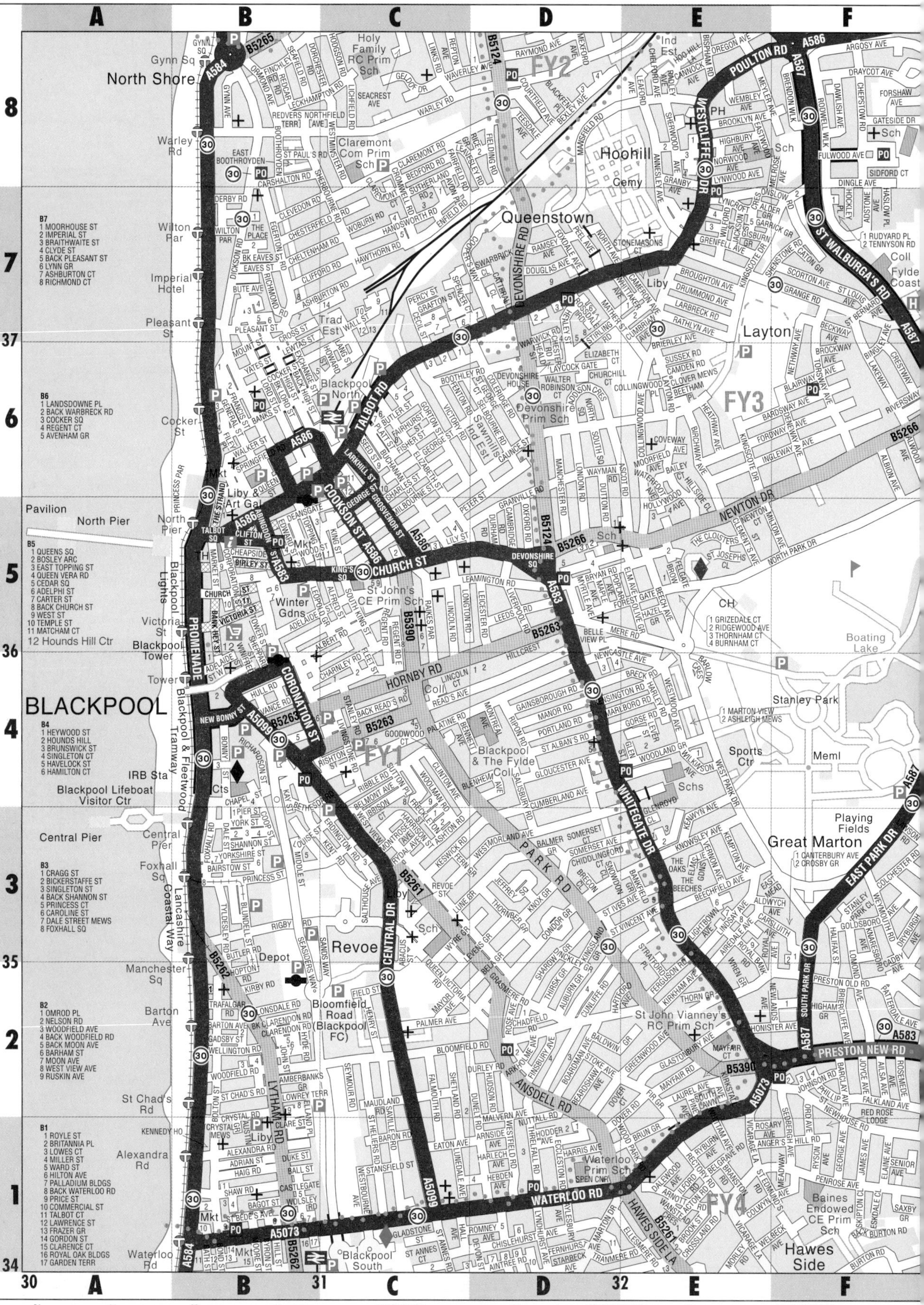


C1
1 PARKINSON WAY
2 LIGHTWOOD AVE
3 EXETER ST

C2
1 ORKNEY RD
2 DUNELT CT

C3
1 ORME ST
2 JAMESON ST
3 CHADWICK ST

C4
1 CONCORDE HO
2 WESTWELL GR
3 COURTFIELDS
4 COLLEGE CT
5 KINGSLEY CT
6 NEW CHURCH HO
7 READS CT
8 PENNINE CL
9 ANDERSON ST

C5
1 WINSTANLEY GR
2 RAIKES HILL
3 PARKER ST
4 DANESBURY PL
5 ADELAIDE CT
6 RAIKES MEWS
7 PRIORY CT
8 ST JOHN'S CT
9 GOODWOOD PL

D1
1 DUNSOP CL
2 DUNSOP CT
3 DOUGLAS LEATHAM HOUSE
4 WESTON PL
5 WINCHESTER AVE
6 SCUDAMORE CRES
7 TRURO ST
8 TAUNTON ST
9 RUGBY ST
10 DORSET ST
11 MIRFIELD GR

110

D2
1 LILAC AVE
2 MARINA AVE
3 DARAM HO
4 BACK CUNLIFFE RD

D4
1 HORNBY PARK CT
2 LAWN CT
3 LYCEUM AVE
4 TYNE AVE
5 GLOUCESTER CT

D5
1 DUTTON CT
2 RIDLEY ST
3 GLENWOOD ST
4 WHITLEY AVE
5 DEVONSHIRE SQ MEWS

E1
1 GARDEN VIEW PL
2 LANE ENDS CT
3 MANOR CT

E3
1 SPRINGFIELD CT
2 OLD MEADOW LA
3 OLD MEADOW CT
4 HOMEFYLDE HO
5 WHITEGATE LODGE
6 HASLEMERE AVE
7 GODWIN AVE
8 HEREFORD AVE
9 LATHAM AVE

F2
1 DUNMAIL AVE
2 MALTBY PL
3 JOHN HILL ST
4 OSCAR ST

153
132

A8
1 ARGOSY CT
2 GATESIDE CT
3 FURNESS CT
4 SHORE FIELDS
5 SLAIDBURN WLK

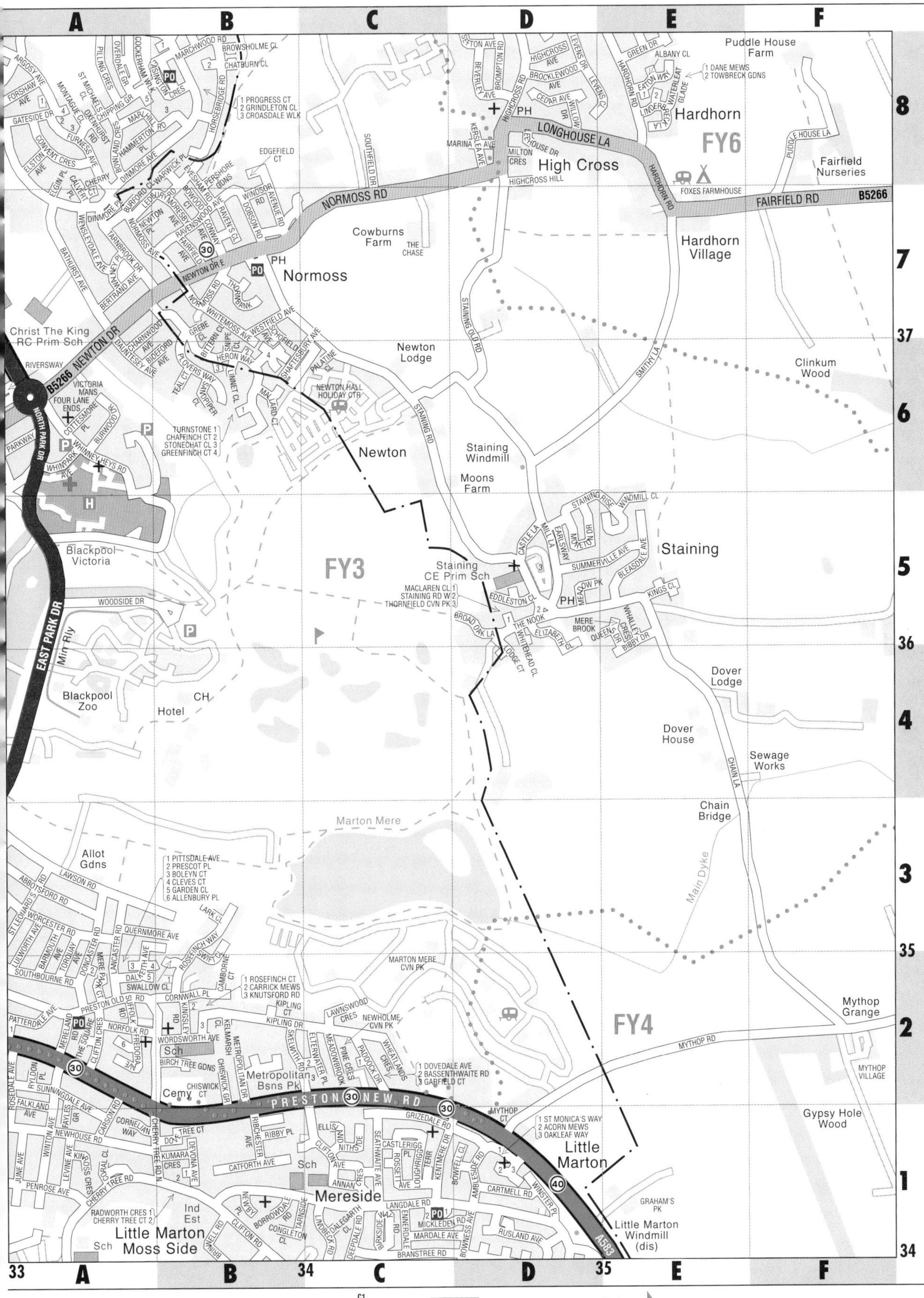


C1
1 LANGDALE PL
2 CRUMMOCK PL

111
132

131
154

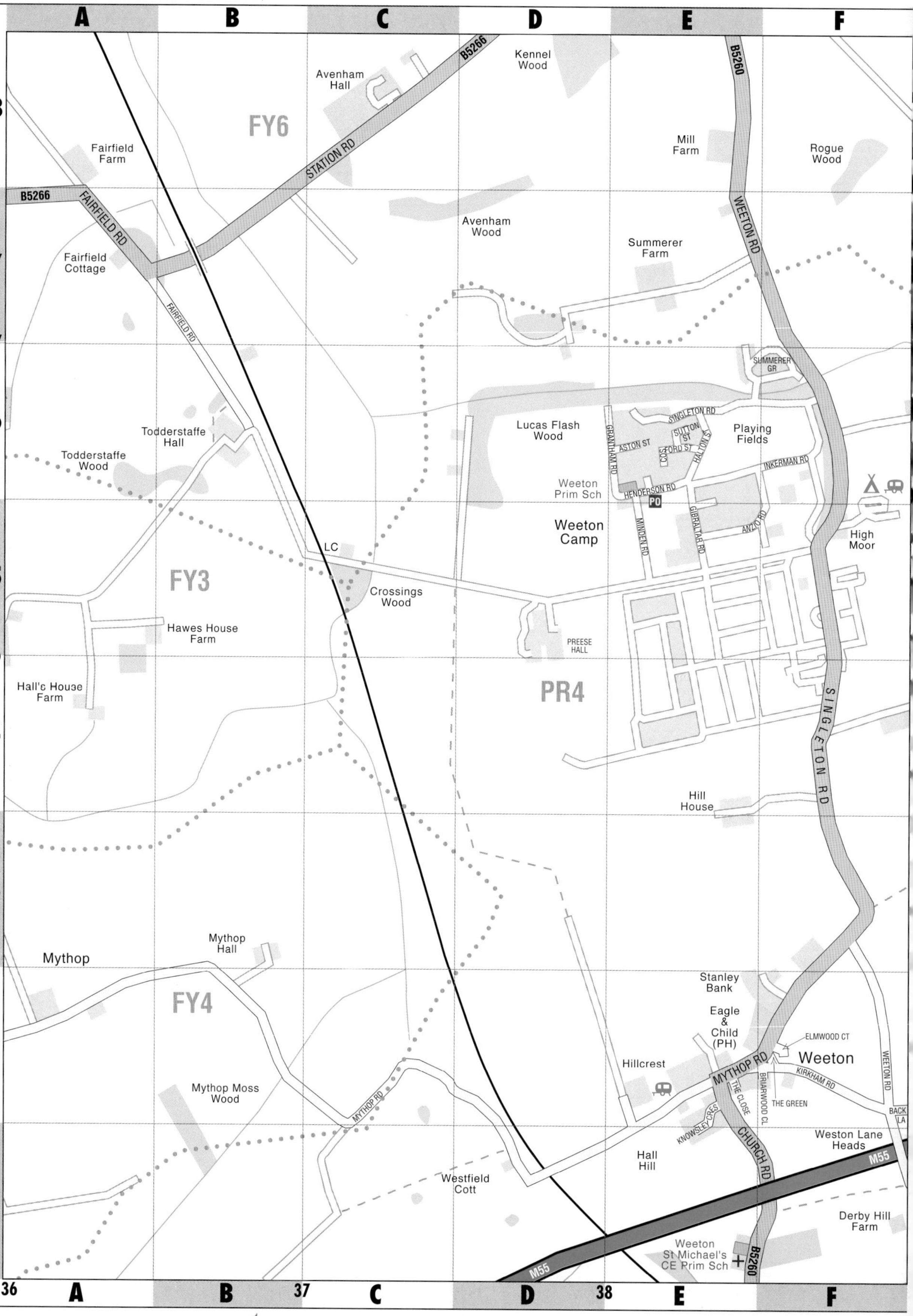
A
B
C
D
E
F
8
7
37
6
5
36
4
3
35
2
1
34
38
B5266
Avenham Hall
Kennel Wood
FY6
STATION RD
Fairfield Farm
B5266
FAIRFIELD RD
Mill Farm
Rogue Wood
B5260
Avenham Wood
WEETON RD
Summerer Farm
Fairfield Cottage
FAIRFIELD RD
SUMMERER GR
SINGLETON RD
Todderstaffe Hall
Lucas Flash Wood
SUTTON ST
ASTON ST
Playing Fields
GRANTHAM RD
FORD ST
COOT
HALTON S
Todderstaffe Wood
INKERMAN RD
Weeton Prim Sch
HENDERSON RD
PO
Weeton Camp
MINDEN RD
GIBRALTAR RD
ANZIO RD
High Moor
LC
FY3
Crossings Wood
Hawes House Farm
PREESE HALL
Hall's House Farm
PR4
SINGLETON RD
Hill House
Mythop Hall
Mythop
Stanley Bank
FY4
Eagle & Child (PH)
ELMWOOD CT
Weeton
MYTHOP RD
Hillcrest
KIRKHAM RD
WEETON RD
Mythop Moss Wood
THE CLOSE
BRIARWOOD CL
THE GREEN
MYTHOP RD
KNOWSLEY CRES
CHURCH RD
BACK LA
Weston Lane Heads
Hall Hill
M55
Westfield Cott
Derby Hill Farm
Weeton St Michael's CE Prim Sch
B5260
M55
36
37
38

131
112

155
134

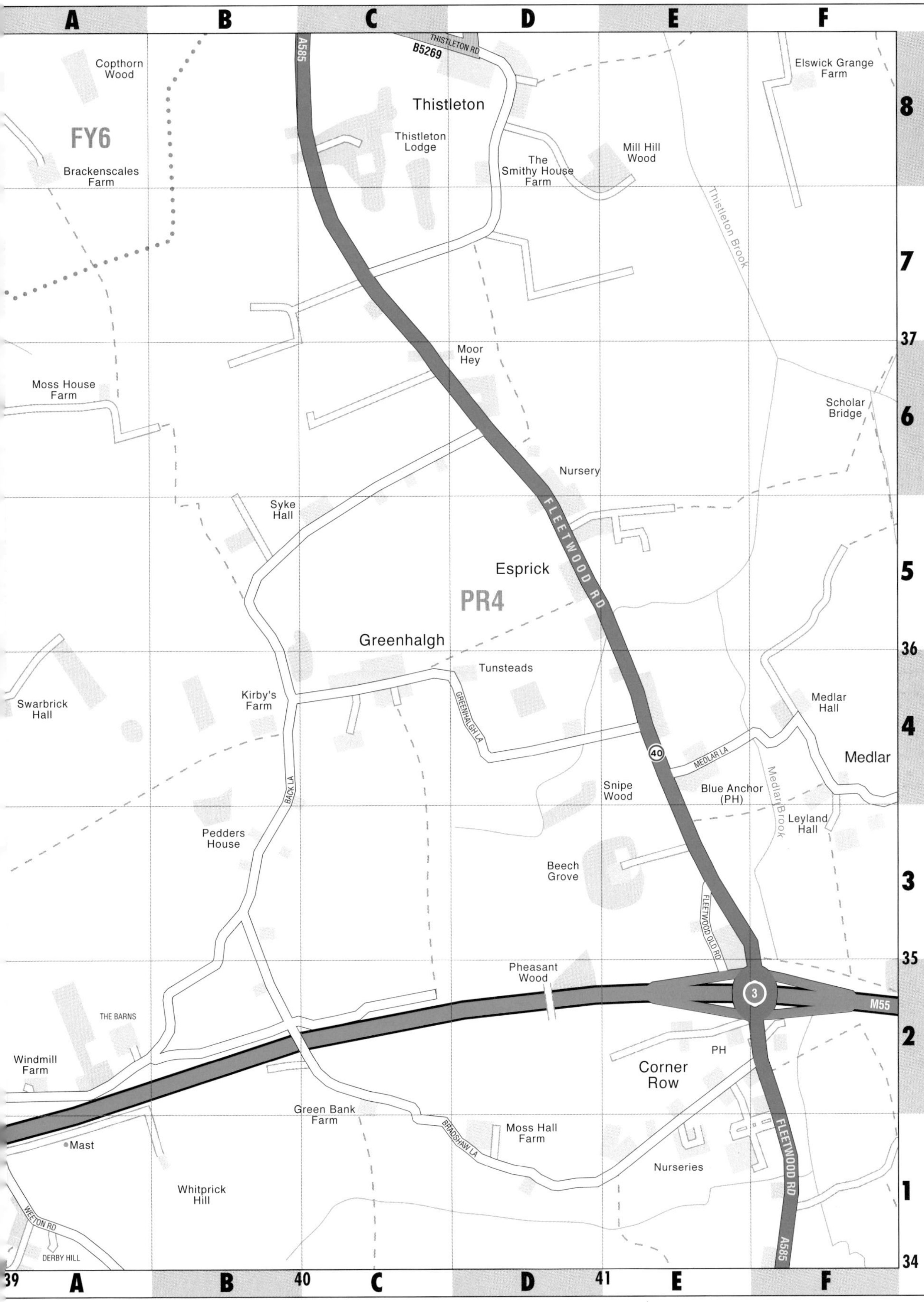


113
134

133
156

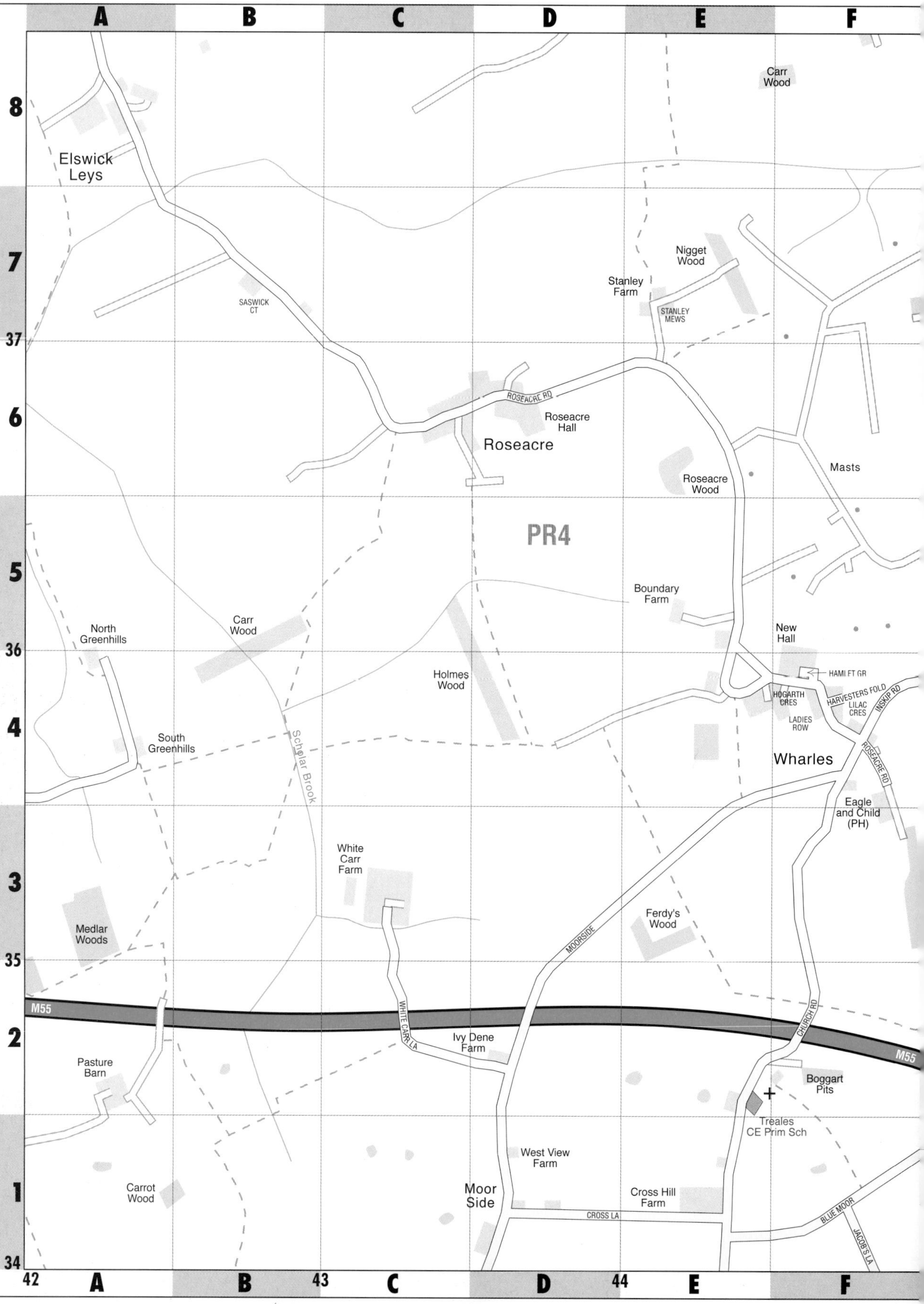
A
B
C
D
E
F
8
7
37
6
5
36
4
3
35
2
1
34
42
43
44
Carr Wood
Elswick Leys
SASWICK CT
Nigget Wood
Stanley Farm
STANLEY MEWS
ROSEACRE RD
Roseacre Hall
Roseacre
Masts
Roseacre Wood
PR4
Boundary Farm
North Greenhills
Carr Wood
New Hall
HAMLET GR
HARVESTERS FOLD
LILAC CRES
INSKIP RD
HOGARTH CRES
LADIES ROW
Holmes Wood
South Greenhills
Scholar Brook
Wharles
ROSEACRE RD
Eagle and Child (PH)
White Carr Farm
MOORSIDE
Ferdy's Wood
Medlar Woods
M55
WHITE CARR LA
CHURCH RD
M55
Ivy Dene Farm
Pasture Barn
Boggart Pits
Treales CE Prim Sch
West View Farm
Carrot Wood
Moor Side
Cross Hill Farm
CROSS LA
BLUE MOOR
JACOBS LA

133
114

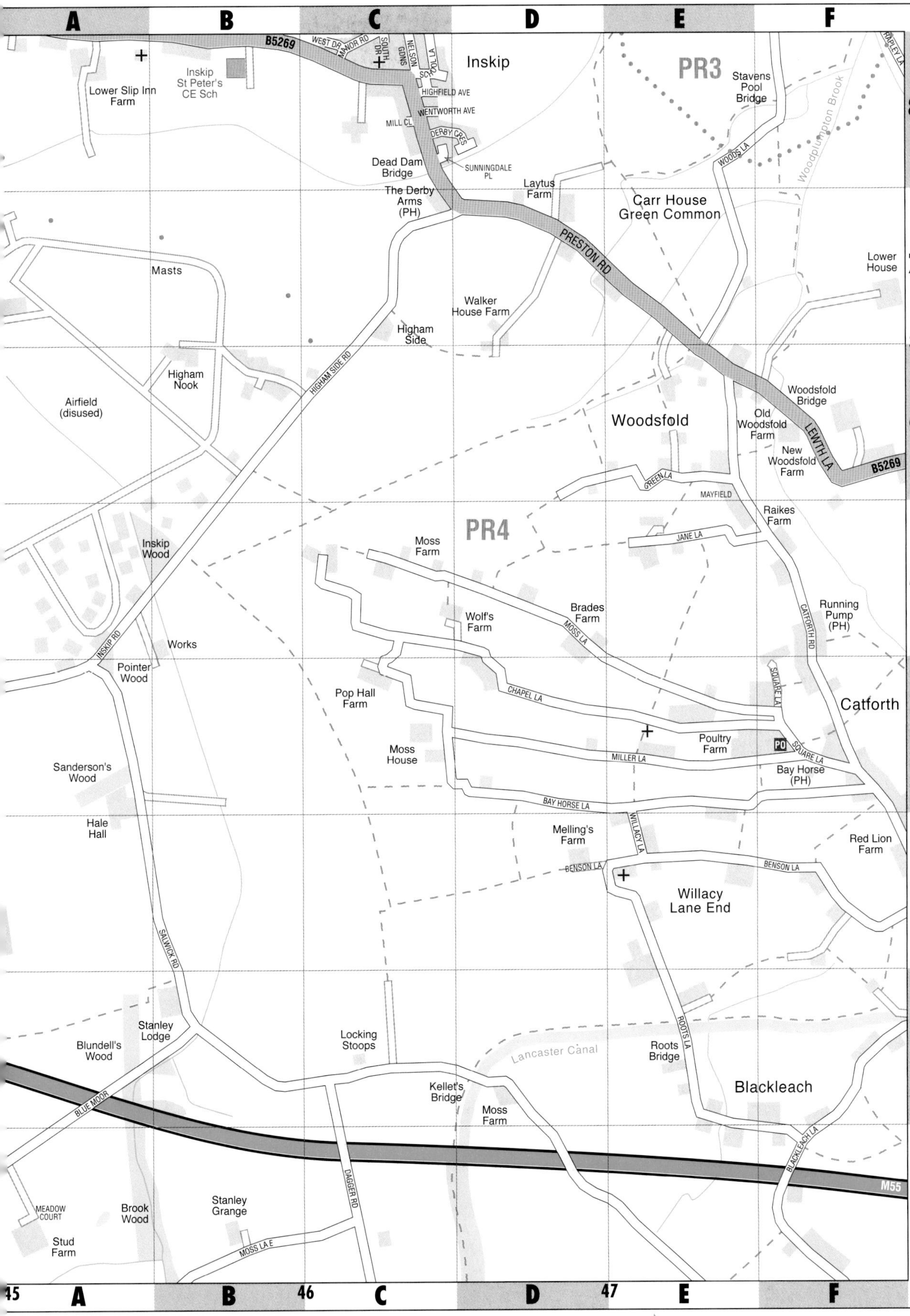
A
B
C
D
E
F
B5269
WEST DR
MANOR RD
SOUTH DR
NELSON GDNS
SCHOOL LA
Inskip
PR3
Stavens Pool Bridge
HAPLEY LA
Lower Slip Inn Farm
Inskip St Peter's CE Sch
HIGHFIELD AVE
WENTWORTH AVE
MILL CL
DERBY CRES
SUNNINGDALE PL
Dead Dam Bridge
The Derby Arms (PH)
Laytus Farm
Carr House Green Common
WOODS LA
Woodplumpton Brook
8
Masts
PRESTON RD
Lower House
7
Walker House Farm
Higham Side
37
Higham Nook
HIGHAM SIDE RD
Airfield (disused)
Woodsfold
Woodsfold Bridge
Old Woodsfold Farm
LEWTH LA
New Woodsfold Farm
B5269
6
GREEN LA
MAYFIELD
PR4
Raikes Farm
JANE LA
Inskip Wood
Moss Farm
5
Wolf's Farm
Brades Farm
Running Pump (PH)
MOSS LA
CATFORTH RD
Works
INSKIP RD
Pointer Wood
36
SQUARE LA
CHAPEL LA
Pop Hall Farm
Catforth
Moss House
Poultry Farm
PO
SQUARE LA
4
MILLER LA
Sanderson's Wood
Bay Horse (PH)
BAY HORSE LA
Hale Hall
WILLACY LA
Melling's Farm
Red Lion Farm
BENSON LA
BENSON LA
Willacy Lane End
3
SALWICK RD
35
Stanley Lodge
Blundell's Wood
Locking Stoops
Lancaster Canal
Roots Bridge
ROOTS LA
2
Kellet's Bridge
Blackleach
Moss Farm
BLUE MOOR
BLACKLEACH LA
DAGGER RD
M55
1
MEADOW COURT
Brook Wood
Stanley Grange
Stud Farm
MOSS LA E
34
45
A
B
46
C
D
47
E
F

135
158

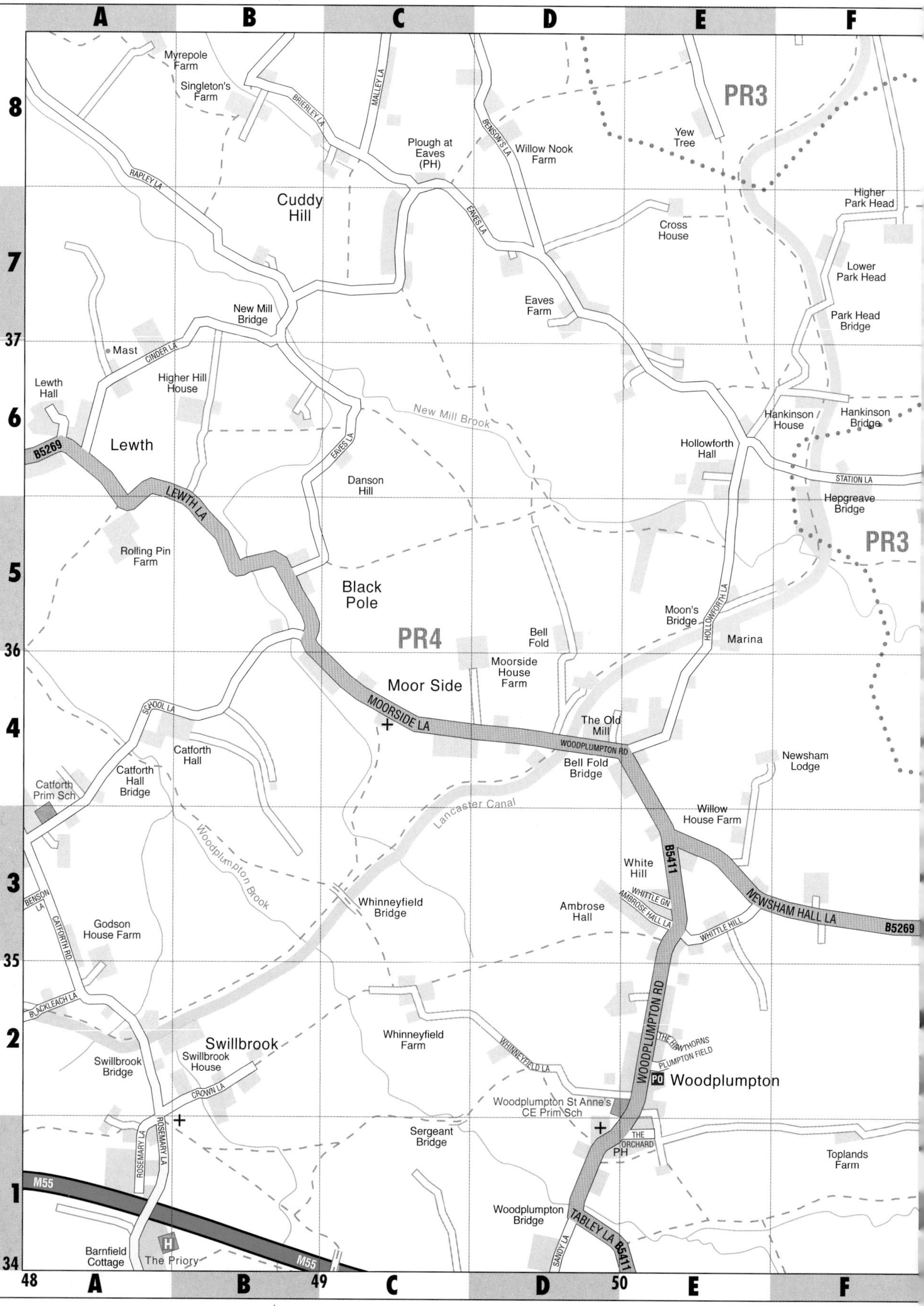


135
116

159
138

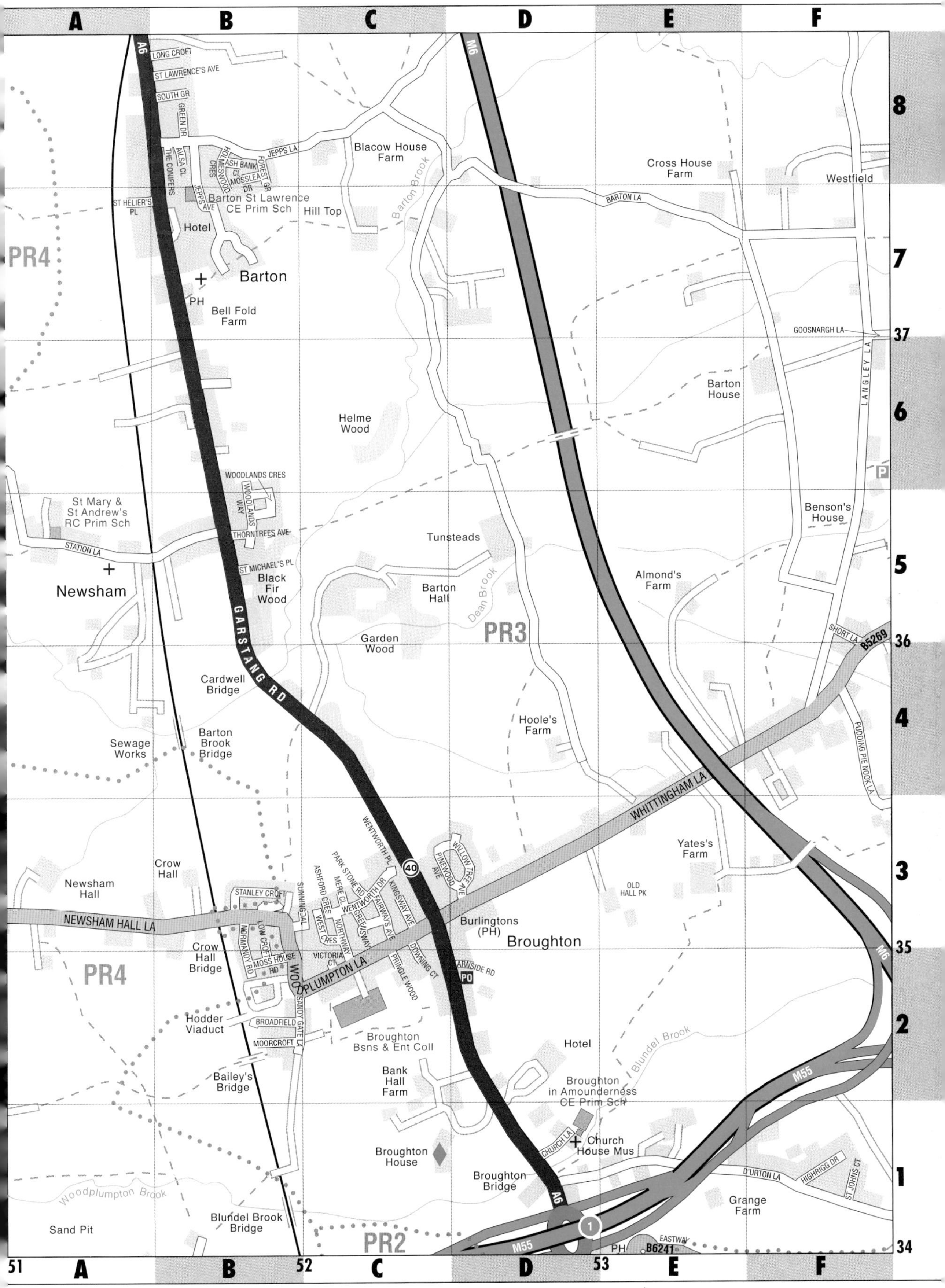


117
138

137 160

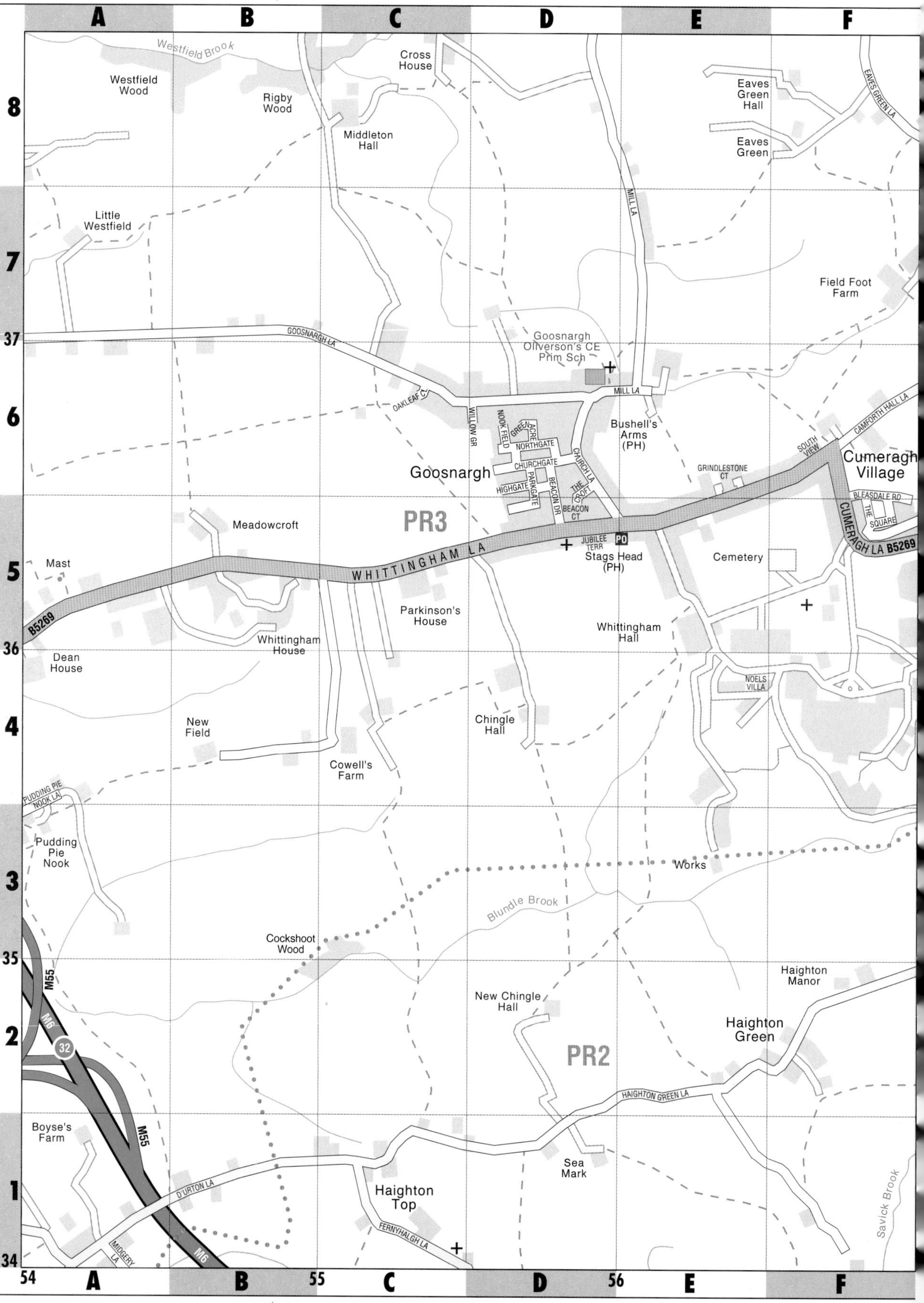
A
B
C
D
E
F
8
7
37
6
5
36
4
3
35
2
1
34
54
55
56
Westfield Brook
Westfield Wood
Rigby Wood
Cross House
Middleton Hall
Eaves Green Hall
Eaves Green
EAVES GREEN LA
Little Westfield
MILL LA
Field Foot Farm
GOOSNARGH LA
Goosnargh Oliverson's CE Prim Sch
OAKLEAF CT
MILL LA
WILLOW GR
NOOK FIELD
GREEN ACRE
NORTHGATE
CHURCHGATE
HIGHGATE
PARKGATE
BEACON DR
THE CROFT
CHURCH LA
BEACON CT
Bushell's Arms (PH)
Goosnargh
GRINDLESTONE CT
SOUTH VIEW
CAMFORTH HALL LA
Cumeragh Village
BLEASDALE RD
THE SQUARE
CUMERAGH LA B5269
PR3
Meadowcroft
WHITTINGHAM LA
JUBILEE TERR
PO
Stags Head (PH)
Cemetery
Mast
B5269
Parkinson's House
Whittingham Hall
Whittingham House
Dean House
NOELS VILLA
New Field
Chingle Hall
Cowell's Farm
PUDDING PIE NOOK LA
Pudding Pie Nook
Works
Blundle Brook
Cockshoot Wood
M55
M6
32
New Chingle Hall
Haighton Manor
Haighton Green
PR2
HAIGHTON GREEN LA
Boyse's Farm
M55
Sea Mark
D'URTON LA
Haighton Top
FERNYHALGH LA
MIDGERY LA
M6
Savick Brook

137 118

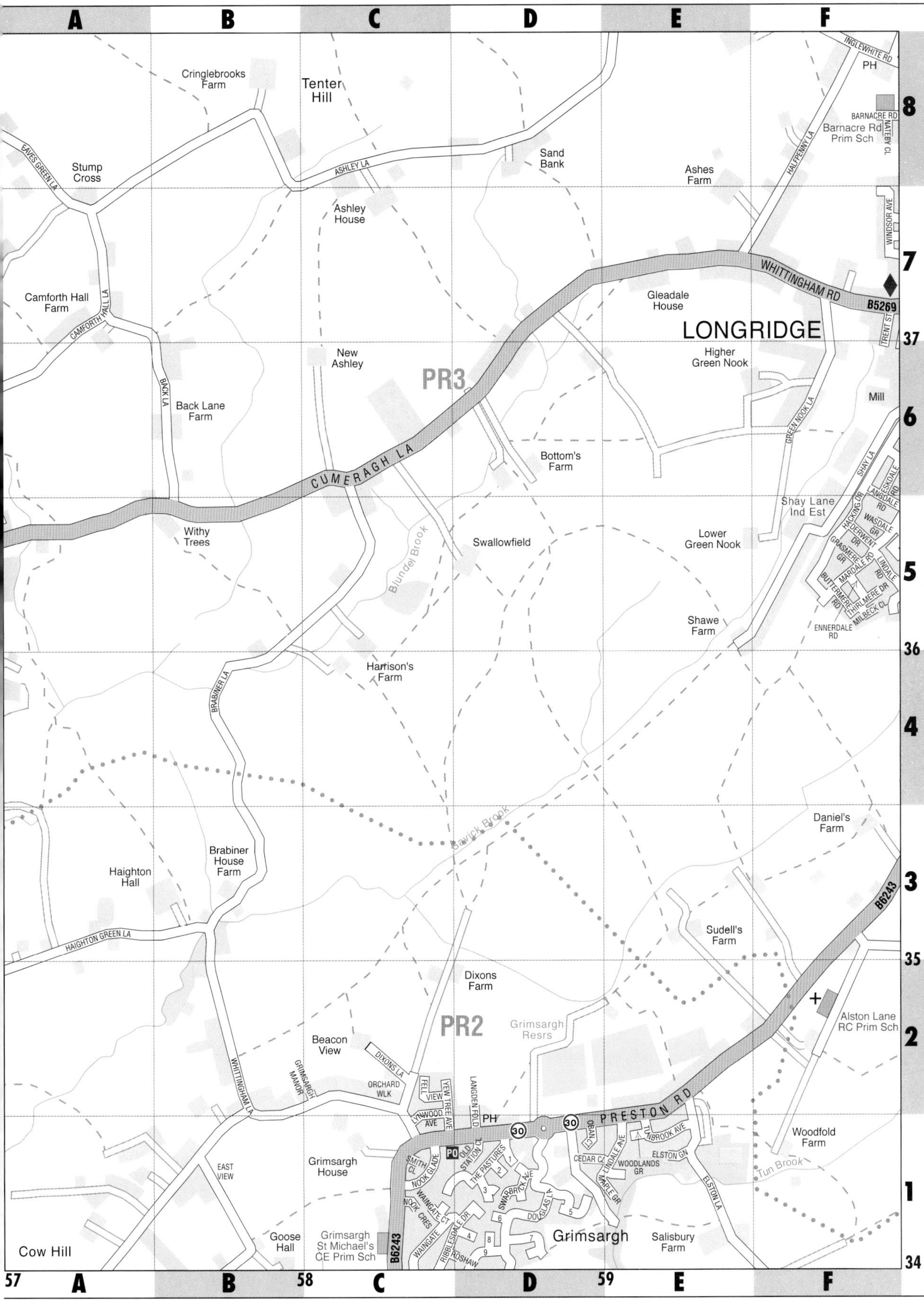




D1
1 PLOUGHMANS CT
2 ALEXANDER PL
3 SWALLOWFOLD
4 BLACKLEACH AVE
5 SALISBURY AVE
6 BRINDLE PL
7 CROFTS DR
8 BILLINGTON CT
9 CARBIS AVE

139
162

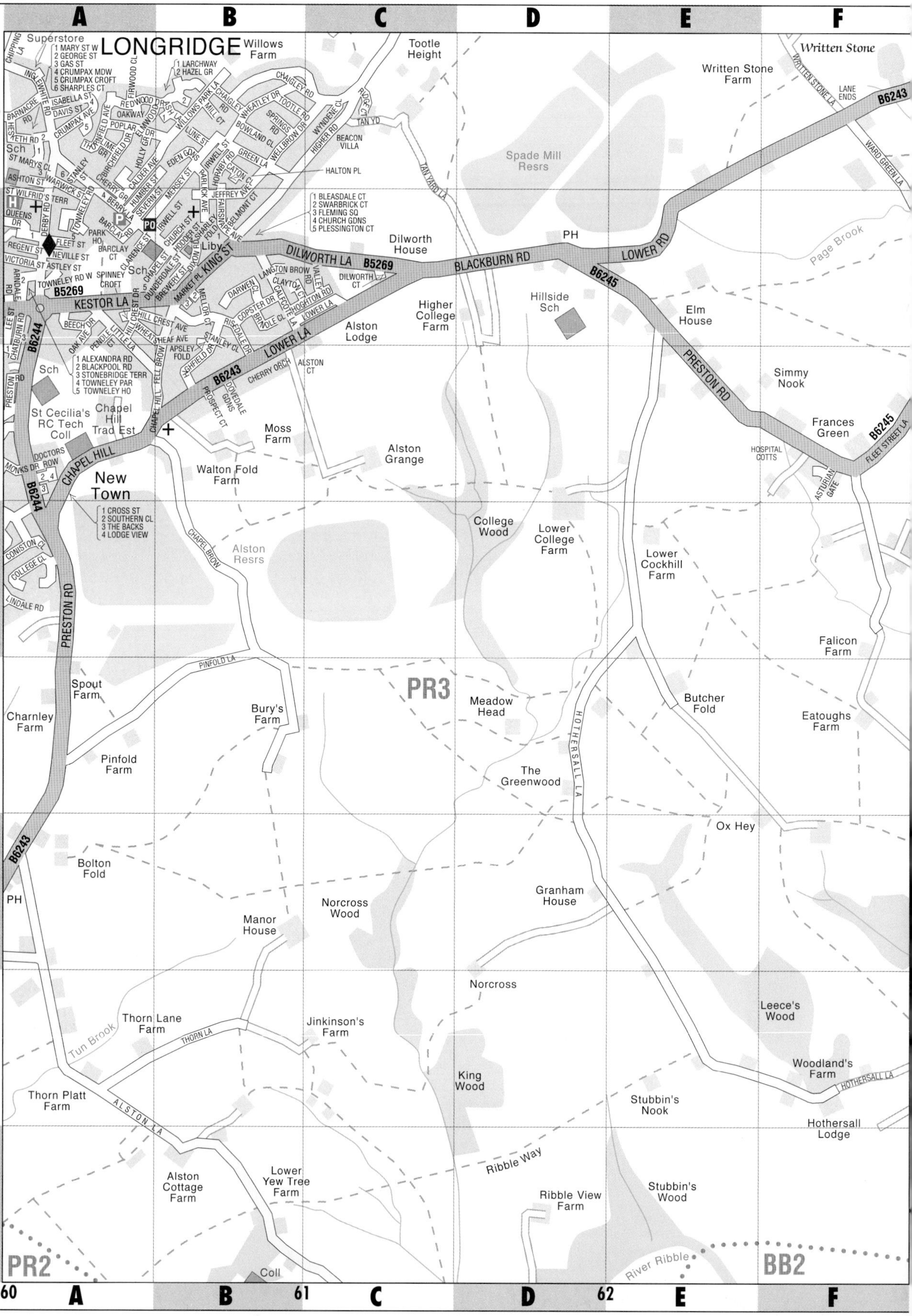


139
120

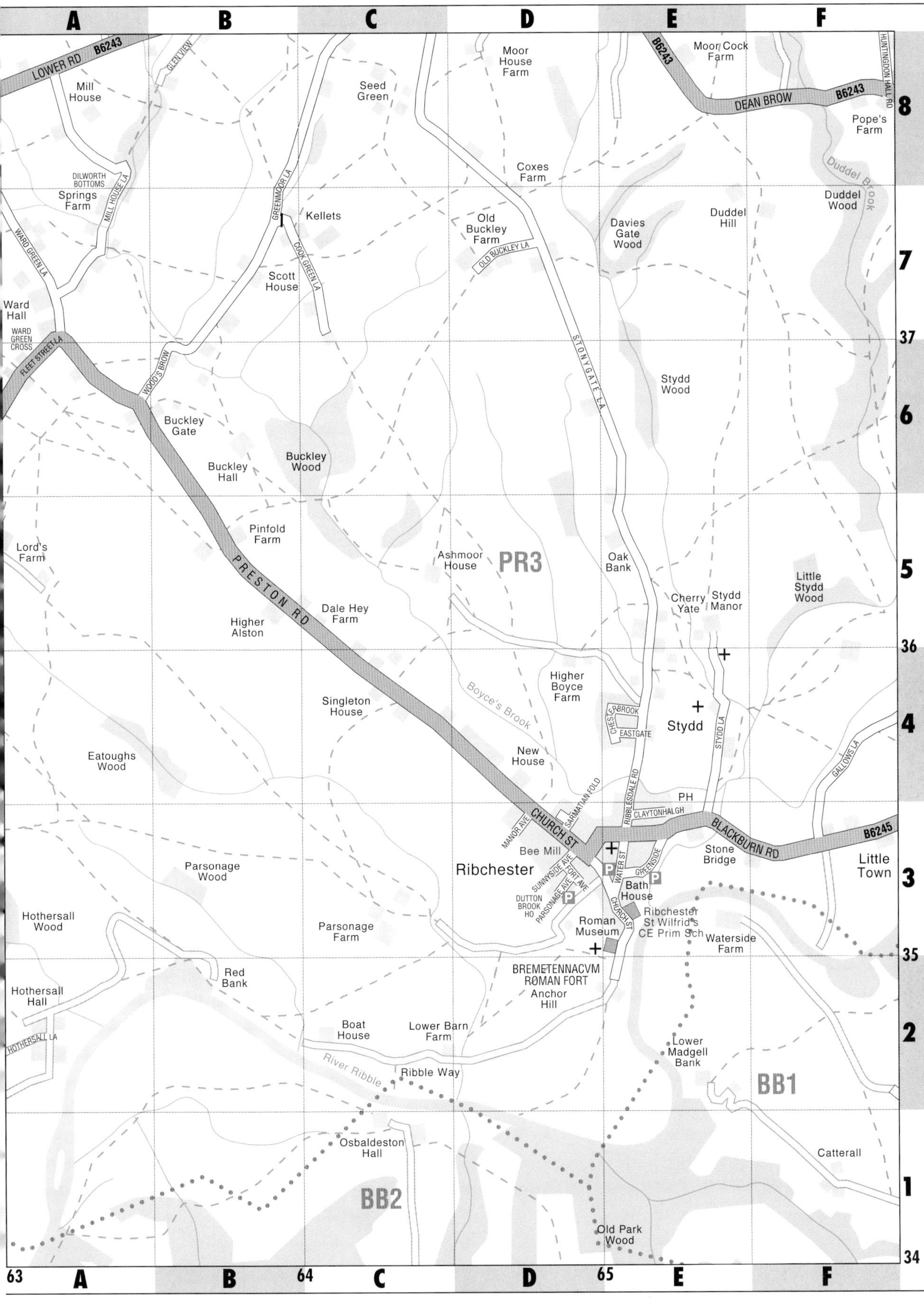
A
B
C
D
E
F
8
7
37
6
5
36
4
3
35
2
1
34
63
64
65
LOWER RD
B6243
GLEN VIEW
Mill House
Seed Green
Moor House Farm
Moor Cock Farm
DEAN BROW
B6243
HUNTINGDON HALL RD
Pope's Farm
Duddel Brook
DILWORTH BOTTOMS
Springs Farm
MILL HOUSE LA
WARD GREEN LA
GREENMOOR LA
Kellets
COOK GREEN LA
Coxes Farm
Old Buckley Farm
OLD BUCKLEY LA
Davies Gate Wood
Duddel Hill
Duddel Wood
Scott House
Ward Hall
WARD GREEN CROSS
FLEET STREET LA
WOOD'S BROW
STONYGATE LA
Stydd Wood
Buckley Gate
Buckley Hall
Buckley Wood
Pinfold Farm
Lord's Farm
Ashmoor House
PR3
Oak Bank
PRESTON RD
Dale Hey Farm
Higher Alston
Cherry Yate
Stydd Manor
Little Stydd Wood
Higher Boyce Farm
Boyce's Brook
Singleton House
CHESTER BROOK
EASTGATE
Stydd
STYDD LA
GALLOWS LA
Eatoughs Wood
New House
SARMATIAN FOLD
RIBBLESDALE RD
CLAYTONHALGH
PH
MANOR AVE
CHURCH ST
BLACKBURN RD
B6245
Bee Mill
Ribchester
SUNNYSIDE AVE
FORT AVE
WATER ST
GREENSIDE
Stone Bridge
Little Town
Parsonage Wood
DUTTON BROOK HO
PARSONAGE AVE
Bath House
Ribchester St Wilfrid's CE Prim Sch
Hothersall Wood
Parsonage Farm
Roman Museum
CHURCH ST
Waterside Farm
BREMETENNACVM ROMAN FORT
Anchor Hill
Red Bank
Hothersall Hall
HOTHERSALL LA
Boat House
Lower Barn Farm
Lower Madgell Bank
BB1
River Ribble
Ribble Way
Osbaldeston Hall
BB2
Catterall
Old Park Wood

141 164

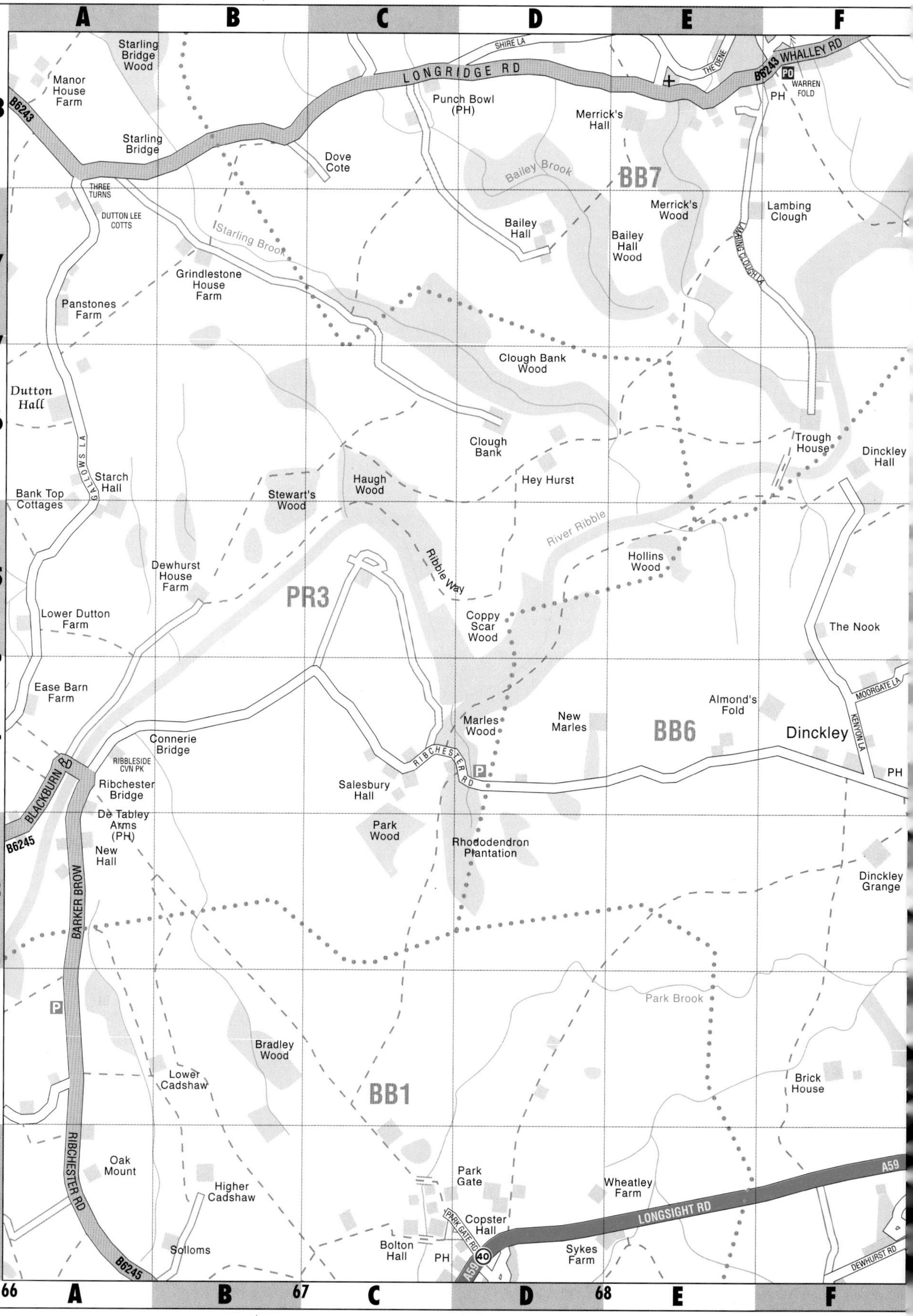


141 122

165
144

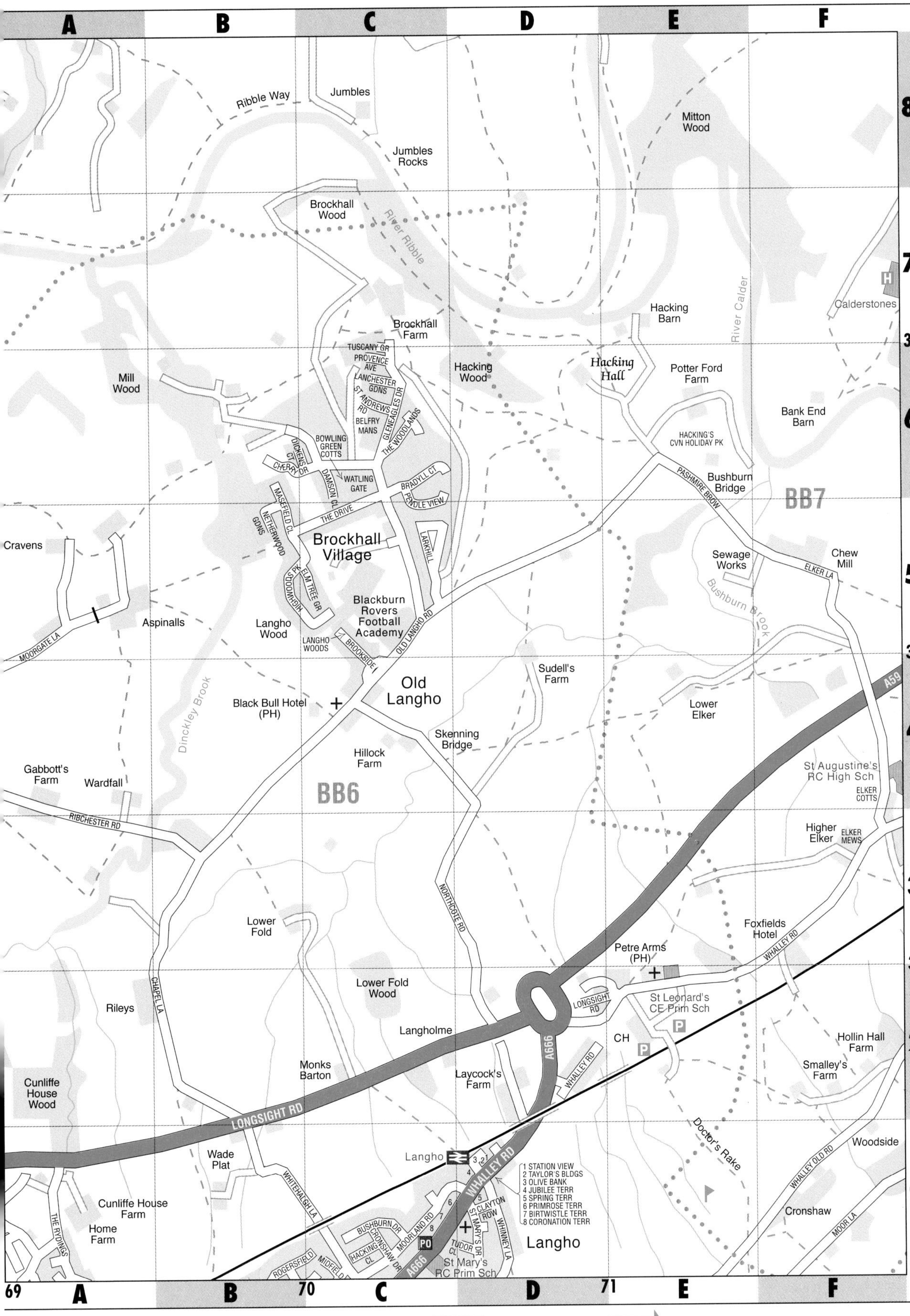


123
144

143
166

143
124

167
146

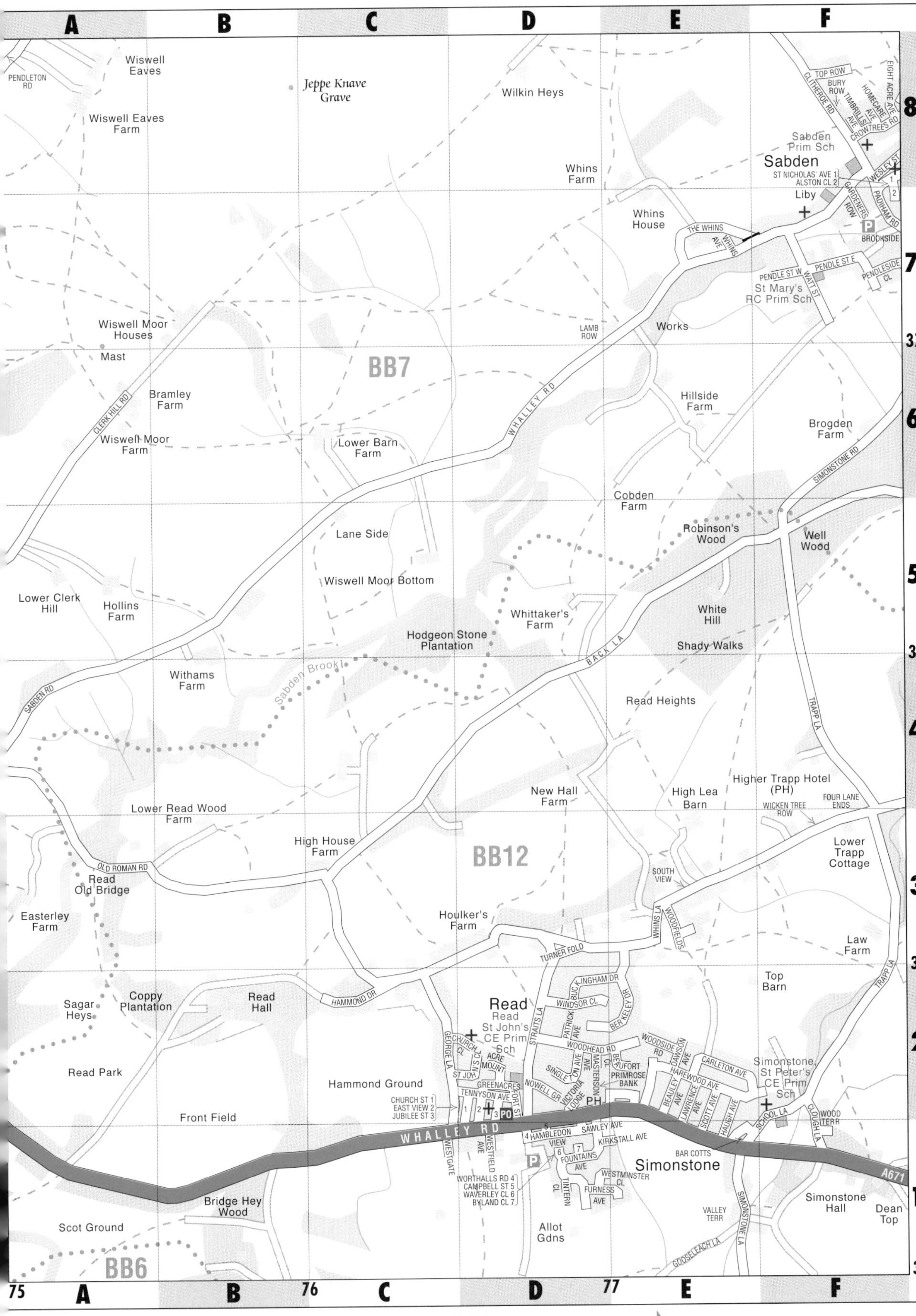
A
B
C
D
E
F
Wiswell Eaves
PENDLETON RD
Jeppe Knave Grave
Wilkin Heys
Wiswell Eaves Farm
Sabden Prim Sch
Sabden
Whins Farm
Whins House
Liby
THE WHINS
St Mary's RC Prim Sch
Works
LAMB ROW
Wiswell Moor Houses
Mast
BB7
Bramley Farm
CLERK HILL RD
Wiswell Moor Farm
WHALLEY RD
Hillside Farm
Brogden Farm
Lower Barn Farm
SIMONSTONE RD
Cobden Farm
Robinson's Wood
Well Wood
Lane Side
Wiswell Moor Bottom
Lower Clerk Hill
Hollins Farm
Whittaker's Farm
White Hill
Hodgeon Stone Plantation
Shady Walks
BACK LA
Withams Farm
Sabden Brook
SABDEN RD
Read Heights
TRAPP LA
Higher Trapp Hotel (PH)
New Hall Farm
High Lea Barn
Lower Read Wood Farm
FOUR LANE ENDS
WICKEN TREE ROW
High House Farm
BB12
Lower Trapp Cottage
OLD ROMAN RD
Read Old Bridge
SOUTH VIEW
Easterley Farm
Houlker's Farm
WHINS LA
WOODFIELDS
Law Farm
TURNER FOLD
Top Barn
Sagar Heys
Coppy Plantation
Read Hall
HAMMOND DR
Read
Read St John's CE Prim Sch
Read Park
Hammond Ground
Simonstone St Peter's CE Prim Sch
Front Field
WHALLEY RD
Simonstone
A671
Bridge Hey Wood
Simonstone Hall
Dean Top
Scot Ground
Allot Gdns
VALLEY TERR
GOOSELEACH LA
SIMONSTONE LA
BB6
8
7
37
6
5
36
4
3
35
2
1
34
75
76
77

125
146

145
168

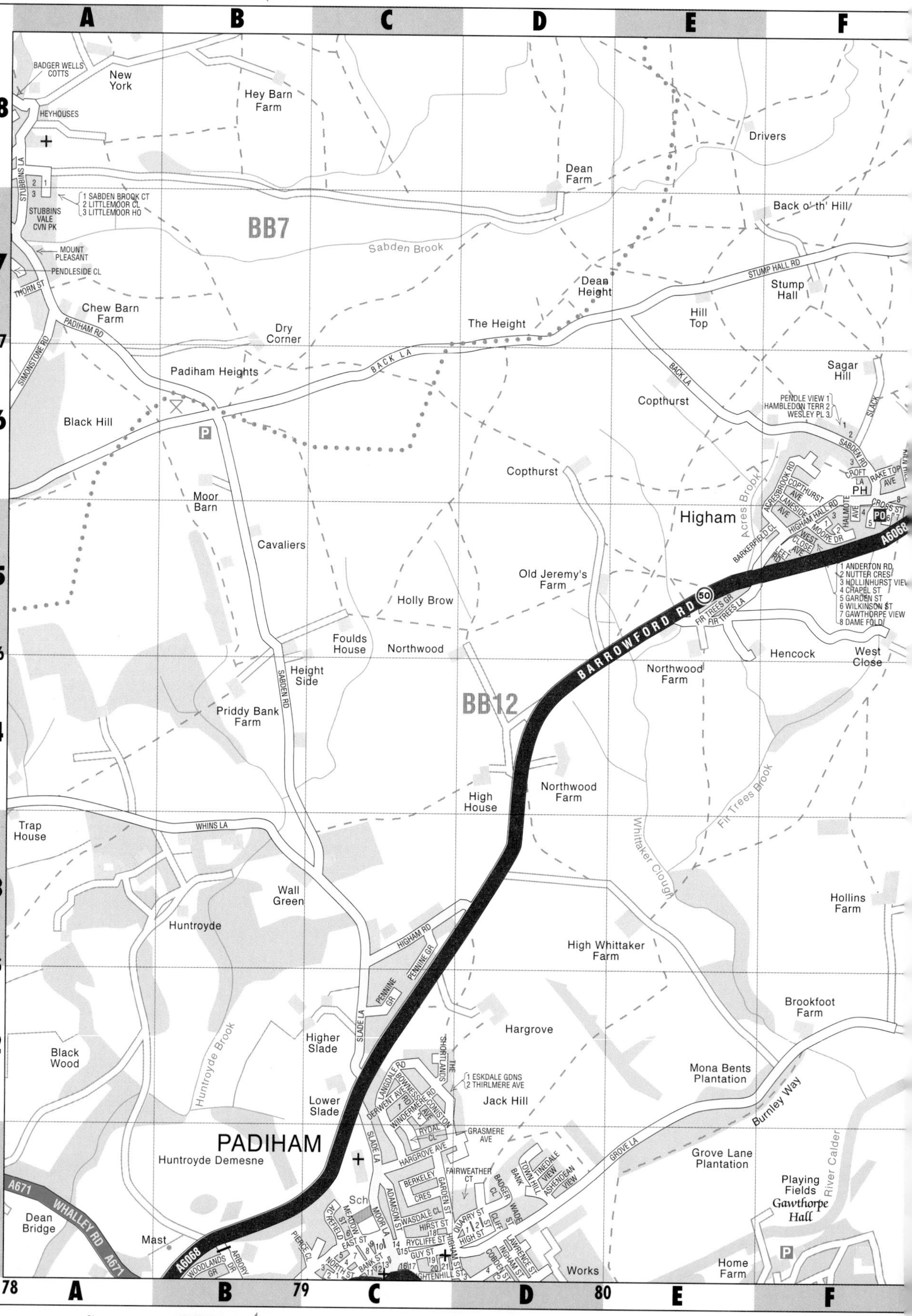
A
B
C
D
E
F
8
7
37
6
5
36
4
3
35
2
1
34
78
79
80
BADGER WELLS COTTS
New York
Hey Barn Farm
HEYHOUSES
STUBBINS LA
1 SABDEN BROOK CT
2 LITTLEMOOR CL
3 LITTLEMOOR HO
STUBBINS VALE CVN PK
BB7
Sabden Brook
MOUNT PLEASANT
PENDLESIDE CL
THORN ST
Chew Barn Farm
PADIHAM RD
SIMONSTONE RD
Dry Corner
Padiham Heights
BACK LA
Black Hill
Dean Farm
Drivers
Back o' th' Hill
STUMP HALL RD
Dean Height
Stump Hall
Hill Top
The Height
BACK LA
Sagar Hill
Copthurst
PENDLE VIEW 1
HAMBLEDON TERR 2
WESLEY PL 3
SLACK
SABDEN RD
Copthurst
Moor Barn
Cavaliers
Higham
Acres Brook
CROFT LA
PH
RAKE TOP AVE
ACRESBROOK RD
COPTHURST AVE
LANGSIDE AVE
HIGHAM HALL RD
HALMOTE AVE
MOORE DR
CROSS ST
PO
WEST CLOSE AVE
BARKERFIELD CL
A6068
1 ANDERTON RD
2 NUTTER CRES
3 HOLLINHURST VIEW
4 CHAPEL ST
5 GARDEN ST
6 WILKINSON ST
7 GAWTHORPE VIEW
8 DAME FOLD
Old Jeremy's Farm
Holly Brow
50
BARROWFORD RD
FIR TREES GR
FIR TREES LA
Foulds House
Northwood
Hencock
West Close
Height Side
SABDEN RD
Northwood Farm
BB12
Priddy Bank Farm
Northwood Farm
High House
Fir Trees Brook
Whittaker Clough
Trap House
WHINS LA
Wall Green
Hollins Farm
Huntroyde
HIGHAM RD
PENNINE GR
PENNINE GR
High Whittaker Farm
SLADE LA
Brookfoot Farm
Hargrove
Black Wood
Higher Slade
Huntroyde Brook
THE SHORTLANDS
1 ESKDALE GDNS
2 THIRLMERE AVE
Mona Bents Plantation
Burnley Way
LANGDALE RD
BOWNESS RD
DERWENT AVE
WINDERMERE RD
CONISTON
RYDAL CL
Lower Slade
Jack Hill
GRASMERE AVE
PADIHAM
SLADE LA
HARGROVE AVE
TINEDALE VIEW
TOWN HILL BANK
ASHENDEAN VIEW
GROVE LA
Grove Lane Plantation
River Calder
Huntroyde Demesne
Sch
BERKELEY CRES
FAIRWEATHER CT
GARDEN ST
BADGER WADE CL
Playing Fields
Gawthorpe Hall
A671
WHALLEY RD
Dean Bridge
MEADOW ST
MOOR LA
ADAMSON ST
WASDALE CL
HIRST ST
QUARRY ST
CLIFF ST
ACREFIELD
EAST ST
RYCLIFFE ST
HIGH ST
HIGHAM ST
LAWRENCE ST
Mast
A6068
WOODLANDS GR
ARBORY DR
PIERCE CL
NORTH ST
BANK ST
GUY ST
COBDEN ST
INGHAM ST
Works
Home Farm
LIGHTENHILL ST

C1
1 THE MEWS
2 CHAPEL WLK
3 SPRING GARDENS TERR
4 HALL HILL ST
5 CROSSHILLS
6 ST GILES TERR
7 ST GILES ST
8 ST LEONARD'S ST
9 CLAYBANK FOLD
10 CLAYBANK
11 HAVELOCK ST
12 CHURCH LA
13 GAWTHORPE ST
14 BARBON ST
15 JOHN O' GAUNT ST
16 CENTRAL BLDGS
17 FACTORY LA
18 COPTHURST ST
19 HABERGHAM ST

145

C1
20 VICTORIA APARTMENTS
21 CLITHEROE ST

126

D1
1 KAY ST
2 DEAN ST
3 CHIPPING ST
4 PARTRIDGE HILL
5 PARTRIDGE HILL ST

169
148

A
B
C
D
E
F
Lower Houses
Higher Town
HADDINGS LA
Croft Top Farm
Hoarstones
MILLBROOK 1
FOREST AVE 2
GREENBANK DR
PO
A6068
Grains Barn
Old Laund Clough
Higher Old Laund
HARPERS LA
LAUND GATE
GREYSTONES DR
DEER CHACE
PH
HEATHGATE
FORESTER DR
WHEATLEY LANE RD
OLD LAUND ST
WHEATCROFT AVE
EVERSHOLT CL
HEATHERLEA RD
Liby
Wheatley Lane Methodist Prim Sch
WHEATLEY CL
Higher Fencegate Farm
Haddings Head
Bank House
STUMP HALL RD
Recn Gd
Height Farm
Pendle Way
Meadow Top
LANE TOP
HOARSTONES AVE
CUCKSTOOL LA
WOODBURY AVE
UPLANDS DR
Wheatlands
B6248
Fence
ST ANNE'S DR
PENDLE FIELDS
ST ANNE'S WAY
GUIDE LA
PH
Raven's Clough
Fence House
BARROWFORD RD
FENCEGATE
Pancakes Farm
Forest Hotel (PH)
BARROWFORD RD
50
Ashlar House
Higher White Lee
The Old Vicarage
Raven's Clough Wood
Lower White Lee
BLIND LA
CUCKSTOOL LA
MONTFORD CT
St John's CE Prim Sch
Waterside
Spurn Clough
HILL ST
Waterside Farm Cottage
MONTFORD RD
B6248 CLITHEROE RD
Heys
M65
New Laund Farm
Moor Isles Clough
FOXENDOLE LA
Pendle Hall Plantation
GREENHEAD LA
BB9
ROBINSON LA
Moor Isles Farm
Greenhead Manor
Monkhey Farm
BB12
Pendle Water
Bronte Way
Round Wood
Holme End Farm
HOLME END
Wood End Farm
Pendle Way
New in Pendle Bridge
River Calder
Smith's Barn
PENDLE BRIDGE
Pendle Hall
WOOD END
BARDEN LA
Sewage Works
HEALDWOOD CL
HEALDWOOD DR
Ingham's Farm
LOWER MANOR LA
Hunters Oak
Adamson's Farm
GARSWOOD CL
LOWER MEAD DR
Springwood House Farm
Hogg Wood
Heald Bridge
Burnley Way
Wks
IGHTENHILL PARK LA
Leeds and Liverpool Canal
Cornfield Farm
Hollins Farm
Royle Hall Farm
Spring Wood
Bronte Way
Cornfield House
Nurseries
Bronte Way
BB10
CORNFIELD GR
YEWBARROW CL
OSWALD ST
NEW HALL ST
Crow Wood House Farm
M65
8
7
37
6
5
36
4
3
35
2
1
34
81
82
83

127
148

D8
1 STOTT ST
2 CUBA ST
3 ALBION ST
4 RAGLAN ST
5 PROSPECT BLDGS
6 RUSSELL ST

147

D8
7 BK SCOTLAND RD
8 SCOTLAND RD
9 MARKET ST
10 BOOTH ST
11 ELLEN ST
12 PLACE-DE-CRIEL

170

D8
13 BROAD ST
14 CLEMENT VIEW
15 MEADOW BANK RD
E8
1 The Galleries
2 The Victory Ctr
3 Trafalgar Mall
4 LEEDS RD
5 Marsden Mall
6 Arndale Ctr
7 Pendle Way
8 BACON ST
9 NETHERFIELD GDNS
10 WARDE ST
11 LLOYD WLK
12 LLOYD CL
13 HARDY CT
14 AUDLEY CL
15 ASHIANA LODGE
16 YORKSHIRE ST
17 BANNISTER CT
18 ROSSER CT
19 Pendle Bsns Ctr

F8
1 HEMINGWAY PL
2 WILLIAMS PL
3 WALVERDEN CRES
4 COLEMAN ST
5 ORMEROD ST
6 MALVERN CT

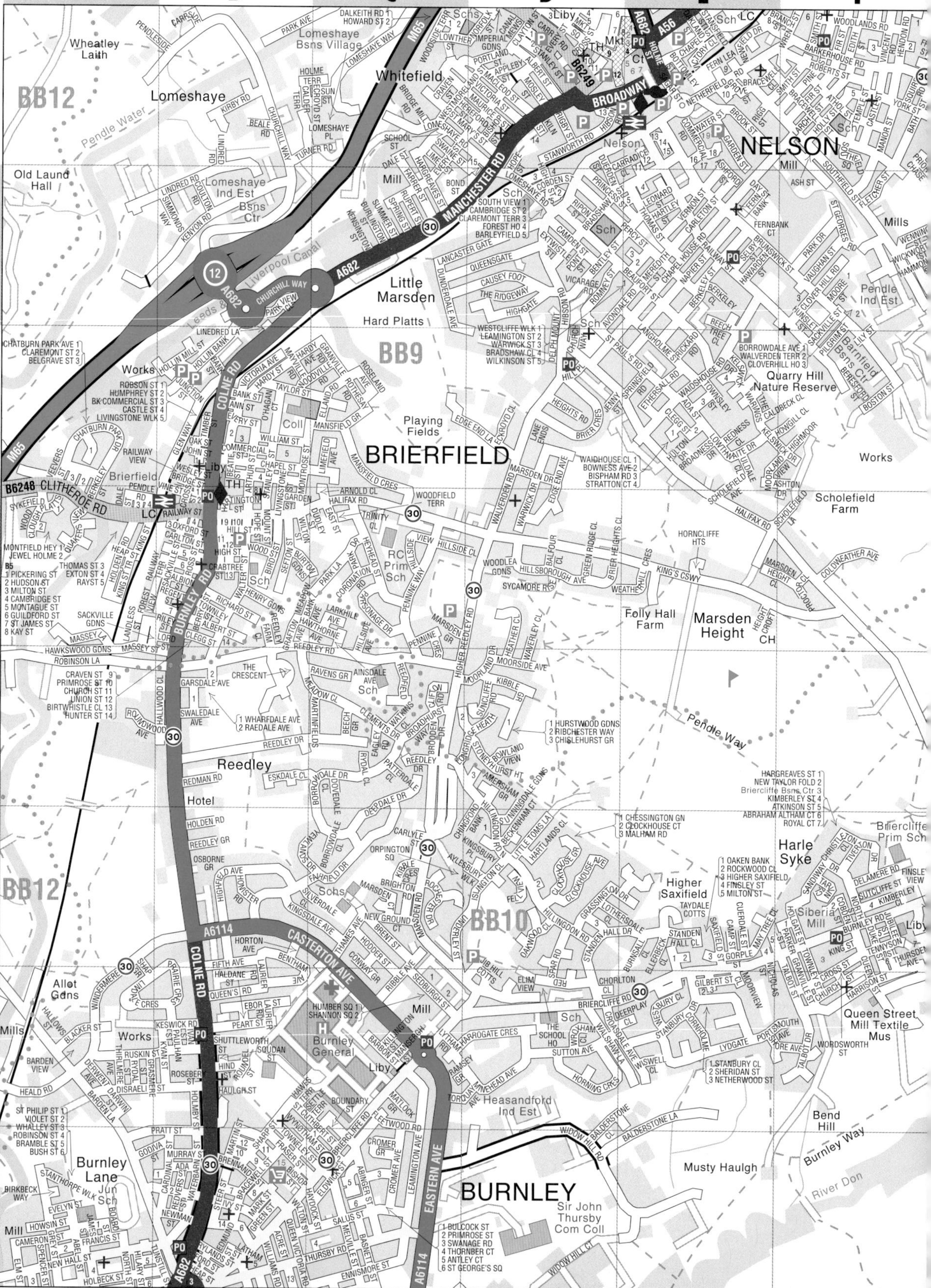

A
B
C
D
E
F
8
7
37
6
5
36
4
3
35
2
1
34
84
85
86
Wheatley Laith
Lomeshaye
BB12
Pendle Water
Old Laund Hall
Lomeshaye Bsns Village
Lomeshaye Ind Est
Whitefield
Leeds & Liverpool Canal
Little Marsden
Hard Platts
BB9
NELSON
BRIERFIELD
Playing Fields
Brierfield
Quarry Hill Nature Reserve
Pendle Ind Est
Barnfield Bsns Ctr
Scholefield Farm
Folly Hall Farm
Marsden Height
Pendle Way
Reedley
Hotel
BB10
Higher Saxifield
Harle Syke
Briercliffe Prim Sch
Siberia Mill
Queen Street Mill Textile Mus
Burnley General
Heasandford Ind Est
Bend Hill
Burnley Way
Musty Haugh
River Don
BURNLEY
Sir John Thursby Com Coll
Burnley Lane
Allot Gdns
M65
A682
A56
B6249
B6248 CLITHEROE RD
A6114
MANCHESTER RD
COLNE RD
BURNLEY RD
CASTERTON AVE
EASTERN AVE
BROADWAY


84
A
B
85
C
D
86
E
F

B1
1 HASLAM CT
2 BRIGHT ST
3 BARDEN ST
4 ST ANDREW'S ST
5 NEW CHURCH MEWS
6 RUSHWORTH ST E
7 FURNESS ST
8 RENSHAW ST
9 WALPOLE ST
10 RANDALL ST
11 PEMBROKE ST
12 RAWSON ST
13 CLAUGHTON ST
14 RUSHWORTH ST W
15 Briercliffe Sh Ctr

147

128

171
150

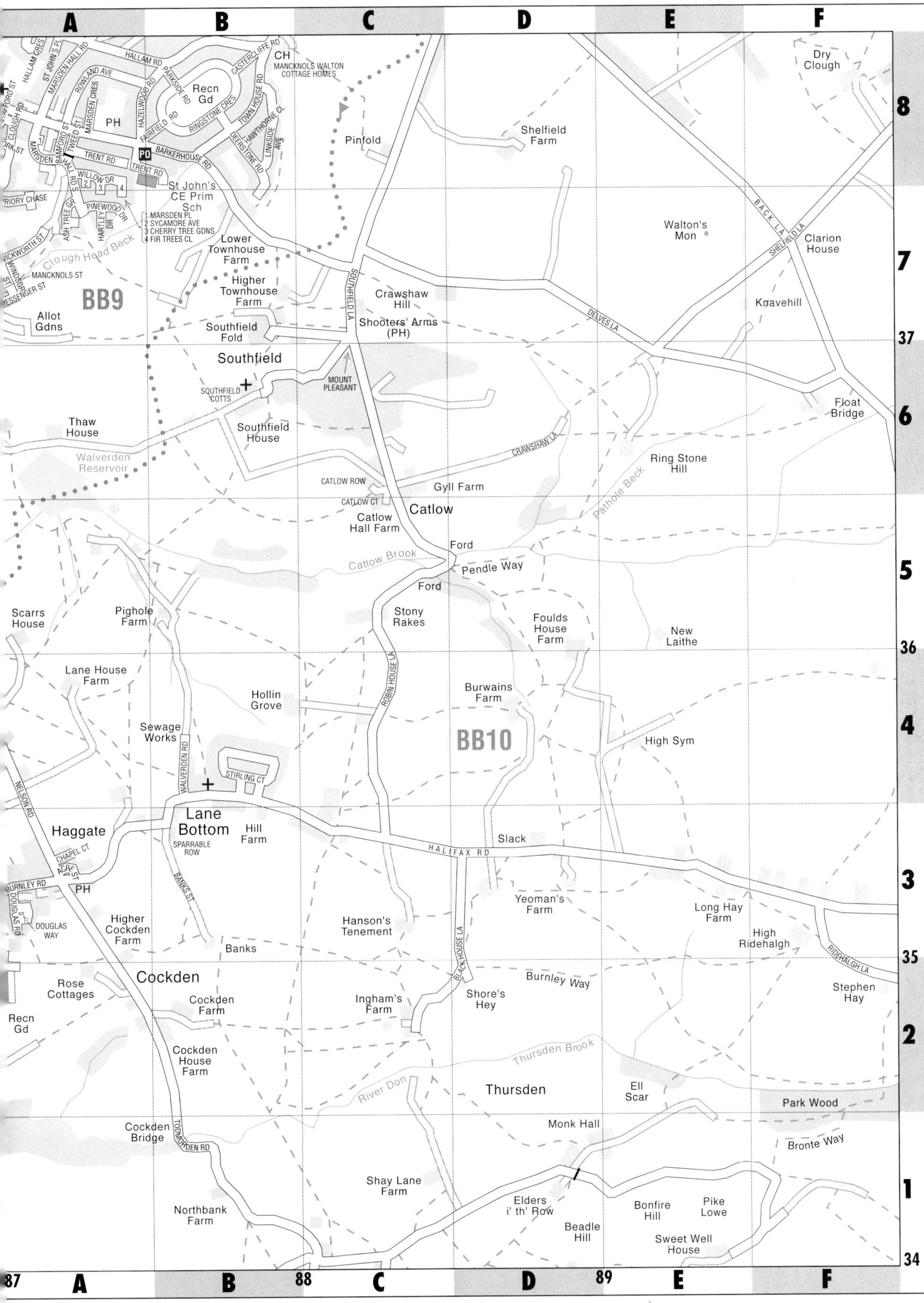
A
B
C
D
E
F
8
7
37
6
5
36
4
3
35
2
1
34
87
88
89
HALLAM CRES
ST JOHN'S PL
MARSDEN HALL RD
HALLAM RD
ROWLAND AVE
MARSDEN CRES
HAZELWOOD RD
PARKSIDE RD
Recn Gd
RINGSTONE CRES
CASTERCLIFFE RD
CH
MANCKNOLS WALTON COTTAGE HOMES
TOWN HOUSE RD
HAWTHORNE CL
LINKSIDE AVE
DEERSTONE RD
PH
FAIRFIELD RD
BAMFORD ST
TWEED ST
CLOUGH RD
MARSDEN
TRENT RD
PO
BARKERHOUSE RD
WILLOW DR
HALL RD S
PRIORY CHASE
PINEWOOD DR
ASH TREE GR
HARTLEY DR
St John's CE Prim Sch
1 MARSDEN PL
2 SYCAMORE AVE
3 CHERRY TREE GDNS
4 FIR TREES CL
Lower Townhouse Farm
Higher Townhouse Farm
Clough Head Beck
WICKWORTH ST
WINDSOR
MANCKNOLS ST
MESSENGER ST
BB9
Allot Gdns
Southfield Fold
Southfield
SOUTHFIELD COTTS
MOUNT PLEASANT
Pinfold
Shelfield Farm
Dry Clough
Walton's Mon
BACK LA
SHELFIELD LA
Clarion House
Knavehill
Crawshaw Hill
SOUTHFIELD LA
Shooters' Arms (PH)
DELVES LA
Float Bridge
Thaw House
Walverden Reservoir
Southfield House
CRAWSHAW LA
Ring Stone Hill
CATLOW ROW
CATLOW CT
Gyll Farm
Catlow
Catlow Hall Farm
Pathole Beck
Ford
Catlow Brook
Pendle Way
Ford
Scarrs House
Pighole Farm
Stony Rakes
Foulds House Farm
New Laithe
Lane House Farm
Hollin Grove
ROBIN HOUSE LA
Burwains Farm
BB10
Sewage Works
WALVERDEN RD
STIRLING CT
High Sym
NELSON RD
Haggate
Lane Bottom
SPARRABLE ROW
Hill Farm
Slack
HALIFAX RD
CHAPEL CT
ACRE ST
BURNLEY RD
PH
DOUGLAS RD
DOUGLAS WAY
BANKS ST
Higher Cockden Farm
Hanson's Tenement
Yeoman's Farm
Long Hay Farm
High Ridehalgh
RIDEHALGH LA
Banks
BLACK HOUSE LA
Cockden
Rose Cottages
Cockden Farm
Ingham's Farm
Shore's Hey
Burnley Way
Stephen Hay
Recn Gd
Cockden House Farm
Thursden Brook
River Don
Thursden
Ell Scar
Park Wood
Cockden Bridge
TODMORDEN RD
Monk Hall
Bronte Way
Shay Lane Farm
Northbank Farm
Elders i' th' Row
Bonfire Hill
Pike Lowe
Beadle Hill
Sweet Well House

129
150

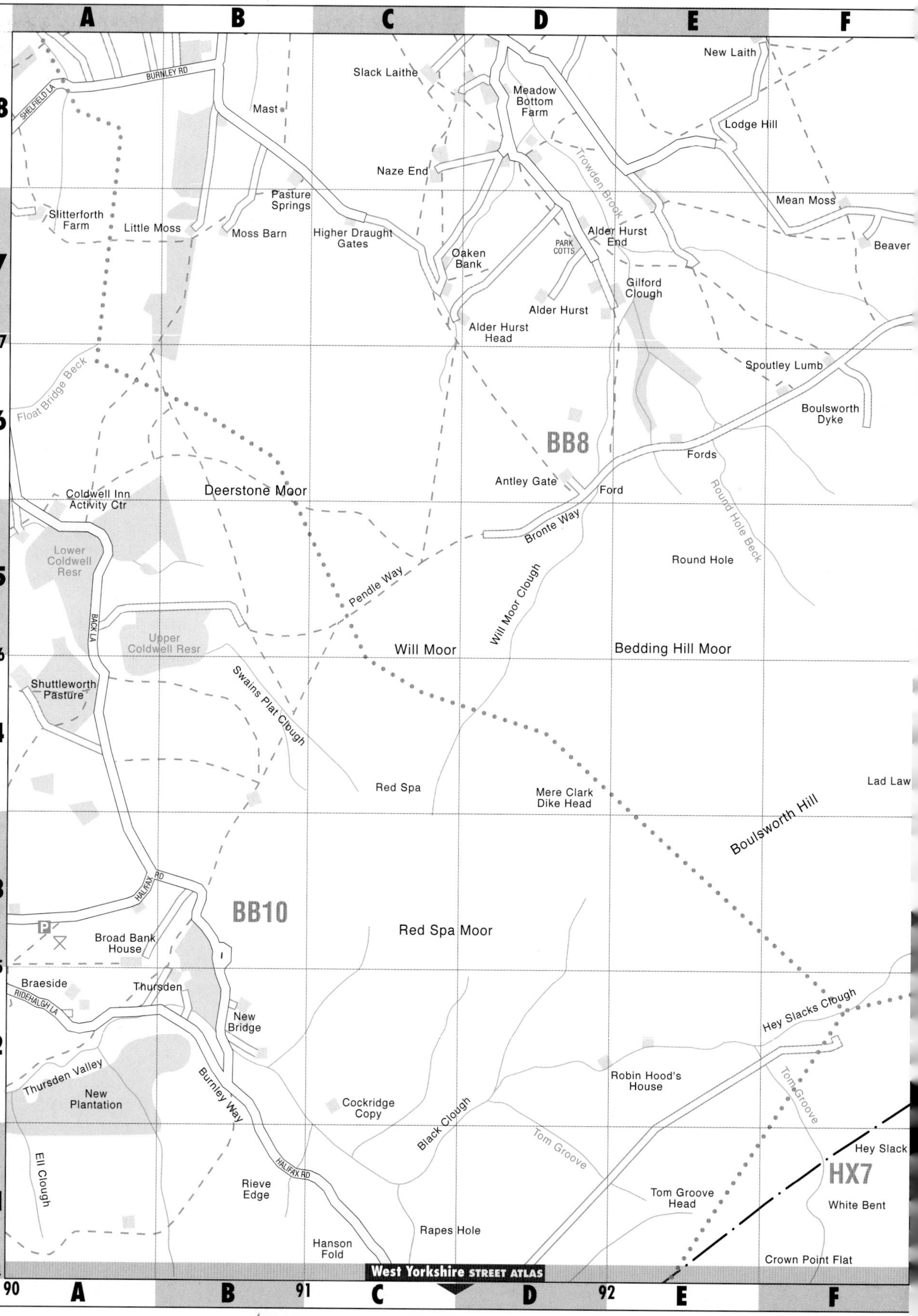
A
B
C
D
E
F
8
7
37
6
5
36
4
3
35
2
1
34
90
91
92
BURNLEY RD
SHELFIELD LA
Slack Laithe
Mast
Meadow Bottom Farm
New Laith
Lodge Hill
Naze End
Trowden Brook
Slitterforth Farm
Little Moss
Pasture Springs
Moss Barn
Higher Draught Gates
Oaken Bank
PARK COTTS
Alder Hurst End
Mean Moss
Beaver
Gilford Clough
Alder Hurst
Alder Hurst Head
Spoutley Lumb
Float Bridge Beck
Boulsworth Dyke
BB8
Fords
Antley Gate
Ford
Coldwell Inn Activity Ctr
Deerstone Moor
Bronte Way
Round Hole Beck
Lower Coldwell Resr
Round Hole
Pendle Way
Will Moor Clough
BACK LA
Upper Coldwell Resr
Will Moor
Bedding Hill Moor
Shuttleworth Pasture
Swains Plat Clough
Red Spa
Mere Clark Dike Head
Lad Law
Boulsworth Hill
HALIFAX RD
BB10
Red Spa Moor
Broad Bank House
Braeside
Thursden
RIDEHALGH LA
New Bridge
Hey Slacks Clough
Robin Hood's House
Thursden Valley
New Plantation
Burnley Way
Cockridge Copy
Black Clough
Tom Groove
Tom Groove
Hey Slack
HX7
Ell Clough
HALIFAX RD
Rieve Edge
Tom Groove Head
White Bent
Rapes Hole
Hanson Fold
Crown Point Flat

173

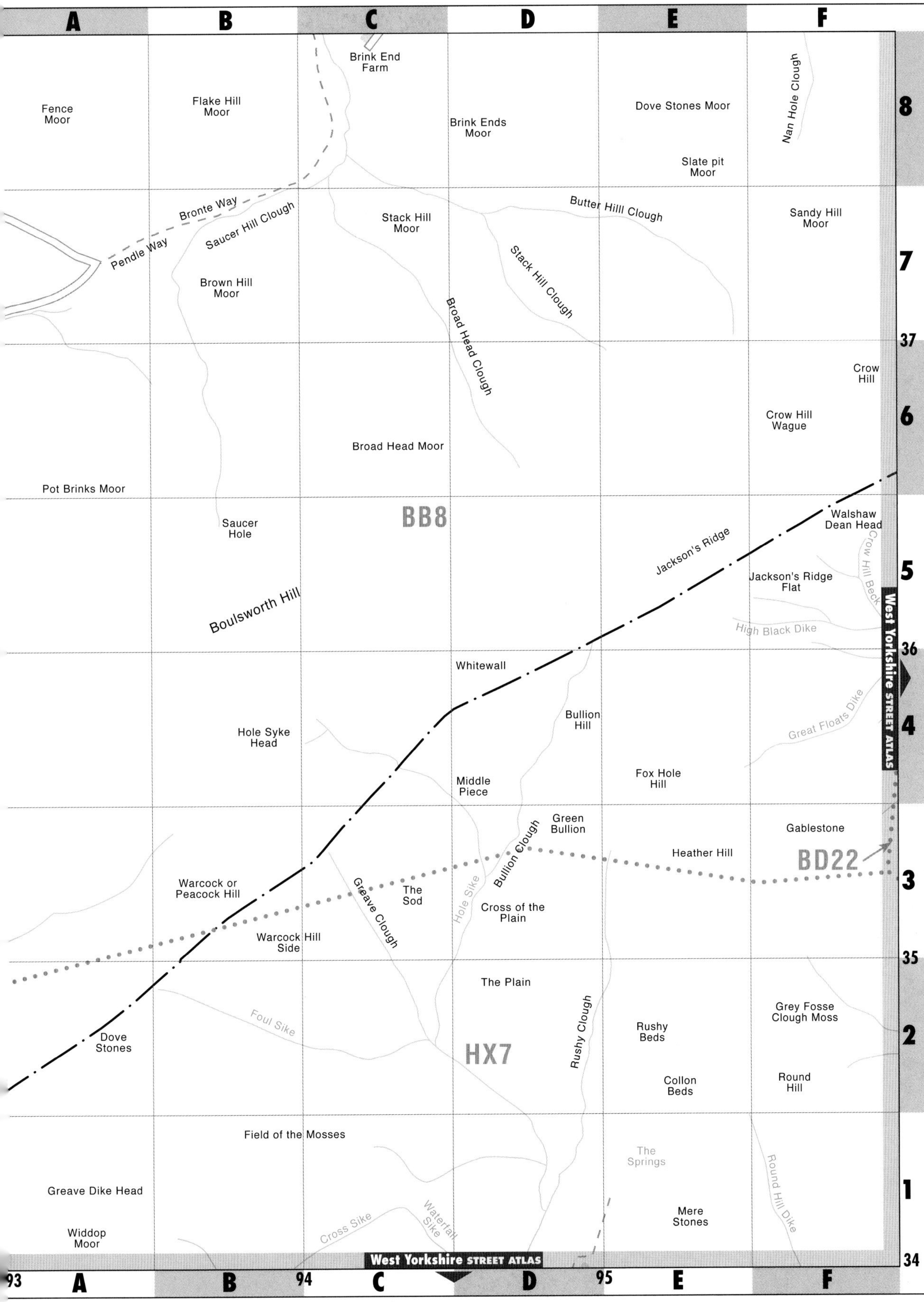


West Yorkshire STREET ATLAS

West Yorkshire STREET ATLAS

175

F7
1 WHEATFIELD CL
2 CHARDONNAY CRES
3 WOODBANK CT
4 GARNET CL
5 MARBLE AVE
6 OPAL CL
7 BRIDGEWATER AVE
8 CRAVEN CNR
9 PRENTON GDNS
10 THE SHAY
11 PRIESTIELD
12 BESCOT WAY
13 SIXFIELDS

F8
1 MELBOURNE CT
2 SEVENOAKS CT
3 QUARRYBANK
4 GRASSINGTON PL
5 LUTON RD
6 SANDERLING CL
7 THORNCROSS
8 ROSEBANK

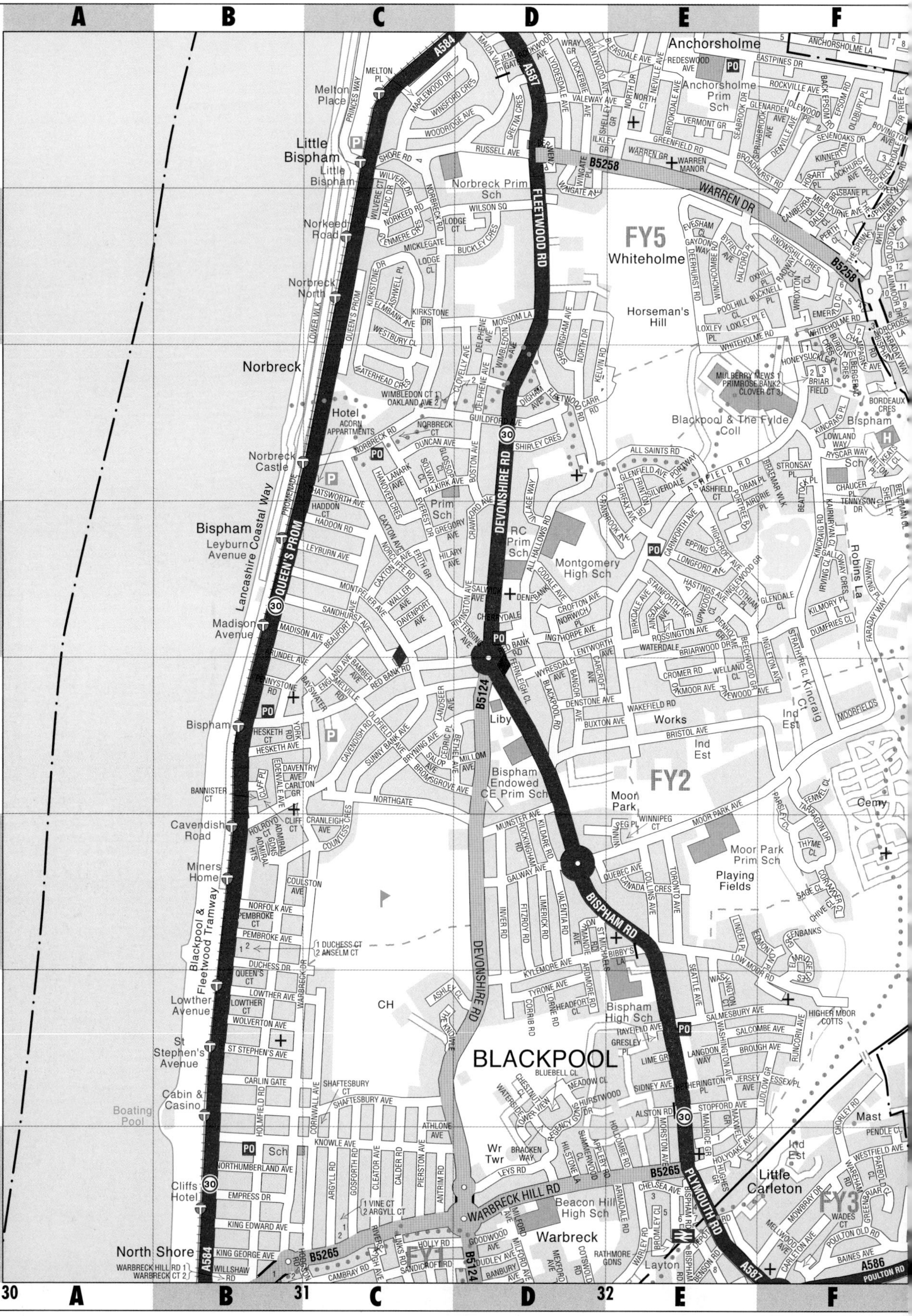


130

E1
1 BRODERICK AVE
2 Fox Ind Est
3 CHELSEA CT
4 CHELSEA MEWS
5 BROMLEY CT
6 PEARL AVE
7 HENLEY CT
8 DELAWARE RD

D3
1 BURLINGTON HO
2 CHURCH ST
3 CHAPEL STREET CT
4 MARKET PL
5 STOCKS CT
6 FALKUS CT

153 177

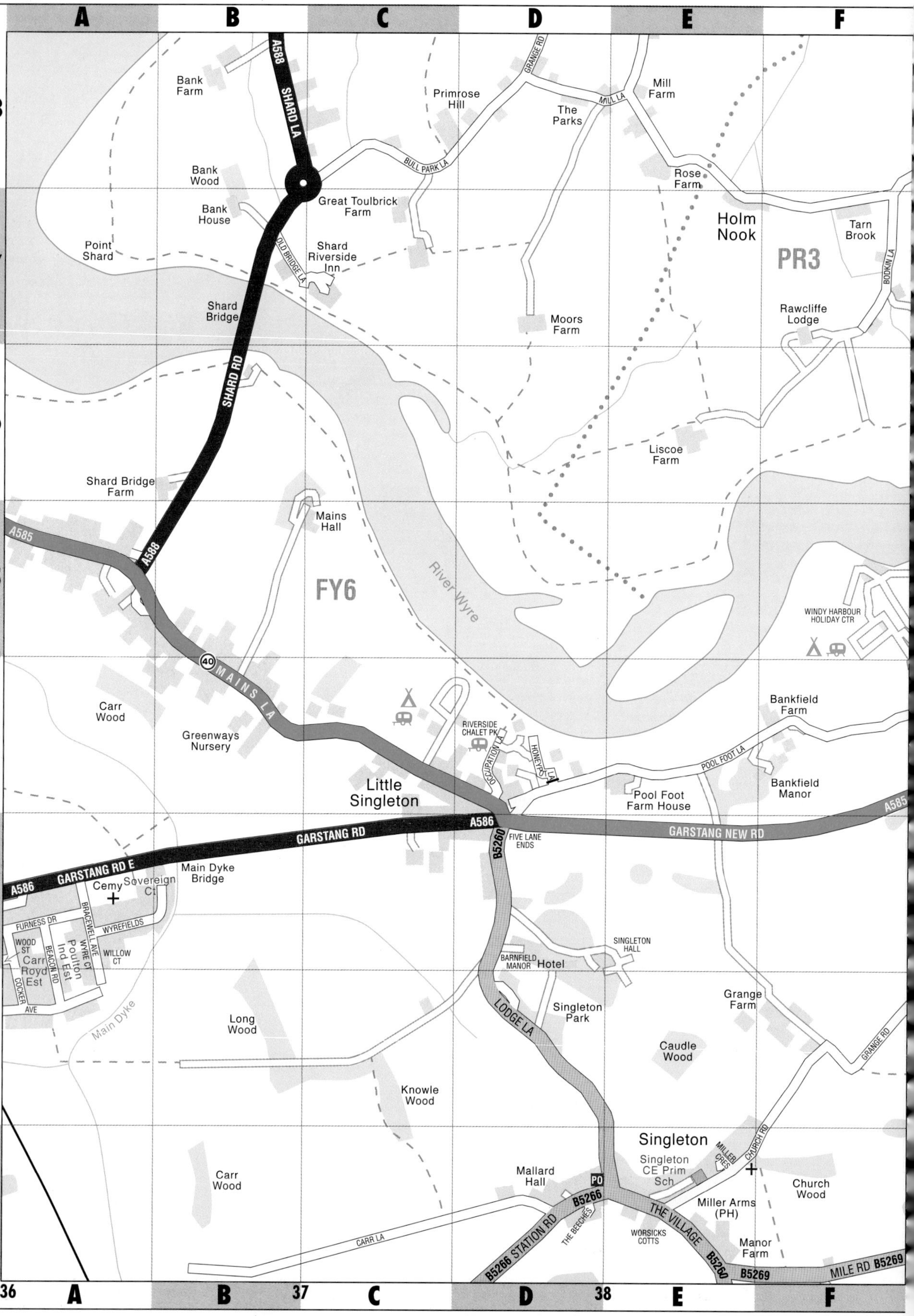
A B C D E F
8 7 41 6 5 40 4 3 39 2 1 38
36 37 38
Bank Farm
A588 SHARD LA
Primrose Hill
GRANGE RD
MILL LA
The Parks
Mill Farm
BULL PARK LA
Bank Wood
Bank House
Great Toulbrick Farm
Rose Farm
Holm Nook
Tarn Brook
Point Shard
OLD BRIDGE LA
Shard Riverside Inn
PR3
BODKIN LA
Shard Bridge
Moors Farm
Rawcliffe Lodge
SHARD RD
Liscoe Farm
Shard Bridge Farm
Mains Hall
A585
A588
FY6
River Wyre
WINDY HARBOUR HOLIDAY CTR
MAINS LA
Carr Wood
Bankfield Farm
RIVERSIDE CHALET PK
Greenways Nursery
OCCUPATION LA
HONEYKS LA
POOL FOOT LA
Little Singleton
Pool Foot Farm House
Bankfield Manor
A586
GARSTANG RD
GARSTANG NEW RD
A585
B5260
FIVE LANE ENDS
A586
GARSTANG RD E
Main Dyke Bridge
Cemy
Sovereign Ct
FURNESS DR
BRACEWELL AVE
WYREFIELDS
WOOD ST
Carr Royd Est
BEACON RD
Poulton Ind Est
WYRE CT
WILLOW CT
COCKER AVE
SINGLETON HALL
BARNFIELD MANOR
Hotel
LODGE LA
Singleton Park
Grange Farm
Main Dyke
Long Wood
Caudle Wood
GRANGE RD
Knowle Wood
Singleton
Singleton CE Prim Sch
MILLER CRES
CHURCH RD
Carr Wood
Mallard Hall
PO
B5266
Church Wood
Miller Arms (PH)
CARR LA
THE BEECHES
B5266 STATION RD
WORSICKS COTTS
THE VILLAGE
B5260
Manor Farm
B5269
MILE RD B5269

153 132

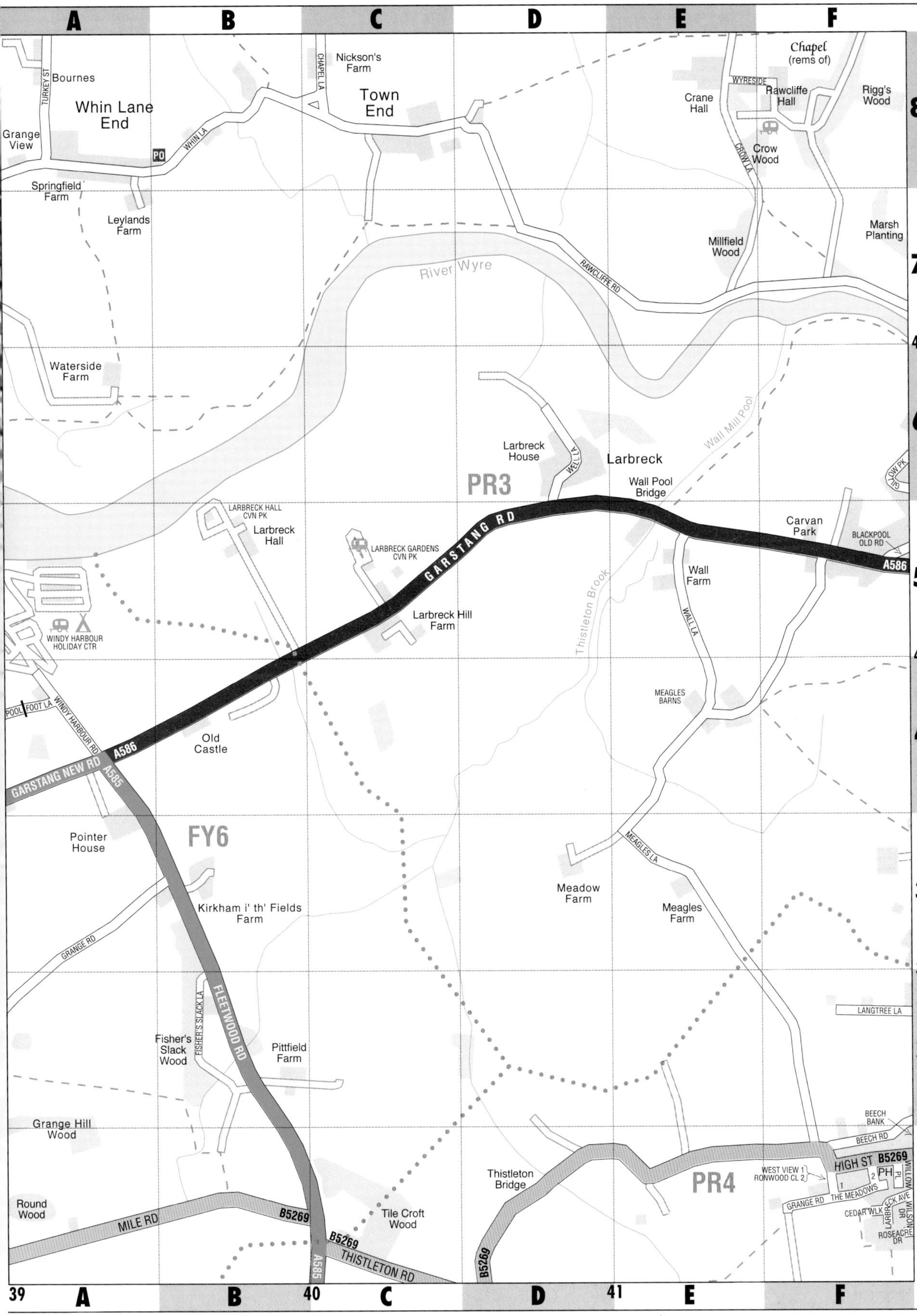
A
B
C
D
E
F
Bournes
TURKEY ST
Whin Lane
End
Grange
View
PO
WHIN LA
CHAPEL LA
Nickson's
Farm
Town
End
Chapel
(rems of)
WYRESIDE
Rawcliffe
Hall
Crane
Hall
Rigg's
Wood
CROW LA
Crow
Wood
8
Springfield
Farm
Leylands
Farm
Millfield
Wood
Marsh
Planting
River Wyre
RAWCLIFFE RD
7
41
Waterside
Farm
Wall Mill Pool
6
Larbreck
House
WELL LA
Larbreck
PR3
Wall Pool
Bridge
LARBRECK HALL
CVN PK
Larbreck
Hall
LARBRECK GARDENS
CVN PK
GARSTANG RD
Carvan
Park
BLACKPOOL
OLD RD
A586
5
WINDY HARBOUR
HOLIDAY CTR
Larbreck Hill
Farm
Thistleton Brook
Wall
Farm
WALL LA
40
POOL FOOT LA
WINDY HARBOUR RD
MEAGLES
BARNS
Old
Castle
A586
4
GARSTANG NEW RD
A585
Pointer
House
FY6
MEAGLES LA
Meadow
Farm
Meagles
Farm
3
Kirkham i' th' Fields
Farm
GRANGE RD
39
LANGTREE LA
FLEETWOOD RD
FISHER'S SLACK LA
Fisher's
Slack
Wood
Pittfield
Farm
2
BEECH
BANK
BEECH RD
Grange Hill
Wood
HIGH ST
B5269
Thistleton
Bridge
PR4
WEST VIEW 1
RONWOOD CL 2
PH
PL
WILLOW
GRANGE RD
THE MEADOWS
CEDAR WLK
LARBRECK AVE
WILSON DR
ROSEACRE DR
Round
Wood
MILE RD
B5269
Tile Croft
Wood
B5269
THISTLETON RD
A585
B5269
1
38
39
A
B
40
C
D
41
E
F

155
179

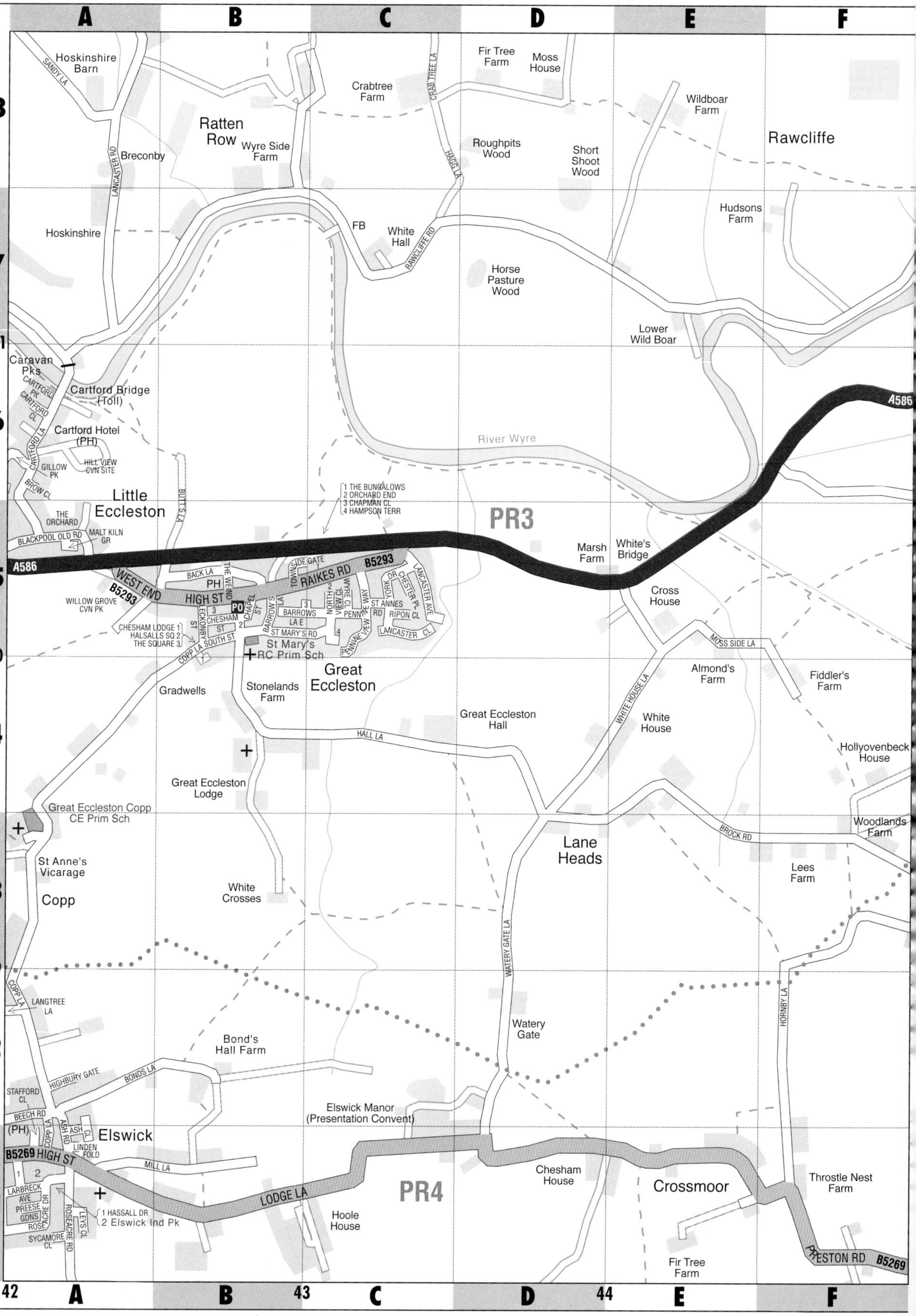
A
B
C
D
E
F
8
7
41
6
5
40
4
3
39
2
1
38
42
43
44
Hoskinshire Barn
SANDY LA
Ratten Row
Wyre Side Farm
Crabtree Farm
Fir Tree Farm
Moss House
CRAB TREE LA
Wildboar Farm
Rawcliffe
LANCASTER RD
Breconby
Roughpits Wood
HAGG LA
Short Shoot Wood
Hudsons Farm
Hoskinshire
FB
White Hall
RAWCLIFFE RD
Horse Pasture Wood
Lower Wild Boar
Caravan Pks
CARTFORD PK
CARTFORD CL
Cartford Bridge (Toll)
A586
CARTFORD LA
Cartford Hotel (PH)
River Wyre
GILLOW PK
HILL VIEW CVN SITE
BROW CL
Little Eccleston
BUTTS LA
1 THE BUNGALOWS
2 ORCHARD END
3 CHAPMAN CL
4 HAMPSON TERR
PR3
THE ORCHARD
MALT KILN GR
BLACKPOOL OLD RD
Marsh Farm
White's Bridge
A586
BACK LA
THE WEND
TOWNSIDE GATE
B5293
RAIKES RD
LANCASTER AVE
WEST END
PH
HIGH ST
B5293
PO
CHAPEL ST
BARROW'S LA
NORTH VIEW
WYRE CL
YORK DR
CHESTER PL
Cross House
WILLOW GROVE CVN PK
LECKONBY ST
CHESHAM ST
BARROWS LA E
PENNINE VIEW
ST ANNES RD
RIPON CL
CHESHAM LODGE 1
HALSALLS SQ 2
THE SQUARE 3
SOUTH ST
ST MARY'S RD
LANCASTER CL
MOSS SIDE LA
COPP LA
St Mary's RC Prim Sch
Great Eccleston
Almond's Farm
Fiddler's Farm
Gradwells
Stonelands Farm
WHITE HOUSE LA
Great Eccleston Hall
White House
HALL LA
Hollyovenbeck House
Great Eccleston Lodge
Great Eccleston Copp CE Prim Sch
Woodlands Farm
BROCK RD
Lane Heads
St Anne's Vicarage
Lees Farm
Copp
White Crosses
WATERY GATE LA
COPP LA
LANGTREE LA
HORNBY LA
Bond's Hall Farm
Watery Gate
HIGHBURY GATE
BONDS LA
STAFFORD CL
BEECH RD
(PH)
COPP LA
ASH RD
ASH CL
Elswick Manor (Presentation Convent)
Elswick
LINDEN FOLD
B5269 HIGH ST
MILL LA
Chesham House
Crossmoor
Throstle Nest Farm
LARBRECK AVE
PREESE GDNS
ROSEACRE DR
ROSE
ROSEACRE RD
LEYS CL
LODGE LA
PR4
Hoole House
1 HASSALL DR
2 Elswick Ind Pk
SYCAMORE CL
Fir Tree Farm
PRESTON RD
B5269

155
134

180
158

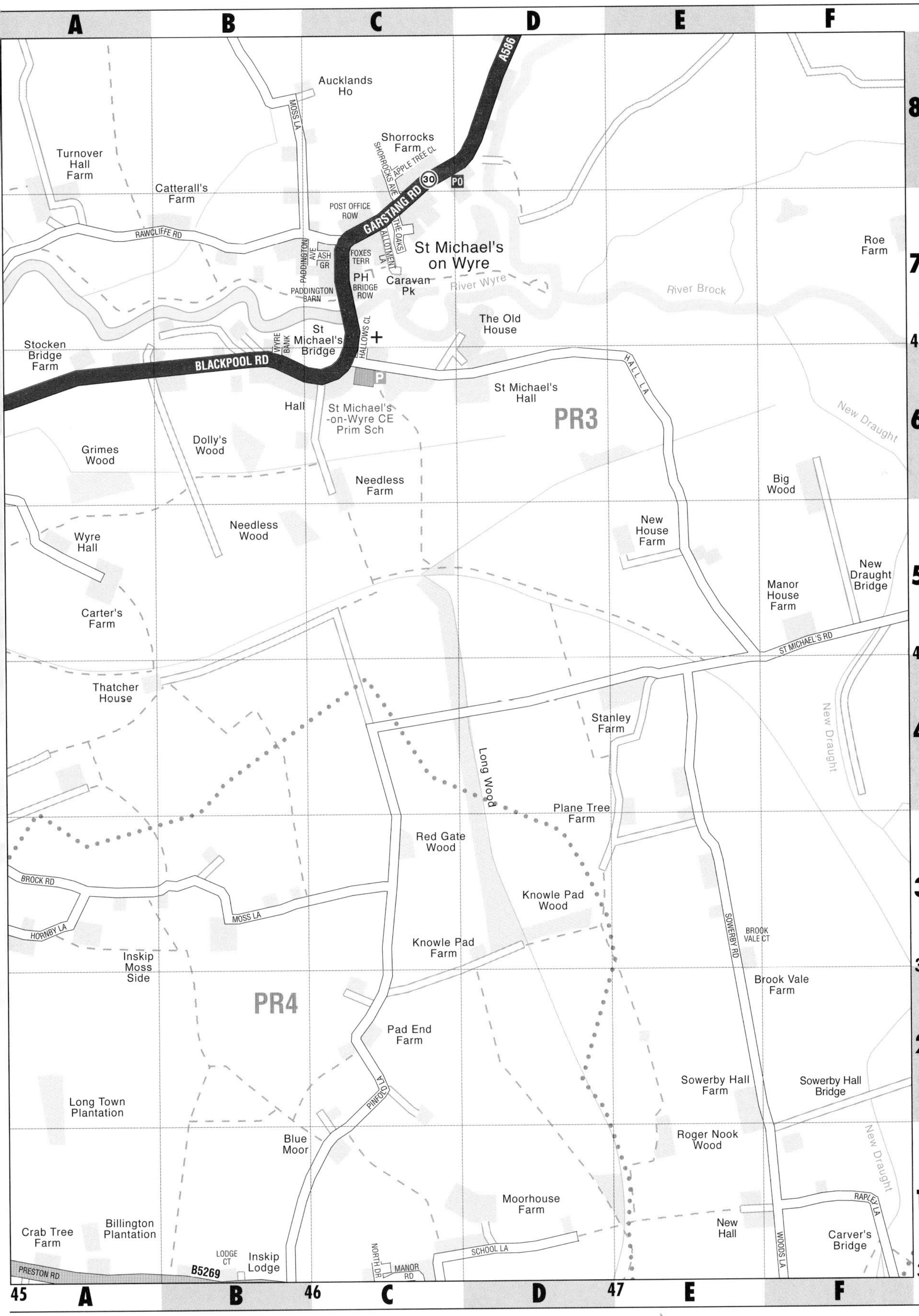


135
158

157
181
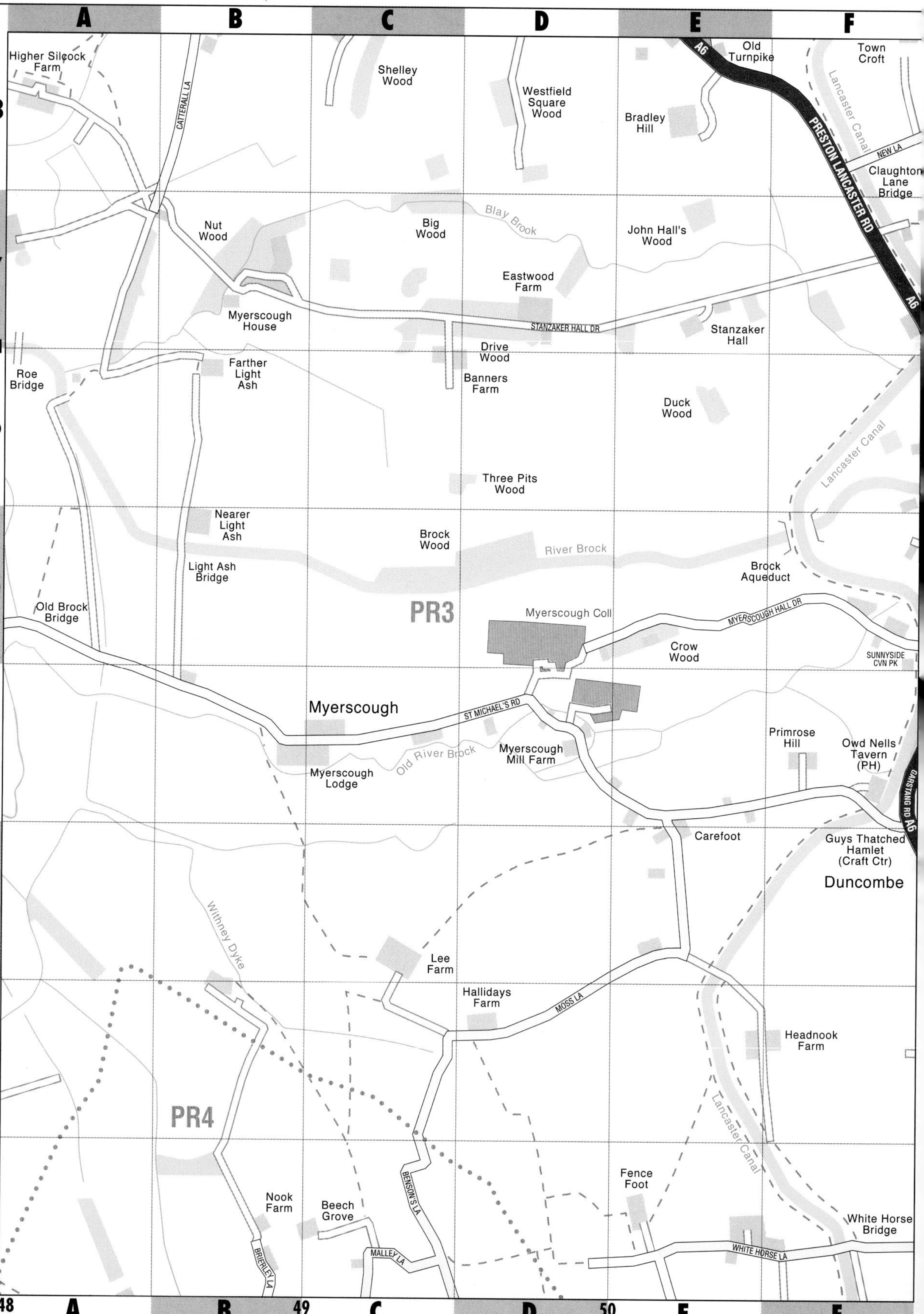

157
136

A B C D E F
8 7 41 6 5 40 4 3 39 2 1 38
51 52 53
Carter House
LODGE RD
OLD LODGE LA
NEW LA
M6
Old Heronry Wood
Bowman House Farm
Manor House Farm
Whinny Plantation
Claughton House
Lofthouse
Duckett's Farm
DUCKETTS LA
MAY LA
WALMSLEY BRIDGE LA
Walmsley Bridge
Lower Brock Wood
Brow Top
River Brock
Poulton's Wood
Brock Side
Higher Barn
BADGERS WOOD
Matshead
BROCK SIDE
New Bridge
LYDIATE LA
Lower House Wood
Lower House
PRESTON LANCASTER RD
LC
Brock
Bull Brook
BOURNE BROW
SCOTCH GREEN LA
BILSBOROW LA
THE HAWTHORNS
WILLOW BANK
BEECH AVE
MOORE RD
THE GROVE
SYCAMORE
Bilsborough Hall
Wrights Farm
Spaddock Hall
PR3
Bilsborrow
BALLOT HILL CRES
John Cross CE Prim Sch
GARSTANG RD
CHURCH LA
PO
MEMORIAL GDNS
DUNCOMBE TERR
40
Bilsborrow Hall Farm
Roebuck Inn (PH)
BILSBORROW LA
Raby's Farm
GREEN LA
Green Lane Farm
Bacchus Brook
GARSTANG RD
Anderton Fold
Mount Pleasant Farm
Fisher's Farm
North Planks
MYERSCOUGH PLANKS
Abbotts Farm
Jack Nook Farm
Park House
Jack Wood
South Planks
Beesley's Farm
Myerscough Cottage
Manor House
Sparling Brook
Blake Hall
White Horse Hotel (PH)
Barton Old Hall Farm
LANGLEY LA
WHITE HORSE LA
Hall
Hoole Fold
Mast
A6

159
183

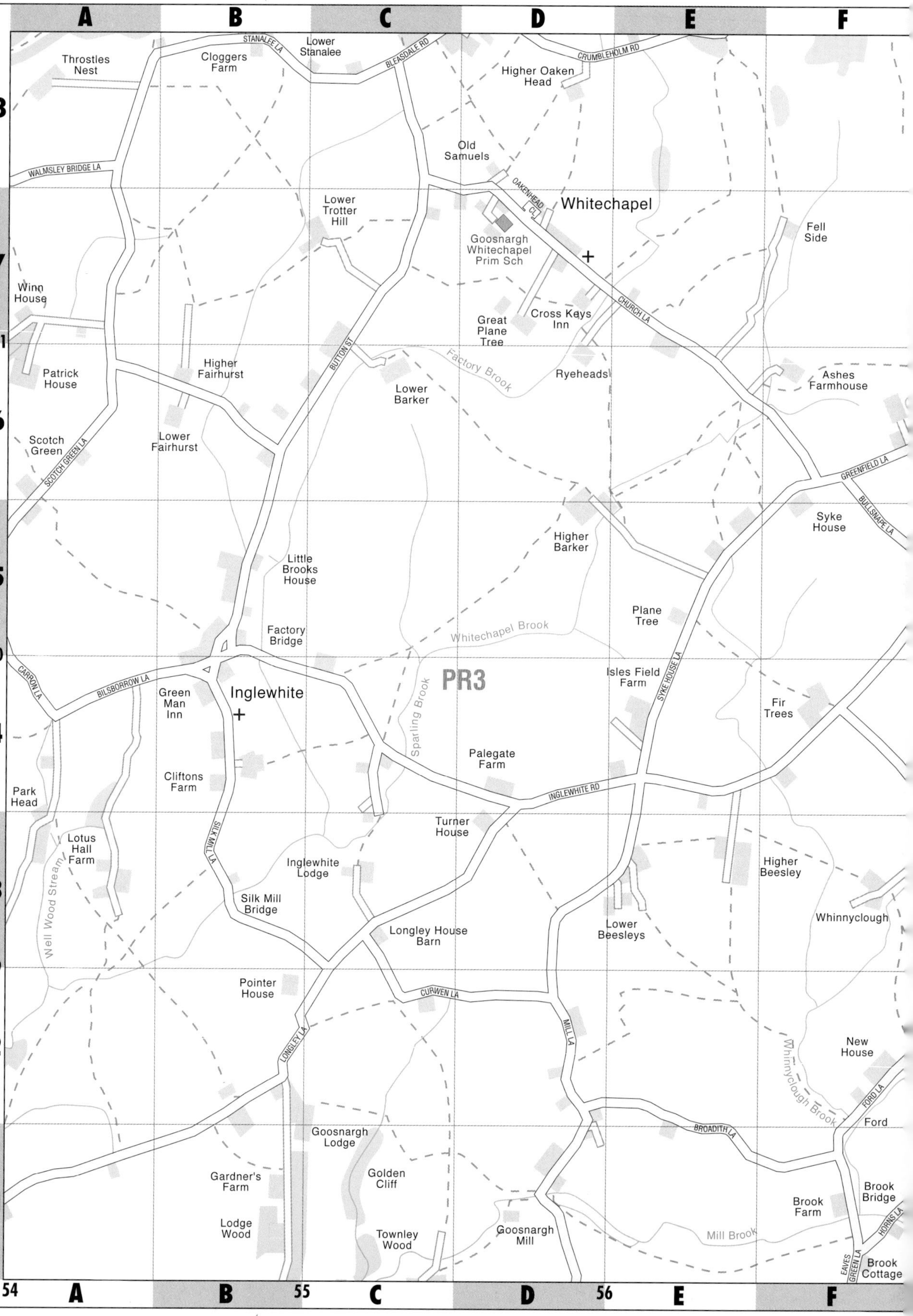


156
138

184
162

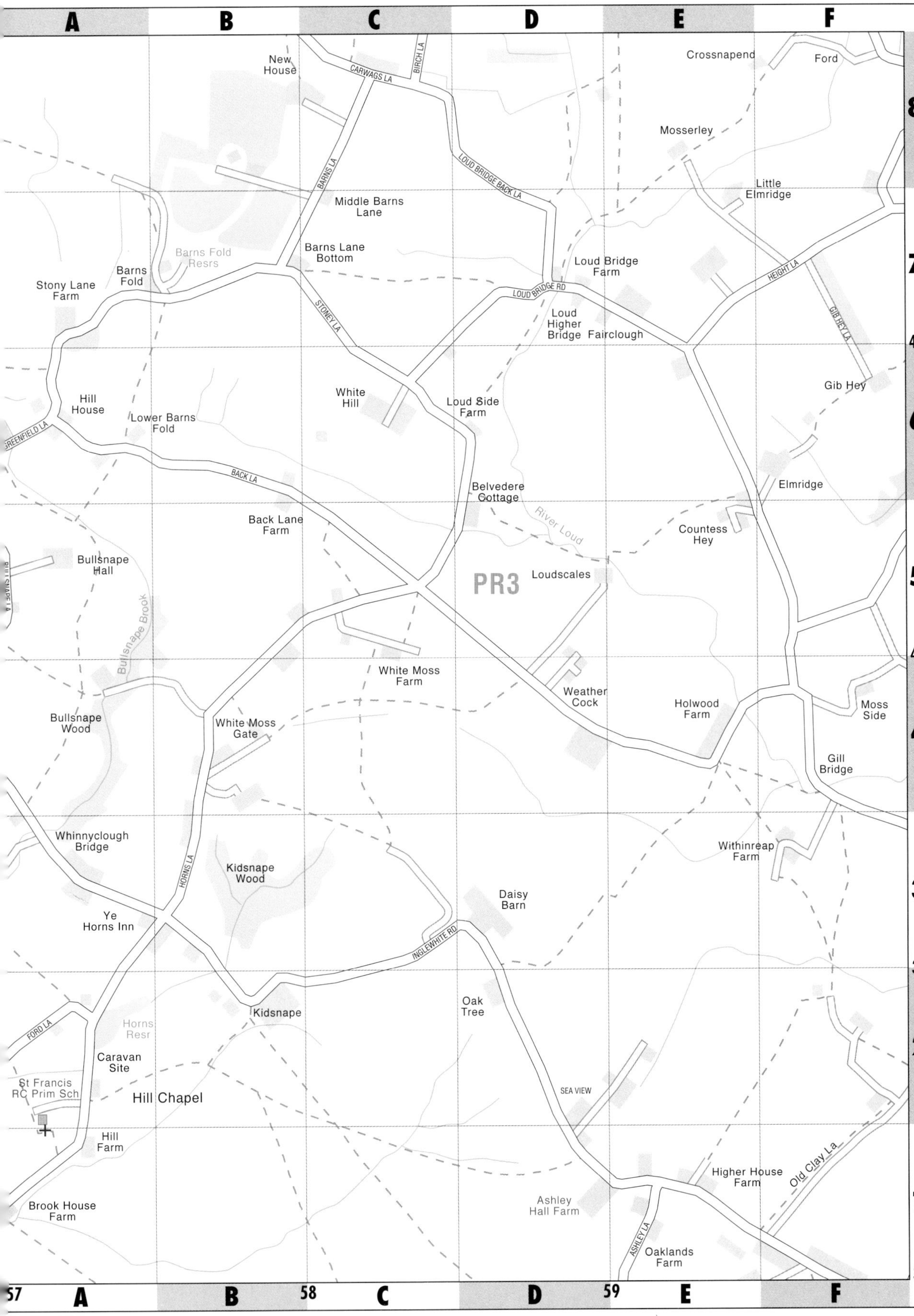
A
B
C
D
E
F
8
7
41
6
5
40
4
3
39
2
1
38
57
58
59
New House
CARWAGS LA
BIRCH LA
Crossnapend
Ford
Mosserley
BARNS LA
LOUD BRIDGE BACK LA
Little Elmridge
Middle Barns Lane
Barns Lane Bottom
Barns Fold Resrs
Barns Fold
Stony Lane Farm
Loud Bridge Farm
LOUD BRIDGE RD
HEIGHT LA
STONEY LA
Loud Higher Bridge
Fairclough
GIB HEY LA
Gib Hey
Hill House
White Hill
Loud Side Farm
Lower Barns Fold
GREENFIELD LA
BACK LA
Belvedere Cottage
Elmridge
River Loud
Back Lane Farm
Countess Hey
Bullsnape Hall
PR3
Loudscales
Bullsnape Brook
White Moss Farm
Weather Cock
Holwood Farm
Moss Side
Bullsnape Wood
White Moss Gate
Gill Bridge
Whinnyclough Bridge
Withinreap Farm
HORNS LA
Kidsnape Wood
Daisy Barn
Ye Horns Inn
INGLEWHITE RD
Oak Tree
Kidsnape
FORD LA
Horns Resr
Caravan Site
St Francis RC Prim Sch
Hill Chapel
SEA VIEW
Hill Farm
Higher House Farm
Old Clay La
Brook House Farm
Ashley Hall Farm
ASHLEY LA
Oaklands Farm

161
185

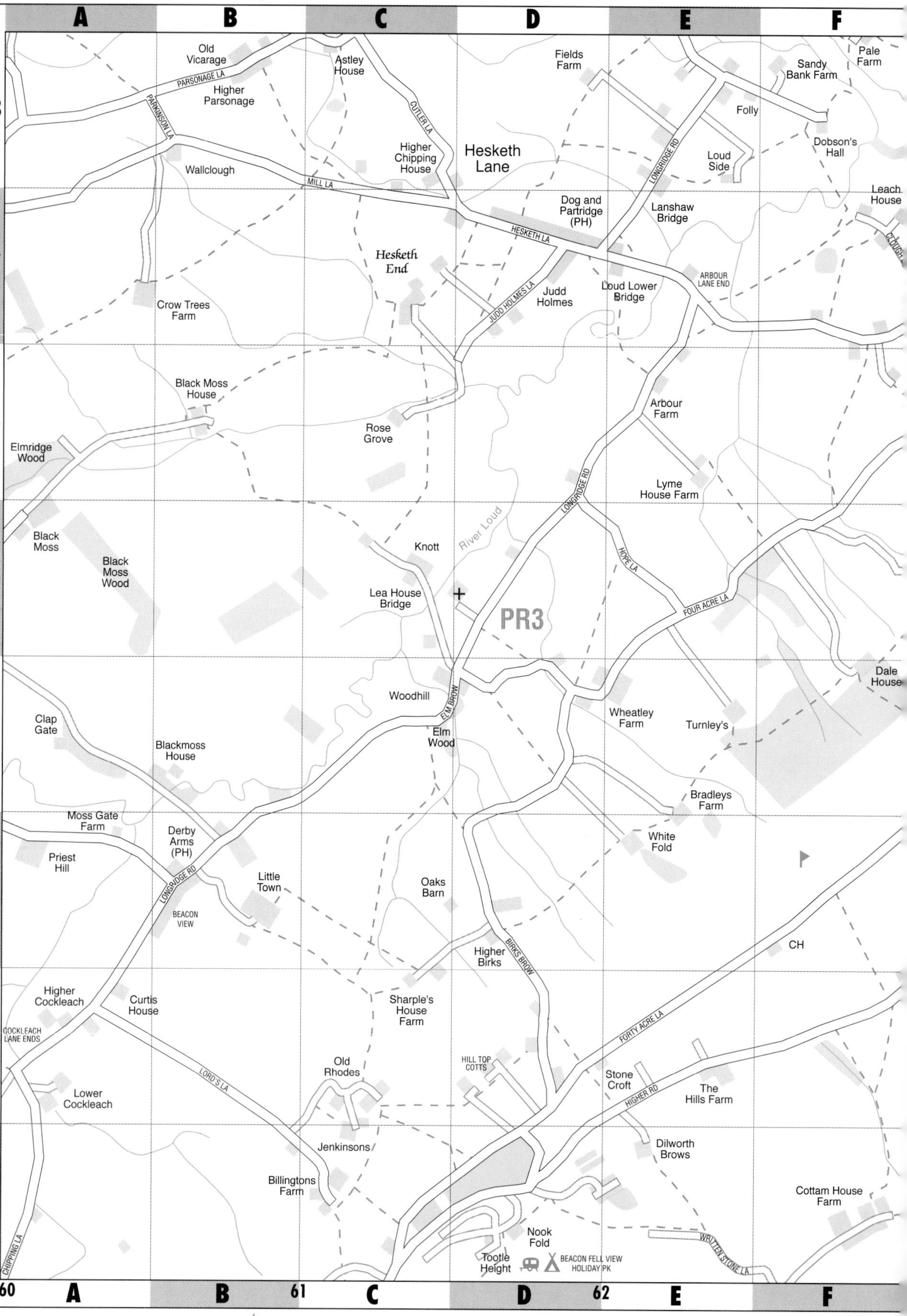
A B C D E F
8 7 6 5 4 3 2 1
41 40 39 38
60 61 62
Old Vicarage
PARSONAGE LA
Higher Parsonage
PARKINSON LA
Astley House
CUTLER LA
Fields Farm
Pale Farm
Sandy Bank Farm
Folly
Loud Side
LONGRIDGE RD
Dobson's Hall
Wallclough
MILL LA
Higher Chipping House
Hesketh Lane
Dog and Partridge (PH)
Lanshaw Bridge
Leach House
CLOUGH
HESKETH LA
Hesketh End
Judd Holmes
JUDD HOLMES LA
Loud Lower Bridge
ARBOUR LANE END
Crow Trees Farm
Black Moss House
Rose Grove
Arbour Farm
Elmridge Wood
Lyme House Farm
Black Moss
Black Moss Wood
Knott
River Loud
HOPE LA
Lea House Bridge
PR3
FOUR ACRE LA
Dale House
Woodhill
ELM BROW
Elm Wood
Wheatley Farm
Turnley's
Clap Gate
Blackmoss House
Bradleys Farm
Moss Gate Farm
Derby Arms (PH)
Priest Hill
White Fold
Little Town
Oaks Barn
BEACON VIEW
Higher Birks
BIRKS BROW
CH
Higher Cockleach
Curtis House
Sharple's House Farm
COCKLEACH LANE ENDS
LORD'S LA
FORTY ACRE LA
Old Rhodes
HILL TOP COTTS
Stone Croft
The Hills Farm
HIGHER RD
Lower Cockleach
Jenkinsons
Dilworth Brows
Billingtons Farm
Cottam House Farm
Nook Fold
Tootle Height
BEACON FELL VIEW HOLIDAY PK
WRITTEN STONE LA
CHIPPING LA

161
140

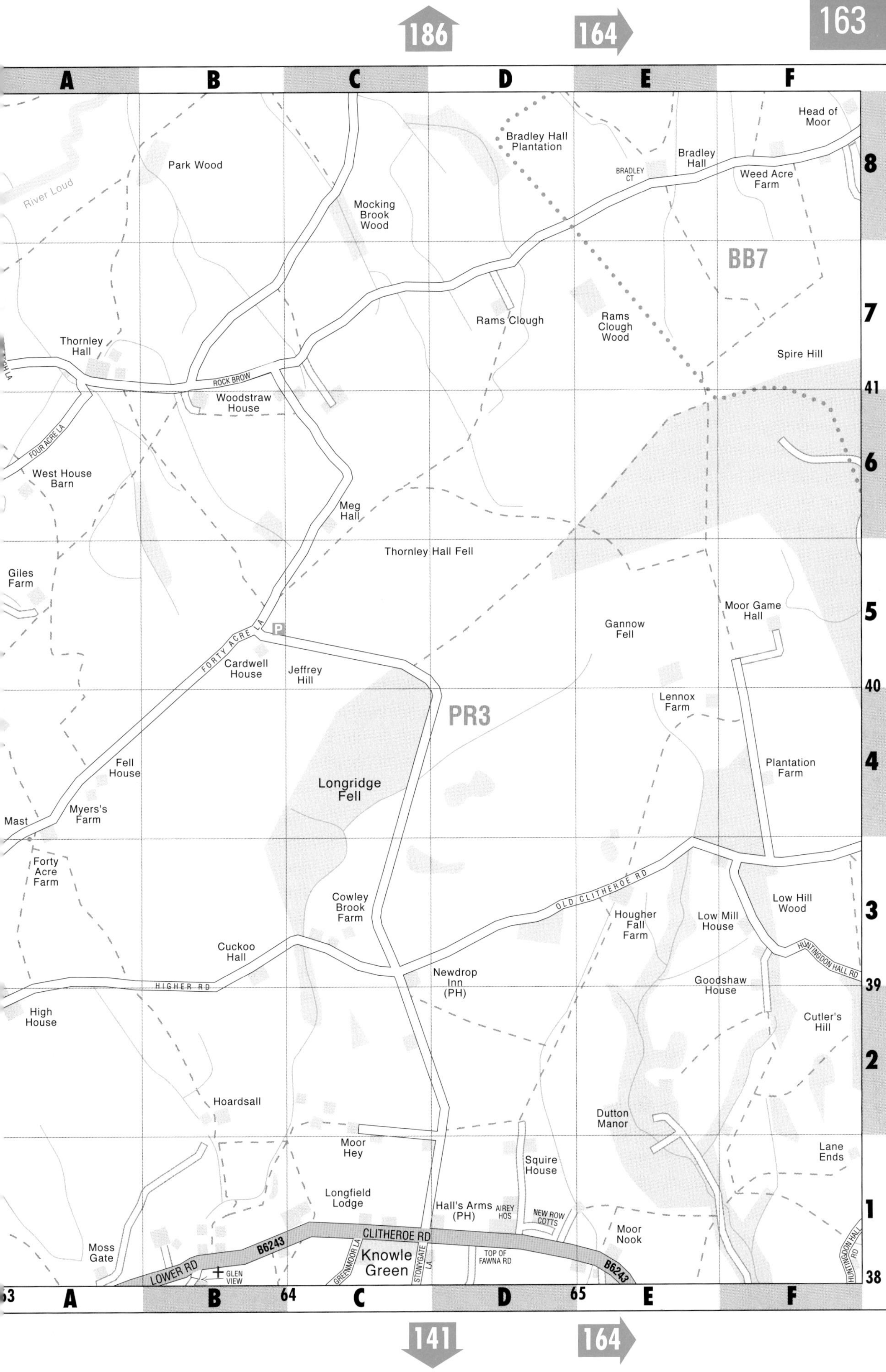
186
164
A
B
C
D
E
F
8
7
41
6
5
40
4
3
39
2
1
38
Head of Moor
Bradley Hall Plantation
Bradley Hall
BRADLEY CT
Weed Acre Farm
Park Wood
River Loud
Mocking Brook Wood
BB7
Thornley Hall
Rams Clough
Rams Clough Wood
Spire Hill
ROCK BROW
Woodstraw House
FOUR ACRE LA
West House Barn
Meg Hall
Thornley Hall Fell
Giles Farm
Moor Game Hall
Gannow Fell
FORTY ACRE LA
Cardwell House
Jeffrey Hill
PR3
Lennox Farm
Fell House
Longridge Fell
Plantation Farm
Myers's Farm
Mast
Forty Acre Farm
OLD CLITHEROE RD
Cowley Brook Farm
Hougher Fall Farm
Low Mill House
Low Hill Wood
Cuckoo Hall
HUNTINGDON HALL RD
HIGHER RD
Newdrop Inn (PH)
Goodshaw House
High House
Cutler's Hill
Hoardsall
Dutton Manor
Moor Hey
Squire House
Lane Ends
Longfield Lodge
Hall's Arms (PH)
AIREY HOS
NEW ROW COTTS
Moor Nook
CLITHEROE RD
B6243
Moss Gate
LOWER RD
GLEN VIEW
GREENMOOR LA
Knowle Green
STONYGATE LA
TOP OF FAWNA RD
HUNTINGDON HALL RD
63
64
65
141
164

163
187

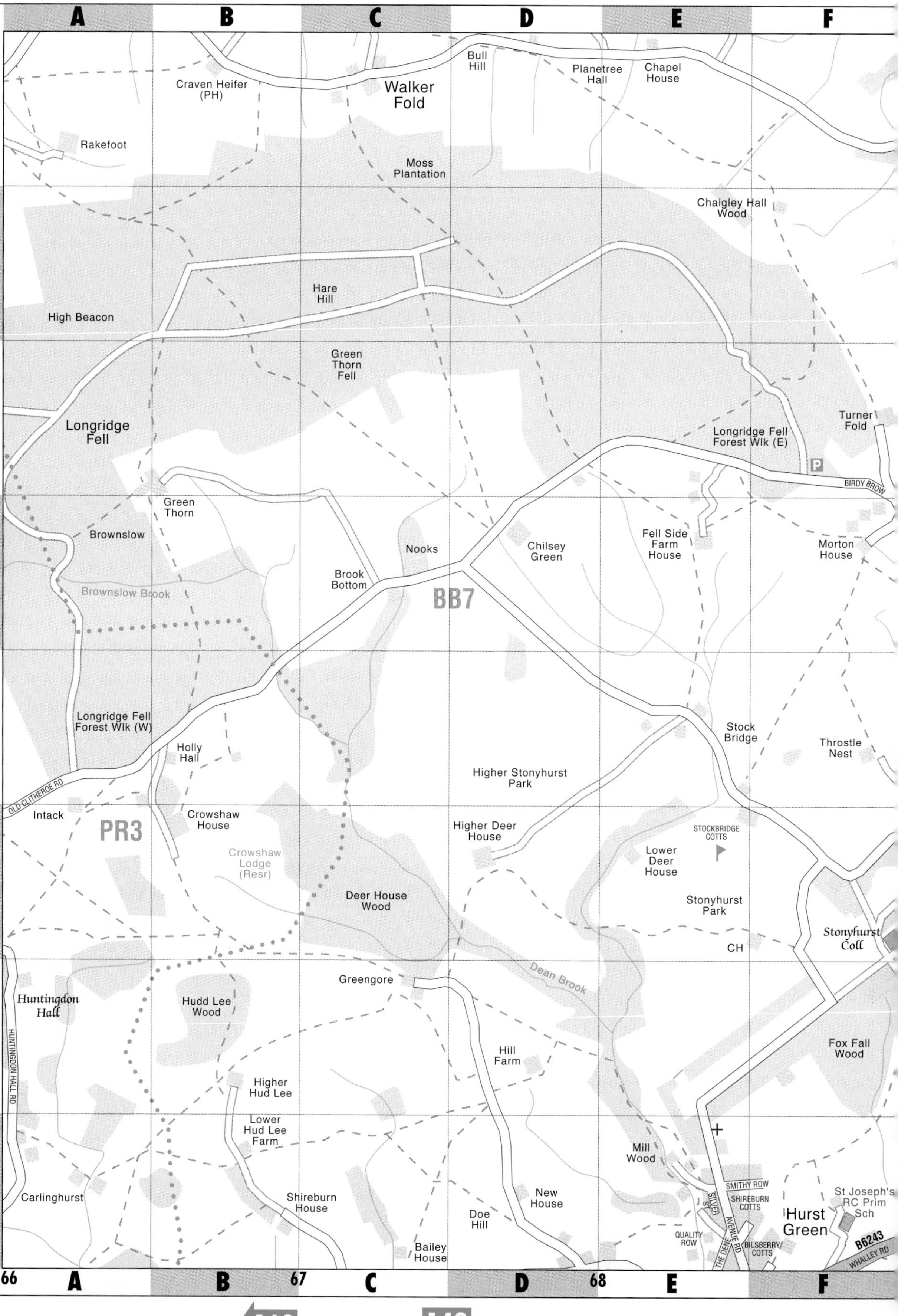


163
142

188
166
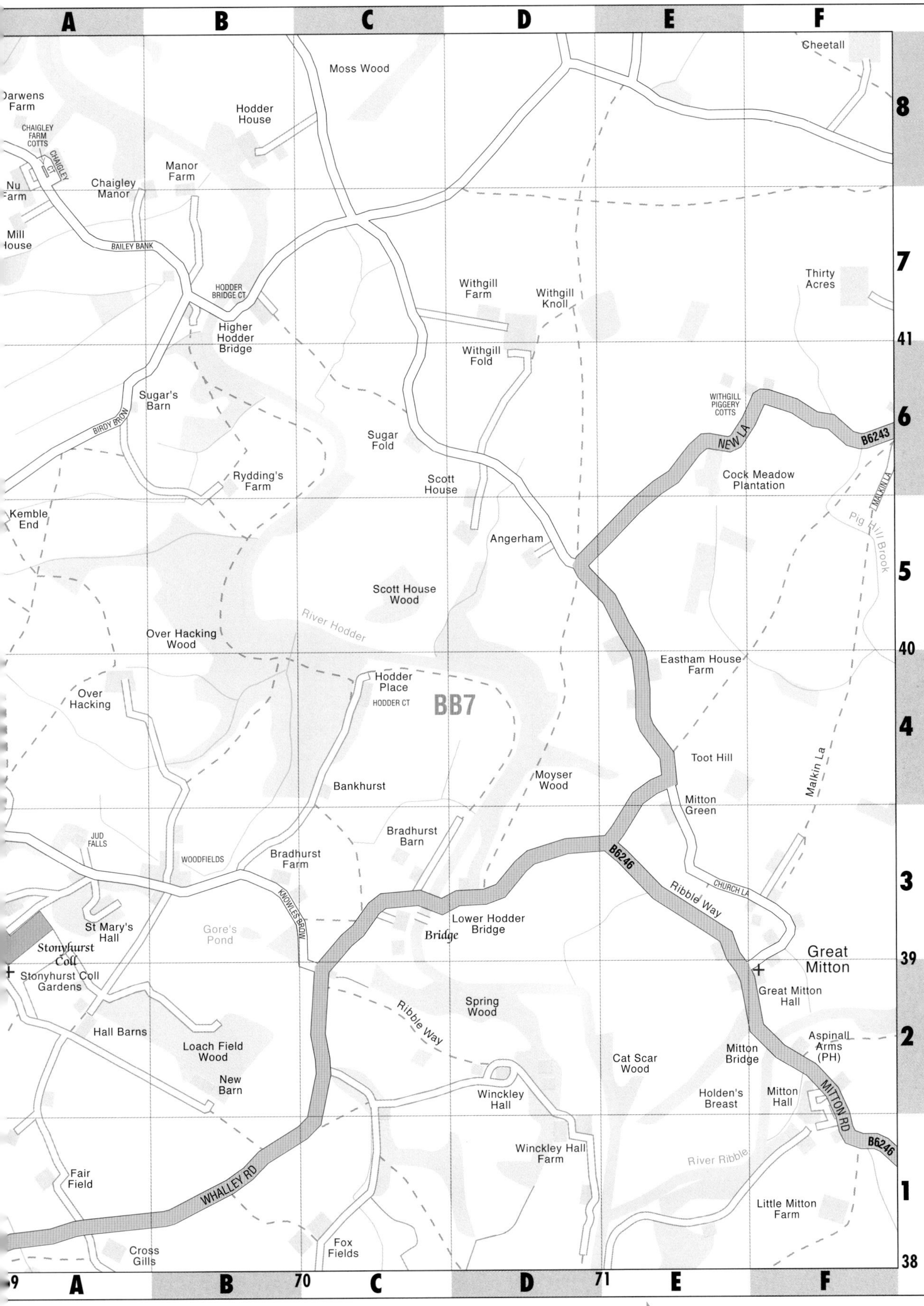

143
166

165
189

D7
1 CURZON ST
2 MONK ST
3 BARN CROFT
4 HENTHORN CL
5 DEAN MDW
6 MAPLE AVE

D7
7 VICTORIA MEWS
D8
1 CARDIGAN CL
2 ALBEMARLE CT
3 BALDWIN HILL
4 MONTAGUE ST

5 WHALLEY ST
6 CORPORATION ST
7 MOSS ST
8 JOHN WALL CT
9 MILLTHORNE HO
E8
1 CHURCH ST

2 HARRIS CT
3 MARKET PL
4 BOWLAND CT
5 SADDLERS MEWS
6 STRANG STEE
7 WILKIN SQ
8 THE EMPORIUM

9 OLD STATION CT
10 PARSONAGE COTTS
11 CARDIGAN AVE
12 CASTLE VIEW HO
13 CASTLEKEEP HO
F8
1 ALBION ST

2 DUCK ST
3 CANDLEMAKERS CROFT
4 SHAW BRIDGE ST
5 PENDLE CT
6 BOLLAND CL
7 BROTHERTON MDWS

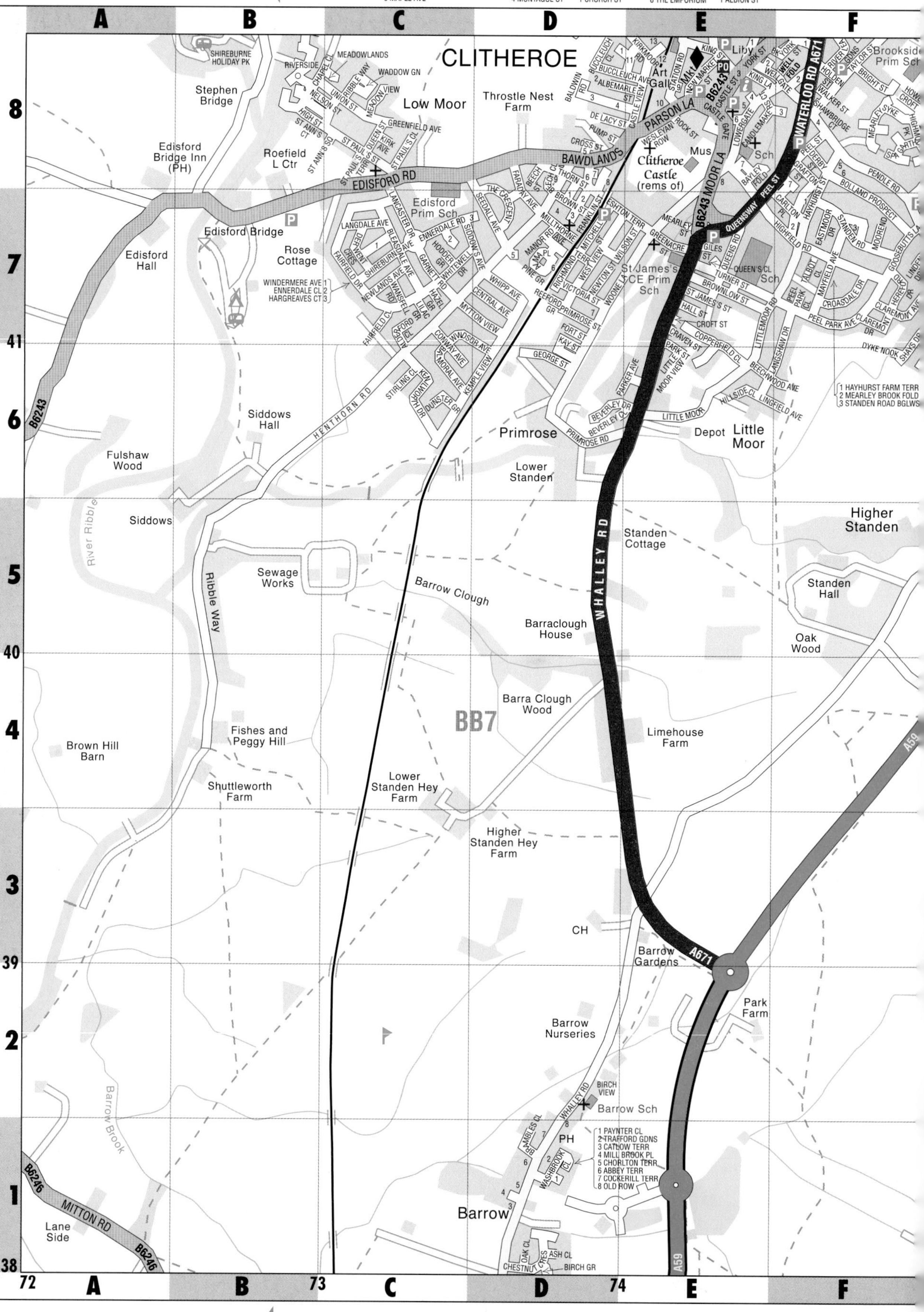


165
144

190
168

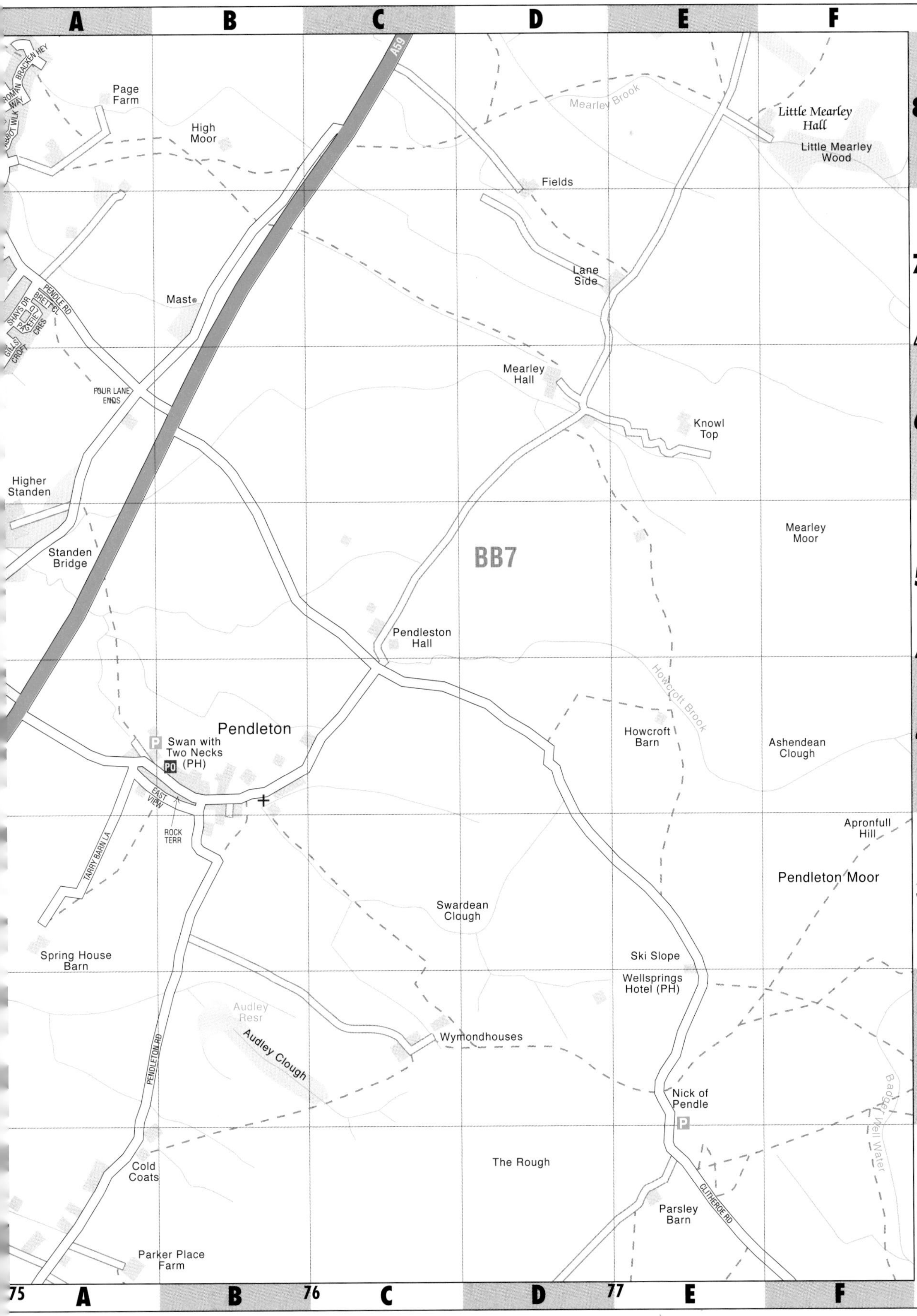
A
B
C
D
E
F
8
7
41
6
5
40
4
3
39
2
1
38
75
76
77
A59
BRACKEN HEY
ABBOT WLK
Page Farm
High Moor
Mearley Brook
Little Mearley Hall
Little Mearley Wood
Fields
Lane Side
Mast
PENDLE RD
BRETT CL
SHAYS DR
FOUR LANE ENDS
Mearley Hall
Knowl Top
Higher Standen
Standen Bridge
Mearley Moor
BB7
Pendleston Hall
Howcroft Brook
Pendleton
Swan with Two Necks (PH)
PO
Howcroft Barn
Ashendean Clough
EAST VIEW
ROCK TERR
TARRY BARN LA
Apronfull Hill
Pendleton Moor
Swardean Clough
Spring House Barn
Ski Slope
Wellsprings Hotel (PH)
Audley Resr
Audley Clough
Wymondhouses
PENDLETON RD
Nick of Pendle
Badger Well Water
Cold Coats
The Rough
CLITHEROE RD
Parsley Barn
Parker Place Farm

145
168

167
191

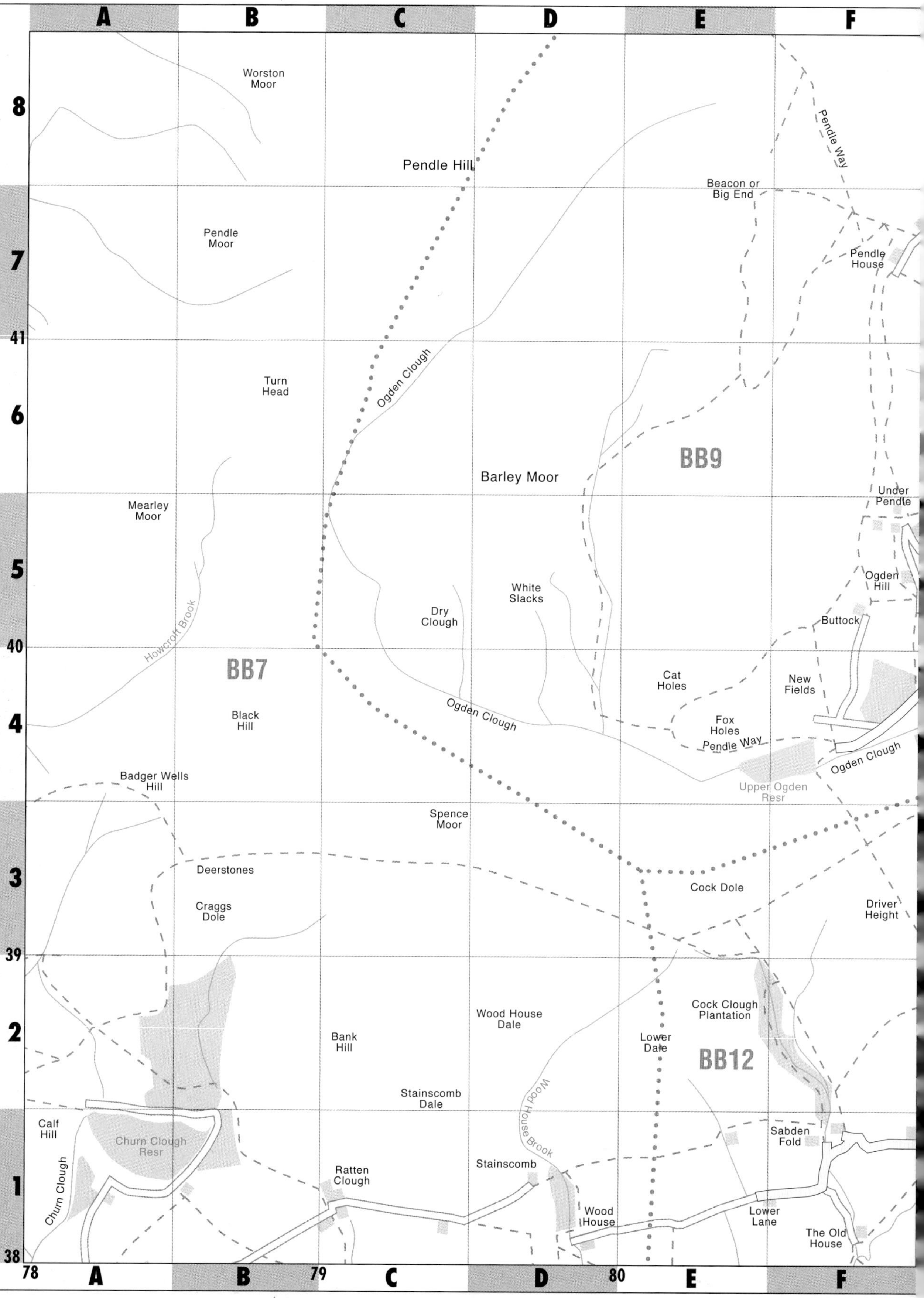
A
B
C
D
E
F
8
7
41
6
5
40
4
3
39
2
1
38
78
79
80
Worston Moor
Pendle Hill
Pendle Way
Beacon or Big End
Pendle Moor
Pendle House
Turn Head
Ogden Clough
BB9
Barley Moor
Mearley Moor
Under Pendle
Ogden Hill
White Slacks
Dry Clough
Howcroft Brook
Buttock
BB7
Cat Holes
New Fields
Black Hill
Ogden Clough
Fox Holes
Pendle Way
Ogden Clough
Badger Wells Hill
Upper Ogden Resr
Spence Moor
Deerstones
Cock Dole
Craggs Dole
Driver Height
Wood House Dale
Cock Clough Plantation
Bank Hill
Lower Dale
BB12
Stainscomb Dale
Wood House Brook
Calf Hill
Churn Clough Resr
Sabden Fold
Stainscomb
Ratten Clough
Churn Clough
Wood House
Lower Lane
The Old House

167
146

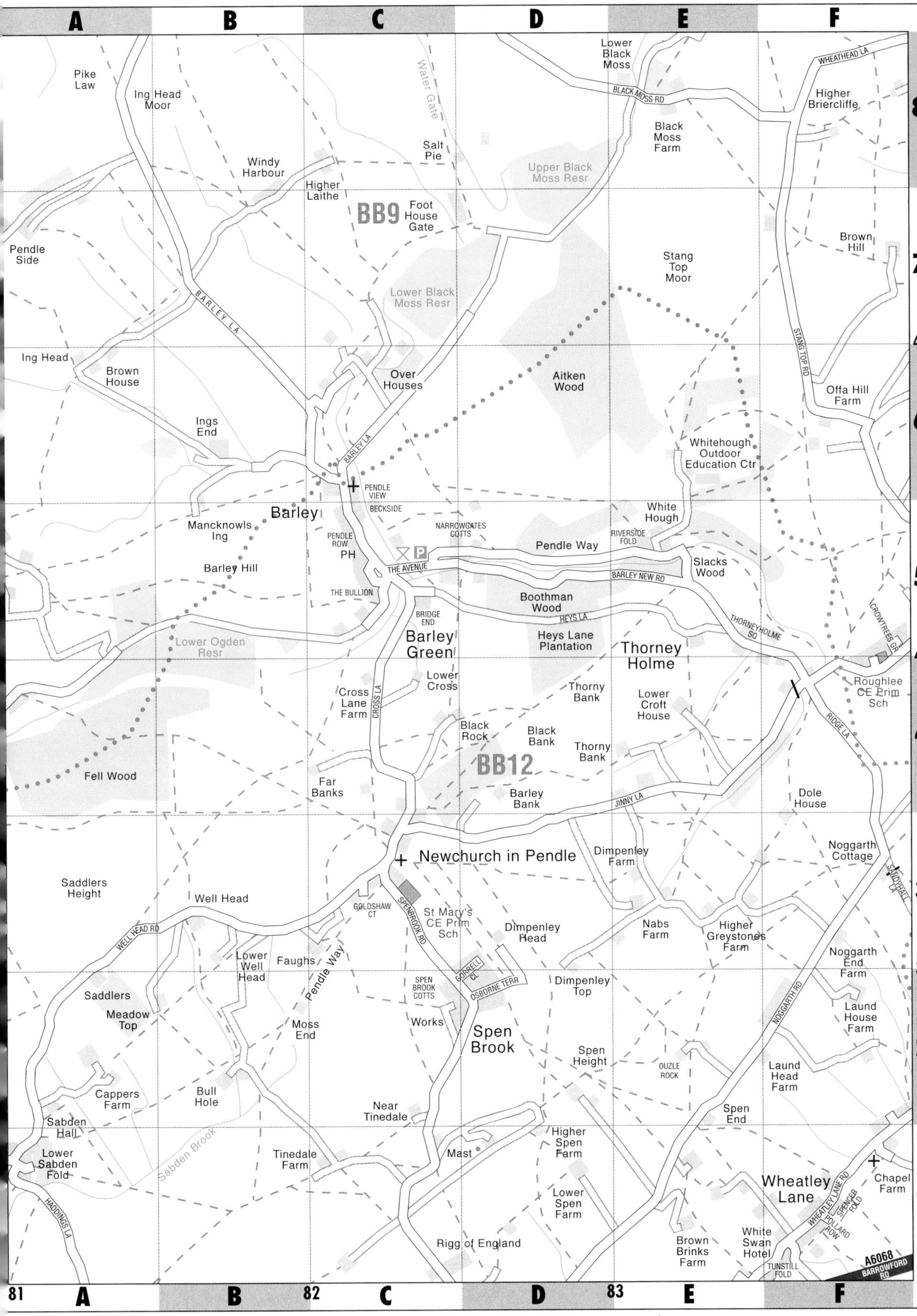
Pike Law
Ing Head Moor
Windy Harbour
Higher Laithe
Water Gate
Salt Pie
Lower Black Moss
BLACK MOSS RD
WHEATHEAD LA
Higher Briercliffe
Black Moss Farm
Upper Black Moss Resr
BB9
Foot House Gate
Pendle Side
Stang Top Moor
Brown Hill
BARLEY LA
Lower Black Moss Resr
Ing Head
Brown House
Over Houses
Aitken Wood
STANG TOP RD
Offa Hill Farm
Ings End
BARLEY LA
Whitehough Outdoor Education Ctr
PENDLE VIEW
BECKSIDE
Barley
Mancknowls Ing
PENDLE ROW
PH
NARROWGATES COTTS
White Hough
RIVERSIDE FOLD
Pendle Way
Slacks Wood
Barley Hill
THE AVENUE
BARLEY NEW RD
THE BULLION
Boothman Wood
BRIDGE END
HEYS LA
Lower Ogden Resr
Barley Green
Heys Lane Plantation
Thorney Holme
THORNEYHOLME SQ
CROWTREES GR
Cross Lane Farm
CROSS LA
Lower Cross
Thorny Bank
Lower Croft House
Roughlee CE Prim Sch
Black Rock
Black Bank
Thorny Bank
RIDGE LA
BB12
Fell Wood
Far Banks
Barley Bank
JINNY LA
Dole House
Newchurch in Pendle
Dimpenley Farm
Noggarth Cottage
Saddlers Height
Well Head
GOLDSHAW CT
St Mary's CE Prim Sch
SPENBROOK RD
Dimpenley Head
Nabs Farm
Higher Greystones Farm
SANDYHALL LA
WELL HEAD RD
Lower Well Head
Faughs
Pendle Way
GORRELL CL
OSBORNE TERR
SPEN BROOK COTTS
Dimpenley Top
Noggarth End Farm
Saddlers
Meadow Top
Moss End
Works
Spen Brook
NOGGARTH RD
Laund House Farm
Spen Height
OUZLE ROCK
Laund Head Farm
Cappers Farm
Bull Hole
Near Tinedale
Spen End
Sabden Hall
Lower Sabden Fold
Sabden Brook
Tinedale Farm
Mast
Higher Spen Farm
Chapel Farm
Wheatley Lane
HADDINGS LA
Lower Spen Farm
WHEATLEY LANE RD
SPENCER FOLD
POLLARD ROW
Rigg of England
Brown Brinks Farm
White Swan Hotel
TUNSTILL FOLD
A6068
BARROWFORD RD
A B C D E F
8 7 41 6 5 40 4 3 39 2 1 38
81 82 83

169
193

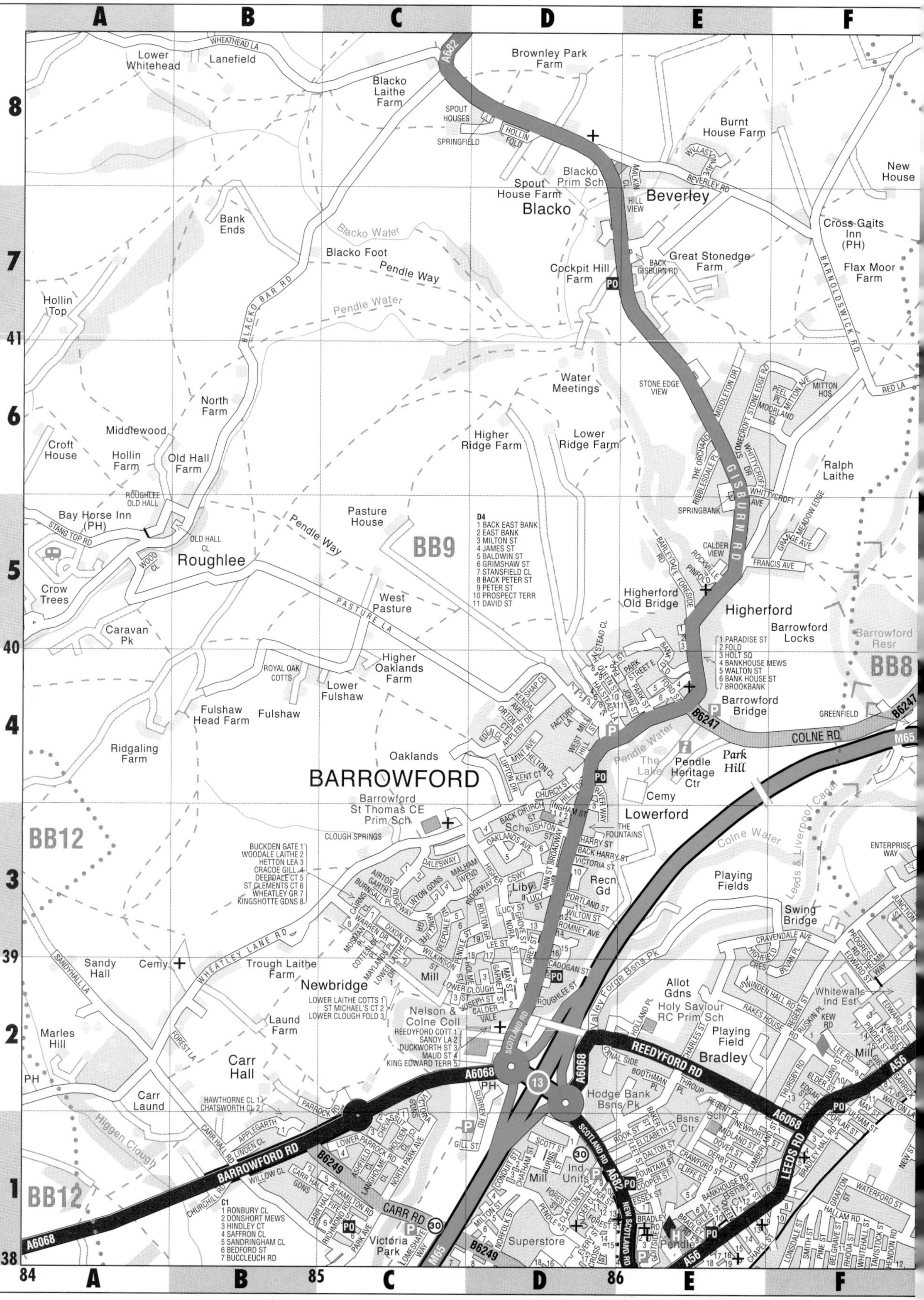
A
B
C
D
E
F
8
7
41
6
5
40
4
3
39
2
1
38
84
85
86
Lower Whitehead
Lanefield
WHEATHEAD LA
Blacko Laithe Farm
A682
Brownley Park Farm
SPOUT HOUSES
SPRINGFIELD
HOLLIN FOLD
Burnt House Farm
New House
Blacko Prim Sch
Spout House Farm
Blacko
Beverley
BEVERLEY RD
WILLASTON AVE
MALKIN CL
HILL VIEW
Cross Gaits Inn (PH)
Bank Ends
Blacko Water
Blacko Foot
Pendle Way
Cockpit Hill Farm
Great Stonedge Farm
BACK GISBURN RD
Flax Moor Farm
BARNOLDSWICK RD
Hollin Top
BLACKO BAR RD
Pendle Water
Water Meetings
STONE EDGE VIEW
MIDDLETON DR
STONE EDGE RD
PEEL PL
MITTON AVE
MITTON HOS
MOORLAND CL
RED LA
North Farm
Middlewood
Croft House
Hollin Farm
Old Hall Farm
Higher Ridge Farm
Lower Ridge Farm
THE ORCHARD
STONECROFT
WHITTYCROFT DR
WHITTYCROFT AVE
RIBBLESDALE PL
GISBURN RD
Ralph Laithe
ROUGHLEE OLD HALL
Bay Horse Inn (PH)
STANG TOP RD
OLD HALL CL
WOOD CL
Roughlee
Pasture House
Pendle Way
BB9
D4
1 BACK EAST BANK
2 EAST BANK
3 MILTON ST
4 JAMES ST
5 BALDWIN ST
6 GRIMSHAW ST
7 STANSFIELD CL
8 BACK PETER ST
9 PETER ST
10 PROSPECT TERR
11 DAVID ST
SPRINGBANK
CALDER VIEW
GRANGE AVE
MEADOW EDGE
FRANCIS AVE
BARLEYDALE RD
ROCKVILLE
PINFOLD
FORESIDE
Crow Trees
West Pasture
PASTURE LA
Higherford Old Bridge
Higherford
Barrowford Locks
Barrowford Resr
Caravan Pk
1 PARADISE ST
2 FOLD
3 HOLT SQ
4 BANKHOUSE MEWS
5 WALTON ST
6 BANK HOUSE ST
7 BROOKBANK
BB8
ROYAL OAK COTTS
Higher Oaklands Farm
Lower Fulshaw
Fulshaw Head Farm
Fulshaw
KENDAL AVE
SHAP CL
ORTON CT
APPLEBY DR
FACTORY LA
WEST MILL
HALSTEAD LA
PARK ST
JOHN ST
PARK STREET E
Barrowford Bridge
B6247
GREENFIELD
COLNE RD
M65
Ridgaling Farm
Oaklands
EDEN CL
MINT AVE
HELTON CL
LUPTON DR
KENT CT
Pendle Water
The Lake
Pendle Heritage Ctr
Park Hill
BARROWFORD
Barrowford St Thomas CE Prim Sch
CHURCH ST
HILL TOP
RIVER WAY
Cemy
Lowerford
Leeds & Liverpool Canal
BB12
CLOUGH SPRINGS
BACK CHURCH ST
Sch
RUSHTON ST
INGHAM ST
THE FOUNTAINS
Colne Water
BUCKDEN GATE 1
WOODALE LAITHE 2
HETTON LEA 3
CRACOE GILL 4
DEEPDALE CT 5
ST CLEMENTS CT 6
WHEATLEY GR 7
KINGSHOTTE GDNS 8
DALESWAY
MALHAM WEND
OAKLANDS AVE
HARRY ST
BACK HARRY ST
VICTORIA ST
Recn Gd
Playing Fields
ENTERPRISE WAY
AIRTON GARTH
BURNSALL PL
RIDGEWAY
LINTON GDNS
Liby
PORTLAND ST
WILTON ST
ROMNEY AVE
Swing Bridge
CRAVENDALE AVE
BOLTON GR
LUCY ST
NORA ST
LEE ST
WILKINSON ST
PENDLE ST
HOLME ST
GARNETT ST
CADOGAN ST
ROUGHLEE ST
Sandy Hall
Cemy
WHEATLEY LANE RD
Trough Laithe Farm
Newbridge
Mill
LOWER CLOUGH ST
JOSEPH ST
CALDER VALE
LOWER LAITHE COTTS 1
ST MICHAEL'S CT 2
LOWER CLOUGH FOLD 3
Valley Forge Bsns Pk
Allot Gdns
Holy Saviour RC Prim Sch
Playing Field
Whitewalls Ind Est
RAKES HOUSE
SWINDEN HALL RD
SANDYHALL LA
Marles Hill
FOREST LA
Laund Farm
Nelson & Colne Coll
REEDYFORD COTT 1
SANDY LA 2
DUCKWORTH ST 3
MAUD ST 4
KING EDWARD TERR 5
SCOTLAND RD
HOLLAND PL
REEDYFORD RD
Bradley
Mill
PH
Carr Hall
A6068
13
Hodge Bank Bsns Pk
BOOTHMAN PL
THROUP PL
A56
Carr Laund
HAWTHORNE CL 1
CHATSWORTH CL 2
PARROCK RD
Higgen Clough
APPLEGARTH
LINDEN CL
CARR HALL RD
BARROWFORD RD
LOWER PARROCK RD
GILL ST
SCOTT ST
Ind Units
Bsns Ctr
Sch
LEEDS RD
DERBY ST
CUMBERLAND ST
WILLOW CL
CHURCHILL RD
CARR HALL GDNS
B6249
CARR RD
C1
1 RONBURY CL
2 DONSHORT MEWS
3 HINDLEY CT
4 SAFFRON CL
5 SANDRINGHAM CL
6 BEDFORD ST
7 BUCCLEUCH RD
Victoria Park
PARK AVE
LOMESHAYE WAY
Mill
Superstore
NEW SCOTLAND RD
Pendle
CHAPEL ST
LONSDALE ST
SMITH ST
PINE ST
BELGRAVE ST
RHODA ST
WHITEHALL ST
TAVISTOCK ST
HENDON RD
WATERFORD ST
HALLAM RD
GRAFTON ST

D1
1 WESTFIELD
2 HENRY ST
3 BALL ST
4 MERTON ST
5 KENDAL ST
6 BEDDINGTON ST
7 WEST ST
8 GORDON RD
9 BACK CLAYTON ST
10 EAST ST
11 CLAYTON CL
12 NILE ST
13 SEEDHILL TERR
14 NORTH ST
15 SCOTLAND RD
16 WELLINGTON ST
17 NEW BROWN ST
18 CLAYTON ST

D3
1 SHARP ST
2 BUTTERFIELD ST
3 FOUNTAIN SQ
4 LONSDALE GDNS
5 HIGHFIELD CRES
6 CORONATION PL
7 BELMONT TERR
8 HOLMEFIELD CT
9 ALBERT TERR

169

D3
10 CORLASS ST
11 CAMDEN ST
12 CROMWELL TERR
13 MOUNT ST
14 FOREST VIEW
15 HOLMEFIELD GDNS
16 GLADSTONE TERR
17 HAWTHORNE GR
18 ASH TREE WLK
19 ST CLEMANCE CT

148

E1
1 SUSSEX ST
2 OAK ST
3 ELEANOR ST
4 POLLARD ST
5 BRADLEY FOLD
6 CALEB ST
7 THROSTLE ST
8 WALTON ST
9 ELM ST
10 BEECH ST
11 BANK ST
12 BRADLEY VIEW
13 ST PHILIP'S ST
14 HARVEY ST
15 SELDON ST
16 BARKERHOUSE RD
17 WILLIAM ST
18 ARTHUR ST
19 PARROCK ST

F1
1 RUTLAND ST
2 EAGLE ST
3 RAVEN ST
4 VULCAN ST
5 PRIORY ST
6 PLANTATION ST
7 HILDROP RD
8 PERTH ST
9 WICKLIFFE ST
10 CANNON ST
11 EARL ST
12 ROSEHILL AVE

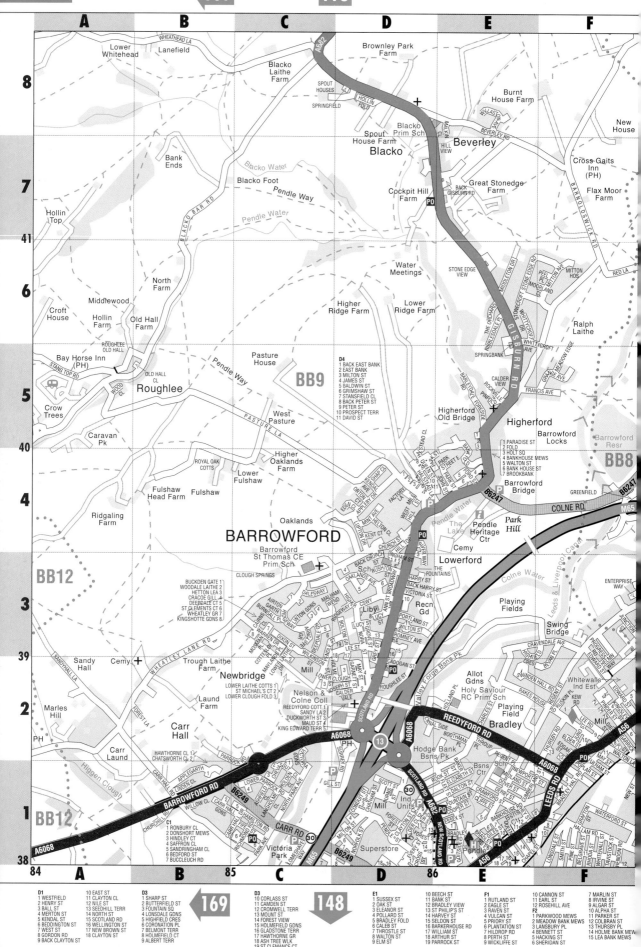

F2
1 PARKWOOD MEWS
2 MEADOW BANK MEWS
3 LANSBURY PL
4 BENNETT ST
5 HACKING ST
6 SHERIDAN ST
7 MARLIN ST
8 IRVINE ST
9 ALGAR ST
10 ALPHA ST
11 PARKER ST
12 COLBRAN ST
13 THURSBY PL
14 HOLME BANK MEWS
15 LEA BANK MEWS

C5
1 FOTHERGILL ST
2 MOORHEAD ST
3 MELLING CT
4 BARROWFORD RD

D5
1 WALLACE HARTLEY MEWS
2 THE EXCHANGE
3 BIRTWISTLE HYDE PK
4 MITCHELL ST
5 SPRING YD
6 BACK DERBY ST
7 NELSON ST
8 ARGYLE ST
9 TURNEY CROOK MEWS
10 SPRING PL
11 NORWAY HO
12 BLACK HORES YD
13 IVEGATE MEWS

194

D5
14 Linden Bsns Ctr
15 SPRING CT

172

E5
1 WATER ST
2 DOCKRAY CT
3 ANGEL WAY
4 DOCKRAY YD
5 CUMBERLAND ST
6 CROSS SKELTON ST
7 BIRTWISTLE FOLD
8 POST OFFICE YD
9 ARCADIA
10 MARKET PL
11 PARLIAMENT ST
12 NINEVEH ST

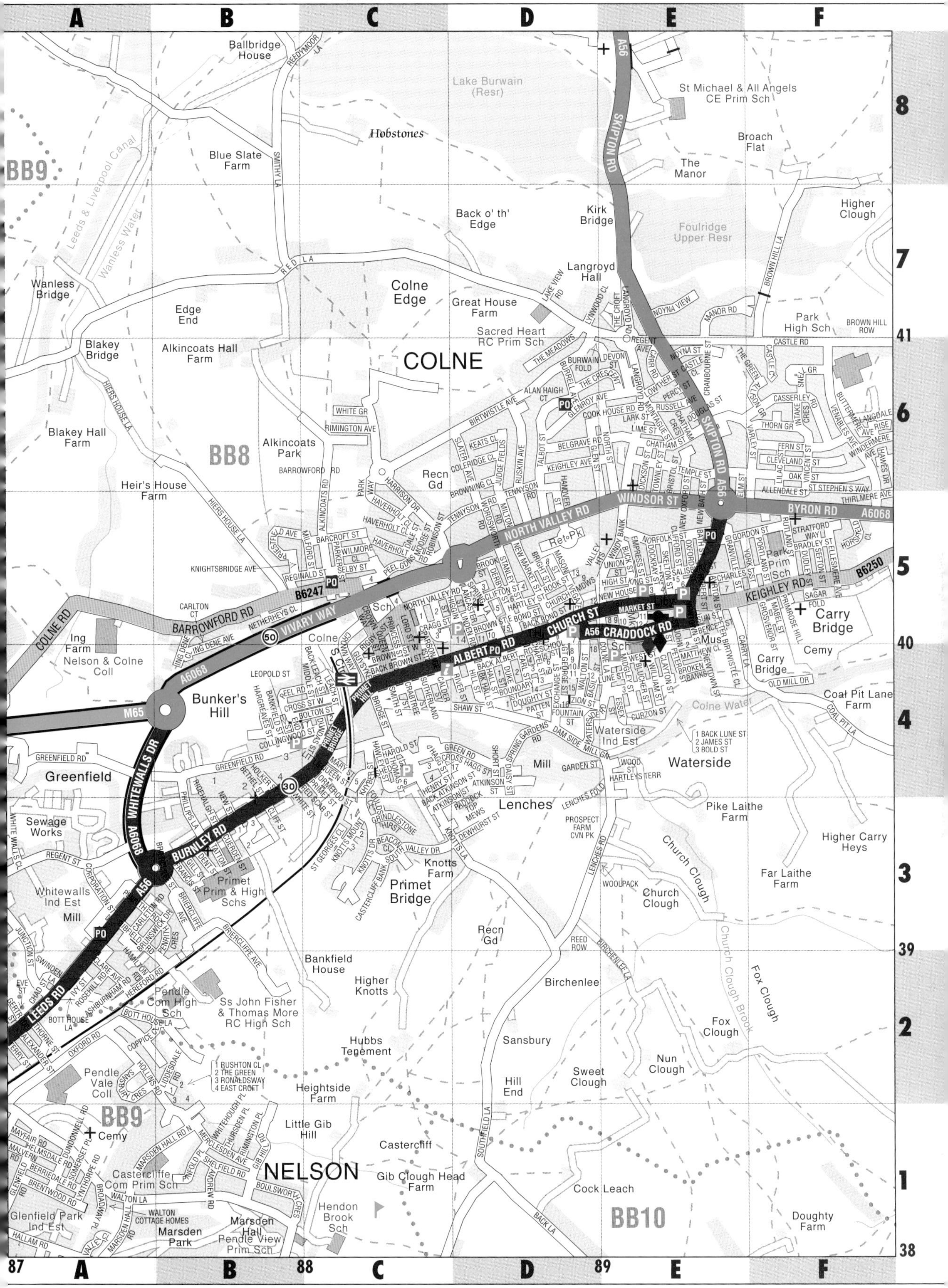


B3
1 JOBLING ST
2 PRIMET HTS
3 WACKERSALL RD

B4
1 Garden Vale Bsns Ctr
2 Holker Bsns Ctr
3 Riverside Mill
4 Primet Bsns Ctr

C4
1 EAST END ST
2 JOHN ST
3 NICHOLAS ST
4 PEERART CT
5 THE SIDINGS
6 LAITHE ST
7 CENTAUR CT

C3
1 PENDLEMIST VIEW
2 COTTON CT
3 ST ANDREWS CL

149

D4
1 BACK DUKE ST
2 BACK EARL ST
3 KNOWSLEY ST
4 BACK CHAPEL ST
5 CROSS SCHOOL ST
6 LOWER SCHOOL ST
7 WEST EXCHANGE ST
8 RAGLAN ST
9 CAMBRIDGE ST

172

D4
10 BACK CAMBRIDGE ST
11 SELDON ST
12 CHAPEL FOLD
13 BLASCOMAY SQ
14 BACK BOUNDARY ST
15 BURRANS MDW
16 BACK ZION ST
17 CROSS HELLIWELL ST
18 WALTON HTS

171
195

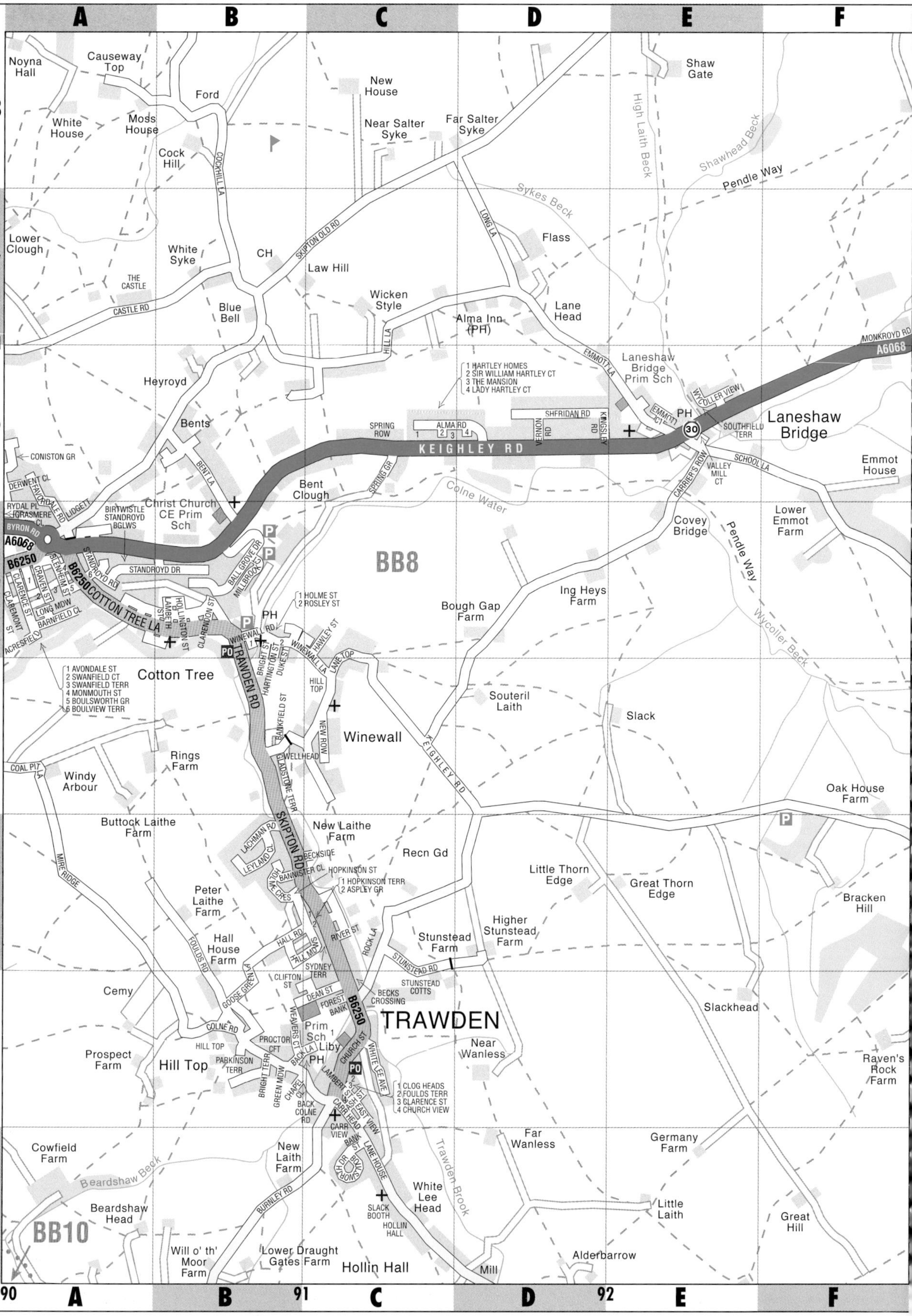


171
150

174

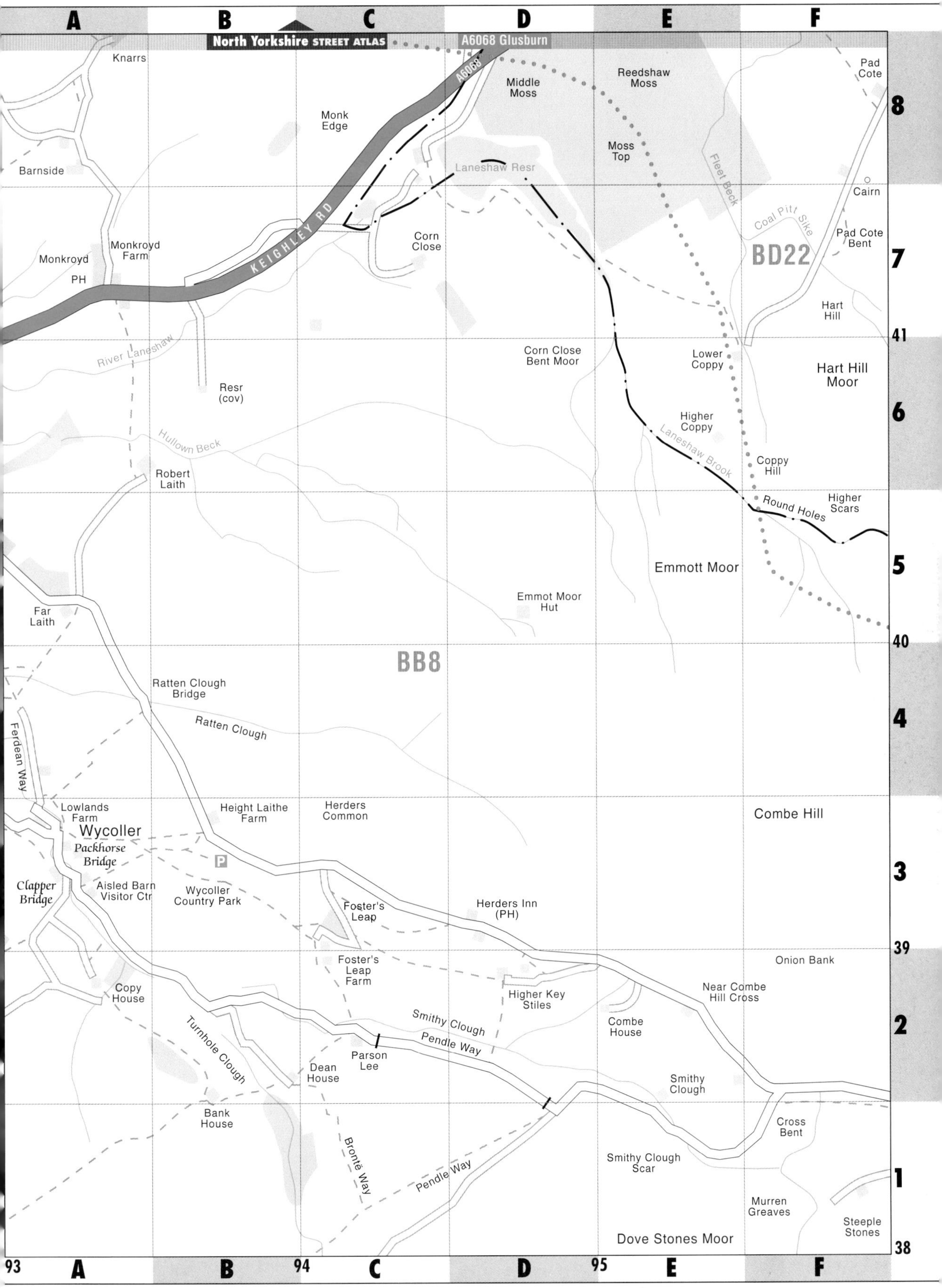

A
B
C
D
E
F
North Yorkshire STREET ATLAS
A6068 Glusburn
Knarrs
A6068
Middle Moss
Reedshaw Moss
Pad Cote
Monk Edge
Barnside
Moss Top
Laneshaw Resr
Fleet Beck
Cairn
Coal Pitt Sike
Pad Cote Bent
KEIGHLEY RD
Monkroyd Farm
Monkroyd
PH
Corn Close
BD22
Hart Hill
River Laneshaw
Corn Close Bent Moor
Lower Coppy
Hart Hill Moor
Resr (cov)
Higher Coppy
Laneshaw Brook
Hullown Beck
Robert Laith
Coppy Hill
Higher Scars
Round Holes
Emmott Moor
Emmot Moor Hut
Far Laith
BB8
Ratten Clough Bridge
Ratten Clough
Ferdean Way
Lowlands Farm
Height Laithe Farm
Herders Common
Combe Hill
Wycoller
Packhorse Bridge
P
Clapper Bridge
Aisled Barn Visitor Ctr
Wycoller Country Park
Foster's Leap
Herders Inn (PH)
Foster's Leap Farm
Onion Bank
Copy House
Higher Key Stiles
Near Combe Hill Cross
Combe House
Smithy Clough
Turnhole Clough
Pendle Way
Parson Lee
Dean House
Smithy Clough
Bank House
Cross Bent
Brontë Way
Smithy Clough Scar
Pendle Way
Murren Greaves
Steeple Stones
Dove Stones Moor
8
7
41
6
5
40
4
3
39
2
1
38
93
94
95


151
174

173

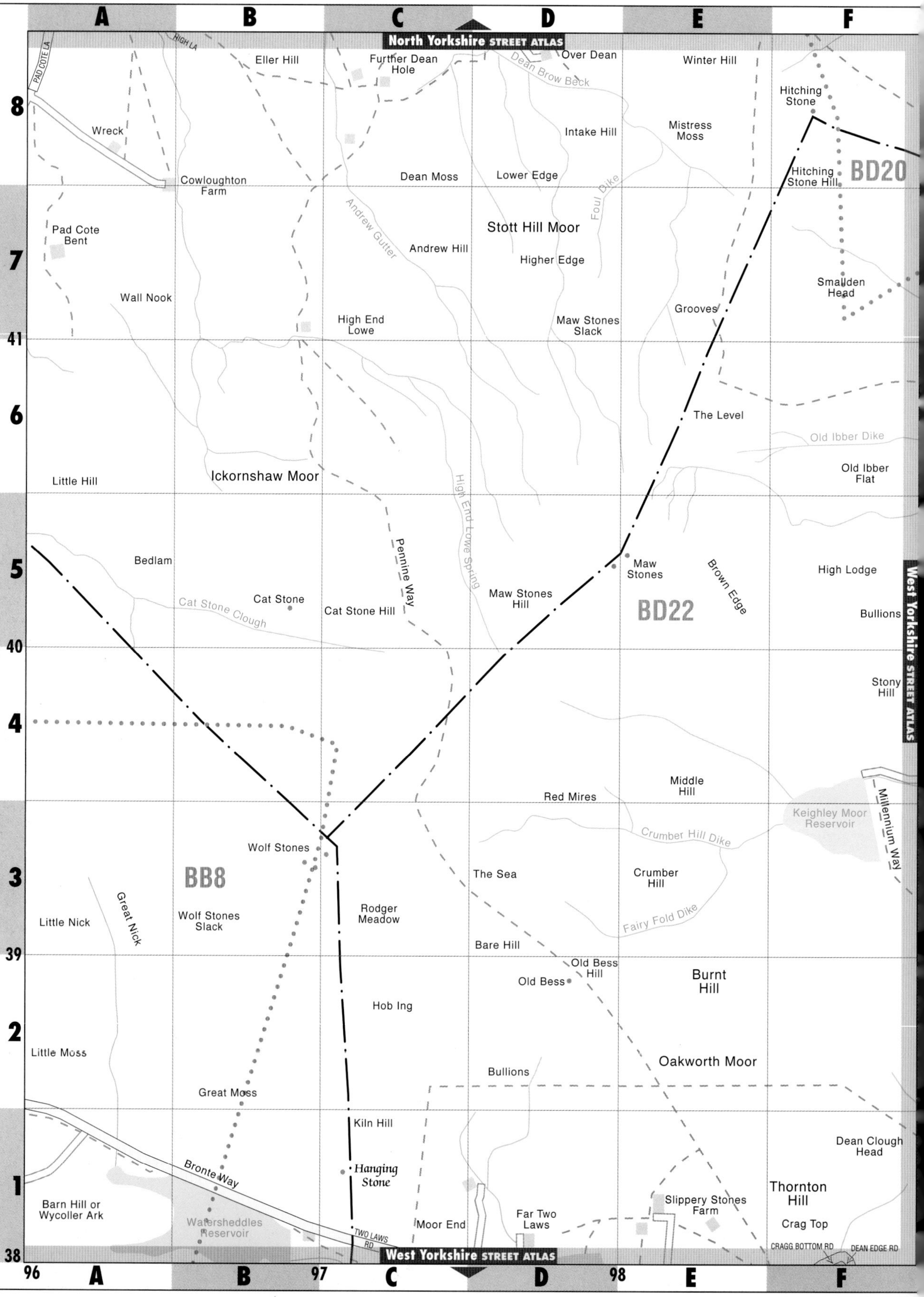

A B C D E F
North Yorkshire STREET ATLAS
8 7 41 6 5 40 4 3 39 2 1 38
96 97 98
PAD COTE LA
HIGH LA
Eller Hill
Further Dean Hole
Over Dean
Dean Brow Beck
Winter Hill
Hitching Stone
Wreck
Intake Hill
Mistress Moss
Cowloughton Farm
Dean Moss
Lower Edge
Hitching Stone Hill
BD20
Foul Dike
Pad Cote Bent
Andrew Gutter
Stott Hill Moor
Andrew Hill
Higher Edge
Smallden Head
Wall Nook
High End Lowe
Maw Stones Slack
Grooves
The Level
Old Ibber Dike
Old Ibber Flat
Little Hill
Ickornshaw Moor
High End Lowe Spring
Pennine Way
Bedlam
Maw Stones
Brown Edge
High Lodge
Cat Stone
Cat Stone Clough
Cat Stone Hill
Maw Stones Hill
BD22
Bullions
West Yorkshire STREET ATLAS
Stony Hill
Middle Hill
Red Mires
Millennium Way
Keighley Moor Reservoir
Crumber Hill Dike
Wolf Stones
BB8
The Sea
Crumber Hill
Rodger Meadow
Little Nick
Great Nick
Wolf Stones Slack
Fairy Fold Dike
Bare Hill
Old Bess Hill
Old Bess
Burnt Hill
Hob Ing
Little Moss
Oakworth Moor
Bullions
Great Moss
Kiln Hill
Dean Clough Head
Bronte Way
Hanging Stone
Thornton Hill
Slippery Stones Farm
Barn Hill or Wycoller Ark
Far Two Laws
Moor End
Watersheddles Reservoir
TWO LAWS RD
Crag Top
CRAGG BOTTOM RD
DEAN EDGE RD
West Yorkshire STREET ATLAS


173

198
176

A
B
C
D
E
F
FLEETWOOD
CLEVELEYS
FY7
FY5
A587
A585
B5409
B5268
B5412
A584
BROADWAY
ROSSALL RD
ROSSALL LA
VICTORIA RD W
FLEETWOOD RD
AMOUNDERNESS WAY
Broadwater
Cardinal Allen RC High Sch
Larkholme Prim Sch
Playing Field
Caravan Pk
Blackpool & The Fylde Coll (Nautical)
Camping Site
Farmer Parr's Animal World (Mus)
Rossall
Rossall Sq
Rifle Range
Rossall Sch
Wyre Way
Fleetwood Farm
Blackpool & Fleetwood Tramway
Woodcock Wood
Westbourne Rd
Rossall Beach
Lancashire Coastal Way
Haven Sch
Northfold Com Prim Sch
Westmorland Ave
Wks
Thornton Gate
Jubilee Gdns
Thornton Cleveleys Manor Beach Prim Sch
Beach Rd
Liby
West Dr
Cleveleys
Lauderdale Ave
St Teresa's RC Prim Sch
Supermarket
Anchorsholme
Anchorsholme La
BLUEBELL CL 1
BLACKTHORN CL 2
ELDERBERRY CL 3
CALENDINE CL 4
SPEEDWELL CL 5
KESTREL CL 6
SANDY CL 1
MANOR HOUSE PK FLATS 2
PEBBLE CT 3
8
7
6
5
4
3
2
1
45
44
43
42
30
31
32

D2
1 ORION BLDGS
2 SANDRINGHAM LODGE

F4
1 REDWING AVE
2 CURLEW CL
3 WHITECREST AVE
4 BARNFIELD CL
5 CORNWALL MEWS
6 COLCHESTER DR
7 PORTSMOUTH CL

F1
1 TUDOR CL
2 SHERWOOD PL
3 RICHARDS WAY
4 POCHARD PL
5 INGLENOOK CL
6 BUNTING PL
7 SANDPIPER PL
8 THROSTLE WAY
9 REDSTART PL
10 KITTIWAKE CL
11 MOORHEN PL
12 THORNCROSS

152
176

175
199

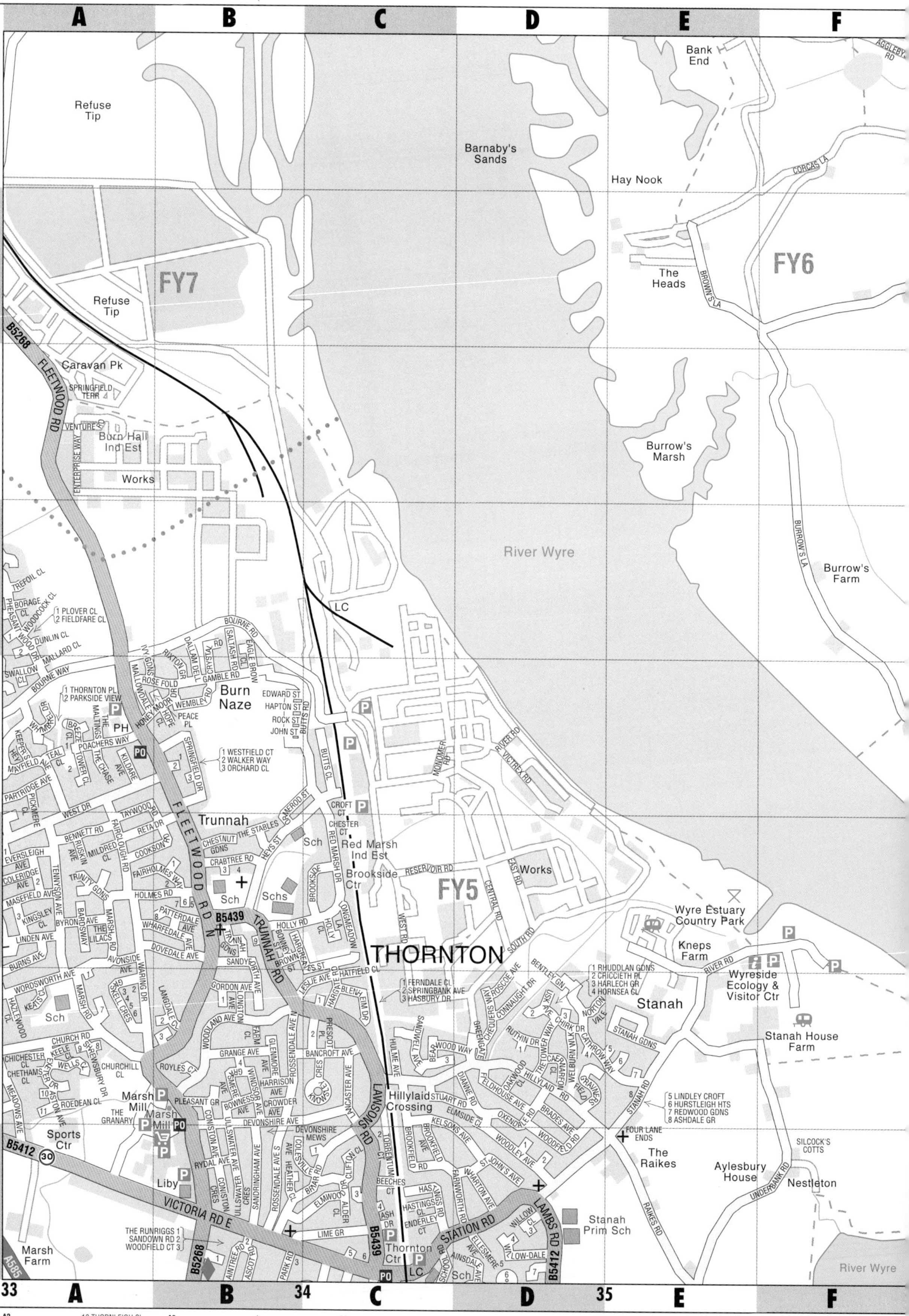


A2
1 BRAMBLE CT
2 MARSH CT
3 TOWN END
4 SANDFIELD
5 CARR HEY
6 VERONA CT
7 PENNYFARTHING LA
8 GORDONSTOUN PL
9 BENENDEN PL
10 THORNLEIGH CL
11 ROEHAMPTON CL

A3
1 GREENMOUNT AVE
2 MILTON AVE
3 BROWNING AVE

175

B2
1 CARLISLE GR
2 CHURCHILL CL
3 COUNSELL CT
4 LINADALE AVE

153

B3
1 FAIRHOLMES CL
2 FAIRHOLMES CT
3 CRABTREE ORCH
4 KINGSTON MEWS
5 LOWES CT
6 LOWESWAY
7 HOUGHTON CT
8 GRIZEDALE CT
9 ROYLES BROOK CL

C1
1 BRIAR MEWS
2 BRAYS HEYS
3 EDGEWAY PL
4 LAWSONS CT
5 MAYFAIR GDNS
6 LAWSWOOD

D1
1 ROSEWOOD CL
2 CHATSWORTH CL
3 WILLOW TREE GDNS
4 ACACIA CL
5 WILLOW CT
6 FAIRHAVEN CL
7 LAMBS HILL CL

200
178

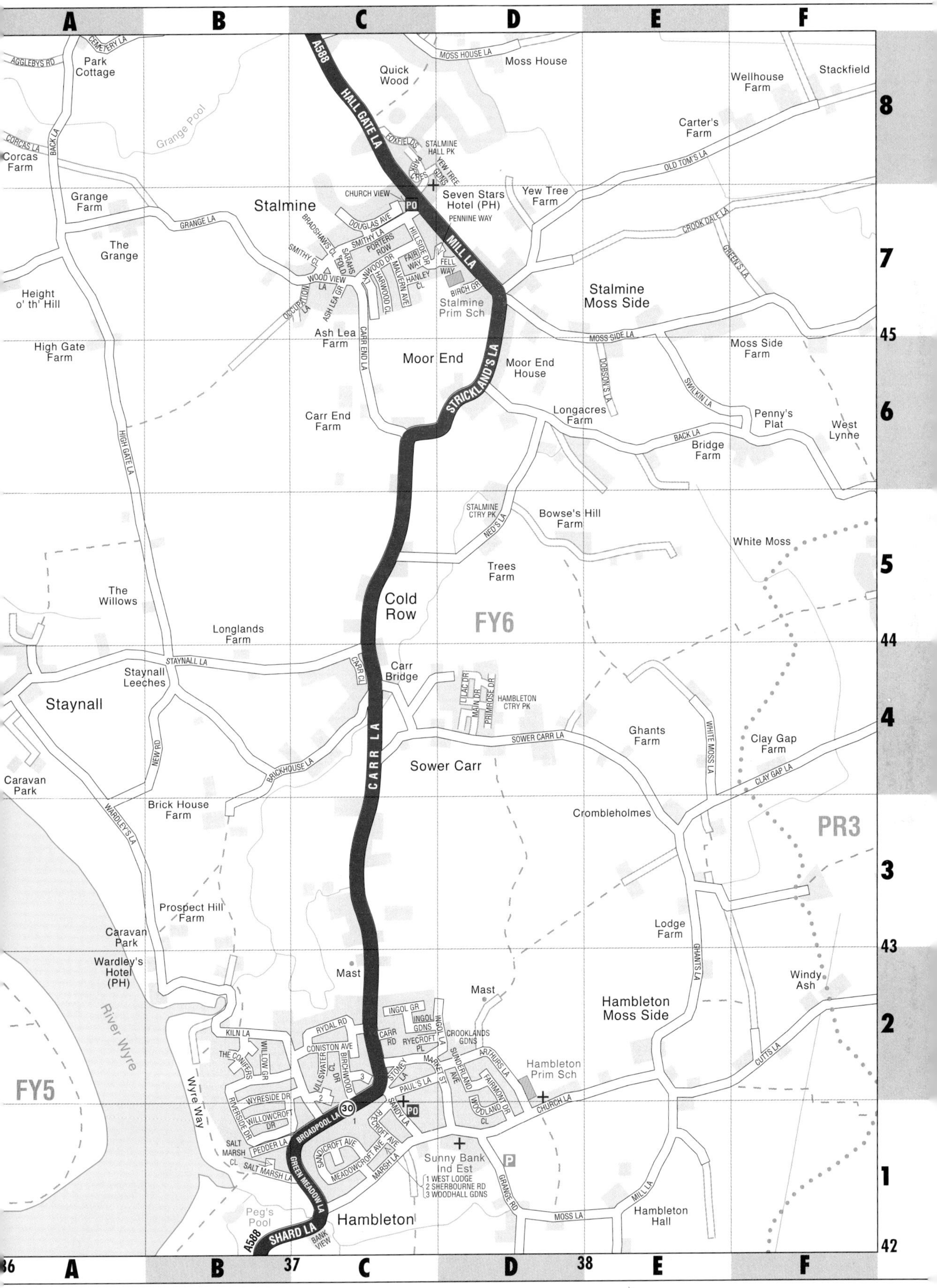
A
B
C
D
E
F
8
7
45
6
5
44
4
3
43
2
1
42
36
37
38
CEMETERY LA
AGGLEBYS RD
Park Cottage
A588
HALL GATE LA
Quick Wood
MOSS HOUSE LA
Moss House
Wellhouse Farm
Stackfield
Grange Pool
CORCAS LA
Corcas Farm
BACK LA
FOXFIELDS
STALMINE HALL PK
PARK CRES
YEW TREE GDNS
Carter's Farm
OLD TOM'S LA
Grange Farm
CHURCH VIEW
PO
Seven Stars Hotel (PH)
Yew Tree Farm
Stalmine
PENNINE WAY
GRANGE LA
DOUGLAS AVE
BRADSHAWS CL
SMITHY LA
PORTERS ROW
HILLSIDE DR
MILL LA
CROOK DALE LA
The Grange
SMITHY CL
SARAHS FOLD
LYNWOOD DR
MALVERN AVE
FAIR WAY
FELL WAY
GREEN'S LA
HARWOOD CL
HANLEY CL
WOOD VIEW
LA
BIRCH GR
Stalmine Moss Side
Height o' th' Hill
ASH LEA GR
OCCUPATION LA
Stalmine Prim Sch
Ash Lea Farm
MOSS SIDE LA
High Gate Farm
CARR END LA
Moor End
STRICKLAND'S LA
Moor End House
DOBSON'S LA
Moss Side Farm
SWILKIN LA
Longacres Farm
Penny's Plat
Carr End Farm
West Lynne
BACK LA
Bridge Farm
HIGH GATE LA
STALMINE CTRY PK
NED'S LA
Bowse's Hill Farm
White Moss
Trees Farm
The Willows
Cold Row
FY6
Longlands Farm
STAYNALL LA
CARR CL
Carr Bridge
Staynall Leeches
LILAC DR
MAIN DR
PRIMROSE DR
HAMBLETON CTRY PK
Staynall
CARR LA
SOWER CARR LA
Ghants Farm
WHITE MOSS LA
Clay Gap Farm
NEW RD
BRICKHOUSE LA
Sower Carr
CLAY GAP LA
Caravan Park
Brick House Farm
WARDLEY'S LA
Crombleholmes
PR3
Prospect Hill Farm
Lodge Farm
Caravan Park
Wardley's Hotel (PH)
GHANTS LA
Mast
Mast
Windy Ash
River Wyre
INGOL GR
INGOL GDNS
Hambleton Moss Side
KILN LA
RYDAL RD
CARR RD
RYECROFT PL
INGOL LA
CROOKLANDS GDNS
CONISTON AVE
MARKET ST
SUNDERLAND AVE
ARTHURS LA
THE CONIFERS
WILLOW GR
ULLSWATER CL
DR
BIRCHWOOD
STONEY LA
FAIRMONT DR
Hambleton Prim Sch
CUTTS LA
FY5
Wyre Way
WYRESIDE DR
PAUL'S LA
RIVERSIDE DR
WILLOWCROFT DR
30
SANDY LA
PO
WOODLAND CL
CHURCH LA
BROADPOOL LA
RYECROFT AVE
SALT MARSH CL
PEDDER LA
SANDICROFT AVE
MEADOWCROFT AVE
Sunny Bank Ind Est
P
SALT MARSH LA
GREEN MEADOW LA
MARSH LA
1 WEST LODGE
2 SHERBOURNE RD
3 WOODHALL GDNS
GRANGE RD
MILL LA
Peg's Pool
Hambleton
MOSS LA
Hambleton Hall
SHARD LA
BANK VIEW

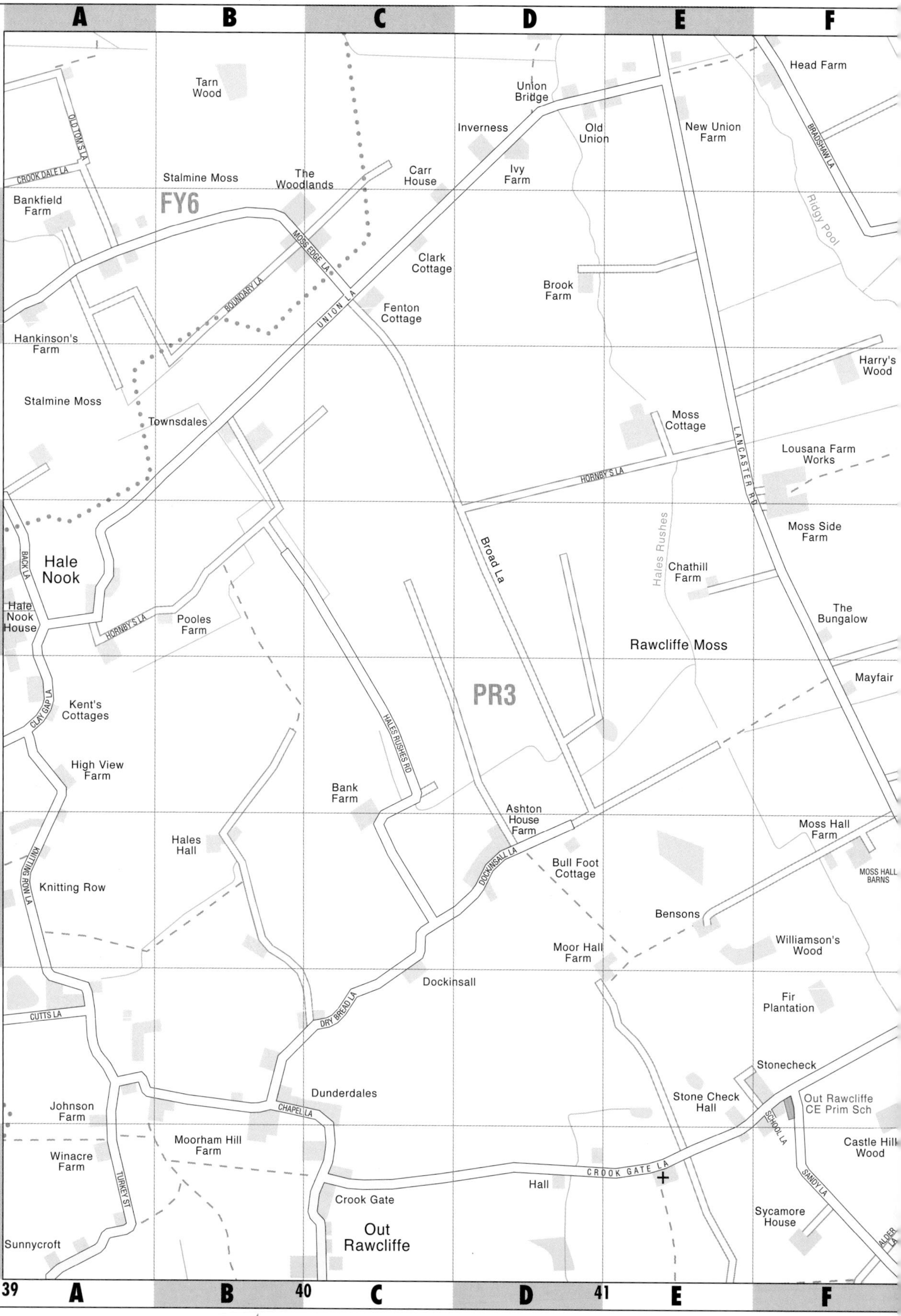
A
B
C
D
E
F
8
7
45
6
5
44
4
3
43
2
1
42
39
40
41
Tarn Wood
Union Bridge
Head Farm
Inverness
Old Union
New Union Farm
OLD TOM'S LA
CROOK DALE LA
Stalmine Moss
The Woodlands
Carr House
Ivy Farm
BRADSHAW LA
Bankfield Farm
FY6
Ridgy Pool
MOSS EDGE LA
BOUNDARY LA
Clark Cottage
Brook Farm
UNION LA
Fenton Cottage
Hankinson's Farm
Harry's Wood
Stalmine Moss
Moss Cottage
Townsdales
Lousana Farm Works
HORNBY'S LA
LANCASTER RD
Moss Side Farm
Broad La
Hales Rushes
BACK LA
Hale Nook
Chathill Farm
Hale Nook House
HORNBY'S LA
Pooles Farm
The Bungalow
Rawcliffe Moss
Mayfair
CLAY GAP LA
Kent's Cottages
PR3
HALES RUSHES RD
High View Farm
Bank Farm
Ashton House Farm
Moss Hall Farm
Hales Hall
KNITTING ROW LA
DOCKINSALL LA
Bull Foot Cottage
MOSS HALL BARNS
Knitting Row
Bensons
Williamson's Wood
Moor Hall Farm
Dockinsall
Fir Plantation
CUTTS LA
DRY BREAD LA
Stonecheck
Dunderdales
Stone Check Hall
Out Rawcliffe CE Prim Sch
Johnson Farm
CHAPEL LA
SCHOOL LA
Moorham Hill Farm
Castle Hill Wood
Winacre Farm
CROOK GATE LA
TURKEY ST
Hall
SANDY LA
Crook Gate
Sycamore House
Out Rawcliffe
Sunnycroft
ALDER LA

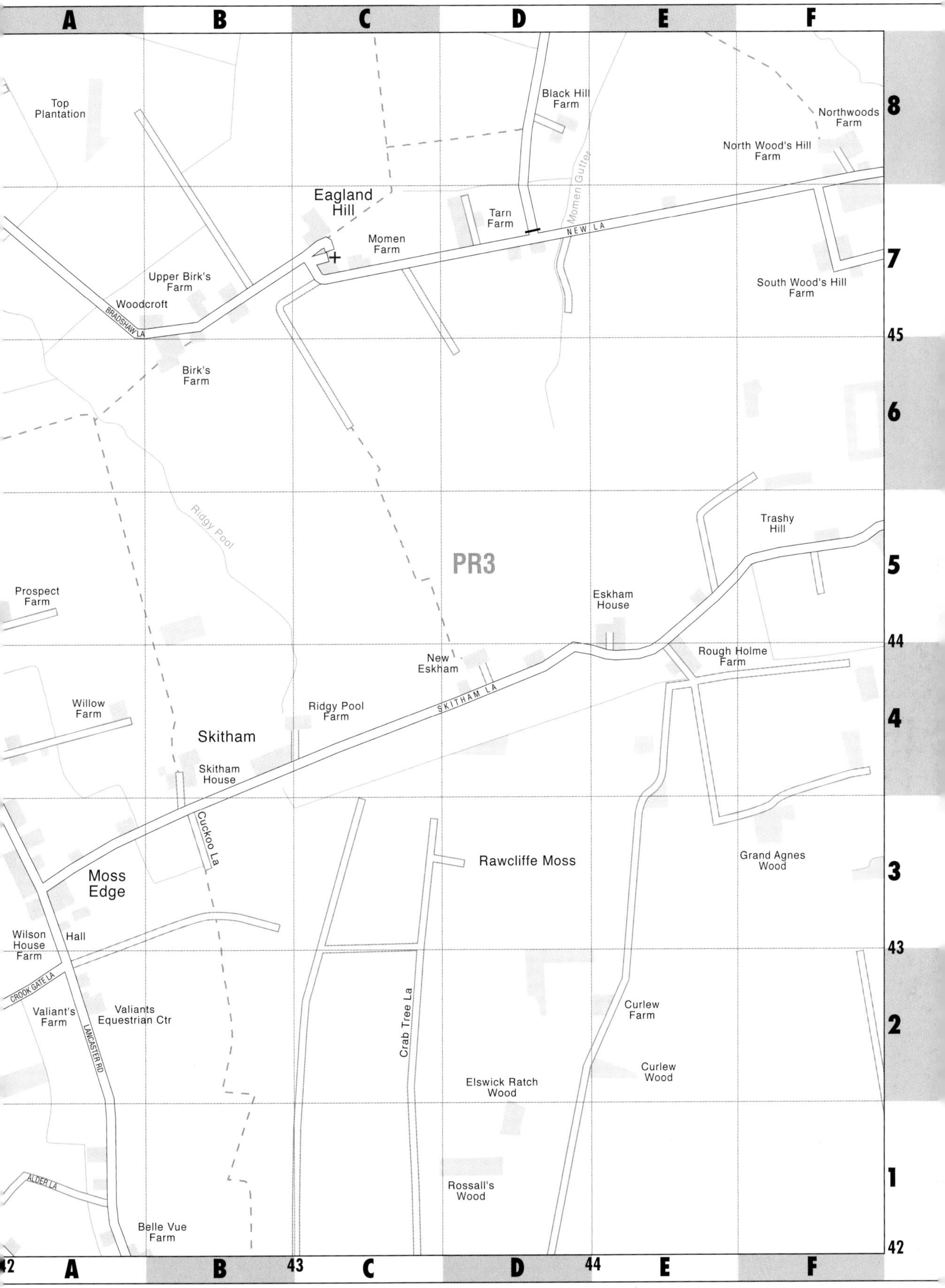
A
B
C
D
E
F
Top Plantation
Black Hill Farm
Northwoods Farm
North Wood's Hill Farm
8
Eagland Hill
Tarn Farm
Momen Gutter
NEW LA
Momen Farm
Upper Birk's Farm
Woodcroft
BRADSHAW LA
South Wood's Hill Farm
7
45
Birk's Farm
6
Ridgy Pool
Trashy Hill
PR3
5
Prospect Farm
Eskham House
44
New Eskham
Rough Holme Farm
SKITHAM LA
Willow Farm
Ridgy Pool Farm
4
Skitham
Skitham House
Cuckoo La
Rawcliffe Moss
Grand Agnes Wood
Moss Edge
3
Wilson House Farm
Hall
43
CROOK GATE LA
Valiant's Farm
Valiants Equestrian Ctr
LANCASTER RD
Crab Tree La
Curlew Farm
Curlew Wood
2
Elswick Ratch Wood
1
ALDER LA
Rossall's Wood
Belle Vue Farm
42
42
43
44

179
203

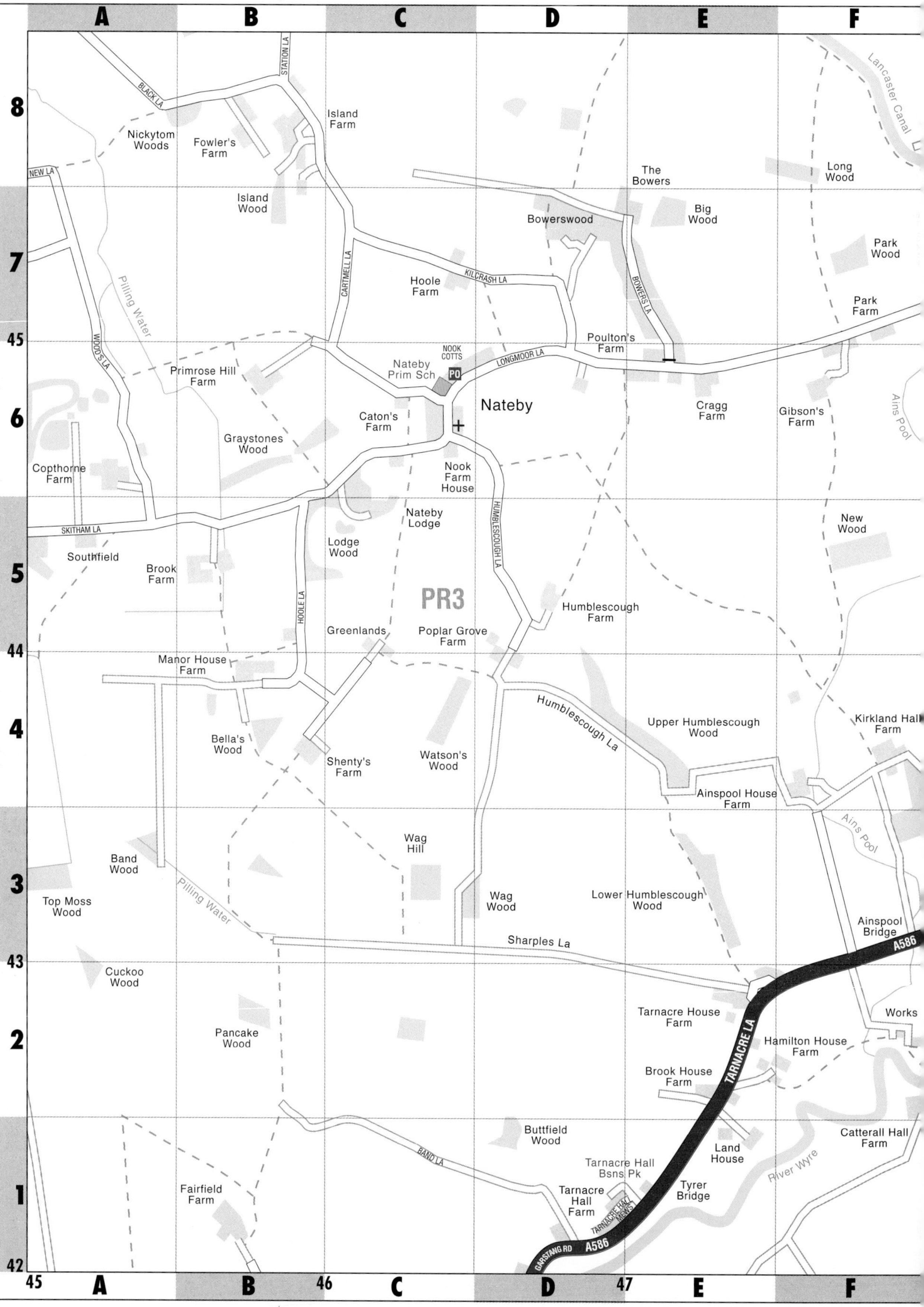
A
B
C
D
E
F
8
7
45
6
5
44
4
3
43
2
1
42
46
47
BLACK LA
STATION LA
Island
Farm
Nickytom
Woods
Fowler's
Farm
NEW LA
Island
Wood
The
Bowers
Long
Wood
Lancaster Canal
Bowerswood
Big
Wood
Park
Wood
CARTMELL LA
KILCRASH LA
Hoole
Farm
BOWERS LA
Park
Farm
Pilling Water
WOODS LA
Poulton's
Farm
NOOK
COTTS
LONGMOOR LA
Primrose Hill
Farm
Nateby
Prim Sch
PO
Nateby
Cragg
Farm
Gibson's
Farm
Ains Pool
Caton's
Farm
Graystones
Wood
Copthorne
Farm
Nook
Farm
House
Nateby
Lodge
HUMBLESCOUGH LA
New
Wood
SKITHAM LA
Southfield
Lodge
Wood
Brook
Farm
PR3
HOOLE LA
Humblescough
Farm
Greenlands
Poplar Grove
Farm
Manor House
Farm
Humblescough La
Upper Humblescough
Wood
Kirkland Hall
Farm
Bella's
Wood
Shenty's
Farm
Watson's
Wood
Ainspool House
Farm
Ains Pool
Wag
Hill
Band
Wood
Pilling Water
Wag
Wood
Lower Humblescough
Wood
Top Moss
Wood
Ainspool
Bridge
Sharples La
A586
Cuckoo
Wood
Tarnacre House
Farm
Works
TARNACRE LA
Pancake
Wood
Hamilton House
Farm
Brook House
Farm
Buttfield
Wood
Land
House
Catterall Hall
Farm
BAND LA
River Wyre
Tarnacre Hall
Bsns Pk
Fairfield
Farm
Tarnacre
Hall
Farm
Tyrer
Bridge
TARNACRE HALL MEWS
GARSTANG RD
A586

179
157

204
182

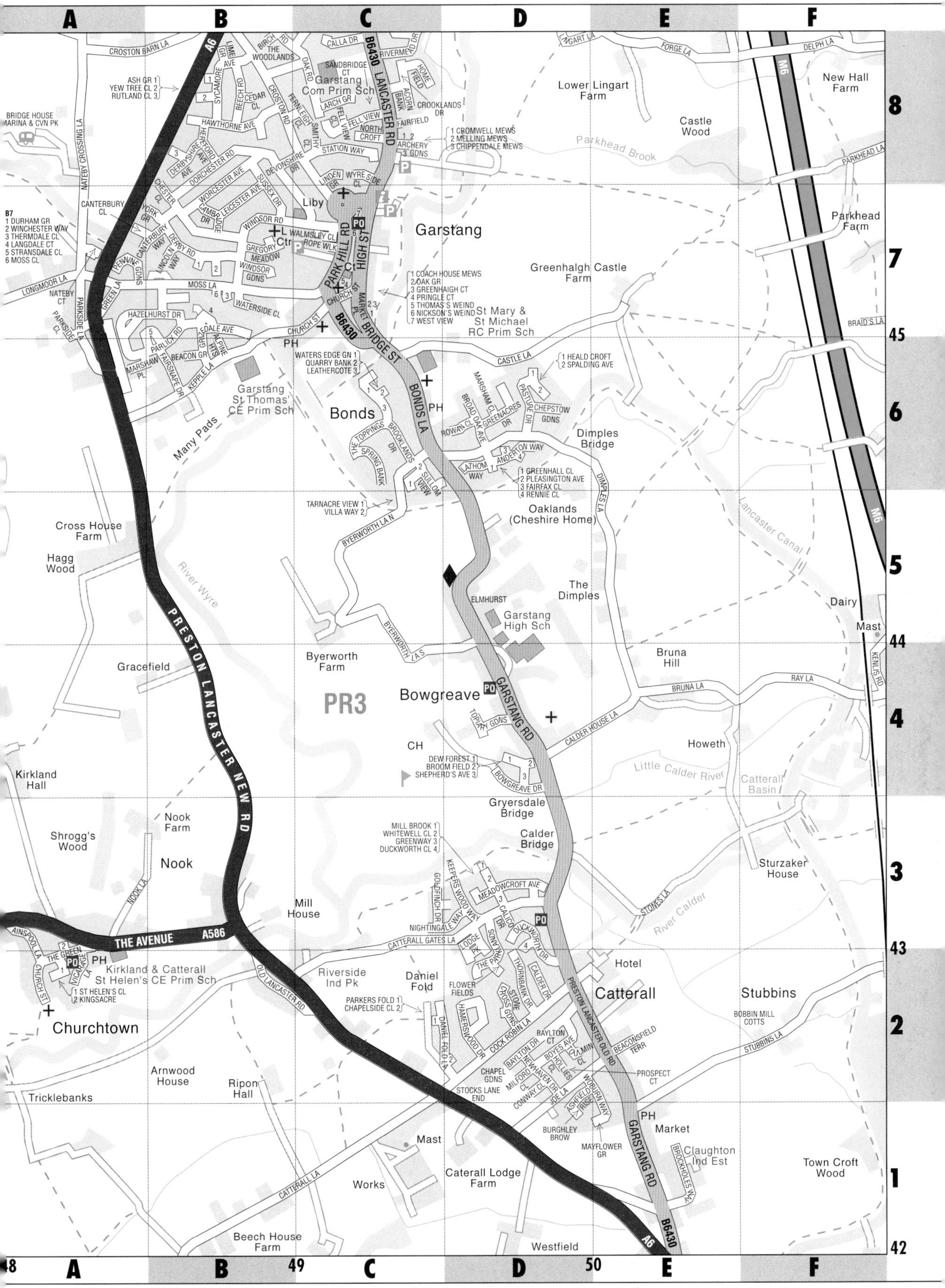
Garstang
Bonds
Bowgreave
Catterall
Churchtown
Nook
PR3
PRESTON LANCASTER NEW RD
THE AVENUE A586
GARSTANG RD
B6430 LANCASTER RD
BONDS LA
M6
Lower Lingart Farm
Castle Wood
New Hall Farm
Parkhead Farm
Greenhalgh Castle Farm
St Mary & St Michael RC Prim Sch
Garstang St Thomas' CE Prim Sch
Garstang Com Prim Sch
Dimples Bridge
Oaklands (Cheshire Home)
The Dimples
Garstang High Sch
Bruna Hill
Howeth
Catterall Basin
Cross House Farm
Hagg Wood
Gracefield
Byerworth Farm
Kirkland Hall
Shrogg's Wood
Nook Farm
Mill House
Gryersdale Bridge
Calder Bridge
Sturzaker House
Riverside Ind Pk
Daniel Fold
Kirkland & Catterall St Helen's CE Prim Sch
Stubbins
Arnwood House
Ripon Hall
Tricklebanks
Mast
Works
Caterall Lodge Farm
Claughton Ind Est
Town Croft Wood
Beech House Farm
Westfield
Market
Hotel
Dairy
Many Pads
River Wyre
Lancaster Canal
Little Calder River
River Calder
Parkhead Brook

181
226

181
159

226
184

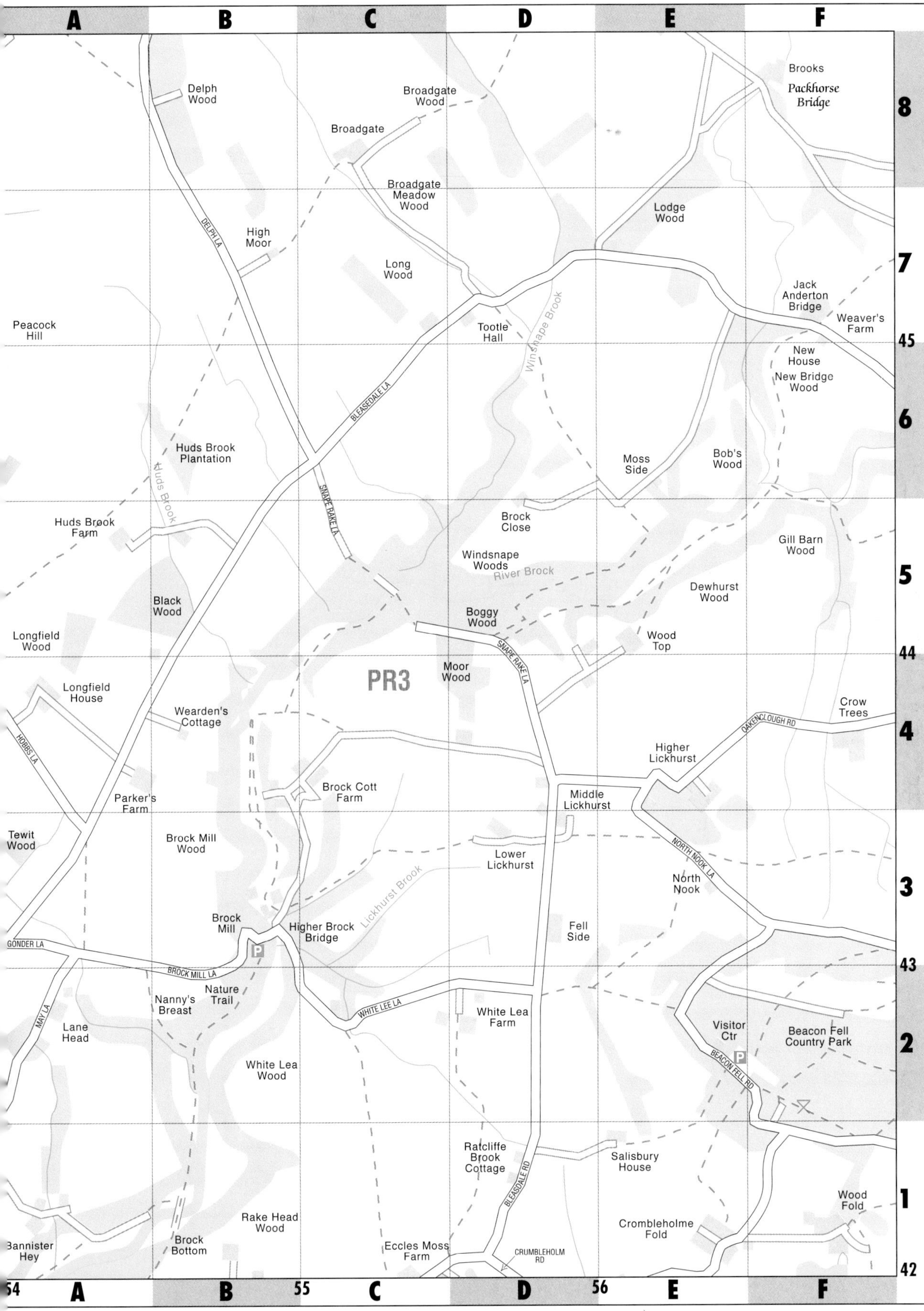
A
B
C
D
E
F
8
7
6
5
4
3
2
1
45
44
43
42
54
55
56
Delph Wood
Broadgate Wood
Broadgate
Brooks
Packhorse Bridge
Broadgate Meadow Wood
Lodge Wood
DELPH LA
High Moor
Long Wood
Jack Anderton Bridge
Weaver's Farm
Peacock Hill
Tootle Hall
Winsnape Brook
New House
New Bridge Wood
BLEASEDALE LA
Huds Brook Plantation
Huds Brook
Moss Side
Bob's Wood
SNAPE RAKE LA
Huds Brook Farm
Brock Close
Gill Barn Wood
Windsnape Woods
River Brock
Black Wood
Dewhurst Wood
Boggy Wood
Longfield Wood
Wood Top
Moor Wood
PR3
Longfield House
Crow Trees
Wearden's Cottage
OAKENCLOUGH RD
HOBBS LA
Higher Lickhurst
Brock Cott Farm
Parker's Farm
Middle Lickhurst
Tewit Wood
Brock Mill Wood
Lower Lickhurst
NORTH NOOK LA
North Nook
Lickhurst Brook
Brock Mill
Higher Brock Bridge
Fell Side
GONDER LA
BROCK MILL LA
Nature Trail
Nanny's Breast
WHITE LEE LA
White Lea Farm
MAY LA
Lane Head
Visitor Ctr
Beacon Fell Country Park
BEACON FELL RD
White Lea Wood
Ratcliffe Brook Cottage
Salisbury House
BLEASDALE RD
Wood Fold
Rake Head Wood
Crombleholme Fold
Bannister Hey
Brock Bottom
Eccles Moss Farm
CRUMBLEHOLM RD

160
184

183
227

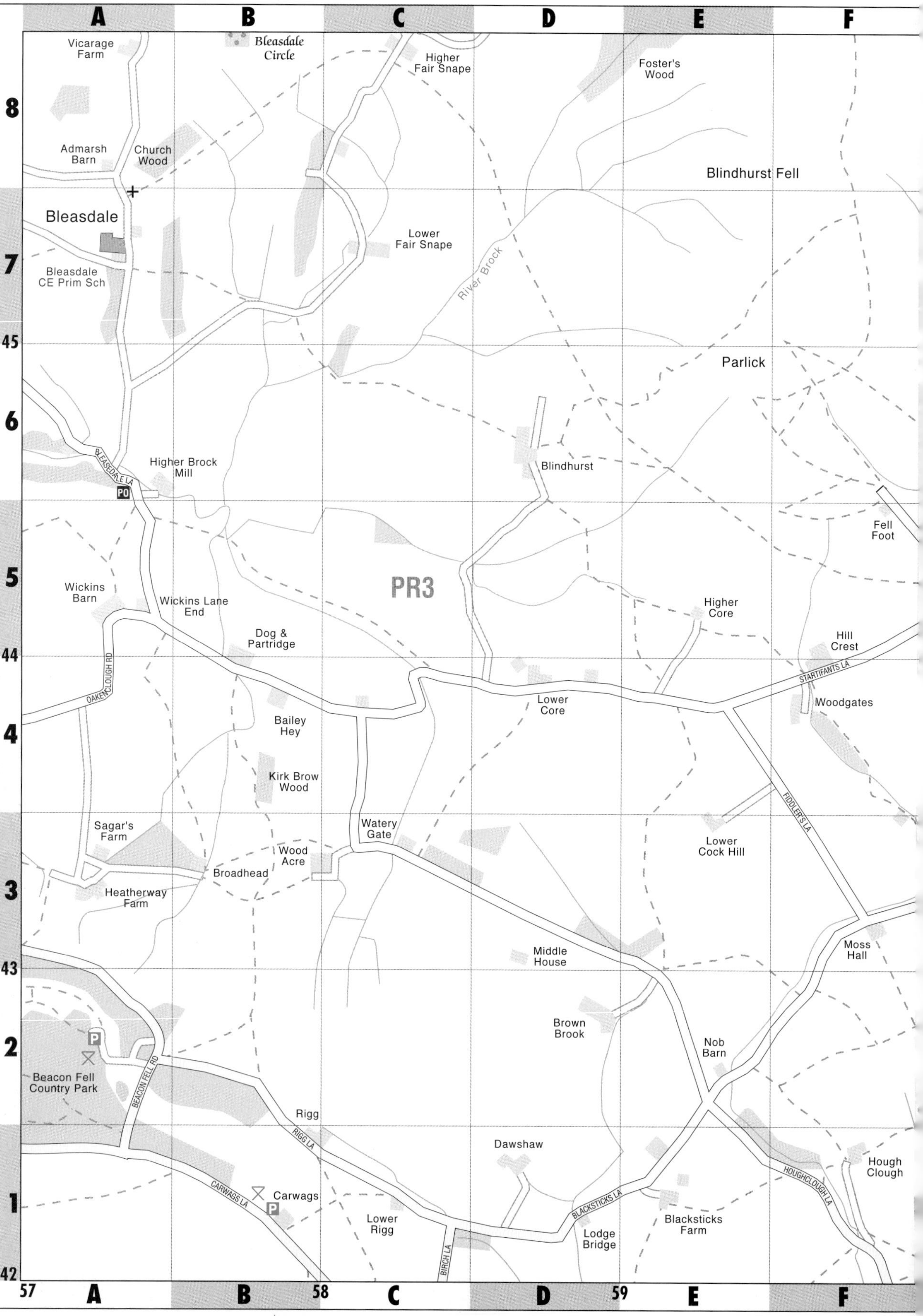
A
B
C
D
E
F
8
7
45
6
5
44
4
3
43
2
1
42
57
58
59
Vicarage Farm
Bleasdale Circle
Higher Fair Snape
Foster's Wood
Admarsh Barn
Church Wood
Blindhurst Fell
Bleasdale
Lower Fair Snape
River Brock
Bleasdale CE Prim Sch
Parlick
Higher Brock Mill
BLEASDALE LA
PO
Blindhurst
Fell Foot
PR3
Wickins Barn
Wickins Lane End
Higher Core
Dog & Partridge
Hill Crest
OAKENCLOUGH RD
STARTIFANTS LA
Lower Core
Woodgates
Bailey Hey
Kirk Brow Wood
Sagar's Farm
Watery Gate
FIDDLER'S LA
Lower Cock Hill
Wood Acre
Broadhead
Heatherway Farm
Middle House
Moss Hall
Brown Brook
P
Nob Barn
Beacon Fell Country Park
BEACON FELL RD
Rigg
RIGG LA
Dawshaw
Hough Clough
HOUGHCLOUGH LA
Carwags
CARWAGS LA
BLACKSTICKS LA
Lower Rigg
Lodge Bridge
Blacksticks Farm
BIRCH LA

183
161

227
186

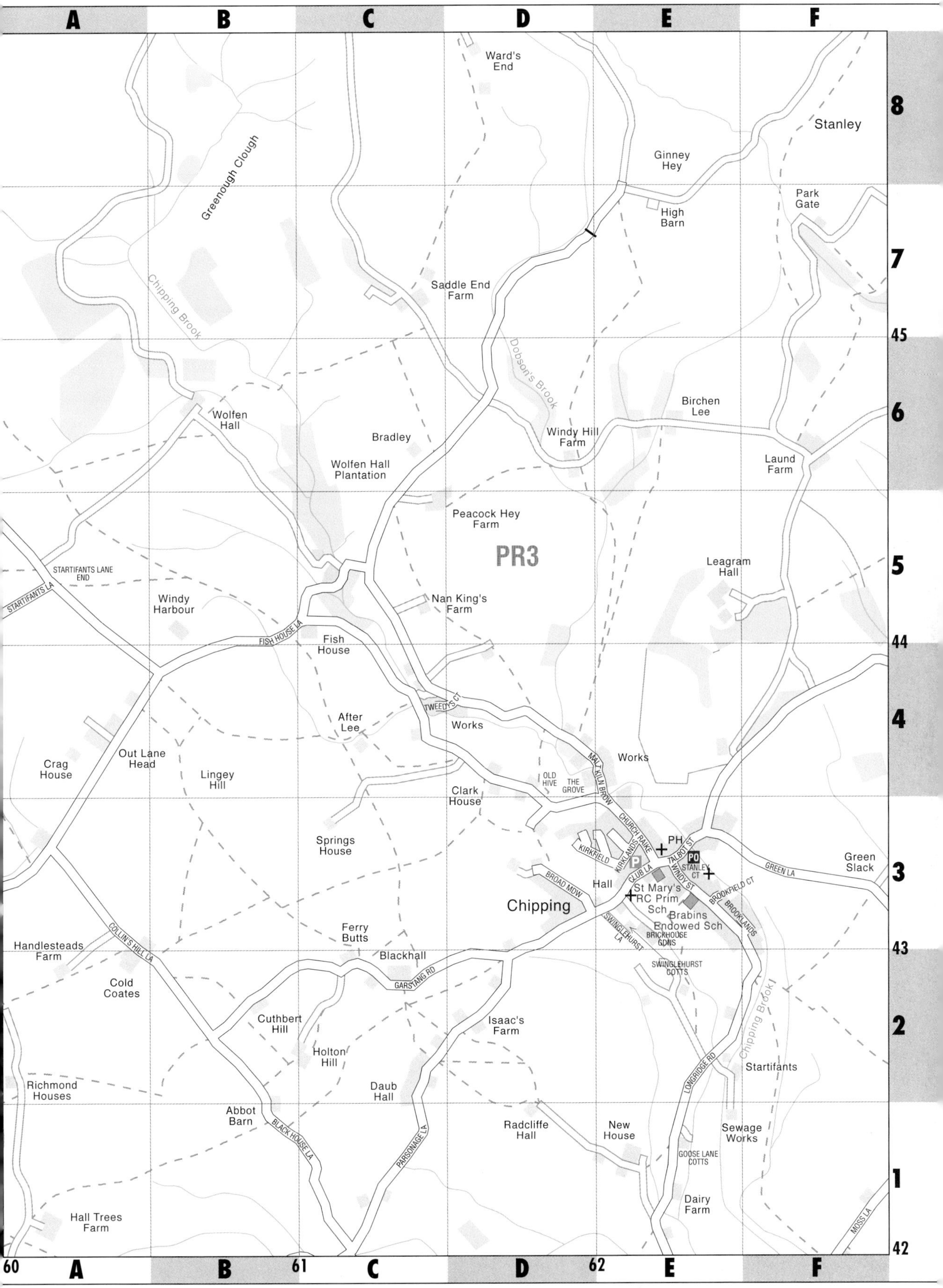


162
186

185
228

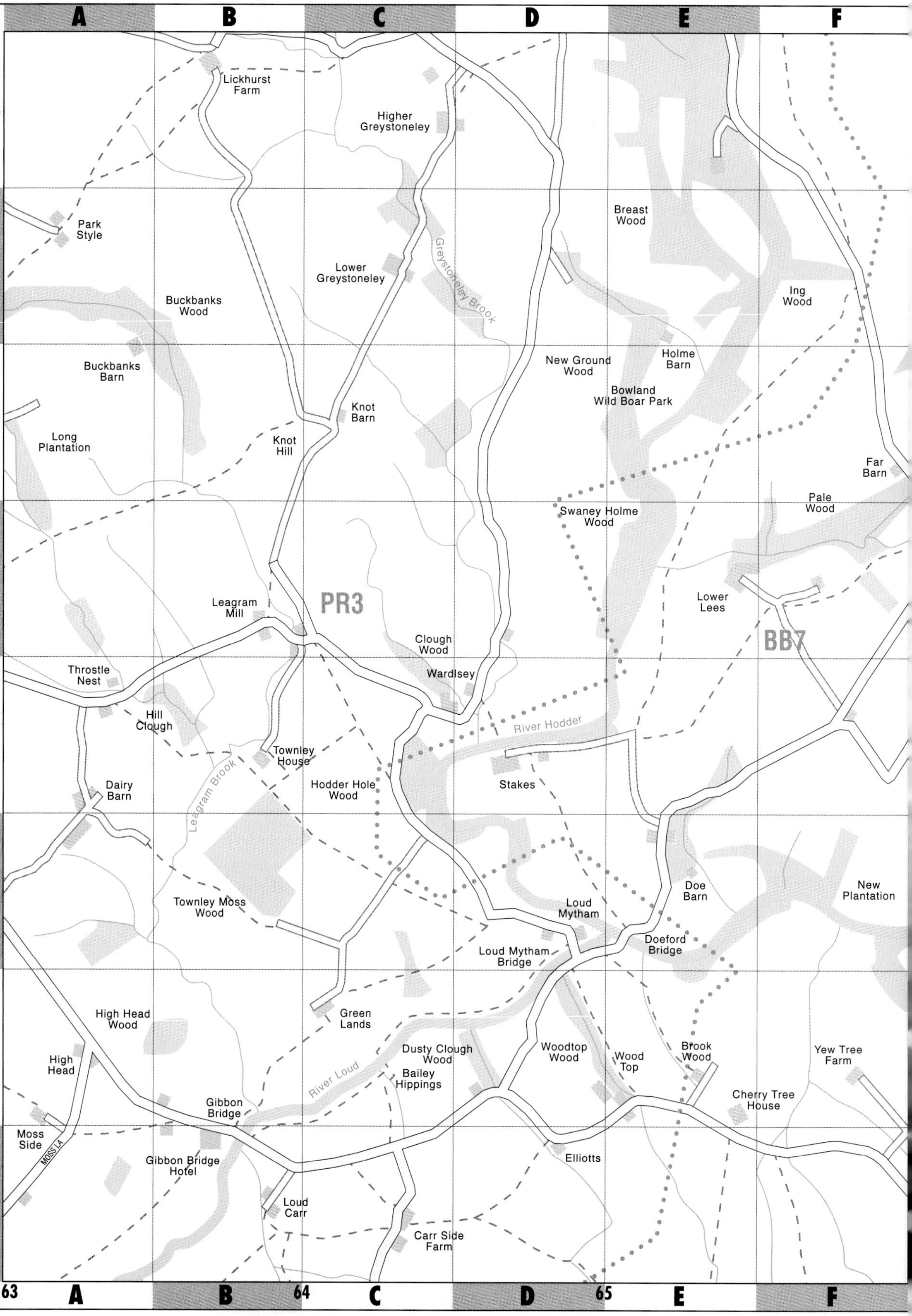
A
B
C
D
E
F
8
7
6
5
4
3
2
1
45
44
43
42
63
64
65
Lickhurst Farm
Higher Greystoneley
Park Style
Breast Wood
Lower Greystoneley
Greystoneley Brook
Buckbanks Wood
Ing Wood
Buckbanks Barn
New Ground Wood
Holme Barn
Bowland Wild Boar Park
Knot Barn
Knot Hill
Long Plantation
Far Barn
Pale Wood
Swaney Holme Wood
Lower Lees
PR3
Leagram Mill
BB7
Clough Wood
Throstle Nest
Wardlsey
Hill Clough
River Hodder
Townley House
Leagram Brook
Dairy Barn
Hodder Hole Wood
Stakes
Doe Barn
New Plantation
Loud Mytham
Townley Moss Wood
Doeford Bridge
Loud Mytham Bridge
High Head Wood
Green Lands
High Head
Dusty Clough Wood
Woodtop Wood
Wood Top
Brook Wood
Yew Tree Farm
Bailey Hippings
River Loud
Cherry Tree House
Gibbon Bridge
Moss Side
MOSS LA
Gibbon Bridge Hotel
Elliotts
Loud Carr
Carr Side Farm

185
163

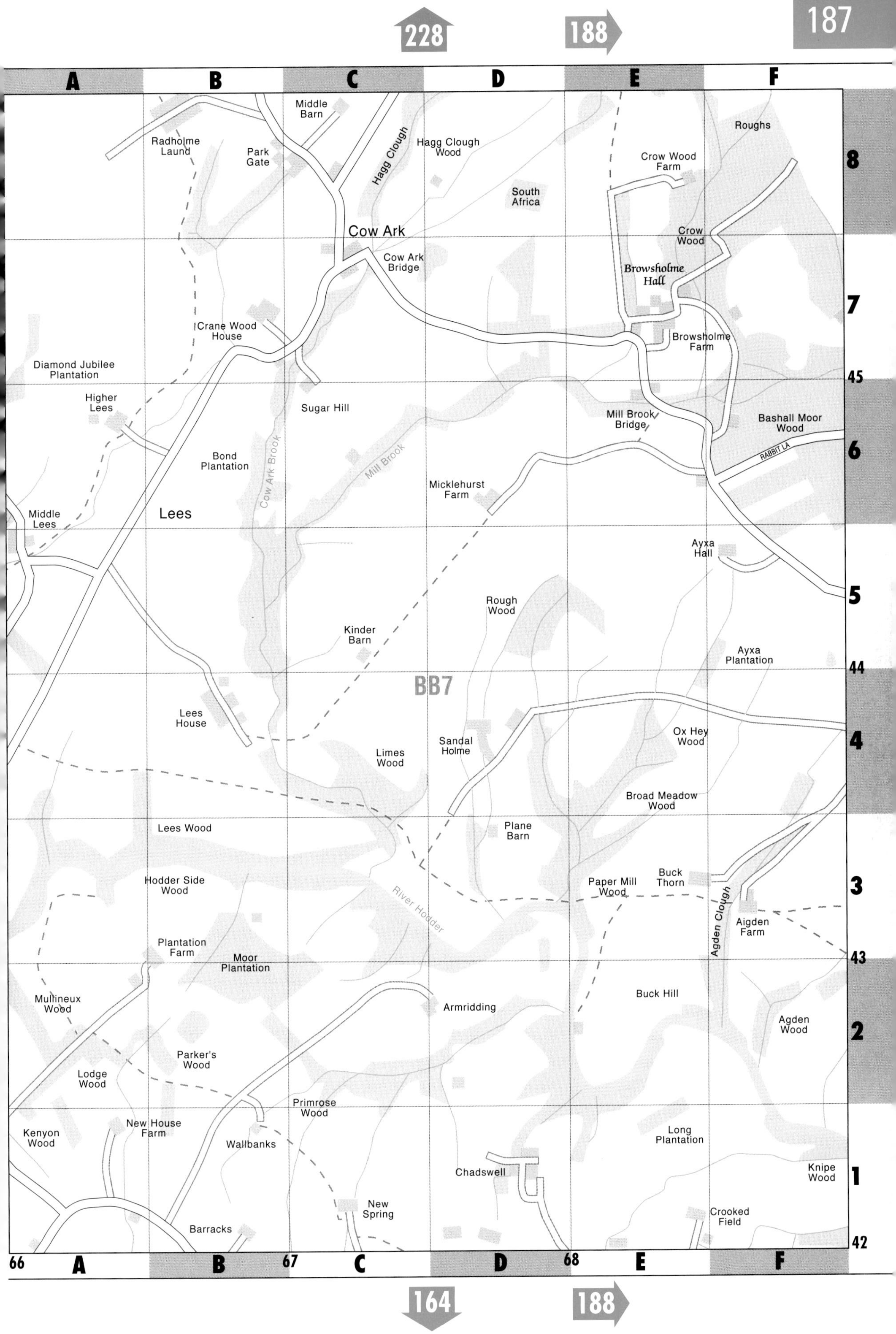
228
188
A
B
C
D
E
F
8
7
45
6
5
44
4
3
43
2
1
42
66
67
68
Radholme Laund
Park Gate
Middle Barn
Hagg Clough
Hagg Clough Wood
South Africa
Crow Wood Farm
Roughs
Cow Ark
Cow Ark Bridge
Crow Wood
Browsholme Hall
Browsholme Farm
Crane Wood House
Diamond Jubilee Plantation
Higher Lees
Sugar Hill
Mill Brook Bridge
Bashall Moor Wood
RABBIT LA
Bond Plantation
Cow Ark Brook
Mill Brook
Micklehurst Farm
Middle Lees
Lees
Ayxa Hall
Rough Wood
Kinder Barn
Ayxa Plantation
BB7
Lees House
Limes Wood
Sandal Holme
Ox Hey Wood
Broad Meadow Wood
Lees Wood
Plane Barn
Hodder Side Wood
River Hodder
Paper Mill Wood
Buck Thorn
Agden Clough
Aigden Farm
Plantation Farm
Moor Plantation
Mullineux Wood
Armridding
Buck Hill
Agden Wood
Parker's Wood
Lodge Wood
Primrose Wood
Kenyon Wood
New House Farm
Wallbanks
Long Plantation
Chadswell
Knipe Wood
New Spring
Barracks
Crooked Field
164
188

187
229

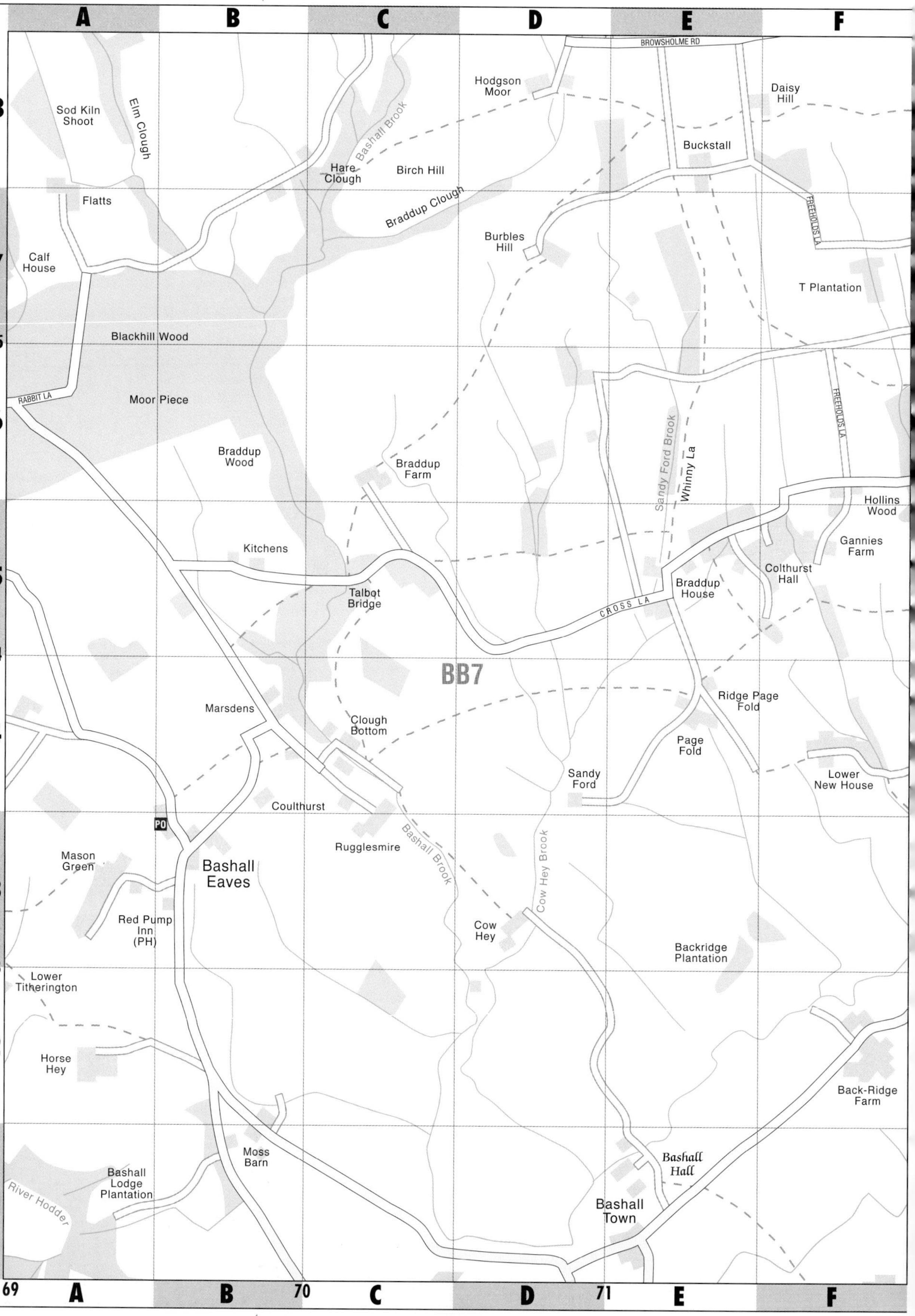
A B C D E F
8 7 6 5 4 3 2 1
45 44 43 42 69 70 71
BROWSHOLME RD
Hodgson Moor
Daisy Hill
Sod Kiln Shoot
Elm Clough
Bashall Brook
Buckstall
Hare Clough
Birch Hill
Flatts
Braddup Clough
FREEHOLDS LA
Burbles Hill
Calf House
T Plantation
Blackhill Wood
RABBIT LA
Moor Piece
Braddup Wood
Braddup Farm
Sandy Ford Brook
Whinny La
Hollins Wood
Gannies Farm
Kitchens
Colthurst Hall
Braddup House
Talbot Bridge
CROSS LA
BB7
Ridge Page Fold
Marsdens
Clough Bottom
Page Fold
Sandy Ford
Lower New House
Coulthurst
PO
Rugglesmire
Mason Green
Bashall Eaves
Cow Hey Brook
Red Pump Inn (PH)
Cow Hey
Backridge Plantation
Lower Titherington
Horse Hey
Back-Ridge Farm
Moss Barn
Bashall Hall
Bashall Lodge Plantation
River Hodder
Bashall Town

187
165

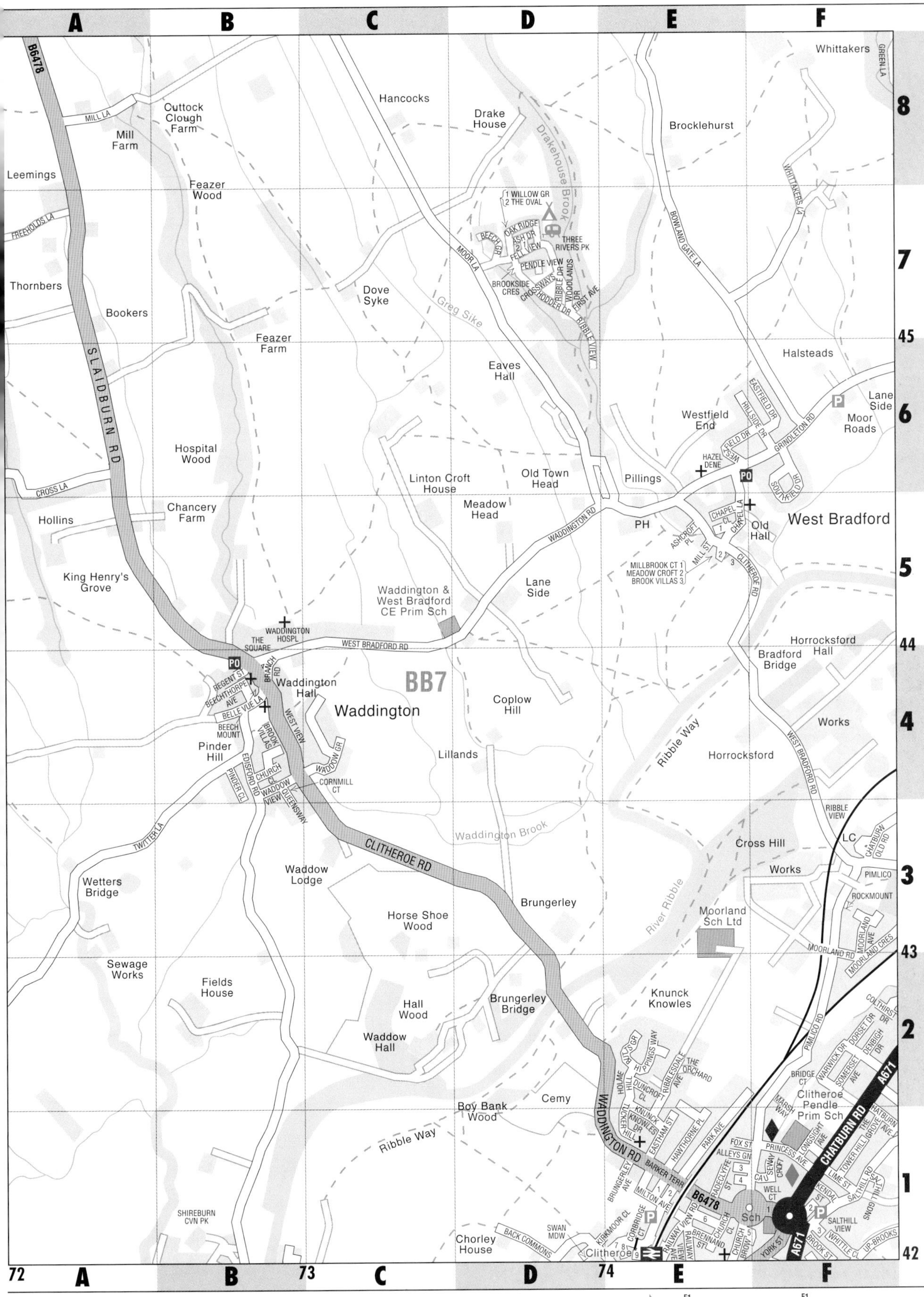
A
B
C
D
E
F
8
7
45
6
5
44
4
3
43
2
1
42
72
73
74
B6478
MILL LA
Cuttock Clough Farm
Mill Farm
Leemings
Feazer Wood
FREEHOLDS LA
Thornbers
Bookers
Feazer Farm
SLAIDBURN RD
Hospital Wood
CROSS LA
Chancery Farm
Hollins
King Henry's Grove
Hancocks
Drake House
Drakehouse Brook
1 WILLOW GR
2 THE OVAL
OAK RIDGE
BEECH GR
ASH DR
FELL VIEW
THREE RIVERS PK
PENDLE VIEW
BROOKSIDE CRES
CROSSWAYS
RIBBLE DR
WOODLANDS DR
HODDER DR
FIRST AVE
RIBBLE VIEW
MOOR LA
Dove Syke
Greg Sike
Eaves Hall
Linton Croft House
Old Town Head
Meadow Head
Brocklehurst
BOWLAND GATE LA
WHITTAKERS LA
Whittakers
GREEN LA
Halsteads
Lane Side
Moor Roads
Westfield End
EASTFIELD DR
HILLSIDE DR
FIELD DR
WEST
GRINDLETON RD
HAZEL DENE
SOUTHFIELD DR
Pillings
PO
PH
CHAPEL CL
CHAPEL LA
West Bradford
Old Hall
ASHCROFT PL
MILL ST
MILLBROOK CT 1
MEADOW CROFT 2
BROOK VILLAS 3
CLITHEROE RD
WADDINGTON RD
Lane Side
Waddington & West Bradford CE Prim Sch
WADDINGTON HOSPL
THE SQUARE
WEST BRADFORD RD
BRANCH RD
REGENT ST
BEECHTHORPE AVE
BELLE VUE LA
BEECH MOUNT
Waddington Hall
Waddington
BB7
Coplow Hill
WEST VIEW
BROOK VILLAS
WADDOW GR
Pinder Hill
EDISFORD RD
PINDER CL
CHURCH CL
WADDOW VIEW
QUEENSWAY
CORNMILL CT
Lillands
Horrocksford Hall
Bradford Bridge
Ribble Way
Works
Horrocksford
WEST BRADFORD RD
RIBBLE VIEW
Waddington Brook
TWITTER LA
CLITHEROE RD
Wetters Bridge
Waddow Lodge
Cross Hill
LC
CHATBURN OLD RD
Works
PIMLICO
ROCKMOUNT
Brungerley
Horse Shoe Wood
River Ribble
Moorland Sch Ltd
MOORLAND RD
MOORLAND AVE
MOORLAND CRES
Sewage Works
Fields House
Brungerley Bridge
Hall Wood
Knunck Knowles
COLTHIRST DR
Waddow Hall
PIMLICO RD
WARWICK DR
DORSET DR
DENBIGH DR
SOMERSET AVE
RIBBLESDALE AVE
THE ORCHARD
HIPPINGS WAY
DUNCROFT CL
KNUNCK KNOWLES DR
EASTHAM ST
HAWTHORNE PL
PARK AVE
BRIDGE CT
Clitheroe Pendle Prim Sch
MARSH WAY
CHATBURN RD
A671
CHATBURN AVE
THE GROVE
TOWER HILL
Cemy
Boy Bank Wood
Ribble Way
WADDINGTON RD
BARKER TERR
FOX ST
ALLEYS GN
PRINCESS AVE
LONGSIGHT AVE
RADECLYFFE ST
CAU SEWAY
CROFT
WELL CT
LIME ST
SALTHILL RD
SALTHILL GDNS
KENDAL ST
SALTHILL VIEW
WHITTLE CL
UP-BROOKS
BROOK ST
YORK ST
B6478
Sch
BRUNGERLEY AVE
MILTON AVE
KIRKMOOR CL
CORBRIDGE CT
RAILWAY VIEW RD
RAILWAY VIEW
BRENNAND ST
CHURCH BROW
SHIREBURN CVN PK
Chorley House
BACK COMMONS
SWAN MDW
Clitheroe
P



E1
1 COWPER AVE
2 CHESTER AVE
3 SPRING MDW
4 ST DENY'S CROFT
5 CHURCH BROW GDNS
6 ST MARY'S ST
7 KIRKMOOR RD
8 CASTLEKEEP VIEW
9 BLACK LA CROFT

F1
1 WELL TERR
2 NORTH ST
3 STAMFORD PL

189
230

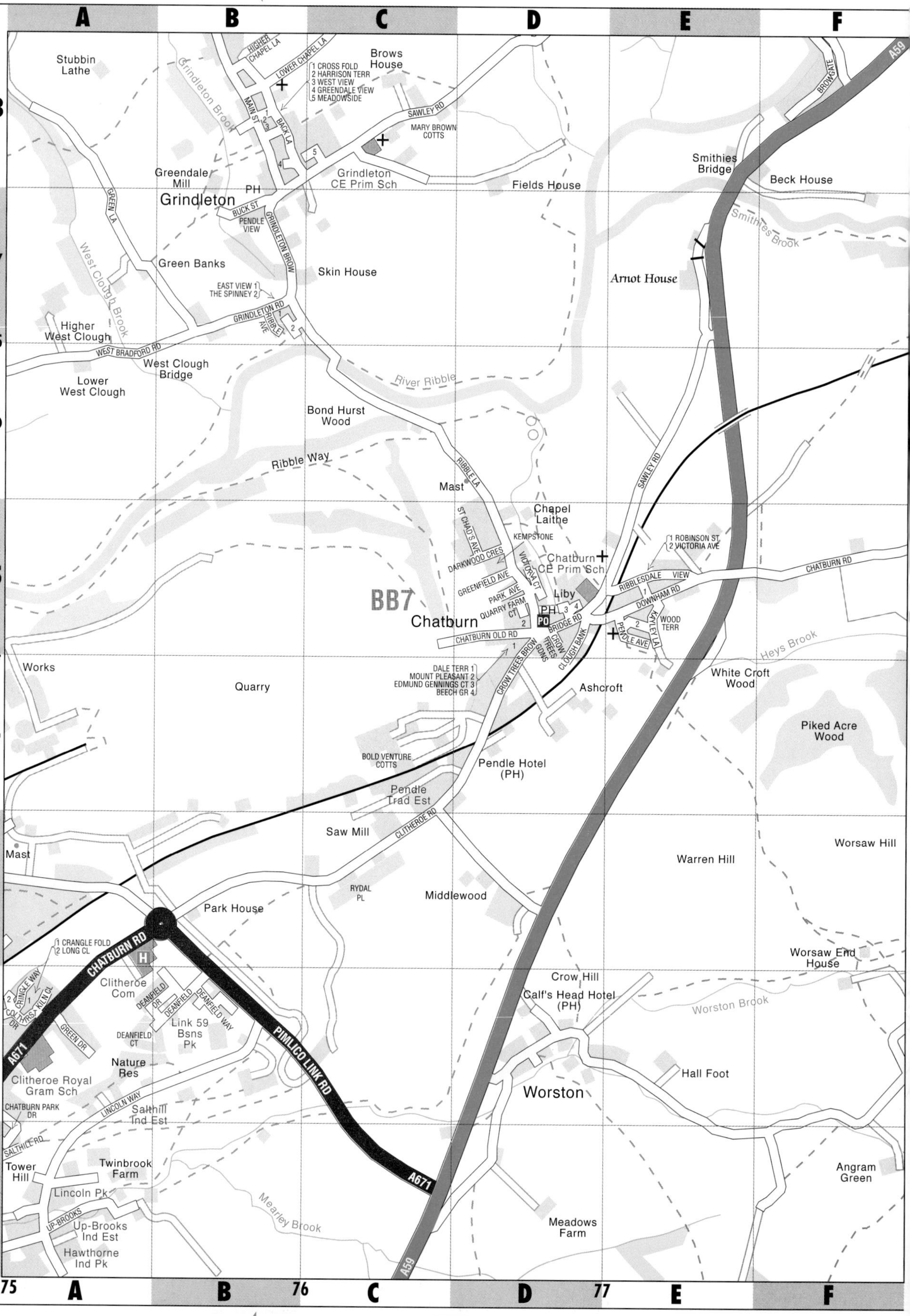


189
167

230
192

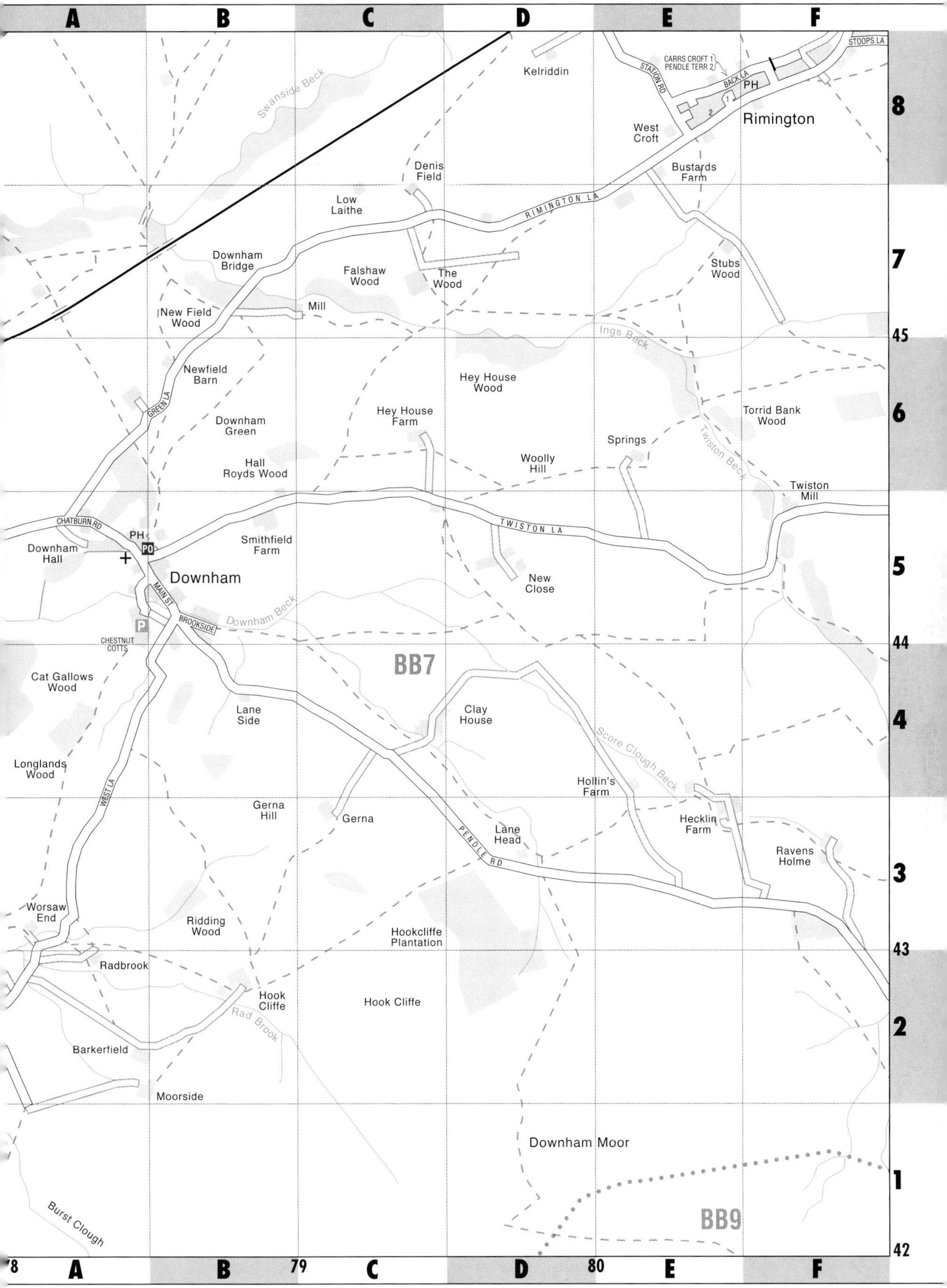


168
192

191
231

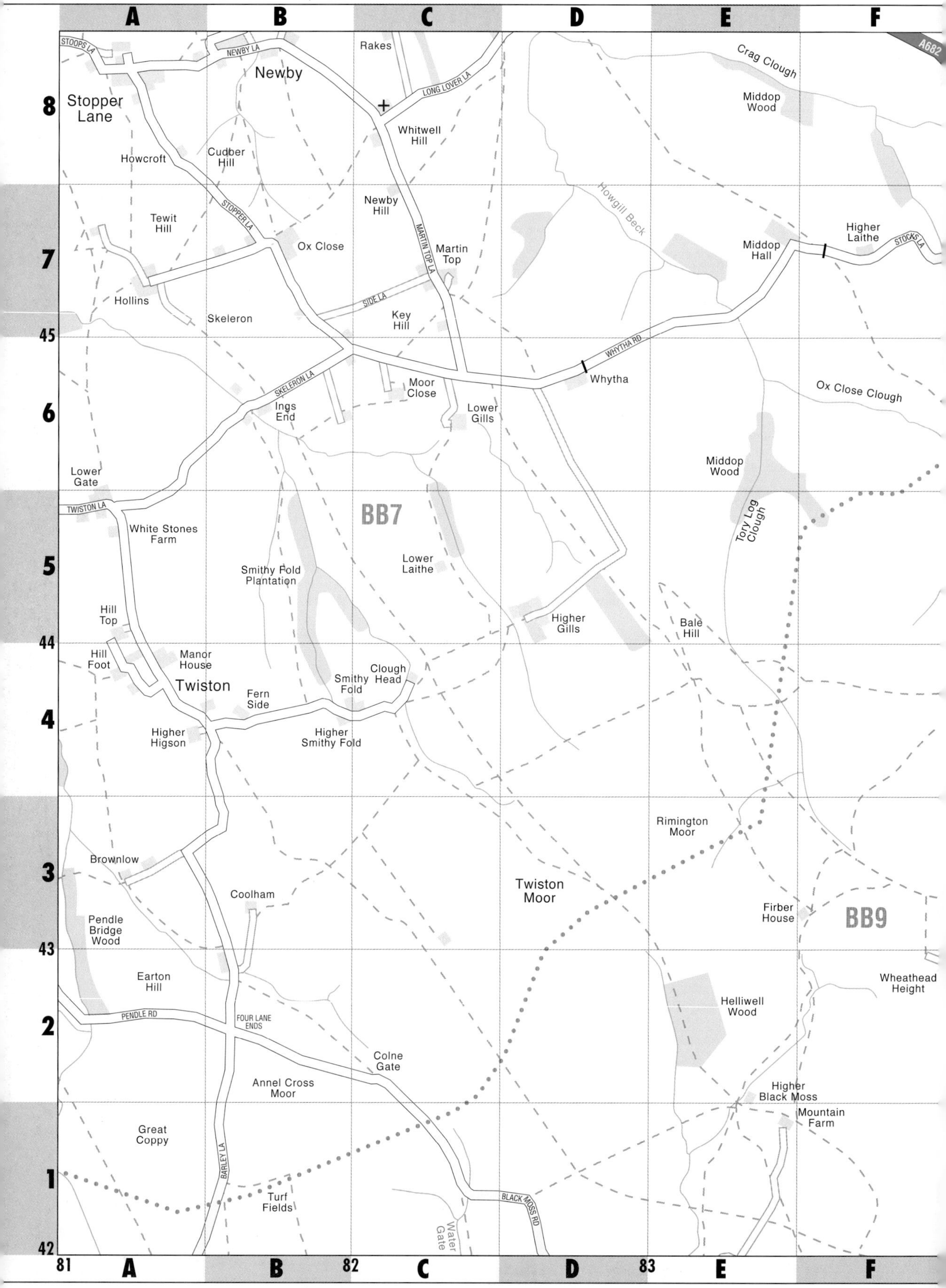


191
169

231
194

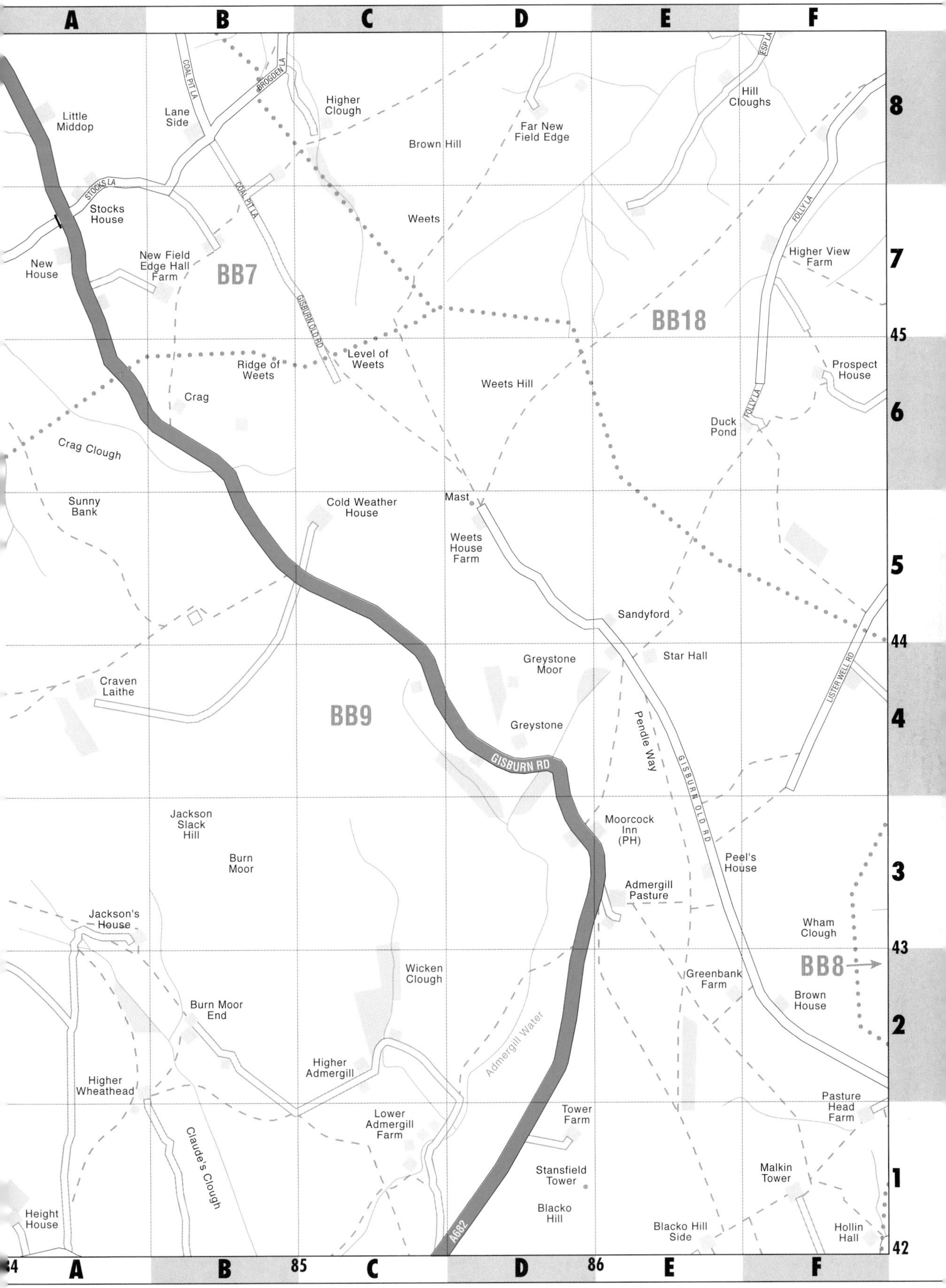


170
194

193
196

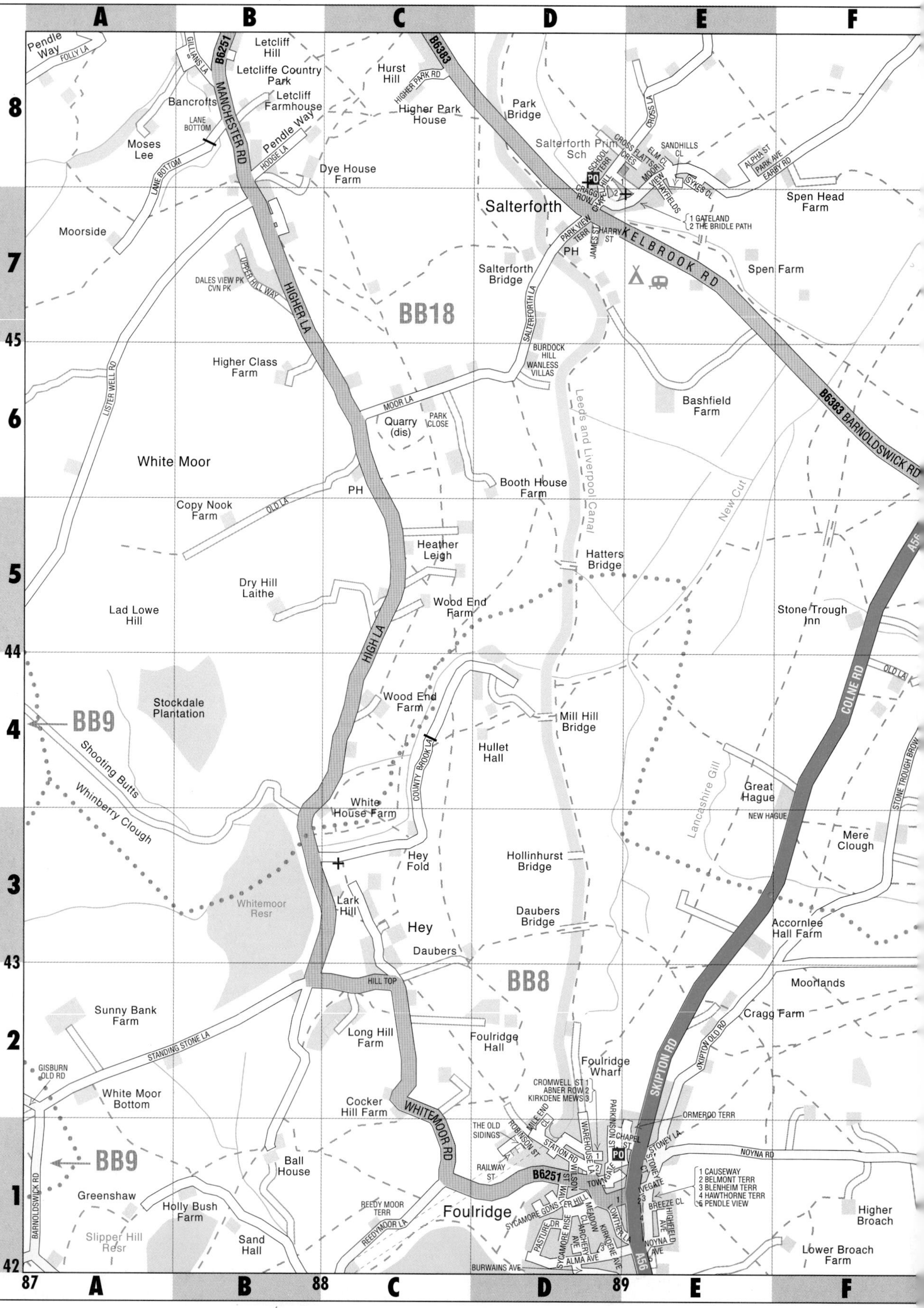
A
B
C
D
E
F
8
7
45
6
5
44
4
3
43
2
1
42
87
88
89
Pendle Way
FOLLY LA
GILLIANS LA
B6251
Letcliff Hill
Letcliffe Country Park
Letcliff Farmhouse
Bancrofts
LANE BOTTOM
MANCHESTER RD
Moses Lee
Pendle Way
HODGE LA
LANE BOTTOM
Hurst Hill
HIGHER PARK RD
B6383
Higher Park House
Park Bridge
Dye House Farm
Salterforth Prim Sch
CROSS LA
CROSS FLATTS CRES
ELM CL
SANDHILLS CL
MOOR VIEW
HAYFIELDS
SYKES CL
ALPHA ST
PARK AVE
EARBY RD
SCHOOL TERR
CRAGG ROW
CHAPEL HILL
Salterforth
Spen Head Farm
1 GATELAND
2 THE BRIDLE PATH
Moorside
PARK VIEW TERR
HARRY ST
JAMES ST
KELBROOK RD
PH
UPPER HILL WAY
DALES VIEW PK CVN PK
HIGHER LA
Salterforth Bridge
Spen Farm
SALTERFORTH LA
BB18
BURDOCK HILL
WANLESS VILLAS
Higher Class Farm
LISTER WELL RD
MOOR LA
Leeds and Liverpool Canal
Bashfield Farm
B6383 BARNOLDSWICK RD
Quarry (dis)
PARK CLOSE
White Moor
Booth House Farm
PH
Copy Nook Farm
OLD LA
New Cut
Heather Leigh
Hatters Bridge
A56
Dry Hill Laithe
Wood End Farm
Stone Trough Inn
Lad Lowe Hill
HIGH LA
OLD LA
COLNE RD
Stockdale Plantation
Wood End Farm
Mill Hill Bridge
BB9
Shooting Butts
COUNTY BROOK LA
Hullet Hall
Lancashire Gill
Great Hague
STONE TROUGH BROW
Whinberry Clough
White House Farm
NEW HAGUE
Mere Clough
Hey Fold
Hollinhurst Bridge
Lark Hill
Whitemoor Resr
Hey
Daubers Bridge
Accornlee Hall Farm
Daubers
HILL TOP
BB8
Moorlands
Sunny Bank Farm
Long Hill Farm
Foulridge Hall
Cragg Farm
SKIPTON OLD RD
STANDING STONE LA
Foulridge Wharf
GISBURN OLD RD
CROMWELL ST
ABNER ROW
KIRKDENE MEWS
SKIPTON RD
White Moor Bottom
Cocker Hill Farm
WHITEMOOR RD
MILE END CL
PARKINSON ST
ORMEROD TERR
THE OLD SIDINGS
ROBINSON ST
WAREHOUSE LA
CHAPEL ST
STONEY LA
BB9
STATION RD
PO
NOYNA RD
Ball House
RAILWAY ST
B6251
WILSON ST
TOWNGATE
1 CAUSEWAY
2 BELMONT TERR
3 BLENHEIM TERR
4 HAWTHORNE TERR
5 PENDLE VIEW
BARNOLDSWICK RD
Greenshaw
Holly Bush Farm
REEDY MOOR TERR
REEDYMOOR LA
Foulridge
BREEZE CL
HIGHFIELD AVE
NOYNA AVE
Higher Broach
Slipper Hill Resr
Sand Hall
SYCAMORE GDNS
PASTURE DR
SYCAMORE RISE
MEADOW CL
ARCHERY AVE
KIRKDENE AVE
ALMA AVE
BURWAINS AVE
Lower Broach Farm

197

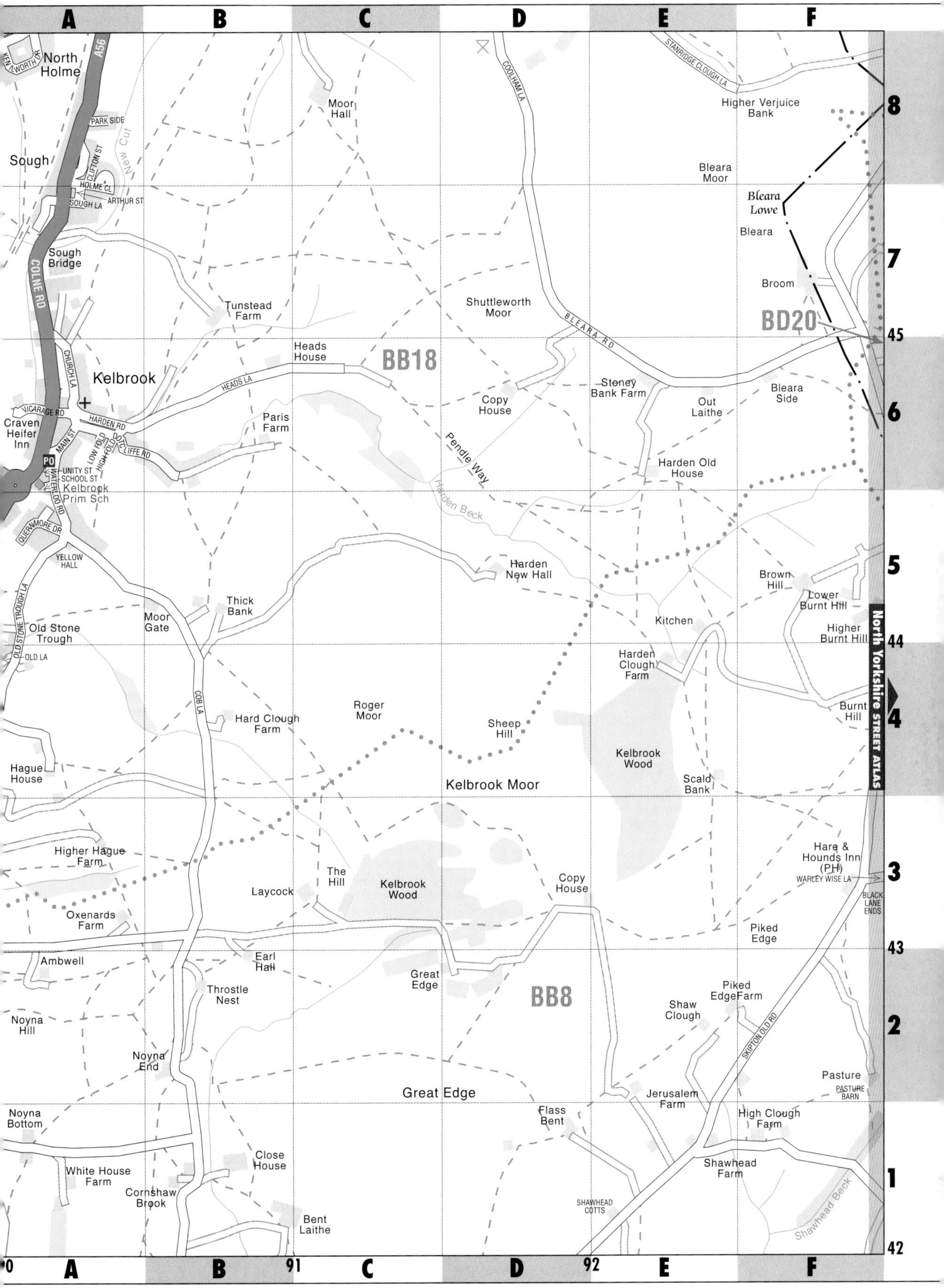
A
B
C
D
E
F
North Holme
A56
KENILWORTH DR
PARK SIDE
New Cut
Sough
CLIFTON ST
HOLME CL
ARTHUR ST
SOUGH LA
Sough Bridge
COLNE RD
Moor Hall
COOLHAM LA
STANRIDGE CLOUGH LA
Higher Verjuice Bank
Bleara Moor
Bleara Lowe
Bleara
Broom
Tunstead Farm
Shuttleworth Moor
BLEARA RD
BD20
Heads House
BB18
CHURCH LA
Kelbrook
HEADS LA
Stoney Bank Farm
Out Laithe
Bleara Side
Copy House
VICARAGE RD
Craven Heifer Inn
HARDEN RD
Paris Farm
MAIN ST
LOW FOLD
HIGH FOLD
DOTCLIFFE RD
Pendle Way
Harden Old House
PO
UNITY ST
SCHOOL ST
WATERLOO RD
Kelbrook Prim Sch
Harden Beck
QUERNMORE DR
YELLOW HALL
Harden New Hall
Brown Hill
Lower Burnt Hill
Thick Bank
Moor Gate
Kitchen
Old Stone Trough
OLD STONE TROUGH LA
OLD LA
Higher Burnt Hill
Harden Clough Farm
North Yorkshire STREET ATLAS
COB LA
Hard Clough Farm
Roger Moor
Sheep Hill
Burnt Hill
Kelbrook Wood
Hague House
Kelbrook Moor
Scald Bank
Higher Hague Farm
Hare & Hounds Inn (PH)
WARLEY WISE LA
The Hill
Kelbrook Wood
Copy House
Laycock
BLACK LANE ENDS
Oxenards Farm
Piked Edge
Ambwell
Earl Hall
Great Edge
Throstle Nest
BB8
Piked EdgeFarm
Shaw Clough
Noyna Hill
SKIPTON OLD RD
Noyna End
Pasture
PASTURE BARN
Great Edge
Jerusalem Farm
Noyna Bottom
Flass Bent
High Clough Farm
Close House
Shawhead Farm
White House Farm
Cornshaw Brook
Shawhead Beck
SHAWHEAD COTTS
Bent Laithe
8
7
45
6
5
44
4
3
43
2
1
42
90
91
92

172

231

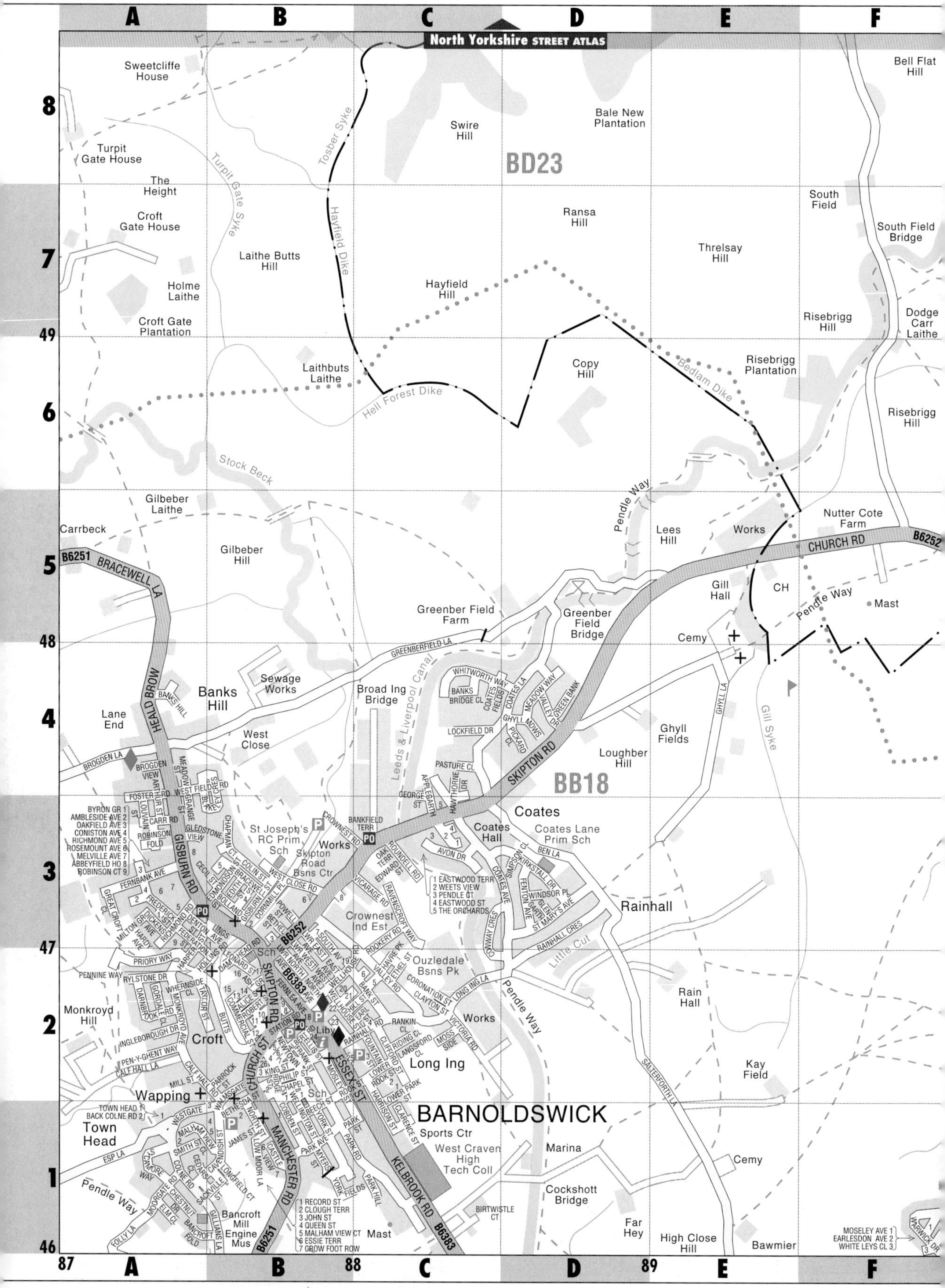


B2
1 BACK CHAPEL ST
2 DAVID CROSLEY HO
3 JEPP HILL
4 BROOK ST
5 ORCHARD ST
6 GARDEN ST
7 MARKET ST
8 BACK SKIPTON RD
9 FORESTER'S BLDGS
10 ST JAMES' RD
11 ST JAMES' SQ
12 GREEN ST
13 BESSIE ST
14 EAST VIEW TERR
15 PLEASANT VIEW
16 FAR EAST VIEW
17 MONTROSE TERR
18 POST OFFICE BLDGS
19 EAST PAR
20 WELLHOUSE SQ
21 EAST HILLS ST
22 CO-OPERATIVE ST
23 RAILWAY ST
24 MAJESTIC BLDGS
25 SUSSEX ST
26 OLD TOWN HALL

231

B3
1 HOLLINS CT
2 DAM SIDE
3 BAIRSTOW ST
4 BROGDEN ST
5 BRUCE ST
6 CORNMILL TERR
7 NORTH PAR
8 MASONS WAY

194

C2
1 MYRTLE GR
2 BEECH GR
3 UNITY ST
4 TURNER ST
5 STUART ST
6 CRAVEN ST

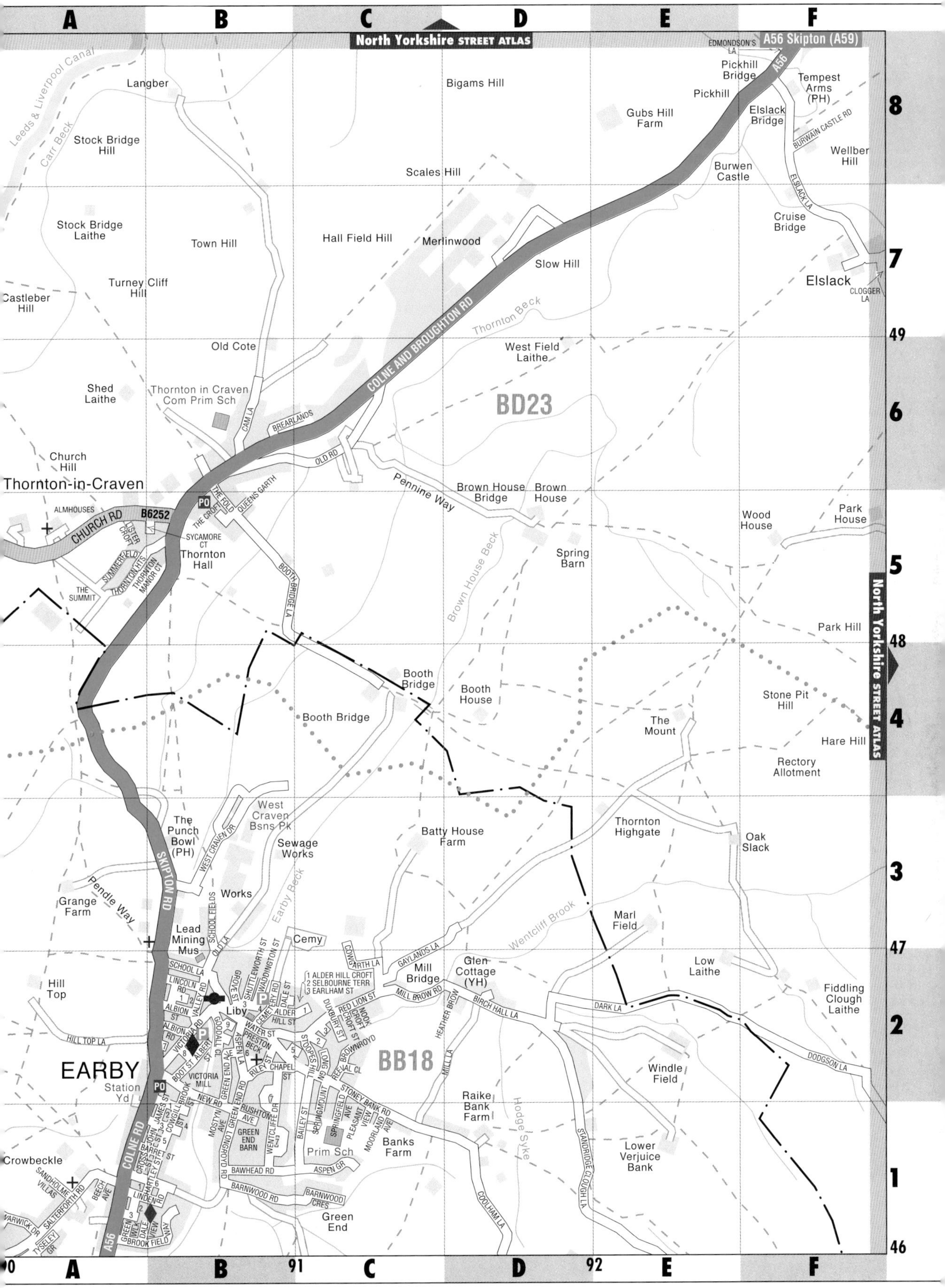


A1
1 LINDEN CT
2 JAGOE MEWS
3 JAGOE RD

B1
1 GEORGE ST
2 CHAPEL MEWS
3 APPLEGARTH ST
4 RIVERSIDE TERR
5 WILLIAM ST
6 ROSTLE TOP RD
7 THE BUNGALOWS

B2
1 HIGHFIELD RD
2 VALLEY GDNS
3 LOWER CROFT ST
4 SHAW SQ
5 WELBURY CL
6 WILKINSON MOUNT
7 VICTORIA ST
8 EDWARD ST
9 VICTORIA MEWS

195

FLEETWOOD
FY7
OUTER PROM
Boating Pool
Marine Gdns
MARINE VIEW APARTMENTS
THE ESPLANADE
LAIDLEY'S WLK
CHARTERHOUSE CT
Cemy
Promenade
Rossall Point
Lancashire Coastal Way
SEA WALL
SHAKESPEARE RD
Shakespeare Prim Sch
MANOR WOOD
POULTON RD
A587
WYREDALE CT
Meml Pk
WEST GATE
LANCASTER GATE
HIGH GATE
ROSSALL GRANGE LA
PH
Prim Sch
CH
D3
1 CURTIS DR
2 GARLAND GR
3 MONROE DR
4 LAMOUR PL
5 KENTMERE CL
6 HONISTER CL
Fleetwood Charles Saer Com Prim Sch
Liby
BROADWAY
BRENTWOOD
HATFIELD AVE
GEORGE WILLIAMS HO
Linden Rd
Lingfield Rd
Heathfield Rd
Blackpool & Fleetwood Tramway
A585
Fleetwood Sports Coll
Larkholme
LARKHOLME PAR
LARKHOLME LA
LARKHOLME AVE
Prim Sch
ROBERTSON CT
Southfleet Ave
KILBANE ST
MEADOW AVE
BENTHAM AVE
THIRLMERE AVE
MARTINDALE AVE
MEDLOCK PL
PO

175

E2
1 HATFIELD WLK
2 HATFIELD GDNS
3 LANGDALE CT
E3
1 MASONS CT
2 WESTWOOD AVE
3 LONSDALE CRES

E4
1 MOWBRAY PL
2 STRATFORD PL
3 GRASMERE AVE
F2
1 WESTHEAD WLK
2 HATFIELD MEWS
3 GREGSON DR

4 EDMONDSEN PL
5 ARMITSTEAD WAY
6 FORSHAW CL
7 CROOKALL CL
8 ARMITSTEAD CT
9 NOBLETT CT
10 MAYFIELD PL
11 HARBOUR CL

12 Copse View Bsns Pk
13 Harbour Trad Est

F3
1 WARRENHURST HO
2 EASTWOOD AVE
3 ADDISON RD
F4
1 ROSE CT
2 SEYMOUR ST
3 ALBANY RD
4 WELBECK HO

200

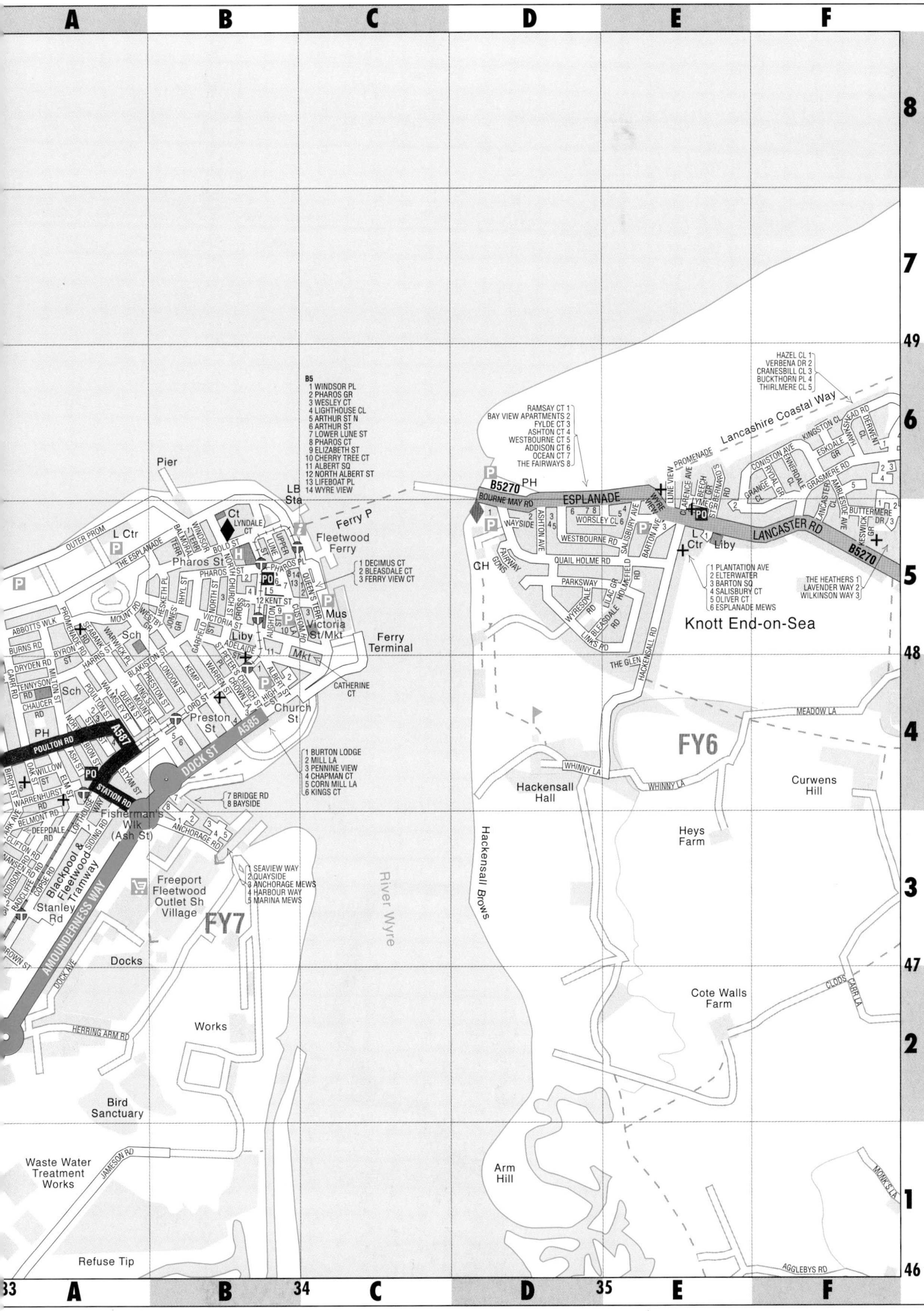

A
B
C
D
E
F
8
7
49
6
5
48
4
3
47
2
1
46
33
34
35
B5
1 WINDSOR PL
2 PHAROS GR
3 WESLEY CT
4 LIGHTHOUSE CL
5 ARTHUR ST N
6 ARTHUR ST
7 LOWER LUNE ST
8 PHAROS CT
9 ELIZABETH ST
10 CHERRY TREE CT
11 ALBERT SQ
12 NORTH ALBERT ST
13 LIFEBOAT PL
14 WYRE VIEW
RAMSAY CT 1
BAY VIEW APARTMENTS 2
FYLDE CT 3
ASHTON CT 4
WESTBOURNE CT 5
ADDISON CT 6
OCEAN CT 7
THE FAIRWAYS 8
HAZEL CL 1
VERBENA DR 2
CRANESBILL CL 3
BUCKTHORN PL 4
THIRLMERE CL 5
Lancashire Coastal Way
PROMENADE
Pier
LB Sta
Ferry P
Fleetwood Ferry
1 DECIMUS CT
2 BLEASDALE CT
3 FERRY VIEW CT
L Ctr
OUTER PROM
THE ESPLANADE
Pharos St
LYNDALE CT
Ct
BOLD ST
PHAROS PL
Liby
Mus
Victoria St/Mkt
Mkt
Ferry Terminal
CATHERINE CT
Sch
ABBOTTS WLK
BURNS RD
DRYDEN RD
TENNYSON RD
CHAUCER RD
MILTON ST
BYRON ST
HARRIS ST
PH
POULTON RD
A587
Preston St
Church St
DOCK ST
A585
STATION RD
1 BURTON LODGE
2 MILL LA
3 PENNINE VIEW
4 CHAPMAN CT
5 CORN MILL LA
6 KINGS CT
7 BRIDGE RD
8 BAYSIDE
Fisherman's Wlk (Ash St)
ANCHORAGE RD
1 SEAVIEW WAY
2 QUAYSIDE
3 ANCHORAGE MEWS
4 HARBOUR WAY
5 MARINA MEWS
Blackpool & Fleetwood Tramway
Stanley Rd
Freeport Fleetwood Outlet Sh Village
FY7
AMOUNDERNESS WAY
Docks
DOCK AVE
HERRING ARM RD
Works
Bird Sanctuary
Waste Water Treatment Works
JAMESON RD
Refuse Tip
River Wyre
B5270
PH
BOURNE MAY RD
ESPLANADE
WAYSIDE
ASHTON AVE
WORSLEY CL
WESTBOURNE RD
QUAIL HOLME RD
PARKSWAY
FAIRWAY GDNS
GH
WYRESDALE RD
BLEASDALE RD
LINKS RD
LILAC GR
HOLMEFIELD RD
SALISBURY AVE
BARTON AVE
WYRE VIEW
LUNE VIEW
CLARENCE AVE
L Ctr
Liby
PO
LANCASTER RD
B5270
1 PLANTATION AVE
2 ELTERWATER
3 BARTON SQ
4 SALISBURY CT
5 OLIVER CT
6 ESPLANADE MEWS
THE HEATHERS 1
LAVENDER WAY 2
WILKINSON WAY 3
Knott End-on-Sea
CONISTON AVE
GRANGE CL
RYDAL GR
GRASMERE RD
KINGSTON CL
ESKDALE GR
LANCASTER CL
AMBLESIDE AVE
BUTTERMERE DR
KESWICK GR
DERWENT CL
THE GLEN
HACKENSALL RD
MEADOW LA
FY6
WHINNY LA
Hackensall Hall
Curwens Hill
Heys Farm
Hackensall Brows
Cote Walls Farm
CLODS CARR LA
Arm Hill
MONK'S LA
AGGLEBYS RD


A3
1 NAVIGATION WAY
2 STANLEY RD
3 KEATING CT
A4
1 ST MARGARET'S CT
2 DELTA LA
3 LANCASTER HO
4 POULTON GR
5 LAWRENCE ROW
6 WARREN AVENUE N

176

200

199

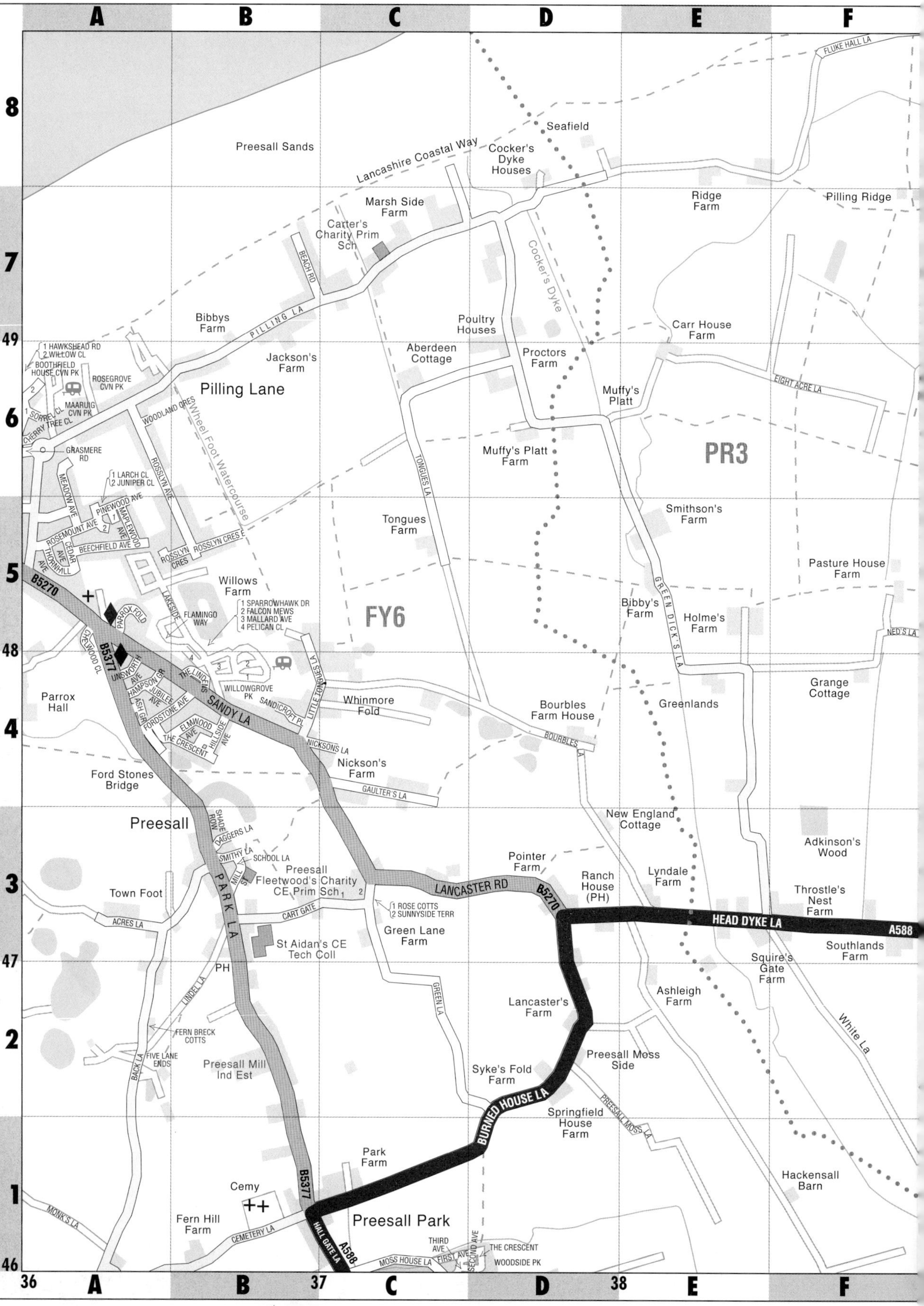
A
B
C
D
E
F
8
7
49
6
5
48
4
3
47
2
1
46
36
37
38
Preesall Sands
Lancashire Coastal Way
Seafield
Cocker's
Dyke
Houses
Marsh Side
Farm
Carter's
Charity Prim
Sch
BEACH RD
FLUKE HALL LA
Ridge
Farm
Pilling Ridge
Cocker's Dyke
Bibbys
Farm
PILLING LA
Poultry
Houses
Carr House
Farm
Aberdeen
Cottage
Proctors
Farm
Jackson's
Farm
1 HAWKSHEAD RD
2 WILLOW CL
BOOTHFIELD
HOUSE CVN PK
ROSEGROVE
CVN PK
MAARUIG
CVN PK
Pilling Lane
SORREL CL
CHERRY TREE CL
WOODLAND GRES
Wheel Foot Watercourse
Muffy's
Platt
EIGHT ACRE LA
GRASMERE
RD
Muffy's Platt
Farm
PR3
1 LARCH CL
2 JUNIPER CL
MEADOW AVE
PINEWOOD AVE
ROSSLYN AVE
TONGUES LA
MAPLEWOOD AVE
ROSEMOUNT AVE
CEDAR AVE
BEECHFIELD AVE
THORNHILL AVE
ROSSLYN CRES
Tongues
Farm
Smithson's
Farm
Pasture House
Farm
Willows
Farm
1 SPARROWHAWK DR
2 FALCON MEWS
3 MALLARD AVE
4 PELICAN CL
FLAMINGO
WAY
LAKESIDE
PARROX FOLD
FY6
GREEN DICK'S LA
Bibby's
Farm
Holme's
Farm
NED'S LA
B5270
B5377
CHELWOOD CL
UNSWORTH AVE
HAMPSON GR
JUBILEE AVE
ASH GR
FORDSTONE AVE
THE LINDENS
WILLOWGROVE
PK
SANDICROFT PL
LITTLE TONGUES LA
Whinmore
Fold
SANDY LA
Parrox
Hall
ELMWOOD AVE
HILLSIDE AVE
THE CRESCENT
Bourbles
Farm House
BOURBLES LA
Greenlands
Grange
Cottage
NICKSONS LA
Nickson's
Farm
GAULTER'S LA
Ford Stones
Bridge
Preesall
SHADE ROW
DAGGERS LA
SMITHY LA
SCHOOL LA
MILL ST
Preesall
Fleetwood's Charity
CE Prim Sch
New England
Cottage
Adkinson's
Wood
Pointer
Farm
Ranch
House
(PH)
Lyndale
Farm
Throstle's
Nest
Farm
Town Foot
PARK LA
LANCASTER RD
1 ROSE COTTS
2 SUNNYSIDE TERR
HEAD DYKE LA
A588
ACRES LA
CART GATE
St Aidan's CE
Tech Coll
Green Lane
Farm
Southlands
Farm
Squire's
Gate
Farm
PH
LINDEL LA
GREEN LA
Lancaster's
Farm
Ashleigh
Farm
White La
FERN BRECK
COTTS
FIVE LANE
ENDS
BACK LA
Preesall Mill
Ind Est
Syke's Fold
Farm
Preesall Moss
Side
BURNED HOUSE LA
Springfield
House
Farm
PREESALL MOSS LA
Park
Farm
Hackensall
Barn
Cemy
MONK'S LA
Fern Hill
Farm
CEMETERY LA
Preesall Park
HALL GATE LA
THIRD AVE
FIRST AVE
SECOND AVE
MOSS HOUSE LA
THE CRESCENT
WOODSIDE PK

199

177

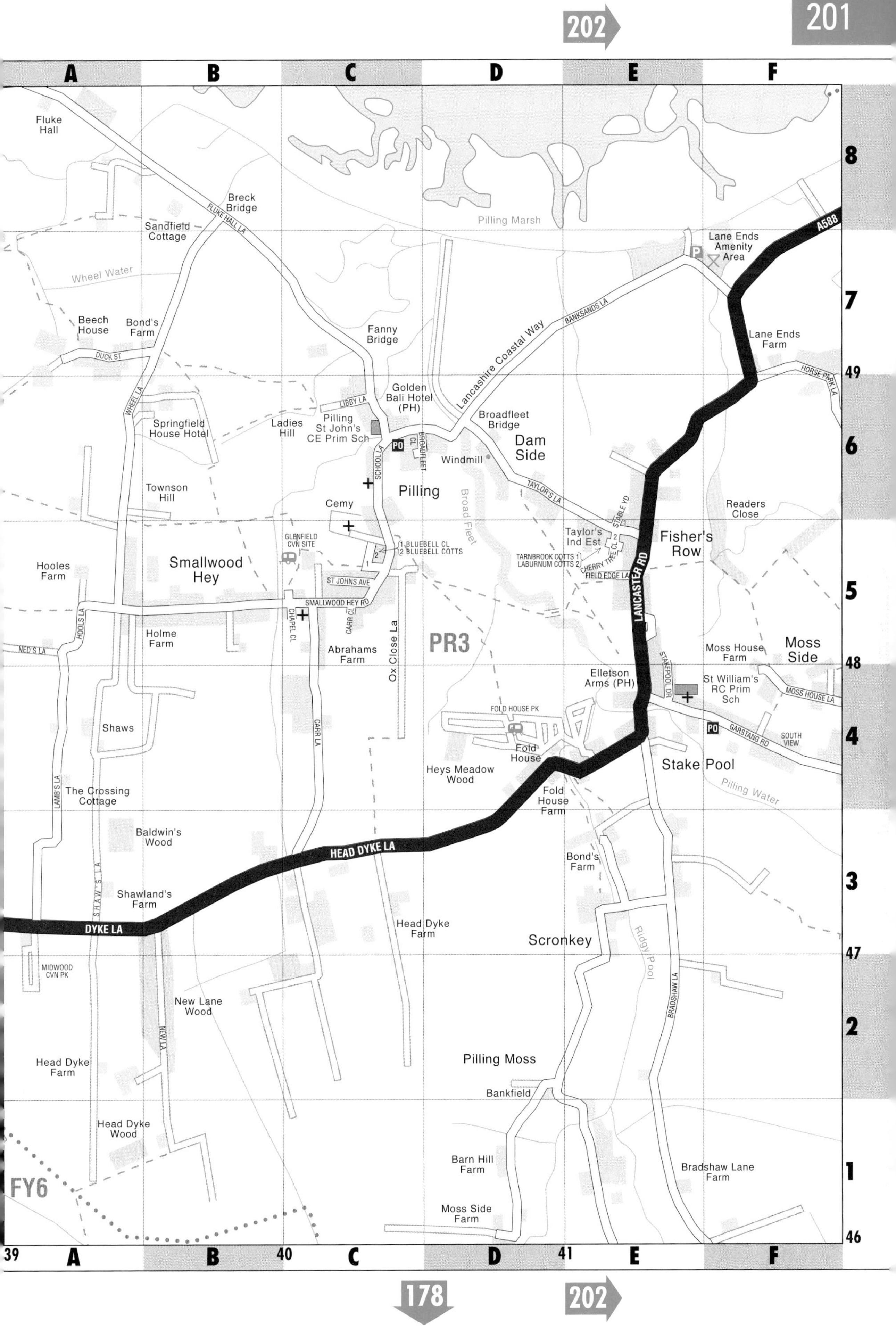
202
A
B
C
D
E
F
8
7
49
6
5
48
4
3
47
2
1
46
39
40
41
178
202
Fluke Hall
Breck Bridge
FLUKE HALL LA
Sandfield Cottage
Wheel Water
Pilling Marsh
Lane Ends Amenity Area
A588
BANKSANDS LA
Lancashire Coastal Way
Beech House
Bond's Farm
DUCK ST
Fanny Bridge
Lane Ends Farm
HORSE PARK LA
WHEEL LA
Golden Bali Hotel (PH)
LIBBY LA
Springfield House Hotel
Ladies Hill
Pilling St John's CE Prim Sch
PO
CL
BROADFLEET
Broadfleet Bridge
Dam Side
Windmill
SCHOOL LA
Townson Hill
Pilling
Broad Fleet
TAYLOR'S LA
Readers Close
Cemy
STABLE YD
Taylor's Ind Est
Fisher's Row
GLENFIELD CVN SITE
1 BLUEBELL CL
2 BLUEBELL COTTS
TARNBROOK COTTS 1
LABURNUM COTTS 2
CHERRY TREE CL
FIELD EDGE LA
Hooles Farm
Smallwood Hey
ST JOHNS AVE
SMALLWOOD HEY RD
LANCASTER RD
HOOLS LA
Holme Farm
CHAPEL CL
CARR CL
Abrahams Farm
Ox Close La
PR3
Moss House Farm
Moss Side
NED'S LA
STAKEPOOL DR
Elletson Arms (PH)
St William's RC Prim Sch
MOSS HOUSE LA
FOLD HOUSE PK
PO
GARSTANG RD
SOUTH VIEW
Shaws
CARR LA
Fold House
Stake Pool
Heys Meadow Wood
Pilling Water
LAMB'S LA
The Crossing Cottage
Fold House Farm
Baldwin's Wood
HEAD DYKE LA
Bond's Farm
SHAW'S LA
Shawland's Farm
DYKE LA
Head Dyke Farm
Scronkey
Ridgy Pool
MIDWOOD CVN PK
BRADSHAW LA
New Lane Wood
NEW LA
Head Dyke Farm
Pilling Moss
Bankfield
Head Dyke Wood
Barn Hill Farm
Bradshaw Lane Farm
FY6
Moss Side Farm

201
205

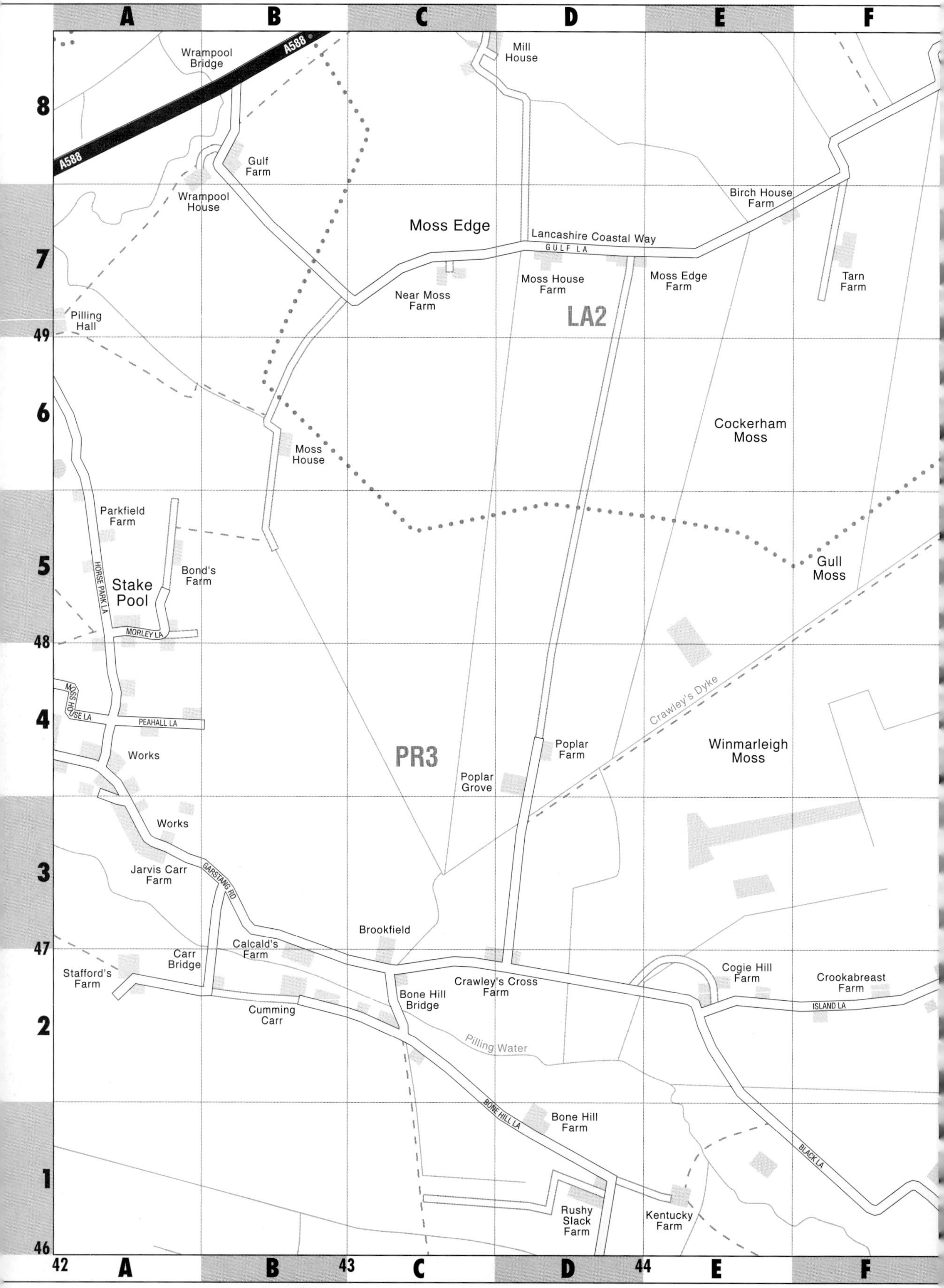


201
179

206
204

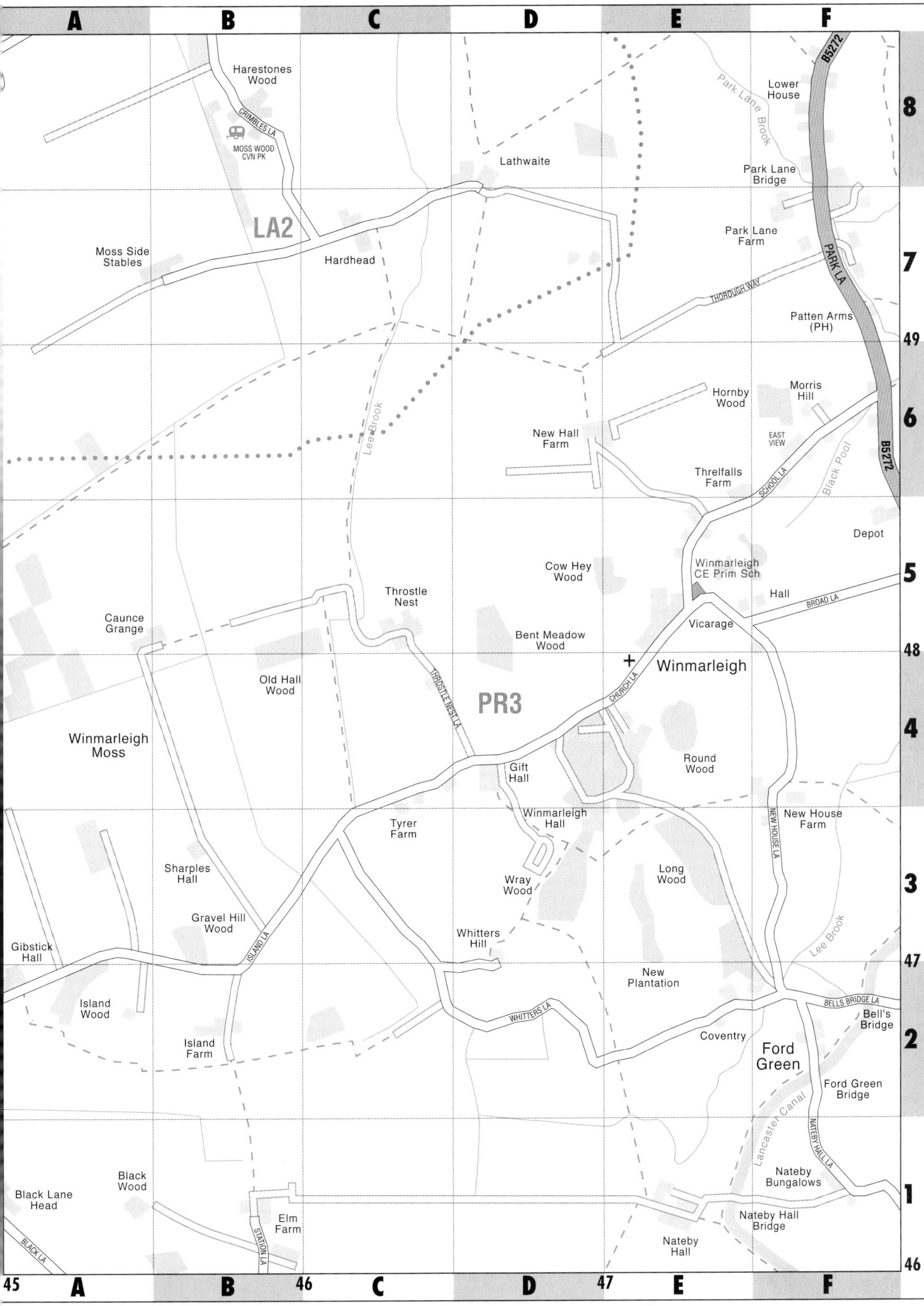
A
B
C
D
E
F
Harestones Wood
CRIMBLES LA
MOSS WOOD CVN PK
B5272
Lower House
Park Lane Brook
8
Lathwaite
Park Lane Bridge
LA2
Park Lane Farm
Moss Side Stables
Hardhead
7
PARK LA
THOROUGH WAY
Patten Arms (PH)
49
Hornby Wood
Morris Hill
Lee Brook
6
New Hall Farm
EAST VIEW
B5272
Threlfalls Farm
SCHOOL LA
Black Pool
Depot
Cow Hey Wood
Winmarleigh CE Prim Sch
5
Throstle Nest
Hall
BROAD LA
Caunce Grange
Vicarage
Bent Meadow Wood
48
Winmarleigh
Old Hall Wood
THROSTLE NEST LA
CHURCH LA
PR3
4
Winmarleigh Moss
Round Wood
Gift Hall
Winmarleigh Hall
New House Farm
Tyrer Farm
NEW HOUSE LA
Sharples Hall
Long Wood
Wray Wood
3
Gravel Hill Wood
Whitters Hill
Lee Brook
Gibstick Hall
ISLAND LA
47
New Plantation
BELLS BRIDGE LA
Island Wood
WHITTERS LA
Bell's Bridge
Coventry
Island Farm
Ford Green
2
Ford Green Bridge
Lancaster Canal
NATEBY HALL LA
Black Wood
Nateby Bungalows
Black Lane Head
1
Elm Farm
Nateby Hall Bridge
STATION LA
BLACK LA
Nateby Hall
46
45
46
47

180
204

203 207 226

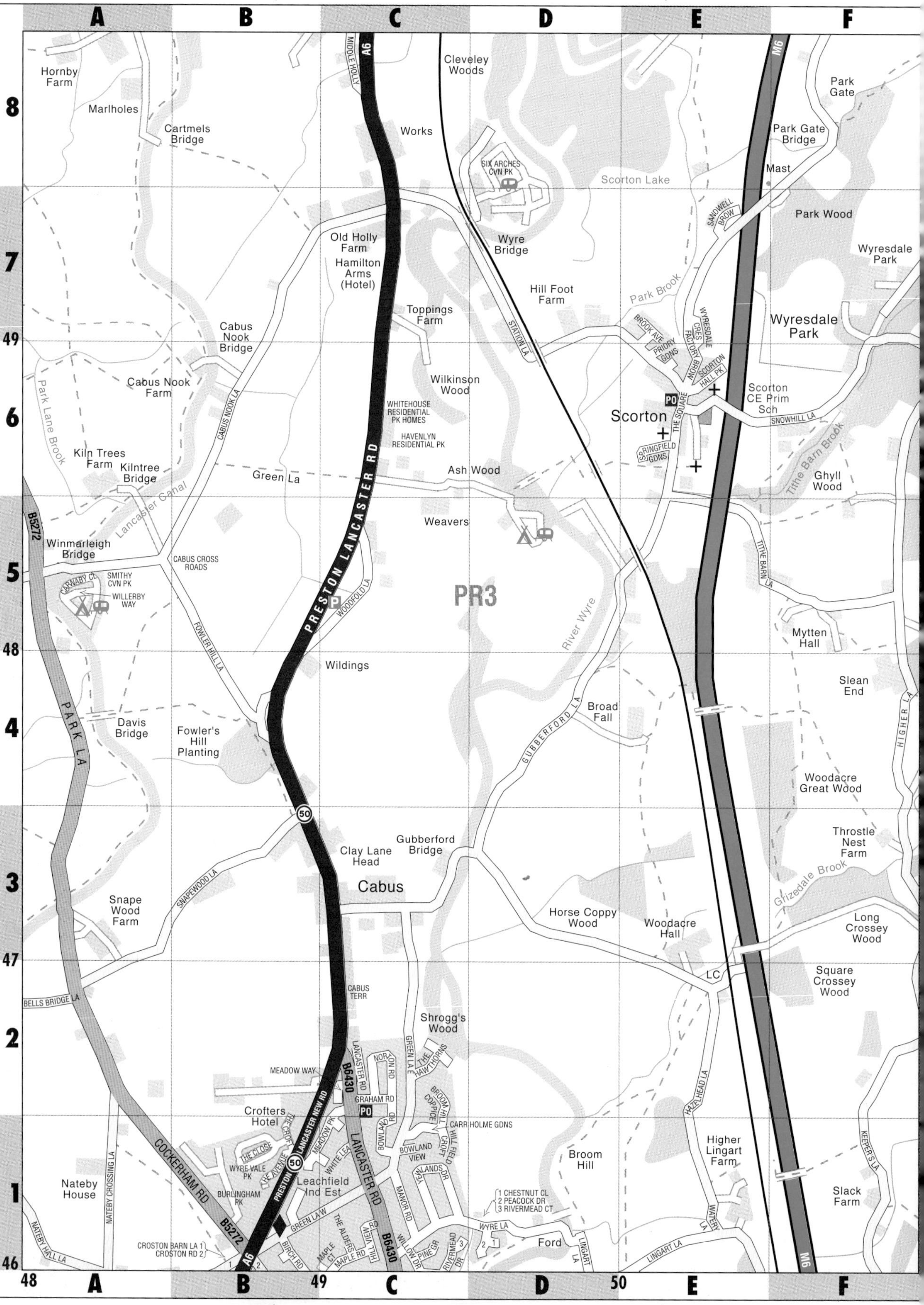


203 181 226

209
206

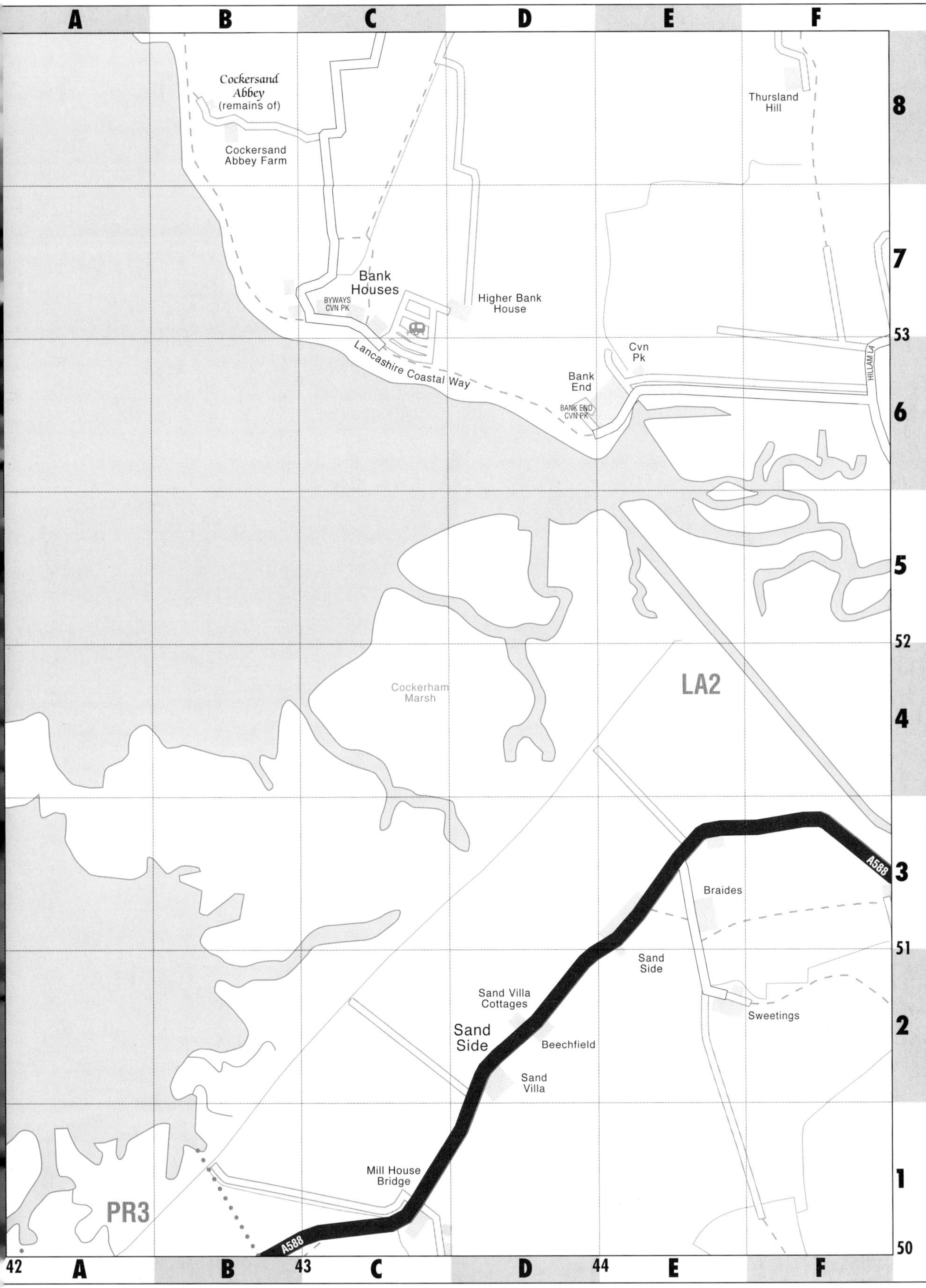


202
206

205
210

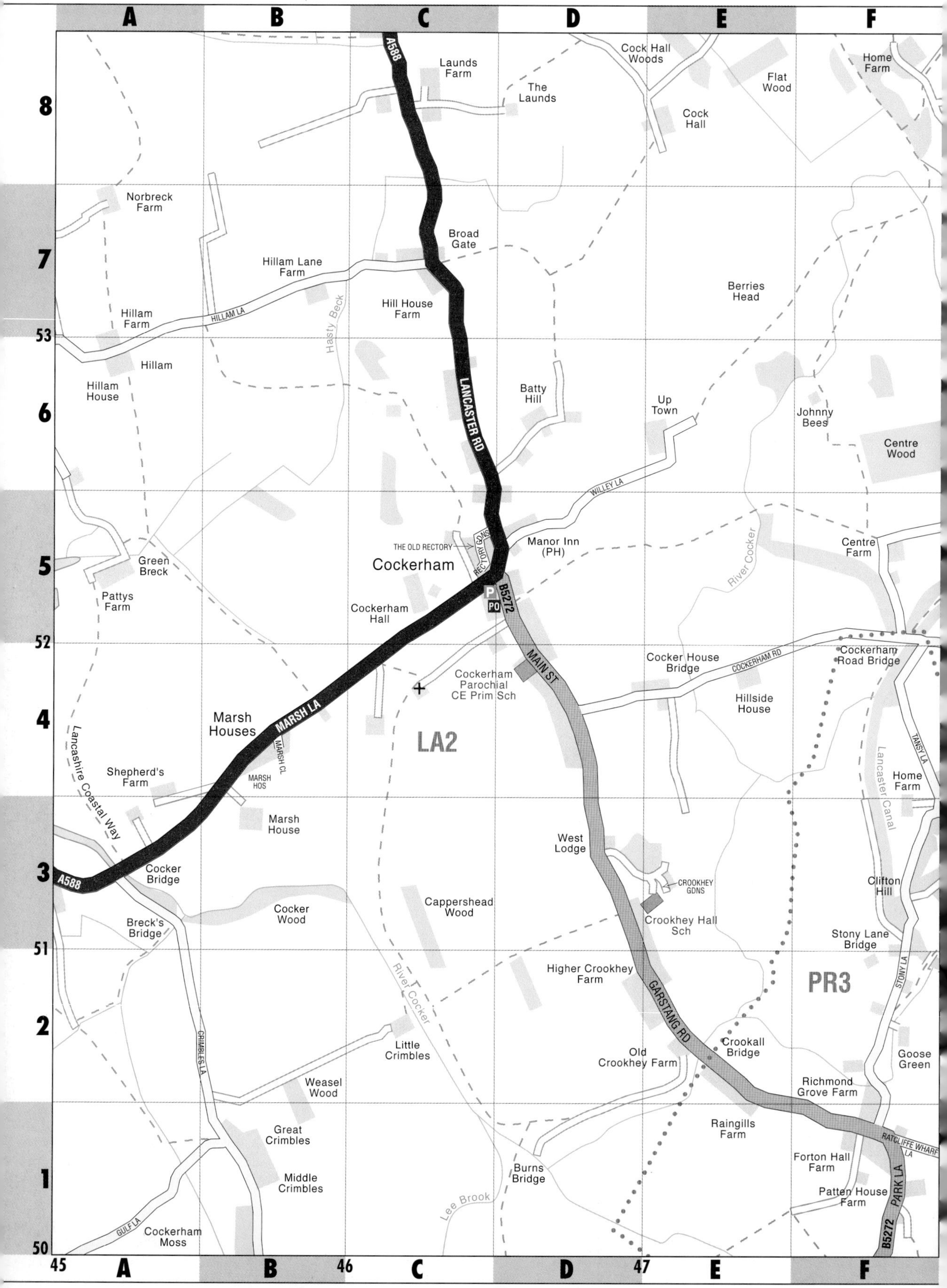


205
203

211
226
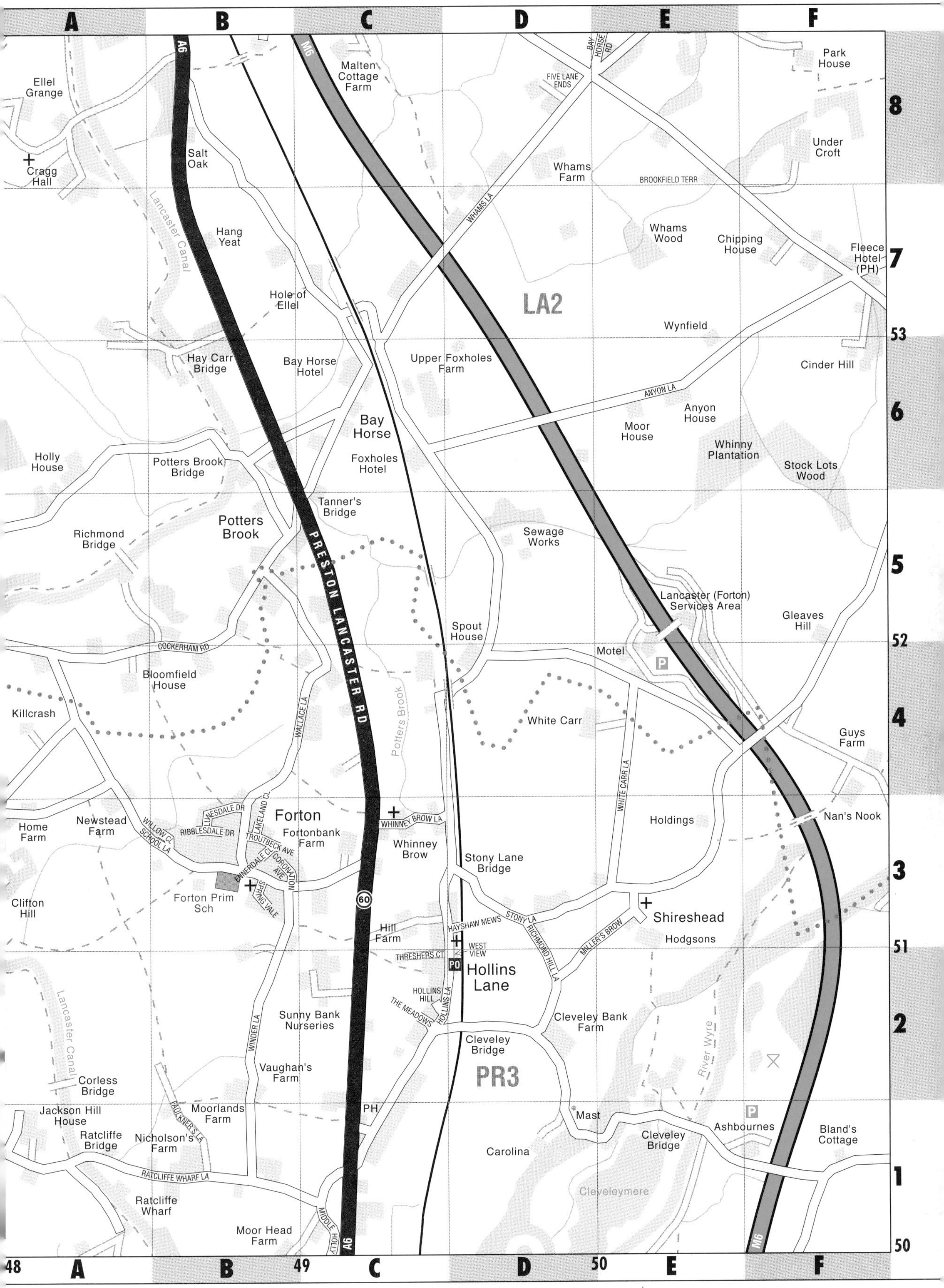

204
226

212

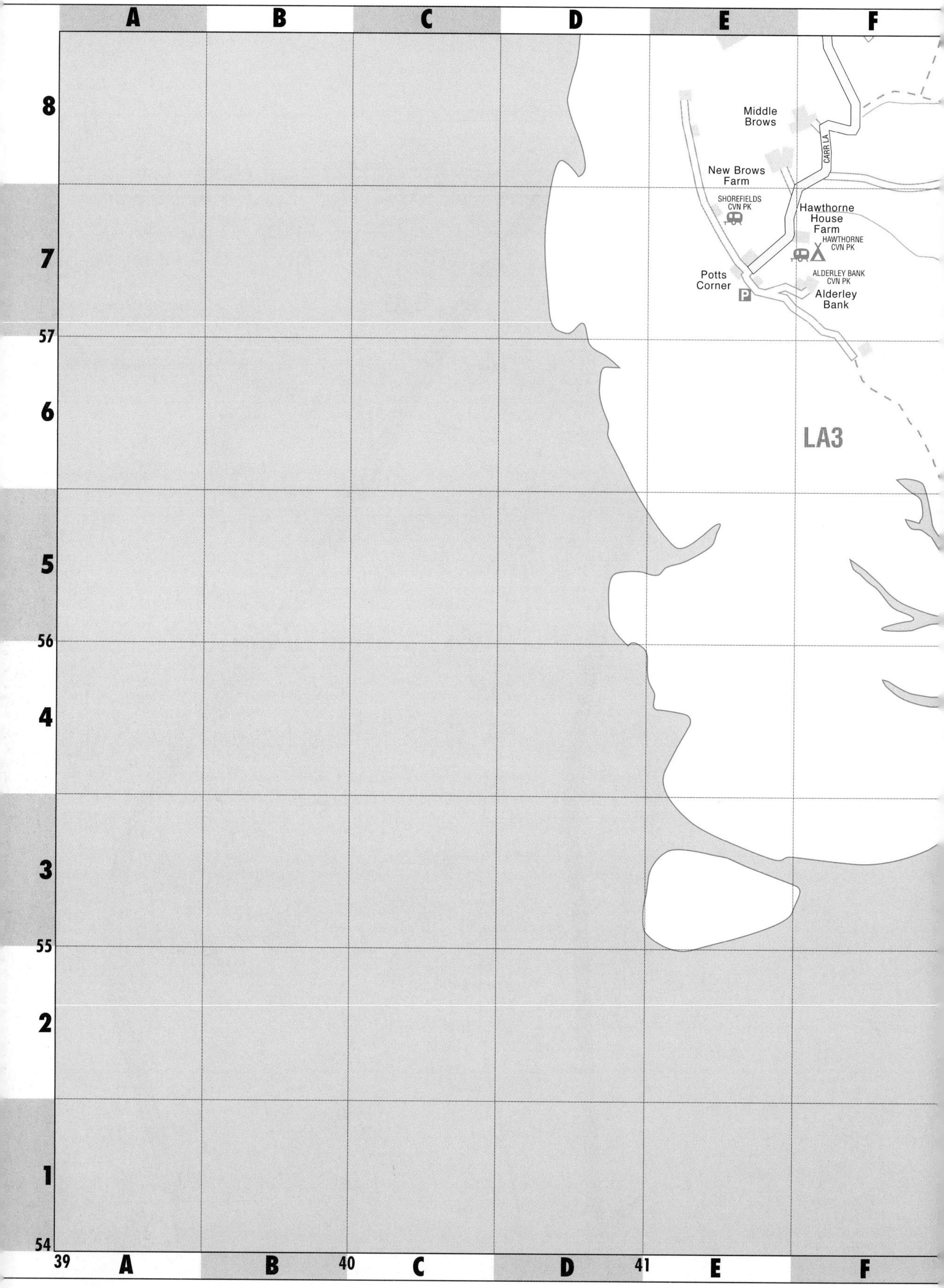
A
B
C
D
E
F
8
7
57
6
5
56
4
3
55
2
1
54
39
40
41
Middle Brows
CARR LA
New Brows Farm
SHOREFIELDS CVN PK
Hawthorne House Farm
HAWTHORNE CVN PK
Potts Corner
ALDERLEY BANK CVN PK
Alderley Bank
P
LA3

213
210

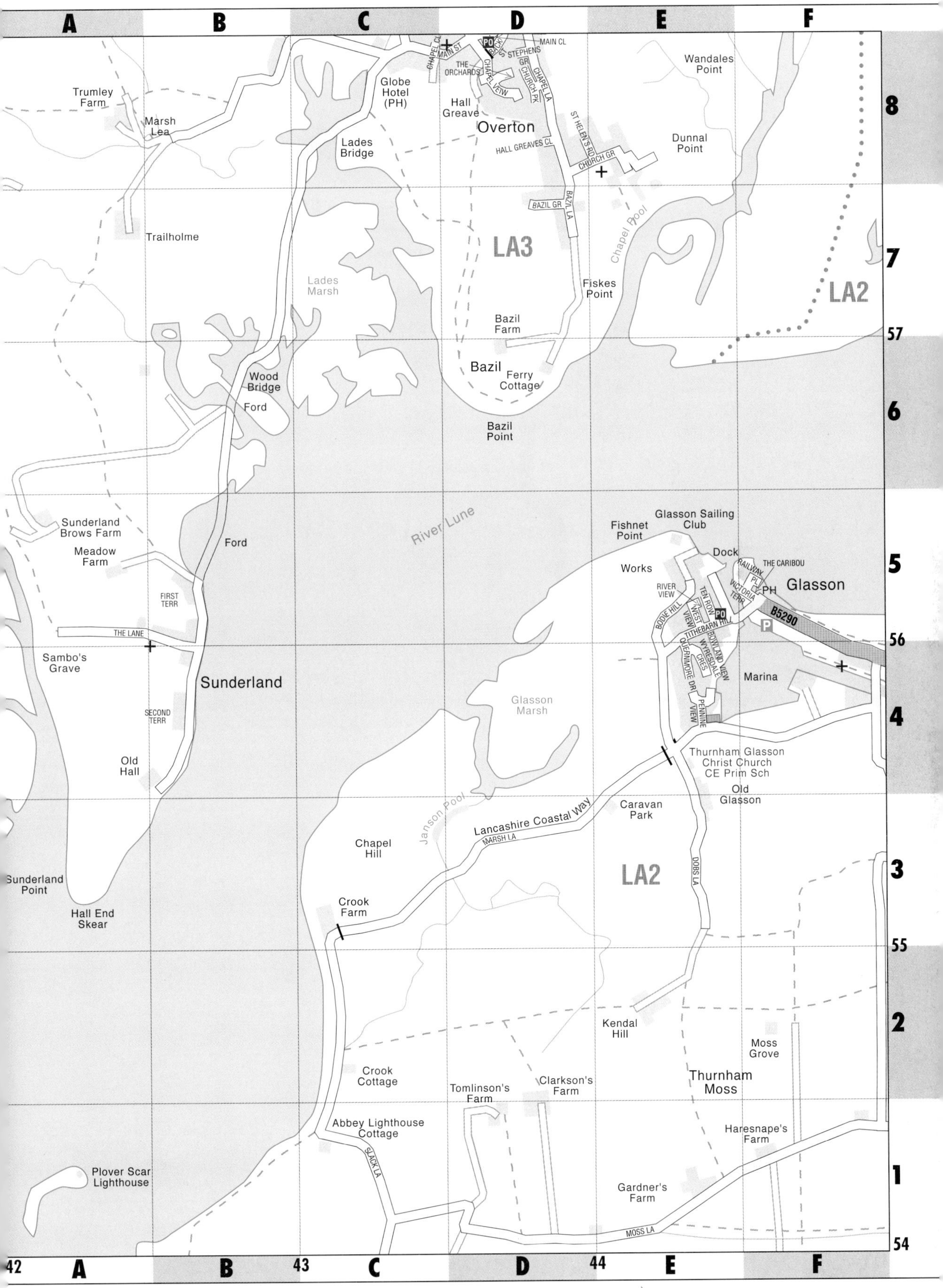


205
210

209
214

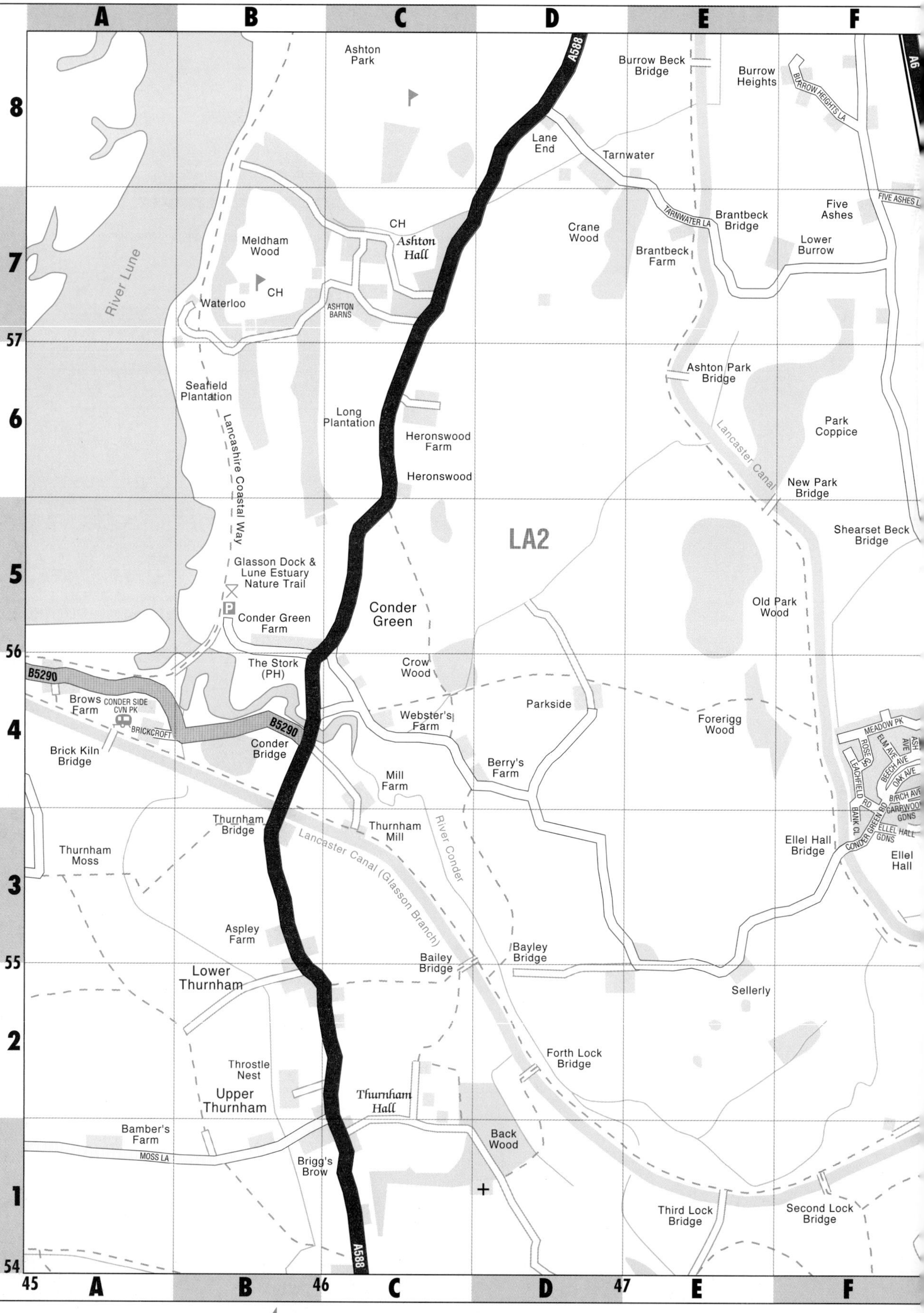
A
B
C
D
E
F
8
7
57
6
5
56
4
3
55
2
1
54
45
46
47
A588
A6
Ashton Park
Burrow Beck Bridge
Burrow Heights
BURROW HEIGHTS LA
Lane End
Tarnwater
TARNWATER LA
FIVE ASHES LA
Five Ashes
Brantbeck Bridge
Brantbeck Farm
Lower Burrow
Crane Wood
CH
Ashton Hall
Meldham Wood
CH
River Lune
Waterloo
ASHTON BARNS
Ashton Park Bridge
Seafield Plantation
Lancashire Coastal Way
Long Plantation
Heronswood Farm
Heronswood
Park Coppice
Lancaster Canal
New Park Bridge
Shearset Beck Bridge
LA2
Glasson Dock & Lune Estuary Nature Trail
Conder Green Farm
Conder Green
Old Park Wood
The Stork (PH)
Crow Wood
B5290
Brows Farm
CONDER SIDE CVN PK
BRICKCROFT
B5290
Conder Bridge
Webster's Farm
Parkside
Forerigg Wood
MEADOW PK
Brick Kiln Bridge
Berry's Farm
Mill Farm
Thurnham Bridge
Thurnham Mill
River Conder
Lancaster Canal (Glasson Branch)
Thurnham Moss
Ellel Hall Bridge
Ellel Hall
CONDER GREEN RD
Aspley Farm
Bayley Bridge
Bailey Bridge
Lower Thurnham
Sellerly
Forth Lock Bridge
Throstle Nest
Upper Thurnham
Thurnham Hall
Bamber's Farm
MOSS LA
Back Wood
Brigg's Brow
Third Lock Bridge
Second Lock Bridge

215
232

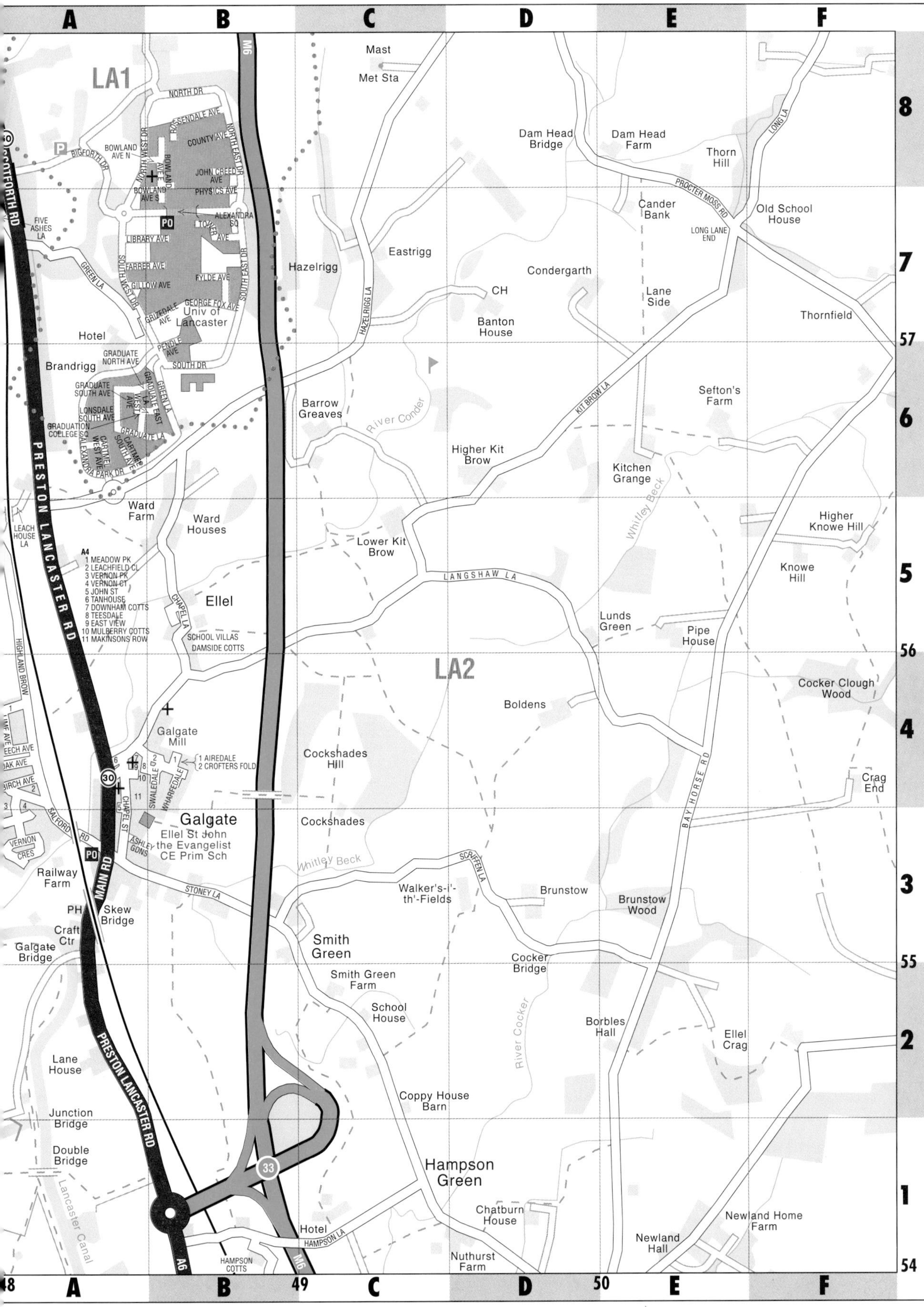


207
232

216

E7
1 WEMYSS CL
2 DUNBAR DR
3 TOWER COTTS
4 HEYSHAM RD
5 MIDDLETON WAY

F8
1 STRAWBERRY MEWS
2 BACK KNOWLYS RD
3 KNOWLYS DR
4 KNOWLYS CRES
5 TARNBROOK RD

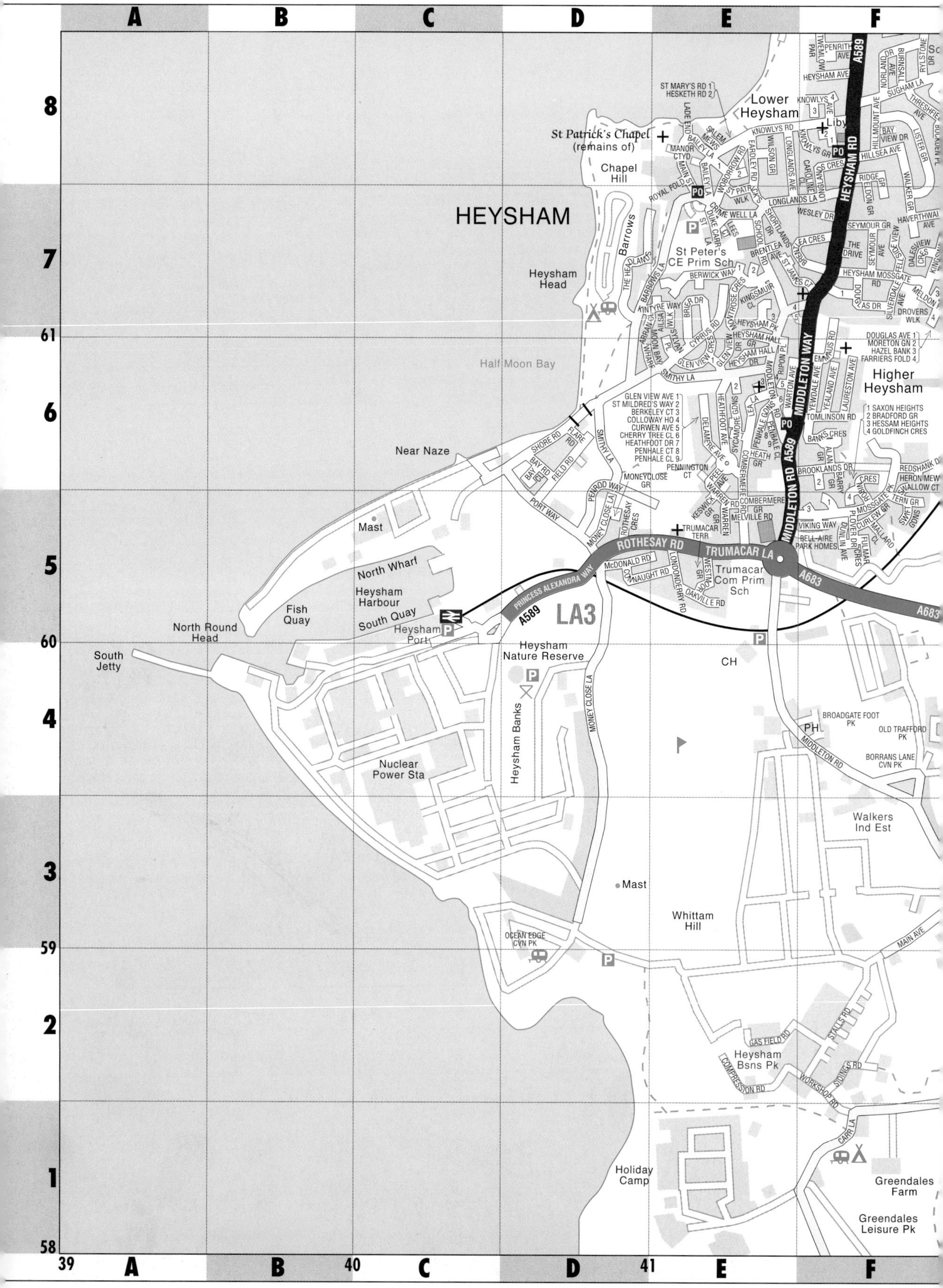

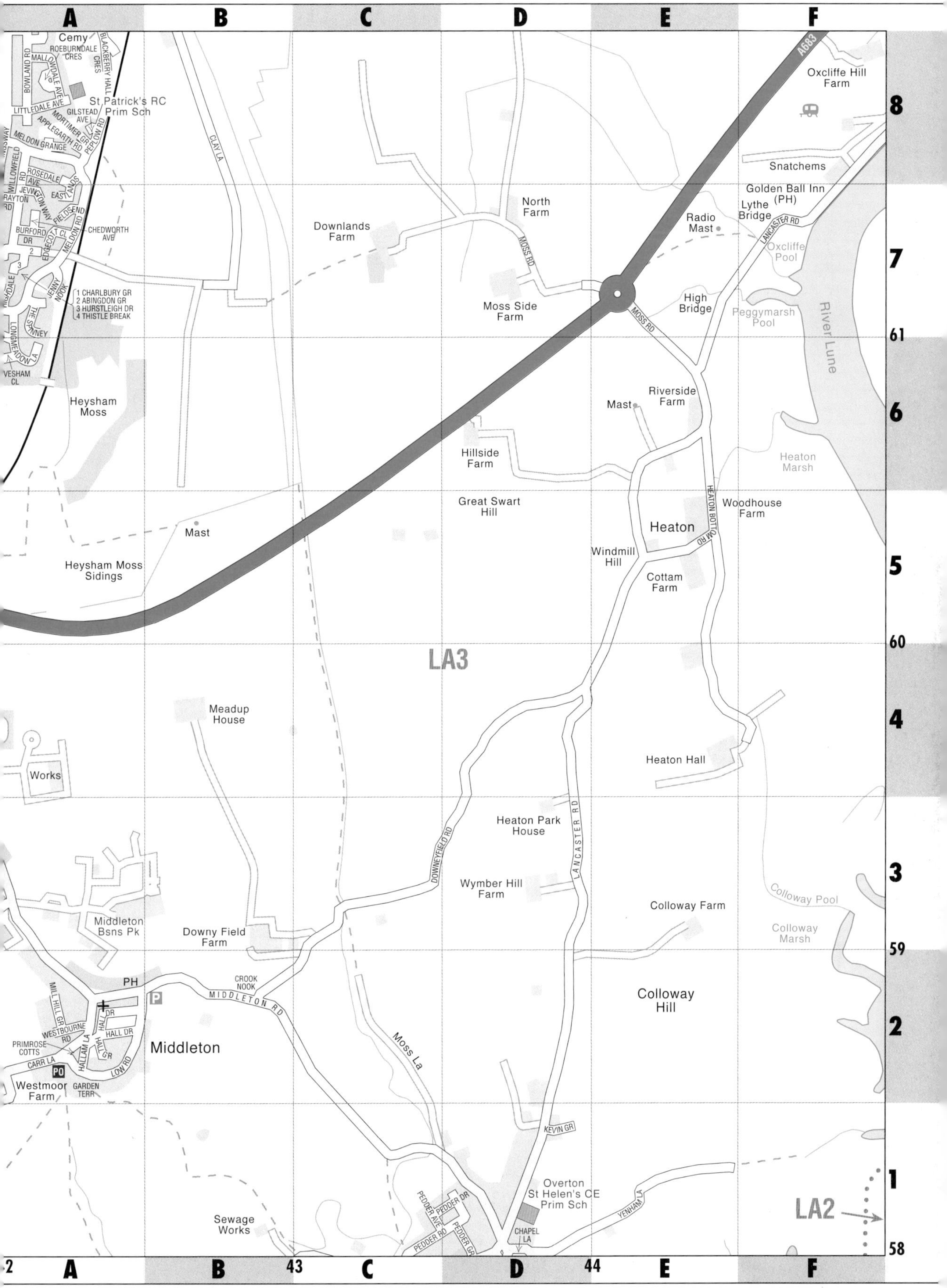
A B C D E F
8 7 61 6 5 60 4 3 59 2 1 58
43 44
Cemy
ROEBURNDALE CRES
BLACKBERRY HALL
BOWLAND RD
MALLOWDALE AVE
St Patrick's RC Prim Sch
LITTLEDALE AVE
GILSTEAD AVE
MORTIMER GR
APPLEGARTH RD
PEPLOW RD
MELDON GRANGE
WILLOWFIELD
ROSEDALE AVE
JEVINGTON WAY
EASTLANDS
FIELDS END
BURFORD DR
EDGECOTT CL
MELDON RD
CHEDWORTH AVE
JENNY NOOK
1 CHARLBURY GR
2 ABINGDON GR
3 HURSTLEIGH DR
4 THISTLE BREAK
THE SPINNEY
LONGMEADOW LA
VESHAM CL
CLAY LA
Heysham Moss
Mast
Heysham Moss Sidings
Downlands Farm
North Farm
MOSS RD
Moss Side Farm
A683
Oxcliffe Hill Farm
Snatchems
Golden Ball Inn (PH)
Lythe Bridge
Radio Mast
LANCASTER RD
Oxcliffe Pool
High Bridge
Peggymarsh Pool
River Lune
Riverside Farm
Mast
Hillside Farm
Heaton Marsh
Great Swart Hill
Woodhouse Farm
HEATON BOTTOM RD
Heaton
Windmill Hill
Cottam Farm
LA3
Meadup House
Works
Heaton Hall
Heaton Park House
DOWNEYFIELD RD
LANCASTER RD
Wymber Hill Farm
Colloway Farm
Colloway Pool
Colloway Marsh
Middleton Bsns Pk
Downy Field Farm
CROOK NOOK
MIDDLETON RD
PH
P
Colloway Hill
MILL HILL GR
WESTBOURNE RD
HALL DR
HALL GR
HALLAM LA
PRIMROSE COTTS
Middleton
CARR LA
LOW RD
PO
Westmoor Farm
GARDEN TERR
Moss La
KEVIN GR
Overton St Helen's CE Prim Sch
YENHAM LA
PEDDER DR
PEDDER AVE
PEDDER RD
PEDDER GR
CHAPEL LA
Sewage Works
LA2

217 213 218

F8
1 WOOD ST
2 BUTTERFIELD ST
3 CHAPEL ST
4 ALEXANDRA CT
5 NILE ST
6 FLEET SQ

F8
7 CALKELD LA
8 ROSEMARY LA
9 BACK SUN ST
10 MARKET SQ
11 CHEAPSIDE
12 ASHTON WLK
13 St Nicholas Arcs
14 LANCASTER GATE
15 RENDSBURG WAY
16 PERPIGNAN WAY
17 STONEWELL
18 ST ANNE'S PL
19 BREWERY LA
20 GREAT JOHN ST
21 ABBOTS HO
22 BRIDGET ST
23 FRIARS PAS
24 FRIAR ST
25 BRYER ST

F8
26 ST CATHERINES CT
27 SIR SIMON'S ARC
28 MARKETGATE
29 SLIP INN LA
30 JAMES ST
31 FFRANCES PAS
32 GAGE ST
33 MOOR ST
34 KINGS ARMS CL
35 ALMSHOUSES
36 WINDYHILL
37 KINGS ARC
38 COMMON GARDEN ST
39 RUSSELL ST
40 RUSSELL MEWS
41 SPRING GARDEN ST
43 ROBERT ST
44 THE ROUNDHOUSE

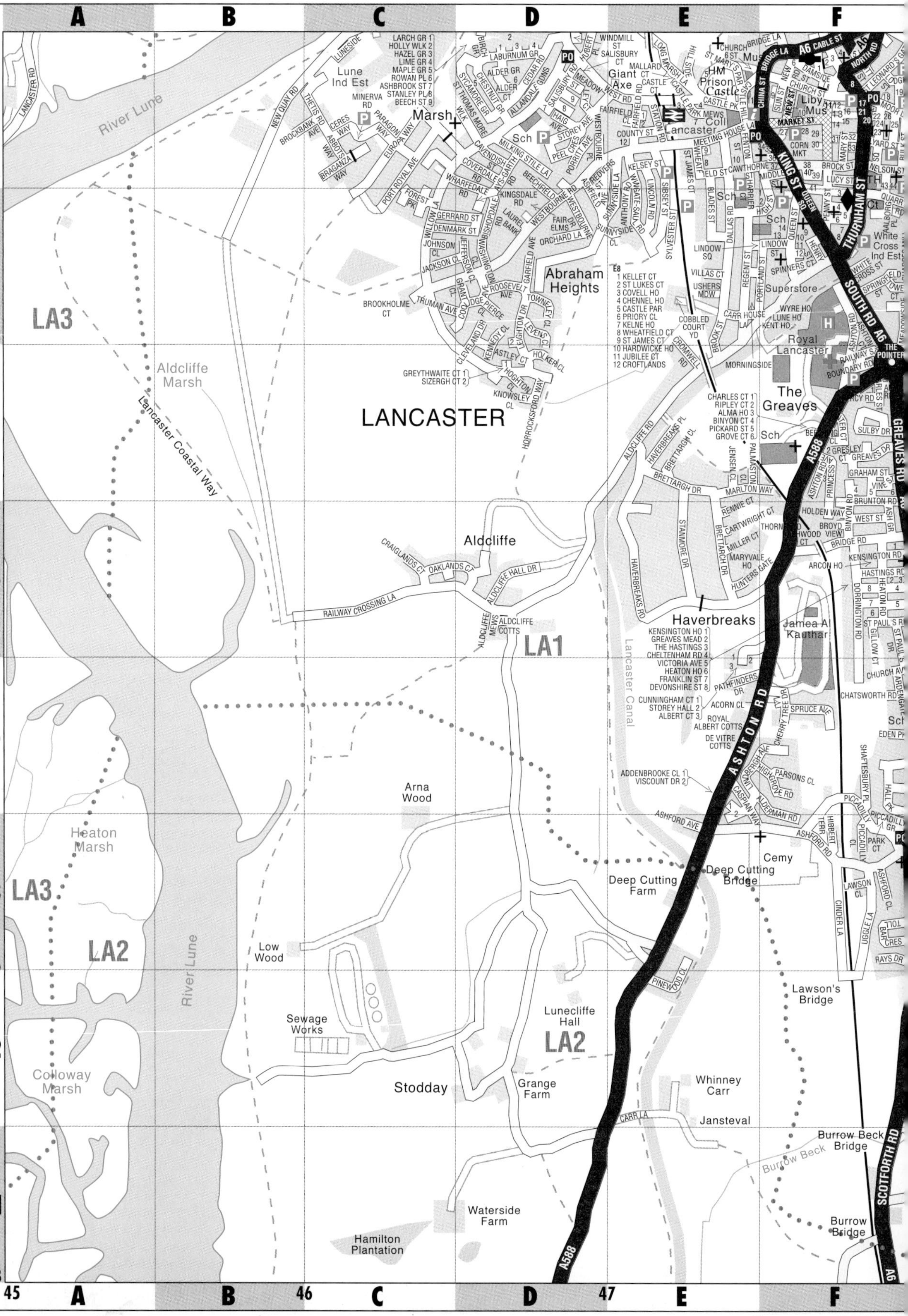

A
B
C
D
E
F
8
7
61
6
5
60
4
3
59
2
1
58
45
46
47
LA3
LA1
LA2
River Lune
Lune Ind Est
Marsh
LANCASTER
Abraham Heights
Aldcliffe Marsh
Lancaster Coastal Way
Aldcliffe
Haverbreaks
Lancaster Canal
Arna Wood
Heaton Marsh
Low Wood
Sewage Works
Stodday
Grange Farm
Lunecliffe Hall
Colloway Marsh
Hamilton Plantation
Waterside Farm
Deep Cutting Farm
Deep Cutting Bridge
Lawson's Bridge
Whinney Carr
Jansteval
Burrow Beck
Burrow Beck Bridge
Burrow Bridge
Cemy
The Greaves
Royal Lancaster
Superstore
HM Prison Castle
Giant Axe
Lancaster
Jamea Al Kauthar
White Cross Ind Est
THE POINTER
ASHTON RD
SCOTFORTH RD
GREAVES RD
SOUTH RD
THURNHAM ST
KING ST
A588
A6
RAILWAY CROSSING LA
CARR LA
ASHFORD AVE
ALDCLIFFE RD
ALDCLIFFE HALL DR
OAKLANDS CT
CRAIGLANDS CT
ALDCLIFFE MEWS
ALDCLIFFE COTTS
PINEWOOD CL
HORROCKSFORD WAY
NEW QUAY RD
LARCH GR 1
HOLLY WLK 2
HAZEL GR 3
LIME GR 4
MAPLE GR 5
ROWAN PL 6
ASHBROOK ST 7
STANLEY PL 8
BEECH ST 9
E8
1 KELLET CT
2 ST LUKES CT
3 COVELL HO
4 CHENNEL HO
5 CASTLE PAR
6 PRIORY CL
7 KELNE HO
8 WHEATFIELD CT
9 ST JAMES CT
10 HARDWICKE HO
11 JUBILEE CT
12 CROFTLANDS
GREYTHWAITE CT 1
SIZERGH CT 2
CHARLES CT 1
RIPLEY CT 2
ALMA HO 3
BINYON CT 4
PICKARD ST 5
GROVE CT 6
KENSINGTON HO 1
GREAVES MEAD 2
THE HASTINGS 3
CHELTENHAM RD 4
VICTORIA AVE 5
HEATON HO 6
FRANKLIN ST 7
DEVONSHIRE ST 8
CUNNINGHAM CT 1
STOREY HALL 2
ALBERT CT 3
ROYAL ALBERT COTTS
DE VITRE COTTS
ADDENBROOKE CL 1
VISCOUNT DR 2


213 210

F7
1 HIGH MOUNT HO
2 HIGH MOUNT CT
3 GEORGE ST
4 MARTON ST
5 PETER ST
6 VICTORIA PL
7 THURNHAM MEWS
8 ALEXANDRA HALL
9 ELIZABETH CT
10 DIANA CT
11 ROYAL CT
12 BACK QUEEN ST
13 LINDOW CL
14 ALMSHOUSES

A8
1 DE VITRE ST
2 SHAW ST
3 GARNET ST
4 SIDNEY TERR
5 SEYMOUR ST
6 PRIORY WLK

218

A8
7 BATH MILL SQ
8 WHITBARROW SQ
9 HAYLOT SQ
10 CROSSDALE SQ
11 MELBOURNE RD
12 GREENFIELD ST
13 NORWOOD CT
14 MOOR GATE
15 DAVIDSON ST
16 ST PETERS MEWS
17 MILL HO MEWS
18 GREENFIELD HO
19 MILL HO
20 GLEBE CT
21 CITY HEIGHTS CL

A7
1 SWAN YD
2 GREENFIELD CT
3 ARGYLE ST
4 ELGIN ST
5 DUNKELD ST
6 PRIMROSE CT
7 BRADSHAW ST
8 VINCENT ST

A6
1 BOWERHAM TERR
2 CUMBERLAND VIEW
3 HANMER PL

219

232

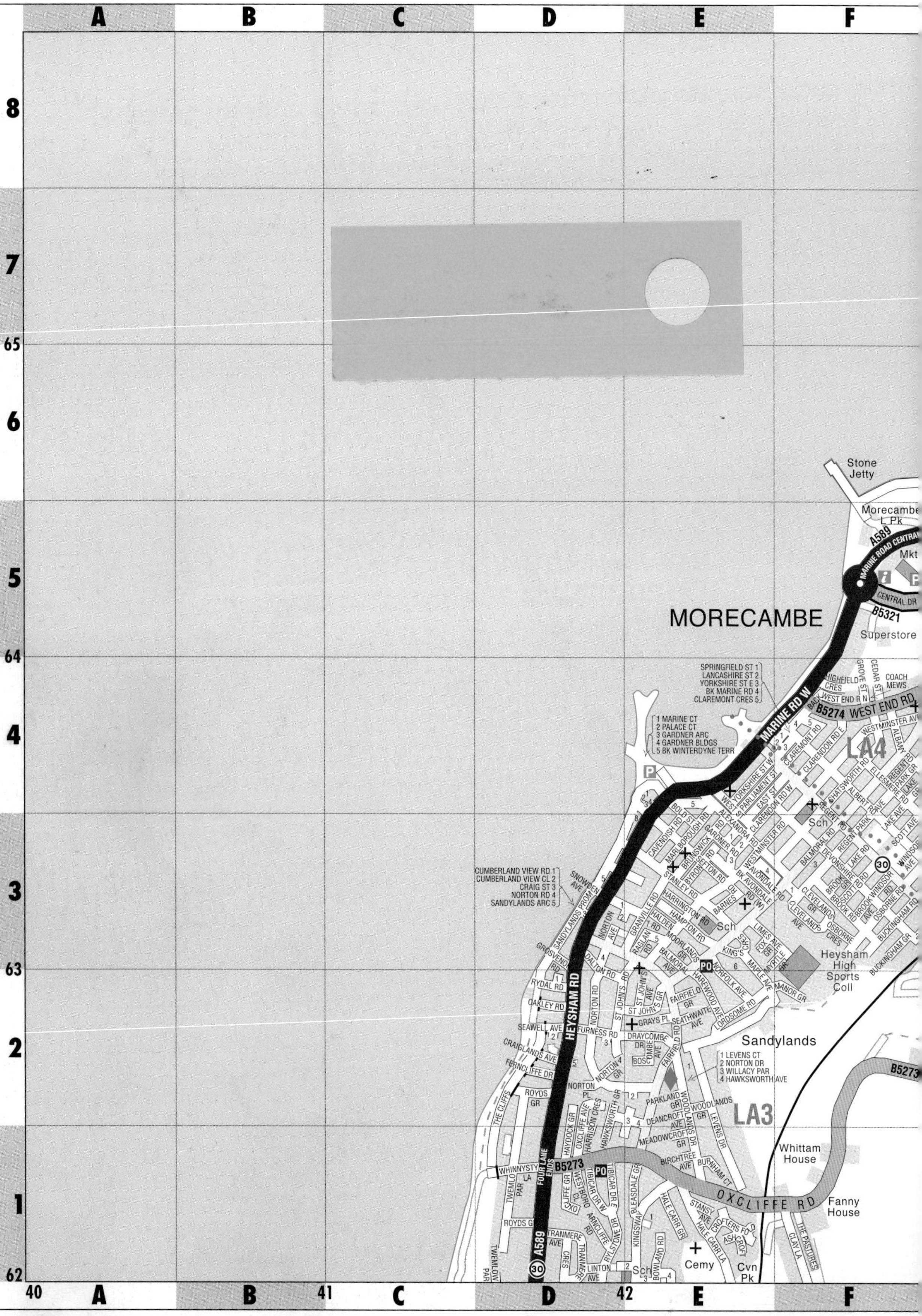
A
B
C
D
E
F
8
7
65
6
5
64
4
3
63
2
1
62
40
41
42
Stone Jetty
Morecambe L Pk
A589
MARINE ROAD CENTRAL
Mkt
CENTRAL DR
B5321
MORECAMBE
Superstore
SPRINGFIELD ST 1
LANCASHIRE ST 2
YORKSHIRE ST E 3
BK MARINE RD 4
CLAREMONT CRES 5
1 MARINE CT
2 PALACE CT
3 GARDNER ARC
4 GARDNER BLDGS
5 BK WINTERDYNE TERR
MARINE RD W
B5274 WEST END RD
COACH MEWS
LA4
Sch
CUMBERLAND VIEW RD 1
CUMBERLAND VIEW CL 2
CRAIG ST 3
NORTON RD 4
SANDYLANDS ARC 5
Heysham High Sports Coll
HEYSHAM RD
Sandylands
1 LEVENS CT
2 NORTON DR
3 WILLACY PAR
4 HAWKSWORTH AVE
LA3
B5273
Whittam House
OXCLIFFE RD
Fanny House
FOUR LANE ENDS
A589
Cemy
Cvn Pk
THE PASTURES
CLAY LA

D2
1 RYDAL GR
2 DREWTON AVE
3 CROOKLEIGH PL
4 DRAYCOMBE CT
5 CROSSDALE AVE

E1
1 KINGSWAY CT
2 KINGSDALE AVE
3 WYRESDALE AVE
4 GRIZEDALE PL

E3
1 CAMBRIDGE RD
2 GRAFTON RD
3 GRAFTON PL
4 BK AVONDALE RD (E)
5 GLOUCESTER DR
6 SUNACRE CT
7 HENLEY MEWS
8 MEARSBECK

F3
1 CLEAVLANDS WLK
2 BUCKINGHAM PL
3 OLDEST BARN MEWS

212
213

**A5**
1 WEST VIEW RD
2 SKIPTON ST
3 CHAPEL ST
4 NEW ST
5 UNION ST
6 GRAHAM ST
7 DERBY ST
8 NELSON ST
9 Arndale Ctr
10 LONGMIRE WAY
11 ALDINGHAM WLK
12 WINTER GARDENS ARC
13 ANDERTON ST

**B5**
1 BACK QUEEN ST
2 BACK LINES ST
3 WASHINGTON AVE
4 RABY ST
5 RIBBLESDALE CT
6 PRIMROSE ST
7 WHITMOOR CL

**B6**
1 OLD TOWN HALL MEWS
2 MORECAMBE ST W
3 OLDHAM ST
4 STANLEY ST
5 MORECAMBE ST E
6 GARNETT ST
7 BK GREEN ST
8 LUCY ST
9 OLD MARKET CT
10 ROSE ST
11 POULTON SQ
12 RABY SQ
13 NEW INN YD

**C5**
1 THORNTON GR
2 THORNTON CRES
3 CROSS ST
4 BACK ROSEBERRY AVE N

**E6**
1 HOME BREEZE HO
2 TUDOR GR
3 PALMER GR
4 PRINCESS CT
5 CLARENCE CT
6 LODGERS CT
7 WHITMOOR CL

218
220

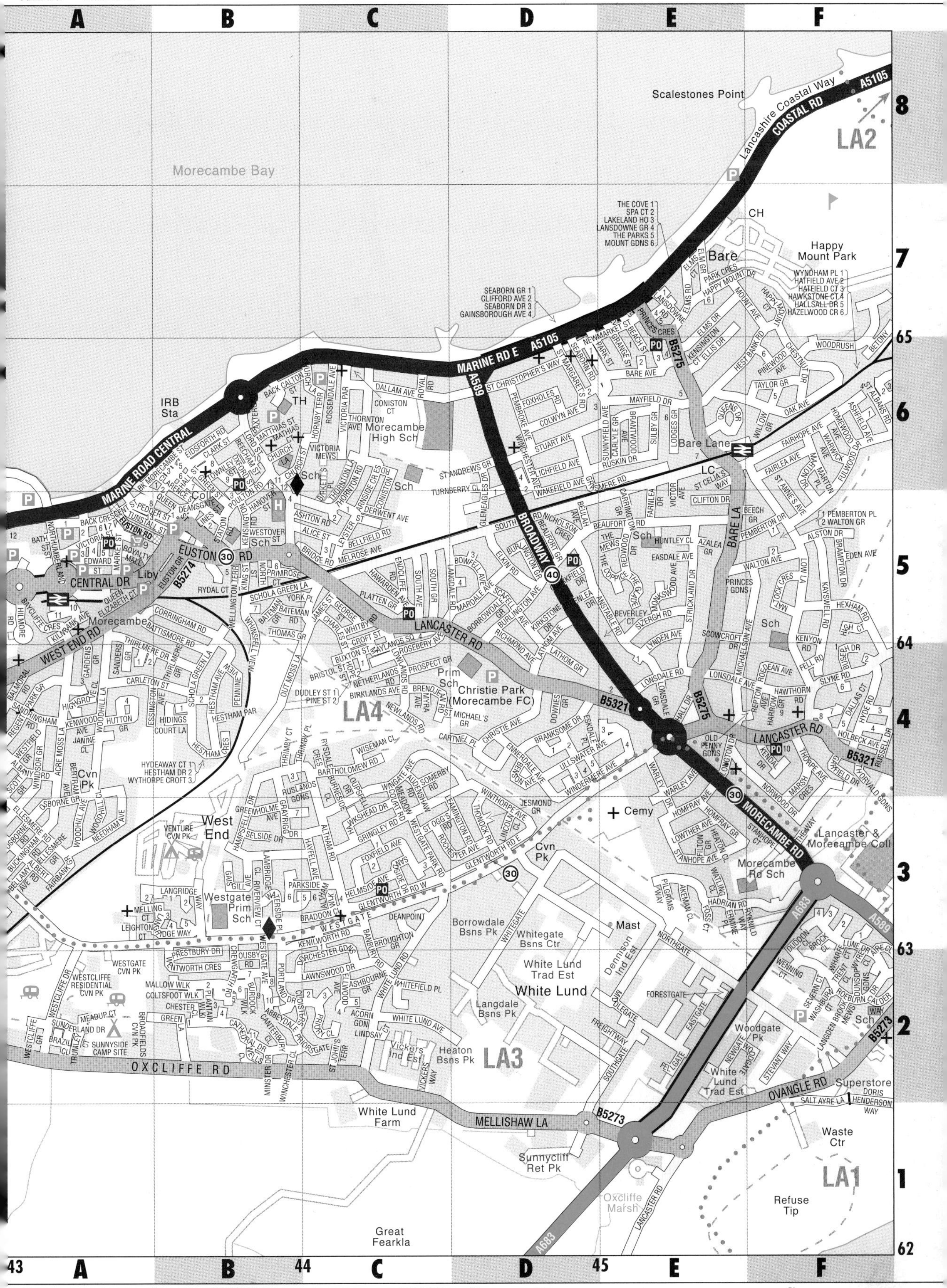


**A3**
1 NEEDHAM RISE
2 THURLAND CT

**A4**
1 LLOYD'S AVE
2 DENNIS GR
3 SANDRINGHAM CT
4 HUTTON CRES

**B2**
1 SALISBURY CL
2 CAMPION WAY
3 RAMSON CT
4 DURHAM CL
5 YARROW WLK
6 TEASEL WLK
7 OUSBY AVE
8 SEDGE CT
9 BRYONY CT
10 REEDMACE WLK
11 WESTMINSTER CL

**B3**
1 ARKHOLME CT
2 ALDINGHAM CT
3 BORWICK CT
4 HALTON CT
5 ALDCLIFFE CT
6 MEADOWSIDE RD
7 WITHERSLACK CL

213

**C2**
1 SAVOY AVE
2 VICARAGE CL
3 PARSONAGE CL
4 ELLWOOD CT
5 ELLWOOD GR

**C3**
1 HERON DR
2 HEVERSHAM CL
3 THURSGILL AVE
4 PIPER COTTS
5 PARKVIEW CL
6 PARKSIDE CT

**D4**
1 KENTMERE GR
2 BUTTERMERE AVE
3 BLEA TARN PL
4 WINDERMERE CT
5 LOWESWATER DR

**D5**
1 FAIRHAVEN WAY
2 BERWYN AVE
3 GABLES PL
4 MICHAEL PL

**E4**
1 STAINTON GR
2 BRAEMAR CT
3 HAWESWATER PL
4 WASTWATER DR

**F3**
1 HODDER AVE
2 HYNDBURN CL
3 BISHOPDALE CL
4 KENT WAY

218
214

**F4**
1 BUSEPH BARROW
2 BUSEPH CT
3 ESSEX RD
4 HARDLANDS AVE
5 DALLAS RD
6 NOVAK PL
7 OLD HALL CL
8 TORRISHOLME SQ
9 ERIC MORECAMBE HO
10 BACK GROVE TERR

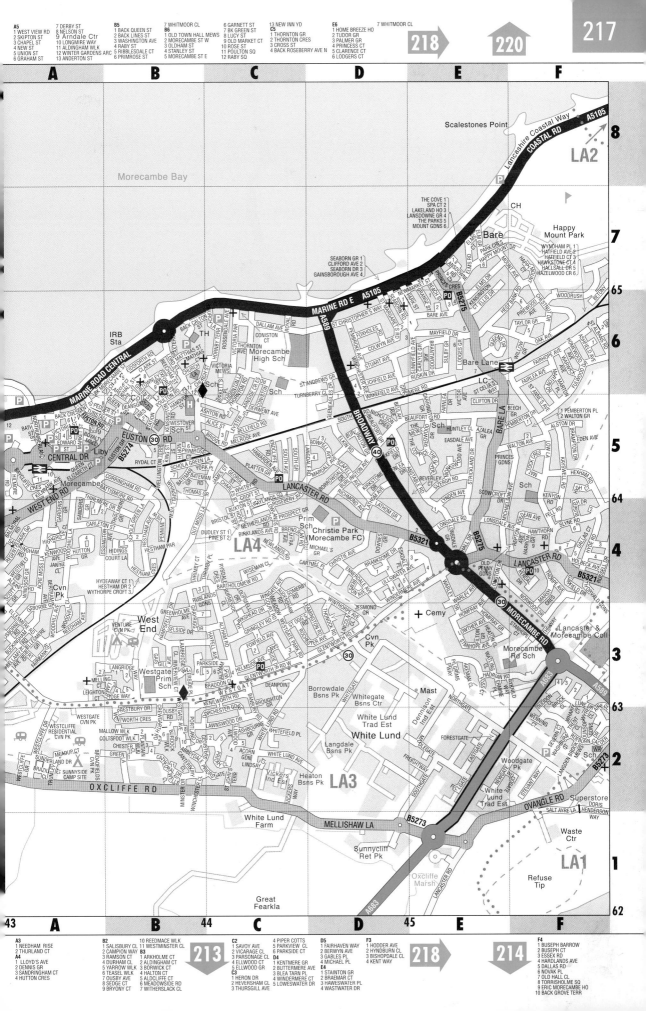

217
220
221

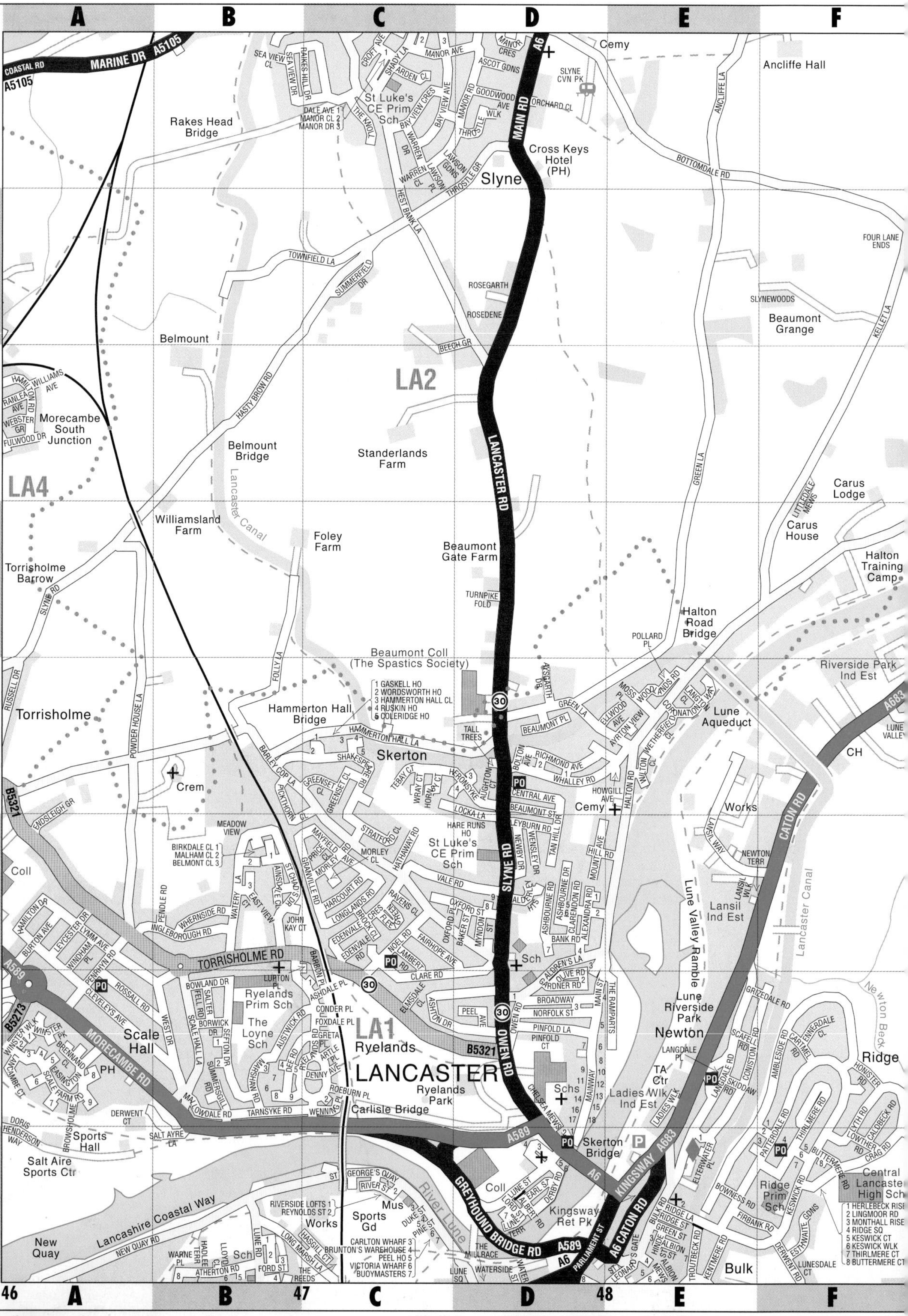
A
B
C
D
E
F
8
7
65
6
5
64
4
3
63
2
1
62
46
47
48
COASTAL RD
MARINE DR
A5105
Cemy
Ancliffe Hall
Rakes Head Bridge
St Luke's CE Prim Sch
Cross Keys Hotel (PH)
Slyne
SLYNE CVN PK
MAIN RD
A6
BOTTOMDALE RD
ANCLIFFE LA
FOUR LANE ENDS
TOWNFIELD LA
SUMMERFIELD DR
ROSEGARTH
ROSEDENE
BEECH GR
SLYNEWOODS
Beaumont Grange
KELLET LA
Belmount
LA2
Morecambe South Junction
HASTY BROW RD
Belmount Bridge
Standerlands Farm
LANCASTER RD
GREEN LA
LA4
Lancaster Canal
Williamsland Farm
Foley Farm
Beaumont Gate Farm
Carus Lodge
Carus House
Halton Training Camp
Torrisholme Barrow
SLYNE RD
TURNPIKE FOLD
Halton Road Bridge
POLLARD PL
Beaumont Coll (The Spastics Society)
Riverside Park Ind Est
RUSSELL DR
FOLLY LA
1 GASKELL HO
2 WORDSWORTH HO
3 HAMMERTON HALL CL
4 RUSKIN HO
5 COLERIDGE HO
Torrisholme
Hammerton Hall Bridge
HAMMERTON HALL LA
POWDER HOUSE LA
Skerton
Lune Aqueduct
A683
CH
Crem
B5321
ENDSLEIGH GR
MEADOW VIEW
HARE RUNS HO
St Luke's CE Prim Sch
Cemy
Works
CATON RD
NEWTON TERR
Coll
BIRKDALE CL 1
MALHAM CL 2
BELMONT CL 3
SLYNE RD
Lune Valley Ramble
Lansil Ind Est
Lancaster Canal
TORRISHOLME RD
A589
Sch
Ryelands Prim Sch
The Loyne Sch
LA1
Ryelands
LANCASTER
Ryelands Park
B5273
MORECAMBE RD
Scale Hall
PH
OWEN RD
Lune Riverside Park
Newton
Newton Beck
Ridge
Schs
TA Ctr
Ladies Wlk Ind Est
LADIES WLK
Carlisle Bridge
Sports Hall
Salt Aire Sports Ctr
SALT AYRE LA
Skerton Bridge
KINGSWAY
A6
Coll
GREYHOUND BRIDGE RD
Central Lancaster High Sch
1 HERLEBECK RISE
2 LINGMOOR RD
3 MONTHALL RISE
4 RIDGE SQ
5 KESWICK CT
6 KESWICK WLK
7 THIRLMERE CT
8 BUTTERMERE CT
Ridge Prim Sch
River Lune
Sports Gd
Mus
Works
Kingsway Ret Pk
A6 CATON RD
PARLIAMENT ST
RIVERSIDE LOFTS 1
REYNOLDS ST 2
CARLTON WHARF 3
BRUNTON'S WAREHOUSE 4
PEEL HO 5
VICTORIA WHARF 6
BUOYMASTERS 7
Lancashire Coastal Way
New Quay
NEW QUAY RD
Sch
THE MILLRACE
LUNE SQ
WATERSIDE
Bulk
LUNESDALE CT

A2
1 KEER BANK
2 GILPIN CL
3 BELA CL
4 CRAKE BANK
5 GREGARETH CL
6 WINDHOLME
7 CROASDALE
8 WHITENDALE
9 BRINDLE CL

B1
1 CHARNLEY ST
2 BRIERY ST
3 FURNESS ST
4 MARSH ST
5 HUTTON WAY
6 BORDER CT
7 RICHARDS WLK
8 COWDREY MEWS

217

B2
1 BURNFELL RD
2 TARNBROOK RD
3 RAYGILL PL
4 AUSTWICK RD
5 RAWTHEY RD
6 MEARBECK PL
7 CROSSGILL PL
8 BROWGILL PL
9 WHITERAY RD

214

C2
1 UDALE PL
2 HINDBURN PL

D1
1 KILN CT
2 HILLS CT
3 CAPTAIN'S ROW
4 PARK HO
5 LUNE HO
6 DERBY HO
7 BACK LORD ST
8 PHOENIX ST

D2
1 SKERTON
2 LABURNUM RD
3 KENT ST
4 RIVERSWAY
5 MILLRACE CT
6 SKERTON HO
7 GREENWATER CT
8 FLEMING HO
9 STEWART CT
10 RIGG HO
11 ACRE CT
12 ELLERSHAW HO
13 GREG HO
14 MILLER CT
15 FRANKLAND HO
16 CHURCH CT
17 SHARDS CT
18 BRIDGE HO

D3
1 BULLER ST
2 RUSKIN RD
3 MILLSTONE CT
4 DAISY ST
5 REGAL TERR
6 ALDEN TERR
7 ASHBOURNE CL
8 LINDETH GDNS
9 RICHMOND HO

D4
1 RIPON AVE
2 SELBY AVE
3 FARLETON CT
4 ESKRIDGGE CL

215

E1
1 MARDALE RD
2 GREBE WHARF
3 GLADSTONE TERR
4 FACTORY HILL
5 ST LEONARD CT
6 DE VITRE ST
7 SWALLOW WHARF

221 237 237

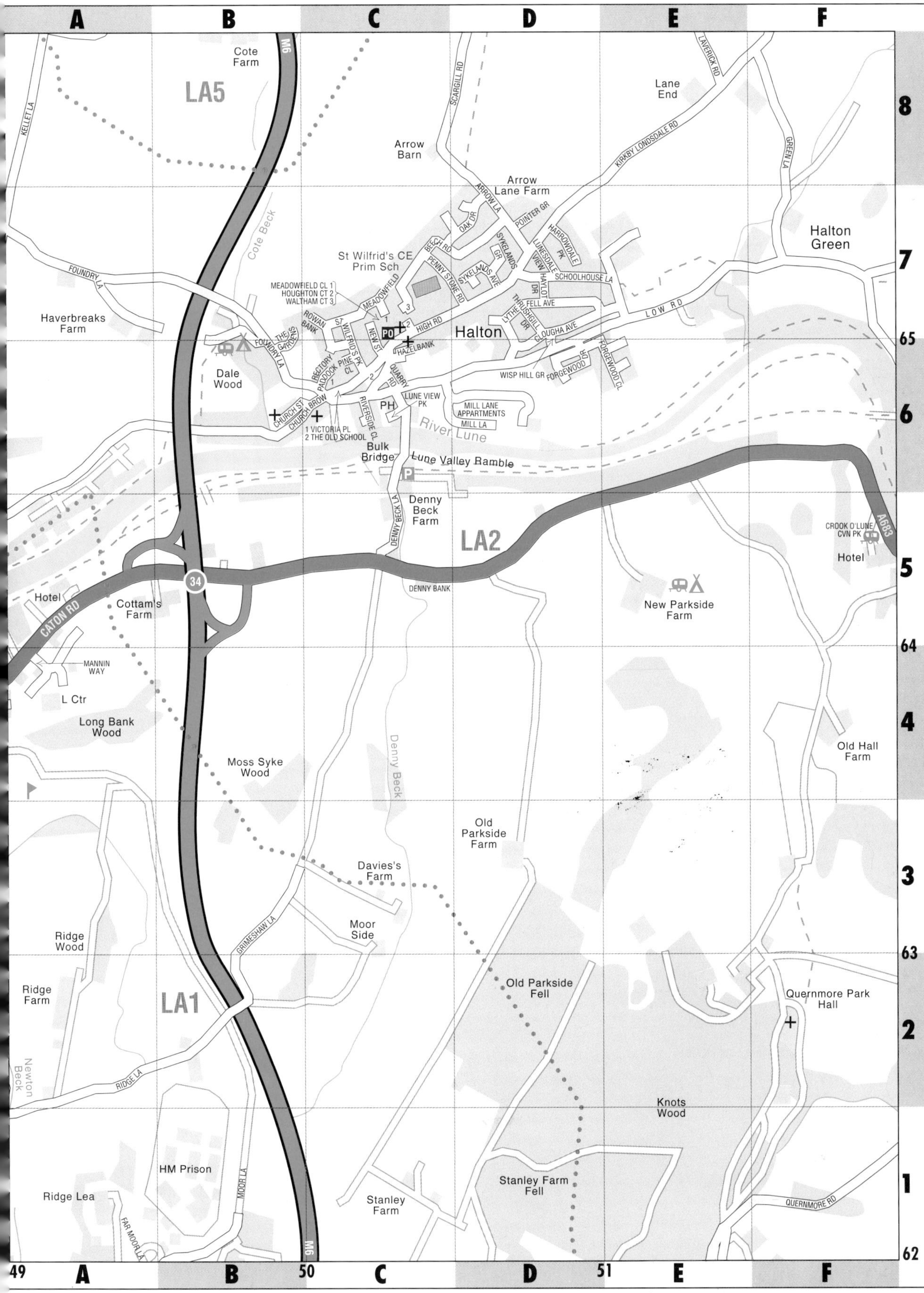

A B C D E F
8 7 6 5 4 3 2 1
65 64 63 62
49 50 51
Cote Farm
LA5
M6
Lane End
LAVERICK RD
KELLET LA
SCARGILL RD
KIRKBY LONSDALE RD
GREEN LA
Arrow Barn
Arrow Lane Farm
ARROW LA
Halton Green
Cote Beck
OAK DR
POINTER GR
HARROWDALE PK
BEECH RD
SYKELANDS
St Wilfrid's CE Prim Sch
PENNY STONE RD
SYKELANDS AVE
SYKELANDS GR
LUNESDALE VIEW
HAYLOT DR
SCHOOLHOUSE LA
FOUNDRY LA
MEADOWFIELD CL 1
HOUGHTON CT 2
WALTHAM CT 3
MEADOWFIELD
FELL AVE
LOW RD
Haverbreaks Farm
ROWAN BANK
ST WILFRID'S PK
NEW ST
HIGH RD
Halton
LYTHE FELL AVE
THRUSHGILL DR
CLOUGHA AVE
THE GARDENS
PO
HAZELBANK
FORGEWOOD DR
FORGEWOOD CL
Dale Wood
RECTORY PADDOCK
PINE CL
QUARRY RD
WISP HILL GR
FORGEWOOD
CHURCH ST
CHURCH BROW
LUNE VIEW PK
PH
MILL LANE APPARTMENTS
MILL LA
RIVERSIDE CL
1 VICTORIA PL
2 THE OLD SCHOOL
River Lune
Bulk Bridge
Lune Valley Ramble
P
Denny Beck Farm
DENNY BECK LA
LA2
A683
CROOK O'LUNE CVN PK
Hotel
34
DENNY BANK
Hotel
CATON RD
Cottam's Farm
New Parkside Farm
MANNIN WAY
L Ctr
Long Bank Wood
Old Hall Farm
Moss Syke Wood
Denny Beck
Old Parkside Farm
Davies's Farm
Moor Side
GRIMESHAW LA
Ridge Wood
Ridge Farm
LA1
Old Parkside Fell
Quernmore Park Hall
Newton Beck
RIDGE LA
Knots Wood
HM Prison
MOOR LA
Stanley Farm Fell
Ridge Lea
Stanley Farm
QUERNMORE RD
FAR MOOR LA


215 237 232

222

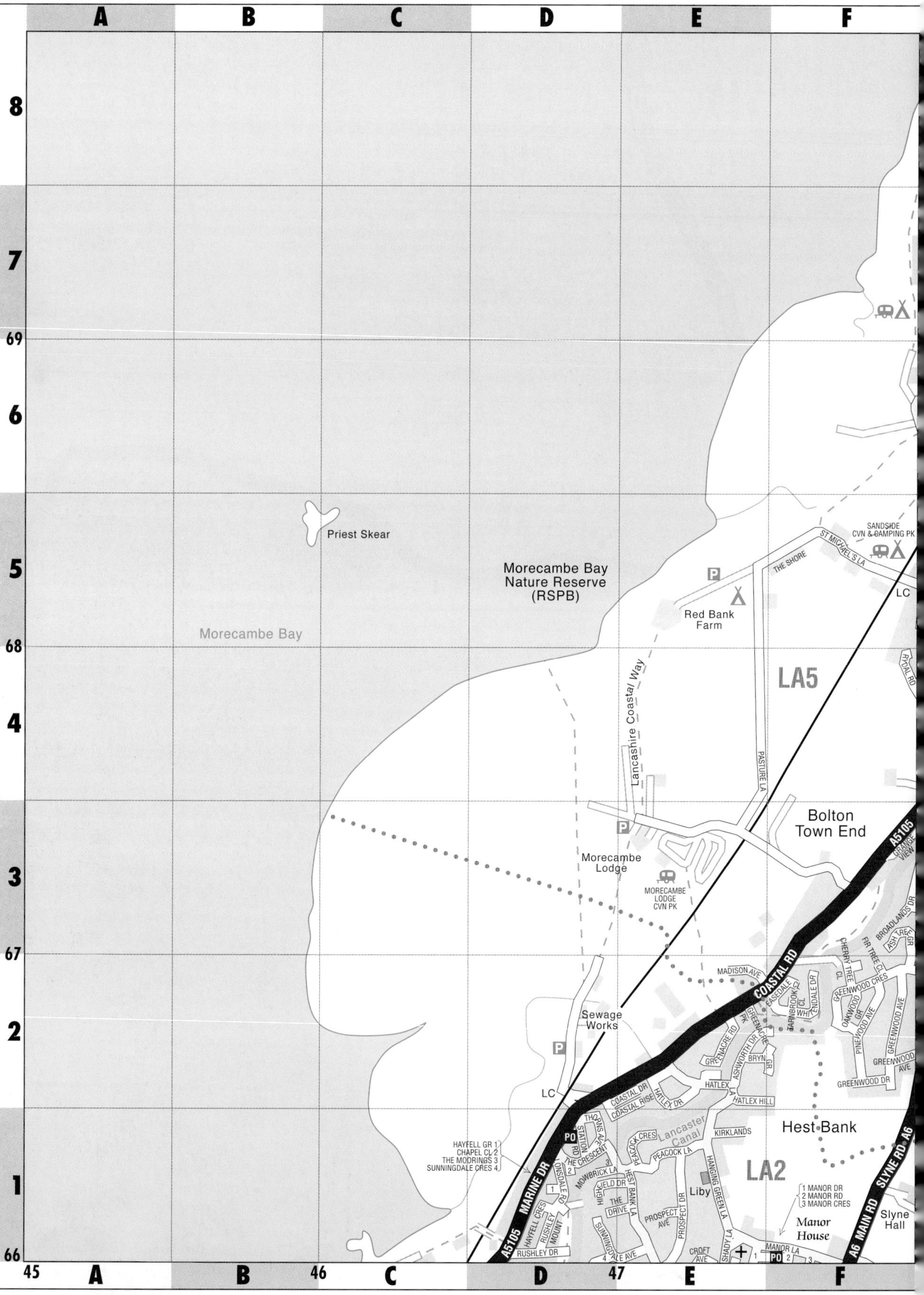
A
B
C
D
E
F
Priest Skear
Morecambe Bay Nature Reserve (RSPB)
Morecambe Bay
SANDSIDE CVN & CAMPING PK
ST MICHAEL'S LA
THE SHORE
LC
Red Bank Farm
LA5
RYDAL RD
Lancashire Coastal Way
PASTURE LA
Bolton Town End
A5105
GRANGE VIEW
Morecambe Lodge
MORECAMBE LODGE CVN PK
BROADLANDS DR
ASH TREE GR
FIR TREE CL
CHERRY TREE CL
MADISON AVE
COASTAL RD
EASEDALE CL
TARNBROOK CL
WHINDALE DR
GREENWOOD CRES
OAKWOOD GR
PINEWOOD AVE
GREENWOOD AVE
GREENWOOD DR
Sewage Works
GREENACRE PK
GREENACRE RD
ASHWORTH DR
BRYN GR
HATLEX LA
HATLEX HILL
HATLEY DR
COASTAL DR
COASTAL RISE
LC
Hest Bank
Lancaster Canal
KIRKLANDS
PEACOCK CRES
PEACOCK LA
STATION RD
THORNS AVE
THE CRESCENT
HAYFELL GR 1
CHAPEL CL 2
THE MODRINGS 3
SUNNINGDALE CRES 4
MARINE DR
LONSDALE RD
MOWBRICK LA
HIGHFIELD DR
THE DRIVE
HEST BANK LA
HANGING GREEN LA
LA2
Liby
PROSPECT AVE
PROSPECT DR
1 MANOR DR
2 MANOR RD
3 MANOR CRES
Manor House
SLYNE RD A6
A6 MAIN RD
Slyne Hall
HAYFELL CRES
RUSHLEY MOUNT
RUSHLEY DR
SUNNINGDALE AVE
CROFT AVE
SHADY LA
MANOR LA
PO
45
46
47
66
67
68
69
1
2
3
4
5
6
7
8

217
218

223
237

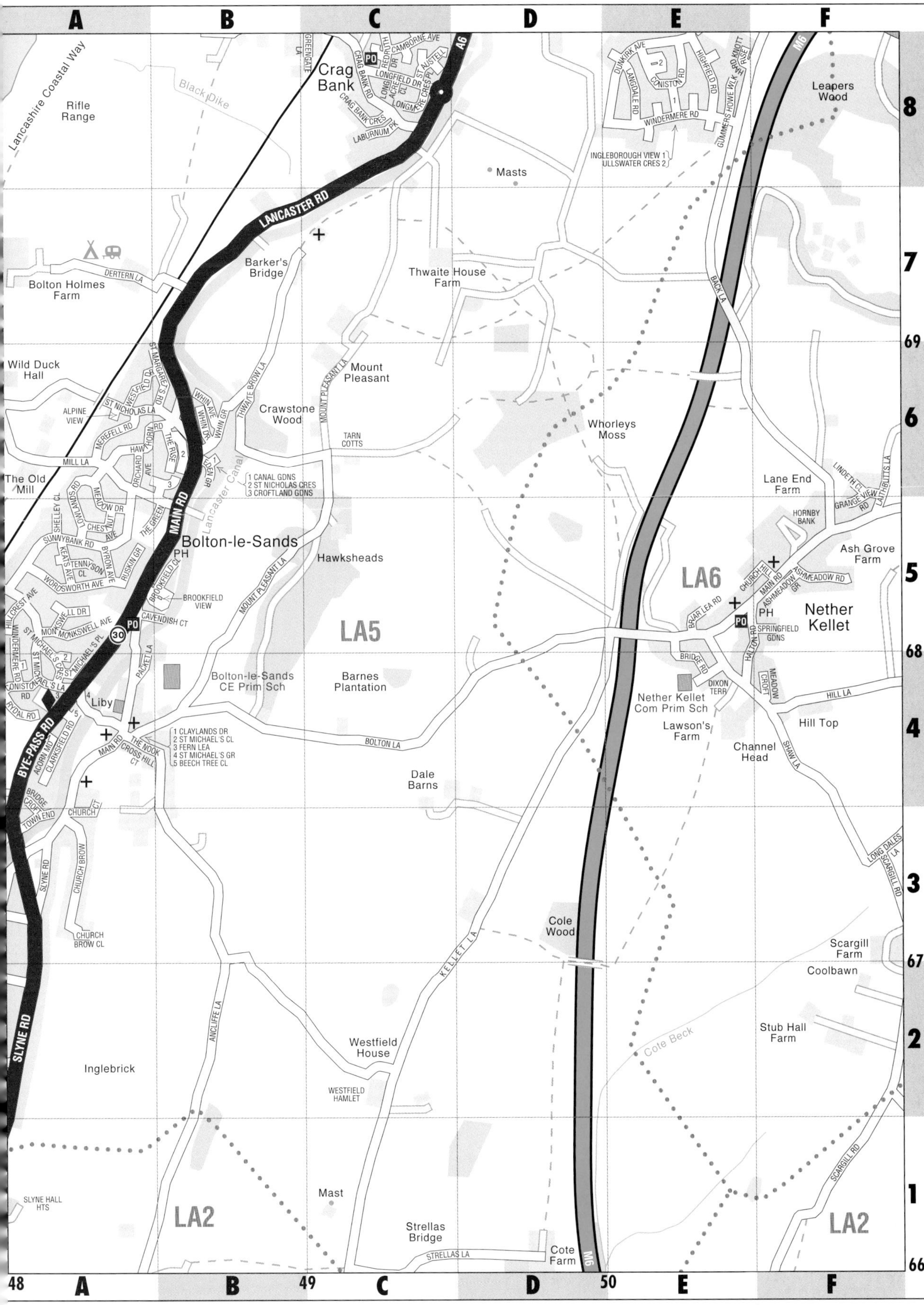
A
B
C
D
E
F
Lancashire Coastal Way
Rifle Range
Black Dike
Crag Bank
GREENGATE LA
CRAG BANK RD
CRAG BANK CRES
LABURNUM PK
LONGFIELD DR
REDRUTH DR
CAMBORNE AVE
ST AUSTELL
A6
LANCASTER RD
Masts
DUNKIRK AVE
LANGDALE RD
CONISTON RD
HIGHFIELD RD
WINDERMERE RD
INGLEBOROUGH VIEW 1
ULLSWATER CRES 2
GUMMERS HOWE WLK
KNOTT RISE
M6
Leapers Wood
8
Bolton Holmes Farm
DERTERN LA
Barker's Bridge
Thwaite House Farm
BACK LA
7
69
Wild Duck Hall
ALPINE VIEW
ST NICHOLAS LA
WESTFIELD DR
ST MARGARET'S RD
MEREFELL RD
MILL LA
The Old Mill
HAWTHORN AVE
ORCHARD AVE
THE ROSE
WHIN AVE
WHIN DR
WHIN GR
THWAITE BROW LA
Crawstone Wood
Mount Pleasant
MOUNT PLEASANT LA
TARN COTTS
1 CANAL GDNS
2 ST NICHOLAS CRES
3 CROFTLAND GDNS
Lancaster Canal
Whorleys Moss
6
Lane End Farm
LINDETH CL
LAITHBUTTS LA
GRANGE VIEW RD
HORNBY BANK
SHELLEY CL
LOWLANDS RD
MEADOW DR
CHESTNUT AVE
THE GREEN
SUNNYBANK RD
KEATS AVE
TENNYSON CL
BYRON AVE
RUSKIN GR
WORDSWORTH AVE
MAIN RD
Bolton-le-Sands
PH
BROOKFIELD CL
BROOKFIELD VIEW
Hawksheads
LA5
HILLCREST AVE
CAVENDISH CT
MONKSWELL DR
MONKSWELL AVE
ST MICHAEL'S CL
ST MICHAEL'S PL
ST MICHAEL'S LA
WINDERMERE RD
CONISTON RD
RYDAL RD
PO
30
PACKET LA
Bolton-le-Sands CE Prim Sch
Barnes Plantation
Liby
LA6
Ash Grove Farm
CHURCH HILL
MAIN RD
ASHMEADOW GR
ASHMEADOW RD
BRIAR LEA RD
Nether Kellet
SPRINGFIELD GDNS
HALTON RD
BRIDGE RD
DIXON TERR
MEADOW CROFT
Nether Kellet Com Prim Sch
HILL LA
Hill Top
5
68
BYE-PASS RD
ACORN MDW
CLARKSFIELD RD
THE NOOK
CROSS HILL CT
1 CLAYLANDS DR
2 ST MICHAEL'S CL
3 FERN LEA
4 ST MICHAEL'S GR
5 BEECH TREE CL
BOLTON LA
Lawson's Farm
Channel Head
SHAW LA
4
Dale Barns
BRIDGE CROFT
TOWN END
CHURCH CT
SLYNE RD
CHURCH BROW
CHURCH BROW CL
LONG DALES LA
SCARGILL RD
3
Cole Wood
KELLET LA
Scargill Farm
Coolbawn
67
SLYNE RD
ANCLIFFE LA
Westfield House
Stub Hall Farm
Cote Beck
2
Inglebrick
WESTFIELD HAMLET
SLYNE HALL HTS
LA2
Mast
Strellas Bridge
STRELLAS LA
Cote Farm
LA2
1
66
48
49
50

218
219
237

224

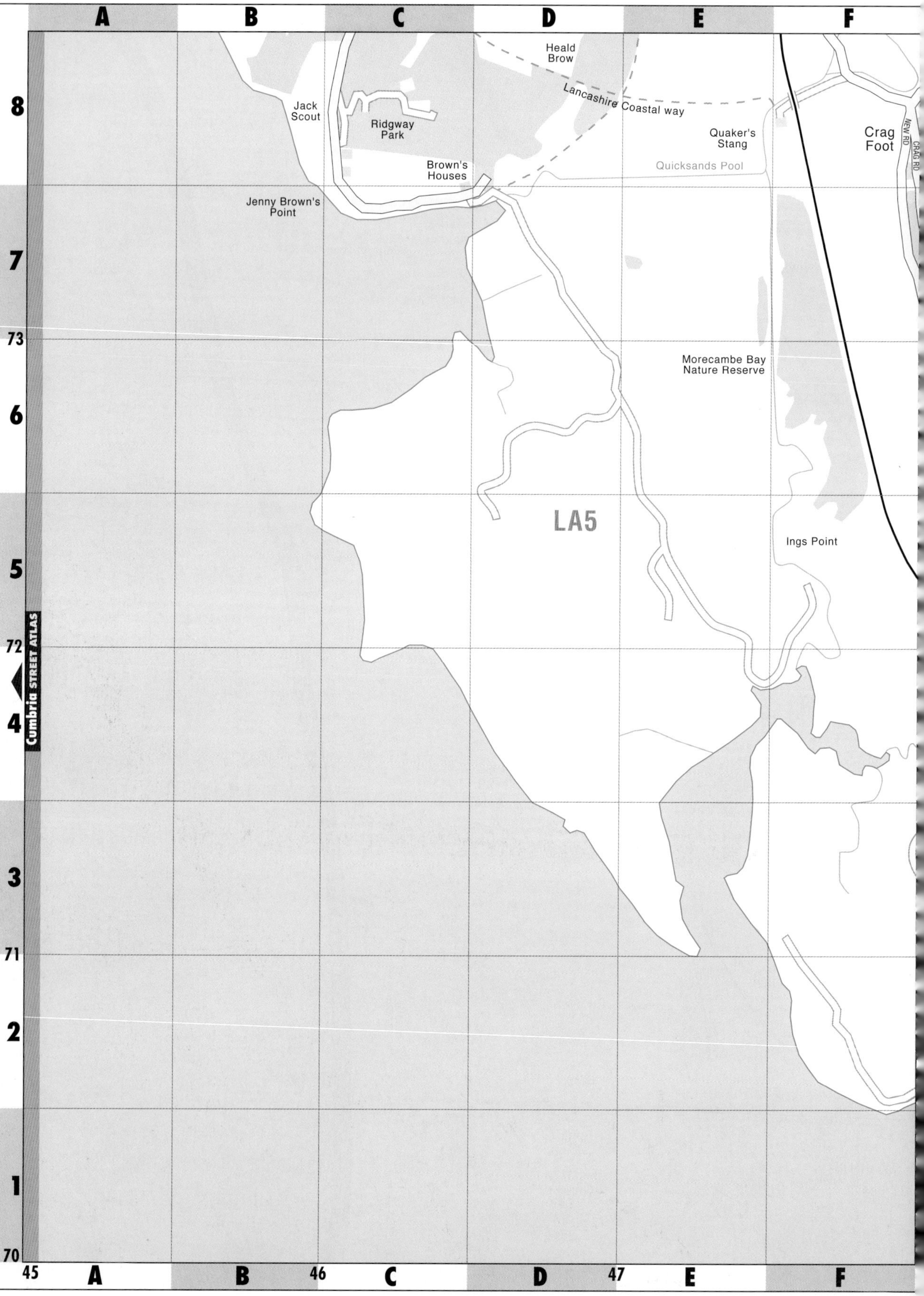
A
B
C
D
E
F
8
7
73
6
5
72
4
3
71
2
1
70
45
46
47
Heald Brow
Lancashire Coastal way
Jack Scout
Ridgway Park
Brown's Houses
Jenny Brown's Point
Quaker's Stang
Quicksands Pool
Crag Foot
NEW RD
CRAG RD
Morecambe Bay Nature Reserve
LA5
Ings Point
Cumbria STREET ATLAS

220

225
240

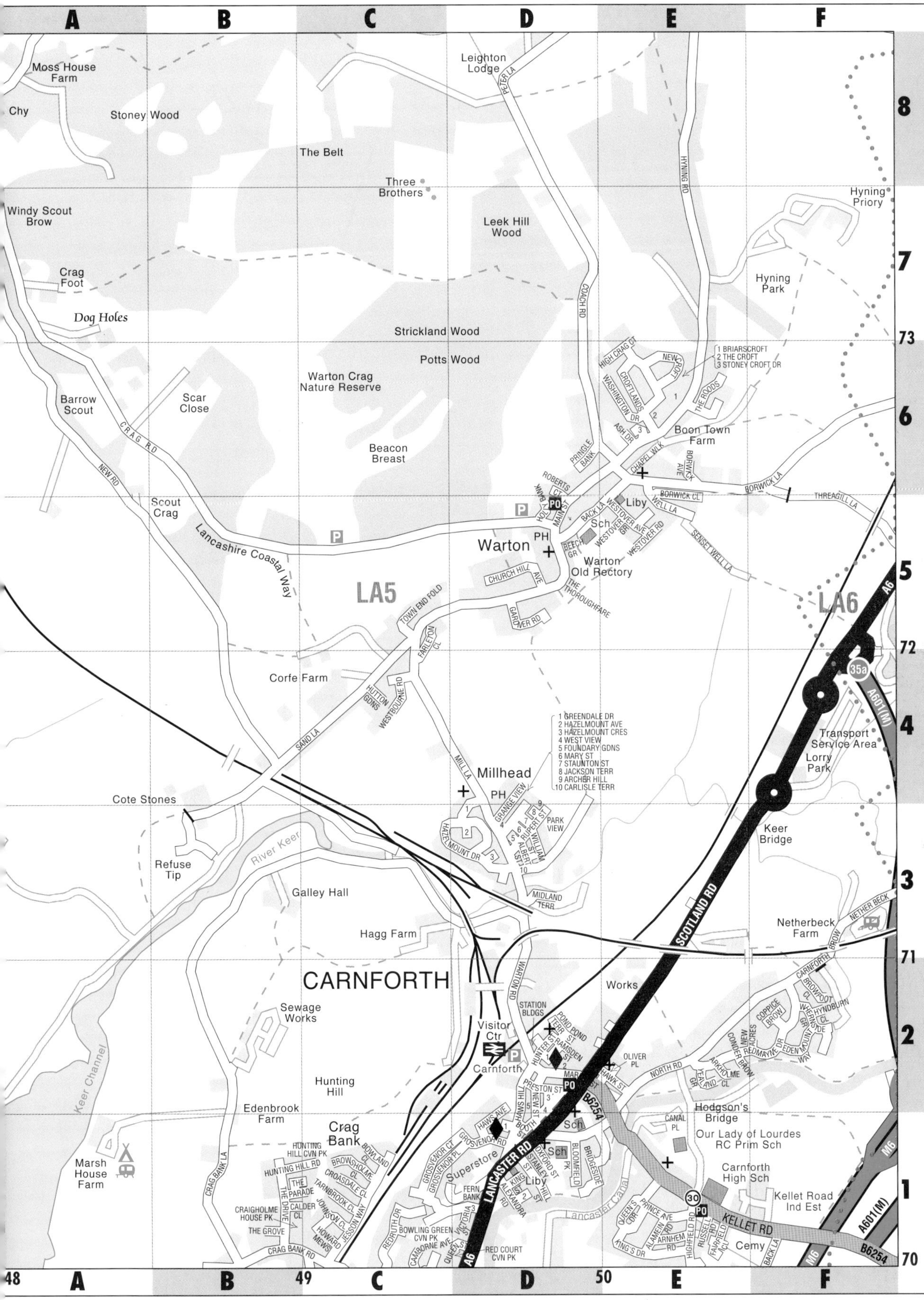
A
B
C
D
E
F
8
7
73
6
5
72
4
3
71
2
1
70
48
49
50
Moss House Farm
Chy
Stoney Wood
The Belt
Three Brothers
Windy Scout Brow
Crag Foot
Dog Holes
Leek Hill Wood
Leighton Lodge
PETER LA
HYNING RD
Hyning Priory
Hyning Park
COACH RD
Strickland Wood
Potts Wood
Warton Crag Nature Reserve
Barrow Scout
Scar Close
CRAG RD
NEW RD
Beacon Breast
HIGH CRAG CT
NEW CROFT
CROFTLANDS
WASHINGTON DR
ASH DR
THE ROODS
1 BRIARSCROFT
2 THE CROFT
3 STONEY CROFT DR
Boon Town Farm
PRINGLE BANK
CHAPEL WLK
BORWICK AVE
BORWICK LA
BORWICK CL
THREAGILL LA
ROBERTS CT
HOLLY BANK
MAIN ST
PO
Liby
BACK LA
WESTOVER AVE
WESTOVER GR
WESTOVER RD
WELL LA
SENSET WELL LA
Sch
Scout Crag
Lancashire Coastal Way
Warton
PH
BEECH GR
Warton Old Rectory
CHURCH HILL AVE
THE THOROUGHFARE
GARNER RD
LA5
LA6
A6
TOWN END FOLD
FARLETON CL
35a
A601(M)
Corfe Farm
HUTTON GDNS
WESTBOURNE RD
SAND LA
1 GREENDALE DR
2 HAZELMOUNT AVE
3 HAZELMOUNT CRES
4 WEST VIEW
5 FOUNDARY GDNS
6 MARY ST
7 STAUNTON ST
8 JACKSON TERR
9 ARCHER HILL
10 CARLISLE TERR
Transport Service Area
Lorry Park
MILL LA
Millhead
PH
Cote Stones
GRANGE VIEW
RUPERT ST
WILLIAM ST
ALBERT ST
PARK VIEW
HAZELMOUNT DR
Keer Bridge
River Keer
Refuse Tip
Galley Hall
MIDLAND TERR
SCOTLAND RD
NETHER BECK
Netherbeck Farm
Hagg Farm
CARNFORTH
WARTON RD
Works
CARNFORTH BROW
BROWFOOT CL
HYNDBURN CL
COPPICE BROW
NEW ACRES
CONDER BROW
REDMAYNE GR
EDEN WAY
Sewage Works
STATION BLDGS
POND TERR
POND ST
HUNTER ST
RAMSDEN ST
Visitor Ctr
Carnforth
OLIVER PL
NORTH RD
HAWK ST
ARKHOLME CL
YEALAND CL
Keer Channel
Hunting Hill
MARKET ST
PRESTON ST
NEW ST
B6254
Hodgson's Bridge
CANAL PL
Our Lady of Lourdes RC Prim Sch
Edenbrook Farm
Crag Bank
HAWS AVE
GROSVENOR RD
BOOTH ST
Marsh House Farm
HUNTING HILL CVN PK
BOWLAND CL
BROWNSHOLME CL
CROASDALE CL
HUNTING HILL RD
THE PARADE
TARNBROOK CL
CALDER CL
JOHNSON CL
JESSON WAY
HOWARD MEWS
CRAIGHOLME HOUSE PK
THE DRIVE
THE GROVE
CRAG BANK RD
CRAG BANK LA
GROSVENOR CT
GROSVENOR PL
Superstore
LANCASTER RD
STANLEY ST
OXFORD ST
KING ST
ALEXANDRA RD
Liby
Sch
BLOOMFIELD PK
BRIDGESIDE
Lancaster Canal
Carnforth High Sch
Kellet Road Ind Est
M6
FERN BANK
REDRUTH DR
BOWLING GREEN CVN PK
CAMBORNE AVE
QUEEN ST
VICTORIA RD
RED COURT CVN PK
QUEEN'S DR
PRINCE AVE
ALAMEIN RD
ARNHEM RD
KING'S DR
HIGHFIELD RD
RUSSELL RD
FAIRFIELD CL
30
PO
KELLET RD
Cemy
BACK LA
B6254
A601(M)

221
240

D1
1 WARTONWOOD VIEW
2 TOWPATH WLK
3 ALBERT ST

D2
1 BACK HUNTER ST
2 ASHTREES WAY
3 EDWARD ST
4 JOHN ST
5 BACK NEW ST

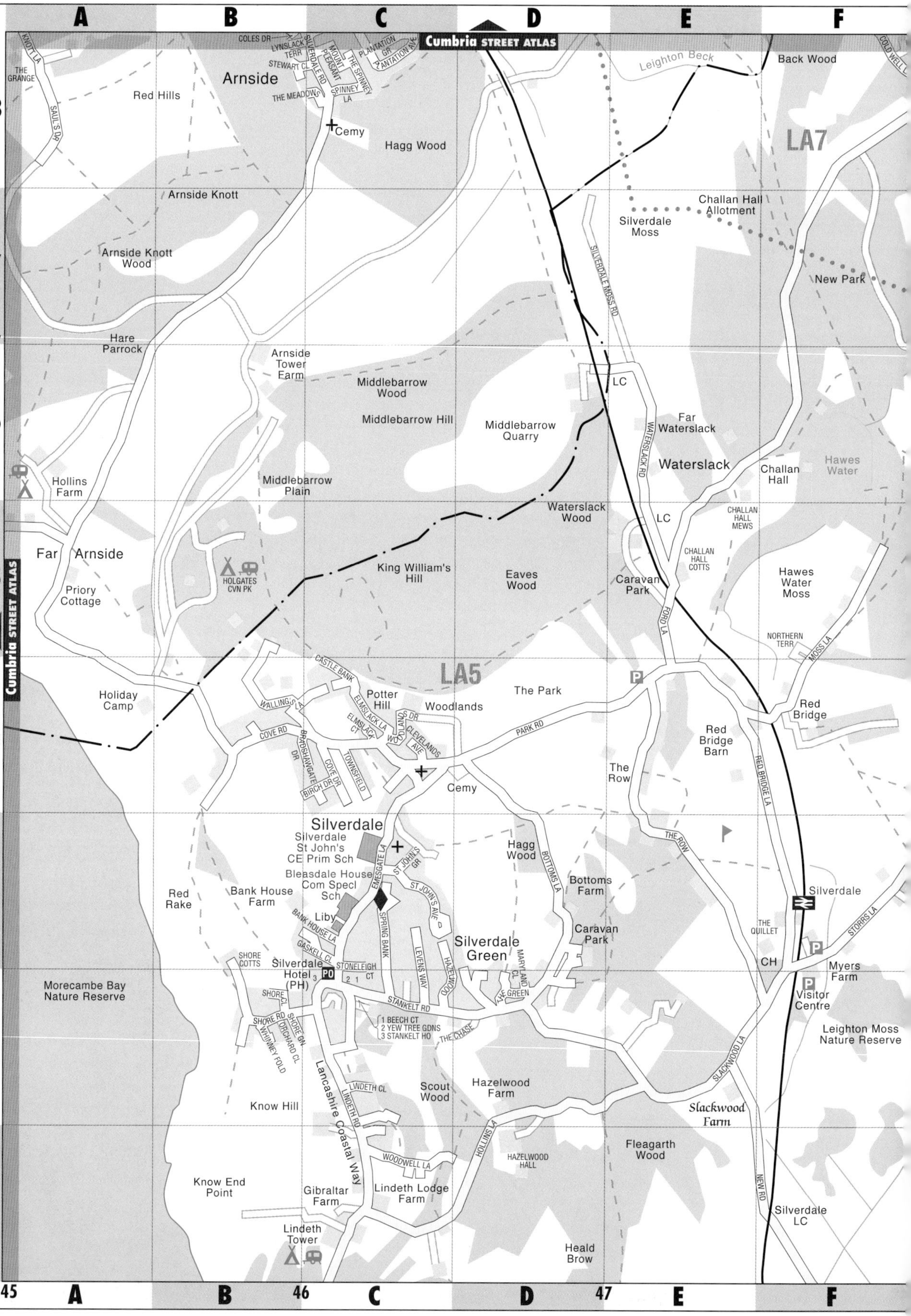
Cumbria STREET ATLAS
A
B
C
D
E
F
8
7
77
6
5
76
4
3
75
2
1
74
45
46
47
KNOTT LA
THE GRANGE
SAUL'S DR
Red Hills
Arnside
COLES DR
LYNSLACK TERR
STEWART CL
SILVERDALE RD
MOUNT PLEASANT
THE SPINNEY
PLANTATION GR
PLANTATION AVE
THE MEADOWS
SPINNEY LA
Cemy
Hagg Wood
Leighton Beck
Back Wood
COLD WELL LA
LA7
Arnside Knott
Arnside Knott Wood
Challan Hall Allotment
Silverdale Moss
SILVERDALE MOSS RD
New Park
Hare Parrock
Arnside Tower Farm
Middlebarrow Wood
Middlebarrow Hill
Middlebarrow Quarry
LC
Far Waterslack
WATERSLACK RD
Waterslack
Challan Hall
Hawes Water
Hollins Farm
Middlebarrow Plain
Waterslack Wood
CHALLAN HALL MEWS
CHALLAN HALL COTTS
Far
Arnside
HOLGATES CVN PK
King William's Hill
Eaves Wood
Caravan Park
Hawes Water Moss
Priory Cottage
FORD LA
NORTHERN TERR
MOSS LA
CASTLE BANK
LA5
Holiday Camp
WALLINGS LA
Potter Hill
Woodlands
The Park
ELMSLACK LA
ELMSLACK CT
WOODLANDS DR
CLEVELANDS AVE
PARK RD
Red Bridge
COVE RD
BRADSHAWGATE DR
COVE DR
TOWNSFIELD
BIRCH DR
Cemy
Red Bridge Barn
The Row
RED BRIDGE LA
Silverdale
Silverdale St John's CE Prim Sch
EMESGATE LA
ST JOHN'S GR
Hagg Wood
BOTTOMS LA
THE ROW
Bleasdale House Com Specl Sch
ST JOHN'S AVE
Bottoms Farm
Red Rake
Bank House Farm
Silverdale
Liby
BANK HOUSE LA
SPRING BANK
Silverdale Green
Caravan Park
THE QUILLET
STORRS LA
GASKELL CL
LEVENS WAY
HAZELWOOD
MARYLAND CL
SHORE COTTS
Silverdale Hotel (PH)
PO
STONELEIGH CT
CH
Myers Farm
Morecambe Bay Nature Reserve
SHORE CL
STANKELT RD
THE GREEN
Visitor Centre
SHORE RD
SHORE GN
ORCHARD CL
WHINNEY FOLD
1 BEECH CT
2 YEW TREE GDNS
3 STANKELT HO
THE CHASE
Leighton Moss Nature Reserve
Lancashire Coastal Way
SLACKWOOD LA
LINDETH CL
Scout Wood
Hazelwood Farm
Know Hill
LINDETH RD
Slackwood Farm
HOLLINS LA
HAZELWOOD HALL
Fleagarth Wood
WOODWELL LA
NEW RD
Know End Point
Gibraltar Farm
Lindeth Lodge Farm
Silverdale LC
Lindeth Tower
Heald Brow

240

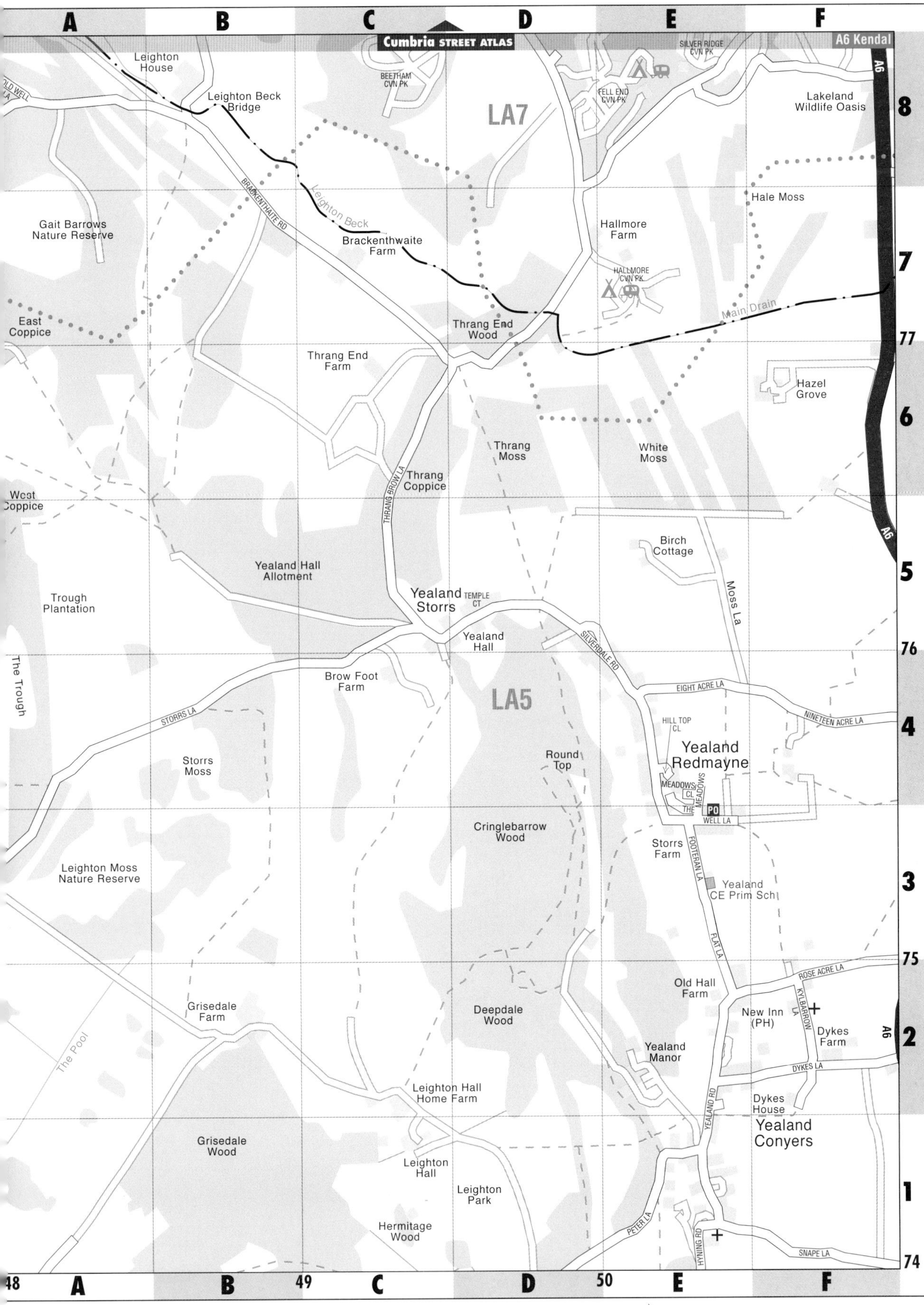
Cumbria STREET ATLAS
A6 Kendal
Leighton House
Leighton Beck Bridge
BEETHAM CVN PK
LA7
SILVER RIDGE CVN PK
FELL END CVN PK
Lakeland Wildlife Oasis
Gait Barrows Nature Reserve
Leighton Beck
BRACKENTHWAITE RD
Brackenthwaite Farm
Hale Moss
Hallmore Farm
HALLMORE CVN PK
Main Drain
East Coppice
Thrang End Wood
Thrang End Farm
Hazel Grove
Thrang Moss
White Moss
Thrang Coppice
THRANG BROW LA
West Coppice
Birch Cottage
Yealand Hall Allotment
Moss La
Trough Plantation
Yealand Storrs
TEMPLE CT
Yealand Hall
SILVERDALE RD
The Trough
Brow Foot Farm
LA5
EIGHT ACRE LA
STORRS LA
HILL TOP CL
NINETEEN ACRE LA
Storrs Moss
Round Top
Yealand Redmayne
MEADOWS CL
THE MEADOWS
PO
WELL LA
Cringlebarrow Wood
Storrs Farm
Leighton Moss Nature Reserve
FOOTERAN LA
Yealand CE Prim Sch
FLAT LA
ROSE ACRE LA
Old Hall Farm
Grisedale Farm
Deepdale Wood
New Inn (PH)
KYLBARROW LA
Dykes Farm
A6
The Pool
Yealand Manor
DYKES LA
Leighton Hall Home Farm
YEALAND RD
Dykes House
Yealand Conyers
Grisedale Wood
Leighton Hall
Leighton Park
PETER LA
Hermitage Wood
HYNING RD
SNAPE LA
A
B
C
D
E
F
8
7
77
6
5
76
4
3
75
2
1
74
48
49
50

207 204
232
Scale: 1¾ inches to 1 mile
0 ¼ ½ mile
0 250m 500m 750m 1 km

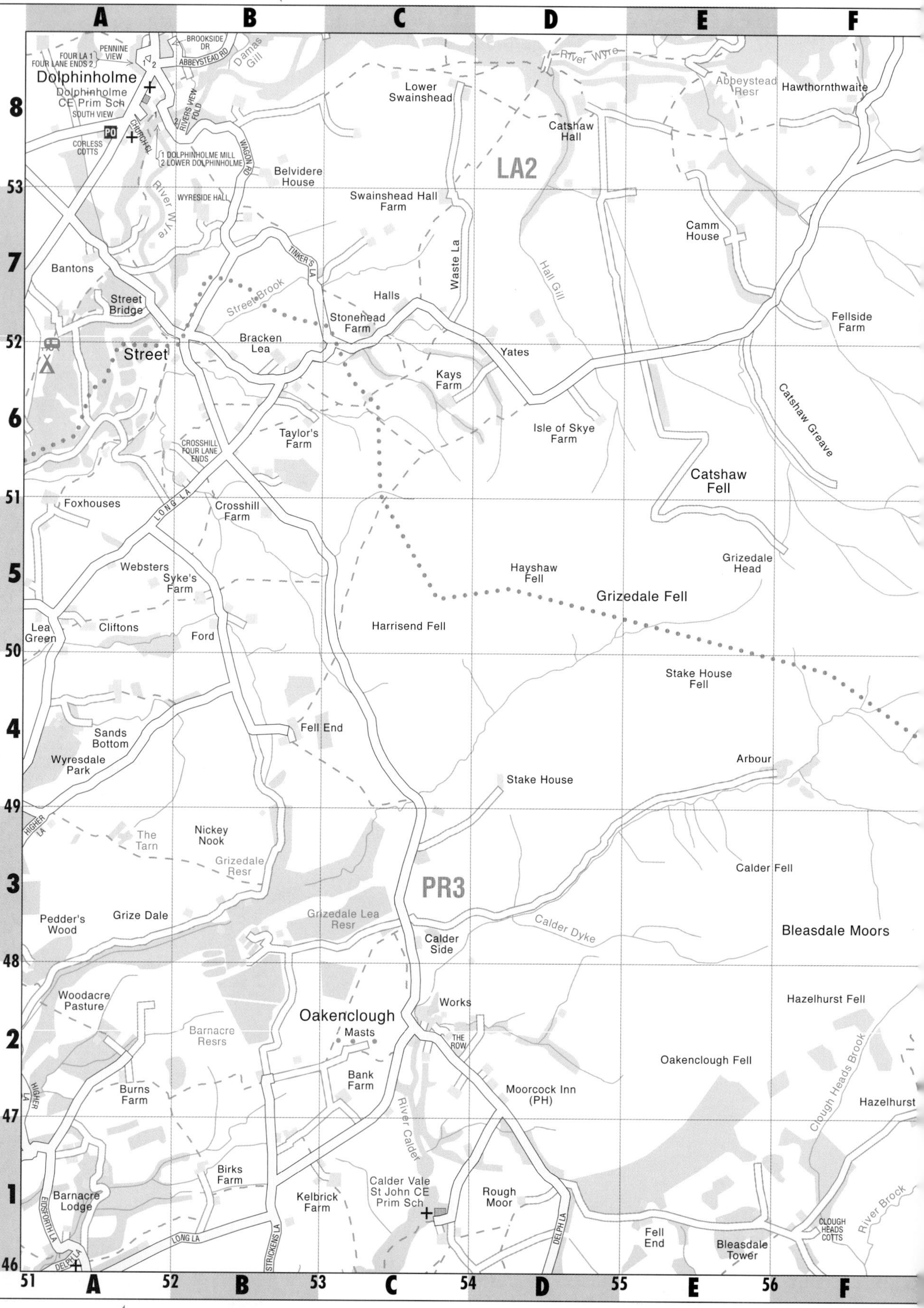
A
B
C
D
E
F
Dolphinholme
Dolphinholme CE Prim Sch
FOUR LA 1
FOUR LANE ENDS 2
PENNINE VIEW
BROOKSIDE DR
ABBEYSTEAD RD
Damas Gill
SOUTH VIEW
PO
CORLESS COTTS
CHURCH CL
RIVERS VIEW FOLD
1 DOLPHINHOLME MILL
2 LOWER DOLPHINHOLME
WAGON RD
WYRESIDE HALL
River Wyre
Lower Swainshead
Belvidere House
Swainshead Hall Farm
Catshaw Hall
LA2
Abbeystead Resr
Hawthornthwaite
Camm House
Bantons
Street Bridge
Street
Street Brook
TINKER'S LA
Halls
Waste La
Hall Gill
Stonehead Farm
Bracken Lea
Yates
Fellside Farm
Kays Farm
Catshaw Greave
Taylor's Farm
Isle of Skye Farm
CROSSHILL FOUR LANE ENDS
Catshaw Fell
Foxhouses
LONG LA
Crosshill Farm
Grizedale Head
Websters
Syke's Farm
Hayshaw Fell
Grizedale Fell
Lea Green
Cliftons
Ford
Harrisend Fell
Stake House Fell
Sands Bottom
Fell End
Wyresdale Park
Arbour
Stake House
HIGHER LA
The Tarn
Nickey Nook
Grizedale Resr
Calder Fell
PR3
Pedder's Wood
Grize Dale
Grizedale Lea Resr
Calder Dyke
Calder Side
Bleasdale Moors
Woodacre Pasture
Works
Hazelhurst Fell
Oakenclough
Barnacre Resrs
Masts
THE ROW
Oakenclough Fell
Clough Heads Brook
Burns Farm
Bank Farm
Moorcock Inn (PH)
HIGHER LA
River Calder
Hazelhurst
Birks Farm
Calder Vale St John CE Prim Sch
Rough Moor
Barnacre Lodge
Kelbrick Farm
River Brock
EIDSFORTH LA
LONG LA
STRICKENS LA
DELPH LA
Fell End
Bleasdale Tower
CLOUGH HEADS COTTS
DELPH LA
8
53
7
52
6
51
5
50
4
49
3
48
2
47
1
46
51
52
53
54
55
56

207 204
182
183

Scale: 1¾ inches to 1 mile
¼ ½ mile
250m 500m 750m 1 km

233
228

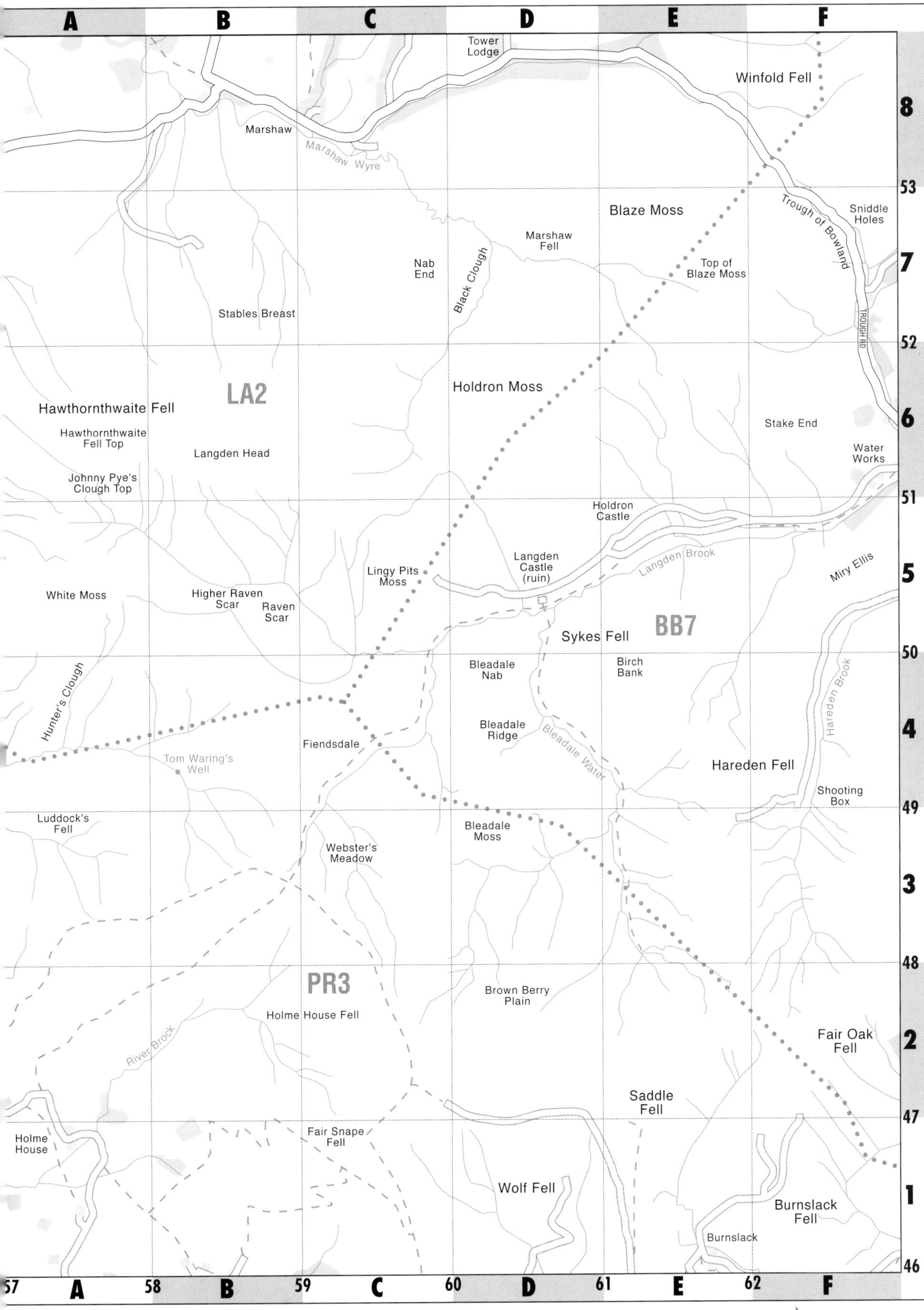
A B C D E F
8 7 6 5 4 3 2 1
53 52 51 50 49 48 47 46
57 58 59 60 61 62
Tower Lodge
Winfold Fell
Marshaw
Marshaw Wyre
Blaze Moss
Sniddle Holes
Trough of Bowland
Marshaw Fell
Nab End
Black Clough
Top of Blaze Moss
Stables Breast
TROUGH RD
LA2
Holdron Moss
Hawthornthwaite Fell
Hawthornthwaite Fell Top
Langden Head
Stake End
Water Works
Johnny Pye's Clough Top
Holdron Castle
Langden Castle (ruin)
Langden Brook
Lingy Pits Moss
Miry Ellis
White Moss
Higher Raven Scar
Raven Scar
Sykes Fell
BB7
Bleadale Nab
Birch Bank
Hunter's Clough
Hareden Brook
Bleadale Ridge
Fiendsdale
Tom Waring's Well
Bleadale Water
Hareden Fell
Shooting Box
Luddock's Fell
Bleadale Moss
Webster's Meadow
PR3
Brown Berry Plain
Holme House Fell
Fair Oak Fell
River Brock
Saddle Fell
Holme House
Fair Snape Fell
Wolf Fell
Burnslack Fell
Burnslack

184
185
228

227
234

Scale: 1¾ inches to 1 mile

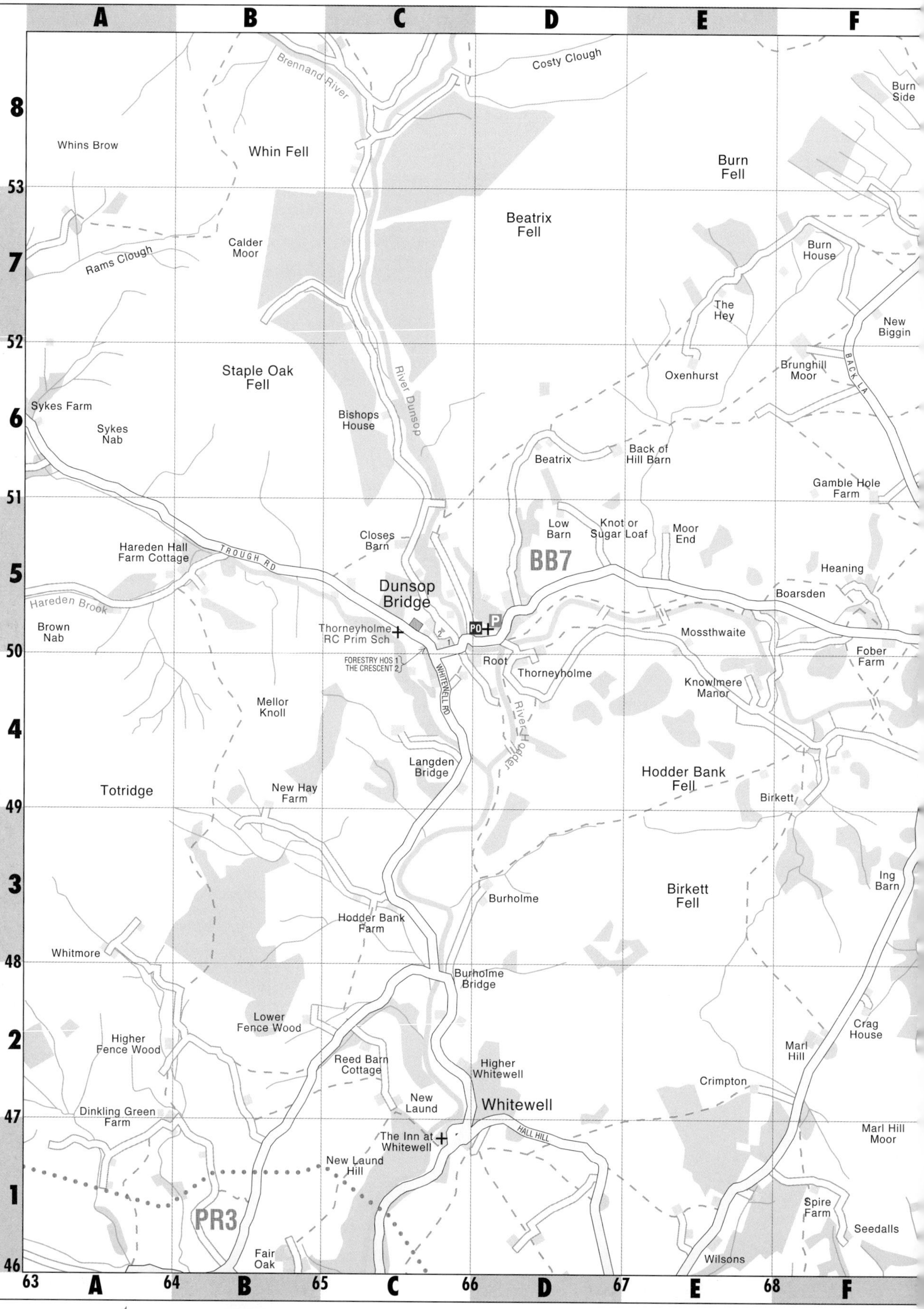
A
B
C
D
E
F
Brennand River
Costy Clough
Burn Side
Whins Brow
Whin Fell
Burn Fell
Beatrix Fell
Calder Moor
Rams Clough
Burn House
The Hey
New Biggin
Staple Oak Fell
River Dunsop
Brunghill Moor
Oxenhurst
BACK LA
Sykes Farm
Sykes Nab
Bishops House
Beatrix
Back of Hill Barn
Gamble Hole Farm
Low Barn
Knot or Sugar Loaf
Moor End
Closes Barn
Hareden Hall Farm Cottage
TROUGH RD
BB7
Heaning
Dunsop Bridge
Boarsden
Hareden Brook
Brown Nab
Thorneyholme RC Prim Sch
Mossthwaite
Fober Farm
FORESTRY HOS 1
THE CRESCENT 2
Root
Thorneyholme
Knowlmere Manor
WHITEWELL RD
Mellor Knoll
River Hodder
Langden Bridge
Hodder Bank Fell
Totridge
New Hay Farm
Birkett
Ing Barn
Birkett Fell
Burholme
Hodder Bank Farm
Whitmore
Burholme Bridge
Lower Fence Wood
Higher Fence Wood
Crag House
Marl Hill
Reed Barn Cottage
Higher Whitewell
Crimpton
New Laund
Whitewell
Dinkling Green Farm
The Inn at Whitewell
HALL HILL
Marl Hill Moor
New Laund Hill
PR3
Spire Farm
Seedalls
Fair Oak
Wilsons
8
53
7
52
6
51
5
50
4
49
3
48
2
47
1
46
63
64
65
66
67
68

227
186
187

Scale: 1¾ inches to 1 mile
¼ ½ mile
250m 500m 750m 1 km
235
230

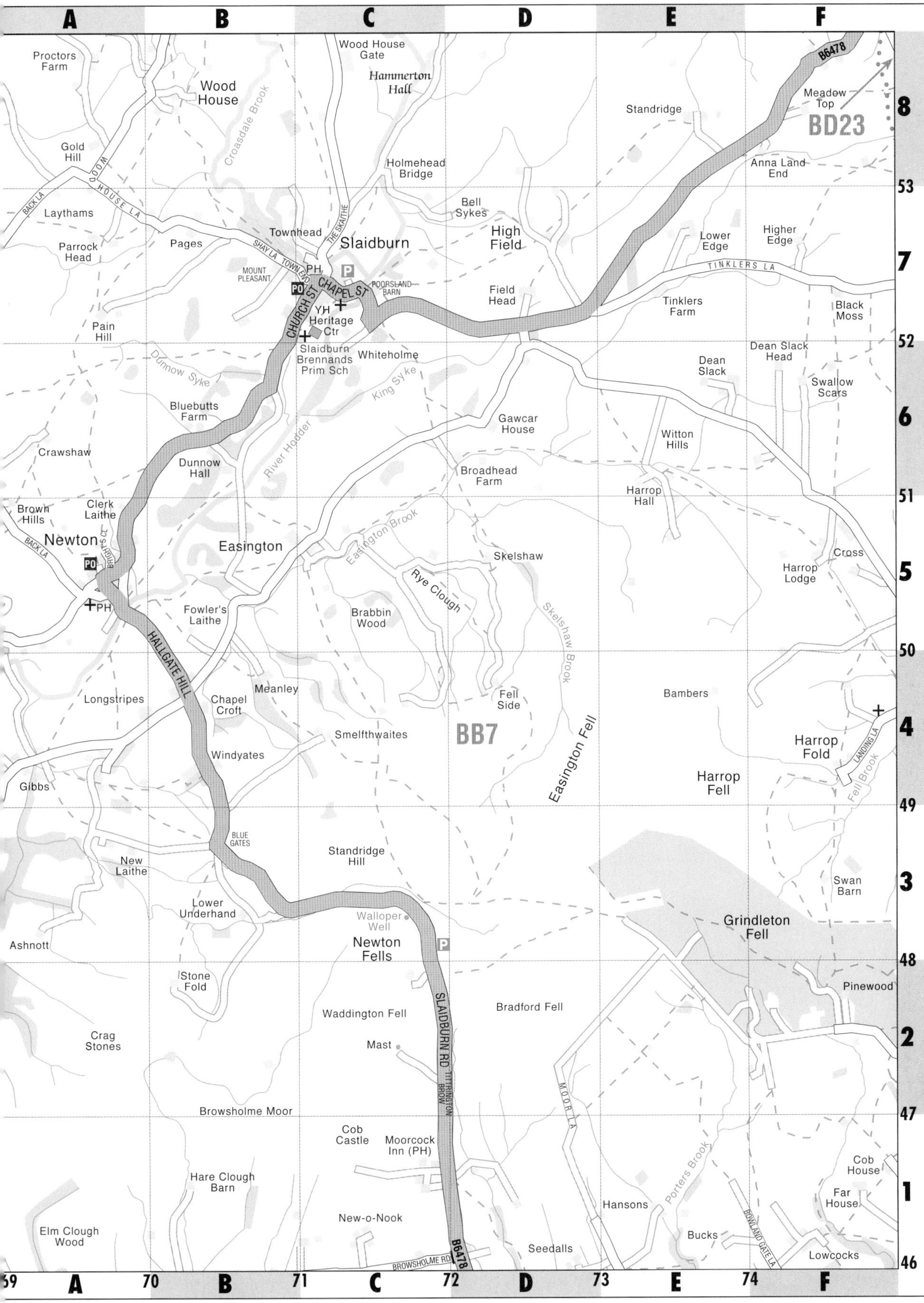

229
236

Scale: 1¾ inches to 1 mile
0 ¼ ½ mile
0 250m 500m 750m 1 km

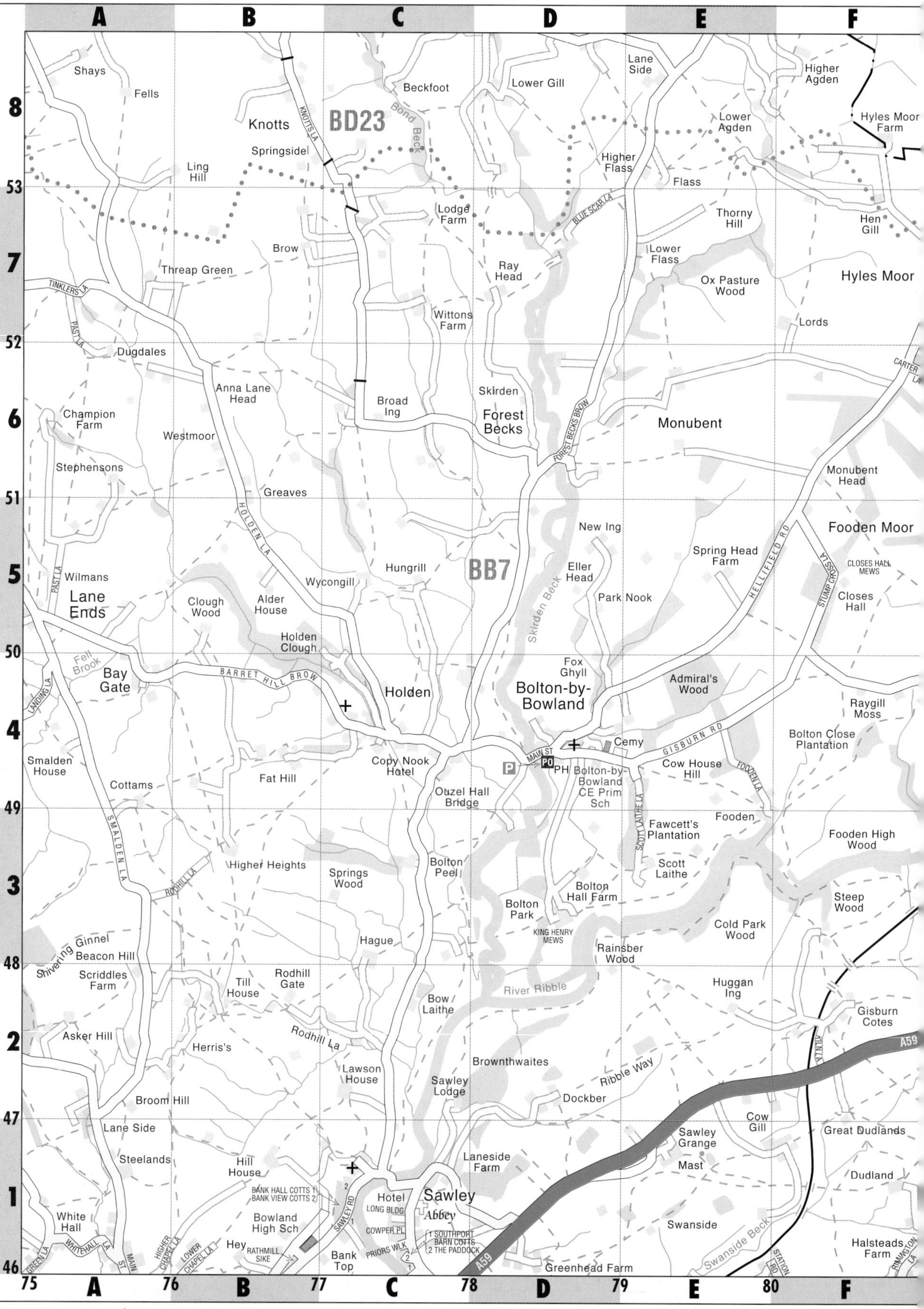


229
190
191

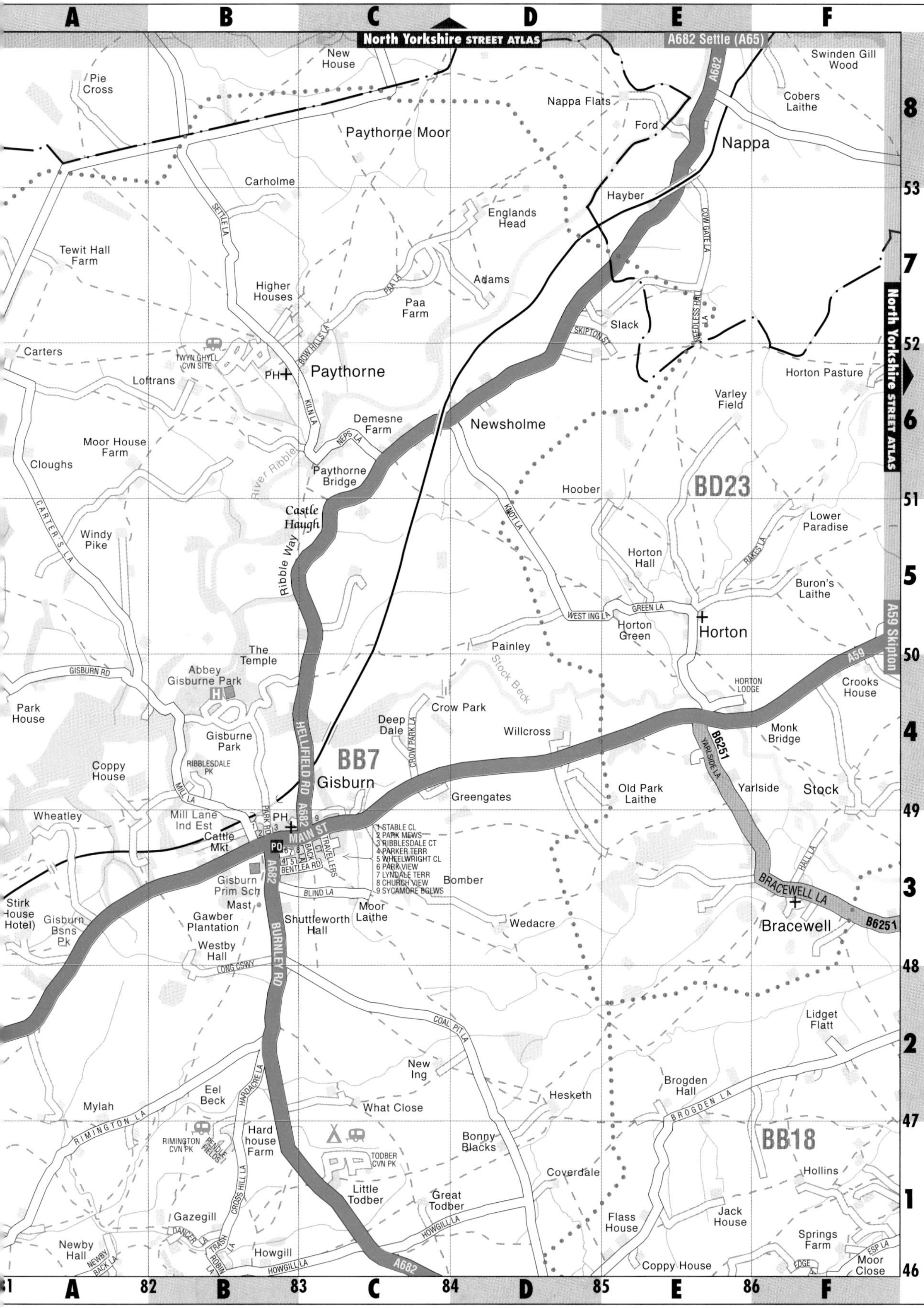
A
B
C
D
E
F
North Yorkshire STREET ATLAS
A682 Settle (A65)
New House
Pie Cross
Swinden Gill Wood
Cobers Laithe
Nappa Flats
Ford
Nappa
Paythorne Moor
Carholme
Hayber
Englands Head
Tewit Hall Farm
SETTLE LA
COW GATE LA
Adams
Higher Houses
PAA LA
Paa Farm
Slack
SKIPTON ST
NEEDLESS HALL LA
Carters
TWYN GHYLL CVN SITE
BOW HILLS LA
PH
Paythorne
Loftrans
Horton Pasture
Varley Field
KILN LA
Demesne Farm
NEPS LA
Newsholme
Moor House Farm
Cloughs
River Ribble
Paythorne Bridge
Hoober
BD23
Castle Haugh
Lower Paradise
CARTER'S LA
Windy Pike
KNOT LA
RAKES LA
Ribble Way
Horton Hall
Buron's Laithe
GREEN LA
WEST ING LA
Horton Green
Horton
A59 Skipton
The Temple
Painley
Abbey
Gisburne Park
GISBURN RD
Stock Beck
HORTON LODGE
A59
Crooks House
Park House
Crow Park
Deep Dale
Willcross
Monk Bridge
Gisburne Park
CROW PARK LA
BB7
B6251
YARLSIDE LA
Coppy House
RIBBLESDALE PK
HELLIFIELD RD
A682
Gisburn
Old Park Laithe
Yarlside
Stock
MILL LA
Greengates
Wheatley
Mill Lane Ind Est
PARK RD
PH
MAIN ST
Cattle Mkt
PO
BACK LA
TRAVELLERS CT
BENTLEA RD
1 STABLE CL
2 PARK MEWS
3 RIBBLESDALE CT
4 PARKER TERR
5 WHEELWRIGHT CL
6 PARK VIEW
7 LYNDALE TERR
8 CHURCH VIEW
9 SYCAMORE BGLWS
HALL LA
Bomber
BRACEWELL LA
Gisburn Prim Sch
BLIND LA
Stirk House (Hotel)
Mast
Moor Laithe
Bracewell
B6251
Gisburn Bsns Pk
Gawber Plantation
Shuttleworth Hall
Wedacre
BURNLEY RD
Westby Hall
LONG CSWY
Lidget Flatt
COAL PIT LA
New Ing
Eel Beck
HARDACRE LA
Brogden Hall
Hesketh
Mylah
What Close
BROGDEN LA
RIMINGTON LA
Hard house Farm
BB18
RIMINGTON CVN PK
PENDLE FIELDS
TODBER CVN PK
Bonny Blacks
Hollins
CROSS HILL LA
Coverdale
Little Todber
Great Todber
Gazegill
Flass House
Jack House
Springs Farm
HOWGILL LA
DANCER LA
Newby Hall
NEWBY BACK LA
TRASH LA
ROBIN LA
Howgill
HOWGILL LA
A682
Coppy House
EDGE
ESP LA
Moor Close
8
53
7
52
6
51
5
50
4
49
3
48
2
47
1
46
81
82
83
84
85
86

215
211
237

Scale: 1¾ inches to 1 mile
0 ¼ ½ mile
0 250m 500m 750m 1 km

A
B
C
D
E
F
8
61
7
60
6
59
5
58
4
57
3
56
2
55
1
54
51
52
53
54
55
56
Mast
QUERNMORE RD
POSTERN GATE RD
FRIAR'S MOSS RD
Corney Hill Farm
Friar's Moss Farm
Knotts Farm
Askew Hill
LITTLEDALE RD
Baines Cragg
The Cragg
Cragg Wood
Littledale Hall
Foxdale Beck
Bellhill Farm
Field Head
Littledale
Stock-a-Bank
River Gander
Greenlot
Windy Clough
Wisp Hill
Udale Beck
Conder Head
Quernmore CE Prim Sch
RIGG LA
Black Fell
Far Lodge
Fell End Farm
Clougha Scar
Clougha
Narr Lodge
Clougha Pike
Brownley Hill
Rowton Brook
WYRESDALE RD
Rowton Brook Fell
Quernmore
PO
QUERNMORE BROW
Brow Top Farm
Shooters Pile
LONG LA
Terrace Farm
Grit Fell
Gibson's Farm
Middle Brow Top
Hare Appletree Fell
Burrow Hill
Grizedale Head
Hare Appletree
BAY HORSE RD
Lower Browtop
LA2
Damas Gill
Abbeystead Fell
Lee Fell
Blackwood End
Rotten Hill
Twr
Westfield House
Longmoor
Castle o' Trim
Higher Moor Head
High Moor Cross
River Grizedale
Yeat House Farm
Gate House Bridge
PROCTER MOSS RD
Grizedale Barn
Lower Moor Head
Damas Gill
Lower Castle o' Trim
Tills Farm
Balderstones
RAKEHOUSE BROW
Lee
Brook House
ABBEYSTEAD LA
Borwicks
Grizedale Bridge
LOWER LEE
Middle Crag
Summer House Head
Lee Bridge
Tarnbrook Wyre
Hollyhead Farm
Gallows Clough
PLANTATION LA
Chapel House Farm
LONG LA
Abbeystead
Ortner
Cawthorne's Endowed Sch
STRAIT LA
ABBEYSTEAD RD
SMITHY BROW
THE RAKE
DOEHOLME RAKE
Doeholme Farm
Lower Green Bank
River Wyre
Starbank
Lentworth Hall
Abbeystead Resr

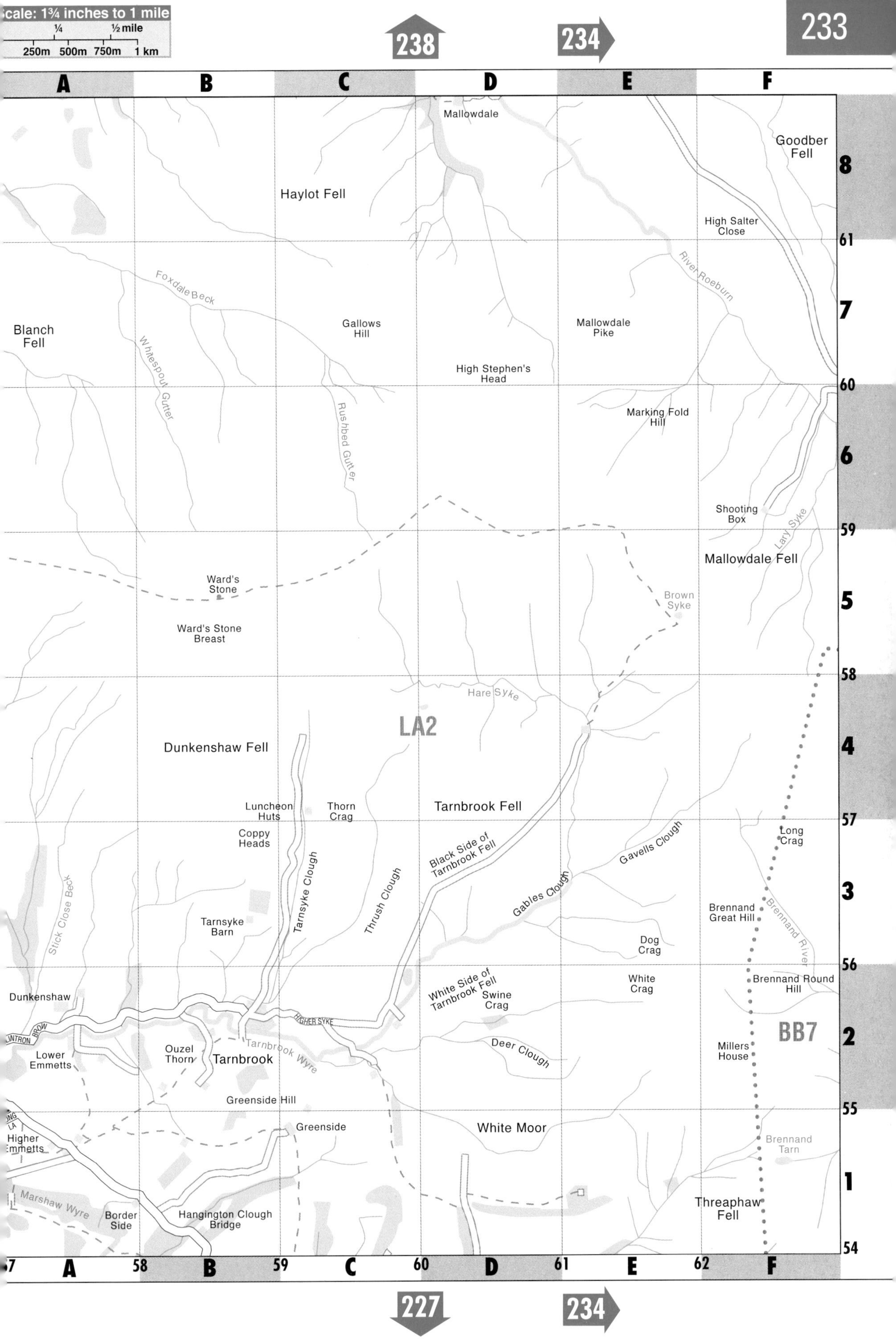
Scale: 1¾ inches to 1 mile
¼
½ mile
250m 500m 750m 1 km
238
234
A
B
C
D
E
F
Mallowdale
Goodber Fell
Haylot Fell
High Salter Close
Foxdale Beck
River Roeburn
Blanch Fell
Whitespout Gutter
Gallows Hill
Mallowdale Pike
High Stephen's Head
Rushbed Gutter
Marking Fold Hill
Shooting Box
Lary Syke
Mallowdale Fell
Ward's Stone
Brown Syke
Ward's Stone Breast
Hare Syke
LA2
Dunkenshaw Fell
Luncheon Huts
Thorn Crag
Tarnbrook Fell
Coppy Heads
Black Side of Tarnbrook Fell
Gavells Clough
Long Crag
Tarnsyke Clough
Thrush Clough
Gables Clough
Stick Close Beck
Tarnsyke Barn
Brennand Great Hill
Brennand River
Dog Crag
White Crag
Brennand Round Hill
Dunkenshaw
White Side of Tarnbrook Fell
Swine Crag
HIGHER SYKE
BB7
Millers House
Lower Emmetts
Ouzel Thorn
Tarnbrook
Tarnbrook Wyre
Deer Clough
Greenside Hill
Greenside
White Moor
Higher Emmetts
Brennand Tarn
Marshaw Wyre
Border Side
Hangington Clough Bridge
Threaphaw Fell
8
61
7
60
6
59
5
58
4
57
3
56
2
55
1
54
57
58
59
60
61
62
227
234

233
239

Scale: 1¾ inches to 1 mil

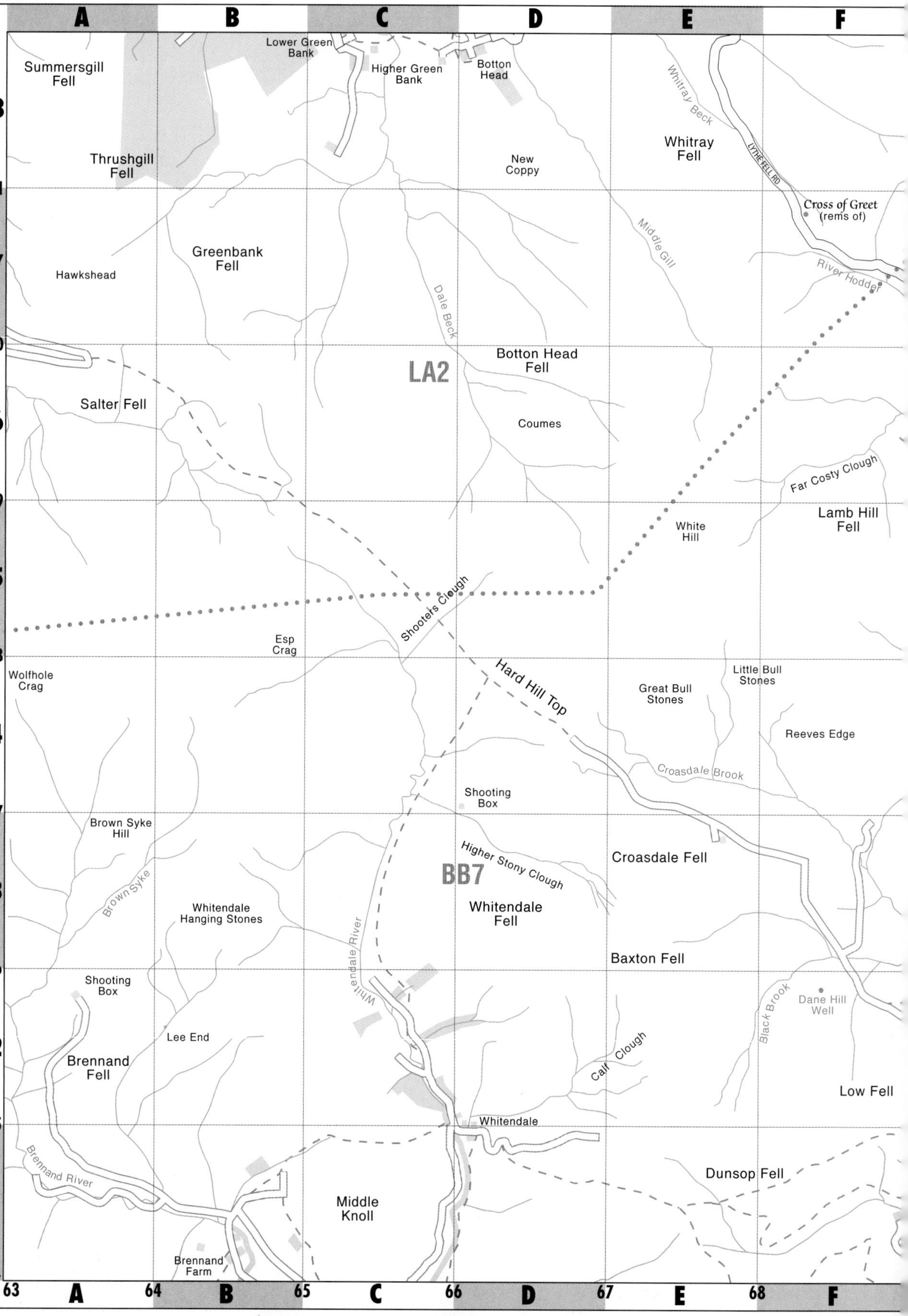
A
B
C
D
E
F
Summersgill Fell
Lower Green Bank
Higher Green Bank
Botton Head
Whitray Beck
Whitray Fell
Lythe Fell Rd
Thrushgill Fell
New Coppy
Cross of Greet (rems of)
Middle Gill
Greenbank Fell
Hawkshead
River Hodder
Dale Beck
Botton Head Fell
LA2
Salter Fell
Coumes
Far Costy Clough
Lamb Hill Fell
White Hill
Shooters Clough
Esp Crag
Wolfhole Crag
Hard Hill Top
Little Bull Stones
Great Bull Stones
Reeves Edge
Croasdale Brook
Shooting Box
Brown Syke Hill
Higher Stony Clough
Croasdale Fell
BB7
Brown Syke
Whitendale Hanging Stones
Whitendale Fell
Whitendale River
Baxton Fell
Shooting Box
Black Brook
Dane Hill Well
Lee End
Brennand Fell
Calf Clough
Low Fell
Whitendale
Brennand River
Dunsop Fell
Middle Knoll
Brennand Farm
8
61
7
60
6
59
5
58
4
57
3
56
2
55
1
54
63
64
65
66
67
68

233
228

Scale: 1¾ inches to 1 mile
¼ ½ mile
250m 500m 750m 1 km

236

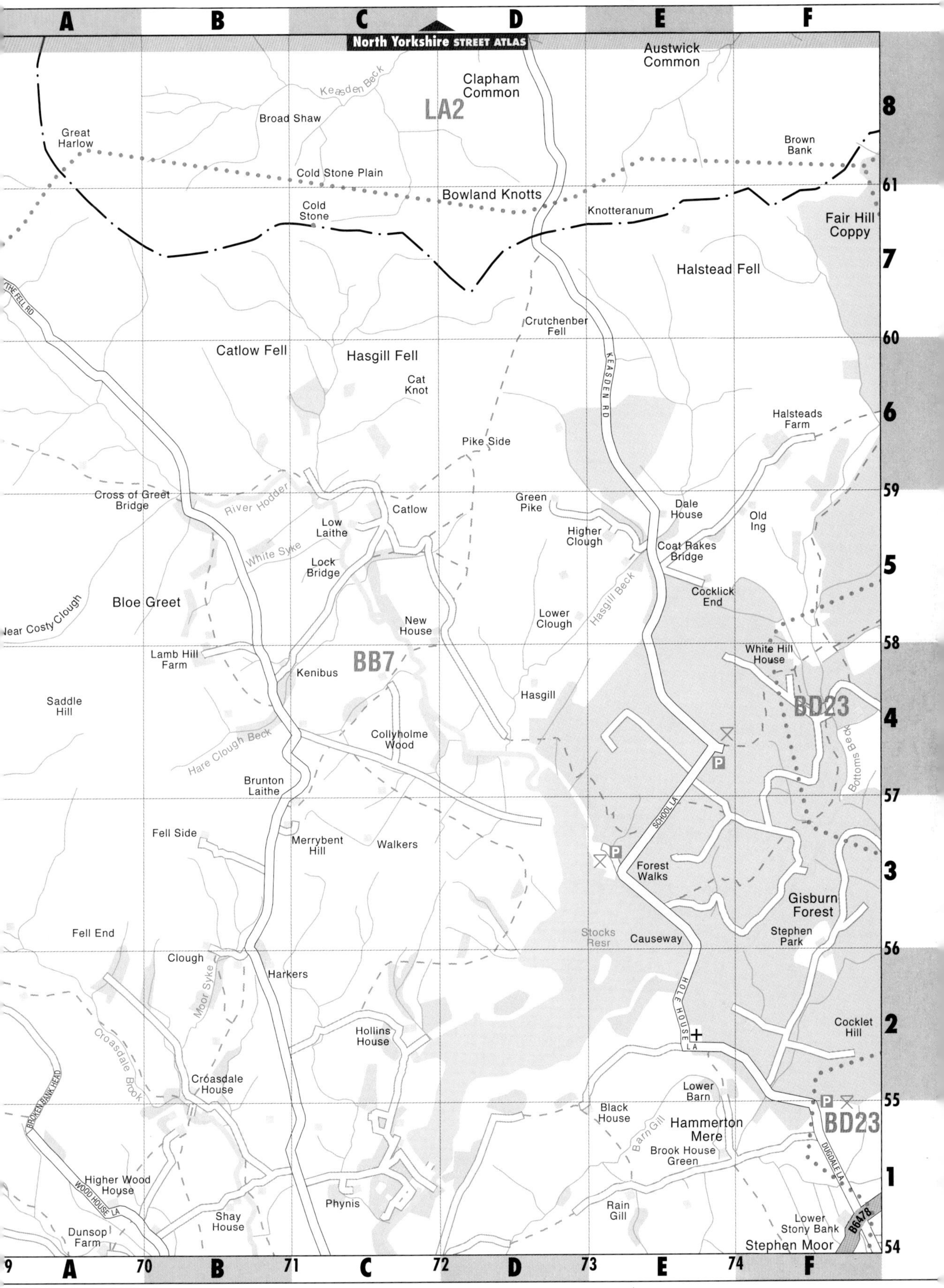


229
236

235

Scale: 1¾ inches to 1 mil
0 ¼ ½ mile
0 250m 500m 750m 1 km

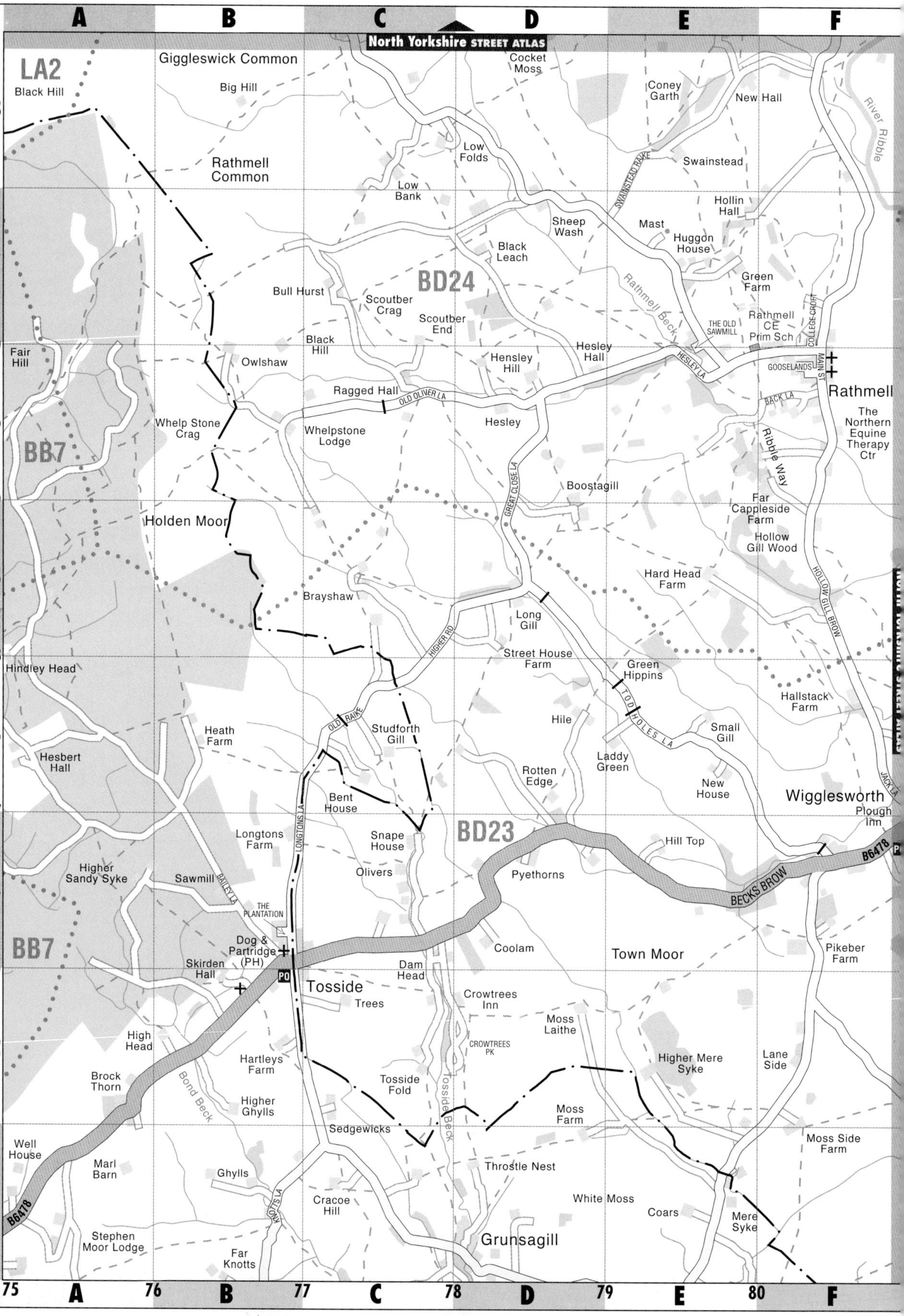

A B C D E F
North Yorkshire STREET ATLAS
8
61
7
60
6
59
5
58
4
57
3
56
2
55
1
54
75 A 76 B 77 C 78 D 79 E 80 F
LA2
Black Hill
Giggleswick Common
Big Hill
Cocket Moss
Coney Garth
New Hall
River Ribble
Low Folds
Rathmell Common
Swainstead
SWAINSTEAD RAKE
Low Bank
Hollin Hall
Sheep Wash
Mast
Huggon House
Black Leach
BD24
Rathmell Beck
Green Farm
Bull Hurst
Scoutber Crag
Scoutber End
COLLEGE CROFT
Rathmell CE Prim Sch
THE OLD SAWMILL
Fair Hill
Black Hill
Hesley Hall
HESLEY LA
GOOSELANDS
MAIN ST
Owlshaw
Hensley Hill
Rathmell
Ragged Hall
OLD OLIVER LA
BACK LA
Whelp Stone Crag
Whelpstone Lodge
Hesley
The Northern Equine Therapy Ctr
BB7
Ribble Way
GREAT CLOSE LA
Boostagill
Holden Moor
Far Cappleside Farm
Hollow Gill Wood
Hard Head Farm
HOLLOW GILL BROW
Brayshaw
Long Gill
Street House Farm
HIGHER RD
Hindley Head
Green Hippins
Hallstack Farm
TOD HOLES LA
OLD RAIKE
Studforth Gill
Hile
Heath Farm
Small Gill
Hesbert Hall
Laddy Green
Rotten Edge
New House
Bent House
JACK LA
Wigglesworth
Plough Inn
Longtons Farm
Snape House
BD23
Hill Top
LONGTONS LA
B6478
Higher Sandy Syke
Olivers
Pyethorns
Sawmill
BAILEY LA
BECKS BROW
THE PLANTATION
BB7
Dog & Partridge (PH)
Coolam
Town Moor
Pikeber Farm
Skirden Hall
Dam Head
PO
Tosside
Trees
Crowtrees Inn
Moss Laithe
High Head
CROWTREES PK
Higher Mere Syke
Lane Side
Hartleys Farm
Brock Thorn
Bond Beck
Tosside Fold
Higher Ghylls
Tosside Beck
Moss Farm
Well House
Sedgewicks
Moss Side Farm
Marl Barn
Ghylls
Throstle Nest
KNOTTS LA
White Moss
Cracoe Hill
Coars
B6478
Mere Syke
Stephen Moor Lodge
Grunsagill
Far Knotts


235

230

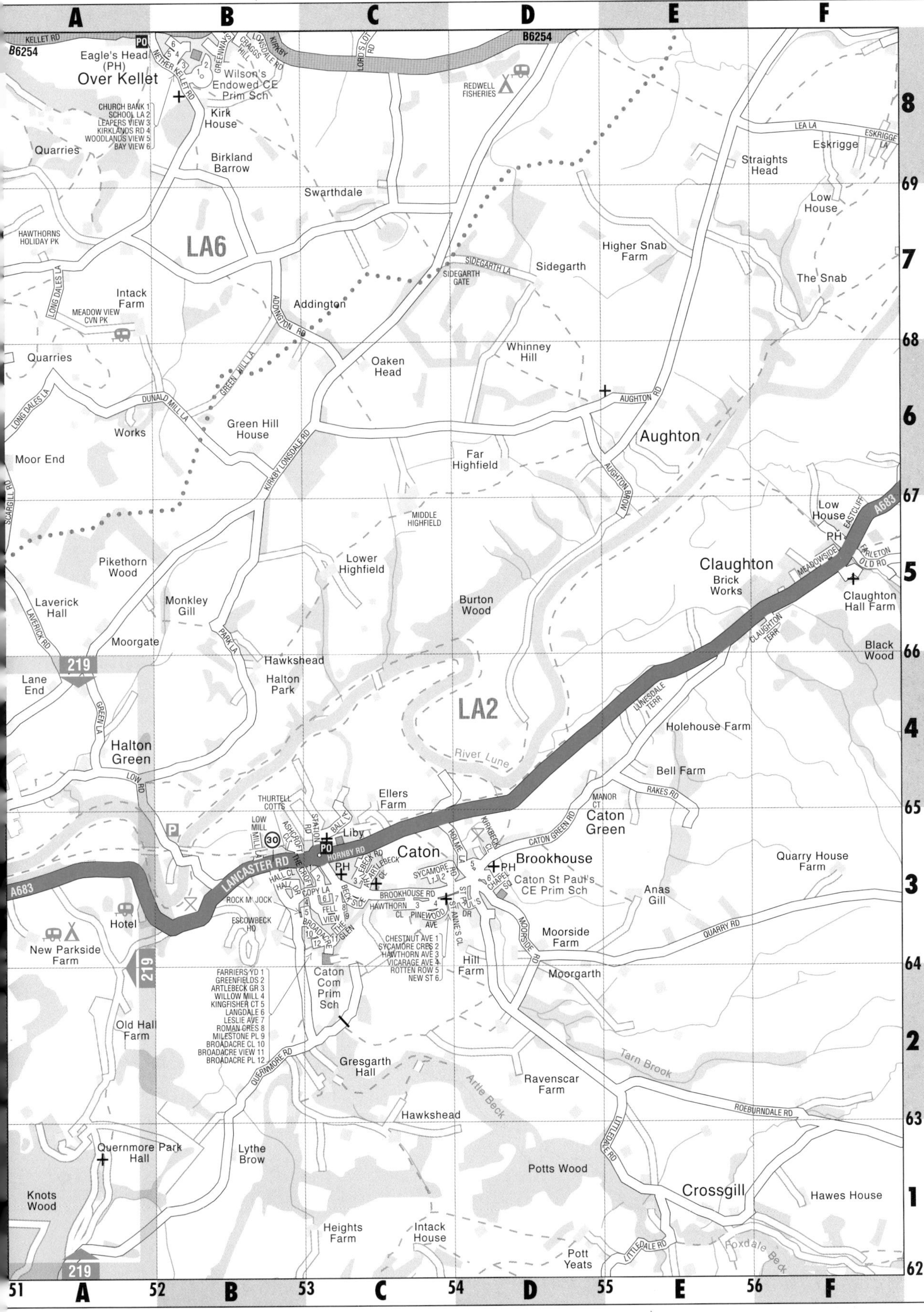
A
B
C
D
E
F
KELLET RD
B6254
Eagle's Head
(PH)
Over Kellet
NETHER KELLET RD
GREENWAYS
CRAGGS HILL
LONSDALE RD
KIRKBY
Wilson's
Endowed CE
Prim Sch
LORD'S LOT RD
B6254
REDWELL
FISHERIES
CHURCH BANK 1
SCHOOL LA 2
LEAPERS VIEW 3
KIRKLANDS RD 4
WOODLANDS VIEW 5
BAY VIEW 6
Kirk
House
Quarries
Birkland
Barrow
Swarthdale
LEA LA
ESKRIGGE LA
Eskrigge
Straights
Head
Low
House
HAWTHORNS
HOLIDAY PK
LA6
Higher Snab
Farm
SIDEGARTH LA
SIDEGARTH
GATE
Sidegarth
The Snab
LONG DALES LA
Intack
Farm
MEADOW VIEW
CVN PK
Addington
ADDINGTON RD
Quarries
Oaken
Head
Whinney
Hill
GREEN HILL LA
DUNALD MILL LA
AUGHTON RD
LONG DALES LA
Works
Green Hill
House
KIRKBY LONSDALE RD
Aughton
Moor End
Far
Highfield
AUGHTON BROW
SCARGILL RD
MIDDLE
HIGHFIELD
Low
House
EASTCLIFF
A683
PH
Lower
Highfield
Claughton
Brick
Works
MEADOWSIDE
FARLETON
OLD RD
Pikethorn
Wood
Claughton
Hall Farm
Laverick
Hall
Monkley
Gill
Burton
Wood
LAVERICK RD
PARK LA
CLAUGHTON TERR
Moorgate
Black
Wood
219
Hawkshead
Lane
End
Halton
Park
GREEN LA
LA2
LUNESDALE TERR
Holehouse Farm
Halton
Green
River Lune
Bell Farm
LOW RD
RAKES RD
THURTELL
COTTS
Ellers
Farm
MANOR CT
Caton
Green
LOW MILL
ASHCROFT CL
STATION RD
BALL LA
Liby
HOLME LA
KIRKBECK CL
CATON GREEN RD
30
PO
HORNBY RD
Caton
Brookhouse
Quarry House
Farm
LANCASTER RD
ARTLEBECK RD
PH
PH
A683
HALL CL
HALL DR
THE CROFT
COPY LA
SYCAMORE RD
Caton St Paul's
CE Prim Sch
CHAPEL SQ
ROCK M' JOCK
BECK SIDE
BROOKHOUSE RD
Anas
Gill
HAWTHORN CL
PINEWOOD AVE
ST ANNE'S CL
ST PAUL'S DR
FELL VIEW
QUARRY RD
Hotel
ESCOWBECK
HQ
BROADACRE
THE GLEN
Moorside
Farm
MOORSIDE RD
New Parkside
Farm
CHESTNUT AVE 1
SYCAMORE CRES 2
HAWTHORN AVE 3
VICARAGE AVE 4
ROTTEN ROW 5
NEW ST 6
Hill
Farm
Moorgarth
219
FARRIERS YD 1
GREENFIELDS 2
ARTLEBECK GR 3
WILLOW MILL 4
KINGFISHER CT 5
LANGDALE 6
LESLIE AVE 7
ROMAN CRES 8
MILESTONE PL 9
BROADACRE CL 10
BROADACRE VIEW 11
BROADACRE PL 12
Caton
Com
Prim
Sch
Old Hall
Farm
Tarn Brook
QUERNMORE RD
Gresgarth
Hall
Ravenscar
Farm
Artle Beck
ROEBURNDALE RD
Hawkshead
LITTLEDALE RD
Quernmore Park
Hall
Lythe
Brow
Potts Wood
Crossgill
Hawes House
Knots
Wood
Heights
Farm
Intack
House
Pott
Yeats
LITTLEDALE RD
Foxdale Beck
219
8
69
7
68
6
67
5
66
4
65
3
64
2
63
1
62
51
52
53
54
55
56

237
241

Scale: 1¾ inches to 1 mile
0 ¼ ½ mile
0 250m 500m 750m 1 km

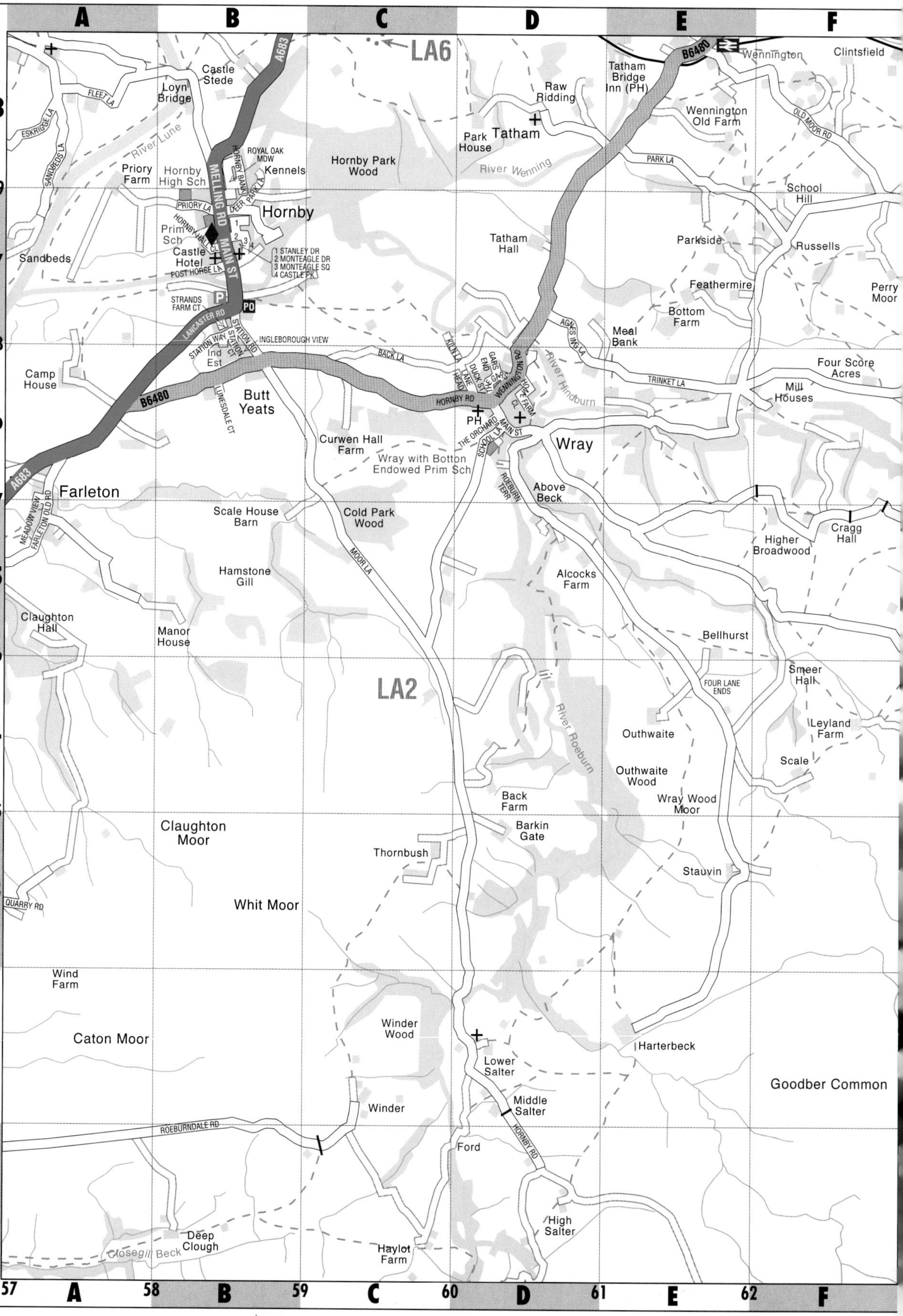
A
B
C
D
E
F
LA6
A683
Castle Stede
Loyn Bridge
FLEET LA
ESKRIGGE LA
SANDBEDS LA
River Lune
Priory Farm
Hornby High Sch
MELLING RD
MAIN ST
HORNBY BANK
ROYAL OAK MDW
Kennels
DEER PARK LA
PRIORY LA
Hornby
HORNBY HALL CL
Prim Sch
Castle Hotel
POST HORSE LA
1 STANLEY DR
2 MONTEAGLE DR
3 MONTEAGLE SQ
4 CASTLE PK
Sandbeds
STRANDS FARM CT
P
PO
LANCASTER RD
STATION WAY
STATION CT
STATION RD
INGLEBOROUGH VIEW
Ind Est
Camp House
B6480
LUNESDALE CT
Butt Yeats
Hornby Park Wood
Raw Ridding
Tatham
Park House
River Wenning
Tatham Hall
Tatham Bridge Inn (PH)
B6480
Wennington
Clintsfield
Wennington Old Farm
OLD MOOR RD
PARK LA
School Hill
Parkside
Russells
Feathermire
Perry Moor
Bottom Farm
Meal Bank
AGNES ING LA
Four Score Acres
TRINKET LA
Mill Houses
BACK LA
KILN LA
LANE HEAD
DUCK ST
GARS END
WENNINGTON RD
HORNBY RD
PH
River Hindburn
HOLME FARM CL
THE ORCHARD
SCHOOL LA
MAIN ST
Wray
Curwen Hall Farm
Wray with Botton Endowed Prim Sch
ROEBURN TERR
Above Beck
Farleton
MEADOW VIEW
FARLETON OLD RD
Scale House Barn
Cold Park Wood
MOOR LA
Higher Broadwood
Cragg Hall
Alcocks Farm
Hamstone Gill
Claughton Hall
Manor House
Bellhurst
Smeer Hall
FOUR LANE ENDS
LA2
River Roeburn
Leyland Farm
Outhwaite
Outhwaite Wood
Scale
Back Farm
Wray Wood Moor
Barkin Gate
Claughton Moor
Thornbush
Stauvin
QUARRY RD
Whit Moor
Wind Farm
Caton Moor
Winder Wood
Harterbeck
Lower Salter
Goodber Common
Middle Salter
Winder
ROEBURNDALE RD
HORNBY RD
Ford
High Salter
Deep Clough
Closegill Beck
Haylot Farm
8
69
7
68
6
67
5
66
4
65
3
64
2
63
1
62
57
58
59
60
61
62

237
233

Scale: 1¾ inches to 1 mile
¼ ½ mile
250m 500m 750m 1 km

242

B8
1 CHEAPSIDE
2 BANK COTT
3 CROWTREES
4 EAST VIEW
5 BAYNES COTTS
6 GREENFOOT
7 GREEN HEAD COTTS
8 THE TERRACE
9 VICTORIA BLDGS
10 COLLINGWOOD DR

D8
1 PINEWOOD COTTS
2 ASHFIELD COTTS
3 TWEED STREET CT
4 TWEED ST
5 SUNNYSIDE
6 MILL GDNS
7 COLLINGWOOD TERR
8 GRASMERE CL
9 GRASMERE DR
10 BANKS RISE
11 LAKEBER CL
12 BANKS WAY
13 LAKEBER DR
14 INGLEBOROUGH VIEW
15 GOODENBER CRES
16 BUTTERBERGH
17 HIGHCROFT
18 POLICE YARD
19 JUBILEE BLDGS

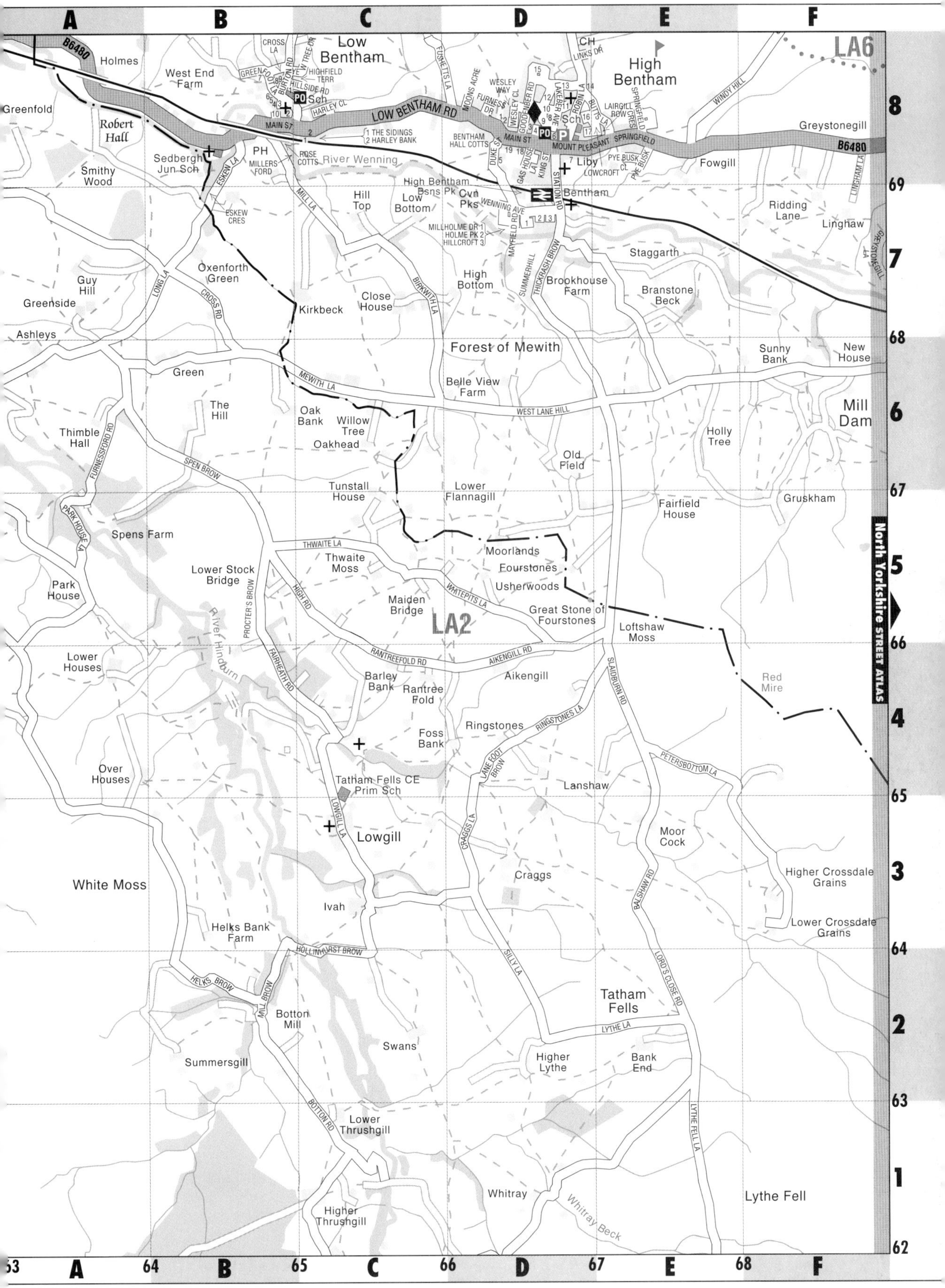


234

Scale: 1¾ inches to 1 mile
0 ¼ ½ mile
0 250m 500m 750m 1 km

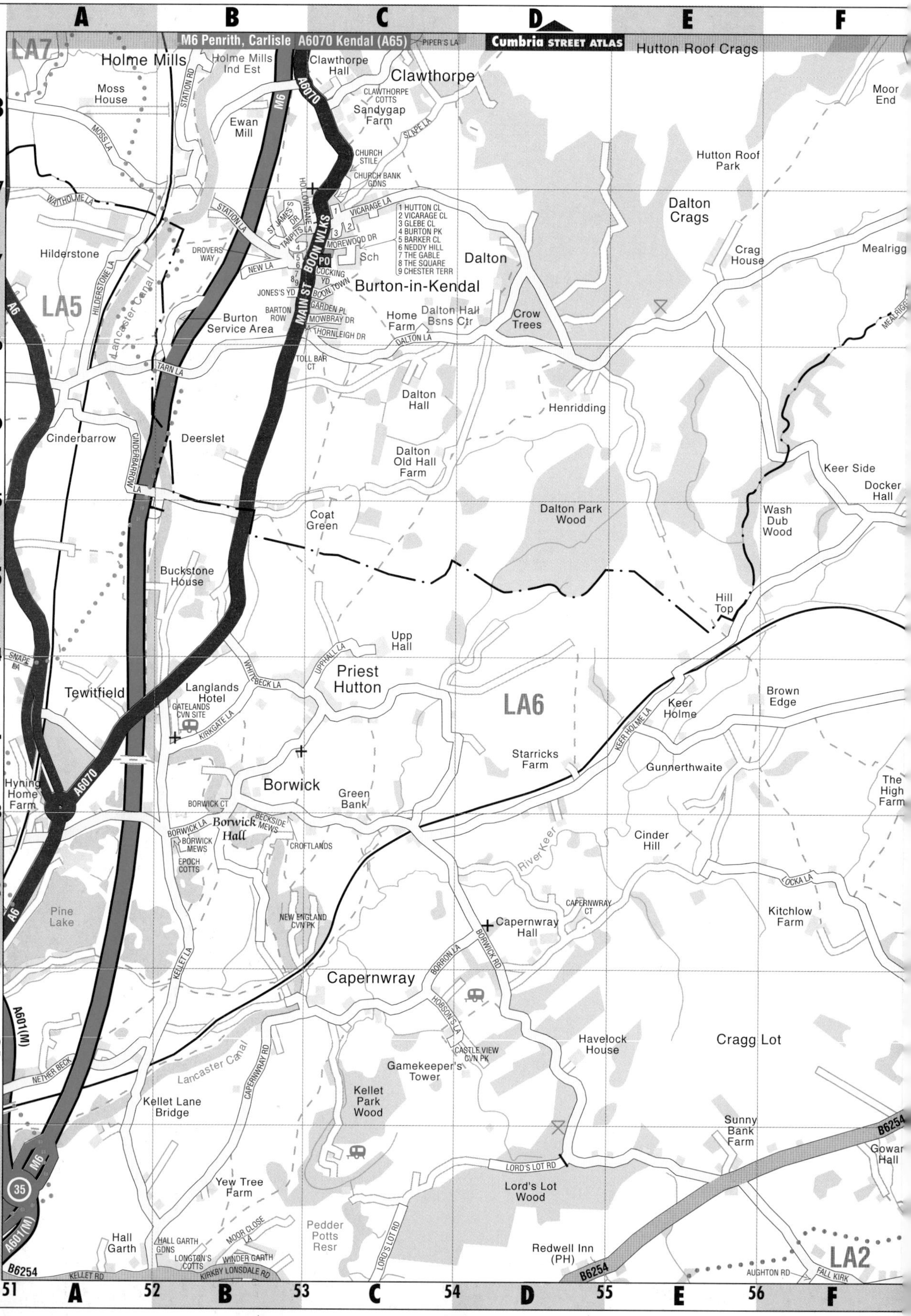
A
B
C
D
E
F
M6 Penrith, Carlisle
A6070 Kendal (A65)
PIPER'S LA
Cumbria STREET ATLAS
Hutton Roof Crags
LA7
Holme Mills
Holme Mills Ind Est
Clawthorpe Hall
Clawthorpe
Moss House
STATION RD
CLAWTHORPE COTTS
Sandygap Farm
Moor End
Ewan Mill
MOSS LA
SLAPE LA
CHURCH STILE
Hutton Roof Park
CHURCH BANK GDNS
HOLLOWAYANE
WATHOLME LA
STATION LA
ST JAMES'S DR
VICARAGE LA
1 HUTTON CL
2 VICARAGE CL
3 GLEBE CL
4 BURTON PK
5 BARKER CL
6 NEDDY HILL
7 THE GABLE
8 THE SQUARE
9 CHESTER TERR
Dalton Crags
TANPITS LA
MOREWOOD DR
Crag House
Mealrigg
Hilderstone
DROVERS WAY
Sch
Dalton
NEW LA
MAIN ST
BOON WLKS
PO
COCKING YD
BOON TOWN
Burton-in-Kendal
LA5
HILDERSTONE LA
JONES'S YD
Lancaster Canal
BARTON ROW
GARDEN PL
MOWBRAY DR
Burton Service Area
Home Farm
Dalton Hall Bsns Ctr
Crow Trees
MEALRIGG
THORNLEIGH DR
DALTON LA
TARN LA
TOLL BAR CT
Dalton Hall
Henridding
Cinderbarrow
CINDERBARROW LA
Deerslet
Dalton Old Hall Farm
Keer Side
Docker Hall
Coat Green
Dalton Park Wood
Wash Dub Wood
Buckstone House
Hill Top
SNAPE LA
Upp Hall
UPPHALL LA
WHITEBECK LA
Priest Hutton
Tewitfield
Langlands Hotel
LA6
Keer Holme
Brown Edge
GATELANDS CVN SITE
KIRKGATE LA
KEER HOLME LA
Starricks Farm
Gunnerthwaite
Hyning Home Farm
A6070
Borwick
Green Bank
The High Farm
BORWICK CT
BORWICK LA
Borwick Hall
BECKSIDE MEWS
BORWICK MEWS
CROFTLANDS
River Keer
Cinder Hill
EPOCH COTTS
A6
COCKA LA
Pine Lake
NEW ENGLAND CVN PK
CAPERNWRAY CT
Capernwray Hall
Kitchlow Farm
KELLET LA
BORRON LA
BORWICK RD
Capernwray
A601(M)
HORSON'S LA
Havelock House
Cragg Lot
CASTLE VIEW CVN PK
NETHER BECK
Lancaster Canal
CAPERNWRAY RD
Gamekeeper's Tower
Kellet Lane Bridge
Kellet Park Wood
Sunny Bank Farm
B6254
Gowan Hall
M6
35
LORD'S LOT RD
Yew Tree Farm
Lord's Lot Wood
Pedder Potts Resr
MOOR CLOSE LA
LORD'S LOT RD
Hall Garth
HALL GARTH GDNS
LONGTON'S COTTS
WINDER GARTH
KIRKBY LONSDALE RD
Redwell Inn (PH)
LA2
B6254
KELLET RD
AUGHTON RD
FALL KIRK
8
77
7
76
6
75
5
74
4
73
3
72
2
71
1
70
51
52
53
54
55
56

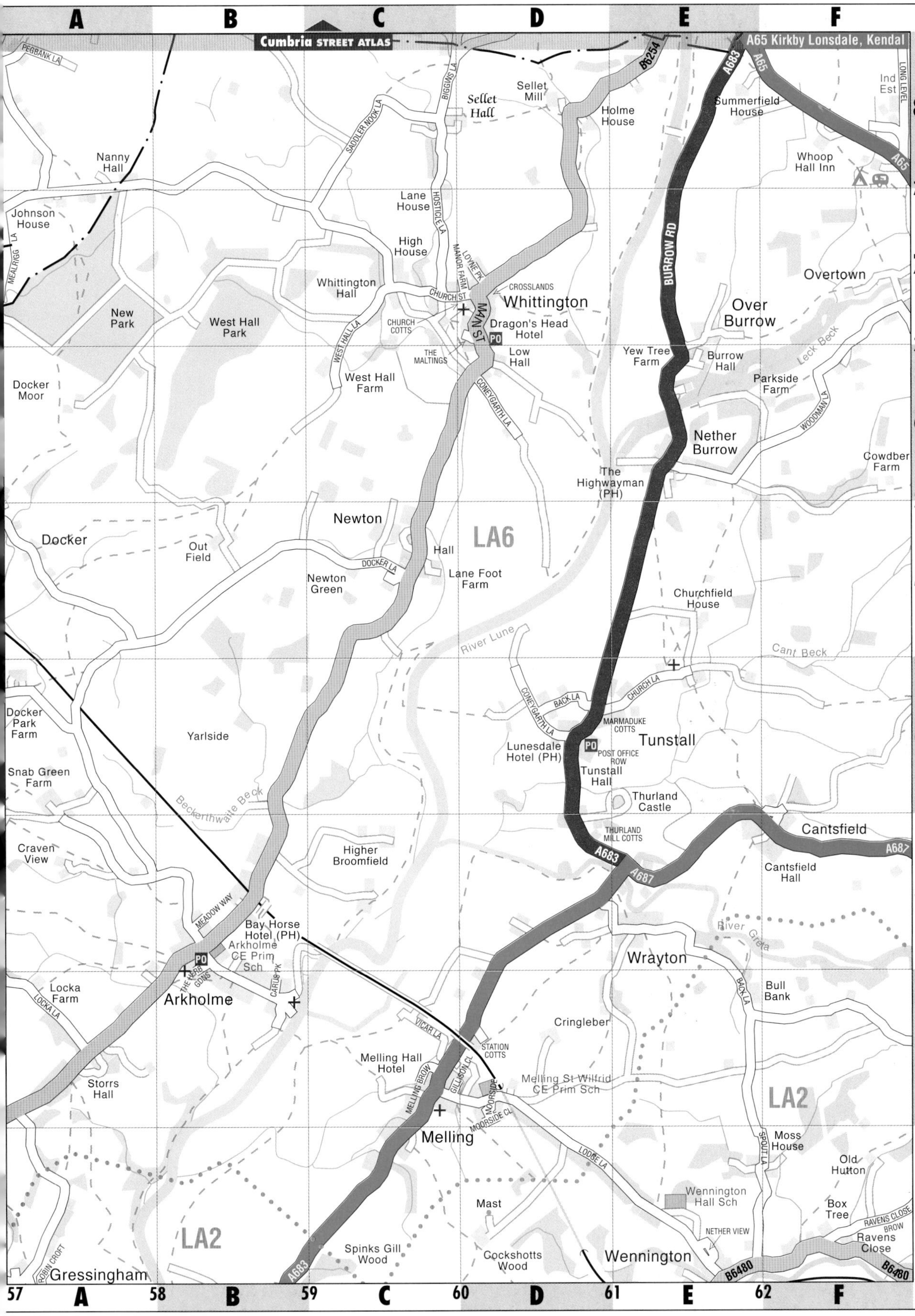
A
B
C
D
E
F
Cumbria STREET ATLAS
A65 Kirkby Lonsdale, Kendal
8
77
7
76
6
75
5
74
4
73
3
72
2
71
1
70
57
58
59
60
61
62
PEGBANK LA
Nanny Hall
SADDLER NOOK LA
BIGGINS LA
Sellet Hall
Sellet Mill
B6254
A683
A65
Holme House
Summerfield House
Ind Est
LONG LEVEL
Whoop Hall Inn
Johnson House
Lane House
HOSTICLE LA
High House
MANOR FARM
LOYNE PK
BURROW RD
MEALRIGG LA
Whittington Hall
CHURCH ST
CROSSLANDS
Whittington
Overtown
New Park
West Hall Park
WEST HALL LA
CHURCH COTTS
MAIN ST
Dragon's Head Hotel
PO
Over Burrow
Leck Beck
THE MALTINGS
Low Hall
Yew Tree Farm
Burrow Hall
Parkside Farm
Docker Moor
West Hall Farm
CONEYGARTH LA
WOODMAN LA
Nether Burrow
Cowdber Farm
The Highwayman (PH)
Newton
LA6
Docker
Out Field
Hall
DOCKER LA
Newton Green
Lane Foot Farm
Churchfield House
River Lune
Cant Beck
CHURCH LA
BACK LA
Docker Park Farm
MARMADUKE COTTS
Tunstall
Yarlside
Lunesdale Hotel (PH)
POST OFFICE ROW
Snab Green Farm
Tunstall Hall
Thurland Castle
Beckerthwaite Beck
THURLAND MILL COTTS
Cantsfield
A687
Craven View
Higher Broomfield
Cantsfield Hall
MEADOW WAY
Bay Horse Hotel (PH)
Arkholme CE Prim Sch
River Greta
Wrayton
Locka Farm
LOCKA LA
THE HERB GDNS
CARUS PK
Arkholme
Bull Bank
Cringleber
VICAR LA
STATION COTTS
Melling Hall Hotel
GILLISON CL
MELLING BROW
MOORSIDE
Melling St Wilfrid CE Prim Sch
Storrs Hall
LA2
MOORSIDE CL
Melling
LODGE LA
SPOUT LA
Moss House
Old Hutton
Mast
Wennington Hall Sch
Box Tree
RAVENS CLOSE BROW
NETHER VIEW
Ravens Close
ROBIN CROFT
Gressingham
Spinks Gill Wood
Cockshotts Wood
Wennington
B6480

241
243

Scale: 1¾ inches to 1 mile
0 ¼ ½ mile
0 250m 500m 750m 1 km

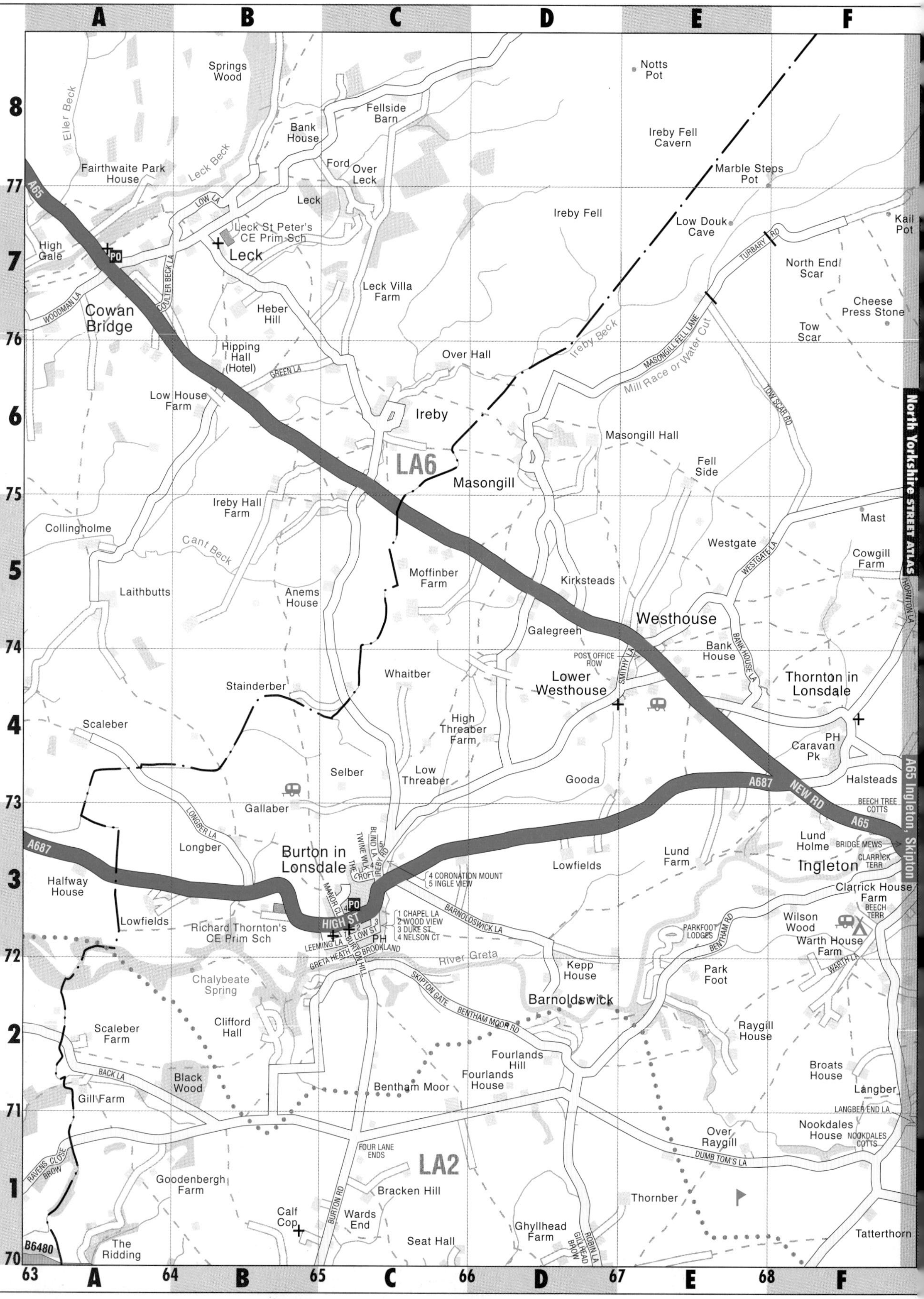
A
B
C
D
E
F
8
77
7
76
6
75
5
74
4
73
3
72
2
71
1
70
63
64
65
66
67
68
Springs Wood
Notts Pot
Eller Beck
Fellside Barn
Bank House
Ireby Fell Cavern
Leck Beck
Fairthwaite Park House
Ford
Over Leck
Marble Steps Pot
A65
Low La
Leck
Ireby Fell
Kail Pot
Low Douk Cave
Leck St Peter's CE Prim Sch
High Gale
PO
Turbary Rd
North End Scar
Coulter Beck La
Leck Villa Farm
Woodman La
Cowan Bridge
Heber Hill
Cheese Press Stone
Tow Scar
Ireby Beck
Masongill Fell Lane
Mill Race or Water Cut
Hipping Hall (Hotel)
Green La
Over Hall
Low House Farm
Ireby
Tow Scar Rd
North Yorkshire STREET ATLAS
Masongill Hall
Fell Side
LA6
Masongill
Ireby Hall Farm
Collingholme
Mast
Cant Beck
Westgate
Cowgill Farm
Westgate La
Laithbutts
Moffinber Farm
Kirksteads
Anems House
Thornton La
Westhouse
Galegreen
Bank House
Post Office Row
Smithy La
Bank House La
Whaitber
Lower Westhouse
Thornton in Lonsdale
Stainderber
High Threaber Farm
Scaleber
PH
Caravan Pk
Selber
Low Threaber
Gooda
Halsteads
A687
New Rd
Gallaber
Beech Tree Cotts
A65
A65 Ingleton, Skipton
Longber La
Blind La
Twine Wlk
Ireby Rd
Lund Holme
Bridge Mews
A687
Longber
Burton in Lonsdale
The Croft
Lund Farm
Clarrick Terr
Lowfields
Ingleton
Halfway House
4 Coronation Mount
5 Ingle View
Manor Cl
PO
Clarrick House Farm
Barnoldswick La
Beech Terr
High St
1 Chapel La
2 Wood View
3 Duke St
4 Nelson Ct
Parkfoot Lodges
Bentham Rd
Wilson Wood
Lowfields
Richard Thornton's CE Prim Sch
Low St
PH
Warth House Farm
Leeming La
Brookland
Greta Heath
Burton Hill
River Greta
Warth La
Chalybeate Spring
Kepp House
Park Foot
Skipton Gate
Barnoldswick
Bentham Moor Rd
Clifford Hall
Raygill House
Scaleber Farm
Fourlands Hill
Broats House
Back La
Black Wood
Fourlands House
Bentham Moor
Langber
Gill Farm
Langber End La
Nookdales House
Nookdales Cotts
Over Raygill
Ravens Close Brow
Four Lane Ends
LA2
Dumb Tom's La
Goodenbergh Farm
Bracken Hill
Thornber
Calf Cop
Burton Rd
Wards End
Ghyllhead Farm
Robin La
Gillhead Brow
Seat Hall
Tatterthorn
B6480
The Ridding

241
239

Scale: 1¾ inches to 1 mile
0 ¼ ½ mile
0 250m 500m 750m 1 km

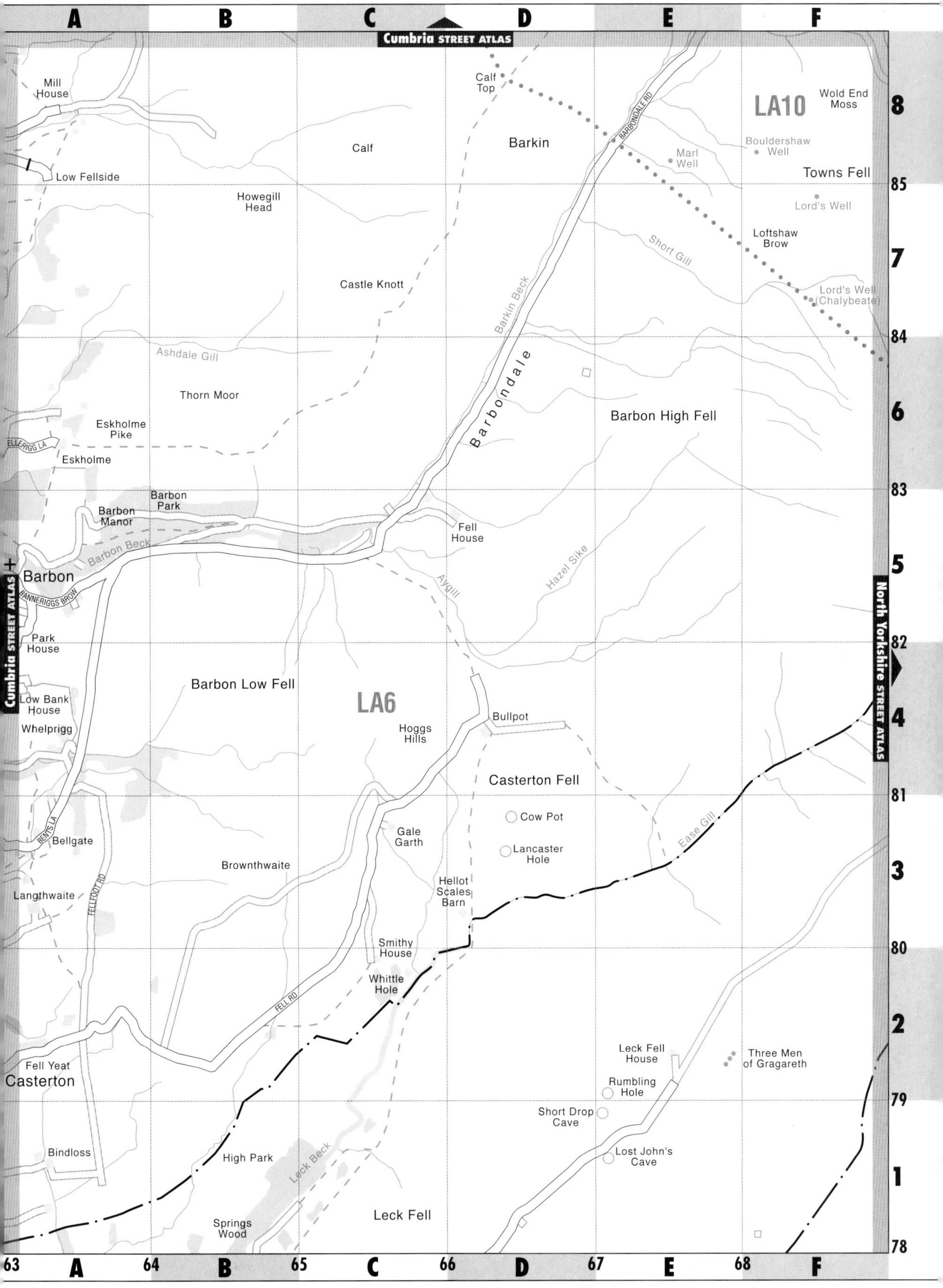
Cumbria STREET ATLAS
North Yorkshire STREET ATLAS
Cumbria STREET ATLAS
A
B
C
D
E
F
8
85
7
84
6
83
5
82
4
81
3
80
2
79
1
78
63
64
65
66
67
68
LA10
LA6
Mill House
Low Fellside
Calf Top
Calf
Barkin
BARBONDALE RD
Wold End Moss
Bouldershaw Well
Marl Well
Towns Fell
Lord's Well
Howegill Head
Loftshaw Brow
Short Gill
Castle Knott
Lord's Well (Chalybeate)
Barkin Beck
Ashdale Gill
Barbondale
Thorn Moor
Barbon High Fell
Eskholme Pike
ELLERIGG LA
Eskholme
Barbon Park
Barbon Manor
Fell House
Barbon Beck
Barbon
BANNERIGGS BROW
Aygill
Hazel Sike
Park House
Barbon Low Fell
Low Bank House
Whelprigg
Hoggs Hills
Bullpot
Casterton Fell
Cow Pot
Lancaster Hole
BENTS LA
Bellgate
Gale Garth
Ease Gill
Brownthwaite
Hellot Scales Barn
Langthwaite
FELLFOOT RD
Smithy House
Whittle Hole
FELL RD
Fell Yeat
Casterton
Leck Fell House
Three Men of Gragareth
Rumbling Hole
Short Drop Cave
Bindloss
High Park
Leck Beck
Lost John's Cave
Springs Wood
Leck Fell

# Index

**Church Rd [6] Beckenham BR2..........53 C6**

- **Place name** May be abbreviated on the map
- **Location number** Present when a number indicates the place's position in a crowded area of mapping
- **Locality, town or village** Shown when more than one place has the same name
- **Postcode district** District for the indexed place
- **Page and grid square** Page number and grid reference for the standard mapping

**Cities, towns and villages are listed in CAPITAL LETTERS**

**Public and commercial buildings** are highlighted in **magenta** **Places of interest** are highlighted in **blue** with a star★

## Abbreviations used in the index

| | | | | | | | | | |
|---|---|---|---|---|---|---|---|---|---|
| Acad | **Academy** | Comm | **Common** | Gd | **Ground** | L | **Leisure** | Prom | **Promenade** |
| App | **Approach** | Cott | **Cottage** | Gdn | **Garden** | La | **Lane** | Rd | **Road** |
| Arc | **Arcade** | Cres | **Crescent** | Gn | **Green** | Liby | **Library** | Recn | **Recreation** |
| Ave | **Avenue** | Cswy | **Causeway** | Gr | **Grove** | Mdw | **Meadow** | Ret | **Retail** |
| Bglw | **Bungalow** | Ct | **Court** | H | **Hall** | Meml | **Memorial** | Sh | **Shopping** |
| Bldg | **Building** | Ctr | **Centre** | Ho | **House** | Mkt | **Market** | Sq | **Square** |
| Bsns, Bus | **Business** | Ctry | **Country** | Hospl | **Hospital** | Mus | **Museum** | St | **Street** |
| Bvd | **Boulevard** | Cty | **County** | HQ | **Headquarters** | Orch | **Orchard** | Sta | **Station** |
| Cath | **Cathedral** | Dr | **Drive** | Hts | **Heights** | Pal | **Palace** | Terr | **Terrace** |
| Cir | **Circus** | Dro | **Drove** | Ind | **Industrial** | Par | **Parade** | TH | **Town Hall** |
| Cl | **Close** | Ed | **Education** | Inst | **Institute** | Pas | **Passage** | Univ | **University** |
| Cnr | **Corner** | Emb | **Embankment** | Int | **International** | Pk | **Park** | Wk, Wlk | **Walk** |
| Coll | **College** | Est | **Estate** | Intc | **Interchange** | Pl | **Place** | Wr | **Water** |
| Com | **Community** | Ex | **Exhibition** | Junc | **Junction** | Prec | **Precinct** | Yd | **Yard** |

## Index of towns, villages, streets, hospitals, industrial estates, railway stations, schools, shopping centres, universities and places of interest

### Aal–Agn

### A


**Aalborg Pl** LA1 214 F7
**Aaron Ct** PR9 53 E1
**Abacus St** FY1 130 C2
**Abbey Cl**
Formby L37 12 B2
Up Holland WN8 10 C7
**Abbey Cres** BB3 65 C8
**Abbeydale** LA3 217 B2
**Abbey Dale**
Appley Bridge WN6 19 D7
Burscough L40 25 F3
**Abbeydale Way** BB5 103 F5
**Abbey Dr** WN5 10 E6
**Abbey Farm** BB7 144 B6
**Abbey Farm Cvn Pk**
L40 16 C8
**Abbeyfield** [3] BB11 128 B4
**Abbeyfield Cl** LA1 215 A3
**Abbeyfield Ho**
Barnoldswick BB18 196 A3
[10] Burnley BB11 127 E5
**Abbey Fields** BB7 144 C5
**Abbey Fold** L40 25 D5
**Abbey Gdns** PR8 35 A4
Abbey Gisburne Park Hospl
BB7 231 B4
**Abbey Gr** PR6 31 B7
**Abbey La**
Burscough L40 25 C1
Ormskirk L40 16 C8
Abbey Lane Ind Est L40 25 C1
**Abbey Mews** BB7 144 C5
**Abbey Pl** [1] BB3 82 C1
**Abbey Rd**
Blackpool FY4 110 D5
Whalley BB7 144 C5
**Abbey St**
Accrington BB5 104 C6
Accrington, Scaitcliffe
BB5 104 C5
Bacup OL13 87 F4
Preston PR2 96 D8
**ABBEYSTEAD** 232 F1
**Abbeystead** WN8 9 C7
**Abbeystead Dr** LA1 215 A3
**Abbeystead Ho** [8] LA1 215 A3
**Abbeystead La** LA2 232 E2
**Abbeystead Rd** LA2 232 C1
**Abbey Terr**
Barrow BB7 166 D1
Billington BB7 144 A3
**Abbey View**
Whalley BB7 144 C4
Withnell PR6 80 A1
**ABBEY VILLAGE** 80 C2
Abbey Village Prim Sch
PR6 80 C1
**Abbeyville** FY4 110 C6
**Abbey Wlk** PR1 96 D3
**Abbeywood** WN8 9 C6
**Abbot Mdw** PR1 96 D4
**Abbots Cl**
Formby L37 12 A1
Kirkham PR4 114 C4
Rawtenstall BB4 86 A4
**Abbots Croft** BB7 144 C5
**Abbotsford** L39 15 F5
**Abbotsford Ave** BB2 101 D1
**Abbotsford Rd** FY3 131 A3
**Abbots Ho** [21] LA1 214 F8
**Abbots Row** FY8 90 D6
**Abbotsway** PR1 96 C6
**Abbots Way**
Formby L37 12 B1
Lancaster LA1 214 C8
**Abbott Brow** BB2 121 E3
**Abbott Clough Ave**
BB1 102 E4
**Abbott Clough Cl** BB1 102 E4
**Abbott Croft** PR2 117 A7
**Abbotts Cl** PR5 97 F3
**Abbott St** [14] BL6 32 B4
**Abbotts Wlk** FY7 199 A5
**Abbot Wlk** BB7 167 A8
**Abel St** BB10 128 A8
**Abercorn Pl** FY4 110 B5
**Abercrombie Rd** FY7 198 F4
**Aberdare Cl** BB1 101 E7
**Aberdeen Dr** BB1 102 A4
**Aberdeen Gdns** OL12 52 D4
**Aberdeen Rd** LA1 215 A7
**Abernethy Ct** BL6 32 D2
**Abernethy St** BL6 32 D2
**Abingdon Dr** PR2 117 B1
**Abingdon Gr** LA3 213 A7
**Abingdon Rd** BB12 126 D7
**Abingdon St** FY1 130 B5
**Abinger St** BB10 148 C1
**Abington Dr** PR9 55 A5
**Abner Row** BB8 194 D1
**Abraham Altham Ct**
BB10 148 F3
**ABRAHAM HEIGHTS** 214 D7
**Abraham St**
[7] Accrington BB5 104 B5
Blackburn BB2 101 E2
[11] Horwich BL6 32 B4
**Abram Ho** PR1 97 A7
**Abrams Fold** PR9 54 F5
**Abrams Gn** PR9 54 F5
**Acacia Cl** [4] FY5 176 D1
**Acacia Rd** PR2 118 E2
**Acacia Wlk** [4] BB1 102 B5
**Academy The** [1] PR9 35 C8
**ACCRINGTON** 104 E6
Accrington Huncoat Prim
Sch BB5 125 F2
**Accrington Rd**
Blackburn BB1 102 C4
Burnley BB11 127 C5
Hapton BB11 126 E3
Whalley BB6, BB7 144 E4
Accrington Sta BB5 104 B6
Accrington Victoria Hospl
BB5 104 B7
**Acer Gr** PR2 118 F3
Ackhurst Bsns Pk & Ind Est
PR7 42 F8
**Ackhurst La** WN5 19 F2
**Ackhurst Rd** PR7 42 F8
**Ackroyd St** OL14 109 B1
**Acorn Appartments**
FY2 152 C6
**Acorn Ave** BB5 103 F3
**Acorn Bank** PR3 181 C8
Acorn Bsns Ctr L33 1 B1
**Acorn Cl**
Kingsfold PR1 96 B2
Lancaster LA1 214 F4
Leyland PR25 60 A8
**Acornfield Rd** L33 1 D2
**Acorn Gdn** LA3 217 C2
**Acorn Mdw** LA5 221 A4
**Acorn Mews** FY4 131 D1
**Acorn St**
Bacup OL13 87 F2
Blackburn BB1 102 B4
**Acorns The** L39 15 C3
Acorn Venture Urban
Farm★ L33 1 D4
**ACRE** 85 B6
**Acre Ave** OL13 70 D8
**Acre Cl** BL0 68 D3
**Acre Ct** [11] LA1 218 D2
**Acrefield**
Blackburn BB2 101 A7
Clayton Brook PR5 78 C5
Newburgh WN8 27 A1
Padiham BB12 146 C1
**Acrefield Dr** BB4 86 A6
**Acregate** WN8 9 C7
**Acre Gate** FY4 110 E7
**Acregate La** PR1 118 D1
**Acre Gr**
Much Hoole PR4 74 F3
Southport PR8 34 F3
**Acre Mill Rd** OL13 70 D8
**Acre Moss La** LA4 217 A4
**Acremount** BB12 145 D2
**Acresbrook Rd** BB12 146 F6
**Acresfield**
Adlington PR7 30 F6
Colne BB8 172 A5
**Acresfield Cl** BL6 31 C3
**Acres La**
Great Altcar L37 3 E8
Maghull L31, L39 4 E7
Preesall FY6 200 A3
**Acre St**
Burnley BB10 148 B1
Burnley, Haggate BB10 149 A3
Whitworth OL12 71 D1
**Acres The** BB6 144 E8
**Acreswood Cl** PR7 29 E8
**Acre View** OL13 70 D7
**Active Way** BB11 128 A6
**Acton Rd** FY4 130 E1
**Adamson St**
Burnley BB12 127 C6
Padiham BB12 146 C1
**Ada St**
Blackburn BB2 101 C5
Burnley BB10 148 B1
Nelson BB9 148 E6
Ramsbottom BL0 50 B5
**Addenbrooke Cl** LA1 214 E4
**Addington Rd** LA2, LA6 237 B7
**Addington St** BB1 102 A4
**Addison Cres** FY3 130 D6
**Addison Ct** FY6 199 D5
**Addison Rd** FY7 199 A3
**Addison St**
Accrington BB5 104 C7
Blackburn BB2 101 C5
**Addle St** LA1 215 A4
**Adelaide Ave** FY5 153 C8
**Adelaide Ct** [5] FY1 130 C5
**Adelaide La** BB5 104 C5
**Adelaide St W** FY1 130 B4
**Adelaide St**
[7] Accrington, Enfield
BB5 125 A1
Accrington, Scaitcliffe
BB5 104 C5
[5] Adlington PR6 31 A8
Blackpool FY1 130 B5
Fleetwood FY7 199 B5
Preston PR1 97 B8
[2] Ramsbottom BL0 50 A4
Rawtenstall BB4 86 A7
**Adelaide Terr** BB2 101 C5
**ADELPHI** 117 E1
**Adelphi Ho** [1] PR1 117 E1
**Adelphi Pl** [2] PR1 96 F8
**Adelphi St**
[6] Blackpool FY1 130 B5
Burnley BB11 128 A7
Lancaster LA1 215 A6
Preston PR1 117 E1
Standish WN6 29 E2
**ADLINGTON** 31 B7
**Adlington Ave** FY6 153 B3
Adlington Prim Sch
PR7 30 F7
Adlington St Paulís CE
Prim Sch PR6 31 A7
Adlington South Bsns
Village PR7 31 A6
**Adlington St** BB11 128 A6
Adlington Sta PR6 31 A7
**Admiral Cl** FY8 110 E1
**Admiral Gdns** FY2 152 B3
**Admiral Hts** FY2 152 B3
**Admirals Sound** FY5 175 C2
**Admiral St** BB10 128 B5
**Admiralty Cl** L40 25 C2
**Admiral Way** PR2 95 D7
**Adrian St** FY1 130 B1
**Adstone Ave** FY3 130 F7
**Agate St** BB1 122 F1
**Ager St** OL13 70 C8
**Agglebys Rd** FY6 176 F8
**Agnes Ing La** LA2 238 D7
**Agnes St**
Blackburn BB2 101 C3
[12] Preston PR1 97 A8
**Agnew Rd** FY7 198 F4
**Agnew St** FY8 91 A3

Aiken Ct PR4 114 A5
Aikengill Rd LA2 239 D4
Ailsa Ave FY4 130 F2
Ailsa Cl PR3 137 B8
Ailsa Rd BB1 102 D3
Ailsa Wlk LA3 212 E7
Aindow Ct PR8 34 F3
Ainley Ct 10 FY1 130 C6
Ainscough Brook Ho 1 PR2 118 F3
Ainscouth Bsns Pk WN6 28 F6
AINSDALE 21 B5
Ainsdale Ave
Blackpool FY2 152 E5
Burnley BB10 148 C5
Edgworth BL7 48 E6
Fleetwood FY7 175 D7
Thornton FY5 176 D1
Ainsdale & Birkdale Sandhills Nature Reserve* PR8 21 B7
Ainsdale Cl LA1 218 B3
Ainsdale Dr
Darwen BB3 65 B5
Preston PR2 116 E2
Whitworth OL12 52 D7
AINSDALE-ON-SEA 20 F6
Ainsdale St John's CE Prim Sch PR8 21 D4
Ainsdale Sand Dunes National Nature Reserve* PR8 20 E3
Ainsdale Sta PR8 21 C5
Ainse Rd BL6 31 B3
Ainslie Cl BB6 124 B5
Ainslie Rd PR2 117 E3
Ainslie St 3 BB12 127 C6
Ainspool La PR3 181 A3
Ainsworth Ave BL6 32 E2
Ainsworth Cl 5 BB3 65 A8
Ainsworth Fold PR4 113 B3
Ainsworth Mall 3 BB1 101 E5
Ainsworth St BB1 101 E5
Aintree Cotts BB2 121 C3
Aintree Cres PR8 35 F4
Aintree Dr BB3 82 A7
Aintree Rd
Blackpool FY4 130 D1
Thornton FY5 153 B8
Airdrie Cres BB11 127 D4
Airdrie Pl FY2 152 E6
Aire Cl LA3 217 F3
Airedale LA2 211 B4
Airedale Ave FY3 130 E3
Airedale Ct FY6 153 C4
Airegate L31 5 B2
Airey Hos PR3 163 D1
Airey St BB5 104 D3
Air Hill Terr 8 OL12 52 C1
Airton Garth BB9 170 C3
Aisled Barn Visitor Ctr* BB8 173 A3
Aitken Cl BL0 50 B5
Aitken St
Accrington BB5 104 C7
Haslingden BL0 68 C5
Ajax St 3 BL0 50 B5
A K Bsns Pk PR9 36 A6
Akeman Cl LA3 217 E3
Alamein Rd LA5 223 E1
Alandale Cl PR25 60 B7
Alan Gr LA3 212 F6
Alan Haigh Ct BB8 171 D6
Alan Ramsbottam Way BB6 124 D4
Alaska St BB2 101 E2
Albany Ave FY4 110 B5
Albany Cl FY6 131 E8
Albany Ct 10 PR7 43 E8
Albany Dr
Bamber Bridge PR5 97 D2
Copster Green BB1 122 C8
Albany Rd
Blackburn BB2 101 B6
3 Fleetwood FY7 198 F4
Lytham St Anne's FY8 90 C5
Morecambe LA4 216 F4
Southport PR9 53 C1
Albany Science Coll PR7 43 E5
Albany The BB3 81 E4
Albatros St PR1 118 B1
Albemarle Ct 2 BB7 166 D8
Albemarle St BB7 166 D8
Alberta Cl BB2 101 B8
Albert Ct
Lancaster LA1 214 E4
Southport PR9 53 D1
Albert Ho BB4 86 D1
Albert Mill BB3 81 F7
Albert Pl
Blackburn BB3 81 F7
Southport PR9 35 B8
Albert Rd
Barnoldswick BB18 196 B2
Blackpool FY1 130 C5
Colne BB8 171 D4
Formby L37 2 B8
Fulwood PR2 117 F3
Lancaster LA1 218 D1
Leyland PR25 60 C8
Lytham St Anne's FY8 90 A7
Morecambe LA4 216 F4
Preston PR1 117 F2
Rawtenstall BB4 86 A8
Rufford L40 39 A3
Albert Rd *continued*
Southport PR9 53 D1
Albert Sq 11 FY7 199 B5
Albert St
Accrington BB5 104 C5
Blackburn BB2 101 C2
Bolton BL7 47 D3
Brierfield BB9 148 B5
Burnley BB11 128 B6
Bury BL9 33 A2
3 Carnforth LA5 223 D1
Carnforth, Millhead LA5 223 D3
1 Chorley PR7 43 D7
Church BB5 103 E6
Clayton-le-M BB5 124 F2
Darwen BB3 65 B5
Earby BB18 197 B2
Fleetwood FY7 199 B4
Great Harwood BB6 124 D4
Hoddlesden BB3 82 F1
Horwich BL6 32 B4
Kirkham PR4 113 F6
Lytham St Anne's FY8 91 C3
Nelson BB9 148 D8
Oswaldtwistle BB5 103 E4
Padiham BB12 126 C8
Ramsbottom BL0 50 B6
Rishton BB1 124 B1
Wheelton PR6 62 A7
Whitewell Bottom BB4 86 E5
Whitworth OL12 52 C8
Albert Terr
Bacup OL13 87 F3
9 Barrowford BB9 170 D3
Calder Vale PR3 182 E8
Higher Walton PR5 98 B3
9 Preston PR1 118 A1
Rawtenstall BB4 86 B2
Southport PR8 35 A5
Albion Ave FY3 130 F6
Albion Ct BB11 127 E4
Albion Mews LA1 218 E1
Albion Mill 8 BB4 86 F2
Albion Rd
Blackburn BB2 101 D1
Earby BB18 197 B2
Albion St
Accrington BB5 104 B6
Bacup, Greave OL13 88 A3
7 Bacup, Stacksteads OL13 70 C8
Blackburn BB2 101 C1
Brierfield BB9 148 B5
Burnley BB11 127 E5
Chorley PR7 43 C7
1 Clitheroe BB7 166 F8
Earby BB18 197 B2
Lancaster LA1 218 E1
3 Nelson BB9 148 D8
7 Padiham BB12 126 D7
Albion Terr 11 BB11 127 F5
Albrighton Cl PR5 77 B7
Albrighton Cres PR5 77 B7
Albrighton Rd PR5 77 C7
Albyn Bank Rd PR1 97 B7
Albyn St E PR1 97 B7
Alcester Ave PR1 96 C5
Alconbury Cres FY5 175 C2
Aldate Gr PR2 117 A2
ALDCLIFFE 214 D5
Aldcliffe Cotts LA1 214 D5
Aldcliffe Ct 5 LA4 217 B3
Aldcliffe Hall Dr LA1 214 D5
Aldcliffe Mews LA1 214 D5
Aldcliffe Rd
Lancaster LA1 214 E6
7 Preston PR2 116 E1
Alden Cl
Haslingden BB4 68 A6
Standish WN1 30 B1
Alden Rd BB4, BL8 67 F5
Alden Rise BB4 68 A6
Alden Terr 6 LA1 218 D3
Alder Ave
Bury BL9 33 C3
Rawtenstall BB4 86 B2
Alderbank BL6 31 F3
Alder Bank
Blackburn BB2 101 B4
20 Rawtenstall BB4 86 A3
Alderbrook Dr WN8 27 C2
Alder Cl
Leyland PR26 59 B8
Newton-w-S PR4 115 A2
Thornton FY5 176 C1
Alder Coppice PR2 116 E3
Alder Ct
Fleetwood FY7 198 C2
Lancaster LA1 214 D8
Alderdale Ave PR8 21 A5
Alder Dr
Charnock Richard PR7 42 D3
Gregson Lane PR5 98 E1
Alderfield PR1 96 D3
Alderford Cl BB7 166 C7
Alder Gr
Blackpool FY3 130 E7
Coppull PR7 42 F1
Fulwood PR2 116 F6
Huncoat BB5 125 E2
Lancaster LA1 214 D8
Lytham St Anne's FY8 91 A4
Poulton-le-F FY6 153 D1
Alder Grange Com & Tech Sch BB4 86 A4
Alder Hill Croft BB18 197 C2
Alder Hill St BB18 197 B2
Alder La
Formby L37, L39 12 E7
Moss Edge PR3 179 A1
Parbold WN8 27 C1
Alderlee Pk Cvn Site PR8 36 A2
Alderley WN8 9 C6
Alderley Ave FY4 110 B5
Alderley Bank Cvn Pk LA3 208 F7
Alderley Hts LA1 218 D3
Alderman Foley Dr OL12 52 A2
Alderman Rd LA1 214 F4
Alder Meadow Cl 1 OL12 52 A1
Alderney Cl BB2 101 B1
Alder Rd PR2 119 A4
Aldersleigh Cres PR5 98 D1
Alderson Cres L37 11 F4
Alder St
Bacup OL13 87 F3
4 Blackburn BB1 102 A7
Burnley BB12 127 C7
Rawtenstall BB4 86 B3
Alders The PR3 204 C1
Alderville Cl PR4 92 F6
Alderway BL0 68 C1
Alderwood BB4 86 B2
Alderwood Gr BL0 68 D4
Aldfield Ave PR2 116 C1
Aldingham Ct 2 LA4 217 B3
Aldingham Wlk 11 LA4 217 A5
Aldon Gr PR4 95 A1
Aldon Rd FY6 153 F2
Aldren's La LA1 218 D3
Aldwych Ave FY3 130 E3
Aldwych Ct PR2 117 A2
Aldwych Dr
Bamber Bridge PR5 77 B7
Preston PR2 117 A2
Aldwych Pl BB1 122 F2
Alert St PR2 117 C1
Alexander Cl
Accrington BB5 104 E1
Burscough L40 25 F3
Alexander Ct FY6 153 D3
Alexander Dr L31 5 D3
Alexander Gr BB12 127 B6
Alexander Mews BB2 101 C6
Alexander Pl 2 PR2 139 D1
Alexander St BB9 171 A2
Alexander Wharf L31 5 C1
Alexandra Cl
Clayton-le-M BB5 124 E3
Skelmersdale WN8 17 E1
Alexandra Ct 4 LA1 214 F8
Alexandra Hall 8 LA1 214 F7
Alexandra Ho 10 PR1 118 C1
Alexandra Mews
1 Ormskirk L39 15 E6
8 Southport PR9 35 C8
Alexandra Park Dr LA1 211 A6
Alexandra Pavilions 6 PR1 118 A1
Alexandra Pl BB6 124 D6
Alexandra Rd
Bamber Bridge PR5 97 D3
Blackburn BB2 101 C6
Blackpool FY1 130 B1
Burscough L40 25 D4
Carnforth LA5 223 D1
8 Darwen BB3 81 F2
Formby L37 11 B1
Kirkham PR4 114 A6
Lancaster LA1 218 D3
Longridge PR3 140 A7
Lytham St Anne's FY8 90 A7
Morecambe LA3 216 E3
Southport PR9 35 D8
Thornton FY5 153 C8
Alexandra Sq LA1 211 B7
Alexandra St
Clayton-le-M BB5 124 E3
Preston PR1 97 C7
Alexandra View 7 BB3 81 F2
Alexandria Dr FY8 89 F5
Alexandria St BB4 85 F4
Alford Fold PR2 117 D7
Alfred St
Blackpool FY1 130 C5
Bolton, Egerton BL7 47 D3
Bury BL9 33 A1
Darwen BB3 65 B6
Lancaster LA1 215 A8
10 Ramsbottom BL0 50 B5
Whitworth OL12 71 D2
Algar St 9 BB9 170 F2
Alice Ave PR25 77 A1
Alice Sq 5 PR1 118 A1
Alice St
Accrington BB5 104 D7
Barnoldswick BB18 196 B2
9 Darwen BB3 65 A8
Morecambe LA4 217 C5
Oswaldtwistle BB5 103 E3
Alicia Ct 1 OL12 52 E1
Alicia Dr OL12 52 E1
Alisan Rd FY6 153 B5
Alker La PR7 61 B3
Alker St PR7 43 C7
Alkincoats Rd BB8 171 C5
Allan Critchlow Way BB1 124 B2
Allandale FY4 110 C5
Allandale Ave FY5 175 F4
Allandale Gdns LA1 214 D8
Allan St OL13 87 F1
Allenbury Pl FY3 131 A2
Allenby Ave PR2 118 B4
Allenby Rd FY8 89 E8
Allen Cl
Cleveleys FY5 175 D1
Fleetwood FY7 198 D2
Allen Ct BB10 128 A8
Allendale Ct 6 BB12 127 B6
Allendale Gr BB10 128 F4
Allendale St
5 Burnley BB12 127 B6
Colne BB8 171 F5
Allengate PR2 117 F4
Allen St BB10 128 A8
Allen Way FY7 198 D2
Allerton Cl BB3 82 A2
Allerton Dr BB12 127 D6
Allerton Rd
Bamber Bridge PR5 97 D4
Southport PR9 53 E1
Alleys Gn BB7 189 E1
ALLEYTROYDS 103 E6
Alleytroyds BB5 103 E5
All Hallows RC High Sch PR1 96 A3
All Hallows Rd FY2 152 D5
Alliance Bsns Pk BB5 104 A5
Alliance St BB5 104 F1
Allington Cl PR5 97 E3
Allison Gr BB8 171 F6
Allonby Ave FY5 175 E4
Allotment La PR3 157 C7
All Saints CE Prim Sch BB5 124 F2
All Saints Cl
Padiham BB12 126 F7
Rawtenstall BB4 106 A1
All Saint's Cl BB5 103 B4
All Saints RC High Sch BB4 85 D1
All Saints Rd FY2 152 E6
All Saints' Rd FY8 89 E6
Allsprings Cl BB6 124 D6
Allsprings Dr BB6 124 D6
Alma Ave BB8 194 D1
Alma Cl WN8 10 C7
Alma Ct
Southport PR8 21 F7
Up Holland WN8 10 C7
Alma Dr PR7 42 E4
Alma Hill WN8 10 C7
Alma Hill Est WN8 10 C7
Alma Ho LA1 214 F6
Alma Ind Est 25 OL12 52 F1
Alma Par WN8 10 C7
Alma Pl
Accrington BB5 84 E8
Clitheroe BB7 166 D7
Alma Rd
Lancaster LA1 214 F6
Laneshaw Bridge BB8 172 C6
Southport PR8 35 A4
Up Holland WN8 10 C7
Alma Row PR5 98 E1
Alma St
Bacup OL13 88 A2
Blackburn BB2 101 D5
9 Clayton-le-M BB5 124 F3
Padiham BB12 126 C8
Preston PR1 118 A1
13 Rochdale OL12 52 F1
Alma Terr BB11 106 B4
Alma Wood Cl PR7 43 A6
Almelo Ho 2 PR1 117 E2
Almhouses BD23 197 A5
Almond Ave
Burscough Bridge L40 25 E6
4 Bury BL9 33 C3
Almond Brook Rd WN6 29 C1
Almond Cl
Abbey Village PR6 80 B2
Fulwood PR2 118 D6
Higher Penwortham PR1 96 B3
Almond Cres BB4 68 F8
Almond St BB3 65 A8
Almonry The L40 17 D7
Alms House Bglws L39 6 A7
Almshouses 14 LA1 214 F7
Alnwick Cl BB12 127 E7
Alpha St
Darwen BB3 65 B8
10 Nelson BB9 170 F2
Salterforth BB18 194 E8
Alpic Dr FY5 152 C7
Alpine Ave
Bamber Bridge PR5 77 B7
Blackpool FY4 110 E5
Alpine Cl
Bamber Bridge PR5 77 B7
Hoddlesden BB3 82 E1
Alpine Gr BB2 81 B8
Alpine Hts PR3 181 B6
Alpine Lo FY8 89 E5
Alpine Rd PR6 61 E3
Alpine View LA5 221 A6
Alsop St PR1 117 F2
Alston Ave FY5 175 D4
Alston Cl BB7 145 F7
Alston Ct
Longridge PR3 140 B6
Southport PR8 21 E6
Alston Dr LA4 217 F5
Alston Hall Coll PR3 120 B8
Alston La PR3 140 A2
Alston Lane RC Prim Sch PR3 139 F2
Alston Rd FY2 152 E2
Alston St PR1 118 D1
Altcar La
Formby L37 11 F1
Haskayne L39 14 A2
Maghull L31 4 F5
Runshaw Moor PR25 59 E5
Altcar Rd L37 12 B2
ALTHAM 125 E6
Altham Bsns Pk BB5 125 E6
Altham Cvn Site BB5 125 C1
Altham Ind Est BB5 125 D6
Altham La BB5 125 F4
Altham Rd
Morecambe LA4 217 C3
Southport PR8 35 E2
Altham St James CE Prim Sch BB5 125 D6
Altham St
2 Burnley BB10 128 A8
6 Padiham BB12 126 D8
Altham Wlk LA4 217 C3
Althorp Cl 6 FY1 130 C7
Althorpe Dr PR8 35 E3
Altom St BB1 101 E6
Alton Cl L38 2 F2
Alt Rd
Formby L37 12 B2
Hightown L38 3 A4
Altys La L39 15 F3
Alum Scar La BB2 100 A6
Alvern Ave PR2 117 D4
Alvern Cres PR2 117 D4
Alvina La L33 1 A5
Alwin St 8 BB11 127 E5
Alwood Ave FY3 130 F6
Amber Ave BB1 122 F2
Amberbanks Gr FY1 130 B2
Amber Dr PR6 43 E6
Ambergate
Fulwood PR2 116 F6
Skelmersdale WN8 9 B7
Amberley St BB2 101 C2
Amberwood PR4 113 F5
Amberwood Dr BB2 101 A1
Ambledene PR5 78 A5
Ambleside Ave
Barnoldswick BB18 196 A3
3 Euxton PR7 60 D1
Knott End-on-S FY6 199 F6
2 Rawtenstall BB4 85 E2
Ambleside Cl
Accrington, Hillock Vale BB5 104 E8
Bamber Bridge PR5 97 E2
Blackburn BB1 102 A6
Ambleside Dr BB3 82 C3
Ambleside Rd
Blackpool FY4 131 D1
Fulwood PR2 118 E5
Lancaster LA1 218 F2
Lytham St Anne's FY8 110 E1
Maghull L31 5 D2
Ambleside Wlk PR2 118 E5
Ambleway PR5 97 C4
Ambrose Ave PR7 60 E6
Ambrose Hall La PR4 136 E3
Ambrose St PR25 77 B2
Amelia St BB1 102 B6
Amersham WN8 9 C7
Amersham Cl PR4 75 F8
Amersham Gr BB10 148 D4
Amethyst St BB1 122 F2
Amounderness Way
Cleveleys FY5 175 F4
Fleetwood FY7 199 A3
Thornton FY5 153 C7
Ampleforth Dr PR5 97 A1
AMS Trad Est PR4 75 D7
Amy Johnson Way FY4 110 E4
Amy St OL12 52 B1
Ancenis Ct PR4 114 B5
ANCHOR 81 F5
Anchorage Ave PR4 72 F1
Anchorage Bsns Pk 3 PR2 95 F8
Anchorage Mews FY7 199 B3
Anchorage Rd FY7 199 B3
Anchor Ave BB3 81 F4
Anchor Ct
Darwen BB3 81 F5
Preston PR1 96 F7
Anchor Dr PR4 95 D2
Anchor Fields PR7 41 B7
Anchor Gr BB3 81 E5
Anchor Ho 1 BB1 101 F4
Anchor Rd BB3 81 F4
Anchor Ret Pk 1 BB11 128 A6
ANCHORSHOLME 175 E1
Anchorsholme La
Cleveleys FY5 152 F8
Thornton FY5 153 A8
Anchorsholme La E FY5 175 E1
Anchorsholme La W FY5 175 C1
Anchorsholme Prim Sch FY5 152 E8
Anchor St PR9 35 B7
Anchor Way FY8 110 E1
Ancliffe La LA2, LA5 221 B2
Andelen Cl BB11 126 C3
Anders Dr L33 1 A5

**Anderson Cl**
Bacup OL13 87 F1
Lancaster LA1 215 B6
**Anderson Rd** BB1 123 A7
**Anderson St** 9 FY1 130 C4
**ANDERTON** 31 C8
**Anderton Cl** BB4 69 F7
**Anderton Cres** PR7 60 E7
**Anderton La** BL6 31 E4
**Anderton Prim Sch** PR6 31 B8
**Anderton Rd**
Euxton PR7 60 D1
Higham BB12 146 F5
**Anderton St Joseph's RC Prim Sch** PR6 31 B8
**Anderton St**
Adlington PR7 31 A7
Chorley PR7 43 C7
13 Morecambe LA4 217 A5
**Andertons Way** PR2 118 D5
**Anderton Way** PR3 181 D6
**Andreas Cl** PR8 35 B4
**Andrew Ave** BB4 85 F1
**Andrew Cl**
Blackburn BB2 81 B8
Ramsbottom BL8 49 F1
**Andrew Rd** BB9 171 B1
**Andrews Cl** L37 11 E1
**Andrews La** L37 11 E1
**Andrew St**
Bury BL9 33 A2
Preston PR1 118 C1
**Andrews Yort** L37 11 E1
**Anemone Dr** BB4 67 F8
**Angela St** BB2 101 B1
**Angelbank** BL6 31 F2
**Angel Way** 3 BB8 171 E5
**Anger's Hill Rd** FY4 130 F1
**Anglesey Ave** BB12 127 A7
**Anglesey St** BB2 81 B8
**Angle St** BB10 128 A8
**Anglezarke Rd** PR6 31 A7
Anglezarke Woodland Trail* PR6 44 D6
**Anglian Cl** BB5 103 C5
**Angus St** OL13 70 C8
**Aniline St** PR6 43 E8
**Annan Cres** FY4 131 C1
**Annandale Gdns** WN8 10 A7
**Annarly Fold** BB10 129 A5
**Annaside Cl** 2 FY4 110 E7
**Anna's Rd** FY4 111 E3
**Anne Ave** PR8 21 E6
**Anne Cl** 6 BB10 128 B5
**Annesley Ave** FY3 130 E8
**Anne St** 2 BB11 128 B5
**Annie St**
Accrington BB5 104 C7
Ramsbottom BL0 50 A4
5 Rawtenstall BB4 86 A2
**Annis St** PR1 97 C8
**Ann St**
Barrowford BB9 170 D3
Brierfield BB9 148 B6
4 Clayton-le-M BB5 124 F3
Skelmersdale WN8 8 E8
**Ansbro Ave** PR4 93 C6
**ANSDELL** 90 C4
**Ansdell & Fairhaven Sta** FY8 90 D4
**Ansdell Gr**
Fulwood PR2 117 C3
Southport PR9 54 A4
**Ansdell Prim Sch** FY8 90 C5
**Ansdell Rd**
Blackpool FY1 130 D2
Horwich BL6 32 C4
**Ansdell Rd N** FY8 90 D4
**Ansdell Rd S** FY8 90 D3
**Ansdell St** 3 PR1 118 C1
**Ansdell Terr** BB2 101 E1
**Anselm Ct** FY2 152 B3
**Anshaw Cl** BL7 46 C5
**Anson Cl** FY8 110 D1
**Anson Rd** PR4 114 B2
**Anstable Rd** LA4 217 E5
**Anthony Rd** LA1 214 E7
**Antigua Dr** BB3 81 F6
**Antley Ct** BB10 148 C1
**Antrim Rd** FY2 152 C1
**Anvil Cl** WN5 10 D5
**Anvil St** OL13 70 E8
**Anyon La** LA2 207 E6
**Anyon St** BB3 82 B2
**Anzio Rd** PR4 132 E5
**Apartments The** PR9 35 B8
**Apex Cl** BB11 127 E2
**Apiary The** PR26 58 A6
**Appealing La** FY8 110 E2
**Appleby Bsns Ctr** BB1 102 A5
**Appleby Cl**
Accrington BB5 104 D5
Gregson Lane PR5 98 E1
**Appleby Dr** BB9 170 D4
**Appleby Rd** FY2 152 D1
**Appleby St**
Blackburn BB1 102 A5
Nelson BB9 148 D8
Preston PR1 117 F1
**Apple Cl** 2 BB2 101 C4
**Applecross Dr** BB10 128 E4
**Apple Ct** 3 BB2 101 C4
**Applefields** PR25 60 B7
**Applegarth**
Barnoldswick BB18 196 C3

**Applegarth** *continued*
Barrowford BB9 170 B1
**Applegarth Rd** LA3 213 A8
**Applegarth St** 3 BB18 197 B1
**Apple Hey** WN6 19 C8
**Applesike** PR4 95 A1
**Apple St** BB2 101 C4
**Appleton Cl** FY6 153 A2
**Appleton Rd** WN8 17 F2
**Appletree Cl**
Kingsfold PR1 96 C2
Lancaster LA1 215 A3
**Apple Tree Cl**
Euxton PR7 60 D3
St Michael's on W PR3 157 C8
**Appletree Dr** LA1 215 A3
**Apple Tree Way** BB5 103 E5
**Applewood Cl** FY8 90 F3
**APPLEY BRIDGE** 19 D8
**Appley Bridge All Saints CE Prim Sch** WN6 28 C1
**Appley Bridge Sta** WN6 19 C7
**Appley Cl** WN6 28 C2
**Appley La N** WN6 28 C1
**Appley La S** WN6, WN8 19 C6
**Approach Way** BB11 127 F2
**Apsley Brow** L31 5 B1
**Apsley Fold** PR3 140 B6
**Aquaduct Street Ind Est** PR1 117 D1
**Aqueduct Mill** PR1 117 D1
**Aqueduct Rd** BB2 101 D1
**Aqueduct St** PR1 117 E1
**Aragon Cl** L31 5 E3
**Arago St** BB5 104 C7
**Arbories Ave** 4 BB12 126 B8
**Arbory Dr** BB12 126 B8
**Arbory The** PR4 112 E7
**Arbour Ct** L33 1 B2
**Arbour Dr** BB2 81 D6
**Arbour La**
Kirkby L33 1 B2
Shevington Moor WN6 29 B1
**Arbour Lane End** PR3 162 E7
**Arbour Pl** L33 1 B2
**Arbour St**
9 Bacup OL13 88 A3
Southport PR8 35 C6
**Arboury St** BB12 126 B8
**Arcade** BB5 104 C5
**Arcade The** 8 BB4 69 E8
**Arcadia** 9 BB8 171 E5
**Arcadia Ave** L31 5 D3
**Archbishop Temple CE High Sch & Tech Coll** PR2 117 F5
**Archer Hill** LA5 223 D3
**Archery Ave** BB8 194 D1
**Archery Gdns** PR3 181 C8
**Arches The** BB7 144 B6
**Arch St**
Burnley BB11 127 F6
4 Darwen BB3 82 A1
**Archway Bldgs** PR2 117 A1
**Arcon Ho**
5 Coppull PR7 42 E1
Lancaster LA1 214 F5
Lytham St Anne's FY8 91 B4
**Arcon Rd** PR7 42 E1
**Ardee Rd** PR1 96 D6
**Arden Cl**
Slyne LA2 218 C8
Southport PR8 21 A5
**Arden Coll** PR9 35 C7
**Ardengate** LA1 214 F4
**Arden Gn** FY7 198 E4
**Ardleigh Ave** PR8 35 E3
**Ardley Rd** BL6 32 C4
**Ardmore Rd** FY2 152 D2
**Ardwick St** BB10 128 A8
**Argameols Cl** PR8 35 F5
**Argarmeols Gr** L37 11 E5
**Argarmeols Rd** L37 11 E6
**Argosy Ave** FY3 130 F8
**Argosy Ct** 1 FY3 131 A8
**Argyle Ct** PR9 53 D1
**Argyle Rd**
7 Leyland PR25 77 A1
Poulton-le-F FY6 153 E3
Southport PR9 53 D2
**Argyle St**
Accrington BB5 104 B6
8 Colne BB8 171 D5
Darwen BB3 81 F3
Heywood OL10 33 F1
3 Lancaster LA1 215 A7
**Argyll Ct** FY2 152 C1
**Argyll Rd**
Blackpool FY2 152 C1
Preston PR1 118 A1
**Ariel Way** FY7 198 E4
**ARKHOLME** 241 B2
**Arkholme Ave** FY1 130 D2
**Arkholme CE Prim Sch** LA6 241 B3
**Arkholme Cl** LA5 223 E2
**Arkholme Ct** 1 LA4 217 B3
**Arkholme Dr** PR4 94 F1
**Arkwright Ct**
Blackpool FY4 111 C7
Darwen BB3 81 E5
**Arkwright Fold** BB2 81 C8
**Arkwright Rd** PR1 117 F2
**Arkwright St**
Burnley BB12 127 C7
Horwich BL6 32 C2
**Arley Gdns** BB12 127 F7
**Arley La** WN1, WN2 30 D2

**Arley Rise** BB2 121 E2
**Arley St** PR6 43 D8
**Arley Wood Dr** PR7 43 A6
**Arlington Ave** FY4 110 B7
**Arlington Cl**
Ramsbottom BL9 50 C2
Southport PR8 21 A5
**Arlington Rd** BB3 64 F8
**Armadale Rd** FY2 152 E1
**Armaside Rd** PR4 116 D4
**Armitstead Ct** 8 FY7 198 F2
**Armitstead Way** 5 FY7 198 F2
**Armstrong St**
Horwich BL6 32 C2
Preston PR2 117 B2
**Arncliffe Ave** BB5 103 F4
**Arncliffe Gr** BB9 170 C3
**Arncliffe Rd**
Burnley BB10 128 E5
Morecambe LA3 216 D1
**Arndale Cl** FY7 198 C2
**Arndale Ctr**
9 Morecambe LA4 217 A5
6 Nelson BB9 148 E8
**Arndale Rd** PR3 140 A7
**Arnhem Rd**
Carnforth LA5 223 E1
Preston PR1 97 D8
**Arnian Ct** L39 6 C7
**Arnold Ave** FY4 110 C7
**Arnold Cl**
Blackburn BB2 102 A1
Brierfield BB9 148 C5
Burnley BB11 127 E2
Fulwood PR2 118 E2
**Arnold Pl** 1 PR7 43 A5
**Arnold Rd** FY8 91 D4
**Arnold Sch** FY4 110 C7
**Arnold St** 2 BB5 104 C6
**Arno St** 9 PR1 97 B7
**Arnott Rd**
Blackpool FY4 130 E1
Fulwood PR2 117 C2
**ARNSIDE** 224 B8
**Arnside Ave**
Blackpool FY1 130 D1
Lytham St Anne's FY8 90 C7
**Arnside Cl**
Clayton-le-M BB5 124 E2
Coupe Green PR5 98 E4
Lancaster LA1 215 B3
**Arnside Cres**
Blackburn BB2 80 E8
Morecambe LA4 217 C6
**Arnside Rd**
Broughton PR3 137 D2
Preston PR2 116 E2
Southport PR9 35 C7
**Arnside Terr** PR9 35 C7
**Arran Ave** BB1 102 D2
**Arran Cl** LA3 212 E7
**Arran St** BB11 127 D5
**Arrow La** LA2 219 D7
**Arrowsmith Cl** PR5 98 E2
**Arrowsmith Ct** 7 BL6 32 E1
**Arrowsmith Dr** PR5 98 E2
**Arrowsmith Gdns** FY5 175 E5
**Arroyo Way** PR2 118 B4
**Arthur St N** 5 FY7 199 B5
**Arthurs La** FY6 177 D2
**Arthur St**
Bacup OL13 88 B3
Barnoldswick BB18 196 A3
Blackburn BB2 101 C4
Brierfield BB9 148 B6
Burnley BB11 127 E6
Clayton-le-M BB5 124 F3
Earby BB18 195 A7
6 Fleetwood FY7 199 B5
Great Harwood BB6 124 D6
18 Nelson BB9 170 E1
Preston PR1 96 E7
**Arthur Way** BB2 101 C4
**Artlebeck Cl** LA2 237 C3
**Artlebeck Gr** LA2 237 C3
**Artlebeck Rd** LA2 237 C3
**Artle Pl** LA1 218 C2
**Arundel Ave** FY2 152 B5
**Arundel Cl** 7 BB12 127 D7
**Arundel Dr** FY6 153 C5
**Arundel Pl** 36 PR1 97 A7
**Arundel Rd**
4 Longton PR4 95 A1
Lytham St Anne's FY8 90 C4
Southport PR8 21 F8
**Arundel St** BB1 124 A2
**Arundel Way** PR25 60 C8
**Ascot Cl**
Lancaster LA1 215 B4
Southport PR8 34 E5
**Ascot Gdns** LA2 218 D8
**Ascot Rd**
Blackpool FY3 130 E6
Thornton FY5 153 B8
**Ascot Way** BB5 104 D5
**Ascroft Lo** PR4 57 A4
**Ash Ave**
Galgate LA2 210 F4
Haslingden BB4 85 C3
Kirkham PR4 114 A4
**Ash Bank Cl** PR3 137 B8
**Ashborne Dr** BL9 50 D2
**Ashbourne Cl** 7 LA1 218 D3
**Ashbourne Cres** PR2 117 A5
**Ashbourne Dr** LA1 218 D3
**Ashbourne Gr** LA3 217 C2
**Ashbourne Rd** LA1 218 D3

**Ashbridge Ind Sch** PR4 95 F2
**Ashbrook Cl** PR4 73 E3
**Ashbrook St** LA1 214 D8
**Ash Brow** WN8 27 B1
**Ashburn Cl** 7 BL6 32 D1
**Ashburnham Rd** BB8 171 A2
**Ashburton Ct** 7 FY1 130 B7
**Ashburton Rd** FY1 130 B7
**Ashby St** PR7 43 D6
**Ash Cl**
Appley Bridge WN6 19 D7
Barrow BB7 166 D1
Elswick PR4 156 A1
Ormskirk L39 15 D5
Rishton BB1 103 B8
**Ashcombe Gate** FY5 153 D7
**Ashcombe Pl** BL7 48 E7
**Ash Coppice** PR2 116 D2
**Ashcroft** LA3 216 E1
**Ashcroft Ave** L39 15 F6
**Ashcroft Cl** LA2 237 B3
**Ashcroft Pl** BB7 189 E5
**Ashcroft Rd**
Formby L37 11 F1
Kirkby L33 1 C3
**Ash Ct** PR4 115 D2
**Ashdale Cl**
Coppull PR7 29 D8
Formby L37 11 C2
**Ashdale Gr** FY5 176 E2
**Ashdale Pl** LA1 218 C2
**Ashdene** OL12 52 D4
**Ashdown Cl**
Carleton FY6 153 B5
Southport PR8 35 E4
**Ashdown Dr** PR6 78 C2
**Ashdown Mews** PR2 118 E6
**Ash Dr**
Freckleton PR4 93 A5
Poulton-le-F FY6 153 E2
Thornton FY5 176 C1
Warton LA5 223 E6
Warton PR4 92 D6
West Bradford BB7 189 D7
**Asheldon St** 1 PR1 118 D1
**Ashen Bottom** BB4 68 D6
**Ashendean View** BB12 146 D1
**Ashfield** PR2 117 F8
**Ash Field** PR6 78 C3
**Ashfield Ave**
Lancaster LA1 214 D7
Morecambe LA4 217 F6
**Ashfield Cl** BB9 170 C1
**Ashfield Cotts** 2 LA2 239 D8
**Ashfield Ct**
Adlington PR6 31 B8
Blackpool FY2 152 E6
Fulwood PR2 116 F6
**Ashfield Rd**
Adlington PR6 31 B8
Blackpool FY2, FY5 152 E6
Burnley BB11 127 F6
Chorley PR7 43 B7
**Ashfield Rise** PR3 181 D2
**Ashfields** PR26 76 B1
**Ashfield Terr** WN6 19 C8
**Ashford Ave** LA1 214 E3
**Ashford Cl** LA1 214 F3
**Ashford Cres** PR3 137 C3
**Ashford Rd**
Lancaster LA1 214 F3
Preston PR2 116 E2
**Ashford St**
Heywood OL10 33 F2
Nelson BB9 148 E7
**Ash Gr**
Bamber Bridge PR5 97 F1
Barnoldswick BB18 196 B2
Chorley PR7 43 C5
Darwen BB3 82 B2
Formby L37 11 C1
Garstang PR3 181 B8
8 Horwich BL6 32 E1
Kirkham PR4 114 B7
Lancaster LA1 214 F5
Longton PR4 74 F8
New Longton PR4 75 F6
Orrell WN5 10 F6
Preesall FY6 200 A4
Ramsbottom BL0 49 F3
3 Rawtenstall BB4 86 A3
Skelmersdale WN8 17 D1
St Michael's on W PR3 157 C7
Water BB4 87 A8
Wrea Green PR4 113 C3
**Ashgrove** PR1 118 E1
**Ash Holme** PR1 118 C3
**Ashiana Lo** 15 BB9 148 E8
**Ash La**
Clifton PR4 115 E2
Great Harwood BB6 124 B6
Longridge PR3 140 B8
**Ashlands Cl** BL0 68 D2
**Ash Lea Gr** FY6 177 C7
**Ashleigh Ct** PR2 118 A7
**Ashleigh Mews** FY3 130 E4
**Ashleigh Prim Sch** BB3 65 A6
**Ashleigh St**
Darwen BB3 65 B6
Preston PR1 97 C7
**Ashley Cl**
Blackpool FY2 152 D2
Thornton FY5 153 B7
**Ashley Ct**
Accrington BB5 103 F5
Poulton-le-F FY6 153 C3
**Ashley Gdns** LA2 211 A3
**Ashley Hall Farm** PR3 161 D2

**Ashley La** PR3 139 C8
**Ashley Mews** PR2 117 C1
**Ashley Rd**
Lytham St Anne's FY8 110 F1
Skelmersdale WN8 18 B3
Southport PR9 35 C7
**Ashley St** BB12 127 F7
**Ash Mdw** PR2 116 E3
**Ashmeadow Gr** LA6 221 F5
**Ashmeadow La** PR6 62 F8
**Ashmeadow Rd** LA6 221 F5
**Ashmead Rd** WN8 18 A4
**Ashmead View** WN8 18 A4
**Ashmoor St** PR1 117 E1
**Ashmore Gr** FY5 175 D1
**Ashmount Dr** OL12 52 F2
**Ashness Cl**
Fulwood PR2 117 F8
Horwich BL6 31 F3
**Ash Rd**
Coppull PR7 29 E8
Elswick PR4 156 A1
**Ash St**
Bacup OL13 87 F3
Blackburn BB1 102 A7
Blackpool FY4 110 C6
Burnley BB11 128 B5
Bury BL9 33 A2
Fleetwood FY7 199 A4
Great Harwood BB6 124 C6
Nelson BB9 148 F8
Oswaldtwistle BB5 103 D4
Southport PR8 35 C5
Trawden BB8 172 C2
**Ashton Ave** FY6 199 D5
**Ashton Barns** LA2 210 C7
**Ashton Cl** PR2 96 A8
**Ashton Com Science Coll** PR2 116 F2
**Ashton Ct**
Knott End-on-S FY6 199 D5
Lancaster LA1 214 F7
**Ashton Dr**
Lancaster LA1 218 C2
Nelson BB9 148 F6
**Ashton Garden Ct** FY8 89 E7
**Ashtongate** PR2 116 F1
**Ashton Ho** BB3 65 B8
**Ashton La** BB3 65 A8
Ashton Meml* LA1 215 B7
**ASHTON-ON-RIBBLE** 117 A1
**Ashton Prim Sch** PR2 116 E2
**Ashton Rd**
Blackpool FY1 130 C3
8 Darwen BB3 65 B8
Lancaster LA1, LA2 214 E4
Morecambe LA4 217 C5
Southport PR8 34 F1
**Ashton St**
Longridge PR3 140 A8
8 Lytham St Anne's FY8 91 A3
7 Preston PR2 96 D8
**Ashton Wlk** 12 LA1 214 F8
**Ashtree Ct**
Fulwood PR2 117 A4
Higher Walton PR5 98 C3
**Ashtree Gr** PR1 96 B4
**Ash Tree Gr**
Hest Bank LA5 220 F3
Nelson BB9 149 A7
**Ashtrees** L40 40 C2
**Ashtrees Way** 2 LA5 223 D2
**Ash Tree Wlk** 18 BB9 170 D3
**ASHURST** 18 A4
**Ashurst Cl** WN8 18 A4
**Ashurst Ct** L37 11 E2
**Ashurst Gdns** WN8 18 B4
**Ashurst Rd**
Clayton-le-W PR25 77 D1
Shevington Moor WN6 29 B2
Skelmersdale WN8 18 B4
**Ashville Terr** BB2 81 D8
**Ashwall St** WN8 8 E8
**Ashwell Pl** FY5 152 C7
**Ashwood** WN8 18 C3
**Ashwood Ave**
Blackburn BB3 81 D6
Ramsbottom BL0 50 D7
**Ashwood Cl** FY8 90 E4
**Ashwood Ct** LA1 214 F5
**Ashwood Rd** PR2 117 D7
**Ashworth Cl** BB2 101 C5
**Ashworth Ct**
5 Blackpool FY3 130 D7
Preston, Fishwick PR1 97 E7
Preston, Frenchwood PR1 97 B6
**Ashworth Dr** LA2 220 E2
**Ashworth Gr** PR1 97 C6
**Ashworth Hospl** L31 6 B2
**Ashworth La**
Newchurch BB4 86 F3
Preston PR1 97 C6
**Ashworth Rd**
Blackpool FY4 111 C8
Newchurch BB4 86 F2
Ramsbottom OL11 51 E2
**Ashworth St**
Accrington BB5 104 E2
15 Bacup, Greave OL13 88 A3
3 Bacup, Stacksteads OL13 70 D8
3 Bamber Bridge PR5 97 F2
1 Preston PR1 97 B7
11 Rawtenstall BB4 69 F8
Rishton BB1 124 B1
Water BB4 87 A7
**Ashworth Terr**
2 Bacup OL13 70 B8

**Ashworth Terr** *continued*
7 Darwen BB3 .......... 82 A1
**Askrigg Cl**
Accrington BB5 ........ 104 E5
Blackpool FY4 ......... 111 A7
**Asland Cl** PR5 .......... 77 F8
**Asland Gdns** PR9 ........ 54 C4
**Asmall Cl** L39 ........... 15 D6
**Asmall La**
Halsall L39, L40 ......... 14 E8
Ormskirk L39, L40 ......... 15 B7
**Asmall Prim Sch** L39 ..... 15 D6
**Aspden St** PR5 .......... 97 E1
**Aspels Cres** PR1 ........ 96 C4
**Aspels Nook** PR1 ........ 96 C4
**Aspels The** PR1 ......... 96 C4
**Aspendale Cl** PR4 ....... 74 F8
**Aspen Dr** BB10 .......... 128 C7
**Aspen Fold** BB5 ......... 103 B5
**Aspen Gdns**
3 Chorley PR7 .......... 43 B6
Rochdale OL12 .......... 52 A1
**Aspen Gr**
Earby BB18 ........... 197 C1
Formby L37 ............ 11 C1
**Aspen La**
Earby BB18 ........... 197 B2
Oswaldtwistle BB5 ...... 103 C4
**Aspen Way** 3 WN8 ...... 17 E2
**Aspinall Cl**
Horwich BL6 ........... 32 D1
Kingsfold PR1 .......... 96 D2
**Aspinall Cres** L37 ....... 12 F1
**Aspinall Fold** BB1 ....... 101 E8
**Aspinall Rd** WN6 ........ 29 B1
**Aspinall St** BL6 ......... 32 D1
**Aspinall Way** BL6 ........ 32 C1
**Aspley Gr** BB8 .......... 172 C3
**Asshawes The** PR6 ....... 43 F1
**Assheton Pl** PR2 ........ 118 E4
**Assheton Rd** BB2 ........ 101 A5
**Astbury Chase** BB3 ....... 82 B2
**Asten Bldgs** 4 BB4 ...... 69 F7
**Aster Chase** BB3 ......... 82 A7
**Aster Ct** L31 ............. 5 C3
**Astland Gdns** PR4 ........ 73 F2
**Astland St** FY8 .......... 89 E6
**Astley Cres** PR4 ......... 93 C6
**Astley Ct** LA1 .......... 214 D6
**Astley Ctr The** 2 PR7 .... 43 D6
**Astley Gate** BB2 ........ 101 E5
Astley Hall★ PR7 ........ 61 A1
**Astley Hall Dr** BL0 ...... 50 C4
**Astley Ho** BB11 ......... 128 B6
**Astley Hts** BB3 .......... 65 A7
**Astley Rd** PR7 ........... 61 C1
**Astley St**
Chorley PR7 ............ 61 C1
Darwen BB3 ............ 65 A7
Longridge PR3 ......... 140 A7
**Astley Terr** BB3 ......... 65 A7
**ASTLEY VILLAGE** ......... 61 A2
**Aston Ave** FY5 .......... 176 A2
**Aston Manor** PR9 ........ 55 A5
**Aston St** PR4 ........... 132 E6
**Aston Way** PR26 ......... 76 C2
**Aston Wlk** BB2 .......... 82 A8
Astronomy Ctr The★
OL14 ................. 88 F4
**Asturian Gate** PR3 ...... 140 F6
**Athelstan Fold** PR2 ..... 117 C3
**Athens View** BB10 ...... 128 C5
**Atherton Cl** 2 PR2 ...... 117 C2
**Atherton Rd** PR25 ........ 59 D8
**Atherton St**
Adlington PR7 .......... 31 A6
Bacup OL13 ............ 70 C8
**Atherton Way** OL13 ...... 70 B8
**Athletic St** BB10 ....... 128 C5
**Athlone Ave** FY2 ....... 152 C2
**Athole Gr** PR9 ........... 35 F7
**Athol Gr** PR6 ............ 43 E6
**Atholl St** 12 PR1 ........ 96 D8
**Athol St N** BB11 ........ 127 D5
**Athol St S** BB11 ........ 127 D5
**Athol St**
Nelson BB9 ........... 148 F8
Ramsbottom BL0 ......... 50 C7
**Atkinson Cl** 15 PR1 ...... 96 F8
**Atkinson St**
Burnley BB10 .......... 148 F3
Colne BB8 ............ 171 D4
**Atlas Rd** BB3 ............ 82 B1
**Atlas St** BB5 ........... 125 A1
**Atrium Ct** 9 BB11 ...... 128 B4
**Aubigny Dr** PR2 ......... 117 D4
**Auburn Gr** FY1 ......... 130 D2
**Auckland St** BB3 ......... 65 B7
**Audenlea** FY5 .......... 175 F3
**Audenshaw Rd** LA4 ..... 217 C4
**Audley Cl**
Lytham St Anne's FY8 ..... 90 D5
14 Nelson BB9 .......... 148 E8
**Audley Inf & Jun Schs**
BB1 ................. 102 A3
**Audley La** BB1 .......... 102 A4
**Audley Range** BB1 ...... 102 B4
**Audley St** BB1 .......... 102 A5
**Audlum Ct** 5 BL9 ......... 33 A2
**AUGHTON**
Hornby ............... 237 E6
Ormskirk ............... 6 A7
**Aughton Brow** LA2 ...... 237 E6
**Aughton Chase** PR8 ...... 35 A5
**Aughton Christ Church CE**
**Prim Sch** L39 .......... 15 C3
**Aughton Ct** LA1 ........ 218 D4
**Aughton Hall Cotts** L39 ... 15 C6
**Aughton Mews** PR8 ....... 35 A5
**AUGHTON PARK** .......... 15 E2
**Aughton Park Dr** L39 ..... 15 D2
**Aughton Park Sta** L39 .... 15 D2
**Aughton Rd**
Aughton LA2 ........... 237 E6
Southport PR8 .......... 35 A5
**Aughton St Michael's CE**
**Prim Sch** L39 .......... 15 B1
**Aughton St**
Fleetwood FY7 ......... 199 B5
Ormskirk L39 ........... 15 E4
**Aughton Town Green Prim**
**Sch** L39 ............... 6 D8
**Aughton Wlk** 2 PR1 .... 117 F1
**Augusta Cl** OL12 ......... 52 E2
**Augusta St**
4 Accrington BB5 ...... 104 C4
4 Rochdale OL12 ........ 52 E1
**Auster Cres** PR4 ........ 114 B2
**Austin Cres** PR2 ........ 117 B4
**Austin Gr** FY1 .......... 130 B1
**Austins Cl** PR25 ......... 60 A8
**Austin's La** BL6 ......... 32 F1
**Austin St**
6 Bacup OL13 .......... 87 F2
5 Burnley BB11 ........ 127 E5
**Austin Way** FY4 ......... 112 A7
**Austwick Rd** 4 LA1 ..... 218 B2
**Austwick Way** BB5 ...... 104 E5
**Avallon Way** BB3 ......... 82 C1
**Avalon Cl** 5 BB12 ...... 126 F7
**Avalon Dr** PR4 ........... 93 C7
**Avalwood Ave** PR4 ....... 75 B8
**Avebury Cl**
Blackburn BB2 .......... 82 A8
Horwich BL6 ........... 32 F1
**Aveling Dr** PR9 .......... 55 A6
**Avelon Cl** L31 ............ 5 B5
**AVENHAM** ............... 97 A6
**Avenham Cl** PR9 ......... 55 B5
**Avenham Colonnade**
PR1 .................. 97 A6
**Avenham Ct** 19 PR1 ...... 97 A7
**Avenham Gr** 5 FY1 ..... 130 B6
**Avenham La** PR1 ......... 97 A7
**Avenham Mills** 23 PR1 .... 97 A7
**Avenham Pl**
Newton-w-S PR4 ....... 114 F2
6 Preston PR1 .......... 97 A6
**Avenham Rd**
1 Chorley PR7 .......... 43 C7
Preston PR1 ............ 97 A7
**Avenham St** PR1 ......... 97 A7
**Avenham Terr** 11 PR1 .... 97 A7
**Avenue Par** BB5 ........ 104 D6
**Avenue Rd**
Hurst Green BB7 ....... 164 E1
Normoss FY3 .......... 131 B7
**Avenue The**
Adlington PR6 .......... 31 A8
Banks PR9 ............. 54 F5
Barley BB12 ........... 169 C5
Burnley BB10, BB11 ..... 128 D3
Carleton FY6 .......... 153 C4
Churchtown PR3 ....... 181 A3
Fulwood PR2 .......... 117 A6
Garstang PR3 ......... 204 B1
Higher Penwortham PR1 ... 96 B5
Leyland PR25 ........... 60 A6
Ormskirk L39 .......... 15 D6
Ormskirk L39 ........... 15 E6
Orrell WN5 ............ 10 D3
Preston PR2 .......... 116 D1
Southport PR8 .......... 36 F5
**Avery Gdns** FY6 ........ 153 B6
**Aviemore Cl**
5 Blackburn BB1 ....... 102 A4
2 Ramsbottom BL0 ...... 50 A2
**Avocet Ct** PR26 .......... 76 A1
**Avon Ave** FY7 .......... 175 D8
**Avon Bridge** PR2 ....... 117 C8
**Avon Cl** BB2 ........... 101 D3
**Avon Ct** BB12 .......... 127 D7
**Avondale Ave**
Blackburn BB1 ......... 102 E5
Burnley BB12 ......... 127 C7
**Avondale Cl** BB3 ......... 81 E2
**Avondale Cres** FY4 ...... 110 F7
**Avondale Dr**
Bamber Bridge PR5 ...... 77 B8
Ramsbottom BL0 ......... 49 F2
Tarleton PR4 ........... 57 A8
**Avondale Mews** BB3 ...... 81 E3
**Avondale Prim Sch** BB3 .. 81 E2
**Avondale Rd**
Chorley PR7 ............ 43 C7
Darwen BB3 ............ 81 E3
Lancaster LA1 ......... 215 A6
Lytham St Anne's FY8 .... 89 C8
Morecambe LA3 ........ 216 E3
Nelson BB9 ........... 148 D7
Southport PR9 .......... 35 B8
**Avondale Rd N** PR9 ...... 53 C1
**Avondale St**
Colne BB8 ............ 172 A5
Standish WN6 .......... 29 E2
**Avon Dr**
Barnoldswick BB18 ..... 196 C3
Bury BL9 .............. 33 A8
**Avon Gdns** PR4 ......... 116 D5
**Avon Gn** FY7 ........... 198 E4
**Avonhead Cl** BL6 ......... 31 F3
**Avon Ho** 12 PR1 .......... 97 D8
**Avon Pl** FY1 ............ 130 C8
**Avonside Ave** FY5 ...... 176 A3
**Avon St** FY8 ............. 89 E6
**Avonwood Cl** BB3 ........ 81 E2
**Avroe Cres** FY4 ......... 110 D4
**Axeholme Ct** BL6 ......... 31 F3
**Aylesbury Ave** FY4 ...... 130 D1
**Aylesbury Ho** L31 .......... 5 B4
**Aylesbury Wlk** BB10 ..... 148 D3
**Ayr Cl** PR8 .............. 35 F4
**Ayr Ct** FY7 ............. 175 E7
**Ayrefield Gr** WN6 ........ 19 D6
**Ayrefield Rd** WN8 ........ 19 C4
**Ayreshire Cl** PR7 ......... 60 F6
**Ayr Gr** BB11 ........... 127 D3
**Ayr Rd** BB1 ............ 102 D3
**Ayr St** LA1 ............. 215 B7
**Ayrton Ave** FY4 ......... 110 D7
**Ayrton St** BB8 .......... 171 E5
**Ayrton View** LA2 ........ 218 E4
**Aysgarth Ave** PR2 ....... 117 F7
**Aysgarth Ct** 1 FY4 ...... 110 F7
**Aysgarth Dr**
Accrington BB5 ........ 104 D6
Darwen BB3 ............ 81 E2
Lancaster LA1 ......... 218 D4
**Ays-Garth Rd** LA1 ...... 214 D8
**Azalea Cl**
Clayton-le-W PR25 ....... 77 E2
Fulwood PR2 .......... 118 C6
**Azalea Gr** LA4 .......... 217 E5
**Azalea Rd** BB2 .......... 101 B6

## B

**Babbacombe Ave** FY4 ... 110 B6
**Babylon La** PR6 .......... 31 B8
**Back Albert Rd** BB8 ..... 171 D4
**Back Albert St**
Bury BL9 .............. 33 A2
10 Padiham BB12 ....... 126 C8
**Back Alfred St** 11 BL0 .... 50 B5
**Back Altham St** 5
BB12 ................. 126 D8
**Back Andrew St N** 13
BL9 .................. 33 A2
**Back Andrew St** 14 BL9 ... 33 A2
**Back Arthur St** 15 BB5 ... 124 F3
**Back Ashburton Rd** 14
FY1 .................. 130 C7
**Back Ashby St** 1 PR7 .... 43 D6
**Back Ash St** 8 BL9 ....... 33 A2
**Back Atkinson St** BB8 ... 171 C4
**Back Avondale Rd (E)** 4
LA3 .................. 216 E3
**Back Avondale Rd (W)**
LA3 .................. 216 E3
**Back Bath St** PR9 ........ 35 B8
**Back Bell La**
8 Bury BL9 ............ 33 A3
Bury BL9 .............. 33 B3
**Back Benson St** BL9 ...... 33 A1
**Back Blackburn Rd E**
BL7 .................. 47 D3
**Back Blackburn Rd W**
BL7 .................. 47 D3
**Back Bolton Rd** BB3 ...... 65 B7
**Back Bond St W** BL9 ..... 33 A2
**Back Bond St** BB8 ...... 171 D5
**Back Boundary St** 14
BB8 ................. 171 D4
**Back Bourne's Row** PR5 .. 98 E1
**Back Bridge St** 2 BL0 .... 50 C6
**Back Broading Terr**
BB4 ................. 106 A3
**Back Brook St N** 13 BL9 .. 33 A4
**Back Brow** WN8 ......... 10 C7
**Back Brown St** BB8 ..... 171 C4
**Back Burnley Rd** BB5 ... 104 C6
**Back Burton Rd** FY4 ..... 130 F1
**Back Calton St** LA4 ...... 217 B6
**Back Cambridge St** 10
BB8 ................. 171 D4
**Back Canada St** BL6 ...... 32 B3
**Back Carr Mill St** BB4 .... 85 B5
**Back Cedar St N** 1 BL9 ... 33 B3
**Back Cedar St** 2 BL9 ..... 33 B3
**Back Cemetery Terr** 9
OL13 ................. 70 D8
**Back Chapel St**
1 Barnoldswick BB18 ... 196 B2
4 Colne BB8 .......... 171 D4
Horwich BL6 ........... 32 C3
**Back Chesham Rd N** 5
BL9 .................. 33 A4
**Back Chesham Rd S**
BL9 .................. 33 A4
**Back Chester St** BL9 ..... 33 A4
**Back Church St**
Barrowford BB9 ........ 170 D3
8 Blackpool FY1 ....... 130 B5
5 Great Harwood BB6 ... 124 C5
3 Hapton BB12 ........ 126 C4
1 Newchurch BB4 ....... 86 E1
**Back Clarendon Rd**
FY1 .................. 130 B2
**Back Clayton St** 9
BB9 ................. 170 D1
**Back Club St** PR5 ........ 77 E7
**Back Colne Rd**
Barnoldswick BB18 ..... 196 A1
Trawden BB8 ......... 172 C2
**Back Commons** BB7 ..... 189 D1
**Back Constablelee** BB4 ... 85 F4
**Back Cookson St** 12
FY1 .................. 130 C6
**Back Cowm La** OL12 ...... 71 C3
**Back Crescent St** LA4 ... 217 A5
**Back Crown St** BL6 ....... 32 A4
**Back Cunliffe Rd** 4
FY1 .................. 130 D2
**Back Curzon St** FY8 ...... 90 A7
**Back Darwen Rd N** 2
BL7 .................. 47 E1
**Back Deal St** BL9 ........ 33 B2
**Back Delamere St S**
BL9 .................. 33 A5
**Back Derby St** 6 BB8 ... 171 D5
**Back Drinkhouse La**
PR26 ................. 58 B1
**Back Duckworth St**
4 Bury BL9 ............ 33 A4
12 Darwen BB3 .......... 82 A1
**Back Duke St** 1 BB8 .... 171 D4
**Back Duncan St** BL6 ..... 32 C3
**Back Earl St** 2 BB8 ..... 171 D4
**Back East Bank** 1
BB9 ................. 170 D4
**Back Eaves St** FY1 ...... 130 B7
**Back Elizabeth St** BB4 .... 86 F4
**Back Elm St** 10 BL9 ...... 33 B2
**Back Emmett St** BL6 ..... 32 B3
**Back Epsom Rd** FY5 ..... 152 F8
**Back Fazakerley St** 14
PR7 .................. 43 C8
**Back Fir St** BL9 .......... 33 B2
**Back Fletcher St** BL9 ..... 33 A2
**Back Forest Rd** PR8 ...... 35 D6
**Back Garston St** BL9 ..... 33 A4
**Back George St** BL6 ...... 32 C3
**Back Gisburn Rd** BB9 ... 170 E7
**Back Glen Eldon Rd**
FY8 .................. 89 E7
**Back Green St** 7 LA4 ... 217 B6
**Back Grimshaw St** 8
PR1 .................. 97 A7
**Back Grove Terr** 10
LA4 ................. 217 F4
**Back Hall St** BB8 ....... 171 D4
**Back Halstead St** 2
BL9 .................. 33 A4
**Back Hamilton St** 1
BL9 .................. 33 A4
**Back Harry St** BB9 ...... 170 D3
**Back Haslam St** BL9 ...... 33 A4
**Back Headroomgate Rd**
FY8 .................. 89 F8
**Back Heys** BB5 ......... 103 E3
**Back Heywood St E** 15
BL9 .................. 33 A2
**Back Heywood St W**
BL9 .................. 33 A1
**Back High St**
Belmont BL7 ........... 46 C5
Blackpool FY1 ......... 130 B6
Chapeltown BL7 ......... 48 C4
**Back Hill St** 17 BB4 ...... 86 A7
**Back Holly St S** 9 BL9 ... 33 A2
**Back Holly St** BL9 ........ 33 A2
**Back Hope St** OL13 ....... 87 F4
**Backhouse St** 1 BB5 .... 103 E4
**Back Hunter St** 1
LA5 ................. 223 D2
**Back Huntley Mount Rd**
BL9 .................. 33 B3
**Back Hurst St** BL9 ........ 33 A1
**Back Ingham St E** BL9 .... 33 A1
**Back Ingham St** BL9 ...... 33 A1
**Back Kershaw St** 10
BL9 .................. 33 A2
**Back Knowlys Rd** 2
LA3 ................. 212 F8
**Back La**
Accrington BB5 ........ 104 E1
Appley Bridge WN6 ...... 19 E8
Bolton Green PR7 ....... 42 B7
Bretherton PR26 ........ 57 E5
Burscough Bridge L40 ..... 25 E6
Carnforth LA5, LA6 ..... 221 E7
Chorley PR6 ........... 44 C5
Clayton Green PR6 ....... 78 A2
Cumeragh Village PR3 ... 139 B6
Gisburn BB7 .......... 231 C3
Great Eccleston PR3 .... 156 B5
Greenhalgh PR4 ....... 133 B4
Grindleton BB7 ........ 190 B8
Haskayne, Clieves Hills
L39 .................. 14 E1
Haskayne L39 ........... 13 D3
Higham BB12 ......... 146 E6
Leyland PR25 ........... 60 C7
Longridge PR3 ........ 161 B6
Longton PR4 ........... 74 E8
Maghull L39 ............ 5 E6
Mawdesley L40 ......... 40 D1
Nelson BB10 .......... 149 F7
Newburgh L40, WN8 ...... 26 E2
Newton BB7 .......... 228 F6
Preesall FY6 .......... 200 A2
Rathmell BD24 ........ 236 F6
Rawtenstall BB4 ......... 86 A3
Rimington BB7 ........ 191 E8
Royal Oak L39 ........... 7 B2
Sabden BB12, BB7 ..... 146 C6
Skelmersdale, Digmoor
WN8 .................. 9 D6
Skelmersdale, Holland Moor
WN8 .................. 9 E7
Stalmine FY6 ......... 177 E6
Trawden BB8 ......... 172 B2
Tunstall LA6 .......... 241 D4
Warton LA5 .......... 223 D5
Whitworth OL12 ......... 71 C3
Wiswell BB7 .......... 144 F8
Wray LA2 ............ 238 C6
Wrayton LA6 .......... 241 E2
**Back La E** L40 ........... 40 F1
**Back Lathom St** 9 BL9 ... 33 A4
**Back Laurel St** 2 BL9 .... 33 B2
**Back Leach St** BB8 ..... 171 C4
**Back Lee St** BB4 ......... 85 B2
**Back Lines St** 2 LA4 ... 217 B5
**Back Longworth Rd**
BL7 .................. 47 D3
**Back Lord St**
Blackpool FY1 ......... 130 B6
7 Lancaster LA1 ....... 218 D1
5 Rawtenstall BB4 ....... 86 A7
**Back Lune St** BB8 ...... 171 E4
**Back Manor St** 1 BL9 .... 33 A2
**Back Marine Rd** LA4 .... 216 F4
**Back Mason St** 17 BL9 .... 33 A2
**Back Moon Ave** 5
FY1 .................. 130 B2
**Back Morecambe St**
LA4 ................. 217 B6
**Back Moss La** L40 ......... 25 F7
**Back Mount St** 5 PR7 .... 43 C8
**Back Myrtle St S** BL9 ..... 33 B2
**Back Myrtle St** 4 BL9 .... 33 B2
**Back Nelson St** BL6 ...... 32 D3
**Back New St** 5 LA5 ..... 223 D2
**Back Nook Terr** 2
OL12 ................. 52 F3
**Back North Cres** FY8 ..... 89 E6
**Back Oddfellows Terr**
BB4 .................. 86 F3
**Back Oram St** BL9 ........ 33 A4
**Back Ormrod St** 11 BL9 ... 33 A2
**Back O The Town La** L38 ... 3 E3
**Back Owen's Row** BL6 .... 32 C3
**Back Oxford St** BL9 ....... 33 A1
**Back Parkinson St**
BB2 ................. 101 B2
**Back Parsonage St** 10
BL9 .................. 33 A3
**Back Patience St** 10
OL12 ................. 52 C1
**Back Percy St** BL9 ........ 33 B3
**Back Peter St**
8 Barrowford BB9 ...... 170 D4
3 Bury BL9 ............ 33 A3
**Back Pine St** 1 BL9 ...... 33 B2
**Back Pleasant St** 5
FY1 .................. 130 B7
**Back Queen St**
Great Harwood BB6 ..... 124 C5
12 Lancaster LA1 ....... 214 F7
1 Morecambe LA4 ...... 217 B5
**Back Railway View** PR7 .. 31 A7
**Back Rawlinson St** 16
BL6 .................. 32 B4
**Back Read's Rd** FY1 ..... 130 C4
**Back Regent St** 1 BB4 .... 85 B3
**Back Rhoden Rd** BB5 ... 103 D2
**Back Richard Burch St** 1
BL9 .................. 33 A3
**Back Rings Row** BB4 .... 106 A1
**Back Rochdale Old Rd N** 1
BL9 .................. 33 C3
**Back Rochdale Old Rd S**
3 Bury BL9 ............ 33 C3
Bury, Fairfield BL9 ....... 33 D3
**Back Rochdale Rd** BL9 ... 33 B2
**Back Rochdale Rd S** 18
BL9 .................. 33 A2
**Back Roseberry Ave N** 4
LA4 ................. 217 C5
**Back Rushton St** 6
OL13 ................. 70 E8
**Back St Anne's Rd W**
FY8 .................. 89 E6
**Back St George's Sq**
FY8 .................. 89 D7
**Back St John St** OL13 ..... 87 F3
**Back Salford St** BL9 ...... 33 A4
**Back Sandy Bank Rd**
BL7 .................. 48 D5
**Back School La**
Skelmersdale WN8 ....... 17 D2
Up Holland WN8 ........ 10 C7
**Back Seed St** 8 PR1 ...... 96 F8
**Back Shannon St** 4
FY1 .................. 130 B3
**Back Shaw-Street** BL9 .... 33 B3
**Back Shuttleworth St** 7
BB12 ................. 126 C8
**Back Skipton Rd** 8
BB18 ................. 196 B2
**Back Skull House La**
WN6 .................. 19 C8
**Back South Cross St E** 16
BL9 .................. 33 A2
**Back Spencer St** BB4 ..... 86 A7
**Back Springfield Rd N**
FY8 .................. 89 E6
**Back Square St** BL0 ...... 50 C6
**Back St** LA3 ............ 209 D8
**Back Stanley St** BL0 ...... 50 B5
**Back Starkie St** PR1 ...... 96 F6
**Backs The** PR3 .......... 140 A6
**Back Sun St** 9 LA1 ..... 214 F8
**Back Teak St** 5 BL9 ...... 33 B2
**Back Tinline St** 12 BL9 ... 33 A2
**Back Union St** 7 BL7 .... 47 D2
**Back Virginia St** PR8 ..... 35 C6
**Back Warbreck Rd** 2
FY1 .................. 130 B6
**Back Wash La** BL9 ....... 33 B2
**Back Wash La S** 7 BL9 ... 33 A2
**Back Waterloo Rd** 8
FY1 .................. 130 B1
**Back Water St**
10 Accrington BB5 ..... 104 C6

**Back Water St** *continued*
5 Bolton BL7 47 D2
**Back Wellington St** BB5 104 C5
**Back West Cres** FY8 89 E6
**Back West End Rd N** LA4 216 F4
**Back Willow St** BB12 127 E6
**Back Winterdyne Terr** LA3 216 E4
**Back Woodfield Rd** 4 FY1 130 B2
**Back Wood St** BL6 32 C3
**Back Wright St** BL6 32 B4
**Back York St**
Clitheroe BB7 166 F8
Rawtenstall BB4 86 A7
**Back Zion St** 16 BB8 171 D4
**Bacon St** 8 BB9 148 E8
**BACUP** 70 E8
Bacup Holy Trinity Stacksteads CE Prim Sch OL13 70 C8
Bacup Mus★ OL13 87 F3
**Bacup Old Rd** OL13 87 F7
Bacup & Rawtenstall Gram Sch BB4 69 F8
**Bacup Rd**
Rawtenstall BB4, OL13 69 E8
Rawtenstall, Lower Cloughfold BB4 86 C2
Todmorden OL14 88 E5
Walk Mill BB11 107 E6
Bacup St Saviour's Com Prim Sch OL13 71 A8
Bacup Thorn Prim Sch OL13 87 F3
**Baden Ct** BB1 122 F3
**Baden Terr** BB2 101 D1
**Badge Brow** BB5 103 E5
**Badger Cl** BB12 146 D1
**Badger Rd** PR26 77 A4
**Badgers Cl** BB5 104 E8
**Badgers Croft** PR2 118 F1
**Badgers Rake** L37 11 C5
**Badger St** BL9 33 A3
**Badgers Way** PR5 97 B3
**Badgers Wlk** PR7 61 A3
**Badgers Wlk E** FY8 91 C3
**Badgers Wlk W** 12 FY8 91 B3
**Badgers Wood** PR3 159 C7
**Badger Wells Cotts** BB7 146 A8
**Bagganley La**
Chorley PR6 61 E1
Great Knowley PR6 61 F2
**Bagnold Rd** PR1 118 D1
**Bagot St** FY1 130 B1
**Baildon Rd** OL12 52 B1
**Bailey Bank** BB7 165 A7
**Bailey Cl** BB2 81 C8
**Bailey Ct** FY3 130 E6
**Bailey La**
Heysham LA3 212 E8
Tosside BD23 236 B3
**Bailey St**
Burnley BB11 127 E5
Earby BB18 197 C1
**Baillie St**
Fulwood PR2 118 C7
Fulwood PR2 118 C7
**BAILRIGG** 215 A1
**Bailrigg Chase** LA1 215 B1
**Bailrigg La** LA1 215 A1
**Baines Ave** FY3 152 F1
Baines Endowed CE Prim Sch FY4 130 F1
**Bainesfield** FY6 153 D1
**Baines Sch** FY6 153 D1
**Bairstow St**
3 Barnoldswick BB18 196 B3
Blackpool FY1 130 B3
14 Preston PR1 96 F7
**Bakers Ct** FY4 110 F7
**Baker's La** PR9 53 F3
**Bakers Mews** PR4 57 A6
**Baker St**
12 Bacup OL13 87 F3
Blackburn BB1 102 B4
Burnley BB11 127 E5
Coppull PR7 42 E1
Lancaster LA1 218 D3
4 Leyland PR25 77 B2
Nelson BB9 170 E1
Ramsbottom BL0 50 B5
**Bala Cl** BB1 101 E6
**Balaclava St** BB1 101 E6
**Balcarres Cl** PR25 77 A1
**Balcarres Pl** PR25 60 A8
**Balcarres Rd**
Chorley PR7 43 B5
Leyland PR25 60 A8
Leyland PR25 77 B1
Preston PR2 117 C2
**BALDERSTONE** 121 A5
**Balderstone Cl** BB10 148 D2
**Balderstone Hall La** BB2 120 C6
**Balderstone La** BB10 148 E2
**Balderstone Rd**
Freckleton PR4 93 B7
Preston PR1 96 D5
**BALDINGSTONE** 50 F1
**Baldwin Gr** FY1 130 D2
**Baldwin Hill** 3 BB7 166 D8
**Baldwin Rd** BB7 166 D8
**Baldwin's Bldgs** 14 BB4 86 A3
**Baldwin St**
Bacup OL13 70 B8
7 Bamber Bridge PR5 97 E1
5 Barrowford BB9 170 D4
Blackburn BB2 101 C3
**Balfour Cl**
Brierfield BB9 148 D5
Thornton FY5 153 D7
**Balfour Ct** 9 PR25 77 A1
**Balfour Ho** 5 BB2 101 C4
**Balfour Rd**
Fulwood PR2 117 E3
5 Rochdale OL12 52 C1
Southport PR8 35 E5
**Balfour St**
Blackburn BB2 101 C4
Great Harwood BB6 124 E5
Leyland PR25 77 A1
**Balham Ave** FY4 110 E5
**BALLADEN** 68 F8
Balladen Com Prim Sch BB4 68 F8
**Ballam Rd**
Lower Ballam FY8 112 C3
Lytham St Anne's FY8 91 B4
Preston PR2 116 E1
**Ballam St** BB11 128 A4
**Ballantrae Rd** BB1 102 D3
**Ballater St** BB11 127 D3
**Balle St** BB3 65 A8
**Ball Grove Dr** BB8 172 B5
**Balliol Cl** BB12 126 D6
**Ball La** LA2 237 C3
**Ballot Hill Cres** PR3 159 A5
**Ball's Pl** PR8 35 B7
**Ball St**
Blackpool FY1 130 B1
3 Nelson BB9 170 D1
Poulton-le-F FY6 153 D3
**Balmer Gr** FY1 130 D3
**Balmoral** PR7 30 E6
**Balmoral Ave**
Blackburn BB1 123 A4
Clitheroe BB7 166 C6
Leyland PR25 60 C8
Morecambe LA3 216 E3
**Balmoral Cl**
Horwich BL6 32 E2
Ramsbottom BL8 50 A1
Southport PR9 54 B3
Walmer Bridge PR4 74 F5
**Balmoral Cres** BB1 102 F4
**Balmoral Ct** PR7 43 B8
**Balmoral Dr**
Brinscall PR6 62 E8
Formby L37 11 E1
Southport PR9 54 B3
**Balmoral Pl** FY5 153 C8
**Balmoral Rd**
Accrington BB5 104 D7
5 Bamber Bridge PR5 97 D3
Blackpool FY4 110 B8
Chorley PR7 43 B8
Darwen BB3 65 B6
Eccleston PR7 41 C7
Haslingden BB4 85 A1
Lancaster LA1 215 A7
Lytham St Anne's FY8 90 A5
Maghull L31 5 C1
Morecambe LA3, LA4 216 F3
New Longton PR4 96 A1
**Balmoral Terr** FY7 199 B5
**Balm St** BL0 50 A4
**Balniel Cl** PR7 43 A7
**Balshaw Ave** PR7 60 D2
**Balshaw Cres** PR25 76 F2
**Balshaw House Gdns** PR7 60 D2
**Balshaw La** PR7 60 D1
Balshaw Lane Com Prim Sch PR7 60 E1
**Balshaw Rd**
Leyland PR25 76 F1
Lowgill LA2 239 E3
Balshaw's CE High Sch PR25 60 B7
**Balshaw St** 4 PR5 97 E2
**Baltic Bldgs** 4 BB4 69 E8
**Baltic Flats** 3 BB4 69 E8
**Baltic Rd** 5 BB4 69 E8
**Baltimore Rd** FY8 90 B6
**Bamber Ave**
Blackpool FY2 152 C4
Buckshaw Village PR7 60 E7
**BAMBER BRIDGE** 97 E1
Bamber Bridge Sta PR5 77 E8
**Bamber Gdns** PR9 36 A8
**Bambers La** FY4 111 C6
**Bambers La N** FY4 111 C7
**Bamber St** 2 PR7 43 B5
**Bamber's Wlk** PR4 113 E7
**Bamburgh Cl** FY4 111 A7
**Bamburgh Dr** BB12 127 E7
**Bamford Cl** BL9 33 E4
**Bamford Cres** BB5 104 D4
**Bamford Pl** 3 OL12 52 E1
**Bamford Rd** BL0 51 B6
**Bamfords Fold** PR26 57 F5
**Bamford St**
Burnley BB11 128 A6
Nelson BB9 149 A8
**Bampton Dr** PR4 116 D4
**Bamton Ave** FY4 110 C7
**Banastre** PR7 61 A2
**Banastre Rd** PR8 35 B5
**Banastre St** 10 BB5 125 A1
**Banbury Ave**
Blackpool FY2 152 D1
Oswaldtwistle BB5 103 C4
**Banbury Cl**
3 Accrington BB5 104 A7
Blackburn BB2 80 F8
**Banbury Dr** PR2 117 E4
**Banbury Rd**
Longshaw WN5 10 D2
Lytham St Anne's FY8 90 A6
Morecambe LA3 217 C3
**Bancroft Ave** FY5 176 C2
**Bancroft Fold** BB18 196 A1
Bancroft Mill Engine Mus★ BB18 196 B1
**Bancroft Rd** BB10 128 C8
**Bancroft St** 4 BB1 101 F5
**Band La** PR3 180 D1
**Bangor Ave** FY2 152 D4
**BANGOR'S GREEN** 14 D7
**Bangor St** BB1 101 F7
**Bank Ave** WN5 10 D5
**Bank Bottom** BB3 82 A1
**Bank Bridge** PR4 57 B5
**Bank Brow** WN8 19 C5
**Bank Cl**
Galgate LA2 210 F3
Longton PR4 75 A8
**Bank Cott** 2 LA2 239 B8
**Bank Cotts** BB7 144 B4
**Bank Croft** PR4 75 A8
**Bankcroft Cl** BB12 126 E8
**Bank End Cvn Pk** LA2 205 D6
**Bankfield**
Burnley BB11 128 A6
Skelmersdale WN8 9 C7
**Bankfield Ct** FY5 153 B8
**Bankfield Gr** FY1 130 E3
**Bankfield La** PR9 54 B2
**Bankfield St**
Bacup OL13 70 D8
Colne BB8 171 B4
Trawden BB8 172 B4
**Bankfield Terr**
1 Bacup OL13 70 D8
Barnoldswick BB18 196 C3
**BANK FOLD** 82 F5
**Bank Fold** BB9 170 E4
**Bank Hall Cotts** BB7 230 C1
**Bank Hall Terr** BB10 128 A7
**Bank Head La** PR5 98 D1
**BANK HEY** 123 A2
**Bank Hey Cl** BB1 123 A1
**Bank Hey La N** BB1 122 F3
**Bank Hey La S** BB1 123 A1
**Bank Hey St** FY1 130 B5
**Bank Hey View** BB2 81 C7
**Bank House La**
Bacup OL13 87 F2
Silverdale LA5 224 C3
Westhouse LA6 242 E4
**Bankhouse Mews** BB9 170 E4
**Bankhouse Rd** BB9 170 E1
**BANK HOUSES** 205 C7
**Bankhouse St**
Burnley BB11 127 F6
Burnley BB11 128 A6
**Bank House St** BB9 170 E4
**Bank La**
Blackburn BB1 102 D4
Warton PR4 92 D4
**BANK LANE** 50 E7
**Bank Mdw** BB3 32 C4
**Bank Mill St** 3 BB4 85 B2
**Bank Nook** PR9 53 F3
**Bank Par**
Burnley BB11 128 A6
Middleforth Green PR1 96 D3
Preston PR1 97 A6
**Bank Pas** PR8 35 A7
**Bank Pl** PR2 117 C1
**Bank Rd**
Lancaster LA1 218 D3
Up Holland WN8 19 D4
**BANKS** 54 F6
**Banksands La** PR3 201 E7
**Banksbarn** WN8 9 C7
**Banks Bridge Cl** BB18 196 C4
**Banks Cres** LA3 212 F6
**Banksfield Ave** PR2 117 C3
**Banksfield Pl** PR5 78 A7
**BANKS HILL** 196 B4
**Banks Hill** BB18 196 A4
**Bankside**
Blackburn BB2 101 E2
Clayton Green PR6 78 B1
Hightown L38 2 F3
Parbold WN8 27 B2
**Bankside Cl**
Bacup OL13 87 E1
Goodshaw Chapel BB4 106 A1
**Bankside La** OL13 87 F2
Banks Meth Sch PR9 55 B7
**Bank Sq** PR9 35 B8
**Banks Rd**
Fulwood PR2 117 C3
Southport PR9 54 D6
**Banks Rise** 10 LA2 239 D8
Banks St Stephens' CE Sch PR9 55 A5
**Banks St**
Blackpool FY1 130 B6
Lane Bottom BB10 149 B3
**Bank St**
Accrington BB5 104 C5
Adlington PR7 31 A7
14 Bacup OL13 87 F2
Bank Lane BL0 50 E7
**Bank St** *continued*
Barnoldswick BB18 196 C2
Brierfield BB9 148 B6
Chapeltown BL7 48 C4
Chorley PR7 43 C8
Church BB5 103 E6
Darwen BB3 82 A1
Haslingden BB4 85 B3
11 Nelson BB9 170 E1
Padiham BB12 146 C1
Rawtenstall BB4 86 A2
Trawden BB8 172 C1
**Banks Way** 12 LA2 239 D8
**Bank Terr**
Heapey PR6 62 C4
Simonstone BB12 125 E8
Whitworth OL12 52 C8
**Bank Top** BL9 50 F1
**BANK TOP** 101 D3
**Bank Top**
Blackburn BB2 101 C4
Burnley BB11 128 A6
**BANK TOP** 19 C4
**Bank View** FY6 177 C1
**Bank View Cotts** BB7 230 C1
**Bankwood** WN6 19 E6
**Banner Cl** PR7 41 B6
**Banneriggs Brow** LA6 243 A5
**Bannerman Terr** PR6 61 D2
**Bannister Brook Ho** PR25 77 A2
**Bannister Cl**
Higher Walton PR5 98 B4
Trawden BB8 172 B3
**Bannister Ct**
Blackpool FY2 152 B4
17 Nelson BB9 148 E8
**Bannister Dr** PR25 76 E1
**Bannister Gn** PR7 41 C3
**Bannister Hall Cres** PR5 98 B4
**Bannister Hall Dr** PR5 98 B4
**Bannister Hall La** PR5 98 B4
**Bannister La**
Eccleston PR7 41 C5
Hill Dale L40, WN6 27 E6
Leyland PR26 76 E4
**Bannister's Bit** 4 PR1 96 C2
**Bannister St**
11 Chorley PR7 43 C7
Lytham St Anne's FY8 91 B3
**Bannistre Cl** 1 FY8 90 A8
**Bannistre Ct** PR4 57 A6
**Bannistre Mews** PR4 57 A6
**Barbara Castle Way** BB1 101 E5
**Barberry Bank** BL7 47 E2
**BARBER'S MOOR** 58 D3
**BARBON** 243 A5
**Barbondale Rd** LA6, LA10 243 E8
**Barbon Pl** LA1 218 C2
**Barbon St**
Burnley BB10 148 C2
14 Padiham BB12 146 C1
**Barbrook Cl** WN6 29 B2
**Barclay Ave**
Blackpool FY4 130 F2
Burnley BB11 127 C4
**Barclay Ct** PR3 140 A7
**Barclay Rd** PR3 140 A7
**Bar Cotts** BB12 145 E1
**Barcroft Gn** BB10 128 E1
**Barcroft St** BB8 171 C5
**Barden Croft** BB5 124 F4
Barden Jun Sch BB10 148 A1
**Barden La** BB10, BB12 148 A2
**Barden Pl** PR2 118 D4
**Barden Rd** BB5 103 F4
**Barden St** 3 BB10 148 B1
**Barden View** BB10 148 A2
**Bardsea Pl** PR2 116 F3
**Bardsley Cl** WN8 10 A7
**Bardsway** FY5 176 A3
**Bardsway Ave** FY3 130 F6
**BARE** 217 E7
**Bare Ave** LA4 217 E6
**Bare La** LA4 217 E5
Bare Lane Sta LA4 217 E6
**Barford Cl**
Southport PR8 21 A6
Up Holland WN8 10 A7
**Barford Gr** BL6 32 F1
**Bargee Cl** BB1 101 F3
**Barham St** 6 FY1 130 B2
**Barker Brow** BB1, PR7 142 A3
**Barker Cl** LA6 240 B7
**Barker Ct** 11 OL13 88 A1
**Barkerfield Cl** BB12 146 F5
**Barkerhouse Rd** BB10, BB9 149 B8
**Barker La** BB2 122 C2
**Barker Terr** BB7 189 E1
**Barkfield Ave** L37 11 E4
**Barkfield La** L37 11 D4
**BARLEY** 169 B5
**Barley Bank St** BB3 81 F2
**Barley Cl** BB2 101 D5
**Barley Cop La** LA1 218 B4
**Barleydale Rd** BB9 170 E5
**Barleyfield**
Clayton Green PR5 78 C3
Nelson BB9 148 D7
**Barley Gr** BB10 128 C6
**BARLEY GREEN** 169 C5
**Barley Holme Rd** BB4 86 A8
**Barley La** BB9 169 B7
**Barley New Rd** BB12 169 E5
**Barley St** BB12 126 C7
**Barley Way** 9 BB2 101 D5
**Barlow Cres** FY3 130 E4
**Barlow Ct** BL7 48 E5
**Barlows Bldgs** 5 BB4 85 F1
**Barlow's La** L39 22 D5
**Barlow St**
Accrington BB5 104 A6
Bacup OL13 70 B7
Horwich BL6 32 C2
Preston, Maudlands PR1 117 E1
Preston PR1 117 F2
11 Rawtenstall BB4 86 A3
**Barmouth Ave** FY3 131 A3
**Barmouth Cres** BB1 122 E1
**Barmouth Ct** PR2 117 A3
**Barmskin La**
Heskin Green PR7 41 B2
Wrightington Bar WN6 28 C8
**Barn Acre** BL6 31 E1
**Barnacre Cl**
Fulwood PR2 118 A8
Lancaster LA1 215 B2
**Barnacre Rd** PR3 140 A8
Barnacre Rd Prim Sch PR3 139 F8
**Barnard Cl** BB5 103 C4
**Barnbrook St** BL9 33 A3
**Barn Cl** PR4 56 A2
**Barn Croft**
3 Clitheroe BB7 166 D7
Higher Penwortham PR1 96 B4
1 Leyland PR26 76 B1
**Barncroft Dr** BL6 32 F3
**Barnes Ave** BB4 85 F2
**Barnes Cl** BL0 50 A3
**Barnes Ct** BB10 128 D4
**Barnes Dr**
Cleveleys FY5 175 E5
Maghull L31 5 C3
**Barnes Rd**
Morecambe LA3 216 E3
Ormskirk L39 15 E3
Skelmersdale WN8 17 E1
**Barnes Sq** 1 BB5 124 F2
**Barnes St**
Accrington BB5 104 C6
Burnley BB11 128 A6
Church BB5 103 E6
Clayton-le-M BB5 124 F3
Haslingden BB4 85 B4
**BARNFIELD** 104 E5
**Barnfield**
6 Bamber Bridge PR5 77 A8
Kirkham PR4 114 A5
Much Hoole PR4 74 E3
**Barnfield Ave** BB10 128 F6
Barnfield Bsns Ctr BB9 148 F6
**Barnfield Cl**
Bolton BL7 47 E2
4 Cleveleys FY5 175 F4
Colne BB8 172 A5
**Barnfield Dr** WN8 9 E7
**Barnfield Manor** FY6 154 D3
**Barnfield St**
Accrington BB5 104 D5
Rochdale OL12 52 F2
**Barnfield Way** BB5 125 E5
**Barnflatt Cl** PR5 98 A4
**Barn Gill Cl** BB1 101 F3
**Barn Hey** PR4 95 A1
**Barn Hey Dr** PR26 76 E3
**Barn Hey Rd** L33 1 A2
**Barn Mdw**
Clayton Brook PR5 78 B6
Edgworth BL7 48 D5
**Barn Meadow Cres** BB1 124 C1
**Barnmeadow La** BB6 124 C5
**BARNOLDSWICK**
Earby 196 C1
Ingleton 242 D2
Barnoldswick CE Prim Sch BB18 196 B2
**Barnoldswick La** LA6 242 D3
**Barnoldswick Rd**
Beverley BB8, BB9 170 F7
Kelbrook BB18 194 F6
**Barnsfold** PR2 117 D6
**Barnside**
Euxton PR7 60 C3
Whitworth OL12 52 B8
**Barns La** PR3 161 C8
**Barnstaple Way** PR4 116 F6
**Barns The** PR4 133 A2
**Barn View** PR6 30 F8
**Barnwood Cres** BB18 197 C1
**Barnwood Rd** BB18 197 B1
**Baron Rd** FY1 130 C1
**Barons Cl** BB3 82 A7
**Baron St**
Darwen BB3 81 F2
Rawtenstall BB4 86 D1
**Barons Way**
Blackburn BB3 82 A6
Euxton PR7 60 D2
Great Harwood BB6 124 D4
**Barracks Rd** BB11 127 D6
**Barret Hill Brow** BB7 230 B4
**Barret St** BB18 197 A1
**Barrett Ave** PR8 35 A2
**Barrett Ct** 6 BL9 33 A2
**Barrett Rd** PR8 35 A2
**Barrett St** 5 BB10 128 A8
**Barrington Ct** BB5 103 F7
**Barrington Dr** PR8 21 B5

Barrison Gn L40 . . . . . . . . . 24 E2
Barritt Rd BB4 . . . . . . . . . . . 85 F2
Barronwood Ct PR4 . . . . . . 57 A5
BARROW . . . . . . . . . . . . . . . 166 D1
Barrowcroft Cl WN1 . . . . . 30 B1
BARROWFORD . . . . . . . . . . 170 C4
Barrowford Rd
Barrowford BB9 . . . . . . . . . 170 B1
Colne BB8 . . . . . . . . . . . . . 171 B5
4 Colne BB8 . . . . . . . . . . . 171 C5
Fence BB12 . . . . . . . . . . . . 147 C7
Barrowford St Thomas CE
Prim Sch BB9 . . . . . . . . . . 170 C3
Barrowford Sch BB9 . . . . 170 D3
BARROW NOOK . . . . . . . . . . . 7 F2
Barrow Nook La L39 . . . . . . . 7 E2
Barrow Sch BB7 . . . . . . . . 166 D2
Barrows La LA3 . . . . . . . . . 212 E7
Barrow's La PR3 . . . . . . . . 156 B5
Barrows La E PR3 . . . . . . . 156 B5
Barry Ave PR2 . . . . . . . . . . 117 A3
Barry Gr LA3 . . . . . . . . . . . . 212 F6
Barry St BB12 . . . . . . . . . . . 127 C7
Bar St BB10 . . . . . . . . . . . . 128 B8
Bar Terr OL12 . . . . . . . . . . . . 52 C7
Bartholomew Rd LA4 . . . . 217 C4
Bartle La PR4 . . . . . . . . . . 116 C7
Bartle Pl PR2 . . . . . . . . . . . 116 E1
Bartle Rd FY8 . . . . . . . . . . . . 90 A8
Bartle St BB11 . . . . . . . . . . 127 D5
Bartlett Ho PR8 . . . . . . . . . . 35 B3
BARTON
Fulwood . . . . . . . . . . . . . . . 137 B7
Ormskirk . . . . . . . . . . . . . . . 13 F6
Barton Ave
Blackpool FY1 . . . . . . . . . . 130 B2
Knott End-on-S FY6 . . . . . . 199 E5
Barton Ct LA1 . . . . . . . . . . 215 A4
Barton Gdns LA1 . . . . . . . . 215 B5
Barton Heys Rd L37 . . . . . . 11 D1
Barton La PR3 . . . . . . . . . . 137 E7
Barton Mans FY8 . . . . . . . . . 89 C7
Barton Rd
Lancaster LA1 . . . . . . . . . . 215 A4
Lytham St Anne's FY8 . . . . . 89 D8
Barton Row LA6 . . . . . . . . . 240 B7
Barton St Lawrence CE
Prim Sch PR3 . . . . . . . . . 137 B7
Bartons Cl PR9 . . . . . . . . . . 54 D5
Barton Sq FY6 . . . . . . . . . . 199 E5
Barton St BB2 . . . . . . . . . . . 101 E5
Barwood Lea Mill 14
BL0 . . . . . . . . . . . . . . . . . . 50 C6
Bashall Gr PR25 . . . . . . . . . . 77 B3
BASHALL TOWN . . . . . . . . . 188 E1
Basil St
Colne BB8 . . . . . . . . . . . . . 171 D4
Preston PR1 . . . . . . . . . . . . 118 C2
Basnett St BB10 . . . . . . . . . 148 C1
Bassenthwaite Rd FY3 . . 131 C2
Bassett Cl OL12 . . . . . . . . . . 52 E3
Bassett Gdns OL12 . . . . . . . 52 E3
Bassett Way OL12 . . . . . . . . 52 E2
Bass La BL9 . . . . . . . . . . . . . 50 D3
BASTWELL . . . . . . . . . . . . . 102 A8
Bastwell Rd BB1 . . . . . . . . . 101 F7
Bateman Gr LA4 . . . . . . . . . 217 B5
Bateman Rd LA4 . . . . . . . . . 217 B5
Bateman St BL6 . . . . . . . . . . 32 D2
Bates St BB5 . . . . . . . . . . . 124 E3
Bath Ho* PR3 . . . . . . . . . . 141 E3
Bath Mill La LA1 . . . . . . . . . 215 A8
Bath Mill Sq 7 LA1 . . . . . 215 A8
Bath Rd FY8 . . . . . . . . . . . . . 91 B3
Bath St N PR9 . . . . . . . . . . . 35 B8
Bath Springs L39 . . . . . . . . 15 F5
Bath Springs Ct L39 . . . . . . 15 F5
Bath St
Accrington BB5 . . . . . . . . . 104 B4
1 Bacup OL13 . . . . . . . . . . . 88 A2
Blackburn BB2 . . . . . . . . . . 101 C4
Blackpool FY4 . . . . . . . . . . 130 B1
Colne BB8 . . . . . . . . . . . . . 171 E5
23 Darwen BB3 . . . . . . . . . . 82 A1
Lancaster LA1 . . . . . . . . . . 215 A8
Lytham St Anne's FY8 . . . . . 91 B3
Morecambe LA4 . . . . . . . . . 217 A5
Nelson BB9 . . . . . . . . . . . . 148 F8
2 Preston PR2 . . . . . . . . . . 117 D1
Southport PR9 . . . . . . . . . . . 35 B8
Bathurst Ave FY3 . . . . . . . 131 A7
Bathurst St 3 BB2 . . . . . . 101 D5
Batridge Rd BL7 . . . . . . . . . 48 A7
Battersby St BL9 . . . . . . . . . 33 D3
Battismore Rd LA4 . . . . . . 217 B5
Battle Way L37 . . . . . . . . . . 12 B2
Bawdlands BB7 . . . . . . . . . 166 D8
Bawhead Rd BB18 . . . . . . . 197 B1
Baxendale Gr 9 PR5 . . . . . 97 E1
BAXENDEN . . . . . . . . . . . . . 104 E1
Baxenden St John's CE
Prim Sch BB5 . . . . . . . . . 104 E1
Baxtergate LA4 . . . . . . . . . 217 B6
Baxter St WN6 . . . . . . . . . . . 29 F1
Bayard St BB12 . . . . . . . . . 127 A6
Bay Cl LA3 . . . . . . . . . . . . . 212 D6
Baycliffe Cres LA4 . . . . . . 217 A5
BAY GATE . . . . . . . . . . . . . 230 A4
BAY HORSE . . . . . . . . . . . . 207 C6
Bay Horse Dr LA1 . . . . . . . 215 B3
Bay Horse La PR4 . . . . . . . 135 D4
Bay Horse Rd LA2 . . . . . . . 211 E4
Bayley Fold BB7 . . . . . . . . 166 E8
Bayley St BB5 . . . . . . . . . . 124 E3
Bayliss Cl PR2 . . . . . . . . . . 118 F3
Baylton Ct PR3 . . . . . . . . . 181 D2
Baylton Dr PR3 . . . . . . . . . 181 D2
Baynes Cotts 5 LA2 . . . . 239 B8
Baynes St BB3 . . . . . . . . . . . 82 F1
Bay Rd
Fulwood PR2 . . . . . . . . . . . 118 E2
Heysham LA3 . . . . . . . . . . . 212 D6
Bayside FY7 . . . . . . . . . . . . 199 B4
Bay St BB1 . . . . . . . . . . . . . 102 A7
Bayswater FY2 . . . . . . . . . . 152 C4
Bay The FY5 . . . . . . . . . . . . 175 C5
Baytree Cl
Bamber Bridge PR5 . . . . . . . 77 C8
Southport PR9 . . . . . . . . . . . 54 D5
Bay Tree Farm PR2 . . . . . . 95 D8
Baytree Gr BL0 . . . . . . . . . . . 50 B2
Bay Tree Rd PR6 . . . . . . . . . 78 B3
Baytree Wlk OL12 . . . . . . . . 71 C1
Bay View LA6 . . . . . . . . . . . 237 B8
Bay View Apartments
FY6 . . . . . . . . . . . . . . . . . . 199 D5
Bay View Ave LA2 . . . . . . . 218 C8
Bay View Cres LA2 . . . . . . 218 C8
Bay View Dr LA3 . . . . . . . . 212 F8
Baywood St BB1 . . . . . . . . . 101 F7
BAZIL . . . . . . . . . . . . . . . . . 209 D6
Bazil Gr LA3 . . . . . . . . . . . . 209 D7
Bazil La LA3 . . . . . . . . . . . . 209 D7
Bazley Rd FY8 . . . . . . . . . . . 90 D3
Beacham Rd PR8 . . . . . . . . . 35 E7
Beach Ave
Cleveleys FY5 . . . . . . . . . . 175 D3
Lytham St Anne's FY8 . . . . . 90 C3
Beachcomber Dr FY5 . . . 175 C3
Beachley Rd PR2 . . . . . . . . 117 A4
Beachley Sq BB12 . . . . . . . 127 D7
Beachmews PR8 . . . . . . . . . 34 F6
Beach Priory Gdns PR8 . . . 35 A6
Beach Rd
Cleveleys FY5 . . . . . . . . . . 175 D3
Fleetwood FY7 . . . . . . . . . . 198 E3
Lytham St Anne's FY8 . . . . . 89 D7
Pilling Lane FY6 . . . . . . . . 200 B7
Southport PR8 . . . . . . . . . . . 34 F6
Beach St
Lytham St Anne's FY8 . . . . . 91 A3
Morecambe LA4 . . . . . . . . . 217 E7
Beacon Ave PR2 . . . . . . . . 117 D5
Beacon Cl BB8 . . . . . . . . . . 171 C3
Beacon Crossing WN8 . . . 27 C2
Beacon Ct PR3 . . . . . . . . . . 138 D5
Beacon Ctry Pk* WN8 . . . 18 F2
Beacon Dr PR3 . . . . . . . . . 138 D6
Beacon Fell Ctry Pk*
PR3 . . . . . . . . . . . . . . . . . . 183 F2
Beacon Fell Rd PR3 . . . . . 183 E2
Beacon Fell View Holiday
Pk PR3 . . . . . . . . . . . . . . . 162 D1
Beacon Gr
Fulwood PR2 . . . . . . . . . . . 117 D4
Garstang PR3 . . . . . . . . . . 181 B6
Beacon Hill High Sch
FY2 . . . . . . . . . . . . . . . . . . 152 D1
Beacon Hts WN8 . . . . . . . . . 10 A8
Beacon La L40, WN8 . . . . . . 18 D4
Beacon Lo 10 PR2 . . . . . . 118 F4
Beacon Rd
Poulton-le-F FY6 . . . . . . . . 154 A3
Shevington Moor WN6 . . . . . 29 B2
Beacon Sch WN8 . . . . . . . . . 9 E8
Beaconsfield Ave PR1 . . . 118 E1
Beaconsfield Ct 4 L39 . . . 15 F5
Beaconsfield Rd PR9 . . . . . 35 F6
Beaconsfield St
3 Accrington BB5 . . . . . . 104 D5
Great Harwood BB6 . . . . . 124 C5
16 Haslingden BB4 . . . . . . . 85 B3
Beaconsfield Terr
Catterall PR3 . . . . . . . . . . 181 E2
Chorley PR6 . . . . . . . . . . . . 61 D2
Beacon St PR7 . . . . . . . . . . . 43 D7
Beacons The WN6 . . . . . . . 19 D7
Beacon View
Appley Bridge WN6 . . . . . . . 19 C8
Longridge PR3 . . . . . . . . . . 162 B3
Standish WN6 . . . . . . . . . . . 29 D1
Beacon View Dr WN8 . . . . . 10 B7
Beacon Villa PR3 . . . . . . . 140 C8
Beale Cl BB1 . . . . . . . . . . . 102 B1
Beale Rd BB9 . . . . . . . . . . . 148 B8
Beamish Ave BB2 . . . . . . . . 81 D8
Beamont Dr PR1 . . . . . . . . . 96 D8
Bean Ave FY4 . . . . . . . . . . . 110 E8
Beardshaw Ave FY1 . . . . . 130 D2
Beardsworth St BB1 . . . . 102 A7
BEARDWOOD . . . . . . . . . . 101 B7
Beardwood BB2 . . . . . . . . . 101 A8
Beardwood Brow BB2 . . . 101 B7
Beardwood Dr BB2 . . . . . . 101 A7
Beardwood Fold BB2 . . . . 101 A7
Beardwood High Sch
BB2 . . . . . . . . . . . . . . . . . . 101 A6
Beardwood Hospl The
BB2 . . . . . . . . . . . . . . . . . . 101 A6
Beardwood Mdw BB2 . . . 101 A7
Beardwood Pk BB2 . . . . . 101 B7
Bearncroft WN8 . . . . . . . . . . 9 D6
Bear St BB12 . . . . . . . . . . . 126 F6
Bearswood Croft PR6 . . . . 78 B2
Bearwood Way FY5 . . . . . 176 C2
Beatie St BB9 . . . . . . . . . . . 148 B6
Beatrice Ave BB12 . . . . . . 127 C7
Beatrice Mews 9 BL6 . . . . 32 B4
Beatrice Pl BB2 . . . . . . . . . . 82 A8
Beatrice St 17 BL6 . . . . . . 32 B4
Beattock Pl FY2 . . . . . . . . . 152 F6
Beatty Ave PR7 . . . . . . . . . . 43 B6
Beatty Cl FY8 . . . . . . . . . . . 110 D1
Beatty Rd PR8 . . . . . . . . . . . 35 E5
Beauclerk Rd FY8 . . . . . . . . 90 B6
Beaufort L37 . . . . . . . . . . . . 12 A2
Beaufort Ave FY2 . . . . . . . 152 C5
Beaufort Cl
Ormskirk L39 . . . . . . . . . . . . 15 A1
Simonstone BB12 . . . . . . . 145 E2
Beaufort Gr LA4 . . . . . . . . 217 D5
Beaufort Rd
Morecambe LA4 . . . . . . . . . 217 E5
Weir OL13 . . . . . . . . . . . . . . 88 A7
Beaufort St
Nelson BB9 . . . . . . . . . . . . 148 E7
Rochdale OL12 . . . . . . . . . . . 52 C1
Beauley Ave BB12 . . . . . . 145 E2
Beauly Cl 3 BL0 . . . . . . . . . 50 A2
Beaumaris Ave BB2 . . . . . 101 A1
Beaumaris Cl 2 BB4 . . . . . 85 B1
Beaumaris Rd PR25 . . . . . . 60 C8
Beaumont Ave BL6 . . . . . . . 32 C4
Beaumont Coll (The
Spastics Society)
LA1 . . . . . . . . . . . . . . . . . . 218 D4
Beaumont Cres L39 . . . . . . 15 D2
Beaumont Ct
8 Blackpool FY1 . . . . . . . . 130 C6
Lytham St Anne's FY8 . . . . . 90 A8
Beaumont Gdns FY6 . . . . 153 A5
Beaumont Ho L39 . . . . . . . . 15 D2
Beaumont Pl LA1 . . . . . . . 218 D4
Beaumont Rd BL6 . . . . . . . . 32 C4
Beaumont St LA1 . . . . . . . 218 D4
Beaumont Way BB3 . . . . . . 82 C1
Beaver Cl BB1 . . . . . . . . . . 122 F5
Beavers La WN8 . . . . . . . . . . 9 D6
Beaver Terr 17 OL13 . . . . . 88 A3
Bebles Rd L39 . . . . . . . . . . . 15 C3
BECCONSALL . . . . . . . . . . . 73 E1
Becconsall La PR4 . . . . . . . 73 F3
Beck Ct FY7 . . . . . . . . . . . . 198 D1
Beckdean Ave FY6 . . . . . . 153 D2
Beckenham Ct BB10 . . . . 148 D3
Beckett Ct 16 PR1 . . . . . . . 96 F8
Beckett St 6 BB3 . . . . . . . . 65 A8
Beck Gr FY5 . . . . . . . . . . . . 175 E4
Becks Brow BD23 . . . . . . . 236 F3
Becks Crossing BB8 . . . . . 172 C2
Beckside
Barley BB12 . . . . . . . . . . . . 169 C5
Trawden BB8 . . . . . . . . . . . 172 C3
Beck Side LA2 . . . . . . . . . . 237 C3
Beckside Mews LA6 . . . . . 240 B3
Beck View 7 LA1 . . . . . . . 215 A3
Beckway Ave FY3 . . . . . . . 130 F7
Bedale Pl FY5 . . . . . . . . . . . 175 E1
Beddington St 6 BB9 . . . 170 D1
Bedford Ave FY5 . . . . . . . . 175 D3
Bedford Cl BB5 . . . . . . . . . 103 C4
Bedford Ct PR8 . . . . . . . . . . 35 A2
Bedford Mews BB3 . . . . . . 81 F4
Bedford Pl
Lancaster LA1 . . . . . . . . . . 215 A4
Padiham BB12 . . . . . . . . . . 126 D7
Bedford Rd
Blackpool FY1 . . . . . . . . . . 130 C8
Fulwood PR2 . . . . . . . . . . . 118 A4
6 Lytham St Anne's FY8 . . . 91 D4
Southport PR8 . . . . . . . . . . . 35 A2
Bedfordshire Ave
BB12 . . . . . . . . . . . . . . . . . 127 B7
Bedford St
6 Barrowford BB9 . . . . . . 170 C1
Blackburn BB2 . . . . . . . . . . 101 C2
Bolton, Egerton BL7 . . . . . . 47 D2
Bury BL9 . . . . . . . . . . . . . . . 33 A4
Darwen BB3 . . . . . . . . . . . . . 81 F4
Bedford Terr BB4 . . . . . . . . 68 A8
Beechacre BL0 . . . . . . . . . . 50 D5
Beecham St LA4 . . . . . . . . 217 B6
Beech Ave
Adlington PR6 . . . . . . . . . . . 31 B8
Bilsborrow PR3 . . . . . . . . . 159 A5
Blackpool FY3 . . . . . . . . . . 130 E5
Darwen BB3 . . . . . . . . . . . . . 82 B2
Earby BB18 . . . . . . . . . . . . 197 A1
Euxton PR7 . . . . . . . . . . . . . 60 C4
Galgate LA2 . . . . . . . . . . . . 210 F4
Horwich BL6 . . . . . . . . . . . . 32 E1
Kirkham PR4 . . . . . . . . . . . 114 B4
Leyland PR25 . . . . . . . . . . . . 60 A7
Parbold WN8 . . . . . . . . . . . . 27 C2
Poulton-le-F FY6 . . . . . . . . 153 D4
Warton PR4 . . . . . . . . . . . . . 92 D6
Beech Bank PR4 . . . . . . . . 155 F1
Beech Cl
Bacup OL13 . . . . . . . . . . . . . 88 A3
Clitheroe BB7 . . . . . . . . . . 166 D8
Oswaldtwistle BB5 . . . . . . 103 C2
Rishton BB1 . . . . . . . . . . . . 103 B8
Rufford L40 . . . . . . . . . . . . . 39 C4
Skelmersdale WN8 . . . . . . . 17 E1
Whitworth OL12 . . . . . . . . . . 71 C1
Wilpshire BB1 . . . . . . . . . . 122 E6
Beech Cres BB5 . . . . . . . . 125 A1
Beechcroft
Cleveleys FY5 . . . . . . . . . . 175 C4
Maghull L31 . . . . . . . . . . . . . . 5 D1
Beech Ct
Fulwood PR2 . . . . . . . . . . . 117 E7
Leyland PR25 . . . . . . . . . . . . 59 F8
Silverdale LA5 . . . . . . . . . . 224 C2
Southport PR9 . . . . . . . . . . . 35 D8
Beech Dr
Formby L37 . . . . . . . . . . . . . 11 D4
Freckleton PR4 . . . . . . . . . . 93 A5
Fulwood PR2 . . . . . . . . . . . 117 D8
Haslingden BB4 . . . . . . . . . . 85 C2
Kirkham PR4 . . . . . . . . . . . 113 E4
Longridge PR3 . . . . . . . . . . 140 A7
Newton-w-S PR4 . . . . . . . . 114 F2
Poulton-le-F FY6 . . . . . . . . 153 D2
Beech Dr *continued*
Whalley BB7 . . . . . . . . . . . 144 A7
Beeches Ct FY5 . . . . . . . . . 176 C1
Beeches The
Blackpool FY3 . . . . . . . . . . 130 E3
Clayton Green PR6 . . . . . . . 78 C3
Singleton FY6 . . . . . . . . . . 154 D1
Tarleton PR4 . . . . . . . . . . . . 57 A7
Beechfield
Hill Dale WN8 . . . . . . . . . . . 27 C5
Lancaster LA1 . . . . . . . . . . 214 D7
Maghull L31 . . . . . . . . . . . . . . 5 E1
Beechfield Ave
Blackpool FY3 . . . . . . . . . . 130 E3
Knott End-on-S FY6 . . . . . . 200 A5
Wrea Green PR4 . . . . . . . . 113 C4
Beechfield Ct PR25 . . . . . . 60 B8
Beechfield Gdns PR8 . . . . . 34 F6
Beechfield Mews PR9 . . . . 35 C7
Beechfield Rd PR25 . . . . . . 60 B8
Beechfields PR7 . . . . . . . . . 41 B6
Beech Gdns PR6 . . . . . . . . . 78 B1
Beech Gr
5 Accrington BB5 . . . . . . 104 A4
2 Barnoldswick BB18 . . . 196 C2
Blackburn BB3 . . . . . . . . . . . 81 D6
Burnley BB10 . . . . . . . . . . . 148 C4
Chatburn BB7 . . . . . . . . . . 190 D5
Knott End-on-S FY6 . . . . . . 199 E6
Morecambe LA4 . . . . . . . . . 217 E5
Preston PR2 . . . . . . . . . . . . 117 B1
Ramsbottom BL8 . . . . . . . . . 50 A1
Slyne LA2 . . . . . . . . . . . . . . 218 C6
Southport PR9 . . . . . . . . . . . 35 F7
Warton LA5 . . . . . . . . . . . . 223 D5
West Bradford BB7 . . . . . . 189 D7
Beech Grove Cl BL9 . . . . . . 33 B4
Beech Ho PR7 . . . . . . . . . . . 42 F6
Beechill Cl PR5 . . . . . . . . . . 97 E3
Beech Ind Est OL13 . . . . . . 88 A3
Beeching Cl LA1 . . . . . . . . 214 F6
Beech Mdw L39 . . . . . . . . . . 16 A4
Beech Mount
Blackburn BB1 . . . . . . . . . . 122 F3
Waddington BB7 . . . . . . . . 189 B4
Beech Rd
Aughton L39 . . . . . . . . . . . . . . 6 A6
Elswick PR4 . . . . . . . . . . . . 155 F1
Garstang PR3 . . . . . . . . . . 181 B8
Halton LA2 . . . . . . . . . . . . . 219 C7
Leyland PR25 . . . . . . . . . . . . 77 A2
Beech St S PR1 . . . . . . . . . . 96 E6
Beech St
Accrington BB5 . . . . . . . . . 104 C5
Bacup OL13 . . . . . . . . . . . . . 88 A3
Barnoldswick BB18 . . . . . . 196 B1
Blackburn BB1 . . . . . . . . . . 102 A7
Bury BL9 . . . . . . . . . . . . . . . 33 B2
Clayton-le-M BB5 . . . . . . . . 124 F1
Clitheroe BB7 . . . . . . . . . . 166 D8
Edgworth BL7 . . . . . . . . . . . 48 D5
Great Harwood BB6 . . . . . . 124 C6
Lancaster LA1 . . . . . . . . . . 214 D8
10 Nelson BB9 . . . . . . . . . . 170 E1
Padiham BB12 . . . . . . . . . . 126 D7
1 Preston PR1 . . . . . . . . . . . 96 D6
Ramsbottom BL0 . . . . . . . . . 50 C3
Rawtenstall BB4 . . . . . . . . . 86 A3
Beech Terr
Ingleton LA6 . . . . . . . . . . . 242 F3
1 Preston PR1 . . . . . . . . . . . 96 E6
Beechthorpe Ave BB7 . . . 189 B4
Beech Tree Ave WN6 . . . . . 19 D8
Beech Tree Cl
Bolton-le-S LA5 . . . . . . . . . 221 A4
Nelson BB9 . . . . . . . . . . . . 148 E7
Beech Tree Cotts LA6 . . . 242 F3
Beechtrees WN8 . . . . . . . . . . 9 D7
Beech Tree Sch PR5 . . . . . . 78 B4
Beechway
Fulwood PR2 . . . . . . . . . . . 118 A4
Higher Penwortham PR1 . . . 96 B3
Maghull L31 . . . . . . . . . . . . . . 6 B2
Beechway Ave L31 . . . . . . . . 6 B2
Beech Wlk PR6 . . . . . . . . . . 61 A7
Beechwood
Kirkham PR4 . . . . . . . . . . . 114 B7
Skelmersdale WN8 . . . . . . . 18 C3
Beechwood Ave
Accrington BB5 . . . . . . . . . 104 D3
Bamber Bridge PR5 . . . . . . . 97 D4
Burnley BB11 . . . . . . . . . . . 127 F3
Clitheroe BB7 . . . . . . . . . . 166 E6
Fulwood PR2 . . . . . . . . . . . 117 C4
Ramsbottom BL0 . . . . . . . . . 50 D6
Shevington WN6 . . . . . . . . . 19 F5
Beechwood Cres WN5 . . . . 10 E6
Beechwood Croft PR6 . . . . 78 A3
Beechwood Ct
Blackburn BB1 . . . . . . . . . . 101 F7
Coppull PR7 . . . . . . . . . . . . . 29 F8
Maghull L31 . . . . . . . . . . . . . . 5 F1
Skelmersdale WN8 . . . . . . . . 9 D6
Beechwood Dr
Blackburn BB2 . . . . . . . . . . . 80 E8
Formby L37 . . . . . . . . . . . . . 11 C1
Ormskirk L39 . . . . . . . . . . . . 15 D5
Thornton FY5 . . . . . . . . . . . 153 B8
Beechwood Gdns LA1 . . . 215 A2
Beechwood Gr FY2 . . . . . . 152 E4
Beechwood Mews BB1,
BB2 . . . . . . . . . . . . . . . . . . . 82 A8
Beechwood Rd
12 Blackburn BB1 . . . . . . . 102 A7
Chorley PR7 . . . . . . . . . . . . . 43 E6
Beeford Dr WN5 . . . . . . . . . 10 E5
Beehive Ind Units FY4 . . . 111 B8
Bee La PR1 . . . . . . . . . . . . . . 96 E1
Bee Mill PR3 . . . . . . . . . . . 141 D3
Beenland St 3 PR1 . . . . . 118 D1
Beeston Ave FY6 . . . . . . . . 153 C5
Beetham Ct BB5 . . . . . . . . 124 E2
Beetham Cvn Pk LA5,
LA7 . . . . . . . . . . . . . . . . . . 225 C8
Beetham Pl FY3 . . . . . . . . . 130 E6
Begonia St BB3 . . . . . . . . . . 82 B1
Begonia View BB3 . . . . . . . 82 A7
Beightons Wlk OL12 . . . . . . 52 D4
Bela Cl 3 LA1 . . . . . . . . . . 218 A2
Bela Gr FY1 . . . . . . . . . . . . 130 D2
Belfield WN8 . . . . . . . . . . . . . 9 D6
Belfield Rd BB5 . . . . . . . . . 104 C4
Belford Ave FY5 . . . . . . . . 175 F4
Belford St BB12 . . . . . . . . . 127 F7
Belfry Cl PR7 . . . . . . . . . . . . 60 D4
Belfry Cres WN6 . . . . . . . . . 29 F2
Belfry Mans BB6 . . . . . . . . 143 C6
Belfry The FY8 . . . . . . . . . . . 91 D5
Belgarth Rd BB5 . . . . . . . . 104 C7
BELGRAVE . . . . . . . . . . . . . . 64 E8
Belgrave Ave
Higher Penwortham
PR1 . . . . . . . . . . . . . . . . . . . 96 B3
Kirkham PR4 . . . . . . . . . . . 114 A7
Belgrave Cl
Blackburn BB2 . . . . . . . . . . 101 B3
3 Lytham St Anne's FY8 . . . 90 D6
Belgrave Cres BL6 . . . . . . . 32 D3
Belgrave Ct
Burnley BB12 . . . . . . . . . . . 127 F7
Leyland PR25 . . . . . . . . . . . . 59 F8
Belgrave Pl
Poulton-le-F FY6 . . . . . . . . 153 B2
Southport PR8 . . . . . . . . . . . 34 F3
Belgrave Rd
Blackpool FY4 . . . . . . . . . . 130 E1
Colne BB8 . . . . . . . . . . . . . 171 D6
Darwen BB3 . . . . . . . . . . . . . 65 A8
5 Leyland PR25 . . . . . . . . . 77 A1
Poulton-le-F FY6 . . . . . . . . 153 B3
Southport PR8 . . . . . . . . . . . 34 F3
Belgrave Sq 9 BB3 . . . . . . 82 A1
Belgrave St
Brierfield BB9 . . . . . . . . . . 148 A6
Burnley BB12 . . . . . . . . . . . 127 F7
Nelson BB9 . . . . . . . . . . . . 170 F1
Rising Bridge BB5 . . . . . . . . 85 A8
Rochdale OL12 . . . . . . . . . . . 52 D1
Belgravia Apartments
PR9 . . . . . . . . . . . . . . . . . . . 53 B1
Belgravia Ho PR9 . . . . . . . . 35 D8
Bell-Aire Park Homes
LA3 . . . . . . . . . . . . . . . . . . 212 F5
Bellamy Ave LA4 . . . . . . . . 217 A3
Belle Field Cl PR1 . . . . . . . 97 A1
Belle Isle Ave OL12 . . . . . . 52 C6
Belle View Pl FY3 . . . . . . . 130 D5
Belle Vue Ave LA1 . . . . . . 215 A5
Belle Vue Dr LA1 . . . . . . . 215 A5
Belle Vue La BB7 . . . . . . . 189 B4
Belle Vue Pl BB11 . . . . . . 127 E6
Belle Vue St
Blackburn BB2 . . . . . . . . . . 101 C5
Burnley BB11 . . . . . . . . . . . 127 E6
Bellfield Rd LA4 . . . . . . . . 217 C5
Bellflower Cl PR25 . . . . . . . 77 E3
Bellingham Rd FY8 . . . . . . . 91 B4
Bellis Ave PR9 . . . . . . . . . . . 53 F2
Bellis Way PR5 . . . . . . . . . . 97 B2
Bell La
Bury BL9 . . . . . . . . . . . . . . . 33 A3
Claughton PR3 . . . . . . . . . . 182 C4
Clayton-le-M BB5 . . . . . . . . 125 B4
Bells Arc 10 BB10 . . . . . . 128 A8
Bells Bridge La PR3 . . . . . 203 F2
Bell's Cl L31 . . . . . . . . . . . . . 5 C4
Bells La PR5 . . . . . . . . . . . . . 98 E3
Bell's La L31 . . . . . . . . . . . . . 5 B3
Bell St BB4 . . . . . . . . . . . . . . 85 B3
Bell Villas PR5 . . . . . . . . . . 99 C3
BELMONT . . . . . . . . . . . . . . . 46 C4
Belmont Ave
Blackpool FY1 . . . . . . . . . . 130 C4
Fulwood PR2 . . . . . . . . . . . 118 D2
Orrell WN5 . . . . . . . . . . . . . . 10 D3
Poulton-le-F FY6 . . . . . . . . 153 B3
Belmont Cl
Brinscall PR6 . . . . . . . . . . . . 62 E8
Burscough L40 . . . . . . . . . . . 25 E3
Fulwood PR2 . . . . . . . . . . . 118 D2
Lancaster LA1 . . . . . . . . . . 218 B3
Belmont Cres PR2 . . . . . . 118 D2
Belmont Ct PR3 . . . . . . . . . 140 B7
Belmont Dr PR6 . . . . . . . . . 61 E1
Belmont Gr BB10 . . . . . . . 128 D5
Belmont Pl PR7 . . . . . . . . . . 29 D6
Belmont Rd
Adlington PR6 . . . . . . . . . . . 31 B7
Belmont BB3, BL7 . . . . . . . . 64 A2
Bolton BL7 . . . . . . . . . . . . . . 47 A1
Fleetwood FY7 . . . . . . . . . . 199 A3
Fulwood PR2 . . . . . . . . . . . 117 C2
Great Harwood BB6 . . . . . . 124 B5
Horwich BL6 . . . . . . . . . . . . 32 C7
Leyland PR25 . . . . . . . . . . . . 59 D8
Lytham St Anne's FY8 . . . . . 90 C5
Rivington BL6 . . . . . . . . . . . 45 C3
Belmont Sch BB4 . . . . . . . . 85 E2
Belmont St PR8 . . . . . . . . . . 35 A5
Belmont Terr
7 Barrowford BB9 . . . . . . 170 D3
Foulridge BB8 . . . . . . . . . . 194 E1
Belmont Way OL12 . . . . . . . 52 E2

Belper St BB1 102 A6
Belsfield Dr PR4 73 E4
Belshaw Ct BB11 127 A3
BELTHORN 82 F6
Belthorn Prim Sch BB1 82 F6
Belthorn Rd BB1 82 E6
Belton Hill PR2 117 D8
Belvedere Ave
Ramsbottom BL8 50 A1
Rawtenstall BB4 87 A1
Belvedere Ct
1 Lytham St Anne's FY8 90 D4
Thornton FY5 153 C8
Belvedere Dr
Chorley PR7 43 B8
Formby L37 11 F1
Belvedere Fold BB4 87 A1
Belvedere Pk L39 6 C7
Belvedere Rd
Adlington PR6 31 B8
Blackburn BB1 123 A3
Burnley BB10 128 B6
2 Leyland PR25 77 B2
Southport PR8 21 C5
Thornton FY5 153 C8
Belverdale Gdns FY4 110 F5
Belvere Ave FY4 110 D6
Belvoir St OL12 52 C1
Benbow Cl FY8 110 D2
Bence Rd PR1 97 B6
Bence St BB8 171 E5
Bench Carr OL12 52 E1
Bendwood Cl BB12 126 D8
Benenden Pl 9 FY5 176 A2
Bengal St PR7 61 D1
Bengarth Rd PR9 35 F8
Benjamin Hargreaves CE Prim Sch BB5 104 D5
Ben La
Barnoldswick BB18 196 D3
Rainford L39 8 A1
Ben Lane Ct L39 8 B2
Bennett Ave FY1 130 C4
Bennett Dr WN5 10 D4
Bennett Rd FY5 176 A3
Bennett's La FY4 110 F6
Bennett St 4 BB9 170 F2
Bennington St BB1, BB2 101 F3
Bennison Ct PR9 53 C1
Benson Ave LA4 217 D4
Benson Ho BB1 102 B7
Benson La PR4 135 F3
Benson Rd FY3 152 E1
Benson's La PR4 158 C1
Benson St
Blackburn BB1 102 B7
Bury BL9 33 A1
Edgworth BL7 48 E5
Bentcliffe Gdns BB5 104 D4
Bent Est OL13 88 A7
Bent Gap La BB2 101 C4
BENT GATE 68 C8
Bentgate Cl BB4 68 D8
Bentham Ave
Burnley BB10 148 B3
Fleetwood FY7 198 C1
Bentham Cl BB2 101 B1
Bentham Hall Cotts LA2 239 D8
Bentham Moor Rd LA6 242 D2
Bentham Pl WN6 29 F2
Bentham Rd
Blackburn BB2 101 B1
Ingleton LA6 242 E3
Lancaster LA1 215 A2
Standish WN6 29 F2
Bentham St
Coppull PR7 42 E1
Southport PR8 35 B5
Bentham Sta LA2 239 D7
Bentham's Way PR8 35 C2
Bentinck Ave FY4 110 B5
Bentinck Rd FY8 89 C8
Bentinck St 9 OL12 52 C1
Bent La
Colne BB8 172 B6
Leyland PR25 60 C8
Bentlea Rd BB7 231 B3
Bentley Brook Cl BL6 32 E4
Bentley Dr
Blackpool FY4 112 A6
Kirkham PR4 113 E5
Bentley Gn FY5 176 D2
Bentley La
Bispham Green L40 27 E8
Bury BL9 51 A1
Heskin Green L40, PR7 41 A1
Bentley Mews OL12 52 E2
Bentley Park Rd PR4 74 F7
Bentley St
7 Bacup OL13 87 F3
Blackburn BB1 102 C5
Darwen BB3 65 C7
Nelson BB9 148 D7
Rochdale OL12 52 E2
Bentley Wood Way BB11 126 F4
Bentmeadows OL12 52 E1
Benton Rd PR2 118 D4
Bents La LA6 243 A3
Bent St
Blackburn BB2 101 D4
Bent St *continued*
Haslingden BB4 68 D8
4 Oswaldtwistle BB5 103 D3
Bentwood Rd BB4 85 A3
Beresford Dr PR9 53 F1
Beresford Gdns PR9 53 F2
Beresford Rd BB1 101 D7
Beresford St
8 Blackpool FY1 130 C7
Nelson BB9 148 F6
Bergen St BB11 127 B5
Bergerac Cres FY5 152 F6
Berkeley Cl
Chorley PR7 43 D5
Nelson BB9 148 E7
Berkeley Colonnade PR2 118 A4
Berkeley Cres BB12 146 C1
Berkeley Ct
Heysham LA3 212 E6
Poulton-le-F FY6 153 E3
Berkeley Dr
Clayton-le-W PR5 77 E4
Simonstone BB12 145 E2
Berkeley St
Brierfield BB9 148 A5
Nelson BB9 148 E7
Preston PR1 117 E1
Berkley Cl PR4 113 E5
Berkshire Ave BB12 127 B7
Berkshire Cl BB1 122 F7
Bernard St OL12 52 E3
Berne Ave BL6 32 A3
Berridge Ave BB12 127 A6
Berriedale Rd BB9 171 A1
Berry Cl WN8 17 F2
Berry Field 3 PR1 96 C3
Berry House Cotts L40 38 A5
Berry House Rd L40 38 A4
Berry La PR3 140 A7
Berrys La BB7 144 C2
Berry's La FY6 153 C4
Berry Sq BL6 31 D3
Berry St
Bamber Bridge PR5 77 A8
Brierfield BB9 148 B5
Burnley BB11 127 F4
Preston PR1 97 A7
Skelmersdale WN8 17 F2
Bertha St BB5 104 D6
Bertram Ave LA4 217 A4
Bertrand Ave FY3 131 A7
Berwick Ave
Cleveleys FY5 175 F4
Southport PR8 21 D5
Berwick Dr
Burnley BB12 127 E7
Fulwood PR2 117 D4
Berwick Rd
Blackpool FY4 110 C5
Lytham St Anne's FY8 89 F7
Preston PR1 97 A6
Berwick St PR1 118 E1
Berwick Way LA3 212 E7
Berwyn Ave 2 LA4 217 D5
Berwyn Cl BL6 32 C5
Berwyn Ct PR8 35 D4
Beryl Ave
Blackburn BB1 122 F2
Cleveleys FY5 175 E1
Besant Cl BB1 102 B1
BESCAR 24 A7
Bescar Brow La L40 23 F7
Bescar La L40 37 B1
Bescar La Sta L40 37 B2
Bescot Way 12 FY5 152 F7
Bessie St 13 BB18 196 B2
Best St PR4 113 F5
Bethel Ave FY2 152 D4
Bethel Rd BB1 102 A7
Bethel St
Barnoldswick BB18 196 B3
Colne BB8 171 B4
Bethesda Cl BB2 101 D3
Bethesda Rd FY1 130 B4
Bethesda St
Barnoldswick BB18 196 B2
Burnley BB11 127 F6
Betjeman Cl FY2 152 F6
Betony LA4 217 F6
Betony Cl OL12 52 D3
Bett La PR6 79 C1
Betty Anne Ct PR9 35 B8
Beulah Ave LA4 217 D5
Bevan Pl BB9 170 F2
BEVERLEY 170 E7
Beverley Ave
Longshaw WN5 10 E1
Poulton-le-F FY6 131 D8
Beverley Cl
Clitheroe BB7 166 E6
Preston PR2 96 C8
Southport PR9 54 C5
Wrea Green PR4 113 A3
Beverley Ct
2 Lytham St Anne's FY8 90 A8
Morecambe LA4 217 E5
Beverley Dr BB7 166 D6
Beverley Gr FY4 110 C7
Beverley Rd BB9 170 E8
Beverley Rd N FY8 90 A8
Beverley Rd S FY8 90 A8
Beverley St
5 Blackburn BB2 101 B1
Burnley BB11 127 E5
Beverly Cl FY5 153 B8
Bevington Cl BB11 127 E5
Bewcastle Dr L40 16 C3
Bexhill Rd PR2 117 A4
Bexley Ave FY2 130 D8
Bexley Pl FY8 90 E5
Bezza La BB2, PR5 120 C5
Bhailok St 3 PR1 96 E8
Bibby Dr FY3 131 E5
Bibby Rd PR9 54 A1
Bibby's La FY2 152 E3
BICKERSTAFFE 7 F5
Bickerstaffe CE Sch L39 7 E5
Bickerstaffe St 2 FY1 130 B3
Bickerton Rd PR8 34 F4
Bicknell St BB1 101 E6
Bideford Ave FY3 131 A6
Bideford Way PR4 116 F6
Bidston St PR1 97 E8
Bigdale Dr L33 1 A3
Big Fold BL6 31 D2
Bigforth Dr LA1 211 A8
Biggins La LA6 241 C8
Billinge Ave BB2 101 B5
Billinge Cl BB2 101 B5
Billinge End BB2 101 A6
Billinge End Rd
Blackburn BB2 100 F5
Pleasington BB2 100 B4
Billinge Hospl WN5 10 D2
Billinge Side BB2 100 F5
Billinge St BB1 102 B4
Billinge View BB2 100 F2
BILLINGTON 144 B3
Billington Ave BB4 86 A5
Billington Ct 8 PR2 139 D1
Billington Gdns BB7 144 A4
Billington Rd BB11 127 B3
Billington St E 3 PR4 113 F6
Billington St 1 PR4 113 F6
Bilsberry Cotts BB7 164 F1
Bilsborough Hey PR1 96 E2
Bilsborough Mdw PR2 116 E3
BILSBORROW 159 A5
Bilsborrow La
Bilsborrow PR3 159 C4
Inglewhite PR3 160 A4
Binbrook Pl PR7 43 A7
Bingley Ave FY3 130 F6
Bingley Cl PR6 78 C2
Binns St BB4 86 A7
Binyon Ct LA1 214 F6
Binyon Rd LA1 214 F5
Birbeck Rd L33 1 A3
Birbeck Wlk L33 1 A3
Birchall Lo 6 PR2 118 F4
Birch Ave
Burscough L40 25 E4
Clayton-le-W PR25 77 D3
Cleveleys FY5 175 E2
Euxton PR7 60 C4
Galgate LA2 211 A4
Haslingden BB4 85 C3
Higher Penwortham PR1 96 A3
Newton-w-S PR4 114 F3
Preston PR2 117 A2
Birchbank Gdns BB1 102 A7
Birch Cl
Huncoat BB5 125 E2
Maghull L31 5 F1
Whitworth OL12 52 C6
Birch Cres
Gregson Lane PR5 98 E1
Oswaldtwistle BB5 103 F3
Birch Dr LA5 224 C4
Birchenlee La BB8 171 E2
Birches End OL12 52 C5
Birches Rd BL7 48 D4
Birches The L37 11 E5
Birchfield PR4 74 F4
Birch Field PR6 78 B3
Birchfield Ave BL9 33 E1
Birchfield Dr PR3 140 A8
Birchfield Mews 9 BB12 127 C6
Birchfield Way L31 5 B5
Birch Gn L37 11 D4
Birch Gr
Barrow BB7 166 D1
Lancaster LA1 214 D8
Ramsbottom BL0 50 A3
Stalmine FY6 177 D7
BIRCH GREEN 18 C2
Birch Green Rd WN8 18 C3
BIRCH HALL 81 E4
Birch Hall Ave BB3 81 D4
Birch Hall La BB18 197 D2
Birch Ho PR7 42 F6
Birchill Rd L33 1 C2
Birchin La PR6 78 D1
Birch's Brow L39 14 E2
Birch La PR3 184 C1
Birchover Cl PR2 117 A5
Birch Rd
Chorley PR6 61 E2
Coppull PR7 42 E1
Garstang PR3 181 C8
Birch St
1 Accrington BB5 104 B6
Bacup OL13 87 F3
Fleetwood FY7 199 A4
5 Lytham St Anne's FY8 91 C3
Skelmersdale WN8 8 E8
Southport PR8 35 B4
Birch Terr BB5 104 D2
Birchtree Ave LA3 216 E1
Birch Tree Gdns FY3 131 B2
Birch Tree Way 4 BL6 32 E1
Birch View BB7 166 D2
Birch Way FY6 153 C4
Birchway Ave FY3 130 E6
Birch Wlk 1 BB1 102 B4
Birchwood PR26 76 C1
Birchwood Ave PR4 95 B1
Birchwood Cl FY8 90 E4
Birchwood Dr
Coppull PR7 42 E2
Fulwood PR2 117 D7
Hambleton FY6 177 C2
Birchwood Way L33 1 A5
Bird i' th' Hand Cotts 2 L39 15 E6
Bird St
Brierfield BB9 148 B5
Preston PR1 96 D6
Birdy Brow BB7 165 A6
BIRKACRE 43 A3
Birkacre Brow PR7 42 F2
Birkacre Rd PR7 42 F4
Birkbeck Pl FY7 198 D2
Birkbeck Way BB10 148 A1
BIRKDALE 34 F2
Birkdale Ave
Blackpool FY2 152 E5
Fleetwood FY7 175 E7
Longton PR4 74 F8
Lytham St Anne's FY8 110 F1
Birkdale Cl
Euxton PR7 60 D4
Lancaster LA1 218 B3
Longton PR4 74 F8
Thornton FY5 153 D8
Birkdale Cop PR8 35 E1
Birkdale Dr PR2 116 E2
Birkdale High Sch PR8 21 E7
BIRKDALE HILLS 21 C7
Birkdale Prim Sch PR8 35 B3
Birkdale Sch for the Hearing Impaired PR8 34 D4
Birkdale Sta PR8 34 F4
Birkdale Trad Est PR8 35 A2
Birkett Dr PR2 119 A3
Birkett Pl PR2 119 A3
Birkett Rd BB5 104 D7
Birkett's Pl LA4 217 C5
Birkey La L37 11 F2
Birklands Ave LA4 217 C4
Birkrig WN8 9 D6
Birks Brow PR3 162 D3
Birkside Way FY4 131 C1
Birk St PR1 96 E7
Birkwith La LA2 239 C7
Birley Cl WN6 19 F8
Birley Ct PR8 35 B5
Birley Pl BB10 128 A8
Birley St
Blackburn BB1 101 F6
Blackpool FY1 130 B5
Kirkham PR4 114 B5
1 Preston PR1 97 A7
Birleywood WN8 9 D6
Birnam Gn FY7 198 E4
Birtle Rd BL9 33 E6
Birtwistle Ave BB8 171 D6
Birtwistle Cl BB9 148 B5
Birtwistle Ct BB18 196 C1
Birtwistle Fold 7 BB8 171 E5
Birtwistle Hyde Pk 3 BB8 171 D5
Birtwistle St
Accrington BB5 104 C5
3 Bamber Bridge PR5 77 B7
Great Harwood BB6 124 B5
Birtwistle Standroyd Bglws BB8 172 A5
Birtwistle Terr BB6 143 C1
Bisham Cl BB3 65 C8
Bishopdale Cl
Blackburn BB2 80 D7
3 Morecambe LA3 217 F3
Bishopdale Rd LA1 214 D7
Bishop David Sheppard CE Prim Sch PR9 36 B7
Bishopgate 15 PR1 97 A8
Bishop Martin CE Prim Sch WN8 9 D6
Bishop Rawstorne CE Language Coll PR26 58 C2
Bishopsgate
Blackpool FY3 153 B1
Lancaster LA1 215 A4
Bishops Gate FY8 90 D7
Bishop St
Accrington BB5 104 C5
Burnley BB10 148 B1
Nelson BB9 148 D8
Bishopstone Cl BB2 82 A8
Bishopsway PR1 96 D3
Bison Pl PR26 76 C2
BISPHAM 152 B5
Bispham Ave PR26 76 E4
Bispham Ct WN5 10 D2
Bispham Endowed CE Jun Sch FY2 152 D4
BISPHAM GREEN 27 B7
Bispham Hall Bsns Pk WN5 10 C2
Bispham High Sch FY2 152 E2
Bispham Hospl FY2 152 F6
Bispham Rd
Blackpool FY2 152 D3
Blackpool, Warbreck FY3 130 E8
Carleton FY5, FY6 153 A6
Cleveleys FY5 175 C2
Bispham Rd *continued*
Cleveleys, Whiteholme FY5 152 F6
Nelson BB9 148 E6
Southport PR9 35 F7
Bispham St 21 PR1 96 F8
Bittern Cl FY3 131 B6
Bivel St BB12 127 D6
Bk Commercial St BB9 148 B6
Bk Dawson St BL9 33 A4
Bk Owen St BB5 104 C7
Bk Scotland Rd 7 BB9 148 D8
Bk Shepherd St BL9 33 A1
Black Abbey St BB5 104 C5
Blackacre La L39, L40 15 E8
BLACKAMOOR 82 B8
Black-A-Moor La L39 14 A2
Blackamoor Rd BB1 82 C8
Blackberry Hall Cres LA3 213 A8
Blackberry Way PR1 96 B2
Blackbrook CL PR6 62 A2
Black Bull La PR2 117 D5
BLACKBURN 101 E1
Blackburn Brow PR6 61 E3
Blackburn Cathedral* BB1 101 E4
Blackburn Coll BB2 101 D5
Blackburn Mus & Art Gall* BB1 101 E5
Blackburn Old Rd
Blackburn BB1 123 D3
Great Harwood BB1, BB6 123 F5
Hoghton PR5 99 C2
Blackburn Rd
Accrington BB5 104 C6
Blackburn BB1 102 E8
Bolton, Egerton BL7 47 C4
Church BB5 103 F6
Clayton-le-M BB5 124 E1
Darwen BB3 81 E4
Edenfield BL0, BB4 68 D5
Edgworth BL7 48 D7
Great Harwood BB6 124 C4
Great Knowley PR6 61 E4
Haslingden BB4, BB5 85 B5
Higher Walton PR5 98 B3
Higher Wheelton PR6 79 C1
Longridge PR3 140 D7
Oswaldtwistle BB5, BB1 103 C5
Padiham BB12 126 A8
Ribchester PR3 141 E3
Rishton BB1 124 A1
Wheelton PR6 61 F6
Whittlestone Head BB3, BL7 66 B2
Blackburn St
Blackburn BB1 101 E6
5 Burnley BB11 127 F6
Chorley PR6 43 E7
Blackburn Sta BB1 101 F4
Blackburn Trad Pk BB1 101 F6
Blackcar La L29 4 B3
Black Croft PR6 78 B3
Blacker St BB10 148 A2
Blackfen Pl FY2 130 D8
Blackfield Rd PR4 93 B6
Blackgate La
Holmes PR4 56 C3
Tarleton PR4 56 E5
Blackhorse Ave BL6 31 C2
Blackhorse Cl BL6 31 C3
Black Horse St
Blackrod BL6 31 C3
4 Chorley PR7 43 B6
Black Horse Yd 12 BB8 171 D5
Black House La
Chipping PR3 185 B1
Lane Bottom BB10 149 D3
Blackhurst Ave PR4 95 F2
Blackhurst Ct PR4 75 B8
Blackhurst Rd L31 5 C5
Black La
Nateby PR3 180 A8
Ramsbottom BL0 51 B7
Black Lane Croft 9 BB7 189 E1
Black Lane Ends BB8 195 F3
BLACKLEACH 135 F2
Blackleach Ave 4 PR2 139 D1
Blackleach La PR4 135 F1
Blackledge Cl WN5 10 E5
Blackley Gr L33 1 A6
Black Moor Rd L40 40 A2
Black Moss La
Ormskirk L39 15 E3
Scarisbrick L40 23 D6
Black Moss Rd BB9 169 E8
BLACKO 170 D7
Blacko Bar Rd BB9 170 B7
Blacko Prim Sch BB9 170 D8
BLACK POLE 136 C5
BLACKPOOL 130 A4
Blackpool Airport FY4 110 D3
Blackpool Central Pier* FY1 130 A3
Blackpool & Fleetwood Tramway* FY2 152 B3
Blackpool Lifeboat Visitor Ctr* FY1 130 A4
Blackpool Lights* FY1 130 B5

Blackpool North Pier★ FY1 . . . 130 A5
Blackpool North Sta FY1 . . . 130 C6
Blackpool Old Rd
Little Eccleston PR3 . . . 156 A5
Poulton-le-F FY6 . . . 153 B2
Blackpool Pleasure Beach★ FY4 . . . 110 B7
Blackpool Pleasure Beach Sta FY4 . . . 110 B6
Blackpool Rd
Blackpool FY2 . . . 152 D4
Carleton FY6 . . . 153 A4
Clifton PR4 . . . 94 E8
Longridge PR3 . . . 140 A7
Lytham St Anne's FY8 . . . 90 D5
Newton-w-S PR4 . . . 115 B2
Preston, Larches PR2 . . . 116 E1
Preston PR1, PR2 . . . 117 C2
St Michael's on W PR3 . . . 157 B6
Wrea Green PR4 . . . 113 C6
Blackpool Rd N FY8 . . . 110 F2
Blackpool Sixth Form Coll FY3 . . . 153 A2
Blackpool South Pier★ FY4 . . . 110 A8
Blackpool South Sta FY4 . . . 130 B1
Blackpool St
5 Church BB5 . . . 103 E5
3 Darwen BB3 . . . 65 B6
Blackpool & The Fylde Coll Ansdell Campus FY8 . . . 90 C5
Blackpool & The Fylde Coll Bispham Campus FY2 . . . 152 E6
Blackpool & The Fylde Coll Central Campus FY1 . . . 130 D4
Blackpool & The Fylde Coll (Nautical) FY7 . . . 175 E8
Blackpool & The Fylde Coll (Park Road Campus) FY1 . . . 130 C4
Blackpool Twr★ FY1 . . . 130 B5
Blackpool Victoria Hospl FY3 . . . 131 A5
Blackpool Zoo★ FY3 . . . 131 A4
BLACKROD . . . 31 D2
Blackrod Anglican/Methodist Prim Sch BL6 . . . 31 C2
Blackrod Brow BL6 . . . 31 B4
Blackrod By-Pass Rd BL6 . . . 31 D2
Blackrod Sta BL6 . . . 31 E2
Blacksmiths Row FY8 . . . 90 D7
Blacksmith Wlk PR7 . . . 60 E6
BLACKSNAPE . . . 65 E8
Blacksnape Rd BB3 . . . 82 D2
Blacksticks La PR3 . . . 184 D1
Blackstone Rd PR6 . . . 61 E1
Blackthorn Cl
Blackburn BB1 . . . 101 F7
Cleveleys FY5 . . . 175 F5
Newton-w-S PR4 . . . 114 F2
Preston PR2 . . . 116 D1
Rochdale OL12 . . . 52 E2
Blackthorn Cres OL13 . . . 87 F3
Blackthorn Croft PR6 . . . 78 A2
Blackthorn Dr PR1 . . . 96 B3
Blackthorn La OL13 . . . 87 F3
Blackthorn Mews
Lytham St Anne's FY8 . . . 90 C5
Rochdale OL12 . . . 52 E2
Blackwood Ct OL13 . . . 70 C8
Blackwood Pl LA1 . . . 215 B5
Blackwood Rd OL13 . . . 70 B7
Blades St LA1 . . . 214 E7
BLAGUEGATE . . . 17 B1
Blaguegate La WN8 . . . 17 B2
Blainscough Rd PR7 . . . 29 E8
Blairgowrie Gdns L39 . . . 16 A4
Blair Gr PR9 . . . 35 F7
Blair St OL12 . . . 52 D1
Blairway Ave FY3 . . . 130 F6
Blake Ave PR5 . . . 77 A7
Blake Gdns BB6 . . . 124 B4
Blakehall WN8 . . . 9 D7
Blakeley Cres BB18 . . . 196 B3
Blake St 6 BB5 . . . 104 B6
Blakewater Coll BB1 . . . 102 C2
Blakewater Rd BB1 . . . 102 C7
Blakey Moor BB2 . . . 101 D5
Blakey St BB11 . . . 128 B6
Blakiston St FY7 . . . 199 A4
Blanche St 6 PR2 . . . 117 C1
Blandford Ave FY5 . . . 175 C1
Blandford Cl PR8 . . . 34 F5
Blandford Rise BL6 . . . 32 F1
Blannel St BB11 . . . 127 E6
Blascomay Sq 13 BB8 . . . 171 D4
Blashaw La PR1 . . . 96 A5
Blaydike Moss PR26 . . . 76 B1
Blaydon Ave FY5 . . . 175 E4
Blaydon Pk WN8 . . . 9 D7
Bleachers Dr 2 PR25 . . . 76 E1
Blea Cl BB12 . . . 127 B8
Bleakholt Rd BL0 . . . 68 F1
Bleak La L40 . . . 26 D5
Bleara Rd BB18 . . . 195 D7
BLEASDALE . . . 184 A7
Bleasdale Ave
Blackpool FY5 . . . 152 E8
Clitheroe BB7 . . . 166 C7
Kirkham PR4 . . . 114 A5
Poulton-le-F FY6 . . . 153 C2
Staining FY3 . . . 131 E5
Bleasdale CE Prim Sch PR3 . . . 184 A7
Bleasdale Cl
2 Bamber Bridge PR5 . . . 77 F8
Leyland PR25 . . . 60 B7
Ormskirk L39 . . . 6 D7
Bleasdale Ct
Fleetwood FY7 . . . 199 C5
Longridge PR3 . . . 140 B7
Bleasdale Gr LA3 . . . 216 E1
Bleasdale House Com Specl Sch LA5 . . . 224 C3
Bleasdale Rd
Cumeragh Village PR3 . . . 138 F6
Knott End-on-S FY6 . . . 199 D5
Lytham St Anne's FY8 . . . 91 C4
Whitechapel PR3 . . . 183 D1
Bleasdale St E PR1 . . . 118 C1
Bleasedale La PR3 . . . 183 C6
Blea Tarn Pl 3 LA4 . . . 217 D4
Blea Tarn Rd LA2 . . . 215 C2
Blelock St PR1 . . . 97 A7
Blenheim Ave
Blackpool FY1 . . . 130 D4
Kirkham PR4 . . . 113 F5
Blenheim Cl
Bamber Bridge PR5 . . . 77 C8
1 Blackburn BB1 . . . 122 E1
Blenheim Dr
Thornton FY5 . . . 176 C2
Warton PR4 . . . 92 D6
Blenheim Pl FY8 . . . 110 E1
Blenheim Rd PR8 . . . 21 B6
Blenheim St
Colne BB8 . . . 172 A5
13 Rochdale OL12 . . . 52 C1
Blenheim Terr BB8 . . . 194 E1
Blenheim Way PR4 . . . 116 E6
Blessed Sacrament RC Prim Sch PR2 . . . 118 F3
Blessed Trinity RC Coll BB11 . . . 127 C3
Blind La
Burton in L LA6 . . . 242 C3
Gisburn BB7 . . . 231 C3
Higham BB12 . . . 147 A6
Blindman's La L39 . . . 15 C7
Bloomfield Ct PR1 . . . 117 E2
Bloomfield Grange PR1 . . . 96 C2
Bloomfield Pk LA5 . . . 223 D1
Bloomfield Rd
Blackpool FY1 . . . 130 C2
Withnell PR6 . . . 80 A1
Bloomfield Road (Blackpool FC) FY1 . . . 130 C2
Bloom St 3 BL0 . . . 50 A4
Blossom Ave
Blackpool FY4 . . . 110 F7
Oswaldtwistle BB5 . . . 103 E5
Blossoms The
Fulwood PR2 . . . 118 C6
Poulton-le-F FY6 . . . 153 F3
BLOWICK . . . 35 E6
Blowick Bsns Pk PR9 . . . 36 A6
Blowick Ind Pk PR9 . . . 36 A6
BLOWICK MOSS . . . 35 E3
Blucher St BB8 . . . 171 E4
Bluebell Ave BB4 . . . 68 A8
Bluebell Cl
Blackpool FY2 . . . 152 D2
Cleveleys FY5 . . . 175 F5
Hesketh Bank PR4 . . . 73 E4
Lucas Green PR6 . . . 61 C5
Pilling PR3 . . . 201 C5
Bluebell Cotts PR3 . . . 201 C5
Bluebell Gr BB11 . . . 127 A5
Blue Bell La OL14 . . . 109 D2
Blue Bell Pl PR1 . . . 97 A7
Bluebell Way
Fulwood PR2 . . . 118 F6
Huncoat BB5 . . . 125 E2
Walton Summit PR5 . . . 78 A8
Bluebell Wood PR25 . . . 76 F3
Bluecoat Cres PR4 . . . 115 A2
Blue Gates BB7 . . . 229 B3
Blue Moor PR4 . . . 135 A2
Blue Scar La BB7 . . . 230 D7
Bluestone La L31 . . . 5 E1
Blue Stone La L40 . . . 40 F4
Blundell Ave
Formby L37 . . . 11 B4
Hightown L38 . . . 2 F3
Southport PR8 . . . 34 F2
Blundell Cres PR8 . . . 34 F2
Blundell Dr PR8 . . . 34 F2
Blundell Gr L38 . . . 2 F3
Blundell La
Blackrod BL6 . . . 31 A2
Higher Penwortham PR1 . . . 96 B6
Southport PR9 . . . 54 C2
Blundell Links Ct PR8 . . . 21 C4
Blundell Rd
Fulwood PR2 . . . 117 E3
Hightown L38 . . . 2 F2
Lytham St Anne's FY8 . . . 110 F1
Blundell St FY1 . . . 130 B3
Blythe Ave FY5 . . . 175 E5
Blythe Cotts L40 . . . 25 E1
Blythe Ct PR9 . . . 54 A2
Blythe La
Burscough L40 . . . 25 E1
Ormskirk L40 . . . 16 D8
Blythe Mdw L40 . . . 25 B1
Blythe Mews PR8 . . . 22 A8
Blythewood WN8 . . . 9 D7
Boarded Barn PR7 . . . 60 C3
Boardman Ave FY1 . . . 130 D2
Boardman St BL6 . . . 31 D2
Board St BB10 . . . 148 A1
Boarsgreave La BB4 . . . 69 F6
Bobbin Cl BB5 . . . 104 A5
Bobbiners La PR9 . . . 55 A3
Bobbin Mill Cl OL14 . . . 109 B1
Bobbin Mill Cotts PR3 . . . 181 F2
Bobbin St OL14 . . . 109 C1
Bobby Langton Way L40 . . . 25 E5
Bocholt Way BB4 . . . 86 A2
Bodiam Rd BL8 . . . 49 F2
Bodie Hill LA2 . . . 209 E5
Bodkin La PR3 . . . 154 F7
Bodmin Ave PR9 . . . 54 B5
Bodmin St PR1 . . . 118 D1
Boegrave Ave PR5 . . . 77 A8
Bogburn La PR7 . . . 29 D6
Bog Height Rd BB3 . . . 81 C6
Boland St BB1 . . . 102 A7
Bold La L39 . . . 6 B7
Bold St
Accrington BB5 . . . 104 D6
Bacup OL13 . . . 87 F1
Blackburn BB1 . . . 101 E6
Bury BL9 . . . 33 A3
Colne BB8 . . . 171 E4
Fleetwood FY7 . . . 199 B5
Morecambe LA3 . . . 216 E4
Preston PR1 . . . 117 D1
Southport PR9 . . . 35 B8
Bold Venture Cotts BB7 . . . 190 C4
Bold Venture Way BB5 . . . 125 A3
Boleyn Ct FY3 . . . 131 A2
Boleyn The L31 . . . 5 E3
Bolland Cl 6 BB7 . . . 166 F8
Bolland Prospect BB7 . . . 166 F7
Bolland St BB18 . . . 196 B3
BOLTON . . . 47 D1
Bolton Ave
Accrington BB5 . . . 125 D1
Carleton FY6 . . . 153 C5
Lancaster LA1 . . . 218 D4
BOLTON-BY-BOWLAND . . . 230 D4
Bolton-by-Bowland CE Prim Sch BB7 . . . 230 D4
Bolton Cl L37 . . . 12 A2
Bolton Com Coll, Horwich Ctr BL6 . . . 32 D2
Bolton Croft PR26 . . . 59 B8
Bolton Gr BB9 . . . 170 D3
BOLTON GREEN . . . 42 C8
Bolton La LA5 . . . 221 C4
BOLTON-LE-SANDS . . . 221 B5
Bolton-le-Sands CE Prim Sch LA5 . . . 221 B4
Bolton Mdw PR26 . . . 59 A8
Bolton Rd
Abbey Village PR6 . . . 80 B3
Adlington BL6, PR6 . . . 31 D6
Blackburn BB2 . . . 101 D2
Blackburn, Ewood BB2 . . . 81 E7
Chorley PR6 . . . 43 E4
Darwen BB3 . . . 65 B7
Darwen, Cadshaw BB3 . . . 65 C3
Edgworth BL7 . . . 48 D5
Ramsbottom BL8 . . . 49 D2
Riley Green PR5, PR6 . . . 79 E6
Southport PR8 . . . 35 A4
Bolton Rd N BL0 . . . 68 D2
Bolton Rd W BL0, BL8 . . . 50 A4
Bolton's Cop PR9 . . . 55 D5
Boltons Croft PR4 . . . 115 E7
Boltons Ct PR1 . . . 97 A7
Bolton's Ct 24 BB1 . . . 101 E5
Bolton's Meanygate PR4 . . . 56 C7
Bolton St
Blackpool FY1 . . . 130 B2
Chorley PR7 . . . 43 C7
Colne BB8 . . . 171 C4
5 Newchurch BB4 . . . 86 E1
Ramsbottom BL0 . . . 50 B6
BOLTON TOWN END . . . 220 F3
Bombay St BB2 . . . 101 C3
Bonchurch St BB1 . . . 102 C4
Bond Cl BL6 . . . 32 C3
Bondís La PR7 . . . 30 F7
BONDS . . . 181 C6
Bonds La
Bonds PR3 . . . 181 C6
Elswick PR4 . . . 156 A2
Bond's La PR9 . . . 55 A7
Bond St
Blackpool FY4 . . . 110 B7
13 Burnley BB10 . . . 128 A8
Bury BL9 . . . 33 A2
Colne BB8 . . . 171 D5
Darwen BB3 . . . 82 A2
Edenfield BL0 . . . 68 E2
Lancaster LA1 . . . 215 A8
Nelson BB9 . . . 148 D7
Bone Croft PR6 . . . 78 B3
Bone Hill La PR3 . . . 202 D1
Bonfire Hill Cl BB4 . . . 86 B7
Bonfire Hill Rd BB4 . . . 86 A7
Bonney St FY5 . . . 176 B3
Bonny Grass Terr BB7 . . . 144 A4
Bonny St FY1 . . . 130 B4
Bonsall St BB2 . . . 101 B2
Boome St FY4 . . . 110 C6
Boon Town LA6 . . . 240 C7
Boon Wlks LA6 . . . 240 C7
Booth Bridge La BD23 . . . 197 B5
Booth Cres BB4 . . . 87 A1
Booth Ct 4 BB10 . . . 128 A8
Boothfield House Cvn Pk FY6 . . . 200 A6
BOOTH FOLD . . . 86 E1
Boothley Rd FY1 . . . 130 D6
Boothman Pl BB9 . . . 170 E2
Boothman St BB2 . . . 101 D2
Booth Rd OL13 . . . 70 B8
Boothroyden FY1 . . . 130 B8
Booth's La L39 . . . 14 F4
Booth's Par PR2 . . . 117 F7
Booth St
Accrington BB5 . . . 104 C4
10 Bacup OL13 . . . 87 F2
Carnforth LA5 . . . 223 D1
Haslingden BB4 . . . 85 A4
10 Nelson BB9 . . . 148 D8
Rawtenstall BB4 . . . 69 E8
Southport PR9 . . . 35 B8
Bootle St PR1 . . . 118 C1
Boot St BB18 . . . 197 B2
Boot Way BB11 . . . 128 A5
Borage Cl FY5 . . . 176 A5
Boran Ct BB11 . . . 126 E4
Bordeaux Cres FY5 . . . 152 F6
Border Ct 6 LA1 . . . 218 B1
Bores Hill WN1 . . . 30 C4
Borough Rd BB3 . . . 82 A1
Borrans Lane Cvn Pk LA3 . . . 212 F4
Borron La LA6 . . . 240 C3
Borrowdale L37 . . . 11 F5
Borrowdale Ave
Blackburn BB1 . . . 102 C3
Fleetwood FY7 . . . 198 E4
Nelson BB9 . . . 148 F7
Borrowdale Bsns Pk LA3 . . . 217 D3
Borrowdale Cl
4 Accrington BB5 . . . 125 D1
Burnley BB10 . . . 148 C3
Borrowdale Dr BB10 . . . 148 C4
Borrowdale Gr LA4 . . . 217 D5
Borrowdale Rd
Blackpool FY4 . . . 131 B1
Lancaster LA1 . . . 215 A8
Leyland PR25 . . . 60 B7
BORWICK . . . 240 B4
Borwick Ave LA5 . . . 223 E6
Borwick Cl LA5 . . . 223 E6
Borwick Ct
Borwick LA6 . . . 240 B4
3 Morecambe LA4 . . . 217 B3
Borwick Dr LA1 . . . 218 B2
Borwick La LA6 . . . 240 B3
Borwick Mews LA6 . . . 240 B3
Borwick Rd LA6 . . . 240 D3
Bosburn Dr BB2 . . . 121 C2
Boscombe Ave LA3 . . . 216 E2
Boscombe Rd FY4 . . . 110 B6
Bosley Arc 2 FY1 . . . 130 B5
Bosley Cl BB3 . . . 65 D8
Bostock St 21 PR1 . . . 97 A7
Boston Ave FY2 . . . 152 D6
Boston Rd
Bacup OL13 . . . 87 F3
Lytham St Anne's FY8 . . . 90 B6
Bostons BB6 . . . 124 B5
Boston St BB9 . . . 148 F6
Boston Way FY4 . . . 110 F8
Bosworth Dr PR8 . . . 21 B4
Bosworth Pl FY4 . . . 110 B4
Bosworth St BL6 . . . 32 B4
Botanic Gardens Mus★ PR9 . . . 54 B2
Botanic Rd PR9 . . . 54 B2
Botany Bay★ PR6 . . . 61 E3
Botany Brow PR6 . . . 61 E2
Bott House La BB8, BB9 . . . 171 A2
Bottomdale Rd LA2 . . . 218 E8
Bottomgate BB1 . . . 102 B5
Bottomley Bank La BB4 . . . 86 B8
Bottomley St BB9 . . . 148 E8
BOTTOM OF HUTTON . . . 94 F3
Bottom o' th' Knotts Brow BL7 . . . 48 E3
Bottom O' Th' Moor BL6 . . . 32 F3
Bottoms La LA5 . . . 224 D3
Botton Rd LA2 . . . 239 C1
Boulder St 12 BB4 . . . 86 A7
Bouldsworth Rd BB10 . . . 128 E5
Boulevard PR1 . . . 97 B5
Boulevard Gdns FY8 . . . 90 A4
Boulevard The
Blackburn BB1 . . . 101 E4
Lytham St Anne's FY8 . . . 90 A4
Boulsworth Cres BB9 . . . 171 B1
Boulsworth Dr BB8 . . . 172 C1
Boulsworth Gr BB8 . . . 172 A5
Boulview Terr BB8 . . . 172 A5
Boundary Cl
Eccleston PR7 . . . 41 B6
New Longton PR4 . . . 75 F8
Boundary Ct FY3 . . . 153 A1
Boundary Edge BL0 . . . 68 E3
Boundary La
Becconsall PR4 . . . 73 E1
Burscough L40 . . . 25 F4
Hale Nook FY6, PR3 . . . 178 B7
Holmes PR4, PR9 . . . 55 E6
Kirkby L33 . . . 1 F2
Shevington Moor WN6 . . . 29 A3
Boundary Meanygate
Becconsall PR4 . . . 73 D1
Holmes PR4 . . . 55 F7
Boundary Prim Sch FY3 . . . 130 F8
Boundary Rd
Accrington BB5 . . . 104 D7
Fulwood PR2 . . . 117 D3
Lancaster LA1 . . . 214 F6
Lytham St Anne's FY8 . . . 91 E5
Boundary St
Burnley BB10 . . . 148 C2
Colne BB8 . . . 171 D4
Leyland PR25 . . . 77 B2
Southport PR8 . . . 35 B4
Bourbles La FY6 . . . 200 D4
Bourne Brow PR3 . . . 159 E5
Bourne May Rd FY6 . . . 199 D5
Bournemouth Rd FY4 . . . 110 B6
Bourne Rd FY5 . . . 176 B5
Bournesfield PR5 . . . 98 E1
Bourne's Row PR5 . . . 98 E1
Bourne Way FY5 . . . 176 A4
Bovington Ave FY5 . . . 152 F8
Bow Brook Rd PR25 . . . 77 C1
Bowden Ave BB2 . . . 100 C1
Bowden Pl FY8 . . . 90 C6
Bowen St BB2 . . . 101 B2
Bower Cl BB2 . . . 101 B2
BOWERHAM . . . 215 B6
Bowerham Com Prim Sch LA1 . . . 215 A6
Bowerham La LA1 . . . 215 B3
Bowerham Rd LA1 . . . 215 A5
Bowerham Terr 1 LA1 . . . 215 A6
Bowers La PR3 . . . 180 E7
Bower St
Blackburn BB2 . . . 101 B2
Bury BL9 . . . 33 C3
Bowers The PR7 . . . 43 D4
Bowes Lyon Pl FY8 . . . 90 C7
Bowfell Ave LA4 . . . 217 D5
Bowfell Cl FY4 . . . 131 D1
Bowfield's La BB2 . . . 120 F4
BOWGREAVE . . . 181 D4
Bowgreave Cl 1 FY4 . . . 111 A6
Bowgreave Dr PR3 . . . 181 D4
Bow Hills La BB7 . . . 231 C6
BOWKER'S GREEN . . . 6 D5
Bowker's Green La L39 . . . 6 E4
Bowker St BL0 . . . 68 C5
Bow La
Leyland PR25 . . . 77 B1
Preston PR1 . . . 96 E7
Bowland Ave
Burnley BB10 . . . 128 E5
Chorley PR6 . . . 43 D8
Fleetwood FY7 . . . 175 D8
Bowland Ave E LA1 . . . 211 B8
Bowland Ave N LA1 . . . 211 B8
Bowland Ave S LA1 . . . 211 B8
Bowland Cl
Crag Bank LA5 . . . 223 C1
Longridge PR3 . . . 140 B8
Bowland Cres FY3 . . . 131 A8
Bowland Ct
4 Clitheroe BB7 . . . 166 E8
9 Southport PR9 . . . 35 C8
Bowland Dr LA1 . . . 218 B2
Bowland Gate La BB7 . . . 189 E7
Bowland High Sch BB7 . . . 230 B1
Bowland Ho 7 BB1 . . . 101 F6
Bowland Pl PR2 . . . 119 A3
Bowland Rd
Fulwood PR2 . . . 119 A3
Garstang PR3 . . . 204 C1
Heysham LA3 . . . 213 A8
Bowland View
Brierfield BB9 . . . 148 D4
Garstang PR3 . . . 204 C1
Glasson LA2 . . . 209 E4
Bowland Wild Boar Pk★ BB7 . . . 186 E6
Bowlers Cl PR2 . . . 118 C5
Bowlers Wlk OL12 . . . 52 F2
Bowlers Wood 11 OL13 . . . 70 D8
Bowlingfield PR2 . . . 117 A6
Bowling Gn The BL0 . . . 68 D3
Bowling Green Cl
Darwen BB3 . . . 65 B7
Southport PR8 . . . 35 F5
Bowling Green Cotts BB6 . . . 143 C6
Bowling Green Cvn Pk LA5 . . . 223 C1
Bowman Ct 5 BB1 . . . 101 F5
Bowness Ave
Blackpool FY4 . . . 131 D1
Fleetwood FY7 . . . 198 C1
Lytham St Anne's FY8 . . . 110 F2
Nelson BB9 . . . 148 E6
Rochdale OL12 . . . 52 C1
Southport PR8 . . . 21 C3
Thornton FY5 . . . 176 B2
Bowness Cl BB1 . . . 102 A6
Bowness Rd
Lancaster LA1 . . . 218 E1
Padiham BB12 . . . 146 C2
Preston PR1 . . . 119 A1
Bowood Ct FY3 . . . 131 B7
Bowran St PR1 . . . 96 F8
Bow St PR25 . . . 77 B2
Bow Wood Cl PR7 . . . 43 A6
Boxer Pl PR26 . . . 76 C2
Box St BL0 . . . 50 D6
Boxwood Dr BB2 . . . 80 F8
Boxwood St BB1 . . . 101 F8
Boyd Cl WN6 . . . 29 F1

Boyes Ave PR3 . . . 181 D2
Boyle St BB1 . . . 101 F6
Boys La PR2 . . . 117 C5
Brabiner La PR2, PR3 . . . 139 B4
Brabins Endowed Sch PR3 . . . 185 E3
Bracebridge Dr PR8 . . . 35 F2
BRACEWELL . . . 231 F3
Bracewell Ave FY6 . . . 154 A3
Bracewell Cl BB9 . . . 148 E8
Bracewell La BD23 . . . 231 F3
Bracewell Rd PR2 . . . 118 E5
Bracewell St
Barnoldswick BB18 . . . 196 B3
Burnley BB10 . . . 148 B1
Nelson BB9 . . . 148 F8
Brackenbury Cl 5 PR5 . . . 77 A7
Brackenbury Rd PR1, PR2 . . . 117 E3
Brackenbury St PR1 . . . 117 F2
Bracken Cl
Blackburn BB2 . . . 80 F8
Chorley PR6 . . . 43 E8
Brackendale BB2 . . . 101 C1
Bracken Dr PR4 . . . 93 D7
Bracken Gr BB4 . . . 68 A8
Bracken Hey BB7 . . . 167 A8
Bracken Lea Fold 3 OL12 . . . 52 B2
Brackenthaite Rd LA5, LA7 . . . 225 B7
Brackenway L37 . . . 12 A6
Bracken Way FY2 . . . 152 D2
Bracknel Way L39 . . . 15 A1
Braconash Rd PR25 . . . 76 E2
Bradda Rd BB2 . . . 101 E1
Braddon Cl LA4 . . . 217 C3
Braddon St 2 PR1 . . . 118 D1
Brades Ave FY5 . . . 176 D2
Brades La PR4 . . . 93 D7
Brade St PR9 . . . 54 C4
Bradford Gr LA3 . . . 212 F6
Bradford St BB5 . . . 104 D6
Bradkirk La PR5 . . . 78 B8
Bradkirk Pl PR5 . . . 78 A7
BRADLEY . . . 170 E2
Bradley Ct BB7 . . . 163 E8
Bradley Fold 5 BB9 . . . 170 E1
Bradley Gdns BB12 . . . 127 B5
Bradley Hall Rd BB9 . . . 170 F1
Bradley Hall Trad Est WN6 . . . 30 A2
Bradley La
Eccleston PR7 . . . 41 D6
Standish WN6 . . . 29 E1
Standish WN6 . . . 29 F2
Bradley Pl 8 PR8 . . . 35 B7
Bradley Prim Sch BB9 . . . 170 E1
Bradley Rd BB9 . . . 170 E1
Bradley Rd E BB9 . . . 170 E1
Bradley Smithy Cl OL12 . . . 52 E2
Bradley St
Colne BB8 . . . 171 F5
Southport PR9 . . . 35 C8
Bradley View 12 BB9 . . . 170 E1
Bradman Rd L33 . . . 1 D3
Bradshaw Brow L40 . . . 40 E2
Bradshaw Cl
Blackburn BB1 . . . 101 E8
Nelson BB9 . . . 148 E7
Standish WN6 . . . 29 D1
Bradshaw Ct PR9 . . . 36 A7
Bradshawgate Dr LA5 . . . 224 C4
Bradshaw La
Corner Row PR4 . . . 133 D1
Eagland Hill PR3 . . . 179 A7
Mawdesley L40 . . . 40 E2
Parbold WN8 . . . 27 C1
Scronkey PR3 . . . 201 E2
Bradshaw Rd BL2, BL7 . . . 48 E1
Bradshaw Row BB5 . . . 103 F6
Bradshaw St E 3 BB5 . . . 104 C6
Bradshaw St W BB5 . . . 103 F6
Bradshaws Cl FY6 . . . 177 C7
Bradshaw's La PR8 . . . 21 D6
Bradshaw St
Church BB5 . . . 103 F6
7 Lancaster LA1 . . . 215 A7
Nelson BB9 . . . 148 D7
Bradwood Ct BB4 . . . 85 A2
Bradyll Ct BB6 . . . 143 C6
Brady St BL6 . . . 32 A4
Braefield Cres PR2 . . . 118 F2
Braemar Ave
Southport PR9 . . . 53 E2
Thornton FY5 . . . 153 C7
Braemar Ct 2 LA4 . . . 217 E4
Braemar Dr BL9 . . . 33 D2
Braemar Wlk FY2 . . . 152 F6
Braeside BB2 . . . 101 C6
Braewood Cl BL9 . . . 33 C3
Braganza Way LA1 . . . 214 C8
Braid Cl PR1 . . . 96 D1
Braidhaven WN6 . . . 19 E7
Braid's La PR3 . . . 182 A7
Braidwood Ct FY8 . . . 89 D7
Braintree Ave PR1 . . . 96 E2
Braith Cl FY4 . . . 110 F8
Braithwaite St 3 FY1 . . . 130 B7
Bramble Cl PR4 . . . 113 E6
Bramble Ct
Kingsfold PR1 . . . 96 E2
1 Thornton FY5 . . . 176 A2
Brambles Cl BB7 . . . 166 D1
Bramble St BB10 . . . 148 A1
Brambles The
Blackburn BB2 . . . 101 A8
Blackpool FY8 . . . 110 B4
Coppull PR7 . . . 42 F2
Fulwood PR2 . . . 118 D6
Bramble Way
Burscough L40 . . . 25 F4
Parbold WN8 . . . 27 C1
Bramblewood PR26 . . . 58 B2
Bramblings The FY6 . . . 153 B2
Bramcote Cl L33 . . . 1 A4
Bramcote Rd L33 . . . 1 A4
Bramhall Rd WN8 . . . 17 F2
Bramley Ave
Burnley BB12 . . . 127 C8
Fleetwood FY7 . . . 198 E4
Bramley Cl 8 BB5 . . . 103 E5
Bramley Ct WN6 . . . 29 E1
Bramley Gdns FY6 . . . 153 A2
Bramley View BB7 . . . 144 D8
Brampton Ave FY5 . . . 175 F4
Brampton Dr
Bamber Bridge PR5 . . . 97 E1
Morecambe LA4 . . . 217 F5
Brampton St 2 PR2 . . . 117 C1
Bramwell Pk L40 . . . 24 B4
Bramwell Rd PR4 . . . 93 B6
Bramworth Ave BL0 . . . 50 B6
Branch Rd
Blackburn BB2, BB3 . . . 81 E7
Burnley BB11 . . . 128 B4
2 Clayton-le-M BB5 . . . 124 F3
Mellor Brook BB2 . . . 121 C2
Waddington BB7 . . . 189 B4
Branch St
Bacup OL13 . . . 70 D8
Nelson BB9 . . . 148 F8
Brancker St 8 PR7 . . . 43 A5
Brandiforth St PR5 . . . 97 F2
Brandlesholme Rd BL8 . . . 50 A1
Brandon Cl WN8 . . . 10 A7
Brandreth Delph WN8 . . . 27 C3
Brandreth Dr WN8 . . . 27 C2
Brandreth Pk WN8 . . . 27 D4
Brandreth Pl WN6 . . . 29 F1
BRANDWOOD . . . 70 B8
Brandwood
Higher Penwortham PR1 . . . 96 A4
6 Newchurch BB4 . . . 86 E1
Brandwood Ct BL7 . . . 48 E5
Brandwood Fold BL7 . . . 48 E5
Brandwood Gr BB10 . . . 128 C6
Brandwood Pk OL13 . . . 70 B8
Brandwood Rd OL13 . . . 70 B8
Brandwood St BB3 . . . 82 B1
Brandy House Brow BB2 . . . 101 F2
Branksome Ave FY5 . . . 175 F3
Branksome Dr LA4 . . . 217 D4
Branston Rd FY4 . . . 130 E1
Branstree Rd FY4 . . . 131 C1
Brant Ct FY7 . . . 198 C1
Brantfell Dr BB12 . . . 127 B8
Brantfell Rd
Blackburn BB1 . . . 101 D7
Great Harwood BB6 . . . 124 D6
Brant Rd PR1 . . . 119 A1
Brantwood BB5 . . . 124 E2
Brantwood Ave
Blackburn BB1 . . . 102 F5
Morecambe LA4 . . . 217 E6
Brantwood Dr
Lancaster LA1 . . . 215 A2
Leyland PR25 . . . 77 B1
Brassey St BB12 . . . 127 C7
Brathay Pl FY7 . . . 198 D2
Braxfield Ct FY8 . . . 89 D6
Brayshaw Pl PR2 . . . 118 E4
Brays Heys 2 FY5 . . . 176 C1
Brays Rd FY8 . . . 112 B1
Bray St PR2 . . . 117 C1
Brazil Cl LA3 . . . 217 A2
Brazley Ave BL6 . . . 32 E1
Bread St 4 BB12 . . . 127 D6
Bream Wood PR4 . . . 113 E4
Brearlands BD23 . . . 197 B6
Brearley St OL13 . . . 70 D8
Brechin Rd L33 . . . 1 A2
Breck Cl FY6 . . . 153 E5
Breck Dr FY6 . . . 153 E5
Breck Prim Sch The FY6 . . . 153 F5
Breck Rd
Blackpool FY3 . . . 130 E4
Poulton-le-F FY6 . . . 153 F6
Breckside Cl FY6 . . . 153 E5
Brecon Ave BB5 . . . 103 C4
Brecon Cl FY1 . . . 130 D3
Brecon Rd BB1 . . . 102 C5
Bredon Ave PR7 . . . 60 E1
Bredon Cl FY8 . . . 91 D5
Bredon Ct L37 . . . 11 E4
Breeze Cl
Foulridge BB8 . . . 194 E1
Thornton FY5 . . . 176 A4
Breeze Mount PR5 . . . 77 C8
Breeze Rd PR8 . . . 34 E2
Brenbar Cres OL12 . . . 71 D1
Brendjean Rd LA4 . . . 217 C4
Brendon Wlk FY3 . . . 130 F8
Brennand Cl
Bamber Bridge PR5 . . . 77 F8
Lancaster LA1 . . . 218 A2
Brennand St
Burnley BB10 . . . 148 B1
Clitheroe BB7 . . . 189 E1
Brentlea Ave LA3 . . . 212 E7
Brentlea Cres LA3 . . . 212 E7
Brenton Bsns Complex 2 BL9 . . . 33 A2
Brent St BB10 . . . 148 C3
Brentwood FY7 . . . 198 E2
Brentwood Ave
Blackpool FY5 . . . 152 D8
Burnley BB11 . . . 127 E3
Poulton-le-F FY6 . . . 153 C3
Brentwood Cl L38 . . . 2 F2
Brentwood Ct PR9 . . . 53 D1
Brentwood Rd
Adlington PR6 . . . 31 B8
Nelson BB9 . . . 171 A1
BRETHERTON . . . 57 E6
Bretherton Cl PR26 . . . 59 C8
Bretherton Cotts FY5 . . . 153 E8
Bretherton Ct L40 . . . 25 F3
Bretherton Endowed CE Prim Sch PR26 . . . 57 F5
Bretherton Rd PR26 . . . 58 B4
Bretherton Terr 9 PR25 . . . 77 B1
Brettarch Dr LA1 . . . 214 E5
Brettargh Cl LA1 . . . 214 E6
Brettargh Dr LA1 . . . 214 E6
Brett Cl BB7 . . . 167 A7
Bretton Fold PR8 . . . 35 F5
Brewery La
Formby L37 . . . 11 F6
19 Lancaster LA1 . . . 214 F8
Brewery St
6 Blackburn BB2 . . . 101 D5
Longridge PR3 . . . 140 B7
Breworth Fold La PR6 . . . 79 A3
Briar Ave PR7 . . . 60 C4
Briar Bank Row PR2 . . . 118 A8
Briar Cl 3 OL12 . . . 52 A1
Briarcroft BB3 . . . 82 A6
Briar Croft PR4 . . . 75 A7
Briarfield BL7 . . . 47 D2
Briar Field FY2 . . . 152 F6
Briarfield Rd FY6 . . . 153 B5
Briar Gr PR2 . . . 117 A4
Briar Hill Cl 3 BB1 . . . 102 A4
Briar Lea Rd LA6 . . . 221 E5
Briar Mews 1 FY5 . . . 176 C1
Briar Rd
Blackburn BB1 . . . 101 F8
Southport PR8 . . . 21 D4
Thornton FY5 . . . 176 C1
Briars Brook L40 . . . 26 A2
Briarscroft LA5 . . . 223 E6
Briars Gn WN8 . . . 18 B4
Briars La
Maghull L31 . . . 5 E1
Ring o'Bells L40 . . . 26 A3
Briar St 5 OL13 . . . 88 A1
Briars The
Fulwood PR2 . . . 118 D6
Southport PR8 . . . 34 F1
Briarwood PR4 . . . 93 A6
Briarwood Cl
Leyland PR25 . . . 59 E8
Thornton FY5 . . . 153 B7
Weeton PR4 . . . 132 F2
Briarwood Ct FY5 . . . 153 B7
Briarwood Dr FY2 . . . 152 E5
Briary Croft L38 . . . 2 F3
Briary Ct PR5 . . . 78 C5
Brickcroft LA2 . . . 210 A4
Brickcroft La PR26 . . . 58 B3
Brickhouse Gdns PR3 . . . 185 E3
Brickhouse La FY6 . . . 177 B4
Brick Kiln La L40 . . . 39 B3
Brickmakers Arms Yd L39 . . . 15 D6
Brick St
9 Burnley BB11 . . . 127 F6
Bury BL9 . . . 33 A3
Bridge Ave L39 . . . 15 E5
Bridge Bank 4 PR5 . . . 97 C6
Bridge Cl
Bamber Bridge PR5 . . . 77 A8
6 Newchurch BB4 . . . 86 F1
Bridge Croft
Bolton-le-S LA5 . . . 221 A4
Clayton-le-M BB5 . . . 124 E4
Bridge Ct
3 Bamber Bridge PR5 . . . 77 A8
Clitheroe BB7 . . . 189 F2
2 Lytham St Anne's FY8 . . . 91 D4
BRIDGE END . . . 68 A7
Bridge End
Bamber Bridge PR5 . . . 77 C8
Barley BB12 . . . 169 C5
Whalley BB7 . . . 144 C4
Bridge End Cl BB4 . . . 68 A7
Bridge Farm Dr L31 . . . 5 F2
Bridgefield Cl BB1 . . . 124 B2
Bridgefield Dr BL9 . . . 33 C2
Bridgefield St 8 BB12 . . . 126 C4
Bridge Gr PR8 . . . 35 B6
Bridgehall Dr WN8 . . . 10 B7
Bridge Hall Dr BL9 . . . 33 C2
Bridge Hall Fold BL9 . . . 33 C2
Bridge Hall La BL9 . . . 33 D2
Bridge Ho
7 Blackburn BB2 . . . 101 B1
18 Lancaster LA1 . . . 218 D2
3 Lytham St Anne's FY8 . . . 91 D4
Ormskirk L39 . . . 15 E4
Rishton BB1 . . . 124 B1
Bridge Hos
Accrington BB5 . . . 84 E8
Whitewell Bottom BB4 . . . 86 F7
Bridge House Marina & Cvn Pk PR3 . . . 181 A8
Bridge House Rd FY4 . . . 110 F8
Bridge La LA1 . . . 214 F8
Bridge Mews
6 Bamber Bridge PR5 . . . 77 E8
Ingleton LA6 . . . 242 F3
Bridge Mill Ct PR6 . . . 43 F6
Bridgemill Rd BB1 . . . 101 F4
Bridge Mill Rd BB9 . . . 148 C8
Bridgend Ct PR2 . . . 116 F3
Bridgend Dr PR8 . . . 21 B4
Bridge Rd
3 Bamber Bridge PR5 . . . 77 C8
Chatburn BB7 . . . 190 D5
Fleetwood FY7 . . . 199 B4
Lancaster LA1 . . . 214 F5
Lytham St Anne's FY8 . . . 90 E4
Morecambe LA4 . . . 217 C5
Nether Kellet LA6 . . . 221 E4
Preston PR2 . . . 117 C2
Bridge Row PR3 . . . 157 C7
Bridgeside
Blackpool FY8 . . . 110 B4
Carnforth LA5 . . . 223 D1
Bridge St
14 Accrington BB5 . . . 104 C6
Bamber Bridge PR5 . . . 77 E7
Blackburn BB1 . . . 101 E4
Brierfield BB9 . . . 148 B5
Burnley BB11 . . . 128 A6
Bury BL9 . . . 33 A3
Church BB5 . . . 103 E6
Colne BB8 . . . 171 C4
Darwen BB3 . . . 82 A1
Garstang PR3 . . . 181 C6
6 Great Harwood BB6 . . . 124 C5
Haslingden BB4 . . . 68 C6
Higher Walton PR5 . . . 98 B3
Horwich BL6 . . . 32 C4
Newchurch BB4 . . . 86 F1
Ormskirk L39 . . . 15 E4
Padiham BB12 . . . 126 B8
Ramsbottom BL0 . . . 50 C6
Rawtenstall BB4 . . . 69 E7
Rishton BB1 . . . 124 B2
Southport PR8 . . . 35 B6
Water BB4 . . . 87 A8
Wheelton PR6 . . . 62 A7
Whitworth OL12 . . . 71 C1
Bridge Terr
6 Preston PR5 . . . 97 C6
Whalley BB7 . . . 144 B7
Bridget St 22 LA1 . . . 214 F8
Bridgewater Ave 7 FY5 . . . 152 F7
Bridgewater Cl BB11 . . . 126 F4
Bridgewater Ct 6 BB2 . . . 101 C4
Bridgeway PR5 . . . 77 C8
Bridge Wills La PR9 . . . 54 C5
Bridle Path The BB18 . . . 194 D7
Bridleway
Lytham St Anne's FY8 . . . 90 E7
Newchurch BB4 . . . 86 F2
Brief St BB10 . . . 128 A8
Briercliffe Ave
Blackpool FY3 . . . 130 F2
Colne BB8 . . . 171 B3
Briercliffe Bsns Ctr BB10 . . . 148 F3
Briercliffe Prim Sch BB10 . . . 148 F3
Briercliffe Rd
Burnley BB10 . . . 148 C1
Burnley, Harle Syke BB10 . . . 148 D2
9 Chorley PR6 . . . 61 D1
Briercliffe Sh Ctr 15 BB10 . . . 148 B1
Briercliffe St BB8 . . . 171 B3
Brier Cres BB9 . . . 148 D6
Brier Dr LA3 . . . 212 E7
BRIERFIELD . . . 148 C6
Brierfield
New Longton PR4 . . . 75 F8
Skelmersdale WN8 . . . 9 D6
Brierfield Sta BB9 . . . 148 B5
Brier Heights Cl BB9 . . . 148 D5
Brierholme Ave 1 BL7 . . . 47 E1
Brierley Ave FY3 . . . 130 E7
Brierley La PR4 . . . 136 B8
Brierley Rd PR5 . . . 78 A7
Brierley St PR2 . . . 117 D1
Briers Brow PR6 . . . 62 B7
Briers The PR7 . . . 41 C6
Briery Cl PR2 . . . 118 C4
Brieryfield Rd PR1 . . . 96 D8
Briery Hey PR5 . . . 78 C6
Briery St 2 LA1 . . . 218 B1
Brigg Field BB5 . . . 124 F4
Briggs Fold BL7 . . . 47 E2
Briggs Fold Cl BL7 . . . 47 E2
Briggs Fold Rd BL7 . . . 47 E2
Briggs Rd PR2 . . . 117 C2
Brighouse Cl L39 . . . 15 D6
Brighton Ave
Blackpool FY4 . . . 110 B8
Cleveleys FY5 . . . 175 D2
Lytham St Anne's FY8 . . . 89 F7
Brighton Cres PR2 . . . 117 A3
Brighton Rd
Burnley BB10 . . . 148 C3
Southport PR8 . . . 35 A3
Brighton St
Bury BL9 . . . 33 B3
7 Chorley PR6 . . . 43 E8
Todmorden OL14 . . . 109 C1
Brighton Terr
Blackburn BB2 . . . 101 B6
Darwen BB3 . . . 81 E2
Bright St Mill BL9 . . . 33 A3
Bright's Cl BB7 . . . 229 A5
Bright St
Blackburn BB1 . . . 102 B6
Blackpool FY4 . . . 110 B8
2 Bolton BL7 . . . 47 D2
2 Burnley BB10 . . . 148 B1
Bury BL9 . . . 33 A3
Clitheroe BB7 . . . 166 F8
Colne BB8 . . . 171 D5
Colne, Cotton Tree BB8 . . . 172 B5
Darwen BB3 . . . 81 F2
Oswaldtwistle BB5 . . . 103 D3
Padiham BB12 . . . 126 D8
13 Rawtenstall BB4 . . . 86 A3
Southport PR9 . . . 35 F7
Brightstone Cl PR9 . . . 55 B5
Bright Terr BB8 . . . 172 B2
Brightwater BL6 . . . 31 F2
Brigsteer Cl BB5 . . . 124 E2
BRINDLE . . . 78 F5
Brindle Cl
Bamber Bridge PR5 . . . 98 A2
9 Lancaster LA1 . . . 218 A2
Longridge PR3 . . . 140 B7
Walton Summit PR5 . . . 78 B8
Brindle Dell 8 BL7 . . . 47 D2
Brindle Fold PR5 . . . 78 C7
Brindle Gregson Lane Prim Sch PR5 . . . 98 E1
Brindle Hts PR6 . . . 78 F5
Brindle Pl 6 PR2 . . . 139 D1
Brindle Rd
Bamber Bridge PR5 . . . 97 F2
Walton Summit PR5, PR6 . . . 78 C7
Brindle St James' CE Prim Sch PR6 . . . 78 F5
Brindle St
Blackburn BB2 . . . 101 C1
Chorley PR7 . . . 43 C6
Preston PR1 . . . 97 C8
Brindley Cl BB11 . . . 126 F4
Brindley St BL6 . . . 32 C2
Brinklow Cl PR8 . . . 21 A5
Brink's Row BL6 . . . 32 D5
BRINSCALL . . . 62 E7
Brinscall Terr PR6 . . . 62 F7
Brinwell Bsns Ctr FY4 . . . 111 B8
Brinwell Rd FY4 . . . 131 B1
Brisbane Pl FY5 . . . 152 F7
Brisbane St 8 BB5 . . . 125 A1
Bristol Ave
Blackpool FY2 . . . 152 E4
Fleetwood FY7 . . . 175 C8
Leyland PR25 . . . 77 C3
Bristol Cl 9 BB1 . . . 102 A4
Bristol St
Burnley BB11 . . . 127 D3
Colne BB8 . . . 171 E5
Morecambe LA4 . . . 217 C4
Bristow Ave PR2 . . . 117 B2
BRITANNIA . . . 71 C8
Britannia Ave OL13 . . . 88 A2
Britannia Com Prim Sch OL13 . . . 71 C8
Britannia Cotts BB5 . . . 103 A1
Britannia Dr PR2 . . . 96 B7
Britannia Mill
14 Bury BL9 . . . 33 A3
1 Rake Foot BB4 . . . 86 A7
Britannia Pl 2 FY1 . . . 130 B1
Britannia St BB6 . . . 124 C5
Britannia Way
Blackpool FY4 . . . 111 E8
Haslingden BB4 . . . 68 A8
Britannia Wlk
1 Burnley BB11 . . . 128 B4
Lytham St Anne's FY8 . . . 90 C8
British Commercial Vehicle Mus★ PR25 . . . 77 A1
British in India Mus★ BB8 . . . 171 E5
British Lawnmower Mus★ PR8 . . . 35 B5
Britten Cl BB2 . . . 102 A2
Britten St BB3 . . . 81 F2
Britwell Cl BB2 . . . 82 A8
Brixey St PR1 . . . 96 D6
Brixham Pl 4 FY4 . . . 110 B6
Brixton Rd PR1 . . . 97 B7
Broadacre
Caton LA2 . . . 237 C3
Shevington Moor WN6 . . . 29 B2
Up Holland WN8 . . . 10 A6
Broadacre Cl LA2 . . . 237 C3
Broadacre Pl LA2 . . . 237 C3
Broadacre View LA2 . . . 237 C3
Broadbent Dr BL9 . . . 33 E4
BROAD CLOUGH . . . 87 F4
Broad Clough Villas OL13 . . . 87 F5
Broad Croft PR4 . . . 95 A1
Broadfield
Accrington BB5 . . . 84 B8
Broughton PR3 . . . 137 B2
BROADFIELD
Leyland . . . 76 E1
Oswaldtwistle . . . 103 F2
Broadfield BB5 . . . 103 F2
Broadfield Ave
Blackpool FY4 . . . 110 F5
Poulton-le-F FY6 . . . 153 F3
Broadfield Ct FY6 . . . 153 F3
Broadfield Dr
Kingsfold PR1 . . . 96 D2

Broadfield Dr *continued*
Leyland PR25 . . . . . 76 E1
**Broadfield Rd** BB5 . . . . . 104 A3
**Broadfields** PR7 . . . . . 61 B2
**Broadfield Sch** BB5 . . . . . 103 F2
**Broadfields Cvn Pk**
LA3 . . . . . 217 A2
**Broadfield St** BB5 . . . . . 103 F3
**Broadfleet Cl** PR3 . . . . . 201 C6
**Broadfold Ave** BB1 . . . . . 102 B7
**BROADGATE** . . . . . 96 E6
**Broadgate** PR1 . . . . . 96 D6
**Broadgate Foot Pk**
LA3 . . . . . 212 F4
**Broadgreen Cl** PR25 . . . . . 76 F1
**Broadhead Rd**
Edgworth BL7 . . . . . 48 E7
Hoddleston BB3, BL7 . . . . . 66 F5
**Broadhurst La** WN6 . . . . . 28 F7
**Broadhurst Rd** FY5 . . . . . 152 E8
**Broadhurst Way** BB9 . . . . . 148 C4
**Broad Ing** OL12 . . . . . 52 C1
**Broad Ing Cl** BB10 . . . . . 128 E1
**Broadith La** PR3 . . . . . 160 E1
**Broad La**
Formby L37 . . . . . 12 F1
Great Altcar L37, L38 . . . . . 4 A8
Haskayne L39 . . . . . 14 B2
Kirkby L33 . . . . . 1 A1
Maghull, Homer Green L29 . . 4 C2
Southport L37 . . . . . 12 C7
Whalley BB7 . . . . . 144 B5
Winmarleigh PR3 . . . . . 203 F5
**Broadlands** PR8 . . . . . 34 E3
**Broadlands Dr** LA5 . . . . . 220 F3
**Broadlands Pl** FY8 . . . . . 90 F4
**Broadlands Sch** BB1 . . . . . 82 B8
**Broadlea Gr** OL12 . . . . . 52 C2
**BROADLEY** . . . . . 52 C5
**Broadley St** BB4 . . . . . 86 A3
**Broad Mdw**
Bamber Bridge PR5 . . . . . 77 A8
Chipping PR3 . . . . . 185 D3
**Broadmead** WN8 . . . . . 27 B2
**Broad Meadow La** PR26 . . 57 F4
**Broadness Dr** BB9 . . . . . 148 E6
**Broad Oak Ave** PR3 . . . . . 181 D6
**Broad Oak Cl** 4 PR6 . . . . . 31 A8
**Broad Oak Cotts** PR6 . . . . . 44 D3
**Broad Oak Gn** PR1 . . . . . 96 B3
**Broad Oak High Sch**
BL9 . . . . . 33 B2
**Broad Oak Ind Est**
BB5 . . . . . 104 D4
**Broad Oak La**
Bury BL9 . . . . . 33 D3
Higher Penwortham PR1 . . . 96 B3
Kingsfold PR4 . . . . . 96 B2
Staining FY3 . . . . . 131 D5
**Broadoak Rd** L31 . . . . . 5 E1
**Broad Oak Rd** BB5 . . . . . 104 D5
**Broadoaks** BL9 . . . . . 33 D3
**Broad Oak Terr** BL9 . . . . . 33 E3
**Broadpool La** FY6 . . . . . 177 C1
**Broadriding Rd** WN6 . . . . . 19 E6
**Broad Sq** 8 PR25 . . . . . 60 A8
**Broad St**
3 Leyland PR25 . . . . . 60 A8
13 Nelson BB9 . . . . . 148 D8
**Broadstone Cl** 4 OL12 . . . 52 A1
**Broadstone Ct** LA1 . . . . . 215 C7
**Broadstone Dr** PR7 . . . . . 60 E7
**Broadtree Cl** BB2 . . . . . 121 C3
**Broadwater Ave** FY7 . . . . . 175 F8
**Broadwater Gdns** FY7 . . . . . 175 E8
**Broadway**
Accrington BB5 . . . . . 104 B6
Blackburn BB1 . . . . . 122 E2
Blackpool FY4 . . . . . 110 C7
Fleetwood FY7 . . . . . 198 E2
Fulwood PR2 . . . . . 117 D7
Haslingden BB4 . . . . . 68 B8
Horwich BL6 . . . . . 32 D3
Lancaster LA1 . . . . . 218 D2
Leyland PR25 . . . . . 60 B8
Morecambe LA4 . . . . . 217 D5
Nelson BB9 . . . . . 148 D8
Preston PR2 . . . . . 116 F2
**Broadway Cl** PR8 . . . . . 21 B5
**Broadway Cres** BB4 . . . . . 68 A8
**Broadway Pl**
Barrowford BB9 . . . . . 170 D3
Nelson BB9 . . . . . 171 A1
**Broadway Prim Sch**
BB4 . . . . . 68 C8
**Broadway St** BB2 . . . . . 101 B1
**Broadwood Cl** PR1 . . . . . 96 B4
**Broadwood Dr** PR2 . . . . . 117 F7
**Broadwood Way** FY8 . . . . . 90 E4
**Brock Ave** FY7 . . . . . 198 D2
**Brock Bank** BB4 . . . . . 86 F4
**Brockbank Ave** LA1 . . . . . 214 C8
**Brock Cl**
Lancaster LA1 . . . . . 218 C3
Morecambe LA3 . . . . . 217 F3
**Brock Clough Rd** BB4 . . . . . 86 F4
**Brockenhurst St** BB10 . . . 128 C5
**BROCKHALL VILLAGE** . . . 143 C5
**Brockholes Brow** PR1,
PR2 . . . . . 119 A1
**Brockholes Cres** FY6 . . . . . 153 E2
**Brockholes View** PR1 . . . . . 97 C7
**Brockholes Way** PR3 . . . . . 181 E1
**Brockholes Wood Com**
**Prim Sch** PR1 . . . . . 119 A1
**Brocklebank Rd** PR9 . . . . . 53 E2
**Brocklehurst Ave** BB5 . . . 104 B3
**Brocklewood Ave** FY6 . . . 131 D8
**Brock Mill La** PR3 . . . . . 183 B2
**Brock Rd**
Chorley PR6 . . . . . 61 D1
Lane Heads PR3, PR4 . . . . . 156 E3
**Brock Side** PR3 . . . . . 159 C6
**Brock St** LA1 . . . . . 214 F8
**Brockway** FY6 . . . . . 153 D2
**Brockway Ave** FY3 . . . . . 130 F6
**Broderick Ave** 1 FY2 . . . 152 E1
**Brodick Rd** BB1 . . . . . 102 D3
**Brodie Cl** FY4 . . . . . 110 F6
**Brogden La** BB18 . . . . . 231 E2
**Brogden St** 4 BB18 . . . . . 196 B3
**Brogden View** BB18 . . . . . 196 A4
**Broken Bank Head**
BB7 . . . . . 235 A2
**Broken Banks** BB8 . . . . . 171 E4
**Broken Stone Rd** BB3 . . . . . 81 A6
**Bromilow Rd** WN8 . . . . . 17 C1
**Bromley Cl** FY2 . . . . . 152 E1
**Bromley Cross** BL7 . . . . . 48 B1
**Bromley Ct** 5 FY2 . . . . . 152 E1
**Bromley Gn** PR6 . . . . . 61 F4
**Bromley Ho** BB2 . . . . . 101 C5
**Bromley Rd** FY8 . . . . . 89 F6
**Bromley St**
Blackburn BB2 . . . . . 101 C5
Preston PR1 . . . . . 96 D8
**Brompton Ave** L33 . . . . . 1 A5
**Brompton Cl** FY8 . . . . . 90 D5
**Brompton Rd**
Poulton-le-F FY6 . . . . . 131 D8
Southport PR8 . . . . . 35 E7
**Bromsgrove Ave** FY2 . . . . . 152 C4
**Bromsgrove Rd** BB10 . . . . . 128 B8
**Bronte Ave** BB10 . . . . . 128 D6
**Bronte Cl** OL12 . . . . . 52 A1
**Brooden Dr** BB9 . . . . . 148 C4
**Brook Ave**
Maghull L31 . . . . . 5 E2
Morecambe LA3 . . . . . 216 F3
Scorton PR3 . . . . . 204 E7
**Brookbank** BB9 . . . . . 170 E4
**Brook Bldg The** BL7 . . . . . 47 D2
**Brook Croft** PR2 . . . . . 117 B4
**Brook Ct** 9 BB4 . . . . . 86 A7
**Brookdale**
Adlington PR6 . . . . . 44 A1
Belmont BL7 . . . . . 46 C5
New Longton PR4 . . . . . 76 A6
Rochdale OL12 . . . . . 52 E3
**Brookdale Ave** FY5 . . . . . 152 E8
**Brookdale Cl** PR25 . . . . . 60 B6
**Brookdale The** PR8 . . . . . 21 D3
**Brooke Cl**
Accrington BB5 . . . . . 104 E2
Southport PR9 . . . . . 36 B7
**Brookes La** BB7 . . . . . 144 C5
**Brookes St** 7 OL13 . . . . . 70 D8
**Brooke St** PR6 . . . . . 43 E7
**Brookes The** 6 PR6 . . . . . 43 E7
**Brook Farm Cl** L39 . . . . . 15 E4
**BROOKFIELD** . . . . . 118 D4
**Brookfield**
Croston PR26 . . . . . 58 B3
Mawdesley L40 . . . . . 40 C2
Mellor BB2 . . . . . 121 E2
Parbold WN8 . . . . . 27 C2
**Brookfield Ave**
Blackpool FY4 . . . . . 111 A6
Fulwood PR2 . . . . . 118 C4
Thornton FY5 . . . . . 176 C1
**Brookfield Cl** LA5 . . . . . 221 B5
**Brookfield Com Prim Sch**
PR2 . . . . . 118 E5
**Brookfield Ct** PR3 . . . . . 185 E3
**Brookfield Dr** PR2 . . . . . 117 E8
**Brookfield Ho** BL0 . . . . . 49 F3
**Brookfield La** L39 . . . . . 6 A5
**Brookfield Park Prim Sch**
WN8 . . . . . 17 D2
**Brookfield Pl** PR5 . . . . . 78 A6
**Brookfield Rd**
Shevington Moor WN6 . . . . . 29 B2
Thornton FY5 . . . . . 176 C1
Up Holland WN8 . . . . . 10 B7
**Brookfield Sch** FY6 . . . . . 153 F5
**Brookfield St**
2 Blackburn BB1 . . . . . 101 E6
Preston PR1 . . . . . 117 F1
Todmorden OL14 . . . . . 109 C1
**Brookfield Terr**
Hampson Green LA2 . . . . . 207 E8
Lytham St Anne's FY8 . . . . . 91 B4
**Brookfield View** LA5 . . . . . 221 B5
**Brook Field Way** BB18 . . . 197 B1
**Brookford Cl** BB12 . . . . . 127 D8
**Brook Gr**
Cleveleys FY5 . . . . . 175 E4
Morecambe LA3 . . . . . 216 F3
**Brook Hey** PR4 . . . . . 74 F8
**Brook Hey Dr** L33 . . . . . 1 A3
**Brook Hey Wlk** L33 . . . . . 1 A3
**Brook Ho**
Lytham St Anne's FY8 . . . . . 91 A3
Southport PR8 . . . . . 35 C5
**Brookholme Ct** LA1 . . . . . 214 C7
**BROOKHOUSE**
Blackburn . . . . . 101 F6
Lancaster . . . . . 237 D3
**Brookhouse Bsns Ctr** 10
BB1 . . . . . 101 F6
**Brookhouse Cl**
Blackburn BB1 . . . . . 101 F6
Gregson Lane PR5 . . . . . 98 F2
**Brookhouse Dr** PR5 . . . . . 98 F2
**Brookhouse Gdns** 12
BB1 . . . . . 101 F6
**Brookhouse La** BB1 . . . . . 101 F6
**Brookhouse Prim Sch**
BB1 . . . . . 101 F7
**Brookhouse Rd**
Caton LA2 . . . . . 237 C3
Ormskirk L39 . . . . . 15 D6
**Brookhouse St** PR2 . . . . . 117 D1
**Brook La**
Charnock Richard PR7 . . . . . 42 C4
Farington PR26, PR4 . . . . . 76 D6
Much Hoole PR4 . . . . . 74 E3
Ormskirk L39 . . . . . 15 E4
**Brookland** LA6 . . . . . 242 C3
**Brookland Cl** BB5 . . . . . 124 F4
**Brooklands**
Chipping PR3 . . . . . 185 F3
Horwich BL6 . . . . . 32 C3
Much Hoole PR4 . . . . . 74 D2
Ormskirk L39 . . . . . 16 A6
Preston PR2 . . . . . 117 A1
**Brooklands Ave**
Burnley BB11 . . . . . 128 B3
Fulwood PR2 . . . . . 117 E7
Haslingden BB4 . . . . . 68 B7
Kirkham PR4 . . . . . 114 A5
**Brooklands Ct** LA1 . . . . . 215 A4
**Brooklands Dr**
Bonds PR3 . . . . . 181 C6
Heysham LA3 . . . . . 212 F6
Orrell WN5 . . . . . 10 D5
**Brooklands Gr** L40 . . . . . 25 F3
**Brooklands Rd**
Burnley BB11 . . . . . 128 B3
Lytham St Anne's FY8 . . . . . 90 C6
Ramsbottom BL0 . . . . . 50 A2
Up Holland WN8 . . . . . 10 C7
**Brookland St** BB4 . . . . . 86 D1
**Brooklands Terr** BB1 . . . . . 102 A7
**Brooklands The** PR4 . . . . . 113 B4
**Brooklands Way** FY4 . . . . . 111 E7
**Brookland Terr** 3 BB4 . . . 69 F7
**Brooklyn Ave** FY3 . . . . . 130 E8
**Brooklyn Cvn Pk** PR9 . . . . . 55 A4
**Brooklyn Rd** BB1 . . . . . 122 F5
**Brook Mdw** PR4 . . . . . 116 F7
**Brook Mill Ind Est** PR4 . . 113 B4
**Brook Pl** PR2 . . . . . 116 D2
**Brook Rd**
Lytham St Anne's FY8 . . . . . 91 C3
Morecambe LA3 . . . . . 216 F3
**Brook St N** PR2 . . . . . 117 D3
**BROOKSBOTTOMS** . . . . . 50 C3
**Brooksbottoms Cl** BL0 . . . 50 C4
**Brookshaw St** BL9 . . . . . 33 A4
**Brookside**
Brockhall Village BB6 . . . . . 143 C5
Coppull PR7 . . . . . 42 F1
Downham BB7 . . . . . 191 B5
Euxton PR7 . . . . . 60 C2
Hurlston Green L40 . . . . . 24 B4
Kirkham PR4 . . . . . 113 F6
Sabden BB7 . . . . . 145 F7
Thornton FY5 . . . . . 176 C3
**BROOK SIDE** . . . . . 103 A3
**Brook Side** L31 . . . . . 5 E1
**Brookside Cl**
Leyland PR26 . . . . . 76 E3
Ramsbottom BL0 . . . . . 50 A3
Whalley BB7 . . . . . 144 C5
**Brookside Cotts** PR6 . . . . . 62 D3
**Brookside Cres**
Ramsbottom BL8 . . . . . 49 E1
West Bradford BB7 . . . . . 189 D7
**Brookside Ctr** FY5 . . . . . 176 C3
**Brookside Dr** LA2 . . . . . 226 A8
**Brookside Ind Est** BB5 . . . 103 C3
**Brookside La** BB5 . . . . . 103 B3
**Brookside Prim Sch**
BB7 . . . . . 166 F8
**Brookside Rd**
Fulwood PR2 . . . . . 117 D7
Southport PR8 . . . . . 35 C2
Standish WN1 . . . . . 30 B1
**Brookside St** BB5 . . . . . 103 C3
**Brookside View** BB5 . . . . . 103 B4
**Brooks Rd** L37 . . . . . 11 D2
**Brook St**
Adlington PR6 . . . . . 44 A1
4 Barnoldswick BB18 . . . 196 B2
Blackburn BB2 . . . . . 101 B2
Blackpool FY4 . . . . . 130 E1
Bury BL9 . . . . . 33 A3
Clitheroe BB7 . . . . . 189 F1
Colne BB8 . . . . . 171 D5
Earby BB18 . . . . . 197 B2
Fleetwood FY7 . . . . . 175 E8
Haslingden BB4 . . . . . 85 B5
Higher Walton PR5 . . . . . 98 B3
Kirkham PR4 . . . . . 113 F6
Lancaster LA1 . . . . . 214 E7
Nelson BB9 . . . . . 148 E8
Oswaldtwistle BB5 . . . . . 103 E4
Padiham BB12 . . . . . 126 D7
Preston PR1 . . . . . 117 E2
Rishton BB1 . . . . . 124 B1
Southport PR9 . . . . . 54 D4
Wheelton PR6 . . . . . 62 A7
**Brooks Way** L37 . . . . . 11 D2
**Brook Vale Ct** PR3 . . . . . 157 E3
**Brookview** PR2 . . . . . 118 B5
**Brook Villas**
Waddington BB7 . . . . . 189 B4
West Bradford BB7 . . . . . 189 E5
**Brookville** OL12 . . . . . 71 C1
**Brookway**
Blackburn BB2 . . . . . 81 B8
Longton PR4 . . . . . 74 F8
Wrea Green PR4 . . . . . 113 A4
**Broom Cl**
Burscough L40 . . . . . 25 F4
Clayton-le-W PR25 . . . . . 77 E3
**Broome Cl** PR8 . . . . . 35 B3
**Broome Rd** PR8 . . . . . 35 B3
**Broom Field** PR3 . . . . . 181 D4
**Broomfield Ho** WN6 . . . . . 29 E2
**Broomfield Mill St**
PR1 . . . . . 117 F1
**Broomfield Pl**
Blackburn BB2 . . . . . 101 B3
Standish WN6 . . . . . 29 E1
**Broomfield Rd**
Fleetwood FY7 . . . . . 198 F2
Standish WN6 . . . . . 29 E2
**Broomflat Cl** WN6 . . . . . 29 E1
**Broom Hill Coppice**
PR3 . . . . . 204 C2
**Broomholme** WN6 . . . . . 19 D7
**Brotherod Hall Rd** OL12 . . 52 C2
**Brothers St** BB2 . . . . . 101 A1
**Brotherston Dr** BB2 . . . . . 81 C8
**Brotherton Mdws** 7
BB7 . . . . . 166 F8
**Brougham St** BB12 . . . . . 127 F7
**Brough Ave** FY2 . . . . . 152 F2
**BROUGHTON** . . . . . 137 D3
**Broughton Ave**
Blackpool FY3 . . . . . 130 E7
Southport PR8 . . . . . 35 D4
**Broughton Bsns & Ent Coll**
PR3 . . . . . 137 C2
**Broughton Cl** BB2 . . . . . 102 A1
**Broughton Gr** LA3 . . . . . 217 C3
**Broughton in**
**Amounderness CE Prim**
**Sch** PR3 . . . . . 137 D1
**Broughton St**
1 Burnley BB12 . . . . . 127 D6
4 Darwen BB3 . . . . . 81 F2
Preston PR1 . . . . . 117 E2
**Broughton Tower Way**
PR2 . . . . . 118 A8
**Broughton Way** FY6 . . . . . 153 C6
**Brow Cl** PR3 . . . . . 156 A6
**Brow Edge** BB4 . . . . . 86 D1
**Browfoot Cl** LA5 . . . . . 223 F2
**Browgate** BB7 . . . . . 190 F8
**Browgill Pl** 8 LA1 . . . . . 218 B2
**Browhead Ct** BB10 . . . . . 128 B8
**Browhead Rd** BB10 . . . . . 128 B8
**Brow Hey** PR5 . . . . . 78 B6
**Brown Birks Rd** BB5 . . . . . 104 E8
**Brown Birks St** 1
OL14 . . . . . 109 B1
**BROWNEDGE** . . . . . 97 D1
**BROWN EDGE** . . . . . 36 A2
**Brownedge Cl** PR5 . . . . . 97 D1
**Brown Edge Cl** PR8 . . . . . 36 A2
**Brownedge La** PR5 . . . . . 97 E1
**Brownedge Rd** PR5 . . . . . 77 B8
**Brownedge Wlk** PR5 . . . . . 97 D1
**BROWNHILL** . . . . . 122 F2
**Brownhill Ave** BB10 . . . . . 128 C6
**Brownhill Dr** BB1 . . . . . 123 A1
**Brownhill La** PR4 . . . . . 75 D7
**Brown Hill La** BB8 . . . . . 171 F7
**Brownhill Rd**
Blackburn BB1 . . . . . 122 F3
Leyland PR25 . . . . . 76 F1
**Brown Hill Row** BB8 . . . . . 171 F7
**Brownhill Sch** OL12 . . . . . 52 E1
**Brownhill View** OL12 . . . . . 52 E1
**Browning Ave**
4 Lytham St Anne's
FY8 . . . . . 91 D4
Oswaldtwistle BB5 . . . . . 103 C5
3 Thornton FY5 . . . . . 176 A3
**Browning Cl** BB8 . . . . . 171 D6
**Browning Cres** PR1 . . . . . 118 D2
**Browning Rd** PR1 . . . . . 118 D2
**Browning St** BB3 . . . . . 82 F1
**Brown La**
Bamber Bridge PR5 . . . . . 98 A2
Higher Walton PR5 . . . . . 98 A3
**Brownley St**
Chorley PR6 . . . . . 43 E7
Clayton Green PR6 . . . . . 78 B1
**BROWNLOW** . . . . . 10 C1
**Brownlow La** WN5 . . . . . 10 C1
**Brownlow Rd** BL6 . . . . . 32 C5
**Brownlow St**
Blackburn BB1 . . . . . 102 D4
Clitheroe BB7 . . . . . 166 E7
**Brownlow Terr** BB2 . . . . . 100 C1
**Brownroyd** BB18 . . . . . 197 C2
**Brown St E** BB8 . . . . . 171 D5
**Brown St W** BB8 . . . . . 171 C4
**Browns Hey** PR7 . . . . . 61 A2
**BROWNSIDE** . . . . . 128 F6
**Brownside Mill** BB10 . . . . . 128 F6
**Brownside Rd** BB10 . . . . . 128 F5
**Brown's La**
Kirkham PR4 . . . . . 113 D3
Thornton FY6 . . . . . 176 E7
**Brown Sq** 9 BB11 . . . . . 128 A6
**Brown St**
Accrington BB5 . . . . . 104 B5
Bacup OL13 . . . . . 87 F4
Bamber Bridge PR5 . . . . . 77 F8
Blackburn BB1 . . . . . 101 E5
Blackrod BL6 . . . . . 31 D2
Burnley BB11 . . . . . 127 F6
Chorley PR6 . . . . . 43 D8
Clitheroe BB7 . . . . . 166 D7
Fleetwood FY7 . . . . . 199 A3
2 Ramsbottom BL0 . . . . . 50 B5
Thornton FY5 . . . . . 176 B3
**Brows Cl** L37 . . . . . 11 E3
**Browsholme** LA1 . . . . . 218 A2
**Browsholme Ave**
Burnley BB10 . . . . . 128 C6
Fulwood PR2 . . . . . 118 F3
**Browsholme Cl**
Crag Bank LA5 . . . . . 223 C1
Normoss FY3 . . . . . 131 B8
Browsholme Hall*
BB7 . . . . . 187 E7
**Browsholme Rd** BB7 . . . . . 229 C1
**Brows La** L37 . . . . . 11 E3
**Brow The** PR4 . . . . . 73 E4
**Brow View** BB10 . . . . . 128 B8
**Broxton Ave** WN5 . . . . . 10 F7
**Broyd View** LA1 . . . . . 214 F5
**Bruce St**
5 Barnoldswick BB18 . . . 196 B3
Blackburn BB1 . . . . . 102 B6
Burnley BB11 . . . . . 127 D5
**Bruna La** PR3 . . . . . 181 E4
**Brundhurst Fold** BB2 . . . . . 121 E2
**Brunel Dr** BB1 . . . . . 102 A4
**Brunel St**
Burnley BB12 . . . . . 127 C7
Horwich BL6 . . . . . 32 C2
**Brunel Way** FY4 . . . . . 111 C7
**Brunel Wlk** BB1 . . . . . 101 F4
**Brungerley Ave** BB7 . . . . . 189 E1
**Brun Gr** FY1 . . . . . 130 E1
**BRUNSHAW** . . . . . 128 D5
**Brunshaw Ave** BB10 . . . . . 128 D5
**Brunshaw Prim Sch**
BB10 . . . . . 128 D4
**Brunshaw Rd** BB10 . . . . . 128 D6
**Brun St** BB11 . . . . . 127 F6
**Brunswick Ave** BL6 . . . . . 32 E2
**Brunswick Dr** BB8 . . . . . 171 A3
**Brunswick Pl** 4 PR2 . . . . . 117 C1
**Brunswick Rd** LA3 . . . . . 216 E3
**Brunswick St**
Blackburn BB2 . . . . . 101 D4
3 Blackpool FY1 . . . . . 130 B4
Burnley BB11 . . . . . 128 A4
2 Chorley PR6 . . . . . 43 D8
Darwen BB3 . . . . . 65 B8
Nelson BB9 . . . . . 148 E7
**Brunswick Terr**
7 Accrington BB5 . . . . . 104 B6
Bacup OL13 . . . . . 70 D8
**Brun Terr** BB10 . . . . . 128 F5
**Brunton Ho** 2 LA1 . . . . . 215 A5
**Brunton Rd** LA1 . . . . . 214 F6
**Brunton's Warehouse**
LA1 . . . . . 218 C1
**Brush St** BB11 . . . . . 127 C5
**Brussels Rd** BB3 . . . . . 82 C1
**Bryan Rd** FY3 . . . . . 130 D5
**Bryan St** BB2 . . . . . 101 E2
**Brydeck Ave** PR1 . . . . . 96 E4
**Bryer's Croft** BB1 . . . . . 122 F6
**Bryer St** 25 LA1 . . . . . 214 F8
**Bryn Gr** LA2 . . . . . 220 E2
**BRYNING** . . . . . 92 C8
**Bryning Ave**
Blackpool FY2 . . . . . 152 C4
Wrea Green PR4 . . . . . 113 B3
**Bryning Fern La** PR4 . . . . . 113 F4
**Bryning Hall La**
Moss Side FY8 . . . . . 112 F1
Warton PR4 . . . . . 92 B8
Wrea Green FY8, PR4 . . . . . 113 A1
**Bryning La**
Newton-w-S PR4 . . . . . 114 F2
Wrea Green PR4 . . . . . 113 B2
**Bryning with Warton St**
**Paul's CE Prim Sch**
PR4 . . . . . 92 D6
**Bryony Cl**
Cleveleys FY5 . . . . . 175 F5
Orrell WN5 . . . . . 10 D5
**Bryony Ct** 9 LA3 . . . . . 217 B2
**Buccleuch Ave** BB7 . . . . . 166 D8
**Buccleuch Cl** BB7 . . . . . 166 D8
**Buccleuch Rd** 7 BB9 . . . . . 170 C1
**Buccleuch St** BB11 . . . . . 127 E5
**Buchanan Ct** PR7 . . . . . 60 E6
**Buchanan St**
Blackpool FY1 . . . . . 130 C6
Chorley PR6 . . . . . 43 D7
7 Ramsbottom BL0 . . . . . 50 B6
**Buckden Cl** FY5 . . . . . 175 C1
**Buckden Gate** BB9 . . . . . 170 C3
**Buckden Pl** LA3 . . . . . 212 F8
**Buckden Rd** 4 BB5 . . . . . 103 F4
**Buckfast Dr** L37 . . . . . 12 B2
**Buckholes La** PR6 . . . . . 79 C1
**Buckhurst Rd** BL9 . . . . . 51 C3
**Buckingham Ave**
Horwich BL6 . . . . . 32 E2
Kingsfold PR1 . . . . . 96 E2
**Buckingham Cl** BB4 . . . . . 85 A1
**Buckingham Dr** BB12 . . . 145 D2
**Buckingham Gr**
Church BB5 . . . . . 103 F7
Formby L37 . . . . . 11 E1
Morecambe LA3 . . . . . 216 F3
**Buckingham Pl** 2 LA3 . . 216 F3
**Buckingham Rd**
Lytham St Anne's FY8 . . . . . 90 D4
Maghull L31 . . . . . 5 C1
Morecambe LA3, LA4 . . . . . 216 F3
**Buckingham St** PR6 . . . . . 43 D7
**Buckingham Way** FY6 . . . 153 C5
**Bucklands Ave** PR2 . . . . . 117 D2

Buckley Cres FY5 . . . . . . . 152 D7
Bucknell Pl FY5 . . . . . . . . 152 F7
Buckshaw Hall Cl PR7 . . . . 61 B2
Buckshaw Prim Sch
PR7 . . . . . . . . . . . . . . . . . . 61 A2
BUCKSHAW VILLAGE . . . . . . 60 E6
Buck St
Burnley BB11 . . . . . . . . . . . 127 E5
Colne BB8 . . . . . . . . . . . . . 171 E5
Grindleton BB7 . . . . . . . . . 190 B7
Buckthorn Pl FY6 . . . . . . . 199 F6
Buckton Cl PR6 . . . . . . . . . . 61 C6
Bude Cl PR4 . . . . . . . . . . . 116 F6
Buffalo Rd PR26 . . . . . . . . . 77 A4
Buff St 3 BB3 . . . . . . . . . . . 65 A8
Bulcock St BB10 . . . . . . . . 148 C1
BULK . . . . . . . . . . . . . . . . . 218 E1
Bulk Rd LA1 . . . . . . . . . . . . 218 E1
Bulk St LA1 . . . . . . . . . . . . 214 F8
Bull Cop L37 . . . . . . . . . . . . 12 B3
Bullens La L40 . . . . . . . . . . . 23 E7
Buller Ave PR1 . . . . . . . . . . . 96 E4
Buller St
1 Lancaster LA1 . . . . . . . 218 D3
Rawtenstall BB4 . . . . . . . . . 86 A2
Bullfinch Dr BL9 . . . . . . . . . 33 B5
Bullfinch St 3 PR1 . . . . . 118 B1
Bullion The BB12 . . . . . . . 169 C5
Bullough Cl BB5 . . . . . . . . 104 A5
Bull Park La FY6 . . . . . . . . 154 C8
Bullsnape La PR3 . . . . . . . 161 A5
Bull St BB11 . . . . . . . . . . . 128 A6
Bulmer St PR2 . . . . . . . . . . 117 C2
Buncer La BB2 . . . . . . . . . . 101 A4
Bungalows The
Burnley BB11 . . . . . . . . . . 127 F4
7 Earby BB18 . . . . . . . . . 197 B1
Great Eccleston PR3 . . . . 156 C5
BUNKER'S HILL . . . . . . . . . 171 B4
Bunkers Hill Cl BB2 . . . . . . 81 B8
Bunker St PR4 . . . . . . . . . . . 93 C6
Bunting Pl 6 FY5 . . . . . . . 175 F1
Bunyan St 24 OL12 . . . . . . . 52 F1
Buoymasters LA1 . . . . . . . 218 C1
Burbank Cl FY4 . . . . . . . . . 110 F5
Burdett St BB11 . . . . . . . . . 127 D5
Burdock Hill BB18 . . . . . . . 194 D6
Burdock Wlk LA3 . . . . . . . 217 B2
Burford Cl
Blackburn BB2 . . . . . . . . . . 80 E8
Blackpool FY3 . . . . . . . . . 131 A7
Burford Dr LA3 . . . . . . . . . 213 A7
Burgate FY4 . . . . . . . . . . . . 110 D5
Burgess Ave FY4 . . . . . . . . 110 E7
Burgess Gdns L31 . . . . . . . . . 5 C2
Burgess' La L37 . . . . . . . . . . 13 A2
Burgess St
2 Blackburn BB1 . . . . . . . 102 C5
6 Haslingden BB4 . . . . . . . 85 B3
Burgh Hall Rd PR7 . . . . . . . 43 A3
Burgh La PR7 . . . . . . . . . . . . 43 C4
Burgh La S PR7 . . . . . . . . . . 43 B2
Burghley Brow PR3 . . . . . 181 D1
Burghley Cl PR6 . . . . . . . . . 78 C2
Burghley Ct 4 PR25 . . . . . 77 B1
Burgh Mdws PR7 . . . . . . . . . 43 C4
Burgh Wood Way PR7 . . . . 43 A6
Burgundy Cres FY5 . . . . . 152 F7
Burholme Cl PR2 . . . . . . . 119 A2
Burholme Pl PR2 . . . . . . . 119 A2
Burholme Rd PR2 . . . . . . . 119 A2
Burleigh Rd 7 PR1 . . . . . . 96 E7
Burleigh St BB12 . . . . . . . 127 F7
Burlingham Pk PR3 . . . . . 204 B1
Burlington Ave
Formby L37 . . . . . . . . . . . . . 12 B3
Morecambe LA4 . . . . . . . . 217 D5
Burlington Ct
Blackpool FY4 . . . . . . . . . 110 B7
Lytham St Anne's FY8 . . . . . 89 C8
Burlington Ctr The FY8 . . . 89 E6
Burlington Gdns PR25 . . . . 60 B8
Burlington Gr LA4 . . . . . . 217 D5
Burlington Ho 1 FY6 . . . 153 D3
Burlington Rd
Blackpool FY4 . . . . . . . . . 110 B6
Southport PR8 . . . . . . . . . . 34 F3
Burlington Rd W FY4 . . . . 110 A6
Burlington St
Blackburn BB2 . . . . . . . . . 101 C5
Chorley PR7 . . . . . . . . . . . . 43 D7
Nelson BB9 . . . . . . . . . . . . 148 C7
Burnage Gdns FY4 . . . . . . 110 D7
Burnedge Cl OL12 . . . . . . . . 71 D2
Burned House La FY6 . . . 200 D2
Burneside Cl LA4 . . . . . . . 217 C4
Burnfell Rd 1 LA1 . . . . . . 218 B2
Burn Gr FY5 . . . . . . . . . . . 175 E4
Burn Hall Ind Est FY7 . . . 176 A6
Burnham Cl BB11 . . . . . . . 127 E5
Burnham Ct
Blackpool FY3 . . . . . . . . . 130 E5
Morecambe LA3 . . . . . . . . 216 E1
Burnham Gate BB11 . . . . . 127 E5
Burnham Trad Pk 4
BB11 . . . . . . . . . . . . . . . . . 127 E6
BURNLEY . . . . . . . . . . . . . . 128 A7
Burnley Ave PR8 . . . . . . . . . 21 D5
Burnley Barracks Sta
BB12 . . . . . . . . . . . . . . . . . 127 E6
Burnley Central Sta
BB12 . . . . . . . . . . . . . . . . . 127 F7
Burnley Cl BB1 . . . . . . . . . 102 B5
Burnley Coll BB11 . . . . . . . 128 A7
Burnley General Hospl
BB10 . . . . . . . . . . . . . . . . . 148 C2
Burnley La BB11, BB5 . . . . 126 A2
BURNLEY LANE . . . . . . . . . 148 A1
Burnley Manchester Road
Sta BB11 . . . . . . . . . . . . . . 127 F5
Burnley Rd
Accrington, Hillock Vale
BB5 . . . . . . . . . . . . . . . . . 104 D8
8 Accrington, Lower Fold
BB5 . . . . . . . . . . . . . . . . . 104 C6
Baldingstone BL9 . . . . . . . . 50 E1
Blackburn BB1 . . . . . . . . . 102 C6
Brierfield BB9, BB10 . . . . . 148 B5
Burnley BB10, BB11 . . . . . 128 D1
Burnley, Harle Syke
BB10 . . . . . . . . . . . . . . . . 148 F3
Clayton-le-M BB5 . . . . . . . 125 C5
Colne BB8, BB9 . . . . . . . . . 171 B3
Edenfield BL0 . . . . . . . . . . . 68 D5
Gisburn BB7 . . . . . . . . . . . 231 B3
Hapton BB11, BB5 . . . . . . . 126 B1
Holme Chapel BB10 . . . . . 108 C4
Padiham BB12 . . . . . . . . . . 126 D8
Rawtenstall BB4 . . . . . . . . . 85 F5
Rawtenstall, Goodshaw Fold
BB4 . . . . . . . . . . . . . . . . . 106 A2
Southport PR8 . . . . . . . . . . . 21 C5
Todmorden OL14 . . . . . . . . 108 C4
Trawden BB8 . . . . . . . . . . . 172 B1
Weir BB11, BB4 . . . . . . . . . 107 C3
Whalley BB6 . . . . . . . . . . . 144 F3
Burnley Rd E
Rawtenstall BB4 . . . . . . . . . 69 E8
Water BB4 . . . . . . . . . . . . . 107 A2
Whitewell Bottom BB4 . . . . . 86 F4
Burnley St BB1 . . . . . . . . . 102 C5
BURNLEY WOOD . . . . . . . . 128 A4
BURN NAZE . . . . . . . . . . . . 176 B4
Burnsall Ave
Blackpool FY3 . . . . . . . . . . 153 A1
Heysham LA3 . . . . . . . . . . . 212 F8
Burnsall Cl BB10 . . . . . . . . 148 E3
Burnsall Pl
Barrowford BB9 . . . . . . . . . 170 C3
Fulwood PR2 . . . . . . . . . . . 118 E4
Burnsall Rd 2 BB5 . . . . . . 103 F4
Burns Ave
Lytham St Anne's FY8 . . . . . 91 D4
Oswaldtwistle BB5 . . . . . . 103 D5
Thornton FY5 . . . . . . . . . . . 176 A3
Burns Cl WN5 . . . . . . . . . . . . 10 D1
Burns Dr BB5 . . . . . . . . . . . 104 E2
Burnside
Edenfield BL0 . . . . . . . . . . . 68 D2
Parbold WN8 . . . . . . . . . . . . 27 B2
Burnside Ave
Blackpool FY4 . . . . . . . . . . 110 E8
Calder Vale PR3 . . . . . . . . . 182 E8
Fleetwood FY7 . . . . . . . . . . 198 C2
Fulwood PR2 . . . . . . . . . . . 118 F3
Burnside Way PR1 . . . . . . . . 96 D3
Burnslack Rd PR2 . . . . . . . 118 F3
Burns Pl FY4 . . . . . . . . . . . 110 F8
Burns Rd FY7 . . . . . . . . . . . 199 A5
Burns St
Burnley BB12 . . . . . . . . . . 127 F7
Hapton BB12 . . . . . . . . . . . 126 C4
Nelson BB9 . . . . . . . . . . . . 170 D1
Padiham BB12 . . . . . . . . . . 126 D7
Preston PR1 . . . . . . . . . . . . 118 D2
Burns Way BB6 . . . . . . . . . 124 B4
Burns Wlk BB3 . . . . . . . . . . . 82 B1
Burrans Mdw 15 BB8 . . . . 171 D4
Burrell Ave BB8 . . . . . . . . . 171 D6
Burrington Cl PR2 . . . . . . . 118 D6
Burrow Heights La
LA2 . . . . . . . . . . . . . . . . . . 210 F8
Burrow Rd
Over Burrow LA6 . . . . . . . . 241 E7
Preston PR1 . . . . . . . . . . . . 118 A1
Burrow's La FY6 . . . . . . . . 176 F5
BURSCOUGH . . . . . . . . . . . . 25 D4
BURSCOUGH BRIDGE . . . . . 25 D5
Burscough Bridge
Methodist Sch L40 . . . . . . 25 E5
Burscough Bridge St
John's CE Prim Sch
L40 . . . . . . . . . . . . . . . . . . . 25 F5
Burscough Bridge Sta
L40 . . . . . . . . . . . . . . . . . . . 25 E5
Burscough Ind Est L40 . . . 25 B5
Burscough Junc Sta
L40 . . . . . . . . . . . . . . . . . . . 25 F4
Burscough Lordsgate
Township CE Prim Sch
L40 . . . . . . . . . . . . . . . . . . . 25 E3
Burscough Priory Science
Coll L40 . . . . . . . . . . . . . . . 25 E5
Burscough Rd L39 . . . . . . . 15 F7
Burscough St L39 . . . . . . . . 15 F6
Burscough Village Prim
Sch L40 . . . . . . . . . . . . . . . 25 F5
Burton Ave LA1 . . . . . . . . . 218 A3
Burton Ct FY7 . . . . . . . . . . 175 C8
Burton Gdns BB9 . . . . . . . . 148 B5
Burton Hill LA6 . . . . . . . . . 242 C3
BURTON-IN-KENDAL . . . . 240 C7
BURTON IN
LONSDALE . . . . . . . . . . . . 242 C3
Burton Lo FY7 . . . . . . . . . . 199 B4
Burton Morewood CE Prim
Sch LA6 . . . . . . . . . . . . . . 240 C7
Burton Pk LA6 . . . . . . . . . . 240 B7
Burton Rd
Blackpool FY4 . . . . . . . . . . 130 F1
Low Bentham LA2 . . . . . . . 239 B8
Burton St
Burnley BB11 . . . . . . . . . . 128 B5
Rishton BB1 . . . . . . . . . . . 124 C1
Burwain Castle Rd
BD23 . . . . . . . . . . . . . . . . . 197 F8
Burwain Fold BB8 . . . . . . . 171 D6
Burwains Ave BB8 . . . . . . . 194 D1
Burwell Ave
Coppull PR7 . . . . . . . . . . . . 29 D8
Formby L37 . . . . . . . . . . . . . 11 D1
Burwell Cl
Kirkby L33 . . . . . . . . . . . . . . . 1 A3
Rochdale OL12 . . . . . . . . . . . 52 D4
Burwen Cl BB11 . . . . . . . . 127 D3
Burwood Cl PR1 . . . . . . . . . 96 F2
Burwood Dr
Blackpool FY3 . . . . . . . . . 131 A6
Fulwood PR2 . . . . . . . . . . . 118 E3
BURY . . . . . . . . . . . . . . . . . . 33 A1
Bury Bsns Ctr BL9 . . . . . . . 33 A4
Bury Fold BB3 . . . . . . . . . . . 65 A6
Bury Fold La BB3 . . . . . . . . 65 A6
Bury La PR6 . . . . . . . . . . . . . 79 F3
Bury New Rd
Heywood BL9, OL10 . . . . . . 33 E2
Ramsbottom BL0 . . . . . . . . . 50 D6
Bury Old Rd
Edenfield BL0 . . . . . . . . . . . 68 F1
Heywood BL9, OL10 . . . . . . 33 E1
Nangreaves BL0, BL9 . . . . . 50 F4
Bury Rd
Edenfield BL0 . . . . . . . . . . . 68 D3
Edgworth BL7 . . . . . . . . . . . 48 E5
Haslingden BB4 . . . . . . . . . 85 B3
Rawtenstall BB4 . . . . . . . . . 68 E7
Southport PR8 . . . . . . . . . . . 35 B3
Bury & Rochdale Old Rd
BL9 . . . . . . . . . . . . . . . . . . . 33 F4
Bury Row BB7 . . . . . . . . . . 145 F8
Bury St
Darwen BB3 . . . . . . . . . . . . . 82 A1
Oswaldtwistle BB5 . . . . . . 103 D3
Buseph Barrow 1 LA4 . . 217 F4
Buseph Ct 2 LA4 . . . . . . . 217 F4
Buseph Dr LA4 . . . . . . . . . 217 F4
Bushburn Dr BB6 . . . . . . . 143 C1
Bushby's La L37 . . . . . . . . . 11 C2
Bushby's Pk L37 . . . . . . . . . 11 D2
Bushell Pl PR1 . . . . . . . . . . . 97 A6
Bushell St PR1 . . . . . . . . . . 117 F1
Bushey La WA11 . . . . . . . . . . 8 E2
Bush La
Freckleton PR4 . . . . . . . . . . 93 B5
Freckleton PR4 . . . . . . . . . . 93 B6
Bush St BB10 . . . . . . . . . . . 148 B1
Bussel Rd PR1 . . . . . . . . . . . 96 E2
Butcher Brow PR5 . . . . . . . . 97 E5
Butchers La L39 . . . . . . . . . . 6 B3
Bute Ave FY1 . . . . . . . . . . . 130 B7
Bute Rd BB1 . . . . . . . . . . . . 102 D3
Bute St BB11 . . . . . . . . . . . 127 D3
Butler Pl PR1 . . . . . . . . . . . 117 F2
Butler Rd FY1 . . . . . . . . . . . 130 B3
Butlers Farm Ct PR25 . . . . 59 D7
Butlers Mdw PR4 . . . . . . . . 92 E6
Butler St
Blackpool FY1 . . . . . . . . . . 130 C6
7 Burnley BB10 . . . . . . . . 128 A8
Preston PR1 . . . . . . . . . . . . . 96 F7
Ramsbottom BL0 . . . . . . . . . 50 A5
Rishton BB1 . . . . . . . . . . . . 124 C1
Butterbergh 16 LA2 . . . . . 239 D8
Buttercross Cl BB11 . . . . . 127 D2
Butterfield Gdns L39 . . . . . 15 D3
Butterfield St
2 Barrowford BB9 . . . . . . 170 D3
2 Lancaster LA1 . . . . . . . 214 F8
Butterlands PR1 . . . . . . . . . 97 F8
Buttermere Ave
Chorley PR7 . . . . . . . . . . . . 43 B6
Colne BB8 . . . . . . . . . . . . . 171 F6
Fleetwood FY7 . . . . . . . . . . 198 C2
2 Morecambe LA4 . . . . . . 217 D4
Buttermere Cl
1 Bamber Bridge PR5 . . . . 97 E2
5 Blackburn BB1 . . . . . . . 101 F6
Formby L37 . . . . . . . . . . . . . 11 D3
Fulwood PR2 . . . . . . . . . . . 118 C4
Maghull L31 . . . . . . . . . . . . . . 5 E1
Buttermere Cres WA11 . . . . . 8 F2
Buttermere Ct LA1 . . . . . . 218 F1
Buttermere Dr
Knott End-on-S FY6 . . . . . . 199 F5
Oswaldtwistle BB5 . . . . . . 103 D5
Ramsbottom BL0 . . . . . . . . . 50 B7
Buttermere Rd
Burnley BB10 . . . . . . . . . . . 128 F5
Lancaster LA1 . . . . . . . . . . 218 F1
Longridge PR3 . . . . . . . . . . 139 F5
Butterwick Fields BL6 . . . . 31 F3
Butterworth Brow
Brinscall PR6 . . . . . . . . . . . 63 A7
Chorley PR7 . . . . . . . . . . . . 43 A4
Butterworth Cl PR4 . . . . . 114 A6
Butt Hill La PR3 . . . . . . . . 182 E4
Buttons Row BB4 . . . . . . . . 69 F6
Button St PR3 . . . . . . . . . . 160 C6
Butts
Barnoldswick BB18 . . . . . . 196 B2
Great Harwood BB6 . . . . . 124 B5
Butts Cl FY5 . . . . . . . . . . . . 176 C4
Butts Gr BB7 . . . . . . . . . . . . 189 E2
Butts La
Freckleton PR4 . . . . . . . . . . 93 C6
High Bentham LA2 . . . . . . . 239 E8
Southport PR8 . . . . . . . . . . . 35 F5
Butt's La PR3 . . . . . . . . . . . 156 B5
Butts Mount BB6 . . . . . . . . 124 C5
Butts Rd FY5 . . . . . . . . . . . 176 C4
BUTT YEATS . . . . . . . . . . . . 238 B6
Buxton Ave FY2 . . . . . . . . . 152 D4
Buxton St
Accrington BB5 . . . . . . . . . 104 A5
Morecambe LA4 . . . . . . . . . 217 C4
Whitworth OL12 . . . . . . . . . . 71 D3
Bye La L39 . . . . . . . . . . . . . . 14 C3
Bye-Pass Rd LA5 . . . . . . . . 221 A4
Bye Rd BL0 . . . . . . . . . . . . . . 50 E8
Byerworth La N PR3 . . . . . 181 C5
Byerworth La S PR3 . . . . . 181 C4
Byfield Ave FY5 . . . . . . . . . 152 E7
Bygone Times* PR7 . . . . . . 41 C5
Byland Cl
Blackpool FY4 . . . . . . . . . . 110 C5
Formby L37 . . . . . . . . . . . . . 12 B2
Read BB12 . . . . . . . . . . . . . 145 D1
Bymbrig Cl PR5 . . . . . . . . . . 77 E8
Byre View PR6 . . . . . . . . . . . 30 F8
Byrom St
Blackburn BB2 . . . . . . . . . . 101 D4
Southport PR9 . . . . . . . . . . . 35 F7
Byron Ave
Bolton-le-S LA5 . . . . . . . . . 221 A5
Lytham St Anne's FY8 . . . . . 91 D4
Thornton FY5 . . . . . . . . . . . 176 A3
Warton PR4 . . . . . . . . . . . . . 92 E6
Byron Cl
Accrington BB5 . . . . . . . . . 104 E2
Formby L37 . . . . . . . . . . . . . 11 F4
3 Orrell WN5 . . . . . . . . . . . 10 F7
Oswaldtwistle BB5 . . . . . . 103 C5
Tarleton PR4 . . . . . . . . . . . . 56 F5
Byron Cres PR7 . . . . . . . . . . 29 F8
Byron Gr BB18 . . . . . . . . . . 196 A3
Byron Rd
Colne BB8 . . . . . . . . . . . . . 171 F5
Maghull L31 . . . . . . . . . . . . . . 5 D3
Morecambe LA3 . . . . . . . . . 216 E3
Ramsbottom BL8 . . . . . . . . . 49 F2
Byron Sq BB6 . . . . . . . . . . . 124 B4
Byron St
Blackpool FY4 . . . . . . . . . . 130 B1
Chorley PR6 . . . . . . . . . . . . . 43 D8
Fleetwood FY7 . . . . . . . . . . 199 A5
Padiham BB12 . . . . . . . . . . 126 F7
Byron Terr BB2 . . . . . . . . . . 101 B3
Byton Wlk L33 . . . . . . . . . . . . 1 A4
Byways Cvn Pk LA2 . . . . . 205 C7


## C


Cabin End Row BB1 . . . . . 102 E4
Cabin La
Halsall Moss L39 . . . . . . . . . 22 C5
Holmeswood L40 . . . . . . . . . 38 A6
Maghull L31 . . . . . . . . . . . . . . 4 F4
Southport PR9 . . . . . . . . . . . 54 F3
Cable Ct PR2 . . . . . . . . . . . 118 B8
Cable Mews 10 PR8 . . . . . . 35 B7
Cable St
Formby L37 . . . . . . . . . . . . . 12 A4
Lancaster LA1 . . . . . . . . . . 214 F8
Southport PR8 . . . . . . . . . . . 35 B7
CABUS . . . . . . . . . . . . . . . . . 204 C3
Cabus Cross Roads
PR3 . . . . . . . . . . . . . . . . . . 204 B5
Cabus Nook La PR3 . . . . . 204 B6
Cabus Terr PR3 . . . . . . . . . 204 C2
Cadby Ave FY3 . . . . . . . . . . 130 F3
CADLEY . . . . . . . . . . . . . . . 117 C4
Cadley Ave PR2 . . . . . . . . . 117 B3
Cadley Cswy PR2 . . . . . . . 117 C4
Cadley Dr PR2 . . . . . . . . . . 117 B3
Cadogan Pl 5 PR1 . . . . . . . 97 A6
Cadogan St BB9 . . . . . . . . . 170 D2
CADSHAW . . . . . . . . . . . . . . 65 D1
Cadshaw Cl BB1 . . . . . . . . . 101 E8
Cadwell Rd L31 . . . . . . . . . . . 5 B5
Caernarfon Cl FY5 . . . . . . 176 D2
Caernarvon Ave BB12 . . . . 127 A7
Caernarvon Cl BL8 . . . . . . . 49 F1
Caernarvon Rd BB4 . . . . . . . 85 A1
Cage La PR4 . . . . . . . . . . . . . 76 B8
Cairn Ct 6 FY4 . . . . . . . . . 110 C5
Cairndale Dr PR25 . . . . . . . 60 B6
Cairn Gr FY4 . . . . . . . . . . . 110 C4
Cairns Cl BB9 . . . . . . . . . . . 170 C3
Cairnsmore Ave PR1 . . . . . 118 F1
Cairo St BB12 . . . . . . . . . . 127 D6
Caister Cl WN8 . . . . . . . . . . . . 9 E8
Calcott St BB11 . . . . . . . . . 127 E2
Caldbeck Cl BB9 . . . . . . . . 148 E6
Caldbeck Rd LA1 . . . . . . . . 218 F1
Calder Ave
Billington BB7 . . . . . . . . . . 144 A4
Chorley PR7 . . . . . . . . . . . . . 43 B5
Cleveleys FY5 . . . . . . . . . . 175 F2
Darwen BB3 . . . . . . . . . . . . . 81 D4
Fleetwood FY7 . . . . . . . . . . 198 D3
Freckleton PR4 . . . . . . . . . . 93 A5
Fulwood PR2 . . . . . . . . . . . 117 F6
Longridge PR3 . . . . . . . . . . 140 A8
Ormskirk L39 . . . . . . . . . . . . 15 F4
Whalley BB7 . . . . . . . . . . . . 144 A7
Calderbank Cl 1 PR26 . . . . 76 A1
Calder Banks BB1 . . . . . . . 101 F7
Calderbrook Ave BB11 . . . 127 E3
Calderbrook Pl BB11 . . . . . 127 E3
Calder Cl
Bury BL9 . . . . . . . . . . . . . . . 33 A8
Crag Bank LA5 . . . . . . . . . . 223 B1
Kirkby L33 . . . . . . . . . . . . . . . 1 A6
Kirkham PR4 . . . . . . . . . . . 114 C5
Lytham St Anne's FY8 . . . . 110 F2
Nelson BB9 . . . . . . . . . . . . 170 D1
Calder Ct BB5 . . . . . . . . . . . 125 E6
Calder Dr
Catterall PR3 . . . . . . . . . . . 181 D2
Maghull L31 . . . . . . . . . . . . . . 5 F2
Calder House La PR3 . . . . 181 D4
Calder Pl
Billington BB7 . . . . . . . . . . 144 A4
Great Harwood BB6 . . . . . 124 E6
Calder Rd
Blackpool FY2 . . . . . . . . . . 152 C1
Rawtenstall BB4 . . . . . . . . . 86 A4
Withnell PR6 . . . . . . . . . . . . 80 A1
CALDERSHAW . . . . . . . . . . . 52 C2
Caldershaw Bsns Ctr
OL12 . . . . . . . . . . . . . . . . . . 52 B2
Caldershaw Ctr The
OL12 . . . . . . . . . . . . . . . . . . 52 B2
Caldershaw La OL12 . . . . . 52 A2
Caldershaw Prim Sch
OL12 . . . . . . . . . . . . . . . . . . 52 A1
Caldershaw Rd OL11,
OL12 . . . . . . . . . . . . . . . . . . 52 A1
Calder St
Blackburn BB1 . . . . . . . . . . 101 F7
Burnley BB11 . . . . . . . . . . . 127 F6
Colne BB8 . . . . . . . . . . . . . 171 C4
Nelson BB9 . . . . . . . . . . . . 170 D1
Padiham BB12 . . . . . . . . . . 126 C8
Preston PR2 . . . . . . . . . . . . 117 C1
Calderstones Dr BB7 . . . . 144 A7
Calderstones Hospl
BB7 . . . . . . . . . . . . . . . . . . 144 A7
Calder Terr BB9 . . . . . . . . . 148 B8
CALDER VALE . . . . . . . . . . 182 E8
Calder Vale
Barrowford BB9 . . . . . . . . . 170 D2
Whalley BB7 . . . . . . . . . . . 144 C4
Caldervale Ave FY6 . . . . . 153 C3
Calder Vale Rd BB12 . . . . 127 F6
Calder Vale St John CE
Prim Sch PR3 . . . . . . . . . 226 C1
Calder View BB9 . . . . . . . . 170 E5
Calder Way LA3 . . . . . . . . . 217 F2
Caldew Ct 5 BB5 . . . . . . . 104 E8
Caldicott Way FY6 . . . . . . 153 C6
Caldy Dr BL8 . . . . . . . . . . . . 50 A3
Caleb St 6 BB9 . . . . . . . . . 170 E1
Caledonian Ave 1
FY3 . . . . . . . . . . . . . . . . . . 130 E7
Calendar St 1 BB1 . . . . . . 101 E5
Calendine Cl FY5 . . . . . . . 175 F5
Calfcote La PR3 . . . . . . . . 140 B7
Calf Croft Pl FY8 . . . . . . . . . 91 A4
Calf Hall La BB18 . . . . . . . 196 A2
Calf Hall Rd BB18 . . . . . . . 196 A2
Calf Hey BB5 . . . . . . . . . . . 124 F4
Calf Hey La OL12 . . . . . . . . 52 D8
Calf Hey Rd BB4 . . . . . . . . . 84 B2
Calgary Ave BB2 . . . . . . . . 101 B8
Calico Cl BB5 . . . . . . . . . . . 103 B4
Calico Dr PR3 . . . . . . . . . . 181 D3
Calico St BB2 . . . . . . . . . . . 101 D1
Calico Wood Ave WN6 . . . 19 F6
Calkeld La 7 LA1 . . . . . . . 214 F8
Calla Dr PR3 . . . . . . . . . . . . 181 C8
Callander Cl PR2 . . . . . . . . 118 C7
Callander Sq OL10 . . . . . . . 33 F1
Callender Ct 9 BL0 . . . . . . 50 B6
Callender St BL0 . . . . . . . . . 50 B6
Callon St PR1 . . . . . . . . . . . . 97 E8
Caltha Dr BB3 . . . . . . . . . . . 82 A7
Caltha St 8 BL0 . . . . . . . . . 50 B6
Calva Cl BB12 . . . . . . . . . . 127 B8
Calverley St 6 PR1 . . . . . 118 D1
Calverley Way OL12 . . . . . . 52 E4
Calvert Ct PR5 . . . . . . . . . . . 97 D5
Calvert Pl FY3 . . . . . . . . . . 131 A7
Cambell's Ct FY8 . . . . . . . . 89 E7
Camberley Cl PR8 . . . . . . . . 34 E5
Camborne Ave LA5 . . . . . . 221 C8
Camborne Ct FY3 . . . . . . . 131 B2
Camborne Pl PR4 . . . . . . . . 93 B6
Cambray Rd FY1 . . . . . . . . 152 C1
Cambrian Cl BB1 . . . . . . . . 122 F3
Cambrian Ct PR9 . . . . . . . . . 35 D8
Cambrian Way BB4 . . . . . . . 85 B1
Cambridge Arc 5 PR8 . . . . 35 B7
Cambridge Ave
Lancaster LA1 . . . . . . . . . . 215 B5
Southport PR9 . . . . . . . . . . . 53 F2
Cambridge Cl
7 Blackburn BB1 . . . . . . . 101 F4
Padiham BB12 . . . . . . . . . . 126 D6
Preston PR1 . . . . . . . . . . . . 117 E2
Cambridge Ct
Preston PR1 . . . . . . . . . . . . 117 F2
Southport PR9 . . . . . . . . . . . 53 F2
Cambridge Dr
Blackburn BB1 . . . . . . . . . . 102 E4
Garstang PR3 . . . . . . . . . . . 181 B7
Padiham BB12 . . . . . . . . . . 126 D6
Cambridge Gdns
Darwen BB3 . . . . . . . . . . . . . 82 C1
Southport PR9 . . . . . . . . . . . 53 F2
Cambridge Rd
9 Bamber Bridge PR5 . . . . 77 F8
Blackpool FY1 . . . . . . . . . . 130 D5
Cleveleys FY5 . . . . . . . . . . 175 C3
Fleetwood FY7 . . . . . . . . . . 198 E3
Formby L37 . . . . . . . . . . . . . 11 D1
Lytham St Anne's FY8 . . . . . 90 E3
1 Morecambe LA3 . . . . . . 216 E3
Orrell WN5 . . . . . . . . . . . . . 10 F8
Skelmersdale WN8 . . . . . . . 17 E1
Southport PR9 . . . . . . . . . . . 53 E2
Cambridge St
Accrington BB5 . . . . . . . . . 104 D6
Blackburn BB1 . . . . . . . . . . 101 F4

Cambridge St *continued*
4 Brierfield BB9 148 B5
3 Burnley BB11 127 D5
10 Chorley PR7 43 C7
9 Colne BB8 171 D4
Darwen BB3 82 C1
Great Harwood BB6 124 D5
Haslingden BB4 85 B1
Nelson BB9 148 D7
Preston PR1 117 E2
**Cambridge Wlk** PR1 117 E2
**Cambridge Wlks** 6 PR8 35 B7
**Cam Cl** 1 PR5 77 F8
**Camden Pl** PR1 96 F6
**Camden Rd** FY3 130 E6
**Camden St**
11 Barrowford BB9 170 D3
Nelson BB9 148 D7
**Camellia Dr** PR25 77 E2
Camelot Theme Pk* PR7 41 F4
**Cameron Ave** FY3 130 E7
**Cameron Croft** 6 PR6 43 D8
**Cameron St** BB10 148 A1
**Camforth Hall La** PR3 139 A7
**Cam La**
Clayton Green PR6 78 A4
Thornton-in-C BD23 197 B6
**Camms View** BB4 68 A8
**Camomile Cl** PR7 61 A3
**Campbell Ave** 2 FY3 130 E7
**Campbell Cl** BB2 81 C7
**Campbell St**
Blackburn BB1 122 F1
4 Padiham BB12 126 F7
Preston PR1 97 B8
Read BB12 145 D1
Rochdale OL12 52 E2
**Campion Cl** FY5 175 F5
**Campion Ct** BB5 103 E4
**Campion Dr**
Haslingden BB4 68 A8
Preston PR2 116 C1
**Campions The** PR2 116 C1
**Campion Way**
2 Morecambe LA3 217 B2
Rochdale OL12 52 C3
**Camp St** BB10 148 E3
**Cam St** PR1 118 C2
**Camwood** PR5 78 B4
**Camwood Dr** PR5 97 B1
**Cam Wood Fold** PR6 78 A3
**Canada Cres** FY2 152 E3
**Canada St** BL6 32 B3
**Canal Bank**
Appley Bridge WN6 19 C7
Burscough Bridge L40 25 B6
Ring o'Bells L40 26 C2
**Canal Bank Cotts** L31 5 C7
**Canal Bank Pygons Hill** L31 5 C7
**Canal Gdns** LA5 221 B6
**Canal Leach** PR26 57 F6
**Canal Mews** BB9 148 D8
**Canal Pl** LA5 223 E1
**Canal Row** WN2 30 D1
**Canalside**
Blackburn BB1 101 F3
Hurlston Green L40 24 B4
**Canal Side** BB9 170 D2
Canalside Craft Ctr* LA2 211 A3
**Canal St**
Adlington PR7 31 A6
3 Blackburn BB2 101 B1
19 Burnley BB11 127 F6
Church BB5 103 E6
Clayton-le-M BB5 124 F2
**Canal Way** BB5 125 B3
**Canal Wlk** PR6 43 F8
**Canberra Cl** FY5 152 F7
**Canberra Ct** FY4 110 E4
**Canberra La** PR4 116 E4
**Canberra Rd** PR25 60 B8
**Canberraway** PR4 92 E6
**Candlemakers Croft** 3 BB7 166 F8
**Candlemakers Ct** BB7 166 E8
**Candlestick Pk** BL9 33 D4
**Cann Bridge St** PR5 98 B4
**Canning Rd** PR9 36 A6
**Canning St**
Burnley BB12 127 F7
Padiham BB12 126 D7
**Cannock Ave** FY3 130 E8
**Cannock Gn** L31 5 B1
**Cannon Hill** PR2 117 C1
**Cannon St**
Accrington BB5 104 B5
11 Chorley PR7 43 C8
10 Nelson BB9 170 F1
Preston PR1 96 F7
6 Ramsbottom BL0 50 A4
**Canon Cl** WN6 29 F2
**Canon St** BL9 33 A4
**Canterbury Ave**
Blackpool FY3 130 F3
Lancaster LA1 215 B5
**Canterbury Cl**
Brinscall PR6 62 E8
Carleton FY6 153 C5
Formby L37 11 F5
Garstang PR3 181 A7
Morecambe LA3 217 B2
Southport PR8 34 F4
**Canterbury Rd** 11 PR1 118 D1
**Canterbury St**
Blackburn BB2 101 E4
Chorley PR6 43 E6
**Canterbury Way** PR3 181 B7
**Cantlow Fold** PR8 21 A4
**CANTSFIELD** 241 F3
**Cantsfield Ave** PR2 117 B4
**Canute St** PR1 118 A1
**CAPERNWRAY** 240 C2
**Capernwray Ct** LA6 240 D3
**Capernwray Rd** LA6 240 B2
**Cape St** BB4 86 A2
**Capesthorne Dr** PR7 43 B3
**Capilano Pk** L39 6 C8
Capitol Trad Est L33 1 C2
**Capitol Way** PR5 97 C5
**Capstan Cl** FY8 110 E1
**Captain's Row** 3 LA1 218 D1
**Captain St**
Horwich BL6 32 B4
4 Weir OL13 88 A7
**Carawood Cl** WN6 19 D7
**Carbis Ave** 9 PR2 139 D1
**Carcroft Ave** FY2 152 D4
**Cardale** PR4 95 D2
**Cardiff St** WN8 17 D1
**Cardigan Ave**
Burnley BB12 127 A7
11 Clitheroe BB7 166 E8
Oswaldtwistle BB5 103 C4
**Cardigan Cl** 1 BB7 166 D8
**Cardigan Pl** FY4 110 A5
**Cardigan Rd** PR8 34 F1
**Cardigan St**
Preston PR2 117 D1
Rochdale OL12 52 E3
Cardinal Allen RC High Sch FY7 175 E8
**Cardinal Gdns** FY8 90 D6
Cardinal Newman Coll PR1 97 B7
**Cardinal Pl** FY5 175 E3
**Cardinal St** BB10 148 B1
**Cardwell Cl** PR4 92 D5
**Cardwell Pl** BB2 101 E5
**Cardwell St** BB12 126 D7
**Carfax Fold** OL12 52 B2
**Carfax Rd** L33 1 A4
**Carfield** WN8 9 E6
**Carham Rd** BB1 101 E8
**Carholme Ave** BB10 128 C6
**Caribou The** LA2 209 F5
**Carisbrooke Ave** FY4 111 A7
**Carisbrooke Cl** FY6 153 C6
**Carisbrooke Dr** PR9 53 F1
**CARLETON** 153 A5
**Carleton Ave**
Blackpool FY3 152 F1
Fulwood PR2 118 D4
Simonstone BB12 145 E2
**Carleton Dr** PR1 96 A4
**Carleton Gate** FY6 153 C4
**Carleton Gdns** FY6 153 B5
Carleton Green Com Prim Sch FY6 153 C6
**Carleton Rd**
Colne BB8 171 A3
Great Knowley PR6 61 F3
Carleton St Hilda's CE Prim Sch FY6 153 B5
**Carleton St**
Morecambe LA4 217 A4
Nelson BB9 148 E7
**Carleton Way** FY6 153 B5
**Carley St** BB3 81 E2
**Carlin Gate** FY2 152 B2
**Carlinghurst Rd** BB2 101 D4
**Carlisle Ave**
Fleetwood FY7 198 D1
Higher Penwortham PR1 96 A4
**Carlisle Gr** 1 FY5 176 B2
**Carlisle Ho** 35 PR1 97 A7
**Carlisle Pl** 3 PR6 31 A8
**Carlisle Rd**
Accrington BB5 104 D7
Southport PR8 35 A2
**Carlisle St**
Blackburn BB1 101 F4
Preston PR1 97 A8
Rochdale OL12 52 E3
**Carlisle Terr** LA5 223 D3
**Carl Oway Ave** PR2 118 C5
**Carl's Way** L33 1 A6
**Carlton Ave**
Clayton Green PR6 78 B2
Up Holland WN8 10 A7
**Carlton Cl** BL6 31 D2
**Carlton Ct** BB8 171 B5
**Carlton Dr** PR1 97 B5
**Carlton Gdns** BB1 101 E6
**Carlton Gr**
Blackpool FY2 152 B4
6 Horwich BL6 32 D1
**Carlton Pl** BB7 166 F7
**Carlton Rd**
Blackburn BB1 101 E6
Burnley BB11 127 E5
Leyland PR25 59 F8
Lytham St Anne's FY8 89 F7
Southport PR8 21 C6
**Carlton St**
3 Bacup OL13 88 A3
Brierfield BB9 148 B5
Preston PR2 96 D8
**Carlton Wharf** LA1 218 C1
**Carluke St** BB1 102 C5
**Carlyle Ave** FY4 110 B6
**Carlyle Gr** LA4 217 E6
**Carlyle St** BB10 148 C3
**Carmel Cl** L39 15 D2
**Carnaby Cl** PR3 204 A5
**Carnarvon Rd**
Blackburn BB2 101 B5
3 Preston PR1 96 D7
Southport PR8 34 F1
**Carneghie Ct** 1 PR8 34 F4
**Carnfield Pl** PR5 78 B8
**CARNFORTH** 223 C2
**Carnforth Ave** FY2 152 E5
**Carnforth Brow** LA5 223 F2
Carnforth Christ Church CE Prim Sch LA5 223 D1
**Carnforth Cl** BB2 102 A1
**Carnforth Dr** BL8 50 A2
Carnforth High Sch LA5 223 E1
Carnforth Sta LA5 223 D2
**Carnoustie Cl**
Fulwood PR2 117 B7
Southport PR8 34 F4
**Carnoustie Ct** PR1 96 A6
**Carnoustie Dr**
Euxton PR7 60 D4
Ramsbottom BL0 50 B5
**Caroline Cl** LA3 212 F8
**Caroline Ct** BB11 127 B4
**Caroline St**
6 Blackpool FY1 130 B3
Preston PR1 97 C8
**CARR** 50 B7
**Carradice Cl** BB9 148 D8
**Carradon Dr** WN6 29 E1
**Carr Bank Ave** BL0 50 B7
**Carr Bank Dr** BL0 50 B7
**Carr Bank Rd** BL0 50 B7
**Carr Barn Brow** PR5 78 C6
**Carr Bridge Residential Pk** FY4 112 A6
**Carr Brook Cl** PR6 61 B8
**Carr Cl**
Cold Row FY6 177 C4
Poulton-le-F FY6 153 E2
Smallwood Hey PR3 201 C5
**CARR CROSS** 36 D1
**Carr Dene Ct** PR4 114 C5
**Carr Dr** PR4 113 E7
**Carr End La** FY6 177 C6
**Carr Field** PR5 78 C4
**Carrfield Villas** OL14 109 A1
**Carr Fold** BL0 50 B7
**Carr Gate** FY5 175 C4
**CARR HALL** 170 B2
**Carr Hall Dr** BB9 170 C1
**Carr Hall Gdns** BB9 170 B1
**Carr Hall Rd** BB9 170 B1
**Carr Hall St** BB4 85 A5
**Carr Head** BB8 172 C2
**Carr Head La** FY6 153 E2
Carr Head Prim Sch FY6 153 E2
**Carr Hey** 5 FY5 176 A2
Carr Hill 11-18 High Sch PR4 114 B4
**Carr Holme Gdns** PR3 204 C1
**CARR HOUSE GREEN COMMON** 135 E7
**Carr House La**
Bretherton PR26 57 D6
Heskin Green WN6 41 F1
Ince Blundell L38 3 E4
Lancaster LA1 214 E7
Wrightington Bar WN6 28 F8
**Carrick Mews** FY3 131 B2
**Carrier's Row** BB8 172 E6
**Carrington Ave** 4 BB2 81 C8
**Carrington Gr** LA4 217 E5
**Carrington Rd**
Adlington PR7 30 F7
Chorley PR7 43 C7
**Carr La**
Blackburn BB2 100 F6
Chorley PR7 43 D5
Cold Row FY6 177 C4
Croston PR26 40 B8
Heysham LA3 212 E7
Kirkham PR4 114 C6
Lancaster LA2 214 E2
Leyland PR25 77 A3
Maghull L31 4 F5
Middleton LA3 212 F1
Much Hoole PR4, PR5 75 A1
Rawtenstall BB4 69 F7
Rawtenstall, Hall Carr BB4 86 A1
Ring o'Bells L40 26 B3
Singleton FY6 154 C1
Smallwood Hey PR3 201 C4
Southport PR8 21 F7
Tarleton PR4 56 F7
Warton PR4 92 B6
**Carr Mdw** PR5 78 C6
**Carr Mill St** BB4 85 B5
**Carr Moss La**
Halsall L39 14 B8
Southport L39 22 D2
**Carr Mount** 7 BB4 85 F1
**Carroll Cres** L39 15 F7
**Carrol St** PR1 118 B1
**Carron La** PR3 160 A4
**Carr Pl** PR5 78 B7
**Carr Rd**
Barnoldswick BB18 196 A3
Barrowford BB9 170 C1
Blackpool FY5 152 D6
Burnley BB11 127 E3
Clayton Green PR6 78 B2
Carr Rd *continued*
Colne BB8 171 E6
Darwen BB3 65 B8
Fleetwood FY7 199 A4
Hambleton FY6 177 C2
Horwich BL6 32 B5
Kirkham PR4 114 B4
Rawtenstall BB4 85 F1
Water BB4 87 C7
**Carr Royd Est** FY6 154 A3
**Carr's Cres** L37 11 E1
**Carr's Cres W** L37 11 D1
**Carrs Croft** BB7 191 E8
**Carrside** BB9 148 B8
**Carr Side La** L29 4 A3
**Carrs Ind Est** BB4 85 A4
**Carr St**
Bamber Bridge PR5 77 E8
Blackburn BB1 101 E6
Chorley PR6 61 E1
Preston PR1 97 B7
Ramsbottom BL0 50 B7
**Carrs Wood** BB2 100 F6
**Carr View** BB8 172 C1
**Carrwood Dr** PR4 114 B4
**Carrwood Gdns** LA2 210 F3
**Carrwood Gn** BB12 126 C8
**Carrwood Hey** BL0 50 A4
**Carrwood Pk** PR8 35 B4
**Carrwood Rd** PR5 97 B3
**Carrwood Way** PR5 97 B2
**CARRY BRIDGE** 171 F5
**Carry La** BB8 171 E4
**Carshalton Rd** FY1 130 B8
**Carsluith Ave** FY3 130 F3
**Carson Rd** FY4 131 A1
**Carter Ave** BB11 126 C4
**Carter Fold** BB2 121 E2
Carter's Charity Prim Sch FY6 200 C7
**Carter's La** BB7 231 A5
**Carter St**
Accrington BB5 104 B4
7 Blackpool FY1 130 B5
Burnley BB12 127 C7
**Carterville Cl** FY4 111 A7
**Cartford Cl** PR3 156 A6
**Cartford Cvn Pk** PR4 156 A6
**Cartford La** PR3 156 A6
**Cartford Pk** PR3 156 A6
**Cart Gate** FY6 200 B3
**Cartmel Ave**
Accrington BB5 104 A3
Fleetwood FY7 198 D1
Maghull L31 5 E2
**Cartmel Cl** PR8 35 F3
**Cartmel Dr**
Burnley BB12 127 B8
Coupe Green PR5 98 E4
Formby L37 12 B2
**Cartmell Fold** FY4 110 D5
**Cartmell La**
Lytham St Anne's FY8 91 E8
Nateby PR3 180 C7
**Cartmell Rd**
Blackpool FY4 131 D1
Lytham St Anne's FY8 89 F5
**Cartmel Pl**
Morecambe LA4 217 D4
Preston PR2 116 E2
**Cartmel Rd**
Blackburn BB2 101 A3
Lancaster LA1 218 F2
Leyland PR25 59 D8
**Cartmel South Ave** LA1 211 A6
**Cartmel West Ave** LA1 211 A6
**Cartwright Ct** LA1 214 E5
**Carus Ave** BB3 82 E1
**Carus Pk** LA6 241 B2
**Carvel Way** L40 25 F3
**Carver Hey Farm** PR4 75 B4
**Carvers Brow** PR26 58 B1
**Carwags La** PR3 161 C8
**Carwood Gr** BL6 32 D1
**Carwood La** PR6 61 C8
**Caryl Rd** FY8 89 D8
**Caspian Way** LA1 214 E4
**Casserley Rd** BB8 171 F6
**Casson Gate** OL12 52 E1
**Castercliff Bank** BB8 171 C3
Castercliffe Com Prim Sch BB9 171 B1
**Castercliffe Rd** BB9 149 B8
**CASTERTON** 243 A2
**Casterton** PR7 60 C2
**Casterton Ave** BB10 148 C3
Casterton Prim Sch BB10 148 C3
**Castle Ave** FY6 153 B6
**Castle Bank** LA5 224 C4
**Castle Cl** BB8 171 E6
**Castle Cres** BL6 32 C5
**Castlecroft Ave** BL6 31 D2
**Castle Ct**
Colne BB8 171 F6
Lancaster LA1 214 E8
**Castle Dr**
Adlington PR7 30 E6
Formby L37 11 F1
**Castle Fold** PR1 96 F2
**Castle Gardens Cres** FY6 153 B5
**Castlegate** FY1 130 B1
**Castle Gate** BB7 166 E8
**Castle Gr** BL0 50 A2
**Castlehey** WN8 9 E6
**Castle Hill** LA1 214 E8
**Castle Hill Rd** BL9 33 D5
**Castle House La** PR7 30 E6
**Castlekeep Ho** 13 BB7 166 E8
**Castlekeep View** 8 BB7 189 E1
**Castle La**
Bonds PR3 181 D6
Staining FY3 131 D5
Westhead L40 16 E5
**Castle Mount** PR2 117 F7
**Castle Par** 5 LA1 214 E8
**Castle Park Mews** LA1 214 E8
**Castle Pk**
Hornby LA2 238 B7
Lancaster LA1 214 E8
**Castle Rd** BB8 172 A7
**Castlerigg Dr** BB12 127 B8
**Castlerigg Pl** FY4 131 C1
**Castle St**
Blackburn BB1 102 B5
Brierfield BB9 148 B6
Burnley BB12 127 F7
6 Chorley PR7 43 D7
Clitheroe BB7 166 E8
7 Hapton BB12 126 C4
Nelson BB9 148 F8
Preston PR1 117 F1
Ramsbottom BL9 50 D2
Southport PR9 35 B8
**Castle The** BB8 172 A7
**Castleton Rd** PR1 118 B1
**Castletown Dr** OL13 88 B1
**Castle View**
Barnoldswick BB18 196 B1
Clitheroe BB7 166 E8
**Castle View Cvn Pk** LA6 240 D2
**Castle View Ho** 12 BB7 166 E8
**Castle Wlk**
Higher Penwortham PR1 96 C7
Southport PR8 35 A6
**Castle Wlks** PR26 58 B2
**Catches La** OL11 52 B1
**CATFORTH** 135 F4
**Catforth Ave** FY4 131 B1
Catforth Prim Sch PR4 136 A4
**Catforth Rd**
Catforth PR4 135 F5
Preston PR2 116 E1
**Catharine's La** L39 15 F1
**Cathedral Dr** LA3 217 B2
Cathedral RC Prim Sch The LA1 215 A7
**Catherine Cl** PR4 113 F7
**Catherine Ct** FY7 199 C4
**Catherine St E** BL6 32 B4
**Catherine St W** BL6 32 B5
**Catherine St**
6 Chorley PR7 43 C6
Kirkham PR4 113 F6
5 Preston PR1 97 B8
**Cathrow Dr** PR4 76 A7
**Cathrow Way** FY5 176 D2
**Catley Cl** PR6 61 C5
**CATLOW** 149 C5
**Catlow Ct** BB10 149 C5
**Catlow Hall St** BB5 103 E4
**Catlow Row** BB10 149 C6
**Catlow Terr** BB7 166 D1
**CATON** 237 C3
**Caton Ave** FY7 198 D1
**Caton Cl**
Longridge PR3 140 B8
Southport PR9 53 F4
Caton Com Prim Sch LA2 237 C3
**Caton Dr** PR25 77 E2
**Caton Gr** FY3 130 F7
**CATON GREEN** 237 D3
**Caton Green Rd** LA2 237 D3
**Caton Rd** LA1 218 F4
Caton St Paul's CE Prim Sch LA2 237 D3
**Cato St** 4 BL0 50 A4
**Cat Tail La** PR8 36 E1
**Cattan Gn** L37 12 B3
**CATTERALL** 181 E2
**Catterall Cl** FY1 130 D7
**Catterall Gates La** PR3 181 C3
**Catterall La** PR3 181 C1
**Catterall St** 3 BB2 81 C8
**Catterick Fold** PR8 35 F3
**Cattle St** BB6 124 C5
**Caunce Ave** PR9 55 A6
**Caunce's Rd** PR9 37 C5
**Caunce St** FY1, FY3 130 D6
**Causeway**
Foulridge BB8 194 D1
Great Harwood BB6 124 B5
**Causeway Ave** PR2 117 C4
**Causeway Croft** BB7 189 F1
**Causeway Head** BB4 68 A8
**Causeway La**
Haskayne L37 13 B1
Rufford L40 39 B2
**Causeway St** 2 BB3 65 C7
**Causeway The**
3 Chorley PR6 43 E8
Southport PR9 54 C5
Wymott PR26 58 F6
**Causey Foot** BB9 148 D7

**Cavalry Way** BB11 127 D6
**Cavell Cl** BB1 102 B1
**Cavendish Cres** PR2 118 F3
**Cavendish Ct**
Bolton-le-S LA5 221 A5
Southport PR9 35 E8
**Cavendish Dr** PR2 118 F3
**Cavendish Mans** FY5 175 C4
**Cavendish Pl**
6 Bamber Bridge PR5 97 D3
Blackburn BB2 101 B3
**Cavendish Rd**
Blackpool FY2 152 C4
Lytham St Anne's FY8 89 D8
Morecambe LA3 216 E3
2 Preston PR1 118 E1
Southport PR8 34 F3
**Cavendish St**
Barnoldswick BB18 196 B1
1 Chorley PR6 43 E7
Darwen BB3 81 F3
Lancaster LA1 214 D8
**Cavendish Wlk** PR9 35 E8
**Cave St**
1 Blackburn BB2 101 B1
2 Preston PR1 97 D8
**Cavour St** BB12 127 F7
**Cawsey The** PR1 97 A2
**Cawthorne's Endowed Sch** LA2 232 F1
**Cawthorne St** LA1 214 E8
**Caxton Ave** FY2 152 C5
**Caxton Rd** PR2 118 B8
**Cecil Ct** FY8 91 A3
**Cecilia Rd** BB2 101 A2
**Cecilia St** PR1 118 D1
**Cecil St**
Barnoldswick BB18 196 B3
Blackpool FY1 130 C7
4 Lytham St Anne's FY8 91 A3
Oswaldtwistle BB5 103 E4
Rishton BB1 124 C2
**Cedar Ave**
5 Bamber Bridge PR5 77 B8
Cleveleys FY5 175 E2
Euxton PR7 60 C4
Fleetwood FY7 175 E8
Haslingden BB4 85 C3
Horwich BL6 32 E1
Knott End-on-S FY6 200 A5
Poulton-le-F FY6 131 D8
Preston PR2 117 A2
Rawtenstall BB4 85 E2
Warton PR4 92 D6
**Cedar Cl**
Garstang PR3 181 B8
Grimsargh PR2 139 D1
Newton-w-S PR4 115 A3
Rishton BB1 103 B8
**Cedar Cres**
Kirkham PR4 114 A4
Ormskirk L39 15 D4
Ramsbottom BL0 50 C7
**Cedar Ct**
Blackburn BB1 101 F7
7 Leyland PR25 77 B1
**Cedar Dr** L37 11 C1
Cedar Farm Galleries* L40 40 C1
**Cedar Field** PR6 78 C2
**Cedar Gr**
Longton PR4 95 A1
Orrell WN5 10 F6
Skelmersdale WN8 17 E1
**Cedar Ho** PR7 42 F6
**Cedar Rd**
Chorley PR6 61 D2
Fulwood PR2 118 E2
Lancaster LA1 214 D8
**Cedars Cl** BB18 196 A1
**Cedars Inf Sch** BB1 101 F8
**Cedar Sq** 5 FY1 130 B5
**Cedar St**
Accrington BB5 104 D6
Blackburn BB1 101 F8
Burnley BB11 128 B5
Bury BL9 33 B3
Morecambe LA4 216 F4
Rochdale OL12 52 F1
Southport PR8 35 D4
**Cedars The**
Chorley PR7 43 B4
Eccleston PR7 41 B7
New Longton PR4 75 F8
**Cedar Way** PR1 96 B3
**Cedar Wlk** PR4 155 F1
**Cedarwood Cl** FY8 90 E4
**Cedarwood Dr** PR25 59 E8
**Cedarwood Pl** LA1 215 C7
**Cedric Pl** FY2 152 C4
**Celia St** BB10 128 C5
**Cemetery La**
Burnley BB11 127 A4
Preesall Park FY6 200 B1
**Cemetery Rd**
Darwen BB3 65 B5
Earby BB18 197 B2
Padiham BB12 126 C7
Preston PR1 118 C1
Ramsbottom BL0 50 A4
Southport PR8 35 C4
**Cemetery View** PR7 31 A6
**Centaur Cl** 7 BB8 171 C4
**Centenary Mill** PR1 97 C8
**Centenary Way** BB11 128 A5
**Central 12 Ret Pk** PR9 35 C6
**Central Ave**
Clitheroe BB7 166 D7
Edenfield BL0 68 D2
Gregson Lane PR5 98 E2
Kirkham PR4 113 F6
Lancaster LA1 218 D4
Oswaldtwistle BB5 103 C4
Southport PR8 21 F8
**Central Ave N** FY5 175 F3
**Central Beach** FY8 91 B3
**Central Bldgs** 16 BB12 146 C1
**Central Dr**
Blackpool FY1 130 C3
Higher Penwortham PR1 96 A4
Lytham St Anne's FY8 90 C5
Morecambe LA4 217 A5
**Central Lancaster High Sch** LA1 218 F1
**Central Rd** FY5 176 D3
**Central Sq**
7 Haslingden BB4 85 B3
Maghull L31 5 D2
**Central St** BL0 50 C6
**Central View** OL13 88 A2
**Centre Dr** PR6 78 B4
**Centurian Way** BB1 82 B6
**Centurion Ct** BB1 82 B7
**Centurion Ho** 1 PR4 114 B5
**Centurion Ind Est** PR25 77 B3
**Centurion Way** PR25, PR26 77 A4
**Ceres Way** LA1 214 C8
**Chadderton Ct** 22 PR1 97 A8
**Chaddock St** 29 PR1 97 A7
**Chadfield Rd** FY1 130 D2
**Chad St** BB8 171 A2
**Chadwick Cl** 5 PR5 77 E8
**Chadwick Gdns** 1 PR5 77 A7
**Chadwick St**
Blackburn BB2 101 D3
3 Blackpool FY1 130 C3
Bury BL9 33 E4
**Chadwick Terr** OL12 52 D4
**Chaffinch Cl** FY5 175 F5
**Chaffinch Ct** FY3 131 B6
**Chaffinch Dr** BL9 33 C4
**Chaigley Ct** BB7 165 A8
**Chaigley Farm Cotts** BB7 165 A8
**Chaigley Rd** PR3 140 B8
**Chain Caul Rd** PR2 95 F8
**Chain Caul Way** PR2 95 F8
**Chain House La** PR4 76 D7
**Chain La** FY3, FY4 131 E4
**Chalfont Ct** PR8 35 A3
**Chalfont Field** PR2 117 C5
**Challan Hall Cotts** LA5 224 E5
**Challan Hall Mews** LA5 224 E5
**Challenge Way** BB1 102 C7
**Chamber St** BB4 87 A8
**Chambres Rd** PR8 35 D5
**Chambres Rd N** PR8 35 D6
**Champagne Ave** FY5 152 F7
**Chancel Pl** BB3 65 C8
**Chancel Way** BB3 65 C8
**Chancery Cl** PR7 42 F1
**Chancery Rd** PR7 61 B2
**Chancery Wlk** 3 BB11 128 A6
**Chandler Bsns Pk** PR25 76 E2
**Chandlers Croft** PR4 73 E4
**Chandlers Ford** FY6 153 E4
**Chandlers Rest** FY8 91 D3
**Chandler St** 6 PR1 96 F8
**Chandley Cl** PR8 21 A5
**Change Cl** OL13 88 B4
**Changford Gn** L33 1 A3
**Changford Rd** L33 1 A3
**Channel Way** PR2 96 C8
**Channing Rd** FY8 90 C4
**Chanters Way** BB3 82 A5
**Chapel Alley** L37 11 F3
**Chapel Brow**
Leyland PR25 77 B2
Longridge PR3 140 B5
**Chapel Cl**
Clitheroe BB7 166 B8
Hest Bank LA2 220 D1
Kirkham PR4 113 F7
Overton LA3 209 C8
Pilling PR3 201 C5
Trawden BB8 172 B2
West Bradford BB7 189 E5
Whalley BB7 144 C5
**Chapel Ct** BB10 149 A3
**Chapel Fields** BL7 48 C4
**Chapel Fold**
12 Colne BB8 171 D4
Wiswell BB7 144 F7
**Chapel Gdns**
Catterall PR3 181 D2
Hesketh Bank PR4 73 E4
Ramsbottom BL8 49 E1
**Chapel Grange** BL7 48 C4
**Chapel Hill**
Longridge PR3 140 A6
Salterforth BB18 194 D7
**Chapel Hill La** BB4 86 B4
**Chapel Hill Trad Est** PR3 140 A6
**Chapel Ho**
Burnley BB11 127 C5
Maghull L31 5 D1
Rishton BB1 124 C1
**Chapel Hos** OL12 71 D4
**CHAPEL HOUSE** 17 E2
**Chapel House Rd** BB9 148 E7
**Chapelhouse Wlk** L37 12 A3
**Chapel La**
Banks PR9 55 B7
Burscough L40 25 E2
Burton in L LA6 242 C3
Catforth PR4 135 D4
Coppull PR7 42 F1
Formby L37 11 F3
Galgate LA2 211 B5
Hoghton PR5 99 D2
Holmeswood L40 38 B6
Langho BB6 143 B2
Longton PR4 75 C8
New Longton PR4 75 E8
Out Rawcliffe PR3 178 B2
Overton LA3 209 D8
Parbold WN8 27 D1
Ramsbottom BL8 50 A6
West Bradford BB7 189 E5
Wheelton PR6 62 B5
**Chapel Mdw** PR4 75 C8
**Chapel Mdws** PR4 57 A5
**Chapel Mews**
2 Earby BB18 197 B1
Ormskirk L39 15 F4
**Chapel Park Rd** PR4 75 D8
**Chapel Rd**
Blackpool FY4 111 B7
Fulwood PR2 118 A4
Hesketh Bank PR4 73 E4
**Chapel Rise** BB7 144 B4
**CHAPELS** 82 A3
**Chapels** BB3 82 A3
**Chapels Brow** BB3 82 A3
**Chapelside** 4 BB10 128 B5
**Chapelside Cl** PR3 181 D2
**Chapels La** BB3 80 F3
**Chapel Sq** LA2 237 D3
**Chapel St**
10 Accrington BB5 104 C5
Adlington PR7 30 F6
14 Bacup OL13 70 C8
Barnoldswick BB18 196 B2
Belmont BL7 46 C5
Belthorn BB1 82 F6
Blackburn BB2 101 D4
Blackpool FY1 130 B4
Blackrod BL6 31 D2
Bolton, Egerton BL7 47 D3
Brierfield BB9 148 B6
Brinscall PR6 62 F8
Burnley BB11 128 A6
Chorley PR7 43 C8
Clayton-le-M BB5 124 E3
Colne BB8 171 D4
Coppull PR7 42 E1
Darwen BB3 65 A8
Earby BB18 197 B2
Foulridge BB8 194 E1
Galgate LA2 211 A3
Great Eccleston PR3 156 B5
Haslingden BB4 85 B3
Higham BB12 146 F5
Horwich BL6 32 C3
3 Lancaster LA1 214 F8
Longridge PR3 140 B7
Lytham St Anne's FY8 91 A3
3 Morecambe LA4 217 A5
Nelson BB9 148 E8
Newchurch BB4 86 E1
Ormskirk L39 15 F4
Oswaldtwistle BB5 103 E4
Poulton-le-F FY6 153 D3
Preston PR1 96 F7
Rawtenstall BB4 86 A8
Rishton BB1 124 C1
Slaidburn BB7 229 C7
Southport PR8 35 B7
Whitworth OL12 52 C8
Worsthorne BB10 129 A5
**Chapel Street Ct** 3 FY6 153 D3
**Chapel The** BB4 86 A3
**CHAPELTOWN** 48 D4
**Chapeltown Rd** BL7 48 C2
**Chapel View**
Goodshaw Chapel BB4 106 A1
Overton LA3 209 D8
**Chapel Way** PR7 29 F8
**Chapel Wlk**
Coppull PR7 42 E1
Longton PR4 75 D8
2 Padiham BB12 146 C1
Warton LA5 223 E6
**Chapel Wlks**
Kirkham PR4 114 B4
5 Preston PR1 96 F7
**Chapel Yd** PR5 97 D5
**Chapman Cl** PR3 156 C5
**Chapman Ct**
Barnoldswick BB18 196 B3
Fleetwood FY7 199 B4
**Chapman Rd**
Fulwood PR2 118 A3
Hoddlesden BB3 82 F1
**Chapter Rd** BB3 65 C8
**Chardonnay Cres** 2 FY5 152 F7
**Charlbury Gr** LA3 213 A7
**Charles Ave** PR8 21 E6
**Charlesbye Ave** L39 16 B6
**Charlesbye Cl** L39 16 B6
**Charles Cl** PR4 73 E3
**Charles Cres** PR5 98 C3
**Charles Ct**
4 Blackpool FY3 130 D7
Lancaster LA1 214 F6
**Charles La** BB4 85 A2
**Charles St**
Blackburn BB2 101 D2
Blackpool FY1 130 C6
1 Bolton, Egerton BL7 47 D2
Clayton-le-M BB5 124 E2
Colne BB8 171 E5
Darwen BB3 82 A2
Great Harwood BB6 124 C4
Lancaster LA1 214 F6
Morecambe LA4 217 C5
Nelson BB9 170 E2
Newchurch BB4 86 F2
Oswaldtwistle BB5 103 E3
**Charleston Ct** 3 PR5 97 E2
**Charles Way** PR2 116 E1
**Charlesway Ct** 1 PR2 116 E1
**Charlesworth Cl** L31 5 B5
**Charley Wood Rd** L33 1 C1
**Charlotte Pl** 33 PR1 97 A7
**Charlotte's La** PR4 56 E2
**Charlotte St**
Blackburn BB1 101 E6
Burnley BB11 127 F5
Preston PR1 97 A7
4 Ramsbottom BL0 50 B5
**Charnley Cl** PR1 96 C2
**Charnley Ct** PR5 97 F2
**Charnley Fold Bglws** PR5 97 F3
**Charnley Fold Ind Est** PR5 97 F3
**Charnley Fold La** PR5 97 F3
**Charnley Rd** FY1 130 C4
**Charnley's La** PR9 54 E7
**Charnley St**
Blackburn BB2 101 C2
1 Lancaster LA1 218 B1
2 Preston PR1 96 F7
**Charnock Ave** PR1 96 E2
**Charnock Brow** PR7 42 C7
**Charnock Fold** PR1 118 A2
**Charnock Gdns** PR1 96 F1
**CHARNOCK GREEN** 42 C6
**Charnock Ho** PR7 61 C2
**Charnock Moss** PR5 76 F8
**CHARNOCK RICHARD** 42 D4
**Charnock St**
Chorley PR6 43 D7
9 Kirkham PR4 113 F6
8 Leyland PR25 77 B1
Preston PR1 117 F2
**Charnocks The** PR6 61 A1
**Charnwood Ave** FY3 131 A7
**Charnwood Cl** BB2 101 A8
**Charter Brook** BB6 124 D5
**Charterhouse Ct** FY7 198 D4
**Charterhouse Pl** BB2 101 B3
**Charter La** PR7 42 D3
**Charter St** BB5 104 A5
**Chartwell Cl** PR6 78 C2
**Chartwell Rd** PR8 21 B6
**Chartwell Rise** 5 PR5 77 C8
**Chasden Cl** PR6 61 C5
**Chase Cl** PR8 34 F4
**Chase Heys** PR9 54 A1
**Chase The**
Burnley BB12 127 D8
Cottam PR4 116 D5
3 Leyland PR25 77 C2
Normoss FY3 131 C7
Silverdale LA5 224 D2
Thornton FY5 176 A4
**CHATBURN** 190 C5
**Chatburn Ave**
Burnley BB10 128 D5
Clitheroe BB7 189 F1
**Chatburn CE Prim Sch** BB7 190 D5
**Chatburn Cl**
Great Harwood BB6 124 E5
Normoss FY3 131 B8
Rawtenstall BB4 86 A4
**Chatburn Gdns** OL10 33 F2
**Chatburn Old Rd** BB7 190 D5
**Chatburn Park Ave** BB9 148 A6
**Chatburn Park Dr**
Brierfield BB9 148 A6
Clitheroe BB7 190 A2
**Chatburn Rd**
Chatburn BB7 190 F5
Clitheroe BB7 190 A3
Fulwood PR2 118 F4
Longridge PR3 140 A7
**Chatburn St** BB2 101 C5
**Chateaux Apartments** PR4 116 D5
**Chatham Ave** FY8 110 E1
**Chatham Cres** BB8 171 E6
**Chatham Pl**
5 Chorley PR6 43 E8
Preston PR1 118 B2
**Chatham St**
Colne BB8 171 E6
Nelson BB9 170 D1
**Chatsworth Ave**
Blackpool FY2 152 C6
Fleetwood FY7 198 D2
Warton PR4 92 D6
**Chatsworth Cl**
Barrowford BB9 170 B1
4 Blackburn BB1 122 E1
Chorley PR7 43 B8
2 Thornton FY5 176 D1
**Chatsworth Ct** PR6 43 F1
**Chatsworth Rd**
Bamber Bridge PR5 97 D3
Lancaster LA1 214 F4
**Chatsworth Rd** *continued*
1 Leyland PR25 77 A1
Lytham St Anne's FY8 89 D7
Morecambe LA4 216 F4
Southport PR8 21 B6
**Chatsworth St**
Preston PR1 97 D8
Rochdale OL12 52 E3
**Chatteris Pl** FY5 175 C1
**CHATTERTON** 68 C1
**Chatterton** BL0 68 C2
**Chatterton Dr** BB5 104 E2
**Chatterton Old La** BL0 68 C2
**Chatterton Rd** BL0 68 C1
**Chaucer Ave** FY5 175 F2
**Chaucer Cl** PR7 41 B6
**Chaucer Gdns** BB6 124 B4
**Chaucer Pl** FY2 152 F6
**Chaucer Rd** FY7 199 A4
**Chaucer St** PR1 118 D2
**Cheam Ave** PR7 43 D6
**Cheapside**
Blackpool FY1 130 B5
6 Chorley PR7 43 C7
Formby L37 12 A2
11 Lancaster LA1 214 F8
1 Low Bentham LA2 239 B8
9 Preston PR1 96 F7
**Cheddar Ave** FY4 110 D6
**Cheddar Dr** PR2 118 D6
**Chedworth Ave** LA3 213 A7
**CHEESDEN** 51 D6
**Cheetham Hill** OL12 71 D3
**Cheetham Mdw** PR26 59 B8
**Cheetham St** BB2 101 C5
**Chelburn Gr** BB10 128 C6
**Chelford Ave** FY3 130 E8
**Chelford Cl** PR1 96 F2
**Chelmsford Cl** LA1 215 B5
**Chelmsford Gr** PR7 43 B7
**Chelmsford Pl** PR7 43 B7
**Chelmsford Wlk** PR26 59 A8
**Chelsea Ave** FY2 152 E1
**Chelsea Ct** 3 FY2 152 E1
**Chelsea Mews**
4 Blackpool FY2 152 E1
Lancaster LA1 218 D2
**Chelston Dr** BB4 68 A7
**Cheltenham Ave** BB5 104 C8
**Cheltenham Cres**
Lytham St Anne's FY8 91 D5
Thornton FY5 153 D8
**Cheltenham Dr** WN5 10 D2
**Cheltenham Rd**
Blackburn BB2 101 C5
Blackpool FY1 130 B7
Lancaster LA1 214 F5
**Cheltenham Way** PR8 35 F3
**Chelwood Cl** FY6 200 A5
**Chennel Ho** 4 LA1 214 E8
**Chepstow Gdns** PR3 181 D6
**Chepstow Rd** FY3 130 F8
**Chequer Cl** WN8 9 F5
**Chequer La** WN8 9 F6
**Chequers** BB5 124 F2
**Chequers Ave** LA1 215 B4
**Chequers Way** FY5 176 D2
**Cheriton Field** PR2 117 C7
**Cheriton Gdns** BL6 32 B5
**Cheriton Pk** PR8 35 E3
**Cherries The** PR7 60 D3
**Cherry Ave** BL9 33 C3
**Cherry Cl**
2 Blackburn BB1 102 B5
Fulwood PR2 118 D6
Kirkham PR4 113 E5
**Cherryclough Way** BB2 81 B8
**Cherry Cres**
Oswaldtwistle BB5 103 D2
Rawtenstall BB4 68 F8
**Cherrycroft** WN8 9 E6
**Cherry Ct** FY3 131 A7
**Cherrydale** FY2 152 D5
**Cherry Dr** BB6 143 C6
**Cherryfields** PR7 60 D4
**Cherryfold Com Prim Sch** BB11 127 D4
**Cherry Gn** L39 15 B1
**Cherry Gr**
Abbey Village PR6 80 B2
Burscough Bridge L40 25 E6
Longridge PR3 140 A7
**Cherry La** PR4 93 B4
**Cherry Lea** BB2 100 F2
**Cherry Orch** PR3 140 B6
**Cherry Rd** PR8 21 D2
**Cherry St** BB1 102 B5
**CHERRY TREE** 100 E1
**Cherry Tree Cl**
Fisher's Row PR3 201 E5
Hest Bank LA5 220 F2
Heysham LA3 212 E6
Knott End-on-S FY6 200 A6
**Cherry Tree Ct**
Blackpool FY4 131 B1
10 Fleetwood FY7 199 B5
Standish WN6 29 D2
**Cherry Tree Dr** LA1 214 F4
**Cherry Tree Gdns**
Blackpool FY4 111 A8
Nelson BB9 149 A8
**Cherry Tree Gr** PR6 61 C3
**Cherry Tree La**
3 Blackburn BB2 80 E8
Hurlston Green L40 24 B4
Ormskirk L39 15 B1
Rawtenstall BB4 68 F8

**Cherry Tree Mews**
BB11 . . . . . . . . . . . . . . . . 127 D3
**Cherry Tree Rd** FY4 . . . . . 131 A1
**Cherry Tree Rd N** FY4 . . . 131 A1
**Cherry Trees** PR5 . . . . . . . . 97 C3
**Cherry Tree Sta** BB2 . . . . . 100 F1
**Cherry Tree Terr** BB2 . . . . 100 F1
**Cherry Tree Way**
Haslingden BB4 . . . . . . . . . 68 B7
5 Horwich BL6 . . . . . . . . . . 32 E1
**Cherry Vale** PR4 . . . . . . . . . 73 F2
**Cherry View** L33 . . . . . . . . . . 1 A5
**Cherry Wood** PR1 . . . . . . . . 96 A3
**Cherrywood Ave**
Cleveleys FY5 . . . . . . . . . . 175 C1
Lytham St Anne's FY8 . . . . . 90 E4
**Cherrywood Cl** PR25 . . . . . . 59 E8
**Cheryl Dr** FY5 . . . . . . . . . . 153 B8
**CHESHAM** . . . . . . . . . . . . . . 33 A5
**Chesham Cres** BL9 . . . . . . . 33 A3
**Chesham Dr** PR4 . . . . . . . . . 75 F8
**Chesham Fold Rd** BL9 . . . . 33 B3
**Chesham Ind Est** BL9 . . . . 33 A4
**Chesham Lo** PR3 . . . . . . . . 156 B5
**Chesham Prim Sch** BL9 . . 33 A5
**Chesham Rd** BL9 . . . . . . . . . 33 A5
**Chesham St** PR3 . . . . . . . . 156 B5
**Cheshire Ct**
Buckshaw Village PR7 . . . . . 60 F6
Ramsbottom BL0 . . . . . . . . . 50 D6
**Cheshire House Cl**
PR26 . . . . . . . . . . . . . . . . . . 76 F7
**Cheshire Lines Path**
L39 . . . . . . . . . . . . . . . . . . . . 12 F6
**Chesmere Croft** PR1 . . . . . 96 B5
**Chesmere Dr** PR1 . . . . . . . . 96 B5
**Chessington Gn** BB10 . . . 148 D3
**Chester Ave**
Chorley PR7 . . . . . . . . . . . . . 43 E4
Cleveleys FY5 . . . . . . . . . . 175 E2
2 Clitheroe BB7 . . . . . . . . 189 E1
Poulton-le-F FY6 . . . . . . . . 153 C4
Southport PR9 . . . . . . . . . . . 35 F8
**Chesterbrook** PR3 . . . . . . 141 E4
**Chester Cl**
Blackburn BB1 . . . . . . . . . . 102 A3
Garstang PR3 . . . . . . . . . . 181 B7
Morecambe LA3 . . . . . . . . . 217 B2
**Chester Cres** BB4 . . . . . . . . 68 B8
**Chester Ct** FY5 . . . . . . . . . 176 C3
**Chester Dr** BL0 . . . . . . . . . . 50 A4
**Chesterfield Cl** PR8 . . . . . . 21 C4
**Chesterfield Rd**
Blackpool FY1 . . . . . . . . . . 130 C7
Southport PR8 . . . . . . . . . . . 21 C5
**Chester Pl**
Adlington PR6 . . . . . . . . . . . 31 A8
Great Eccleston PR3 . . . . . 156 C5
Lancaster LA1 . . . . . . . . . . 215 A5
**Chester Rd**
Blackpool FY3 . . . . . . . . . . 130 D6
Preston PR1 . . . . . . . . . . . . 118 C1
Southport PR9 . . . . . . . . . . . 35 F8
**Chester St**
Accrington BB5 . . . . . . . . . 104 A5
Blackburn BB1 . . . . . . . . . . 102 A4
Bury BL9 . . . . . . . . . . . . . . . 33 A4
**Chester Terr** LA6 . . . . . . . 240 B7
**Chestnut Ave**
Blackpool FY4 . . . . . . . . . . 110 F5
Bolton-le-S LA5 . . . . . . . . . 221 A5
Bury BL9 . . . . . . . . . . . . . . . 33 B2
Caton LA2 . . . . . . . . . . . . . 237 C3
Chorley PR6 . . . . . . . . . . . . . 61 E2
Euxton PR7 . . . . . . . . . . . . . 60 C4
Higher Penwortham PR1 . . . 96 A4
**Chestnut Bsns Pk**
BB11 . . . . . . . . . . . . . . . . . 127 B5
**Chestnut Cl**
Bamber Bridge PR5 . . . . . . . 97 E2
Blackpool FY2 . . . . . . . . . . 152 D2
Garstang PR3 . . . . . . . . . . 204 D1
Halsall L39 . . . . . . . . . . . . . . 23 C1
Kirkham PR4 . . . . . . . . . . . 114 B5
**Chestnut Cotts** BB7 . . . . . 191 A5
**Chestnut Cres**
Barrow BB7 . . . . . . . . . . . . 166 D1
Fulwood PR2 . . . . . . . . . . . 118 E2
Longton PR4 . . . . . . . . . . . . 74 F8
**Chestnut Ct**
Leyland PR25 . . . . . . . . . . . . 60 A7
3 Ormskirk L39 . . . . . . . . . 15 F6
**Chestnut Dr**
Barnoldswick BB18 . . . . . . 196 A1
Fulwood PR2 . . . . . . . . . . . 117 D7
Morecambe LA4 . . . . . . . . . 217 F6
Rawtenstall BB4 . . . . . . . . . 68 F8
Whalley BB7 . . . . . . . . . . . 144 A7
**Chestnut Gdns**
Blackburn BB1 . . . . . . . . . . 101 F7
Thornton FY5 . . . . . . . . . . . 176 B3
**Chestnut Gr**
4 Accrington BB5 . . . . . . 104 A4
Clayton-le-M BB5 . . . . . . . . 125 A4
Darwen BB3 . . . . . . . . . . . . . 65 A5
Lancaster LA1 . . . . . . . . . . 214 D8
**Chestnut Grange** L39 . . . . 15 D3
**Chestnut Rise** BB11 . . . . . 127 F4
**Chestnut St** PR8 . . . . . . . . . 35 C5
**Chestnuts The** PR7 . . . . . . . 42 F2
**Chestnut Way** L37 . . . . . . . . 11 C1
**Chestnut Wlk** 5 BB1 . . . . 102 B5
**Chethams Cl** FY5 . . . . . . . 176 A2
**Chevassut Cl** BB9 . . . . . . . 170 C1
**Cheviot Ave**
Burnley BB10 . . . . . . . . . . . 128 E5
Cleveleys FY5 . . . . . . . . . . 175 F4
Lytham St Anne's FY8 . . . . . 91 E5
**Cheviot Cl**
Horwich BL6 . . . . . . . . . . . . 32 C5
Ramsbottom BL0 . . . . . . . . . 50 C4
**Cheviot St** PR1 . . . . . . . . . . 96 C8
**Chew Gdns** FY6 . . . . . . . . . 153 B3
**Chichester Cl**
Burnley BB10 . . . . . . . . . . . 128 B6
Thornton FY5 . . . . . . . . . . . 176 A2
**Chicken St** BB2 . . . . . . . . . 101 C4
**Chiddlingford Ct** FY1 . . . . 130 D3
**Childrey Wlk** BB2 . . . . . . . . 82 A8
**Chilgrove Ave** BL6 . . . . . . . 31 D1
**Chiltern Ave**
Blackpool FY4 . . . . . . . . . . 110 D7
Burnley BB10 . . . . . . . . . . . 128 E5
Euxton PR7 . . . . . . . . . . . . . 60 D1
Poulton-le-F FY6 . . . . . . . . 153 C3
**Chiltern Cl**
Horwich BL6 . . . . . . . . . . . . 32 C5
Lytham St Anne's FY8 . . . . . 91 D5
Ramsbottom BL0 . . . . . . . . . 50 C4
**Chiltern Ct** 4 LA1 . . . . . . 215 A5
**Chiltern Mdw** PR25 . . . . . . 77 D1
**Chiltern Rd**
Ramsbottom BL0 . . . . . . . . . 50 C4
Southport PR8 . . . . . . . . . . . 21 B6
**Chilton Cl** L31 . . . . . . . . . . . . 5 D1
**Chilton Ct** L31 . . . . . . . . . . . . 5 D1
**Chilton Mews** L31 . . . . . . . . . 5 D1
**Chimes The**
Kirkham PR4 . . . . . . . . . . . 114 A4
Tarleton PR4 . . . . . . . . . . . . 57 A5
**China St**
Accrington BB5 . . . . . . . . . 103 F6
Lancaster LA1 . . . . . . . . . . 214 F8
**Chindit Cl** L37 . . . . . . . . . . . 11 D2
**Chindits Way** PR2 . . . . . . . 118 B4
**Chines The** PR2 . . . . . . . . . 117 E4
**Chingford Bank** BB10 . . . 148 D3
**Chingle Cl** PR2 . . . . . . . . . 118 E6
**Chippendale Mews**
PR3 . . . . . . . . . . . . . . . . . . 181 C8
**CHIPPING** . . . . . . . . . . . . . 185 D3
**Chipping Ave** PR8 . . . . . . . . 21 A5
**Chipping Gr**
Burnley BB10 . . . . . . . . . . . 128 D4
Normoss FY3 . . . . . . . . . . . 131 A8
**Chipping La** PR3 . . . . . . . . 140 A8
**Chipping Manor** PR9 . . . . . 55 A6
**Chipping St** 3 BB12 . . . . 146 D1
**Chirk Dr** FY5 . . . . . . . . . . . 176 D2
**Chisacre Dr** WN6 . . . . . . . . 19 D7
**Chisholm Cl** WN6 . . . . . . . . 29 B2
**Chisholme Cl** BL8 . . . . . . . . 49 F2
**Chislehurst Ave** FY4 . . . . . 130 D1
**Chislehurst Gr** BB10 . . . . . 148 D4
**Chislehurst Pl** FY8 . . . . . . . 90 E5
**Chislett Cl** L40 . . . . . . . . . . 25 D4
**Chisnall Ave** WN6 . . . . . . . . 28 F6
**Chisnall La**
Coppull PR7 . . . . . . . . . . . . . 29 C6
Heskin Green PR7 . . . . . . . . 41 F2
Wrightington Bar WN6 . . . . 29 A5
**Chiswell Gr** FY5 . . . . . . . . 153 D8
**Chiswick Ct** FY3 . . . . . . . . 131 B2
**Chiswick Gr** FY3 . . . . . . . . 131 B2
**Chive Cl** FY2 . . . . . . . . . . . 152 F3
**Chorcliffe Ho** 7 PR7 . . . . . 43 C8
**CHORLEY** . . . . . . . . . . . . . . . 43 C6
**Chorley All Saints CE Prim Sch** PR7 . . . . . . . . . . . . . . 43 B5
**Chorley Astley Park Sch**
PR7 . . . . . . . . . . . . . . . . . . . 43 B8
**Chorley Bsns & Tech Ctr**
PR7 . . . . . . . . . . . . . . . . . . . 60 E4
**Chorley Cl** PR9 . . . . . . . . . . 54 F5
**Chorley Hall Rd** PR7 . . . . . . 61 C2
**Chorley La** PR7 . . . . . . . . . . 42 D3
**CHORLEY MOOR** . . . . . . . . . 43 D6
**Chorley New Rd** BL6 . . . . . 32 C2
**Chorley New Road Prim Sch** BL6 . . . . . . . . . . . . . . . 32 D2
**Chorley North Ind Est**
PR6 . . . . . . . . . . . . . . . . . . . 61 D3
**Chorley Old Rd**
Clayton Green PR6 . . . . . . . 78 C2
Horwich BL6 . . . . . . . . . . . . 32 E3
Whittle-le-W PR6 . . . . . . . . . 61 C8
**Chorley Rd**
Adlington PR6 . . . . . . . . . . . 31 A8
Bamber Bridge PR5 . . . . . . . 97 D3
Blackpool FY3 . . . . . . . . . . 152 F2
Blackrod BL6, PR7 . . . . . . . . 31 B5
Hill Dale L40, WN8 . . . . . . . 27 D6
Ollerton Fold BB2, PR6 . . . . 79 E4
Parbold WN8 . . . . . . . . . . . . 27 C4
Standish WN1 . . . . . . . . . . . 30 C3
**Chorley St James CE Prim Sch** PR6 . . . . . . . . . . . . . . . 43 E7
**Chorley Southlands High Sch** PR7 . . . . . . . . . . . . . . . 43 A5
**Chorley & South Ribble District Hospl** PR7 . . . . . . 61 C2
**Chorley St** PR6 . . . . . . . . . . 31 B8
**Chorley Sta** PR6 . . . . . . . . . 43 D8
**Chorley West Bsns Pk**
PR7 . . . . . . . . . . . . . . . . . . . 42 F8
**Chorlton Cl** BB10 . . . . . . . 148 D2
**Chorlton Gdns** BB1 . . . . . . 101 F7
**Chorlton St** BB1 . . . . . . . . 101 F7
**Chorlton Terr** BB7 . . . . . . 166 D1
**Christ Church CE Prim Sch**
BB8 . . . . . . . . . . . . . . . . . . 172 B5
**Christ Church Charnock Richard CE Prim Sch**
PR7 . . . . . . . . . . . . . . . . . . . 42 D4
**Christ Church Hall** 3
BB5 . . . . . . . . . . . . . . . . . . 104 C4
**Christ Church Sq** 1
BB5 . . . . . . . . . . . . . . . . . . 104 C5
**Christ Church St**
2 Accrington BB5 . . . . . . 104 C5
4 Bacup OL13 . . . . . . . . . . 88 A3
Preston PR1 . . . . . . . . . . . . . 96 E7
**Christiana Hartley Maternity Hospl** PR8 . . . . 35 E4
**Christian Rd** PR1 . . . . . . . . . 96 E7
**Christie Ave** LA4 . . . . . . . . 217 D4
**Christie Park (Morecambe FC)** LA4 . . . . . . . . . . . . . . 217 D4
**Christines Cres** L40 . . . . . . 25 E4
**Christleton Cl** BB10 . . . . . 148 F3
**Christ The King RC High Sch & Sixth Form Ctr**
PR8 . . . . . . . . . . . . . . . . . . . 35 B3
**Christ The King RC Maths & Computing Coll**
PR1 . . . . . . . . . . . . . . . . . . . 97 B6
**Christ The King RC Prim Sch**
Blackpool FY3 . . . . . . . . . . 131 A7
Burnley BB11 . . . . . . . . . . . 127 E3
**Chromolyte Ind Est** PR8 . . 35 B5
**CHURCH** . . . . . . . . . . . . . . 103 E7
**Church Alley** BB5 . . . . . . . 124 F2
**Church Ave**
Accrington BB5 . . . . . . . . . 104 E2
Higher Penwortham PR1 . . . 96 C6
Lancaster LA1 . . . . . . . . . . 214 F4
Preston PR1 . . . . . . . . . . . . . 97 E8
**Church Bank**
Church BB5 . . . . . . . . . . . . 103 E7
Over Kellet LA6 . . . . . . . . . 237 B8
**Church Bank Gdns**
LA6 . . . . . . . . . . . . . . . . . . 240 C7
**Church Bank St** 20 BB3 . . . 82 A1
**Church Brook Ho** 8
PR1 . . . . . . . . . . . . . . . . . . . 96 E4
**Church Brow**
Bolton-le-S LA5 . . . . . . . . . 221 A3
Clitheroe BB7 . . . . . . . . . . 189 E1
Halton LA2 . . . . . . . . . . . . . 219 C6
Walton-le-D PR5 . . . . . . . . . 97 E5
**Church Brow Cl** LA5 . . . . . 221 A3
**Church Brow Gdns** 5
BB7 . . . . . . . . . . . . . . . . . . 189 E1
**Church Cl**
Clitheroe BB7 . . . . . . . . . . 189 E1
Dolphinholme LA2 . . . . . . . 226 A8
Formby L37 . . . . . . . . . . . . . 12 A3
Freckleton PR4 . . . . . . . . . . 93 A6
Mellor BB2 . . . . . . . . . . . . . 121 E2
Ramsbottom BL0 . . . . . . . . . 50 B5
Read BB12 . . . . . . . . . . . . . 145 D2
Southport PR9 . . . . . . . . . . . 36 A8
Waddington BB7 . . . . . . . . 189 B4
**Church Close Ct** L37 . . . . . . 12 A3
**Church Cotts** LA6 . . . . . . . 241 C7
**Church Ct**
Bolton-le-S LA5 . . . . . . . . . 221 A3
6 Bury BL9 . . . . . . . . . . . . . 33 A3
Edenfield BL0 . . . . . . . . . . . 68 D4
Kirkham PR4 . . . . . . . . . . . 114 A5
16 Lancaster LA1 . . . . . . . 218 D2
Preston PR1 . . . . . . . . . . . . 118 C2
**Church Dr**
Lytham St Anne's FY8 . . . . . 90 F3
Orrell WN5 . . . . . . . . . . . . . . 10 D5
Whalley BB7 . . . . . . . . . . . 144 A7
**Churchfield** PR2 . . . . . . . . 117 F6
**Churchfields**
Bescar L40 . . . . . . . . . . . . . . 23 F7
Southport PR8 . . . . . . . . . . . 34 F3
**Church Fields** L39 . . . . . . . . 15 E5
**Church Fold**
Charnock Richard PR7 . . . . . 42 E4
Coppull PR7 . . . . . . . . . . . . . 29 F8
**Churchgate**
Goosnargh PR3 . . . . . . . . . 138 D6
Southport PR9 . . . . . . . . . . . 53 F1
**Churchgate Mews** PR9 . . . 54 A1
**Church Gdns**
Longridge PR3 . . . . . . . . . . 140 B7
Warton PR4 . . . . . . . . . . . . . 92 E6
**Church Gn**
Formby L37 . . . . . . . . . . . . . 11 C2
Skelmersdale WN8 . . . . . . . 17 F1
**Church Gr** LA3 . . . . . . . . . 209 E8
**Church Hall** BB5 . . . . . . . . 103 F7
**Church Hill**
Nether Kellet LA6 . . . . . . . 221 F5
Whittle-le-W PR6 . . . . . . . . . 61 C7
**Church Hill Ave** LA5 . . . . . 223 D5
**Church Hill Rd**
Blackburn BB1 . . . . . . . . . . 102 A7
Ormskirk L39 . . . . . . . . . . . . 15 D6
**Church Ho** 7 L39 . . . . . . . . 15 E5
**Church House Mus**
PR3 . . . . . . . . . . . . . . . . . . 137 D1
**Churchill Ave**
Rishton BB1 . . . . . . . . . . . . 103 A8
Southport PR9 . . . . . . . . . . . 53 F2
**Churchill Cl** 2 FY5 . . . . . . 176 B2
**Churchill Ct** FY3 . . . . . . . . 130 D6
**Churchill Dr** PR2 . . . . . . . . 118 D4
**Churchill Rd**
Barrowford BB9 . . . . . . . . . 170 B1
Brinscall PR6 . . . . . . . . . . . . 63 A8
Fulwood PR2 . . . . . . . . . . . 118 C4
**Churchill St** OL11, OL12 . . . 52 C1
**Churchill Way**
Burnley BB9 . . . . . . . . . . . . 148 B7
Leyland PR25 . . . . . . . . . . . . 77 A2
Nelson BB9 . . . . . . . . . . . . 148 B8
**Church La**
Accrington BB5 . . . . . . . . . 125 A1
**Church La** *continued*
Aughton L39 . . . . . . . . . . . . . 6 A7
Bilsborrow PR3 . . . . . . . . . 159 A4
Broughton PR3 . . . . . . . . . 137 D1
Charnock Richard PR7 . . . . . 42 D4
Edenfield BL0 . . . . . . . . . . . 68 D4
Farington PR4, PR26 . . . . . . 76 F7
Goosnargh PR3 . . . . . . . . . 138 D6
Great Harwood BB6 . . . . . 124 C6
Great Mitton BB7 . . . . . . . 165 E3
Hambleton FY6 . . . . . . . . . 177 D1
Kelbrook BB18 . . . . . . . . . 195 A6
Maghull L31 . . . . . . . . . . . . . 5 A8
Mellor BB2 . . . . . . . . . . . . . 121 E2
Morecambe LA4 . . . . . . . . . 217 B6
Newchurch BB4 . . . . . . . . . . 86 E1
Newton-w-S PR4 . . . . . . . . 115 B3
12 Padiham BB12 . . . . . . . 146 C1
Tunstall LA6 . . . . . . . . . . . 241 E4
Whalley BB7 . . . . . . . . . . . 144 C5
Whitechapel PR3 . . . . . . . . 160 E7
Winmarleigh PR3 . . . . . . . . 203 E4
Wrightington Bar WN6 . . . . 28 D8
**Churchlands La** WN6 . . . . . 29 F2
**Church Mdws** BB8 . . . . . . 171 D5
**Church Mews**
Bamber Bridge PR5 . . . . . . . 77 F7
Great Harwood BB6 . . . . . 124 D5
Southport PR9 . . . . . . . . . . . 36 A7
**Church & Oswaldtwistle Sta** BB5 . . . . . . . . . . . . . . . 103 E5
**Church Pk**
Overton LA3 . . . . . . . . . . . 209 D8
Salwick PR4 . . . . . . . . . . . . 115 F3
**Church Raike** PR3 . . . . . . . 185 E3
**Church Rd**
Bamber Bridge PR5 . . . . . . . 77 E7
Banks PR9 . . . . . . . . . . . . . . 55 A6
Bickerstaffe L39 . . . . . . . . . . 7 E6
Formby L37 . . . . . . . . . . . . . 12 A4
Kirkham PR4 . . . . . . . . . . . 113 F7
Leyland PR25 . . . . . . . . . . . . 60 A8
Lytham St Anne's FY8 . . . . . 90 B6
Lytham St Anne's, Lytham
FY8 . . . . . . . . . . . . . . . . . . . 90 F3
Rufford L40 . . . . . . . . . . . . . 39 C4
Shuttleworth BL0 . . . . . . . . . 50 E8
Singleton FY6 . . . . . . . . . . 154 F1
Skelmersdale WN8 . . . . . . . 17 F1
Tarleton PR4 . . . . . . . . . . . . 57 A5
Thornton FY5 . . . . . . . . . . . 176 A2
Thornton-in-C BD23 . . . . . 197 A5
Walton Summit PR5 . . . . . . . 77 F6
Warton PR4 . . . . . . . . . . . . . 92 E6
Weeton PR4 . . . . . . . . . . . . 132 F1
Wharles PR4 . . . . . . . . . . . 134 F2
**Church Row**
Preston PR1 . . . . . . . . . . . . . 97 A7
Wrea Green PR4 . . . . . . . . 113 B4
**Church Row Chambers**
PR4 . . . . . . . . . . . . . . . . . . . 75 A8
**Churchside** PR4 . . . . . . . . . . 75 F8
**Church Sq** BB10 . . . . . . . . 129 B5
**Church St**
Accrington BB5 . . . . . . . . . 104 C5
Adlington PR7 . . . . . . . . . . . 31 A7
Bacup OL13 . . . . . . . . . . . . . 70 C8
Barnoldswick BB18 . . . . . . 196 B2
Barrowford BB9 . . . . . . . . . 170 D4
Belmont BL7 . . . . . . . . . . . . 46 C4
Blackburn BB1 . . . . . . . . . . 101 E5
Blackpool FY1 . . . . . . . . . . 130 C5
Blackrod BL6 . . . . . . . . . . . . 31 C2
Brierfield BB9 . . . . . . . . . . 148 B5
Burnley BB11 . . . . . . . . . . . 128 A6
Burnley, Harle Syke
BB10 . . . . . . . . . . . . . . . . . 148 F2
Bury BL9 . . . . . . . . . . . . . . . 33 A3
Chorley PR7 . . . . . . . . . . . . . 43 C7
Church BB5 . . . . . . . . . . . . 103 E6
Churchtown PR3 . . . . . . . . 181 A2
Clayton-le-M BB5 . . . . . . . . 124 F2
1 Clitheroe BB7 . . . . . . . 166 E8
Colne BB8 . . . . . . . . . . . . . 171 D5
Croston PR26 . . . . . . . . . . . . 58 B1
Darwen BB3 . . . . . . . . . . . . . 82 A1
Fleetwood FY7 . . . . . . . . . . 199 B4
Garstang PR3 . . . . . . . . . . 181 C7
Goodshaw Chapel BB4 . . . 106 A1
Great Harwood BB6 . . . . . 124 C5
Halton LA2 . . . . . . . . . . . . . 219 B6
2 Hapton BB12 . . . . . . . . 126 C4
Haslingden BB4 . . . . . . . . . . 85 B4
Higher Walton PR5 . . . . . . . 98 B3
Horwich BL6 . . . . . . . . . . . . 32 C3
Kirkham PR4 . . . . . . . . . . . 114 B5
Lancaster LA1 . . . . . . . . . . 214 F8
Leyland PR25 . . . . . . . . . . . . 77 B2
Longridge PR3 . . . . . . . . . . 140 B7
Morecambe LA4 . . . . . . . . . 217 B6
Newchurch BB4 . . . . . . . . . . 86 E1
Ormskirk L39 . . . . . . . . . . . . 15 E5
Orrell WN5 . . . . . . . . . . . . . . 10 E5
Oswaldtwistle BB5 . . . . . . 103 D3
Padiham BB12 . . . . . . . . . . 126 C8
2 Poulton-le-F FY6 . . . . . . 153 D3
Preston PR1 . . . . . . . . . . . . . 97 A7
5 Ramsbottom BL0 . . . . . . 50 C6
Rawtenstall BB4 . . . . . . . . . 69 E8
Read BB12 . . . . . . . . . . . . . 145 D2
Ribchester PR3 . . . . . . . . . 141 D3
Rishton BB1 . . . . . . . . . . . . 124 A1
Slaidburn BB7 . . . . . . . . . . 229 C7
Southport PR9 . . . . . . . . . . . 35 C7
Standish WN6 . . . . . . . . . . . 29 E1
Trawden BB8 . . . . . . . . . . . 172 C2
Up Holland WN8 . . . . . . . . . 10 C7
Whittington LA6 . . . . . . . . . 241 C7
**Church St** *continued*
Whitworth OL12 . . . . . . . . . . 52 C8
**Church Stile** LA6 . . . . . . . 240 C8
**Church Terr**
21 Darwen BB3 . . . . . . . . . . 82 A1
Higher Walton PR5 . . . . . . . 98 B3
**CHURCHTOWN**
Catterall . . . . . . . . . . . . . . . 181 A2
Southport . . . . . . . . . . . . . . . 54 A1
**Churchtown Cres** OL13 . . . 88 B1
**Churchtown Ct** PR9 . . . . . . 54 A2
**Churchtown Gdns** PR9 . . . 54 A2
**Churchtown Prim Sch**
PR9 . . . . . . . . . . . . . . . . . . . 54 B2
**Church View**
Aughton L39 . . . . . . . . . . . . . 6 A7
Gisburn BB7 . . . . . . . . . . . 231 B3
Salesbury BB1 . . . . . . . . . . 122 E6
Stalmine FY6 . . . . . . . . . . . 177 C7
Tarleton PR4 . . . . . . . . . . . . 57 A5
Trawden BB8 . . . . . . . . . . . 172 C2
**Church View Ct** 1 L39 . . . 15 E5
**Churchward Sq** BL6 . . . . . . 32 C2
**Church Way**
Formby L37 . . . . . . . . . . . . . 11 C2
Nelson BB9 . . . . . . . . . . . . 148 D6
**Church Wlk**
Blackburn BB1 . . . . . . . . . . 122 F3
Euxton PR7 . . . . . . . . . . . . . 60 C2
Fulwood PR2 . . . . . . . . . . . 118 F5
Kirkham PR4 . . . . . . . . . . . 113 F7
Tarleton PR4 . . . . . . . . . . . . 57 A6
**Church Wlks** 3 L39 . . . . . 15 E5
**Churton Gr** WN6 . . . . . . . . . 29 B2
**Cicely Ct** 6 BB1 . . . . . . . . 101 F4
**Cicely La** BB1 . . . . . . . . . . 101 F5
**Cicely St** BB1 . . . . . . . . . . 101 F4
**Cinderbarrow La** LA5,
LA6 . . . . . . . . . . . . . . . . . . 240 A6
**Cinder La**
Lancaster LA1 . . . . . . . . . . 214 F3
Lewth PR4 . . . . . . . . . . . . . 136 A6
Mere Brow PR4 . . . . . . . . . . 55 F2
**Cinnamon Brow** WN8 . . . . 10 C6
**Cinnamon Ct** 3 PR1 . . . . . 96 C2
**Cinnamon Hill Dr N**
PR5 . . . . . . . . . . . . . . . . . . . 97 D3
**Cinnamon Hill Dr S**
PR5 . . . . . . . . . . . . . . . . . . . 97 D3
**Cintra Ave** PR2 . . . . . . . . . 117 D3
**Cintra Terr** PR2 . . . . . . . . 117 D3
**Circus The** 10 BB3 . . . . . . 82 A1
**Cirrus Dr** L39 . . . . . . . . . . . 15 A1
**City Ct** PR1 . . . . . . . . . . . . . 97 A8
**City Heights Cl** 21 LA1 . . 215 A8
**City of Preston High Sch**
PR2 . . . . . . . . . . . . . . . . . . 118 F3
**City Space Ho** PR1 . . . . . . . 96 F6
**City Views** PR1 . . . . . . . . . . 97 A7
**Clairane Ave** PR2 . . . . . . . 117 E6
**Clairville** PR8 . . . . . . . . . . . 34 F5
**Clancut La** PR7 . . . . . . . . . . 42 F2
**Clanfield** PR2 . . . . . . . . . . 117 E7
**Clara St**
Preston PR1 . . . . . . . . . . . . . 97 C7
Whitworth OL12 . . . . . . . . . . 71 D1
**Clare Ave** BB8 . . . . . . . . . . 171 A2
**Claremont Ave**
Chorley PR7 . . . . . . . . . . . . . 43 B7
Clitheroe BB7 . . . . . . . . . . 166 F7
Southport PR8 . . . . . . . . . . . 35 A4
**Claremont Com Prim Sch**
FY1 . . . . . . . . . . . . . . . . . . 130 C8
**Claremont Cres** LA4 . . . . . 216 F4
**Claremont Ct**
Blackpool FY1 . . . . . . . . . . 130 C7
Lytham St Anne's FY8 . . . . . 89 E5
**Claremont Dr**
Clitheroe BB7 . . . . . . . . . . 166 F7
Ormskirk L39 . . . . . . . . . . . . 15 D3
**Claremont Gdns** PR8 . . . . . 35 A4
**Claremont Pl** FY8 . . . . . . . . 89 E8
**Claremont Rd**
Accrington BB5 . . . . . . . . . 104 B8
Blackpool FY1 . . . . . . . . . . 130 C8
Chorley PR7 . . . . . . . . . . . . . 43 B5
Morecambe LA4 . . . . . . . . . 216 F4
Southport PR8 . . . . . . . . . . . 35 A4
**Claremont St**
Brierfield BB9 . . . . . . . . . . 148 A6
Burnley BB12 . . . . . . . . . . . 127 D6
Colne BB8 . . . . . . . . . . . . . 172 A5
**Claremont Terr** BB9 . . . . . 148 D7
**Claremount Ave** PR25 . . . . 60 B8
**Clarence Ave**
Cleveleys FY5 . . . . . . . . . . 175 D3
4 Haslingden BB4 . . . . . . . 85 A1
Knott End-on-S FY6 . . . . . . 199 E5
**Clarence Cl** 10 BL9 . . . . . . 33 A4
**Clarence Ct**
15 Blackpool FY4 . . . . . . . 130 B1
5 Morecambe LA4 . . . . . . 217 E6
Southport PR8 . . . . . . . . . . . 35 A4
**Clarence High Sch** L37 . . . 11 F6
**Clarence Pk** BB2 . . . . . . . . 101 B7
**Clarence Rd**
Accrington BB5 . . . . . . . . . 104 A4
Southport PR8 . . . . . . . . . . . 35 A4
**Clarence St**
Barnoldswick BB18 . . . . . . 196 C1
Blackburn BB1 . . . . . . . . . . 101 D6
Burnley BB11 . . . . . . . . . . . 128 B4
4 Chorley PR7 . . . . . . . . . . 43 D7
Colne BB8 . . . . . . . . . . . . . 172 A5
Darwen BB3 . . . . . . . . . . . . . 81 F3

**Clarence St** *continued*
Lancaster LA1 .......... 215 A7
Leyland PR25 .......... 77 B2
Longridge PR3 .......... 140 A8
Morecambe LA4 .......... 217 B5
Oswaldtwistle BB5 .......... 103 C3
Rawtenstall BB4 .......... 86 A7
Rochdale OL12 .......... 52 D2
Trawden BB8 .......... 172 C2
**Clarendon Gr** L31 .......... 5 C5
**Clarendon Rd**
Blackburn BB1 .......... 101 F8
Blackpool FY1 .......... 130 B2
Lancaster LA1 .......... 218 D3
Lytham St Anne's FY8 .......... 90 A8
**Clarendon Rd E**
Blackburn BB1 .......... 102 A8
Morecambe LA4 .......... 216 F4
**Clarendon Rd N** FY8 .......... 89 F8
**Clarendon Rd W** LA3 .......... 216 E4
**Clarendon St**
Accrington BB5 .......... 104 D6
Bury BL9 .......... 33 A4
10 Chorley PR6 .......... 43 E7
Colne BB8 .......... 172 B5
Preston PR1 .......... 97 A6
**Clare Rd** LA1 .......... 218 C2
**Clare St**
Blackpool FY1 .......... 130 B1
Burnley BB11 .......... 127 D6
**Claret St** BB5 .......... 104 A5
**Clarke Holme St** 3 BB4 .......... 86 F2
**Clarke's Cotts** L40 .......... 27 A8
**Clarkes Croft** BL9 .......... 33 C3
**Clarke's La** OL12 .......... 52 E1
**Clarke St** BB1 .......... 124 B1
**Clarke Wood Cl** BB7 .......... 144 F8
**Clarkfield Cl** L40 .......... 25 F3
**Clarkfield Dr** LA4 .......... 217 D5
**Clarksfield Rd** LA5 .......... 221 A4
**Clark St**
Morecambe LA4 .......... 217 B6
Poulton-le-F FY6 .......... 153 F3
**Clarrick Terr** LA6 .......... 242 F3
**CLAUGHTON**
Catterall .......... 182 D1
Hornby .......... 237 E5
**Claughton Ave** PR25 .......... 77 E1
**Claughton Dr** LA1 .......... 215 A3
**Claughton Ind Est** PR3 .......... 181 E1
**Claughton Mans** 5
FY4 .......... 110 D8
**Claughton St** 13 BB10 .......... 148 B1
**Claughton Terr** LA2 .......... 237 F5
**CLAWTHORPE** .......... 240 C8
**Clawthorpe Cotts** LA6 .......... 240 C8
**Claybank** 10 BB12 .......... 146 C1
**Claybank Fold** 9
BB12 .......... 146 C1
**Clay Brow Rd** WN8 .......... 9 E6
**Clayburn Cl** PR6 .......... 61 E2
**Clay Gap La** FY6, PR3 .......... 177 F4
**Clay La** LA3 .......... 213 B8
**Claylands Dr** LA5 .......... 221 A4
**Claypool Prim Sch** BL6 .......... 32 F1
**Claypool Rd** BL6 .......... 32 E1
**Clay St** BB11 .......... 127 C5
**Clayton Ave**
Leyland PR25 .......... 59 D7
Rawtenstall BB4 .......... 68 E8
**CLAYTON BROOK** .......... 78 A5
**Clayton Brook Ho** BB5 .......... 125 A1
**Clayton Brook Prim Sch**
PR5 .......... 78 B5
**Clayton Brook Rd** PR5 .......... 78 C6
**Clayton Cl** 11 BB9 .......... 170 D1
**Clayton Cres** FY4 .......... 110 E6
**Clayton Ct** PR3 .......... 140 B7
**Claytongate**
Blackpool FY4 .......... 111 A7
Coppull PR7 .......... 42 F2
**Claytongate Dr** PR1 .......... 97 A2
**Clayton Gdns** L40 .......... 25 E4
**Clayton Gr** BB1 .......... 122 D6
**CLAYTON GREEN** .......... 78 A3
**Clayton Green Bsns Pk**
PR6 .......... 78 B4
**Clayton Green Rd** PR6 .......... 78 B3
**Claytonhalgh** PR3 .......... 141 E3
**Clayton Hall Dr** BB5 .......... 124 F4
**CLAYTON-LE-DALE** .......... 122 C7
**CLAYTON-LE-MOORS** .......... 124 E2
**Clayton-le-Moors Ind Est**
BB5 .......... 124 F1
**CLAYTON-LE-WOODS** .......... 77 D2
**Clayton-le-Woods CE Prim Sch**
Clayton Green PR6 .......... 78 A2
Clayton-le-W PR6 .......... 77 F2
**Clayton-le-Woods Manor Road Prim Sch** PR6 .......... 78 B2
**Clayton Lo** BB5 .......... 124 F4
**Clayton Mews** WN8 .......... 17 D1
**Clayton Row** BB6 .......... 143 D1
**Clayton's Gate** 11 PR1 .......... 96 F8
**Clayton St**
1 Accrington BB5 .......... 125 A1
6 Bamber Bridge PR5 .......... 97 E1
Barnoldswick BB18 .......... 196 C2
Blackburn BB2 .......... 101 E4
Colne BB8 .......... 171 E4
Great Harwood BB6 .......... 124 C5
18 Nelson BB9 .......... 170 D1
7 Oswaldtwistle BB5 .......... 103 E5
**Clayton St** *continued*
Skelmersdale WN8 .......... 17 D1
**Clayton Street Ind Units**
BB9 .......... 170 D1
**Clayton Villa Fold** PR6 .......... 78 A3
**Clayton Way**
Blackburn BB2 .......... 81 D7
Clayton-le-M BB5 .......... 125 A3
**Cleator Ave** FY2 .......... 152 C1
**Cleaver Cotts** L38 .......... 3 A6
**Cleaver St**
Blackburn BB1 .......... 101 F5
Burnley BB10 .......... 128 B8
**Clecken La** PR3 .......... 182 D2
**Clegg Ave** FY5 .......... 175 D3
**Cleggís Ct** OL12 .......... 71 C2
**Clegg St E** 9 BB10 .......... 128 A8
**Clegg St**
6 Bacup OL13 .......... 70 C8
Brierfield BB9 .......... 148 B5
Burnley BB10 .......... 128 A8
Haslingden BB4 .......... 85 B3
Kirkham PR4 .......... 114 A5
Nelson BB9 .......... 148 E6
Skelmersdale WN8 .......... 17 D1
Whitworth OL12 .......... 71 C2
Worsthorne BB10 .......... 129 A5
**Clematis Cl** PR7 .......... 61 A3
**Clematis St** BB2 .......... 101 B6
**Clemens Ct** BB3 .......... 81 E3
**Clementina St** OL12 .......... 52 F1
**Clements Dr** BB9 .......... 148 C4
**Clement St**
Accrington BB5 .......... 104 C5
4 Darwen BB3 .......... 65 A8
**Clement View** 14 BB9 .......... 148 D8
**Clengers Brow** PR9 .......... 54 A3
**Clent Ave** L31 .......... 5 C3
**Clent Gdns** L31 .......... 5 C3
**Clent Rd** L31 .......... 5 C3
**Clerk Hill Rd** BB7 .......... 144 F5
**Clerkhill St** BB1 .......... 102 B5
**Clery St** BB12 .......... 127 A5
**Clevedon Rd**
Blackpool FY1 .......... 130 B7
Fulwood PR2 .......... 117 A4
**Cleveland Ave** PR2 .......... 118 C4
**Cleveland Cl** BL0 .......... 50 C3
**Cleveland Dr** LA1 .......... 214 D7
**Cleveland Rd**
Leyland PR25 .......... 76 F2
Lytham St Anne's FY8 .......... 91 B3
**Clevelands Ave**
Morecambe LA3 .......... 216 F3
Silverdale LA5 .......... 224 C4
**Clevelands Gr**
Burnley BB11 .......... 127 E4
Morecambe LA3 .......... 216 F3
**Clevelands Mt** BB11 .......... 127 E4
**Clevelands Rd** BB11 .......... 127 F4
**Cleveland St**
Chorley PR7 .......... 43 C8
Colne BB8 .......... 171 F6
2 Coppull PR7 .......... 42 E1
Todmorden OL14 .......... 109 B1
**Clevelands Wlk** 1 LA3 .......... 216 F3
**CLEVELEYS** .......... 175 C3
**Cleveleys Ave**
Cleveleys FY5 .......... 175 D3
Fulwood PR2 .......... 117 C4
Lancaster LA1 .......... 218 A2
Southport PR9 .......... 54 A4
**Cleveleys Rd**
Accrington BB5 .......... 104 B8
Blackburn BB2 .......... 101 F1
Coupe Green PR5 .......... 98 E3
Southport PR9 .......... 54 A3
**Cleves Ct** FY3 .......... 131 A2
**Cleves The** L31 .......... 5 E3
**Cleve Way** L37 .......... 12 B2
**CLIEVES HILLS** .......... 14 F3
**Clieves Hills La** L39 .......... 14 E3
**Clieves Viewpoint**★
L39 .......... 14 E3
**Clifden Ct** L37 .......... 11 F3
**Cliff Ave** BL9 .......... 50 C2
**Cliff Bank Hamlet** BB4 .......... 86 E2
**Cliff Ct** FY2 .......... 152 B4
**CLIFFE** .......... 124 C6
**Cliffe Ct** PR1 .......... 97 D8
**Cliffe Dr** PR6 .......... 61 B8
**Cliffe La** BB6 .......... 124 C6
**Cliffe Pk** BB6 .......... 124 C6
**Cliffe St** BB9 .......... 170 E1
**Cliff Mount** BL0 .......... 50 B7
**Clifford Ave**
Longton PR4 .......... 95 A1
Morecambe LA4 .......... 217 D6
**Clifford Rd**
Blackpool FY1 .......... 130 C7
Southport PR8 .......... 35 A2
**Clifford St**
Barnoldswick BB18 .......... 196 C2
Chorley PR7 .......... 43 D8
Colne BB8 .......... 171 E5
**Cliff Pl** FY2 .......... 152 B4
**Cliff Rd** PR9 .......... 53 D1
**Cliff St**
Colne BB8 .......... 171 B3
Padiham BB12 .......... 146 D1
Preston PR1 .......... 96 E6
Rishton BB1 .......... 124 B2
**Cliffs The** LA3 .......... 216 D2
**CLIFTON** .......... 115 D1
**Clifton Ave**
Accrington BB5 .......... 104 C7
Blackpool FY4 .......... 131 C1
Leyland PR25 .......... 60 B8
**Clifton Ave** *continued*
Preston PR2 .......... 117 A2
Warton PR4 .......... 92 E6
**Clifton Bsns Pk** PR4 .......... 94 B7
**Clifton Cl** FY5 .......... 176 C1
**Clifton Cres**
Blackpool FY3 .......... 131 A2
Preston PR1 .......... 118 C2
**Clifton Ct**
1 Blackpool FY4 .......... 110 B6
3 Lytham St Anne's, Lytham
FY8 .......... 91 C3
2 Lytham St Anne's, St Annes
FY8 .......... 89 E6
**Clifton Dr**
Blackpool FY4 .......... 110 B5
Blackrod BL6 .......... 31 C3
Great Harwood BB6 .......... 124 C6
Higher Penwortham PR1 .......... 96 C5
Lytham St Anne's FY8 .......... 90 D3
Morecambe LA4 .......... 217 E5
**Clifton Dr N** FY8 .......... 110 B2
**Clifton Dr S** FY8 .......... 89 E5
**Clifton Gate** FY8 .......... 91 B4
**Clifton Gdns** FY8 .......... 90 C6
**Clifton Gn** PR4 .......... 115 D2
**Clifton Gr**
Chorley PR7 .......... 43 B7
Preston PR1 .......... 118 C3
Wilpshire BB1 .......... 122 F4
**Clifton Grange** FY8 .......... 89 D7
**Clifton Ho** PR2 .......... 118 C4
**Clifton Hospl** FY8 .......... 90 B5
**Clifton La** PR4 .......... 115 D2
**Clifton Lo** FY8 .......... 89 E5
**Clifton Par** 4 FY8 .......... 91 B3
**Clifton Pk Ret Ctr** FY4 .......... 111 D8
**Clifton Pl**
Freckleton PR4 .......... 93 B6
Fulwood PR2 .......... 117 B2
**Clifton Prim Sch** FY8 .......... 90 C6
**Clifton Rd**
Blackpool FY4 .......... 111 C8
Brierfield BB9 .......... 148 C4
Burnley BB12 .......... 127 C7
Fleetwood FY7 .......... 199 A3
Formby L37 .......... 12 A5
Southport PR8 .......... 35 F6
**Clifton Sq** 5 FY8 .......... 91 B3
**Clifton St**
Accrington BB5 .......... 104 A4
Blackpool FY1 .......... 130 B5
Burnley BB12 .......... 127 F6
Colne BB8 .......... 171 D5
Darwen BB3 .......... 81 F4
Earby BB18 .......... 195 A8
Lytham St Anne's FY8 .......... 91 B3
5 Preston PR1 .......... 96 D6
Rishton BB1 .......... 124 B1
Trawden BB8 .......... 172 C2
**Clifton Terr** BB3 .......... 82 E2
**Clifton Windmill**★
PR4 .......... 115 C3
**Clifton Wlk** 8 FY8 .......... 91 B3
**Clifton Wlk Sh Ctr** 14
FY8 .......... 91 B3
**Clinkham Rd** BB6 .......... 124 A5
**Clinning Rd** PR8 .......... 35 A2
**Clinton Ave** FY1 .......... 130 C4
**Clinton St** BB1 .......... 102 A6
**Clippers Quay** 2 BB1 .......... 101 F4
**CLITHEROE** .......... 166 D8
**Clitheroe Castle**★
BB7 .......... 166 E8
**Clitheroe Castle Mus**★
BB7 .......... 166 E8
**Clitheroe Com Hospl**
BB7 .......... 190 A3
**Clitheroe Pendle Prim Sch**
BB7 .......... 189 F1
**Clitheroe Pl** FY4 .......... 111 A8
**Clitheroe Rd**
Brierfield BB9 .......... 148 A5
Chatburn BB7 .......... 190 C3
Knowle Green PR3 .......... 163 C1
Lytham St Anne's FY8 .......... 90 C6
Sabden BB7 .......... 167 E1
Waddington BB7 .......... 189 C3
West Bradford BB7 .......... 189 F5
Whalley BB7 .......... 144 C7
**Clitheroe Royal Gram Sch**
Clitheroe BB7 .......... 189 F1
Clitheroe BB7 .......... 190 A2
**Clitheroes La** PR4 .......... 93 B6
**Clitheroe St**
3 Padiham BB12 .......... 126 C8
Preston PR1 .......... 97 C7
**Clitheroe Sta** BB7 .......... 189 E1
**Clive Ave** FY8 .......... 110 E1
**Clive Lo** PR8 .......... 34 F2
**Clive Rd**
Higher Penwortham
PR1 .......... 96 B6
Southport PR8 .......... 34 F2
**Clive St** BB12 .......... 127 F8
**Clockhouse Ave** BB10 .......... 148 D3
**Clockhouse Ct** BB10 .......... 148 D3
**Clockhouse Gr** BB10 .......... 148 D3
**Clod La** BB4 .......... 68 C8
**Clods Carr La** FY6 .......... 199 F2
**Clogger La** BD23 .......... 197 F7
**Clog Heads** BB8 .......... 172 C2
**Cloister Dr** BB3 .......... 82 C1
**Cloister Gn** L37 .......... 12 B2
**Cloisters** LA3 .......... 217 C2
**Cloisters The**
Blackpool FY3 .......... 130 E5
Formby L37 .......... 11 F3
**Cloisters The** *continued*
2 Leyland PR25 .......... 77 C2
6 Preston PR2 .......... 96 D8
6 Rawtenstall BB4 .......... 69 E8
2 Southport PR9 .......... 35 C8
Tarleton PR4 .......... 57 A6
Whalley BB7 .......... 144 D5
**Clone Primet High Sch**
BB8 .......... 171 B3
**Clone Primet Prim Sch**
BB8 .......... 171 B3
**Clorain Cl** L33 .......... 1 A3
**Clorain Rd** L33 .......... 1 A3
**Closes Hall Mews** BB7 .......... 230 F5
**Close The**
Banks PR9 .......... 55 A5
Clayton-le-M BB5 .......... 124 F4
Cleveleys FY5 .......... 175 D2
Cleveleys, Rossall Beach
FY5 .......... 175 D4
Fulwood PR2 .......... 118 E6
Garstang PR3 .......... 204 B1
Ince Blundell L38 .......... 3 E3
Kirkham PR4 .......... 114 B4
New Longton PR4 .......... 76 A7
Rising Bridge BB5 .......... 85 A8
Weeton PR4 .......... 132 E2
Withnell Fold PR6 .......... 79 C3
**Clougha Ave**
Halton LA2 .......... 219 D7
Lancaster LA1 .......... 215 B6
**Clough Acre** PR7 .......... 61 A2
**Clough Ave**
Bamber Bridge PR5 .......... 97 B3
Burscough L40 .......... 25 F4
**Clough Bank** BB7 .......... 190 D5
**Clough End Rd** BB4 .......... 85 B5
**Clough End View** BB4 .......... 85 B5
**Cloughfield** PR1 .......... 96 D1
**CLOUGHFOLD** .......... 86 D2
**Clough Gdns** BB4 .......... 85 B5
**Clough Heads Cotts**
PR3 .......... 226 F1
**Clough Head Visitor Ctr**★
BB4 .......... 84 A3
**Clough La**
Hesketh Lane PR3 .......... 163 A7
Simonstone BB12 .......... 145 F1
**Clough Rd**
Bacup OL13 .......... 88 A3
Nelson BB9 .......... 149 A8
**Clough Springs** BB9 .......... 170 C3
**Clough St**
8 Bacup OL13 .......... 70 D8
Burnley BB11 .......... 127 D5
Darwen BB3 .......... 65 C6
5 Newchurch BB4 .......... 86 F1
**Clough Terr** BB18 .......... 196 B1
**Clough The**
Clayton Green PR6 .......... 78 A3
Darwen BB3 .......... 65 C6
**Cloughwood Cres** WN6 .......... 19 D6
**Clovelly Ave**
Blackpool FY5 .......... 152 D6
Fulwood PR2 .......... 117 D3
**Clovelly Dr**
Higher Penwortham
PR1 .......... 96 A5
Newburgh WN8 .......... 27 A1
Skelmersdale WN8 .......... 18 A8
Southport PR8 .......... 21 E8
**Clover Ave** FY8 .......... 111 A1
**Clover Cres** BB12 .......... 127 D8
**Clover Ct**
Blackpool FY2 .......... 152 F6
Southport PR8 .......... 35 C5
**Clover Dr** PR4 .......... 93 D7
**Cloverfield** PR1 .......... 96 B4
**Clover Field** PR6 .......... 78 B2
**Cloverfields** 5 BB1 .......... 102 A6
**Cloverhill Ho** BB9 .......... 148 F7
**Clover Hill Rd** BB9 .......... 148 F7
**Clover Mews** FY3 .......... 130 E6
**Clover Rd** PR7 .......... 43 A5
**Clover St** OL13 .......... 88 A3
**Clover Terr** BB3 .......... 82 A3
**CLOW BRIDGE** .......... 106 C5
**Club La** PR3 .......... 185 E3
**Club St**
Bamber Bridge PR5 .......... 77 F7
Todmorden OL14 .......... 109 B1
**Clucas Gdns** L39 .......... 15 E6
**Clydesdale Pl** PR26 .......... 76 C2
**Clyde St**
Blackburn BB2 .......... 101 B3
4 Blackpool FY1 .......... 130 B7
Preston PR2 .......... 96 C8
**Clyffes Farm Cl** L40 .......... 24 A7
**Coach Ho** PR7 .......... 60 A5
**Coach House Ct** L40 .......... 25 E3
**Coach House Mews**
PR3 .......... 181 C7
**Coach Mews** LA4 .......... 216 F4
**Coach Rd**
Bickerstaffe L39 .......... 7 F1
Church BB5 .......... 103 E5
Warton LA5 .......... 223 D7
**Coal Clough La** BB11 .......... 127 E4
**Coal Clough Rd** OL14 .......... 109 B2
**Coal Hey** 12 BB4 .......... 85 B3
**Coal Hey St** 13 BB4 .......... 85 B3
**Coal Pit La**
Accrington BB5 .......... 103 F4
Bacup OL13 .......... 88 B3
Barnoldswick BB7 .......... 193 B7
Colne BB8 .......... 171 F4
Gisburn BB7 .......... 231 D2
Rawtenstall BB4 .......... 87 A4
**Coal Pit La** *continued*
Skelmersdale L39 .......... 8 D4
Tockholes BB3 .......... 81 B3
**Coal Rd** BL0 .......... 51 C8
**Coal St** 12 BB11 .......... 127 F6
**Coastal Dr** LA2 .......... 220 E2
**Coastal Rd**
Hest Bank LA2, LA5 .......... 220 F2
Morecambe LA4 .......... 217 F8
Southport, Birkdale PR8 .......... 34 C3
Southport, Woodvale PR8 .......... 21 A4
**Coastal Rise** LA2 .......... 220 E2
**Coastline Mews** PR9 .......... 54 A4
**COATES** .......... 196 D3
**Coates Ave** BB18 .......... 196 C3
**Coates Fields** BB18 .......... 196 C4
**Coates La** BB18 .......... 196 D4
**Coates Lane Prim Sch**
BB18 .......... 196 D3
**Cobbís Brow Cotts** L40 .......... 17 F5
**Cobbled Court Yd** LA1 .......... 214 E7
**Cobb's Brow La** L40,
WN8 .......... 18 B6
**Cobbs Brow Prim Sch**
WN8 .......... 18 A3
**Cobb's Clough Rd** L40 .......... 17 F5
**Cobbs La** BB5 .......... 83 E8
**Cob Castle Rd** BB4 .......... 84 E3
**Cobden Ct** 4 BB1 .......... 101 E5
**Cobden Ho** BB4 .......... 86 D1
**Cobden Rd** PR9 .......... 36 A6
**Cobden St**
Barnoldswick BB18 .......... 196 B1
3 Bolton, Egerton BL7 .......... 47 D2
Britannia OL13 .......... 71 B8
Burnley, Harle Syke
BB10 .......... 148 F3
Burnley, Heasandford
BB10 .......... 128 B8
4 Bury BL9 .......... 33 A3
Chorley PR6 .......... 61 E1
11 Darwen BB3 .......... 65 A8
Hapton BB12 .......... 126 C4
Nelson BB9 .......... 148 D7
Padiham BB12 .......... 146 D1
**Cobham Ct** 2 BB4 .......... 86 E1
**Cobham Rd** BB5 .......... 104 D5
**Cob La** BB8, BB18 .......... 195 B4
**Cob Moor Ave** WN5 .......... 10 D1
**Cob Moor Rd** WN5 .......... 10 D1
**Cobourg Cl** BB2 .......... 101 F2
**COB WALL** .......... 102 A7
**Cob Wall** BB1 .......... 102 A6
**Cochran St** 26 BB3 .......... 82 A1
**COCKDEN** .......... 149 B2
**Cocker Ave** FY6 .......... 154 A2
**COCKER BAR** .......... 75 F1
**Cocker Bar Rd** PR26 .......... 58 D8
**COCKERHAM** .......... 206 C5
**Cockerham Parochial CE Prim Sch** LA2 .......... 206 D4
**Cockerham Rd**
Forton LA2, PR3 .......... 207 B4
Garstang PR3 .......... 204 B1
**Cockerham Wlk** FY3 .......... 131 A8
**Cockerill St** BB4 .......... 85 B4
**Cockerill Terr** BB7 .......... 166 D1
**Cocker La** PR26 .......... 76 C1
**Cocker Rd** PR5 .......... 78 B7
**Cockersand Ave** PR4 .......... 95 C1
**Cockersand Dr** LA1 .......... 215 A3
**Cocker Sq** 3 FY1 .......... 130 B6
**Cocker St**
Blackpool FY1 .......... 130 B6
Darwen BB3 .......... 65 C7
**Cocker Trad Est** FY1 .......... 130 C7
**Cockhall La** OL12 .......... 71 C1
**Cock Hall La** OL12 .......... 52 C8
**Cockhill La** BB8 .......... 172 B8
**Cocking Yd** LA6 .......... 240 C7
**Cockleach Lane Ends**
PR3 .......... 162 A2
**Cockle Dick's La** PR9 .......... 53 E2
**Cockridge Cl** BB2 .......... 81 B7
**Cock Robin** PR26 .......... 58 C2
**Cock Robin La** PR3 .......... 181 D2
**Codale Ave** FY2 .......... 152 D5
**Coddington St** BB1 .......... 102 B5
**Coe La** PR4 .......... 57 A5
**Cog La** BB11 .......... 127 D4
**Cog St** BB11 .......... 127 D5
**Colbran St**
Burnley BB10 .......... 128 B8
12 Nelson BB9 .......... 170 F2
**Colburne Cl** L40 .......... 25 E5
**Colchester Ave** LA1 .......... 215 B5
**Colchester Dr** 6 FY5 .......... 175 F4
**Colchester Rd**
Blackpool FY3 .......... 130 F3
Southport PR8 .......... 35 F3
**Coldale Ct** 5 FY4 .......... 110 B6
**Cold Bath St** 4 PR1 .......... 96 E8
**COLD ROW** .......... 177 C5
**Coldstream Pl** BB2 .......... 101 E2
**Coldweather Ave** BB9 .......... 148 F5
**Cold Well La** LA7 .......... 224 F8
**Colebatch** PR2 .......... 117 D5
**Cole Cres** L39 .......... 6 C8
**Coleman St** 4 BB9 .......... 148 F8
**Colenso Rd**
Blackburn BB1 .......... 101 D7
Fulwood PR2 .......... 117 C2
**Coleridge Ave** FY5 .......... 176 A3
**Coleridge Cl**
Colne BB8 .......... 171 D6
Cottam PR4 .......... 116 E4
**Coleridge Dr** BB5 .......... 104 E2
**Coleridge Ho** LA2 .......... 218 C4

Coleridge Pl BB6 124 B4
Coleridge Rd
Blackpool FY1 130 D6
Longshaw WN5 10 D1
Ramsbottom BL8 49 F2
Coleridge St BB2 101 C3
Coles Dr LA5 224 B8
Coleshill Ave BB10 128 D5
Colesville Ave FY5 176 B1
Colinmander Gdns L39 15 C3
Colin St
Barnoldswick BB18 196 B3
Burnley BB11 127 D5
Colinton WN8 9 E7
Colldale Terr BB4 85 B2
College Ave
Cleveleys FY5 175 C1
Formby L37 11 E4
College Cl
Formby L37 11 D4
Longridge PR3 140 A5
Padiham BB12 126 D6
Southport PR8 35 A3
College Croft BD24 236 F7
College Ct
5 Accrington BB5 104 A6
4 Blackpool FY1 130 C4
Preston PR1 117 F2
College Farm WN8 19 A1
College Gate FY5 175 C5
College La BB4 86 D2
College Path L37 11 D5
College Rd WN8 10 B8
College St
2 Accrington BB5 104 A6
Todmorden OL14 109 C1
Collegiate High Sch Sports Coll FY3 153 A1
Collier's Row BB1 102 F1
Colliers St BB5 103 E5
Collier St 6 BB5 104 E2
Collinge Fold La BB4 85 F4
Collinge St
Padiham BB12 126 C7
Rawtenstall BB4 85 F4
Collingham Pk LA1 215 A2
Colling St 9 BL0 50 B5
Collingwood BB5 124 E2
Collingwood Ave
Blackpool FY3 130 E6
Lytham St Anne's FY8 110 E1
Collingwood Dr 10 LA2 239 B8
Collingwood Pl FY3 130 E6
Collingwood Rd PR7 43 B7
Collingwood St
Colne BB8 171 C4
Standish WN6 29 E1
Collingwood Terr 7 LA2 239 D8
Collins Ave FY2 152 E3
Collins Dr BB5 104 E2
Collin's Hill La PR3 185 A3
Collinson St PR1 118 C1
Collins Rd PR5 97 F1
Collins Rd N PR5 97 F2
Collisdene Rd WN5 10 E6
Collison Ave PR7 43 C8
Colloway Ho LA3 212 E6
Collyhurst Ave FY4 110 E6
Colman Ct PR1 96 D6
Colnbrook WN6 29 B1
COLNE 171 C6
Colne & Broughton Rd BD23 197 C6
COLNE EDGE 171 C7
Colne La BB8 171 E4
Colne Lord Street Sch BB8 171 C5
Colne Rd
Barnoldswick BB18 196 A1
Barrowford BB8, BB9 170 F4
Brierfield BB9 148 B6
Burnley BB10, BB11 128 A8
Burnley, Burnley Lane BB10 148 B3
Kelbrook BB18 195 A7
Trawden BB8 172 B2
Colne Sta BB8 171 C4
Colonnade The LA1 215 C7
Colthirst Dr BB7 190 A2
Colt House Cl PR25 60 A7
Coltsfoot Dr PR6 61 D2
Coltsfoot Wlk LA3 217 B2
Columbia Way BB2 101 B8
Columbine Cl
Chorley PR7 61 A3
Rochdale OL12 52 C3
Colville Ave 1 FY4 110 C5
Colville Rd BB3 81 E4
Colville St BB10 128 A8
Colwall Cl L33 1 A2
Colwall Rd L33 1 A2
Colwall Wlk L33 1 A2
Colwyn Ave
Blackpool FY4 130 E1
Morecambe LA4 217 D6
Colwyn Pl PR2 117 A3
Colyton Cl PR6 43 E8
Colyton Rd PR6 43 E8
Colyton Rd E 2 PR6 43 E8
Combermere Gr LA3 212 E5
Combermere Rd LA3 212 E6
Comer Gdns L31 5 C3
Comet Rd PR26 76 C2
Comet St 8 OL13 88 A7
Commerce St
Bacup OL13 87 F2
Commerce St *continued*
Haslingden BB4 85 A4
Commercial Rd
Chorley PR7 61 C1
Darwen BB3 81 F5
Great Harwood BB6 124 C5
Nelson BB9 148 E8
Commercial St
Bacup OL13 70 D8
Barnoldswick BB18 196 B2
10 Blackpool FY1 130 B1
Brierfield BB9 148 B6
Church BB5 103 E6
12 Great Harwood BB6 124 C5
Oswaldtwistle BB5 103 D3
Rawtenstall BB4 106 A3
Rishton BB1 124 B1
Common Bank Employment Area PR7 42 F8
Common Bank La PR7 42 F8
COMMON EDGE 110 F6
Common Edge Rd FY4 110 F6
Common End PR7 30 E5
Common Garden St 38 LA1 214 F8
Common La PR9 55 C1
Commonside FY8 90 D4
Commons La BB2 121 B5
Common The
Adlington PR7 30 E5
Parbold WN8 27 C3
Commonwealth Cl FY8 90 C8
Como Ave BB11 127 C4
Company St BB1 124 B1
Compley Ave FY6 153 C2
Compley Gn FY6 153 C2
Compression Rd LA3 212 E2
Compston Ave BB4 106 A1
Compton Cl FY6 153 C5
Compton Gn PR2 117 D7
Compton Rd PR8 35 B3
Comrie Cres BB11 127 D3
Concorde Ho 1 FY1 130 C4
Concourse Sh Ctr The WN8 18 B1
Conder Ave FY5 175 F2
Conder Brow LA5 223 E2
CONDER GREEN 210 C5
Conder Green Rd LA2 210 F3
Conder Pl LA1 218 C2
Conder Rd PR2 116 E1
Conder Side Cvn Pk LA2 210 A4
Condor Gr
Blackpool FY1 130 D3
Lytham St Anne's FY8 89 E8
Condor Way PR1 97 A2
Conduit St BB9 170 D1
Coneygarth La
Tunstall LA6 241 D4
Whittington LA6 241 D6
Congleton Cl FY4 131 B1
Congress St PR7 61 C1
Conifer Ct L37 12 A2
Conifers The
Barton PR3 137 B8
Hambleton FY6 177 B2
Kirkham PR4 114 B5
Maghull L31 5 C3
Conisber Cl BL7 47 E1
Coniston Ave
Accrington BB5 103 F4
Adlington PR6 31 B8
Barnoldswick BB18 196 A3
Carleton FY6 153 B4
Euxton PR7 60 D1
Fleetwood FY7 198 E4
Hambleton FY6 177 C2
Knott End-on-S FY6 199 F6
Lytham St Anne's FY8 110 F2
Orrell WN5 10 F7
Padiham BB12 146 C2
Preston PR2 117 D2
Thornton FY5 176 B1
Coniston Cl
Longridge PR3 140 A5
Ramsbottom BL0 50 C7
Coniston Cres FY5 176 B1
Coniston Ct
Morecambe LA4 217 C6
Southport PR8 21 C3
Coniston Dr
Bamber Bridge PR5 97 E2
Darwen BB3 82 C2
Coniston Gr BB8 172 A6
Coniston Ho PR1 96 B4
Coniston Rd
Blackburn BB1 102 A8
Blackpool FY4 110 C7
Blackrod BL6 31 D3
Bolton-le-S LA5 221 A4
Carnforth LA5 221 E8
Chorley PR7 43 B6
Formby L37 11 D2
Fulwood PR2 118 C4
Lancaster LA1 218 E2
Maghull L31 5 E2
Morecambe LA4 217 C6
Coniston St 8 BB12 127 C6
Coniston Way
Bacup OL13 88 A4
Croston PR26 58 B3
Rainford WA11 8 F2
Rishton BB1 123 F1
Connaught Dr FY5 176 D2
Connaught Rd
Heysham LA3 212 D5
Lancaster LA1 215 B5
Connaught Rd *continued*
Preston PR1 96 E5
Consett Ave FY5 175 E5
Constable Ave
Bamber Bridge PR5 77 A7
Burnley BB11 127 F3
CONSTABLE LEE 86 B4
Constable Lee Cres BB4 86 A4
Constable St 8 PR1 97 A8
Convent Cl
Bamber Bridge PR5 97 D1
Leyland PR25 77 C2
Ormskirk L39 15 E2
Convent Cres FY3 131 A8
Conway Ave
Bamber Bridge PR5 97 A1
Blackburn BB1 101 E7
Cleveleys FY5 175 D2
Clitheroe BB7 166 C6
Leyland PR25 60 C8
Normoss FY3 131 B7
Conway Cl
Catterall PR3 181 D2
Euxton PR7 60 E1
Haslingden BB4 85 B1
Ramsbottom BL0 50 B6
Conway Cres
Barnoldswick BB18 196 C3
Ramsbottom BL8 49 F2
Conway Ct
Gregson Lane PR5 98 D2
4 Lytham St Anne's FY8 89 E6
Conway Dr
Bury BL9 33 D2
Fulwood PR2 117 C6
Oswaldtwistle BB5 103 B4
Conway Gr BB10 148 C3
Conway Ho 7 PR1 97 D8
Conway Rd
Eccleston PR7 41 C7
Rawtenstall BB4 86 C2
Conyers Ave PR8 34 F3
Cooke St BL6 32 D4
Cook Gdns BB1 102 B4
Cook Green La PR3 141 C7
Cook House Rd BB8 171 E6
Cookson Cl PR4 93 B6
Cookson Rd FY5 176 B3
Cookson St FY1 130 C5
Cook St BL9 33 A2
Cookwood Ho 13 PR1 96 D8
Coolham La BB18 197 D1
Coolidge Ave LA1 214 D7
Coombes The PR2 117 F5
Cooperage The BB5 103 D3
Co-operation St
2 Bacup OL13 88 A2
1 Newchurch BB4 86 F2
Rawtenstall, Cloughfold BB4 86 B2
4 Rawtenstall, Crawshawbooth BB4 86 A7
Co-operative Bldgs
5 Rawtenstall BB4 69 F7
Walk Mill BB10 107 F8
Co-operative St
1 Bamber Bridge PR5 77 E8
22 Barnoldswick BB18 196 B2
Haslingden BB4 67 F7
Cooper Ct FY5 175 D3
Cooper Hill Cl PR5 97 D5
Cooper Hill Dr PR5 97 D5
Cooperís La PR7 28 B8
Cooper Rd PR1 96 D8
Coopers Cl 5 BB5 103 D3
Coopers Fold PR2 119 A2
Cooper St
Bacup OL13 87 F4
Burnley BB11 128 A5
Horwich BL6 32 B4
Nelson BB9 170 E1
Cooper's Way FY1 130 D7
Coop St FY1 130 B3
Coote La PR4, PR5 76 F7
Copeland Dr WN6 29 F2
Copeland Pl FY8 91 C4
Cop La PR1 96 C4
Cop Lane CE Prim Sch PR1 96 C3
COPP 156 A3
Copperas La BL6 31 B1
Copper Beech Cl PR4 74 E3
Copper Beeches
Blackburn BB2 101 A6
Kingsfold PR1 96 D2
Copperfield Cl BB10 128 F6
Copperfield St BB1 101 F3
Copperwood Way PR7 42 F7
Coppice Ave BB5 104 D7
Coppice Brow LA5 223 F2
Coppice Cl
Chorley PR6 61 E1
Nelson BB9 171 A2
Coppice Dr
Longshaw WN5 10 D2
Whitworth OL12 52 D7
Coppice La PR6 62 C3
Coppice Leys L37 11 E3
Coppice Sch The PR5 97 F1
Coppice St BL9 33 C3
Coppice The
Blackburn BB2 101 A7
Burnley BB11 127 E4
Clayton-le-M BB5 124 F4
Fulwood PR2 117 B4
Kirkham PR4 114 A6
Longton PR4 75 A7
Coppice The *continued*
Morecambe LA4 217 E5
Ramsbottom BL0 50 A4
Coppingford Cl OL12 52 A2
Coppins Gn FY6 153 E1
Copp La PR3, PR4 156 A2
COPPULL 42 E2
Coppull Cross Rds PR7 29 F7
Coppull Ent Ctr PR7 42 E2
Coppull Hall La PR7 30 B8
COPPULL MOOR 29 D6
Coppull Moor La PR7 29 E6
Coppull Parish CE Prim Sch PR7 42 F1
Coppull Prim Sch PR7 42 E1
Coppull Rd
Chorley PR7 43 A4
Maghull L31 5 C4
Coppull St John's CE Prim Sch PR7 29 D6
Cop Royd Terr BB10 128 F1
Copse Cl BB1 101 F7
Copse Rd FY7 198 F2
Copse The
Accrington BB5 103 F5
Chapeltown BL7 48 C2
Chorley PR7 43 B4
Copse View Bsns Pk 12 FY7 198 F2
Copster Dr PR3 140 B7
COPSTER GREEN 122 D8
Copster Hill Cl BB1 82 D8
Cop The FY5 175 D6
Copthurst Ave BB12 146 F6
Copthurst La PR6 61 F7
Copthurst St 18 BB12 146 C1
Coptrod Head Cl OL12 52 E4
Copy Bottom BB10 108 C4
Copy La LA2 237 C3
Copy Nook BB1 102 A5
Coral Cl FY4 131 A1
Corbridge Cl
Blackpool FY4 111 A7
Carleton FY6 153 C5
Corbridge Ct BB7 189 E1
Corcas La FY6 176 F8
Cordwainers Ct PR7 60 E6
Coriander Cl FY2 152 F3
Corka La FY8 112 F1
Cork Rd LA1 215 B5
Cork St BL9 33 A2
Corlass St 10 BB9 170 D3
Corless Cotts LA2 226 A8
Cornbrook WN8 9 E7
Corncroft PR1 96 C3
Cornel Gr BB11 127 C4
Cornelian St BB1 122 F2
Cornelian Way FY3 131 A1
Corner Bank Cl PR4 112 F7
Cornerhouse The 13 BL0 50 C6
CORNER ROW 133 E2
Corners The FY5 175 C4
Cornfield PR4 116 E6
Cornfield Cl PR4 73 E4
Cornfield Gr BB12 127 A8
Cornfield St BB3 82 B2
Cornflower Cl PR6 61 D2
Cornford Rd FY4 111 B8
Cornhill Arc BB5 104 B6
CORNHOLME 109 B1
Cornholme BB10 148 E2
Cornholme Jun & Inf Sch OL14 109 A1
Cornholme Terr 7 OL14 109 B1
Cornmill Ct
Altham BB5 125 E6
Waddington BB7 189 B4
Corn Mill La FY7 199 B4
Corn Mill Lo L31 5 C2
Corn Mill Mews BB7 144 C5
Cornmill Pl BB18 196 B3
Cornmill Terr 6 BB18 196 B3
Corn Mill Yd BB5 124 F2
Corn Mkt LA1 214 F8
Cornthwaite Rd PR2 117 E3
Cornwall Ave
Blackburn BB1 102 E4
Blackpool FY2 152 C2
Buckshaw Village PR7 60 F6
Cleveleys FY5 175 F4
Cornwall Cres WN1 30 B1
Cornwall Mews 5 FY5 175 F4
Cornwall Pl
Blackpool FY3 131 B2
Church BB5 103 F7
Cornwall Rd BB1 124 A1
Cornwall Way PR8 21 C2
Corona Ave L31 5 C5
Coronation Ave
Blackburn BB2 80 C7
Formby L37 12 A2
Forton PR3 207 B3
Padiham BB12 126 C7
Coronation Cres 5 PR1 97 B7
Coronation Ct PR26 58 B3
Coronation Gr BB4 86 E1
Coronation Mount LA6 242 C3
Coronation Pl 6 BB9 170 D3
Coronation Rd
Brierfield BB9 148 C5
Cleveleys FY5 175 C2
Kirkham PR4 114 A5
Lytham St Anne's FY8 90 C4
Maghull L31 5 D3
Coronation St
Barnoldswick BB18 196 C2
Blackpool FY1 130 B4
Great Harwood BB6 124 D6
Coronation Terr BB6 143 C1
Coronation Way LA1 218 E4
Coronation Wlk PR8 35 A7
Coronet Cl WN6 19 C7
Corporation Ct 10 OL13 70 D8
Corporation St
Accrington BB5 104 A5
11 Blackburn BB2 101 E5
Blackpool FY1 130 B5
Chorley PR6 61 D1
6 Clitheroe BB7 166 D8
Colne BB8 171 A3
Preston PR1 96 F8
4 Southport PR8 35 B7
Corpus Christi RC Sports Coll PR2 117 E5
Corranstone Cl BL6 32 B3
Corrib Rd FY2 152 D2
Corringham Rd LA4 217 B5
Corston Gr BL6 31 D1
Corwen Cl BB1 101 E7
Cosford St PR4 132 E6
Cosgate Cl 1 WN5 10 E5
COTE HOLME 103 D6
Cotman Cl OL13 71 B8
Cotswold Ave PR7 60 D1
Cotswold Cl
Eccleston PR7 41 D6
Ramsbottom BL0 50 C4
Cotswold Dr BL6 32 C5
Cotswold Rd
Blackpool FY2 152 D1
Chorley PR7 43 C6
Lytham St Anne's FY8 91 D5
Cottage Cl L39 15 D4
Cottage Fields PR7 43 B5
Cottage Gdns PR5 78 B8
Cottage La
Bamber Bridge PR5 97 F3
Ormskirk L39 15 D5
Cottage Mews L39 15 E5
Cottage Mus* LA1 214 E8
Cottage View OL12 52 C7
Cottage Wlk OL12 52 C4
COTTAM 116 D5
Cottam Ave PR2 117 A4
Cottam Cl
Lytham St Anne's FY8 110 F2
Whalley BB7 144 C5
Cottam Ct PR2 117 A2
Cottam Gn PR4 116 F6
Cottam Hall La PR2 116 F5
Cottam La PR2 117 A2
Cottam Pl FY6 153 C2
Cottam Prim Sch PR4 116 D5
Cottam St PR7 43 C6
Cottam Way PR4 116 D4
Cottesloe Pl BB9 170 C3
Cottesmore Cl OL12 52 C6
Cottesmore Pl FY3 131 A6
Cotton Croft BB5 124 F4
Cotton Ct
2 Colne BB8 171 C3
Preston PR1 97 A8
Cotton Dr L39 15 D6
Cotton Hall St BB3 82 A2
Cotton Spinners Ct BB3 82 B1
Cotton St
Accrington BB5 104 B5
Burnley BB12 127 D7
Padiham BB12 126 C7
COTTON TREE 172 B4
Cotton Tree La BB8 172 A5
Cottys Brow PR9 53 F3
Coudray Rd PR9 53 E1
Coulston Ave FY2 152 B3
Coulston Rd LA1 215 B6
Coultate St 7 BB12 127 C6
Coulter Beck La LA6 242 A7
Coulthurst St 1 BL0 50 B6
Coulton Rd BB9 148 B7
Counsell Ct 3 FY5 176 B2
Countess Cl PR4 114 A7
Countess Cres FY2 152 C3
Countess Rd BB3 82 A7
Countess St BB5 104 A6
Countessway 3 PR5 97 E1
Countess Way PR7 60 D2
Country Mews BB2 100 F8
County Ave LA1 211 B8
County Brook La BB8, BB18 194 C4
County Cl PR26 77 A4
County Rd
Kirkby L33 1 A1
Ormskirk L39 15 E6
County St LA1 214 E8
Coupe Gn PR5 98 E4
COUPE GREEN 98 E4
Coupe Green Prim Sch PR5 98 E4
Coupland Cl OL12 52 C8
Courage Low La WN6 28 D5
Course La L40, WN8 26 D1
Courtfield L39 15 D7
Courtfield Ave FY2 130 D8
Courtfields 3 FY1 130 C4
Court Gr BB1 122 E6
Courtgreen L39 15 D7
Court Hey L31 5 E1
Court Mews PR9 54 A1

Court Rd PR9 35 C8
Court Royal FY8 90 E3
Court The
Fulwood PR2 117 C7
Higher Penwortham PR1 96 C4
Southport PR9 35 B8
Courtyard The
7 Bacup OL13 88 A3
11 Burnley BB11 128 B4
Cleveleys FY5 175 D1
1 Kirkham PR4 113 F5
Courtyard Works L33 1 C2
Cousin's La L40 39 A3
Cove Dr LA5 224 C4
Covell Ho 3 LA1 214 E8
Coventry St 2 PR7 43 C6
Cove Rd LA5 224 B4
Coverdale Dr BB2 80 D7
Coverdale Rd LA1 214 D8
Coverdale Way 4 BB12 127 D7
Covert Cl PR8 36 A2
Covertside Rd PR8 36 A2
Covert The FY5 175 F4
Cove The
Cleveleys FY5 175 C4
Lytham St Anne's FY8 90 D3
Morecambe LA4 217 E7
Coveway Ave FY3 130 E6
Cowan Brae BB1 101 D6
COWAN BRIDGE 242 A7
COW ARK 187 C8
Cowdrey Mews 8 LA1 218 B1
Cowell Way 8 BB2 101 D5
Cowes Ave 2 BB4 85 C2
Cowgarth La BB18 197 C2
Cow Gate La BD23 231 E7
Cowgill St
14 Bacup OL13 88 A3
Earby BB18 197 B1
COW HILL 119 A8
Cowhill La BB1 102 F7
Cow La BB11 127 F6
Cowley Cres BB12 126 E7
Cowley Rd
Blackpool FY4 110 F8
Fulwood PR2 118 E4
COWLING 43 F6
Cowling Brow PR6 43 E7
Cowling Brow Ind Est PR6 43 F6
Cowling Bsns Pk PR6 43 F6
Cowling La PR25 76 D1
Cowling Rd PR6 43 F6
Cowm Park Way N OL12 71 D2
Cowm Park Way S OL12 71 C1
Cowm St OL12 71 E5
COWPE 69 F6
Cowper Ave 1 BB7 189 E1
Cowpe Rd BB4 69 F7
Cowper Pl BB7 230 C1
Cowper St
Blackburn BB1 101 F7
Burnley BB11 127 C5
Cowslip Way PR6 61 D2
Cowtoot La OL13 88 A4
Cow Well La PR6 61 B8
Coxfield Gr WN6 19 D7
Cox Green Cl BL7 47 D3
Cox Green Rd BL7 47 E2
Coyford Dr PR9 54 A4
Crabtree Ave
Bacup OL13 88 A1
Higher Penwortham PR1 96 A3
Newchurch BB4 86 F2
Crabtree Bldgs BB4 86 F4
Crabtree Cl L40 25 D4
Crabtree La L40 25 D6
Crabtree Orch 3 FY5 176 B3
Crabtree Rd FY5 176 B3
Crabtree St
Blackburn BB1 102 B5
Brierfield BB9 148 B5
Colne BB8 171 C4
Whitewell Bottom BB4 86 F4
Cracoe Gill BB9 170 C3
Craddock Rd BB8 171 E5
Crag Ave BL9 50 D2
CRAG BANK 221 C8
Crag Bank Cres LA5 221 C8
Crag Bank La LA5 223 B1
Crag Bank Rd LA5 221 C8
CRAG FOOT 222 F8
Cragg Bottom Rd BD22 174 F1
Cragg Row BB18 194 D7
Craggs Hill LA6 237 B8
Craggs La LA2 239 D3
Cragg's Row 13 PR1 96 F8
Cragg St
1 Blackpool FY1 130 B3
Colne BB8 171 C5
Crag La BL9 50 D2
Crag Rd
Lancaster LA1 218 F1
Warton LA5 223 A6
Craigflower Ct PR5 78 C7
Craigholme House Pk LA5 223 B1
Craiglands Ave LA3 216 D2
Craiglands Ct LA1 214 C5
Craig St LA3 216 D3
Crail Pl OL10 33 F1
Crake Ave FY7 198 C2
Crake Bank 4 LA1 218 A2
Crambe Hts BB3 82 A7
Cranberry Bottoms BB3 65 E5
Cranberry Chase 4 BB3 65 C7
Cranberry Cl BB3 65 D6
CRANBERRY FOLD 65 D5
Cranberry Fold Ct BB3 65 D5
Cranberry La BB3 65 D6
Cranberry Rise BB4 106 A2
Cranborne Cl
Horwich BL6 32 F1
Standish WN6 29 D1
Cranborne St 10 PR1 97 C8
Cranborne Terr BB2 101 C6
Cranbourne Dr
Chorley PR6 43 E7
Church BB5 104 A8
Cranbourne Gr FY5 153 E7
Cranbourne St
7 Bamber Bridge PR5 77 E8
Chorley PR6 43 D7
Colne BB8 171 E6
Cranbrook Ave
Blackpool FY2 152 E5
Oswaldtwistle BB5 103 C4
Cranbrook St BB2 101 D2
Cranbury Ct FY5 175 D3
Cranesbill Cl FY6 199 F6
Cranes La L40 16 E7
Crane St PR7 29 D6
Cranfield View BB3 65 C6
Crangle Fold BB7 190 A2
Crank Rd WN5 10 D1
Crankshaw St 22 BB4 86 A3
Cranleigh Ave FY2 152 C3
Cranleigh Cl BL6 31 D1
Cranmer St 5 BB11 127 E6
Cranshaw Dr BB1 101 F8
Cranston Rd L33 1 C2
Cranwell Ave LA1 215 B5
Cranwell Cl 2 BB1 102 A4
Cranwell Ct PR4 113 F5
Craven Cl PR2 117 F7
Craven Cnr 8 FY5 152 F7
Craven Ct BL6 32 D2
Cravendale Ave BB9 170 F3
Craven Dr PR5 77 D7
Craven St E BL6 32 D2
Craven's Ave BB2 81 E7
Craven's Brow BB2 81 E7
Cravens Hollow BB2 81 D6
Cravens Hollows BB2 81 E6
Craven St
Accrington BB5 104 A5
6 Barnoldswick BB18 196 C2
Brierfield BB9 148 B5
Burnley BB11 128 A5
Bury BL9 33 C3
Clitheroe BB7 166 E7
Colne BB8 172 A5
Nelson BB9 148 C8
Rawtenstall BB4 85 F2
Cravenwood Cl BB5 103 F5
CRAWFORD 9 E2
Crawford Ave
Adlington PR7 30 E5
Blackpool FY2 152 D5
Chorley PR7 43 B7
Leyland PR25 60 B8
Maghull L31 5 B3
Preston PR1 118 F1
Crawford Rd WN8 9 D2
Crawford St BB9 170 E1
Crawford Village Prim Sch WN8 9 E3
CRAWSHAWBOOTH 86 A8
Crawshawbooth Prim Sch BB4 86 A8
Crawshaw Dr BB4 86 A6
Crawshaw Grange BB4 86 A7
Crawshaw La BB10 149 D6
Crawshaw's Bldgs BB4 86 A1
Crawshaw St 2 BB5 104 B6
Crediton Ave PR9 54 B5
Crediton Cl 5 BB2 81 C8
Crescent Ave
Cleveleys FY5 175 D2
Formby L37 11 E1
Crescent Ct FY4 110 A5
Crescent E FY5 175 D2
Crescent Gn L39 15 B1
Crescent Rd
Poulton-le-F FY6 153 E4
Southport PR8 34 F3
Crescent St PR1 118 C1
Crescent The
Bamber Bridge PR5 77 C8
Bamber Bridge, School Lane PR5 97 F2
Blackburn BB2 100 E1
Blackpool FY4 110 B7
Burnley BB10 148 B4
Carleton FY6 153 C4
Chorley PR7 61 C2
Clitheroe BB7 166 D7
Colne BB8 171 E6
Dunsop Bridge BB7 228 C5
Fleetwood FY7 175 E8
Freckleton PR4 93 C5
Hest Bank LA2 220 D1
Horwich BL6 32 E1
Lytham St Anne's FY8 89 E6
Preesall FY6 200 B4
Preesall Park FY6 200 D1
Preston, Ashton-on-R PR2 117 B2
Crescent The *continued*
1 Preston, Lea PR2 116 D1
Southport PR9 54 C3
Warton PR4 92 C4
Whalley BB7 144 A6
Whitworth OL12 52 C8
Worsthorne BB10 129 A5
Crescent W FY5 175 D2
Cressell Pk WN6 29 B1
Cresswood Ave FY5 175 D1
Crestway
Blackpool FY3 130 F6
Tarleton PR4 57 A8
Creswell Ave PR2 116 F3
Creswick Ave BB11 127 F3
Creswick Cl BB11 127 F3
Crewdson St BB3 81 F2
Crewgarth Rd LA3 217 B2
Cribden End La BB4 85 D4
Cribden La BB4 85 E5
CRIBDEN SIDE 85 C5
Cribden St BB4 85 F4
Criccieth Cl 3 BB4 85 B1
Criccieth Pl FY5 176 D2
Crichton Pl FY4 110 B5
Cricketers Cl BB5 103 C2
Cricketers Gn PR7 41 B6
Cricket Path
Formby L37 11 F5
Southport PR8 34 F3
Crimbles La LA2 206 B2
Crimea St 5 OL13 88 A2
Crime Well La LA3 212 E7
Crinan Sq OL10 33 F1
Cringle Way BB7 190 A2
Cripple Gate WN6 29 A2
Cripple Gate La PR5 99 C4
Critchley Cl PR4 74 F3
Croasdale 7 LA1 218 A2
Croasdale Ave
Burnley BB10 148 E2
Fulwood PR2 118 E4
Croasdale Cl LA5 223 C1
Croasdale Dr
Cleveleys FY5 175 F4
Clitheroe BB7 166 F7
Parbold WN8 27 C3
Croasdale Sq BB1 102 A3
Croasdale Wlk FY3 131 B8
Crockleford Ave PR8 35 E3
Crocus Cl BB4 67 F8
Crocus Field PR25 60 A7
CROFT 196 B2
Croft Acres BL0 68 D2
Croft Ave
Burscough L40 25 F3
Orrell WN5 10 D5
Slyne LA2 218 C8
Croft Bank PR1 96 C3
Croft Cl BB4 86 A5
Croft Ct
Fleetwood FY7 198 E2
Freckleton PR4 93 B6
Southport PR9 54 C4
Thornton FY5 176 C4
Crofters Bank BB4 106 A1
Crofters Fold
Galgate LA2 211 B4
Morecambe LA3 216 E1
Crofters Gn
Euxton PR7 60 C3
Preston PR1 117 E2
Crofters La L33 1 A5
Crofters Mdw PR26 76 E3
Crofters Mews 12 FY1 130 C7
Crofters Wlk
4 Kingsfold PR1 96 D2
Lytham St Anne's FY8 90 E7
Croft Field L31 5 E1
Croftgate PR2 117 F5
Croft Head Rd BB1 123 B1
Croft Hey L40 39 B4
Croft Heys L39 15 B1
Croft Ho FY6 153 D4
Croft La BB12 146 F6
Croftland Gdns LA5 221 B6
Croftlands
Borwick LA6 240 B3
12 Lancaster LA1 214 E8
Orrell WN5 10 D4
1 Ramsbottom BL0 50 A3
Warton LA5 223 E6
Croft Manor PR4 93 C6
Croft Mdw PR5 78 C6
Crofton Ave FY2 152 D5
Croft Pk PR25 77 D1
Croft Rd PR6 43 E7
Crofts Cl PR4 114 C5
Crofts Dr 7 PR2 139 D1
Croftson Ave L39 15 F7
Croft St
Bacup OL13 87 F3
Burnley BB11 128 A5
Bury BL9 33 A2
Clitheroe BB7 166 E7
18 Darwen BB3 82 A1
Earby BB18 197 C2
Great Harwood BB6 124 C4
Morecambe LA4 217 C5
Preston PR1 96 E8
Crofts The PR4 95 A1
Croft The
Blackburn BB1 101 D7
Burton in L LA6 242 C3
Caton LA2 237 C3
Cleveleys FY5 175 D2
Colne BB8 171 E7
Eccleston PR7 41 C7
Croft The *continued*
Euxton PR7 60 B3
Fleetwood FY7 198 E2
Garstang PR3 204 B1
Goosnargh PR3 138 D6
Great Plumpton PR4 112 E7
Hoghton PR5 99 B2
Lytham St Anne's FY8 111 B1
Maghull L31 5 B5
Orrell WN5 10 D3
Poulton-le-F FY6 153 D2
Thornton-in-C BD23 197 B5
Warton LA5 223 E6
Croft Way FY5 153 C8
Croftwood Terr BB2 101 A1
Croichbank BL8 49 B2
Croichley Fold BL8 49 D2
Cromarty Sq OL10 33 F1
Crombleholme Rd PR1 118 E1
Cromer Ave BB10 148 C1
Cromer Gr BB10 148 C1
Cromer Pl
Blackburn BB1 101 E7
Fulwood PR2 117 A4
Cromer Rd
Blackpool FY2 152 E4
Lytham St Anne's FY8 111 A1
Southport PR8 34 E2
Cromfield L39 15 C2
Cromford Wlk 9 PR1 97 C8
Crompton Ave FY4 110 E7
Crompton Ct 23 PR1 97 A8
Crompton Pl BB2 101 C5
Crompton St PR1 118 C1
Cromwell Ave 1 PR1 96 C3
Cromwell Cl L39 15 C2
Cromwell Mews PR3 181 C8
Cromwell Rd
Blackpool FY1 130 C7
Fulwood PR2 118 D3
Higher Penwortham PR1 96 C3
Lancaster LA1 214 E6
Cromwell St
Accrington BB5 104 B8
20 Blackburn BB1 102 A4
Burnley BB12 127 F8
Foulridge BB8 194 D1
4 Preston PR1 118 A1
Cromwell Terr 12 BB9 170 D3
Cromwell Way PR1 96 F1
Cronkeyshaw Ave OL12 52 E2
Cronkeyshaw Rd OL12 52 F1
Cronkshaw St BB10 128 A7
Cronshaw Dr BB6 143 C1
Crookall Cl 7 FY7 198 F2
Crook Dale La FY6 177 E7
Crooked La 19 PR1 97 A8
Crooked Shore OL13 87 F3
Crookfield Rd BL7 64 B3
Crook Gate La PR3 178 E1
Crookhalgh Ave BB10 128 F6
Crookhey Gdns LA2 206 E3
Crookhey Hall Sch LA2 206 E3
Crookings La PR1 96 A6
Crooklands Dr PR3 181 C8
Crooklands Gdns FY6 177 D2
Crookleigh Pl 3 LA3 216 D2
Crook Nook LA3 213 B2
Crook O'Lune Cvn Pk LA2 219 F5
Crook St
Adlington PR7 30 F7
Chorley PR7 43 B5
Preston PR1 97 B8
Cropper Gdns PR4 73 D3
Cropper Rd FY4 111 C6
Cropper Rd N FY4 111 C7
Cropper's La L39 16 A1
Cropton Rd L37 11 F3
Crosby Cl BB3 65 B6
Crosby Ct FY8 110 F1
Crosby Gr FY3 130 F3
Crosby Pl PR2 117 A4
Crosby Rd
Blackburn BB2 101 E1
Lytham St Anne's FY8 110 F1
Southport PR8 35 A3
Crosby St 1 OL12 52 F2
Crosfield Ave BL9 50 C2
Crosier Wlk PR4 116 E5
Crosland Rd L32 1 A1
Crosland Rd N FY8 90 A8
Crosland Rd S FY8 90 A8
Crosley Cl BB5 104 B3
Cross Bank 9 BB12 126 D8
Cross Barn Gr BB3 65 B8
Cross Barn La L38 3 E3
Cross Barn Wlk 5 BB3 65 B8
Cross Bldgs 19 BB4 86 A7
Cross Brow PR7 42 C8
Crossdale Ave 5 LA3 216 D2
Crossdale Sq 10 LA1 215 A8
Cross Edge BB5 104 A1
Crosse Hall La PR6 43 F7
Crosse Hall St PR6 43 F7
CROSSENS 54 C4
Crossens Way PR9 54 C6
Cross Field PR4 95 C1
Crossfield Rd WN8 9 C8
Crossfield St BB2 101 F3
Cross Flatts Cres BB18 194 E8
Cross Fold
Blackburn BB1 101 F2
Grindleton BB7 190 B8
Cross Gates BB6 124 C5
CROSSGILL 237 E1
Crossgill Pl 7 LA1 218 B2
Cross Gn L37 12 A2
Cross Green Cl L37 12 A2
Cross Green Rd PR2 117 E6
Cross Hagg St BB8 171 C4
Crosshall Brow L40 16 C4
Cross Hall Ct L39 16 A4
Cross Halls PR1 96 C3
Cross Helliwell St 17 BB8 171 D4
Cross Hill Ct LA5 221 A4
Cross Hill Four Lane Ends PR3 226 B6
Cross Hill La BB7 231 B1
Crosshill Rd BB2 101 B5
Crosshills 5 BB12 146 C1
Crosshill Specl Sch BB1 102 C2
Cross Hos PR7 42 C8
Crossings The PR5 99 B2
Cross Keys Dr PR6 61 C7
Cross La
Barley Green BB12 169 C4
Halsall L39 23 C1
Low Bentham LA2 239 B8
Orrell WN5 10 D3
Ramsbottom BL8 50 A6
Salterforth BB18 194 E8
Treales PR4 134 D1
Waddington BB7 188 E5
Crossland Rd FY4 130 E1
Crosslands LA6 241 D7
Crossland St BB5 104 A5
Crossley Fold BB11 127 D4
Crossley House Ind Est PR1 96 E4
Cross Meanygate L40 38 C5
CROSSMOOR 156 E1
Cross Rd LA2 239 B7
Cross St N BB4 85 B5
Cross St S BB4 85 B4
Cross St W BB8 171 B4
Cross School St 5 BB8 171 D4
Cross Skelton St 6 BB8 171 E5
Cross St
Accrington BB5 104 C5
11 Bacup OL13 88 A3
Blackburn BB3 81 F7
Blackpool FY1 130 B7
Brierfield BB9 148 B5
Burnley, Harle Syke BB10 148 F3
Chorley PR7 61 C1
Clayton-le-M BB5 124 E3
Clitheroe BB7 166 D8
Darwen BB3 65 B7
Earby BB18 197 A1
Fleetwood FY7 199 B5
Great Harwood BB6 124 D5
Higham BB12 146 F6
3 Leyland PR25 77 B2
Longridge PR3 140 A6
Lytham St Anne's FY8 89 D8
3 Morecambe LA4 217 C5
Nelson BB9 148 D8
Oswaldtwistle BB5 103 D4
Preston PR1 96 F7
Ramsbottom BL0 50 C6
18 Rawtenstall BB4 86 A7
Southport PR8 35 B6
Standish WN6 29 E1
Worsthorne BB10 129 B6
Cross Swords Cl PR7 43 A5
Cross The L38 3 E4
Cross Way FY5 175 D4
Crossways BB7 189 D7
CROSTON 58 B2
Croston Ave PR6 31 A8
Croston Barn La PR3 181 A8
Croston Cl 6 BB1 102 B5
Croston Close Rd BL9, OL12 51 C4
Croston Dr L40 39 B6
Croston La PR7 42 B2
Croston Rd
Croston L40, PR26 39 C7
Farington PR26 76 F6
Garstang PR3 181 B8
Leyland PR26 76 E4
Croston's Brow PR9 53 F3
Croston St BB1 102 C5
Croston Sta PR26 58 B3
Crowborough Cl BL6 32 F1
Crowder Ave FY5 176 B2
Crowell Way PR5 97 E3
Crow Foot Row BB18 196 B1
Crow Hills Rd PR1 96 A6
Crow La
Ramsbottom BL0 50 C6
Skelmersdale WN8 18 F3
Town End PR3 155 E8
Crowland Cl PR9 36 A6
Crowland St PR9 36 A6
Crowland Way L37 12 B2
Crowle St PR1 97 D8
Crown Bldgs PR8 21 F8
Crown Cl L37 12 A2
Crowndale BL7 48 D7
Crownest Ind Est BB18 196 C3
Crownest Rd BB18 196 C3
Crown Gdns BL7 48 D6
Crown La
Fleetwood FY7 199 B4
Horwich BL6 32 A4

Crown La *continued*
Swillbrook PR4 . . . . . . . . . 136 B2
Crownlee PR1 . . . . . . . . . . . 96 A3
Crown Mews 3 PR4 . . . . 114 A5
Crown Point BL7 . . . . . . . . 48 D6
Crown Point Rd BB11 . . . 127 E1
Crown St
Accrington BB5 . . . . . . . . . 104 A5
3 Chorley PR7 . . . . . . . . . . 43 C8
Darwen BB3 . . . . . . . . . . . . 65 A8
Leyland PR25 . . . . . . . . . . . 77 B3
Preston PR1 . . . . . . . . . . . . 96 F8
Crown Way BB8 . . . . . . . . 171 C5
Crow Orchard Prim Sch
WN8 . . . . . . . . . . . . . . . . . . 17 F2
Crow Orchard Rd WN6 . . . 29 A1
Crow Park La BB7 . . . . . . 231 C4
Crowshaw Dr OL12 . . . . . . . 52 E3
Crowther Ct BB10 . . . . . . . 129 B6
Crowther St
Burnley BB11 . . . . . . . . . . 128 B4
Clayton-le-M BB5 . . . . . . . 124 E3
Crowthorn Rd BL7 . . . . . . . 67 A1
Crow Tree Ave 4 OL13 . . . 70 B8
Crowtrees 3 LA2 . . . . . . . 239 B8
Crow Trees Brow BB7 . . . 190 D4
Crow Trees Gdns BB7 . . . 190 D5
Crowtrees Gr BB9 . . . . . . . 169 F5
Crow Trees La BL7 . . . . . . . 48 C7
Crowtrees Pk BD23 . . . . . 236 D2
Crowtrees Rd BB7 . . . . . . 145 F8
Crow Wood Ave BB12 . . . 127 D7
Crow Wood Ct BB12 . . . . . 127 E7
Crow Wood Rd BB4 . . . . . . 68 D6
Croxteth Cl L31 . . . . . . . . . . . 5 E3
Croxton Wlk 8 BL6 . . . . . . 32 B4
Croyde Cl PR9 . . . . . . . . . . . 54 B5
Croyde Rd FY8 . . . . . . . . . . 90 A5
Croydon Rd 5 FY3 . . . . . . 130 E7
Croydon St BB2 . . . . . . . . . 101 C5
Crummock Pl 2 FY4 . . . . 131 C1
Crummock Rd PR1 . . . . . . 119 A1
Crumpax Ave PR3 . . . . . . . 140 A8
Crumpax Croft PR3 . . . . . 140 A8
Crumpax Gdns PR3 . . . . . 140 A7
Crumpax Mdw PR3 . . . . . . 140 A8
Crystal Gr FY8 . . . . . . . . . . 89 E8
Crystal Lo 3 FY8 . . . . . . . . 90 C4
Crystal Mews FY1 . . . . . . . 130 B1
Crystal Rd
Blackpool FY1 . . . . . . . . . . 130 B1
Thornton FY5 . . . . . . . . . . 176 B5
Cuba Ind Est BL0 . . . . . . . . 50 C8
Cuba St 2 BB9 . . . . . . . . . . 148 D8
Cub St PR26 . . . . . . . . . . . . 77 A4
Cuckoo Brow BB1 . . . . . . . 101 D8
Cuckoo La
Bury, Heap Bridge BL9 . . . . 33 C2
Bury, Topping Fold BL9 . . . . 33 C3
Cuckstool La BB12 . . . . . . 147 E6
CUDDY HILL . . . . . . . . . . . 136 B7
Cudworth Rd FY8 . . . . . . . 110 F1
Cuerdale La PR5 . . . . . . . . . 98 D6
Cuerdale St BB10 . . . . . . . 148 E3
Cuerden Ave PR25 . . . . . . . 59 D7
Cuerden Church Sch
PR5 . . . . . . . . . . . . . . . . . . . 77 F8
Cuerden Cl PR5 . . . . . . . . . . 77 E4
CUERDEN GREEN . . . . . . . . . 77 C6
Cuerden Green Mills 7
PR5 . . . . . . . . . . . . . . . . . . . 77 B7
Cuerden Residential Cvn
Pk PR25 . . . . . . . . . . . . . . . 77 E3
Cuerden Rise PR5 . . . . . . . . 77 C7
Cuerden St
Chorley PR6 . . . . . . . . . . . . 43 E7
Colne BB8 . . . . . . . . . . . . . 171 B3
Cuerden Valley Pk★
PR5 . . . . . . . . . . . . . . . . . . . 77 F3
Cuerden Way PR5 . . . . . . . . 77 D7
Culbeck La PR7 . . . . . . . . . . 59 F2
Culshaw St
3 Blackburn BB1 . . . . . . . 102 A5
Burnley BB10 . . . . . . . . . . 128 C5
Culshaw Way L40 . . . . . . . . 23 F7
Culvert La WN8 . . . . . . . . . . 27 A2
Cumberland Ave
Blackpool FY1 . . . . . . . . . . 130 D4
Burnley BB12 . . . . . . . . . . 127 A6
Clayton-le-M BB5 . . . . . . . 125 A3
Cleveleys FY5 . . . . . . . . . . 175 E4
Leyland PR25 . . . . . . . . . . . 59 E7
Cumberland Cl BB3 . . . . . . 65 C6
Cumberland Rd PR8 . . . . . 35 D5
Cumberland St
12 Blackburn BB1 . . . . . . . 102 A4
5 Colne BB8 . . . . . . . . . . . 171 E5
Nelson BB9 . . . . . . . . . . . . 170 E1
Cumberland View 2
LA1 . . . . . . . . . . . . . . . . . . 215 A6
Cumberland View Cl
LA3 . . . . . . . . . . . . . . . . . . 216 D3
Cumberland View Rd
LA3 . . . . . . . . . . . . . . . . . . 216 D3
Cumbria Ct PR9 . . . . . . . . . . 35 C7
Cumbrian Ave FY3 . . . . . . 130 E7
Cumbrian Way BB12 . . . . 127 B8
Cumeragh La PR3 . . . . . . . 139 C6
CUMERAGH VILLAGE . . . . . 138 F6
Cummins Ave L37 . . . . . . . . 11 E5
Cunliffe Ave BL0 . . . . . . . . . 50 A4
Cunliffe Cl BB1 . . . . . . . . . 123 B1
Cunliffe Ct BB5 . . . . . . . . . 124 F2
Cunliffe Ho BB4 . . . . . . . . . 86 D1
Cunliffe La BB7 . . . . . . . . . 144 F8
Cunliffe Rd
Blackburn BB1 . . . . . . . . . . 123 C1
Blackpool FY1 . . . . . . . . . . 130 D2
Cunliffe St
Chorley PR7 . . . . . . . . . . . . . 43 D7
11 Preston PR1 . . . . . . . . . . 97 A8
Ramsbottom BL0 . . . . . . . . 50 C7
Cunnery Mdw PR25 . . . . . . 77 E1
Cunningham Ave PR7 . . . . 43 A6
Cunningham Ct LA1 . . . . . 214 E5
Cunningham Gr BB12 . . . 127 B6
Cunscough La L31, L39 . . . . 6 D3
Curate St
Chorley PR6 . . . . . . . . . . . . . 61 E1
Great Harwood BB6 . . . . . 124 C5
Curlew Cl
Blackburn BB1 . . . . . . . . . . 101 E8
2 Cleveleys FY5 . . . . . . . . 175 F4
Leyland PR25 . . . . . . . . . . . . 59 C7
Oswaldtwistle BB5 . . . . . . 103 D3
Curlew Gdns BB11 . . . . . . 127 C5
Curlew Gr LA3 . . . . . . . . . . 212 F5
Curlew La L40 . . . . . . . . . . . 38 E2
Curteis St BL6 . . . . . . . . . . . 32 B4
Curtis Dr 1 FY7 . . . . . . . . 198 D3
Curtis St 8 BB4 . . . . . . . . . 86 A3
Curven Edge BB4 . . . . . . . . 68 A7
Curve St OL13 . . . . . . . . . . . 87 F1
Curwen Ave LA3 . . . . . . . . 212 E6
Curwen La PR3 . . . . . . . . . 160 C2
Curwen St 7 PR1 . . . . . . . 118 C1
Curzon Pl BB2 . . . . . . . . . . 101 C3
Curzon Rd
Lytham St Anne's FY8 . . . . . 90 A7
Poulton-le-F FY6 . . . . . . . . 153 E3
Southport PR8 . . . . . . . . . . . 35 E5
Curzon St
10 Burnley BB11 . . . . . . . . 127 F6
1 Clitheroe BB7 . . . . . . . . 166 D7
Colne BB8 . . . . . . . . . . . . . 171 E4
Cusson Rd L33 . . . . . . . . . . . . 1 B1
Custom House La FY7 . . . 199 C5
Customs Way PR2 . . . . . . . 96 C8
Cutgate Rd OL12 . . . . . . . . . 52 B1
Cuthbert FY8 . . . . . . . . . . . . 90 E3
Cut La
Haskayne L39, L40 . . . . . . . 14 F6
Rishton BB1 . . . . . . . . . . . 123 F1
Rochdale OL12 . . . . . . . . . . 52 A1
Cutler Cl BB2 . . . . . . . . . . . 101 C5
Cutler Cres OL13 . . . . . . . . 70 D7
Cutler La
Bacup OL13 . . . . . . . . . . . . . 70 D7
Hesketh Lane PR3 . . . . . . 162 C8
Cutt Cl PR26 . . . . . . . . . . . . 58 F6
Cutts La FY6 . . . . . . . . . . . 177 F2
Cyclamen Cl PR25 . . . . . . . 77 E2
Cygnet Cl L39 . . . . . . . . . . . 15 C2
Cygnet Ct L33 . . . . . . . . . . . . 1 A2
Cypress Ave FY5 . . . . . . . 175 E2
Cypress Cl
Clayton-le-W PR25 . . . . . . . 77 E2
Fulwood PR2 . . . . . . . . . . . 119 A4
Cypress Gr
Bamber Bridge PR5 . . . . . . . 77 B8
7 Blackpool FY3 . . . . . . . . 130 D7
Cypress Rd PR8 . . . . . . . . . . 35 F6
Cypress Ridge BB2 . . . . . . . 80 F8
Cyprus Ave FY8 . . . . . . . . . . 90 B4
Cyprus Rd LA3 . . . . . . . . . 212 E7
Cyprus St BB3 . . . . . . . . . . . 65 B6

D

Dacre Way PR4 . . . . . . . . . 116 D5
Daffodil Cl
Haslingden BB4 . . . . . . . . . . 68 A8
Rochdale OL12 . . . . . . . . . . 52 E3
Dagger Rd PR4 . . . . . . . . . 115 C8
Daggers Hall La FY4 . . . . 110 E8
Daggers La FY6 . . . . . . . . . 200 B3
Dahlia Cl
Blackburn BB3 . . . . . . . . . . . 82 B7
Clayton-le-W PR25 . . . . . . . 77 E2
Rochdale OL12 . . . . . . . . . . 52 D3
Dailton Rd WN8 . . . . . . . . . . 10 A7
Daisy Bank
11 Bacup OL13 . . . . . . . . . . 87 F3
Lancaster LA1 . . . . . . . . . . 215 D7
6 Rawtenstall BB4 . . . . . . . 69 F7
Daisy Bank Cl PR25 . . . . . . 76 D1
Daisy Bank Cres BB10 . . . 128 E5
Daisy Bank St 2 OL14 . . . 109 B1
Daisy Croft PR2 . . . . . . . . . 95 D8
DAISYFIELD . . . . . . . . . . . 102 A6
Daisyfield 9 BL6 . . . . . . . . 32 D1
Daisyfield Mill BB1 . . . . . 102 A5
Daisyfield Prim Sch
BB1 . . . . . . . . . . . . . . . . . . 102 A6
Daisyfields PR4 . . . . . . . . 116 F7
Daisyfield St BB3 . . . . . . . . 81 E5
Daisy Fold PR6 . . . . . . . . . . 61 E2
DAISY HILL . . . . . . . . . . . . . 60 D1
Daisy Hill BB4 . . . . . . . . . . . 86 A3
Daisy Hill Ct BB5 . . . . . . . 125 E1
Daisy Hill Dr PR6 . . . . . . . . 31 A8
Daisy Hill Fold PR7 . . . . . . 60 D1
Daisy La
Blackburn BB1 . . . . . . . . . . 101 F6
Preston PR1 . . . . . . . . . . . 118 C3
Ring o'Bells L40 . . . . . . . . . 26 B4
Daisy Mdw PR5 . . . . . . . . . . 78 B5
Daisy St
Blackburn BB1 . . . . . . . . . . 102 A6
Colne BB8 . . . . . . . . . . . . . 171 D4
4 Lancaster LA1 . . . . . . . . 218 D3
Daisy Way PR8 . . . . . . . . . . 35 C2
Dalby Cl
Blackpool FY5 . . . . . . . . . . 152 F7
Preston PR1 . . . . . . . . . . . . 118 D3
Dalby Cres BB2 . . . . . . . . . 101 A1
Dalby Lea BB2 . . . . . . . . . . 101 A1
Dale Ave
1 Euxton PR7 . . . . . . . . . . . 60 D1
Longton PR4 . . . . . . . . . . . . 74 E8
Slyne LA2 . . . . . . . . . . . . . . 218 C8
Dale Cl
Burnley BB12 . . . . . . . . . . . 127 D6
Maghull L31 . . . . . . . . . . . . . . 5 C2
Parbold WN8 . . . . . . . . . . . . 27 B2
Dale Cres BB2 . . . . . . . . . . . 80 E7
Dalecrest WN5 . . . . . . . . . . 10 D1
Dale Dyke Wlk FY6 . . . . . . 153 B3
Daleford Cl FY5 . . . . . . . . 153 C8
Dalegarth Cl FY4 . . . . . . . . 131 C1
Dalehead Rd PR25 . . . . . . . 60 B7
Dale La L33 . . . . . . . . . . . . . . 1 B4
Dale Mill BB4 . . . . . . . . . . . . 86 F2
Dale St E BL6 . . . . . . . . . . . . 32 D2
Dale St W BL6 . . . . . . . . . . . 32 D2
Dales Ct FY4 . . . . . . . . . . . 110 D6
Dalesford BB4 . . . . . . . . . . . 85 B1
Dale St
Accrington BB5 . . . . . . . . . 104 A6
Bacup OL13 . . . . . . . . . . . . . 87 F3
8 Bacup, Stacksteads
OL13 . . . . . . . . . . . . . . . . . . 70 C8
Blackburn BB2 . . . . . . . . . . 101 D4
Blackpool FY1 . . . . . . . . . . 130 B3
Brierfield BB9 . . . . . . . . . . 148 A5
Burnley BB12 . . . . . . . . . . . 127 D6
Colne BB8 . . . . . . . . . . . . . 171 C5
Earby BB18 . . . . . . . . . . . . 197 B2
Haslingden BB4 . . . . . . . . . . 85 B3
Lancaster LA1 . . . . . . . . . . 215 A7
Nelson BB9 . . . . . . . . . . . . 148 C8
4 Oswaldtwistle BB5 . . . . 103 E4
Preston PR1 . . . . . . . . . . . . . 97 B8
Ramsbottom BL0 . . . . . . . . . 68 C1
Dales The BB6 . . . . . . . . . . 123 A8
Dale Street Mews 7
FY1 . . . . . . . . . . . . . . . . . . . 130 B3
Dalesview Cres LA3 . . . . . 212 F7
Dales View Pk Cvn Pk
BB18 . . . . . . . . . . . . . . . . . 194 B7
Dalesway BB9 . . . . . . . . . . 170 C3
Dales Wlk L37 . . . . . . . . . . . 12 A6
Dale Terr BB7 . . . . . . . . . . 190 D5
Dale View
Billington BB7 . . . . . . . . . . 144 B4
Blackburn BB2 . . . . . . . . . . . 81 E6
Chorley PR7 . . . . . . . . . . . . . 43 C4
Earby BB18 . . . . . . . . . . . . 197 A1
6 Rawtenstall BB4 . . . . . . . 85 F1
Dalewood Ave FY4 . . . . . . 130 E1
Dalglish Dr BB2 . . . . . . . . . 81 D7
Dalkeith Ave FY3 . . . . . . . 131 A2
Dalkeith Rd BB9 . . . . . . . . 148 C8
Dallam Ave LA4 . . . . . . . . . 217 C6
Dallam Dell FY5 . . . . . . . . 176 B4
Dallas Ct LA4 . . . . . . . . . . 217 F4
Dallas Rd
Lancaster LA1 . . . . . . . . . . 214 E7
5 Morecambe LA4 . . . . . . 217 F4
Dallas St PR1 . . . . . . . . . . . 117 E2
Dall St BB11 . . . . . . . . . . . 128 A4
Dalmore Rd PR2 . . . . . . . . 117 A3
DALTON
Burton-in-Kendal . . . . . . . . 240 D7
Skelmersdale . . . . . . . . . . . . 18 C5
Dalton Ave FY4 . . . . . . . . . 110 D5
Dalton Cl
Blackburn BB1 . . . . . . . . . . 102 B5
Ramsbottom BL0 . . . . . . . . . 50 A4
Dalton Ct BB3 . . . . . . . . . . . 81 F5
Dalton Hall Bsns Ctr
LA6 . . . . . . . . . . . . . . . . . . 240 C7
Dalton La LA6 . . . . . . . . . . 240 C7
Dalton Rd
Lancaster LA1 . . . . . . . . . . 215 A8
Morecambe LA3 . . . . . . . . . 216 D3
Dalton St Michael's CE
Prim Sch WN8 . . . . . . . . . . 18 D5
Dalton Sq LA1 . . . . . . . . . . 214 F8
Dalton St
Burnley BB11 . . . . . . . . . . . 127 D3
Lytham St Anne's FY8 . . . . . 89 D8
Nelson BB9 . . . . . . . . . . . . 170 E1
Dalweb Ind Pk PR9 . . . . . . 55 C3
Dame Fold
Higham BB12 . . . . . . . . . . . 146 F6
12 Padiham BB12 . . . . . . . 126 C8
Damfield La L31 . . . . . . . . . . 5 C1
Dam Head Rd BB18 . . . . . 196 B2
Dam La L40 . . . . . . . . . . . . . 24 C6
DAM SIDE . . . . . . . . . . . . . 201 D6
Dam Side
2 Barnoldswick BB18 . . . 196 B3
Colne BB8 . . . . . . . . . . . . . 171 D4
Damside Cotts LA2 . . . . . . 211 B5
Damside St LA1 . . . . . . . . . 214 F8
Damson Cl BB6 . . . . . . . . . 143 C6
Dam Top BB4 . . . . . . . . . . . . 86 B2
Dam Wood La L40 . . . . . . . 24 C5
Danbers WN8 . . . . . . . . . . . . 9 F6
Dancer La BB7 . . . . . . . . . . 231 B1
Dandy Row BB3 . . . . . . . . . . 82 C3
Dandy's Meanygate
PR4 . . . . . . . . . . . . . . . . . . . 56 A8
Dandy Wlk BB1 . . . . . . . . . 101 E4
Dane Mews FY6 . . . . . . . . . 131 E8
Danesbury Pl 4 FY1 . . . . 130 C5
Danes Cl PR4 . . . . . . . . . . . 114 C5
Danes Dr PR5 . . . . . . . . . . . . 97 D1
Daneshouse Rd BB10 . . . . 128 A8
Danesmoor Dr BL9 . . . . . . . 33 B4
Dane St BB10 . . . . . . . . . . . 128 A7
Danesway
Adlington PR7 . . . . . . . . . . . 43 F1
Bamber Bridge PR5 . . . . . . . 97 D1
Higher Penwortham PR1 . . . 96 A4
Daneswood Ave OL12 . . . . 52 C8
Daneswood Cl OL12 . . . . . . 52 C8
Daneswood Fold OL12 . . . . 52 C8
Daneway PR8 . . . . . . . . . . . . 21 B6
Danewerke St 9 PR1 . . . . 97 A8
DANGEROUS CORNER . . . . . 28 C2
Daniel Fold OL12 . . . . . . . . 52 B2
Daniel Fold La PR3 . . . . . . 181 D2
Daniell St BB1 . . . . . . . . . . 124 A2
Daniels La WN8 . . . . . . . . . . . 9 C7
Daniel St
10 Clayton-le-M BB5 . . . . . 124 F3
Whitworth OL12 . . . . . . . . . 71 D2
Daniel Street Ind Est
OL12 . . . . . . . . . . . . . . . . . . 71 D2
Danson Gdns 3 FY2 . . . . . 130 D8
Danvers St BB1 . . . . . . . . . 124 B2
Danvers Way PR2 . . . . . . . 118 C7
Daram Ho 3 FY1 . . . . . . . 130 D2
Darbishire Rd FY7 . . . . . . 198 F4
Daresbury Ave PR8 . . . . . . . 21 A5
Darfield WN8 . . . . . . . . . . . . . 9 F7
Darkinson La
Preston PR4 . . . . . . . . . . . . 116 B2
Salwick PR4 . . . . . . . . . . . . 115 F1
Dark La
Blackrod BL6 . . . . . . . . . . . . 31 B3
Earby BB18 . . . . . . . . . . . . 197 E2
Johnson's Hillock PR6 . . . . . 61 E6
Maghull L31 . . . . . . . . . . . . . . 5 E1
Mawdesley L40 . . . . . . . . . . . 40 E3
Newchurch BB4 . . . . . . . . . . 86 E1
Ormskirk L40 . . . . . . . . . . . . 16 C6
Darkwood Cres BB7 . . . . . 190 D5
Dark Wood La PR5 . . . . . . . 99 B6
Darley Ave FY4 . . . . . . . . . 110 E7
Darley Ct FY8 . . . . . . . . . . . 89 D7
Darley St BL6 . . . . . . . . . . . . 32 B5
Darlington St PR7 . . . . . . . . 42 E1
Darmond Rd L33 . . . . . . . . . . 1 A3
Darnbrook Rd BB18 . . . . . 196 A2
DARN HILL . . . . . . . . . . . . . 33 F2
Darnley St BB10 . . . . . . . . 128 C5
Dartford Cl 1 BB1 . . . . . . 102 A4
Dartmouth Cl PR4 . . . . . . 113 F5
Dart St PR2 . . . . . . . . . . . . . 96 C8
Darul-Uloom Islamic Coll
BL8 . . . . . . . . . . . . . . . . . . . 49 F4
DARWEN . . . . . . . . . . . . . . . 81 E2
Darwen Cl PR3 . . . . . . . . . 140 B7
Darwen Ent Ctr BB3 . . . . . . 82 A2
Darwen L Ctr BB3 . . . . . . . . 82 A1
Darwen Moorland High
Sch BB3 . . . . . . . . . . . . . . . 82 B3
Darwen Rd 3 BL7 . . . . . . . . 47 E1
Darwen St Barnabas CE
Prim Sch BB3 . . . . . . . . . . . 65 C6
Darwen St Peter's CE Prim
Sch BB3 . . . . . . . . . . . . . . . 65 B8
Darwen St
Blackburn BB2 . . . . . . . . . . 101 E4
Higher Walton PR5 . . . . . . . 98 B4
2 Padiham BB12 . . . . . . . 126 C8
Preston PR1 . . . . . . . . . . . . . 97 C7
Darwen Sta BB3 . . . . . . . . . . 82 A1
Darwen Vale High Sch
BB3 . . . . . . . . . . . . . . . . . . . 81 E5
Darwen View PR5 . . . . . . . . 97 E5
Darwin Ct PR9 . . . . . . . . . . . 53 E1
Darwin St BB10 . . . . . . . . . 148 A2
Daub Hall La PR5 . . . . . . . . 98 E3
Daub La L40 . . . . . . . . . . . . . 40 A1
Dauntesey Ave FY3 . . . . . . 131 A6
Davenham Rd
Darwen BB3 . . . . . . . . . . . . . 81 E3
Formby L37 . . . . . . . . . . . . . . 11 F3
Davenport Ave FY2 . . . . . . 152 C5
Daventry Ave FY2 . . . . . . . 152 B4
David Crosley Ho 2
BB18 . . . . . . . . . . . . . . . . . 196 B2
David St N 15 OL12 . . . . . . 52 F1
Davidson St 15 LA1 . . . . . 215 A8
David St
Bacup OL13 . . . . . . . . . . . . . 70 D8
11 Barrowford BB9 . . . . . . 170 D4
Burnley BB11 . . . . . . . . . . . 127 F4
16 Rochdale OL12 . . . . . . . 52 F1
Davies Rd BB1 . . . . . . . . . . 102 D6
Davis St PR3 . . . . . . . . . . . 140 A8
Davitt Cl 4 BB4 . . . . . . . . . 85 B3
Davy Field Brow BB1 . . . . . 82 B6
Davy Field Rd BB1 . . . . . . . 82 B6
Dawber Delph WN6 . . . . . . . 19 D8
Dawber's La PR7 . . . . . . . . 59 E2
Dawlish Ave FY3 . . . . . . . . 130 F8
Dawlish Cl BB2 . . . . . . . . . . 81 C8
Dawlish Dr PR9 . . . . . . . . . . 54 A5
Dawlish Lo FY8 . . . . . . . . . . 89 D7
Dawlish Pl PR2 . . . . . . . . . 117 A3
Dawnay Rd PR2 . . . . . . . . . 118 E3
Dawson Ave
Simonstone BB12 . . . . . . . 145 E2
Southport PR9 . . . . . . . . . . . 54 C5
Dawson Gdns L31 . . . . . . . . . 5 C2
Dawson La PR6, PR7 . . . . . . 60 E7
Dawson Pl PR5 . . . . . . . . . . . 78 A7
Dawson Rd
Lytham St Anne's FY8 . . . . 110 F1
Ormskirk L39 . . . . . . . . . . . . 15 F7
Dawson Sq BB11 . . . . . . . . 128 A7
Dawson St BL9 . . . . . . . . . . . 33 A4
Dawson Wlk PR1 . . . . . . . . 117 F1
Daybrook WN8 . . . . . . . . . . . . 9 F7
Dayfield WN8 . . . . . . . . . . . . 10 B7
Day St BB9 . . . . . . . . . . . . . 148 E7
Dayton Pl FY4 . . . . . . . . . . 110 C6
Deakins Bsns Pk BL7 . . . . . 47 D1
Deakins Mill Way BL7 . . . . . 47 D2
Deakin's Terr BL7 . . . . . . . . 46 C5
Deal Pl FY8 . . . . . . . . . . . . . 110 F1
Deal St 9 BL9 . . . . . . . . . . . 33 B2
DEAN . . . . . . . . . . . . . . . . . . 87 C8
Dean Brow PR3 . . . . . . . . . 141 F8
Dean Cl
Edenfield BL0 . . . . . . . . . . . . 68 D3
Up Holland WN8 . . . . . . . . . 10 C7
Deancroft Ave LA3 . . . . . . 216 E2
Dean Ct
Bamber Bridge PR5 . . . . . . . 97 E1
Fleetwood FY7 . . . . . . . . . . 175 D8
Dean Edge Rd BD22 . . . . . 174 F1
Deanfield BB7 . . . . . . . . . . 190 B2
Deanfield Ct BB7 . . . . . . . . 190 A2
Deanfield Dr BB7 . . . . . . . 190 B2
Deanfield Way BB7 . . . . . . 190 B2
Dean Fold BB4 . . . . . . . . . . . 87 A8
Dean Hall La PR7 . . . . . . . . 59 D2
Dean Head La BL6 . . . . . . . 45 A4
Dean La
Billington BB6, BB7 . . . . . . 144 C1
Samlesbury PR5 . . . . . . . . . 119 F3
Tockholes BB3 . . . . . . . . . . . 81 B1
Water BB4 . . . . . . . . . . . . . . 87 B8
Dean Mdw 5 BB7 . . . . . . . 166 D7
Dean Mill BB11 . . . . . . . . . 128 A5
Deanpoint LA3 . . . . . . . . . . 217 C3
Dean Rd
Haslingden, Helmcroft
BB4 . . . . . . . . . . . . . . . . . . . 85 B1
Haslingden, Helmshore
BB4 . . . . . . . . . . . . . . . . . . . 68 B8
Deans Ct L37 . . . . . . . . . . . . 11 F5
Deansgate
Blackpool FY1 . . . . . . . . . . 130 B5
Morecambe LA4 . . . . . . . . . 217 B5
Deansgate La L37 . . . . . . . . 12 B5
Deansgate La N L37 . . . . . . 12 A6
Deansgrave BB4 . . . . . . . . . 85 B1
Deansgreave Rd OL13 . . . . 71 B7
Deansgreave Terr OL13 . . 71 B7
Deans La L40, WN8 . . . . . . . 26 E3
Dean St
Bamber Bridge PR5 . . . . . . . 97 E1
Blackpool FY4 . . . . . . . . . . 110 B8
Burnley BB11 . . . . . . . . . . . 127 E6
Darwen BB3 . . . . . . . . . . . . . 81 F4
2 Padiham BB12 . . . . . . . 146 D1
Trawden BB8 . . . . . . . . . . . 172 C2
Dean Terr 4 PR4 . . . . . . . 114 A5
Dean Wood Ave WN5 . . . . 10 E8
Dean Wood Cl PR7 . . . . . . . 43 A6
Dearden Clough BL0 . . . . . 68 E2
Dearden Fold BL0 . . . . . . . . 68 E2
Deardengate BB4 . . . . . . . . 85 B3
Deardengate Croft 11
BB4 . . . . . . . . . . . . . . . . . . . 85 B3
Dearden Nook BB4 . . . . . . . 86 A1
Dearden Way WN8 . . . . . . . 10 A7
Deben Cl WN6 . . . . . . . . . . . 29 D1
Deborah Ave PR2 . . . . . . . 118 A7
Decimus Ct FY7 . . . . . . . . 199 C5
DEEPDALE . . . . . . . . . . . . . 118 A2
Deepdale Ave FY6 . . . . . . 153 B5
Deepdale Ct BB9 . . . . . . . . 170 C3
Deepdale Dr BB10 . . . . . . 148 C4
Deepdale Gn BB9 . . . . . . . 170 C3
Deepdale Ho 5 PR1 . . . . 118 B1
Deepdale Inf Sch PR1 . . . 118 B2
Deepdale Jun Sch
PR1 . . . . . . . . . . . . . . . . . . 118 B2
Deepdale La PR4 . . . . . . . 115 E3
Deepdale Mill PR1 . . . . . . 118 B1
Deepdale Mill St PR1 . . . 118 B1
Deepdale Rd
Blackpool FY4 . . . . . . . . . . 131 C1
Fleetwood FY7 . . . . . . . . . . 199 A3
Preston PR1 . . . . . . . . . . . 118 B2
Deepdale Sh Pk PR1 . . . . 118 C3
Deepdale St PR1 . . . . . . . . . 97 B8
Deeply Vale La BL9,
OL11 . . . . . . . . . . . . . . . . . . 51 C2
Deer Chace BB12 . . . . . . . 147 D8
Dee Rd LA1 . . . . . . . . . . . . 218 B2
Deerfold PR7 . . . . . . . . . . . . 61 B2
Deerhurst Rd FY5 . . . . . . . 152 E7
Deer Park La LA2 . . . . . . . 238 B7
Deer Park Rd BB10 . . . . . . 128 E4
Deer Pk BB5 . . . . . . . . . . . 104 E8
Deerplay Cl BB10 . . . . . . . 148 E2
Deerplay Ct OL13 . . . . . . . . 88 A8
Deerplay Dr OL13 . . . . . . . . 88 A8
Deer St 6 OL13 . . . . . . . . . . 88 A7
Deerstone Ave BB10 . . . . 128 C6
Deerstone Rd BB9 . . . . . . 149 B8
Deeside FY4 . . . . . . . . . . . . 110 E5
Dee St FY8 . . . . . . . . . . . . . . 89 E6
Deganwy Ave BB1 . . . . . . . 101 E7
De-Haviland Way WN8 . . . . 9 E8
Deighton Ave 6 PR25 . . . . 60 A8
Deighton Cl WN5 . . . . . . . . 10 E6
Deighton Rd PR7 . . . . . . . . . 43 B6
De Lacy Ho BB2 . . . . . . . . . 101 C5
De Lacy St
Clitheroe BB7 . . . . . . . . . . 166 D8
Preston PR2 . . . . . . . . . . . . 117 D2
Delamere Ave LA3 . . . . . . 212 E6
Delamere Cl
Accrington BB5 . . . . . . . . . 125 B1
Blackburn BB2 . . . . . . . . . . 101 B2

Delamere Pl PR6 43 D8
Delamere Rd
  Burnley BB10 148 F3
  Skelmersdale WN8 17 F2
  Southport PR8 21 B5
Delamere St BL9 33 A5
Delamere Way WN8 10 A7
Delany Dr PR4 93 A6
Delaware Rd 8 FY3 152 E1
Delaware St PR1 118 D1
Delfby Cres L32 1 A1
Delf La
  Haskayne L39 14 A4
  Todmorden OL14 109 D3
Delius Cl BB2 102 A1
Dellar Fold 20 OL12 52 C1
Dellar St 19 OL12 52 C1
Dellfield La L31 5 E1
Dell Gdns OL12 52 B2
Dell La 4 BB12 126 C4
Dell Mdw OL12 52 C5
Dell Rd OL12 52 B3
Dell Side Way OL12 52 C2
Dell The
  Appley Bridge WN6 19 D7
  Blackburn BB2 81 D6
  Fulwood PR2 117 D7
  Knowley PR6 62 A3
  Up Holland WN8 10 B7
  Wrea Green PR4 113 B3
Dellway The PR4 95 D2
Delma Rd BB10 128 E5
Delph App BB1 102 C4
Delph Ave BL7 47 D3
Delph Brook Way BL7 47 D2
Delph Cl
  Blackburn BB1 102 C4
  Ormskirk L39 15 C1
Delph Common Rd L39 15 C1
Delph Ct 3 BB6 124 C5
Delph Dr L40 25 F4
Delphene Ave FY5 152 D6
Delphinium Way BB3 82 A7
Delph La
  Blackburn, Queen's Park BB1 102 C4
  Blackburn, Shadsworth BB1 102 C3
  Charnock Green PR7 42 D6
  Coppull PR7 42 E5
  Formby L37 11 C3
  Garstang PR3 181 F8
  Oakenclough PR3 183 B7
  Ormskirk L39 15 C1
Delph Lane Est BB1 102 C4
Delph Mount
  Great Harwood BB6 124 B6
  Nelson BB9 148 D6
Delph Park Ave L39 15 B1
Delph Rd BB6 124 C5
Delphside Cl WN5 10 D5
Delph Side Com Prim Sch WN8 9 C8
Delphside Rd WN5 10 D5
Delph St
  Darwen BB3 82 B3
  Haslingden BB4 85 B4
Delph The WN8 27 C3
Delph Top L39 16 A6
Delph Way PR6 61 C7
Delta La 2 FY7 199 A4
Delta Park Ave PR4 73 E4
Delta Park Dr PR4 73 E4
Deltic Pl L33 1 B1
Deltic Way L33 1 B1
Delves La BB10 149 E7
Demming Cl PR2 95 C8
Denbigh Ave
  Cleveleys FY5 175 E1
  Southport PR9 53 F3
Denbigh Cl PR25 77 B1
Denbigh Dr BB7 189 F2
Denbigh Gr BB12 127 A7
Denby Cl PR5 97 C3
Denebank FY2 152 D5
Dene Bank Rd BB5 103 E3
Denefield Ho PR8 35 B6
Dene The
  Blackburn BB2 101 B7
  Hurst Green BB7 142 E8
Deneway Ave FY3 130 F6
Denford Ave
  Leyland PR25 60 B8
  Lytham St Anne's FY8 90 A4
Denham La PR6 78 E2
Denham Way FY7 198 F2
Denham Wood Cl PR7 42 F6
Denholme
  Skelmersdale WN8 9 F7
  1 Up Holland WN8 10 A7
Denholme Gr FY2 152 E5
Denis St LA1 215 A8
Denmark Rd
  Lytham St Anne's FY8 90 D4
  Southport PR9 54 A2
Denmark St LA1 214 D7
Dennis Gr 2 LA4 217 A4
Dennison Ind Est LA3 217 E2
Denny Ave LA1 218 C2
Denny Bank LA2 219 C5
Denny Beck La LA2 219 C5
Denshaw WN8 9 F7
Denstone Ave FY2 152 D4
Dent Dale BB5 104 D5
Dentdale Cl BB2 80 D7
Denton St
  Barnoldswick BB18 196 A3
  7 Rochdale OL12 52 F1
Dent Row 8 BB11 127 F5
Dent St BB8 171 B3
Denville Ave FY5 152 F8
Denville Rd
  Blackburn BB2 101 D5
  Preston PR1 118 C1
Denville St 5 BB2 101 D5
Depot Rd
  Blackpool FY3 152 E1
  Kirkby L33 1 D4
Derbe Rd FY8 89 F5
Derby Cl BB3 65 B5
Derby Cres PR4 135 C8
Derby Ct L37 11 E5
Derby Hill PR4 133 A1
Derby Hill Cres L39 16 A5
Derby Hill Rd L39 16 A5
Derby Ho
  Kirkham PR4 114 A6
  6 Lancaster LA1 218 D1
  2 Ormskirk L39 15 F5
Derby Pl PR6 31 A8
Derby Rd
  Blackpool FY1 130 B7
  Cleveleys FY5 175 C3
  Formby L37 11 E5
  Fulwood PR2 117 E3
  Garstang PR3 181 B7
  Kirkham PR4 114 A6
  Lancaster LA1 218 D1
  Longridge PR3 140 A7
  Lytham St Anne's FY8 90 C5
  Poulton-le-F FY6 153 D4
  Skelmersdale WN8 8 C8
  Southport PR9 35 C7
Derby St W L39 15 E5
Derbyshire Almshouses The BB2 101 B6
Derbyshire Ave PR3 181 B8
Derby Sq PR1 97 D8
Derby St
  Accrington BB5 104 C6
  Blackburn BB1 102 A6
  Brinscall PR6 63 A8
  Burnley BB11 127 F5
  Clitheroe BB7 166 F8
  Colne BB8 171 D5
  Horwich BL6 32 D1
  Leyland PR25 77 B2
  7 Morecambe LA4 217 A5
  Nelson BB9 170 E1
  Ormskirk L39 15 F5
  Preston PR1 97 A8
  Ramsbottom BL0 50 D6
  Rishton BB1 124 C1
Derek Rd PR6 78 C1
Derham St BB2 101 E3
Derry Rd PR2 118 E3
Dertern La LA5 221 A7
Derwent Ave
  Burnley BB10 148 A2
  Fleetwood FY7 198 D2
  Formby L37 11 D2
  Morecambe LA4 217 C5
  Padiham BB12 146 C2
  Southport PR9 53 F1
Derwent Cl
  Colne BB8 172 A6
  3 Darwen BB3 82 C1
  Freckleton PR4 93 A6
  Haslingden BB4 85 B4
  Horwich BL6 32 C2
  Knott End-on-S FY6 199 F6
  Maghull L31 5 F2
  Rishton BB1 123 F1
Derwent Cres BB7 166 C7
Derwent Ct LA1 218 A2
Derwent Dr
  Freckleton PR4 93 A6
  Longridge PR3 139 F5
Derwent Hall 3 PR1 117 E1
Derwent Ho 9 PR1 97 D8
Derwent Pl
  Blackpool FY5 152 D8
  Poulton-le-F FY6 153 D1
Derwent Rd
  Chorley PR7 43 B5
  Lancaster LA1 215 B8
  Lytham St Anne's FY8 111 A1
  Orrell WN5 10 F8
Derwent St
  6 Darwen BB3 81 F2
  11 Rochdale OL12 52 F1
Derwentwater Pl PR1 117 F2
Dever Ave PR25 76 D1
Devere Gdns FY8 89 E5
De Vitre Cotts LA1 214 E4
De Vitre St 7 LA1 218 E1
Devona Ave FY4 131 B1
Devon Ave
  Fleetwood FY7 198 E3
  Oswaldtwistle BB5 103 B6
  Up Holland WN8 10 B6
Devon Cl PR5 97 D3
Devon Cres BB4 68 B8
Devon Dr WN1 30 B1
Devon Farm Way L37 12 B3
Devon Gr BB12 127 A7
Devon Pl
  1 Church BB5 103 E5
  Lancaster LA1 215 A4
Devonport Cl PR5 97 E3
Devonport Ct BB2 101 C5
Devonport Rd BB2 101 C5
Devonport Way PR6 43 E8
Devon Rd BB1 102 C5
Devonshire Ave FY5 176 B2
Devonshire Ct
  9 Blackpool FY3 130 D7
  17 Chorley PR7 43 C8
Devonshire Dr
  Clayton-le-M BB5 125 A3
  Garstang PR3 181 B8
Devonshire Ho FY3 130 D6
Devonshire Mews FY5 176 B1
Devonshire Pl PR1 118 E1
Devonshire Prim Sch FY3 130 D6
Devonshire Rd
  Blackpool FY2 152 D2
  Burnley BB10 128 A8
  Chorley PR7 43 C7
  Fulwood PR2 118 A4
  Lytham St Anne's FY8 89 D7
  Morecambe LA3 216 F3
  Rishton BB1 124 A1
  Southport PR9 36 A8
Devonshire Sq FY3 130 D5
Devonshire Square Mews 5 FY3 130 D5
Devonshire St
  Accrington BB5 104 B7
  Lancaster LA1 214 F5
Devon St
  Blackpool FY4 130 D1
  Colne BB8 171 E6
  Darwen BB3 65 B6
Devron Mill BB6 124 D4
Dewan Ind Est BB4 68 B8
Dewberry Fields WN8 10 B7
Dew Forest PR3 181 D4
Dewhirst Rd OL12 52 F4
Dewhirst Way OL12 52 F4
Dewhurst Ave FY4 110 E8
Dewhurst Cl BB3 65 C6
Dewhurst Clough Rd BL7 47 D2
Dewhurst Ct BL7 47 D3
Dewhurst Ind Est PR2 117 D1
Dewhurst Rd BB6 142 F1
Dewhurst Row PR5 77 D7
Dewhurst St
  Blackburn BB1 102 A4
  Colne BB8 171 D3
  Darwen BB3 65 B6
  Preston PR2 117 D1
Dew Meadow Cl OL12 52 E2
Dexter Way WN8 10 B6
Deycroft Ave L33 1 A4
Deycroft Wlk L33 1 A4
Deyes Ct L31 5 E1
Deyes End L31 5 E1
Deyes High Sch L31 5 D1
Deyes La
  Maghull L31 5 D1
  Maghull, Moss Side L31 5 F1
Diamond Jubilee Rd L40 39 C4
Diana Ct 10 LA1 214 F7
Dianne Rd FY5 176 D2
Dibbs Pocket PR4 93 D7
Dib Rd PR4 73 B5
Dicconson's La L39 14 D4
Dicconson Terr 13 FY8 91 B3
Dicconson Way L39 16 A5
Dickens Ave BB18 196 A3
Dickens Ct BB6 143 C6
Dickensons Field 3 PR1 96 E2
Dickens Rd PR7 29 E8
Dickens St BB1 102 A3
Dicket's Brow L40 16 F3
Dicket's La L40, WN8 17 A2
Dickie's La FY4 111 B7
Dickie's La S FY4 111 C6
Dickinson Cl
  Blackburn BB2 101 C3
  Formby L37 11 F2
Dickinson Ct
  1 Horwich BL6 32 B4
  Southport PR8 35 A2
Dickinson Rd L37 11 F2
Dickinson St W BL6 32 B4
Dick La PR6 62 E7
Dick's La L40 16 F4
Dickson Ave PR1 118 D2
Dickson Hey PR4 75 F8
Dickson Rd FY1 130 B7
Dickson St W BL6 32 B4
Dickson St
  Burnley BB12 127 C6
  Colne BB8 171 E6
  8 Preston PR1 97 B7
Didsbury St BB1 102 C5
Digham Ave FY5 152 D6
DIGMOOR 9 D6
Digmoor Dr WN8 9 C7
Digmoor Rd WN8 9 D6
DILL HALL 104 A8
Dill Hall La BB5 103 F7
Dilworth Bottoms PR3 141 A8
Dilworth Ct PR3 140 C7
Dilworth La PR3 140 C7
Dimmock St BB2 101 C2
Dimple Pk BL7 47 D3
Dimple Rd BL7 47 C4
Dimples La PR3 181 E5
DINCKLEY 142 F4
Dinckley Gr FY1 130 D3
Dinckley Sq BB2 101 B6
Dinely St BB5 103 F6
Dingle Ave
  Appley Bridge WN6 19 E8
Dingle Ave *continued*
  Blackpool FY3 130 F8
  Up Holland WN8 10 C8
Dingle Cl L39 15 C1
Dingle Rd WN8 10 B7
Dingle The
  Fulwood PR2 117 D7
  Knowley PR6 62 A3
Dinmore Ave FY3 131 A8
Dinmore Pl FY3 131 A7
Dinorwic Rd PR8 35 A2
Dirty Leech OL12 52 F6
Disraeli St BB10 148 A2
Ditchfield L37 12 A2
Division La FY4 111 C3
Dixey St BL6 32 A3
Dixon Rd
  Kirkby L33 1 B1
  Longridge PR3 140 B7
Dixon's Farm Mews PR4 115 D1
Dixons La PR2 139 C2
Dixon St
  Barrowford BB9 170 C3
  Blackburn BB2 101 C4
  Horwich BL6 32 B3
DOALS 87 F7
Doals Farm OL13 87 F7
Doals Gate OL13 88 A8
Dobbin Cl BB4 86 C2
Dobbin Ct BB4 86 C2
Dobbin La BB4 86 C2
Dob Brow PR7 42 F4
Dobbs Dr L37 12 A4
Dob La PR4 75 A4
Dobs La LA2 209 E3
Dobson Ave FY8 89 E8
Dobson Cl WN6 28 E2
Dobson Rd FY3 131 B7
Dobson's La FY6 177 E6
Dobson St 2 BB3 81 F2
Dock Ave FY7 199 A2
DOCKER 241 A5
Docker La LA6 241 C5
Docker Park Farm* LA6 241 A4
Dockinsall La PR3 178 D3
Dockray Ct 2 BB8 171 E5
Dockray St BB8 171 E5
Dockray Yd 4 BB8 171 E5
Dock Rd FY8 91 D4
Dock St
  Blackburn BB1 102 A5
  Fleetwood FY7 199 B4
Docky Pool La FY4 111 A6
Doctor's La
  Eccleston PR7 41 B6
  Great Altcar L37 12 E2
  Sollom PR4 56 F3
Doctors Row PR3 140 A6
Dodd's La L31 5 D2
Dodd Way PR5 78 A6
Dodgeons Cl FY6 153 C2
Dodgson La BB18 197 F2
Dodgson Pl PR1 118 C1
Dodgson Rd PR1 118 C1
Dodney Dr PR2 116 C1
Dodworth Ave PR8 35 E5
Doeholme Rake LA2 232 F1
Doe Mdw WN8 27 A1
Dog Pits La OL13 88 A6
Dole La
  Abbey Village PR6 80 C1
  Chorley PR7 43 C8
Doles La PR26 58 A7
Dolls House & Fleetwood Mus The* FY7 199 C5
Dolly's La PR9 36 D8
DOLPHINHOLME 226 A8
Dolphinholme CE Prim Sch LA2 226 A8
Dolphinholme Mill LA2 226 A8
Dombey St BB1 102 A4
Dominica Ave BB3 81 F6
Dominion Ct BB11 127 B4
Dominion Rd BB2 101 C8
Doncaster Rd FY3 131 A3
Donnington Lo PR8 34 F6
Donnington Rd
  Carleton FY6 153 C6
  Lytham St Anne's FY8 89 F7
Donshort Mews 2 BB9 170 C1
Don St FY8 89 E7
Doodstone Ave PR5 97 B1
Doodstone Cl PR5 97 B1
Doodstone Dr PR5 97 B1
Doodstone Nook PR5 97 B1
Dora St BL0 50 A4
Dorchester Ave
  Bamber Bridge PR5 97 B2
  Oswaldtwistle BB5 103 C4
Dorchester Cl
  Blackburn BB1 102 B3
  Thornton FY5 153 C8
Dorchester Dr L33 1 A5
Dorchester Gdns LA3 217 C2
Dorchester Rd
  Blackpool FY1 130 B8
  Garstang PR3 181 B8
  Up Holland WN8 10 A7
Doric Gn WN5 10 D3
Doris Henderson Way LA1 217 F1
Doris St
  Burnley BB11 128 B7
  Chorley PR6 61 D1
Dorking Rd PR6 61 F4
Dorman Cl 1 PR2 117 C2
Dorman Rd PR2 118 E3
Dorothy Ave 11 PR25 77 A1
Dorothy St
  1 Blackburn BB2 81 C8
  13 Ramsbottom BL0 50 B5
Dorrington Rd LA1 214 F5
Dorritt Rd FY4 110 E6
Dorritt St 19 BB1 102 A4
Dorset Ave
  3 Bamber Bridge PR5 97 D3
  Cleveleys FY5 175 D4
  Darwen BB3 81 F3
  Padiham BB12 126 D7
  Southport PR8 21 C2
Dorset Dr
  Blackburn BB1 102 E4
  Clitheroe BB7 189 F2
  Haslingden BB4 68 A8
Dorset Rd
  Lytham St Anne's FY8 89 F8
  Preston PR1 118 A1
  Rishton BB1 124 A1
  Standish WN1 30 B1
Dorset St
  10 Blackpool FY4 130 D1
  Burnley BB12 127 A6
Dotcliffe Rd BB18 195 A6
Double Row 1 BB12 126 B8
Doughty St BB8 171 D4
Douglas Ave
  Becconsall PR4 73 F1
  Blackpool FY3 130 D7
  Heysham LA3 212 F7
  Horwich BL6 32 C5
  Stalmine FY6 177 C7
  Up Holland WN8 10 B7
Douglas Cl
  Bamber Bridge PR5 77 F7
  Blackburn BB2 81 D7
  Horwich BL6 32 C5
  Rufford L40 39 C3
Douglas Ct
  2 Fulwood PR2 117 D3
  Southport PR8 21 C5
Douglas Dr
  Freckleton PR4 93 B6
  Heysham LA3 212 F7
  Maghull L31 5 F2
  Ormskirk L39 15 D7
  Orrell WN5 10 F7
  Shevington WN6 19 F5
Douglas Gr BB3 81 D4
Douglas Hall 4 PR1 117 E1
Douglas Ho PR7 43 D5
Douglas La PR2 139 D1
Douglas Leatham Ho 3 FY1 130 D1
Douglas Mill WN6 30 A3
Douglas Pl
  Blackburn BB1 122 F1
  Fleetwood FY7 198 D3
Douglas Rd
  Bacup OL13 88 A1
  Burnley BB10 149 A3
  Fulwood PR2 117 D3
  Shevington Moor WN6 29 B2
  Southport PR9 54 C4
Douglas Rd N PR2 117 D3
Douglas Sq 4 OL10 33 F1
Douglas St
  Colne BB8 171 E6
  Lytham St Anne's FY8 89 D6
  Preston PR2 96 C8
  Ramsbottom BL0 50 B6
Douglas View
  Adlington PR7 31 A6
  Hesketh Bank PR4 73 E4
Douglas Way BB10 149 A3
Doultons The PR5 97 C3
Dove Ave 2 PR1 96 E4
Dove Cl FY5 175 F1
Dovecote PR6 78 A3
Dovedale Ave
  Blackpool FY3 131 C2
  Fulwood PR2 117 A5
  Maghull L31 5 C2
  Thornton FY5 176 B3
Dovedale Cl
  Burnley BB10 148 C4
  Fulwood PR2 117 A4
  Leyland PR25 60 A6
Dovedale Dr
  Burnley BB12 127 C8
  Standish WN6 29 E2
Dovedale Gdns PR3 140 B6
Dove Dr BL9 33 B4
Dove La BB3 81 E1
Dover Cl
  Blackburn BB1 102 C4
  Ramsbottom BL8 50 A1
  Warton PR4 92 E7
Dover Ct FY1 130 D2
Dover Gdns FY6 153 B5
Dover La PR5, PR6 79 C8
Dover Rd
  Blackpool FY1 130 E2
  Lytham St Anne's FY8 89 F8
  Southport PR8 34 F2
Dover St
  Accrington BB5 104 A4
  Blackburn BB3 81 F7
  Nelson BB9 170 E1
Dove St
  Lytham St Anne's FY8 89 D6
  Preston PR1 118 B1
Dovestone Dr FY6 153 B3

Dovetree Cl PR5 97 A3
Dove Tree Ct FY4 131 B1
Dove Villas OL13 70 B7
DOWBRIDGE 114 D4
Dowbridge PR4 114 C4
Dowbridge Way PR4 114 C5
Downes Gr LA4 217 D4
Downeyfield Rd LA3 213 C3
Downfield Cl BL0 50 B6
DOWNHAM 191 B5
Downham Ave
Great Harwood BB6 124 F6
Rawtenstall BB4 86 A4
Downham Cotts 7 LA2 211 A4
Downham Dr BB5 104 A3
Downham Gr BB10 128 D5
Downham Pl
Lytham St Anne's FY8 90 C6
3 Preston PR2 116 E2
Downham Rd
Chatburn BB7 190 E5
Leyland PR25 76 D1
Downham St BB2 101 C4
Downham Wlk WN5 10 D1
DOWNHOLLAND CROSS 14 A2
Downholland-Haskayne CE Prim Sch L39 13 E3
Downholland Moss La L37 12 C4
Downing Ct PR3 137 C3
Downing St PR1 97 E8
Downley Cl OL12 52 B2
Downs The FY6 153 D4
Dowry St BB5 104 C6
Dragon Cl WN8 9 E8
Dragon St 8 BB12 126 C8
Drake Cl
Lytham St Anne's FY8 110 E1
Ormskirk L39 15 C2
Drakelowe Ave FY4 110 F6
Drakes Croft PR2 117 C3
Drakes Hollow PR5 97 D4
Drammen Ave BB11 127 B5
Draperfield PR7 43 A4
Drapers Ave PR7 41 C6
Draw Well Rd L33 1 D2
Draycombe Ct 4 LA3 216 D2
Draycombe Dr LA3 216 E2
Draycot Ave FY3 130 F8
Drayton Rd LA3 213 A7
Drewitt Cres PR9 54 D4
Drew St BB11 127 B5
Drewton Ave 2 LA3 216 D2
DRINK HOUSE 58 A1
Drinkhouse La PR26 58 A1
Drinkhouse Rd PR26 58 B1
Driscoll St 1 PR1 97 B8
Driver St 16 BB4 86 A7
Drive The
Bacup OL13 87 F2
Brockhall Village BB6 143 C5
Crag Bank LA5 223 B1
Edenfield BL0 68 D3
Fulwood PR2 118 B4
Hest Bank LA2 220 E1
Heysham LA3 212 F7
Longton PR4 75 A8
Walton-le-D PR5 97 F5
Driving Gate BB4 106 A1
Dronsfield Rd FY7 198 F4
Drovers Way
Burton-in-K LA6 240 B7
Lytham St Anne's FY8 90 E7
Drovers Wlk LA3 212 F7
Druids Cl BL7 47 D3
Drumacre La E PR4 75 D6
Drumacre La W PR4 75 A6
Drumhead Rd PR6 61 D2
DRUMMERSDALE 24 C7
Drummersdale La L40 24 D7
Drummond Ave FY3 130 E7
Dry Bread La PR3 178 C2
Dryburgh Ave FY3 130 F3
Dryden Gr BB6 124 C4
Dryden Rd FY7 199 A4
Dryden St
6 Clayton-le-M BB5 124 F3
Padiham BB12 126 E7
Dryfield La BL6 32 A5
Duchess Ct FY2 152 B3
Duchess Dr FY2 152 B3
Duchess St BB3 81 F7
Duchy Ave PR2 118 B4
Ducie Pl PR1 118 F1
Ducie St BL0 50 B7
Ducketts La PR3 159 B8
Duckett St 3 BB11 127 E6
Duckshaw Rd BB3 64 F6
Duck St
2 Clitheroe BB7 166 F8
Smallwood Hey PR3 201 A7
Wray LA2 238 D6
Duckworth Cl PR3 181 D3
Duckworth Dr PR3 181 D3
Duckworth Hall BB5 103 A2
Duckworth Hall Brow BB5 103 A1
Duckworth Hill La BB5 103 B1
Duckworth La
Rawtenstall BB4 68 E8
Tarleton PR4 56 F8
Duckworth St
Barrowford BB9 170 D2
Blackburn BB2 101 D3
3 Bury BL9 33 A4
Duckworth St *continued*
Church BB5 103 E6
Darwen BB3 81 F2
Duddle La PR5 97 D2
Duddon Ave
Darwen BB3 81 E3
Fleetwood FY7 198 D2
Maghull L31 5 F2
Duddon Cl LA3 217 F3
Dudley Ave
Blackpool FY2 152 D1
Oswaldtwistle BB5 103 C4
Dudley Cl PR4 95 A1
Dudley Pl PR2 116 F2
Dudley St
Brierfield BB9 148 C5
Colne BB8 171 F5
Morecambe LA4 217 C4
Duerden St BB9 148 D7
Duffins Cl OL12 52 D3
Dugdale Ct FY4 110 F5
Dugdale La BB7, BD23 235 F1
Dugdale Rd BB12 127 C7
Dugdales Cl FY4 111 E7
Dugdale St BB11 128 A5
Duke Ave PR8 35 C4
Duke of Sussex St BB2 81 B8
Duke St Prim Sch PR7 43 C6
Dukes Brow
Blackburn BB2 101 C6
Great Harwood BB6 124 B5
Dukes Ct BB2 101 B6
Dukes Dr BB3 82 F1
Dukes Mdw PR2 117 A5
Duke St
Bamber Bridge PR5 77 E7
Blackburn BB2 101 D5
Blackpool FY1 130 B1
Burnley BB10 148 F3
Burton in L LA6 242 C3
Chorley PR7 43 C6
Clayton-le-M BB5 125 A2
Colne BB8 171 D4
Colne, Cotton Tree BB8 172 B5
Formby L37 11 F2
Great Harwood BB6 124 B5
Heysham LA3 212 E7
High Bentham LA2 239 D8
Lancaster LA1 218 C1
Oswaldtwistle BB5 103 D3
Preston PR1 97 B7
Ramsbottom BL0 50 A4
Rawtenstall BB4 69 E8
Rochdale OL12 52 F1
Southport PR8 35 B5
Dukes Way L37 11 F2
Duke's Wood La WN8 9 D3
Dulas Gn L32 1 A1
Dulas Rd L32 1 A1
Dumbarton Cl 2 FY4 111 A6
Dumbarton Rd LA1 215 A7
Dumb Tom's La LA2, LA6 242 E1
Dumfries Cl FY2 152 F5
Dunald Mill La LA2, LA6 237 B6
Dunbar Cl FY4 111 A6
Dunbar Cres PR8 21 F8
Dunbar Dr
Fulwood PR2 117 D4
2 Heysham LA3 212 E7
Dunbar Rd
Fulwood PR2 116 F3
Southport PR8 34 F1
Duncan Ave FY2 152 C6
Duncan Cl
Brownside BB10 128 F5
Lytham St Anne's FY8 110 D1
Duncan Pl FY7 198 E4
Duncan St
Burnley BB12 127 A5
Horwich BL6 32 C3
DUNCOMBE 158 F3
Duncombe Terr PR3 159 A4
Duncroft Cl BB7 189 E2
Dundas St BB8 171 C4
Dundee Cl OL10 33 F1
Dundee Dr BB1 102 A4
Dundee La BL0 50 B6
Dundee St LA1 215 A7
Dunderdale Ave BB9 148 C7
Dunderdale St PR3 140 B7
Dundonald St PR1 97 D8
Dundonnell Rd BB9 171 A1
Dunedin Rd BL8 49 F2
Dunelt Ct 2 FY1 130 C2
Dunelt Rd FY1 130 D2
Dune Point FY8 110 B2
Dunes Ave FY4 110 B5
Dunes Dr L37 11 C4
Dunes Ho FY8 89 F5
Dungeon La WN8 18 C7
Dunham Dr PR6 61 C6
Dunkeld St 5 LA1 215 A7
Dunkenhalgh Way
Church BB5 103 E7
Clayton-le-M BB5 124 E1
Dunkenshaw Cres LA1 215 B2
Dunkirk Ave
Carnforth LA5 221 E8
Fulwood PR2 117 C3
Dunkirk La
Leyland PR26 59 C8
New Longton PR26 76 A1
Dunkirk Mews PR25 59 D8
Dunkirk Rd PR8 34 F2
Dunlin Ave LA3 212 F5
Dunlin Cl FY5 176 A5
Dunlin Dr FY8 90 E7
Dunlop Ave PR8 21 C2
Dunmail Ave 1 FY3 130 F2
Dunmore St PR1 97 B8
Dunnock La PR4 116 E4
DUNNOCKSHAW 106 B4
Dunnockshaw Community Woodland Trail* BB11 106 E6
DUNNYSHOP 103 E3
Dunny Shop Ave BB5 104 A4
Dunoon Cl PR2 116 F4
Dunoon Dr BB1 102 D3
Dunoon St BB11 127 D5
Dunrobin Dr PR7 60 D1
Dunscar Dr PR6 61 E1
DUNSOP BRIDGE 228 C5
Dunsop Cl
3 Bamber Bridge PR5 77 F8
1 Blackpool FY1 130 D1
Dunsop Ct 2 FY1 130 D1
Dunsop Gdns LA3 217 F2
Dunsop Rd PR2 118 D4
Dunsop St BB1 101 F7
Dunster Ave BB5 103 C5
Dunster Gr BB7 166 C6
Dunster Rd PR8 21 E8
Dunvegan Cl 3 FY4 111 A6
Durban Ct FY5 175 C4
Durban Gr BB11 127 E4
Durham Ave
Burnley BB12 127 B7
Cleveleys FY5 175 E3
Lancaster LA1 215 A4
Lytham St Anne's FY8 89 E7
Durham Cl
Blackburn BB1 101 F4
Leyland PR25 59 E7
4 Morecambe LA3 217 B2
Durham Dr
Buckshaw Village PR7 60 E6
Oswaldtwistle BB5 103 F3
Ramsbottom BL0 50 B3
Wilpshire BB1 122 F6
Durham Gr 1 PR3 181 B7
Durham Rd
Blackpool FY1 130 D5
Darwen BB3 81 F2
Wilpshire BB1 122 F7
Durham St
Accrington BB5 104 D7
Skelmersdale WN8 17 D2
Durley Rd FY1 130 D2
Durn St OL14 109 A1
D'urton La PR2, PR3 137 F1
Dutch Barn Cl PR7 61 B2
Dutton Brook Ho PR3 141 D3
Dutton Ct 1 FY3 130 D5
Duttonfield Cl PR26 76 E3
Dutton Lee Cotts PR3 142 A7
Dutton Rd FY3 130 D5
Dutton St 15 BB5 104 C6
Duttons Way BB1 102 D1
Duxbury Cl L31 5 E3
Duxbury Dr BL9 33 C2
Duxbury Hall Rd PR7 43 E3
Duxbury Ho 8 PR6 43 D7
Duxbury Jubilee Pk* PR7 43 D3
Duxbury St
Darwen BB3 65 B6
Earby BB18 197 C2
Dyers La L39 15 E4
Dyer St PR4 113 F5
Dyke La PR3 201 A3
Dyke Nook BB7 166 F6
Dykes La LA5 225 F2
Dymock Rd PR1 118 D1
Dymock Rd N PR1 118 D1
Dyneley Ave BB10 128 F4
Dyneley Rd BB1 102 C7
Dyson St BB2 101 E2

## E

Eachill Gdns BB1 103 B8
Eachill Rd BB1 124 B1
Eager La L31 5 B8
EAGLAND HILL 179 C7
Eagle Brow Cl FY5 176 B4
Eagle St
Accrington BB5 104 B5
Blackburn BB1 102 C4
2 Nelson BB9 170 F1
Oswaldtwistle BB5 103 C2
Eagles The FY6 153 E5
Eagleton Way PR1 97 A2
Eagley Bank OL12 71 E6
Eagley Rd BB9 148 C6
Ealand Chase BL6 31 F3
Ealing Gr PR6 61 F3
Eamont Ave PR9 54 B5
Eamont Pl FY7 198 D2
Eanam BB1 101 F5
Eanam Old Rd BB1 101 F5
EARBY 197 A2
Earby Lead Mining Mus* BB18 197 B2
Earby Rd BB18 194 F8
Earby Springfield Prim Sch BB18 197 C1
EARCROFT 81 E6
Earcroft Way BB3 81 E5
Eardley Rd LA3 212 E8
Earhart Cl WN8 9 E8
Earlesdon Ave BB18 196 F1
Earlham St BB18 197 C2
Earl Rd BL0 50 B6
Earls Ave PR5 77 E8
Earls Dr BB3 82 E1
Earl St
Barnoldswick BB18 196 C2
Blackburn BB1 101 E6
Burnley BB10 128 B8
Clayton-le-M BB5 124 F2
Colne BB8 171 D4
Great Harwood BB6 124 B5
Lancaster LA1 218 D1
11 Nelson BB9 170 F1
Preston PR1 96 F8
Ramsbottom BL0 50 D6
Earlsway FY3 131 D5
Earls Way PR7 60 D2
Earlswood WN8 18 E1
Earnsdale Ave BB3 81 D2
Earnsdale Cl BB3 81 E2
Earnsdale Rd BB3 81 E3
Earnshaw Ave OL12 52 E3
EARNSHAW BRIDGE 76 E2
Earnshaw Dr PR25 76 D1
Earnshaw Rd OL13 87 F3
Earnshaw Row 18 OL13 87 F3
Easby Cl L37 12 A2
Easdale Ave LA4 217 E5
Easedale Cl
Burnley BB12 127 B8
Hest Bank LA5 220 F2
Easedale Dr PR8 21 B4
EASINGTON 229 B5
Easington LA1 218 A2
Easington Cres FY3 131 B8
East Ave BB18 196 B2
East Bank
2 Barrowford BB9 170 D4
Water BB4 107 A1
Eastbank Ave FY4 111 A7
East Bank Ave BB4 85 B2
East Bank Rd FY8 89 E5
Eastbank St PR8 35 B6
Eastbank Street Sq 9 PR8 35 B7
East Beach FY8 91 C3
East Boothroyden FY1 130 B8
Eastbourne Cl PR2 116 F5
Eastbourne Rd
Blackpool FY4 110 B6
Southport PR8 35 A3
East Cecil St FY8 91 A3
East Chorley Business Ctr 3 PR6 43 D8
Eastcliff LA2 237 F5
East Cliff PR1 96 F6
East Cliffe FY8 91 C3
East Cliff Rd PR1 96 F6
Eastcott Cl BB2 82 A8
East Cres BB5 104 B8
East Croft BB9 171 B2
East Ct FY5 175 D5
East Dene WN8 27 B2
East End St 1 BB8 171 C4
Eastern Ave BB10 148 C1
Eastfield Dr
Longton PR4 95 A1
West Bradford BB7 189 F6
Eastgate
Accrington BB5 104 C6
Fulwood PR2 117 E4
Morecambe LA3 217 E2
Ribchester PR3 141 E4
Whitworth OL12 52 C7
East Gate BB4 85 B3
East Gate Cl FY8 110 C4
EAST GILLIBRANDS 9 A8
Eastham Hall Cvn Pk FY8 91 E6
Eastham Pl BB11 128 B6
Eastham St
Burnley BB10 128 B5
Clitheroe BB7 189 E1
Lancaster LA1 215 A7
Preston PR1 117 E1
East Hills St 21 BB18 196 B2
East Holme FY8 91 C4
East La L29 4 B2
East Lancashire Rd BB1 122 F3
East Lancashire Rly* BL0 50 C5
Eastlands
Heysham LA3 213 A7
Leyland PR26 59 C7
East Leigh WN8 18 D1
East Lodge Pl BB10 128 E1
East Mead
Blackpool FY3 130 F3
Ormskirk L39 15 B2
East Meade L31 5 C2
Eastmoor Dr BB7 166 F7
East Mount WN5 10 F6
Easton Cl PR2 118 D6
East Par
19 Barnoldswick BB18 196 B2
17 Rawtenstall BB4 86 A3
East Park Ave
Blackburn BB1 101 D7
Darwen BB3 64 F8
East Park Ct BB1 101 D6
East Park Dr FY3 131 A5
East Park Rd BB1 101 D6
EAST PIMBO 9 E5
Eastpines Dr FY5 152 F8
East Rd
Fulwood PR2 118 A3
Lancaster LA1 215 A8
Maghull L31 5 F1
East Rd *continued*
Thornton FY5 176 D3
Eastside FY4 110 F8
East Sq PR4 95 A1
East St
Bamber Bridge PR5 77 E7
Blackburn BB2 101 C3
Blackburn, Feniscowles BB2 80 D8
Brierfield BB9 148 C5
Edenfield BL0 68 D4
Farington PR25 77 B2
Hapton BB12 126 C4
Haslingden BB4 68 A7
Leyland PR25 77 B1
Morecambe LA3 216 E4
10 Nelson BB9 170 D1
Padiham BB12 146 C1
13 Preston PR1 97 A8
Rawtenstall BB4 85 F5
Southport PR9 35 D7
East Terr PR7 60 D4
East Topping St 3 FY1 130 B5
East View
Bacup OL13 87 F2
3 Bamber Bridge PR5 77 A7
Fulwood PR2 118 F5
9 Galgate LA2 211 A4
Grimsargh PR2 139 B1
Grindleton BB7 190 B7
4 Low Bentham LA2 239 B8
Pendleton BB7 167 B4
9 Preston, Frenchwood PR5 97 C6
Preston PR1 97 A8
Ramsbottom BL0 50 C3
Ramsbottom, Chatterton BL0 68 C1
Read BB12 145 D2
Rising Bridge BB5 85 A8
Trawden BB8 172 C2
Whitworth OL12 71 D2
Winmarleigh PR3 203 F6
East View Ct LA1 218 B3
East View Terr
Abbey Village PR6 80 B3
14 Barnoldswick BB18 196 B2
East Ward Com Prim Sch BL9 33 B2
Eastway
Freckleton PR4 93 A6
Fulwood PR2 118 B6
Maghull L31 5 E1
East Way PR6 43 D8
Eastway Bsns Village PR2 118 B8
East Wlk BL7 47 D2
Eastwood Ave
Blackpool FY3 130 E8
2 Fleetwood FY7 198 F3
Eastwood Cl BL9 33 B2
Eastwood Cres BB4 86 C2
Eastwood Ct 11 BL9 33 B2
Eastwood Rd PR25 76 F1
Eastwood St
Barnoldswick BB18 196 C3
2 Blackburn BB1 102 A6
Rawtenstall BB4 86 C2
Eastwood Terr BB18 196 C3
Eaton Ave
Blackpool FY1 130 C1
Leyland PR7 60 D7
Eaton Ct FY8 89 F6
Eaton Pl PR4 113 F5
Eaton Way FY6 131 E8
Eaves Ave BB11 127 D2
Eaves Cl BB5 125 F1
Eavesdale WN8 9 E8
Eaves Green La PR3 138 F8
Eaves Green Rd PR7 43 B5
Eavesham Cl PR1 97 A1
Eaves La
Chorley PR6 43 E8
Cuddy Hill PR4 136 D7
Fulwood PR2 117 E3
Eaves Rd FY8 111 A1
Eaves St FY1 130 B7
Eaveswood Cl PR5 97 E1
Ebenezer Terr BB7 144 B4
Ebony St 11 BB1 102 A7
Ebor Lo PR8 35 A5
Ebor St BB10 148 B2
Ecclesgate Rd FY4 111 A5
Eccleshill Cotts BB3 82 C4
Eccleshill Gdns BB3 82 C4
Eccleshill Rd BB3 81 F6
Eccleshill St 1 BB12 126 C8
Eccles La L40 27 B7
Eccles Rd L37 11 D1
Eccles St
Accrington BB5 104 B7
Blackburn BB2 101 E3
Preston PR1 118 C1
Ramsbottom BL0 50 B6
ECCLESTON 41 C6
Eccleston Prim Sch PR7 41 B6
Eccleston Rd FY1 130 D1
Eckersley Cl BB2 81 D8
Eckroyd Cl BB9 148 D6
Eclipse Rd BB2 80 D8
Ecroyd Rd PR2 117 C2
Ecroyd St
Leyland PR25 77 A1

**Ecroyd St** *continued*
Nelson BB9 ... 148 C8
**Edale Ave** 1 BB4 ... 85 C2
**Edale Cl** PR25 ... 60 A7
**Edale Ct** PR1 ... 117 F1
**Edale Dr** WN6 ... 29 E2
**Eddington Rd** FY8 ... 90 B4
**Eddleston Cl** FY3 ... 131 D5
**Edelston Rd** 5 FY1 ... 130 C6
**Eden Ave**
Edenfield BL0 ... 68 D3
Fleetwood FY7 ... 198 D2
Lytham St Anne's FY8 ... 90 E3
Morecambe LA4 ... 217 F5
Southport PR9 ... 53 F2
**Eden Cl** BB9 ... 170 D4
**Eden Ct** BL0 ... 68 D2
**EDENFIELD** ... 68 D3
**Edenfield**
Lytham St Anne's FY8 ... 90 E3
Much Hoole PR4 ... 74 F4
**Edenfield Ave** FY6 ... 153 F2
**Edenfield CE Prim Sch**
BL0 ... 68 D4
**Edenfield Cl** PR8 ... 35 E3
**Edenfield Rd**
Ramsbottom OL11,
OL12 ... 51 E4
Rochdale OL12 ... 52 A1
**Edenfield St** OL11, OL12 ... 52 C1
**Eden Gdns** PR3 ... 140 B8
**Eden Gr** LA5 ... 221 B6
**Eden Hall** PR1 ... 117 E1
**Edenhurst**
Haslingden BB4 ... 68 D8
Skelmersdale WN8 ... 9 E8
**Edenhurst Cl** L37 ... 11 C2
**Edenhurst Dr** L37 ... 11 C2
**Eden Mount Way** LA5 ... 223 F2
**Eden Pk**
Blackburn BB2 ... 101 A8
Lancaster LA1 ... 214 F4
**Edensor Terr** BB3 ... 81 F2
**Eden St**
Accrington BB5 ... 104 A5
Blackburn BB1 ... 102 A5
9 Blackpool FY1 ... 130 C6
Edenfield BL0 ... 68 D2
Leyland PR25 ... 60 A8
**Edenvale Ave** FY2 ... 152 B4
**Edenvale Cres** LA1 ... 218 C3
**Edenvale Rd** LA1 ... 218 C3
**Edenway** PR2 ... 117 D7
**Edgar St W** 17 BL0 ... 50 B5
**Edgar St**
Accrington BB5 ... 104 B6
Huncoat BB5 ... 125 E2
Nelson BB9 ... 170 F2
16 Ramsbottom BL0 ... 50 B5
**Edgecott Cl** LA3 ... 213 A7
**EDGE END** ... 124 B6
**Edge End** BB6 ... 124 B5
**Edge End Ave** BB9 ... 148 D6
**Edge End La**
Burnley BB9 ... 148 D6
Great Harwood BB6 ... 124 B6
**Edge End Rd** BB6 ... 124 B5
**Edge End Terr** BB2 ... 80 B3
**Edgefield** PR7 ... 61 B2
**Edgefield Ct** FY3 ... 131 B8
**Edge Gate La** PR6 ... 63 A6
**Edge Hall Rd** WN5 ... 10 E5
**Edgehill Cl** PR2 ... 117 D4
**Edge Hill Coll** PR7 ... 43 A8
**Edgehill Cres** PR25 ... 76 E2
**Edgehill Dr** PR2 ... 117 D4
**Edge Hill Univ** L39 ... 16 A3
**Edge La**
Barnoldswick BB18 ... 231 F1
Britannia OL13 ... 71 C8
Entwistle BL7 ... 48 A8
Rawtenstall BB4 ... 86 D3
**Edgeley Ct** 1 BB12 ... 127 D7
**Edgemoor Cl** OL12 ... 71 E5
**EDGESIDE** ... 86 F2
**Edgeside** BB6 ... 124 B5
**Edgeside La** BB4 ... 86 F2
**Edgeware Rd** BB2 ... 101 C6
**Edgeway Pl** 3 FY5 ... 176 C1
**Edgeway Rd** FY4 ... 110 E5
**Edge Yate La** BB4 ... 86 B5
**Edgley Ct** PR4 ... 95 E2
**Edgley Dr** L39 ... 16 A5
**EDGWORTH** ... 48 D6
**Edgworth Gr** BB10 ... 128 C6
**Edgworth Vale** BL7 ... 48 E6
**Edgworth Views** BL7 ... 48 D8
**Edinburgh Cl** PR25 ... 77 C1
**Edinburgh Dr** BB5 ... 103 F3
**Edinburgh Rd**
Formby L37 ... 11 E1
Haslingden BB4 ... 84 F1
**Edisford Prim Sch**
BB7 ... 166 C7
**Edisford Rd**
Clitheroe BB7 ... 166 C8
Waddington BB7 ... 189 B4
**Edison St** BB3 ... 81 F1
**Edith St**
Barnoldswick BB18 ... 196 B3
Blackburn BB1 ... 102 A4
Nelson BB9 ... 148 F8
Shuttleworth BL0 ... 50 E8
**Edleston Lo** 2 PR2 ... 118 F4
**Edleston St** BB5 ... 103 F4
**Edmondsen Pl** 4 FY7 ... 198 F2
**Edmondson's La** BD23 ... 197 F8
**Edmondson St** BB18 ... 196 B3
**Edmonton Dr** BB2 ... 101 A8
**Edmonton Pl** FY2 ... 152 F3
**Edmund Gennings Ct**
BB7 ... 190 D5
**Edmundson St**
Blackburn BB2 ... 101 C5
Church BB5 ... 103 E6
**Edmund St**
5 Accrington BB5 ... 104 C5
Blackburn BB2 ... 81 D7
Burnley BB10 ... 148 B1
Darwen BB3 ... 82 B1
3 Preston PR1 ... 97 B8
**Edward Cl** PR4 ... 57 A5
**Edward Ct** BB5 ... 103 E6
**Edward Sq** 10 PR1 ... 118 A1
**Edward St**
Accrington BB5 ... 104 E1
18 Bacup OL13 ... 88 A3
Bamber Bridge PR5 ... 77 E8
Barnoldswick BB18 ... 196 C3
Blackpool FY1 ... 130 B5
Burnley BB11 ... 128 A6
3 Carnforth LA5 ... 223 D2
Chorley PR6 ... 43 D7
Church BB5 ... 103 E6
Darwen BB3 ... 82 A2
8 Earby BB18 ... 197 B2
7 Great Harwood BB6 ... 124 C5
Haslingden BB4 ... 85 B6
Horwich BL6 ... 32 A3
Lancaster LA1 ... 215 A8
2 Leyland PR25 ... 60 A8
Lytham St Anne's FY8 ... 89 F7
Morecambe LA4 ... 217 A5
Nelson BB9 ... 170 F2
Preston PR1 ... 96 F8
Rawtenstall BB4 ... 86 A8
Rishton BB1 ... 124 B1
Thornton FY5 ... 176 B4
Walton-le-D PR5 ... 97 C5
Whitworth OL12 ... 71 D2
**Edward VII Quay** PR2 ... 96 B7
**Edwell Ave** FY4 ... 110 D8
**Edwinstowe Rd** FY8 ... 90 D6
**Edwin Waugh Gdns**
OL12 ... 52 D3
**Egan St** PR1 ... 97 A8
**Egbert St** PR1 ... 118 A1
**EGERTON** ... 47 E2
**Egerton** WN8 ... 9 D8
**Egerton Gr** PR7 ... 43 B6
**Egerton Lo** BL7 ... 47 E1
**Egerton Prim Sch** BL7 ... 47 D3
**Egerton Rd**
Belmont BL7 ... 46 E4
Blackpool FY1 ... 130 B7
Leyland PR25 ... 76 F2
Preston PR2 ... 117 B1
**Egerton Vale** BL7 ... 47 D2
**Egremont Ave** FY5 ... 175 D5
**Egypt Mount** BB4 ... 85 D2
**Egypt Terr** 3 BB4 ... 85 E2
**Eider Cl** FY5 ... 175 F5
**Eidsforth La** PR3 ... 226 A1
**Eidsforth Rd** LA4 ... 217 B6
**Eight Acre Ave** BB7 ... 145 F8
**Eight Acre La**
Formby L37 ... 12 B6
Preesall PR3 ... 200 F6
Yealand Redmayne LA5 ... 225 E4
**Eildon Dr** FY6 ... 153 D1
**Elaine Ave** FY4 ... 130 F1
**Eland Way** PR4 ... 114 B2
**Elbow La** L37 ... 11 F3
**Elbow St** PR7 ... 43 C7
**Elbut La** BL9 ... 33 F5
**Elcho St** PR1 ... 118 A2
**Elder Ave** L40 ... 25 F4
**Elderberry Cl** FY5 ... 175 F5
**Elderbrook Cl** PR4 ... 73 E4
**Elder Cl**
Clayton Green PR6 ... 78 C2
Fulwood PR2 ... 118 D6
Warton PR4 ... 92 E6
**Elder Ct** 2 BB5 ... 104 E8
**Elder St** BB9 ... 170 F2
**Elderwood Ave** FY5 ... 153 B7
**Eldon Ct** FY8 ... 89 F7
**Eldon Gr** LA3 ... 212 F7
**Eldon Ho** PR6 ... 43 D7
**Eldon Prim Sch** PR1 ... 117 E2
**Eldon Rd** BB1 ... 101 D7
**Eldons Croft** PR8 ... 21 D5
**Eldon St**
Chorley PR6 ... 43 D7
Preston PR1, PR2 ... 117 D2
**Eldwick St** BB10 ... 148 C1
**Eleanor St**
Blackburn BB1 ... 101 F5
3 Nelson BB9 ... 170 E1
**Electricity St** BB5 ... 104 B6
**Elgar Cl** BB2 ... 102 A2
**Elgin Cres** BB11 ... 127 D4
**Elgin Pl** FY3 ... 131 A7
**Elgin St**
4 Lancaster LA1 ... 215 A7
Preston PR1 ... 118 A2
**Elijah St** 4 PR1 ... 97 D8
**Elim Ct** 4 FY8 ... 91 C3
**Elim Gdns** BB2 ... 101 C1
**Elim Pl** BB2 ... 101 C1
**Elim View** BB10 ... 148 D2
**Elizabeth Ave** PR8 ... 21 E6
**Elizabeth Cl** FY3 ... 131 D5
**Elizabeth Ct**
Blackpool FY3 ... 130 D6
9 Lancaster LA1 ... 214 F7
Poulton-le-F FY6 ... 153 D3
**Elizabeth Dr** BB4 ... 68 A8
**Elizabeth Ho** BB3 ... 82 B1
**Elizabeth Sq** 8 PR1 ... 118 A1
**Elizabeth St**
Accrington BB5 ... 103 F5
Blackburn BB1 ... 101 F5
Blackpool FY1 ... 130 C6
Burnley BB11 ... 128 A5
Edenfield BL0 ... 68 D3
9 Fleetwood FY7 ... 199 B5
Nelson BB9 ... 170 E1
Padiham BB12 ... 126 C7
Preston PR1 ... 96 F8
Whitewell Bottom BB4 ... 86 F4
**Eliza St**
Burnley BB10 ... 128 B5
Ramsbottom BL0 ... 50 D6
**Elker Cotts** BB7 ... 143 F4
**Elker La** BB7 ... 143 F5
**Elker Mews** BB7 ... 143 F3
**Elkfield Dr** FY3 ... 153 A1
**Elkin Rd** LA4 ... 217 D5
**Elland Pl** FY1 ... 130 B1
**Elland Rd** BB9 ... 148 C6
**ELLEL** ... 211 B5
**Ellel Hall Gdns** LA2 ... 210 F3
**Ellel St John the**
**Evangelist CE Prim Sch**
LA2 ... 211 A3
**Ellen Ct** PR1 ... 117 F2
**Ellenrod Dr** OL12 ... 52 A2
**Ellenrod La** OL12 ... 52 A2
**Ellenshaw Cl**
Darwen BB3 ... 82 B1
Rochdale OL12 ... 52 A2
**Ellenshaw St** BB3 ... 82 B1
**Ellen St**
Bamber Bridge PR5 ... 97 E1
Darwen BB3 ... 65 A7
11 Nelson BB9 ... 148 D8
Preston, Maudlands
PR1 ... 117 E1
Preston PR1 ... 117 F2
**Ellerbeck Ave** PR2 ... 118 E5
**Ellerbeck Cl** BB10 ... 148 E3
**Ellerbeck Rd**
Accrington BB5 ... 104 B7
Cleveleys FY5 ... 175 C2
Darwen BB3 ... 82 B1
**Eller Brook Cl** PR6 ... 43 F1
**Ellerbrook Dr** L40 ... 25 F3
**Eller Brook Ho** L39 ... 15 E6
**Ellerbrook Way** L39 ... 15 E6
**Ellerigg La** LA6 ... 243 A6
**Ellershaw Ho** 12 LA1 ... 218 D2
**Ellerslie Rd** PR2 ... 117 B1
**Ellesmere Ave**
Colne BB8 ... 171 F5
Thornton FY5 ... 176 D1
**Ellesmere Gr** LA4 ... 217 A3
**Ellesmere Rd**
Blackpool FY4 ... 130 E1
Darwen BB3 ... 81 E3
Morecambe LA4 ... 216 F4
**Elletson St** FY6 ... 153 D4
**Elliott Ave** BB3 ... 65 B6
**Elliott Cl** PR1 ... 117 E2
**Elliott St**
Burnley BB10 ... 128 C5
Preston, Adelphi PR1 ... 117 E1
Preston PR1 ... 117 E2
**Elliott Wlk** PR1 ... 117 E2
**Ellis Dr** LA4 ... 217 E6
**Ellisland** FY4 ... 131 C1
**Ellison Fold** BB5 ... 124 E3
**Ellison Fold La** BB3 ... 82 C1
**Ellison Fold Terr** BB3 ... 82 B1
**Ellison St**
Accrington BB5 ... 104 B6
Darwen BB3 ... 82 A2
**Ellis St**
Barnoldswick BB18 ... 196 B2
1 Burnley BB11 ... 127 E5
19 Ramsbottom BL0 ... 50 B5
**Ellwood Ave**
Lancaster LA1 ... 218 E4
Morecambe LA3 ... 217 C2
**Ellwood Ct** 4 LA3 ... 217 C2
**Ellwood Gr** 5 LA3 ... 217 C2
**Elm Ave**
Blackpool FY3 ... 130 E5
Galgate LA2 ... 210 F4
Poulton-le-F FY6 ... 153 D3
Preston PR2 ... 117 A2
Warton PR4 ... 92 D6
**Elmbank Ave** FY5 ... 152 C7
**Elm Brow** PR3 ... 162 C4
**Elm Cl**
Barnoldswick BB18 ... 196 A1
Haslingden BB4 ... 85 B3
Rishton BB1 ... 103 B8
Salterforth BB18 ... 194 E8
**Elmcroft La** L38 ... 3 A3
**Elm Ct**
Poulton-le-F FY6 ... 153 D3
Skelmersdale WN8 ... 17 E1
**Elmdale Cl** L37 ... 11 D2
**Elm Dr**
3 Bamber Bridge PR5 ... 97 F1
Formby L37 ... 11 D1
**Elmers Gn** WN8 ... 18 D2
**ELMERS GREEN** ... 18 D2
**Elmer's Green La** WN8 ... 18 C4
**Elmers Wood Rd** WN8 ... 18 D2
**Elmfield Dr** PR5 ... 78 C6
**Elmfield Hall** BB5 ... 103 F7
**Elmfield St** BB5 ... 103 F7
**Elm Gr**
Chorley PR6 ... 61 E2
Clayton-le-W PR25 ... 77 D3
Darwen BB3 ... 82 B3
Fulwood PR2 ... 118 E2
6 Horwich BL6 ... 32 E1
Kirkham PR4 ... 114 B7
Morecambe LA4 ... 217 E7
Skelmersdale WN8 ... 17 E1
**Elmhurst** PR3 ... 181 D5
**Elmhurst Rd** FY8 ... 90 B8
**Elm Mill** BB10 ... 128 A8
**Elm Park Dr** PR8 ... 21 E5
**Elmpark Gate** OL12 ... 52 B3
**Elmpark Gr** OL12 ... 52 B3
**Elmpark Vale** OL12 ... 52 B3
**Elmpark View** OL12 ... 52 B3
**Elmpark Way** OL12 ... 52 B3
**Elm Pl** L39 ... 15 E4
**Elm Rd**
Burscough L40 ... 25 E3
Southport PR8 ... 35 B4
**Elmridge** WN8 ... 9 D8
**Elmridge Cres** FY2 ... 152 F3
**Elms Ave**
Cleveleys FY5 ... 175 E2
Lytham St Anne's FY8 ... 90 E3
**Elms Ct** LA4 ... 217 E7
**Elmsdale Cl** LA1 ... 218 C2
**Elms Dr**
Morecambe LA4 ... 217 E7
Wrea Green PR4 ... 113 B4
**Elmsfield Pk** L39 ... 6 A6
**Elmside Cl** FY5 ... 176 D2
**Elmslack Ct** LA5 ... 224 C4
**Elmslack La** LA5 ... 224 C4
**Elmsley St** PR1 ... 117 E2
**Elmslie Gdns** FY3 ... 130 E3
**Elms Rd** LA4 ... 217 E7
**Elms Sch** PR1 ... 118 A3
**Elm St**
6 Bacup OL13 ... 88 A3
Blackburn BB1 ... 102 A7
Burnley BB10 ... 128 A8
Bury BL9 ... 33 B2
Colne BB8 ... 171 E6
Edenfield BL0 ... 68 E3
Fleetwood FY7 ... 199 A4
Great Harwood BB6 ... 124 C4
Haslingden BB4 ... 85 B3
9 Nelson BB9 ... 170 E1
Ramsbottom BL0 ... 50 D6
Rawtenstall BB4 ... 86 A3
Rochdale OL12 ... 52 F1
Whitworth OL12 ... 71 D2
**Elmstead** WN8 ... 9 D8
**Elms The**
Clayton Green PR6 ... 78 C1
Maghull L31 ... 5 D3
Southport, Birkdale PR8 ... 34 F6
Southport, Blowick PR8 ... 35 C5
**Elmswood Cl** FY8 ... 90 F4
**Elm Tree Gr** BB6 ... 143 C5
**Elmwood**
Chorley PR7 ... 61 B1
Longridge PR3 ... 140 A8
Skelmersdale WN8 ... 18 C3
**Elmwood Ave**
1 Leyland PR25 ... 76 E1
Preesall FY6 ... 200 B4
**Elmwood Cl** BB5 ... 104 D6
**Elmwood Ct** PR4 ... 132 F2
**Elmwood Dr**
Higher Penwortham
PR1 ... 96 B4
Thornton FY5 ... 176 C1
**Elmwood Gdns** LA1 ... 215 A2
**Elmwood St** BB11 ... 127 D5
**Elsby Ave** FY5 ... 153 C8
**Elsie St** 10 BL0 ... 50 A4
**Elsinore Cl** FY7 ... 198 F5
**ELSLACK** ... 197 F7
**Elslack La** BD23 ... 197 F7
**Elson Rd** L37 ... 11 D1
**ELSTON** ... 120 A6
**Elston Ave** FY3 ... 131 A8
**Elston Gn** PR2 ... 139 E1
**Elston La** PR2 ... 119 F7
**Elston Lo** 7 PR2 ... 118 F4
**ELSWICK** ... 156 A1
**Elswick** WN8 ... 9 C8
**Elswick Gdns** BB2 ... 121 D3
**Elswick Gn** PR9 ... 54 A5
**Elswick Ind Pk** PR4 ... 156 A1
**ELSWICK LEYS** ... 134 A8
**Elswick Lo** BB2 ... 121 E3
**Elswick Pl**
Blackpool FY4 ... 110 E5
Lytham St Anne's FY8 ... 90 B8
**Elswick Rd**
Leyland PR25 ... 59 D8
Preston PR2 ... 116 E1
Southport PR9 ... 53 F4
**Elswick St** BB3 ... 82 B1
**Elsworth Cl** L37 ... 2 C8
**Elterwater** FY6 ... 199 E5
**Elterwater Pl**
Blackpool FY3 ... 131 C2
Lancaster LA1 ... 218 E1
**Eltham Ct** FY3 ... 153 B1
**Elton Rd** BB1, BB4 ... 83 B5
**Elton St** 3 PR2 ... 117 C1
**Elvaston Rd** FY6 ... 153 C6
**Elvington Rd** L38 ... 3 A2
**Elwood Grange** FY8 ... 89 C8
**Ely Cl**
Darwen BB3 ... 82 C1
Wilpshire BB1 ... 122 F6
**Ely Mews** PR9 ... 54 A2
**Embankment Rd** BL7 ... 48 C5
**Emerald Ave** BB1 ... 122 F2
**Emerald Cl**
Blackburn BB1 ... 122 F2
Blackpool FY5 ... 152 F7
**Emerald Cotts** BL8 ... 49 F3
**Emerald St** BB1 ... 122 F2
**Emerson Ave** FY4 ... 110 D7
**Emerson Cl** L38 ... 3 A4
**Emerson Rd** PR1 ... 118 D2
**Emerson St** LA1 ... 215 A4
**Emesgate La** LA5 ... 224 C3
**Emily St**
Bamber Bridge PR5 ... 77 A8
Blackburn BB1 ... 102 A6
Burnley BB11 ... 128 A4
**Emlsett Rd** PR5 ... 97 F3
**Emmanuel Christian Sch**
OL12 ... 52 D2
**Emmanuel Holcombe CE**
**Prim Sch** BL8 ... 50 A6
**Emmanuel Rd** PR9 ... 53 F2
**Emmanuel St** PR1, PR2 ... 117 E2
**Emma St** BB5 ... 103 F6
**Emmaus Rd** LA3 ... 212 F6
**Emmett St**
Horwich BL6 ... 32 B3
Preston PR1 ... 117 F1
**Emmott Ct** BB8 ... 172 E6
**Emmott La** BB8 ... 172 D6
**Emmsix** L40 ... 24 B4
**Emnie La** PR26, PR25 ... 59 C7
**Empire Gr** 2 FY3 ... 130 D7
**Empire Ho** 3 BB5 ... 104 B6
**Empire St** BB6 ... 124 D6
**Emporium The** 8 BB7 ... 166 E8
**Empress Ave** PR2 ... 117 E4
**Empress Cl** L31 ... 5 B1
**Empress Dr** FY2 ... 152 B1
**Empress St**
Accrington BB5 ... 103 F6
Blackburn BB3 ... 81 F7
Colne BB8 ... 171 E5
**Empress Way** PR7 ... 60 E2
**Endcliffe Rd** LA4 ... 217 C5
**Endeavour Cl** PR2 ... 96 B7
**Enderley Ct** FY5 ... 176 C1
**Ending Rake** OL12 ... 52 C4
**Endsleigh Gdns** FY4 ... 110 E6
**Endsleigh Gr** LA1 ... 218 A3
**End St** BB8 ... 171 B4
**ENFIELD** ... 125 A2
**Enfield Cl** PR7 ... 41 C5
**Enfield Rd**
Accrington BB5 ... 125 E2
Blackpool FY1 ... 130 C7
**Engel Cl** BL0 ... 50 A5
**Engine La** L37 ... 3 E8
**England Ave**
Blackburn BB2 ... 81 D8
Blackpool FY2 ... 152 C4
**English Martyrs' Pl**
PR1 ... 117 F2
**English Martyrs RC Prim**
**Sch** PR1 ... 117 E1
**Ennerdale** WN8 ... 9 D8
**Ennerdale Ave**
Blackburn BB1 ... 102 C3
Fleetwood FY7 ... 198 C1
Maghull L31 ... 5 E2
Morecambe LA4 ... 217 D4
**Ennerdale Cl**
Clitheroe BB7 ... 166 C7
Formby L37 ... 11 D3
Forton PR3 ... 207 B3
Knott End-on-S FY6 ... 199 F6
Lancaster LA1 ... 218 F2
Leyland PR25 ... 60 A7
Oswaldtwistle BB5 ... 103 D5
**Ennerdale Dr**
Ormskirk L39 ... 15 B2
Walton-le-D PR5 ... 97 E5
**Ennerdale Rd**
Blackpool FY4 ... 131 C1
Burnley BB10 ... 128 E5
Chorley PR7 ... 43 A6
Clitheroe BB7 ... 166 C7
Formby L37 ... 11 E3
Longridge PR3 ... 139 F5
**Ennismore Gdns** PR9 ... 53 E1
**Ennismore St** BB10 ... 148 C1
**Enoch Brow** BB2 ... 80 C8
**Ensign Ct** FY8 ... 110 C4
**Enstone** WN8 ... 18 D1
**Enterprise Ct** BB5 ... 125 D1
**Enterprise Dr** PR26 ... 77 A4
**Enterprise Way**
Fleetwood FY7 ... 176 A6
Nelson BB8 ... 170 F3
**Enterprise Workshops**
L33 ... 1 B1
**Entwisle Rd** BB5 ... 104 B8
**ENTWISTLE** ... 48 B7
**Entwistle Hall La** BL7 ... 48 B8
**Entwistle St** BB3 ... 82 A1
**Entwistle Sta** BL7 ... 48 B8
**Ephraim St** PR1 ... 97 C7
**Epoch Cotts** LA6 ... 240 B3
**Epping Ave** BB5 ... 125 B1
**Epping Cl** FY2 ... 152 E5
**Epping Pl** PR6 ... 43 D8
**Epsom Cl** PR6 ... 61 F4
**Epsom Croft** PR6 ... 31 B7
**Epsom Gr** L33 ... 1 A6

Epsom Rd FY5 . . . . . 152 F8
Epsom Way BB5 . . . . . 104 D5
Epworth St BB3 . . . . . 65 B6
Equity St BB3 . . . . . 65 A8
Erdington Rd FY1 . . . . . 130 C3
Eric Morecambe Ho 9 LA4 . . . . . 217 F4
Ericson Dr PR8 . . . . . 35 B5
Erith Gr FY2 . . . . . 152 C5
Ermine Cl BB2 . . . . . 82 A8
Ermine Pl LA3 . . . . . 217 E3
Ernest St
Britannia OL13 . . . . . 71 C8
Church BB5 . . . . . 103 E6
Clayton-le-M BB5 . . . . . 124 F1
Todmorden OL14 . . . . . 109 C1
Ernlouen Cl BB2 . . . . . 81 A8
Erskine Rd PR6 . . . . . 61 E1
Escar St 9 BB11 . . . . . 127 F5
Escott Gdns 11 BB10 . . . . . 128 A8
Escowbeck Ho LA2 . . . . . 237 B3
Esher Pond PR2 . . . . . 117 C6
Eshton Terr BB7 . . . . . 166 D7
Esk Ave
Edenfield BL0 . . . . . 68 D5
Fleetwood FY7 . . . . . 198 D2
Eskbank WN8 . . . . . 9 C8
Eskbrook WN8 . . . . . 18 C1
Eskdale WN8 . . . . . 9 B8
Eskdale Ave
Fleetwood FY7 . . . . . 198 D1
Ormskirk L39 . . . . . 15 C2
Eskdale Cl
Blackpool FY4 . . . . . 130 F1
Burnley BB10 . . . . . 148 B4
Formby L37 . . . . . 11 D2
Fulwood PR2 . . . . . 117 F8
Eskdale Cres BB2 . . . . . 80 E8
Eskdale Ct FY5 . . . . . 175 D1
Eskdale Dr
Formby L37 . . . . . 11 D2
Kirkham PR4 . . . . . 114 A7
Maghull L31 . . . . . 5 E2
Eskdale Gdns BB12 . . . . . 146 C2
Eskdale Gr FY6 . . . . . 199 F6
Eskdale Pl LA4 . . . . . 217 D4
Eskdale Rd
Leyland PR25 . . . . . 60 C7
Longridge PR3 . . . . . 139 F6
Eskew Cres LA2 . . . . . 239 B7
Eskew La LA2 . . . . . 239 B8
Eskham Cl PR4 . . . . . 113 E6
Eskrigge Cl 4 LA1 . . . . . 218 D4
Eskrigge La LA2 . . . . . 238 A8
Esp La BB18 . . . . . 231 F1
Esplanade
Knott End-on-S FY6 . . . . . 199 D6
Preston PR1 . . . . . 97 B5
Southport PR8 . . . . . 34 F7
Esplanade Mews FY6 . . . . . 199 E5
Esplanade The
Fleetwood FY7 . . . . . 199 A5
Rishton BB1 . . . . . 103 A8
ESPRICK . . . . . 133 D5
Essex Ave
Burnley BB12 . . . . . 127 B7
Heywood BL9 . . . . . 33 E1
Essex Cl BB2 . . . . . 101 D3
Essex Pl FY2 . . . . . 152 F2
Essex Rd
3 Morecambe LA4 . . . . . 217 F4
4 Rishton BB1 . . . . . 124 A1
Southport PR8 . . . . . 22 A8
Standish WN1 . . . . . 30 B1
Essex St
Accrington BB5 . . . . . 104 D6
Barnoldswick BB18 . . . . . 196 B2
Colne BB8 . . . . . 171 E4
Darwen BB3 . . . . . 82 C1
Horwich BL6 . . . . . 32 D1
Nelson BB9 . . . . . 170 E1
Preston PR1 . . . . . 118 A1
Essie Terr BB18 . . . . . 196 B1
Essington Ave LA4 . . . . . 217 A4
Est Bank Rd BL0 . . . . . 50 A3
Esther St BB1 . . . . . 102 C5
Esthwaite Gdns LA1 . . . . . 218 F1
Ethel St
Barnoldswick BB18 . . . . . 196 C2
Whitworth OL12 . . . . . 71 D2
Ethersall Rd BB9 . . . . . 148 E6
Eton Ave BB5 . . . . . 104 C7
Eton Cl BB12 . . . . . 126 E6
Eton Ct PR9 . . . . . 53 C1
Eton Pk PR2 . . . . . 118 C5
Eton Way WN5 . . . . . 10 F8
Ettington Dr PR8 . . . . . 21 A5
Ettrick Ave FY7 . . . . . 198 D3
Europa Dr PR26 . . . . . 77 A4
Europa Way LA1 . . . . . 214 C8
Euston Gr LA4 . . . . . 217 B5
Euston Rd LA4 . . . . . 217 B5
Euston St PR1 . . . . . 96 E7
EUXTON . . . . . 60 D2
Euxton Balshaw La Sta PR7 . . . . . 60 D1
Euxton CE Prim Sch PR7 . . . . . 60 C2
Euxton Ct FY4 . . . . . 110 E8
Euxton Hall Ct PR7 . . . . . 60 C2
Euxton Hall Gdns PR7 . . . . . 60 C1
Euxton Hall Hospl PR7 . . . . . 60 C1
Euxton Hall Mews PR7 . . . . . 60 C2
Euxton La
Chorley PR7 . . . . . 61 B3
Euxton PR7 . . . . . 60 E4
Euxton St Mary's RC Prim Sch PR7 . . . . . 60 C3
Evans St
Burnley BB11 . . . . . 127 F4
Horwich BL6 . . . . . 32 D4
Preston PR2 . . . . . 117 D1
Evanstone Cl BL6 . . . . . 32 B3
Evelyn Rd BB3 . . . . . 81 E5
Evelyn St BB10 . . . . . 148 A1
Evenwood WN8 . . . . . 18 D1
Evenwood Ct WN8 . . . . . 18 C1
Everard Cl L40 . . . . . 23 F7
Everard Rd PR8 . . . . . 35 D4
Everest Cl FY8 . . . . . 111 A1
Everest Ct 2 PR4 . . . . . 113 F6
Everest Dr FY2 . . . . . 152 C5
Everest Rd FY8 . . . . . 111 A2
Evergreen Ave
Horwich BL6 . . . . . 32 B3
Leyland PR25 . . . . . 60 A7
Evergreen Cl PR7 . . . . . 43 B5
Evergreens The
Blackburn BB2 . . . . . 80 F8
Cottam PR4 . . . . . 116 E4
Formby L37 . . . . . 11 D4
Horwich BL6 . . . . . 32 E1
Eversham Cl PR9 . . . . . 55 A5
Eversholt Cl BB12 . . . . . 147 D7
Eversleigh Ave FY5 . . . . . 176 A3
Eversleigh St PR1 . . . . . 117 E1
Eversley WN8 . . . . . 18 D1
Everton BB2 . . . . . 102 A1
Everton Rd
Blackpool FY4 . . . . . 110 C6
Southport PR8 . . . . . 35 A4
Everton St BB3 . . . . . 81 F1
Every St
Brierfield BB9 . . . . . 148 B6
Burnley BB11 . . . . . 127 E5
Nelson BB9 . . . . . 148 D8
Ramsbottom BL0 . . . . . 50 D6
Evesham Ave PR1 . . . . . 96 E2
Evesham Cl
5 Accrington BB5 . . . . . 104 A7
Blackpool FY5 . . . . . 152 E7
Heysham LA3 . . . . . 213 A6
Hutton PR4 . . . . . 95 C1
Evesham Manor PR9 . . . . . 55 A6
Evesham Rd
Lytham St Anne's FY8 . . . . . 90 A5
Normoss FY3 . . . . . 131 B7
Eve St BB9 . . . . . 171 A2
Evington WN8 . . . . . 18 D1
Ewell Cl PR6 . . . . . 61 F4
EWOOD . . . . . 81 D8
Ewood BB2 . . . . . 101 D1
EWOOD BRIDGE . . . . . 68 C6
Ewood Cvn Site BB2 . . . . . 101 D1
Ewood La BB4 . . . . . 68 C7
Ewood Park (Blackburn Rovers FC) BB2 . . . . . 81 D8
Exchange St
Accrington BB5 . . . . . 103 F5
18 Blackburn BB1 . . . . . 101 E5
Blackpool FY1 . . . . . 130 B6
Colne BB8 . . . . . 171 D4
Darwen BB3 . . . . . 82 A2
Edenfield BL0 . . . . . 68 D3
Exchange The 2 BB8 . . . . . 171 D5
Exe St PR1 . . . . . 118 B2
Exeter Ave LA1 . . . . . 215 B6
Exeter Dr FY5 . . . . . 176 A2
Exeter Pl 2 PR2 . . . . . 116 E2
Exeter St
Blackburn BB2 . . . . . 101 D2
3 Blackpool FY4 . . . . . 130 C1
Exmoor Cl PR9 . . . . . 54 B6
Exmouth St BB11 . . . . . 128 A5
Exton St BB9 . . . . . 148 A5
Extwistle Rd BB10 . . . . . 129 B7
Extwistle Sq BB10 . . . . . 128 E5
Extwistle St
Burnley BB10 . . . . . 128 B8
Nelson BB9 . . . . . 148 D7
Eyes La
Bretherton PR26 . . . . . 57 E3
Newburgh WN8 . . . . . 27 A3

## F

FACIT . . . . . 71 D2
Factory Brow
Blackrod BL6 . . . . . 31 D3
Scorton PR3 . . . . . 204 E6
Factory Hill
Horwich BL6 . . . . . 32 D4
5 Lancaster LA1 . . . . . 218 E1
Factory La
Adlington PR6 . . . . . 31 B8
Barrowford BB9 . . . . . 170 D4
Middleforth Green PR1 . . . . . 96 F3
17 Padiham BB12 . . . . . 146 C1
Factory St BL0 . . . . . 50 C7
Fairacres WN6 . . . . . 29 B1
Fairbairn Ave BB12 . . . . . 127 C8
Fairbairn St BL6 . . . . . 32 B3
Fairbank Gr LA4 . . . . . 217 A3
Fairbank Wlk BB4 . . . . . 106 A2
Fairburn WN8 . . . . . 18 B3
Fairclough Rd
Accrington BB5 . . . . . 104 A3
Thornton FY5 . . . . . 176 A3
Fair Elms LA1 . . . . . 214 D7
Fairfax Ave FY2 . . . . . 152 E5
Fairfax Cl PR3 . . . . . 181 D6
Fairfax Pl PR5 . . . . . 97 D2
Fairfax Rd PR2 . . . . . 118 E4
FAIRFIELD . . . . . 33 E3
Fairfield PR3 . . . . . 181 C8
Fairfield Ave
Newchurch BB4 . . . . . 86 F2
Normoss FY3 . . . . . 131 B7
Poulton-le-F FY6 . . . . . 153 D3
Fairfield Cl
Carnforth LA5 . . . . . 223 E1
Clitheroe BB7 . . . . . 166 C7
Lancaster LA1 . . . . . 214 E8
Ormskirk L39 . . . . . 15 E7
Fairfield Com Prim Sch BL9 . . . . . 33 D3
Fairfield Ct
Fleetwood FY7 . . . . . 198 F2
Poulton-le-F FY6 . . . . . 153 D4
Fairfield Dr
Burnley BB10 . . . . . 148 C3
Bury BL9 . . . . . 33 D3
Clitheroe BB7 . . . . . 166 C7
Ormskirk L39 . . . . . 15 E7
Preston PR2 . . . . . 117 B2
Fairfield General Hospl BL9 . . . . . 33 E4
Fairfield Gr LA3 . . . . . 216 E2
Fairfield Rd
Blackpool FY1 . . . . . 130 C8
Fulwood PR2 . . . . . 118 A4
Lancaster LA1 . . . . . 214 E8
Leyland PR25 . . . . . 59 F8
Morecambe LA3 . . . . . 216 E2
Nelson BB9 . . . . . 149 B8
Poulton-le-F FY6 . . . . . 131 F7
Southport PR8 . . . . . 21 C5
Fairfield St
Accrington BB5 . . . . . 103 F4
5 Bamber Bridge PR5 . . . . . 77 B7
Fairham Ave 6 PR1 . . . . . 96 D2
FAIRHAVEN . . . . . 90 A3
Fairhaven WN8 . . . . . 18 C3
Fairhaven Ave FY7 . . . . . 175 D7
Fairhaven Cl 6 FY5 . . . . . 176 D1
Fair Haven Ct 2 FY8 . . . . . 90 D4
Fairhaven La FY8 . . . . . 89 E5
Fairhaven Lake★ FY8 . . . . . 90 C3
Fairhaven Rd
Blackburn BB2 . . . . . 101 F1
Leyland PR25 . . . . . 76 D1
Lytham St Anne's FY8 . . . . . 89 F5
Middleforth Green PR1 . . . . . 96 E5
Southport PR9 . . . . . 54 B4
Fairhaven Way 1 LA4 . . . . . 217 D5
Fairheath Rd LA2 . . . . . 239 B4
Fair Hill BB4 . . . . . 68 A7
Fairhill Terr BB4 . . . . . 68 A7
Fairholme Rd BB11 . . . . . 128 B3
Fairholmes Cl 1 FY5 . . . . . 176 B3
Fairholmes Ct 2 FY5 . . . . . 176 B3
Fairholmes Way FY5 . . . . . 176 B3
Fairhope Ave
Lancaster LA1 . . . . . 218 C3
Morecambe LA4 . . . . . 217 F6
Fairhope Ct BB2 . . . . . 101 C6
Fairhurst Ave WN6 . . . . . 29 D3
Fairhurst Ct FY5 . . . . . 175 D3
Fairhurst's Dr WN8 . . . . . 27 B2
Fairhurst St FY1 . . . . . 130 C6
Fairlawn Rd FY8 . . . . . 90 F3
Fairlea Ave LA4 . . . . . 217 F6
Fairlie WN8 . . . . . 18 C3
Fairmont Dr FY6 . . . . . 177 D2
Fair Oak Cl PR2 . . . . . 118 F3
Fairsnape Ave PR3 . . . . . 140 B7
Fairsnape Dr PR3 . . . . . 181 B6
Fairsnape Rd FY8 . . . . . 91 D4
Fairstead WN8 . . . . . 18 C3
Fairthorn Wlk L33 . . . . . 1 A3
FAIRVIEW . . . . . 44 A1
Fairview BB4 . . . . . 85 F5
Fair View OL13 . . . . . 71 C8
Fairview Ave FY8 . . . . . 90 A7
Fairview Cl PR4 . . . . . 74 F5
Fair View Cres OL13 . . . . . 88 B3
Fairview Dr
Adlington PR6 . . . . . 44 A1
Adlington PR6, PR7 . . . . . 30 F8
Fair View Rd BB11 . . . . . 128 B5
Fairway
Chorley PR7 . . . . . 61 C2
Fleetwood FY7 . . . . . 198 C1
Higher Penwortham PR1 . . . . . 96 B6
Poulton-le-F FY6 . . . . . 153 A2
Southport PR9 . . . . . 53 C2
Whitworth OL12 . . . . . 52 C7
Fair Way FY6 . . . . . 177 C7
Fairway Gdns FY6 . . . . . 199 D5
Fairway Rd FY4 . . . . . 110 E8
Fairways
Fulwood PR2 . . . . . 118 A6
Horwich BL6 . . . . . 32 C3
Lytham St Anne's FY8 . . . . . 90 A6
Fairways Ave PR3 . . . . . 137 C3
Fairways Ct
Formby L37 . . . . . 11 C5
Wilpshire BB1 . . . . . 122 F5
Fairways Dr BB11 . . . . . 127 E2
Fairways The
Knott End-on-S FY6 . . . . . 199 D5
Skelmersdale WN8 . . . . . 18 D3
Fairweather Ct BB12 . . . . . 146 D1
Fairwinds Ave PR4 . . . . . 73 D4
Falcon Ave BB3 . . . . . 81 E3
Falcon Cl
Blackburn BB1 . . . . . 101 D8
Bury BL9 . . . . . 33 B4
Falcon Ct BB5 . . . . . 124 F2
Falcon Dr FY6 . . . . . 153 B2
Falcon Ho BL9 . . . . . 33 A4
Falcon Mews FY6 . . . . . 200 B4
Falcon St PR1 . . . . . 118 B2
FALINGE FOLD . . . . . 52 D1
Falinge Fold OL12 . . . . . 52 D1
Falinge Park High Sch OL12 . . . . . 52 D1
Falinge Rd OL12 . . . . . 52 E1
Falkirk Ave FY2 . . . . . 152 C6
Falkland WN8 . . . . . 18 C3
Falkland Ave FY4 . . . . . 130 F2
Falkland Rd PR8 . . . . . 35 D5
Falkland St PR1 . . . . . 96 F7
Falkus Ct 6 FY6 . . . . . 153 D3
Fallbarn Cres BB4 . . . . . 86 A1
Fallbarn Fold BB4 . . . . . 86 B2
Fall Barn Rd BB4 . . . . . 86 B2
Fall Kirk LA2 . . . . . 240 F1
Fallowfield Cl PR4 . . . . . 113 E6
Fallowfield Dr
Burnley BB12 . . . . . 127 D8
Rochdale OL12 . . . . . 52 D2
Fallowfield Rd FY8 . . . . . 90 C6
Falmouth Ave
Fleetwood FY7 . . . . . 175 C8
Haslingden BB4 . . . . . 85 C2
Falmouth Rd FY1 . . . . . 130 C2
Falshaw Dr BL9 . . . . . 50 E1
Falstone Ave BL0 . . . . . 50 C4
Faraday Ave BB7 . . . . . 166 D8
Faraday Dr PR2 . . . . . 118 C7
Faraday Rise OL12 . . . . . 52 B1
Faraday St BB12 . . . . . 127 D7
Faraday Way FY2, FY6 . . . . . 153 A6
FAR ARNSIDE . . . . . 224 A5
FAR BANKS . . . . . 55 C8
Far Croft PR5 . . . . . 97 A1
Far East View 16 BB18 . . . . . 196 B2
Fareham Cl
Bamber Bridge PR5 . . . . . 97 F3
Fulwood PR2 . . . . . 118 A4
Fareham Dr PR9 . . . . . 55 A5
Far Field PR1 . . . . . 96 D3
Farfield Dr BB3 . . . . . 81 F6
Farholme La OL13 . . . . . 70 D8
Faringdon Ave FY4 . . . . . 110 E5
FARINGTON
Bamber Bridge . . . . . 76 F6
Leyland . . . . . 77 B3
Farington Ave PR25 . . . . . 59 D7
Farington Gate PR25 . . . . . 77 B2
Farington Prim Sch PR25 . . . . . 77 B3
Farington Rd PR5, PR26 . . . . . 77 A6
Farington St Paul's CE Prim Sch PR26 . . . . . 76 F7
Far La PR1 . . . . . 96 C2
FARLETON . . . . . 238 A6
Farleton Cl LA5 . . . . . 223 C5
Farleton Ct 3 LA1 . . . . . 218 D4
Farleton Old Rd LA2 . . . . . 238 A5
Farley La
Skelmersdale WN8 . . . . . 18 F3
Up Holland WN8 . . . . . 19 A3
Farm Ave
Adlington PR6 . . . . . 31 A8
Bacup OL13 . . . . . 87 F4
Farm Cl
Southport PR9 . . . . . 36 A8
Thornton FY5 . . . . . 176 B2
Farmdale Dr L31 . . . . . 5 E1
Farmdale Rd LA1 . . . . . 215 B5
Farmend Cl PR4 . . . . . 75 B8
Farmer Parr's Animal World (Mus)★ FY7 . . . . . 175 F7
Farmer's Row BB2 . . . . . 81 B7
Farmer Ted's Farm Pk★ L39 . . . . . 13 E1
Farm House Cl
Blackburn BB1 . . . . . 102 C4
Lucas Green PR6 . . . . . 61 C6
Farm Meadow Rd WN5 . . . . . 10 E5
FAR MOOR . . . . . 10 E4
Far Moor La LA1 . . . . . 215 C8
Farnborough Rd PR8 . . . . . 21 F8
Farnborough Road Inf & Jun Schs PR8 . . . . . 22 A8
Farnell Pl FY4 . . . . . 110 D6
Farnham Way FY6 . . . . . 153 C5
Farnlea Dr LA4 . . . . . 217 E5
Far Nook PR6 . . . . . 61 B7
Farnworth Rd FY5 . . . . . 176 D1
Faroes Cl BB2 . . . . . 101 F1
Farrer Ave LA1 . . . . . 211 A7
Farrer St BB9 . . . . . 148 C7
Farrier Rd L33 . . . . . 1 A2
Farriers Fold LA3 . . . . . 212 F7
Farriers Way
Buckshaw Village PR7 . . . . . 60 E6
Poulton-le-F FY6 . . . . . 153 E4
Farriers Yd LA2 . . . . . 237 C3
Farrier Way WN6 . . . . . 19 C7
Farringdon Cl PR1 . . . . . 118 F1
Farringdon Cres PR1 . . . . . 118 F1
Farringdon La PR2 . . . . . 118 F3
Farringdon Pl PR1 . . . . . 118 F1
Farrington Cl
1 Blackburn BB2 . . . . . 101 C1
Burnley BB11 . . . . . 127 C3
Farrington Ct
Burnley BB11 . . . . . 127 C3
Leyland PR25 . . . . . 77 C4
Farrington Dr L39 . . . . . 15 E6
Farrington Pl BB11 . . . . . 127 C3
Farrington Rd
Britannia OL13 . . . . . 71 B8
Burnley BB11 . . . . . 127 B3
Farrington St PR7 . . . . . 43 C8
Farthings The PR7 . . . . . 60 F1
Faulkner Cl PR8 . . . . . 21 C6
Faulkner Gdns PR8 . . . . . 21 C6
Faulkner's La PR3 . . . . . 207 B1
Favordale Rd BB8 . . . . . 172 A5
Fawcett WN8 . . . . . 18 B3
Fawcett Cl BB2 . . . . . 101 D3
Fawcett Rd L31 . . . . . 5 D3
Fayles Gr FY4 . . . . . 131 A1
Fazackerley Cl BB2 . . . . . 81 D7
Fazackerley St PR2 . . . . . 117 C1
Fazakerley St 13 PR7 . . . . . 43 C8
Fearn Dene 2 OL12 . . . . . 52 B2
Fearnhead Ave BL6 . . . . . 32 B5
Fearns Com Sports Coll OL13 . . . . . 87 A1
Fearns Moss
Bacup OL13 . . . . . 70 A8
Rawtenstall BB4, OL13 . . . . . 87 A1
Fecit La BL0 . . . . . 51 C8
Fecitt Brow BB1 . . . . . 102 D4
Fecitt Rd BB2 . . . . . 101 B6
Federation St BB18 . . . . . 196 A3
Feilden Pl BB2 . . . . . 80 D8
Feildens Farm La BB2 . . . . . 121 B3
Feilden St BB2 . . . . . 101 D5
Felgate Brow FY3 . . . . . 130 E5
Felix St BB11 . . . . . 128 B7
Fellborough Lo 5 FY8 . . . . . 90 A8
Fell Brow PR3 . . . . . 140 B6
Fell Cl 5 PR5 . . . . . 77 F8
Fell End Cvn Pk LA7 . . . . . 225 E8
Fellery St PR7 . . . . . 43 C8
Fellfoot Lo PR2 . . . . . 119 A4
Fellfoot Rd LA6 . . . . . 243 A3
Fellgate LA3 . . . . . 217 E2
Fell Rd
Casterton LA6 . . . . . 243 B2
Morecambe LA4 . . . . . 217 F4
Fellside Cl BL8 . . . . . 49 F1
Fellside View LA3 . . . . . 212 F7
Fellstone Vale PR6 . . . . . 80 A1
Fells View BB7 . . . . . 144 A4
Fellview PR9 . . . . . 54 D6
Fell View
Burnley BB10 . . . . . 148 D3
Caton LA2 . . . . . 237 C3
Chorley PR6 . . . . . 43 E6
Garstang PR3 . . . . . 181 C8
Grimsargh PR2 . . . . . 139 C2
Weir OL13 . . . . . 88 A8
West Bradford BB7 . . . . . 189 D7
Whalley BB7 . . . . . 144 A7
Fell View Cl PR3 . . . . . 181 C8
Fell Way FY6 . . . . . 177 D7
Fellway Cl 7 PR5 . . . . . 77 C8
Felstead WN8 . . . . . 18 B2
Felstead St PR1 . . . . . 97 D8
Feltons WN8 . . . . . 18 B2
Felton Way PR4 . . . . . 74 F3
Fenber Ave FY4 . . . . . 110 C7
FENCE . . . . . 147 E7
Fencegate BB12 . . . . . 147 D7
Fengrove PR4 . . . . . 75 A8
Fenham Carr La LA1 . . . . . 215 C7
FENISCLIFFE . . . . . 101 A2
Feniscliffe Dr BB2 . . . . . 101 A2
FENISCOWLES . . . . . 80 D8
Feniscowles Prim Sch BB2 . . . . . 80 C8
Fennel Cl FY2 . . . . . 152 F4
Fenney Ct WN8 . . . . . 18 C1
Fennyfold Terr BB12 . . . . . 126 C6
Fensway PR4 . . . . . 95 D2
Fenton Ave BB18 . . . . . 196 D3
Fenton Rd
Blackpool FY1 . . . . . 130 C6
Fulwood PR2 . . . . . 118 C4
Fenton St LA1 . . . . . 214 E8
Fenwick St BB11 . . . . . 127 D3
Ferguson Gdns OL12 . . . . . 52 F3
Ferguson Rd FY1 . . . . . 130 E2
Ferguson St BB2 . . . . . 81 D7
Fermor Rd
Becconsall PR4 . . . . . 73 E1
Preston PR1 . . . . . 118 E1
Fern Ave BB5 . . . . . 103 F3
Fern Bank
Carnforth LA5 . . . . . 223 D1
Chorley PR6 . . . . . 61 D3
Lancaster LA1 . . . . . 215 A5
Maghull L31 . . . . . 5 E1
Nelson BB9 . . . . . 148 E7
Fernbank Ave BB18 . . . . . 196 A3
Fernbank Ct BB9 . . . . . 148 E7
Fern Breck Cotts FY6 . . . . . 200 A2
Fern Cl
2 Bamber Bridge PR5 . . . . . 77 B8
Skelmersdale WN8 . . . . . 17 E1
Ferncliffe Dr LA3 . . . . . 216 D2
Fern Ct FY7 . . . . . 198 C1
Ferndale
4 Blackburn BB1 . . . . . 102 A6
Fulwood PR2 . . . . . 117 E6
Skelmersdale WN8 . . . . . 18 C2
Ferndale Ave FY4 . . . . . 110 D7
Ferndale Cl
Freckleton PR4 . . . . . 93 D7
Leyland PR25 . . . . . 60 B7
Thornton FY5 . . . . . 176 C2
Ferndale Dr WN6 . . . . . 19 E7
Ferndale St BB10 . . . . . 128 C8
FERN GORE . . . . . 104 A3
Fern Gore Ave BB5 . . . . . 104 A3
Fern Gr FY1 . . . . . 130 C3
Ferngrove BL9 . . . . . 33 B4
FERN GROVE . . . . . 33 C4
Fernhill Ave OL13 . . . . . 70 E8

Fernhill Cl OL13 70 E8
Fernhill Cres 1 OL13 70 E8
Fernhill Dr OL13 70 E8
Fernhill Gr 2 OL13 70 E8
Fern Hill La OL12 52 A3
Fernhill Pk OL13 70 E8
Fernhills BL7 47 E2
Fernhill Way 4 OL13 70 E8
Fernhurst Ave FY4 130 D1
Fernhurst Gate L39 15 B1
Fernhurst Sec SEBD Sch BB2 81 C7
Fernhurst St BB2 81 D8
Fern Isle Cl OL12 52 B6
Fern Lea
Bolton-le-S LA5 221 A4
Nelson BB9 148 E8
Fernlea Ave
Barnoldswick BB18 196 B2
Oswaldtwistle BB5 104 A3
Fernlea Cl
Blackburn BB2 81 B8
1 Rochdale OL12 52 B2
Fernlea Dr BB5 124 F4
Fern Lea St BB4 69 D8
Fernleigh
10 Horwich BL6 32 D1
Leyland PR26 59 A8
Fernleigh Cl
Blackpool FY2 152 D4
Garstang PR3 181 C8
Fernley Rd PR8 35 A5
Fern Mdw PR6 78 C2
Fern Rd BB11 127 E4
Fernside Way OL12 52 A1
Fern St
Bacup OL13 87 F3
Colne BB8 171 F6
Newchurch BB4 86 F1
Ramsbottom BL0 50 D7
Ferns The
3 Bacup OL13 88 A1
Bamber Bridge PR5 97 C3
Britannia OL13 71 A8
Kirkham PR4 113 F4
Preston PR2 117 C2
Fernstone Cl BL6 32 A3
Fern Terr BB4 85 A3
Fernview Dr BL0 50 A1
Fernville Terr 6 OL13 70 D8
Fernwood Ave FY5 153 B8
Fernwood Cl FY8 90 E4
Fernyhalgh Ct PR2 118 D6
Fernyhalgh Gdns PR2 118 D6
Fernyhalgh Gr PR2 118 D6
Fernyhalgh La PR2 118 D7
Fernyhalgh Pl PR2 118 D6
Ferny Knoll Rd WA11 8 F4
Ferrier Bank PR4 92 D5
Ferrier Cl 1 BB1 102 C5
Ferrier Ct BB1 102 C5
Ferry Rd PR2 95 F8
Ferry Road Office Pk 4 PR2 95 F8
Ferryside La PR9 54 C5
Ferry View Ct FY7 199 C5
Ffrances Pas 31 LA1 214 F8
FIDDLER'S FERRY 54 D6
Fiddlers Fold Ct PR4 116 C4
Fiddler's La
Chipping PR3 184 F4
Clayton Green PR6 78 B2
Fidler La PR26 76 F5
Field Cl L40 25 F3
Field Edge La PR3 201 E5
Fielden St
Burnley BB11 127 D5
Chorley PR6 43 E8
5 Leyland PR25 76 D1
Fieldfare Cl
Middleforth Green PR1 96 E3
Thornton FY5 176 A5
Fieldfare Ct PR7 42 F5
Fieldfare Way OL13 88 A1
Fieldhouse Ave FY5 176 D2
Fieldhouse Ind Est OL12 52 F2
Fieldhouse Rd OL12 52 F2
Fielding Cres BB2 101 A1
Fielding La
Great Harwood BB6 124 B5
Oswaldtwistle BB5 103 E3
Fielding Pl PR6 31 B8
Fielding Rd FY1 130 D8
Fielding's Bldgs 9 BB4 85 E2
Fielding St BB1 124 C1
Fieldings The
Fulwood PR2 117 D3
Maghull L31 5 B4
Fieldlands PR8 36 A2
Field Maple Dr PR2 118 F3
Field Rd LA3 212 D6
Fieldsend LA3 213 A7
Fields End BB6 123 C8
Fieldside Ave PR7 60 C1
Fieldside Cl PR5 97 C3
Fields Rd BB4 85 C1
Field St
Blackburn BB2 101 B2
Blackpool FY1 130 C2
Padiham BB12 126 C7
Skelmersdale WN8 17 D2
Fields The PR7 41 B7
Field Top 2 OL13 88 A7
Fieldview 2 WN8 10 A7
Fieldway FY8 110 E2
Field Wlk L39 16 B5
Fife Cl PR6 43 E6
Fife St
Accrington BB5 104 A4
Barrowford BB9 170 C1
Fifth Ave
Blackpool FY4 110 C7
Burnley BB10 148 B3
Bury BL9 33 D4
Filberts Cl PR2 117 C3
Filberts The PR2 117 C3
File St PR7 43 C7
Filey Pl
Blackpool FY1 130 B6
Fulwood PR2 117 A4
Filey Rd FY8 111 A1
Filton Gr LA3 217 E3
Finch Cl BB1 101 E6
Finches The FY6 153 B2
Finch La
Appley Bridge WN6 28 B1
Cottam PR4 116 E4
Finchley Rd FY1 130 B8
Finch Mill Ave WN6 19 D7
Finch's Cotts 6 PR1 96 E4
Finch St 5 BB3 81 F2
Findon WN8 18 C2
Fine Jane's Way PR9 36 B8
Finney Park Dr PR2 95 D8
Finnington Cotts BB2 80 A6
Finnington La BB2 80 A6
Finsbury Ave
Blackpool FY1 130 D2
Lytham St Anne's FY8 90 B4
Finsbury Pl BB2 81 D7
Finsley Gate BB11 128 A5
Finsley St BB10 148 E3
Finsley View BB10 148 F3
Firbank
1 Bamber Bridge PR5 97 D1
Euxton PR7 60 C2
Firbank Ave PR4 57 A7
Firbank Rd LA1 218 E1
Firbeck WN8 18 C1
Fir Cl FY7 198 C2
Fir Cotes L31 5 E1
Fircroft WN6 29 A2
Fir Ct 4 BB5 104 E8
Firfield Cl PR4 113 E5
Fir Gr
Blackpool FY1 130 E2
Warton PR4 92 D6
Fir Grove Rd 10 BB11 128 B4
Fir Mount 10 OL13 88 A1
Firs Cl L37 11 D5
Firs Cres L37 11 D5
Firshill Cl FY5 153 B8
Firs La L39 14 E3
Firs Link L37 11 D4
Fir St
Burnley BB10 128 B5
Bury BL9 33 A2
Haslingden BB4 85 B3
Nelson BB9 148 F8
Ramsbottom BL0 50 D7
Southport PR8 35 F6
First Ave
Blackpool FY4 110 C7
Church BB5 104 A8
Clifton PR4 115 C1
Poulton-le-F FY6 153 E3
Preesall Park FY6 200 C1
Preston PR2 117 A2
West Bradford BB7 189 D7
Wrea Green PR4 113 B4
First Terr LA3 209 B5
Firswood Cl FY8 90 E4
Firswood Rd L40, WN8 17 C3
Fir Tree Ave PR2 117 B4
Firtree Cl PR7 43 C3
Fir Tree Cl
Hest Bank LA5 220 F2
Much Hoole PR4 74 E3
Skelmersdale WN8 9 D7
Fir Tree La
Haskayne L39 14 F3
Ormskirk L39 15 A2
Fir Tree Pl FY5 152 F8
Fir Trees Ave
Bamber Bridge PR5 77 A8
Fulwood PR2 119 A4
Fir Trees Cl BB9 149 A8
Fir Trees Cres 1 PR5 77 A8
Firtrees Dr BB2 80 F8
Fir Trees Gr BB12 146 E5
Fir Trees La BB12 146 E5
Fir Trees Pl PR2 118 F4
Fir Trees Rd PR5 97 A1
Fir Tree Way 3 BL6 32 E1
Firwood WN8 18 D3
Firwood Cl PR3 140 A8
Firwood La PR5 99 B5
Fisher Dr
Orrell WN5 10 E7
Southport PR9 35 F7
Fishergate PR1 96 F7
Fishergate Ct 13 PR1 96 E7
Fishergate Ctr PR1 96 F7
Fishergate Hill PR1 96 E6
Fishergate Wlk 7 PR1 96 F7
Fishermans Cl L37 11 E6
Fishermans Reach PR4 113 D4
Fishermans Way FY7 175 C8
Fisher's La FY4 111 A5
FISHER'S ROW 201 E5
Fisher's Slack La FY6 155 B2
Fisher St FY1 130 C6
Fish House La PR3 185 B5
Fish La L40 38 B2
Fishmoor Dr BB2 81 F8
Fish Rake La BL0, BB4 68 E6
Fish St 5 PR1 117 F1
FISHWICK 97 C8
Fishwick La PR6 79 B1
Fishwick Par PR1 97 D8
Fishwick Prim Sch PR1 118 E1
Fishwick Rd PR1 97 C8
Fishwick View PR1 97 D8
Fitchfield PR1 96 F2
Fitzgerald St PR1 118 C1
Fitzroy Rd FY2 152 D3
Fitzroy St PR1 96 E7
Five Acres PR26 76 E4
Five Ashes La LA2 210 F7
Five Lane Ends
Hampson Green LA2 207 D8
Preesall FY6 200 A2
Singleton FY6 154 D3
Flag La
Bamber Bridge PR1 96 F1
Bretherton PR26 58 A5
Chorley PR6 43 F5
Runshaw Moor PR26, PR7 59 D4
Flag St OL13 70 E8
Flakefleet Ave FY7 198 E1
Flamingo Way FY6 200 B5
Flamstead WN8 18 C1
Flare Rd LA3 212 D6
Flash La L40 39 B4
Flatfield Way L31 5 E1
Flat La LA5 225 E3
Flatman's La L39 13 E1
Flats Ret Pk The PR5 97 C5
Flats The
Chorley PR7 43 B6
Kirkham PR4 114 B4
3 Kirkham PR4 114 B5
Flax Cl BB4 68 A8
Flaxfield Rd L37 12 A3
Flaxfields L40 25 F3
Flaxfield Way PR4 114 A5
Flax La L40 25 F2
FLAX MOSS 68 A8
Flax Moss Cl BB4 68 A8
Flax St 8 BL0 50 A4
Flaxton WN8 18 C1
Fleetgreen LA1 218 C3
Fleet La LA2 238 A8
Fleet Sq 6 LA1 214 F8
Fleet St
Blackpool FY1 130 C4
Chorley PR7 43 C7
Horwich BL6 32 D3
Longridge PR3 140 A7
Lytham St Anne's FY8 89 D8
Nelson BB9 170 E1
4 Preston PR1 96 F7
Fleet Street La PR3 141 A6
Fleet Wlk 6 BB11 128 A6
FLEETWOOD 198 E5
Fleetwood Charles Saer Com Prim Sch FY7 198 D3
Fleetwood Chaucer Com Prim Sch FY7 199 A4
Fleetwood Cl
Blackburn BB2 101 F1
Southport PR9 53 F3
Fleetwood Cres PR9 55 A6
Fleetwood Ct PR9 53 D1
Fleetwood Dr PR9 55 A6
Fleetwood Flakefleet Prim Sch FY7 198 E2
Fleetwood Hospl FY7 199 B5
Fleetwood Old Rd PR4 133 E3
Fleetwood Rd
Blackpool FY5 152 D7
Burnley BB10 148 C2
Carleton FY6 153 B5
Esprick PR4 133 D5
Fleetwood FY7 175 E8
Kirkham PR4 113 F7
Padiham BB12 126 D8
Southport PR9 53 E3
Fleetwood Rd N FY5 176 B3
Fleetwood Rd S FY5 153 B7
Fleetwood Sports Coll FY7 198 D2
Fleetwood St
6 Leyland PR25 77 B2
Preston PR2 117 D1
Fleming Ho 8 LA1 218 D2
Fleming Sq
Blackburn BB2 101 E4
Longridge PR3 140 B7
Flensburg Way PR26 76 D4
Fletcher Ave PR4 57 A6
FLETCHER BANK 50 D6
Fletcher Rd
Preston PR1 118 C1
Rishton BB1 103 A8
Fletcher's Dr L40 25 E4
Fletcher St
Blackburn BB2 101 D3
Bury BL9 33 A2
Nelson BB9 148 F7
Fletton Cl OL12 52 E2
Fletton Mews OL12 52 E2
Flett St PR2 117 C1
Flimby WN8 18 D1
Flimby Cl BB2 81 F8
Flintoff Way PR1 118 B3
Flintron Brow LA2 233 A2
Flip Rd BB4 85 A2
Flockton Ct 7 BL6 32 B4
Floodgates Rd L38 2 F5
Flordon WN8 18 D2
Florence Ave
Burnley BB11 127 C4
Warton PR4 92 D5
Florence Pl 1 BB1 102 A6
Florence St
Blackburn BB1 102 A6
Blackpool FY4 111 A6
Burnley BB11 127 C5
Church BB5 103 E6
Flowerfield PR4 116 E6
Flower Fields PR3 181 D2
Flower Scar Rd OL13 88 E6
Flowers Cl BB2 81 D7
Floyd Rd PR2 118 E3
Floyer St PR1 97 B7
Fluke Hall La PR3 201 B8
Flyde Road Ind Est PR9 54 B4
Fold BB9 170 E5
Fold Gdns OL12 52 B3
Fold House Pk PR3 201 D4
Fold La OL12 52 C4
Folds BL6 31 C3
Foldside PR4 93 C7
Folds St BB12 127 F8
Fold The BD23 197 B5
Fold View BL7 47 E1
Folkestone Cl
Cleveleys FY5 175 F4
Warton PR4 92 E7
Folkestone Rd
Lytham St Anne's FY8 89 F8
Southport PR8 35 F3
Folly La
Barnoldswick BB8 193 F7
Lancaster LA1, LA2 218 B4
Folly Terr BB4 86 B8
Folly Wlk 20 OL12 52 F1
Folly Wood Dr PR7 43 A6
Fontwell Cl WN6 29 F1
Fooden La BB7 230 E4
Footeran La LA5 225 E3
Foot Mill Cres OL12 52 D2
Foot Wood Cres OL12 52 D2
Forbes Ct BB11 127 A3
FORD GREEN 203 F2
Fordham Cl PR8 35 E3
Ford La
Goosnargh PR3 160 F2
Silverdale LA5 224 E5
Fordside Ave BB5 124 E4
Ford St
Barrowford BB9 170 E4
Burnley BB10 148 B1
Lancaster LA1 218 B1
Fordstone Ave FY6 200 A4
Fordway Ave FY3 130 F6
Foregate PR2 117 E4
Foreside BB9 170 E5
Fore St BB3 81 F7
Forest Ave BB12 147 E8
Forest Bank
Rawtenstall BB4 86 A7
Trawden BB8 172 C2
Forest Bank Rd BB4 86 A7
FOREST BECKS 230 D6
Forest Becks Brow BB7 230 D6
Forest Brook Ho PR2 117 F3
Forest Cl PR5 97 C3
Forest Dr
Lytham St Anne's FY8 90 F4
Shevington Moor WN6 29 A2
Skelmersdale WN8 18 C3
Forester Dr BB12 147 D8
Forester's Bldgs 9 BB18 196 B2
Foresters Hall 12 PR1 96 F8
Forest Fold WN6 19 E6
Forest Gate FY3 130 E5
Forest Gr PR3 137 B8
Forest Ho BB9 148 D7
FOREST HOLME 87 A7
Forest Holme Cl BB4 87 A7
Forest La BB9 170 B2
FOREST OF MEWITH 239 D6
Forest Pk LA1 214 C7
Forest Rd PR8 35 D6
Forestry Hos BB7 228 C5
Forest St
Burnley BB11 128 B6
Nelson BB9 170 D1
Water BB4 87 A7
Forest View
14 Barrowford BB9 170 D3
Brierfield BB9 148 A5
Rochdale OL12 52 D2
Forestway PR25 59 F8
Forest Way PR2 117 F6
Forfar Gr BB11 127 D3
Forfar St BB11 127 D3
Forge Cl L40 16 E4
Forge Cnr BB7 144 C5
Forge La PR3 181 E8
Forge St
3 Bacup OL13 87 F2
13 Leyland PR25 77 A1
Forgewood Cl LA2 219 E6
Forgewood Dr LA2 219 D6
FORMBY 11 E3
Formby Ave FY7 175 D7
Formby Bridge L37 11 E2
Formby Bsns Pk L37 12 B3
Formby By-Pass
Formby L37 12 B5
Formby By-Pass *continued*
Hightown L37, L38 3 B8
Formby Cl BB2 81 F8
Formby Cres PR4 74 F8
Formby Fields L37 12 A2
Formby Gdns L37 11 F4
Formby High Sch L37 11 E4
Formby La
Formby L37 12 B2
Haskayne L39 14 F1
Formby Pl PR2 116 E2
Formby Point Cvn Pk L37 11 B1
Formby Rd FY8 110 F1
Formby St L37 11 E2
Formby Sta L37 11 E2
Forrest Ct 4 FY3 130 E8
Forrester Cl PR25 76 E1
Forrestside BB2 81 D7
Forrest St BB1 102 A5
Forshaw Ave
Blackpool FY3 130 F8
Lytham St Anne's FY8 89 D8
Forshaw Cl 6 FY7 198 F2
Forshaw Rd 3 PR1 96 D2
Forsythia Dr PR6 78 B4
Fort Ave PR3 141 D3
FORTON 207 B3
Forton Primary Sch PR3 207 B3
Forton Rd 8 PR2 116 E1
Fort St
Accrington BB5 104 B6
Blackburn BB1 102 A5
11 Clayton-le-M BB5 124 F3
Clitheroe BB7 166 D7
Read BB12 145 D2
Fort Street Ind Est BB1 102 A6
Forty Acre La PR3 163 B5
Forward Ind Est PR25 76 E2
Foscote Rd L33 1 A4
Foss Ct LA3 217 E2
Fossdale Moss PR26 76 C1
Fosse Bank Ct BB2 82 A8
Fosse Cl BB2 82 A8
Fosse Ct LA3 217 E3
Foster Croft PR1 96 C6
Foster Ct
Bury BL9 33 D4
Chorley PR6 61 E1
Fosterfield Pl PR6 61 E1
Foster Rd
Barnoldswick BB18 196 A3
Formby L37 11 D2
Fosters Cl PR9 36 B8
FOSTERS GREEN 18 D3
Fosters Green Rd WN8 18 D3
Foster St
Accrington BB5 104 C7
Chorley PR6 61 E1
Fothergill St 1 BB8 171 C5
Fouldrey Ave FY6 153 F5
Foulds Cl BB8 171 C3
Foulds Rd BB8 172 B3
Foulds Terr BB8 172 C2
Foul La PR8, PR9 36 A5
FOULRIDGE 194 D1
Foulridge Wharf* BB8 194 D2
Foundary Gdns LA5 223 D3
Foundry Ct 8 PR1 117 E1
Foundry La LA2 219 B6
Foundry St
1 Bacup OL13 87 F2
Blackburn BB2 101 D4
3 Burnley BB11 127 F6
15 Chorley PR7 43 C8
24 Darwen BB3 82 A1
Haslingden BB4 85 B2
Rawtenstall BB4 85 F1
Fountain Cl BB12 126 D8
Fountain Pl 1 BB5 104 B5
Fountain St N 12 BL9 33 A3
Fountains Ave
Blackburn BB1 102 B8
Read BB12 145 D1
Fountains Cl PR7 43 D5
Fountain Sq 3 BB9 170 D3
Fountains Reach PR5 97 D1
Fountain St
Accrington BB5 104 A5
Barnoldswick BB18 196 C2
Bury BL9 33 A2
Colne BB8 171 D4
Darwen BB3 65 A8
Nelson BB9 170 E1
Fountains The
Barrowford BB9 170 D3
Ormskirk L39 15 E6
Fountains Way
Formby L37 12 B2
Oswaldtwistle BB5 103 B5
Fouracre BB2 121 E2
Four Acre La PR3 162 E5
Fourfields PR5 97 E2
Four La LA2 226 A8
FOUR LANE ENDS 101 D8
Four Lane Ends
Barley BB7 192 B2
Blackpool FY3 131 A6
Bretherton PR26 58 A7
Burton in L LA2 242 C1
Carleton FY6 153 B5
Charnock Richard PR7 42 C4
Clitheroe BB7 167 A6
Dolphinholme LA2 226 A8
Gregson Lane PR5 98 D2

**Four Lane Ends** *continued*
Halsall L39 23 D3
Halton LA2 218 F7
Heapey PR6 62 C4
Morecambe LA3 216 D1
Simonstone BB12 145 F4
Thornton FY5 176 E1
Wray LA2 238 E4
**Four Lanes End Rd** OL13 70 B8
**Four Oaks Rd** PR5 78 B7
**Fourth Ave**
Blackpool FY4 110 C7
Bury BL9 33 D4
**Fowler Ave** PR26 77 B6
**Fowler Cl** PR5 99 C2
**Fowler Height Cl** BB2 81 B7
**Fowler Hill La** PR3 204 B5
**Fowler Ind Pk** BL6 32 C2
**Fowler La**
Farington PR26 76 F6
Leyland PR5, PR26 77 B5
**Fowler St** 4 PR2 117 D3
**Foxcote** PR7 61 C2
**Foxcroft** BB12 127 D8
**Foxdale Ave** FY3 130 D7
**Foxdale Cl**
1 Bacup OL13 88 A1
Edgworth BL7 48 E7
Southport PR8 35 E3
**Foxdale Gr** PR1 118 D3
**Foxdale Pl** LA1 218 C2
**Foxen Dole La** BB12 147 A5
**Foxes Farmhouse** FY6 131 E7
**Foxes Terr** PR3 157 C7
**Foxfield Ave** LA4 217 C3
**Foxfield Cl** BB5 103 D4
**Foxfield Dr** BB4 86 F4
**Foxfields** FY6 177 C8
**Foxfold** WN8 18 D3
**Foxglove Ave** L40 25 F4
**Foxglove Cl**
Burnley BB11 128 B3
Hesketh Bank PR4 73 E4
Standish WN6 29 D2
Walton Summit PR5 78 B8
**Foxglove Ct** OL12 52 D3
**Foxglove Dr**
Bury BL9 33 D3
Lucas Green PR6 61 C5
**Foxglove Way** PR4 93 D7
**Fox Gr** LA3 216 E3
**Foxhall Rd** FY1 130 B3
**Foxhall Sq** 8 FY1 130 B3
**FOXHILL BANK** 103 D5
**Foxhill Bank Brow** BB5 103 E5
**Foxhill Cl** L37 11 C3
**Foxhill Dr** BB4 86 F4
**Foxhill Terr** BB5 103 E4
**Foxhole Rd**
Chorley PR7 42 F8
Euxton PR7 60 F1
**Foxholes Rd**
Horwich BL6 32 D4
Morecambe LA4 217 D6
**Foxhouse La** L31 5 F1
**Foxhouse St** BB2 101 C5
**Fox Ind Est** 2 FY2 152 E1
**Fox La**
Coupe Green PR5 98 E3
Leyland PR25 59 E7
**Fox Lane Ends** PR4 113 A5
**Fox St**
Accrington BB5 104 B6
Clitheroe BB7 189 E1
Horwich BL6 32 C2
Padiham BB12 126 F6
Preston PR1 96 F7
**Foxstones Cres** BB2 81 A8
**Foxstones La** BB10 129 B2
**Foxwell Cl** BB4 85 C2
**Foxwood Chase**
6 Accrington, Hillock Vale BB5 104 E8
Little Plumpton PR4 112 C6
**Foxwood Cl** WN5 10 E5
**Foxwood Dr** PR4 113 E5
**Foxwood The** PR7 42 C1
**Frailey Cl** PR8 21 C4
**Frances Darlington Ct** PR7 42 D4
**Frances St** 3 BB3 81 F2
**France St**
Blackburn BB2 101 D4
Church BB5 103 E6
**Francis Ave** BB9 170 E5
**Francis St**
Blackburn BB2 101 B1
Blackpool FY1 130 B6
Burnley BB10 148 A1
3 Clayton-le-M BB5 124 F3
Colne BB8 171 B3
Preston PR2 117 C1
**Frankland Ho** 15 LA1 218 D2
**Franklands** PR4 95 A1
**Franklands Dr** PR2 119 A5
**Franklands Fold** PR4 75 A8
**Franklin Ainsworth Ho** 2 BB6 124 C5
**Franklin Rd** BB2 101 B3
**Franklin St**
2 Burnley BB12 127 C6
Clitheroe BB7 166 D7
28 Darwen BB3 82 A1
Lancaster LA1 214 F5
**Frank St**
4 Accrington BB5 125 A1

**Frank St** *continued*
Barnoldswick BB18 196 B2
Preston PR1 117 F1
**Fraser Ave** PR1 96 E5
**Fraser Eagle Stadium (Accrington Stanley FC)** BB5 104 B8
**Fraser St**
3 Accrington BB5 104 A4
Burnley BB10 148 B1
**Frazer Gr** 18 FY4 130 B1
**FRECKLETON** 93 C7
**Freckleton CE Prim Sch** PR4 93 C7
**Freckleton Ct** FY8 91 C3
**Freckleton Dr** L33 1 A5
**Freckleton Rd**
Kirkham PR4 114 B3
Southport PR9 53 F4
**Freckleton St**
Blackburn BB2 101 E4
Blackpool FY1 130 C3
Kirkham PR4 114 B4
2 Lytham St Anne's FY8 91 C3
**Freckleton Strike Lane Prim Sch** PR4 93 B8
**Frederick Row** BB1 102 B5
**Frederick St**
Accrington BB5 104 A6
Barnoldswick BB18 196 A3
5 Blackburn BB2 101 E3
2 Blackpool FY4 110 D8
Chorley PR6 43 E7
Darwen BB3 82 A2
Oswaldtwistle BB5 103 E4
12 Ramsbottom BL0 50 B5
**Fredora Ave** FY3 131 A2
**FREEHOLD** 215 A8
**Freeholds La** BB7 188 F6
**Freeholds Rd** OL12 71 E6
**Freeholds Terr** OL12 71 E6
**Free La** BB4 68 A6
**Freeman Cl** BB1 102 C4
**Freeman's La** PR7 42 E3
**Freemantle Ave** FY4 110 B4
**Freeport Fleetwood Outlet Sh Village** FY7 199 A3
**FREE TOWN** 33 A4
**Freetown Bsns Pk** 11 BL9 33 A4
**Free Trade St** 16 BB11 127 F6
**Freightway** LA3 217 E2
**French Cl** BB2 101 B4
**French Rd** BB2 101 B4
**FRENCHWOOD** 97 B6
**Frenchwood Ave**
Lytham St Anne's FY8 90 F3
Preston PR1 97 B6
**Frenchwood Com Prim Sch** PR1 97 B6
**Frenchwood Knoll** PR1 97 B6
**Frenchwood St** 4 PR1 97 A6
**FRESHFIELD** 11 E5
**Freshfield Ave** BB5 124 E3
**Freshfield Ct** L37 11 E4
**Freshfield Cvn Pk** L37 11 B6
**Freshfield Gdns** L37 11 E4
**Freshfield Prim Sch** L37 12 A4
**Freshfield Rd** L37 11 E4
**Freshfields** PR2 116 D3
**Freshfield Sta** L37 11 E5
**Friargate** PR1 96 F8
**Friargate Wlk** 6 PR1 96 F7
**Friar's Moss Rd** LA2 232 A8
**Friar's Pas** 23 LA1 214 F8
**Friar St** 24 LA1 214 F8
**Friars The** PR2 117 E4
**Friars Wlk** L37 12 B2
**Friary Cl** PR4 114 C4
**Friday St** PR6 43 D8
**Frieldhurst Rd** OL14 109 C1
**Frinton Gr** FY2 152 E6
**Friths Ave** PR5 98 E1
**Frith's Ct** PR5 98 F1
**Frobisher Dr** FY8 110 D1
**Frog La** L40 26 D3
**Frome St** PR1 118 D1
**Froom St** PR6 43 F8
**Frostholme** OL14 109 B1
**Fryent Cl** BL6 31 D2
**Fryer Cl** PR1 96 D1
**Fry St** BB9 148 F8
**Fulford Ave** 1 PR2 116 C1
**Fulham St** BB9 170 F2
**FULLEDGE** 128 C5
**Fullers Terr** OL13 87 F1
**Full View** BB2 81 B8
**Fulmar Cres** LA3 212 F5
**Fulmars The** FY6 153 B2
**Fulmar Terr** BB5 103 E3
**Fulshaw Rd** PR2 117 B2
**FULWOOD** 117 D5
**Fulwood Ave**
Becconsall PR4 73 F1
Blackpool FY3 130 F8
Southport PR8 35 D4
**Fulwood & Cadley Prim Sch** PR2 117 D4
**Fulwood Dr** LA4 217 F6
**Fulwood Hall Hospl** PR2 118 C5
**Fulwood Hall La** PR2 118 B4
**Fulwood High Sch & Arts Coll** PR2 117 D6
**Fulwood Hts** PR2 118 C5
**Fulwood Pk** PR2 118 B7
**FULWOOD ROW** 118 E5
**Fulwood Row** PR2 118 E6
**Funchal Ave** L37 11 D1
**Furlong Cres** FY3 153 A1
**Furlong Gn** FY5 153 E8
**Furlong La** FY6 153 D5
**Furness Ave**
Blackburn BB1 102 B8
Fleetwood FY7 198 D1
Formby L37 11 F3
Normoss FY3 131 A8
Ormskirk L39 15 E4
Read BB12 145 D1
**Furness Cl**
Chorley PR7 43 D5
Southport PR8 21 B3
**Furness Ct** 3 FY3 131 A8
**Furness Dr**
High Bentham LA2 239 D8
Poulton-le-F FY6 154 A3
**Furnessford Rd** LA2 239 A6
**Furness Rd** LA3 216 D2
**Furness St**
7 Burnley BB10 148 B1
3 Lancaster LA1 218 B1
**Furnival Dr** L40 25 D4
**Further Ends Rd** PR4 93 B6
**Further Field** PR5 78 A8
**Furthergate** BB1 102 B5
**Furthergate Bsns Pk** BB1 102 B5
**Furthergate Ind Est** BB1 102 B5
**Further Heights Rd** 1 OL12 52 F1
**Further La** BB2, PR5 100 A8
**Further Wilworth** BB1 122 E2
**Fushetts La** LA2 239 D8
**Fusiliers Cl** PR7 60 F6
**Futura Pk** BL6 32 C1
**Futures Pk** OL13 70 E8
**Fylde Ave**
Lancaster LA1 211 B7
Leyland PR26 76 E4
**Fylde Coast Hospl** FY3 130 F7
**Fylde Ct** FY6 199 D5
**Fylde Rd**
Lytham St Anne's FY8 90 D5
Poulton-le-F FY6 153 E4
Preston PR1, PR2 117 D1
Southport PR9 54 B4
**Fylde Road Ind Est** PR1 117 D1
**Fylde St**
Kirkham PR4 114 A4
Preston PR1 96 E8
**Fylde View Cl** FY6 153 D2


## G


**Gabbot St** PR7 31 A7
**Gable Mews** L37 12 A1
**Gables Pl** 3 LA4 217 D5
**Gables The** PR4 116 E4
**Gable The** LA6 240 B7
**Gadfield St** 2 BB3 65 B8
**Gadsby St** FY1 130 B2
**Gage St** 32 LA1 214 F8
**Gaghills Rd** BB4 86 F1
**Gaghills Terr** 3 BB4 86 F1
**Gainsborough Ave**
Bamber Bridge PR5 77 A7
Blackburn BB2 101 C6
Burnley BB11 127 F3
Morecambe LA4 217 D6
**Gainsborough Rd**
Blackpool FY1 130 D4
Ramsbottom BL0 50 B1
Southport PR8 34 E3
**Gaisgill Ave** LA4 217 B3
Gait Barrows Nature Reserve* LA7 225 A7
**Gales La** L40 40 A3
**Gale St** OL12 52 F3
**GALGATE** 211 B3
**Galgate Mill** LA2 211 B4
**Galleries The** 1 BB9 148 E8
**Gallery The** L37 11 F3
**Galligreaves St** BB2 101 D3
**Galligreaves Way** BB2 101 D3
**Gall La** OL14 109 C3
**Galloway Cl** 2 OL10 33 F1
**Galloway Cres** FY2 152 F5
**Galloway Dr** WN8 10 B6
**Galloway Rd** FY7 198 F5
**Gallows La** PR3 142 A6
**Galway Ave** FY2 152 D3
**Gamble Rd** FY5 176 B4
**Gambleside Cl** BB4 106 A1
**Game St** BB6 124 C5
**Gamull La** PR2 118 F5
**Gandy La** OL12 52 D4
**Gannet Way** PR4 114 B2
**Gannow Bsns Pk** BB12 127 B6
**Gannow La** BB12 127 C6
**Gantley Ave** WN5 10 D3
**Gantley Cres** WN5 10 D3
**Gantley Rd** WN5 10 D4
**Ganton Cl** PR8 35 E3
**Ganton Ct** PR1 96 A6
**Garbett St** BB5 104 A4
**Garden Ave** PR4 113 B4
**Garden City** BL0 50 A2
**Garden Cl**
Blackpool FY3 131 A2
Poulton-le-F FY6 153 F3
**Garden Ct**
8 Preston PR2 117 C1

**Garden Ct** *continued*
Ramsbottom BL0 50 C7
**Gardeners Mews** 10 FY1 130 C7
**Gardeners Row** BB7 145 F7
**Gardeners View** L33 1 A6
**Gardenia Cl** PR6 78 B4
**Garden Pl** LA6 240 C7
**Garden Row** OL12 52 D2
**Gardens Gr** LA4 217 A4
**Garden St**
Abbey Village PR6 80 C2
Accrington BB5 104 B7
11 Bacup OL13 70 C8
1 Bamber Bridge PR5 77 B7
6 Barnoldswick BB18 196 B2
Blackburn BB2 101 C4
Brierfield BB9 148 B5
Colne BB8 171 D4
Great Harwood BB6 124 C4
Higham BB12 146 F5
Kirkham PR4 114 A4
Lytham St Anne's FY8 89 E6
Nelson BB9 148 E8
Oswaldtwistle BB5 103 D4
Padiham BB12 146 C1
Preston PR1 96 F7
Ramsbottom BL0 50 C6
Ramsbottom, Brooksbottoms BL0 50 C3
**Gardens The**
Edgworth BL7 48 D4
Halton LA2 219 B6
**Garden Terr**
17 Blackpool FY4 130 B1
Chorley PR7 61 C1
Middleton LA3 213 A2
**Garden Vale Bsns Ctr** 1 BB8 171 B4
**Garden View Pl** 1 FY4 130 E1
**Garden Wlk**
Cleveleys FY5 175 D5
Preston PR2 117 B1
**Gardinar Cl** WN1 30 B1
**Gardiners Pl** WN8 8 E8
**Gardner Arc** LA3 216 E4
**Gardner Bldgs** LA3 216 E4
**Gardner Rd**
Formby L37 12 B4
Lancaster LA1 218 D2
Morecambe LA3 216 E3
Warton LA5 223 D5
**Gardner's La** PR3 182 D3
**Gardner St** 18 PR1 96 F8
**Garfield Ave** LA1 214 D7
**Garfield Ct** FY3 131 C2
**Garfield Dr** LA4 217 F4
**Garfield St**
Accrington BB5 104 D5
Fleetwood FY7 199 B5
Todmorden OL14 109 C1
**Garfield Terr** PR6 61 D2
**Garforth Cres** 9 PR5 77 E8
**Garland Gr** 2 FY7 198 D3
**Garner Ave** BB2 81 D7
**Garnet Cl** 4 FY5 152 F7
**Garnet St** 3 LA1 215 A8
**Garnett Gn** L39 15 D4
**Garnett Pl** WN8 9 A7
**Garnett Rd** BB7 166 C7
**Garnett St**
Barrowford BB9 170 D2
Darwen BB3 82 B1
6 Morecambe LA4 217 B6
Ramsbottom BL0 50 B5
**Garrick Gr** FY3 130 E7
**Garrick Par** PR8 35 A6
**Garrick St** BB9 170 F2
**Garrison Rd** PR2 118 B3
**Garsdale Ave** BB10 148 B4
**Garsdale Cl** PR5 97 E5
**Garsdale Rd** PR2 118 E4
**Garsden Ave** BB1 102 E3
**Gars End** LA2 238 D6
**GARSTANG** 181 C7
**Garstang Cl** FY6 153 C3
**Garstang Com Prim Sch** PR3 181 C8
**Garstang High Sch** PR3 181 D5
**Garstang New Rd** FY6 154 E3
**Garstang Rd**
Bilsborrow PR3 159 A4
Bowgreave PR3 181 D4
Catterall PR3 181 E1
Chipping PR3 185 C2
Cockerham LA2, PR3 206 E2
Fisher's Row PR3 202 B3
Fulwood PR1, PR2, PR3 117 E5
Little Eccleston PR3, FY6 155 D5
Newsham PR3 137 B4
Singleton FY6 154 C3
Southport PR9 54 A5
St Michael's on W PR3 157 C7
**Garstang Rd E** FY6 153 E3
**Garstang Rd N** PR4 113 F7
**Garstang Rd S** PR4 113 F6
**Garstang Rd W** FY3, FY6 153 B2
**Garstang St Thomas' CE Prim Sch** PR3 181 B6
**Garstang St** BB3 82 A2
**Gars The** LA2 238 D6
**Garstone Croft** PR2 117 D6
**Garston St** BL9 33 A4
**Garswood Cl**
Brierfield BB12 147 F2
Maghull L31 5 E3
**Garton Ave** FY4 110 D6
**Gas Field Rd** LA3 212 E2
**Gas House La** LA2 239 D8
**Gaskell Cl** LA5 224 C3
**Gaskell Cres** FY5 176 A2
**Gaskell Ho** LA1 218 C4
**Gaskell Rd** PR1 96 E5
**Gaskell St** PR6 43 E8
**Gas St**
Adlington PR7 31 A6
Bacup OL13 87 F2
8 Burnley BB11 127 F6
Haslingden BB4 84 F1
Longridge PR3 140 A8
**Gas Terr** PR25 77 B2
**Gatefield Ct** BB11 128 A4
**Gategill Gr** WN5 10 D3
**Gate Ho** PR1 96 E7
**Gate House Ct** BL9 33 C2
**Gateland** BB18 194 D8
**Gatelands Cvn Site** LA6 240 B4
**Gatesgarth Ave** PR2 117 F7
**Gateside Ct** 2 FY3 131 A8
**Gateside Dr** FY3 130 F8
**Gates La** L29 4 C1
**Gate St** BB1 102 A5
**Gateway Cl** FY5 153 D7
**Gathurst La** WN6 19 F4
**Gathurst Rd**
Fulwood PR2 117 C2
Orrell WN5 10 E8
**Gaulter's La** FY6 200 C4
**Gaw Hill La** L39 15 B3
**Gaw Hill View** L39 15 B3
**Gawthorpe Edge** BB12 126 F8
Gawthorpe Hall* BB12 146 F1
**Gawthorpe Rd** BB12 127 D7
**Gawthorpe St** 13 BB12 146 C1
**Gawthorpe View** BB12 146 F5
**Gaydon Way** FY5 152 E7
**Gaylands La** BB18 197 C2
**Gayle Way** 1 BB5 103 F4
**Gaythorne Ave** PR1 97 F8
**GEC Bsns Pk** BB5 124 E2
**Geddes St** BB2 100 F2
**Geldof Dr** FY1 130 C8
**Gem Apartments** 9 OL14 109 B1
**General St** FY1 130 B6
**Geneva Rd** PR2 118 C4
**Genoa St** BB11 127 C4
**Geoffrey Lo** 13 PR2 118 F4
**Geoffrey St**
Bury BL9 33 A4
Chorley PR6 61 D1
Preston PR1 97 C8
Ramsbottom BL0 50 A4
**George Ave**
Blackpool FY4 130 F1
Great Harwood BB6 124 B4
**George Dr** PR8 21 E5
**George Fox Ave** LA1 211 B7
**George La** BB12 145 C2
**George Rd** BL0 50 B5
**George St W** BB2 101 D4
**George's La**
Banks PR9 55 A7
Horwich BL6 32 E5
**George's Rd** PR1 96 F7
**George's Row** 2 BB4 69 F8
**George St**
Accrington BB5 103 F4
4 Bacup OL13 70 C8
Barnoldswick BB18 196 C4
Blackburn BB2 101 E4
Blackpool FY1 130 C6
Burnley BB11 127 F5
Chorley PR7 43 C7
13 Clayton-le-M BB5 124 F3
Clitheroe BB7 166 D6
Darwen BB3 82 A2
1 Earby BB18 197 B1
Great Harwood BB6 124 C5
Haslingden BB4 85 B3
Horwich BL6 32 C3
3 Lancaster LA1 214 F7
Leyland PR25 77 B2
Longridge PR3 140 A8
11 Lytham St Anne's FY8 91 B3
Morecambe LA4 217 C5
Oswaldtwistle BB5 103 E5
Preston PR1 97 B7
Rishton BB1 124 B1
Whalley BB7 144 C5
Whitworth OL12 52 C8
**George Terr** WN5 10 D5
**George Trad Est** PR8 35 B4
**George Williams Ho** FY7 198 F2
**Georgian Pl** L37 11 E1
**Gerald Ct** 4 BB11 128 B4
**Gerard Way** L33 1 A2
**German La**
Bolton Green PR7 42 D7
1 Coppull PR7 42 E1
**Gerrard Pl** WN8 8 F7
**Gerrard's Fold** PR6 80 B2
**Gerrard St**
Lancaster LA1 214 D7
Preston PR1 96 E7

Gerrard's Terr FY6 153 C4
Gertrude St
Nelson BB9 171 A2
Shawforth OL12 71 E6
Ghants La FY6 177 E2
Ghyll La BB18 196 E4
Ghyll Mdws BB18 196 D4
Gibfield Rd BB8 171 A3
Gib Hey La PR3 161 F7
Gib Hill La BB4 106 B2
Gib Hill Rd BB9 171 B1
Gib La
Blackburn BB2 81 A7
Hoghton PR5 99 C3
Gibraltar Rd PR4 132 E5
Gibraltar St BB2 101 B6
Gibson St BB9 170 F2
Giddygate La L31 6 B1
Gidlow Ave PR6 31 A7
Gifford Way BB3 82 B2
Gilbert Pl L40 25 B4
Gilbertson Rd PR7 43 E2
Gilbert St
Burnley BB10 148 E2
4 Chorley PR7 43 C6
Ramsbottom BL0 68 C1
Rawtenstall BB4 86 D1
Gildabrook Rd FY4 110 D5
Gilderdale Ct 2 FY8 91 C4
Gildow St 1 PR1 96 E8
Gilescroft Ave L33 1 A4
Giles St
Clitheroe BB7 166 E7
Nelson BB9 170 E1
Gilett Farm Cvn Pk
FY4 111 F5
Gilhouse Ave PR2 116 C1
Gillcroft PR7 41 B7
Gill Ct FY4 110 B5
Giller Cl PR1 96 F2
Giller Dr PR1 96 F2
Giller Fold PR1 96 F2
Gillett St 6 PR1 118 C1
Gillhead Brow LA2 242 D1
Gillians La BB18 194 B8
Gillibrand Cl PR1 96 C1
Gillibrand Ho PR7 61 C2
Gillibrand Prim Sch
PR7 43 B6
Gillibrands Rd WN8 9 A7
Gillibrand St
Chorley PR7 43 C7
Darwen BB3 81 F3
Walton-le-D PR5 97 D5
Gillibrand Wlks PR7 43 C7
Gillies St
Accrington BB5 104 C6
Blackburn BB2 101 F3
Gillison Cl LA6 241 C2
Gill La PR4 75 C5
Gill Nook PR4 75 A5
Gillow Ave LA1 211 A7
Gillow Ct LA1 214 F5
Gillow Pk PR3 155 F6
Gillow Rd PR4 113 F5
Gills Croft BB7 167 A7
Gill St
Burnley BB12 127 E6
Colne BB8 171 B3
Nelson BB9 170 D1
Gilpin Ave L31 5 E2
Gilpin Cl 2 LA1 218 A2
Gilstead Ave LA3 213 A8
Gin Bow PR7 43 D6
Gin Croft La BL0 68 E4
Gingham Brow BL6 32 E4
Girvan Gr BB11 127 D5
Girvan Wlk 1 OL10 33 F1
GISBURN 231 C4
Gisburn Ave FY8 90 C6
Gisburn Bsns Pk BB7 231 A3
Gisburn Gr
Blackpool FY3 130 E7
Burnley BB10 128 D5
Gisburn Old Rd
Barnoldswick BB7,
BB9 193 C7
Blacko BB9 193 E4
Gisburn Prim Sch BB7 231 B3
Gisburn Rd
Barnoldswick BB18 196 A3
Barrowford BB9 170 E5
Blacko BB9 193 D4
Bolton-by-B BB7 230 E4
Fulwood PR2 118 E4
Gisburn Road Com Prim
Sch BB18 196 B2
Gisburn St
Barnoldswick BB18 196 B3
Blackburn BB2 101 C4
Gladden Pl WN8 8 E8
Glades The FY8 91 C4
Gladeswood Rd L33 1 B1
Glade The
Blackburn BB2 81 E6
Morecambe LA4 217 E5
Gladeway FY5 153 D7
Gladstone Cl BB2 100 F1
Gladstone Cres 3 OL13 88 A2
Gladstone Ho BB2 100 F1
Gladstone Rd PR9 35 F6
Gladstone St
Bacup OL13 88 A2
Blackburn BB1 102 B6
Blackpool FY4 130 C1
Gladstone St *continued*
Bury BL9 33 B3
Great Harwood BB6 124 C5
12 Todmorden OL14 109 B1
Gladstone Terr
Abbey Village PR6 80 C1
16 Barrowford BB9 170 D3
Blackburn BB2 100 F1
3 Lancaster LA1 218 E1
Trawden BB8 172 B4
Gladstone Way FY5 175 F1
Glaisdale Dr PR8 35 F3
Glamis Dr
Chorley PR7 43 B8
Southport PR9 54 B3
Glamis Rd PR25 60 C8
Glamorgan Gr BB12 127 A7
GLASSON 209 F5
Glasson Cl BB2 101 F1
Glasson Dock & Lune
Estuary Nature Trail*
LA2 210 B5
Glastonbury Ave FY1 130 E2
Glebe Cl
6 Accrington BB5 104 B5
Burton-in-K LA6 240 C7
Fulwood PR2 117 F4
Maghull L31 5 B1
Standish WN6 29 F1
Glebe Cotts BB4 85 A6
Glebe Ct 20 LA1 215 A8
Glebe La
Banks PR9 55 A7
Kirkham PR4 114 C4
Glebelands PR4 57 A5
Glebe Pl PR8 35 B7
Glebe Rd
Skelmersdale WN8 9 A8
Standish WN6 29 F1
Glebe St
Burnley BB11 128 B4
Great Harwood BB6 124 C5
Glebe The PR26 59 B8
Gleb Mews PR4 115 D2
Gledhill Way BL7 48 A1
Gledstone View BB18 196 A3
Glegside Rd L33 1 A2
Glenapp Ave FY4 111 A6
Glenarden Ave FY5 152 F8
Glenavon Dr OL12 52 D3
Glenbeck Cl BL6 32 D1
Glenborough Ave OL13 70 C8
Glenbrook Cl BB2 81 B8
Glenburn Rd
Skelmersdale WN8 17 F2
Skelmersdale WN8 18 A1
Glenburn Sports Coll
WN8 9 B8
Glencarron Cl BB3 65 F8
Glencoe Ave
Blackpool FY3 153 A1
Hoddlesden BB3 82 E1
Glencoe Cl OL10 33 F1
Glen Cottage (Youth
Hostel)* BB18 197 D2
Glencourse Dr PR2 118 D5
Glencoyne Dr PR9 54 B5
Glen Cres OL13 70 A8
Glencroft PR7 60 C3
Glencross Pl FY4 110 E7
Glendale Ave PR5 97 C1
Glendale Cl
Blackpool FY2 152 F5
Burnley BB11 128 A3
Leyland PR25 60 B7
Poulton-le-F FY6 153 C3
Glendale Cres PR5 97 C1
Glendale Dr BB2 121 E2
Glendale Gr
Fulwood PR2 118 D2
Kirkby L33 1 A5
Glendale Way L37 11 F2
Glendene Pk BB1 122 E5
Glenden Foot OL12 52 D2
Glendor Rd BB10 128 E5
Glen Dr WN6 19 E8
Gleneagles FY8 90 A6
Gleneagles Ave BB3 82 E1
Gleneagles Ct
Blackburn BB1 102 C3
Kirkham PR4 114 B4
Gleneagles Dr
Brockhall Village BB6 143 C6
Euxton PR7 60 D4
Fulwood PR2 117 B7
Higher Penwortham PR1 96 A6
Lancaster LA1 215 C7
Morecambe LA4 217 D6
Southport PR8 21 C3
Gleneagles Way 1 BL0 50 B5
Glen Eldon Rd FY8 89 E7
Glenfield Ave FY2 152 E6
Glenfield Cl BB1 102 B7
Glenfield Cvn Site
PR3 201 C5
Glenfield Park Ind Est
Blackburn BB1 102 B7
Nelson BB9 171 A1
Glenfield Park One
BB1 102 B8
Glenfield Park Two
BB1 102 B7
Glenfield Rd BB9 171 A1
Glengarry 7 FY8 91 C3
Glen Garth BB18 196 D3
Glen Gdns OL12 52 F2
Glen Gr PR2 118 F5
Glengreave Ave BB1 122 E3
Glenholme Gdns FY6 153 C2
Glenluce Cres BB1 102 D3
Glenluce Dr PR1 97 F8
Glenmarsh Way L37 12 B3
Glenmere Cres FY5 152 C7
Glenmore PR6 78 A3
Glenmore Ave FY5 176 B2
Glenmore Cl 4 BB5 104 E2
Glenmore Rd BL0 49 F2
Glenpark Dr PR9 54 B4
Glen Park Dr PR4 73 D4
Glen Rd BB4 69 F8
Glenrose Terr PR8 35 A5
Glenroy Ave BB8 171 D6
Glen Royd 1 OL12 52 C1
Glenroyd Cl FY3 130 E3
Glenroyd Dr L40 25 E4
Glenshiels Ave BB3 65 E8
Glenside WN6 28 B2
Glen Sq BB11 127 F2
Glen St
Bacup OL13 70 E8
Blackpool FY3 130 E4
Burnley BB11 127 E6
Colne BB8 171 D6
Ramsbottom BL0 50 B7
Glen Terr BB4 69 F8
Glen The
Blackburn BB2 81 E6
Caton LA2 237 C3
Fulwood PR2 118 F2
Knott End-on-S FY6 199 E4
GLEN TOP 70 A8
Glentworth Rd E LA4 217 D3
Glentworth Rd W LA4 217 C3
Glen View PR3 141 B8
Glen View Ave LA3 212 E6
Glenview Cl PR2 119 A3
Glen View Cres LA3 212 E6
Glenview Ct PR2 119 A3
Glen View Dr LA3 212 E6
Glen View Rd BB11 127 E2
Glen View St OL14 109 B1
Glenway PR1 96 C4
Glen Way BB9 148 B6
Glenwood St 3 FY3 130 D5
Global Way BB3 82 A5
Globe La BL7 47 D3
Globe Mill 7 BB4 86 F2
Glossop Cl FY2 152 C6
Gloucester Ave
Accrington BB5 104 A7
Blackpool FY1 130 D4
8 Clayton-le-M BB5 124 F3
Cleveleys FY5 175 D3
Horwich BL6 32 D2
Lancaster LA1 215 A4
Leyland PR25 77 C3
Gloucester Ct
5 Blackpool FY1 130 D4
Horwich BL6 32 D2
Gloucester Dr 5 LA3 216 E3
Gloucester Rd
Blackburn BB1 102 D5
Chorley PR7 43 C6
Lytham St Anne's FY8 90 D4
Rishton BB1 103 A8
Southport PR8 34 F5
Glover Cl PR26 58 F6
Glover Rd PR7 29 D7
GLOVERS BRIDGE 26 B3
Glover's Ct 23 PR1 97 A7
Glover St
Horwich BL6 32 B4
Preston PR1 97 A7
Glynn St BB5 103 F7
Godiva St BB10 148 A1
Godley St BB11 128 B6
Godwin Ave 7 FY3 130 E3
Goe La PR4 93 B6
Goitside BB9 170 E1
Goit St
Blackburn BB2 101 C2
Newchurch BB4 86 F1
Golbourne Cl FY7 198 D2
Golbourne St PR1 118 B1
Goldacre La BB6 124 A7
Goldburn Cl PR2 116 F6
Goldcrest Ave OL13 88 A2
Goldcrest Dr PR5 98 A2
GOLDEN HILL 77 A2
Golden Hill 9 PR25 77 B2
Golden Hill La PR25 76 F2
Golden Hill PRU PR25 76 E2
Golden Way PR1 96 C3
Goldfield Ave BB10 128 F6
Goldfinch Cres LA3 212 F5
Goldfinch Ct PR7 42 F5
Goldfinch Dr
Bury BL9 33 C4
Catterall PR3 181 C3
Goldfinch St PR1 118 B1
Goldhey St 13 BB1 102 A7
Goldsboro Ave FY3 130 F3
Goldshaw Ct BB12 169 C3
Goldstone Dr FY5 152 F7
Goldthread Works 27
PR1 97 A7
Golf Rd L37 11 E5
Golf View PR2 117 A6
GOLGOTHA 215 B7
Golgotha Rd LA1 215 A6
Golgotha Village LA1 215 B7
Gollinrod BL9 50 E4
Gonder La PR3 182 E3
Gooch St BL6 32 C2
Goodall Cl BB18 197 B2
Goodenber Cres 15
LA2 239 D8
Goodenber Rd LA2 239 D8
Goodier St PR1 97 C8
GOODSHAW 85 F8
Goodshaw Ave
Blackburn BB1 122 E1
Goodshaw Chapel BB4 106 A1
Goodshaw Ave N BB4 106 A2
GOODSHAW CHAPEL 106 B1
Goodshaw Chapel*
BB4 106 B1
Goodshaw Cl BB1 101 E8
GOODSHAW FOLD 105 F2
Good Shaw Fold Cl
BB4 106 A2
Goodshaw Fold Rd
BB4 105 F2
Goodshaw La
Accrington BB5 105 C1
Goodshaw Chapel BB4 106 B2
Good St PR1 96 E7
Goodwood Ave
Blackpool FY2 152 D1
Fulwood PR2 117 F7
Slyne LA2 218 D8
Goodwood Ct
Blackpool FY1 130 C4
Lancaster LA1 215 B4
Goodwood Pl 9 FY1 130 C5
Goodwood Rd LA1 215 B4
Goosebutts La BB7 166 F7
Goose Cote Hill BL7 47 E1
Goose Foot PR5 99 D5
Goose Foot Cl PR5 99 D7
Goose Foot La PR5 99 C6
Goose Green Ave PR7 42 F1
Goose Green La BB8 172 B2
Goose Hill St 13 OL13 87 F3
Goose House La BB3 82 A3
Gooselands BD24 236 F6
Goose Lane Cotts PR3 185 E1
Gooseleach La BB12 145 E1
GOOSNARGH 138 C6
Goosnargh La PR3 138 B7
Goosnargh Oliverson's CE
Prim Sch PR3 138 D6
Goosnargh Whitechapel
Prim Sch PR3 160 D7
Gordale Cl
Barnoldswick BB18 196 A2
Blackpool FY4 111 A8
Gordon Ave
2 Accrington BB5 104 A4
Maghull L31 5 C3
Southport PR9 53 C1
Thornton FY5 176 B2
Gordon Rd
Fleetwood FY7 198 F3
Lytham St Anne's FY8 90 D4
8 Nelson BB9 170 D1
Gordon St
Bacup OL13 87 F4
14 Blackpool FY4 130 B1
Burnley BB12 127 F7
Chorley PR6 43 D7
Church BB5 103 E5
Clayton-le-M BB5 125 A2
Colne BB8 171 F5
Darwen BB3 82 A3
Preston PR1 117 E1
Rawtenstall BB4 85 F2
Southport PR9 35 C8
Worsthorne BB10 129 B6
Gordonstoun Cres WN5 10 F7
Gordonstoun Pl
Blackburn BB2 101 C3
8 Thornton FY5 176 A2
Gordon Terr 1 LA1 215 A5
Gordon Way OL10 33 F1
Gore Cl BL9 33 C1
Gore Dr L39 15 E3
Gores La L37 11 F5
Gores Rd L33 1 B1
Goring St PR7 43 D7
Gornall's Bldgs 7 BB4 85 E2
Gorple Gn BB10 129 B5
Gorple Rd BB10 129 D5
Gorple St BB10 148 E3
Gorrell Cl BB12 169 D2
Gorse Ave FY5 175 F3
Gorse Bank BL9 33 C3
Gorse Cl
Great Knowley PR6 61 E5
Tarleton PR4 57 A6
Gorsefield L37 12 A6
Gorse Gr
Fulwood PR2 118 E3
Haslingden BB4 68 A8
3 Longton PR4 95 A1
Gorse La PR4 56 D5
Gorse Rd
Blackburn BB2 101 B5
Blackpool FY3 130 E4
Gorse St BB1 102 B6
Gorse Way L37 11 C4
Gorsewood Rd PR25 76 E1
Gorsey Brow WN6 29 B2
Gorsey La
Banks PR9 55 C7
Haskayne L39 13 B7
Hightown L38 3 B2
Mawdesley L40 40 C1
Gorsey Pl WN8 9 B7
Gorst La L40, PR9 25 A6
Gorsuch La L39, L40 23 D4
Gorton Fold BL6 32 C3
Gorton St FY1 130 C6
Gosforth Rd
Blackpool FY2 152 C1
Southport PR9 35 F8
Goudhurst Ct BL6 32 E4
Gough La
Clayton Brook PR5 78 C5
Walton Summit PR5 78 B6
Goulding Ave PR25 77 B1
Goulding St PR7 43 D6
Gowans La PR6 79 A8
Gower Ct PR26 76 D3
Gower Gdns L40 25 F3
Gower Gr PR4 75 A5
Gowery The 4 L37 12 A3
Goyt St FY8 89 F7
Grab La LA1 215 C7
Graburn Rd L37 11 F4
Gracamy Ave PR4 92 D5
Grace St BL6 32 B3
Graduate East La LA1 211 A6
Graduate La LA1 211 A6
Graduate North Ave
LA1 211 A6
Graduate South Ave
LA1 211 A6
Graduation College Sq
LA1 211 A6
Gradwell St 2 PR1 96 E8
Grafton Ave
Accrington BB5 104 E2
Burnley BB10 148 B5
Grafton Ct
3 Chorley PR7 43 B5
12 Darwen BB3 81 F2
Grafton Dr PR8 21 A5
Grafton Gdns BB5 104 E3
Grafton Pl 3 LA3 216 E3
Grafton Rd
Fulwood PR2 118 F4
2 Morecambe LA3 216 E3
Grafton St
Adlington PR7 30 F6
Blackburn BB2 101 D2
Blackpool FY1 130 C7
Clitheroe BB7 166 F8
Nelson BB9 170 F1
Preston PR1 96 E6
Grafton Terr 11 BB3 81 F2
Grafton Villas OL13 87 F1
Graham Ave
Appley Bridge WN6 28 C2
Bamber Bridge PR5 77 C8
Graham Rd PR3 204 C2
Graham's Pk FY4 131 E1
Graham St
Hoddlesden BB3 82 F1
Lancaster LA1 214 F6
6 Morecambe LA4 217 A5
1 Padiham BB12 126 D7
4 Preston PR1 118 B1
Grammar School Ct
L39 15 F4
Grammar School La
PR4 113 F5
Grampian Way FY8 91 D5
Granary The FY5 176 A2
Granby Ave FY3 130 E8
Granby Cl PR9 53 F3
Granby St BB12 127 D6
Grand Manor Dr FY8 90 D7
Grane Pk BB4 85 A2
Grane Rd BB4 84 C2
Grane St BB4 85 B2
GRANGE 119 A4
Grange PR7 29 D8
Grange Ave
Barrowford BB9 170 F5
Fulwood PR2 118 F4
Great Harwood BB6 124 E6
Rawtenstall BB4 86 B3
Southport PR9 35 E8
Thornton FY5 176 B2
Grange Cl
Great Harwood BB6 124 C6
Knott End-on-S FY6 199 F6
Oswaldtwistle BB5 104 A3
Rawtenstall BB4 86 B2
Grange Cres BB4 86 A2
Grange Ct 13 FY1 130 C7
Grange Dr
Coppull PR7 29 D8
Coupe Green PR5 98 E4
Euxton PR7 60 C4
Grange Farm Cotts PR4 93 E5
Grangefield PR4 94 F1
Grange Gdns FY6 153 D2
Grange Hts 7 BB4 84 F1
Grange La
Accrington BB5 104 C5
Formby L37 11 E5
Hutton PR4 94 D3
Newton-w-S PR4 114 F2
Stalmine FY6 177 B7
Grange Park Cl PR1 96 A6
Grange Park Way 5
BB4 84 F1
Grange Pl PR2 118 F4
Grange Rd
Blackburn BB2 101 B2
Blackpool FY3 130 F7
Bolton BL7 48 C1
Elswick PR4 155 F1
Fleetwood FY7 198 D3
Fulwood PR2 117 C3
Hambleton FY6 177 D1
Hightown L38 2 E6
Holme Chapel BB10 108 A7
Leyland PR25 76 D2

**Grange Rd** *continued*
Lytham St Anne's FY8 . . . . . 89 E7
Rawtenstall BB4 . . . . . . . . . 86 B2
Singleton FY6. . . . . . . . . . . 155 A3
Southport PR9 . . . . . . . . . . 35 E7
Whitworth OL12. . . . . . . . . . 71 D3
**Grange St**
Accrington BB5 . . . . . . . . . 104 C5
Barnoldswick BB18 . . . . . . 196 A3
Burnley BB11. . . . . . . . . . . 127 E5
Clayton-le-M BB5. . . . . . . . 124 E3
Morecambe LA4. . . . . . . . . 217 E6
2 Rawtenstall BB4. . . . . . . 86 A2
**Grange Terr** 19 BB4 . . . . . . 86 A3
**Grange The**
Arnside LA5. . . . . . . . . . . . 224 A8
Cottam PR4 . . . . . . . . . . . 116 E5
Lytham St Anne's FY8 . . . . . 90 E3
Southport PR9. . . . . . . . . . . 54 C3
Wilpshire BB1 . . . . . . . . . . 122 F5
**Grange View**
Carnforth LA5 . . . . . . . . . . 223 D3
Hest Bank LA5. . . . . . . . . . 220 F3
**Grange View Rd** LA6 . . . . 221 F6
**Granings The** PR4. . . . . . . 116 D6
**Granny's Bay** FY8 . . . . . . . . 90 C3
**Grant Cl** LA1. . . . . . . . . . . 214 D7
**Grant Dr** PR4 . . . . . . . . . . . 75 A5
**Grantham Cl** PR8 . . . . . . . . 35 A1
**Grantham Rd**
5 Blackpool FY1. . . . . . . . 130 C7
Southport PR8 . . . . . . . . . . . 35 A1
Weeton Camp PR4. . . . . . . . 132 E6
**Grantham St** BB2 . . . . . . . 101 B2
**Grant Mews** BL0 . . . . . . . . . 50 B7
**Granton Cl** L37 . . . . . . . . . . 11 E3
**Granton Wlk** PR2 . . . . . . . 117 A4
**Grant Rd** BB2. . . . . . . . . . . 101 B3
**Grants La** BL0 . . . . . . . . . . 50 C6
**Grant St**
Accrington BB5 . . . . . . . . . 104 A6
Burnley BB11. . . . . . . . . . . 127 E5
**Granville Ave**
Becconsall PR4 . . . . . . . . . . 73 E2
Maghull L31. . . . . . . . . . . . . . 5 C2
**Granville Cl** L39. . . . . . . . . . . 6 B8
**Granville Ct**
Chorley PR6. . . . . . . . . . . . . 61 E1
Southport PR9 . . . . . . . . . . . 53 D1
**Granville Gdns** BB5 . . . . . 104 D3
**Granville Ho**
Blackburn BB2. . . . . . . . . . 100 F1
Formby L37 . . . . . . . . . . . . . 11 E4
**GRANVILLE PARK**. . . . . . . . . . 6 B8
**Granville Pk** L39 . . . . . . . . . 6 C8
**Granville Pk W** L39. . . . . . . . 6 B8
**Granville Rd**
Accrington BB5 . . . . . . . . . 104 D3
Blackburn BB2. . . . . . . . . . 101 B5
Blackpool FY1 . . . . . . . . . . 130 D5
Brierfield BB9 . . . . . . . . . . 148 C6
Chorley PR6. . . . . . . . . . . . . 61 E1
Darwen BB3. . . . . . . . . . . . . 64 F8
Great Harwood BB6 . . . . . 124 D6
Lancaster LA1 . . . . . . . . . . 218 C3
Morecambe LA3. . . . . . . . . 216 E3
Southport PR8 . . . . . . . . . . . 34 D4
**Granville St**
Adlington PR6 . . . . . . . . . . . 31 A7
Burnley, Harle Syke
BB10. . . . . . . . . . . . . . . . 148 F2
14 Burnley, Stoneyholme
BB10. . . . . . . . . . . . . . . . 128 A8
Colne BB8 . . . . . . . . . . . . . 171 E5
Haslingden BB4. . . . . . . . . . 68 A7
**Grape La** PR26. . . . . . . . . . . 58 C1
**Grasmere Ave**
Blackburn BB1. . . . . . . . . . 122 C1
3 Fleetwood FY7 . . . . . . . 198 E4
Leyland PR25. . . . . . . . . . . . 77 A3
Orrell WN5. . . . . . . . . . . . . . 10 F8
Padiham BB12 . . . . . . . . . . 146 C1
Thornton FY5. . . . . . . . . . . 176 B2
Up Holland WN8 . . . . . . . . . 10 B7
**Grasmere Cl**
Accrington, Hillock Vale
BB5. . . . . . . . . . . . . . . . . 104 E8
Bamber Bridge PR5. . . . . . . 97 D2
Colne BB8 . . . . . . . . . . . . . 172 A5
Euxton PR7 . . . . . . . . . . . . . 60 E1
Fulwood PR2 . . . . . . . . . . . 118 C4
8 High Bentham LA2 . . . 239 D8
Rishton BB1. . . . . . . . . . . . 124 A1
**Grasmere Dr** 9 LA2. . . . . 239 D8
**Grasmere Gr**
Longridge PR3. . . . . . . . . . 139 F5
Whittle-le-W PR6. . . . . . . . . 61 B7
**Grasmere Rd**
Blackpool FY1 . . . . . . . . . . 130 D2
Formby L37 . . . . . . . . . . . . . 11 D3
Haslingden BB4. . . . . . . . . . 68 C8
Hightown L38. . . . . . . . . . . . . 3 A4
Knott End-on-S FY6 . . . . . . 199 F6
Lancaster LA1 . . . . . . . . . . 215 A8
Lytham St Anne's FY8 . . . . 110 E1
Maghull L31. . . . . . . . . . . . . . 5 D2
Morecambe LA4. . . . . . . . . 217 E6
**Grasmere St**
Burnley BB10. . . . . . . . . . . 148 A2
10 Rochdale OL12. . . . . . . . 52 F1
**Grasmere Terr**
Bacup OL13 . . . . . . . . . . . . . 87 F4
Chorley PR7. . . . . . . . . . . . . 43 B5
**Grasscroft Cl** FY7 . . . . . . . 198 D2
**Grassington Dr**
Burnley BB10. . . . . . . . . . . 148 D3
Bury BL9 . . . . . . . . . . . . . . . 33 D1
**Grassington Pl** 4 FY5. . . 152 F8
**Grassington Rd** FY8 . . . . . . 90 C7
**Gratton Pl** WN8. . . . . . . . . . . 9 A8
**Gravel Cl** PR9. . . . . . . . . . . . 54 F5
**Gravel La**
Banks PR9 . . . . . . . . . . . . . . 54 F5
Banks PR9 . . . . . . . . . . . . . . 55 B3
**Gravel The** PR4 . . . . . . . . . . 55 F2
**Graver Weir Terr** BB4 . . . 107 A1
**Grave-Yard La** L39. . . . . . . . 7 A6
**Graving Dock Rd** FY8. . . . . . 91 D4
**Gravners Field** FY5. . . . . . 176 D2
**Grayrigg Dr** LA4 . . . . . . . . 217 B3
**Grays Pl** LA3. . . . . . . . . . . . 216 E2
**GREAT ALTCAR** . . . . . . . . . . 12 E1
**Great Arley Sch** FY5. . . . . 176 B3
**Great Avenham St** 3
PR1 . . . . . . . . . . . . . . . . . . . . 97 A6
**Great Bolton St** BB2. . . . . 101 E3
**Great Close La** BD23,
BD24 . . . . . . . . . . . . . . . . . 236 D6
**Great Croft Cl** BB18 . . . . . 196 A3
**Great Eaves Rd** BL0 . . . . . . 50 C7
**GREAT ECCLESTON**. . . . . . 156 C4
**Great Eccleston Copp CE Prim Sch** PR3 . . . . . . . . . 156 A3
**Great Flatt** OL12 . . . . . . . . . 52 B1
**Great George St**
Colne BB8 . . . . . . . . . . . . . 171 D5
Preston PR1. . . . . . . . . . . . 118 A1
**Great Gill** PR4 . . . . . . . . . . . 75 A5
**Great Greens La** PR5 . . . . . 78 C5
**Great Hanover St** PR1 . . . 118 A1
**GREAT HARWOOD** . . . . . . 124 D4
**Great Harwood Prim Sch**
BB6. . . . . . . . . . . . . . . . . . 124 B5
**Great Hay** PR4 . . . . . . . . . . . 74 E2
**Great Hey** PR4. . . . . . . . . . . . 74 E2
Great House Barn*
BL6 . . . . . . . . . . . . . . . . . . . 31 F8
**Great John St** 20 LA1. . . . 214 F8
**GREAT KNOWLEY** . . . . . . . . 61 E3
**Great Lee** OL12 . . . . . . . . . . 52 D3
**Great Lee Wlk** OL12 . . . . . . 52 D2
**GREAT MARTON**. . . . . . . . . 130 F3
**GREAT MARTON MOSS** . . . . . . . . . . . . . . . 111 B4
**GREAT MARTON MOSS SIDE** . . . . . . . . . . . . . . . . 111 B7
**Great Mdw**
Bamber Bridge PR5. . . . . . . 77 A8
Chorley PR7. . . . . . . . . . . . . 61 A2
**GREAT MITTON** . . . . . . . . . 165 F2
**Great Park Dr** PR25 . . . . . . 77 A2
**GREAT PLUMPTON** . . . . . . 112 E7
**Great Shaw St** PR1. . . . . . . 96 F8
Great Stone of Fourstones*
LA2 . . . . . . . . . . . . . . . . . . 239 D5
**Great Stones Cl** BL7. . . . . . 47 E2
**Great Townley St** PR1 . . . . 97 D8
**Great Tunstead** PR4. . . . . . 75 A7
**Great Wood Cl** PR7 . . . . . . 42 F6
**Great Wood Prim Sch**
LA4 . . . . . . . . . . . . . . . . . . 217 E5
**GREAVE**. . . . . . . . . . . . . . . . 88 B3
**Greave Cl**
4 Bacup OL13 . . . . . . . . . . 88 B3
Rawtenstall BB4 . . . . . . . . . 86 A4
**Greave Clough Cl** 1
OL13 . . . . . . . . . . . . . . . . . . 88 B3
**Greave Clough Dr** OL13 . . 88 B3
**Greave Cres** 8 OL13 . . . . . . 88 A3
**Greave Fold** 6 OL13 . . . . . 88 B3
**Greave Rd** OL13. . . . . . . . . 88 B3
**Greaves Cl**
Appley Bridge WN6 . . . . . . . 19 F8
Banks PR9 . . . . . . . . . . . . . . 55 A6
**Greaves Ct** 3 LA1. . . . . . . 215 A5
**Greaves Dr** LA1 . . . . . . . . . 214 F6
**Greaves Hall Ave** PR9 . . . . 55 A5
**Greaves Mdw** PR1 . . . . . . . 96 E2
**Greaves Mead** LA1 . . . . . . 214 F5
**Greaves Rd** LA1. . . . . . . . . 214 F6
**Greaves St**
Great Harwood BB6 . . . . . 124 C4
Haslingden BB4. . . . . . . . . . 84 F2
9 Preston PR1. . . . . . . . . . 97 A7
**Greaves The** LA1. . . . . . . . 215 A6
**Greaves Town La** PR2 . . . 116 E1
**Greave Terr** 2 OL13 . . . . . . 88 B3
**Grebe Cl** FY3. . . . . . . . . . . 131 B7
**Grebe Wharf** 2 LA1. . . . . . 218 E1
**Greenacre**
Blackburn BB3. . . . . . . . . . . 81 F6
Westhead L40 . . . . . . . . . . . 16 E4
**Green Acre** PR3. . . . . . . . . 138 D6
**Greenacre Cl** BL0 . . . . . . . . 50 E7
**Greenacre Ct** LA1 . . . . . . . 215 B3
**Greenacre Pk** LA2. . . . . . . 220 E2
**Greenacre Rd** LA2 . . . . . . 220 E2
**Greenacres**
Chorley PR7. . . . . . . . . . . . . 43 C5
Edgworth BL7 . . . . . . . . . . . 48 E6
Fulwood PR2 . . . . . . . . . . . 117 B7
Read BB12. . . . . . . . . . . . . 145 D2
**Green Acres** PR4. . . . . . . . . 93 C7
**Greenacres Ave** PR4 . . . . 114 A4
**Greenacres Dr** PR3 . . . . . 181 D6
**Greenacre St** BB7. . . . . . . 166 E7
**Greenacres The** PR4 . . . . . 95 D2
**Green Ave** FY4. . . . . . . . . . 110 C6
**Greenbank**
3 Horwich BL6. . . . . . . . . . 32 D1
Ormskirk L39. . . . . . . . . . . . 15 C2
Poulton-le-F FY6 . . . . . . . . 153 E3
Whitworth OL12. . . . . . . . . . 52 C5
**GREEN BANK** . . . . . . . . . . 102 B6
**Green Bank**
Bacup OL13 . . . . . . . . . . . . . 70 D8
Barnoldswick BB18 . . . . . . 196 D4
**Greenbank Ave**
Maghull L31. . . . . . . . . . . . . . 5 C3
Orrell WN5. . . . . . . . . . . . . . 10 D3
Preston PR1. . . . . . . . . . . . 117 D2
**Green Bank Bsns Pk**
BB1. . . . . . . . . . . . . . . . . . 102 C7
**Greenbank Dr**
Fence BB12 . . . . . . . . . . . . 147 E8
Southport PR8. . . . . . . . . . . 34 E2
**Greenbank High Sch**
PR8. . . . . . . . . . . . . . . . . . . 34 E1
**Greenbank Pk** BB4. . . . . . . 86 B2
**Greenbank Pl** 6 PR1. . . . . 117 E1
**Greenbank Prim Sch**
OL12. . . . . . . . . . . . . . . . . . 52 F1
**Greenbank Rd**
Blackburn BB1. . . . . . . . . . 102 B6
Middleforth Green PR1 . . . . 96 E4
Rochdale OL12. . . . . . . . . . . 52 F2
**Greenbanks** FY2 . . . . . . . . 152 F3
**Greenbank St**
Preston, Maudlands
PR1. . . . . . . . . . . . . . . . . 117 D2
Preston PR1. . . . . . . . . . . . 117 E1
Rawtenstall BB4 . . . . . . . . . 86 B2
**Greenbank Tech Pk**
BB1. . . . . . . . . . . . . . . . . . 102 C7
**Greenbank Terr** BB3 . . . . . 81 F6
**Greenbank Way** BB1 . . . . 102 C6
**Greenbarn Way** BL6. . . . . . 31 D1
**Greenberfield La**
BB18 . . . . . . . . . . . . . . . . 196 C4
**Greenbriar Cl** FY3. . . . . . . 152 F1
**Green Bridge N** BB4. . . . . . 69 E7
**Green Bridge S** BB4. . . . . . 69 E7
**Greenbrook Cl**
Bury BL9 . . . . . . . . . . . . . . . 33 A4
Padiham BB12 . . . . . . . . . . 126 F6
**Greenbrook Rd** BB12. . . . 126 F6
**Greenbrook St** 6 BL9. . . . 33 A4
**Green Cl** BB11 . . . . . . . . . . 127 E2
**Greencliffe La** BB10. . . . . . 129 A1
**Greencroft** PR1. . . . . . . . . . 96 D3
**Greendale Ave** BB4 . . . . . . 86 E2
**Greendale Cl**
Fleetwood FY7. . . . . . . . . . 198 C2
Holme Chapel BB10. . . . . . 108 A7
**Greendale Dr** LA5. . . . . . . 223 D3
**Greendale Mews** 1
PR2 . . . . . . . . . . . . . . . . . . 116 E2
**Greendale View** BB7 . . . . 190 B8
**Green Dick's La** PR3 . . . . 200 E5
**Green Dr**
Bamber Bridge PR5. . . . . . . 97 C1
Barton PR3 . . . . . . . . . . . . 137 B8
Cleveleys FY5 . . . . . . . . . . 175 C5
Clitheroe BB7 . . . . . . . . . . 190 A2
Fulwood PR2 . . . . . . . . . . . 117 E7
Higher Penwortham PR1. . . 96 B5
Lytham St Anne's FY8 . . . . . 91 C5
Poulton-le-F FY6 . . . . . . . . 131 E8
**Green End** PR5 . . . . . . . . . . 99 E7
**Green End Ave** BB18 . . . . . 197 B2
**Green End Barn** BB18 . . . . 197 B1
**Green End Cl** 10 OL13 . . . . 88 A3
**Green End Rd** BB18 . . . . . 197 B1
**GREENFIELD**. . . . . . . . . . . 171 A4
**Greenfield Ave**
Chatburn BB7 . . . . . . . . . . 190 D5
Clitheroe BB7 . . . . . . . . . . 166 C8
Parbold WN8 . . . . . . . . . . . . 27 B2
**Greenfield Cl** PR9. . . . . . . . 54 A3
**Green Field Cl** 10 PR1. . . . 97 A6
**Greenfield Ct** 2 LA1 . . . . 215 A7
**Greenfield Dr** PR5 . . . . . . . 77 A8
**Greenfield Gdns** 1 BB4 . . 85 B2
**Greenfield Ho** 18 LA1 . . . 215 A8
**Greenfield La** PR3 . . . . . . 161 A6
**Greenfield Pk** PR4 . . . . . . . 93 F8
**Greenfield Rd**
Adlington PR6 . . . . . . . . . . . 31 A8
Blackpool FY5 . . . . . . . . . . 152 E8
Burnley BB10. . . . . . . . . . . 128 D4
Chorley PR6. . . . . . . . . . . . . 43 E8
Colne, Bunker's Hill BB8 . . 171 B4
Colne, Greenfield BB8 . . . . 171 A4
Fleetwood FY7. . . . . . . . . . 198 F2
Southport PR8. . . . . . . . . . . 36 C1
**Greenfields**
Blackburn BB2. . . . . . . . . . . 81 D7
Caton LA2 . . . . . . . . . . . . . 237 C3
Hesketh Bank PR4. . . . . . . . 73 D4
**Greenfields Cres** PR4 . . . 113 E6
**Greenfield St**
Darwen BB3. . . . . . . . . . . . . 65 C6
Haslingden BB4. . . . . . . . . . 85 B3
12 Lancaster LA1 . . . . . . . 215 A8
Rawtenstall BB4 . . . . . . . . . 86 A3
**Greenfield Terr**
Oswaldtwistle BB5 . . . . . . 103 A1
Todmorden OL14. . . . . . . . 109 A1
**Greenfield View** BB3 . . . . . 82 A7
**Greenfield Way** PR2. . . . . . 117 B5
**Greenfinch Ct** FY3 . . . . . . 131 B6
**Greenfold Dr** BB4 . . . . . . . 106 A2
**Greenfoot** 6 LA2 . . . . . . . 239 B8
**Greenfoot La** LA2 . . . . . . . 239 B8
**Greenford Cl** WN5 . . . . . . . 10 D6
**Greenford Rd** PR8 . . . . . . . 21 C4
**Greengate** FY5. . . . . . . . . . 176 D2
**Green Gate**
Fulwood PR2 . . . . . . . . . . . 117 C3
Hutton PR4 . . . . . . . . . . . . . 95 C1
**Greengate Cl**
6 Burnley BB12 . . . . . . . . 127 D7
**Greengate Cl** *continued*
Bury BL9 . . . . . . . . . . . . . . . 33 C2
Rawtenstall BB4 . . . . . . . . . 86 A5
**Greengate La** LA5. . . . . . . 221 C8
**Greenhaigh Ct** PR3. . . . . . 181 C7
**GREENHALGH**. . . . . . . . . . . 133 C5
**Greenhalgh La**
Adlington PR6 . . . . . . . . . . . 31 B8
Greenhalgh PR4. . . . . . . . . 133 D4
**Greenhall Cl** PR3 . . . . . . . 181 D6
**Greenham Ave** L33. . . . . . . . 1 A6
**Greenhaven** WN8 . . . . . . . . 10 B7
**GREEN HAWORTH** . . . . . . . 104 B1
**Green Haworth CE Prim Sch** BB5. . . . . . . . . . . . . . . 104 B1
**Greenhead Ave** BB1. . . . . 102 B7
**Green Head Cotts** 7
LA2. . . . . . . . . . . . . . . . . . . 239 B8
**Greenhead La** BB12 . . . . . 147 D5
**Green Hey**
Lytham St Anne's FY8 . . . . . 91 D4
Much Hoole PR4 . . . . . . . . . 74 E3
**Greenhey Pl** WN8. . . . . . . . . 8 F8
**Greenheys Ave** FY6 . . . . . 153 B4
**Greenheys Cres** BL8. . . . . . 49 F1
**Green Heys Dr** L31. . . . . . . . 5 F1
**Greenhill** BB6 . . . . . . . . . . 124 B5
**Green Hill** 9 OL13 . . . . . . . 88 A1
**Greenhill Ave** PR4 . . . . . . 114 A6
**Green Hill La** LA2, LA6 . . . 237 B6
**Greenhill Pl** 2 FY1 . . . . . . 130 C6
**Green Hill Rd** 8 OL13 . . . . 88 A1
**Greenholme Ave** LA4. . . . 217 B3
**Green Howarth View**
BB5 . . . . . . . . . . . . . . . . . . 104 A3
**Greenhurst Cl** BB2 . . . . . . 101 D4
**Greenings La** PR9. . . . . . . . 37 C3
**Green La**
Banks PR9 . . . . . . . . . . . . . . 55 C4
Bilsborrow PR3 . . . . . . . . . 159 B2
Bispham Green L40 . . . . . . . 27 B7
Blackburn BB2. . . . . . . . . . 101 A1
Bretherton PR26 . . . . . . . . . 58 C7
Chipping PR3 . . . . . . . . . . . 185 F3
Coppull PR7 . . . . . . . . . . . . . 30 A8
Cowan Bridge LA6. . . . . . . 242 B6
Downham BB7 . . . . . . . . . . 191 B6
Farington PR26 . . . . . . . . . . 76 E7
Formby L37 . . . . . . . . . . . . . 11 F5
Freckleton PR4 . . . . . . . . . . 93 B6
Garstang PR3 . . . . . . . . . . . 181 A7
Grindleton BB7 . . . . . . . . . 190 A7
Halton LA2. . . . . . . . . . . . . 219 F8
Holmes PR4. . . . . . . . . . . . . 56 C4
Horton BD23 . . . . . . . . . . . 231 E5
Horwich BL6 . . . . . . . . . . . . 32 B5
Kingsfold PR4 . . . . . . . . . . . 96 C1
Lancaster, Bailrigg LA1,
LA2 . . . . . . . . . . . . . . . . . 211 A7
Lancaster LA1, LA2 . . . . . . 218 E6
Longridge PR3. . . . . . . . . . 140 B8
Maghull L31. . . . . . . . . . . . . . 5 A2
Maghull L31. . . . . . . . . . . . . . 5 C1
Morecambe LA3. . . . . . . . . 217 B2
Ormskirk L39. . . . . . . . . . . . 15 E6
Orrell WN5. . . . . . . . . . . . . . 10 D3
Padiham BB12 . . . . . . . . . . 126 C8
Preesall FY6 . . . . . . . . . . . 200 C2
Riley Green PR5. . . . . . . . . . 79 E8
Samlesbury Bottoms PR5 . . 99 B7
Skelmersdale L40 . . . . . . . . 18 A6
Skelmersdale L40, WN8 . . . 17 F6
Sollom PR4 . . . . . . . . . . . . . 56 D1
Woodsfold PR4 . . . . . . . . . 135 E6
**Green La E** PR3 . . . . . . . . . 204 C2
**Greenland Ave** WN6. . . . . . . 29 E1
**Greenland La** PR6. . . . . . . . 31 D5
**Greenlands Cres** PR2. . . . . 118 E3
**GREEN LANE**. . . . . . . . . . . . . 81 A8
**Green Lane Ave** L39. . . . . . . 15 E6
**Green La The** L40 . . . . . . . . 25 F4
**Green La W**
Freckleton PR4 . . . . . . . . . . 93 B5
Garstang PR3 . . . . . . . . . . . 204 B1
**Greenlea Cl** WN5 . . . . . . . . 10 D5
**Greenlea Dr** LA4 . . . . . . . . 217 D5
**Green Link** L31 . . . . . . . . . . . 5 B2
**Greenloon's Dr** L37 . . . . . . 11 C3
**Greenloon's Wlk** L37. . . . . 11 C2
**Green Mdw** BB8 . . . . . . . . 172 B2
**Greenmead Cl** PR4 . . . . . 116 E5
**Green Meadow La**
FY6. . . . . . . . . . . . . . . . . . . 177 C1
**Greenmoor La** PR3. . . . . . 141 B7
**GREENMOUNT** . . . . . . . . . . 49 E1
**Green Mount** BB6. . . . . . . 144 D8
**Greenmount Ave**
1 Kirkham PR4 . . . . . . . . 114 A5
1 Thornton FY5 . . . . . . . . 176 A3
**Greenmount Cl** BL8 . . . . . . 49 F2
**Greenmount Dr** BL8. . . . . . 49 F2
**Greenmount Prim Sch**
BL8 . . . . . . . . . . . . . . . . . . . 49 F2
**Green Nook La** PR3 . . . . . 139 F6
**Green Oak Pl** FY5 . . . . . . . 153 A8
**Greenock Cl** BB11. . . . . . . 127 D4
**Greenock Dr** OL10 . . . . . . . 33 F1
**Greenock St** BB11. . . . . . . 127 D4
**Greenpark Cl** BL8 . . . . . . . . 49 F1
**Green Park Cl** BB2 . . . . . . 101 C2
**Green Park Ct** BB7 . . . . . . 144 D8
**Green Park Dr** L31. . . . . . . . . 5 B1
**Green Park Prim Sch**
L31 . . . . . . . . . . . . . . . . . . . . 5 B2
**Green Pk** BB7. . . . . . . . . . . 144 C5
**Green Pl** PR5 . . . . . . . . . . . . 78 A6
**Green Rd** BB8 . . . . . . . . . . 171 D4
**Green Ridge Cl** BB9 . . . . . 148 D5
**Green Row** BB3. . . . . . . . . . . 81 B6
**Green St E** 17 BB3 . . . . . . . 82 A1
**Greens Arms Rd** BB3,
BL7. . . . . . . . . . . . . . . . . . . . 47 E7
**Greenset Cl** LA1 . . . . . . . . 218 C4
**Greenside**
Cottam PR4 . . . . . . . . . . . . 116 D4
Euxton PR7 . . . . . . . . . . . . . 60 C3
Ribchester PR3 . . . . . . . . . 141 E3
**Greenside Ave**
Blackburn BB2. . . . . . . . . . . 81 A8
Preston PR2. . . . . . . . . . . . 116 C1
**Greenside Cl**
Hawkshaw BL8 . . . . . . . . . . 49 B3
Kirkby L33 . . . . . . . . . . . . . . . 1 A6
**Greenside Dr** BL8. . . . . . . . 49 F1
**Greenside Gdns** PR26 . . . . 59 B7
**Greens La**
Bacup, Greave OL13 . . . . . . 88 A3
Bacup, Nun Hills OL13. . . . . 70 D7
Haslingden BB4. . . . . . . . . . 68 C7
**Green's La**
Haskayne L31 . . . . . . . . . . . 14 C1
Stalmine FY6 . . . . . . . . . . . 177 F7
**Greenslate Ave** WN6 . . . . . 19 E8
**Greenslate Ct** WN5. . . . . . . 10 E3
**Greenslate Rd** WN5 . . . . . . 10 E3
**Greensnook La** OL13 . . . . . 88 A3
**Greensnook Mews** 2
OL13 . . . . . . . . . . . . . . . . . . 88 A3
**Greensnook Terr** 1
OL13 . . . . . . . . . . . . . . . . . . 88 A3
**Green St**
Adlington PR6 . . . . . . . . . . . 31 B8
12 Barnoldswick BB18 . . . 196 B2
Burnley BB10. . . . . . . . . . . 148 B1
Chorley PR7. . . . . . . . . . . . . 43 A5
Darwen BB3. . . . . . . . . . . . . 82 A1
Edenfield BL0. . . . . . . . . . . . 68 E3
Great Harwood BB6 . . . . . 124 B5
Lancaster LA1 . . . . . . . . . . 218 E1
Lytham St Anne's FY8 . . . . . 91 A3
Morecambe LA4. . . . . . . . . 217 B6
Oswaldtwistle BB5 . . . . . . 103 C2
Padiham BB12 . . . . . . . . . . 126 C7
Rawtenstall BB4 . . . . . . . . . 86 A3
**Greens The** OL12. . . . . . . . . 71 C1
**Greenstone Ave** BL6 . . . . . . 32 B3
**Greensward Cl** WN6. . . . . . 29 B1
**Greensway** PR3. . . . . . . . . 137 C3
**Green The**
Adlington PR6 . . . . . . . . . . . 43 F2
Bispham Green L40. . . . . . . 27 B8
Bolton-le-S LA5 . . . . . . . . . 221 B5
Churchtown PR3 . . . . . . . . 181 A2
Colne BB8 . . . . . . . . . . . . . 171 F6
5 Darwen BB3. . . . . . . . . . . 82 A1
Eccleston PR7 . . . . . . . . . . . 41 C6
Fulwood PR2 . . . . . . . . . . . 118 F2
Hesketh Bank PR4. . . . . . . . 73 E3
Nelson BB9 . . . . . . . . . . . . 171 B2
Parbold WN8 . . . . . . . . . . . . 27 B2
Ramsbottom BL8. . . . . . . . . 49 F1
Silverdale LA5 . . . . . . . . . . 224 D2
Weeton PR4. . . . . . . . . . . . 132 F2
Wrea Green PR4 . . . . . . . . 113 B3
**Greenthorn Cres** PR2 . . . 119 A2
**Greenthorne Cl** BL7. . . . . . 48 E7
**Greenthorne Terr** 2
BB3 . . . . . . . . . . . . . . . . . . . 65 A8
**Greenvale** WN6 . . . . . . . . . . 19 F4
**Greenville Dr** L31. . . . . . . . . 5 C1
**Greenwater Ct** 7 LA1 . . . 218 D2
**Greenway**
Catterall PR3. . . . . . . . . . . 181 D3
Eccleston PR7 . . . . . . . . . . . 41 B7
Fulwood PR2 . . . . . . . . . . . 117 D7
Higher Penwortham PR1. . . 96 B4
Horwich BL6 . . . . . . . . . . . . 32 F3
**Green Way** 4 FY4 . . . . . . . 110 F7
**Greenway Ave** WN8 . . . . . . . 9 B8
**Greenway Cl** WN8. . . . . . . . 17 E2
**Greenway Ho** FY6. . . . . . . 153 E3
**Greenway Mews** BL0 . . . . . 50 C4
**Greenways**
Becconsall PR4 . . . . . . . . . . 73 F1
Lytham St Anne's FY8 . . . . . 90 B6
Orrell WN5. . . . . . . . . . . . . . 10 D3
Over Kellet LA6 . . . . . . . . . 237 B8
**Greenway St** BB3 . . . . . . . . 81 F3
**Greenwich Dr** FY8 . . . . . . . 90 D5
**Green Wlk**
Blackrod BL6 . . . . . . . . . . . . 31 D1
Earby BB18 . . . . . . . . . . . . 197 A1
Southport PR8. . . . . . . . . . . 21 D5
**Greenwood** PR5 . . . . . . . . . . 78 B4
**Greenwood Ave**
Blackpool FY1 . . . . . . . . . . 130 E2
Hest Bank LA5. . . . . . . . . . 220 F2
Horwich BL6 . . . . . . . . . . . . 32 D1
**Greenwood Cl**
Lytham St Anne's FY8 . . . . . 90 E4
Ormskirk L39. . . . . . . . . . . . 15 C1
**Greenwood Cres** LA5. . . . . 220 F2
**Greenwood Ct** PR25. . . . . . 77 A1
**Greenwood Dr** LA5. . . . . . 220 F2
**Greenwood Gdns** PR8. . . . . 35 A5
**Greenwood Rd** WN6 . . . . . 29 E2
**Greenwood St**
1 Bamber Bridge PR5 . . . . 97 E1
Preston PR1. . . . . . . . . . . . . 97 B7
**Greenwood The** BB2 . . . . . 81 D7
**Greetby Hill** L39, L40. . . . . 16 A6
**Greetby Pl** WN8. . . . . . . . . . 9 A8
**Gregareth Cl** 5 LA1. . . . . 218 A2

Greg Ho 13 LA1 218 D2
Gregory Ave FY2 152 C5
Gregory Fold BB4 68 A7
Gregory La L39 23 B3
Gregory Mdw PR3 181 B7
Gregory Pl FY8 91 A3
Gregory's Ct LA1 215 A4
Gregson Cl 5 FY4 110 F7
Gregson Dr 3 FY7 198 F2
Gregson La
7 Blackburn BB2 101 D5
Gregson Lane PR5 98 E1
Higher Walton PR5 98 C2
GREGSON LANE 98 E2
Gregson Rd LA1 215 A7
Gregson's Ave L37 11 E5
Gregson St
Darwen BB3 65 A8
Lytham St Anne's FY8 91 A3
Gregson Way PR2 118 B5
Grenada Cl BB3 81 F6
Grenfell Ave FY3 130 E7
Grenville Ave
Bamber Bridge PR5 97 D2
Lytham St Anne's FY8 110 E1
Gresham Rd FY5 175 D1
Gresham St BB4 86 F1
Gresley Ave BL6 32 B3
Gresley Ct LA1 214 F6
Gresley Pl FY2 152 E2
GRESSINGHAM 241 A1
Gressingham Dr LA1 215 A4
Gressingham Ho 3
LA1 215 A3
Gressingham Wlk LA1 215 B3
Greta Heath LA6 242 C3
Greta Pl
Fleetwood FY7 198 D3
Lancaster LA1 218 C2
Gretdale Ave FY8 89 E8
Gretna Cres FY5 152 D8
Gretna Rd BB1 122 F1
Gretna Wlk BB1 122 F1
Greyfriars Ave PR2 117 D5
Greyfriars Cres PR2 117 D5
Greyfriars Dr PR1 96 C5
Greyfriars Rd PR8 21 B6
Grey Heights View PR6 43 E8
Greyhound Bridge Rd
LA1 218 D1
Grey St
Barrowford BB9 170 D3
Burnley BB10 128 A8
Greystock Ave PR2 117 E6
Greystock Cl PR5 78 B8
Greystock Pl PR2 117 E6
Greystoke Ave BB2 80 E8
Greystoke Ct FY4 110 B5
Greystoke Pl FY4 110 B5
Greystokes L39 15 D2
Greystonegill La LA2 239 F7
Greystones PR26 76 B1
Greystones Dr BB12 147 E8
Greythwaite Ct LA1 214 D6
Greywood Ave BL9 33 B2
GRIFFIN 101 C3
Griffin Cl
Burnley BB11 127 B5
Bury BL9 33 B4
Huncoat BB5 125 F1
Griffin Ho BL9 33 A4
Griffin Park Prim Sch
BB2 101 B3
Griffin St BB2 101 B3
Griffiths Dr PR9 35 F8
Griffon Ho PR9 53 F2
Grimeford La BL6, PR6 31 C5
GRIMEFORD VILLAGE 31 D6
Grimeshaw La LA1 219 B3
Grime St
Chorley PR7 43 D6
Darwen BB3 81 F2
7 Ramsbottom BL0 50 A4
Grimrod Pl WN8 9 A7
GRIMSARGH 139 D1
Grimsargh Manor PR2 139 C2
Grimsargh St Michael's CE
Sch PR2 139 C1
Grimsargh St 10 PR1 118 D1
GRIMSHAW GREEN 27 B5
Grimshaw Green La L40,
WN8 27 C6
Grimshaw La L39 15 E7
GRIMSHAW PARK 101 F2
Grimshaw Pk BB2 101 F3
Grimshaw Pl PR1 97 A7
Grimshaw Rd WN8 9 D8
Grimshaw Ret Pk BB2 101 F3
Grimshaw St
Accrington BB5 104 A5
6 Barrowford BB9 170 D4
Burnley BB11 128 A5
Church BB5 103 E6
2 Clayton-le-M BB5 124 F2
Darwen BB3 65 B7
Great Harwood BB6 124 C5
Preston PR1 97 A7
Grindlestone Ct PR3 138 E6
Grindlestone Hirst
BB8 171 C3
GRINDLETON 190 B7
Grindleton Brow BB7 190 B7
Grindleton CE Prim Sch
BB7 190 C8
Grindleton Cl FY3 131 B8
Grindleton Gr BB10 128 D5
Grindleton Rd
1 Blackburn BB2 101 C4
Grindleton BB7 190 B7
West Bradford BB7 189 F6
Gringley Rd LA4 217 C3
Grinstead Cl PR8 34 F1
Grisedale Ave BB1 102 C2
Grisedale Cl L37 11 E3
Grisedale Dr BB12 127 B8
Grisedale Pl PR7 43 B5
Gristlehurst La BL9 33 F5
Grizedale Ave
Garstang PR3 181 B7
Lancaster LA1 211 B7
Poulton-le-F FY6 153 C3
Grizedale Cl
Clayton-le-M BB5 124 E2
Fulwood PR2 118 F2
Grizedale Cres PR2 119 A2
Grizedale Ct
Blackpool FY3 130 E5
8 Thornton FY5 176 B3
Grizedale Pl
Fulwood PR2 118 F2
4 Morecambe LA3 216 E1
Grizedale Rd
Blackpool FY4 131 C1
Lancaster LA1 218 F2
Grosvenor Cl PR8 34 E3
Grosvenor Ct
Carnforth LA5 223 C1
Cleveleys FY5 175 C2
6 Lytham St Anne's FY8 90 A8
Southport PR8 34 E3
Grosvenor Gdns PR8 34 F3
Grosvenor Lo BB1 122 F6
Grosvenor Mews PR4 114 B4
Grosvenor Park Prim Sch
LA3 217 F2
Grosvenor Pl
Carnforth LA5 223 C1
Preston PR2 117 B2
Southport PR8 34 F3
Grosvenor Rd
Carnforth LA5 223 D1
Chorley PR7 43 B6
Morecambe LA3 216 D3
Southport PR8 34 E4
Grosvenor St
Blackpool FY1 130 C5
Burnley BB12 127 F7
Colne BB8 171 F5
Lytham St Anne's FY8 91 C3
Preston PR1 97 B7
Grosvenor Way
5 Blackburn BB1 101 E5
Horwich BL6 32 C3
Grouse St OL12 52 F1
Grove Ave
Adlington PR6 31 A7
Longton PR4 74 F8
Grove Cres PR6 31 A7
Grove Ct
Lancaster LA1 214 F6
Oswaldtwistle BB5 103 C3
Grove La BB12 146 E1
Grove Mead L31 5 F1
Grove Mill PR7 41 C5
Grove Park Ind Est PR7 41 C5
Grove Pk
Ormskirk L39 15 F7
Southport PR9 35 F8
Grove Rd
Preston PR5 97 C6
Up Holland WN8 10 C8
Grove St
Accrington BB5 104 A6
Bacup OL13 88 A3
12 Bamber Bridge PR5 77 F8
Barrowford BB9 170 D3
Blackburn BB2 101 E2
4 Burnley BB11 127 D5
Earby BB18 197 B2
Leyland PR25 59 D8
Lytham St Anne's FY8 89 F7
Morecambe LA4 216 F4
Nelson BB9 148 E8
Oswaldtwistle BB5 103 D3
Southport PR8 35 A4
Grove Terr PR8 35 A5
Grove The
Appley Bridge WN6 28 C2
Bilsborrow PR3 159 A5
4 Burnley BB12 127 B6
Chipping PR3 185 D4
Chorley PR7 61 C2
Cleveleys FY5 175 E3
Clitheroe BB7 189 F1
Crag Bank LA5 223 B1
Higher Penwortham PR1 96 B4
Lancaster LA1 215 A7
Ormskirk L39 6 C7
Oswaldtwistle BB5 103 E5
Preston PR2 117 B1
Rufford L40 39 A3
Whalley BB7 144 C5
Grovewood PR8 34 E5
Grovewood Dr WN6 19 E8
Grovewood Ho PR7 61 C2
Grundy Cl
Bury BL9 33 A1
Southport PR8 35 E5
Grundy La BL9 33 A1
Grundy Mews FY4 110 C7
Grundy's La PR7 43 D1
Grundy St 7 PR25 77 B2
GRUNSAGILL 236 D1
Guardian Cl PR2 118 A4
Gubberford La PR3 204 D4
Guernsey Ave
Blackburn BB2 101 F1
Buckshaw Village PR7 60 F6
GUIDE 82 D8
Guide La BB12 147 A7
Guide Rd PR4 73 E6
Guildford Ave
Blackpool FY2 152 D6
Great Knowley PR6 61 E4
Guildford Rd
30 Preston PR1 97 A7
Southport PR8 22 A8
Guildford St 6 BB9 148 B5
Guildford Way FY6 153 C6
Guild Hall Arc 5 PR1 97 A7
Guildhall St PR1 96 F7
Guild Row 7 PR1 97 A7
Guild Trad Est 9 PR1 97 B8
Guild Way PR1 96 D7
Guinea Hall Cl PR9 55 A5
Guinea Hall La PR9 55 A5
Guinea Hall Mews PR9 55 A5
Gulf La LA2, PR3 202 D7
Gummers Howe Wlk
LA5 221 E8
Gurney St BB2 101 B3
Gutter La BL0 50 B7
Guys Ind Est L40 25 B2
Guy St BB12 146 C1
Guys Thatched Hamlet
(Craft Ctr)* PR3 158 F3
Guysyke BB8 171 C4
Gynn Ave FY1 130 B8
Gynn Sq FY1 130 B8

H

HABERGHAM 126 F7
Habergham Dr BB12 126 F8
Habergham St 19
BB12 146 C1
Hackensall Rd FY6 199 E5
Hacking Cl BB6 143 C1
Hacking Dr PR3 139 F5
Hacking's Cvn Holiday Pk
BB7 143 E6
Hacking St
Bury BL9 33 A2
Darwen BB3 81 F1
5 Nelson BB9 170 F2
Hacklands Ave PR2 116 C1
Haddings La BB12 147 A8
Haddon Ct FY2 152 C5
Haddon Pl PR2 117 D3
Haddon Rd FY2 152 C5
Hadlee Terr LA1 218 B1
Hadleigh Rd FY6 153 C6
Hadrian Rd LA3 217 E3
Hadstock Ave L37 11 D1
HAGGATE 149 A3
Hagg La PR3 156 C8
Hagg St BB8 171 C4
Haig Ave
Lancaster LA1 214 D8
Leyland PR25 76 F1
Preston PR2 117 D2
Southport PR8 35 E5
Tarleton PR4 57 A7
Haigh Cl PR7 43 A7
Haigh Cres
Chorley PR7 43 B7
Maghull L31 5 C4
Haigh Ct PR8 35 F6
Haigh Hall Cl BL0 50 B4
Haighton Ct PR2 118 A7
Haighton Dr PR2 118 E6
HAIGHTON GREEN 138 E2
Haighton Green La
PR2 138 E2
HAIGHTON TOP 138 C1
Haig Rd FY1 130 B1
Hail St BL0 50 A4
Hala Cres LA1 215 A3
Hala Gr LA1 215 A3
Hala Hill LA1 215 B3
Hala Rd LA1 215 A3
Hala Sq LA1 215 A3
Halcyon Cl 6 OL12 52 B2
Haldane Rd BB3 81 E4
Haldane St BB10 148 B2
Halden Rd LA3 216 E3
Hale Carr Gr LA3 216 E1
Hale Carr La LA3 216 E1
HALE NOOK 178 A5
Hales Rushes Rd PR3 178 C4
Hale St BB11 128 A4
Half Acre PR5 77 A8
Half Acre La BL6 31 C2
Halford Pl FY5 152 E7
Halfpenny La
Heskin Green PR7 41 B3
Longridge PR3 139 F8
Halifax Rd
Brierfield BB9 148 C5
Lane Bottom BB10 149 D3
Nelson BB9, BB10 148 E5
Southport PR8 21 C5
Halifax St FY3 130 F3
Hallam Cres BB9 149 A8
Hallam La LA3 213 A2
Hallam Rd BB9 149 A8
Hallam St 11 BB5 125 A1
Hallam Way FY4 111 E7
Hall Ave FY4 130 C1
Hallbridge Gdns WN8 10 B8
Hall Brow Cl L39 16 B4
HALL CARR 86 A1
Hall Carr La PR4 74 D6
Hall Carr Mill Cotts
BB4 86 B2
Hall Carr Rd BB4 86 A1
Hall Cl
Caton LA2 237 B3
Rawtenstall BB4 86 A6
Hall Coppice The BL7 47 E1
Hallcroft WN8 18 C2
Hall Croft PR4 95 D2
HALL CROSS 114 A1
Hall Dr
Caton LA2 237 B3
Middleton LA3 213 A2
Morecambe LA4 217 E4
Halley Rd BB3 81 E3
Halley St 5 OL13 88 A7
Hallfield Rd BB6 124 D6
Hall Fold OL12 52 C8
Hall Garth Gdns LA6 240 B1
Hall Gate PR7 61 A2
Hallgate Hill BB7 229 B4
Hall Gate La FY6 177 C8
Hall Gdns OL12 52 C2
Hall Gn WN8 10 B7
Hall Gr LA3 213 A2
Hall Greaves Cl LA3 209 D8
HALL GREEN 10 A7
Hall Green Cl WN8 10 B7
Hall Green La L40, PR7 41 A3
Hall Hill BB7 228 D1
Hall Hill St 4 BB12 146 C1
Halliwell Cres PR4 95 E1
Halliwell Ct 7 PR7 43 C7
Halliwell Hts PR5 97 F3
Halliwell La PR6 61 C4
Halliwell Pl 8 PR7 43 C7
Halliwell St
3 Accrington BB5 104 E2
Chorley PR7 43 C7
Hall La
Appley Bridge WN6 28 D2
Bickerstaffe L39 7 E4
Bispham Green L40, WN8 27 A6
Bracewell BD23 231 F3
Great Eccleston PR3 156 C4
Ince Blundell L38 3 F3
Kirkby L33 1 A8
Leyland PR25 76 F2
Longton PR4 74 E7
Maghull, Lydiate L31 5 B7
Mawdesley L40 40 D3
Orrell WN5 10 F4
Rivington BL6 45 A2
Skelmersdale L40 17 A6
St Michael's on W PR3 157 E6
Hall Mdws BB8 172 C3
Hallmoor Cl L39 15 E2
Hallmore Cvn Pk LA7 225 E7
Hallows Cl PR3 157 C6
Hallows Farm Ave OL12 52 D2
Hallows St BB10 148 A2
Hall Park Ave BB10 128 F4
Hall Park Ctr FY8 90 F4
Hall Park Dr FY8 90 E6
Hall Pk
Haslingden BB4 85 A6
Lancaster LA1 214 F4
Hall Rd
Bescar L40 23 F6
Bescar L40 24 B6
Fulwood PR2 117 E5
Middleforth Green PR1 96 E3
Trawden BB8 172 B3
Hallsall Dr LA4 217 F6
Hall's Cotts FY4 111 A6
Hall St
Bacup OL13 87 F3
Blackburn BB2 101 E2
Burnley BB11 128 A6
Clitheroe BB7 166 E7
Colne BB8 171 D4
Haslingden BB4 85 B2
Morecambe LA4 217 B6
Preston PR2 117 C1
Ramsbottom BL0 50 C2
12 Rawtenstall BB4 86 A3
Southport PR9 35 C7
Whitworth OL12 52 B8
Whitworth OL12 52 C8
Worsthorne BB10 129 A5
Hallwell St BB10 128 A8
Hallwood Cl BB10 148 B4
Hallwood Rd PR7 43 A5
Halmot Ct 3 BB4 86 E1
Halmote Ave BB12 146 F5
HALSALL 23 C1
Halsall Bldgs 6 PR9 35 C8
Halsall Ct L39 15 D6
Halsall Hall L39 23 B1
Halsall Hall Dr L39 23 B1
Halsall La
Formby L37 11 F3
Haskayne L39 14 D6
Ormskirk L39 15 D6
Halsall Manor Ct L39 23 B1
HALSALL MOSS 22 F4
Halsall Rd
Halsall L39 23 C2
Southport PR8 22 A8
Halsalls Sq PR3 156 B5
Halsbury St PR1 97 B6
Halstead Cl BB9 170 D4
Halstead La BB9 170 D4
Halstead Rd PR2 118 E5
Halstead St
Burnley BB11 127 F5
Bury BL9 33 A4
Worsthorne BB10 129 A6
Halstead Wlk BL9 33 A5
HALTON 219 D7
Halton Ave
Clayton-le-W PR25 77 D1
Cleveleys FY5 175 E4
Halton Chase L40 16 E4
Halton Ct 4 LA4 217 B3
Halton Gdns
Blackpool FY4 110 F8
Cleveleys FY5 175 F4
HALTON GREEN 219 F7
Halton Pl
Fulwood PR2 118 F4
Longridge PR3 140 B8
Halton Rd
Lancaster LA1 218 E4
Maghull L31 5 D3
Nether Kellet LA6 221 E5
Halton St PR4 132 E6
Hambledon Dr 6 PR1 96 E2
Hambledon St 10
BB12 126 D8
Hambledon Terr
Higham BB12 146 F6
2 Padiham BB12 126 F7
Hambledon View
Padiham BB12 126 F7
Read BB12 145 D1
HAMBLETON 177 C1
Hambleton Cl PR4 94 F1
Hambleton Ctry Pk
FY6 177 D4
HAMBLETON MOSS
SIDE 177 E2
Hambleton Prim Sch
FY6 177 D2
Hameldon App BB11 127 D5
Hameldon Ave 1 BB5 104 E2
Hameldon Cl BB11 126 C2
Hameldon Com Coll
BB12 126 F7
Hameldon Rd
Goodshaw Chapel BB4 106 A2
Hapton BB11 126 D2
Hameldon View BB6 124 D5
Hamer Ave
Blackburn BB1 102 D5
Goodshaw Chapel BB4 106 A1
Hamer Rd PR2 117 D3
Hamer St
21 Darwen BB3 65 A8
Ramsbottom BL0 50 B2
Rawtenstall BB4 86 A2
Hamerswood Dr PR3 181 D2
Hamer Terr BL0 50 C3
Hamilton Cl 8 FY8 91 D4
Hamilton Ct 6 FY1 130 B4
Hamilton Dr LA1 218 A3
Hamilton Gr PR2 118 E3
Hamilton Rd
Barrowford BB9 170 C1
Chorley PR7 43 C7
Fulwood PR2 118 D4
Morecambe LA4 218 A6
Nelson BB8 171 A2
Hamilton St BB2 101 D2
Hamilton Way OL10 33 E1
Hamlet Cl BB2 101 C3
Hamlet Gr PR4 134 F4
Hamlet Rd FY7 198 F4
Hamlet The
Adlington PR7 43 F1
Lytham St Anne's FY8 110 F2
Hammerton Gn 17 OL13 87 F3
Hammerton Hall Cl
LA1 218 C4
Hammerton Hall La
LA1 218 C4
HAMMERTON MERE 235 E1
Hammerton Pl FY3 131 A8
Hammerton St
Bacup OL13 87 F4
Burnley BB11 127 F5
Hammond Ave OL13 70 D8
Hammond Ct PR1 117 E1
Hammond Dr BB12 145 C2
Hammond Rd L33 1 C3
Hammond's Row 20
PR1 97 A8
Hammond St
Nelson BB9 148 F7
Preston, Adelphi PR1 117 E2
Preston, Maudlands
PR1 117 E1
Preston PR1 117 F2
Hampden Ave BB3 65 B7
Hampden Rd PR25 77 A2
Hampden St
5 Burnley BB11 128 B4
Hapton BB12 126 C4
Hampsfell Dr LA4 217 B3
Hampshire Cl BB1 123 A7
Hampshire Pl FY4 110 F6
Hampshire Rd
Bamber Bridge PR5 97 E3
Rishton BB1 124 A1
Hampson Ave PR25 77 D1
Hampson Cotts LA2 211 B1
Hampson Gr FY6 200 A4
HAMPSON GREEN 211 D1
Hampson La LA2 211 C1
Hampson St BL6 32 B4
Hampson Terr PR3 156 C5
Hampstead Cl FY8 90 E6

Hampstead Mews 3 FY1 130 C7
Hampstead Rd
Fulwood PR2 118 D2
Standish WN6 29 D1
Hampton Cl PR7 43 B8
Hampton Ct FY8 90 C8
Hampton Pl FY5 175 E3
Hampton Rd
Blackpool FY4 110 C8
Formby L37 11 E1
Morecambe LA3 216 E3
Southport PR8 35 C5
Hampton St PR2 117 C2
Hamptons The FY6 153 D1
Hanbury St PR2 117 C1
Hancock St BB2 101 C3
Handbridge The PR2 117 E5
Handel St OL12 52 B8
Hand La L40 40 F5
Handley Rd 4 FY1 130 C6
Handshaw Dr PR1 97 A2
Handsworth Ct 4 FY1 130 C7
Handsworth Rd FY1 130 C7
Handsworth Wlk PR8 35 F3
Hanging Green La LA2 220 E1
Hanley Cl FY6 177 C7
Hanmer Pl 3 LA1 215 A6
Hannah Ct PR7 60 E6
Hannah St
3 Accrington BB5 104 B5
16 Bacup OL13 88 A3
Darwen BB3 65 B8
Hanover Cres FY2 152 C5
Hanover Ct PR2 116 F6
Hanover St
Colne BB8 171 D5
Morecambe LA4 217 B5
4 Preston PR1 117 F1
Hansby Cl WN8 9 E8
Hanson Bldgs 5 BB12 126 C8
Hanson St
Adlington PR7 30 F5
Great Harwood BB6 124 C4
Rishton BB1 124 C1
Hanstock Cl WN5 10 E5
Hants La L39 15 E6
Happy Mount Ct LA4 217 F7
Happy Mount Dr LA4 217 E7
HAPTON 126 B4
Hapton CE Methodist Prim Sch BB11 126 C4
Hapton Rd BB12 126 C7
Hapton St
7 Padiham BB12 126 D8
Thornton FY5 176 B4
Hapton Sta BB11 126 C4
Hapton Way BB4 106 A2
Harbour Ave PR4 92 E6
Harbour Cl 11 FY7 198 F2
Harbour Ho 7 FY8 91 D4
Harbour La
Brinscall PR6 62 D7
Edgworth BL7 48 D5
Warton PR4 92 E6
Harbour Trad Est 13 FY7 198 F2
Harbour Way FY7 199 B3
Harbury Ave PR8 21 A4
Harcles Dr BL0 50 B2
Harcourt Mews 10 BL6 32 B4
Harcourt Rd
Accrington BB5 104 D3
Blackburn BB2 101 C6
Blackpool FY4 110 D8
Lancaster LA1 218 C3
Harcourt St
14 Bacup OL13 87 F3
2 Burnley BB11 127 D5
Preston PR1 117 E1
Hardacre La
Lucas Green PR6 61 C5
Rimington BB7 231 B2
Hardacre St L39 15 F6
Hardaker Ct 1 FY8 89 E6
Hardcastle Rd PR2 117 E3
Harden Rd BB18 195 A6
HARDHORN 131 E8
Hardhorn Ct FY6 153 D3
Hardhorn Rd FY6 153 D2
HARDHORN VILLAGE 131 E7
Hardhorn Way FY6 153 D2
Harding Rd L40 25 D4
Harding St PR6 31 B8
Hard Knott Rise LA5 221 E8
Hardlands Ave 4 LA4 217 F4
Hardman Ave BB4 86 A1
Hardman Cl
Blackburn BB1 102 F4
Rawtenstall BB4 69 F7
Hardman Dr BB4 69 F7
Hardmans Bsns Ctr BB4 85 E1
Hardman St
Blackburn BB2 101 C3
3 Blackpool FY1 130 C6
Hardman Terr OL13 70 D8
Hardman Way 25 BB3 82 A1
Hardsough La BL0 68 D5
Hardwen Ave 7 PR2 116 C1
Hardwicke Ho 10 LA1 214 E8
Hardwicke St 4 PR1 97 A8
Hardy Ave
Barnoldswick BB18 196 A3
Brierfield BB9 148 B6
Hardy Cl PR2 95 F8
Hardy Ct 13 BB9 148 E8
Hardy Dr PR7 43 A7
Hardy St
Blackburn BB1 122 F1
Brierfield BB9 148 B6
Harebell Cl
Blackburn BB2 80 D8
Formby L37 11 F1
Rochdale OL12 52 D3
Hare Clough Cl BB2 101 F3
Hareden Brook Cl BB1 101 F3
Hareden Cl 4 PR5 77 F8
Hareden Rd PR2 118 F2
Harefield Rise BB12 127 D7
HAREHOLME 86 D1
Hareholme La BB4 86 D2
Hare Runs Ho LA1 218 D3
Hares La PR8 36 D1
Harestone Ave PR7 43 A5
Harewood PR7 61 B2
Harewood Ave
Blackpool FY3 153 A1
Lancaster LA1 215 A3
Morecambe LA3 216 E2
Simonstone BB12 145 E2
Southport PR8 21 C6
Harewood Cl FY6 153 C5
Harewood Rd PR1 118 C2
Hargate Ave OL12 52 A2
Hargate Cl BL9 50 C2
Hargate Rd FY5 176 C2
Hargher St BB11 127 D5
Hargreaves Ave PR25 60 B8
Hargreaves Ct
Clitheroe BB7 166 C7
Fulwood PR2 116 F4
Whitewell Bottom BB4 86 F6
Hargreaves Dr BB4 85 F2
HARGREAVES FOLD 87 A7
Hargreaves Fold La BB4 87 A7
Hargreaves La 2 BB2 101 E3
Hargreaves Rd BB5 103 C4
Hargreaves St
9 Accrington BB5 104 C5
14 Burnley BB11 127 F6
Burnley, Harle Syke BB10 148 F3
Colne BB8 171 B4
Haslingden BB4 85 B3
Hoddlesden BB3 82 F1
Nelson BB9 148 C7
Southport PR8 35 C6
Thornton FY5 176 B3
Whitewell Bottom BB4 86 E5
Hargrove Ave
Burnley BB12 127 D7
Padiham BB12 146 C1
Harington Cl L37 11 D3
Harington Gn L37 11 D3
Harington Rd L37 11 D4
Harland St PR2 117 D3
Harland Way OL12 52 B2
Harlech Ave FY1 130 D1
Harlech Cl BB4 85 B1
Harlech Dr
Leyland PR25 77 C1
Oswaldtwistle BB5 103 C4
Harlech Gr FY5 176 D2
Harleston Rd L33 1 A3
Harleston Wlk L33 1 A3
HARLE SYKE 148 F3
Harley Bank LA2 239 C8
Harley Cl LA2 239 C8
Harley Rd FY3 130 E4
Harley St BB12 127 C6
Harling Rd PR1 118 D1
Harling St BB12 127 B6
Harold Ave
8 Blackpool FY4 111 A6
Burnley BB11 127 C4
Harold St
Burnley BB11 127 D5
Colne BB8 171 C4
Harold Terr PR5 77 A8
Harperley PR7 61 B2
Harpers La BB12 147 D8
Harper's La PR6 61 D1
Harper St BB18 196 A3
Harridge Ave OL12 52 C3
Harridge La
Halsall L39 14 F8
Hurlston L39, L40 24 A1
Harridge St OL12 52 C3
Harridge The OL12 52 C3
Harrier Ct LA1 214 E8
Harrier Dr
Blackburn BB1 101 D8
Skelmersdale WN8 9 E8
Harriet St BB11 127 E5
Harrington Ave FY4 110 B5
Harrington Rd
Chorley PR7 43 B8
Morecambe LA3 216 E3
Harrington St
Accrington BB5 125 A1
Preston PR1 117 F1
Harris Ave FY1 130 D1
Harris Cl OL10 33 E1
Harris Ct 2 BB7 166 E8
Harris Mus & Art Gallery* PR1 97 A7
Harrison Ave FY5 176 B2
Harrison Cres
Blackrod BL6 31 C3
Morecambe LA3 216 D1
Harrison Dr BB8 171 C6
Harrison La PR4 96 B2
Harrison Rd
Adlington PR7 31 A6
Harrison Rd *continued*
Chorley PR7 43 C6
Fulwood PR2 117 E6
Harrison St
Barnoldswick BB18 196 C1
Blackburn BB2 101 D4
Blackpool FY1 130 C3
Britannia OL13 71 B8
Burnley BB10 148 F2
Horwich BL6 32 B4
Ramsbottom BL0 50 C7
Todmorden OL14 109 B1
Harrison Terr BB7 190 B8
Harrison Trading Est PR1 118 C1
Harris Pk PR2 117 E5
Harris Prim Sch PR2 117 B7
Harris Rd WN6 29 B3
Harris St
Fleetwood FY7 199 A4
2 Preston PR1 97 A7
Harrock La
Appley Bridge WN6 28 A5
Hill Dale L40, WN6 27 F6
Harrock Rd PR25 77 D1
Harrod Dr PR8 34 E3
Harrogate Cres BB10 148 D2
Harrogate Rd FY8 90 C7
Harrogate Way PR9 54 C6
HARROP FOLD 229 F4
Harrop Pl PR2 118 E4
Harrow Ave
Accrington BB5 104 C7
Fleetwood FY7 198 F3
Harrow Cl
Orrell WN5 10 F8
Padiham BB12 126 E6
Harrowdale Pk LA2 219 D7
Harrow Dr BB1 102 B3
Harrow Gr LA4 217 F4
Harrow Pl
Blackpool FY4 110 A5
Lytham St Anne's FY8 90 E5
Harrowside FY4 110 B6
Harrowside Brow 3 FY4 110 B6
Harrowside W FY4 110 A5
Harrow St BB5 103 E4
Harrow Stiles La OL13 107 E1
Harry Potts Way BB10 128 B5
Harry St
Barrowford BB9 170 D3
Salterforth BB18 194 D7
Harsnips WN8 18 C2
Harswell Cl WN5 10 E5
Hartford Ave FY1 130 D2
Hartington Rd
Brinscall PR6 63 A8
Darwen BB3 81 E4
Preston PR1 96 D7
Hartington St
Brierfield BB9 148 B5
Colne, Cotton Tree BB8 172 B5
Lancaster LA1 215 B8
Rishton BB1 124 A1
Hartland WN8 18 C2
Hartland Ave PR9 54 B5
Hartlands Cl BB10 148 D3
Hartley Ave BB5 104 A3
Hartley Cres PR8 34 F2
Hartley Dr BB9 149 A7
Hartley Homes BB8 172 C6
Hartley Rd PR8 34 F2
Hartley St
3 Blackburn BB1 101 E6
2 Burnley BB11 127 C5
Colne BB8 171 D5
Earby BB18 197 B1
Great Harwood BB6 124 D6
2 Haslingden BB4 85 B3
Horwich BL6 32 B3
Nelson BB9 148 E7
2 Oswaldtwistle BB5 103 E4
Rochdale OL12 52 B1
Hartleys Terr BB8 171 E4
Hartmann St BB5 104 A6
Hartshead WN8 18 C2
Hart's Hos BL6 32 D5
Hart's La WN8 9 F8
Hart St
Blackburn BB1 101 F4
Burnley BB11 128 A6
Southport PR8 35 E6
HARTWOOD 61 C3
Hartwood Gn PR6 61 C3
Hartwood Rd PR9 35 D7
Harvest Dr PR6 61 C6
Harvesters Fold PR4 134 F4
Harvey Longworth Ct BB4 106 A1
Harvey St
14 Nelson BB9 170 E1
Oswaldtwistle BB5 103 D4
Harvington Dr PR8 21 B5
Harwich Rd FY8 111 A1
Harwin Cl OL12 52 D3
Harwood Ave FY8 89 E8
HARWOOD BAR 124 F6
Harwood Cl FY6 177 C7
Harwood Gate BB1 102 B6
Harwood La BB6 124 E6
Harwood New Rd BB6 124 E6
Harwood Rd
Rishton BB1 124 A2
Wilpshire BB1 123 D4
Harwood's La BB3 82 E1
Harwood St
14 Blackburn, Cob Wall BB1 102 A7
Blackburn, Green Bank BB1 102 B6
Darwen BB3 81 E2
Hasbury Dr FY5 176 C2
Hasgill Ct LA1 218 C1
HASKAYNE 13 F4
Haskoll St BL6 32 D1
Haslam Ct 1 BB10 148 B1
Haslam Dr L39 15 D7
Haslam St BL9 33 A4
Haslemere Ave 6 FY3 130 E3
Haslemere Ind Est PR25 76 F3
HASLINGDEN 85 B4
HASLINGDEN GRANE 84 B2
Haslingden Grane (Trail)* BB4 84 A2
Haslingden High Sch BB4 68 B8
Haslingden Old Rd
Blackburn BB1, BB5 102 E3
Rawtenstall BB4 85 E2
Haslingden Prim Sch BB4 85 B2
Haslingden Rd
Blackburn BB1, BB2 102 B2
Oswaldtwistle BB5 83 D7
Rawtenstall BB4 85 E2
Haslingden St James CE Prim Sch BB4 85 B3
Haslow Pl FY3 130 F7
Hassall Dr PR4 156 A1
Hassett Cl PR1 96 E6
Hastings Ave
Blackpool FY2 152 E5
Warton PR4 92 E7
Hastings Cl
Blackburn BB1 102 C4
Thornton FY5 176 C1
Hastings Pl FY8 91 A3
Hastings Rd
Kirkham PR4 114 B2
Lancaster LA1 214 F5
Leyland PR25 77 B2
Preston PR2 117 B1
Southport PR8 34 E1
Thornton FY5 176 C1
Hastings The LA1 214 F5
Haston Lee Ave BB1 122 F3
Hasty Brow Rd LA2 218 B6
Hatfield Ave
Fleetwood FY7 198 F3
Morecambe LA4 217 F6
Hatfield Cl FY5 176 C2
Hatfield Ct LA4 217 F6
Hatfield Gdns 2 FY7 198 E2
Hatfield Mews 2 FY7 198 F2
Hatfield Rd
Accrington BB5 104 D7
Fulwood PR2 118 E3
Southport PR8 21 C6
Hatfield Wlk 1 FY7 198 E2
Hathaway FY4 110 E8
Hathaway Fold 4 BB12 126 D7
Hathaway Rd
Fleetwood FY7 198 E4
Lancaster LA1 218 C3
Hatlex Dr LA2 220 E2
Hatlex Hill LA2 220 E2
Hatlex La LA2 220 E2
Hattersley St BB11 127 E6
Hatton St PR7 30 F6
Haugh Ave BB12 145 E2
Haulgh St BB10 148 B2
Haunders La PR4 74 B1
Havelock Cl BB2 101 D3
Havelock Rd
Bamber Bridge PR5 77 E7
Middleforth Green PR1 96 E5
Havelock St
Blackburn BB2 101 C2
5 Blackpool FY1 130 B4
Burnley BB12 127 B6
Lancaster LA1 215 A6
Oswaldtwistle BB5 103 D3
11 Padiham BB12 146 C1
Preston, Adelphi PR1 117 E2
Preston, Maudlands PR1 117 D2
Preston PR1 117 F2
Havenbrook Gr BL0 50 A3
Haven Brow L39 6 C8
Havenlyn Residential Pk PR3 204 C6
Haven Rd FY8 91 C3
Haven Sch FY5 175 E4
Haven St BB10 128 C5
Haven Wlk L31 5 C4
HAVERBREAKS 214 E5
Haverbreaks Pl LA1 214 E6
Haverbreaks Rd LA1 214 E5
Haverholt Cl BB8 171 C5
Haverholt Rd BB8 171 C5
Haverthwaite Ave LA3 212 F7
Havre Pk BB18 196 C2
Hawarden Ave LA4 217 C5
Hawarden Rd 1 PR1 118 E1
Hawarden St BB9 148 E7
Hawes Dr BB8 171 F6
HAWES SIDE 130 F1
Hawes Side La FY4 110 E8
Hawes Side Prim Sch FY4 110 E7
Hawesside St PR9 35 C7
Hawes Terr BB10 148 B2
Haweswater Ave PR7 43 B6
Haweswater Gr L31 5 F2
Haweswater Pl 3 LA4 217 E4
Haweswater Rd 1 BB5 125 D1
Hawfinch Cl OL13 88 A2
Hawick Gr OL10 33 E1
Hawk Cl BL9 33 B4
Hawker Dr WN8 9 E8
Hawkeshead Cl BB2 101 B4
Hawkhurst Ave PR2 117 D6
Hawkhurst Cres PR2 117 D6
Hawkhurst Rd
Middleforth Green PR1 96 E5
Preston PR1 118 B1
Hawking Pl FY2 152 F5
Hawkins Cl PR1 117 E1
Hawkins St
Blackburn BB2 101 B2
Preston PR1 117 E1
Hawksbury Dr PR1 96 D2
Hawksclough WN8 18 D2
Hawks Gr BB4 86 A1
HAWKSHAW
Darwen 81 D3
Ramsbottom 49 C2
Hawkshaw Ave BB3 81 E3
Hawkshaw Bank Rd BB1 101 D8
Hawkshaw Cl BL8 49 B3
Hawkshaw La BL8 49 B5
Hawkshaw St BL6 32 B3
Hawkshead PR1 96 E3
Hawkshead Ave PR7 60 D1
Hawkshead Cl L31 5 E2
Hawkshead Dr LA4 217 C3
Hawkshead Rd
Fulwood PR2 118 E5
Knott End-on-S FY6 199 F6
Hawkshead St
Blackburn BB2 101 B4
Southport PR8, PR9 35 D7
Hawkshead Terr FY4 111 D8
Hawksheath Cl BL7 47 E1
Hawksley St BL6 32 D2
HAWKS STONES 109 E3
Hawk St
Burnley BB11 128 A6
Carnforth LA5 223 E2
Hawkstone Cl
Huncoat BB5 125 F1
Thornton FY5 153 D8
Hawkstone Ct LA4 217 F6
Hawkswood PR7 41 B6
Hawkswood Gdns BB9 148 A4
Hawksworth Ave LA3 216 E2
Hawksworth Cl L37 12 A6
Hawksworth Dr L37 12 A6
Hawksworth Gr LA3 216 D2
Hawksworth Rd BB5 104 B8
Hawley Gn OL12 52 D2
Hawley St
Colne BB8 171 C4
Colne, Cotton Tree BB8 172 C5
Haworth Art Gallery* BB5 104 D3
Haworth Ave
Accrington BB5 104 D3
Ramsbottom BL0 50 A2
Rawtenstall BB4 85 F2
Haworth Dr OL13 70 C8
Haworth St
Accrington BB5 125 B1
Edgworth BL7 48 D5
Oswaldtwistle BB5 103 E4
Rishton BB1 124 B1
Haws Ave LA5 223 D1
Haws Hill LA5 223 D1
Hawthorn Ave
Burscough L40 25 F4
Caton LA2 237 C3
Darwen BB3 82 C2
Edenfield BL0 68 D2
Fleetwood FY7 175 E8
Orrell WN5 10 F6
Oswaldtwistle BB5 103 F3
Ramsbottom BL0 50 A2
Hawthorn Bank BB5 125 A3
Hawthorn Cl
Caton LA2 237 C3
Kirkham PR4 113 E6
Langho BB6 123 D8
Leyland PR26 76 D2
New Longton PR4 76 A7
Whalley BB7 144 A7
Hawthorn Cres
Preston PR2 116 D1
Skelmersdale WN8 17 E1
Hawthorn Dr BB1 103 B8
Hawthorne Ave
Burnley BB10 148 C5
Garstang PR3 181 B8
Higher Walton PR5 98 C3
Horwich BL6 32 E1
Newton-w-S PR4 114 F3
Hawthorne Cl
Barrowford BB9 170 B1
Clayton Green PR6 78 B3
Nelson BB9 149 B8
Hawthorne Cres L37 12 A2
Hawthorne Ct PR6 30 F8
Hawthorne Cvn Pk LA3 208 F7
Hawthorne Dr BB18 196 C4

**Hawthorne Gr**
17 Barrowford BB9 170 D3
Carleton FY6 153 B5
Southport PR9 35 F7
**Hawthorne Ind Pk**
BB7 190 A1
**Hawthorne Lea** FY5 153 C8
**Hawthorne Mdws** BB4 106 A1
**Hawthorne Pl** BB7 189 E1
**Hawthorne Rd**
Burnley BB11 127 F4
Thornton FY5 153 C8
**Hawthorne St** BB1 101 F8
**Hawthornes The** L40 39 B3
**Hawthorne Terr** BB8 194 E1
**Hawthorn Gdns** BB5 125 A3
**Hawthorn Rd**
Bacup OL13 88 A2
Blackpool FY1 130 C7
Bolton-le-S LA5 221 A6
Fulwood PR2 118 E2
Morecambe LA4 217 F4
**Hawthorns Holiday Pk**
LA6 237 A7
**Hawthorns Jun Sch**
BB1 101 F8
**Hawthorns The**
Bilsborrow PR3 159 A5
Eccleston PR7 41 B7
3 Formby L37 12 A3
Fulwood PR2 117 F6
Garstang PR3 204 C2
Lancaster LA1 215 A2
Lytham St Anne's FY8 110 F2
Newburgh WN8 27 A1
1 Newchurch BB4 86 F1
Wilpshire BB1 122 F6
Woodplumpton PR4 136 E2
**Haxey Wlk** BL6 31 F3
**Haydock Ave** PR25 60 A8
**Haydock Gr** LA3 216 D1
**Haydock La** BL7 48 A1
**Haydock Rd** LA1 215 B3
**Haydocks La** PR4 116 D5
**Haydock Sq** 1 BB6 124 C5
**Haydock St**
6 Bamber Bridge PR5 97 E2
3 Blackburn BB1 122 E1
Burnley BB10 148 C1
**Haydon Ave** PR5 77 A7
**Hayfell Ave** LA4 217 C3
**Hayfell Cres** LA2 220 D1
**Hayfell Gr** LA2 220 D1
**Hayfield** BB2 101 A7
**Hayfield Ave**
Blackpool FY2 152 E2
Gregson Lane PR5 98 E1
Poulton-le-F FY6 153 E3
**Hayfield Cl**
Gregson Lane PR5 98 E1
Ramsbottom BL8 49 F1
**Hayfield Rd** L39 15 E7
**Hayfields** BB18 194 E8
**Hayhurst Cl** BB7 144 C6
**Hayhurst Farm Terr**
BB7 166 F7
**Hayhurst Rd** BB7 144 C6
**Hayhurst St** BB7 166 F7
**Haylemere Ct** PR8 34 E5
**Hayling Pl** PR2 117 A4
**Haylot Dr** LA2 219 D7
**Haylot Sq** 9 LA1 215 A8
**Haymans Gn** L31 5 E1
**Haymarket** FY8 90 B6
**Haymarket Lo** PR9 53 D1
**Hayshaw Mews** PR3 207 D3
**Haysworth St** PR1 117 F2
**Hayward Ct** L37 12 A4
**Hayward Gr** WN6 29 D2
**Haywood Cl**
Accrington BB5 104 B8
Fulwood PR2 118 A8
**Haywood Rd** BB5 104 B8
**Hazel Ave**
Bamber Bridge PR5 98 A1
Bury BL9 33 B2
Clayton-le-M BB5 124 F2
Darwen BB3 82 B2
Fleetwood FY7 175 F8
Ramsbottom BL0 50 B1
**Hazelbank** LA2 219 C6
**Hazel Bank** LA3 212 F7
**Hazelbank Gdns** L37 11 E5
**Hazel Cl**
Bamber Bridge PR5 97 F1
Blackburn BB2 101 C4
Higher Penwortham PR1 96 B3
Knott End-on-S FY6 199 F6
**Hazel Coppice** PR2 116 E3
**Hazel Ct**
Fulwood PR2 117 E7
Ormskirk L39 15 E5
**Hazel Dene** BB7 189 E6
**Hazeldene Ave** 2 BB4 85 B2
**Hazeldene Rd** FY7 198 F2
**Hazel Gr**
Bacup OL13 88 B3
Bamber Bridge PR5 98 A1
Blackburn BB1 102 F5
Blackpool FY3 130 E5
Chorley PR6 61 C3
Clayton-le-M BB5 125 A2
Clitheroe BB7 166 C7
Fulwood PR2 119 A4
Lancaster LA1 214 D8
**Hazel Gr** *continued*
Longridge PR3 140 B8
Rawtenstall BB4 85 F4
Southport PR8 35 E7
Tarleton PR4 56 F8
**Hazel Hall La** BL0 50 B1
**Hazelhead La** PR3 204 E2
**HAZELHURST** 50 B4
**Hazelhurst Cl** BL0 50 B4
**Hazelhurst Com Prim Sch**
BL0 50 A4
**Hazelhurst Dr** PR3 181 A7
**Hazelhurst Lo** 12 PR2 118 F4
**Hazelhurst Rd** PR2 119 A2
**Hazel La** WN8 18 B4
**Hazelmere Rd**
Fulwood PR2 117 D8
Preston PR2 117 A1
**Hazelmoor** BB1 122 E6
**Hazel Mount** BL7 47 E2
**Hazelmount Ave** LA5 223 D3
**Hazelmount Cres** LA5 223 D3
**Hazelmount Dr** LA5 223 C3
**Hazelrigg La** LA2 211 C7
**Hazel St**
Ramsbottom BL0 50 A4
Rising Bridge BB5 85 A8
**Hazels The**
Coppull PR7 42 E1
Wilpshire BB1 122 E6
**Hazelwood**
Silverdale LA5 224 C2
Southport PR8 34 F1
**Hazelwood Ave** L40 25 E4
**Hazelwood Cl**
Blackburn BB1 123 A1
Leyland PR25 76 E1
**Hazelwood Dr**
Hesketh Bank PR4 73 E4
Morecambe LA4 217 F6
**Hazelwood Gdns** LA1 215 A2
**Hazelwood Hall** LA5 224 D1
**Hazelwood Rd** BB9 149 A8
**Hazlehurst Cl** L37 11 C2
**Hazlewood Cl** FY5 176 A2
**Headbolt La**
Kirkby L33 1 A5
Southport, Hillside PR8 22 B7
Southport L39 22 A4
**Head Dyke La** PR3 201 C3
**Headfort Cl** FY2 152 D2
**Headingley Cl** BB5 125 F1
**Headingly Ave** WN8 17 D1
**Headlands St** 2 OL12 52 E1
**Headlands The** LA3 212 D7
**Headley Rd** PR25 76 E1
**Headroomgate Rd** FY8 89 F8
**Heads La** BB18 195 B6
**Heald Brow** BB18 196 A4
**Heald Cl**
Rochdale OL12 52 C3
Weir OL13 88 A8
**Heald Croft** PR3 181 D6
**Heald Dr** OL12 52 C3
**Heald House Rd** PR25 60 C7
**Heald La** OL13 88 A8
**Heald Rd** BB10, BB12 148 A2
**Heald St**
Blackpool FY3 130 D6
6 Chorley PR6 43 E8
**Healdwood Cl** BB12 147 F3
**Healdwood Dr** BB12 147 F3
**Healey Ave** OL12 52 D4
**Healey Ct** BB11 127 F5
**Healey Dell Cotts** OL12 52 B4
Healey Dell Nature Reserve★ OL12 52 B6
**Healey Foundation Prim Sch** OL12 52 E3
**Healey Gr** OL12 52 C5
**Healey Hall Farm** OL12 52 C4
**Healey Hall Mews** OL12 52 C4
**Healey La** OL12 52 E3
**Healey Mount** BB11 127 F4
**Healey Row** BB11 127 F5
**Healey St** FY3 130 D7
**Healey Stones** OL12 52 E4
**Healey Wood Rd** BB11 127 F4
**Healey Wood Road Ind Est**
BB11 127 F5
**Heaning Ave**
Accrington BB5 104 D8
Blackburn BB1 102 D4
**Heanor Dr** PR8 35 F3
**HEAP BRIDGE** 33 C1
**Heap Bridge Village Prim Sch** BL9 33 D1
**Heap Brow** BL9 33 D1
**Heap Clough** BB4 84 C3
**Heap Ct** PR9 35 E8
**HEAPEY** 62 A6
**Heapey Fold La** PR6 44 C7
**Heapey Ho** PR6 62 A3
**Heapey Rd** PR6 61 F2
**Heapfold** 4 OL12 52 B2
**Heaplands** BL8 49 F1
**Heap St**
Brierfield BB9 148 A5
Burnley BB10 148 B1
Bury BL9 33 D1
Rawtenstall BB4 86 A8
Worsthorne BB10 129 B6
**Heapworth Ave** BL0 50 B6
**Heartwood Cl** BB2 101 A8
**HEASANDFORD** 128 C8
**Heasandford Ind Est**
Burnley BB10 148 D2
**Heasandford Ind Est** *continued*
Burnley, Heasandford
BB10 128 D8
**Heasandford Prim Sch**
BB10 128 B8
**Heath Ave** BL0 50 B1
**Heathbourne Rd** OL13 70 C8
**HEATH CHARNOCK** 43 F2
**Heather Bank**
Burnley BB11 127 C4
Rawtenstall BB4 68 F8
**Heather Brow** BB18 197 D2
**Heather Cl**
Brierfield BB9 148 D4
Burscough L40 25 E4
Chorley PR6 43 E8
Formby L37 12 B5
Haslingden BB4 68 A8
Horwich BL6 32 B4
Southport PR8 21 D2
Thornton FY5 176 B1
**Heatherfield** BL7 48 E6
**Heatherfield Pl** PR2 117 C1
**Heather Gr** PR2 118 E3
**Heatherlands** OL12 71 D4
**Heatherlea Cl** WN8 10 C7
**Heather Lea Dr** PR6 62 F8
**Heatherlea Rd** BB12 147 D7
**Heatherleigh** PR26 76 D3
**Heatherleigh Gdns** BB2 81 D6
**Heatherside Rd** BL0 50 C7
**Heathers The**
Clayton Brook PR5 78 C4
Knott End-on-S FY6 199 F5
**Heatherway** PR2 118 E6
**Heatherways** L37 12 A6
**Heathey La** L39, PR8 23 A7
**Heathfield** PR6 43 F1
**Heathfield Ave** OL13 70 C8
**Heathfield Cl** L37 12 A6
**Heathfield Dr** PR2 118 E4
**Heathfield Pk** BB2 100 F6
**Heathfield Rd**
Bacup OL13 70 C8
Fleetwood FY7 198 E2
Southport PR8 21 F6
**Heathfoot Ave** LA3 212 E6
**Heathfoot Dr** LA3 212 E6
**Heathgate**
Fence BB12 147 D8
Skelmersdale WN8 18 C2
**Heath Gr** LA3 212 E6
**Heath Hill Dr** OL13 70 C8
**Heathland** WN8 10 B7
**Heathland Coll** BB5 104 D5
**Heathrow Pl** PR7 43 A7
**Heath St** BB10 128 B8
**Heathway** PR2 117 F5
**Heathway Ave** FY3 130 E6
**Heathy La** L39 13 B8
**Heatley Cl** BB2 101 D3
**Heatley St** PR1 96 F8
**HEATON** 213 E5
**Heaton Bottom Rd**
LA3 213 E5
**Heaton Bsns Pk** LA3 217 C2
**Heaton Cl**
Bamber Bridge PR5 97 D4
Burscough L40 25 D4
Carleton FY6 153 C5
Morecambe LA3 217 E3
Thornton FY5 153 C8
Up Holland WN8 10 A7
**Heaton Ho** LA1 214 F5
**Heaton Mount Ave**
PR2 117 F7
**Heaton Pl** PR1 118 E1
**Heaton Rd**
Lancaster LA1 214 F5
Lytham St Anne's FY8 90 A8
**HEATON'S BRIDGE** 24 D4
**Heatons Bridge Rd** L40 24 D3
**Heaton St**
3 Blackburn BB2 101 E4
Leyland PR25 76 E2
Standish WN6 29 E1
**Heaviley Gr** BL6 32 A5
**Hebden Ave** FY1 130 D1
**Heber St** BB11 106 B4
**Hebrew Rd** BB10 128 A8
**Hebrew Sq** 12 BB10 128 A8
**Heckenhurst Ave**
BB10 129 A6
**Hector Rd** BB3 81 E5
**Hedge Row** PR4 113 B3
**Hedge Rows** OL12 71 C1
**Hedgerows Rd** PR26 59 A8
**Hedgerow The** BB2 101 A8
**Hedgeview** L40 24 B4
**Heeley Rd** FY8 89 E8
**Height Barn La** OL13 71 A8
**Height Croft** BB9 148 E5
**HEIGHT END** 85 D3
**Height La** PR3 161 F7
**Heights Ave** OL12 52 E2
**Heights Cl** OL12 52 E2
**Heights Cotts** BB5 104 F4
**Heights Ct** OL12 52 E1
**Heightside Ave** BB4 86 E2
**Height Side La** BB4 86 B7
**Heightside Mews** BB4 86 E2
**Heights La** OL12 52 E1
**Heights Rd** BB9 148 D6
**Heights The** BL6 32 D1
**Helena St** BB10 128 B5
**Helen's Cl** FY4 110 E6
**Helks Brow** LA2 239 B2
**Hellifield** PR2 117 F7
**Hellifield Rd**
Bolton-by-B BB7 230 E5
Gisburn BB7 231 C4
**Helm Cl** BB11 127 D2
**HELMCROFT** 85 B1
**Helmcroft** 5 BB4 85 A1
**Helmcroft Ct** 1 BB4 85 B1
**Helmn Way** BB9 170 F2
**Helmsdale** WN8 18 C2
**Helmsdale Cl** BL0 50 A4
**Helmsdale Rd**
Blackpool FY4 110 F7
Nelson BB9 171 A1
**HELMSHORE** 68 B7
**Helmshore Prim Sch**
BB4 68 A7
**Helmshore Rd**
Haslingden BB4 68 A7
Ramsbottom BL0, BL8,
BB4 68 A3
Helmshore Textile Mus★
BB4 67 F8
**Helmside Ave** LA4 217 C3
**Helmsley Gn** 2 PR25 77 B1
**Helston Cl**
Burnley BB11 127 B4
Southport PR9 54 B5
**Helton Cl** BB9 170 D4
**Helvellyn Dr** BB12 127 C8
**Hemingway** FY4 110 D8
**Hemingway Pl** 1 BB9 148 F8
**Hempshaw Ave** BB4 106 A2
**Hemp St** OL13 87 F1
**Henderson Rd**
Fleetwood FY7 198 F2
Weeton Camp PR4 132 E6
**Henderson St** PR1 117 E2
**Hendon Brook Sch**
BB8 171 C1
**Hendon Pl** PR2 116 E2
**Hendon Rd** BB9 148 F8
**Hendriff Pl** 4 OL12 52 F1
**Hendry La** BB2 81 D7
**Henfield Cl** BB5 125 A3
**Henley Ave** FY5 175 D2
**Henley Ct**
7 Blackpool FY2 152 E1
Southport PR9 53 E1
**Henley Dr** PR9 53 F1
**Henley Mews** 7 LA3 216 E3
**Henley St** 9 OL12 52 F1
**Hennel Ho** PR5 97 C4
**Hennel La** PR5 97 C3
**Henrietta St**
Bacup OL13 87 F2
Blackburn BB2 101 C5
Preston PR1 97 B8
**Henrietta Street Ind Est** 2
OL13 87 F2
**Henry Gdns** BB9 148 B5
**Henry St**
Accrington BB5 104 D3
Bank Lane BL0 50 D7
Blackpool FY1 130 C2
Church BB5 103 F6
Clayton-le-M BB5 125 A2
Colne BB8 171 C4
Lancaster LA1 214 F7
Lytham St Anne's FY8 91 A3
2 Nelson BB9 170 D1
Rawtenstall BB4 85 F2
Rishton BB1 124 B1
**Henry Whalley St** BB2 101 A2
**Henson Ave** FY4 110 E6
**Henthorn Cl** 4 BB7 166 D7
**Henthorne St** 1 FY1 130 C6
**Henthorn Rd** BB7 166 C6
**Henwick Hall Ave** BL0 50 B4
**Herbert St**
Bacup OL13 70 D8
Blackburn BB2 101 D2
Burnley BB11 127 E5
Horwich BL6 32 B4
Leyland PR25 77 A1
Padiham BB12 126 D7
Preston PR1 118 B1
**Herb Gdns The** LA6 241 B3
**Hereford Ave**
8 Blackpool FY3 130 E3
Burnley BB12 127 B7
Garstang PR3 181 B8
**Hereford Cl** BB5 104 B7
**Hereford Dr** BB7 166 F7
**Hereford Gr**
Buckshaw Village PR7 60 F6
Cottam PR4 116 D5
Up Holland WN8 10 B6
**Hereford Rd**
Blackburn BB1 102 C5
Nelson BB8, BB9 171 A2
Southport PR9 35 F7
**Hereford St** BB9 148 C8
**Herevale Hall Dr** BL0 50 B4
**Heriot Cl** FY5 175 F1
**Heritage The** PR25 76 F3
**Heritage Way**
Cleveleys FY5 175 F1
Tarleton PR4 57 A5
**Herkomer Ave** BB11 127 E2
**Herlebeck Rise** LA1 218 F2
**Hermitage Cl** WN6 19 E7
**Hermitage St** BB1, BB5 124 C1
**Hermitage The** FY5 175 F2
**Hermitage Way** FY8 90 D6
**Hermon Ave** FY5 175 E1
**Hermon St** 2 PR1 118 C1
**Hern Ave** PR5 77 A8
**Heron Cl**
Blackburn BB1 101 D8
Cleveleys FY5 175 F5
**Heron Ct** BB11 127 C5
**Heron Dr** 1 LA4 217 C3
**Heron Mews** LA3 212 F6
**Herons Ct** L31 5 B4
**Herons Wharf** WN6 19 D7
**Heronsyke** LA1 218 D4
**Heron Way**
Blackpool FY3 131 B6
Kirkham PR4 114 B2
Oswaldtwistle BB5 103 E3
**Herring Arm Rd** FY7 199 A2
**Herschel Ave** BB12 127 C8
**Herschell St**
2 Blackburn BB2 101 B1
Preston PR1 97 B6
**Hertford St** BB2 101 C2
**Hesketh Ave**
Banks PR9 55 A6
Blackpool FY2 152 B4
**HESKETH BANK** 73 D4
**Hesketh Cl**
Darwen BB3 65 C6
Fulwood PR2 118 E1
**Hesketh Ct**
Blackpool FY2 152 B4
Great Harwood BB6 124 E6
**Hesketh Dr**
Maghull L31 5 F1
Rufford L40 39 A3
Shevington Moor WN6 29 A2
Southport PR9 53 F1
**Hesketh Gn** L40 39 B4
**Hesketh La**
Becconsall PR4 73 F1
Hesketh Lane PR3 162 D7
Tarleton PR4 57 A7
**HESKETH LANE** 162 D8
**Hesketh Links Ct** PR9 53 E2
**Hesketh Lo** L37 11 E3
**Hesketh Pl** FY7 199 B5
**Hesketh Rd**
Burscough L40 25 D4
Fulwood PR2 118 E1
Heysham LA3 212 E8
Longridge PR3 140 A8
Lytham St Anne's FY8 111 A1
Southport PR9 53 D2
**Hesketh St**
Great Harwood BB6 124 C5
Preston PR2 117 C1
**Hesketh-with-Becconsall All Saints CE Sch** PR4 73 E4
**Heskin Cl** L31 5 D4
**HESKIN GREEN** 41 E3
**Heskin Hall Ct** L39 15 D8
**Heskin La** L39 15 D8
**Heskin Pemberton's CE Prim Sch** PR7 41 E2
**Hesley La** BD24 236 E6
**Hessam Hts** LA3 212 F5
**Hesse St** 1 BB3 65 A8
**HEST BANK** 220 F1
**Hest Bank La** LA2 218 C7
**Hest Bank Rd** LA4 217 E6
**Hester Cl** L38 2 F4
**Hestham Ave** LA4 217 B4
**Hestham Cres** LA4 217 B4
**Hestham Dr** LA4 217 B4
**Hestham Par** LA4 217 B4
**Hetherington Pl** FY2 152 E2
**Hetton Lea** BB9 170 C3
**Heversham** WN8 18 C2
**Heversham Ave** PR2 117 F7
**Heversham Cl**
Lancaster LA1 215 B3
2 Morecambe LA4 217 C3
**Hewart Dr** BL9 33 C3
**Hewart St** BB12 127 A7
**Hewitt Bsns Pk** WN5 10 E4
**Hewitt Cl** PR4 95 E1
**Hewitt St** 8 PR25 77 B2
**Hewlett Ave** PR7 42 D1
**Hewlett Ct** BL8 50 A1
**Hewlett St** PR7 42 D1
**Hewngate** PR5 98 E1
**Hexham Ave** FY5 175 E4
**Hexham Cl** BB5 104 E3
**Hexham Rd** LA4 217 F5
**HEY** 194 C3
**Hey Bottom La** OL12 52 F6
**Heycrofts View** BL0 68 E3
**Heydon Cl** L37 11 D1
**Hey End** PR4 75 F8
**Heyescroft** L39 7 D6
**Heyes Rd** WN5 10 E6
**Heyes St** WN6 19 C7
**Heyes The** PR6 78 B2
**Heyfold Gdns** BB3 81 F3
**HEY HEAD** 87 A1
**Hey Head Ave** BB4 70 A8
**Heyhead St** BB9 148 C5
**Hey House Mews** BL8 49 F4
**Heyhouses** BB7 146 A8
**HEY HOUSES** 90 D7
**Heyhouses Ct** FY8 90 B8
**Heyhouses Endowed CE Prim Sch** FY8 89 F8
**Heyhouses La** FY8 90 C7
**Heyhurst Rd** BB2 101 D5
**Heymoor Ave** BB6 124 D6
**Heys** BB5 103 D3
**Heys Ave** 5 BB4 85 A3
**Heys Cl**
Blackburn BB2 81 C7
Rawtenstall BB4 86 C1

**Heys Ct**
Blackburn BB2 81 C8
Oswaldtwistle BB5 103 E3
**HEYSHAM** 212 D7
**Heysham Ave** LA3 212 F8
**Heysham Bsns Pk** LA3 212 E2
**Heysham Cres** BB2 101 F1
**Heysham Hall Dr** LA3 212 E6
**Heysham Hall Gr** LA3 212 E7
**Heysham High Sports Coll** LA3 216 F3
**Heysham Mossgate Rd** LA3 212 F7
**Heysham Nature Reserve*** LA3 212 D4
**Heysham Pk** LA3 212 E7
**Heysham Port Sta** LA3 212 C5
**Heysham Rd**
[4] Heysham LA3 212 E7
Morecambe LA3 216 D2
Southport PR9 35 F7
**Heysham St** [2] PR1 117 E1
**Heys Hunt Ave** PR25 77 A2
**Heys La**
Barley Green BB12 169 D5
Blackburn BB2, BB3 81 C7
Darwen BB3 81 F2
Great Harwood BB6 124 E5
Oswaldtwistle BB5 103 E3
**Heys Lo** PR6 61 E6
**Heys St**
Bacup OL13 87 F1
Haslingden BB4 85 A3
Rawtenstall BB4 86 C1
Thornton FY5 176 B3
**Hey St** BB9 170 E1
**Heys The**
Coppull PR7 42 F2
Parbold WN8 27 C3
Southport PR8 34 D4
**HEYWOOD** 33 F2
**Heywood Cl** L37 11 E3
**Heywood Com High Sch** OL10 33 E1
**Heywood Rd** PR2 116 E2
**Heywood St**
[1] Blackpool FY1 130 B4
Bury BL9 33 A1
Great Harwood BB6 124 C4
**Heyworth Ave** BB2 81 C7
**Hibbert Terr** LA1 214 F3
**Hibson Rd**
Nelson BB9 148 D8
Nelson, Little Marsden BB9 148 D7
**Hic Bibi La** PR7 29 E6
**Hickory St** BB1 101 F7
**Hickson Ave** L31 5 C3
**Hick's Terr** BB1 124 B1
**Hidings Court La** LA4 217 B4
**Hiers House La** BB8 171 B5
**Higgin's La** L40 25 C4
**Higgin St**
Burnley BB10 128 B5
Colne BB8 171 D5
Worsthorne BB10 129 B5
**HIGHAM** 146 E5
**Higham Gr** FY3 130 F2
**Higham Hall Rd** BB12 146 F5
**Higham Rd** BB12 146 C3
**Higham Side Rd** PR4 135 C6
**Higham St** BB12 146 D1
**Highbank** BB1 122 F1
**High Bank** PR6 62 A3
**Highbank Ave** FY4 111 A8
**High Bank Cres** BB3 65 A7
**Highbank Hotel** [7] PR2 117 C1
**Highbanks** L31 5 C3
**High Barn La** OL12 71 C3
**HIGH BENTHAM** 239 E8
**High Bentham Bsns Pk** LA2 239 D7
**High Bentham Com Prim Sch** LA2 239 D8
**High Booths Cl** BB4 106 A1
**Highbury Ave**
Blackpool FY3 130 E8
Fleetwood FY7 198 F3
**Highbury Gate** PR4 156 A2
**Highbury Pl** BB1 101 D6
**Highbury Rd** FY8 110 E1
**Highbury Rd E** FY8 110 E1
**Highbury Rd W** FY8 110 D1
**High Cl** BB12 126 E6
**High Cop** PR6 78 F4
**High Crag Ct** LA5 223 E6
**Highcroft** [17] LA2 239 D8
**Highcroft Ave** FY2 152 E5
**Highcroft Way** OL12 52 F4
**HIGH CROSS** 131 D8
**Highcross Ave** FY6 131 D8
**Highcross Hill** FY6 131 D8
**Highcross Rd** FY6 153 D1
**High Ct** LA4 217 F5
**Highdale** LA3 213 A7
**Higher Antley St** BB5 104 A5
**HIGHER AUDLEY** 102 A4
**Higher Audley St** BB1 101 F4
**Higher Austin's** BL6 32 F1
**HIGHER BALLAM** 111 F1
**Higher Bank Rd** PR2 117 F3
**Higher Bank St**
Blackburn BB2 101 B6
Withnell PR6 80 A1
**Higher Barn** BL6 32 F3
**Higher Barn St** [2] BB1 102 A5
**HIGHER BARTLE** 116 E7
**HIGHER BAXENDEN** 104 F2
**Higher Blackthorn** OL13 87 F4
**HIGHER BOARSGREAVE** 70 A6
**Higher Bold Venture** BB3 65 A6
**Higher Booths La** BB4 106 A1
**HIGHER BROAD CLOUGH** 87 F5
**HIGHER BROADHALGH** 80 E7
**Higherbrook Cl** BL6 32 D1
**HIGHER CHANGE** 88 B4
**Higher Change Villas** OL13 88 B4
**Higher Chapel La** BB7 230 A1
**Higher Church St** BB3 82 B1
**HIGHER CLOUGHFOLD** 86 D2
**Higher Cockcroft** [14] BB1 101 E5
**Higher Commons La** BB2 121 C4
**HIGHER COPTHURST** 61 E7
**HIGHER CROFT** 101 F1
**Higher Croft** PR1 96 C2
**Higher Croft Cotts** BB3 81 F8
**Higher Croft Rd** BB2, BB3 81 F8
**Higher Cross Row** [8] OL13 87 F3
**Higher Cswy** BB9 170 D3
**Higher Dunscar** BL7 47 E1
**Higher Eanam** BB1 102 A5
**HIGHER END** 10 D3
**Higher Feniscowles La** BB2 80 B8
**Higherfield** BB6 123 C8
**Higher Firs Dr** BB5 125 A3
**Higher Fold La** BL0 50 E7
**Higher Furlong** PR4 74 F6
**Higher Gate** BB5 125 F1
**Highergate Cl** BB5 125 F2
**Higher Gate Rd** BB5 125 F1
**Higher Gn** FY6 153 E3
**Higher Greenfield** PR2 117 B5
**Higher Heys** BB5 103 E3
**HIGHER HEYSHAM** 212 F6
**Higher Hill** BB3 80 F2
**Higher House Cl** BB2 81 A7
**Higher House La** PR6 62 B2
**Higher Knowles** BL6 32 E2
**Higher La**
Haslingden BB4 85 B4
Holmes PR4 56 C3
Salterforth BB18 194 B7
Scorton PR3 204 F4
Skelmersdale WN8 18 C7
Up Holland WN8 10 C7
**Higher Lawrence St** [14] BB3 81 F2
**Higher London Terr** BB3 82 B2
**Higher Mdw** PR25 77 E1
**Higher Mill St** BB4 86 A3
**Higher Moor Cotts** FY2 152 F2
**Higher Moor Rd** FY3 153 A2
**Higher Moss La** L37 13 A2
**Higher Moulding** BL9 33 E5
**Higher Park Rd** BB18 194 C8
**Higher Peel St** [8] BB5 103 D3
**HIGHER PENWORTHAM** 96 C4
**Higher Perry St** BB3 82 B2
**Higher Ramsgreave Rd** BB1 122 C3
**Higher Rd**
Knowle Green PR3 163 B3
Longridge PR3 162 E2
Tosside BD23 236 C5
**Higher Reedley Rd** BB9, BB10 148 D5
**Higher Row** BL9 33 B3
**Higher Saxifield** BB10 148 E3
**Higher South St** BB3 82 A1
**HIGHER STANDEN** 166 F5
**HIGHER STANHILL** 103 B4
**HIGHER SUMMERSEAT** 50 B1
**Higher Summerseat** BL0 50 B2
**Higher Syke** LA2 233 C2
**Higher Tentre** BB11 128 B5
**Higher View** WN8 10 C6
**HIGHER WALTON** 98 B4
**Higher Walton CE Prim Sch** PR5 98 C3
**Higher Walton Mill** PR5 98 B4
**Higher Walton Rd** PR5 97 E4
**Higher Waterside** BB3 82 E3
**HIGHER WHEELTON** 79 B1
**Higher Witton Rd** BB2 101 B4
**Highfield**
Bacup OL13 87 F2
Brinscall PR6 62 F8
Great Harwood BB6 124 B5
Rawtenstall BB4 86 A7
**Highfield Ave**
Bamber Bridge PR5 97 C1
Burnley BB10 148 B3
Foulridge BB8 194 E1
Fulwood PR2 118 C4
Inskip PR4 135 C8
Leyland PR25 77 C3
**Highfield Cl**
Adlington PR6 31 A7
Clifton PR4 115 C1
Oswaldtwistle BB5 103 F3
**Highfield Cl** *continued*
Tarleton PR4 57 A5
**Highfield Cres**
[5] Barrowford BB9 170 D3
Morecambe LA4 216 F4
Nelson BB9 170 E3
**Highfield Ct**
Darwen BB3 82 D1
Haslingden BB4 85 A2
**Highfield Dr**
Fulwood PR2 117 E8
Hest Bank LA2 220 D1
Kingsfold PR1 96 D2
Longridge PR3 140 B6
Longton PR4 74 F6
**Highfield Gdns** BB2 101 E2
**Highfield Gr** PR5 97 C2
**Highfield Humanities Coll** FY4 110 E6
**Highfield Ind Est** PR7 61 D2
**Highfield La** L40 24 D7
**Highfield Mews** BB3 65 B8
**Highfield Pk**
Haslingden BB4 85 A1
Maghull L31 5 F1
**Highfield Prim Sch** PR6 43 E8
**Highfield Priory Sch** PR2 118 F5
**Highfield Rd**
Adlington PR6 31 A7
Blackburn BB2 101 E3
Blackpool FY4 110 E6
Blackrod BL6 31 E1
Carnforth LA5 221 E8
Clitheroe BB7 166 F7
Croston PR26 58 D2
Darwen BB3 82 B1
[1] Earby BB18 197 B2
Edenfield BL0 68 D3
Ormskirk L39 15 E7
Rawtenstall BB4 86 D1
[5] Rishton BB1 124 A1
Southport PR9 54 B3
**Highfield Rd N**
Adlington PR6 31 A8
Chorley PR7 61 C2
**Highfield Rd S** PR7 61 C1
**Highfield St**
[4] Darwen BB3 65 B8
Haslingden BB4 85 A2
**Highfield Terr**
Kirkham PR4 114 B4
Low Bentham LA2 239 C8
**High Fold** BB18 195 A6
**HIGHFURLONG** 153 A2
**Highfurlong Sch** FY3 153 A2
**Highgale Gdns** PR5 77 C7
**Highgate**
Blackpool FY4 110 D5
Goosnargh PR3 138 D6
Higher Penwortham PR1 96 B5
Nelson BB9 148 D7
**High Gate** FY7 198 D3
**Highgate Ave** PR2 117 E4
**Highgate Cl**
Fulwood PR2 117 F4
Newton-w-S PR4 114 F3
**Highgate Cres** WN6 19 E7
**Highgate La**
Warton PR4 92 E6
Whitworth OL12 52 C5
**High Gate La** FY6 177 A6
**Highgate Pl** FY8 90 D6
**Highgate Rd**
Maghull L31 5 D3
Up Holland WN8 10 B7
**High Gn** PR25 76 F1
**Highgrove Ave** PR7 41 F3
**Highgrove Cl** LA4 217 A4
**Highgrove Ct** PR26 58 F8
**Highgrove Rd** LA1 214 F4
**High La**
Bickerstaffe L39 7 C8
Laneshaw Bridge BD22 174 A8
Ormskirk L39, L40 16 A8
Salterforth BB18 194 C5
**Highland Ave** PR1 96 B4
**Highland Brow** LA2 211 A4
**Highland Dr** PR7 60 E6
**Highland Lo** WN6 29 D1
**Highland Rd** BL6 32 E1
**High Lea** PR6 31 A8
**High Legh** FY8 90 C3
**High Mdw** PR25 97 B2
**Highmeadow** WN8 10 A6
**Highmoor** BB9 148 F6
**HIGH MOOR** 27 F4
**High Moor La** WN6 28 B4
**Highmoor Pk** BB7 166 F8
**High Moss** L39 15 E3
**High Mount Ct** [2] LA1 214 F7
**High Mount Ho** [1] LA1 214 F7
**HIGH PARK** 36 A8
**High Park Pl** PR9 36 A8
**High Park Rd** PR9 36 A8
**High Peak Rd** OL12 52 C6
**High Rd**
Halton LA2 219 C7
Lowgill LA2 239 C5
**Highrigg Dr** PR3 137 F1
**Highsands Ave** L40 39 A3
**High St**
Accrington BB5 104 B4
Belmont BL7 46 C5
Blackburn BB1 101 E5
Blackpool FY1 130 B6
Brierfield BB9 148 B5
Burton in L LA6 242 C3
**High St** *continued*
Chapeltown BL7 48 C4
[10] Chorley PR7 43 C8
Clitheroe BB7 166 B8
Colne BB8 171 E5
Darwen BB3 82 A1
Elswick PR4 155 F1
Fleetwood FY7 199 B4
Garstang PR3 181 C7
Great Eccleston PR3 156 B5
Haslingden BB4 85 B4
Horwich BL6 32 B4
Lancaster LA1 214 F7
Mawdesley L40 40 B1
Nelson BB9 148 D7
Oswaldtwistle BB5 103 F3
Padiham BB12 146 D1
[14] Preston PR1 97 A8
Rishton BB1 124 B1
Skelmersdale WN8 17 E1
Standish WN6 29 E1
**HIGHTOWN** 2 F3
**Hightown** BB4 86 E4
**Hightown Rd** BB4 86 F4
**Hightown Sta** L38 3 A4
**Highways Ave** PR7 60 D1
**Highwoods Pk** BB6 143 B5
**Higson St** BB2 101 D5
**Hilary Ave** FY2 152 F5
**Hilary St** BB10 148 A1
**Hilbre Cl** PR9 53 F1
**Hilbre Dr** PR9 53 F1
**Hilderstone La** LA5 240 A7
**Hildrop Rd** [7] BB9 170 F1
**Hillam La** LA2 206 B7
**Hillary Cres** L31 5 D1
**Hillary Ct** L37 11 E2
**Hillbrook Rd** PR25 76 F2
**HILL CHAPEL** 161 A2
**Hill Cl** WN6 19 E8
**Hillcliffe** FY8 89 E5
**Hill Cres** PR4 115 A2
**Hillcrest**
Blackpool FY3 130 D5
Maghull L31 5 F1
Skelmersdale WN8 9 B8
**Hill Crest** OL13 87 D1
**Hillcrest Ave**
Bolton-le-S LA5 221 A5
Fulwood PR2 117 A4
**Hill Crest Ave**
Burnley BB10 128 F4
Fulwood PR2 117 E8
Longridge PR3 140 A7
**Hillcrest Cl** PR4 57 A8
**Hillcrest Dr**
Bescar L40 23 F7
Longridge PR3 140 A7
Tarleton PR4 57 A8
**Hillcrest Rd**
Blackburn BB2 100 F2
Blackpool FY4 110 B4
Langho BB6 123 C8
Ormskirk L39 15 E6
**Hillcroft**
Fulwood PR2 117 C7
High Bentham LA2 239 D7
**Hill Croft**
Clayton Green PR6 78 A2
Kirkham PR4 114 B5
**HILL DALE** 27 D5
**Hilldean** WN8 10 C8
**Hill End La** BB4 86 C1
**Hill Field Croft** PR3 204 C1
**Hill Hos** [19] BB3 65 A8
**Hill House Fold La** WN6 28 C5
**Hill House La**
Appley Bridge WN6 28 C5
Jack Green PR6 79 A7
**Hillingdon Rd** BB10 148 D3
**Hillingdon Rd N** BB10 148 D3
**Hillkirk Dr** OL12 52 C3
**Hill La**
Blackrod BL6 31 C2
Colne BB8 172 C7
Nether Kellet LA6 221 F4
**Hillmount Ave** LA3 212 F8
**Hillock Cl** L40 24 A7
**Hillock La**
Bescar L40 24 A7
Skelmersdale WN8 18 D7
Warton PR4 92 E8
**Hillocks The** PR26 58 B1
**HILLOCK VALE** 104 E8
**Hillpark Ave**
Fulwood PR2 117 D4
Gregson Lane PR5 98 D1
**Hill Pl** BB9 148 D6
**Hill Rd**
Higher Penwortham PR1 96 C5
Lancaster LA1 218 D3
Leyland PR25 77 C1
**Hill Rd S** PR1 96 D3
**Hill Rise**
Haslingden BB4 85 C1
[1] Ramsbottom BL0 50 A4
**Hill Rise View** L39 15 A1
**Hillsborough Ave** BB9 148 D5
**Hills Ct** [2] LA1 218 D1
**Hillsea Ave** LA3 212 F8
**HILLSIDE** 34 F1
**Hillside**
Burnley BB11 127 D3
Tarleton PR4 57 A6
**Hill Side** LA1 214 E8
**Hillside Ave**
Blackburn BB1 102 D4
Blackrod BL6 31 E1
Bolton BL7 48 B1
Burnley BB10 148 C5
[18] Darwen BB3 65 A8
Farington PR26 76 F7
Fulwood PR2 117 D4
Hill Dale WN8 27 D5
Horwich BL6 32 C4
Kirkham PR4 114 C5
Ormskirk L39 15 D3
Preesall FY6 200 B4
**Hillside Cl**
Blackburn BB1 102 C4
Blackpool FY3 130 E6
Brierfield BB9 148 C5
Burnley BB11 127 D2
Clitheroe BB7 166 E6
Euxton PR7 60 C1
Goodshaw Chapel BB4 106 A1
Great Harwood BB6 124 C6
Thornton FY5 153 D8
**Hillside Com Prim Sch** WN8 9 D8
**Hillside Cres**
Horwich BL6 32 C4
Weir OL13 87 F7
Whittle-le-W PR6 61 C8
**Hillside Ct** L39 15 D3
**Hillside Dr**
Newchurch BB4 86 E2
Stalmine FY6 177 C7
West Bradford BB7 189 F6
**Hillside Gdns** BB3 65 A7
**Hillside Rd**
Haslingden BB4 85 C3
Low Bentham LA2 239 C8
[2] Preston PR1 97 C6
Ramsbottom BL0 50 A5
Southport PR8 34 E1
**Hillside Sch** PR3 140 D7
**Hillside Sta** PR8 34 E1
**Hillside View** BB9 148 C5
**Hillside Way** OL12 71 C1
**Hillside Wlk**
Blackburn BB1 102 C4
Rochdale OL12 52 D4
**Hill St**
[3] Accrington, Enfield BB5 125 A1
Accrington, Scaitcliffe BB5 104 C5
Barnoldswick BB18 196 C2
Blackburn BB1 102 B5
Blackpool FY4 130 B1
Brierfield BB9 148 B5
Carnforth LA5 223 D1
Colne BB8 171 D4
Fence BB9 147 F6
Oswaldtwistle BB5 103 D5
Padiham BB12 126 C8
Preston PR1 96 F8
Ramsbottom BL9 50 C3
Rawtenstall BB4 86 A7
Southport PR9 35 B7
**Hills The** PR2 119 C7
**Hillstone Ave** OL12 52 D4
**Hillstone Cl** BL8 49 F2
**Hillsview Rd** PR8 21 C4
**Hilltop** OL12 52 C5
**HILL TOP** 172 B2
**Hill Top**
Barrowford BB9 170 D4
Colne, Cotton Tree BB8 172 C4
Foulridge BB8 194 C2
New Longton PR4 76 A6
Trawden BB8 172 B2
**Hill Top Cl**
Freckleton PR4 93 D7
Yealand Redmayne LA5 225 E4
**Hill Top Cotts** PR3 162 D2
**Hilltop Dr** BB4 68 C7
**Hill Top La**
Earby BB18 197 A2
Whittle-le-W PR6 61 D8
**Hilltop Wlk** L39 15 C3
**Hill View**
Beverley BB9 170 E7
[7] Blackburn BB1 122 E1
[2] Rawtenstall BB4 85 F1
**Hill View Cvn Site** PR3 156 A6
**Hill View Dr** PR7 29 D8
**Hillview Rd** PR4 114 A6
**Hill View Rd** PR3 204 C1
**Hill Wlk** PR25 77 A2
**Hillylaid Rd** FY5 176 D2
**Hilmont Terr** BB1 101 F7
**Hilmore Rd** LA4 217 A5
**Hilstone La** FY2 152 D1
**Hilton Ave**
[6] Blackpool FY1 130 B1
Horwich BL6 32 A3
Lytham St Anne's FY8 90 C6
**Hilton Ct** FY8 89 E5
**Hilton Rd** BB3 65 B8
**Hilton's Brow** PR6 79 B4
**Hilton St** BB3 65 A8
**Hinchley Gn** L31 5 B1
**Hindburn Ave** L31 5 F2
**Hindburn Pl** [2] LA1 218 C2
**Hinde St** LA1 218 E1
**Hindís Head Ave** WN6 28 F6
**Hindle Fold La** BB6 124 C6

Hindle St
Accrington BB5 104 B6
12 Bacup OL13 70 D8
Darwen BB3 81 F2
Haslingden BB4 85 B3
Hindley Beech 1 L31 5 C2
Hindley Cl PR2 118 C7
Hindley Ct 3 BB9 170 C1
Hindley St 5 PR7 43 C6
Hind St
Burnley BB10 148 B2
4 Preston PR1 96 E6
Hinton St BB10 128 B5
Hippings La BB4 86 F1
Hippings Meth Prim Sch BB5 103 E3
Hippings Vale BB5 103 D4
Hippings Way BB7 189 E2
Hirst St
Padiham BB12 146 C1
Todmorden OL14 109 B1
Hoarstones Ave BB12 147 D7
Hobart Pl FY5 152 F8
Hobart St BB11 128 B6
Hobberley Dr WN8 9 E8
Hobbs La PR3 183 A4
Hobcross La L40 26 A2
Hob Gn BB2 121 F2
Hob La BL7 48 C7
Hobson's La LA6 240 C2
Hobson St BB4 85 F4
Hockley Pl FY3 130 F7
Hodder Ave
Blackpool FY1 130 D1
Chorley PR7 43 B5
Fleetwood FY7 198 D2
Maghull L31 5 F2
1 Morecambe LA3 217 F3
Hodder Bridge Ct BB7 165 B7
Hodder Brook PR2 119 A3
Hodder Cl
6 Bamber Bridge PR5 77 F8
Fleetwood FY7 198 C2
Hodder Ct BB7 165 C4
Hodder Dr
Lytham St Anne's FY8 90 C7
West Bradford BB7 189 D7
Hodder Gr
Clitheroe BB7 166 C7
Darwen BB3 81 E4
Hodder Pl
Blackburn BB1 101 F6
Lancaster LA1 215 B5
Hodder St
Accrington BB5 104 D6
1 Blackburn BB1 101 E6
Burnley BB10 148 C3
Longridge PR3 140 B7
Hodder Way FY6 153 D2
HODDLESDEN 82 F1
Hoddlesden Fold BB3 82 F1
Hoddlesden Rd BB3 82 E1
Hoddlesden St Paul's CE Prim Sch BB3 82 F1
Hodge Bank Bsn Pk BB9 170 D2
Hodge Brow BL6 44 F4
Hodgefield BB7 144 A4
Hodge La BB18 194 B8
Hodge St PR8 35 B7
Hodgson Ave PR4 93 A5
Hodgson High Sch Tech Coll FY6 153 F3
Hodgson Pl FY6 153 D2
Hodgson Rd FY1 130 C8
Hodgson's Bldgs 2 BB4 69 F7
Hodgson St
Darwen BB3 82 B1
3 Oswaldtwistle BB5 103 E4
Hodson St
Bamber Bridge PR5 97 E1
Southport PR8 35 C6
Hogarth Ave BB11 127 F3
Hogarth Cres PR4 134 F4
Hoggs Hill La L37 11 F1
Hogg's La PR7 43 E5
HOGHTON 99 B2
Hoghton Ave OL13 71 A8
Hoghton Cl
Lancaster LA1 214 D6
Lytham St Anne's FY8 110 F2
Hoghton Gr PR9 35 C8
Hoghton La PR5 98 D3
Hoghton Pl 3 PR9 35 B7
Hoghton Rd
Leyland PR25 76 D1
Longridge PR3 140 C7
Hoghton St
8 Bamber Bridge PR5 77 A8
Southport PR9 35 C7
Hoghton Twr* PR5 99 E1
Hoghton View PR1 97 C6
Holbeck Ave
Blackpool FY4 110 F8
Morecambe LA4 217 F4
Rochdale OL12 52 D4
Holbeck St BB10 148 A1
Holborn Dr L39 15 C3
Holborn Hill L39 15 C4
HOLCOMBE 50 A6
HOLCOMBE BROOK 50 B2
Holcombe Brook Prim Sch BL0 50 A2
Holcombe Ct BL0 49 F2
Holcombe Dr BB10 128 B6
Holcombe Gr PR6 61 E1
Holcombe Lee BL0 50 A4
Holcombe Mews BL0 49 F3
Holcombe Old Rd BL8, BL0 50 A5
Holcombe Prec BL0 49 F3
Holcombe Rd
Blackpool FY2 152 E1
Haslingden BB4 67 F8
Ramsbottom BL8 49 F2
Holcombe Village BL8 50 A6
Holcroft FY8 90 E3
Holcroft Pl FY8 90 F4
HOLDEN 230 C4
Holden Ave
Bury BL9 33 E4
Ramsbottom BL0 50 A5
Holden Cl BB9 170 C1
Holden Fold BB3 82 B3
Holden La BB7 230 B5
Holden Pl BB4 84 F1
Holden Rd
Brierfield BB9 148 A5
Burnley, Reedley BB10 148 B3
Holden St
4 Accrington BB5 104 B5
Adlington PR7 30 F7
Belthorn BB1 82 F6
Blackburn BB2 101 C4
Burnley BB11 127 F5
Clitheroe BB7 166 F8
HOLDEN VALE 85 A5
Holden Way LA1 214 F5
Holden Wood Dr BB4 84 F1
HOLE HOUSE 102 C6
Hole House La BB7 235 E2
Hole House St BB1 102 C5
Holgate FY4 110 F6
Holgate Dr WN5 10 E6
Holgates Cvn Pk LA5 224 B5
Holgate St
Burnley BB10 148 F3
Great Harwood BB6 124 C5
Holhouse La BL8 49 F2
Holker Bsns Ctr 2 BB8 171 B4
Holker Cl
Coupe Green PR5 98 E3
Lancaster LA1 214 D6
Holker La PR26 59 B4
Holker St
Colne BB8 171 B4
Darwen BB3 65 B8
Holland Ave
Bamber Bridge PR5 97 E2
Rawtenstall BB4 85 F3
Holland Bsns Pk L40 17 C4
Holland Ct WN8 9 D2
Holland Ho WN8 10 C6
Holland House Ct PR5 97 E3
Holland House Rd PR5 97 E3
Holland Lo 4 PR2 118 F4
HOLLAND MOOR 9 F7
Holland Moor Prim Sch WN8 9 E7
Holland Moss WN8 9 A5
Holland Pl BB9 170 E2
Holland Rd PR2 117 C1
Holland's La WN8 17 A1
HOLLAND SLACK 97 E2
Holland St
Accrington BB5 103 F6
Blackburn BB1 101 D6
3 Burnley BB12 126 B8
Holliers Cl L31 5 E1
Hollies Cl
Blackburn BB2 80 F8
Catterall PR3 181 D2
Hollies Rd BB1 123 A7
Hollies The
Ormskirk L39 15 A4
Southport PR8 34 F6
HOLLIN BANK 68 A6
Hollin Bank BB9 148 B6
Hollin Bridge St BB2 101 D2
Hollin Cl BB4 86 F4
Hollin Fold BB9 170 D8
Hollin Gr BB4 86 A4
Hollingreave Dr BB4 86 A5
Hollingreave Rd BB11 128 A4
Hollings PR4 75 F7
Hollington St BB8 172 B5
HOLLIN HALL 172 C1
Hollin Hall BB8 172 C1
Hollinhead Cres PR2 117 B4
Hollin Hill BB11 128 B3
Hollinhurst Ave PR1 96 C6
Hollinhurst Brow LA2 239 C2
Hollinhurst Ct PR1 96 C6
Hollinhurst View BB12 146 F5
Hollin La
Knowley PR6 62 C2
Rawtenstall BB4 86 A4
Hollin Mill St BB9 148 B6
HOLLINS 81 F4
Hollins Ave BB10 128 F4
Hollins Cl
Accrington BB5 104 C4
Hoghton PR5 99 C3
Hollins Ct 1 BB18 196 B3
Hollins Gr PR2 117 B3
HOLLINS GROVE 81 F3
Hollins Grove St BB3 81 F3
Hollinshead Ho FY8 90 A4
Hollinshead St PR7 43 C8
Hollinshead Terr BB3 64 B7
Hollins Hill PR3 207 C2
Hollins La
Accrington BB5 104 D3
Edenfield BL0 68 E2
Hollins Lane PR3 207 C2
Runshaw Moor PR26 59 C4
Silverdale LA5 224 D1
HOLLINS LANE 207 D2
Hollins Rd
Barnoldswick BB18 196 A2
Darwen BB3 81 F4
Nelson BB9 171 A2
Preston PR1 118 B2
Hollin St BB2 101 C2
Hollins Tech Coll The BB5 104 D2
Hollinview Cl BB4 86 A5
Hollin Way
Rawtenstall, Constable Lee BB4 86 A4
Rawtenstall, Rush Bed BB4 86 A6
Hollinwood Dr BB4 86 A5
Hollowbrook Way 4 OL12 52 D2
Hollowell La BL6 32 D1
Hollowford La L40 26 D2
Hollowforth La PR4 136 E5
Hollow Gill Brow BD23, BD24 236 F5
Hollowhead Ave BB1 122 F5
Hollowhead Cl BB1 122 F5
Hollowhead La BB1 123 A5
Hollowrane LA6 240 C7
Holly Ave BB4 85 C1
Holly Bank
1 Accrington BB5 104 C4
Entwistle BL7 48 B7
Fulwood PR2 117 C5
Warton LA5 223 D5
Hollybank Cl PR2 116 F5
Hollybrook Rd PR8 35 A5
Holly Cl
Clayton Green PR6 78 B2
Skelmersdale WN8 17 E1
Thornton FY5 176 C3
Westhead L40 16 E4
Holly Cres PR7 42 E2
Holly Ct
Blackburn BB1 101 F7
10 Bury BL9 33 A2
Holly Fold La L39, WA11 8 E3
Holly Gr
Longridge PR3 140 A8
Tarleton PR4 57 A7
Holly Ho
8 Burnley BB11 128 B5
Chorley PR7 42 F6
Holly La
Ormskirk L39 15 B4
Rufford L40 39 C3
Skelmersdale L39, WA11 8 E4
Holly Mews FY8 110 F2
Holly Mount BB4 68 A7
Holly Mount La BL8 49 E1
Holly Mount RC Prim Sch BL8 49 D1
Holly Pl PR5 78 B6
Holly Rd
Blackpool FY1 152 C1
Thornton FY5 176 B3
Holly St
Blackburn BB1 101 F7
Burnley BB10 128 B5
Bury BL9 33 A2
Nelson BB9 148 F8
Oswaldtwistle BB5 103 D4
Ramsbottom BL0 50 C3
Holly Terr BB1 101 F8
Holly Tree Cl
Darwen BB3 65 A6
Rawtenstall BB4 85 F5
Holly Tree Way BB2 80 F8
Holly Wlk LA1 214 D8
Hollywood Ave
Blackpool FY3 130 E5
Higher Penwortham PR1 96 C3
Hollywood Gr FY7 198 F4
Holman St 5 PR1 118 C1
Holmbrook Cl BB2 81 F8
Holmby St BB10 148 B2
Holmdale Ave PR9 54 C4
Holme Ave FY7 175 D8
Holme Bank BB4 85 F1
Holme Bank Mews 14 BB9 170 F2
Holmebrook Dr BL6 32 D1
HOLME CHAPEL 108 A6
Holme Cl BB18 195 A7
Holme Cotts 7 BB4 69 F7
Holme Cres BB8 172 B3
Holme End BB12 147 F4
Holmefield Ave FY5 175 E2
Holmefield Cl FY5 175 E2
Holmefield Ct 8 BB9 170 D3
Holmefield Gdns 15 BB9 170 D3
Holmefield Gr L31 5 C1
Holmefield Rd
Knott End-on-S FY6 199 E5
Lytham St Anne's FY8 90 A7
Holme Hill BB7 189 E2
Holmehouse Lo 15 PR2 118 F4
Holme House Rd OL14 109 C1
Holme La
Caton LA2 237 D3
Haslingden BB4 68 D8
Rawtenstall BB4 68 E8
Holme Lea BB5 124 F4
HOLME MILLS 240 A8
Holme Mills Ind Est LA6 240 B8
Holme Pk LA2 239 D7
Holme Rd
Bamber Bridge PR5 77 E8
Burnley BB12 127 E7
Clayton-le-M BB5 124 E4
Higher Penwortham PR1, PR2 96 C7
HOLMES 56 D3
Holmes Ct PR1 117 E3
Holmes Dr OL13 87 F4
Holmes La OL13 87 F3
HOLME SLACK 118 C3
Holme Slack Com Prim Sch PR1 118 C3
Holme Slack La PR1 118 C3
Holmes Mdw 3 PR26 76 B1
Holmes Rd FY5 176 B3
Holmes Sq 7 BB11 128 B5
Holmes St
Burnley BB11 128 B5
Padiham BB12 126 D8
Rawtenstall BB4 86 B3
Water BB4 87 A7
Holme St
Accrington BB5 104 C6
Bacup OL13 70 D8
Barrowford BB9 170 D2
Colne, Cotton Tree BB8 172 B5
Darwen BB3 65 A8
Nelson BB9 148 E8
Holmes Terr BB4 85 F5
Holmes The BB4 85 F5
Holmestrand Ave BB11 127 B4
HOLMESWOOD 38 C6
Holmeswood PR4 114 A5
Holmeswood Cres PR3 137 B8
Holmeswood Meth Sch L40 38 C6
Holmeswood Pk BB4 68 E8
Holmeswood Rd L40 38 D6
Holme Terr
Haslingden BB4 68 D8
Nelson BB9 148 C8
Holme The PR3 182 E8
Holme Vale BB4 68 A6
Holmfield Cres 2 PR2 116 D1
Holmfield Pk L37 11 D4
Holmfield Rd
Blackpool FY2 152 B2
Fulwood PR2 118 A4
HOLM NOOK 154 E7
Holmrook Rd PR1 118 B1
Holmsley St BB10 128 B5
Holmwood Cl L37 11 D3
Holmwood Dr L37 11 D4
Holmwood Gdns L37 11 D4
Holroyd Ct FY2 152 B3
Holsands Cl PR2 118 E6
Holstein Ave OL12 52 D4
Holstein St PR1 97 A8
Holst Gdns BB2 102 A1
Holt Ave PR7 42 F2
Holt Brow PR25 60 A6
Holt Coppice L39 6 A7
HOLT GREEN 6 A7
Holtís Terr OL12 52 E2
Holt La PR6 78 E3
Holt Mill Rd BB4 69 D8
Holt St W BL0 50 B5
Holts La FY6 153 F2
Holt Sq BB9 170 E5
Holt St
Orrell WN5 10 D5
Ramsbottom BL0 50 D6
9 Rawtenstall BB4 69 E8
Rishton BB1 124 C1
Whitworth OL12 71 C1
Holy Cross RC High Sch PR7 43 C4
Holy Family RC Prim Sch
Blackpool FY1 130 C8
Fulwood PR2 116 F4
Southport PR9 35 E7
Warton PR4 92 E6
Holyoake Ave FY2 152 E1
Holyoake St
Burnley BB12 127 A6
Todmorden OL14 109 A1
Holy Saviour RC Prim Sch BB9 170 E2
Holy Souls RC Prim Sch BB1 122 E1
Holy Trinity CE Prim Sch
Burnley BB11 127 E5
Southport PR9 35 C8
Holy Trinity RC Prim Sch BB9 148 C5
Holy Trinity Sch BB3 82 A1
Homeacre Ave BB7 145 F8
Home Breeze Ho 1 LA4 217 E6
Homechase Ho 3 PR8 34 F4
Home Farm Cl LA2 238 D6
Home Farm Mews PR26 58 D1
Home Field PR3 181 C8
Homefylde Ho 4 FY3 130 E3
Homelinks Ho FY8 90 D3
Homer Ave PR4 56 F7
HOMER GREEN 4 C1
Homer St 1 BB11 127 C5
Homesands Ho PR9 35 D8
Homestead PR5 78 B4
Homestead Cl 4 PR25 76 D1
Homestead Dr FY7 198 E1
Homestead The 9 FY8 91 A3
Homestead Way FY7 198 E1
Homewood Ave LA4 217 F6
Homfray Ave LA3 217 E3
Homfray Gr LA3 217 E3
Honey Hole BB2 101 E2
Honey Holme La BB10 107 F7
Honey Moor Dr FY5 176 B4
Honeypot La FY6 154 D4
Honeysuckle Cl PR6 61 B5
Honeysuckle Ct BB5 125 E1
Honeysuckle Gr PR4 73 E4
Honeysuckle Pl FY2 152 F6
Honeysuckle Row PR2 118 E2
Honeysuckle Way OL12 52 D3
Honeywood Cl BL0 50 A3
Honister Ave FY3 130 F2
Honister Cl 6 FY7 198 D3
Honister Rd
Burnley BB10 148 B3
Lancaster LA1 218 F2
Honister Sq FY8 110 F2
Honiton Ave BB2 81 C8
Honiton Way PR4 116 F6
Hoodhouse St BB11 127 E4
Hood St 4 BB5 104 C6
HOOHILL 130 E8
Hoo Hill Ind Est FY3 130 E8
Hoo Hill La FY3 130 E8
Hookwood Ave FY5 175 D1
Hoole La
Banks PR9 55 A6
Nateby PR3 180 B5
Hoole St Michael CE Prim Sch PR4 74 C1
Hools La PR3 201 A5
Hope Cl FY5 176 B4
Hope La PR3 162 E5
Hope St N BL6 32 B5
Hope Sq PR9 35 D7
Hope St
Accrington BB5 104 B5
Adlington PR6 31 B8
Bacup OL13 87 F4
Blackburn BB2 101 D5
Brierfield BB9 148 B5
Chorley PR7 61 C1
Darwen BB3 81 F1
Great Harwood BB6 124 C4
Haslingden BB4 85 B2
Horwich BL6 32 B4
Lancaster LA1 215 A7
Lytham St Anne's FY8 90 A7
Morecambe LA4 217 C4
Nelson BB9 148 D8
12 Padiham BB12 126 D8
4 Preston PR1 96 F8
Ramsbottom BL0 50 B5
Rawtenstall BB4 86 C1
Southport PR9 35 C7
Worsthorne BB10 129 B6
Hope Terr
10 Bamber Bridge PR5 77 A8
Blackburn BB2 101 C6
Hopkinson St BB8 172 B3
Hopkinson Terr BB8 172 C3
Hopton Rd FY1 130 B2
Hopwood Ave BL6 32 C4
Hopwood St
Accrington BB5 104 B4
4 Bamber Bridge PR5 77 E8
Bamber Bridge PR5 77 F7
7 Burnley BB11 127 E6
Preston PR1 97 A8
Horace St 7 BB12 127 D6
Horden Rake BB2 80 E7
Horden View BB2 80 E7
Hordley St BB12 127 A6
Horeb Cl 5 BB12 126 D7
Hornbeam Cl PR1 96 B3
HORNBY 238 B7
Hornby Ave
Fleetwood FY7 175 D8
Fulwood PR2 118 E4
Hornby Bank
Hornby LA2 238 B8
Nether Kellet LA6 221 F5
Hornby Croft PR26 59 B8
Hornby Ct
4 Blackburn BB2 101 C4
Kirkham PR4 114 B4
Lancaster LA1 218 C4
Hornby Dr
Lancaster LA1 215 A4
Newton-w-S PR4 114 F2
Hornby Hall Cl LA2 238 B7
Hornby High Sch LA2 238 B7
Hornby La PR4 156 F2
Hornby Park Ct 1 FY3 130 D4
Hornby Rd
Blackpool FY1 130 C4
Caton LA2 237 C3
Chorley PR6 43 E6
Longridge PR3 140 B8
Lytham St Anne's FY8 89 E5
Southport PR9 54 A4
Wray LA2 238 D1
Wray LA2 238 D6
Hornby St Margaret's CE Prim Sch LA2 238 B7
Hornby's La
Hale Nook PR3 178 A5
Moss Edge PR3 178 D6

Hornby St
Burnley BB11 . . . . . 128 A5
Oswaldtwistle BB5 . . . . . 103 E3
Hornby Terr LA4 . . . . . 217 C6
Hornchurch Dr PR7 . . . . . 43 A7
Horncliffe Cl BB4 . . . . . 68 E8
Horncliffe Hts BB9 . . . . . 148 E5
Horncliffe Rd FY4 . . . . . 110 B6
Horncliffe View BB4 . . . . . 68 B8
Horne St BB5 . . . . . 104 C7
Horning Cres BB10 . . . . . 148 D2
Hornsea Cl
Fulwood PR2 . . . . . 117 A4
Thornton FY5 . . . . . 176 D2
Hornsey Ave FY8 . . . . . 110 B4
Horns La PR3 . . . . . 161 B3
Horridge Fold BL7 . . . . . 47 E3
Horrobin Fold BL7 . . . . . 48 C2
Horrobin La
Chapeltown BL7 . . . . . 48 C2
Rivington PR6, BL6 . . . . . 44 E1
Horrocks Fold PR4 . . . . . 74 E3
Horrocksford Way
LA1 . . . . . 214 D6
Horrocks Rd BL7 . . . . . 48 D6
Horsebridge Rd FY3 . . . . . 131 B8
Horsefield Ave OL12 . . . . . 52 C6
Horse Park La PR3 . . . . . 202 A5
Horsfall Ave 2 FY8 . . . . . 91 A3
Horsfall Cl BB5 . . . . . 104 B7
Horsfield Cl BB8 . . . . . 171 F5
HORTON . . . . . 231 E5
Horton Ave BB10 . . . . . 148 B3
Horton Lo BD23 . . . . . 231 E4
HORWICH . . . . . 32 D4
Horwich Bsns Pk BL6 . . . . . 32 B2
Horwich Heritage Ctr*
BL6 . . . . . 32 C4
Horwich L Ctr* BL6 . . . . . 32 C3
Horwich Parish CE Prim
Sch BL6 . . . . . 32 C4
HOSCAR . . . . . 26 D4
Hoscar Moss Rd L40 . . . . . 26 D3
Hoscar Sta L40 . . . . . 26 D4
Hospital Cotts PR3 . . . . . 140 F6
Hosticle La LA6 . . . . . 241 C7
Hothersall La PR3 . . . . . 140 D4
Houghclough La PR3 . . . . . 184 F1
Hough La PR25 . . . . . 77 A1
Houghton Ave 6 FY4 . . . . . 110 D8
Houghton Cl PR1 . . . . . 96 C3
Houghton Ct
Halton LA2 . . . . . 219 C7
7 Thornton FY5 . . . . . 176 B3
Houghton La WN6 . . . . . 19 F6
Houghton Rd PR1 . . . . . 96 C3
Houghton's La WN8 . . . . . 18 C1
Houghtons Rd WN8 . . . . . 18 B3
Houghton St 8 PR6 . . . . . 43 D8
Houldsworth Rd PR2 . . . . . 117 E3
Hounds Hill 2 FY1 . . . . . 130 B4
Hounds Hill Ctr 12
FY1 . . . . . 130 B5
Houseman Pl FY4 . . . . . 110 E7
Hove Ave FY7 . . . . . 175 C8
Hove Cl BL8 . . . . . 49 F1
Hove Rd FY8 . . . . . 89 F6
Howard Brook Ho PR1 . . . . . 118 F1
Howard Cl
Accrington BB5 . . . . . 103 F5
Lytham St Anne's FY8 . . . . . 110 E1
Maghull L31 . . . . . 5 F1
Howard Ct PR9 . . . . . 53 D1
Howard Dr PR4 . . . . . 56 F7
Howard Mews LA5 . . . . . 223 C1
Howard Rd PR7 . . . . . 43 C5
Howards La WN5 . . . . . 10 F7
Howard St
Blackpool FY1 . . . . . 130 C6
Burnley BB11 . . . . . 127 D5
Nelson BB9 . . . . . 148 C8
Rishton BB1 . . . . . 124 A1
27 Rochdale OL12 . . . . . 52 F1
Howarth Ave BB5 . . . . . 103 F7
Howarth Cres FY6 . . . . . 153 E3
Howarth Rd PR2 . . . . . 117 D3
Howden Hts FY6 . . . . . 153 B3
Howe Ave FY4 . . . . . 110 E8
Howe Croft BB7 . . . . . 166 F8
Howe Dr BL0 . . . . . 50 B2
Howe Gr PR7 . . . . . 43 A7
Howells Cl L31 . . . . . 5 D2
Howe Wlk 4 BB11 . . . . . 128 A6
Howgill Ave LA1 . . . . . 218 E4
Howgill Cl BB9 . . . . . 148 F6
Howgill La BB7 . . . . . 231 C1
Howgills The PR2 . . . . . 118 A7
Howgill Way FY8 . . . . . 91 D5
Howick CE Prim Sch
PR1 . . . . . 95 F3
HOWICK CROSS . . . . . 96 A5
Howick Cross La PR1 . . . . . 95 E5
Howick Moor La PR1 . . . . . 96 A3
Howick Park Ave PR1 . . . . . 95 F4
Howick Park Cl PR1 . . . . . 95 F4
Howick Park Dr PR1 . . . . . 95 F4
Howick Row PR2 . . . . . 95 D5
Howorth Cl BB11 . . . . . 128 A3
Howorth Rd BB11 . . . . . 128 A3
Howsin St BB10 . . . . . 148 A1
Hoylake Cl PR2 . . . . . 117 B6
Hoyle Ave FY8 . . . . . 110 F2
Hoyle Bottom BB5 . . . . . 103 E1
Hoyles La PR4 . . . . . 116 D6
Hoyle St
Bacup OL13 . . . . . 70 E8
Rising Bridge BB5 . . . . . 85 A8
Whitworth OL12 . . . . . 71 D3
Hozier St BB1 . . . . . 102 C5
Hubert Pl LA1 . . . . . 214 D8
Hubie St BB12 . . . . . 127 F7
Huck La FY8 . . . . . 91 E7
Hudcar La BL9 . . . . . 33 A4
HUD HEY . . . . . 85 A6
Hud Hey Ind Est BB4 . . . . . 85 B5
Hud Hey Rd BB4 . . . . . 85 B5
Hud Rake BB4 . . . . . 85 B4
Hudson Cl BB2 . . . . . 101 B8
Hudson Ct PR5 . . . . . 78 C8
Hudson Rd FY1 . . . . . 130 D2
Hudson St
Accrington BB5 . . . . . 104 C4
2 Brierfield BB9 . . . . . 148 B5
Burnley BB11 . . . . . 127 D5
9 Preston PR1 . . . . . 97 A6
Todmorden OL14 . . . . . 109 C1
Hufling Ct 7 BB11 . . . . . 128 B4
Hufling La BB11 . . . . . 128 B4
Hugh Barn La PR4 . . . . . 75 F7
Hugh Bsns Pk BB4 . . . . . 69 F8
Hughes Ave BL6 . . . . . 32 A4
Hughes Cl 11 BL9 . . . . . 33 A3
Hughes Gr FY2 . . . . . 152 E1
Hughes St BB11 . . . . . 128 A5
Hugh La PR26 . . . . . 76 D3
HUGH MILL . . . . . 69 F7
Hugh Rake BB4 . . . . . 85 F6
Hullet Cl WN6 . . . . . 19 E8
Hull Rd FY1 . . . . . 130 B4
Hull St
Burnley BB11 . . . . . 128 B5
Preston PR2 . . . . . 96 C8
Hulme Ave FY5 . . . . . 176 C2
Hulme Ct BB3 . . . . . 81 E5
Hulmes Bridge Bsns Ctr
L39 . . . . . 23 D2
Hulme St PR8 . . . . . 35 A7
Hulton Dr BB9 . . . . . 148 E6
Humber Ave 2 FY3 . . . . . 130 E8
Humber Sq BB10 . . . . . 148 C2
Humber St PR3 . . . . . 140 A7
Humblescough La
PR3 . . . . . 180 D5
Humphrey St BB9 . . . . . 148 B6
HUNCOAT . . . . . 125 E2
Huncoat Ind Est BB5 . . . . . 125 C1
Huncoat Ind Pk BB5 . . . . . 125 D1
Huncoat Sta BB5 . . . . . 125 E2
HUNDRED END . . . . . 72 F1
Hundred End La PR4,
PR9 . . . . . 72 F1
Hungerford Rd FY8 . . . . . 89 F5
HUNGER HILL . . . . . 28 F4
Hunniball Ct 3 PR2 . . . . . 117 C2
Hunslet St
Burnley BB11 . . . . . 128 B6
Nelson BB9 . . . . . 148 F7
Hunstanton Cl PR7 . . . . . 60 D5
Hunter Ave PR4 . . . . . 57 A6
Hunter Rd PR4 . . . . . 114 B2
Hunters Chase WN5 . . . . . 10 E1
Hunters Dr BB12 . . . . . 127 D8
Hunters Fold PR4 . . . . . 75 A5
Hunters Gate LA1 . . . . . 214 E5
Hunters Gn BL0 . . . . . 49 F3
Hunter's La PR4 . . . . . 56 B3
Hunters Lo
Bamber Bridge PR5 . . . . . 97 D3
Blackburn BB2 . . . . . 100 F1
Hunters Rd PR25 . . . . . 77 D1
Hunter St
Brierfield BB9 . . . . . 148 B5
Carnforth LA5 . . . . . 223 D2
Hunters Wood Ct PR7 . . . . . 42 F6
Hunt Fold Dr BL8 . . . . . 49 F1
Huntingdon Gr L31 . . . . . 5 C4
Huntingdon Hall Rd
PR3 . . . . . 164 A2
Huntingdon Rd FY5 . . . . . 175 C1
Hunting Hill Cvn Pk
LA5 . . . . . 223 C1
Hunting Hill Rd LA5 . . . . . 223 B1
Huntington Dr BB3 . . . . . 65 A7
Huntís Cotts PR9 . . . . . 54 A1
Huntley Ave 4 FY3 . . . . . 130 E7
Huntley Cl LA4 . . . . . 217 E5
Huntley La PR5 . . . . . 120 D2
Huntley Mount Rd BL9 . . . . . 33 B3
Huntley St BL9 . . . . . 33 B3
Huntly Way OL10 . . . . . 33 E1
Hunt Rd L31 . . . . . 5 D1
Huntroyde Ave BB12 . . . . . 126 B8
Huntroyde Cl 2 BB12 . . . . . 127 D7
Hunts Field PR6 . . . . . 78 C2
Huntsmans Chase PR4 . . . . . 114 F6
Hunt St 2 PR1 . . . . . 96 D7
HURLSTON . . . . . 24 C3
Hurlston Ave WN8 . . . . . 9 C8
Hurlston Dr L39 . . . . . 15 F7
HURLSTON GREEN . . . . . 24 B3
Hurlston La L40 . . . . . 24 C1
Hurn Gr PR7 . . . . . 43 A7
Hurst Brook PR7 . . . . . 42 F1
Hurst Cres BB4 . . . . . 86 B3
Hurstdene Cl FY6 . . . . . 153 F3
Hurstead St BB5 . . . . . 104 E1
Hurst Gn L40 . . . . . 40 C2
HURST GREEN . . . . . 164 F1
Hurst La BB4 . . . . . 86 B3
Hurstleigh Dr LA3 . . . . . 213 A7
Hurstleigh Hts FY5 . . . . . 176 E2
Hurstmere Ave FY4 . . . . . 110 E8
Hurst Pk PR1 . . . . . 96 C4
Hurst's La L39 . . . . . 7 B2
Hurst St BL9 . . . . . 33 A2
Hurstway PR2 . . . . . 117 D7
Hurstway Cl PR2 . . . . . 117 D7
HURSTWOOD . . . . . 129 C4
Hurstwood L37 . . . . . 11 E5
Hurstwood Ave
Blackburn BB2 . . . . . 101 A1
Burnley BB10 . . . . . 128 D5
Hurstwood Dr FY2 . . . . . 152 D2
Hurstwood Ent Pk BB4 . . . . . 85 A2
Hurstwood Gdns BB9 . . . . . 148 D4
Hurstwood La BB10 . . . . . 129 B4
Hurtley St BB10 . . . . . 128 A8
HUTCH BANK . . . . . 84 F2
Hutch Bank Rd BB4 . . . . . 84 F2
Hutchinson Ct BB3 . . . . . 82 A2
Hut La PR6 . . . . . 44 B3
Huttock End La OL13 . . . . . 70 D8
HUTTOCK TOP . . . . . 87 E2
HUTTON . . . . . 95 D2
Hutton CE Gram Sch
PR4 . . . . . 95 D2
Hutton Cl LA6 . . . . . 240 C7
Hutton Cres 4 LA4 . . . . . 217 A4
Hutton Ct WN8 . . . . . 17 D1
Hutton Dr BB12 . . . . . 127 E7
Hutton Gdns LA5 . . . . . 223 C4
Hutton Gr LA4 . . . . . 217 A4
Hutton Hall Ave PR4 . . . . . 95 E1
Hutton Rd WN8 . . . . . 17 D1
Hutton St
Blackburn BB1 . . . . . 102 B5
Standish WN1 . . . . . 30 A3
Hutton Way
5 Lancaster LA1 . . . . . 218 B1
Ormskirk L39 . . . . . 15 E5
Huyton Rd BL6, PR7 . . . . . 31 A6
Huyton Terr PR6 . . . . . 31 B6
Hyacinth Ave BB5 . . . . . 125 E2
Hyacinth Cl BB4 . . . . . 67 F8
Hyatt Cres WN6 . . . . . 29 C3
Hydeaway Ct LA4 . . . . . 217 B4
Hyde Rd
Blackpool FY1 . . . . . 130 B2
Morecambe LA4 . . . . . 217 F4
Hygiene BB5 . . . . . 124 E2
Hynd Brook Ho BB5 . . . . . 104 A5
Hyndburn Bridge BB5 . . . . . 124 F5
Hyndburn Cl
Carnforth LA5 . . . . . 223 F2
2 Morecambe LA3 . . . . . 217 F3
Hyndburn Dr BB3 . . . . . 81 D4
Hyndburn Park Prim Sch
BB5 . . . . . 104 A6
Hyndburn Rd
Accrington BB5 . . . . . 104 A6
Church BB5 . . . . . 103 F6
Great Harwood BB6 . . . . . 124 F5
Hyndburn St BB5 . . . . . 103 F6
Hyning Rd LA5 . . . . . 223 E8
Hynings The BB6 . . . . . 124 B6
Hythe Cl
Blackburn BB1 . . . . . 102 C4
Southport PR8 . . . . . 35 E3

## I

Ibbison Ct FY1 . . . . . 130 C3
Icconhurst Cl BB5 . . . . . 104 E2
Ice St BB1 . . . . . 101 E7
Iddesleigh Rd 3 PR1 . . . . . 118 E1
Iddon Ct 6 FY1 . . . . . 130 C6
Idlewood Pl FY5 . . . . . 152 F8
Idstone Cl BB2 . . . . . 82 A8
Ightenhill Cty Prim Sch
BB12 . . . . . 127 C6
Ightenhill Park La
BB12 . . . . . 127 C8
Ightenhill Pk Mews 1
BB12 . . . . . 127 C7
Ightenhill St BB12 . . . . . 146 C1
Ilex Mill BB4 . . . . . 86 A2
Ilford Rd FY4 . . . . . 130 E1
Ilkley Ave
Lytham St Anne's FY8 . . . . . 90 C6
Southport PR9 . . . . . 54 C6
Ilkley Gr FY5 . . . . . 152 E8
Illawalla The FY5 . . . . . 153 E6
Illingworth Rd PR1 . . . . . 118 E1
Ilway PR5 . . . . . 97 E3
Imam Muhammad Zakariya
Sch PR1 . . . . . 96 F7
Imperial Gdns BB9 . . . . . 148 D8
Imperial St 2 FY1 . . . . . 130 B7
INCE BLUNDELL . . . . . 3 E4
Ince Cres L37 . . . . . 11 D3
Ince La PR7 . . . . . 41 C6
Inchfield WN8 . . . . . 18 B2
Inch Field BB10 . . . . . 129 B6
India Mill Bsns Ctr BB3 . . . . . 65 A8
India St
Accrington BB5 . . . . . 103 F6
Darwen BB3 . . . . . 65 B8
Ramsbottom BL0 . . . . . 50 C3
Industrial Cotts 10 BB4 . . . . . 69 F8
Industrial Pl 4 OL13 . . . . . 87 F2
Industrial St
Bacup OL13 . . . . . 88 A2
Ramsbottom BL0 . . . . . 68 C1
Industry Rd 8 OL12 . . . . . 52 F1
Industry St
Darwen BB3 . . . . . 82 B2
Whitworth OL12 . . . . . 71 D2
Infant St 11 BB5 . . . . . 104 C6
Infirmary Cl BB2 . . . . . 101 D2
Infirmary Rd BB2 . . . . . 101 D2
Infirmary St BB2 . . . . . 101 E2
Ing Dene Ave BB8 . . . . . 171 B4
Ing Dene Cl BB8 . . . . . 171 B4
Ingfield Terr OL14 . . . . . 109 C1
Ingham St
Barrowford BB9 . . . . . 170 D3
Bury BL9 . . . . . 33 A1
Padiham BB12 . . . . . 146 D1
Inglby Cl BB1 . . . . . 102 D5
Ingleborough Dr BB18 . . . . . 196 A2
Ingleborough Rd LA1 . . . . . 218 B3
Ingleborough View
Brinscall PR6 . . . . . 63 A8
Carnforth LA5 . . . . . 221 E8
14 High Bentham LA2 . . . . . 239 D8
Hornby LA2 . . . . . 238 B6
Ingleborough Way
PR25 . . . . . 77 C2
Ingleby Cl
Cleveleys FY5 . . . . . 175 F5
Standish WN6 . . . . . 29 D2
Ingle Cl 5 PR6 . . . . . 61 D1
Ingle Head PR2 . . . . . 117 D6
Inglehurst Rd BB11 . . . . . 127 B5
Ingle Nook BB10 . . . . . 128 F4
Inglenook Cl 5 FY5 . . . . . 175 F1
Inglesby Cnr L40 . . . . . 24 B4
INGLETON . . . . . 242 F3
Ingleton Ave FY2 . . . . . 152 F4
Ingleton Cl 1 BB5 . . . . . 104 D5
Ingleton Dr LA1 . . . . . 215 A4
Ingleton Ho 2 LA1 . . . . . 215 A3
Ingleton Rd
Fulwood PR2 . . . . . 118 E4
Southport PR8 . . . . . 35 E3
Ingle View LA6 . . . . . 242 C3
Ingleway FY5 . . . . . 175 F3
Ingleway Ave FY3 . . . . . 130 F6
INGLEWHITE . . . . . 160 B4
Inglewhite WN8 . . . . . 18 A2
Inglewhite Fold 2
BB12 . . . . . 126 D7
Inglewhite Rd PR3 . . . . . 161 C3
Inglewood Cl
Bury BL9 . . . . . 33 C4
Fleetwood FY7 . . . . . 198 C1
Warton PR4 . . . . . 92 D6
Inglewood Gr FY2 . . . . . 152 E5
INGOL . . . . . 117 A4
Ingol Com Prim Sch
PR2 . . . . . 116 F4
Ingol Gdns FY6 . . . . . 177 C2
Ingol Gr FY6 . . . . . 177 C2
Ingol La FY6 . . . . . 177 D2
Ingot St PR1 . . . . . 96 D8
Ingram WN8 . . . . . 18 B2
Ings Ave
Barnoldswick BB18 . . . . . 196 B3
Rochdale OL12 . . . . . 52 B2
Ings La OL12 . . . . . 52 C2
Ingthorpe Ave FY2 . . . . . 152 D5
Inkerman Rd PR4 . . . . . 132 F6
Inkerman St
6 Bacup OL13 . . . . . 88 A2
Blackburn BB1 . . . . . 101 E6
9 Padiham BB12 . . . . . 126 C8
Preston PR2 . . . . . 117 D2
12 Rochdale OL12 . . . . . 52 F1
Inner Prom FY8 . . . . . 90 B3
INSKIP . . . . . 135 D8
Inskip WN8 . . . . . 18 A2
Inskip Ct WN8 . . . . . 18 B2
Inskip Pl
Blackpool FY4 . . . . . 110 E5
Lytham St Anne's FY8 . . . . . 90 A8
Inskip Rd
Leyland PR25 . . . . . 76 D2
Preston PR2 . . . . . 116 E1
Southport PR9 . . . . . 54 A4
Wharles PR4 . . . . . 135 A5
Inskip St Peter's CE Sch
PR4 . . . . . 135 B8
Inskip St BB12 . . . . . 126 C8
Institute St BB12 . . . . . 126 D8
INTACK . . . . . 102 D5
Intack La BB2 . . . . . 121 B2
Intack Prim Sch BB1 . . . . . 102 D5
Intack Rd PR4 . . . . . 75 B8
Intake Cres BB8 . . . . . 171 F6
Intake La
Maghull L39 . . . . . 4 E8
Skelmersdale L39 . . . . . 8 B2
Inverness Rd BB3 . . . . . 64 F8
Inver Rd FY2 . . . . . 152 D3
Ipswich Pl FY5 . . . . . 175 C2
Ipswich Rd PR2 . . . . . 118 D2
IREBY . . . . . 242 C6
Ireby Rd LA6 . . . . . 242 C3
Irene Pl BB2 . . . . . 101 B5
Irene St BB10 . . . . . 128 C5
Iris St BL0 . . . . . 50 B6
Irongate PR5 . . . . . 77 C8
Ironside Cl PR2 . . . . . 118 B4
Iron St
Blackburn BB2 . . . . . 101 E3
Horwich BL6 . . . . . 32 C2
Irton Rd PR9 . . . . . 35 E8
Irvin Ave PR9 . . . . . 54 C5
Irvine St 8 BB9 . . . . . 170 F2
Irving Cl FY2 . . . . . 152 F5
Irving Pl BB2 . . . . . 101 B5
Irving St PR9 . . . . . 53 B1
Irvin St PR1 . . . . . 118 B1
Irwell WN8 . . . . . 18 A3
Irwell Rd WN5 . . . . . 10 F7
Irwell St
7 Bacup OL13 . . . . . 87 F2
Burnley BB12 . . . . . 127 A6
Longridge PR3 . . . . . 140 B7
Longridge PR3 . . . . . 140 B8
Lytham St Anne's FY8 . . . . . 89 F7
Irwell St *continued*
Ramsbottom BL0 . . . . . 50 C6
Irwell Terr 12 OL13 . . . . . 87 F2
IRWELL VALE . . . . . 68 C5
Irwell Vale Rd BB4, BL0 . . . . . 68 C6
Irwell Vale Sta BL0 . . . . . 68 C5
Isabella St
Longridge PR3 . . . . . 140 A8
Rochdale OL12 . . . . . 52 F2
Isa St 5 BL0 . . . . . 50 A4
Isherwood Fold BL7 . . . . . 48 D7
Isherwood St
Blackburn BB2 . . . . . 101 D1
Preston PR1 . . . . . 118 C1
Island Cotts BL9 . . . . . 50 C2
Island La PR3 . . . . . 203 B3
Islay Cl 5 FY4 . . . . . 110 F6
Islay Rd FY8 . . . . . 90 E6
Isle of Man BB1 . . . . . 122 E4
Isle of Man St BB4 . . . . . 87 A7
Isleworth Dr PR7 . . . . . 43 B7
Islington BB2 . . . . . 101 E3
Islington Cl BB10 . . . . . 148 D3
Ivan St BB10 . . . . . 148 B2
Ivegate
Colne BB8 . . . . . 171 D5
Foulridge BB8 . . . . . 194 E1
Ivegate Mews 13 BB8 . . . . . 171 D5
Ivinson Rd BB3 . . . . . 82 B3
Ivory St 1 BB12 . . . . . 127 C6
Ivy Ave
Blackpool FY4 . . . . . 110 E5
Haslingden BB4 . . . . . 85 C3
Ivy Bank PR2 . . . . . 118 D6
Ivybridge WN8 . . . . . 18 B2
Ivy Cl
Clayton-le-W PR25 . . . . . 77 E2
13 Rawtenstall BB4 . . . . . 69 F8
Ring o'Bells L40 . . . . . 26 A3
Ivy Cotts
12 Rawtenstall BB4 . . . . . 69 F8
Tockholes BB3 . . . . . 80 F3
Ivydale WN8 . . . . . 18 B2
Ivy Gdns FY5 . . . . . 176 A4
Ivy Gr 2 BB4 . . . . . 86 A3
Ivy House Cl PR5 . . . . . 78 B7
Ivy Pl OL14 . . . . . 108 F1
Ivy St
Blackburn BB2 . . . . . 101 E2
Burnley BB10 . . . . . 148 B1
Nelson BB8 . . . . . 171 A2
Ramsbottom BL0 . . . . . 49 F3
1 Rawtenstall BB4 . . . . . 69 F8
Southport PR8 . . . . . 35 D6
Ivy Terr BB3 . . . . . 65 B6

## J

j2 Bsns Pk BL9 . . . . . 33 C2
Jackdaw Rd BL8 . . . . . 49 F2
JACK GREEN . . . . . 78 F8
Jack La BD23 . . . . . 236 F4
Jacks Key Dr BB3 . . . . . 65 C5
Jacksmere La L40, PR8 . . . . . 23 B8
Jackson Cl
Haskayne L39 . . . . . 13 F5
Lancaster LA1 . . . . . 214 C7
Jackson Heights Rd
BB1 . . . . . 83 B4
Jackson Rd
2 Chorley PR7 . . . . . 43 A5
1 Leyland PR25 . . . . . 76 D1
Jackson's Banks Rd
BB2 . . . . . 120 E6
Jackson's Common La
L40 . . . . . 24 B1
Jackson's La L40 . . . . . 27 E7
Jackson St
8 Bamber Bridge PR5 . . . . . 77 F8
Blackpool FY3 . . . . . 130 E7
6 Burnley BB10 . . . . . 128 A8
Chorley PR7 . . . . . 43 D6
5 Clayton-le-M BB5 . . . . . 124 F3
Jackson Terr LA5 . . . . . 223 D3
Jack Walker Way BB2 . . . . . 81 D7
Jacob Brigth Mews 5
OL12 . . . . . 52 F2
Jacob's La PR4 . . . . . 115 A7
Jacob St BB5 . . . . . 104 C5
Jacson St 3 PR1 . . . . . 97 A7
Jade Cl L33 . . . . . 1 A3
Jagoe Mews 2 BB18 . . . . . 197 A1
Jagoe Rd 3 BB18 . . . . . 197 A1
Jamea Al Kauthar LA1 . . . . . 214 F5
James Ave
Blackpool FY4 . . . . . 130 F1
Great Harwood BB6 . . . . . 124 B5
Jameson Rd FY7 . . . . . 199 A1
Jameson St 2 FY1 . . . . . 130 C3
James Pl
Coppull PR7 . . . . . 29 E8
Standish WN6 . . . . . 29 D2
James St W 6 BB3 . . . . . 82 A1
James Sq WN6 . . . . . 29 D2
James St
Bacup OL13 . . . . . 70 B7
Bamber Bridge PR5 . . . . . 97 E1
Barnoldswick BB18 . . . . . 196 B1
4 Barrowford BB9 . . . . . 170 D4
Belthorn BB1 . . . . . 82 F6
Blackburn BB1 . . . . . 101 E5
Bolton BL7 . . . . . 47 D3
Burnley BB10 . . . . . 148 A1
Bury BL9 . . . . . 33 A1

**James St** *continued*
12 Clayton-le-M BB5 . . . . . 124 F3
Colne BB8 . . . . . 171 E4
1 Darwen BB3 . . . . . 82 A1
Earby BB18 . . . . . 197 B1
Great Harwood BB6 . . . . . 124 B5
Haslingden BB4 . . . . . 85 A2
Horwich BL6 . . . . . 31 F3
Huncoat BB5 . . . . . 125 E2
30 Lancaster LA1 . . . . . 214 F8
Morecambe LA4 . . . . . 217 C5
Oswaldtwistle BB5 . . . . . 103 D3
Preston PR1 . . . . . 97 B7
Rawtenstall BB4 . . . . . 86 A2
Rishton BB1 . . . . . 124 C1
Salterforth BB18 . . . . . 194 D7
Whitworth OL12 . . . . . 71 D2
**Jameston Rise** 18 BL6 . . . . 32 B4
**Jane La**
Catforth PR4 . . . . . 135 E5
Leyland PR26 . . . . . 76 A3
**Jane's Brook Rd** PR8 . . . . 35 E4
**Jane's Mdw** PR4 . . . . . 57 A5
**Jane St** OL12 . . . . . 71 E6
**Janice Dr** PR2 . . . . . 117 D7
**Janine Cl** LA4 . . . . . 217 A4
**Jannat Cl** 2 BB5 . . . . . 104 B5
**Jarrett Rd** L33 . . . . . 1 A4
**Jarrett Wlk** L33 . . . . . 1 A4
**Jarvis St** OL12 . . . . . 52 F1
**Jasmine Rd** PR5 . . . . . 97 A3
**Jasper St** BB1 . . . . . 122 F1
**Jefferson Cl** LA1 . . . . . 214 D7
**Jefferson Way** OL12 . . . . . 52 F3
**Jeffrey Ave** PR3 . . . . . 140 B7
**Jeffrey Hill Cl** PR2 . . . . . 119 C7
**Jeffrey Sq** FY1 . . . . . 130 D3
**Jellicoe Cl** FY8 . . . . . 110 E1
**Jem Gate** FY5 . . . . . 152 D8
**Jemmett St** PR1 . . . . . 117 E2
**Jenny La**
Blackpool FY4 . . . . . 111 C7
Higher Wheelton PR6 . . . . . 79 C1
**Jenny Nook** LA3 . . . . . 213 A7
**Jenny St** BB9 . . . . . 148 D6
**Jensen Cl** LA1 . . . . . 214 E6
**Jensen Dr** FY4 . . . . . 112 A6
**Jepheys Pl** 17 OL12 . . . . . 52 F1
**Jepheys St** OL12 . . . . . 52 F1
**Jepp Hill** 3 BB18 . . . . . 196 B2
**Jepps Ave** PR3 . . . . . 137 B7
**Jepps La** PR3 . . . . . 137 B8
**Jepson St** 10 BB3 . . . . . 65 A8
**Jepson Way** FY4 . . . . . 110 F4
**JERICHO** . . . . . 33 F4
**Jericho Rd** BL9 . . . . . 33 E4
**Jersey Ave** FY2 . . . . . 152 E2
**Jersey Fold** PR7 . . . . . 60 E6
**Jersey St** BB2 . . . . . 101 B1
**Jervis Cl** FY8 . . . . . 110 D1
**Jesmond Ave** FY4 . . . . . 110 B7
**Jesmond Ct** FY8 . . . . . 89 F8
**Jesmond Gr** LA4 . . . . . 217 D3
**Jessel St** BB2 . . . . . 101 B2
**Jesson Way** LA5 . . . . . 223 C1
**Jevington Way** LA3 . . . . . 213 A7
**Jewel Holme** BB9 . . . . . 148 A5
**Jib Hill Cotts** BB10 . . . . . 148 D2
**Jinny La** BB12 . . . . . 169 E4
**Jobling St** 1 BB8 . . . . . 171 B3
**Jockey St** BB11 . . . . . 127 C5
**Joe Connolly Way** 1
BB4 . . . . . 69 E8
**Joe La** PR3 . . . . . 181 D2
**John Creed Ave** LA1 . . . . 211 B8
**John Cross CE Prim Sch**
PR3 . . . . . 159 A4
**John Henry St** OL12 . . . . . 71 D4
**John Hill St** 3 FY4 . . . . . 130 F2
**John Kay Ct** LA1 . . . . . 218 B3
**Johnny Barn Cl** BB4 . . . . . 86 D2
**Johnny Barn Cotts** BB4 . . . 86 D2
**John o' Gaunt St** 15
BB12 . . . . . 146 C1
**Johnson Cl**
Crag Bank LA5 . . . . . 223 C1
Lancaster LA1 . . . . . 214 C7
**Johnson New Rd** BB3 . . . . 82 E2
**Johnson Rd**
Blackpool FY4 . . . . . 130 F2
Darwen BB3 . . . . . 82 D4
**JOHNSON'S HILLOCK** . . . . . 61 E6
**Johnson's Meanygate**
PR4 . . . . . 56 D7
**Johnson St** PR9 . . . . . 35 B8
**Johnson Way** BB1 . . . . . 102 C1
**Johnspool** PR2 . . . . . 117 C6
**John St**
2 Bamber Bridge PR5 . . . . 97 E1
Barnoldswick BB18 . . . . . 196 B1
Barrowford BB9 . . . . . 170 E4
Blackpool FY1 . . . . . 130 B2
Brierfield BB9 . . . . . 148 B6
4 Carnforth LA5 . . . . . 223 D2
Church BB5 . . . . . 103 E7
Clayton-le-M BB5 . . . . . 124 F3
2 Colne BB8 . . . . . 171 C4
Coppull PR7 . . . . . 42 E1
Darwen BB3 . . . . . 81 F1
Earby BB18 . . . . . 197 B1
5 Galgate LA2 . . . . . 211 A4
Haslingden BB4 . . . . . 85 B3
Leyland PR25 . . . . . 77 A1
Newchurch BB4 . . . . . 86 F1
Oswaldtwistle BB5 . . . . . 103 D3
**John St** *continued*
Thornton FY5 . . . . . 176 B4
Whitworth OL12 . . . . . 71 D2
**Johnston Cl** BB2 . . . . . 101 C5
**Johnston St** BB2 . . . . . 101 C5
**Johnsville Ave** FY4 . . . . . 110 E7
**Johns Wood Cl** PR7 . . . . . 42 F6
**John Wall Ct** 8 BB7 . . . . 166 D8
**John William St** 7 PR1 . . 97 C8
**Joiners Alley** 10 BB6 . . . . 124 C5
**Joiner's Row** BB2 . . . . . 101 E3
**Jolly Tar La** PR7 . . . . . 30 B7
**Jonathan Cl** BB4 . . . . . 68 A8
**Jones' Gr** FY7 . . . . . 199 B5
**Jones St** BL6 . . . . . 32 B4
**Jones's Yd** LA6 . . . . . 240 B7
**Joseph St**
Barrowford BB9 . . . . . 170 D2
Darwen BB3 . . . . . 82 B1
3 Rochdale OL12 . . . . . 52 D2
**Joyce Ave** FY4 . . . . . 130 F2
**Joy Pl** 3 OL12 . . . . . 52 F2
**Joy St**
Ramsbottom BL0 . . . . . 50 B6
Rochdale OL12 . . . . . 52 F2
**Jubilee Almshouses**
PR26 . . . . . 58 B1
**Jubilee Ave**
Ormskirk L39 . . . . . 15 F6
Orrell WN5 . . . . . 10 D4
Preesall FY6 . . . . . 200 A4
Preston PR2 . . . . . 116 D1
**Jubilee Bldgs** 19 LA2 . . . . 239 D8
**Jubilee Cl**
Darwen BB3 . . . . . 82 D1
Haslingden BB4 . . . . . 85 A1
**Jubilee Ct**
1 Haslingden BB4 . . . . . 85 A1
11 Lancaster LA1 . . . . . 214 E8
**Jubilee Cts** PR25 . . . . . 59 E8
**Jubilee Dr**
Cleveleys FY5 . . . . . 175 C4
Skelmersdale WN8 . . . . . 8 E8
**Jubilee La** FY4 . . . . . 111 B5
**Jubilee La N** FY4 . . . . . 111 B6
**Jubilee Pl** PR6 . . . . . 61 D1
**Jubilee Rd**
9 Bamber Bridge PR5 . . . . 77 A8
Church BB5 . . . . . 103 F7
Formby L37 . . . . . 11 D1
Haslingden BB4 . . . . . 85 A1
Walmer Bridge PR4 . . . . . 74 F4
**Jubilee St**
Accrington BB5 . . . . . 125 A1
Blackburn BB1 . . . . . 101 E4
Burnley BB10 . . . . . 148 F3
Darwen BB3 . . . . . 82 A1
Oswaldtwistle BB5 . . . . . 103 E4
Read BB12 . . . . . 145 D2
**Jubilee Terr**
Clifton PR4 . . . . . 115 C1
Freckleton PR4 . . . . . 93 C7
Goosnargh PR3 . . . . . 138 D5
Langho BB6 . . . . . 143 D1
**Jubilee Trad Est** PR1 . . . . 117 E1
**Jubilee Way**
Croston PR26 . . . . . 58 B3
Lytham St Anne's FY8 . . . . . 90 C8
**Judd Ho** PR1 . . . . . 96 E6
**Judd Holmes La** PR3 . . . . 162 D7
**Judeland** PR7 . . . . . 61 A2
**Jude St** BB9 . . . . . 148 D8
**Jud Falls** BB7 . . . . . 165 A3
**Judge Fields** BB8 . . . . . 171 D6
**Judges Lodgings Mus**★
LA1 . . . . . 214 E8
**Judith St** OL12 . . . . . 52 C3
**Julia Mews** 4 BL6 . . . . . 32 B4
**Julia St** BL6 . . . . . 32 B4
**July St** 17 BB1 . . . . . 102 A4
**Jumbles Beck** BL7 . . . . . 48 D4
**Jumbles Ctry Pk**★ BL7 . . . 48 D2
**Junction La** L40 . . . . . 25 E3
**Junction Rd**
Preston PR2 . . . . . 96 D7
Rainford WA11 . . . . . 8 F1
**Junction St**
Brierfield BB9 . . . . . 148 B6
Burnley BB12 . . . . . 127 E6
Burnley, Whittlefield
BB12 . . . . . 127 E7
Colne BB8 . . . . . 171 A3
Darwen BB3 . . . . . 65 B7
**Junction Terr** PR7 . . . . . 60 C5
**June Ave** FY4 . . . . . 131 A1
**June St** 16 BB1 . . . . . 102 A4
**June's Wlk** PR4 . . . . . 75 A5
**Juniper Cl** FY6 . . . . . 200 A5
**Juniper Croft** PR6 . . . . . 78 A1
**Juniper Ct** 3 BB5 . . . . . 104 E8
**Juniper St** 6 BB1 . . . . . 102 A7
**Juno St** BB9 . . . . . 170 F2
**Jutland St** PR1 . . . . . 97 A8

# K

**Kairnryan Cl** FY2 . . . . . 152 F5
**Kale Gr** L33 . . . . . 1 A5
**Kane St** PR2 . . . . . 117 C1
**Kateholm** OL13 . . . . . 88 A7
**Kate St** 3 BL0 . . . . . 50 B6
**Kay Brow** BL0 . . . . . 50 C6
**Kay Fold Lo** BB1 . . . . . 122 D2
**Kay Gdns** BB11 . . . . . 128 B5
**Kayley La** BB7 . . . . . 190 E5
**Kaymar Ind Est** PR1 . . . . . 97 C7
**Kay St**
Blackpool FY1 . . . . . 130 B4
8 Brierfield BB9 . . . . . 148 B5
Bury BL9 . . . . . 33 A3
Chapeltown BL7 . . . . . 48 C4
Clitheroe BB7 . . . . . 166 D6
Darwen BB3 . . . . . 82 B1
3 Oswaldtwistle BB5 . . . . 103 D3
1 Padiham BB12 . . . . . 146 D1
1 Preston PR1 . . . . . 96 E7
Ramsbottom BL0, BL9 . . . . . 50 C3
Rawtenstall BB4 . . . . . 86 A2
**Kayswell Rd** LA4 . . . . . 217 F5
**Kearsley Ave** PR4 . . . . . 57 A6
**Keasden Ave** FY4 . . . . . 110 D7
**Keasden Rd** BB7 . . . . . 235 E6
**Keating Ct** 3 FY7 . . . . . 199 A3
**Keats Ave**
Bolton-le-S LA5 . . . . . 221 A5
Longshaw WN5 . . . . . 10 D1
Rochdale OL12 . . . . . 52 A1
Warton PR4 . . . . . 92 E6
**Keats Cl**
Accrington BB5 . . . . . 104 E2
Blackpool FY2 . . . . . 152 F6
Colne BB8 . . . . . 171 D6
Eccleston PR7 . . . . . 41 D5
Thornton FY5 . . . . . 176 A2
**Keats Fold** 3 BB12 . . . . . 126 F7
**Keats Rd** BL8 . . . . . 49 F2
**Keats Terr** PR8 . . . . . 35 F6
**Keats Way** PR4 . . . . . 116 D4
**Kebs Rd** OL14 . . . . . 109 D3
**Keele Cl** FY5 . . . . . 176 A2
**Keele Wlk** BB1 . . . . . 101 F4
**Keen Cl** PR4 . . . . . 95 E2
**Keepers Gate** FY8 . . . . . 90 D7
**Keeper's Hey** FY5 . . . . . 176 A4
**Keeper's La** PR3 . . . . . 204 F1
**Keepers Wood Way**
Catterall PR3 . . . . . 181 D3
Chorley PR7 . . . . . 42 F6
**Keer Bank** 1 LA1 . . . . . 218 A2
**Keer Holme La** LA6 . . . . . 240 E4
**Keighley Ave** BB8 . . . . . 171 D6
**Keighley Rd**
Colne BB8 . . . . . 171 F5
Laneshaw Bridge BB8 . . . . 172 D6
Trawden BB8 . . . . . 172 C4
**Keirby Wlk** BB11 . . . . . 128 A6
**Keith Gr** FY5 . . . . . 175 D1
**Keith St** BB12 . . . . . 127 C6
**KELBROOK** . . . . . 195 A6
**Kelbrook Dr** BB11 . . . . . 127 E3
**Kelbrook Prim Sch**
BB18 . . . . . 195 A6
**Kelbrook Rd** BB18 . . . . . 194 E7
**Kelk Beck Cl** L31 . . . . . 5 F2
**KELLAMERGH** . . . . . 92 D7
**Kellet Acre** 4 PR5 . . . . . 77 A7
**Kellet Ave** PR25 . . . . . 77 D1
**Kellet Ct** 1 LA1 . . . . . 214 E8
**Kellet La**
Bolton-le-S LA5, LA2 . . . . . 221 C3
Borwick LA6 . . . . . 240 B3
Walton Summit PR5 . . . . . 78 B7
**Kellet Rd**
Carnforth LA5 . . . . . 223 E1
Over Kellet LA6 . . . . . 240 A1
**Kellet Road Ind Est**
LA5 . . . . . 223 F1
**Kellett St** 8 PR7 . . . . . 43 C8
**Kelley Cl** BB2 . . . . . 81 C8
**Kelmarsh Cl** FY3 . . . . . 131 B2
**Kelne Ho** 7 LA1 . . . . . 214 E8
**Kelsall Ave** BB1 . . . . . 102 B8
**Kelsey St** LA1 . . . . . 214 E8
**Kelso Ave** FY5 . . . . . 175 D1
**Kelsons Ave** FY5 . . . . . 176 C2
**Kelswick Dr** BB9 . . . . . 148 E6
**Kelverdale Rd** FY5 . . . . . 152 F8
**Kelvin Rd** FY5 . . . . . 152 D6
**Kelvin St** BB3 . . . . . 81 F1
**Kelwood Ave** BL9 . . . . . 33 D5
**Kemble Cl** BL6 . . . . . 32 B5
**Kem Mill La** PR6 . . . . . 61 B8
**Kemp Ct** BB1 . . . . . 122 F3
**Kemple View** BB7 . . . . . 166 D6
**Kemp St** FY7 . . . . . 199 B4
**Kempstone** BB7 . . . . . 190 D5
**Kempton Ave** FY3 . . . . . 130 E3
**Kempton Park Fold**
PR8 . . . . . 35 F3
**Kempton Rd** LA1 . . . . . 215 B4
**Kempton Rise** BB1 . . . . . 101 F3
**Kenbury Cl** L33 . . . . . 1 A4
**Kenbury Rd** L33 . . . . . 1 A4
**Kendal Ave**
Barrowford BB9 . . . . . 170 D4
Blackpool FY3 . . . . . 153 A1
Cleveleys FY5 . . . . . 175 D4
**Kendal Cl** WA11 . . . . . 8 F2
**Kendal Dr**
Maghull L31 . . . . . 5 E2
Morecambe LA4 . . . . . 217 F4
Rainford WA11 . . . . . 8 F2
**Kendall Cl** BB2 . . . . . 81 D8
**Kendal Rd**
Lytham St Anne's FY8 . . . . 110 D1
Ramsbottom BL0 . . . . . 50 A2
**Kendal Rd W** BL0 . . . . . 49 F2
**Kendal Row** BB1 . . . . . 82 F6
**Kendal St**
Blackburn BB1 . . . . . 101 E6
Clitheroe BB7 . . . . . 189 F1
5 Nelson BB9 . . . . . 170 D1
Preston PR1 . . . . . 96 E8
**Kendal Way** PR8 . . . . . 21 B3
**Kenilworth Ave** FY7 . . . . . 198 E3
**Kenilworth Cl** BB12 . . . . . 126 E8
**Kenilworth Ct** FY8 . . . . . 89 F6
**Kenilworth Dr**
Clitheroe BB7 . . . . . 166 C6
Earby BB18 . . . . . 195 A8
**Kenilworth Gdns** FY4 . . . . 110 B7
**Kenilworth Pl**
Fleetwood FY7 . . . . . 198 E3
Lancaster LA1 . . . . . 215 A5
**Kenilworth Rd**
Lytham St Anne's FY8 . . . . . 89 F6
Morecambe LA3 . . . . . 217 C3
Southport PR8 . . . . . 21 B4
**Kenlis Rd** PR3 . . . . . 181 F4
**Kenmay Way** L33 . . . . . 1 A3
**Kenmure Pl** PR1 . . . . . 117 F2
**Kennedy Cl** LA1 . . . . . 214 D6
**Kennedy Ho** FY1 . . . . . 130 B1
**Kennelwood Ave** L33 . . . . . 1 A3
**Kennet Dr** PR2 . . . . . 117 F8
**Kennett Dr** PR25 . . . . . 77 B2
**Kennington Prim Sch**
PR2 . . . . . 118 A4
**Kennington Rd** PR2 . . . . . 118 A4
**Kensington Ave** PR1 . . . . . 96 B6
**Kensington Cl** BL8 . . . . . 50 A1
**Kensington Ct**
1 Formby L37 . . . . . 12 A3
Morecambe LA4 . . . . . 217 E6
**Kensington Dr** BL6 . . . . . 32 D3
**Kensington Gdns** PR5 . . . . 97 C1
**Kensington Ho** LA1 . . . . . 214 F5
**Kensington Ind Pk** PR9 . . . 35 C6
**Kensington Pl** BB11 . . . . . 127 D4
**Kensington Rd**
Blackpool FY3 . . . . . 130 E4
Chorley PR7 . . . . . 43 B7
Cleveleys FY5 . . . . . 175 C3
Formby L37 . . . . . 11 E1
Lancaster LA1 . . . . . 214 F5
Lytham St Anne's FY8 . . . . . 90 D4
Morecambe LA4 . . . . . 217 B5
Southport PR9 . . . . . 35 C6
**Kensington St** BB9 . . . . . 148 C7
**Kent Ave**
2 Bamber Bridge PR5 . . . . 97 D3
Cleveleys FY5 . . . . . 175 E4
Formby L37 . . . . . 12 A1
**Kent Ct** BB9 . . . . . 170 D4
**Kent Dr**
Blackburn BB1 . . . . . 102 E4
Clayton-le-W PR25 . . . . . 77 D1
**Kent Ho** LA1 . . . . . 214 F7
**Kentmere Ave**
Bamber Bridge PR5 . . . . . 97 E1
Leyland PR25 . . . . . 77 A3
**Kentmere Cl**
Burnley BB12 . . . . . 127 B8
5 Fleetwood FY7 . . . . . 198 D3
**Kentmere Dr**
Blackburn BB2 . . . . . 80 E8
Blackpool FY4 . . . . . 131 C1
Longton PR4 . . . . . 75 B8
**Kentmere Gr** 1 LA4 . . . . . 217 D4
**Kentmere Rd** LA1 . . . . . 218 E1
**Kenton Cl** L37 . . . . . 11 F6
**Kent Rd**
Blackpool FY1 . . . . . 130 C3
Formby L37 . . . . . 12 A1
Southport PR8 . . . . . 35 A4
**Kent's Cl** PR4 . . . . . 113 E7
**Kent St**
Blackburn BB1 . . . . . 101 F4
Burnley BB12 . . . . . 127 F7
Fleetwood FY7 . . . . . 199 B5
3 Lancaster LA1 . . . . . 218 D2
Preston PR1 . . . . . 117 E2
**Kent Way** 4 LA3 . . . . . 217 F3
**Kent Wlk** BB4 . . . . . 68 A8
**Kenwood Ave** LA4 . . . . . 217 A4
**Kenwood Grange** PR9 . . . . 35 C8
**Kenworthys Flats** PR9 . . . . 35 B8
**Kenwyn Ave** FY3 . . . . . 130 E3
**Kenyon Bsns Ctr** BB9 . . . . 148 B7
**Kenyon La**
Dinckley BB6 . . . . . 142 F4
Whittle-le-W PR6 . . . . . 61 F7
**Kenyon Rd**
Morecambe LA4 . . . . . 217 F5
Nelson BB9 . . . . . 148 B7
Standish WN6 . . . . . 29 D2
**Kenyons Farm Units**
PR5 . . . . . 78 B6
**Kenyons La** L31 . . . . . 5 E3
**Kenyon's La** L37 . . . . . 12 A3
**Kenyons Lo** L31 . . . . . 5 E3
**Kenyon St**
6 Accrington BB5 . . . . . 104 C6
Blackburn BB1 . . . . . 102 C5
Britannia OL13 . . . . . 71 B8
Bury BL9 . . . . . 33 A3
Ramsbottom BL0 . . . . . 50 C6
Rawtenstall BB4 . . . . . 86 A3
**Keppel Pl** BB11 . . . . . 127 E6
**Kepple La** PR3 . . . . . 181 B6
**Kerenhappuch St** 5
BL0 . . . . . 50 B5
**Kerfoot's La** WN8 . . . . . 8 C8
**Kerr Pl** PR1 . . . . . 96 D8
**Kershaw Cl** 7 BB4 . . . . . 86 A7
**Kershaw St**
8 Bacup OL13 . . . . . 87 F2
Bury BL9 . . . . . 33 A2
Chorley PR6 . . . . . 61 E1
Church BB5 . . . . . 103 E7
**Kerslake Way** L38 . . . . . 3 A4
**Kerslea Ave** FY3 . . . . . 131 D8
**Kerton Row** PR8 . . . . . 34 F4
**Keston Gr** FY4 . . . . . 110 C5
**Kestor La** PR3 . . . . . 140 A7
**Kestrel Cl**
Blackburn BB1 . . . . . 101 D8
Cleveleys FY5 . . . . . 175 F5
Knowley PR6 . . . . . 62 A3
**Kestrel Ct** PR9 . . . . . 35 D7
**Kestrel Dr**
Bury BL9 . . . . . 33 B4
Darwen BB3 . . . . . 81 D3
**Kestrel Mews** WN8 . . . . . 18 C4
**Kestrel Pk** WN8 . . . . . 18 C4
**Kestrel Terr** BB5 . . . . . 103 E3
**Keswick Cl**
Accrington BB5 . . . . . 125 D1
Maghull L31 . . . . . 5 E2
Southport PR8 . . . . . 21 C3
**Keswick Ct** LA1 . . . . . 218 F1
**Keswick Dr** BB2 . . . . . 80 E8
**Keswick Gr**
Heysham LA3 . . . . . 212 E5
Knott End-on-S FY6 . . . . . 199 F5
**Keswick Rd**
Blackpool FY1 . . . . . 130 C3
Burnley BB10 . . . . . 148 B2
Lancaster LA1 . . . . . 218 F1
Lytham St Anne's FY8 . . . . . 89 E8
**Keswick Way** WA11 . . . . . 8 F2
**Keswick Wlk** LA1 . . . . . 218 F1
**Kettering Rd** PR8 . . . . . 21 B5
**Kevin Ave** FY6 . . . . . 153 F5
**Kevin Gr** LA3 . . . . . 213 D1
**Kew Gdns**
Higher Penwortham
PR1 . . . . . 96 B5
Leyland PR25 . . . . . 77 B3
**Kew Gr** FY5 . . . . . 175 D1
**Kew House Dr** PR8 . . . . . 36 A2
**Kew Rd**
Formby L37 . . . . . 11 D1
Nelson BB9 . . . . . 170 F2
Southport PR8 . . . . . 35 B3
**Kew Ret Pk** PR8 . . . . . 36 A4
**Kew Woods Prim Sch**
PR8 . . . . . 35 F3
**Keynsham Gr** BB12 . . . . . 127 D7
**Keystone Ct** FY4 . . . . . 111 D6
**Key View** BB3 . . . . . 65 C5
**Khyber St** BB8 . . . . . 171 C4
**Kibble Cres** BB10 . . . . . 148 C3
**Kibble Gr** BB9 . . . . . 148 D4
**Kibboth Crew** BL0 . . . . . 50 B7
**Kidbrooke Ave** FY4 . . . . . 110 B4
**Kidder St** BB2 . . . . . 81 D8
**Kiddlington Cl** PR5 . . . . . 77 D8
**Kiddrow La** BB12 . . . . . 127 A7
**Kidsgrove** PR2 . . . . . 116 F5
**Kielder Ct** 3 FY8 . . . . . 91 C4
**Kielder Dr** BB12 . . . . . 127 E7
**Kiers Ct** BL6 . . . . . 32 E4
**Kilbane St** FY7 . . . . . 198 F1
**Kilburn Rd** WN5 . . . . . 10 C5
**Kilcrash La** PR3 . . . . . 180 D7
**Kildale Cl** L31 . . . . . 5 C2
**Kildare Ave** FY5 . . . . . 176 A4
**Kildare Rd** FY2 . . . . . 152 D3
**Kildonan Ave** 6 FY4 . . . . . 111 A6
**Kilgrimol Gdns** FY8 . . . . . 110 C1
**Kilkerran Cl** PR6 . . . . . 43 D8
**Killer St** 1 BL0 . . . . . 50 C6
**Killiard La** BB2 . . . . . 100 E5
**Killingbeck Cl** L40 . . . . . 25 D4
**Killington St** BB10 . . . . . 148 C2
**Killingworth Mews** 4
BL6 . . . . . 32 D1
**Killon St** BL9 . . . . . 33 A1
**Kilmory Pl** FY2 . . . . . 152 F5
**Kilmuir Cl** PR2 . . . . . 118 C5
**Kiln Bank** OL12 . . . . . 71 C2
**Kilnbank Ave** LA4 . . . . . 217 A5
**Kiln Bank La** OL12 . . . . . 71 C2
**Kiln Cl** BB7 . . . . . 190 A2
**Kiln Croft** PR6 . . . . . 78 B3
**Kiln Ct** 1 LA1 . . . . . 218 D1
**Kilngate** PR5 . . . . . 97 C3
**Kiln Hill** BB12 . . . . . 146 F6
**Kilnhouse La** FY8 . . . . . 111 A1
**Kiln House Way** BB5 . . . . 104 A3
**Kiln La**
Hambleton FY6 . . . . . 177 B2
Paythorne BB7 . . . . . 231 C6
Rimington BB7 . . . . . 230 F2
Skelmersdale WN8 . . . . . 17 E1
Wray LA2 . . . . . 238 D6
**Kiln St**
Nelson BB9 . . . . . 148 D8
Ramsbottom BL0 . . . . . 50 B5
**Kilns The** BB11 . . . . . 128 B3
**Kiln Terr** 5 OL13 . . . . . 70 D8
**Kiln Wlk** OL12 . . . . . 52 E2
**Kilruddery Rd** PR1 . . . . . 96 E5
**Kilsby Cl** PR5 . . . . . 97 E3
**Kilworth Ht** PR2 . . . . . 117 C5
**Kimberley Ave** FY4 . . . . . 110 D5
**Kimberley Cl** BB10 . . . . . 148 F3
**Kimberley Rd** PR2 . . . . . 117 C2
**Kimberley St**
Bacup OL13 . . . . . 70 A7
Burnley BB10 . . . . . 148 F3
Coppull PR7 . . . . . 42 E1
**Kimberly Cl** PR4 . . . . . 93 B6
**Kimble Cl** BL8 . . . . . 49 F2
**Kime St** BB12 . . . . . 127 C6
**Kincardine Ave** 7
FY4 . . . . . 111 A6
**Kincraig Ct** FY2 . . . . . 152 F4
**Kincraig Pl** FY2 . . . . . 152 F6

Kincraig Prim Sch FY2 152 F6
Kincraig Rd FY2 152 F5
Kinder Cnr FY6 153 B3
King Edward Ave
Blackpool FY2 152 B1
Lytham St Anne's FY8 90 A4
King Edward St BB5 103 C3
King Edward Terr BB9 170 D2
King Edward VII & Queen Mary Inf Sch FY8 90 A4
King Edward VII & Queen Mary Sch FY8 90 B4
Kingfisher Bank BB11 127 C4
Kingfisher Cl
Blackburn BB1 101 E8
Chorley PR7 42 F5
Kingfisher Ct
Caton LA2 237 C3
Maghull L31 5 B4
Oswaldtwistle BB5 103 E3
Preston PR1 96 D8
Southport PR9 35 D8
Kingfisher Ctr
Bacup OL13 70 E8
10 Rawtenstall BB4 86 A3
Kingfisher Dr
Bury BL9 33 B4
Poulton-le-F FY6 153 B2
Kingfisher Mews FY6 153 B2
Kingfisher Pk WN8 18 C4
Kingfisher St PR1 118 B1
Kingfisher Way
Bamber Bridge PR5 98 A2
Fleetwood FY7 198 E3
King George Ave FY2 152 B1
King George Ct 19 OL13 87 F3
King George V Coll PR8 35 E5
King Henry Mews BB7 230 D3
King La BB7 166 E8
Kingsacre PR3 181 A3
Kings Arc 37 LA1 214 F8
Kings Arms Cl 34 LA1 214 F8
Kings Ave BB4 86 A1
Kingsbarn Cl PR2 118 D7
Kingsbridge Cl PR1 96 E2
King's Bridge Cl 4 BB2 101 B1
Kingsbridge Ct 6 BB2 101 B1
King's Bridge St BB2 101 B1
Kingsbridge Wharf BB2 101 B1
Kingsbury Cl PR8 21 B4
Kingsbury Ct WN8 18 C4
Kingsbury Pl BB10 148 D3
Kingsbury Prim Spec Sch WN8 17 D1
Kings Cl
Buckshaw Village PR7 60 F6
Formby L37 11 E2
Staining FY3 131 E5
King's Cl FY6 153 E3
Kingscote Dr FY3 130 E7
Kings Cres PR25 77 A1
King's Cres LA3 216 E3
King's Croft PR5 97 D5
King's Cswy BB9 148 E5
Kings Ct
Fleetwood FY7 199 B4
Leyland PR25 77 A1
King's Ct 12 PR25 77 A1
Kingsdale Ave
Burnley BB10 148 C3
Fulwood PR2 118 D5
2 Morecambe LA3 216 E1
Kingsdale Cl
Leyland PR25 60 B6
Walton-le-D PR5 97 F5
Kingsdale Rd LA1 214 D7
Kings Dr
Fulwood PR2 117 D5
Hoddlesden BB3 82 F1
Padiham BB12 126 E6
King's Dr LA5 223 E1
KINGSFOLD 96 D2
Kingsfold Christian Sch The PR4 73 E2
Kingsfold Dr PR1 96 D2
Kingsfold Prim Sch PR1 96 D2
Kingshaven Dr PR1 96 E2
Kings Hey Dr PR9 53 F1
King's Highway
Accrington BB5 105 B2
Huncoat BB5 104 F8
Kingshotte Gdns BB9 170 C3
Kingsland Gr
Blackpool FY1 130 D3
12 Burnley BB11 128 B4
Kingsland Rd BB11 128 B4
Kingslea PR7 30 F8
Kingsley Ave BB12 126 E7
Kingsley Cl
Blackburn BB2 80 D7
Church BB5 103 F7
Maghull L31 5 C5
Thornton FY5 176 A3
Kingsley Ct 5 FY1 130 C4
Kingsley Dr PR7 43 A5
Kingsley Rd
Blackpool FY3 131 B2
Cottam PR4 116 E6
Laneshaw Bridge BB8 172 D6
Kingsley St BB9 170 F2
Kings Mdw PR8 21 D3
Kingsmead
Blackburn BB1 102 D4
Chorley PR7 43 C5
Kings Meadow Prim Sch PR8 21 D3
Kingsmede FY4 110 E6
Kingsmere Ave FY8 110 F1
Kingsmill Ave BB7 144 A8
Kingsmuir Ave PR2 118 D4
Kingsmuir Cl LA3 212 E7
Kings Rd
Cleveleys FY5 175 C2
Formby L37 11 E2
King's Rd
Accrington BB5 104 B7
Blackburn BB2 101 B1
Lytham St Anne's FY8 89 E5
King's Sq FY1 130 C5
King St
Accrington BB5 104 B6
5 Bacup OL13 87 F2
6 Bamber Bridge PR5 77 B7
Barnoldswick BB18 196 B2
Blackburn BB2 101 D4
Blackpool FY1 130 C5
Brierfield BB9 148 A5
Burnley, Harle Syke BB10 148 F3
Carnforth LA5 223 D1
Chorley PR7 43 D6
5 Clayton-le-M BB5 124 F2
Clitheroe BB7 166 E8
Colne BB8 171 E5
Fleetwood FY7 199 A4
15 Great Harwood BB6 124 C5
Haslingden BB4 85 B4
High Bentham LA2 239 D8
Horwich BL6 32 A4
Lancaster LA1 214 F8
Leyland PR25 77 A1
Longridge PR3 140 B7
Morecambe LA4 217 B5
Padiham BB12 126 C8
Ramsbottom BL0 50 C6
Rawtenstall BB4 69 E8
Southport PR8 35 A6
Whalley BB7 144 C5
Whitworth OL12 71 D3
Kingston Ave
Accrington BB5 104 A4
Blackpool FY4 110 C5
Kingston Cl FY6 199 F6
Kingston Cres
Haslingden BB4 68 A7
Southport PR9 54 C5
Kingston Dr FY8 90 D6
Kingston Mews 4 FY5 176 B3
Kingston Pl BB3 81 F7
King Street Terr BB9 148 A5
Kingsway
Accrington BB5 104 A8
Bamber Bridge PR5 77 E8
Blackburn BB3 82 A7
Blackpool FY4 110 C7
Burnley BB11 128 A6
Cleveleys FY5 175 C2
Euxton PR7 60 E2
Great Harwood BB6 124 F6
Hapton BB11 126 C3
Haslingden BB4 84 F1
Heysham LA3 213 A8
Higher Penwortham PR1 96 B6
Huncoat BB5 125 F1
Lancaster LA1 218 E1
Leyland PR25 59 E7
Lytham St Anne's FY8 90 C4
Preston PR2 116 F2
Southport PR8 35 A7
Kingsway Ave PR3 137 C3
Kingsway Ct
2 Lytham St Anne's FY8 90 C4
1 Morecambe LA3 216 E1
Kingsway Ret Pk LA1 218 E1
Kingsway W PR1 96 B6
King's Wlk FY5 175 D5
Kingswood PR7 43 B5
Kingswood Cl FY8 90 E4
Kingswood Coll L40 24 A6
Kingswood Ho PR8 34 F5
Kingswood Pk PR8 34 F5
Kingswood Rd PR25 77 A2
Kingswood St 6 PR1 96 E7
King William St BB1 101 E5
Kinloch Way L39 15 D6
Kinnerton Pl FY5 152 F8
Kinross Cl
Blackburn BB1 102 A4
1 Ramsbottom BL0 50 A2
Kinross Cres FY4 131 A1
Kinross St BB11 127 D4
Kinross Wlk 7 BB1 102 A4
Kintbury Rd FY8 89 F4
Kintour Rd FY8 90 E6
Kintyre Cl FY4 110 F7
Kintyre Way LA3 212 E7
Kipling Dr FY3 131 B2
Kipling Pl BB6 124 B4
Kirby Dr PR4 93 B6
Kirby Rd
Blackburn BB2 101 D1
Blackpool FY1 130 B2
Nelson BB9 148 B8
Kirby's Cotts L31 6 B3
Kirk Ave BB7 166 C8
Kirkbeck Cl LA2 237 D3
KIRKBY 1 B3
Kirkby Ave
Clayton-le-W PR25 77 E1
Cleveleys FY5 175 E4
Kirkby Bank Rd L33 1 C2
Kirkby Lonsdale Rd LA2 219 D7
Kirkby Lonsdale Rd
Caton LA2, LA6 237 B6
Over Kellet LA6 240 B1
Kirkdale Ave
Lytham St Anne's FY8 89 F7
Newchurch BB4 86 E1
Kirkdale Cl BB3 65 C6
Kirkdale Gdns WN8 10 A7
Kirkdale Rd BB6 123 C8
Kirkdene Ave BB8 194 D1
Kirkdene Mews BB8 194 D1
Kirkes Rd LA1 215 A7
Kirkfell Dr BB12 127 C8
Kirkfield PR3 185 D3
Kirkgate
Burnley BB11 128 B4
Kirkham PR4 114 B4
Kirkgate La LA6 240 B4
KIRKHAM 114 A5
Kirkham Ave FY1 130 E2
Kirkham By-Pass PR4 114 B4
Kirkham Cl PR25 76 D1
Kirkham Gram Jun Sch PR4 113 F4
Kirkham Gram Sch PR4 113 F5
Kirkham Mus★ PR4 114 A5
Kirkham Rd
Freckleton PR4 93 B8
Kirkham PR4 114 E6
Southport PR9 54 A4
Weeton PR4 132 F2
Kirkham St PR1 96 E8
Kirkham Trad Pk PR4 114 B4
Kirkham & Wesham Prim Sch PR4 113 F5
Kirkham & Wesham Sta PR4 113 F6
Kirk Head PR4 74 E2
Kirkhill Ave BB4 85 C3
Kirk Hill Rd BB4 85 C3
Kirk Ho BB5 103 E6
Kirklake Bank L37 11 C2
Kirklake Rd L37 11 D2
Kirkland & Catterall St Helen's CE Prim Sch PR3 181 A2
Kirkland Pl PR2 95 E8
Kirklands
Chipping PR3 185 E3
Hest Bank LA2 220 E1
Kirklands Rd LA6 237 B8
Kirklees Rd PR8 34 F1
Kirkmoor Cl BB7 189 D1
Kirkmoor Rd BB7 166 E8
Kirk Rd BB5 103 E7
Kirkside View BB11 126 C4
Kirkstall Ave
Blackpool FY1 130 E2
Read BB12 145 D1
Kirkstall Cl PR7 43 D5
Kirkstall Dr
Barnoldswick BB18 196 D3
Chorley PR7 43 D5
Formby L37 12 B2
Kirkstall Rd
Chorley PR7 43 D5
Southport PR8 34 F2
Kirkstone Ave
Blackburn BB2 80 E8
Fleetwood FY7 198 D1
Kirkstone Dr
Blackpool FY5 152 C7
Morecambe LA4 217 D5
Kirkstone Rd FY8 110 D1
Kirk View BB4 87 A1
Kirton Cres FY8 90 C6
Kirton Pl FY5 175 E1
Kit Brow La LA2 211 D6
Kittiwake Cl 10 FY5 175 F1
Kittiwake Rd PR6 62 A3
Kittlingborne Brow PR5 98 A3
Kitty La FY4 111 B4
Knacks La OL12 52 A5
Knaresboro Ave FY3 130 F3
Knaresborough Cl FY6 153 D5
Knebworth Cl PR6 78 C2
Knight Cres BB3 82 A6
Knighton Ave BB2 101 C8
Knightsbrdige Cl PR4 113 E6
Knightsbridge Ave
Blackpool FY4 110 D6
Colne BB8 171 B5
Knightsbridge Cl
Kirkham PR4 113 E6
2 Lytham St Anne's FY8 90 D6
Knights Cl FY5 175 F1
Knightscliffe Cres WN6 19 D6
Knitting Row La PR3 178 A3
Knob Hall Gdns PR9 53 F3
Knob Hall La PR9 53 F3
Knoll La PR4 75 A4
Knoll The LA2 218 C8
Knot Acre PR4 76 A8
Knot La
Paythorne BB7, BD23 231 D5
Walton-le-D PR5 97 F5
KNOTT END-ON-SEA 199 E5
Knott Hill St OL12 71 E6
Knott La LA5 224 A8
KNOTTS 230 B8
Knotts Brow BL7 48 F4
Knotts Dr BB8 171 C3
Knotts La
Bolton-by-B BB7, BD23 230 B8
Colne BB8 171 D3
Padiham BB12 126 E6
Knotts Mount BB8 171 C3
Knott St BB3 82 A1
Knotwood Ct BB5 103 E5
Knowe Hill Cres LA1 215 B3
Knowl Cl BL0 50 C4
Knowle Ave
Blackpool FY2 152 C1
Cleveleys FY5 175 E1
Southport PR8 21 C6
KNOWLE GREEN 163 C1
Knowle La BB3 82 A3
Knowles Brow BB7 165 B3
Knowlesly Mdws BB3 65 C6
Knowlesly Rd BB3 65 B6
Knowles Rd FY8 89 E7
Knowles St
1 Chorley PR7 43 C6
Preston PR1 97 D8
Rishton BB1 124 B1
Knowles Wood Dr PR7 43 A6
Knowle The FY2 152 C2
KNOWLEY 61 F2
Knowley Brow PR6 61 E2
Knowl Gap Ave BB4 85 A1
Knowl Mdw BB4 68 A6
Knowlmere St BB5 104 B7
Knowlys Ave LA3 212 F8
Knowlys Cres 4 LA3 212 F8
Knowlys Dr 3 LA3 212 F8
Knowlys Gr LA3 212 F8
Knowlys Rd LA3 212 E8
Knowsley Ave
Blackpool FY3 130 E3
Leyland PR25 77 C4
Knowsley Cl
Gregson Lane PR5 98 F2
Lancaster LA1 214 D6
Knowsley Cres
Shawforth OL12 71 E6
Thornton FY5 176 C2
Weeton PR4 132 E2
Knowsley Dr PR5 98 F2
Knowsley Gate FY7 198 D4
Knowsley Gr 5 BL6 32 D1
Knowsley Ind Pk L33 1 C2
Knowsley La
Edgworth BL7 66 E4
Rivington PR6 44 E4
Knowsley Park Way BB4 68 B8
Knowsley Rd
Haslingden BB4 68 B8
Leyland PR25 60 C8
Ormskirk L39 15 F5
Southport PR9 53 C1
Wilpshire BB1 122 F5
Knowsley Rd Ind Est BB4 68 B8
Knowsley Rd W BB1 122 E5
Knowsley Road Ind Est BB4 85 B1
Knowsley St
3 Colne BB8 171 D4
32 Preston PR1 97 A7
Knox Gr FY1 130 D3
Knunck Knowles Dr BB7 189 E1
Knutsford Rd FY3 131 B2
Knutsford Wlk L31 5 D4
KNUZDEN BROOK 102 F4
Knuzden Brook BB1 102 D4
Knuzden St Oswald's CE Prim Sch BB1 102 E4
Korea Rd PR2 118 B4
Kumara Cres FY4 131 B1
Kyan St BB10 148 B2
Kylbarrow La LA5 225 F2
Kylemore Ave FY2 152 D3
Kyston Cl 1 FY1 130 D7


## L


Laburnum Ave
Bamber Bridge PR5 77 B8
Lytham St Anne's FY8 91 B5
Laburnum Cl
Burnley BB11 127 D3
Preston PR1 118 C3
Laburnum Cotts PR3 201 E5
Laburnum Dr
Fulwood PR2 117 D8
Oswaldtwistle BB5 103 F3
Skelmersdale WN8 17 D1
Laburnum Gr
Burscough Bridge L40 25 E6
Horwich BL6 32 E1
Lancaster LA1 214 D8
Maghull L31 5 F1
Southport PR8 35 F7
Laburnum Pk LA5 221 C8
Laburnum Rd
Blackburn BB1 102 A8
Chorley PR6 61 D3
Haslingden BB4 68 A7
2 Lancaster LA1 218 D2
Laburnum St
6 Blackpool FY3 130 D7
Haslingden BB4 85 A3
Lacey Ct 19 BB4 85 B3
Lachman Rd BB8 172 B3
Lacy Ave PR1 96 E2
Ladbrooke Gr BB11 127 E2
Lade End LA3 212 E8
Ladies Row PR4 134 F4
Ladies Wlk LA1 218 E2
Ladies Wlk Ind Est LA1 218 E2
Lady Acre PR5 78 A8
Lady Alice's Dr L40 16 E8
Lady Anne Cl L40 24 B7
Ladybank Ave PR2 118 D7
Ladybower La FY6 153 B3
Lady Cl BB3 82 A6
Lady Crosse Dr PR6 61 C7
LADY GREEN 3 D4
Lady Green Ct L38 3 E3
Lady Green La L38 3 D4
Lady Hartley Ct BB8 172 D6
Lady Hey Cres PR2 116 C1
Ladyman St 10 PR1 96 E7
Lady Pl PR5 97 E4
Ladysmith Ave BL9 33 A5
Ladysmith Rd PR2 117 C2
Lady St PR1 96 F8
Lady's Wlk L40 16 C6
Lady Well Dr PR2 118 C7
Ladywell St PR1 96 E8
Lafford La
Up Holland, Roby Mill WN8 19 C2
Up Holland WN8 10 C8
Lagonda Dr FY4 111 F6
Lagonda Way FY4 111 F6
Laidley's Wlk FY7 198 E5
Lairgill Row LA2 239 E8
Laister Ct 7 LA4 217 E6
Laithbutts La LA6 221 F5
Laithe St
Burnley BB11 127 F4
6 Colne BB8 171 C4
Lake Ave LA4 216 F4
Lakeber Ave LA2 239 D8
Lakeber Cl 11 LA2 239 D8
Lakeber Dr 13 LA2 239 D8
Lake Gr LA4 216 F4
Lakeland Cl
Billington BB7 144 A3
Forton PR3 207 B3
Lakeland Dr BB7 144 A8
Lakeland Gdns PR7 43 A5
Lakeland Ho LA4 217 E7
Lakeland Way BB12 127 B8
Lakeland Wildlife Oasis★ LA7 225 F8
Lake Point FY8 90 D3
Lake Rd
Lytham St Anne's FY8 90 C4
Morecambe LA3 216 F3
Lake Rd N FY8 90 C4
Lakes Dr WN5 10 E6
Lakeside FY6 200 B5
Lakeside Ave WN5 10 E3
Lake Side Cotts WN1 30 C1
Lake View BL7 46 C5
Lakeview Ct PR9 35 B8
Lake View Rd BB8 171 D7
Lakeway FY3 130 F6
Lakewood Ave FY5 175 D1
Lamaleach Dr PR4 93 A6
Lamaleach Residential Pk PR4 93 A5
Lambert Cl PR2 118 E3
Lambert Rd
Fulwood PR2 118 E3
Lancaster LA1 218 C3
Lamberts Mill Footwear Mus★ BB4 86 B2
Lambert St BB8 172 C2
Lambeth Cl
Blackburn BB1 102 A4
Horwich BL6 32 D3
Lambeth Ct PR2 117 E5
Lambeth St
Blackburn BB1 102 A4
Colne BB8 172 B5
Lambing Clough La BB7 142 E7
Lambourne WN8 18 B4
Lambridge Cl LA4 217 B3
Lamb Row BB7 145 E7
Lambshear La L31 5 C4
Lambs Hill Cl 7 FY5 176 D1
Lamb's La PR3 201 A4
Lambs Rd FY5 153 D8
Lambton Gates BB4 86 C2
Lamlash Rd BB1 102 D4
LAMMACK 101 C8
Lammack Prim Sch BB1 122 C1
Lammack Rd BB1 101 C8
Lamour Pl 4 FY7 198 D3
Lanark Ave FY2 152 C6
Lanark Cl OL10 33 F1
Lanark St BB11 127 D4
Lancambe Ct LA1 218 A2
Lancashire Coll PR7 43 A8
Lancashire Constabulary HQ PR4 95 E1
Lancashire Dr PR7 60 F6
Lancashire Enterprise Bsns Pk PR26 77 A4
Lancashire Fire & Rescue HQ PR2 117 D8
Lancashire Rd PR26 77 A4
Lancashire St LA4 216 E4
LANCASTER 214 C6

Lancaster Ave
Accrington BB5 104 B7
Clayton-le-W PR25 77 E1
Great Eccleston PR3 156 C5
Haslingden BB4 68 B8
Horwich BL6 32 D2
Lytham St Anne's FY8 89 F4
Ramsbottom BL0 50 A4
Thornton FY5 176 C2
Lancaster Castle★ LA1 214 E8
Lancaster Christ Church CE Prim Sch LA1 215 B8
Lancaster City Mus★ LA1 214 F8
Lancaster Cl
Adlington PR6 31 B7
Great Eccleston PR3 156 C5
Knott End-on-S FY6 199 F5
Maghull L31 5 F1
Southport PR8 34 E4
Lancaster Cres WN8 17 E1
Lancaster Ct
Chorley PR7 61 C2
Parbold WN8 27 C2
Lancaster Dallas Road Com Prim Sch LA1 214 E7
Lancaster Dr
Banks PR9 54 F5
Brinscall PR6 62 E8
Clayton-le-M BB5 125 A3
Clitheroe BB7 166 C7
Padiham BB12 126 D6
Lancastergate PR25 59 F8
Lancaster Gate
Banks PR9 54 F5
Fleetwood FY7 198 D4
14 Lancaster LA1 214 F8
Nelson BB9 148 D7
Lancaster Gdns PR8 34 E4
Lancaster Girls' Gram Sch LA1 214 F7
Lancaster Ho
3 Fleetwood FY7 199 A4
Southport PR8 34 E4
Lancaster La
Clayton-le-W PR25 77 E2
Parbold WN8 27 C3
Lancaster & Lakeland Nuffield Hospl The LA1 215 A7
Lancaster Lane Com Prim Sch PR25 77 D1
Lancaster Maritime Mus★ LA1 218 C1
Lancaster & Morecambe Coll LA1 217 F3
Lancaster & Morecambe Coll (Annexe) LA4 217 B5
Lancaster Pl
Adlington PR6 31 A8
Blackburn BB2 101 B5
Lancaster Rd
Blackpool FY3 131 A3
Caton LA2 237 B3
Cockerham LA2 206 C6
Crag Bank LA5 221 B7
Fisher's Row PR3 201 E5
Formby L37 11 E1
Garstang PR3 204 C1
Hornby LA2 238 B7
Knott End-on-S FY6 199 F5
Lancaster LA3 213 D3
Morecambe LA4 217 C5
Morecambe, Torrisholme LA4 217 F4
Moss Edge PR3 178 E6
Preesall FY6 200 C3
Preston, Adelphi PR1 96 F8
Preston, Avenham PR1 97 A8
Ratten Row PR3 156 A8
Slyne LA2 218 D6
Southport PR8 34 E4
Lancaster Rd N PR1 117 F1
Lancaster Road Prim Sch LA4 217 D4
Lancaster Royal Gram Sch LA1 215 A8
Lancaster Royal Gram Sch (Annexe) LA1 215 B7
Lancaster St
Blackburn BB2 101 C4
Colne BB8 171 D5
Coppull PR7 42 F1
Oswaldtwistle BB5 103 C3
Lancaster Sta LA1 214 E8
Lancaster Steiner Sch LA1 218 B1
Lancaster Way 17 PR1 97 A8
Lanchester Ct PR25 59 D6
Lanchester Gdns BB6 143 C6
Lancia Cres FY4 112 A6
Lancing Pl BB2 101 C3
Landcrest Cl PR4 114 B2
Land End L31 6 C1
Land Gate OL12 71 F5
Landing La BB7 229 F4
Land La
New Longton PR4 75 D5
Southport PR9 54 D4
Landless St BB9 148 A5
Landseer Ave FY2 152 C4
Landseer Cl BB11 127 E3
Landseer St PR1 118 C1
Landsmoor Dr PR4 95 A1
LANE BOTTOM 149 B3
Lane Bottom BB18 194 B8
Lanedale PR4 75 A8
Lane End BB11 126 C2
Lane End Rd
Bacup OL13 88 A1
Britannia OL13 71 A8
LANE ENDS 230 A5
Lane Ends
Burnley BB9 148 D6
Longridge PR3 140 F8
Rivington PR6 44 D4
Lane Ends Ct 2 FY4 130 E1
Lanefield Dr FY5 175 C4
Lane Foot Brow LA2 239 D4
LANE HEAD 87 F4
Lane Head LA2 238 D6
Lane Head La OL13 87 F3
LANE HEADS 156 D3
Lane Ho BB8 172 C1
Lane House Cl BB2 81 B8
LANESHAW BRIDGE 172 F6
Laneshaw Bridge Prim Sch BB8 172 E6
Laneshaw Cl BB3 81 E4
LANESIDE 104 C8
Laneside
Altham BB5 125 D6
Great Harwood BB6 124 A6
LANE SIDE 85 B2
Lane Side OL13 88 A4
Laneside Ave
Accrington BB5 104 B8
Higham BB12 146 F6
Laneside Cl BB7 144 A7
Laneside Ho 5 BB4 85 B2
Laneside Rd BB4 85 C2
Lane Side Terr BB5 125 D6
Lane The
Carleton FY6 153 A3
Sunderland LA3 209 A5
Lane Top
Colne, Cotton Tree BB8 172 C5
Fence BB12 147 D7
Langber End La LA6 242 F1
Langcliffe Rd PR2 118 E4
Langdale LA2 237 C3
Langdale Ave
Clitheroe BB7 166 C7
Croston PR26 58 B3
Formby L37 11 D2
Hesketh Bank PR4 73 D4
Rawtenstall BB4 85 E2
Langdale Bsns Pk LA3 217 D3
Langdale Cl
3 Accrington BB5 125 D1
Bamber Bridge PR5 97 D1
Blackburn BB2 80 E8
Formby L37 11 D2
Freckleton PR4 93 A6
Thornton FY5 176 B2
Langdale Cres PR2 118 E3
Langdale Ct
Cleveleys FY5 175 F1
3 Fleetwood FY7 198 E2
4 Garstang PR3 181 B7
Higher Penwortham PR1 96 C4
Langdale Dr
Burscough L40 25 E4
Maghull L31 5 E2
Langdale Gdns PR8 34 F1
Langdale Gr PR6 61 B7
Langdale Pl
1 Blackpool FY4 131 C1
Lancaster LA1 218 E2
Langdale Prep Sch FY2 152 B1
Langdale Rd
Blackburn BB2 80 E8
Blackpool FY4 131 C1
Carnforth LA5 221 E8
Fulwood PR2 118 E3
Lancaster LA1 218 E2
Leyland PR25 60 B6
Longridge PR3 139 F5
Lytham St Anne's FY8 110 D1
Morecambe LA4 217 D5
Padiham BB12 146 C2
Langdale Rise BB8 171 F6
Langden Brook Mews LA3 217 F2
Langden Brook Sq BB1 102 A3
Langden Cres PR5 77 F8
Langden Dr PR2 119 A3
Langden Fold PR2 139 D1
Langdon Way FY2 152 E2
Langfield BB10 129 B6
Langfield Ave FY4 110 C5
Langfield Cl PR2 117 F8
Langford St BB5 104 E1
Langham Ave BB5 104 B8
Langham Rd
Blackburn BB1 101 D7
Standish WN6 29 D1
Langham St BB12 127 B6
LANGHO 143 D1
Langholm Cl 6 PR25 76 D1
Langholme Cl BB9 170 C1
Langholme Rd PR1 96 B4
Langholme St BB9 148 E6
Langholme Way OL10 33 F1
Langho St BB2 101 C1
Langho Sta BB6 143 C1
Langho Woods BB6 143 C5
Langley Cl
Hightown L38 2 F2
Langley Cl *continued*
Standish WN6 29 E2
Langley Ct L40 25 B5
Langley La PR3 137 F6
Langley Pl L40 25 B4
Langley Rd
Burscough L40 25 B4
Lancaster LA1 215 A7
Langport Cl PR2 117 F8
Langridge Way LA4 217 B3
Langroyd Rd BB8 171 E6
Langsford Cl BB18 196 C2
Langshaw Dr BB7 166 F6
Langshaw La LA2 211 D5
Lang St
3 Accrington BB5 104 A6
Blackpool FY1 130 C6
Langstone Cl BL6 32 B3
Langthwaite Rd LA1, LA2 215 E5
Langton Ave WN6 29 E1
Langton Brow
Eccleston PR7 41 D5
Longridge PR3 140 B7
Langton Cl
Blackburn BB2 81 C8
Eccleston PR7 41 D5
Lancaster LA1 218 E4
Leyland PR26 59 C8
Langton Pl WN6 29 E1
Langton Rd PR4 114 A5
Langton St PR1 96 D7
Langtree WN8 18 B3
Langtree La
Elswick PR4 155 F2
Standish WN6 29 D3
Langwood FY7 198 E2
Langwood Ave 3 BB4 85 C2
Langwood Cl 4 BB4 85 C2
Langwood Ct 6 BB4 85 C2
Langwood Gdns 5 BB4 85 C2
Langwood La WA11 9 C1
Langwyth Rd BB10 128 E5
Lansborough Cl PR26 59 B8
Lansbury Pl 3 BB9 170 F2
Lansdowne Cl
Burnley BB11 127 F4
Ramsbottom BL0 50 B5
Lansdowne Gr LA4 217 E7
Lansdowne Pl 1 FY1 130 B6
Lansdowne Rd
Lytham St Anne's FY8 90 D5
Morecambe LA4 217 E7
Southport PR8 35 E6
Lansdowne St BB2 101 B3
Lansdown Hill PR2 117 C7
Lansdown Rd PR4 114 A7
Lansil Ind Est LA1 218 E3
Lansil Way LA1 218 E3
Lansil Wlk LA1 218 E3
Lanterns The FY6 153 D4
Lapford Cres L33 1 A4
Lapford Wlk L33 1 A4
Lappet Gr PR4 116 E5
Lapwing Row FY8 90 E7
Lapwings The FY6 153 B2
LARBRECK 155 E6
Larbreck Ave PR4 156 A1
Larbreck Gardens Cvn Pk PR3 155 C5
Larbreck Hall Cvn Pk PR3 155 B5
Larbreck Rd FY3 130 E7
Larch Ave PR6 61 E2
Larch Cl
Blackburn BB2 80 F8
Freckleton PR4 93 A5
Knott End-on-S FY6 200 A5
Rawtenstall BB4 68 F8
Skelmersdale WN8 17 E1
Larch Dr PR6 62 F7
LARCHES 116 F1
Larches Ave PR2 116 F1
Larches La PR2 116 E1
Larches The BB1 101 F7
Larchgate PR2 118 C7
Larch Gate PR5 98 E2
Larch Gr
Bamber Bridge PR5 97 F1
Garstang PR3 181 C8
Lancaster LA1 214 D8
Larch Rd BB5 103 F3
Larch St
Blackburn BB1 102 A7
Burnley BB12 127 C7
Bury BL9 33 B2
Nelson BB9 148 F8
Southport PR8 35 E6
Larchway PR3 140 B8
Larch Way L37 11 D4
Larchwood
Higher Penwortham PR1 96 B4
Lancaster LA1 215 B4
Preston PR2 116 E1
Larchwood Cl FY8 90 F4
Larchwood Cres PR25 76 E1
Largs Rd BB1 102 C3
Lark Ave 3 PR1 96 E4
Lark Cl FY3 131 B3
Lark Ct FY7 198 D1
Larkfield PR7 41 B6
Larkfield Cl BL8 49 F1
Larkfield Ct PR9 54 A3
Larkfield La PR9 54 A3
Larkfield Prim Sch PR9 54 A3
Larkhill
Brockhall Village BB6 143 C5
Larkhill *continued*
Skelmersdale WN8 18 B4
Lark Hill
Blackburn BB1 101 F6
Higher Walton PR5 98 B3
Rawtenstall BB4 86 A3
Larkhill Ave BB10 148 C5
Larkhill Gr L38 2 F3
Larkhill La L37 11 C4
Lark Hill Pl 6 OL12 52 E1
Larkhill Rd PR1 97 B7
Larkhill St
Blackpool FY1 130 C6
Preston PR1 97 B7
LARKHOLME 198 D1
Larkholme Ave FY7 198 E1
Larkholme La FY7 198 E1
Larkholme Par FY7 198 D1
Larkholme Prim Sch FY7 175 D8
Larkspur Cl
Blackburn BB2 80 D8
3 Southport PR8 35 D6
Lark St
4 Burnley BB12 127 C7
Colne BB8 171 E6
Darwen BB3 65 B5
Last Drop Village The★ BL7 48 A1
Latham Ave
9 Blackpool FY3 130 E3
Ormskirk L39 16 A5
Latham Cres PR4 57 A6
Latham Rd BL6 31 C3
Latham Row BL6 32 F3
Latham St
Burnley BB10 148 B1
Preston PR1 97 A6
LATHOM 26 B1
Lathom Ave
Morecambe LA4 217 D4
Parbold WN8 27 B3
Lathom Cl L40 25 E4
Lathom Dr L31 5 E3
Lathom Gr LA4 217 D4
Lathom High Sch WN8 17 F3
Lathom Ho L40 17 B7
Lathom La L40 16 C7
LATHOM PARK 17 C7
Lathom Rd
Bickerstaffe L39 7 F8
Southport PR9 53 C1
Lathom St 8 BL9 33 A4
Lathom Way PR3 181 D6
Latimer Cl 2 WN5 10 F7
Latimer Dr PR4 75 F7
Lauderdale Ave FY5 175 D1
Lauderdale Cres 1 PR2 118 F4
Lauderdale Rd PR2 118 F4
Lauderdale St PR1 96 E6
LAUND 85 F4
Laund Gate BB12 147 D8
Laund Gr BB5 104 D3
Laund Hey View BB4 85 B1
Laund La
Haslingden BB4 85 C3
Ollerton Fold PR6 79 E4
Laund Rd BB5 104 D3
Laundry Rd N FY4 111 A5
Laund St BB4 85 F4
Laund The PR26 76 A1
Laura St BL0 50 C2
Laurel Ave
Blackpool FY1 130 E2
Burscough Bridge L40 25 E6
Darwen BB3 82 B2
Euxton PR7 60 B3
Fleetwood FY7 175 F8
Lytham St Anne's FY8 91 B5
Laurel Bank LA1 214 D7
Laurel Bank Ave PR2 117 C3
Laurel Bank Terr BB2 80 B7
Laurel Dr
Skelmersdale WN8 17 E2
Thornton FY5 153 B8
Laurel Gr PR8 35 E7
Laurel St
4 Bacup OL13 87 F3
Burnley BB11 128 B4
3 Bury BL9 33 B2
10 Preston PR1 97 A7
Laurels The
Coppull PR7 42 F3
Kirkham PR4 113 D4
Poulton-le-F FY6 153 F3
Laureston Ave LA3 212 F6
Laurie Pl 2 OL12 52 F1
Laurier Ave 3 FY4 110 C6
Laurier Rd BB10 148 B2
Lauriston Cl 4 FY4 111 A6
Lavender Cl PR2 118 C6
Lavender Gr PR7 43 C5
Lavender Hill BB4 68 F8
Lavender Way FY6 199 F5
Laverick Rd LA2 237 A5
Laverton Cl BL9 33 E1
Laverton Rd FY8 90 A4
Lawley Rd BB2 101 A5
Lawn Ct 2 FY1 130 D4
Lawns Ave WN5 10 C5
Lawnsdale Cvn Pk FY8 112 E1
Lawn St BB10 128 A8
Lawns The PR9 53 F2
Lawnswood Ave
Lancaster LA1 215 A3
Poulton-le-F FY6 153 C2
Lawnswood Cres FY3 131 C2
Lawnswood Dr LA3 217 C2
Lawn Tennis Ct FY4 110 D5
Lawnwood Ave PR7 43 A5
Lawrence Ave
Bamber Bridge PR5 97 D2
Burnley BB11 127 C4
Lytham St Anne's FY8 90 A6
Preston PR1 97 B5
Simonstone BB12 145 E2
Lawrence Cl 2 OL12 52 A1
Lawrence La PR7 41 C7
Lawrence Rd
Chorley PR7 43 B7
Higher Penwortham PR1 96 B5
Lawrence Row 5 FY7 199 A4
Lawrence St
Blackburn BB2 101 C4
12 Blackpool FY4 130 B1
3 Fulwood PR2 117 D3
Padiham BB12 146 D1
Whitewell Bottom BB4 86 F4
Lawrie Ave BL0 50 B5
Lawson Ave BL6 32 C4
Lawson Cl LA1 214 F3
Lawson Gdns LA2 218 C8
Lawson Pl LA2 218 C8
Lawson Rd
Blackpool FY3 131 A3
Lytham St Anne's FY8 111 A2
Lawsons Ct 4 FY5 176 C1
Lawsons Rd FY5 176 C2
Lawson St
3 Chorley PR6 43 E7
Preston PR1 96 F8
Rawtenstall BB4 86 A8
Southport PR9 36 A7
Law St
Newchurch BB4 86 F1
Todmorden OL14 109 B1
Lawswood
Formby L37 11 E5
6 Thornton FY5 176 C1
Lawton Cl PR6 79 B1
Laxey Gr PR1 118 D3
Laxey Rd BB2 101 E1
Laycock Gate FY3 130 D6
LAYTON 130 E7
Layton Prim Sch FY3 130 E8
Layton Rd
Blackpool FY3 130 E6
Preston PR2 116 E1
Layton Sta FY2 152 E1
Lazenby Ave FY7 198 C2
LEA 116 D1
Lea Bank BB4 86 D2
Lea Bank Mews 15 BB9 170 F2
Leach Cres FY8 110 F2
Leaches Rd BL0 50 D8
Leachfield Cl 2 LA2 211 A4
Leachfield Ind Est PR3 204 B1
Leachfield Rd LA2 210 F4
Leach House La LA2 211 A5
Leach La FY8 110 E1
Leach Pl PR5 78 B8
Leach St
Blackburn BB2 101 E2
Colne BB8 171 C4
Lea Com Prim Sch PR2 116 D1
Lea Cres L39 15 F7
Leacroft BB3 82 A6
Lea Ct L39 15 E7
Leadale PR2 116 D2
Leadale Cl WN6 29 D1
Leadale Gn PR25 76 E1
Leadale Rd PR25 76 E1
Lead Mines Clough★ PR6 45 A7
Lea Dr BB2 81 E6
Leaford Ave FY3 130 E8
Leafy Cl PR25 60 B7
Leagram Cres PR2 119 A3
Lea La
Cottam PR4 116 B5
Gressingham LA2 237 F8
Heysham LA3 212 E6
Leamington Ave
Baldingstone BL9 50 E1
Burnley BB10 148 C1
Southport PR8 21 D5
Leamington Rd
Blackburn BB2 101 B6
Blackpool FY1 130 D5
Lytham St Anne's FY8 89 F6
Morecambe LA4 217 D3
Southport PR8 21 D5
Leamington St BB9 148 E7
Lea Mount Dr BL9 33 D4
Leander Gdns FY6 153 D2
Lea Neeld's Endowed CE Prim Sch PR4 116 C4
Leapers View LA6 237 B8
Lea Rd
Lucas Green PR6 61 C5
Preston PR2, PR4 116 D3
Lea St Mary's RC Primary Sch PR4 115 F2
Leaside Cl OL12 52 D2
Leathercote PR3 181 C6
LEA TOWN 115 F3
Leavengreave Ct OL12 71 D4
Leaverholme Cl BB10 108 A7
Leaver St BB12 127 A5
Leavesley Rd FY1 130 D8
Lea Way Cl FY5 153 D7
Lebanon St BB10 128 C5
LECK 242 B7

Leckhampton Rd FY1 130 B8
Leck Ho 11 LA1 215 A3
Leckonby St PR3 156 B5
Leck St Peter's CE Prim Sch LA6 242 B7
Ledburn WN8 18 B3
Ledbury Ave FY8 90 B5
Ledbury Rd FY3 131 B7
Ledson Gr L39 6 B7
LEE 232 F2
Lee Brook Cl BB4 86 A4
Leebrook Rd BB4 85 F4
Leeds Cl 15 BB1 102 A4
Leeds Rd
Blackpool FY1 130 D5
4 Nelson BB9 148 E8
Nelson, Bradley BB9 170 F1
Lee Gr BB10 128 F4
Lee Green St 3 BB10 128 A8
Leehouse Dr FY6 131 D8
Leeís St OL13 71 C8
Leek St PR1 97 E8
Lee La
Bispham Green L40 27 C7
Great Harwood BB1 124 B3
Horwich BL6 32 B4
Whittlestone Head BL7 66 B2
Leeming La LA6 242 C3
Lee Rd
Bacup OL13 70 E8
Blackpool FY4 111 B8
Nelson BB9 170 F2
LEES 187 B6
Leesands Cl PR2 118 E5
Lees Cotts BL7 48 C2
Lees Ct LA3 212 E7
Lees La WN8 18 E7
Leeson Ave PR7 42 D4
Lees Rd
Adlington PR6 31 B8
Kirkby L33 1 B2
Lee St
Accrington BB5 104 C6
Bacup OL13 87 F2
Barrowford BB9 170 D3
Burnley BB10 128 A8
Longridge PR3 140 A7
Rawtenstall BB4 86 A4
Lees The BB10 108 A7
Leeswood WN8 18 B3
Leet Rd BB12 146 F5
Lee View 2 OL13 88 A1
Leeward Cl BB3 81 F6
Leeward Rd PR2 95 F8
Legh La PR4 56 B4
Leicester Ave
Cleveleys FY5 175 E3
Garstang PR3 181 B7
Horwich BL6 32 A3
Leicester Gate FY5 175 E3
Leicester Lo 3 PR2 118 F4
Leicester Rd
Blackburn BB1 102 C5
Blackpool FY1 130 D5
Preston PR1 118 A1
Leicester St PR9 35 B8
Leigh Brow PR5 97 B2
Leigh Pk BB11 126 C3
Leigh Row PR7 43 C7
Leighton Ave
Fleetwood FY7 198 D3
Maghull L31 5 D2
Leighton Ct LA4 217 A3
Leighton Dr LA1 214 D7
Leighton Hall★ LA5 225 C1
Leighton Moss Nature Reserve★ LA5 225 A3
Leighton Moss Visitor Ctr★ LA5 224 F2
Leighton St PR1 96 E8
Leinster Rd LA1 215 A5
Leisure Lakes Cvn Pk PR4 55 E1
Leith Ave FY5 175 D2
Lemonius St BB5 104 C4
Lemon Tree Ct FY8 110 B4
LENCHES 171 D3
Lenches Fold BB8 171 D4
Lenches Rd BB8 171 D3
Lench Rd BB4 69 D8
Lench St 5 BB4 69 F8
Lendel Cl L37 11 E3
Lennon St 3 PR7 43 C7
Lennox Ct FY4 110 D6
Lennox Gate FY4 110 D7
Lennox Rd OL14 109 A1
Lennox St
18 Preston PR1 97 A7
Worsthorne BB10 129 A6
Lennox Wlk OL10 33 F1
Lenton Ave L37 11 D4
Lentworth Ave FY2 152 D5
Lentworth Dr LA1 215 A4
Lentworth Ho 5 LA1 215 A3
Leo Case Ct 5 PR1 97 D8
Leonard St
Barnoldswick BB18 196 B2
Nelson BB9 148 E7
Leonard Terr BB3 82 E3
Leopold Gr FY1 130 B5
Leopold Rd BB2 101 B6
Leopold St BB8 171 B4
Leopold Way BB2 82 A8
Lesley Rd PR8 35 E7
Leslie Ave
Caton LA2 237 C3
Thornton FY5 176 C2
Letchworth Dr PR7 43 B6
Letchworth Pl 2 PR7 43 B6
Letcliffe Ctry Pk★ BB18 194 B8
Lethbridge Rd PR8 35 D5
Letitia St BL6 32 A3
Levant St BB12 126 C7
Leven Ave FY7 198 D3
Leven Gr BB3 81 E4
Levens Cl
Banks PR9 55 A5
Blackburn BB2 81 F8
Lancaster LA1 214 D7
Poulton-le-F FY6 131 E8
Levens Ct LA3 216 E2
Levens Dr
Clayton-le-W PR25 77 D2
Morecambe LA3 216 E2
Poulton-le-F FY6 153 D1
Levensgarth Ave PR2 117 F8
Levens Gr FY1 130 D3
Levens St 12 PR1 118 D1
Leven St BB11 128 B4
Levens Way LA5 224 C3
Lever Cl BB2 100 F8
Lever Ct FY8 90 A7
Lever House La PR25 77 C2
Lever House Prim Sch PR25 77 C3
Lever Park Ave BL6 32 B5
Lever Park Sch BL6 32 C3
Lever St
Blackpool FY3 130 E4
16 Ramsbottom BL0 50 C6
Rawtenstall BB4 86 B2
Levine Ave FY4 131 A1
Lewis Cl PR7 30 E6
Lewis Ct PR9 35 D8
Lewis Dr OL10 33 F1
Lewis St BB6 124 D5
Lewis Textile Mus★ BB1 101 E5
Lewtas St FY1 130 B6
LEWTH 136 A6
Lewth La PR4 136 B5
Lex St PR1 97 C8
Lexton Dr PR9 54 B3
Leybourne Ave PR8 21 F7
Leyburn Ave
Blackpool FY2 152 C5
Fleetwood FY7 198 E2
Leyburn Cl
Accrington BB5 104 E5
Fulwood PR2 118 E5
Leyburn Rd
Blackburn BB2 81 C7
Lancaster LA1 218 D3
Leycester Dr LA1 218 A3
Ley Ct LA1 214 D8
Leyfield PR1 96 E2
Leyfield Cl FY3 153 A1
Leyfield Rd PR25 59 F8
LEYLAND 76 F2
Leyland Cl
Southport PR9 54 E5
Trawden BB8 172 B3
Leyland La
Leyland PR25 76 D2
Runshaw Moor PR26, PR25 59 D4
Leyland Meth Inf Sch PR25 77 B1
Leyland Meth Jun Sch PR25 77 B1
Leyland Rd
Burnley BB11 128 B6
Middleforth Green PR1 96 E3
Southport PR9 53 C1
Leyland St Andrew's CE Inf Sch PR25 59 F8
Leyland St James CE Prim Sch PR26 59 B8
Leyland St Mary's RC Prim Sch PR25 76 F1
Leyland St Mary's RC Tech Coll PR25 59 E7
Leyland St BB5 103 F5
Leyland Sta PR25 77 B2
Leylands The FY8 90 F2
Leyland Way
Leyland PR25 77 C1
Ormskirk L39 15 F5
Leys Cl
Elswick PR4 156 A1
Wiswell BB7 144 F8
Leys Rd FY2 152 D1
Ley St 5 BB5 104 E2
Leyster St LA4 217 C5
Leyton Ave PR25 59 D7
Leyton St OL12 52 F2
Libby La PR3 201 C6
Library Ave LA1 211 A7
Library Mews FY4 110 E7
Library Rd PR6 78 B4
Library St
Chorley PR7 43 C7
Church BB5 103 E6
15 Preston PR1 97 A7
Lichen Cl PR7 42 D4
Lichfield Ave LA4 217 D6
Lichfield Rd
Blackpool FY1 130 C8
Chorley PR7 43 C6
Preston PR2 116 F2
Liddesdale Rd BB9 171 B2
Liddington Cl BB2 82 A8
Liddington Hall Dr BL0 50 B4
Lidget Ave PR2 116 C1
Lidgett BB8 172 A5
Lidum Park Ind Est FY8 91 E5
Liege Rd 4 PR25 60 A8
Lifeboat Pl 13 FY7 199 B5
Lifeboat Rd L37 11 B1
Lifton Rd L33 1 A2
Liggard Ct FY8 91 C4
Lightbown Ave FY3 130 E3
Lightbown Cotts BB3 81 E2
Lightbown St BB3 82 A3
Lightburne Ave FY8 89 F5
Lightfoot Cl PR2 117 D8
Lightfoot Green La PR4 117 B8
Lightfoot La PR2, PR4 117 B7
Lighthorne Dr PR8 21 A4
Lighthouse Cl 4 FY7 199 B5
Lighthouse La L37 12 A1
Lighthurst Ave PR7 43 C6
Lighthurst La PR7 43 D5
Lightwood Ave
2 Blackpool FY4 130 C1
Lytham St Anne's FY8 90 D3
Lilac Ave
1 Blackpool FY1 130 D2
Haslingden BB4 85 B3
Kingsfold PR1 96 F2
Lytham St Anne's FY8 91 B5
Southport PR8 21 D2
Lilac Cl PR4 92 D5
Lilac Cres PR4 134 F4
Lilac Dr FY6 177 D4
Lilac Gr
Abbey Village PR6 80 C2
Clitheroe BB7 166 C7
Darwen BB3 82 B3
Knott End-on-S FY6 199 E5
Preston PR1 118 C3
Skelmersdale WN8 17 E1
Lilac Rd BB1 102 A8
Lilac St BB8 171 F6
Lilacs The
Poulton-le-F FY6 153 F3
Thornton FY5 176 A3
Lilac Terr 2 OL13 70 D8
Lilburn Cl BL0 50 C4
Lilford Cl PR4 57 A5
Lilford Rd BB1 101 D6
Lily Gr
Lancaster LA1 215 A5
Preston PR1 118 C3
Lily St
16 Bacup OL13 87 F2
Blackpool FY1 130 C5
Darwen BB3 82 B1
Nelson BB9 148 F6
Lima Rd FY8 90 B6
Lima St BL9 33 B3
LIMBRICK 44 A6
Limbrick BB1 101 E6
Limbrick Rd PR6 43 E7
Lime Ave
Galgate LA2 211 A4
Kirkham PR4 114 B4
Oswaldtwistle BB5 103 D2
Limebrest Ave FY5 153 D8
Lime Chase PR2 117 C8
Limechase Cl 9 FY4 111 A6
Lime Cl PR1 96 B4
Lime Ct WN8 17 E1
Limefield BB2 101 B5
Limefield Ave
Brierfield BB9 148 C6
Whalley BB7 144 C6
Limefield Ct BB2 101 B5
Limefield Dr WN8 9 E7
Limefield St BB5 104 D5
Lime Gr
Blackpool FY2 152 E2
Chorley PR7 43 C5
Garstang PR3 181 B8
Lancaster LA1 214 D8
Longridge PR3 140 A8
Lytham St Anne's FY8 89 D8
Poulton-le-F FY6 153 E2
Preston PR2 116 F2
Ramsbottom BL0 50 D7
Skelmersdale WN8 17 E1
Thornton FY5 176 C1
Lime Rd
Accrington BB5 104 C7
Haslingden BB4 85 C3
Limerick Rd FY2 152 D3
Limers Gate
Rochdale OL12 52 F5
Todmorden OL14 88 E4
Limers La BB6 124 A6
Limes Ave
Darwen BB3 65 A8
Euxton PR7 60 C4
Morecambe LA3 216 E3
Lime St
Blackburn BB1 101 E6
Clitheroe BB7 189 F1
Colne BB8 171 E6
Great Harwood BB6 124 C6
Nelson BB9 148 C8
Southport PR8 35 E6
Limestone Trail★ BB10 108 E6
Lime Tree Gr BB4 86 A4
Lime Tree Way L37 11 C2
Limewood Cl
Accrington BB5 104 D6
Bridge End BB4 68 A7
Limey La BB11 106 E6
Limont Rd PR8 21 D5
Linacre La L37 4 B7
Linadale Ave 4 FY5 176 B2
Linaker Dr L39 14 B8
Linaker Prim Sch PR8 35 B5
Linaker St PR8 35 B5
Lina St BB5 103 F6
Linby St BB10 128 B5
Lincoln Ave
Cleveleys FY5 175 E3
Fleetwood FY7 198 E3
Lincoln Chase PR2 116 C1
Lincoln Cl
Blackburn BB1 102 B4
Morecambe LA4 217 D3
Lincoln Ct
1 Accrington BB5 104 A7
Blackpool FY1 130 C4
Padiham BB12 126 C8
Lincoln Ho 7 PR1 97 B7
Lincoln Pk BB7 190 A1
Lincoln Pl BB4 85 A3
Lincoln Rd
Blackburn BB1 102 B4
Blackpool FY1 130 C5
Earby BB18 197 B2
Lancaster LA1 214 E7
Southport PR8 35 A1
Lincoln St
Burnley BB11 128 A4
3 Haslingden BB4 85 A3
Preston PR1 118 B1
Todmorden OL14 109 B1
Lincoln Way
Clitheroe BB7 190 A2
Garstang PR3 181 B7
Lincoln Wlk PR1 118 B1
Lindadale Ave BB5 104 A3
Lindadale Cl BB5 104 A3
Lindale Ave PR2 139 E1
Lindale Cres BB10 148 A2
Lindale Gdns FY4 110 E6
Lindale Rd
Fulwood PR2 118 A4
Longridge PR3 139 F5
Lindbeck Ct FY4 111 C8
Lindbeck Rd FY4 131 C1
Lindbergh Ave LA1 214 E4
Lindel La FY6 200 B2
Lindel Rd FY7 198 F2
Linden Ave
Blackburn BB1 101 D6
Cleveleys FY5 175 F3
Orrell WN5 10 E6
Ramsbottom BL0 50 D6
Linden Bsns Ctr 14 BB8 171 D5
Linden Cl
Bamber Bridge PR5 97 B1
Barrowford BB9 170 B1
Cleveleys FY5 175 F2
Clifton PR4 115 D1
Edenfield BL0 68 D2
Linden Cres BB3 82 C2
Linden Ct
1 Earby BB18 197 A1
Orrell WN5 10 E6
Linden Dr
Bamber Bridge PR5 97 B1
Clitheroe BB7 166 F7
Linden Fold PR4 156 A1
Linden Gn FY5 175 F2
Linden Gr
Chorley PR6 61 D3
Fulwood PR2 118 E3
Garstang PR3 181 C8
Orrell WN5 10 E6
Linden Lea
Blackburn BB2 80 F8
Rawtenstall BB4 68 F8
Linden Mews FY8 110 F2
Linden Pl FY2 152 E3
Linden Rd
Colne BB8 171 D5
Earby BB18 197 B1
Lindens WN8 18 B4
Linden St BB10 128 B5
Lindens The FY6 200 B4
Linden Wlk WN5 10 E6
Linderbreck La FY6 131 E8
Lindeth Cl
Nether Kellet LA6 221 F6
Silverdale LA5 224 C2
Lindeth Gdns 8 LA1 218 D3
Lindeth Rd LA5 224 C2
Lindholme WN8 18 C3
Lindisfarne Ave BB2 101 F1
Lindisfarne Cl BB12 127 E7
Lindle Ave PR4 95 E2
Lindle Cl PR4 95 E2
Lindle Cres PR4 95 E2
Lindle La PR4 96 A2
Lindley Ave WN5 10 C5
Lindley Croft FY5 176 E2
Lindley Dr WN8 27 C3
Lindley St
Bamber Bridge PR5 77 B8
Blackburn BB2 101 B2
Lindon Park Rd BB4 68 C7
Lindow Cl 13 LA1 214 F7
Lindow Sq LA1 214 E7
Lindow St LA1 214 F7
Lindred Rd BB9 148 B7
Lindsay Ave
Blackpool FY3 130 E3
Leyland PR25 77 B1
Lytham St Anne's FY8 90 B6
Poulton-le-F FY6 153 D2
Lindsay Ct
Blackpool FY8 110 B4
Morecambe LA3 217 C2
Lindsay Dr PR7 43 A7
Lindsay Pk BB10 128 F5
Lindsay St
Burnley BB11 128 A6
Horwich BL6 32 D1
Lindsey Ho 2 BB5 104 A7
Linedred La BB9 148 B7
Lines St LA4 217 B5
Linfield Terr FY4 110 E6
Lingart La PR3 204 D1
Lingdales L37 12 B5
Lingfield Ave BB7 166 E6
Lingfield Cl LA1 215 B3
Lingfield Ct BB2 80 C8
Lingfield Rd FY7 198 F2
Lingfield Way BB2 80 D8
Lingham La LA2 239 F8
Lingmoor Dr BB12 127 A8
Lingmoor Rd LA1 218 F1
Lingwell Cl PR6 61 C5
Link 59 Bsns Pk BB7 190 B2
Links Ave PR9 53 F3
Links Ct FY8 89 E5
Links Dr LA2 239 D8
Links Field PR2 117 C3
Links Gate
Fulwood PR2 117 C3
Lytham St Anne's FY8 90 A6
Thornton FY5 153 D7
Linkside Ave BB9 149 B8
Links La BB2 80 C8
Links Lo FY8 90 A6
Links Rd
Blackpool FY1 130 C8
Higher Penwortham PR1 96 B6
Kirkby L32 1 A1
Knott End-on-S FY6 199 D5
Lytham St Anne's FY8 89 E5
Links The FY5 175 C4
Links View FY8 90 C5
Linley Gr BL0 50 A2
Linnet Cl FY3 131 B6
Linnet Dr BL9 33 B4
Linnet La FY8 90 E7
Linnet St PR1 118 B2
Linslade Cres L33 1 A4
Linton Ave LA3 216 D1
Linton Dr BB12 127 D3
Linton Gdns BB9 170 C3
Linton Gr PR1 96 B5
Linton St PR2 117 D3
Lion Ct BB5 103 E6
Lionel St BB12 127 C6
Lion La BL6 31 C2
Lions Ct 1 FY8 91 D4
Lions Dr BB1 102 D1
Lion St BB5 103 E6
Liptrott Rd PR7 43 A5
Lisbon Dr
Burnley BB11 127 E5
Darwen BB3 82 C1
Lisbon St 17 OL12 52 C1
Lismore Ave 6 FY4 110 F6
Lismore Pk PR8 34 E4
Lister Croft BD23 197 A5
Lister Gr LA3 212 F8
Lister St
Accrington BB5 104 A6
3 Blackburn BB2 101 E3
Lister Well Rd BB18 194 A6
Litchford Ho BB4 86 C2
Little Acre
Longton PR4 75 A8
Thornton FY5 153 D8
LITTLE ALTCAR 12 A1
Little Banks Cl PR5 78 B6
LITTLE BISPHAM 152 C8
Little Brewery La L37 11 F6
LITTLE CARLETON 152 F1
Little Carr La PR7 43 D5
Little Cl
Leyland PR26 76 E3
Middleforth Green PR1 96 C3
Little Coppins La FY6 153 E1
Littledale Ave LA3 213 A8
Littledale Mews LA2 218 F6
Littledale Rd
Crossgill LA2 237 E1
Quernmore LA2 232 C8
Little Digmoor Prim Sch WN8 9 B6
LITTLE ECCLESTON 156 A5
Little Fell La LA2 215 E3
Little Fell Rd LA1, LA2 215 F6
Little Flatt OL12 52 B1
LITTLE HARWOOD 102 B8
Little Hey La L37 12 B4
LITTLE HOOLE MOSS HOUSES 75 B4
Little Hoole Prim Sch PR4 75 A5
LITTLE KNOWLEY 61 F3
Little La
Banks PR9 55 B7
Longridge PR3 140 A7
Southport PR9 54 B1
LITTLE MARSDEN 148 C7
LITTLE MARTON 131 D1
LITTLE MARTON MOSS SIDE 131 B1
Little Meadow La L40 39 D4
LITTLE MOOR 166 E6
Little Moor BB7 166 E6
Littlemoor Cl BB7 146 A8
Little Moor Clough BL7 47 E2

LITTLE MOOR END 103 C3
Littlemoor Ho BB7 146 A7
Littlemoor Rd BB7 166 E7
Little Moor View BB7 166 E6
LITTLE PLUMPTON 112 D5
LITTLE POULTON 153 F4
Little Poulton La FY6 153 F4
Little Queen St BB8 171 C4
LITTLE SCOTLAND 31 B2
Little Scotland BL6 31 B2
LITTLE SINGLETON 154 C4
Little St 4 BB5 104 A6
Little Stones Rd BL7 47 E2
LITTLE THORNTON 153 E7
Little Toms La BB10 148 D3
Littleton Gr WN6 29 E2
Little Tongues La FY6 200 B4
Littleton Manor PR9 55 A5
LITTLE TOWN 141 F3
Little Twining PR4 75 A7
Littlewalk Ct BB5 103 E5
Littlewood FY7 198 E3
Little Wood Cl PR7 42 F6
Littondale Gdns BB2 80 D7
Liverpool Ave PR8 21 D5
Liverpool New Rd PR4 74 F5
Liverpool Old Rd
Much Hoole PR4 74 E3
Sollom PR4 57 B2
Walmer Bridge PR4 74 F5
Liverpool Rd
Bickerstaffe L39 7 C5
Birkdale Hills PR8 21 E6
Blackpool FY1 130 D5
Burnley BB12 127 A6
Formby L37 12 A1
Higher Penwortham PR1 96 B5
Hightown L37 3 A8
Longton PR4 74 F7
Maghull L31 5 D4
Much Hoole PR4 74 D2
Ormskirk L39 15 B2
Preston, Howick Cross PR1, PR4 95 F3
Preston PR1 96 D6
Royal Oak L39 6 F4
Rufford L40 39 C5
Skelmersdale WN8 8 C8
Sollom PR4 57 A3
Southport PR8 35 A3
Liverpool Rd N
Burscough Bridge L40 25 E5
Maghull L31 5 C2
Liverpool Rd S
Burscough L40 25 D2
Maghull L31 5 C1
Livesey Branch Rd BB2 81 B8
LIVESEY FOLD 81 F2
Livesey Fold PR6 80 A1
Livesey Hall Cl BB2 100 E1
Livesey St Francis CE Prim Sch BB2 100 F1
Livesey St
11 Lytham St Anne's FY8 91 A3
Padiham BB12 126 C8
Preston PR1 97 B7
Rishton BB1 124 B2
Livesley's La
Great Altcar L37 12 F2
Haskayne L37 13 A2
Livet Ave FY4 110 D7
Livingstone Rd
Accrington BB5 104 B8
Blackburn BB2 101 B4
Blackpool FY1 130 C4
Livingstone St BB9 148 B5
Livingstone Wlk BB9 148 B6
Lloyd Cl
Lancaster LA1 218 B1
12 Nelson BB9 148 E8
Lloyd's Ave 1 LA4 217 A4
Lloyd St
Darwen BB3 81 F3
Whitworth OL12 71 C1
Lloyd Wlk 11 BB9 148 E8
Lobden Cres OL12 52 D8
Lochinch Cl FY4 111 A6
Locka La
Gressingham LA6 240 F3
Lancaster LA1 218 D4
Locke Ind Est BL6 32 B3
Lockerbie Ave FY5 152 D8
Lockfield Dr BB18 196 C4
Lock Gate BB4 85 C1
Lockhart Rd PR1 117 F2
Lockhurst Ave FY5 152 F8
Lock La PR4 57 B2
Lockside BB2 101 D2
Lockside Rd PR2 95 F8
Lock St 10 BB5 103 E4
Lockwood Ave FY6 153 D4
Lockyer Ave BB12 127 B7
Lodge Bank
Brinscall PR6 62 F7
Horwich BL6 31 F2
Lodge Bank Est BL6 31 F3
Lodge Cl
2 Bamber Bridge PR5 97 F1
Blackpool FY5 152 C7
Freckleton PR4 93 B7
Lodge Ct
Blackpool FY5 152 C7
Inskip PR4 157 B1
Staining FY3 131 D5
Lodge Hill La BL0 51 A8
Lodge La
Bacup OL13 87 F1
Clifton PR4 115 D1
Elswick PR4 156 B1
Farington PR26 76 E6
Lytham St Anne's FY8 91 F5
Melling LA2, LA6 241 D1
Rainford L39, WA11 8 D1
Singleton FY6 154 D2
Lodge Mill La BL0 69 A1
Lodge Pk PR3 181 D3
Lodge Rd
Catterall PR3 182 A1
Orrell WN5 10 E4
Lodges Ct 6 LA4 217 E6
Lodges Gr LA4 217 E6
Lodgeside BB5 124 F3
Lodge St
Accrington BB5 104 C7
Lancaster LA1 214 F8
Preston PR1 96 E8
Ramsbottom BL0 50 C6
Shuttleworth BL0 50 E8
Lodge Terr BB5 103 E5
Lodge The
Great Harwood BB6 124 B5
Lytham St Anne's FY8 90 E7
Lodge View
Farington PR26 76 E7
Longridge PR3 140 A6
Ramsbottom BL0 51 A8
Lodge Wood Cl PR7 43 A6
Lodgings The PR2 118 C5
Lodore Rd FY4 110 C6
Loelands The BL8 49 E3
Lofthouse Way FY7 199 A4
Loftos Ave FY4 110 D8
Logwood St BB1 101 F7
Lois Pl BB2 101 C5
Lomas La BB4 68 F8
Lomax Cl BB6 124 D6
Lomax Sq BB6 124 D5
Lomax St
7 Bury BL9 33 A3
Darwen BB3 82 A2
Great Harwood BB6 124 C5
Ramsbottom BL8 49 F1
Rochdale OL12, OL16 52 F1
LOMESHAYE 148 B8
Lomeshaye Bsns Village BB9 148 C8
Lomeshaye Ind Est BB9 148 B7
Lomeshaye Jun Sch BB9 148 C8
Lomeshaye Pl BB9 148 C8
Lomeshaye Rd BB9 148 D7
Lomeshaye Way BB9 148 C8
Lomond Ave
Blackpool FY3 130 F2
Lytham St Anne's FY8 90 B5
Lomond Cl PR7 60 D4
Lomond Gdns BB2 100 F1
Londonderry Rd LA3 212 E5
London La PR8 22 D8
London Rd
Blackburn BB1 101 E6
Blackpool FY3 130 D6
Preston PR1 97 C6
London Sq 2 PR8 35 B7
London St
Fleetwood FY7 199 B4
Southport PR8, PR9 35 B7
London Terr BB3 82 B2
London Way PR5 97 C3
London Wlk BB1 101 E6
Longacre
Clayton Brook PR5 78 C5
Longton PR4 74 F8
Southport PR9 53 F3
Long Acre Cl LA5 221 C8
Long Acre Pl FY8 91 A4
Long Acres Dr OL12 71 D2
Longacres La OL12 71 D2
Long Barn Brow PR5 99 E2
Long Barn Row PR5 99 E2
Longber La LA6 242 B3
Long Bldg BB7 230 C1
Longbrook Ave PR5 97 E1
Long Butts PR1 96 D2
Long Cl
Clitheroe BB7 190 A2
Leyland PR26 59 A8
Longcliffe Dr PR8 21 C4
Long Copse PR7 60 F1
Long Croft
Barton PR3 137 B8
Longton PR4 95 A1
Longcroft Cotts BL9 50 F1
Long Croft Mdw PR7 61 B2
Long Cswy BB7 231 B2
Long Cswy The BB10 108 D7
Long Dales La
Caton LA6 237 A6
Over Kellet LA6 237 A7
Longfield
Formby L37 12 B5
Fulwood PR2 117 F8
Higher Penwortham PR1 96 B4
Longfield Ave
Coppull PR7 42 E2
Poulton-le-F FY6 153 D4
Longfield Ct BB18 196 B1
Longfield Dr LA5 221 C8
Longfield Manor PR7 43 A5
Longfield Pl FY6 153 D4
Longfield Terr BB10 107 E8
Longfold
Maghull L31 5 E1
Mere Brow PR4 55 F2
Longford Ave FY2 152 E5
Longford Rd PR8 35 A2
Long Gn BB18 197 C2
Longhey WN8 18 C4
Long Hey La BB1, BB3 83 A2
Long Heys La WN8 18 F5
Long Heys or Back La WN8 19 A6
LONGHOLME 86 A2
Longholme Rd 9 BB4 86 A2
Longhouse La FY6 131 D8
LONG ING 196 C2
Long Ing La BB18 196 C2
Long La
Abbeystead LA2 232 F1
Banks PR9 55 B6
Bickerstaffe L39 7 B7
Chorley PR6 44 B4
Formby L37 11 E4
Laneshaw Bridge BB8 172 D7
Low Bentham LA2 239 B7
Maghull L29 4 B1
Oakenclough PR3 226 B1
Ormskirk L39 6 F8
Pleasington BB2 100 B2
Quernmore LA2 232 A5
Skelmersdale WN8 9 E3
Street PR3 226 B5
Tockholes BB3 81 A3
Longlands Ave LA3 212 E8
Longlands Cres LA3 212 F8
Longlands La LA3 212 E7
Longlands Rd LA1 218 C3
Long Lane End LA2 211 E7
Long Level LA6 241 F8
Longley Cl PR2 117 F8
Longley La PR3 160 B2
Long Lover La BB7 192 C8
Long Marsh La LA1 218 B1
Long Mdw
Chorley PR7 43 A5
Colne BB8 172 A5
Kirkham PR4 113 E5
Mellor Brook BB2 121 B2
Much Hoole PR4 74 F4
Longmeadow La
Heysham LA3 213 A7
Thornton FY5 176 C3
Longmeanygate
Leyland, Midge Hall PR26 76 A2
Leyland PR26 76 D2
Long Meanygate
Mere Brow PR9 37 C7
Southport PR9 36 F8
Longmere Cres LA5 221 C8
Longmire Way 10 LA4 217 A5
Longmoor La PR3 180 E6
Long Moss PR26 59 A8
Long Moss La PR4 76 A6
Long Moss Mdws PR4 75 F6
LONGRIDGE 140 A8
Longridge Ave FY4 110 E5
Longridge CE Prim Sch PR3 140 A7
Longridge Community Hospl PR3 140 A7
Longridge Dr OL10 33 F2
Longridge Fell Forest Wlk (E)★ BB7 164 F6
Longridge Fell Forest Wlk (W)★ PR3 164 A4
Longridge Heath BB9 148 D4
Longridge High Sch PR3 140 A6
Longridge Lo 14 PR2 118 F4
Longridge Rd
Hesketh Lane PR3 162 D6
Hurst Green BB7, PR3 142 D8
Longridge PR3 162 B3
Red Scar PR2 119 B6
Longridge St Wilfrid's RC Prim Sch PR3 140 A8
Long Row
Blackburn BB2 122 B2
Calder Vale PR3 182 E8
Longroyd Rd BB18 197 B1
Longsands Com Prim Sch PR2 118 D5
Longsands La PR2 118 E6
LONGSHAW
Blackburn 101 D1
Orrell 10 E1
Longshaw Ave WN5 10 E1
Longshaw Cl
Longshaw WN5 10 E1
Rufford L40 39 A5
Longshaw Com Jun Sch BB2 101 E1
Longshaw Comm WN5 10 E1
Longshaw Inf Sch BB2 81 E8
Longshaw La BB2 101 D2
Longshaw Old Rd WN5 10 E1
Longshaw St BB2 101 D1
LONGSHOOT 85 C3
Longsight Ave
Accrington, Hillock Vale BB5 104 E8
Clitheroe BB7 189 F1
Longsight Rd
Langho BB6 143 B2
Osbaldeston BB1, BB2 121 E4
Ramsbottom BL0 50 A2
Longstock Hall Moor Hey Sch PR5 97 A1
LONGTON 75 A8
Longton Ave FY5 176 B2
Longton Brickcroft Nature Reserve★ PR4 74 F6
Longton Brickcroft Visitor Ctr★ PR4 74 F7
Longton Bsns Pk PR4 74 E4
Longton By-Pass PR4 75 C6
Longton Cl BB1 102 C5
Longton Ct PR8 21 C5
Longton Dr
Formby L37 12 A6
Morecambe LA4 217 E4
Longton Prim Sch PR4 75 A8
Longton Rd
Blackpool FY1 130 C5
Burnley BB12 127 E8
Longton's Cotts LA6 240 B1
Longtons La BD23 236 B3
Longton St
Blackburn BB1 102 C5
Chorley PR6 43 E8
Longway FY4 110 F8
Long Wham La PR4 75 D1
Longwood Cl FY8 90 E4
Longworth Ave
Blackrod BL6 31 C3
Burnley BB10 128 D6
Coppull PR7 42 F2
Longworth Clough BL7 47 D2
Longworth La BL7 47 C2
Longworth Rd
Billington BB7 144 B4
Bolton BL7 47 B3
Horwich BL6 32 C4
Longworth Rd N BL7 46 D5
Longworth St
5 Bamber Bridge PR5 97 E2
Chorley PR7 43 B6
Preston PR1 118 C1
Lonmore PR5 97 D3
Lonmore Cl PR9 55 A5
Lonsdale Ave
Fleetwood FY7 198 E3
Morecambe LA4 217 E4
Ormskirk L39 15 F7
Lonsdale Cl PR25 60 A6
Lonsdale Cres 3 FY7 198 E3
Lonsdale Dr PR26 58 B3
Lonsdale Gdns 4 BB9 170 D3
Lonsdale Gr LA4 217 E4
Lonsdale Mews 5 PR5 77 A8
Lonsdale Pl LA1 215 A5
Lonsdale Rd
Blackpool FY1 130 B2
Formby L37 11 F3
Hest Bank LA2 220 D1
Morecambe LA4 217 E4
Preston PR1 118 C1
Southport PR8 35 D4
Lonsdale South Ave LA1 211 A6
Lonsdale St
Accrington BB5 103 F5
Burnley BB12 127 C7
Nelson BB9 170 F1
Lord Ave OL13 87 C1
Lord St W
12 Blackburn BB2 101 E5
Southport PR8 35 A6
Lord's Ave PR5 77 B7
Lord's Close Rd LA2 239 E2
Lord's Cres BB3 82 A6
Lords Croft PR6 78 A2
Lord Sefton Way L37 12 E2
Lordsgate Dr L40 25 E3
Lordsgate La L40 25 C2
Lord's La
Kingsfold PR1 96 E1
Longridge PR3 162 B2
Lord's Lot Rd
Capernwray LA6 240 D1
Over Kellet LA6 240 C1
Lordsome Rd LA3 216 E2
Lord Sq BB1 101 E5
Lord St
Accrington BB5 104 B6
Bacup OL13 87 F2
Blackburn BB2 101 E5
Blackpool FY1 130 B6
Brierfield BB9 148 B5
Burscough Bridge L40 25 E5
Bury BL9 33 A2
Bury, Heap Bridge BL9 33 C1
Chorley PR6 43 D7
Clayton Green PR6 78 C1
Colne BB8 171 C5
Darwen BB3 82 A2
Eccleston PR7 41 C5
Fleetwood FY7 199 B4
Great Harwood BB6 124 C4
Horwich BL6 32 B4
Lancaster LA1 218 D1
Lytham St Anne's FY8 89 E7
Morecambe LA4 217 B6
Oswaldtwistle BB5 103 E4
Preston PR1 97 A8
Rawtenstall BB4 86 A2
Rawtenstall, Crawshawbooth BB4 86 A7
Rishton BB1 124 B1
Southport PR8, PR9 35 B7
Lord Street Mall 10 BB1 101 E5
Lord Street Prim Sch BL6 32 B4
Lord's Wlk PR1 97 A8
Lords Wood Cl PR7 43 A6
Lorne Rd FY2 152 D2
Lorne St
Chorley PR7 43 C7
Darwen BB3 81 F2
Lytham St Anne's FY8 91 D4
Lorne Way OL10 33 F1
Lorraine Ave PR2 117 E3
Lorton Cl
Burnley BB12 127 B8
Fulwood PR2 117 F6
Lostock Gdns FY4 110 E6
LOSTOCK HALL 77 B7
Lostock Hall Com High Sch & Art Coll PR5 97 C1
Lostock Hall Com Prim Sch PR5 97 B1
Lostock Hall Com Prim Sch Avondale Unit PR5 77 B8
Lostock Hall Sta PR5 77 B8
Lostock La PR5 77 D7
Lostock Mdw PR6 78 A1
Lostock Rd PR26 58 C3
Lostock Sq PR5 77 B7
Lostock View PR5 77 B7
Lothersdale Cl BB10 148 D3
Lothian Ave FY7 198 D3
Lothian Pl FY2 152 E5
Lottice La BB5, BB1 103 A1
Lotus Dr FY4 112 A6
Loud Bridge Back La PR3 161 D8
Loud Bridge Rd PR3 161 D7
Loughlin Dr L33 1 A5
Loughrigg Cl BB12 127 B7
Loughrigg Terr FY4 131 C1
Louie Pollard Cres BB6 124 D6
Louise St FY1 130 B3
Louis St BL0 68 D5
Louis William St BB1 82 D8
Loupsfell Dr LA4 217 C4
Lourdes Ave PR5 97 A1
Louvain St BB18 196 A3
Lovat Rd PR1 117 F2
LOVE CLOUGH 106 A3
Loveclough Pk BB4 106 A3
Love Clough Rd BB4 105 F2
Love La BL0 68 E1
Lovely Hall La BB1 122 D7
Low Bank BB12 126 E6
LOW BENTHAM 239 C8
Low Bentham Com Prim Sch LA2 239 B8
Low Bentham Rd LA2 239 C8
Lowcroft
High Bentham LA2 239 E8
Skelmersdale WN8 18 C3
Low Croft PR3 137 B2
Lowcross Rd FY6 153 E2
Lower Alt Rd L38 2 F4
Lower Antley St BB5 103 F5
Lower Ashworth Cl BB2 101 C4
Lower Audley Ind Est BB2 101 F3
Lower Audley St BB1, BB2 101 F4
LOWER BALLAM 112 A3
Lower Bank Rd PR2 117 F3
Lower Bank St PR6 80 A1
Lower Barnes St BB5 124 E4
Lower Barn St BB3 65 C7
LOWER BARTLE 116 D8
LOWER BAXENDEN 104 F1
LOWER BOARSGREAVE 70 A6
Lowerbrook Cl BL6 32 D1
Lower Burgh Rd PR7 43 A4
Lower Burgh Way PR7 43 B4
Lower Carr La L37 4 B7
Lower Chapel La BB7 190 B8
LOWER CLOUGHFOLD 86 C2
Lower Clough Fold BB9 170 C2
Lower Clough St BB9 170 D2
Lower Clowes BB4 68 E8
Lower Clowes Rd BB4 68 E8
Lower Cockcroft 13 BB2 101 E5
LOWER COPTHURST 61 E7
Lower Copthurst La PR6 61 E7
Lower Cribden Ave BB4 85 D2
Lower Croft 1 PR1 96 D2
Lower Croft St 3 BB18 197 B2
Lower Cross St 27 BB3 82 A1
LOWER DARWEN 81 F7
Lower Darwen Prim Sch BB3 82 A6
Lower Dolphinholme LA2 226 A8
Lower East Ave BB18 196 B3
Lower Eccleshill Rd BB3 82 A5
Lowerfield BB6 123 C8
Lower Field PR26 76 F6
Lowerfields BB12 126 F6
Lowerfold BB6 124 C6
LOWER FOLD
Accrington 104 C6
Great Harwood 124 C6
Rochdale 52 C3
Lowerfold Cl OL12 52 C4
Lowerfold Cres OL12 52 C4
Lowerfold Dr OL12 52 C4
Lowerfold Rd BB6 124 C6

Lowerfold Way OL12 52 C4
LOWERFORD 170 E3
Lowergate BB7 166 E8
Lower Gate Rd BB5 125 F2
Lower Gn
Poulton-le-F FY6 153 E3
3 Rochdale OL12 52 C1
LOWER GREEN BANK 232 B1
Lower Greenfield PR2 117 B5
Lower Hazel Cl BB2 101 C4
LOWER HEALEY 52 E4
Lower Hey PR4 95 A1
LOWER HEYSHAM 212 E8
Lower Hill BB3 80 F2
Lower Hill Dr PR6 44 A1
Lower Hollin Bank St BB2 101 D2
LOWERHOUSE 126 F6
LOWER HOUSE 59 D8
Lowerhouse Cres BB12 127 A6
Lowerhouse Fold BB12 127 A6
Lower House Gn BB4 87 A8
Lowerhouse Jun Sch BB12 127 A6
Lowerhouse La
Burnley, Rose Grove BB12 127 B6
Padiham BB12 126 F6
Lower House Rd PR26 59 D8
Lower La
Freckleton PR4 93 D7
Haslingden BB4 85 B4
Kirkham PR4 114 C1
Longridge PR3 140 B7
Lower Laithe Cotts BB9 170 C2
Lower Laithe Dr BB9 170 C3
Lower Lee LA2 232 F2
Lower Lune St 7 FY7 199 B5
Lower Makinson Fold 1 BL6 32 D1
Lower Manor La BB12 147 F2
Lower Mdw BL7 48 D6
Lower Mead BL7 47 F1
Lower Mead Dr BB12 147 F2
Lower North Ave BB18 196 B2
Lower Park St BB18 196 C2
Lower Parrock Rd BB9 170 C1
LOWER PENWORTHAM 96 E5
Lower Philips Rd BB1 102 C8
Lower Prom PR9 35 B8
Lower Rd
Longridge PR3 140 E7
Shuttleworth BL0 50 E8
Lower Ridge Cl BB10 128 B6
Lower Rook St BB18 196 C2
Lower Rosegrove La BB12 127 A5
Lower School St 6 BB8 171 D4
LOWER SUMMERSEAT 50 C1
Lower Tentre BB11 128 B5
LOWER THURNHAM 210 B2
Lower Timber Hill La BB11 128 A2
Lower West Ave BB18 196 B2
LOWER WESTHOUSE 242 D4
Lower Wilworth BB1 122 E1
Lower Wlk FY2 152 C7
Lowesby Cl PR5 97 E3
Lowes Ct
3 Blackpool FY1 130 B1
5 Thornton FY5 176 B3
Lowes Gn L37 12 B3
Lowe's La WN8 17 F8
Lowes Rd BL9 33 A6
Loweswater Cl BB5 104 F8
Loweswater Cres BB12 127 B8
Loweswater Dr 5 LA4 217 D4
Lowesway
Blackpool FY4 110 F8
6 Thornton FY5 176 B3
Lowe View BB4 87 A1
Lowfield Cl PR4 114 F2
Lowfield Rd FY4 110 F7
Low Fold BB18 195 A6
LOWGILL 239 C3
Lowgill La LA2 239 C3
Low Gn PR25 76 F1
Low Hill BB3 65 A6
Lowick Cl PR5 98 E4
Lowick Dr FY6 153 D1
Low La
Leck LA6 242 B7
Morecambe LA4 217 F5
Lowlands Rd
Bolton-le-S LA5 221 A5
Morecambe LA4 217 C4
Lowland Way FY2 152 F6
Low Mill LA2 237 B3
LOW MOOR 166 C8
Low Moor La BB18 196 B1
Low Moor Rd FY2 152 E3
Lowndes St PR1 117 E2
Lowood Gr PR2 116 D1
Lowood Lo 7 FY8 91 A3
Lowood Pl BB2 101 A6
Low Rd
Halton LA2 237 A4
Middleton LA3 213 A2
Lowrey Terr FY1 130 B2
Lowry Cl PR5 77 A7
Lowry Hill La L40 26 B2
Low St LA6 242 C3
Lowstead Pl FY4 110 E6
Lowstern Cl BL7 47 E1
Lowther Ave
Blackpool FY2 152 B2
Maghull L31 5 F2
Morecambe LA3 217 E3
Lowther Cres PR26 76 D2
Lowther Ct
Blackpool FY2 152 B2
5 Lytham St Anne's FY8 91 A3
Lowther Dr PR26 76 D3
Lowther La BB8 194 D1
Lowther Pl BB1 102 A8
Lowther Rd
Fleetwood FY7 198 F4
Lancaster LA1 218 F1
Lowther St
Colne BB8 171 E6
Nelson BB9 148 C8
Preston PR2 117 C1
Lowther Terr
Appley Bridge WN6 19 C8
Lytham St Anne's FY8 91 A3
Lowthian St 25 PR1 96 F8
Lowthorpe Cres PR1 118 B2
Lowthorpe Pl PR1 118 B2
Lowthorpe Rd PR1 118 B2
Lowthwaite Dr BB9 148 E6
Lowton Rd FY8 90 A8
Loxham Gdns FY4 110 D6
Loxley Gdns BB12 126 F6
Loxley Gn PR2 118 C6
Loxley Pl FY5 152 E7
Loxley Pl E FY5 152 F7
Loxley Rd PR8 35 D4
Loxwood Cl PR5 97 A3
Loynd St
11 Great Harwood BB6 124 C5
Ramsbottom BL0 50 D6
Loyne Pk LA6 241 D7
Loyne Sch The LA1 218 B2
Lubbock St BB12 127 C6
Lucas Ave PR7 42 D8
LUCAS GREEN 61 C6
Lucas La E PR6 61 C6
Lucas La W PR6 61 C5
Lucas St BL9 33 A3
Lucerne Cl PR2 118 C4
Lucerne Rd PR2 118 C4
Lucy St
Barrowford BB9 170 D3
Lancaster LA1 214 F8
8 Morecambe LA4 217 B6
Ludlow WN8 18 C4
Ludlow Dr L39 15 D7
Ludlow Gr FY2 152 F2
Ludlow St WN6 29 D3
Luke St 18 OL13 70 C8
Lulworth WN8 18 C4
Lulworth Ave
Blackpool FY3 131 A3
Preston PR2 117 D2
Lulworth Lo PR8 34 F5
Lulworth Pl PR5 97 D2
Lulworth Rd
Fulwood PR2 118 A4
Southport PR8 34 F5
LUMB
Haslingden 68 B4
Rawtenstall 86 F6
Lumb Carr Ave BL0, BL8 50 A4
Lumb Carr Rd BL0, BL8 50 A4
Lumb Cotts BL0 68 B4
Lumb Flats BL0 68 B4
Lumb Holes La BB4 69 E7
Lumb La BB4 86 F4
Lumb Scar 9 OL13 87 F2
Lunds Cl L40 16 E4
Lunds La PR4 74 D1
Lund St
Blackburn BB2 101 C4
2 Preston PR1 97 A8
Lune Ave L31 5 E2
Lune Cl PR4 114 C5
Lunedale Ave FY1 130 C1
Lune Dr
Clayton-le-W PR25 77 E2
Morecambe LA3 217 F3
Lune Gr FY1 130 C3
Lune Ho
Lancaster, Abraham Heights LA1 214 F7
5 Lancaster LA1 218 D1
Lune Ind Est LA1 214 C8
Lune Rd
Fleetwood FY7 198 F4
Lancaster LA1 218 B1
Lunesdale Cl FY8 90 C7
Lunesdale Ct
Butt Yeats LA2 238 B6
Lancaster LA1 218 F1
Lunesdale Dr PR3 207 B3
Lunesdale Rd 2 PR4 114 A5
Lunesdale Terr LA2 237 E4
Lunesdale View LA2 219 D7
Luneside LA1 214 C8
Lune Sq LA1 218 D1
Lune St
Colne BB8 171 E4
Lancaster LA1 218 D1
Longridge PR3 140 B8
Padiham BB12 126 D8
Preston PR1 96 F7
Lune Terr LA1 218 D1
Lune Valley LA1 218 F4
Lune View FY6 199 E6
Lune View Cvn Pk LA2 219 C6
Lune View Pk LA2 219 C6
Lunt Rd L29 4 C1
Lupin Cl
Accrington BB5 104 A7
Lucas Green PR6 61 B5
Lupin Rd BB5 104 B7
Lupton Dr BB9 170 D4
Lupton Pl LA1 218 B3
Lupton St PR7 43 C6
Lutner St BB11 128 A5
Luton Rd
Cleveleys FY5 175 E1
Preston PR2 116 F2
Lutwidge Ave PR1 118 C1
Lyceum Ave 3 FY3 130 D4
Lychfield Dr PR5 77 E7
Lychgate 24 PR1 97 A8
Lyddesdale Ave FY5 152 D8
Lydd Gr PR7 43 A7
Lydgate
Burnley BB10 148 E2
Chorley PR7 43 A5
Lydia St BB5 104 B4
LYDIATE 5 D4
Lydiate La
Bilsborrow PR3 159 C6
Leyland PR25 77 C4
Ulnes Walton PR7 59 B1
Lydiate Lane End PR7 59 B2
Lydiate Prim Sch L31 5 C4
Lydiate Station Rd L31 4 E5
Lydric Ave PR5 98 E2
Lyelake La L40 16 F2
Lymbridge Dr BL6 31 D1
Lyme Gr FY6 199 E5
Lymm Ave LA1 218 A3
Lynbridge Cl WN5 10 E5
Lyncroft Cres FY3 130 E7
Lyndale WN8 18 B4
Lyndale Ave
Bamber Bridge PR5 97 C2
Haslingden BB4 85 B2
Wilpshire BB1 123 A7
Lyndale Cl
Leyland PR25 60 B6
Rawtenstall BB4 86 A7
Wilpshire BB1 123 A7
Lyndale Ct FY7 199 B5
Lyndale Gr PR5 97 C2
Lyndale Rd BB11 126 C3
Lyndale Res Cvn Pk FY4 111 F6
Lyndale Terr BB7 231 B3
Lynden Ave LA4 217 E5
Lyndeth Cl PR2 118 E6
Lyndhurst
Maghull L31 5 D1
Skelmersdale WN8 18 B4
Lyndhurst Ave
Blackburn BB1 102 E5
Blackpool FY4 130 D1
Lyndhurst Dr PR2 116 E2
Lyndhurst Gr BB6 124 E6
Lyndhurst Rd
Blackburn BB2 101 E2
Burnley BB10 128 C5
Darwen BB3 81 F3
Southport PR8 35 B2
Lyndon Ave BB6 124 E6
Lyndon Ct BB6 124 E6
Lyndon Ho BB6 124 E6
Lynfield Rd BB6 124 E6
Lynn Gr 6 FY1 130 B7
Lynn Pl PR2 118 D2
Lynslack Terr LA5 224 B8
Lynthorpe Rd
Blackburn BB2 101 E2
Nelson BB9 171 A1
Lynton Ave
Blackpool FY4 110 D8
Leyland PR25 60 C8
Lynton Ct FY7 175 C8
Lynton Dr PR8 34 E1
Lynton Rd
Accrington BB5 103 F4
Southport PR8 34 E1
Lynwood Ave
Blackpool FY3 130 E8
Clayton-le-M BB5 124 F4
Darwen BB3 81 E4
Grimsargh PR2 139 C2
Ormskirk L39 15 C3
Lynwood Cl
Clayton-le-M BB5 124 F4
Colne BB8 171 D7
Darwen BB3 81 E3
Skelmersdale WN8 9 D7
Whalley BB7 144 A7
Lynwood Dr FY6 177 C7
Lynwood End L39 15 C3
Lynwood Pk PR4 92 F6
Lynwood Rd
Blackburn BB2 101 B6
Huncoat BB5 125 E2
Lyons La PR6 43 D7
Lyons La S PR7 43 D7
Lyons Rd PR8 35 A5
Lystra Ct FY8 89 F5
Lythall Ave FY8 91 D4
LYTHAM 91 B3
Lytham CE Prim Sch FY8 91 B4
Lytham Cl
Fulwood PR2 117 D3
Lancaster LA1 215 C7
Lytham Ct PR7 60 D4
Lytham Hall★ FY8 90 F4
Lytham Hall Park Prim Sch FY8 90 F3
Lytham Heritage Ctr★ FY8 91 B3
Lytham Rd
Blackburn BB2 101 F1
Blackpool FY1, FY4 110 C6
Burnley BB10 148 C2
Freckleton PR4 93 B6
Fulwood PR2 117 D3
Moss Side FY8 112 E1
Southport PR9 54 A4
Warton FY8, PR4 92 D5
LYTHAM ST ANNE'S 90 B5
Lytham St Anne's High Tech Coll FY8 90 C5
Lytham St Anne's Local Nature Reserve★ FY8 110 B1
Lytham St Annes Way FY8 90 D7
Lytham St
Chorley PR6 43 E7
Rochdale OL12 52 E3
Lytham Sta FY8 91 A3
Lytham Windmill (Mus)★ FY8 91 C2
Lythcoe Ave PR2 117 C4
Lythe Fell Ave LA2 219 D7
Lythe Fell Rd LA2 234 F8
Lythe La LA2 239 E2
Lyth Rd LA1 218 F2
Lytles Cl L37 12 A2
Lytton St BB12 126 F7

## M

Maaruig Cvn Pk FY6 200 A6
Mabel Ct FY4 110 B8
Mabel St
Colne BB8 171 F5
2 Rochdale OL12 52 D2
Maberry Cl WN6 19 D7
MacAuley Ave FY4 110 F8
MacAuley St BB11 127 C5
Macbeth Rd FY7 198 E4
McCall Cl PR4 113 A3
McDonald Rd LA3 212 D5
Mackay Croft 4 PR6 43 D8
McKenzie St PR5 77 F8
Mackenzie Cl 5 PR6 43 D8
MacLaren Cl FY3 131 D5
MacLeod St BB9 148 D8
Maddy St 2 PR1 96 D8
Madeley Gdns OL12 52 C1
Maden Rd OL13 87 F2
Maden St BB5 103 E6
Maden Way OL13 87 F2
Madison Ave
Blackpool FY2 152 B5
Hest Bank LA5 220 E2
Madison Ctr The BB4 68 B8
Madison Hts FY8 90 D7
Madryn Ave L33 1 A2
Maesbrook Cl PR9 55 B5
Mafeking Ave BL9 33 A5
Mafeking Rd PR2 117 C2
Magdalen Ave FY5 175 D1
Maggots Nook Rd WA11 9 A1
MAGHULL 5 B1
Maghull La L31 6 B1
Maghull Smallholdings Est L31 5 F3
Magnolia Cl PR2 118 C6
Magnolia Dr PR25 77 E2
Magnolia Rd PR1 96 B3
Magpie Cl BB11 127 C5
Maharishi School of the Age of Enlightenment L40 18 A5
Maida Vale FY5 152 D8
Maiden Cl
Rawtenstall BB4 69 F8
Skelmersdale WN8 17 C2
Maiden St BB4 85 B6
Main Ave LA3 212 F3
Main Cl LA3 209 D8
Main Dr
Cold Row FY6 177 D4
Poulton-le-F FY6 153 E2
Main Rd
Bolton-le-S LA5 221 B5
Galgate LA2 211 A3
Hest Bank LA2 220 F1
Nether Kellet LA6 221 F5
Mains La
Bispham Green L40 27 A6
Poulton-le-F FY6 154 B4
Main Sprit Weind PR1 97 A7
Main Sq PR7 60 E6
Main St
Bolton-by-B BB7 230 D4
Buckshaw Village PR7 60 E6
Burton-in-K LA6 240 B7
Cockerham LA2 206 D4
Downham BB7 191 B5
Gisburn BB7 231 C3
Grindleton BB7 190 B8
Heysham LA3 212 E8
High Bentham LA2 239 D8
Hornby LA2 238 B7
Kelbrook BB18 195 A6
Lancaster LA1 218 D2
Low Bentham LA2 239 B8
Overton LA3 209 D8
Rathmell BD24 236 F6
Warton LA5 223 D5
Main St *continued*
Whittington LA6 241 D7
Wray LA2 238 D6
Mainway LA1 218 D2
Mairscough La L39 14 B1
Maitland Ave FY5 175 D1
Maitland Cl 5 PR1 97 C8
Maitland Pl BB4 86 A1
Maitland St
18 Bacup OL13 87 F2
4 Preston PR1 97 C8
1 Preston PR1 97 D8
Majestic Bldgs 24 BB18 196 B2
Majestic Mews WN5 10 D5
Major Bottoms PR6 44 D1
Major St
Accrington BB5 104 B4
Ramsbottom BL0 50 B6
Rawtenstall BB4 86 A7
Makinson Ave BL6 32 E1
Makinson La BL6 32 F4
Makinsons Row 11 LA2 211 A4
Malcolm Pl FY7 198 E4
Malcolm St PR1 118 D1
Malden St PR25 77 A1
Maldern Ave FY6 153 C5
Maldon Pl PR2 118 D2
Malham Ave
5 Accrington BB5 103 F4
Blackpool FY4 110 D8
Malham Cl
Lancaster LA1 218 B3
Southport PR8 35 E3
Malham Gdns BB1 101 F3
Malham Pl PR2 118 E4
Malham Rd BB10 148 D3
Malham View Cl BB18 196 A1
Malham View Ct BB18 196 B1
Malham Wend BB9 170 C3
Malkin Cl BB9 170 E8
Malkin La BB7 165 F6
Mallard Ave FY6 200 B4
Mallard Cl
Heysham LA3 212 F5
Leyland PR25 59 D8
Ormskirk L39 15 C2
Thornton FY5 176 A4
Mallard Ct
Blackpool FY3 131 B6
Lancaster LA1 214 E8
Mallard Dr BL6 32 A3
Mallard Ho L31 5 B4
Mallard Pl BB5 103 D3
Mallards The PR9 54 C3
Mallards Wlk PR5 78 A5
Mallee Ave PR9 54 A3
Mallee Cres PR9 54 A3
Malley La PR4 136 C8
Mallom Ave PR7 60 E1
Mallory Ave L31 5 B4
Mallowdale FY5 176 A4
Mallow Dale PR2 117 B6
Mallowdale Ave LA3 213 A8
Mallowdale Rd LA1 218 B2
Mallow Wlk LA3 217 B2
Mall The
Burnley BB11 128 A6
Fulwood PR2 118 E2
Lytham St Anne's FY8 90 C7
Maltby Pl 2 FY4 130 F2
Malthouse Bsns Pk The L39 15 E6
Malthouse Ct
Ormskirk L39 15 E6
3 Preston PR2 117 D1
Malthouse The 4 PR2 117 D1
Malthouse Way PR1 96 D3
Maltings The
Longton PR4 74 F8
Middleforth Green PR1 96 D4
Thornton FY5 176 A4
Whittington LA6 241 D7
Malt Kiln Brow PR3 185 E4
Malt Kiln Gr PR3 156 A5
Maltkiln La
Bispham Green L40, WN8 27 C7
Ormskirk L39 6 E8
Malton Dr PR5 77 A7
Malt St BB5 104 B7
Malvern Ave
Blackburn BB2 101 D1
Blackpool FY1 130 D2
Lancaster LA1 215 A6
Oswaldtwistle BB5 103 E3
Padiham BB12 126 D6
Preston PR1 97 B6
Stalmine FY6 177 C7
Malvern Cl
6 Accrington BB5 104 A7
Bamber Bridge PR5 77 C8
Horwich BL6 32 C5
Malvern Ct 6 BB9 148 F8
Malvern Rd
Lytham St Anne's FY8 90 D5
Nelson BB9 171 A1
Preston PR1 97 B6
Malvern St
Preston PR1 97 B5
Standish WN6 29 D3
Malvern Way BB4 68 A7
Manby Cl PR5 98 E3

Manchester Mill Ind Est PR1 97 C8
Manchester Rd
Accrington BB5 104 D3
Barnoldswick BB18 196 B1
Blackpool FY3 130 D6
Blackrod BL6 31 E1
Burnley BB11 127 E3
Clow Bridge BB11 106 D6
Hapton BB11, BB12 126 C4
Haslingden, Ewood Bridge BB4 68 D7
Haslingden, Lane Side BB4 85 B2
Nelson BB9 148 D7
Preston PR1 97 B7
Ramsbottom BL0, BL9 50 E4
Southport PR9 35 C7
Mancknols St BB9 149 A7
Mancknols Walton Cottage Homes BB9 149 B8
Mandela Ct BB1 101 E6
Mandeville Rd PR8 21 B5
Mandeville Terr BL8 49 B2
Manfield WN8 18 A3
Manion Ave L31 5 B5
Manion Cl L31 5 B5
Manitoba Cl BB2 101 B8
Manley Cl BL9 50 C2
Manner Sutton St BB1 101 F5
Manning Rd
4 Preston PR1 118 E1
Southport PR8 35 E6
Mannin Way LA1 219 A4
Manor Ave
Burscough L40 25 D2
Fulwood PR2 118 B4
Higher Penwortham PR1 96 B4
Ribchester PR3 141 D3
Slyne LA2 218 C8
Manor Brook 1 BB5 104 C6
Manor Cl
Burton in L LA6 242 C3
Coupe Green PR5 98 F3
Slyne LA2 218 C8
Manor Complex L33 1 B2
Manor Cres
Burscough L40 25 D2
Slyne LA2 218 D8
Manorcroft PR4 74 F8
Manor Ct
11 Blackpool FY1 130 C7
3 Blackpool, Hawes Side FY4 130 E1
Caton LA2 237 D4
Fulwood PR2 117 B7
Manor Ctyd LA3 212 E8
Manor Dr
Burscough L40 25 D2
Cleveleys FY5 175 D3
Kirkham PR4 114 C4
Slyne LA2 218 C8
Manor Farm LA6 241 D7
Manor Fields BB7 144 C5
Manor Gdns L40 25 D2
Manor Gr
Higher Penwortham PR1 96 A4
Morecambe LA3 216 F2
Skelmersdale WN8 17 F1
Manor House Cl
Leyland PR26 59 B8
Maghull L31 5 C1
Manor House Cotts BB3 65 E8
Manor House Cres PR1 118 B3
Manor House Dr WN8 9 E3
Manor House La PR1 118 C3
Manor House Park Flats FY5 175 C3
Manor La
Hest Bank LA2 220 F1
Higher Penwortham PR1 96 B4
Manor Lo L37 11 E4
Manor Mews FY6 153 E4
Manor Pk PR2 118 C4
Manor Pl BB5 103 F7
Manor Rd
Blackburn BB2 101 B5
Blackpool FY1 130 D4
Burnley BB12 127 B7
Burscough L40 25 D2
Clayton Green PR6 78 B3
Clitheroe BB7 166 D7
Colne BB8 171 E7
Darwen BB3 64 F8
Fleetwood FY7 198 E4
Garstang PR3 204 C1
Horwich BL6 32 D4
Inskip PR4 135 C8
Shevington WN6 19 F6
Slyne LA2 218 D8
Southport PR9 54 A2
Whalley BB7 144 C5
Wrea Green PR4 113 B4
Manor St
Accrington BB5 104 D7
Bacup OL13 87 F1
Bury BL9 33 A2
Nelson BB9 148 F8
Ramsbottom BL0 50 B7
Manor Way
Coppull PR7 29 D8
Wrea Green PR4 113 B3
Manor Wood
Fleetwood FY7 198 E4
Kirkham PR4 114 B7
Manse Ave WN6 28 F5
Mansell Way BL6 32 D1
Mansergh St BB10 148 C2
Mansfield Ave BL0 50 B2
Mansfield Cres BB9 148 C6
Mansfield Dr PR5 98 E3
Mansfield Gr BB9 148 C6
Mansfield Rd FY3 130 D8
Mansion House Bldgs 3 BB4 86 A7
Mansion St S BB5 104 D6
Mansion The BB8 172 C6
Manston Gr PR7 43 A7
Manx Jane's La PR9 54 A4
Manxman Rd BB2 101 F1
Many Brooks Ho PR5 98 E1
Maple Ave
Blackpool FY3 130 D5
Brinscall PR6 62 F7
Burscough L40 25 E4
7 Bury BL9 33 B2
6 Clitheroe BB7 166 D7
Fleetwood FY7 175 F8
Haslingden BB4 85 C3
Horwich BL6 32 E1
Morecambe LA3 216 E2
Thornton FY5 153 C8
Maplebank 3 PR2 116 C1
Maple Bank BB10 128 C7
Maple Cl
Formby L37 11 C1
Newton-w-S PR4 114 F2
Whalley BB7 144 D6
Wilpshire BB1 122 E6
Maple Cres
9 Preston PR1 96 E7
Rishton BB1 103 B8
Maple Ct
Clayton-le-W PR25 77 D3
Garstang PR3 204 C1
Maple Dr
Bamber Bridge PR5 97 F1
Oswaldtwistle BB5 103 F3
Poulton-le-F FY6 153 E2
Maple Gr
Chorley PR6 61 D3
Fulwood PR2 119 A4
Grimsargh PR2 139 D1
Higher Penwortham PR1 96 B4
Lancaster LA1 214 D8
Ramsbottom BL0 50 D6
Warton PR4 92 D6
Maple Ho PR7 42 F6
Maple Leaf Cl PR2 116 F6
Maple Mews BB3 82 D1
Maple Rd PR3 204 C1
Maple St
Blackburn BB1 102 A7
Clayton-le-M BB5 124 F1
Great Harwood BB6 124 D6
Rishton BB1 124 B1
Southport PR8 35 E6
Maples The PR26 58 F6
Maple View WN8 8 F6
Maplewood
Skelmersdale WN8 18 A4
Southport PR9 53 F2
Maplewood Ave FY6 200 A5
Maplewood Cl
Chorley PR7 43 E6
Leyland PR25 59 E8
Lytham St Anne's FY8 90 F4
Maplewood Dr FY5 152 C8
Maplewood Gdns LA1 215 A2
Marabou Dr BB3 81 E3
Marathon Pl PR26 76 C3
Marble Ave 5 FY5 152 F7
Marble Place Sh Ctr PR8 35 B7
Marble St BB5 103 E4
Marchbank Rd WN8 17 D1
March St BB12 127 F8
Marchwood Rd FY3 131 B8
Marcroft Ave FY4 110 E7
Mardale Ave
Blackpool FY4 131 C1
Morecambe LA4 217 D5
Mardale Cl PR8 21 B4
Mardale Cres PR25 60 B7
Mardale Rd
1 Lancaster LA1 218 E1
Longridge PR3 139 F5
Preston PR1 119 A1
Maresfield Rd PR1 96 E5
Margaret Ct FY8 90 A4
Margaret Rd PR1 96 E4
Margaret St
Blackburn BB1 102 D4
Oswaldtwistle BB5 103 C2
1 Preston PR1 97 A8
Rawtenstall BB4 85 F4
Margate Ave FY4 110 E6
Margate Rd
Fulwood PR2 117 A4
Lytham St Anne's FY8 89 F8
Maria Ct 8 BB11 128 B4
Marians Dr L39 15 E7
Maria Sq BL7 46 D4
Maria St BB3 65 B6
Maricourt Ave BB1 102 D5
Marilyn Ave 4 PR5 77 B8
Marina Ave
2 Blackpool FY1 130 D2
Poulton-le-F FY3 131 D8
Marina Cl PR5 97 A1
Marina Dr
Bamber Bridge PR5 97 A1
Fulwood PR2 117 E7
Marina Gr PR5 97 A1
Marina Mews FY7 199 B3
Marina Rd L37 11 F1
Marine Ave BB11 127 C4
Marine Cres PR7 60 F6
Marine Ct LA3 216 E4
Marine Dr
Hest Bank LA2 220 D1
Lytham St Anne's FY8 90 D3
Southport, Birkdale PR8 34 E7
Southport, Marshside PR8, PR9 53 D4
Marine Gate Mans PR9 35 B8
Marine Ind Ctr FY8 91 D4
Marine Par
Fleetwood FY7 198 C1
Southport PR8 35 A8
Marine Rd E LA4 217 C6
Marine Rd W LA3, LA4 216 F4
Marine Road Central LA4 217 A5
Mariners Cl FY7 198 E1
Mariners Way PR2 96 B8
Marine View Apartments FY7 198 F5
Marino Cl FY5 153 D8
Maritime Ct PR9 35 B8
Maritime St FY7 198 F2
Maritime Way PR2 95 F7
Markazul Uloom Sch BB2 101 F2
Mark Cl PR1 96 F1
Market Ave 2 BB1 101 E5
Market Chambers BL0 50 C7
Market Cross 5 L39 15 E5
Marketgate 23 LA1 214 F8
Market Pl
Adlington PR7 31 A7
12 Chorley PR7 43 C8
3 Clitheroe BB7 166 E8
10 Colne BB8 171 E5
Edenfield BL0 68 D3
Garstang PR3 181 C7
Longridge PR3 140 B7
4 Poulton-le-F FY6 153 D3
Ramsbottom BL0 50 C7
Standish WN6 29 E1
Market Prom 5 BB11 128 A6
Market St W PR1 96 F8
Market Sq
Burnley BB11 128 A6
4 Kirkham PR4 114 B5
10 Lancaster LA1 214 F8
Lytham St Anne's FY8 91 A3
Nelson BB9 148 D8
Market St
Adlington PR7 31 A6
Bacup OL13 87 F2
7 Barnoldswick BB18 196 B2
Blackpool FY1 130 B5
Carnforth LA5 223 D2
Chorley PR7 43 C7
Church BB5 103 E5
Colne BB8 171 E5
Darwen BB3 82 A1
Edenfield BL0 68 D4
Hambleton FY6 177 C2
Kirkham PR4 113 F6
Lancaster LA1 214 F8
Morecambe LA4 217 A5
9 Nelson BB9 148 D8
Preston PR1 96 F8
11 Rawtenstall BB4 69 E8
Southport PR8 35 B7
Standish WN6 29 E1
Whitworth OL12, OL13 71 D4
Market Street La 7 BB2 101 E4
Market Way
8 Blackburn BB1 101 E5
6 Ormskirk L39 15 E5
Market Wlk PR7 43 C8
Markham Dr PR8 35 E2
Markham Rd BB2 101 B3
Markham St PR2 117 C1
Marklands Rd BL6 32 E5
Markland St
3 Preston PR1 96 E7
6 Ramsbottom BL0 50 C6
Mark Rd L38 2 F4
Markross St BB4 86 A2
Mark's Ave PR26 76 E5
Mark Sq PR4 57 A6
Mark St
Bacup OL13 70 C8
Burnley BB10 148 B1
Marland WN8 18 A4
Marl Ave PR1 96 B4
Marlboro Rd FY3 130 E4
Marlborough Ave
Cleveleys FY5 175 D5
Maghull L31 5 D3
Warton PR4 92 D6
Marlborough Cl
Ramsbottom BL0 50 C3
Whitworth OL12 52 C7
Marlborough Ct 1 WN8 18 B4
Marlborough Dr
Bamber Bridge PR5 97 D3
Fulwood PR2 117 D7
Marlborough Gdns
Skelmersdale WN8 18 A4
5 Southport PR9 35 C8
Marlborough Rd
Accrington BB5 104 C7
Lytham St Anne's FY8 110 E1
Morecambe LA3 216 E3
Southport PR9 35 C7
Marlborough St
Burnley BB11 128 A4
Chorley PR6 61 E1
14 Rochdale OL12 52 C1
Marl Cop PR26 58 A6
Marl Croft PR1 96 D2
Marled Hey BL7 48 D5
Marles Ct BB10 128 B8
Marlfield PR4 74 F4
Marlfield Cl PR2 116 F5
Marl Gr WN5 10 D4
Marl Hill Cres PR2 119 A2
Marlhill Rd FY3 131 B8
Marlin St 7 BB9 170 F2
Marlow Ct PR7 30 F6
Marlowe Ave
Accrington BB5 104 E2
Padiham BB12 126 F7
Marlowe Cres BB6 124 B4
Marl Pits BB4 86 B3
Marl Rd L33 1 C3
Marlton Rd BB2 101 D1
Marlton Way LA1 214 E6
Marmaduke Cotts LA6 241 D4
Marple Cl WN6 29 B2
Marquis Cl BB3 81 F7
Marquis Dr PR4 93 C7
Marquis St PR4 113 F5
Marron Cl PR25 59 E8
Marsden Cl PR7 41 B7
Marsden Com Prim Sch BB9 148 D7
Marsden Cres BB9 149 A8
Marsden Ct BB10 148 C3
Marsden Dr BB9 148 D6
Marsden Gr BB9 148 C5
Marsden Hall Rd BB9 149 A8
Marsden Hall Rd N BB9 171 B1
Marsden Hall Road S BB9 149 A8
MARSDEN HEIGHT 148 E5
Marsden Height Cl BB9 148 F5
Marsden Heights Com Coll BB9 148 B6
Marsden Mall 5 BB9 148 E8
Marsden Pl BB9 149 A8
Marsden Rd
Blackpool FY4 110 D8
Burnley BB10 148 C3
Southport PR9 35 E7
Marsden Sq BB4 85 B4
Marsden St
Accrington BB5 104 B4
Blackburn BB2 101 B2
6 Haslingden BB4 85 A3
Kirkham PR4 114 B5
Marsett Cl OL12 52 A1
Marsett Pl PR2 118 E5
MARSH 214 C8
Marshall Ave BB5 125 F2
Marshall Gr PR2 117 A4
Marshallsay L37 12 A2
Marshall's Brow PR1 96 E3
Marshall's Cl
Maghull L31 5 C4
5 Middleforth Green PR1 96 E4
Marsham Cl PR3 181 D6
Marsham Gr BB3 82 C1
Marshaw Pl PR3 181 A6
Marshaw Rd LA1 218 B2
Marsh Brows L37 11 E2
Marsh Cl LA2 206 B4
Marsh Cres LA4 217 F4
Marsh Ct 2 FY5 176 A2
Marshdale Rd FY4 110 F7
Marsh Dr PR4 93 D7
Marshes La The PR4 38 A8
Marsh Gate BB3 82 D1
Marsh Gates PR4 93 D7
Marsh Hos LA2 206 B4
MARSH HOUSE 82 C1
Marsh House La BB3 82 C1
MARSH HOUSES 206 B4
Marsh La
Brindle PR6 79 B5
Cockerham LA2 206 B4
Glasson LA2 209 D3
Hambleton FY6 177 C1
Hightown L37, L38 3 E6
Hurlston L40 24 D1
Longton PR4 74 D8
Preston PR1 96 E7
Withnell Fold PR6 79 A4
Marsh Mill★ FY5 176 B2
Marsh Mill FY5 176 B2
Marsh Moss La L40 25 C7
Marsh Rd
Banks PR9 72 D1
Hesketh Bank PR4 73 F4
Thornton FY5 176 A2
MARSHSIDE 53 E4
Marshside Nature Reserve★ PR9 53 E5
Marshside Prim Sch PR9 54 A5
Marshside Rd PR9 53 F4
Marsh St
Blackburn BB1 101 E6
Horwich BL6 32 A4
4 Lancaster LA1 218 B1
Marsh Terr BB3 82 A2
Marsh View PR4 114 F2
Marsh Way
Clitheroe BB7 189 F2
Kingsfold PR1 96 C2
Mars St BL7 48 E6
Marston Cl PR2 117 C7
Marston Cres L38 3 A2
Marston Moor PR2 117 C7
Martholme Ave BB5 125 A3
Martholme Cl BB6 124 D6
Martholme La BB6 124 F8
Martin Ave FY8 110 C4
Martin Croft Rd BB4 85 A5
Martindale Ave FY7 198 C2
Martindale Cl BB1 102 C2
Martindales The PR6 78 B3
Martin Dr BB3 65 C6
Martinfield PR2 117 F8
Martin Field Rd PR1 96 E2
Martinfields BB10 148 C4
Martinique Dr BB3 81 F6
Martin La
Drummersdale L40 24 E6
Rochdale OL12 52 B1
Martin Mere★ L40 38 B1
Martin Mere Visitor Ctr★ L40 38 B2
Martins Ave PR7 43 E2
Martins La WN8 9 D7
Martin St
Burnley BB10 148 B1
Bury BL9 33 D3
Edgworth BL7 48 D4
Martin Top La BB7 192 C7
Mart La L40 25 E5
Martland Ave WN6 19 F5
Marton Dr
Blackpool FY4 110 D8
Burnley BB11 127 E3
Morecambe LA4 217 F6
Marton Fold FY4 111 A4
Marton Mere Cvn Pk FY3, FY4 131 C2
Marton Pl LA4 217 F6
Marton Prim Sch FY4 110 F7
Marton Rd PR2 95 F8
Marton St 4 LA1 214 F7
Marton View FY3 130 E4
Marton Wlk 4 BB3 65 B6
Marwick Cl WN6 29 D2
Mary Ave PR8 21 E6
Marybank Cl PR2 118 C5
Mary Brown Cotts BB7 190 C8
Maryland Cl LA5 224 D2
Mary St E BL6 32 B4
Mary St W
Horwich BL6 32 A4
Longridge PR3 140 A8
Mary St
Blackburn BB1 102 A4
5 Burnley BB10 128 B5
Carnforth LA5 223 D3
Colne BB8 171 C4
Lancaster LA1 214 F8
Ramsbottom BL0 50 B5
Rishton BB1 124 B1
Mary Towneley Fold BB10 128 C4
Maryvale Ho LA1 214 E5
Masefield Ave
Padiham BB12 126 E7
Thornton FY5 176 A3
Masefield Cl
Brockhall Village BB6 143 B5
Great Harwood BB6 124 B4
Masefield Pl PR5 97 D2
Mason Cl PR4 93 C6
Masonfield PR5 78 B5
Masonfield Cres LA1 215 D7
MASONGILL 242 D6
Masongill Fell La LA6 242 E7
Mason Hill View PR2 118 A4
Mason House Cres PR2 117 A5
Mason Row BL7 47 E2
Masons Ct 1 FY7 198 E3
Mason St
7 Accrington BB5 104 C6
Bolton BL7 47 E1
Bury BL9 33 A2
Chorley PR6 61 E2
Colne BB8 171 D5
Horwich BL6 32 B3
Oswaldtwistle BB5 103 D3
Masons Way 8 BB18 196 B3
Masonwood PR2 118 A6
Massam's La L37 11 F6
Massey Croft OL12 52 C8
Massey La BB9 148 A5
Massey St
Brierfield BB9 148 A4
Bury BL9 33 B3
Masterson Ave BB12 145 D2
Matcham Ct 11 FY1 130 B5
Matchmoor La BL6 32 F4
Mather Ave BB5 104 B8
Mather St FY3 130 D7
Mathias Ct LA4 217 B6
Matlock Ave PR8 35 B4
Matlock Cl PR8 35 B4
Matlock Cres PR8 35 B4
Matlock Ct BL6 32 E4
Matlock Gr BB10 148 C2
Matlock Pl PR2 117 A5
Matlock Rd PR8 35 B4
Matlock St 13 BB3 81 F2

Matrix Pk PR7 60 D7
Matterdale Rd PR25 60 B7
Matthew Cl BB8 171 E4
Matthews Ct FY4 110 D7
Matthew St BB2 101 B2
Matthias St LA4 217 B6
Mattock Cres LA4 217 F5
Maudland Bank PR1 96 E8
Maudland Ho PR1 96 E8
Maudland Rd
Blackpool FY1 130 C2
Preston PR1 96 E8
MAUDLANDS 117 D1
Maudsley St
Accrington BB5 104 C6
Blackburn BB1 101 F5
Maud St
Barrowford BB9 170 D2
Chorley PR7 43 B6
Maureen Ave 3 PR5 77 B8
Maurice Gr FY2 152 E1
Maurice St BB9 148 D8
Mavis Dr PR7 42 E2
Mavis Rd BB2 101 A5
MAWDESLEY 40 C2
Mawdesley St Peter's CE Prim Sch L40 40 C3
Mawdsley Cl L37 12 B3
Mawdsley Terr L39 15 F7
Maxwell Gr FY2 152 E2
Maxwell St BL9 33 B3
Maybank Cl PR9 54 A1
May Bell Ave FY5 175 F3
Maybury Ave BB12 127 B7
Maybury Cl 21 BL0 50 B5
Maycroft Ave FY6 153 B5
Mayfair BL6 32 D3
Mayfair Cl
Haslingden BB4 68 A7
Hightown L38 2 F2
Lytham St Anne's FY8 90 D6
Mayfair Cotts WN1 30 C1
Mayfair Cres BB1 122 F5
Mayfair Ct FY1 130 E2
Mayfair Dr FY5 153 C8
Mayfair Gdns 5 FY5 176 C1
Mayfair Rd
Blackpool FY1 130 E2
Burnley BB10 128 E5
Nelson BB9 171 A1
Mayfayre Ave L31 5 B5
Mayfield
Darwen BB3 65 B7
Woodsfold PR4 135 E6
Mayfield Ave
Adlington PR6 31 A7
Bamber Bridge PR5 77 C8
Blackpool FY4 110 C5
Clitheroe BB7 166 F7
Formby L37 11 C1
Fulwood, Ingol PR2 117 B4
Fulwood PR2 117 A5
Haslingden BB4 85 A1
5 Kirkham PR4 114 A5
Lancaster LA1 218 C3
Oswaldtwistle BB5 103 F4
Thornton FY5 176 A4
Mayfield Cl
Middleforth Green PR1 96 E4
Ramsbottom BL0 50 A2
Mayfield Ct L37 11 F5
Mayfield Dr LA4 217 E6
Mayfield Fold BB11 128 B3
Mayfield Gdns BB5 103 F4
Mayfield Pl 10 FY7 198 F2
Mayfield Prim Sch FY8 89 E8
Mayfield Rd
Blackburn BB1 122 E3
8 Chorley PR6 61 D1
High Bentham LA2 239 D7
Leyland PR25 60 A7
Lytham St Anne's FY8 89 E8
Preston PR2 117 B1
Ramsbottom BL0 50 A2
Up Holland WN8 10 B7
Mayfield Sch PR7 43 C6
Mayfield St BB2 101 E3
Mayfield Terr PR5 99 D5
Mayflower Ave PR1 96 A3
Mayflower Cres PR7 60 F7
Mayflower Gr PR3 181 E1
Mayflower Ind Est L37 12 A1
Mayflower St BB2 101 B2
Mayhall Ct L31 5 D2
May La
Bilsborrow PR3 159 C8
Claughton PR3 182 E1
Maylands Pl BB9 170 C3
Maylands Sq LA4 217 C4
Maynard St PR1, PR2 117 D2
Mayo Dr PR4 57 A6
Mayor Ave FY1 130 C2
Maypark PR5 78 A5
Mayson St BB1 101 E4
May St
Barrowford BB9 170 D2
Blackburn BB1 102 A4
Edgworth BL7 48 E6
Nelson BB9 170 F2
May Terr BB7 144 A4
May Tree Cl BB10 148 E3
Maytree Ct PR6 30 F8
Maytree Wlk WN8 18 B4
Mayville Rd BB9 148 B6
Mead Ave PR25 60 B8
Meadow Ave
Fleetwood FY7 198 E1
Knott End-on-S FY6 200 A6
Meadow Ave *continued*
Southport PR8 35 C4
Meadoway
Accrington BB5 104 A7
Longton PR4 74 F8
Tarleton PR4 57 A5
Meadow Bank
Kingsfold PR1 96 C3
Maghull L31 5 B2
6 Ormskirk L39 15 F5
Meadow Bank Ave
BB10 148 B5
Meadow Bank Cotts
BB4 85 E3
Meadow Bank Mews 2
BB9 170 F2
Meadow Bank Rd 15
BB9 148 D8
Meadowbarn Cl PR4 116 E5
Meadowbridge Cl L40 16 E4
Meadowbrook
Blackpool FY3 131 C2
Burscough L40 25 D2
Meadowbrook Cl BL9 33 C4
Meadow Brook Ho 1
PR1 118 A1
Meadow Brow PR9 54 D5
Meadow Cl
Billington BB7 144 A3
Blackburn BB1 102 B4
Blackpool FY2 152 D2
Burnley BB10 148 C4
Clifton PR4 115 D2
Foulridge BB8 194 D1
Huncoat BB5 125 F1
Skelmersdale WN8 9 D7
Westhead L40 16 E4
Wrea Green PR4 113 B3
Meadow Clough WN8 18 B4
Meadow Cotts OL12 71 D3
Meadow Court Rd LA4 217 C3
Meadow Cr PR4 113 F6
Meadow Cres FY6 153 A3
Meadowcroft
Blackburn BB3 82 A6
Euxton PR7 60 B3
Formby L37 11 F2
Lytham St Anne's FY8 111 A1
Skelmersdale WN8 18 B4
Meadow Croft
Nether Kellet LA6 221 F4
West Bradford BB7 189 E5
Meadowcroft Ave
Catterall PR3 181 D3
Cleveleys FY5 175 E2
Hambleton FY6 177 C1
Meadowcroft Bsns Pk
PR4 96 B1
Meadowcroft Cl BB4 86 A5
Meadowcroft Gr LA3 216 E1
Meadowcroft Rd PR25 59 D7
Meadow Ct
11 Oswaldtwistle BB5 103 E4
Preston PR1 96 E6
Treales PR4 135 A1
Meadow Dr
Bolton-le-S LA5 221 A5
Ormskirk L39 15 C2
Warton PR4 92 C5
Meadow Edge BB9 170 F5
Meadowfield
Fulwood PR2 117 F8
Halton LA2 219 C7
3 Up Holland WN8 10 A7
Meadow Field PR1 96 E2
Meadowfield Cl
Halton LA2 219 C7
Whalley BB7 144 A7
Meadowfields BB2 81 D7
Meadow Gdns BB1 124 B1
Meadow Head Ave
OL12 52 D6
Meadow Head Cl BB2 101 A1
Meadowhead Dr BB1 124 B1
Meadowhead Inf Sch
BB2 101 B1
Meadowhead Jun Sch
BB2 81 B8
Meadow Head La
Longton PR4 74 F7
Tockholes BB3 81 B4
Meadow Ho 7 PR1 97 A8
Meadow Hts BL0 50 D6
Meadow La
Clayton Brook PR5 78 B4
Croston PR26 57 E1
Hesketh Bank PR4 73 F4
Hoscar L40 26 C6
Knott End-on-S FY6 199 F4
Lytham St Anne's FY8 91 E4
Maghull L31 5 F1
Rufford L40 39 D3
Southport PR8 21 D3
Meadowland Cl PR26 76 E3
Meadowlands
Charnock Richard PR7 42 D4
Clitheroe BB7 166 C8
Meadow Pk
Galgate LA2 210 F4
Garstang PR3 204 C1
Haslingden BL0 68 C4
Kirkham PR4 113 E6
Staining FY3 131 D5
Tarleton PR4 57 B6
Meadow Reach PR1 96 B2
Meadow Rise BB2 81 A8
Meadows Ave
Bacup OL13 87 F4
Meadows Ave *continued*
Cleveleys FY5 175 F2
Haslingden BB4 85 C2
Meadows Cl LA5 225 E4
Meadows Dr BB4 106 A1
Meadowside
Claughton LA2 237 F5
Croston PR26 58 A2
Grindleton BB7 190 C8
Lancaster LA1 214 F7
Walmer Bridge PR4 75 A5
Meadowside Ave BB5 124 E3
Meadowside Dr
Gregson Lane PR5 98 E1
Kirkby L33 1 A6
Meadowside Rd 6
LA4 217 B3
Meadow St
Accrington BB5 104 C6
Adlington PR7 31 A6
Barnoldswick BB18 196 A4
17 Burnley BB11 127 F6
Darwen BB3 65 B6
Great Harwood BB6 124 C4
Lancaster LA1 214 D8
Leyland PR25 77 A1
Padiham BB12 146 C1
Preston PR1 97 A8
Wheelton PR6 62 A7
Meadows The
Arnside LA5 224 C8
Bamber Bridge PR5 97 F3
Billington BB7 144 A4
Burnley BB12 127 D8
Cleveleys FY5 175 F2
Colne BB8 171 D6
Darwen BB3 81 E5
Elswick PR4 155 F1
Heskin Green PR7 41 E2
Hollins Lane PR3 207 C2
2 Leyland PR26 76 B1
Maghull L31 5 D1
Oswaldtwistle BB5 103 F5
Whitworth OL12 71 C1
Yealand Redmayne LA5 225 E3
Meadow Terr BB3 81 E5
Meadow Vale
Blackburn BB2 81 E6
Leyland PR26 59 A8
Meadow View
Adlington PR6 30 F8
Clitheroe BB7 166 C8
Farleton LA2 238 A6
Great Plumpton PR4 112 F7
Lancaster LA1 218 B3
Orrell WN5 10 E8
Rochdale OL12 52 A1
Southport PR8 35 D4
Meadow View Cvn Pk
LA6 237 A7
Meadow Way
Arkholme LA6 241 B3
Bacup OL13 87 F2
Barnoldswick BB18 196 D4
Blackrod BL6 31 E1
Coppull PR7 29 D8
Edgworth BL7 48 E6
Garstang PR3 204 C2
Ramsbottom BL9 50 C2
Meads Rd PR2 117 B1
Meadup Ct LA3 217 A2
Meadway
Becconsall PR4 73 F2
Blackpool FY4 130 F1
Clayton Green PR6 78 B3
Higher Penwortham PR1 96 A5
Padiham BB12 126 B7
Ramsbottom BL0 68 C1
Skelmersdale WN8 18 A4
Meadway Cl BL6 32 D3
Meagles Barns PR3 155 E4
Meagles La PR3, PR4 155 E3
Mealhouse La 6 PR7 43 C8
Mealrigg La LA6 241 A7
Meanwood Ave FY4 110 F7
Meanwood Brow 15
OL12 52 C1
Meanwood Com Prim Sch
OL12 52 C1
Meanygate PR5 97 E1
Mearbeck Pl 6 LA1 218 B2
Mearley Brook Fold
BB7 166 F7
Mearley Rd PR2 118 E4
Mearley St BB7 166 E7
Mearley Syke BB7 166 F8
Mearsbeck 8 LA3 216 E3
Meath Rd PR1 96 D6
Mede The PR4 114 B3
Medina Cl 5 BB5 104 B5
MEDLAR 133 F4
Medlar Cl PR4 113 E6
Medlar Ct PR4 114 A6
Medlar Gate PR4 114 A6
Medlar La PR4 133 E4
Medlar-with-Wesham CE Prim Sch PR4 113 F6
Medley St OL12 52 F1
Medlock Ave FY7 198 D2
Medlock Pl FY7 198 D2
Medway PR2 117 F6
Medway Ave FY7 175 D8
Medway Cl PR5 97 B1
Medway Dr BL6 32 D3
Medway Ho 6 PR1 97 D8
Meeting House La LA1 214 E8
Meins Croft BB2 101 A6
Meins Rd BB2 100 F6
Melba Rd PR2 118 E3
Melbert Ave PR2 117 C3
Melbourne Ave
Blackpool FY5 152 F7
Fleetwood FY7 175 E8
Melbourne Cl BL6 32 C3
Melbourne Ct 1 FY5 152 F8
Melbourne Gr BL6 32 C3
Melbourne Rd 11 LA1 215 A8
Melbourne St
6 Accrington BB5 125 A1
7 Darwen BB3 65 B6
2 Newchurch BB4 86 F1
Oswaldtwistle BB5 103 D3
Padiham BB12 126 D7
19 Preston PR1 96 F8
Melbreck WN8 18 A4
Melbury Dr BL6 32 F1
Meldon Grange LA3 213 A8
Meldon Rd LA3 213 A7
Meldreth Cl L37 11 C1
Melford Cl PR6 61 F3
Melford Dr WN5 10 D3
Melfort Cl BB2 100 F1
Melia Cl BB4 85 F2
Melita St 6 BB3 65 B8
MELLING 241 C1
Melling Brow LA6 241 C2
Melling Cl PR6 31 B7
Melling Ct
3 Colne BB8 171 C5
Morecambe LA4 217 A3
Melling Ho 4 LA1 215 A3
Melling Mews PR3 181 C8
Melling Rd
Hornby LA2 238 B7
Southport PR9 35 E7
Melling St Wilfrid CE Prim Sch LA6 241 D2
Mellings Ave WN5 10 E1
Mellings Fold 3 PR1 97 C6
Melling's La FY8 111 A1
Melling St 17 PR1 96 F8
Mellings Wood FY8 111 A1
Mellishaw La LA3 217 D1
MELLOR 121 F2
MELLOR BROOK 121 C3
Mellor Brow BB2 121 D2
Mellor Cl
Blackburn BB2 100 F8
Burnley BB11 127 D3
Standish WN6 29 E2
Mellor Ct PR3 140 B7
Mellor La BB2 121 F3
Mellor Pl 6 PR1 97 B7
Mellor Rd
Kirkham PR4 114 A5
Leyland PR25 76 D2
Mellors Cl PR8 35 F5
Mellwood Ave FY3 152 F1
Melrose Ave
Blackpool FY3 130 E8
Burnley BB11 127 D4
Fulwood PR2 118 C5
Morecambe LA4 217 C5
Oswaldtwistle BB5 103 F3
Southport PR9 54 B5
Melrose Gdns PR26 58 C2
Melrose St
10 Darwen BB3 81 F2
Lancaster LA1 215 A7
Ramsbottom BL0 50 B2
Melrose Terr 11 OL13 88 A7
Melrose Way PR7 43 D5
Melton Gr FY8 90 E3
Melton Pl
Blackpool FY5 152 C8
Leyland PR25 77 B1
Melville Ave
Barnoldswick BB18 196 A3
Darwen BB3 65 A7
Melville Dr BB2 101 D5
Melville Gdns BB3 65 A8
Melville Rd
Blackpool FY2 152 C4
Heysham LA3 212 E5
Melville St
Burnley BB10 148 C1
Darwen BB3 65 A8
Memorial Gdns PR3 159 A4
Memory Cl PR4 93 B7
Menai Dr PR2 117 D7
Mendip Cl
Horwich BL6 32 C5
Lytham St Anne's FY8 91 E5
Mendip Rd PR25 77 D1
Menivale Cl PR9 54 B5
Meols Cl L37 11 E2
Meols Cop High Sch
PR8 35 F5
Meols Cop Rd PR8, PR9 35 F4
Meols Cop Retail Pk
PR9 36 A4
Meols Cop Sta PR9 35 F7
Meols Ct PR9 55 A6
Meolsgate Ave PR4 57 A7
Meols View Cl PR8 36 A3
Mercer Cres BB4 68 A8
Mercer Ct
Adlington PR7 43 F1
Maghull L31 5 A3
Mercer Dr BB6 124 E6
Mercer Ho 5 BB5 125 A1
Mercer Rd PR5 97 A1
Mercer's La L39 7 B4
Mercer St
16 Clayton-le-M BB5 124 F3
Great Harwood BB6 124 D5
Mercer St *continued*
1 Padiham BB12 126 F7
Preston PR1 97 C8
Mercer Way BB1 102 D1
Merchants Ho 4 BB1 101 F4
Merchants Landing
BB1 101 F3
Merchants Quay 1
BB1 101 F3
Merclesden Ave BB9 171 B1
Mercury Way WN8 9 E8
Mere Ave
Burscough Bridge L40 25 E6
Fleetwood FY7 198 D1
Mere Brook FY3 131 E5
MERE BROW 55 E2
Mere Brow La PR4 56 A2
Mere Cl
Broughton PR3 137 C3
Skelmersdale WN8 17 F2
MERECLOUGH 129 A1
Mere Ct
Burnley BB11 127 B4
Burscough Bridge L40 25 E5
Meredith St BB9 148 E7
Merefell Rd LA5 221 A6
Merefield PR7 61 A1
Merefield Sch PR8 21 B4
Merefold BL6 31 F3
Mere Fold PR7 42 D3
Mere La
Banks PR9 55 A2
Holmeswood PR4 38 A7
Rufford L40 38 E3
Mereland Cl WN5 10 E6
Mereland Rd FY3 131 A2
Mere Park Ct FY3 131 A2
Merepark Dr PR9 54 B4
Mere Rd
Blackpool FY3 130 D5
Formby L37 11 D2
Mere Sands Wood Nature Reserve* L40 38 F4
MERESIDE 131 C1
Mereside Cl PR4 74 F7
Mereside Prim Sch
FY4 131 C1
Meres Way PR8 35 B2
Merewood WN8 18 A4
Meriden Cl PR8 21 B5
Merlecrest Dr PR4 57 A8
Merlewood BL0 68 E3
Merlewood Ave PR9 54 B3
Merlin Cl PR6 62 A3
Merlin Ct BB5 103 D3
Merlin Dr BB5 103 D3
Merlin Gr
Leyland PR25 59 C8
Padiham BB12 126 E6
Merlin Rd BB2 101 B6
Merlyn Rd FY5 175 E1
Merrick Ave PR1 97 F8
Merrilox Ave L31 5 D3
Merryburn Cl PR2 118 A4
Merry Trees La PR4 116 E5
Merscar La L40 24 D6
Mersey Ave
Darwen BB3 81 D3
Formby L37 11 E6
Maghull L31 5 F2
Mersey Rd
Blackpool FY4 110 B8
Fleetwood FY7 198 F4
Orrell WN5 10 F7
Mersey St
4 Bacup OL13 88 A1
Burnley BB12 127 A6
Longridge PR3 140 B8
Preston PR2 96 C8
Merton Ave PR2 117 F6
Merton Ct PR2 117 F6
Merton Gr PR6 61 F3
Merton St
Burnley BB12 127 F7
4 Nelson BB9 170 D1
Messenger St BB9 149 A7
Meta St BB2 101 E2
Metcalf Dr BB5 125 D6
Metcalfe Cl BB2 81 D8
Metcalfe St BB12 127 B5
Mete St PR1 97 D8
Methuen Ave
Coupe Green PR5 98 E3
Fulwood PR2 117 E6
Methuen Cl PR5 98 E3
Methuen Dr PR5 98 F3
Metropolitan Bsns Pk
FY3 131 B2
Metropolitan Dr FY3 131 B2
Mettle Cote OL13 88 A1
Mewith La LA2 239 C6
Mews The
1 Darwen BB3 65 C7
Lancaster LA1 215 B6
Morecambe LA4 217 E5
1 Padiham BB12 146 C1
Southport, Birkdale PR8 35 A4
Southport PR8 35 A5
11 Southport PR8 35 B7
Mexford Ave FY2 130 D8
Meyler Ave FY3 130 E8
Michael Pl 4 LA4 217 D5
Michaels Cl L37 11 E3
Michael's La L39 22 C3
Michaelson Ave LA4 217 E4

Michael Wife La
Edenfield BL0 68 F2
Edenfield BL0 68 F3
Mickering La L39 6 C5
Mickleden Ave PR2 117 F7
Mickleden Rd FY4 131 C1
Micklefield Ct 2 PR25 76 D1
Micklegate FY5 152 C7
Micklehurst Cres BB11 127 D2
Mickleton Dr PR8 21 A5
Middlecot Cl 2 WN5 10 E5
Middlefield PR26 59 A8
Middleforth Gn PR1 96 E4
MIDDLEFORTH GREEN 96 E3
Middleforth Ind Est 4 PR1 96 E4
Middlegate LA3 217 E2
Middlegate Gn BB4 106 A1
MIDDLE HEALEY 52 D4
Middle Hey PR4 74 E3
Middle Highfield LA2 237 C5
Middle Hill OL12 52 F4
Middle Holly PR3 204 C8
Middle Meanygate PR4 56 C7
Middle Moss La
Great Altcar L37 12 F3
Haskayne L37 13 A2
Middlesex Ave BB12 127 B7
Middle St
Blackpool FY1 130 B3
Colne BB8 171 C4
Lancaster LA1 214 F8
Whitworth OL12 71 D1
MIDDLETON 213 B2
Middleton Ave FY7 198 D1
Middleton Bsns Pk LA3 213 A3
Middleton Dr BB9 170 E6
Middleton Rd
Fulwood PR2 118 C7
Heysham LA3 212 E5
Middleton LA3 213 B2
Middleton Way LA3 212 F6
Middle Turn BL7 48 D7
Middle Withins La L37, L38 4 A7
Middlewood WN8 18 A4
Middlewood Cl
Eccleston PR7 41 C6
Ormskirk L39 6 C7
Middlewood Dr L39 6 C7
Middlewood Rd L39 6 C7
Midfield BB6 123 C8
MIDGE HALL 76 A3
Midge Hall La
Bescar PR9 37 C3
Leyland PR4, PR5 75 F4
Midgeland Rd FY4 111 B5
Midgeland Terr FY4 111 C5
Midgery La PR2 118 B7
Midgley St BB8 171 E4
Midhurst Dr PR8 21 B4
Midland St
12 Accrington BB5 104 C5
Nelson BB9 170 E1
Midland Terr LA5 223 D3
Midsummer St BB2 101 C5
Midville Pl 15 BB3 82 A1
Midwood Cvn Pk PR3 201 A2
Milbanke Ave PR4 114 A5
Milbeck Cl PR3 139 F5
Milbourne Rd BL9 33 A6
Milbourne St FY1 130 C5
Milbrook Cl BB11 127 B5
Milburn Ave FY5 175 F5
Mildred Cl FY5 176 A3
Mile End Cl BB8 194 D1
Mile End Row BB2 101 B6
Mile Rd FY6 155 A1
Miles Ave OL13 70 D8
Miles La
Appley Bridge WN6 19 E6
Shevington WN6 19 F6
Miles St PR1 117 F2
Milestone Mdw PR7 60 D4
Mile Stone Mdw PR7 60 D4
Milestone Pl LA2 237 C3
Miles Wlk PR1 117 E2
Miletas Pl FY8 90 C4
Milford Ave FY2 152 D1
Milford Cl
Catterall PR3 181 D2
Formby L37 11 C1
Milford St
Colne BB8 171 C5
6 Rochdale OL12 52 F1
Milking La BB3 82 A6
Milking Stile La LA1 214 D8
Milk St BL0 50 B5
Millar Barn La BB4 69 F8
Millar's Pace PR9 54 B5
Millbank
Fulwood PR2 117 C3
4 Preston PR1 97 B8
Mill Bank WN6 19 D7
Millbank Brow L40 25 F3
Millbank La L31, L39 5 F3
Millbrook BB12 147 E8
Mill Brook PR3 181 D3
Millbrook Cl
Oswaldtwistle BB5 103 D2
Skelmersdale WN8 17 E2
Wheelton PR6 62 A7
Millbrook Ct
Colne BB8 172 B5
West Bradford BB7 189 E5
Mill Brook Ho BB5 124 E3
Millbrook Mews 1 FY8 91 C3
Mill Brook Pl BB7 166 D1
Millbrook Row PR6 44 B1
Millbrook St BB3 81 F7
Millbrook Way PR1 96 C3
Mill Brow
Haskayne L39 14 A7
Lowgill LA2 239 B2
Mill Brow Rd BB18 197 C2
Mill Cl PR4 135 C8
Millcombe Way PR5 97 E3
Mill Cotts BB3 82 F3
Millcroft
Chorley PR7 61 A2
Fulwood PR2 117 D4
Millcroft Ave WN5 10 D5
Mill Ct PR3 140 B8
Mill Dam Cl L40 25 C2
Mill Dam La L40 16 D8
Milldyke Cl 2 FY4 110 F6
Millenium Ct FY8 110 B4
Mill Entrance BB5 124 F2
Miller Ave PR6 80 B2
Miller Cl BB5 103 C5
Miller Cres FY6 154 E1
Miller Ct
Lancaster, Haverbreaks LA1 214 E5
14 Lancaster LA1 218 D2
Miller Field PR2 116 E3
MILLER FOLD 104 B3
Miller Fold Ave BB5 104 B3
Miller Ho 4 PR1 97 A7
Miller La
Catforth PR4 135 E4
Cottam PR4 116 E5
Miller Rd PR1, PR2 118 E2
Miller's Brow PR3 207 E3
Millers Cl FY8 90 D7
Millers Ct L39 15 F5
Millersdale Cl FY5 153 E7
Millers Ford LA2 239 B8
Millersgate PR4 116 E4
Millers Nook WN8 10 B7
Miller St
4 Blackpool FY1 130 B1
11 Preston PR1 97 C8
Ramsbottom BL9 50 C2
Millers Vale 6 BB4 84 F1
Millet Terr BL9 33 E7
Millett St BL0 50 D7
Mill Field
Clayton-le-M BB5 124 F4
Parbold WN8 27 C1
Millfield Cl PR4 92 F6
Millfield High Sch FY5 153 C8
Millfield Rd
Blackpool FY4 110 F6
Chorley PR7 61 C1
Millfold OL12 71 D2
Mill Gap St 20 BB3 65 A8
MILLGATE 71 D4
Millgate BL7 47 D2
Mill Gate
Fulwood PR2 117 D3
15 Rawtenstall BB4 86 A3
Millgate Rd 18 BB4 86 A3
Millgate Terr OL12 71 E5
Mill Gdns 6 LA2 239 D8
Mill Gn BB8 171 D4
Millgreen Cl WN8 10 A7
Millham St BB1 101 E6
Mill Haven PR2 117 D3
MILLHEAD 223 D4
Mill Hey Ave FY6 153 E1
Mill Hey La L40 39 C3
MILL HILL 101 C1
Mill Hill
Oswaldtwistle BB5 103 E4
Preston PR1 96 E8
Mill Hill Bridge St BB2 101 B2
Mill Hill Cotts BL6 44 F1
Mill Hill Gr LA3 213 A2
Mill Hill La BB11 126 B3
Mill Hill St BB2 101 B2
Mill Hill Sta BB2 101 B2
Mill Ho 19 LA1 215 A8
Millholme Dr LA2 239 D7
Mill Ho Mews 17 LA1 215 A8
Mill House La
Jack Green PR6 78 F8
Longridge PR3 141 A8
Millhouse Lo PR8 21 D5
Millhouse St BL0 50 E8
Mill House View WN8 10 C7
Millington Ave FY4 110 E8
Millionaire Row L40 24 B4
Mill La
Appley Bridge WN6 19 D7
Bacup OL13 88 B3
Becconsall PR4 73 F2
Blackburn BB2 101 E4
Bolton Green PR7 42 A8
Bolton-le-S LA5 221 A6
Burscough L40 25 E4
Carnforth LA5 223 D4
Caton LA2 237 B3
Clayton Green PR6 78 C1
Coppull PR7 42 E2
Darwen BB3 64 A5
Earby BB18 197 D2
Elswick PR4 156 B1
Fleetwood FY7 199 B4
Fulwood PR2 117 C4
Mill La *continued*
Gisburn BB7 231 B4
Goosnargh PR3 138 E6
Great Harwood BB6 125 A6
Halton LA2 219 D6
Hambleton FY6 177 E1
Haskayne L39 14 F1
Hesketh Lane PR3 162 C8
Heskin Green PR7 42 A2
Horwich BL6 32 D4
Leyland, Earnshaw Bridge PR26 76 E3
Leyland PR25 59 D8
Low Bentham LA2 239 C7
Parbold WN8 27 C1
Skelmersdale, Elmers Green WN8 18 F1
Skelmersdale, Pennylands WN8 17 F2
Skelmersdale, Tawd Valley Park WN8 18 A3
Southport PR9 54 A1
Staining FY3 131 D5
Stalmine FY6 177 D7
Up Holland WN8 10 A8
Waddington BB7 189 A8
Walton-le-D PR5 97 D5
Warton PR4 92 F6
Wrea Green PR4 113 A3
Mill Lane Appartments LA2 219 D6
Mill Lane Cres PR9 54 A1
Mill Lane Ind Est BB7 231 B3
Mill Leat Cl WN8 27 C2
Mill Leat Mews WN8 27 C2
Mill Lo PR4 75 F8
Mill Nook OL12 52 F3
Millom Ave FY2 152 D4
Millom Cl FY7 175 C8
Millrace Ct 5 LA1 218 D2
Millrace The LA1 218 D1
Mill Rd
Orrell WN5 10 D5
Southport PR8 21 D5
Millrose Cl WN8 17 F2
Mill Row BB4 85 F5
Mills St OL12 71 D1
Mill St
Accrington BB5 104 F1
Adlington PR6 31 B8
Bacup OL13 87 F3
Barnoldswick BB18 196 A2
Barrowford BB9 170 D4
Church BB5 103 F6
Clayton-le-M BB5 124 F2
4 Coppull PR7 42 E1
Great Harwood BB6 124 C5
Haslingden BB4 85 B5
Kirkham PR4 114 A5
Lancaster LA1 215 A8
Leyland PR25 77 B3
Leyland, Seven Stars PR25 59 D8
Ormskirk L39 15 F5
Oswaldtwistle BB5 103 D3
Padiham BB12 126 C8
Preesall FY6 200 B3
Preston PR1 96 D8
Ramsbottom BL0 50 A4
Southport PR8 35 C6
West Bradford BB7 189 E5
Wheelton PR6 62 A7
Millstone Ct 3 LA1 218 D3
Mill The
Leyland PR26 76 D2
Preston PR1 96 F8
Millthorne Ave BB7 166 D7
Millthorne Ho 9 BB7 166 D8
Mill View PR4 93 B7
Mill View Ct L39 7 E7
Mill View La BL6 32 E4
Millwood Cl BB2 101 A1
Mill Wood Cl PR6 79 C3
Millwood Glade PR7 61 B1
Millwood Rd PR5 97 B3
Mill Yd BL9 33 A3
Milman Cl L39 15 D3
Milner Rd
Darwen BB3 81 E4
Lytham St Anne's FY8 90 E4
Milner St
Burnley BB10 128 A8
Preston PR1 118 A2
Whitworth OL12 52 C8
Milne St BL0 68 C5
MILNSHAW 104 A6
Milnshaw Gdns BB5 104 B7
Milnshaw La BB5 104 B6
Milnthorpe Ave FY5 175 D5
Milton Ave
Blackpool FY3 130 F5
Clitheroe BB7 189 E1
2 Thornton FY5 176 A3
Milton Cl
Bamber Bridge PR5 97 D2
Darwen BB3 82 C1
Great Harwood BB6 124 B4
Haslingden BB4 68 A7
Milton Cres
Kirkham PR4 114 A5
Poulton-le-F FY6 131 D8
Milton Ct PR7 42 E1
Milton Dr L39 16 A4
Milton Gr
Barnoldswick BB18 196 A3
Longshaw WN5 10 D1
Orrell WN5 10 F6
Milton Pl FY2 152 F6
Milton Rd
Colne BB8 171 D5
Coppull PR7 29 E8
Milton St
3 Barrowford BB9 170 D4
1 Blackburn BB1 102 A5
3 Brierfield BB9 148 B5
Burnley, Harle Syke BB10 148 F3
Clayton-le-M BB5 124 F3
Fleetwood FY7 199 A4
Nelson BB9 170 D1
Oswaldtwistle BB5 103 E4
Padiham BB12 126 E7
Ramsbottom BL0 50 B6
Southport PR9 36 A7
Milton Terr PR6 61 D2
Milton Way L31 5 B1
Mimosa Cl PR7 61 A3
Mimosa Rd PR2 118 E2
Mincing La BB2 101 E4
Minden Rd PR4 132 E5
Minehead Ave BB10 148 D2
Minerva Rd LA1 214 C8
Minnie St OL12 71 D2
Minnie Terr BB2 101 C6
Minor St 15 BB4 86 A7
Minstead Ave L33 1 A2
Minster Cres BB3 65 C8
Minster Dr LA3 217 B2
Minster Pk PR4 116 E5
Minstrel Wlk FY6 153 D4
Mint Ave BB9 170 D4
Mintholme Ave PR5 98 E2
Mintor Rd L33 1 A2
Mint St BL0 68 C2
Mire Ash Brow BB2 121 D1
Mire Ridge BB8 172 A3
Mirfield Gr 11 FY4 130 D1
Miry La WN8 27 D2
Mission Cotts L40 26 B8
Mitcham Rd FY4 111 B8
Mitchell St
Burnley BB12 127 C6
Clitheroe BB7 166 D7
4 Colne BB8 171 D5
Mitella St BB10 128 C5
Mitre St BB11 127 E6
Mitten's La L37 12 B3
Mitton Ave
Barrowford BB9 170 F6
Rawtenstall BB4 86 A4
Mitton Cl
Blackburn BB2 101 C1
Heywood OL10 33 F2
Mitton Dr PR2 119 A3
Mitton Gr BB10 128 D5
Mitton Hos BB9 170 F6
Mitton Rd
Great Mitton BB7 165 F2
Whalley BB7 144 B7
Mitton St BB1 101 F7
Mizpah St BB10 128 C5
Mizzy Rd OL12 52 F1
Moira Cres PR2 118 F4
Moleside Cl BB5 104 D6
Mollington Rd BB2 101 B7
Molly Wood La BB11 126 F5
Molyneaux FY8 90 E3
Molyneux Ct 21 PR1 97 A8
Molyneux Dr FY4 110 D7
Molyneux Pl FY8 91 A4
Molyneux Rd L39 6 C7
Mona Pl PR1 96 E8
Monarch Cres FY8 90 B8
Monarch St BB5 103 E4
Mona Rd BB2 101 E1
Moneyclose Gr LA3 212 D5
Money Close La LA3 212 D4
Monk Hall St BB10 128 A7
Monkroyd Ave BB18 196 A2
Monkroyd Rd BB8 172 F7
Monks Carr La L37, L38 4 A6
Monks Cl L37 12 A1
Monks Dr
Formby L37 12 A1
Longridge PR3 140 A6
Withnell PR6 80 A1
Monks Gate FY8 90 D7
Monks La L40 25 D7
Monk's La FY6 200 A1
Monk St
Accrington BB5 104 A6
2 Clitheroe BB7 166 D7
Monkswell Ave LA5 221 A5
Monkswell Dr LA5 221 A5
Monks Wlk PR1 96 C6
Monkswood Ave LA4 217 E5
Monmouth Ct PR2 116 F3
Monmouth Rd BB1 102 C5
Monmouth St
5 Burnley BB12 127 D6
Colne BB8 172 A5
Monomer Rd FY5 176 C4
Monroe Dr 3 FY7 198 D3
Montague Cl
Blackburn BB2 101 D4
Normoss FY3 131 A8
Montague Rd BB11 127 E5
Montague St
Blackburn BB2 101 D5
Blackpool FY4 110 B8
5 Brierfield BB9 148 B5
4 Clitheroe BB7 166 D8
Colne BB8 171 E6
Montagu Mews L37 11 E5
Montagu Rd L37 11 E5
Montcliffe Rd PR6 61 E1
Monteagle Dr LA2 238 B7
Monteagle Sq LA2 238 B7
Montfield Hey BB9 148 A5
Montford Ct BB12 147 F6
Montford Rd BB9 147 F6
Montgomery Ave PR9 36 B6
Montgomery Cl BB5 104 E2
Montgomery Gr BB12 127 C7
Montgomery High Sch FY2 152 D5
Montgomery St 7 PR5 77 F8
Monthall Rise LA1 218 F1
Montjoly St PR1 97 C7
Monton Rd BB3 81 E4
Montpelier Ave FY2 152 C5
Montreal Ave FY1 130 D4
Montreal Rd BB2 101 C8
Montrose Ave
Blackpool FY1 130 C3
Ramsbottom BL0 50 A2
Montrose Cl PR6 43 E6
Montrose Cres LA3 212 E7
Montrose Dr PR9 53 F1
Montrose St
Blackburn BB2 101 C3
Brierfield BB9 148 B6
Burnley BB11 127 F4
Montrose Terr 17 BB18 196 B2
MONUBENT 230 E6
Moody La L40 40 E1
Moody St WN6 29 E1
Moon Ave 7 FY1 130 B2
Moon Bay Wharf LA3 212 D6
Moons Acre LA2 239 D8
Moon St PR5 77 E8
Moor Ave
Appley Bridge WN6 19 E8
Higher Penwortham PR1 96 A4
Moorbottom Rd BL8 49 E5
Moorbrook Sch PR2 117 E3
Moorbrook St PR1 117 E1
Moor Cl
Darwen BB3 65 D8
Lancaster LA1 215 A8
Southport PR8 21 D2
Moor Close La LA6 240 B1
Moorcroft
Blackburn BB3 82 A6
Broughton PR3 137 B2
Edenfield BL0 68 D2
Moorcroft Cres PR2 118 D3
Moorcroft Ho WN8 27 A1
Moor Dr WN8 9 D7
Moor Edge BB7 144 B6
Moore Dr BB12 146 F5
Moorend BB7 166 F7
MOOR END 177 D6
Moor End Prim Sch BB5 103 D4
Moores La WN6 29 D2
Moore St
Blackpool FY4 130 B1
Colne BB8 171 C5
Nelson BB9 148 F7
Padiham BB12 126 F7
Preston PR1 97 C7
Moore Tree Dr FY4 111 A8
Moorfield BL7 48 D6
Moor Field
New Longton PR4 76 A7
Whalley BB7 144 B6
Moorfield Ave
Accrington, Hillock Vale BB5 104 F8
Blackburn BB1 122 E3
Blackpool FY3 130 E6
Carleton FY6 153 B4
Moorfield Cl
Clayton-le-M BB5 125 B3
Fulwood PR2 117 E8
Preston PR1 96 A2
Moorfield Dr
Clayton-le-M BB5 125 B3
Fulwood PR2 118 E3
Lytham St Anne's FY8 91 A4
Moorfield Ind Est BB5 125 B3
Moorfield La L40 24 C3
Moorfield Pl 3 OL12 52 F1
Moorfield Rd PR25 59 C8
Moorfields
Blackpool FY2 152 F4
Chorley PR6 61 E1
Moorfields Ave PR2 117 E8
Moorfield Sch PR1 118 A3
Moorfield Way BB5 125 B3
MOORGATE 101 D1
Moorgate
Accrington BB5 104 B2
Blackpool FY4 110 F6
Bury BL9 33 A3
Fulwood PR2 117 F5
Ormskirk L39 15 E4
Moor Gate 14 LA1 215 A8
Moorgate Gdns 2 BB2 101 C1
Moorgate La BB6 143 A5
Moorgate Rd BB18 196 A1
Moorgate Ret Pk 13 BL9 33 A3
Moorgate St BB2 101 C1
Moor Hall La PR4 114 F4
Moor Hall St PR1 117 E2
Moorhead Gdns PR4 92 E7
Moorhead High Sch BB5 104 A7
Moorhead St 2 BB8 171 C5
Moorhen Pl 11 FY5 175 F1

Moor Hey Cotts PR26 58 A6
Moorhey Cres
Higher Penwortham PR1 96 B5
Walton Summit PR5 78 A8
Moorhey Dr PR1 96 B5
Moorhouse Ave BB5 104 A4
Moorhouse Cl BB5 104 A4
Moorhouses L38 2 F3
Moorhouse St
Accrington BB5 104 A4
1 Blackpool FY1 130 B7
Burnley BB11 127 C5
Moorings The
Burnley BB12 127 E7
4 Chorley PR6 43 E8
Hest Bank LA2 220 D1
Maghull L31 5 B4
Moor La
Billington BB6, BB7 144 B2
Butt Yeats LA2 238 C5
Clitheroe BB7 166 E8
Darwen BB3 82 B3
Haslingden BB4 84 F6
Hutton PR4 95 D1
Ince Blundell L38, L23 3 E2
Lancaster LA1 215 A8
Langho BB6 123 E8
Maghull L29 4 D1
Padiham BB12 146 C1
Preston PR1 117 F1
Salterforth BB18 194 C6
Southport PR8 21 C2
Waddington BB7 229 D2
West Bradford BB7 189 D7
Whalley BB7 144 B6
Wiswell BB7 144 F7
Moorland Ave
Blackburn BB2 80 D7
Clitheroe BB7 189 F3
Darwen BB3 81 D2
Earby BB18 197 C1
Fulwood PR2 118 D4
Poulton-le-F FY6 153 E4
Whitworth OL12 52 C7
Moorland Cl BB9 170 F6
Moorland Cres
Clitheroe BB7 189 F2
Fulwood PR2 118 D4
Whitworth OL12 52 C7
Moorland Dr
Brierfield BB9 148 D4
Horwich BL6 32 F3
Moorland Gate PR6 43 F6
Moorland Gdns FY6 153 E4
Moorland Rd
Blackburn BB2 81 C7
Burnley BB11 127 F3
Clitheroe BB7 189 F2
Langho BB6 143 C1
Lytham St Anne's FY8 90 A7
Poulton-le-F FY6 153 F4
Moorland Rise BB4 85 C2
MOORLANDS 215 B7
Moorlands PR1 117 E3
Moorland Sch Ltd BB7 189 E3
Moorlands Ct BB3 65 D7
Moorlands Gr LA3 216 E3
Moorland St OL12 52 E1
Moorlands Terr 6 OL13 88 A1
Moorlands The OL13 88 A8
Moorlands View BL0 68 D5
Moorland Terr OL12 52 A1
Moorland View BB9 148 E6
Moor Nook Com Prim Sch PR2 119 A3
Moor Park Ave
Blackpool FY2 152 E4
Preston PR1 118 A2
Moor Park Bsns & Ent Sch PR1 118 A2
Moor Park Prim Sch FY2 152 E3
Moor Platt Cl BL6 32 F3
Moor Rd
Barber's Moor PR26 58 D3
Chorley PR7 43 B5
Haslingden BB4 67 F5
Orrell WN5 10 E6
Ramsbottom BL8 50 A6
Rivington PR6 44 E7
Moorside
Melling LA6 241 D2
Wharles PR4 134 D3
MOOR SIDE
Broughton 136 C4
Kirkham 134 D1
Moorside Ave
Blackburn BB1 102 D4
Brierfield BB9 148 D4
Fulwood PR2 118 F3
Horwich BL6 32 C4
Moorside Cl LA6 241 D2
Moorside Com Prim Sch WN8 9 E7
Moorside Cres OL13 88 A4
Moorside Dr
Clayton-le-M BB5 125 A2
Preston PR1 96 B2
Moorside Fold PR4 75 B5
Moorside La PR4 136 C4
Moor Side La
Ramsbottom BL0 51 A7
Wiswell BB7 144 F8
Moorside Prim Sch LA1 215 B4
Moorside Rd
Caton LA2 237 D3
Edgworth BL7 66 D1
Moor St
Clayton-le-M BB5 124 F3
Kirkham PR4 114 A5
33 Lancaster LA1 214 F8
Ormskirk L39 15 F5
Moorsview BL0 50 B6
Moorthorpe Cl BB3 65 A6
Moor View
Bacup, Brandwood OL13 70 B7
Bacup, Greave OL13 88 A4
Rawtenstall BB4 69 F6
Salterforth BB18 194 E8
Moorview Cl BB10 148 E2
Moorview Ct 2 FY4 110 F7
Moorway FY6 153 F4
Moor Way BL8 49 C3
Moray Cl BL0 50 A4
MORECAMBE 216 E5
Morecambe Bay Com Prim Sch LA4 217 B5
Morecambe Bay Nature Reserve (RSPB)* LA5 220 D5
Morecambe High Sch LA4 217 C6
Morecambe Lodge Cvn Pk LA5 220 E3
Morecambe Rd
Blackburn BB2 101 F1
Lancaster LA3, LA1 218 A2
Morecambe Rd Sch LA3 217 F3
Morecambe St E 5 LA4 217 B6
Morecambe St W 2 LA4 217 B6
Morecambe Sta LA4 217 A5
Moresby Ave FY3 131 B7
Moreton Dr
Poulton-le-F FY6 153 D2
Staining FY3 131 D5
Moreton Gn LA3 212 F7
Moreton Pk BB7 144 E2
Moreton St BB5 104 B6
Morewood Dr LA6 240 C7
Morland Ave
Bamber Bridge PR5 77 A7
Kirkham PR4 113 F7
Morley Ave BB2 101 A1
Morley Cl LA1 218 C3
Morley Croft PR26 76 E3
Morley La PR3 202 A5
Morley Rd
Blackpool FY4 130 E1
Lancaster LA1 218 C3
Southport PR9 35 E8
Morley St 1 BB12 126 D8
Morningside LA1 214 E7
Mornington Ct PR1 118 F1
Mornington Rd
Adlington PR6 31 B8
Higher Penwortham PR1 96 B5
Lytham St Anne's FY8 91 E4
Preston PR1 118 F1
Southport PR9 35 C7
Morris Cl PR25 60 A8
Morris Cres PR2 118 D2
Morris Ct PR2 118 D2
Morris La L39 23 E3
Morrison St PR6 61 D2
Morris Rd
Chorley PR6 61 E1
Fulwood PR2 118 D2
Up Holland WN8 10 A7
Morse St BB10 128 D5
Morston Ave FY2 152 E1
Mortimer Gr LA3 213 A8
Mortimer Ho BL6 32 B3
Morton St 22 BB1 101 E5
Mort St BL6 32 B4
Morven Gr PR8 35 E7
Moscow Mill St BB5 103 E5
Mosedale Dr BB12 127 B8
Moseley Ave BB18 196 F1
Moseley Cl BB11 128 A2
Moseley Rd BB11 128 A3
Mosley Ave BL0 50 B2
Mosley St
Barnoldswick BB18 196 B2
Blackburn BB2 101 E2
4 Leyland PR25 77 A1
Nelson BB9 148 D8
Preston PR1 97 C8
Southport PR8 35 B4
Mosman Pl BB9 170 C3
Moss Acre Rd PR1 96 E2
Moss Ave
Orrell WN5 10 D3
Preston PR2 117 A2
Mossbank 7 BB1 102 A6
Moss Bank
Coppull PR7 42 E1
Ormskirk L39 15 D2
Moss Bank Ct L39 15 D2
Moss Bank Pl FY4 110 F8
Mossbourne Rd FY6 153 C2
MOSS BRIDGE 81 E5
Moss Bridge L40 26 C3
Moss Bridge La L40 26 C2
Moss Bridge Pk PR5 77 C8
Mossbrook Dr PR4 116 F5
Moss Cl
Chorley PR6 43 E8
6 Garstang PR3 181 B7
Moss Cl *continued*
Haslingden BB4 68 A8
Moss Cotts L40 17 A3
Mossdale 6 BB1 102 A6
Mossdale Ave PR2 118 D4
Moss Delph La L39 15 C1
Moss Dr BL6 32 F3
MOSS EDGE 179 A3
Moss Edge Cotts FY8 111 A2
Moss Edge La
Blackpool FY4 111 A3
Hale Nook FY6, PR3 178 C7
Lytham St Anne's FY8 111 B2
Moss End Way L33 1 D3
Mossfield Cl
Bamber Bridge PR5 77 B8
Bury BL9 33 B3
Mossfield Rd PR6 43 E8
Mossfields WN6 28 F6
Moss Fold Rd BB3 81 E5
Moss Gate BB1 102 B6
Mossgate Pk LA3 212 F5
Mossgate Prim Sch LA3 216 E1
Moss Gdns PR8 35 C2
Mossgiel Ave PR8 21 B5
Moss Gn L37 12 B4
Moss Hall Barns PR3 178 F3
Moss Hall La FY8 90 E7
Moss Hall Rd
Accrington BB5 104 C8
Bury BL9 33 D1
Moss Hey La PR4 56 A3
Mosshill Cl L31 5 C3
Moss House La
Fisher's Row PR3 202 A4
Great Plumpton PR4 112 C7
Much Hoole PR4 75 B2
Stalmine FY6 177 D8
Moss House Rd
Blackpool FY4 111 A6
Broughton PR4 137 B2
Moss La
Appley Bridge WN6 28 E3
Bamber Bridge PR5 77 B8
Banks PR9 55 D6
Becconsall PR4 73 C1
Bickerstaffe L39 7 F2
Blackburn BB1, BB5 102 F3
Bretherton PR26 58 C8
Burscough L40 26 A7
Catforth PR4 135 D5
Chipping PR3 186 A1
Clayton-le-W PR25 77 D2
Coppull PR7 42 E1
Croston PR26 40 A8
Duncombe PR3 158 D2
Farington PR26 76 D5
Formby L37, L39 12 E5
Garstang PR3 181 B7
Glasson LA2 209 E1
Hambleton FY6 177 D1
Hightown L38, L23 3 C2
Holme Mills LA5 240 A8
Horwich BL6 31 F2
Inskip PR4 157 B3
Kingsfold PR1 96 E1
Kirkby L33 1 B3
Leyland PR25 77 C2
Lucas Green PR6 61 D5
Maghull L31 5 E2
Maghull, Lydiate L31 5 D5
New Longton PR4 75 E7
Silverdale LA5 224 F5
Skelmersdale WN8 8 F6
Southport PR9 36 D8
St Michael's on W PR3 157 B8
Walmer Bridge PR4 75 C4
Whitworth OL12 52 B7
Wymott PR26 58 F5
Moss La E PR4 115 A8
Mosslands PR25 76 D1
Moss Lane View WN8 8 F6
Moss La W PR4 114 F7
Mosslawn Rd L32 1 A1
Moss Lea PR4 57 A7
Mosslea Dr PR3 137 B8
Moss Nook
Burscough Bridge L40 25 E6
Ormskirk L39 15 C2
Mossom La FY5 152 D7
Moss Pl LA1 218 E4
Moss Rd
Lancaster LA3 213 E7
Orrell WN5 10 D3
Southport PR8 35 C2
Moss Side
Barnoldswick BB18 196 C2
Formby L37 12 B4
MOSS SIDE
Leyland 59 B8
Lytham St Anne's 112 E1
Maghull 6 A1
Pilling 201 F5
Moss Side La
Lane Heads PR3 156 E5
Mere Brow PR4 55 F4
Stalmine FY6 177 E7
Wrea Green PR4 113 A3
Moss Side Prim Sch PR26 76 B1
Moss Side St OL12 71 E5
Moss Side Sta FY8 112 D1
Moss Side Way PR26 59 C8
Moss St
Bamber Bridge PR5 77 B8
Blackburn BB1 102 A6
7 Clitheroe BB7 166 D8
Moss St *continued*
Great Harwood BB6 124 C4
Preston PR1 96 E8
Ramsbottom BL9 50 D2
Moss Terr PR6 61 E5
Moss View
Maghull L31 5 F1
Ormskirk L39 15 E4
Mossway PR4 75 F7
Moss Way 3 FY4 110 F7
Moss Wood Cl PR7 43 A6
Moss Wood Cvn Pk PR3 203 B8
MOSSY LEA 28 F6
Mossy Lea Fold WN6 29 A3
Mossy Lea Rd WN6 28 F5
Mostyn Ave BB18 197 B1
Mostyn St BB3 81 E4
Motherwell Cres PR8 35 F3
Mottram Cl PR6 61 C5
Mottram Mews 6 BL6 32 B4
Mottram St BL6 32 B4
Moulden Brow BB2 80 B7
Moulding Cl BB2 101 B4
Mounsey Rd PR5 77 F8
Mountain Ash OL12 52 B3
Mountain Ash Cl OL12 52 B3
Mountain La 2 BB5 104 C4
Mountain Rd PR7 29 E8
Mount Ave
Lancaster LA1 218 D3
Morecambe LA4 217 F7
Rawtenstall BB4 69 F8
Mountbatten Cl PR2 96 B7
Mountbatten Rd PR7 43 B6
Mount Carmel Prep Sch L39 15 D2
Mount Carmel RC High Sch BB5 104 A4
Mount Cres
Holme Chapel BB10 108 A8
Orrell WN5 10 F6
Mountfield Ct WN5 10 F7
Mount Gdns LA4 217 E7
Mount House Cl L37 12 B5
Mount House Rd L37 12 B5
Mount La
Burnley BB10 128 F1
Holme Chapel BB10 108 A8
Todmorden OL14 109 C3
Mount Pleasant
Adlington PR6 31 A8
Arnside LA5 224 C8
16 Bacup OL13 70 C8
Blackburn BB1 101 F5
Brinscall PR6 63 A8
Chatburn BB7 190 D5
Edgworth BL7 48 D5
High Bentham LA2 239 D8
Nangreaves BL9 50 F3
Nelson BB10 149 C6
7 Preston PR1 96 F8
Rawtenstall BB4 85 E2
Sabden BB7 146 A7
Slaidburn BB7 229 B7
Sollom PR4 57 A3
Whittle-le-W PR6 61 C8
Worsthorne BB10 129 A5
Mount Pleasant La LA5 221 B5
Mount Pleasant Prim Sch BB5 124 F2
Mount Pleasant St
3 Burnley BB11 127 F5
2 Horwich BL6 32 D1
6 Oswaldtwistle BB5 103 E4
Todmorden OL14 109 A1
Mount Rd
Burnley BB11 127 F4
Fleetwood FY7 199 A5
Mount St James BB1 102 F4
Mountside Cl OL12 52 F2
Mount St
Accrington BB5 104 B4
13 Barrowford BB9 170 D3
Blackpool FY1 130 B6
Brierfield BB9 148 B5
Clayton-le-M BB5 125 A2
Fleetwood FY7 199 A4
Great Harwood BB6 124 C6
Horwich BL6 32 D2
Preston PR1 96 F7
Ramsbottom BL0 50 B6
Rawtenstall BB4 85 E2
Southport PR9 35 D7
Mount Terr BB4 86 A2
Mount The
Blackburn BB2 101 C6
1 Rawtenstall BB4 69 F7
Skelmersdale WN8 9 B8
Mount Trinity 3 BB1 101 F5
Mountwood WN8 18 A4
Mountwood Lo PR8 21 C5
Mount Zion Ct OL14 109 A1
Mowbray Ave BB2 101 F2
Mowbray Dr
Blackpool FY3 152 F1
Burton-in-K LA6 240 C7
Mowbray Pl 1 FY7 198 E4
Mowbray Rd FY7 198 E4
Mowbreck Ct PR4 114 A6
Mowbreck La PR4 114 B7
Mowbreck Park Cvn Pk PR4 114 B7
Mowbrick La LA2 220 D1
Mowgrain View 2 OL13 87 F3
MUCH HOOLE 74 D3
MUCH HOOLE MOSS HOUSES 75 A2
Muirfield PR1 96 A6
Muirfield Cl
Euxton PR7 60 D4
Fulwood PR2 117 B6
Muirfield Dr PR8 21 C4
Mulberry Ave PR1 96 A3
Mulberry Cl PR4 115 C1
Mulberry Cotts 10 LA2 211 A4
Mulberry Ct 8 BL6 32 D1
Mulberry La LA1 215 A2
Mulberry Mews
Blackpool FY2 152 F6
5 Kirkham PR4 114 B5
Mulberry St BB1 102 B5
Mulberry Wlk 3 BB1 102 B5
Mulgrave Ave PR2 117 A1
Mullion Cl PR9 54 B5
Muncaster Rd PR1 117 F2
Munro Ave WN5 10 E6
Munro Cres PR2 118 E3
Munster Ave FY2 152 D3
Murchison Gr FY5 175 E1
Murdock Ave PR2 117 D2
Murdock St BB2 101 B4
Murray Ave PR26 76 E5
Murray St
Burnley BB10 148 B1
Leyland PR25 77 B1
Preston PR1 117 E1
Musbury Cres BB4 86 A1
Musbury Mews 4 BB4 84 F1
Musbury Rd BB4 67 F7
Musbury View 2 BB4 84 F1
Musden Ave BB4 68 A7
Museum of Lancashire* PR1 97 B8
Museum St 19 BB1 101 E5
MYERSCOUGH 158 C4
Myerscough Ave
Blackpool FY4 110 F5
Lytham St Anne's FY8 89 D8
Myerscough Coll PR3 158 D5
Myerscough Hall Dr PR3 158 E5
Myerscough Planks PR3 159 A2
MYERSCOUGH SMITHY 120 E3
Myerscough Smithy Rd BB2 120 E4
Myers St
Barnoldswick BB18 196 B1
Burnley BB10 128 A8
Myndon St LA1 218 D3
Myra Ave LA4 217 C4
Myra Rd FY8 90 B4
Myrtle Ave
Blackpool FY3 130 D5
Burnley BB11 127 D4
Cleveleys FY5 175 F5
Poulton-le-F FY6 153 E5
Myrtle Bank Rd
9 Bacup OL13 87 F3
Blackburn BB2 81 C8
Myrtle Cotts 8 OL13 88 A2
Myrtle Dr PR4 114 C4
Myrtle Gdns BL9 33 B2
Myrtle Gr
1 Barnoldswick BB18 196 C2
Burnley BB10 128 F4
Haslingden BB4 85 A1
Morecambe LA3 216 F3
Southport PR9 35 E7
Myrtle Grove Mill BB4 86 D1
Myrtle St N BL9 33 B2
Myrtle St S 8 BL9 33 B2
Mystic Mews 9 L39 15 E5
MYTHOP 132 A3
Mythop Ave FY8 91 C4
Mythop Cl 1 FY8 91 C4
Mythop Ct FY4 131 D1
Mythop Pl PR2 116 F1
Mythop Rd
Lytham St Anne's FY8 91 C4
Weeton FY4, PR4 132 C2
Mythop Village FY4 131 F2
Mytton St BB12 126 D8
Mytton View BB7 166 D7

## N

Naarian Ct BB1 101 F7
Nabbs Fold BL8 49 F3
Nabbs Way BL8 50 A1
Nab La
Blackburn BB2 101 D5
Oswaldtwistle BB5 103 B4
Nab Rd PR6 61 E1
NAB'S HEAD 99 E7
Nab's Head La PR5 99 E8
Naburn Dr WN5 10 E5
Nab View BB7 144 A4
Nab Wood Dr PR7 43 A6
Nailers Gn BL8 49 F1
Nairn Ave WN8 18 B5
Nairn Cl
Blackpool FY4 111 A7
Standish WN6 29 D1
Nairne St BB11 127 D5
Nancy St BB3 82 B1
NANGREAVES 50 F2

Nansen Rd
Blackburn BB2 101 B3
Fleetwood FY7 199 A3
Nantwich Ave OL12 52 F3
Napier Ave
Blackpool FY4 110 B6
Tarleton PR4 56 F8
Napier Cl FY8 110 E1
Napier St
6 Accrington BB5 104 C5
Nelson BB9 148 E7
Napier Terr PR8 35 A5
Naples Rd BB3 82 C1
NAPPA 231 E8
Naptha La PR4 76 C6
Narcissus Ave BB4 68 A8
Nares Rd BB2 101 B3
Nares St PR2 117 C1
Narrow Croft Rd L39 15 B1
Narrowgates Cotts BB12 169 C5
Narrow La
Leyland PR5 75 F2
Ormskirk L39 15 B1
Narrow Lane (Clieves Hills) L39 14 E6
Narrow Moss La L39, L40 15 E8
Narvik Ave BB11 127 B4
Nasmyth St BL6 32 C3
NATEBY 180 D6
Nateby Ave FY4 110 E5
Nateby Cl
Longridge PR3 139 F8
Lytham St Anne's FY8 90 B7
Nateby Crossing La PR3 181 A8
Nateby Ct
2 Blackpool FY4 110 B6
Garstang PR3 181 A7
Nateby Hall La PR3 203 F1
Nateby Pl PR2 116 F1
Nateby Prim Sch PR3 180 C6
National Football Mus The★ PR1 118 B2
Nave Cl BB3 82 C1
Navena Ave FY7 198 E2
Navigation Bsns Village PR2 96 A8
Navigation Ho 6 BB1 101 F3
Navigation Way
Blackburn BB1 101 F3
1 Fleetwood FY7 199 A3
Preston PR2 96 A7
Naylorfarm Ave WN6 19 F5
Naylor's Terr BL7 46 C5
Naze Ct
Freckleton PR4 93 B6
4 Newchurch BB4 86 E1
Naze La PR4 93 B6
Naze La E PR4 93 C5
Naze Lane Ind Est PR4 93 C4
Naze Rd BB4 86 E1
Naze View Ave 4 BB4 86 F2
Neales Fold PR9 54 D5
Neapsands Cl PR2 118 D5
Neargates PR7 42 D3
Near Mdw PR6 78 C3
Neath Cl
Bamber Bridge PR5 97 E3
Blackburn BB1 101 E7
Neddy Hill LA6 240 B7
Neddy La BB7 144 A4
Nedens Gr L31 5 C3
Nedens La L31 5 C3
Ned's La
Smallwood Hey PR3 201 A5
Stalmine FY6 177 D5
Needham Ave LA4 217 A3
Needham Rise 1 LA4 217 A3
Needham Way WN8 18 B5
Needless Hall La BD23 231 E7
Nell Carrs BL0 50 E8
Nell La PR5 77 E4
Nell's La L39 5 F5
NELSON 148 E8
Nelson Ave PR25 77 B1
Nelson & Colne Coll
Barrowford BB9 170 D2
Colne BB8 171 A5
Nelson Court Bsns Ctr 2 PR2 95 F8
Nelson Cres PR2 116 D2
Nelson Ct
Burton in L LA6 242 C3
Fleetwood FY7 198 F3
Southport PR8 34 F4
Nelson Dr PR2 116 D2
Nelson Gdns PR4 135 C8
Nelson Rd
2 Blackpool FY1 130 B2
Burnley BB10 149 A4
Chorley PR7 43 C7
Fleetwood FY7 198 F3
Nelson Sq BB11 127 F5
Nelson St
Accrington BB5 104 C5
3 Bamber Bridge PR5 77 E8
Britannia OL13 71 C8
Clitheroe BB7 166 B8
7 Colne BB8 171 D5
1 Darwen BB3 81 F2
Great Harwood BB6 124 D6
Horwich BL6 32 D3
7 Kirkham PR4 113 F5
Nelson St *continued*
Lancaster LA1 214 F8
Lytham St Anne's FY8 91 D3
8 Morecambe LA4 217 A5
Southport PR8 35 A6
Nelson Sta BB9 148 E8
Nelson Terr
Church BB5 103 F6
Preston PR1 96 D8
Nelson Way PR2 95 E8
Nene Cl PR25 60 B7
Neps La BB7 231 C6
Neptune Ct FY4 111 D6
Neptune St BB11 127 F6
Neptune Way BB3 82 B6
Nesswood Ave FY4 110 E6
Neston St PR1 97 E8
Nether Beck LA6 240 A2
NETHER BURROW 241 E6
Netherby St BB11 127 E4
Netherfield Cl BB12 127 D7
Netherfield Gdns 9 BB9 148 E8
Netherfield Rd BB9 148 E8
Netherheys Cl BB8 171 B5
NETHER KELLET 221 F5
Nether Kellet Com Prim Sch LA6 221 E4
Nether Kellet Rd LA6 237 B8
Netherlands Rd LA4 217 C4
Netherley Rd PR7 29 E8
Netherton Ho 18 BB6 124 C5
NETHERTOWN 144 A6
Nethertown Cl BB7 144 B6
Nether View LA2 241 E1
Netherwood Gdns BB6 143 B5
Netherwood Rd BB10 128 D7
Netherwood St BB10 148 E2
Nethway Ave FY3 130 F6
Netley Ave OL12 52 F3
Network 65 Bsns Pk BB11 126 F4
Neverstitch Cl WN8 17 F2
Neverstitch Rd WN8 17 D2
Nevett St PR1 97 D8
Neville Ave FY5 175 E1
Neville Dr FY5 153 B8
Neville St PR3 140 A7
Nevill St PR8 35 B7
Nevy Fold Ave BL6 32 F3
New Acres
Carnforth LA5 223 F2
Newburgh WN8 27 A1
Newark Pl
Fulwood PR2 117 D8
4 Preston PR2 116 E2
Newark Rd OL12 52 F3
Newark Sq OL12 52 F3
Newark St BB5 103 F5
Newarth La PR4 73 E3
New Bank Rd BB2 101 B6
New Barn BB4 68 B6
New Barn Ct BB1 101 F2
New Barn La BB4 69 A8
New Bath St BB8 171 E6
Newbeck Cl BL6 32 D1
Newbigging Ave 5 BB4 86 F2
New Bonny St FY1 130 B4
NEWBRIDGE 170 C2
Newbridge Farm L33 1 E7
New Briggs Fold BL7 47 E2
New Brown St 17 BB9 170 D1
New Brunswick St BL6 32 B3
NEWBURGH 27 A2
Newburgh CE Prim Sch WN8 27 A1
Newburn Cl WN8 18 B5
Newbury Ave 3 FY4 110 D8
Newbury Cl PR2 117 C8
New Bury Cl BB5 103 C3
Newbury Gn PR2 117 C8
Newbury Rd
Lytham St Anne's FY8 90 A4
Skelmersdale WN8 18 B5
NEWBY 192 B8
Newby Ave
Fleetwood FY7 198 D1
Poulton-le-F FY6 153 D1
Newby Back La BB7 231 A1
Newby Cl
Burnley BB11 127 E2
Southport PR8 21 B3
Newby Ct L37 11 F3
Newby Dr
Clayton-le-W PR25 77 E2
Lancaster LA1 218 D3
Skelmersdale WN8 18 B5
Newby La BB7 192 B8
Newby Pl
Blackpool FY4 131 B1
Fulwood PR2 118 D4
Newby Rd 7 BB5 104 E8
New Carr La L31 4 E7
Newcastle Ave
Blackpool FY3 130 D4
Cleveleys FY5 175 F4
Newcastle St BB2 101 C3
New Century Apartments BL0 50 C7
New Chapel La BL6 32 F2
New Chapel St BB2 101 B2
NEWCHURCH 86 F1
Newchurch Cl BB2 101 F2
New Church Cl 14 BB5 124 F3
New Church Ho 6 FY1 130 C4
NEWCHURCH IN PENDLE 169 C3
New Church Mews 5 BB10 148 B1
Newchurch Old Rd OL13 87 E1
Newchurch Rd
Bacup OL13 70 C8
Rawtenstall BB4 86 C2
New Cock Yd 25 PR1 97 A7
Newcombe Rd BL0 50 B2
New Court Dr BL7 47 E3
New Court Way L39 15 F5
Newcroft LA5 223 E6
New Cswy L37, L38 3 B8
New Cut Cl PR8 22 A8
New Cut La L39, PR8 22 D6
New England Cvn Pk LA6 240 B3
Newfield Ct FY8 89 F6
Newfield Dr
Blackburn BB2 82 A8
Nelson BB9 148 E8
Newfield Rd PR5 78 A7
Newfield Sch BB1 102 C2
New Fold WN5 10 C4
New Foul La PR8 36 A4
New Garden Fields BB4 87 A7
New Garden St 1 BB2 101 E3
NEWGATE 10 A6
Newgate
Fulwood PR2 117 E4
Morecambe LA3 217 E2
NEW GATE 76 C8
Newgate Ave WN6 19 E8
Newgate La PR4 76 C8
Newgate Rd WN8 9 F7
New Ground Ct BB10 148 C3
New Hague BB18 194 F3
New Hall Ave FY4 111 B5
New Hall Ave N FY4 111 B6
New Hall Dr PR8 36 C1
NEW HALL HEY 85 F1
New Hall Hey Bsns Pk BB4 85 F1
New Hall Hey Rd BB4 85 F1
New Hall La PR1 97 C8
New Hall Rd BL9 33 E4
New Hall St BB10, BB12 148 A1
New Hampshire Ct FY8 90 D7
Newhaven Dr PR3 181 D2
New Hey La PR4 114 E5
Newholme Cvn Pk FY3 131 C2
New House La PR3 203 F3
Newhouse Rd
Accrington BB5 125 D1
Blackpool FY4 130 F2
New House St BB8 171 E5
Newington Ave BB1 122 F3
New Inn Yd 13 LA4 217 B6
New La
Burscough Bridge L40 25 B6
Burton-in-K LA6 240 B7
Duncombe PR3 158 F8
Eagland Hill PR3 179 D7
Great Mitton BB7 165 E6
Haskayne L39 13 E3
Middleforth Green PR1 96 E3
Ormskirk L39 15 E2
Oswaldtwistle BB5 103 C2
Smallwood Hey PR3 201 B2
Southport PR9 54 E3
Tarleton PR4 56 D6
Thornton FY5 153 C7
Ulnes Walton PR7 59 A1
NEWLANDS 215 C5
Newlands PR7 41 C6
Newlands Ave
Blackpool FY3 130 F2
Burscough L40 25 F4
Clitheroe BB7 166 C7
Higher Penwortham PR1 96 B5
Lancaster LA1 215 B5
Rochdale OL12 52 F3
Newlands Cl
5 Blackburn BB2 80 E8
Rochdale OL12 52 F3
Newlands Rd
Lancaster LA1 215 C5
Lytham St Anne's FY8 90 C5
Morecambe LA4 217 C4
Quernmore LA1 215 E6
Newlands Way FY6 153 C1
NEW LANE 25 B6
New Lane Head PR26 59 A2
New Lane Pace PR9 55 B8
New Lane Sta L40 25 B7
New Line OL13 71 B8
New Line Ind Est OL13 71 A8
New Links Ave PR2 117 A6
NEW LONGTON 75 F8
New Longton All Saints CE Prim Sch PR4 75 F7
Newlyn Ave
Blackpool FY4 110 E5
Maghull L31 5 E1
Newlyn Ct FY4 110 E5
Newlyn Dr WN8 9 D7
Newlyn Pl PR2 116 F5
Newman Gr FY5 175 E5
Newman Rd 2 FY1 130 D8
Newman St BB10 148 B1
Newmarket Ave LA1 215 B3
Newmarket St LA4 217 E7
New Market St
15 Blackburn BB1 101 E5
Chorley PR7 43 C8
Clitheroe BB7 166 E8
Colne BB8 171 D5
New Market The FY1 130 B1
New Meadow Cl BB1 82 A8
New Meadow La L37 3 F8
New Miles La WN6 19 F5
New Mill Ind Est PR5 77 F7
New Mill St
Blackburn BB1 101 F6
Eccleston PR7 41 C6
New Moss La PR6 61 C5
New Oxford St BB8 171 E6
New Palace Ct BB12 127 B7
New Park St 2 BB2 101 D5
New Pastures 4 PR5 77 C8
New Plough Yd BB6 124 D5
Newport Ct PR2 116 F3
Newport St BB9 170 E1
New Quay Rd LA1 214 B8
New Rd
Adlington PR6 31 D8
Bamber Bridge PR5 97 B1
Blackpool FY8 110 B4
Burnley BB11 128 B2
Coppull PR7 42 F3
Croston PR26 40 B7
Earby BB18 197 B2
Formby L37 12 A5
Ingleton LA6 242 F4
Lancaster LA1 214 F8
Newchurch BB4 86 F2
Rufford L40 39 B3
Silverdale LA5 224 F1
Staynall FY6 177 B4
Thornton FY5 153 C7
Warton LA5 223 A6
Whitworth OL12 71 B1
New Rough Hey PR2 116 F6
New Row
Altham BB5 125 E6
Trawden BB8 172 C4
New Row Cotts PR3 163 D1
New Scotland Rd BB9 170 E1
NEWSHAM 137 A5
Newsham Hall La PR4 136 F3
Newsham Pl LA1 215 A5
Newsham Rd LA1 215 A5
Newsham St 1 PR2 117 D1
NEWSHOLME 231 D6
News La WA11 8 F2
Newsome St 10 PR25 77 A1
New South Prom FY4 110 A6
New St
Blackrod BL6 31 D2
Brinscall PR6 62 F8
2 Burnley BB12 126 B8
Carnforth LA5 223 D2
Caton LA2 237 D3
Colne BB8 171 B3
Eccleston PR7 41 C6
Halsall L39 14 B8
Halton LA2 219 C6
14 Haslingden BB4 85 B3
Lancaster LA1 214 F8
Mawdesley L40 40 C2
4 Morecambe LA4 217 A5
Nelson BB9 170 F1
Rochdale OL12 52 E2
Newstead Dr WN8 18 B5
Newstet Rd L33 1 C2
New Taylor Fold BB10 148 F3
Newthorn BB5 104 A1
NEWTON
Blackpool 131 C6
Lancaster 218 E2
Slaidburn 229 A5
Whittington 241 C5
Newton Ave
Poulton-le-F FY6 153 C2
Preston PR1 98 A8
Newton Bluecoat CE Prim Sch PR4 115 A2
Newton Cl
Freckleton PR4 93 C7
Leyland PR26 59 B8
Newton Ct
Blackpool FY3 130 E5
2 Preston PR2 117 B1
Newton Dr
Accrington BB5 104 D3
Blackpool FY3 130 E5
Holme Chapel BB10 108 A7
Ramsbottom BL8 50 A1
Skelmersdale WN8 18 B5
Newton Dr E FY3 131 B7
NEWTON FELLS 229 C3
Newton Gr FY5 153 D7
Newton Hall Holiday Ctr FY3 131 C6
Newton Ho PR1 97 A8
Newton Pl FY3 131 A7
Newton Rd
Lytham St Anne's FY8 90 A7
Preston PR2 117 B2
Newton St
Blackburn BB1 102 B5
Burnley BB12 127 C7
Clitheroe BB7 166 D7
Darwen BB3 82 B2
Oswaldtwistle BB5 103 C5
2 Preston PR1 97 B8
Southport PR9 36 A7
Newton Terr LA1 218 E3
NEWTON-WITH-SCALES 114 F2
Newtown BB18 196 B2
NEW TOWN 140 A6
Newtown St BB8 171 E5
New Way
Royal Oak L39 7 C2
Whitworth OL12 71 C1
New Wellington Cl BB2 101 C1
New Wellington Gdns BB2 101 C1
New Wellington St BB2 101 C1
Nib La PR1 76 E8
Nicholas St
Burnley BB11 128 A5
Burnley, Harle Syke BB10 148 E3
3 Colne BB8 171 C4
Darwen BB3 81 F1
Nicholl St 1 BB10 128 A8
Nicholson Cres LA4 217 D5
Nichol St PR7 61 C1
Nickey La BB2 121 F2
Nick Hilton's Brow PR6 44 D3
Nick Hilton's La PR6 44 D3
Nickleton Brow PR6 44 C2
Nicksons La FY6 200 B4
Nickson's Weind PR3 181 C7
Nicola Cl OL13 88 A3
Nicoll Ct FY8 89 D7
Nightfield La BB2 120 F6
Nightingale Cl
Blackburn BB1 102 B1
Whalley BB7 144 A7
Nightingale Cres 4 BB11 127 C5
Nightingale Dr FY6 153 B2
Nightingale Rd BL6 31 C3
Nightingale St 2 PR6 31 A8
Nightingale Way
Catterall PR3 181 D3
Chorley PR7 42 F5
Nile Cl PR2 95 E8
Nile St
5 Lancaster LA1 214 F8
12 Nelson BB9 170 D1
Preston PR1 97 A7
Nimes St PR1 97 D8
Nine Elms PR2 117 C6
Nineteen Acre La LA5 225 F4
Nineveh St 12 BB8 171 E5
Nipe La WN8 9 B5
Nithside FY4 131 C1
Niton Cl BB4 85 C1
Nixon La PR26 59 A8
Nixons Ct PR26 58 F8
Nixons La WN8 9 D7
Nixon's La PR8 21 E7
Noble St
15 Darwen BB3 65 A8
Great Harwood BB6 124 C4
Rishton BB1 124 B1
Noblett Ct 9 FY7 198 F2
Noblett St BB1 101 F5
Noel Gate L39 15 B1
Noel Jones Ct FY8 89 E7
Noel Rd LA1 218 C3
Noel Sq PR2 118 E1
Noggarth Rd BB12 169 F2
NOG TOW 116 F7
Nolan St PR8 35 C5
NOOK 181 B3
Nook Cotts PR3 180 C6
Nook Cres PR2 139 C1
Nook Croft BB18 197 C2
Nookdales Cotts LA6 242 F1
Nook Farm Ave OL12 52 F3
Nookfield PR26 76 A1
Nook Field PR3 138 D6
Nookfield Cl FY8 91 A4
Nook Glade PR2 139 C1
Nook La
Bamber Bridge PR5 77 D6
Blackburn BB2 100 F1
Churchtown PR3 181 A3
Mawdesley L40 40 E5
Oswaldtwistle BB5 103 B2
NOOKLANDS 117 D4
Nooklands PR2 117 E4
Nook Terr
Blackburn BB2 101 A1
1 Rochdale OL12 52 F3
Nook The
Appley Bridge WN6 19 E7
Bolton-le-S LA5 221 A4
Staining FY3 131 D5
Noon Sun St OL12 52 F1
Noor St PR1 118 A1
Nora St BB9 170 D3
NORBRECK 152 B6
Norbreck Cl BB2 81 F8
Norbreck Ct FY5 152 C6
Norbreck Dr PR2 116 E1
Norbreck Prim Sch FY5 152 D8
Norbreck Rd FY5 152 C7
Norburn Cres L37 11 F2
Norbury Cl PR9 54 C5
Norcliffe Rd FY2 152 C5
Norcote Lo L37 11 E4
NORCROSS 153 A7
Norcross Brow PR6 63 B8
Norcross La FY5 153 A7
Norcross Pl PR2 116 F1
NORDEN 124 A2
Norden Ct BB6 124 E5
Norden Ct BB1 124 B1

**Norden High Sch & Sports Coll** BB1 . . . 124 A2
**Norden View** BB1 . . . 124 A2
**Norfield** L39 . . . 15 F5
**Norfolk Ave**
Blackpool FY2 . . . 152 B3
Burnley BB12 . . . 127 B7
Cleveleys FY5 . . . 175 E3
Morecambe LA3 . . . 216 E2
Padiham BB12 . . . 126 D6
**Norfolk Cl**
7 Clayton-le-M BB5 . . . 124 F3
Leyland PR25 . . . 59 E7
**Norfolk Gr**
Accrington BB5 . . . 104 A7
Southport PR8 . . . 34 F1
**Norfolk Rd**
Bamber Bridge PR5 . . . 97 D4
Blackpool FY3 . . . 131 A2
Longshaw WN5 . . . 10 E1
Lytham St Anne's FY8 . . . 91 C5
Preston PR1 . . . 118 A1
Southport PR8 . . . 34 F1
**Norfolk St**
Accrington BB5 . . . 104 D7
Blackburn BB2 . . . 101 C2
Colne BB8 . . . 171 E5
Darwen BB3 . . . 82 B1
Lancaster LA1 . . . 218 D2
Nelson BB9 . . . 170 D1
Rishton BB1 . . . 124 A1
**Norham Cl** BB12 . . . 127 E7
**Norkeed Rd** FY5 . . . 152 C7
**Norland Dr** LA3 . . . 212 F8
**Norman Cl** FY5 . . . 175 F1
**Normandie Ave** FY2 . . . 152 D3
**Normandy Rd** PR4 . . . 137 B3
**Normanhurst** L39 . . . 16 A4
**Norman Rd** BB5 . . . 103 C5
**Norman St**
Blackburn BB2 . . . 101 C3
Burnley BB10 . . . 128 A7
Bury BL9 . . . 33 B4
**Normington Cl** L31 . . . 5 C4
**NORMOSS** . . . 131 B7
**Normoss Ave** FY3 . . . 131 A7
**Normoss Rd** FY3 . . . 131 C7
**Norris House Dr** L39 . . . 6 C8
**Norris St**
3 Chorley PR7 . . . 43 C6
Darwen BB3 . . . 82 B1
Fulwood PR2 . . . 117 D3
Preston PR1 . . . 117 E2
**Norris Way** L37 . . . 12 B3
**Norse Cotts** PR26 . . . 57 E6
**North Albert St** 12 FY7 . . . 199 B5
**North Albion St** FY7 . . . 199 A4
**Northall** PR4 . . . 74 E2
**Northam Cl**
Southport PR9 . . . 54 A5
Standish WN6 . . . 29 D1
**North Ave**
Barnoldswick BB18 . . . 196 B2
Blackpool FY3 . . . 130 D7
Ramsbottom BL8 . . . 49 F1
**North Bank Ave** BB1 . . . 122 E1
**Northbrook Gdns** PR25 . . . 76 E1
**Northbrook Prim Sch** PR25 . . . 76 F1
**Northbrook Rd** PR25 . . . 76 F1
**North Church St** FY7 . . . 199 B5
**Northcliffe** BB6 . . . 124 B6
**North Cliffe Sch** BB6 . . . 124 B6
**North Cliff St** 6 PR1 . . . 96 E6
**North Clifton St** 7 FY8 . . . 91 B3
**Northcote Rd**
Langho BB6 . . . 143 C3
Preston PR1 . . . 96 D7
**Northcote St**
Darwen BB3 . . . 65 B6
4 Haslingden BB4 . . . 85 B2
8 Leyland PR25 . . . 77 A1
**North Cres** FY8 . . . 89 E6
**North Croft** PR3 . . . 181 C8
**North Ct**
Blackpool FY5 . . . 152 E8
Cleveleys FY5 . . . 175 D5
**Northdene** WN8 . . . 27 B2
**North Dr**
Appley Bridge WN6 . . . 28 C2
Blackpool FY5 . . . 152 D6
Cleveleys FY5 . . . 175 E2
Inskip PR4 . . . 157 C1
Kirkham PR4 . . . 113 F6
Lancaster LA1 . . . 211 B8
**North Dunes** L38 . . . 2 F4
**North East Ave** PR6 . . . 63 A8
**North East Dr** LA1 . . . 211 B8
**NORTH END** . . . 3 B6
**Northenden Rd** PR7 . . . 42 E1
North End Football Gd (Preston North End FC) PR1 . . . 118 B2
**North End La** L38 . . . 3 A6
**Northern Ave** PR4 . . . 74 E2
Northern Equine Therapy Ctr The★ BD24 . . . 236 F6
Northern Prim Sch OL13 . . . 87 F6
**Northern Terr** LA5 . . . 224 F5
**Northfield** WN8 . . . 18 B4
**Northfield Ave** FY1 . . . 130 B8
**Northfield Cl** L33 . . . 1 A4
**Northfield Rd**
Blackburn BB1 . . . 101 E7
Rising Bridge BB5 . . . 85 A8
**Northfleet Ave** FY7 . . . 198 E2
Northfold Com Prim Sch FY5 . . . 175 E4
**Northgate**
Blackburn BB2 . . . 101 E5
Blackpool FY2 . . . 152 C4
Goosnargh PR3 . . . 138 D6
Leyland PR25 . . . 77 B2
Lytham St Anne's FY8 . . . 89 D6
Morecambe LA3 . . . 217 E2
Whitworth OL12 . . . 52 C7
**Northgate Cl** BL6 . . . 32 C1
**Northgate Dr** PR6 . . . 61 E2
**North Gr** 1 PR5 . . . 77 C8
**NORTH HAG** . . . 85 A4
**North Highfield** PR2 . . . 118 E6
**NORTH HOLME** . . . 195 A8
**North Houses La** FY8 . . . 111 D1
**Northlands**
Fulwood PR2 . . . 117 E6
Leyland PR26 . . . 59 C7
**Northleach Ave** PR1 . . . 96 F2
**Northleach Dr** PR8 . . . 21 A5
**North Meade** L31 . . . 5 C2
**North Meadowside** PR4 . . . 75 A6
North Mersey Bsns Ctr L33 . . . 1 D4
**North Moor La** L39 . . . 23 E2
**North Moss La** L37 . . . 12 D7
**North Nook La** PR3 . . . 183 E3
**North Par** 7 BB18 . . . 196 B3
**North Park Ave** BB9 . . . 170 C1
**North Park Dr** FY3 . . . 130 F5
**North Perimeter Rd** L33 . . . 1 D4
**North Prom** FY8 . . . 89 D7
North Quarry Bsns Pk WN6 . . . 28 D1
**North Rd**
Blackburn BB1 . . . 102 C3
Bretherton PR26 . . . 58 B7
Carnforth LA5 . . . 223 E2
Lancaster LA1 . . . 214 F8
Preston PR1 . . . 117 F1
Rawtenstall BB4 . . . 86 C2
Southport PR9 . . . 54 C4
**North Ribble St** 7 PR5 . . . 97 C6
North Road Prim Sch LA5 . . . 223 D1
**NORTH SHORE** . . . 130 B8
**Northside** PR7 . . . 60 C3
**North Sq**
Blackpool FY3 . . . 130 D6
Cleveleys FY5 . . . 175 D5
**North St**
Barnoldswick BB18 . . . 196 B1
Burnley BB10 . . . 148 A1
Burnley, Harle Syke BB10 . . . 148 F3
Chorley PR7 . . . 61 D2
2 Clitheroe BB7 . . . 189 F1
Colne BB8 . . . 171 E6
Fleetwood FY7 . . . 199 B5
Hapton BB12 . . . 126 C5
Haslingden BB4 . . . 85 C1
Morecambe LA4 . . . 217 B5
14 Nelson BB9 . . . 170 D1
Newchurch BB4 . . . 86 E1
Padiham BB12 . . . 146 C1
Preston PR1 . . . 96 F8
Ramsbottom BL0 . . . 68 C2
Rawtenstall BB4 . . . 86 A2
Southport PR9 . . . 35 C8
Water BB4 . . . 87 A8
Whitworth OL12 . . . 71 C1
**North Syke Ave** PR2 . . . 116 C1
**Northumberland Ave**
Blackpool FY2 . . . 152 B1
Cleveleys FY5 . . . 175 F5
**Northumberland Cl**
BB3 . . . 65 C6
**Northumberland St**
2 Chorley PR7 . . . 43 D7
Morecambe LA4 . . . 217 A5
**North Union View** PR5 . . . 76 F8
**North Vale** PR6 . . . 43 F1
**North Valley Rd** BB8 . . . 171 D5
North Valley Ret Pk BB8 . . . 171 D5
**North View**
Kirkham PR4 . . . 113 F5
Leyland PR25 . . . 59 F8
Ramsbottom BL0 . . . 50 B2
Ramsbottom, Strongstry BL0 . . . 68 C2
Rawtenstall BB4 . . . 86 A8
**North View Cl** PR3 . . . 156 C5
**North Warton St** FY8 . . . 91 C3
**Northway**
Broughton PR3 . . . 137 C3
Fleetwood FY7 . . . 198 D1
Fulwood PR2 . . . 117 D7
Maghull L31, L39 . . . 5 E4
Ormskirk L39 . . . 15 A1
Skelmersdale WN8 . . . 18 B2
Northway Prim Sch L31 . . . 5 E3
**Northways** WN6 . . . 29 D2
North West Bsns Coll PR9 . . . 35 B7
**North West Dr** LA1 . . . 211 A8
**NORTHWOOD** . . . 1 A3
**Northwood Cl**
Burnley BB12 . . . 127 D7
Lytham St Anne's FY8 . . . 90 E4
**Northwood Way** FY6 . . . 153 D2
**Norton Ave** LA3 . . . 216 D3
**Norton Ct** FY8 . . . 89 F4
**Norton Dr** LA3 . . . 216 E2
**Norton Gr** LA3 . . . 216 D2
**Norton Pl** LA3 . . . 216 D2
**Norton Rd**
Garstang PR3 . . . 204 C2
Morecambe LA3 . . . 216 D2
Rochdale OL12 . . . 52 F3
**Norton St** 1 BB12 . . . 126 C4
**Norton Vale** FY5 . . . 176 D2
**Norway Ho** 11 BB8 . . . 171 D5
**Norwich Pl**
Blackpool FY2 . . . 152 D5
34 Preston PR1 . . . 97 A7
**Norwich St** BB1 . . . 101 F7
**Norwood Ave**
Becconsall PR4 . . . 73 F2
Blackburn BB2 . . . 101 E2
Blackpool FY3 . . . 130 E8
Southport PR9 . . . 35 E7
**Norwood Cl** PR6 . . . 31 A8
**Norwood Cres** PR9 . . . 35 E7
**Norwood Ct** 13 LA1 . . . 215 A8
**Norwood Dr** LA4 . . . 217 F3
**Norwood Gdns** PR9 . . . 35 F7
Norwood Prim Sch PR9 . . . 35 E7
**Norwood Rd**
Lytham St Anne's FY8 . . . 89 C8
Southport PR8, PR9 . . . 35 F6
**Notre Dame Gdns** BB1 . . . 102 A6
**Nottingham Rd** PR1 . . . 118 A1
**Nottingham St** BB1 . . . 102 A4
**Novak Pl** 6 LA4 . . . 217 F4
**NOVA SCOTIA** . . . 101 E3
Nova Scotia Ret Pk BB2 . . . 101 E3
**Nowell Gr** BB12 . . . 145 D2
**Nowell St** 17 BB6 . . . 124 C5
**Noyna Ave** BB8 . . . 194 E1
**Noyna Rd** BB8 . . . 194 E1
**Noyna St** BB8 . . . 171 E6
**Noyna View** BB8 . . . 171 E7
**NUN HILLS** . . . 70 C7
**Nun's St** LA1 . . . 215 A8
**Nurseries The**
Blackpool FY4 . . . 110 F5
Formby L37 . . . 12 A2
Hesketh Bank PR4 . . . 73 E3
**Nursery Ave** L39 . . . 16 A6
**Nursery Cl**
Coppull PR7 . . . 42 E4
Leyland PR25 . . . 59 F8
**Nursery Dr**
Becconsall PR4 . . . 73 F1
Formby L37 . . . 11 F2
**Nursery La** PR4 . . . 75 E8
**Nursery Nook** BB3 . . . 82 D5
**Nursery Rd** L31 . . . 5 C4
**Nuthall Rd** PR8 . . . 35 F3
**NUTTALL** . . . 50 C4
**Nuttall Ave**
Great Harwood BB6 . . . 124 C4
Horwich BL6 . . . 32 A3
**Nuttall Cl** BL0 . . . 50 C5
**Nuttall Hall Cotts** BL0 . . . 50 D5
**Nuttall Hall Rd** BL0 . . . 50 D5
**Nuttall La** BL0 . . . 50 C4
**NUTTALL LANE** . . . 50 C5
**Nuttall Rd**
Blackpool FY1 . . . 130 D2
Ramsbottom BL0 . . . 50 D4
**Nuttall St Mews** 3 BB5 . . . 104 C5
**Nuttall St**
Accrington BB5 . . . 104 C5
3 Bacup OL13 . . . 88 B3
Blackburn BB2 . . . 101 D1
Blackburn, Ewood BB2 . . . 81 D8
6 Burnley BB11 . . . 128 B4
Bury BL9 . . . 33 A1
Rawtenstall BB4 . . . 86 B3
**Nuttalls Way** BB1 . . . 102 C2
**Nutter Cres** BB12 . . . 146 F5
**Nutter Rd**
Accrington BB5 . . . 104 C7
Cleveleys FY5 . . . 175 D3
2 Preston PR1 . . . 96 E7
**NUTTER'S PLATT** . . . 96 C1

## O

**Oak Ave**
Blackpool FY4 . . . 110 D8
Euxton PR7 . . . 60 D3
Galgate LA2 . . . 210 F4
Higher Penwortham PR1 . . . 96 B3
9 Horwich BL6 . . . 32 E1
Kirkham PR4 . . . 114 B4
Longridge PR3 . . . 140 A7
Morecambe LA4 . . . 217 F6
Ormskirk L39 . . . 15 D4
Ramsbottom BL0 . . . 50 A2
Rising Bridge BB5 . . . 85 A8
Thornton FY5 . . . 153 C8
**Oak Bank**
Accrington BB5 . . . 125 D2
Gregson Lane PR5 . . . 98 E1
**Oakbank Dr** BB5 . . . 103 E5
**Oak Cl**
Barrow BB7 . . . 166 D1
Rishton BB1 . . . 103 B8
Whalley BB7 . . . 144 A7
Whitworth OL12 . . . 71 D4
**Oak Cres** WN8 . . . 17 D1
**Oak Croft** PR6 . . . 78 B2
**Oakdene Ave** BB5 . . . 125 E1
**Oak Dr**
Burscough L40 . . . 25 F3
Chorley PR6 . . . 61 C3
Freckleton PR4 . . . 93 A5
Halton LA2 . . . 219 D7
**Oaken Bank** BB10 . . . 148 E3
**Oaken Cl** OL13 . . . 88 B3
**OAKENCLOUGH** . . . 226 C2
**Oakenclough Rd**
Bacup OL13 . . . 88 B3
Bleasdale PR3 . . . 183 F4
**Oakeneaves Ave** BB11 . . . 127 D2
**Oakengate** PR2 . . . 118 C7
**Oakengates** WN6 . . . 29 F1
**Oakenhead Cl** PR3 . . . 160 D7
**Oakenhead St** PR1 . . . 118 E1
**OAKENHEAD WOOD** . . . 85 E3
**Oakenhead Wood Old Rd** BB4 . . . 85 E3
**Oakenhurst Rd** BB2 . . . 101 D4
**OAKENSHAW** . . . 124 E3
**Oakenshaw Ave** OL12 . . . 52 C6
**Oakenshaw Croft** BB5 . . . 124 E3
**Oakenshaw View** OL12 . . . 52 C6
**Oakfield**
Fulwood PR2 . . . 117 F7
Preston PR2 . . . 117 B1
**Oakfield Ave**
Barnoldswick BB18 . . . 196 A3
Clayton-le-M BB5 . . . 124 E3
Huncoat BB5 . . . 125 E1
**Oakfield Cl** BL6 . . . 32 F2
**Oakfield Cres** BB5 . . . 103 F4
**Oakfield Dr**
Formby L37 . . . 11 D4
Leyland PR26 . . . 59 B8
Oakfield House Sch PR4 . . . 115 C4
**Oakfield Rd**
Blackburn BB2 . . . 81 D7
Hightown L38 . . . 2 F2
**Oakfields** L39 . . . 16 A5
**Oakford Cl** PR9 . . . 55 B5
**Oakgate Cl** PR4 . . . 56 F5
**Oak Gates** BL7 . . . 47 E1
**Oak Gn** L39 . . . 15 F5
**Oak Gr**
Darwen BB3 . . . 82 B2
Garstang PR3 . . . 181 C7
New Longton PR4 . . . 76 A6
**Oakgrove** FY4 . . . 110 D6
**Oakham Ct**
12 Preston PR1 . . . 97 A7
Southport PR9 . . . 35 C8
**Oakhill Cl** L31 . . . 5 D2
**Oak Hill Cl** BB5 . . . 104 C4
**Oakhill Coll** BB7 . . . 144 D6
**Oakhill Cottage La** L31 . . . 5 D4
**Oakhill Dr** L31 . . . 5 D4
**Oakhill Rd** L31 . . . 5 D3
**Oak Ho** PR7 . . . 42 F6
**Oakhurst Ave** BB5 . . . 125 E1
**Oak La**
Accrington BB5 . . . 104 D5
Newton-w-S PR4 . . . 114 F2
**Oakland Ave** FY5 . . . 152 D6
**Oakland Cl** LA1 . . . 215 D8
**Oakland Glen** PR5 . . . 97 A3
**Oaklands Ave**
Barrowford BB9 . . . 170 D3
Tarleton PR4 . . . 57 A7
**Oaklands Ct** LA1 . . . 214 C5
**Oaklands Dr**
Higher Penwortham PR1 . . . 96 A4
Rawtenstall BB4 . . . 85 E2
**Oaklands Gr** PR2 . . . 116 F1
**Oaklands Rd** BL0 . . . 68 D2
**Oakland St**
4 Bamber Bridge PR5 . . . 97 E1
Nelson BB9 . . . 148 E8
**Oaklands Terr** BB1 . . . 101 F7
**Oaklea** WN6 . . . 29 A2
**Oakleaf Cl** PR3 . . . 138 C6
**Oakleaf Ct** FY5 . . . 175 D4
**Oakleaf Way** FY4 . . . 131 D1
**Oaklee Gr** L33 . . . 1 A4
**Oakleigh** WN8 . . . 9 D2
**Oakleigh Terr** 8 OL14 . . . 109 B1
**Oakley Rd**
Morecambe LA3 . . . 216 D2
Rawtenstall BB4 . . . 85 F2
**Oakley St** BB4 . . . 85 E2
**Oakmere** PR6 . . . 78 C3
**Oakmere Ave** PR6 . . . 79 D2
**Oakmere Cl** BB2 . . . 81 D6
**Oakmoor Ave** FY2 . . . 152 E4
**Oak Rd** PR3 . . . 181 B8
**Oak Ridge** BB7 . . . 189 D7
**Oakridge Cl** PR2 . . . 117 F7
**Oaks Bar** BB1 . . . 122 C8
**Oaks Brow** BB1 . . . 122 C7
**Oaksfield** BB3 . . . 81 E5
**Oakshaw Dr** OL12 . . . 52 A1
**Oakshott Pl** PR5 . . . 78 B7
**Oak St**
Accrington BB5 . . . 104 C5
5 Bacup OL13 . . . 88 A3
Blackburn BB1 . . . 101 F7
Brierfield BB9 . . . 148 B6
Burnley BB12 . . . 127 C6
Clayton-le-M BB5 . . . 124 F1
Clow Bridge BB11 . . . 106 B4
Colne BB8 . . . 171 F6
Fleetwood FY7 . . . 199 A4
Great Harwood BB6 . . . 124 C6
2 Nelson BB9 . . . 170 E1
Oswaldtwistle BB5 . . . 103 D3
Preston PR1 . . . 97 A7
Ramsbottom BL0 . . . 50 B5
Southport PR8 . . . 35 E6
Whitworth OL12 . . . 71 D5
**Oaks The**
Bamber Bridge PR5 . . . 97 B3
Blackpool FY3 . . . 130 E3
Chorley PR7 . . . 43 B4
Leyland PR26 . . . 59 A7
Poulton-le-F FY6 . . . 153 D4
Southport PR8 . . . 34 F6
St Michael's on W PR3 . . . 157 C7
**Oak Terr**
Barnoldswick BB18 . . . 196 C3
Rawtenstall BB4 . . . 68 E8
**Oaktree Ave**
Clayton-le-W PR25 . . . 77 D4
Fulwood PR2 . . . 117 A4
**Oaktree Cl** PR2 . . . 117 A4
**Oak Tree Ct** WN8 . . . 18 D3
**Oak Tree Dr** PR4 . . . 113 E4
**Oak View**
Leyland PR25 . . . 76 E2
Whitworth OL12 . . . 71 D4
**Oakville Rd** LA3 . . . 212 E5
**Oakway** PR3 . . . 140 A8
**Oakwood** WN8 . . . 18 D3
**Oakwood Ave**
Bamber Bridge PR5 . . . 97 C4
Blackburn BB1 . . . 123 B1
Lytham St Anne's FY8 . . . 90 E4
Shevington WN6 . . . 19 F5
Southport PR8 . . . 21 D6
**Oakwood Cl**
Blackpool FY4 . . . 110 F4
Burnley BB10 . . . 148 D3
Darwen BB3 . . . 81 E5
Thornton FY5 . . . 176 D2
**Oakwood Dr**
Fulwood PR2 . . . 117 D8
Southport PR8 . . . 21 E5
**Oakwood Gdns** LA1 . . . 215 A2
**Oakwood Gr** LA5 . . . 220 F2
**Oakwood Rd**
Accrington BB5 . . . 104 D3
Chorley PR7 . . . 43 B6
Coppull PR7 . . . 42 F2
**Oakwood View** PR7 . . . 43 B4
**Oakworth Ave** PR2 . . . 118 F5
**Oasis Cl** L40 . . . 39 B3
**Oat St** BB12 . . . 126 D7
**Oban Cres** PR1 . . . 118 D3
**Oban Ct** PR2 . . . 139 D1
**Oban Dr** BB1 . . . 102 C3
**Oban Pl** FY2 . . . 152 E6
**Oban St** BB10 . . . 128 C8
**Observatory Rd** BB2 . . . 102 A2
**Occupation La**
Singleton FY6 . . . 154 D4
Stalmine FY6 . . . 177 C7
**Ocean Bvd** FY4 . . . 110 A7
**Ocean Ct** FY6 . . . 199 D5
Ocean Edge Cvn Pk LA3 . . . 212 D3
Ocean Plaza PR8 . . . 35 A8
Ocean View Apartments FY5 . . . 175 C2
**Ocean Way** FY5 . . . 175 C3
**Odell Way** PR5 . . . 97 E3
**Off Botanic Rd** PR9 . . . 54 A1
**Offerton St** BL6 . . . 32 A3
**Off Mount Pleasant St** 7 BB5 . . . 103 E4
**Ogden Cl** BB4 . . . 68 A7
**Ogden Dr** BB4 . . . 68 A7
**O'Hagan Ct** BB9 . . . 148 B6
**Old Acre** L38 . . . 2 F3
**Old Back La** BB7 . . . 144 F7
**Old Bank La**
Blackburn, Shadsworth BB1, BB2 . . . 102 B2
Blackburn, Whinny Heights BB2 . . . 102 A2
**Old Bank St** 4 BB2 . . . 101 E4
**OLD BIRTLE** . . . 33 E7
**Old Boundary Way** L39 . . . 15 F6
Old Brewery Trad Est 9 PR1 . . . 96 E8
**Old Bridge La** FY6 . . . 154 B7
**Old Bridge Way** PR6 . . . 61 D1
**Old Buckley La** PR3 . . . 141 D7
**Oldbury Pl** FY5 . . . 152 F8
**Old Carr Mill St** BB4 . . . 85 B5
**Old Clitheroe Rd** PR3 . . . 163 E3
**Old Cock Yd** PR1 . . . 97 A7
**Old Croft** PR2 . . . 117 D8
**Old Dawber's La** PR7 . . . 60 B1
**Olde Back La** BB11 . . . 127 C3
**Old Engine Ho The** 12 BL0 . . . 50 C6
**Old Engine La**
Ramsbottom BL0 . . . 50 D6
Skelmersdale WN8 . . . 17 C2
**Oldest Barn Mews** 3 LA3 . . . 216 F3
**Olde Stoneheath Ct** PR6 . . . 44 B4
**Old Farmside** BB2 . . . 81 D7
**Oldfield**
7 Kingsfold PR1 . . . 96 D2
Much Hoole PR4 . . . 74 F4
**Oldfield Ave**
Blackpool FY2 . . . 152 C4
Darwen BB3 . . . 81 E3
**Oldfield Carr La** FY6 . . . 153 E1
**Oldfield Cl** FY6 . . . 153 E1
**Oldfield Cres** FY6 . . . 153 E3
**Oldfield Rd** PR5 . . . 78 A7
**Old Forge** FY8 . . . 90 D7

Old Gates Dr BB2 . . . . 80 F8
Old Gn BL8 . . . . 49 F1
Old Greaves Town La PR2 . . . . 116 E1
Old Greenwood La BL6 . . . 32 D1
Old Ground St 8 BL0 . . . . 50 C6
Old Hall Cl
Bamber Bridge PR5 . . . . 77 E8
7 Morecambe LA4 . . . . 217 F4
Roughlee BB9 . . . . 170 B5
Old Hall Dr
Bamber Bridge PR5 . . . . 77 E8
Huncoat BB5 . . . . 125 F1
Old Hall Farm Bsns Pk PR9 . . . . 36 A5
Old Hall La
Charnock Green PR7 . . . . 42 B6
Pleasington BB2 . . . . 100 C2
Old Hall Pk PR3 . . . . 137 E3
Old Hall Sq BB10 . . . . 129 A5
Old Hall St BB10 . . . . 128 A8
Oldham St
Burnley BB11 . . . . 127 F4
3 Morecambe LA4 . . . . 217 B6
Old Hey Croft 5 PR1 . . . . 96 D2
Old Hive PR3 . . . . 185 D4
Old House La FY4 . . . . 111 D7
Old Kiln OL13 . . . . 70 D8
Old La
Bispham Green L40 . . . . 27 D8
Earby BB18 . . . . 197 B2
Formby L37 . . . . 11 F6
Haskayne L39 . . . . 13 E3
Horwich BL6 . . . . 32 F2
Kelbrook BB18 . . . . 194 F4
Maghull L31 . . . . 5 E4
Salterforth BB18 . . . . 194 B5
Shawforth OL12, OL13 . . . . 71 E6
Old Lancaster La PR2 . . . 117 D1
Old Lancaster Rd PR3 . . . 181 B2
OLD LANGHO . . . . 143 C4
Old Langho Rd BB6 . . . . 143 C5
Old Laund St BB12 . . . . 147 E8
Old Links Cl PR9 . . . . 36 B8
Old Lodge La PR3 . . . . 159 A8
Old Lord's Cres BL6 . . . . 32 B5
Old Lostock La PR5 . . . . 77 E7
Old Mains La FY6 . . . . 153 F6
Old Market Ct 9 LA4 . . . . 217 B6
Old Meadow Ct 3 FY3 . . . . 130 E3
Old Meadow La 2 FY3 . . . . 130 E3
Old Meadows Rd OL13 . . . 88 A5
Old Mill Ct PR4 . . . . 74 F5
Old Mill Dr BB8 . . . . 171 F4
Old Mill Hill L39 . . . . 15 D3
Old Mill Ind Est PR5 . . . . 97 F2
Old Mill La
Formby L37 . . . . 11 F4
Hill Dale L40 . . . . 27 F6
Old Mill St BB1 . . . . 101 F6
Old Millstones PR1 . . . . 96 D7
Old Mill Terr PR6 . . . . 61 E1
Old Moor Rd LA2 . . . . 238 F8
Old Moss La L39 . . . . 13 C5
Old Nab Rd BB6 . . . . 123 E8
Old Oak Gdns PR5 . . . . 97 B2
Old Oliver La BD24 . . . . 236 C6
Old Orch PR2 . . . . 117 D5
Old Park La PR9 . . . . 36 A8
Old Parsonage La BB12 . . . . 126 B8
Old Penny Gdns LA4 . . . . 217 E4
Old Pepper La WN6 . . . . 29 B2
Old Pope La PR4 . . . . 76 B8
Old Prescot Cl L31 . . . . 6 C2
Old Quarry La BL7 . . . . 47 F1
Old Raike BD23 . . . . 236 C4
Old Rake BL6 . . . . 32 E5
Old Rd BD23 . . . . 197 C6
Old Rectory Gn L39 . . . . 6 A7
Old Rectory The LA2 . . . . 206 C5
Old Roman Rd BB12, BB7 . . . . 145 A3
Old Rough La L33 . . . . 1 A2
Old Row
Barrow BB7 . . . . 166 D1
Kirkham PR4 . . . . 114 B4
4 Rawtenstall BB4 . . . . 85 E2
Old Sawmill The
16 Darwen BB3 . . . . 65 A8
Rathmell BD24 . . . . 236 E7
Old Sch Mews 8 BB4 . . . . 85 B3
Old School Cl PR26 . . . . 59 A8
Old School Dr PR4 . . . . 75 B8
Old School Ho The
Blackburn BB1 . . . . 82 D8
Darwen BB3 . . . . 82 B1
Higher Walton PR5 . . . . 98 B3
Old School La
Adlington PR7 . . . . 30 E5
Bamber Bridge PR5 . . . . 77 C6
Euxton PR7 . . . . 60 D3
Tockholes BB3 . . . . 80 F2
Old School Mews
12 Bacup OL13 . . . . 70 C8
Chorley PR7 . . . . 43 C5
Old School Row 3 BB12 . . . . 127 B6
Old School Sq 8 PR1 . . . . 96 E7
Old School The LA2 . . . . 219 C6
Old Sidings The BB8 . . . . 194 D1
Old St BB4 . . . . 86 F1
Old Stables The BB7 . . . . 144 B8
Old Station Cl PR2 . . . . 139 D1
Old Station Ct 9 BB7 . . . 166 E8
Old Stone Trough La BB18 . . . . 195 A5
Old Swan Cl BL7 . . . . 47 E2
Old Swan Cotts BL7 . . . . 47 E2
Old TH 28 BB18 . . . . 196 B2
Old Tom's La FY6 . . . . 177 E8
Old Town Cl WN8 . . . . 8 D8
Old Town Ct L37 . . . . 11 E4
Old Town Hall Mews 1 LA4 . . . . 217 B6
Old Town La L37 . . . . 11 E4
Old Town Way WN8 . . . . 8 D8
Old Trafford Pk LA3 . . . . 212 F4
Old Tram Rd PR1, PR5 . . . . 97 A4
Old Tramway The PR5 . . . . 78 B6
Old Vicarage 16 PR1 . . . . 97 A8
Old Vicarage Ct FY8 . . . . 89 F5
Old Vicarage Rd BL6 . . . . 32 F3
Old Will's La BL6 . . . . 32 B6
Old Worden Ave PR7 . . . . 60 E7
Olivant St BB12 . . . . 127 C7
Olive Bank BB6 . . . . 143 D1
Olive Cl PR6 . . . . 61 C5
Olive Gr
Blackpool FY3 . . . . 130 E5
Skelmersdale WN8 . . . . 17 E1
Southport PR8 . . . . 35 E7
Warton PR4 . . . . 92 D6
Olive La BB3 . . . . 82 B2
Oliver Ct FY6 . . . . 199 E5
Olive Rd LA1 . . . . 218 D2
Oliver Pl LA5 . . . . 223 E2
Olivers Pl PR2 . . . . 118 A8
Oliver's Pl PR2 . . . . 118 B8
Oliver St 10 OL13 . . . . 70 C8
Olive St OL13 . . . . 70 E8
Olive Terr BB4 . . . . 85 F5
OLLERTON FOLD . . . . 79 D5
Ollerton La PR6 . . . . 79 E4
Ollerton Rd FY8 . . . . 90 D5
Ollerton St PR6 . . . . 44 A1
Ollerton Terr PR6 . . . . 79 E3
Olympian Way PR25 . . . . 77 A2
Olympia St BB10 . . . . 128 C5
Olympic Way FY4 . . . . 111 C8
Omerod St BB4 . . . . 87 A8
Omrod Pl 1 FY1 . . . . 130 B2
Onchan Dr OL13 . . . . 88 B1
Onchan Rd BB2 . . . . 101 E1
One Ash Cl OL12 . . . . 52 F2
Onslow Cres PR8 . . . . 35 A2
Onslow Rd FY3 . . . . 130 F7
Ontario Cl BB2 . . . . 101 A8
Oozebooth Terr BB1 . . . . 101 E7
Oozehead La BB2 . . . . 101 B5
Opal Cl 6 FY5 . . . . 152 F7
Opal St BB1 . . . . 122 F2
Openshaw Dr BB1 . . . . 101 E8
Openshaw St BL9 . . . . 33 A1
Oporto Cl BB11 . . . . 127 E5
Oram Rd PR5 . . . . 78 F8
Oram St BL9 . . . . 33 A4
Orange St BB5 . . . . 104 B8
Orchard Ave
Blackpool FY4 . . . . 110 C6
Bolton-le-S LA5 . . . . 221 A6
New Longton PR4 . . . . 76 A7
Poulton-le-F FY6 . . . . 153 E1
Orchard Bridge 6 BB11 . . . . 127 F6
Orchard Cl
Becconsall PR4 . . . . 73 F3
Blackburn BB2 . . . . 81 D6
Euxton PR7 . . . . 60 D3
Freckleton PR4 . . . . 93 A6
Fulwood PR2 . . . . 117 A5
Silverdale LA5 . . . . 224 B2
Slyne LA2 . . . . 218 D8
Thornton FY5 . . . . 176 B4
Wrea Green PR4 . . . . 113 B3
Orchard Croft 2 PR5 . . . . 77 A8
Orchard Ct
Fulwood PR2 . . . . 117 D5
Leyland PR25 . . . . 59 D7
Maghull L31 . . . . 5 F1
Orrell WN5 . . . . 10 D3
Orchard Dr
Fleetwood FY7 . . . . 198 E1
Lucas Green PR6 . . . . 61 C5
Oswaldtwistle BB5 . . . . 103 F5
Orchard End PR3 . . . . 156 C5
Orchard Gdns
Mossy Lea WN6 . . . . 28 F6
Much Hoole PR4 . . . . 74 E3
Orchard Grange PR1 . . . . 96 A5
Orchard La
Lancaster LA1 . . . . 214 D7
Longton PR4 . . . . 74 F8
Southport PR8 . . . . 21 D4
Orchard Lo 1 L39 . . . . 15 F6
Orchard Mill Dr PR26 . . . . 58 B2
Orchard Pk 16 BB3 . . . . 81 F2
Orchard Pl PR4 . . . . 74 E3
Orchard Rd FY8 . . . . 89 E6
Orchard St
5 Barnoldswick BB18 . . . . 196 B2
Great Harwood BB6 . . . . 124 C4
1 Leyland PR25 . . . . 77 B1
28 Preston PR1 . . . . 96 F8
Orchards The
Barnoldswick BB18 . . . . 196 C3
Carleton FY6 . . . . 153 B5
3 Orrell WN5 . . . . 10 E5
Overton LA3 . . . . 209 D8
Southport PR8 . . . . 21 D4
Orchard The
Barrowford BB9 . . . . 170 E6
Burnley BB11 . . . . 127 C4
Clitheroe BB7 . . . . 189 E2
Croston PR26 . . . . 58 C3
Kirkham PR4 . . . . 114 E6
Leyland PR26 . . . . 76 B1
Little Eccleston PR3 . . . . 156 A5
Ormskirk L39 . . . . 15 D5
Warton PR4 . . . . 92 E6
Woodplumpton PR4 . . . . 136 E1
Wray LA2 . . . . 238 D6
Orchard View L39 . . . . 15 D1
Orchard Wlk
Grimsargh PR2 . . . . 139 C2
Ramsbottom BL8 . . . . 49 F1
Orchid Cl WN8 . . . . 10 B6
Orchid Way OL12 . . . . 52 D3
Ord Ave FY4 . . . . 130 F1
Orders La PR4 . . . . 114 A4
Ordnance St BB1 . . . . 102 A5
Ord Rd PR2 . . . . 117 C2
Oregon Ave FY3 . . . . 130 E8
Oriole Cl 9 BB1 . . . . 101 F6
Orion Bldgs 1 FY5 . . . . 175 D2
Orkney Cl BB1 . . . . 102 D3
Orkney Rd 1 FY1 . . . . 130 C2
Orme Ho L39 . . . . 16 A5
Ormerod Rd BB10, BB11 . . . . 128 B7
Ormerod St
Accrington BB5 . . . . 104 B5
Burnley BB11 . . . . 128 A5
Colne BB8 . . . . 171 C4
Haslingden BB4, BB5 . . . . 85 B7
5 Nelson BB9 . . . . 148 F8
Rawtenstall BB4 . . . . 86 A2
Thornton FY5 . . . . 176 B4
Worsthorne BB10 . . . . 129 A5
Ormerod Terr
Barrow BB6 . . . . 144 D8
Foulridge BB8 . . . . 194 E1
Orme St 1 FY1 . . . . 130 C3
Ormond Ave
Blackpool FY1 . . . . 130 B8
Westhead L40 . . . . 16 E4
Ormonde Cres L33 . . . . 1 A2
Ormond St BL9 . . . . 33 A3
Ormont Ave FY5 . . . . 175 E2
Ormrod Ct 20 BL9 . . . . 33 A2
Ormrod St BL9 . . . . 33 A2
Ormrods The BL9 . . . . 33 F5
Ormsby Cl WN6 . . . . 29 E2
ORMSKIRK . . . . 15 C6
Ormskirk Bsns Pk 2 L39 . . . . 15 F6
Ormskirk CE Prim Sch L39 . . . . 16 A6
Ormskirk Coll L39 . . . . 15 E6
Ormskirk & District General Hospl L39 . . . . 16 A4
Ormskirk Ind Pk L39 . . . . 16 A6
Ormskirk Lathom Park CE Prim Sch L40 . . . . 17 A8
Ormskirk Old Rd L39 . . . . 7 F7
Ormskirk Rd
Bickerstaffe L39 . . . . 7 E7
Preston PR1 . . . . 97 A8
Rainford WA11 . . . . 8 D1
Skelmersdale, Tanhouse WN8 . . . . 9 D7
Skelmersdale WN8 . . . . 17 C1
Up Holland WN8 . . . . 10 A7
Ormskirk Sch L39 . . . . 16 B5
Ormskirk Sta L39 . . . . 15 F5
Ormston Ave BL6 . . . . 32 C5
Orms Way L37 . . . . 11 E3
Orpen Ave BB11 . . . . 127 F3
Orpington Sq BB10 . . . . 148 C3
ORRELL . . . . 10 E6
Orrell Cl 3 PR25 . . . . 76 D1
Orrell Gdns WN5 . . . . 10 F6
Orrell Hill La L38 . . . . 3 C4
Orrell Holgate Prim Sch WN5 . . . . 10 E5
Orrell La L40 . . . . 25 D5
Orrell Newfold Com Prim Sch WN5 . . . . 10 D4
ORRELL POST . . . . 10 E7
Orrell Rd WN5 . . . . 10 E7
Orrell Sta WN5 . . . . 10 E4
Orrell Water Pk* WN5 . . . 10 E4
Orrest Rd PR1 . . . . 119 A1
ORTNER . . . . 232 C1
Orton Ct BB9 . . . . 170 D4
Orwell Cl L37 . . . . 11 D1
OSBALDESTON . . . . 121 D4
OSBALDESTON GREEN . . . . 121 D6
Osbaldeston La BB2 . . . . 121 D5
Osbert Croft PR4 . . . . 95 A1
Osborne Ave FY5 . . . . 175 F1
Osborne Cres LA3 . . . . 216 F3
Osborne Dr PR6 . . . . 78 C2
Osborne Gr
Burnley BB10 . . . . 148 B3
Cleveleys FY5 . . . . 175 D5
Morecambe LA4 . . . . 217 A3
Osborne Rd
Bamber Bridge PR5 . . . . 97 D3
Blackburn BB2 . . . . 101 B6
Cleveleys FY5 . . . . 175 D5
Formby L37 . . . . 11 E1
Lytham St Anne's FY8 . . . . 89 F5
Morecambe LA3, LA4 . . . . 216 F3
Southport PR8 . . . . 21 B6
Osborne St 12 PR1 . . . . 96 E7
Osborne Terr
Bacup OL13 . . . . 70 D8
Darwen BB3 . . . . 81 E2
1 Rawtenstall BB4 . . . . 85 E2
Spen Brook BB12 . . . . 169 D2
Whitewell Bottom BB4 . . . . 86 F4
Osborne Way BB4 . . . . 85 A1
Osbourne Rd FY4 . . . . 110 B8
Osbourne Way PR1 . . . . 118 A1
Oscar St 4 FY4 . . . . 130 F2
Oslo Rd BB11 . . . . 127 B5
Osprey Cl
Blackburn BB1 . . . . 101 D8
Knowley PR6 . . . . 62 A3
Oswald Rd
Lytham St Anne's FY8 . . . . 91 D4
Preston PR2 . . . . 117 C1
Oswald St
Accrington BB5 . . . . 104 D6
Blackburn BB1 . . . . 101 E6
Burnley BB12 . . . . 127 F8
Oswaldtwistle BB5 . . . . 103 D3
Rishton BB1 . . . . 124 C2
OSWALDTWISTLE . . . . 103 B3
Oswaldtwistle Mills Shopping Village* BB5 . . . . 103 E4
Otley Rd FY8 . . . . 90 B7
Ottawa Cl BB2 . . . . 101 A8
Otterburn Cl FY3 . . . . 153 B1
Otterburn Gr BB10 . . . . 128 D6
Otterburn Rd BB2 . . . . 81 C7
Otters Cl PR2 . . . . 118 F2
Ottershaw Gdns BB1 . . . . 101 E8
Ottery Cl PR9 . . . . 54 A5
Otway St PR1 . . . . 117 E2
Oulton Cl L31 . . . . 5 B4
Our Lady & All Saints RC Prim Sch WN8 . . . . 27 C2
Our Lady of Compassion RC Prim Sch L37 . . . . 12 A3
Our Lady of Lourdes RC Prim Sch
Carnforth LA5 . . . . 223 E1
Southport PR8 . . . . 35 A1
Our Lady of Perpetual Succour RC Prim Sch BB2 . . . . 81 E8
Our Lady of the Assumption RC Prim Sch FY4 . . . . 110 F5
Our Lady Queen of Peace RC High Sch WN8 . . . . 17 F4
Our Lady & St Anselm's RC Prim Sch OL12 . . . . 71 D2
Our Lady & St Edward's RC Prim Sch PR2 . . . . 117 D8
Our Lady & St Gerard's RC Prim Sch PR5 . . . . 77 A8
Our Lady & St Hubert's RC Prim Sch BB6 . . . . 124 E6
Our Lady & St John RC Arts Coll BB1 . . . . 102 C3
Our Lady & St Paul's RC Prim Sch OL10 . . . . 33 F1
Our Lady's RC Coll LA1 . . . . 218 D1
Our Lady's RC High Sch PR2 . . . . 117 C4
Our Lady Star of the Sea RC Prim Sch FY8 . . . . 89 F6
Ousby Ave 7 LA3 . . . . 217 B2
Ousby Rd LA3 . . . . 217 B2
Ouseburn Rd BB2 . . . . 81 C8
Outer Prom FY7 . . . . 198 E5
Outgate Rd PR4 . . . . 116 D4
Out La PR26 . . . . 58 C2
Outlet La L31, L39 . . . . 6 F1
Outlook The L38 . . . . 2 F4
Out Moss La LA4 . . . . 217 B4
Outram Ho PR5 . . . . 97 D1
Outram La 2 BB1 . . . . 122 E1
Outram Way PR5 . . . . 77 E8
OUT RAWCLIFFE . . . . 178 C1
Out Rawcliffe CE Prim Sch PR3 . . . . 178 F2
Outterside St PR7 . . . . 31 A6
Outwood Rd BB11 . . . . 128 B4
Ouzledale Bsns Pk BB18 . . . . 196 C2
Ouzle Rock BB12 . . . . 169 E2
Oval The
Burnley BB11 . . . . 127 C3
Shevington WN6 . . . . 19 F5
West Bradford BB7 . . . . 189 D7
Ovangle Rd LA3 . . . . 217 F2
OVER BURROW . . . . 241 E7
Overdale Gr FY3 . . . . 131 A8
Overdell Dr OL12 . . . . 52 C4
Overfield Way OL12 . . . . 52 F2
Over Hos BL7 . . . . 48 B6
OVER KELLET . . . . 237 A8
Overshores Rd BL7 . . . . 48 B8
OVERTON . . . . 209 D8
Overton Rd PR2 . . . . 95 E8
Overton St Helen's CE Prim Sch LA3 . . . . 213 D1
OVERTOWN . . . . 241 F7
OVER TOWN . . . . 108 A8
Over Town BB10 . . . . 129 A1
Ovington Dr PR8 . . . . 35 E3
Owen Ave L39 . . . . 15 F6
Owen Ct BB5 . . . . 124 F3
Owen Rd LA1 . . . . 218 D2
Owen's La L39 . . . . 13 E2
Owen's Row BL6 . . . . 32 C3
Owens St PR6 . . . . 43 E7
Owen St
Accrington BB5 . . . . 104 C7
Burnley BB12 . . . . 127 A5
Darwen BB3 . . . . 82 A3
Preston PR1 . . . . 97 B8
Owlet Hall Rd BB3 . . . . 81 E2
Owsten Ct BL6 . . . . 31 F3
Owtram St 2 PR1 . . . . 97 C8
Oxcliffe Ave LA3 . . . . 216 D1
Oxcliffe Gr LA3 . . . . 216 D1
Oxcliffe Rd LA3 . . . . 216 F2
Oxendale Rd FY5 . . . . 176 D2
Oxenholme Ave FY5 . . . . 175 D4
Oxenhurst Rd FY3 . . . . 131 A8
Oxford Ave BB5 . . . . 125 A3
Oxford Cl
Blackburn BB1 . . . . 101 F4
Padiham BB12 . . . . 126 D6
Oxford Ct
4 Lytham St Anne's FY8 . . . . 90 D4
6 Southport PR8 . . . . 34 F6
Oxford Dr
Blackburn BB1 . . . . 102 E4
Kirkham PR4 . . . . 114 C4
Oxford Gdns PR8 . . . . 34 E4
Oxford Mews PR7 . . . . 60 E6
Oxford Pl
9 Burnley BB11 . . . . 128 B5
Lancaster LA1 . . . . 218 C3
Oxford Rd
Bamber Bridge PR5 . . . . 77 F8
Blackpool FY1 . . . . 130 D5
Burnley BB11 . . . . 128 B5
Cleveleys FY5 . . . . 175 D3
Fleetwood FY7 . . . . 198 E3
Fulwood PR2 . . . . 117 D4
Lytham St Anne's, Ansdell FY8 . . . . 90 D4
Lytham St Anne's FY8 . . . . 89 E8
Nelson BB9 . . . . 171 A2
Orrell WN5 . . . . 10 F8
Skelmersdale WN8 . . . . 17 E1
Southport PR8 . . . . 34 E4
Oxford St
Accrington BB5 . . . . 104 B6
Adlington PR7 . . . . 31 A6
Brierfield BB9 . . . . 148 B5
Bury BL9 . . . . 33 A1
Carnforth LA5 . . . . 223 D1
9 Chorley PR7 . . . . 43 C7
Colne BB8 . . . . 171 E5
Darwen BB3 . . . . 81 F4
Lancaster LA1 . . . . 218 D3
Morecambe LA4 . . . . 217 B6
Preston PR1 . . . . 97 A6
Oxford Way
Fleetwood FY7 . . . . 198 E3
Rochdale OL12 . . . . 52 E2
Ox Hey BB5 . . . . 124 F4
Ox Hey Ave PR2 . . . . 116 C1
Oxhey Cl BB10 . . . . 128 F6
Ox Hey Cl BL0 . . . . 50 C7
Oxheys Ct 1 PR1 . . . . 117 E2
Oxheys Ind Est PR1 . . . . 117 D2
Oxheys St PR1 . . . . 117 D2
Oxhill Pl FY5 . . . . 152 F7
Oxhouse Rd WN5 . . . . 10 D4
Oxley Cl PR4 . . . . 113 F5
Oxley Rd PR1 . . . . 118 D1
Oxley Rd N PR1 . . . . 118 D1
Ox St 15 BL0 . . . . 50 B5
Oystercatcher Gate FY8 . . 90 E7

## P

Paa La BB7 . . . . 231 C7
Packet La LA5 . . . . 221 A4
Pad Cote La BD22 . . . . 174 A8
Paddington Ave PR3 . . . . 157 C7
Paddington Barn PR3 . . . 157 C7
Paddock Ave PR26 . . . . 59 A8
Paddock Dr FY3 . . . . 131 C2
Paddock La BB1 . . . . 102 D4
Paddock Rd WN8 . . . . 9 C5
Paddock St 9 BB5 . . . . 103 E4
Paddock The
Blackburn BB2 . . . . 101 A8
Carleton FY6 . . . . 153 C5
Formby L37 . . . . 12 A5
Fulwood PR2 . . . . 118 A6
4 Kingsfold PR1 . . . . 96 E2
Ormskirk L39 . . . . 15 C3
Oswaldtwistle BB5 . . . . 103 E4
Ramsbottom BL0 . . . . 50 B7
Rufford L40 . . . . 39 C4
Sawley BB7 . . . . 230 C1
Southport PR8 . . . . 21 C4
Thornton FY5 . . . . 153 B8
Paddock Top Mews BB8 . . . . 171 D3
Padgate Pl BB11 . . . . 127 B4
PADIHAM . . . . 126 B7
Padiham Green CE Prim Sch BB12 . . . . 126 C8
Padiham Prim Sch BB12 . . . . 126 D8
Padiham Prim Sch Annexe BB12 . . . . 126 E8
Padiham Rd
Burnley BB12 . . . . 127 E6
Burnley, Habergham BB12 . . . . 127 B7
3 Burnley, Whittlefield BB12 . . . . 127 D6
Padiham BB12 . . . . 126 F7
Sabden BB7 . . . . 146 A7

Padstow Cl PR9 54 A5
Padway PR1 96 D2
Page Ct L37 11 F3
Pagefield Cres BB7 167 A7
Pages Ct PR5 77 B7
Paignton Rd BB1 101 D7
Painley Cl FY8 91 A4
Painter Wood BB7 144 B4
Paisley St BB11 127 D5
Palace Ct LA3 216 E4
Palace Gdns BB12 127 B7
Palace Rd PR8 34 E5
Palace St
  Burnley BB12 127 C7
  Bury BL9 33 A2
Palais Bldgs L40 25 E5
Palatine Ave LA1 215 A5
Palatine Cl FY3 131 C6
Palatine Com Sports Coll FY4 110 C8
Palatine Rd
  Blackburn BB2 101 C5
  Blackpool FY1 130 C4
  Cleveleys FY5 175 D4
  Southport PR8 34 F5
Palatine Sq BB11 127 E5
Palatine St 10 BL0 50 C6
Paley Rd 1 PR1 96 D7
Palfrey Cl FY6 153 B6
Palladium Bldgs 7 FY1 130 B1
Pall Mall
  Blackburn BB2 100 E5
  Chorley PR7 43 C6
Palma St 10 OL14 109 B1
Palmaston Cl LA1 214 E6
Palm Ct WN8 17 E2
Palm Dr FY6 153 B6
Palmer Ave FY1 130 C2
Palmer Gr 3 LA4 217 E6
Palmer St BB1 101 D6
Palmerston Cl BL0 50 C4
Palmerston Rd PR9 35 F6
Palmerston St BB12 126 D7
Palmetto View FY8 90 D7
Palm Gr PR8 35 E6
Palm St
  Blackburn BB1 102 A7
  5 Burnley BB11 127 D5
Pankhurst Cl BB1 102 B1
Pansy St N BB5 104 B7
Pansy St S BB5 104 B7
Panton St BL6 32 D1
Parade The LA5 223 B1
Paradise Cl PR6 61 C8
Paradise La
  1 Blackburn BB2 101 E4
  Formby L37 12 A6
  Leyland PR26 76 B1
Paradise St
  Accrington BB5 104 B5
  Barrowford BB9 170 E5
  Blackburn BB2 101 D4
  11 Burnley BB11 127 F6
  Knowley PR6 61 F3
  2 Newchurch BB4 86 F2
  Ramsbottom BL0 50 C7
Paradise Terr 2 BB2 101 E4
Paragon Way LA1 214 C8
PARBOLD 27 D2
Parbold Cl
  Blackpool FY3 152 F1
  Burscough L40 25 E3
Parbold Douglas CE Prim Sch WN8 27 D3
Parbold Hill WN8 27 E2
Parbold Sta WN8 27 C2
Pardoe Cl PR4 73 E3
Pardoe Ct L40 25 F3
Paris BB1 122 E4
Parish Gdns PR25 77 A2
Parish St 11 BB12 126 C8
Park Ave
  Barnoldswick BB18 196 B1
  Barrowford BB9 170 C1
  Blackburn BB1 101 D6
  Burnley BB11 127 E4
  Chatburn BB7 190 D5
  Clitheroe BB7 189 E1
  Euxton PR7 60 D2
  Fleetwood FY7 198 F3
  Formby L37 11 F1
  Great Harwood BB6 124 D6
  Haslingden BB4 85 B1
  Lancaster LA1 215 B7
  Longshaw WN5 10 E1
  Lytham St Anne's FY8 90 E3
  Maghull L31 5 D3
  Much Hoole PR4 74 E2
  New Longton PR4 75 F8
  Ormskirk L39 15 E5
  Preston PR1 118 B2
  Ramsbottom BL0 50 D6
  Salterforth BB18 194 E8
  Southport PR9 35 E8
Parkbourn L31 6 A2
Parkbourn Dr L31 6 A2
Parkbourn N L31 6 A2
Parkbourn Sq L31 6 A2
Park Bridge Rd BB10 128 D3
Park Cl
  Fulwood PR2 118 D3
  Hightown L37 2 E8
  Middleforth Green PR1 96 D4
  Parbold WN8 27 D3
  Salterforth BB18 194 C6
Park Cotts BB8 150 D7
Park Cres
  Accrington BB5 104 A4
  Bacup OL13 70 F8
  Blackburn BB2 101 C6
  Haskayne L39 13 F4
  Haslingden BB4 85 C1
  Morecambe LA4 217 E7
  Southport PR9 53 D1
  Stalmine FY6 177 C8
Park Ct LA1 214 F3
Parkdale Gdns BB2 81 D6
Park Dr
  Brierfield BB9 148 C5
  Nelson BB9 148 F7
  Preston PR2 116 D1
Parke Mews PR6 79 C3
Parker Ave BB7 166 E6
Parker Cres L39 15 F7
Parke Rd PR6 62 E8
Parker La
  Burnley BB11 128 A5
  New Longton PR4 76 C6
Parkers Fold PR3 181 C2
Parker St
  Accrington, Higher Baxenden BB5 104 E2
  Accrington, Hillock Vale BB5 104 E8
  3 Blackpool FY1 130 C5
  Burnley BB11 128 A6
  Burnley, Harle Syke BB10 148 F3
  Bury BL9 33 A2
  Chorley PR7 61 C1
  Colne BB8 171 C5
  Lancaster LA1 215 A8
  11 Nelson BB9 170 F2
  Preston PR2 117 D2
  Rishton BB1 124 C2
Parkers Wood Cl PR7 43 A6
Parker Terr BB7 231 B3
Parkes Way BB2 81 D7
Park Farm Cl PR4 74 F8
Park Farm Rd BB2 80 D8
Parkfield Ave PR2 117 B2
Parkfield Cl
  Leyland PR26 59 C8
  Ormskirk L39 15 C4
  5 Preston PR2 116 C1
Parkfield Cres 6 PR2 116 C1
Parkfield Dr
  Lancaster LA1 215 A6
  Preston PR2 95 C8
Parkfield Gr L31 5 C1
Parkfield View PR2 95 C8
Parkfoot Lodges LA6 242 E3
Parkgate PR3 138 D5
Parkgate Dr
  Lancaster LA1 215 C7
  Leyland PR25 59 F7
Park Gate Rd BB1 142 D1
Park Hall L Ctr PR7 42 A4
Park Hall Rd PR7 41 F3
Park Head BB7 144 F2
Parkhead La PR3 182 A8
Park Hey Dr WN6 19 E7
Park High Sch BB8 171 F6
PARK HILL 8 D2
Park Hill
  Barnoldswick BB18 196 C1
  21 Rochdale OL12 52 F1
Parkhill Bsns Ctr BB12 127 A8
Park Hill Rd PR3 181 C7
Park Ho
  4 Lancaster LA1 218 D1
  Longridge PR3 140 A7
Park House La LA2 239 A5
Parkinson La PR3 162 B8
Parkinson St
  Blackburn BB2 101 C2
  Burnley BB11 128 A4
  Foulridge BB8 194 D1
  Haslingden BB4 85 A3
Parkinson Terr BB8 172 B2
Parkinson Way 1 FY4 130 C1
Park La
  Brierfield BB9 148 C5
  Caton LA2 237 B5
  Garstang PR3 204 A4
  Great Harwood BB6 124 D6
  Holmes PR4 56 B2
  Horwich BL6 32 D3
  Kirkham PR4 114 A7
  Maghull L31 5 F3
  Middleforth Green PR1 96 E3
  Oswaldtwistle BB5 103 E3
  Preesall FY6 200 B3
  Wennington LA2 238 E8
Parkland Cl FY5 175 C1
Parkland Gr LA3 216 E2
Parklands
  Skelmersdale WN8 18 D2
  Southport PR9 35 E8
Parklands Ave PR1 96 A4
Parklands Cl PR1 96 A4
Parklands Dr PR2 117 E8
Parklands Gr PR2 117 E8
Parklands High Sch PR7 43 A8
Parklands The PR3 181 D3
Parklands Way BB2 81 B8
Parkland View BB11 127 E2
Park Lane Dr L31 6 B2
Park Lee Rd BB2 101 E2
Park Link L39 15 B1
Park Lo BB2 101 A7
Park Mews BB7 231 B3
Park Mill Pl PR1 118 A1
Park Pl
  Blackburn BB2 101 B3
  Blackburn, Feniscowles BB2 80 D7
  24 Preston PR1 97 A7
  Walton-le-D PR5 97 E4
PARK PLACE 101 F3
Park Prim Sch BB8 171 F5
Park Rd
  Accrington BB5 104 A6
  Adlington PR7 30 F6
  Bacup OL13 87 F1
  Barnoldswick BB18 196 B1
  Blackburn BB2 101 E3
  Blackpool FY1 130 D3
  Burnley BB10 128 E1
  Chorley PR7 43 C8
  Coppull PR7 42 E1
  Darwen BB3 65 B6
  Edgworth BL7 48 E5
  Formby L37 11 E1
  Fulwood PR2 118 A4
  Gisburn BB7 231 B3
  Great Harwood BB6 124 D5
  Haslingden BB4 67 F7
  Kirkham PR4 113 F4
  Lancaster LA1 215 A8
  Leyland PR25 60 A7
  Longshaw WN5 10 F1
  Lytham St Anne's FY8 89 E6
  Mellor Brook BB2, PR5 121 A1
  Middleforth Green PR1 96 D4
  Newchurch BB4 86 F1
  Ormskirk L39 15 E5
  Padiham BB12 126 C8
  Poulton-le-F FY6 153 E4
  Ramsbottom BL0 49 F3
  Rishton BB1 124 C1
  Silverdale LA5 224 D4
  Southport PR9 35 D8
  Southport PR9 53 D1
  Thornton FY5 176 B1
Park Rd W PR9 53 C1
Park Road Ind Est OL13 87 F1
Park Sch FY3 130 E4
Parkside
  Morecambe LA4 217 C3
  Preston, Holme Slack PR1 118 B3
  Preston, Lea PR2 116 D2
  Whitworth OL12 71 D2
Park Side BB18 195 A8
Parkside Ave
  Chorley PR7 43 C8
  Skelmersdale WN8 8 D8
Parkside Cl
  Garstang PR3 181 A7
  Todmorden OL14 109 B1
Parkside Cres WN5 10 F6
Parkside Ct
  6 Morecambe LA4 217 C3
  Southport PR9 53 D1
Parkside Dr PR6 61 B6
Parkside La PR3 181 A7
Parkside Rd
  Lytham St Anne's FY8 90 A7
  Nelson BB9 149 B8
  Todmorden OL14 109 B1
Parkside View FY5 176 A4
Park Sq LA1 215 A8
Park St
  Accrington BB5 104 C6
  Barnoldswick BB18 196 B1
  Barrowford BB9 170 D4
  Chorley PR7 61 C1
  Clitheroe BB7 166 E7
  Eccleston PR7 41 C6
  Great Harwood BB6 124 D5
  Haslingden BB4 85 B3
  Haslingden, Bridge End BB4 67 F7
  Lytham St Anne's FY8 91 B3
  Morecambe LA4 217 E6
Parks The LA4 217 E7
Parkstone Ave
  Carleton FY6 153 B5
  Thornton FY5 153 D8
Park Stone Rd PR3 137 C3
Park Street E BB9 170 E4
Parksway FY6 199 D5
Park Terr
  Blackburn BB1 101 D7
  Great Harwood BB6 124 D6
Parkthorn Rd PR2 95 C8
Park View
  Accrington BB5 104 A7
  Carnforth LA5 223 D3
  Gisburn BB7 231 B3
  Middleforth Green PR1 96 D4
  Newchurch BB4 86 F1
  Padiham BB12 126 C8
Park View Ave PR2 117 B2
Parkview Cl 5 LA3 217 C3
Park View Cl
  Nelson BB9 148 B7
  Rawtenstall BB4 85 F5
Park View Ct 2 FY4 110 C6
Parkview Flats FY8 89 D6
Park View Rd FY8 91 B4
Park View Terr
  Abbey Village PR6 80 C1
  Salterforth BB18 194 D7
Park Wall Rd L29, L38 4 B2
Parkway
  Blackpool FY3 131 A6
  Shevington Moor WN6 29 A2
Park Way
  Colne BB8 171 C6
  Formby L37 11 F1
  Middleforth Green PR1 96 D4
Park Wlk PR2 118 A4
Parkwood BL7 47 D2
Parkwood Ave BB12 127 D7
Parkwood Ct 6 BB4 85 E2
Park Wood Dr BB4 85 E2
Parkwood Mews 1 BB9 170 F2
Parliament St
  Burnley BB11 128 B5
  11 Colne BB8 171 E5
  19 Darwen BB3 82 A1
  Lancaster LA1 218 D1
  Morecambe LA3 216 E4
  Up Holland WN8 10 C7
Parlick Ave PR3 140 B7
Parlick Rd
  Fulwood PR2 119 A2
  Garstang PR3 181 B6
Parramatta St 8 BB4 86 A2
Parr Cottage Cl PR7 41 C7
Parr La PR7 41 C7
Parrock Cl PR1 96 E3
Parrock Par 10 BB4 86 A7
Parrock Rd BB9 170 C2
Parrock St
  Barnoldswick BB18 196 B2
  19 Nelson BB9 170 E1
  11 Rawtenstall BB4 86 A7
Parrox Fold FY6 200 A5
Parrox La PR4 114 E2
Parr's La L39 15 D1
Parrys Way FY6 153 E4
Parsley Cl FY2 152 F3
Parsonage Ave PR3 141 D3
Parsonage Brow WN8 10 A8
Parsonage Cl
  3 Bury BL9 33 A2
  Morecambe LA3 217 C2
  Up Holland WN8 10 A7
Parsonage Cotts 10 BB7 166 E8
Parsonage Dr BB9 148 C5
Parsonage Gdns PR4 57 A5
Parsonage La PR3 185 C1
Parsonage Rd
  Blackburn BB1 123 A4
  Up Holland WN8 10 A7
Parsonage St
  Bury BL9 33 A3
  2 Church BB5 103 E5
  Colne BB8 171 C4
Parson La BB7 166 E8
Parson's Brow 4 PR7 43 C7
Parson's Bullough Rd PR6, BL6 44 E5
Parsons Cl LA1 214 F4
Parth St BL9 33 D1
Partnership Way BB1 102 D2
Partridge Ave FY5 176 A4
Partridge Dr BB5 104 F1
Partridge Hill 4 BB12 146 D1
Partridge Hill St 5 BB12 146 D1
Part St PR8 35 B6
Pashmire Brow BB7 143 E6
PASSMONDS 52 B1
Passmonds Cres OL11, OL12 52 B1
Past La
  Lane Ends, Bay Gate BB7 230 A5
  Lane Ends BB7 230 A7
Pasture Barn BB8 195 F2
Pasture Cl
  Barnoldswick BB18 196 C4
  Burnley BB11 127 E3
Pasture Dr
  Bonds PR3 181 D6
  Foulridge BB8 194 D1
Pasture Field FY6 153 B6
Pasture Field Cl PR26 76 C1
Pasturegate BB11 127 E3
Pasturegate Ave BB11 127 E4
Pasture Gr BB7 144 A7
Pasture La
  Barrowford BB9 170 C5
  Hest Bank LA5 220 E4
Pasturelands BB4 106 A1
Pasturelands Dr BB7 144 A3
Pastures The
  Blackburn BB2 101 A8
  Grimsargh PR2 139 D1
  Morecambe LA3 216 F1
  Southport PR9 54 D5
Paterson St BB2 101 E3
Pathfinders Dr LA1 214 E4
Patience St 11 OL12 52 C1
Patmos St BL0 50 D6
Paton St OL12 52 D3
Patrick Ave BB12 145 D2
Patrick Cres BB4 86 C2
Patten St
  Blackburn BB1 102 C5
  Colne BB8 171 D4
  Preston PR1 96 F8
Patterdale Ave
  Blackburn BB1 102 C3
  Blackpool FY3 130 F2
  Fleetwood FY7 198 D1
  Oswaldtwistle BB5 103 D5
  Thornton FY5 176 B3
Patterdale Cl
  Burnley BB10 148 C4
  Southport PR8 21 B3
Patterdale Cres L31 5 E2
Patterdale Rd LA1 218 F1
Patterson Ct 8 FY8 91 C3
Pattison Cl OL12 52 D3
Paulhan St BB10 148 B2
Paul's La
  Hambleton FY6 177 C2
  Southport PR9 53 F3
Pavey Cl FY4 110 F8
Pavilion Cl 2 OL12 52 F2
Pavilions The
  Blackpool FY4 110 D4
  Bury BL9 33 D2
  Preston PR2 96 C7
Pavilion View PR26 58 B2
Paxton Pl WN8 9 C4
Paxton St BB5 104 B6
Paynter Cl
  Barrow BB7 166 D1
  Clayton-le-M BB5 125 A2
PAYTHORNE 231 C6
Paythorne Ave BB10 128 D5
Paythorne Cl FY3 153 B1
Peabody St BB3 82 A2
Peacehaven WN8 17 E1
Peace Pl FY5 176 B4
Peace St BB11 127 D5
Peachtree Cl PR2 118 D6
Peacock Cres LA2 220 E1
Peacock Dr PR3 204 D1
Peacock Hall Rd PR25 59 D7
Peacock Hill Cl PR2 119 C7
Peacock La LA2 220 E1
Peahall La PR3 202 A4
Pear Ave BL9 33 C3
Pearfield PR25 77 A2
Pearl Ave 6 FY2 152 E1
Pearl Brook Ind Est BL6 32 B3
Pearl St
  Accrington BB5 103 F5
  Blackburn BB1 122 F1
Pear Pl 3 OL14 109 B1
Pearson St
  Blackburn BB2 101 D4
  Bury BL9 33 B3
Pear St 4 OL14 109 B1
Pear Tree Ave PR7 42 F3
Pear Tree Cl 2 PR5 97 E2
Pear Tree Cres PR5 97 E2
Pear Tree Croft PR4 75 A8
Pear Tree Ctyd PR4 115 E2
Pear Tree La PR7 60 E3
Peartree Rd PR26 58 B3
Pear Tree Rd PR6 78 B3
Pear Tree Sch PR4 114 A5
Pear Tree St 7 PR5 97 E2
Peart St BB10 148 B2
Pebble Ct FY5 175 C3
Pechell St 5 PR2 117 C1
Pedder Ave LA3 213 C1
Pedder Dr LA3 213 D1
Pedder Gr LA3 213 D1
Pedder La FY6 177 B1
Pedder Rd LA3 213 C1
Pedders Gr PR2 96 A8
Pedders La PR2 96 A8
Pedder's La
  Blackpool FY4 110 D7
  Preston PR2 117 A1
Pedder St
  Morecambe LA4 217 A5
  Preston PR2 96 E8
Pedders Way PR2 96 A8
Peebles Gr BB11 127 D3
Peel Ave
  Blackpool FY3 130 D7
  Heysham LA3 212 E6
  Lancaster LA1 218 D2
  Ramsbottom BL0 50 A5
PEEL BANK 103 E7
Peel Bank Rd BB5 103 B4
PEEL BROW 50 D7
Peel Brow BL0 50 D6
Peel Brow Sch BL0 50 D6
Peel Cl BB2 81 E8
Peel Cres LA1 214 D8
Peel Ct FY4 111 D6
Peel Dr OL13 88 B1
Peel Gdns BB8 171 C5
Peel Hall Rd BL0 50 B2
Peel Hall St PR1 118 B1
PEEL HILL 111 E7
Peel Hill FY4 111 E7
Peel Ho LA1 218 C1
Peel Leisure & Ret Pk BB1 101 F4
Peel Mount
  Blackburn BB1 102 F4
  Ramsbottom BL0 50 A4
Peel Mount Cl BB1 102 F4
Peel Park Ave
  Accrington BB5 104 D7
  Clitheroe BB7 166 F7
Peel Park Cl
  Accrington BB5 104 D7
  Clitheroe BB7 166 F7
Peel Park Prim Sch BB5 104 D7
Peel Pl BB9 170 F6
Peel Rd
  Blackpool FY4 111 F4
  Colne BB8 171 B4
  Fleetwood FY7 198 F3
  Skelmersdale WN8 9 E5

**Peel St**
Accrington BB5 104 C6
Adlington PR6 31 B8
Blackburn BB2 101 C2
Chorley PR7 43 C7
Clitheroe BB7 166 E8
Haslingden BB4 85 A3
6 Oswaldtwistle BB5 103 D3
Padiham BB12 126 D8
Preston PR2 96 E8
Rawtenstall BB4 86 C2
Southport PR8 35 F6
Peel Twr★ BL8 49 F5
**Peel Wlk** L31 5 B2
**Peerart Ct** 4 BB8 171 C4
**Peers Clough Rd** BB4 86 F7
**Peet Ave** L39 15 D4
**Peet's La** PR9 54 A1
**Pegbank La** LA6 241 A8
**Peg's La** FY8 91 B8
**Peg Way** PR4 92 F6
**Pelham Ave** 3 FY3 130 E8
**Pelham St** 3 BB1 102 A6
**Pelican Cl** FY6 200 B4
**Pemberton Dr** LA4 217 F5
**Pemberton Pl** LA4 217 F5
**Pemberton St** BB1 122 E1
**Pembroke Ave**
Blackpool FY2 152 B3
Morecambe LA4 217 D6
**Pembroke Cl** BL6 32 A4
**Pembroke Ct**
Blackpool FY2 152 B3
13 Darwen BB3 82 A1
14 Rochdale OL12 52 F1
**Pembroke Pl**
Chorley PR7 43 B6
Leyland PR25 60 A8
**Pembroke Rd** FY8 90 D4
**Pembroke St**
Accrington BB5 104 D6
Bacup OL13 87 F1
Blackburn BB2 101 E3
11 Burnley BB10 148 B1
**Pembury Ave** PR1 96 F3
**Penarth Ct** PR2 116 F3
**Pendle Ave**
Bacup OL13 88 A3
Chatburn BB7 190 E5
Clayton-le-M BB5 124 F4
Lancaster LA1 211 B6
**Pendle Bridge** BB12 147 F3
Pendle Bsns Ctr 19 BB9 148 E8
**Pendlebury Cl** PR4 75 B8
**Pendle Cl**
Bacup OL13 88 A2
Blackpool FY3 152 F1
Pendle Com High Sch BB8 171 B2
Pendle Com Hospl BB9 170 E1
**Pendle Ct**
Barnoldswick BB18 196 C3
5 Clitheroe BB7 166 F8
Kirkham PR4 114 A6
Longridge PR3 140 A7
Skelmersdale WN8 9 D3
**Pendle Dr**
Blackburn BB2 101 F2
Horwich BL6 32 C5
Ormskirk L39 16 A6
Whalley BB7 144 A7
**Pendle Fields**
Fence BB12 147 D7
Rimington BB7 231 B1
Pendle Heritage Ctr★ BB9 170 E4
**Pendle Hill Cl** PR2 119 C7
**Pendle Ho** BB1 101 F5
**Pendlehurst St** BB11 127 E4
Pendle Ind Est BB9 148 F7
**Pendlemist View** 1 BB8 171 C3
**Pendle Pl**
Lytham St Anne's FY8 91 C4
Skelmersdale WN8 9 D4
**Pendle Rd**
Brierfield BB9 148 A5
Clayton-le-W PR25 77 D1
Clitheroe BB7 167 A7
Downham BB7 191 D3
Great Harwood BB6 124 F6
Lancaster LA1 218 B3
**Pendle Row** BB12 169 C5
**Pendle St E** BB7 145 F7
**Pendle St W** BB7 145 F8
**Pendleside** BB9 148 B8
**Pendleside Cl** BB7 145 F7
**Pendle St**
Accrington BB5 104 A5
Barrowford BB9 170 C3
Blackburn BB1 102 A5
Nelson BB9 170 D1
Padiham BB12 126 D8
**Pendle Terr** BB7 191 E8
**PENDLETON** 167 B4
**Pendleton Ave**
Accrington BB5 103 F4
Rawtenstall BB4 86 A4
**Pendleton Rd**
Pendleton BB7 167 A2
Wiswell BB7 144 F8
Pendle Trad Est BB7 190 C4
Pendle Vale Coll BB9 171 A2
**Pendle View**
Barley BB12 169 C6
Brockhall Village BB6 143 C6
Clayton-le-M BB5 125 A3
Foulridge BB8 194 E1
Grindleton BB7 190 B7
Higham BB12 146 F6
Huncoat BB5 125 F2
West Bradford BB7 189 D7
Pendle View Prim Sch BB8 171 B1
**Pendle Way** BB12 127 E6
**Pendle Way** 7 BB9 148 E8
**Penfold** L31 5 E1
**Pengarth Rd** BL6 32 C4
**Penguin St** PR1 118 B2
**Penhale Cl** LA3 212 E6
**Penhale Ct** LA3 212 E6
**Penhale Gdns** LA3 212 E6
**Penhill Cl** 4 FY2 130 D8
**Penistone St** 6 BB12 127 D6
**Penketh Pl** WN8 9 C5
**Pennine Ave** PR7 60 D1
**Pennine Cl**
8 Blackpool FY1 130 C4
Horwich BL6 32 C5
**Pennine Cres** BB9 148 C5
**Pennine Gdns** PR3 181 A7
**Pennine Gr** BB12 146 C2
**Pennine Pl** WN8 9 B6
**Pennine Rd**
Bacup OL13 88 A2
Chorley PR6 43 E8
Horwich BL6 32 C5
**Pennines The** PR2 118 A7
**Pennine View**
Dolphinholme LA2 226 A8
Fleetwood FY7 199 B4
Glasson LA2 209 E4
Great Eccleston PR3 156 C5
Kirkham PR4 114 C5
Morecambe LA4 217 B4
**Pennine Way**
Barnoldswick BB18 196 A2
Brierfield BB9 148 C5
Great Eccleston PR3 156 C5
Stalmine FY6 177 D7
**Pennington Ave** L39 15 E6
**Pennington Ct**
Heysham LA3 212 E6
4 Ormskirk L39 15 F6
**Pennington La** WN2 30 E1
**Penn St** BL6 32 C3
**Pennyfarthing La** 7 FY5 176 A2
**Penny House La** BB5 104 C7
**PENNYLANDS** 17 E1
**Penny Lodge View** BB4 105 F3
**Penny's Hospital Almshouses** 35 LA1 214 F8
**Penny St**
Blackburn BB1 101 F5
Lancaster LA1 214 F7
3 Preston PR1 97 A8
**Pennystone Rd** FY2 152 B4
**Penny Stone Rd** LA2 219 C7
**Penrhos Ave** FY7 198 E1
**Penrhyn Rd** LA1 218 A2
**Penrith Ave**
Cleveleys FY5 175 D4
Heysham LA3 212 F8
Southport PR8 21 C3
**Penrith Cres**
Colne BB8 171 B3
Maghull L31 5 E2
**Penrith Rd** BB8 171 A3
**Penrod Way** LA3 212 D6
**Penrose Ave** FY4 130 F1
**Penrose Pl** WN8 9 E4
**Penshaw Cl** 6 BB1 122 E1
**Penswick Ave** FY5 175 E1
**Pentland Rd** L33 1 A4
**Penwell Fold** WN8 9 E8
Penwortham Broad Oak Prim Sch PR1 96 C2
**Penwortham Brow** PR1 96 C6
**Penwortham Ct** PR1 96 D4
Penwortham Girls' High Sch PR1 96 C5
**Penwortham Hall Gdns** PR1 96 E3
**PENWORTHAM LANE** 96 F2
Penwortham Middleforth CE Prim Sch PR1 96 D3
Penwortham Prim Sch PR1 96 A5
**Penwortham Residential Pk** PR1 96 D4
Penwortham St Teresa's RC Prim Sch PR1 96 A5
**Penwortham Way**
Farington PR26, PR4 76 D7
Kingsfold PR1 96 C1
**Pen-Y-Ghent Way** BB18 196 A2
**Penzance St** BB2 101 B2
**Peplow Rd** LA3 213 A8
**Pepper La** WN6 29 B3
**Perch Pool La** PR9 36 F4
**Percival Ct** 2 PR8 35 A6
**Percival St**
Accrington BB5 103 F5
Blackburn BB1 101 F7
Darwen BB3 81 F3
**Percliff Way** BB1 102 B7
**Percy Rd** LA1 214 F6
**Percy St**
Accrington BB5 104 D6
Blackburn BB2 101 B2
Blackpool FY1 130 C7
Bury BL9 33 B3
9 Chorley PR7 43 D7
Colne BB8 171 E6
Fleetwood FY7 198 F4
Nelson BB9 148 E7
Oswaldtwistle BB5 103 B5
Preston PR1 97 A8
Ramsbottom BL0 50 B5
Shawforth OL12 71 E6
**Peregrine Dr** BB3 81 D3
**Peregrine Pl** PR25 76 D2
**Peridot Cl** BB1 122 F2
**Perimeter Rd** L33 1 E2
**Peronne Cres** BB1 102 D5
**Perpignan Way** 16 LA1 214 F8
**Perryn Pl** WN6 29 F1
**Perry St** BB3 82 B2
**Pershore Gdns** FY3 131 B8
**Pershore Gr** PR8 21 A4
**Pershore Rd** FY8 90 B5
**Persia St** BB5 103 F6
**Perth Cl** FY5 152 F7
**Perthshire Gr** PR7 60 F6
**Perth St**
Accrington BB5 104 B4
Blackburn BB2 101 C3
Burnley BB11 127 D5
Lancaster LA1 215 A7
8 Nelson BB9 170 F1
**Peter Birtwistle Cl** BB8 171 E5
**Peterfield Rd** 1 PR1 96 E2
**Peter Grime Row** BB5 125 F2
Peterhouse Sch PR9 54 B3
**Peter La** LA5 225 E1
**Peter Martin St** 2 BL6 32 B4
**Petersan Ct** PR6 61 C3
**Peters Ave** L40 25 E4
**Petersbottom La** LA2 239 E4
**Peter St**
9 Barrowford BB9 170 D4
Blackburn BB1 102 A6
Blackpool FY1 130 D5
Chorley PR7 43 C8
Colne BB8 171 E4
5 Lancaster LA1 214 F7
Rawtenstall BB4 86 A2
**Petre Cres** BB1 103 B8
**Petrel Cl** BB1 101 D8
**Petre Rd** BB5 124 F2
**Petunia Cl** PR25 77 E2
**Petworth Rd** PR8 21 B6
**Pharos Ct** 8 FY7 199 B5
**Pharos Gr** 2 FY7 199 B5
**Pharos Pl** FY7 199 B5
**Pharos St** FY7 199 B5
**Pheasantford Gn** BB10 128 B8
**Pheasantford St** BB10 128 B8
**Pheasant Wood Dr** FY5 175 F5
**Philip Ave** PR4 114 B4
**Philip Dr** PR8 21 F6
**Philips Rd**
Blackburn BB1 102 B8
Weir OL13 88 A7
**Philip St**
Barnoldswick BB18 196 B2
Darwen BB3 82 B1
**Phillip's Cl** L37 11 F2
**Phillips La** BB8 171 B3
**Phillip's La** L37 11 F2
**Phillip St** FY4 130 F2
**Phillipstown** BB4 86 E4
**Phoenix St**
8 Lancaster LA1 218 D1
Rochdale OL12 52 C1
**Phoenix Way** BB11 127 C5
**Phyllis St** OL12 52 B1
**Physics Ave** LA1 211 B7
**Piazza The** LA1 215 C7
**Piccadilly** LA1 214 F3
**Piccadilly Cl** LA1 214 F3
**Piccadilly Gr** LA1 214 F3
**Piccadilly Rd** BB11 127 E5
**Piccadilly Sq** 2 BB11 127 E5
**Piccadilly St** 4 BB4 85 B3
**Pickard Cl** BB18 196 D4
**Pickard St** LA1 214 F6
**Pickering Cl** FY8 90 B7
**Pickering Fold** BB1 82 B7
**Pickering St** 1 BB9 148 B5
**Pickerings The** 2 PR5 77 C8
**Pickles Dr** L40 25 D4
**Pickles St** BB12 127 D7
**Pickmere Ave** FY4 110 E8
**Pickmere Cl** FY5 176 A4
**Pickthorn Cl** LA1 218 B4
**PICKUP BANK** 83 A2
**Pickup Fold** 3 BB3 65 C7
**Pickup Fold Rd** BB3 65 C7
**Pickup Rd** BB1 103 A8
**Pickup St**
Accrington BB5 103 F5
11 Bacup OL13 87 F2
Blackburn BB1 102 A5
Clayton-le-M BB5 124 F3
**Picton St** BB2 81 B8
**Pierce Cl**
Lancaster LA1 214 D7
Padiham BB12 146 C1
**Piercefield Ct** L37 12 A5
**Piercefield Rd** L37 11 F5
**Pier Ct** FY8 89 D7
**PIERCY** 86 F2
**Piercy Higher Mount** BB4 86 F3
**Piercy Mdw** BB4 86 F3
**Piercy Mount** BB4 86 F3
**Piercy Rd** BB4 86 F3
**Piercy Terr** BB4 86 F3
**Pier Ho** 3 BB1 101 F3
**Pierpoint II** FY8 89 D7
**Pier St** FY1 130 B3
**Pierston Ave** FY2 152 C1
**Pike Ct** FY7 198 C2
**PIKE HILL** 128 E5
**Pikelaw Pl** WN8 9 C5
**PIKE LOWE** 79 E1
**Pikestone Ct** 9 PR6 43 E8
**Pike View** BL6 32 D4
**Pilgrim St** BB9 148 F6
**Pilgrims Way** LA3 217 E3
**Pilkington Dr** BB5 125 A3
**Pilkington Rd** PR8 35 D5
**Pilkington St**
6 Blackburn BB1 101 E4
14 Ramsbottom BL0 50 B5
Pilkington Tech Ctr L40 17 C6
**PILLING** 201 C6
**Pilling Ave**
Accrington BB5 104 E2
Lytham St Anne's FY8 90 C7
**Pilling Cl**
Chorley PR7 43 D6
Southport PR9 53 F5
**Pilling Cres** FY3 131 A8
**Pilling Ct** FY3 153 A1
**Pilling Field** BL7 47 E1
**Pilling La**
Chorley PR7 43 D6
Maghull L31 5 A5
Pilling Lane FY6 200 B7
**PILLING LANE** 200 B6
**Pilling Pl** WN8 9 C5
Pilling St John's CE Prim Sch PR3 201 C6
**Pilling St**
Haslingden BB4 85 B6
3 Rawtenstall BB4 69 F8
**Pilmuir Rd** BB2 101 E1
**Pilot St** BB5 104 B7
**Pimbo La** WN8 9 F3
**Pimbo Rd** WN8 9 C5
**PIMHOLE** 33 A1
Pimhole Bsns Pk BL9 33 A1
**Pimhole Rd** BL9 33 B2
**Pimlico** BB7 189 F3
**Pimlico Link Rd** BB7 190 C2
**Pimlico Rd** BB7 189 F2
**Pinch Clough Rd** BB4 86 F5
**PINCOCK** 42 C8
**Pincock Brow** PR7 42 C8
**Pincock St** PR7 42 C8
**Pinder Cl** BB7 189 B4
**Pinder St** BB9 170 F2
**Pine Ave**
Blackpool FY1 130 E2
Much Hoole PR4 74 D4
Ormskirk L39 15 F7
**Pine Cl**
Fulwood PR2 118 F4
Halton LA2 219 C6
Newburgh WN8 27 A1
Rishton BB1 103 B8
Skelmersdale WN8 17 F1
**Pine Cres**
Blackpool FY3 131 C2
Oswaldtwistle BB5 103 F3
Poulton-le-F FY6 153 E2
**Pine Crest** L39 15 B2
**Pine Dr** L39 15 F6
**Pine Gr**
Chorley PR6 61 D3
Clitheroe BB7 166 D7
Garstang PR3 204 C1
Ormskirk L39 15 F7
Southport PR9 35 D7
Pine Lake Resort★ LA6 240 A3
**Pine St N** BL9 33 B3
**Pine St S** BL9 33 B2
**Pines Cl** PR5 78 C4
**Pine St**
7 Bacup OL13 88 A1
Blackburn BB1 102 A7
Burnley BB11 128 B5
Bury BL9 33 B2
Darwen BB3 65 B8
Haslingden BB4 85 C3
Lancaster LA1 218 C1
Morecambe LA4 217 C4
Nelson BB9 148 F8
**Pines The**
Leyland PR26 59 A8
Southport PR8 34 F6
**Pineway** PR2 117 C4
**Pine Way** PR4 114 B7
**Pine Wlks** PR2 116 C1
**Pinewood**
Blackburn BB2 80 F8
Skelmersdale WN8 18 D3
**Pinewood Ave**
Blackpool FY2 152 E4
Broughton PR3 137 C3
Caton LA2 237 C3
Formby L37 11 D1
Hest Bank LA5 220 F2
Knott End-on-S FY6 200 A5
Morecambe LA4 217 F6
Thornton FY5 153 B7
**Pinewood Cl**
Formby L37 11 D2
Lancaster LA2 214 E2
Southport PR8 36 C1
**Pinewood Cotts** 1 LA2 239 D8
**Pinewood Cres**
Leyland PR25 59 E8
Lytham St Anne's FY8 90 D4
Orrell WN5 10 E6
Ramsbottom BL0 50 B2
**Pinewood Dr**
Accrington BB5 104 E6
Nelson BB9 149 A7
**Pinewood Rd** PR1 97 A2
**PINFOLD** 23 F4
**Pinfold**
Barrowford BB9 170 E5
Longton PR4 75 A8
**Pinfold Cl**
Fulwood PR2 118 E5
Southport PR8 21 B3
**Pinfold La**
Inskip PR4 157 C2
Lancaster LA1 218 D2
Longridge PR3 140 B4
Pinfold L40 23 F3
Southport PR8 21 B3
**Pinfold Pl**
5 Kirkham PR4 113 F5
Nelson BB9 171 B1
Skelmersdale WN8 9 D4
Pinfold Prim Sch L40 24 A3
**Pinfold St** PR1 97 E8
**Pingle Croft** PR6 78 A2
**Pingwood La** L33 1 A5
**Pink Pl** BB2 101 B3
**Pink St** BB12 127 C6
**Pinnacle Dr** BL7 47 E2
**Pinner La** BB4 85 F7
**Pinners Cl** BL0 50 B7
**Pintail Cl**
Leyland PR26 76 A1
5 Rochdale OL12 52 B2
**Pintail Way** FY8 90 E7
**Pioneer Cl** BL6 32 C4
**Pioneer St** BL6 32 C4
**Piper Cotts** 4 LA4 217 C3
**Piper Lea** BB4 87 A1
**Piper's La** LA6 240 C8
**Pippin Bank** OL13 87 F1
Pippin Bank Mill OL13 87 F1
**Pippin St**
Burscough L40 25 A2
Thorpe Green PR6 78 E5
**PIPPIN STREET** 78 E6
**Pit Hey Pl** WN8 9 C5
**Pittman Ct** PR2 118 B8
**Pittman Way** PR2 118 C7
**Pittsdale Ave** FY3 131 A2
**Pitts House La** PR9 36 B8
**Pitt St**
Lancaster LA1 214 F8
11 Padiham BB12 126 D8
Preston PR1 96 E7
Southport PR9 35 D6
**Pitville St** BB3 81 F3
**Place-de-Criel** 12 BB9 148 D8
**Place The** FY1 130 B7
**Plainmoor Dr** FY5 152 F7
**Plain Pl** BB2 101 E3
**Plane St**
Bacup OL13 87 F4
Blackburn BB1 102 A7
Planet Earth Ctr★ OL14 88 F4
**Plane Tree Cl** BB11 127 D3
**Plane Tree Rd** 7 BB1 102 A7
**Plantain Wlk** LA3 217 B2
**Plantation Ave**
Arnside LA5 224 C8
Knott End-on-S FY6 199 E5
**Plantation Gr** LA5 224 C8
**Plantation La** LA2 232 D1
**Plantation Rd**
Accrington BB5 104 E6
Blackburn BB2 101 B1
Burscough L40 25 B4
Edgworth BL7 48 F7
**Plantation Sq** BB5 104 D6
**Plantation St**
Accrington BB5 104 D6
Bacup OL13 70 C8
Burnley BB10 128 A7
6 Nelson BB9 170 F1
Rawtenstall BB4 86 B2
**Plantation The** BD23 236 B3
**Plantation View**
Bacup OL13 87 F6
Ramsbottom BL0 50 C3
**Plant St**
Oswaldtwistle BB5 103 D3
Preston PR2 117 C1
Platform Gall The★ BB7 166 E8
**Platt Cl** BB5 104 A5
**Platten Gr** LA4 217 C5
**Platt La** WN1 30 B3
**Platts La** L40 25 D2
Platts Lane Ind Est L40 25 D2
**Platt St** FY1 130 C6
**Pleasant Gr** FY5 176 B2
**Pleasant Pl** 4 BB11 127 F5
**Pleasant St**
Blackpool FY1 130 B7
Haslingden BB4 85 B3
3 Lytham St Anne's FY8 91 B3

**Pleasant View**
Bacup OL13 . . . . 70 C7
15 Barnoldswick BB18 . . . 196 B2
Billington BB7 . . . . 144 B4
Blackpool FY4 . . . . 111 A4
Coppull PR7 . . . . 42 F2
Earby BB18 . . . . 197 C1
Hoddlesden BB3 . . . . 82 F1
Leyland PR26 . . . . 76 C3
Newchurch BB4 . . . . 86 F1
Tockholes BB3 . . . . 81 A1
Withnell PR6 . . . . 80 A1
**PLEASINGTON** . . . . 100 C1
**Pleasington Ave** PR3 . . . . 181 D6
**Pleasington Cl**
Blackburn BB2 . . . . 101 B4
Blackpool FY4 . . . . 111 A8
**Pleasington Gr** BB10 . . . . 128 D5
**Pleasington La** BB2 . . . . 80 C8
Pleasington Old Hall Nature Reserve* BB2 . . . . 100 D3
**Pleasington St** BB2 . . . . 101 B4
**Pleasington Sta** BB2 . . . . 100 C1
Pleasure Island* FY8 . . . . 89 E5
**Pleck Farm Ave** BB1 . . . . 101 E8
**PLECKGATE** . . . . 122 D1
**Pleckgate Fold** BB1 . . . . 122 E1
Pleckgate High Sch BB1 . . . . 122 D1
**Pleckgate Rd** BB1 . . . . 122 E1
**Pleck Pl** FY6 . . . . 153 B6
**Pleck Rd** BB5 . . . . 104 C6
**Plessington Ct** PR3 . . . . 140 A7
**Plevna Rd** PR1 . . . . 97 C8
**Plex La** L39 . . . . 14 C5
**Plex Moss La** L39 . . . . 13 D8
**Plock Gn** PR7 . . . . 43 C5
**Plough La** L40 . . . . 17 A4
**Ploughlands The** 2 PR2 . . . . 116 E1
**Ploughmans Ct** 1 PR2 . . . . 139 D1
**Plover Cl** FY5 . . . . 176 A5
**Plover Dr**
Bury BL9 . . . . 33 B4
Heysham LA3 . . . . 212 F5
**Plover St**
Burnley BB12 . . . . 127 D6
Preston PR1 . . . . 118 B1
**Plovers Way** FY3 . . . . 131 B6
**Plover View** 2 BB12 . . . . 127 D6
**Plox Brow** PR4 . . . . 57 A6
**Plumbe St** BB11 . . . . 128 A5
**Plumpton Ave** FY4 . . . . 110 F5
**Plumpton Field** PR4 . . . . 136 E2
**Plumpton La**
Great Plumpton PR4 . . . . 112 E7
Shirdley Hill L39 . . . . 22 E2
**Plumpton Rd** PR2 . . . . 117 C2
**Plumtree Cl** PR2 . . . . 118 C6
**Plunge Rd** BL0 . . . . 68 E3
**Plungington Rd** PR1, PR2 . . . . 117 E2
**Plymouth Ave** FY7 . . . . 175 C8
**Plymouth Gr** PR6 . . . . 43 E8
**Plymouth Rd** FY2, FY3 . . . 152 E1
**Poachers Trail** FY8 . . . . 90 D7
**Poachers Way** FY5 . . . . 176 A4
**Pochard Pl** 4 FY5 . . . . 175 F1
**Pocklington St** BB5 . . . . 104 D2
**Poets' Rd** BB12 . . . . 126 F7
**Point 65 Bsns Ctr** BB1 . . . . 102 B6
**Pointer Ct** LA1 . . . . 214 F6
**Pointer Gr** LA2 . . . . 219 D7
**Pointer The** LA1 . . . . 214 F6
**Poland St** BB5 . . . . 103 F5
**Polefield** PR2 . . . . 117 E7
**Pole La** BB3 . . . . 65 C8
**Pole St**
Preston PR1 . . . . 97 A8
Standish WN6 . . . . 29 E1
**Police St** BB3 . . . . 82 A1
**Police Yd** 18 LA2 . . . . 239 D8
**Pollard Pl** LA1 . . . . 218 E4
**Pollard Row** BB12 . . . . 169 F1
**Pollards La** BL9 . . . . 50 C2
**Pollard St**
Accrington BB5 . . . . 104 C7
Burnley BB11 . . . . 127 D5
4 Nelson BB9 . . . . 170 E1
6 Preston PR1 . . . . 96 E8
**Pollux Gate** FY8 . . . . 90 C4
**Polperro Dr** PR4 . . . . 93 A6
**Pomfret St**
Blackburn BB2 . . . . 101 D3
Burnley BB11 . . . . 127 E6
**Pompian Brow** PR26 . . . . 57 E6
**Pond Cl** PR4 . . . . 57 A5
**Pond Gdns** FY6 . . . . 153 B6
**Pond St** LA5 . . . . 223 D2
**Pond Terr** LA5 . . . . 223 D2
**Pont St** BB9 . . . . 148 D7
Pontville Residential Sch L39 . . . . 15 D3
**Pool Ct** FY7 . . . . 198 D1
**Poole Rd** PR2 . . . . 118 A4
**Poole St** BB1 . . . . 102 C5
**Pool Foot La** FY6 . . . . 154 E4
**POOL HEY** . . . . 36 B3
**Pool Hey La** PR8, PR9 . . . . 36 B3
**Poolhill Cl** FY5 . . . . 152 E7
Pool House Com Prim Sch PR2 . . . . 117 A6
**Pool House Ct** PR2 . . . . 117 A6
**Pool House La** PR2 . . . . 117 A5
**Pool La** PR4 . . . . 93 A4
**Poolside** PR4 . . . . 93 C6
**Poolside Wlk** PR9 . . . . 54 C4
**Pool St** PR9 . . . . 54 D5
**Poorsland Barn** BB7 . . . . 229 C7
**Poot Hall** OL12 . . . . 52 F3
**Pope La**
Fulwood PR2 . . . . 119 A3
Kingsfold PR1 . . . . 96 C2
White Stake PR4 . . . . 76 B8
**Pope Wlk** PR1 . . . . 96 D3
**Poplar Ave**
Bamber Bridge PR5 . . . . 97 F1
Blackpool FY3 . . . . 130 D5
Bury BL9 . . . . 33 B3
Euxton PR7 . . . . 60 C4
Great Harwood BB6 . . . . 124 D6
Horwich BL6 . . . . 32 E1
Kirkham PR4 . . . . 114 A4
Longton PR4 . . . . 75 B8
Poulton-le-F FY6 . . . . 153 E2
4 Rochdale OL12 . . . . 52 C1
Warton PR4 . . . . 92 D6
**Poplar Bank** PR9 . . . . 53 D1
**Poplar Cl**
Bamber Bridge PR5 . . . . 97 F1
Oswaldtwistle BB5 . . . . 103 F3
Rishton BB1 . . . . 103 B8
**Poplar Ct** FY8 . . . . 89 E5
**Poplar Dr**
Coppull PR7 . . . . 42 F1
Freckleton PR4 . . . . 93 A5
Higher Penwortham PR1 . . . 96 C5
Longridge PR3 . . . . 140 A8
Skelmersdale WN8 . . . . 17 F1
**Poplar Gr**
Bamber Bridge PR5 . . . . 97 F1
Fulwood PR2 . . . . 119 A4
Ramsbottom BL0 . . . . 50 D7
**Poplar St**
2 Blackburn BB1 . . . . 102 A7
Chorley PR7 . . . . 43 D6
Haslingden BB4 . . . . 85 B3
Nelson BB9 . . . . 170 F1
Southport PR8 . . . . 35 E6
**Poplars The**
Adlington PR7 . . . . 30 F6
Burscough L40 . . . . 25 E2
**Poplar Terr** BB4 . . . . 85 F6
**Poppy Ave** PR6 . . . . 61 D2
**Poppy Cl** PR8 . . . . 35 B2
**Poppyfield** PR4 . . . . 116 F6
**Poppyfields** PR4 . . . . 73 E4
**Poppy La** L39 . . . . 16 B1
**Porritt Ave** LA1 . . . . 214 D8
**Porritt Ct** FY8 . . . . 89 E6
**Porritt St**
Bury BL9 . . . . 33 B4
Bury, Free Town BL9 . . . . 33 A4
**Porritt Way** BL0 . . . . 50 C7
**Portal Gr** BB12 . . . . 127 B6
**Porter Pl** 2 PR1 . . . . 97 A6
**Porter St E** 4 PR4 . . . . 113 F6
**Porters Row** FY6 . . . . 177 C7
**Porter St**
Accrington BB5 . . . . 103 F5
Preston PR1 . . . . 118 B1
**Portfield Bar** BB7 . . . . 144 F3
**Portfield La** BB6 . . . . 144 F3
**Portfield Rd** BB7 . . . . 144 E4
**Porthcawl Ct** PR2 . . . . 116 F3
**Portland Cotts** PR6 . . . . 62 D8
**Portland Ct** FY4 . . . . 111 A1
**Portland Dr** LA3 . . . . 217 B2
Portland Ind Est 12 BL9 . . 33 A4
**Portland Pl** BL6 . . . . 32 C3
**Portland Rd**
Blackpool FY1 . . . . 130 D4
Langho BB6 . . . . 123 C8
**Portland St**
Accrington BB5 . . . . 104 A6
Barrowford BB9 . . . . 170 D3
Blackburn BB2 . . . . 101 C3
Bury BL9 . . . . 33 A4
1 Chorley PR6 . . . . 43 D8
Colne BB8 . . . . 171 F5
Darwen BB3 . . . . 65 B6
Lancaster LA1 . . . . 214 F7
Nelson BB9 . . . . 148 D8
Preston PR1 . . . . 96 D7
Southport PR8 . . . . 35 B5
**Portman St** PR1 . . . . 118 B1
**Portree Cl** PR2 . . . . 118 C5
**Portree Cres** BB1 . . . . 102 D3
**Portree Rd** FY2 . . . . 152 E5
**Port Royal Ave** LA1 . . . . 214 C8
**PORTSMOUTH** . . . . 108 F1
**Portsmouth Ave** BB10 . . . 148 E2
**Portsmouth Cl** 7 FY5 . . . . 175 F4
**Portsmouth Dr** PR6 . . . . 43 E8
**Portway** FY2 . . . . 152 E6
**Port Way**
Heysham LA3 . . . . 212 D5
Preston PR2 . . . . 96 C7
**Postern Gate Rd** LA2 . . . . 232 A8
**Post Horse La** LA2 . . . . 238 B7
**Post La** PR4 . . . . 92 F6
**Post Office Ave** 1 PR9 . . . 35 B7
**Post Office Bldgs** 18 BB18 . . . . 196 B2
**Post Office Row**
St Michael's on W PR3 . . . 157 C7
Tunstall LA6 . . . . 241 D4
Westhouse LA6 . . . . 242 E4
**Post Office Yd** 8 BB8 . . . . 171 E5
**Pot Gn** BL0 . . . . 50 A3
**POT HOUSE** . . . . 82 C3
**Pot House La**
Darwen BB3 . . . . 82 C3
Oswaldtwistle BB5 . . . . 103 F2
**Potter La**
Coupe Green PR5 . . . . 98 D5
Samlesbury PR5 . . . . 119 E2
**Potter Pl** WN8 . . . . 9 D5
**POTTERS BROOK** . . . . 207 B5
**Potter St** 5 BL9 . . . . 33 A3
**Poulton Ave**
Accrington BB5 . . . . 104 A8
Lytham St Anne's FY8 . . . . 90 B8
**Poulton Cres** PR5 . . . . 98 D3
**Poulton Ct** PR9 . . . . 35 F7
**Poulton Dr** FY6 . . . . 153 F3
**Poulton Gdns** FY6 . . . . 153 F3
**Poulton Gr** 4 FY7 . . . . 199 A4
Poulton Ind Est FY6 . . . . 154 A3
**POULTON-LE-FIELD** . . . . 153 E2
Poulton-le-Fylde Sta FY6 . . . . 153 D4
Poulton-le-Sands CE Prim Sch LA4 . . . . 217 B6
**Poulton Old Rd** FY3 . . . . 152 F1
**Poulton Plaiz Holiday Pk** FY6 . . . . 153 C2
**Poulton Rd**
Blackpool FY3 . . . . 130 E8
Carleton FY6 . . . . 153 C5
Fleetwood FY7 . . . . 198 F4
Morecambe LA4 . . . . 217 B5
Southport PR9 . . . . 35 F7
**Poulton Sq** 11 LA4 . . . . 217 B6
**Poulton St**
Fleetwood FY7 . . . . 199 A4
Kirkham PR4 . . . . 114 B5
Preston PR2 . . . . 117 C1
**Powder House La** LA1, LA4 . . . . 218 A4
**Powderworks La** L31 . . . . 6 C3
**Powell Ave** FY4 . . . . 110 D8
**Powell St**
Barnoldswick BB18 . . . . 196 B3
Burnley BB11 . . . . 127 E4
Darwen BB3 . . . . 82 A2
**Powis Dr** PR4 . . . . 57 A8
**Powis Rd** PR2 . . . . 96 B8
**Powys Cl** BB4 . . . . 85 B1
**Poynter St** 4 PR1 . . . . 118 C1
**Poynton St** BL9 . . . . 33 A1
**Prairie Cres** BB10 . . . . 148 B2
**Pratt St** BB10 . . . . 148 B1
**PREESALL** . . . . 200 A3
**Preesall Cl**
Lytham St Anne's FY8 . . . . 90 B7
Preston PR2 . . . . 116 E1
Southport PR9 . . . . 53 F4
Preesall Fleetwood's Charity CE Prim Sch FY6 . . . . 200 B3
Preesall Mill Ind Est FY6 . . . . 200 B2
**Preesall Moss La** FY6 . . . 200 D2
**PREESALL PARK** . . . . 200 C1
**Preesall Rd** PR2 . . . . 116 E1
**Preese Gdns** PR4 . . . . 156 A1
**Preese Hall** PR4 . . . . 132 D5
**Premier Way** FY6 . . . . 153 F3
**Prenton Gdns** FY5 . . . . 153 A7
**Prescot Cl** BL9 . . . . 33 A1
**Prescot Gn** L39 . . . . 15 D3
**Prescot Pl**
Blackpool FY3 . . . . 131 A2
Thornton FY5 . . . . 176 C2
**Prescot Rd** L31, L39 . . . . 6 D6
**Prescott Ave** L40 . . . . 39 A3
**Prescott Rd** WN8 . . . . 9 F4
**Prescott St** BB10 . . . . 128 C5
Presfield Sch PR9 . . . . 54 A3
**Press Rd** FY8 . . . . 89 D8
**Prestbury Ave**
Blackpool FY4 . . . . 110 C5
Southport PR8 . . . . 21 B5
**Prestbury Cl** BL9 . . . . 33 A1
**Prestbury Dr** LA3 . . . . 217 B2
**PRESTON** . . . . 96 C8
**Preston Beck** BB18 . . . . 197 B2
Preston College Park Campus PR1 . . . . 117 F2
Preston Coll Fulwood Campus PR2 . . . . 117 F5
Preston Ent Ctr 6 PR1 . . . . 117 F1
Preston Grange Prim Sch PR2 . . . . 119 A4
Preston Greenlands Com Prim Sch PR2 . . . . 118 E3
**Preston Lancaster New Rd** PR3 . . . . 181 B4
**Preston Lancaster Old Rd** PR3 . . . . 181 D2
**Preston Lancaster Rd**
Bilsborrow PR3 . . . . 159 A6
Cabus PR3 . . . . 204 C5
Forton LA2, PR3 . . . . 207 C5
Galgate LA2 . . . . 211 A5
**Preston New Rd**
Blackburn BB2 . . . . 101 B5
Blackpool FY3, FY4 . . . . 131 C2
Clifton PR4 . . . . 94 C7
Freckleton PR4 . . . . 93 D7
Little Plumpton PR4 . . . . 112 C6
Mellor Brook BB2, PR5 . . . 120 D1
Samlesbury PR2, PR5 . . . . 119 E1
Southport PR9 . . . . 54 B4
**Preston Nook** PR7 . . . . 41 C5
**Preston Old Rd**
Blackburn BB2 . . . . 80 D8
Blackpool FY3 . . . . 131 A2
Clifton PR4 . . . . 115 C1
Freckleton PR4 . . . . 93 C6
**Preston Rd**
Charnock Richard PR7 . . . . 42 C4
Chorley PR6, PR7 . . . . 61 C2
Clayton Brook PR5, PR6, PR7 . . . . 78 B4
Grimsargh PR2, PR3 . . . . 139 E2
Inskip PR4 . . . . 135 D7
Leyland PR25 . . . . 77 B2
Longridge, New Town PR3 . . . . 140 A5
Longridge PR3 . . . . 140 E6
Lucas Green PR6 . . . . 61 C4
Lytham St Anne's FY8 . . . . 91 D4
Ribchester PR3 . . . . 141 B5
Southport PR9 . . . . 35 E8
Standish PR7, WN6 . . . . 29 D5
**Preston St**
Carnforth LA5 . . . . 223 D2
1 Chorley PR6 . . . . 61 D1
Darwen BB3 . . . . 81 F3
Fleetwood FY7 . . . . 199 B4
Kirkham PR4 . . . . 114 B5
16 Rochdale OL12 . . . . 52 C1
Preston Sta PR1 . . . . 96 E7
Preston Tech Ctr PR1 . . . . 96 D8
**Preston Temple** PR6 . . . . 61 C4
**Prestwich St** BB11 . . . . 127 E5
**Prestwood Pl** WN8 . . . . 9 F4
**Pretoria St** 2 OL12 . . . . 52 C1
**PRETTYWOOD** . . . . 33 E2
**Price Cl** LA1 . . . . 218 C3
**Price St**
9 Blackpool FY1 . . . . 130 B1
Bury BL9 . . . . 33 A1
**Prickshaw** OL12 . . . . 52 B6
**Prickshaw La** OL12 . . . . 52 B6
**Priestfield Ave** BB8 . . . . 171 B5
**Priesthouse Cl** L37 . . . . 12 A3
**Priesthouse La** L37 . . . . 12 A3
**PRIEST HUTTON** . . . . 240 C4
**Priestfield** FY5 . . . . 153 A7
**Priestley Nook** 4 BB5 . . . 104 C5
**PRIMET BRIDGE** . . . . 171 C3
**Primet Bridge** BB8 . . . . 171 C4
Primet Bsns Ctr 4 BB8 . . . . 171 B4
**Primet Hill** BB8 . . . . 171 C4
**Primet Hts** 2 BB8 . . . . 171 B3
**Primet St** BB8 . . . . 171 C4
**PRIMROSE** . . . . 166 D6
**Primrose Ave** FY4 . . . . 110 D6
**Primrose Bank**
1 Bacup OL13 . . . . 70 C8
Blackburn BB1 . . . . 101 F6
Blackpool FY2 . . . . 152 F6
Read BB12 . . . . 145 D2
**Primrose Cl**
Blackburn BB2 . . . . 101 B2
Formby L37 . . . . 12 B5
Hesketh Bank PR4 . . . . 73 E4
Southport PR9 . . . . 54 C6
**Primrose Cotts**
Calder Vale PR3 . . . . 182 E7
Middleton LA3 . . . . 213 A2
**Primrose Ct**
1 Blackburn BB1 . . . . 101 F5
6 Lancaster LA1 . . . . 215 A7
Morecambe LA4 . . . . 217 B5
**Primrose Dr**
2 Blackburn BB1 . . . . 101 F5
Bury BL9 . . . . 33 D4
Cold Row FY6 . . . . 177 D4
**Primrose Gr** PR1 . . . . 118 C3
**PRIMROSE HILL** . . . . 14 F8
**Primrose Hill**
Colne BB8 . . . . 171 F5
Mellor BB1, BB2 . . . . 122 A3
3 Preston PR1 . . . . 97 B7
Primrose Hill Prim Sch PR7 . . . . 60 B4
**Primrose Hill Rd** PR7 . . . . 60 B4
**Primrose La**
Preston PR1 . . . . 118 C3
Standish WN6 . . . . 29 D2
**Primrose Rd**
Clitheroe BB7 . . . . 166 D6
Preston PR1 . . . . 118 C3
**Primrose Row** PR7 . . . . 59 F1
**Primrose St**
Accrington BB5 . . . . 104 A4
9 Bacup OL13 . . . . 70 C8
Brierfield BB9 . . . . 148 B5
Burnley BB10 . . . . 148 C1
Chorley PR6 . . . . 43 D8
Clitheroe BB7 . . . . 166 D7
Darwen BB3 . . . . 65 B8
Lancaster LA1 . . . . 215 A7
6 Morecambe LA4 . . . . 217 B5
**Primrose Terr**
Blackburn BB2 . . . . 101 B2
Blackpool FY4 . . . . 111 A4
1 Darwen BB3 . . . . 65 B8
Langho BB6 . . . . 143 C1
**Primrose Way**
Carleton FY6 . . . . 153 B6
Church BB5 . . . . 103 E7
**Primula Dr** BB3 . . . . 82 A7
**Prince Ave** LA5 . . . . 223 E1
**Prince Charles Gdns** PR8 . . . . 34 F4
**Prince Lee Mdws** BB3 . . . . 65 B8
**Princes Cres** LA4 . . . . 217 E7
**Princes Ct**
Higher Penwortham PR1 . . . . 96 B6
4 Morecambe LA4 . . . . 217 E6
18 Ramsbottom BL0 . . . . 50 C6
**Princes Dr** PR2 . . . . 117 E6
**Princes Gdn** PR8 . . . . 35 E6
**Princes Gdns** LA4 . . . . 217 E5
**Prince's Pk** WN6 . . . . 19 F4
**Princes Rd**
Higher Penwortham PR1 . . . . 96 B6
Lytham St Anne's FY8 . . . . 90 D4
**Prince's Rd** PR5 . . . . 97 E5
**Princes Reach** PR2 . . . . 96 A7
**Princess Alexandra Way** LA3 . . . . 212 D5
**Princess Ave**
Clitheroe BB7 . . . . 189 F1
Kirkham PR4 . . . . 113 F6
Lancaster LA1 . . . . 214 F6
Poulton-le-F FY6 . . . . 153 D3
**Princess Ct** 5 FY1 . . . . 130 B3
**Princess Gdns** BB2 . . . . 80 D7
**Princess Par** FY1 . . . . 130 B6
**Princess Rd**
Adlington PR6 . . . . 31 B8
Cleveleys FY5 . . . . 175 C2
**Princess St**
Accrington BB5 . . . . 103 F6
17 Bacup OL13 . . . . 87 F2
2 Bamber Bridge, Lostock Hall PR5 . . . . 77 B7
10 Bamber Bridge PR5 . . . . 77 F8
Blackburn BB2 . . . . 101 C2
Blackpool FY1 . . . . 130 B3
Burnley BB12 . . . . 126 B8
Chorley PR7 . . . . 43 D6
Church BB5 . . . . 103 E6
Colne BB8 . . . . 171 C4
Great Harwood BB6 . . . . 124 D5
Haslingden BB4 . . . . 85 B2
Leyland PR25 . . . . 77 B1
Nelson BB9 . . . . 148 D7
Preston PR1 . . . . 97 B7
26 Rochdale OL12 . . . . 52 F1
Whalley BB7 . . . . 144 C5
Whitworth OL12 . . . . 52 C8
**Princes St**
Rishton BB1 . . . . 124 B1
Southport PR8 . . . . 35 A6
**Prince's St** BB2 . . . . 101 D4
**Princess Way**
Burnley BB12 . . . . 127 F7
Euxton PR7 . . . . 60 E2
**Prince St**
Britannia OL13 . . . . 71 D7
11 Burnley BB11 . . . . 127 E5
Darwen BB3 . . . . 81 F1
Ramsbottom BL0 . . . . 50 C6
**Princes Way**
Cleveleys FY5 . . . . 175 C1
Fleetwood FY7 . . . . 198 D3
**Princeton Sq** FY8 . . . . 90 D7
**Princeway** FY4 . . . . 110 C7
**Pringle Bank** LA5 . . . . 223 D6
**Pringle Ct** PR3 . . . . 181 C7
**Pringle St** BB1 . . . . 102 A3
**Pringle Wood** PR3 . . . . 137 C2
**Prinny Hill Rd** BB4 . . . . 85 A3
**Printers Fold** BB12 . . . . 126 E6
**Printshop La** BB3 . . . . 65 A6
**Prior's Cl** BB2 . . . . 101 A6
**Priorsgate** 3 LA3 . . . . 217 C2
**Prior's Oak Cotts** PR1 . . . . 96 C6
**Priors Wlk** BB7 . . . . 230 C1
**Priorswood Pl** WN8 . . . . 9 F4
**Priory Chase** BB9 . . . . 148 F8
**Priory Cl**
Blackburn BB1 . . . . 102 E4
Burscough L40 . . . . 25 D5
Formby L37 . . . . 12 B2
Higher Penwortham PR1 . . . 96 C6
6 Lancaster LA1 . . . . 214 E8
Leyland PR25 . . . . 77 C2
Morecambe LA3 . . . . 217 C2
Newchurch BB4 . . . . 86 E2
Pleasington BB2 . . . . 100 C2
Tarleton PR4 . . . . 57 A6
**Priory Cres** PR1 . . . . 96 C6
**Priory Ct**
7 Blackpool FY1 . . . . 130 C5
Burnley BB11 . . . . 128 B2
Lytham St Anne's FY8 . . . . 89 E7
**Priory Dr** BB3 . . . . 65 C8
**Priory Gate** FY4 . . . . 110 C5
**Priory Gdns**
Scorton PR3 . . . . 204 E6
Southport PR8 . . . . 34 F4
**Priory Gr** L39 . . . . 15 D4
**Priory Grange**
Darwen BB3 . . . . 65 C8
Southport PR8 . . . . 35 A4
Priory Hospl Preston The PR4 . . . . 136 A1
**Priory La**
Higher Penwortham PR1 . . . . 96 C6
Hornby LA2 . . . . 238 B7
**Priory Mews**
Lytham St Anne's FY8 . . . . 90 D7
Southport PR8 . . . . 34 F6
**Priory Nook** WN8 . . . . 10 C7
**Priory Pl** BB3 . . . . 65 C8
**Priory Rd** WN8 . . . . 10 C7
Priory Sports & Tech Coll PR1 . . . . 96 A5
**Priory St**
5 Nelson BB9 . . . . 170 F1
Preston PR2 . . . . 96 D8
**Priory Way** BB18 . . . . 196 A2

Priory Wlk 6 LA1 215 A8
Pritchard St
Blackburn BB2 101 E2
Burnley BB11 127 E5
Private La BB4 68 C8
Procter Moss Rd
Lower Green Bank LA2 232 B3
Quernmore LA2 215 D1
Procter's Brow LA2 239 B5
Procter St BB2 101 F3
Proctor Cft BB8 172 B2
Proctor Cl BB9 148 F5
Proctor Rd L37 11 C4
Progress Ave BB1 102 A7
Progress Bsns Pk PR4 114 A4
Progress Ct FY3 131 B8
Progress Rd BB9 170 F3
Progress St
Chorley PR6 43 E8
Darwen BB3 82 B1
Progress Way FY4 111 B6
Promenade
Blackpool, Bispham FY2 152 B6
Blackpool FY1, FY4 130 B5
Cleveleys FY5 175 C5
Knott End-on-S FY6 199 E6
Southport, Ainsdale-on-S PR8 20 F6
Southport PR9 35 B8
Promenade N FY5 175 C3
Promenade Rd FY7 199 A5
Promenade S FY5 175 C2
Prospect Ave
Bamber Bridge PR5 77 B8
Darwen BB3 81 E2
Hest Bank LA2 220 E1
Prospect Bldgs 5 BB9 148 D8
Prospect Ct
Catterall PR3 181 D2
Longridge PR3 140 B6
Prospect Dr LA2 220 E1
Prospect Farm Cvn Pk BB8 171 D3
Prospect Gdns BB3 81 E2
Prospect Gr LA4 217 C4
Prospect Hill
Haslingden BB4 85 A2
4 Rawtenstall BB4 86 A3
Prospect Pl
7 Middleforth Green PR1 96 E4
Preston PR2 117 B1
Skelmersdale WN8 9 F5
Prospect Rd BB4 86 A3
Prospect St
Great Harwood BB6 124 D5
Lancaster LA1 215 A7
Newchurch BB4 86 F1
Prospect Terr
Bacup OL13 70 E7
10 Barrowford BB9 170 D4
Belthorn BB1 82 F6
Brinscall PR6 63 A8
Clow Bridge BB11 106 B4
Huncoat BB5 125 E2
Newchurch BB4 86 F1
Prospect View
Bamber Bridge PR5 77 A7
9 Rawtenstall BB4 86 A3
Provence Ave BB6 143 C6
Providence St BB1 102 A8
Prudy Hill FY6 153 D4
Prunella Dr BB3 82 A7
Pudding La OL14 109 C2
Pudding Pie Nook La PR3 137 F4
Puddle House La FY6 131 F8
PUDSEY 109 B2
Pudsey Rd OL14 109 B2
Pump House La PR26 58 F6
Pump St
Blackburn BB2 101 D4
Burnley BB11 127 E6
Clitheroe BB7 166 D8
Preston PR1 97 A8
Punnell's La L31 4 F5
Punstock Rd BB3 81 F1
Pupil Learning Ctr (New Summerseat Ho) BL0 50 B2
Purbeck Dr BL6 32 F1
Purlbrook Ct BL6 32 B4
Pye Busk LA2 239 E8
Pye Busk Cl LA2 239 E8
Pye's Cotts L39 5 E7
Pygon's Hill La L31 5 D6

Q

Quail Holme Rd FY6 199 D5
Quaker Brook La PR5 99 A3
Quakerfields BB3 82 A2
Quaker La BB3 82 A2
Quakers' Pl WN6 29 E1
Quakers Terr WN6 29 D3
Quakers View BB9 148 A5
Quality Row BB7 164 E1
Quarlton Dr BL8 49 B3
Quarrybank 3 FY5 152 F8
Quarry Bank
Garstang PR3 181 C6
Haslingden BB4 84 F1
Quarry Bank St 3 BB12 127 C7
Quarry Dr L39 15 C1
Quarry Farm Ct BB7 190 D5
Quarry Hill OL12 52 E3
Quarry Hill Nature Reserve* BB9 148 F6
Quarry Mount L39 16 A6
Quarry Mount Mews LA1 215 A7
Quarry Rd
Brinscall PR6 62 F7
Caton LA2 237 E3
Chorley PR6 43 E6
Halton LA2 219 C6
Lancaster LA1 215 A7
Quarryside Dr L33 1 A3
Quarry St
13 Accrington BB5 104 C5
Blackburn BB1 101 F5
Hapton BB11 126 C2
Padiham BB12 146 D1
Ramsbottom BL0 50 D6
Rochdale OL12 52 E1
Shawforth OL12 71 E6
Quayle Ave FY4 110 E8
Quayside
5 Blackburn BB1 101 F4
Fleetwood FY7 199 B3
Quayside Ct PR2 96 A8
Quays The L40 25 E5
Quay W FY8 89 E5
Quebec Ave FY2 152 E3
Quebec Rd BB2 101 B8
Queen Anne St
4 Haslingden BB4 85 A3
Southport PR8 35 B7
Queen Charlotte Villas PR8 21 C5
Queen Elizabeth Cres BB5 104 D5
Queen Elizabeth Ct LA4 217 A5
Queen Elizabeth's Gram Sch BB2 101 C6
Queen Elizabeth's Gram Sch (Annexe) BB2 101 D6
Queen Ho BB4 86 D1
Queen Mary Ave FY8 90 A5
Queen Mary Terr BB7 144 B7
Queen St E 3 PR7 43 D6
Queens Ave L37 11 E5
Queensberry Rd BB11 127 E5
Queensborough Rd BB5 104 B7
Queensbury Rd FY5 175 C2
Queen's Cl
Clitheroe BB7 166 E7
Poulton-le-F FY6 153 E3
Queenscourt Ave PR1 96 E2
Queen's Cres PR4 114 B4
Queens Croft L37 11 D2
Queens Ct
Fulwood PR2 117 E3
Ormskirk L39 15 E4
Queen's Ct FY2 152 B2
Queens Ctyd 7 PR9 35 C8
Queensdale Cl PR5 97 E4
Queens Dr
Fulwood PR2 117 D6
Longridge PR3 140 A7
Morecambe LA4 217 E6
Staining FY3 131 E5
Queen's Dr
Carnforth LA5 223 E1
Oswaldtwistle BB5 103 F3
Queens Drive Prim Sch PR2 117 D5
Queens Garth BD23 197 B5
Queensgate
Chorley PR7 43 B7
Nelson BB9 148 D7
Queens Gn L39 13 F5
Queen's Gr PR7 43 C8
Queens Hotel Ct PR9 35 B8
Queens Jubilee Nature Trail* PR8 34 E5
Queen's Lancashire Regiment Mus The* PR2 118 B4
Queen's Lancashire Way BB11 127 F6
QUEEN'S PARK 102 B4
Queens Park Cl BB1 102 A3
Queen's Park Rd
Blackburn BB1 102 A3
Burnley BB10 128 C7
Queens Pl
Kirkham PR4 113 F7
Ramsbottom BL9 50 C2
Queen's Prom FY2 152 B5
Queen Sq LA1 214 F7
Queens Rd
Clitheroe BB7 166 E7
Orrell WN5 10 C5
Southport PR9 35 C8
Queen's Rd
Accrington BB5 104 C7
Blackburn BB1 102 B3
Burnley BB10 148 B2
Chorley PR7 43 C8
Darwen BB3 65 B6
Formby L37 11 D2
Fulwood PR2 117 E3
Lytham St Anne's FY8 89 F5
Walton-le-D PR5 97 E4
Queens Rd W BB5 104 A7
Queens Ret Pk PR1 97 B7
Queens Sq 1 FY1 130 B5
Queen's Sq
Hoddlesden BB3 82 F1
Poulton-le-F FY6 153 D3
7 Rawtenstall BB4 86 A2
Queen St
12 Accrington BB5 104 C6
Bacup, Rockliffe OL13 87 F2
5 Bacup, Stacksteads OL13 70 C8
4 Bamber Bridge PR5 77 B7
Barnoldswick BB18 196 B1
Barrowford BB9 170 D4
Blackpool FY1 130 B6
Burnley BB11 127 F5
Burnley, Harle Syke BB10 148 F2
Bury BL9 33 A2
Carnforth LA5 223 D1
Clayton-le-M BB5 124 F3
Clitheroe BB7 166 C8
Colne BB8 171 C4
Darwen BB3 81 F2
Fleetwood FY7 199 A4
Great Harwood BB6 124 D5
Hoddlesden BB3 82 F1
Horwich BL6 32 B3
Lancaster LA1 214 F7
Lytham St Anne's FY8 91 A3
Morecambe LA4 217 B5
Nelson BB9 170 E1
Ormskirk L39 15 E4
Oswaldtwistle BB5 103 E4
Padiham BB12 126 C8
Preston PR1 97 B7
Ramsbottom BL0 50 B6
Rawtenstall BB4 86 A2
Whalley BB7 144 C5
Queen's Terr
3 Bacup OL13 70 E8
Blackburn BB2 101 B1
Fleetwood FY7 199 C5
QUEENSTOWN 130 D7
Queen Street Mill Textile Mus* BB10 148 F2
Queensway
Bamber Bridge PR5 97 E1
Blackburn BB2 81 A8
Blackpool FY4 110 C7
Brinscall PR6 62 F8
Church BB5 103 F7
Clitheroe BB7 166 E7
Euxton PR7 60 E2
Higher Penwortham PR1 96 B6
Leyland PR25 59 E7
Lytham St Anne's FY4, FY8 111 B2
Newchurch BB4 86 E1
Poulton-le-F FY6 153 D3
Preston PR2 116 F2
Shevington WN6 19 F4
Waddington BB7 189 B4
Warton PR4 92 E7
Queensway Cl PR1 96 B6
Queensway Ct FY8 111 A1
Queensway Ind Est FY8 111 A2
Queens Wlk FY5 175 D4
Queen Vera Rd 4 FY1 130 B5
Queen Victoria Ctr LA4 217 B5
Queen Victoria Rd
Blackpool FY1 130 C2
Burnley BB10 148 B1
Queen Victoria St BB2 101 B2
Quenby Cnr FY6 153 B3
QUERNMORE 232 A6
Quernmore Ave FY3 131 A3
Quernmore Brow LA2 232 B5
Quernmore CE Prim Sch LA2 232 A7
Quernmore Dr
Glasson LA2 209 E4
Kelbrook BB18 195 A5
Quernmore Ind Est PR4 93 C6
Quernmore Rd
Caton LA2 237 B2
Kirkby L33 1 A3
Lancaster LA1, LA2 215 D7
Quernmore Wlk L33 1 A3
Quillet The LA5 224 F3
Quins Croft PR25 76 F2
Quin St PR25 77 A1
Quinton Cl PR8 21 A4

R

Rabbit La
Burscough L40 24 F4
Cow Ark BB7 187 F6
Raby Sq 12 LA4 217 B6
Raby St
4 Morecambe LA4 217 B5
1 Rawtenstall BB4 86 A2
Rachel Ho 5 BL9 33 C3
Radburn Brow PR6 78 B3
Radburn Cl PR6 78 B3
Radcliffe Ct BB12 127 A6
Radcliffe Rd FY7 198 F2
Radeclyffe St BB7 189 E1
Radfield Ave 17 BB3 65 A8
Radfield Head BB3 64 F8
Radfield Rd BB3 64 F8
RADFORD 65 A8
Radford Bank Gdns 13 BB3 65 A8
Radford Bank Ho 14 BB3 65 A8
Radford Gdns BB3 65 A7
Radford St BB3 65 A8
Radley Ave FY3 130 E8
Radnor Ave
Burnley BB12 127 A7
Cleveleys FY5 175 F1
Radnor Cl BB5 103 C4
Radnor Dr PR9 53 F3
Radnor St
Accrington BB5 104 B7
5 Preston PR1 96 E8
Radway Cl FY5 152 F7
Radworth Cres FY4 131 B1
Raeburn Ave BB11 127 E3
Raedale Ave BB10 148 B4
Raeside Ct FY8 90 A4
Raglan Rd
Burnley BB11 127 E5
Morecambe LA3 216 E3
Raglan St
8 Colne BB8 171 D4
4 Nelson BB9 148 D8
Preston PR2 117 D2
Raikes Hill 2 FY1 130 C5
Raikes Hill Dr LA2 218 C8
Raikes Mews 6 FY1 130 C5
Raikes Par FY1 130 C5
Raikes Rd
Great Eccleston PR3 156 C5
Preston PR1 118 C1
Thornton FY5 153 E8
Rail Cl WA11 8 F2
Railgate
Britannia OL13 71 C8
Whitworth OL13 88 C1
Railton Ave BB2 81 A8
Railway App L39 15 F5
Railway Ave PR9 54 F5
Railway Cotts
Coppull PR7 42 F1
Preston PR4 116 C3
Salwick PR4 115 C4
Railway Crossing La LA1 214 C5
Railway Gr 5 BB1 102 A7
Railway Path L39 15 E4
Railway Pl LA2 209 F5
Railway Rd
Adlington PR6, PR7 31 A7
Blackburn BB1 101 E5
Brinscall PR6 63 A8
Chorley PR6 61 D1
Darwen BB3 82 A1
Haslingden BB4 85 B4
Ormskirk L39 15 F5
Skelmersdale WN8 8 E8
Railway St
Bacup OL13 70 B8
23 Barnoldswick BB18 196 B2
Brierfield BB9 148 B5
Burnley BB11 127 F7
Chorley PR7 43 D7
Foulridge BB8 194 D1
Lancaster LA1 214 F6
Leyland PR25 77 B2
Nelson BB9 148 E7
Ramsbottom BL0 50 C6
Ramsbottom, Summerseat BL0, BL9 50 C2
Southport PR8 35 B5
Railway Terr
Brierfield BB9 148 B5
Entwistle BL7 48 B8
Great Harwood BB6 124 C4
10 Kirkham PR4 113 F6
Rawtenstall BB4 85 F1
Simonstone BB12 125 E8
Southport PR8 35 A5
Railway View
5 Accrington BB5 104 C6
Billington BB7 144 B4
Blackburn BB2 101 B2
Brierfield BB9 148 B6
Croston PR26 58 A2
3 Darwen BB3 65 B8
Railway View Ave BB7 189 E1
Railway View Rd BB7 189 E1
RAINFORD JUNCTION 8 F2
Rainford Rd L39, WA11 8 C4
Rainford Sta WA11 8 F2
RAINHALL 196 D3
Rainhall Cres BB18 196 D2
Rainhall Rd BB18 196 B2
Rake 4 BL0 50 B6
Rake Fold BL0 50 A6
RAKE FOOT 86 A7
Rake Foot BB4 85 B3
RAKE HEAD 70 A7
Rakehead La OL13 70 B8
Rakehouse Brow LA2 232 F2
Rake La PR4 92 D5
Rakes Bridge BB3 82 A7
Rakes House Rd BB9 170 E2
Rakes La BD23 231 F5
Rakes Rd LA2 237 E4
Rake The LA2 232 E1
Rake Top Ave BB12 146 F6
Raleigh Ave FY4 110 B5
Raleigh Cl FY8 110 D1
Raleigh Rd PR2 117 E6
Raleigh St BB12 126 E7
Ralph St BB5 104 C8
Ralph's Wife's La PR9 54 E6
Ramparts The LA1 218 E2
Ramper Gate FY5 175 D2
Ramsay Ct FY6 199 D5
RAMSBOTTOM 50 C5
Ramsbottom Cottage Hospl BL0 50 C5
Ramsbottom Heritage Ctr* BL0 50 C6
Ramsbottom La BL0 50 C7
Ramsbottom Rd
Hawkshaw BL8, BL7 49 A3
Horwich BL6 32 C3
Ramsbottom St BB5 104 B7
Ramsbottom Sta* BL0 50 C6
Ramsbottom Stubbins Prim Sch BL0 68 D1
Rams Clough La BB5 84 A8
Ramsden St LA5 223 D2
Ramsey Ave
Bacup OL13 88 A1
Blackpool FY3 130 D7
Preston PR1 118 D3
Ramsey Cl FY8 110 D1
Ramsey Gr BB10 148 C2
Ramsey Rd BB2 101 D1
Ramsgate Cl PR4 92 E7
Ramsgate Rd FY8 90 A8
Ramsgreave Ave BB1 122 D2
Ramsgreave Bsns Pk BB1 122 E2
Ramsgreave Dr BB1 122 D1
Ramsgreave Rd BB1 122 E4
Ramsgreave & Wilpshire Sta BB1 122 F4
Ramshill Ave FY6 153 B5
Ramson Ct 3 LA3 217 B2
Ranaldsway PR25 59 D8
Randall St 10 BB10 148 B1
Randal St BB1 101 E6
Randolph St 21 BB1 102 A4
Ranelagh Dr PR8 21 F7
Range High Sch L37 2 C8
Ranger St BB5 104 B5
Rangeway Ave FY4 110 C7
Ranglet Rd PR5 78 B7
Rangletts Ave PR7 43 C6
Ranglit Ave PR2 116 C1
Rankin Ave PR4 73 F2
Rankin Cl BB18 196 C2
Rankin Dr BB3 82 E1
Ranlea Ave LA4 218 A6
Ranleigh Dr
Newburgh WN8 27 A1
Skelmersdale WN8 18 A8
RANN 82 E6
Rannoch Dr BB2 100 F1
Ranslett Ct L37 12 A3
Rantreefold Rd LA2 239 C4
Rapley La PR4 136 A8
Ratcliffe Fold 5 BB4 85 B3
Ratcliffe St
Darwen BB3 65 B8
10 Haslingden BB4 85 B3
Ratcliffe Wharf La PR3 207 B1
Rathbone Rd L38 2 F4
Rathlyn Ave FY3 130 E7
RATHMELL 236 F6
Rathmell CE Prim Sch BD24 236 E7
Rathmell Cl FY3 153 B1
Rathmill Sike BB7 230 B1
Rathmore Cres PR9 54 B3
Rathmore Gdns FY2 152 E1
Ratten La PR4 95 D3
RATTEN ROW 156 B8
Raven Ave BB4 68 A7
Raven Cl PR7 42 F5
Raven Croft BB4 68 B8
Ravendale Cl OL12 52 A1
Ravenglass Ave L31 5 D2
Ravenglass Cl
Blackburn BB2 102 A1
Blackpool FY4 110 E7
Kirkham PR4 114 A7
Ravenhead Dr WN8 10 A7
Ravenhead Way WN8 9 F6
Ravenhill Dr PR7 61 C1
Raven Meols Hills Nature Reserve* L37 2 B7
Raven Meols La L37 11 F2
Raven Meols Lo L37 11 E2
Ravenoak La BB10 129 B5
Raven Pk BB4 68 B8
Raven Rd BB2 101 B5
Ravens Cl LA1 218 C3
Raven's Cl FY3 131 B7
Ravens Close Brow LA2 241 F1
Ravenscroft L37 11 F2
Ravenscroft Ave L39 15 E4
Ravenscroft Cl BB1 123 A1
Ravenscroft Way BB18 196 C3
Ravens Gr BB10 148 C4
Raven St
3 Nelson BB9 170 F1
Preston PR1 118 C2
Ravens The L37 11 F2
Ravensthorpe PR7 61 A1
Ravenswing Ave BB2 101 B7
Ravenswood
Fulwood PR2 118 E2
Great Harwood BB6 124 B6
Ravens Wood BB2 101 B5
Ravenswood Ave FY3 131 B7
Ravenwood Ave FY4 110 D5
Rawcliffe Dr PR2 95 E8
Rawcliffe Rd
12 Chorley PR7 43 C7
Ratten Row PR3 156 C7

Rawcliffe St
Blackpool FY4 110 B8
Burnley BB11 128 A6
Rawlinson Ct PR9 35 D8
Rawlinson Gr PR9 53 F1
Rawlinson La PR6 43 E1
Rawlinson Rd PR9 53 E1
Rawlinson St
[1] Darwen BB3 65 B6
[13] Horwich BL6 32 B4
[5] Kirkham PR4 113 F6
Rawson Ave BB5 104 A4
Rawsons Rake BL0, BL8 50 A6
Rawson St [12] BB10 148 B1
Raws St BB11 128 A6
Rawsthorne Ave
Edenfield BL0 68 D2
Haslingden BB4 85 B2
Rawstorne Cl PR4 93 A6
Rawstorne Cres PR4 95 E1
Rawstorne Rd PR1 96 B5
Rawstorne St BB2 101 C4
Rawstron St OL12 71 C1
RAWTENSTALL 86 B1
Rawtenstall Cribden House Com Specl Sch BB4 85 E1
Rawtenstall Newchurch CE Prim Sch BB4 86 E1
Rawtenstall Rd BB4 85 C1
Rawtenstall St Anne's CE Prim Sch BB4 86 F3
Rawtenstall St Paul's Constable Lee CE Prim Sch BB4 86 A4
Rawtenstall Sta BB4 85 F1
Rawtenstall Water Prim Sch BB4 87 A8
Rawthey Rd [5] LA1 218 B2
Raybourne Ave FY6 153 C3
Raygill Ave BB11 127 D3
Raygill Pl [3] LA1 218 B2
Ray La PR3 181 F4
Raylees BL0 50 C4
Raymond Ave FY2 130 D8
Raynor St BB2 101 D5
Rays Dr LA1 214 F3
Ray St BB9 148 A5
READ 145 D2
Reading Cl [14] BB1 102 A4
Read St John's CE Prim Sch BB12 145 D2
Read's Ave FY1 130 C4
Reads Ct [7] FY1 130 C4
Read St [2] BB5 125 A1
Reaney Ave [3] FY4 110 E7
Record St BB18 196 B1
Rectory Cl
Chorley PR7 43 C8
Croston PR26 58 C2
Darwen BB3 65 C8
Newchurch BB4 86 E1
Tarleton PR4 57 A5
Rectory Gdns LA2 206 C5
Rectory Hill BL9 33 D4
Rectory La
Bury BL9 33 D4
Standish WN1, WN6 30 A1
Rectory Paddock LA2 219 C6
Rectory Rd
Blackpool FY4 130 E1
Burnley BB12 127 F7
Southport PR9 54 A1
RED BANK 43 E5
Red Bank BL9 33 E6
Red Bank Rd FY2 152 C4
Red Barnes L37 11 F5
Red Bridge La LA5 224 F4
Redcar Ave
Cleveleys FY5 175 F5
Fulwood PR2 117 A4
Redcar Cl PR8 35 F3
Redcar Rd
Blackpool FY1 130 B8
Lancaster LA1 215 B3
Red Cat La L40 25 E7
Redcliffe Gdns L39 15 E3
Red Court Cvn Pk LA5 223 D1
Redcross St N OL12 52 F1
Redcross St OL12 52 F1
Red Cross St [5] PR1 96 E7
Red Delph La WA11 8 E1
Redearth Rd BB3 65 A8
Redearth St BB3 65 A8
Rede Ave FY7 198 C2
Redeemer CE Prim Sch The BB2 81 D7
Redeswood Ave FY5 152 E8
Redfearn Wood OL12 52 B2
Red Fold L39 15 C2
Redgate
Formby L37 12 A2
Ormskirk L39 15 D5
Redgate Cl BB11 128 B3
Redgate Dr L37 12 B2
Redgate Prim Sch L37 12 A2
Redgrave Ct BB12 127 A6
Redhill PR4 95 C1
Redhill Gr PR6 61 E3
Redhills Dr PR8 35 F3
Redhouse Cl BB5 125 A2
Red House La PR7 41 B6
Redisher Cl BL0 49 F3
Redisher Croft BL0 49 F3
Redisher La BL8 49 E3
Red La
Colne BB8 171 B7
Eccleston PR7 41 E6
Redlam BB2 101 B3
Redlam Brow BB2 101 C3
Red Lees Ave BB10 128 F4
Red Lees Rd BB10 129 A2
Red Lion Cl L31 5 C1
Red Lion Sh Ctr L31 5 D1
Red Lion St
Burnley BB11 128 A5
Earby BB18 197 C2
Redman Rd BB10 148 B4
Red Marsh Dr FY5 176 C3
Red Marsh Ind Est FY5 176 C3
Redmayne Dr LA5 223 F2
Redmayne St [3] PR1 97 D8
Redness Cl BB9 148 E6
Red Rake BB1 101 C7
Red Rose Ct BB2 101 D4
Red Rose Lo FY4 130 F1
Redruth Dr
Carnforth LA5 223 C1
Crag Bank LA5 221 C8
Redruth St BB12 127 D6
Red Sands L39 15 D3
Redsands Dr PR2 118 D5
RED SCAR 119 B5
Red Scar Ind Est PR2 119 B5
Red Scar St BB8 171 C4
Redshank Dr LA3 212 F6
Red Shell La BB1, BB5 83 B7
Red Spar Rd BB10 148 D3
Redstart Pl [9] FY5 175 F1
Redvers Rd BB3 81 E5
Redvers St
Burnley BB10 148 B1
Lancaster LA1 214 D8
Redvers Terr FY1 130 B8
Redwell Fisheries LA6 237 D8
Redwing Ave
[1] Cleveleys FY5 175 F4
Great Harwood BB6 124 B6
Redwing Dr PR7 42 F5
Redwing Rd BL8 49 F2
Redwood Ave
Leyland PR25 76 E1
Maghull L31 5 C3
Redwood Chase PR4 113 E4
Redwood Cl
Blackpool FY4 110 C4
Rochdale OL12 52 B3
Redwood Dr
Chorley PR7 43 D6
Longridge PR3 140 A8
Morecambe LA4 217 E5
Ormskirk L39 15 D4
Rawtenstall BB4 68 F8
Redwood Gdns FY5 176 E2
Redwood Hts LA1 215 C7
Reedfield
Burnley BB10 148 C4
Clayton Brook PR5 78 C4
Reedfield Pl PR5 78 A6
REEDLEY 148 B4
Reedley Dr
Burnley BB10 148 C4
Burnley, Reedley BB10 148 B4
Reedley Farm Cl BB10 148 B5
Reedley Gr BB10 148 B3
Reedley Prim Sch BB10 148 C4
Reedley Rd BB9, BB10 148 C5
Reedmace Wlk [10] LA3 217 B2
Reed Row BB8 171 D3
Reeds Brow WA11 9 C1
Reeds Cl BB4 86 A6
REEDS HOLME 85 F5
Reedsholme Cl BB4 86 A6
Reeds La BB4 86 A6
Reed St
Bacup OL13 88 A3
Burnley BB11 128 A4
Reeds The
Lancaster LA1 218 C1
Ormskirk L39 15 D6
Reedy Acre Pl FY8 90 F4
Reedyford Cott BB9 170 D2
Reedyford Rd BB9 170 E2
Reedymoor La BB8 194 C1
Reedy Moor Terr BB8 194 C1
Reeford Gr BB7 166 D7
Rees Pk L40 25 F3
Reeth Way [3] BB5 103 F4
Reeval Cl BB18 197 C2
Reeveswood PR7 41 B6
Regal Ave FY4 110 E6
Regal Ct PR8 21 D5
Regal Terr [5] LA1 218 D3
Regency Ave PR5 77 D8
Regency Cl
Kirkham PR4 113 E5
Whalley BB7 144 A7
Regency Gdns
Blackpool FY2 152 D2
Euxton PR7 60 D1
Southport PR8 34 E4
Southport PR9 53 D1
Regent Ave
Colne BB8 171 E6
Lytham St Anne's FY8 90 D6
Regent Cl
Padiham BB12 126 C7
Southport PR8 34 F4
Regent Ct
[4] Blackpool FY1 130 B6
Fulwood PR2 117 E5
Lytham St Anne's FY8 89 D8
[12] Southport PR9 35 C8
Regent Dr PR2 117 D4
Regent Gr PR2 117 E5
Regent Mews PR8 34 F4
Regent Park Ave LA3, LA4 216 F3
Regent Park Gr LA4 217 A4
Regent Pk PR2 117 E5
Regent Pl BB9 170 E2
Regent Rd
Bamber Bridge PR5 97 D4
Blackpool FY1 130 C5
Chorley PR7 43 C7
Church BB5 103 F7
[6] Leyland PR25 77 A1
Morecambe LA3 216 F3
Southport PR8 34 F4
Regent Rd E FY1 130 C5
Regents Cl BB2 100 C2
Regent St
[4] Bacup OL13 88 A2
Blackburn BB1 101 E5
Brierfield BB9 148 B5
Coppull PR7 42 E1
Haslingden BB4 85 B3
Lancaster LA1 214 E7
Longridge PR3 140 A7
Nelson BB9 170 F2
Preston PR1 96 F6
Ramsbottom BL0 50 A5
Rochdale OL12 52 F1
Waddington BB7 189 B4
Regents Terr FY6 153 E3
Regents View BB1 122 E1
Regentsway [8] PR5 77 E8
Regents Way PR7 60 D2
Regiment Dr PR7 60 F6
Reginald St BB8 171 C5
Reigate PR6 61 F3
Reiver Rd PR26 76 C3
Renacres Hall Hospl (private) L39 23 B5
Renacres La L39 23 B5
Rendel St BB12 127 C7
Rendsburg Way [15] LA1 214 F8
Renfrey Cl L39 15 E8
Rennie Cl PR3 181 D6
Rennie Ct LA1 214 E5
Rennie St BB10 128 C5
Renshaw Dr
Bamber Bridge PR5 97 E2
Bury BL9 33 C3
Renshaw St [8] BB10 148 B1
Renwick Ave FY4 110 D8
Repton Ave
Blackpool FY1 130 C8
Morecambe LA4 217 F4
Reservoir Rd FY5 176 C3
Reservoir St
Burnley BB11 127 F4
Darwen BB3 81 F1
Reta Dr FY5 176 A3
Retford Rd L33 1 A2
REVIDGE 101 C7
Revidge Rd BB1, BB2 101 C7
REVOE 130 C3
Revoe Com Prim Sch FY1 130 C3
Revoe St FY1 130 C3
Rewe Cl [6] BB2 81 C8
Rexington Bldgs BB11 127 C5
Reynolds St
Burnley BB11 127 E3
Lancaster LA1 218 C1
Rhoda St BB9 170 F1
Rhoden Rd
Leyland PR26 76 C1
Oswaldtwistle BB5 103 D2
Rhodes Ave
Blackburn BB1 101 D8
Haslingden BB4 68 A7
Rhodesway PR5 98 E2
Rhuddlan Cl BB4 85 B1
Rhuddlan Gdns FY5 176 D2
Rhyddings Bsns & Ent Sch BB5 103 E4
Rhyddings St BB5 103 E4
Rhyddings The BL9 33 E7
Rhyl Ave BB1 101 E7
Rhyl St FY7 199 B5
Ribble Ave
Burnley BB10 148 C2
Darwen BB3 81 E4
Freckleton PR4 93 A6
Great Harwood BB6 124 E6
Grindleton BB7 190 B7
Maghull L31 5 E2
Southport PR9 54 C4
Whalley BB7 144 A7
Ribble Bank PR1 96 B6
Ribble Bank St PR1 96 E7
Ribble Brook Ho PR1 117 F1
Ribble Bsns Pk BB1 102 B8
Ribble Cl
Freckleton PR4 93 A6
Middleforth Green PR1 96 E4
[3] Preston PR1 96 E6
Withnell PR6 80 A1
Ribble Cres
Kirkham PR4 114 B5
[5] Preston PR5 97 C6
Ribble Ct [2] PR1 96 D6
Ribble Discovery Ctr* FY8 90 C3
Ribble Dr
Baldingstone BL9 50 F1
Hesketh Bank PR4 73 E4
West Bradford BB7 189 D7
Ribble Hall PR1 117 F1
Ribble Ho
Blackburn BB1 101 F5
[11] Preston PR1 97 D8
Ribble La BB7 190 D6
Ribble Lo [10] FY8 91 A3
Ribble Point FY8 90 C3
Ribble Rd
Blackpool FY1 130 C4
Fleetwood FY7 198 F4
Leyland PR25 59 D8
Shevington Moor WN6 29 B2
Ribblesdale Ave
Accrington BB5 104 B8
Clitheroe BB7 189 E2
Wilpshire BB1 123 A7
Ribblesdale Cl
Blackpool FY4 111 A8
Kirkham PR4 114 A5
Ribblesdale Ct
Gisburn BB7 231 B3
[5] Morecambe LA4 217 B5
Ribblesdale Dr
Forton PR3 207 B3
Grimsargh PR2 139 C1
Ribblesdale High Sch Tech Coll BB7 166 E7
Ribblesdale Pk BB7 231 B4
Ribblesdale Pl
Barrowford BB9 170 E6
Blackburn BB2 101 C5
Chorley PR7 43 B7
Preston PR1 96 F6
Ribblesdale Rd PR3 141 E3
Ribblesdale St BB10 128 B8
Ribblesdale View BB7 190 E5
Ribbleside Cvn Pk PR3 142 A4
Ribble St
Blackburn BB1 101 E6
Britannia OL13 71 A8
Lytham St Anne's FY8 89 D6
Padiham BB12 126 D8
Preston PR1 96 E7
Ribble Steam Rly* PR2 95 E7
Ribble Steam Rly Mus* PR2 95 E7
RIBBLETON 118 E2
Ribbleton Ave PR2 118 E2
Ribbleton Avenue Inf Sch PR1 118 D2
Ribbleton Avenue Meth Jun Sch PR1 118 D2
Ribbleton Dr BB5 104 C8
Ribbleton Gr BB7 144 A7
RIBBLETON HALL 119 B2
Ribbleton Hall Cres [2] PR2 118 F3
Ribbleton Hall Dr PR2 118 F3
Ribbleton Hospl PR2 118 F2
Ribbleton La PR1 118 C1
Ribbleton Pl [6] PR1 97 B8
Ribbleton St [8] PR1 97 B8
Ribbleton Trad Est [10] PR1 97 B8
Ribble View BB7 189 F4
Ribble View Cl PR4 92 F6
Ribble Way BB7 166 C8
RIBBY 113 D4
Ribby Ave
Kirkham PR4 113 F5
Wrea Green PR4 113 C4
Ribby Pl
Blackpool FY4 131 B1
Preston PR2 116 F1
Ribby Rd
Kirkham PR4 113 F4
Wrea Green PR4 113 C4
Ribby-with-Wrea CE Prim Sch PR4 113 B4
RIBCHESTER 141 D3
Ribchester Ave
Blackpool FY4 131 B1
Burnley BB10 128 D5
Ribchester Rd
Copster Green BB1 142 A1
Dinckley BB6, PR3 142 C4
Lytham St Anne's FY8 91 D4
Wilpshire BB1 122 E6
Ribchester St Wilfrid's CE Prim Sch PR3 141 E3
Ribchester Way BB9 148 D4
Rice Gr FY1 130 D8
Richard Burch St [2] BL9 33 A3
Richard Durning's Endowed Prim Sch L40 27 D7
Richardson Cl PR4 93 C6
Richardson St FY1 130 B4
Richards Rd WN6 29 B3
Richard's St [7] PR4 113 F6
Richard St
Brierfield BB9 148 B5
Burnley BB11 128 B5
Shuttleworth BL0 50 E7
[7] Weir OL13 88 A7
Richards Way [3] FY5 175 F1
Richard's Way FY8 110 E2
Richards Wlk [7] LA1 218 B1
Richard Thornton's CE Prim Sch LA6 242 B3
Richmond Ave
Accrington BB5 104 B5
Barnoldswick BB18 196 A3
Burnley BB10 128 F4
Burscough L40 25 E3
Cleveleys FY5 175 E2
Haslingden BB4 85 C2
Richmond Ave *continued*
Lancaster LA1 218 D4
Morecambe LA4 217 D4
Wrea Green PR4 113 B3
Richmond Cl
Brinscall PR6 62 E8
Hightown L38 2 F2
Richmond Cres BB1 102 E5
Richmond Ct
[8] Blackpool FY1 130 B7
Burscough L40 25 E3
Chorley PR7 43 C6
Leyland PR26 76 B1
Richmond Gr L31 5 E3
Richmond Hill [23] BB1 101 E5
Richmond Hill La PR3 207 D2
Richmond Hill St BB5 104 B5
Richmond Ho
Chorley PR7 43 C6
[9] Lancaster LA1 218 D3
[11] Preston PR1 97 A7
Richmond Ind Est BB5 104 B5
Richmond Mews L40 25 E3
Richmond Pk BB3 82 A2
Richmond Rd
Accrington BB5 104 A4
Barnoldswick BB18 196 A3
Barrowford BB9 170 C1
Blackpool FY1 130 B7
Chorley PR6 43 E6
Eccleston PR7 41 C7
Lytham St Anne's FY8 89 E6
Southport PR8 34 F2
Richmond St
Accrington BB5 104 A5
Burnley BB11 127 E5
Horwich BL6 32 B3
[2] Preston PR1 97 B7
Richmond Terr
[17] Blackburn BB1 101 E5
Clitheroe BB7 166 D7
Darwen BB3 82 A2
Rickard Rd BB9 148 E6
Ridding La BB7 144 B5
Riddings Ave BB10 128 F6
Riddings La BB7 144 C6
Ridehalgh La BB10 149 F2
Ridehalgh St BB8 171 B3
Riders Gate BL9 33 F4
RIDGE 218 F2
Ridge Ave BB10 128 D6
Ridge Cl PR9 54 C5
Ridge Ct
Burnley BB10 128 C7
Longridge PR3 140 C8
Ridgeford Gdns PR2 117 D5
Ridge Gr LA3 212 F8
Ridge La
Lancaster LA1 218 E1
Lancaster, Ridge LA1 219 A2
Roughlee BB12 169 F4
Ridgemont PR2 117 C6
Ridge Prim Sch LA1 218 F1
Ridge Rd
Burnley BB11 128 B6
Chorley PR6 43 E7
Ridge Row BB10 128 D6
Ridge Sq LA1 218 F1
Ridge St
Barnoldswick BB18 196 B2
Lancaster LA1 218 E1
Ridgeway
Barrowford BB9 170 C3
Great Harwood BB6 124 B6
Ridge Way PR1 96 E4
Ridgeway Ave BB2 82 A8
Ridgeway Dr
Maghull L31 5 E3
Thornton FY5 153 D8
Ridgeways BB4 85 C2
Ridgeway The
Fleetwood FY7 198 D3
Nelson BB9 148 D7
Ridgmont Cl BL6 32 F3
Ridgmont Dr BL6 32 F3
Ridgway BL6 31 C2
Ridgway Ct FY8 90 A7
Ridgwood Ave FY3 130 E5
Riding Barn St BB5 103 F7
Riding Cl
Barnoldswick BB18 196 C2
Haskayne L39 13 F4
Riding Head La BL0 50 F8
Riding La L39 13 E4
Riding St
Burnley BB11 127 E5
Preston PR1 117 F1
Southport PR8 35 B6
Ridings The
Burnley BB12 127 D8
Lucas Green PR6 61 C6
Southport PR9 54 A3
Ridley La
Barber's Moor PR26 58 D3
Maghull L31 5 D1
Mawdesley L40 40 F2
Ridley Rd PR2 117 C2
Ridley St [2] FY3 130 D5
Rifle St BB4 85 B2
Rigby Ave BL6 31 C2
Rigby Cl PR4 93 C6
Rigby Rd
Blackpool FY1 130 B3
Maghull L31 5 B3

**Rigby St**
Colne BB8 . . . . 171 C5
Nelson BB9 . . . . 148 D8
Preston PR1 . . . . 97 C8
**Rigg Ho** 10 LA1 . . . . 218 D2
**Rigg La**
Quernmore LA2 . . . . 232 B7
Whitechapel PR3 . . . . 184 B1
**Rigg St** BB9 . . . . 148 E8
**Riley Ave** FY8 . . . . 89 F5
**Riley Cl** PR25 . . . . 60 A8
**Riley Ct** FY8 . . . . 89 F4
**RILEY GREEN** . . . . 79 E8
**Riley Green Switch Rd** BB2, PR5 . . . . 79 F7
**Riley St**
Accrington BB5 . . . . 104 B4
Bacup OL13 . . . . 87 F5
Brierfield BB9 . . . . 148 B5
Burnley BB11 . . . . 128 B4
Earby BB18 . . . . 197 B2
**RIMINGTON** . . . . 191 F8
**Rimington Ave**
Accrington BB5 . . . . 104 A3
Burnley BB10 . . . . 128 D5
Colne BB8 . . . . 171 C6
**Rimington Cl** BB2 . . . . 101 F2
**Rimington Cvn Pk** BB7 . . . . 231 B1
**Rimington La** BB7 . . . . 191 D7
**Rimington Pl**
Lytham St Anne's FY8 . . . . 90 B6
Nelson BB9 . . . . 171 B1
**Rimmer Gn** PR8 . . . . 36 D1
**Rimmer's Ave**
Formby L37 . . . . 11 E6
Southport PR8 . . . . 35 B6
**Ring Dyke Way** FY8 . . . . 91 A4
**Ring Lows La** OL12 . . . . 52 F4
**RING O'BELLS** . . . . 26 B2
**Ring O'Bells La** L40 . . . . 26 B2
**Rings St** BB4 . . . . 106 A2
**Ringstone Cres** BB9 . . . . 149 B8
**Ringstones La** LA2 . . . . 239 D4
**Ringtail Ct** L40 . . . . 25 B4
**Ringtail Ind Est** L40 . . . . 25 B2
**Ringtail Pl** L40 . . . . 25 B4
**Ringtail Rd** L40 . . . . 25 B4
**RINGTON** . . . . 153 B6
**Rington Ave** FY6 . . . . 153 B6
**Ringway**
Chorley PR7 . . . . 43 A7
Cleveleys FY5 . . . . 175 E4
**Ring Way** PR1 . . . . 96 F7
**Ringwood Ave** BL0 . . . . 50 A4
**Ringwood Cl**
Accrington BB5 . . . . 125 B1
Lytham St Anne's FY8 . . . . 90 F3
**Ringwood Rd** PR1 . . . . 118 C2
**Ripley Cl** L31 . . . . 5 E1
**Ripley Ct** LA1 . . . . 214 F6
**Ripley Dr** FY8 . . . . 90 B6
**Ripley St Thomas CE High Sch** LA1 . . . . 214 F6
**Ripon Ave** 1 LA1 . . . . 218 D4
**Ripon Brook** PR1 . . . . 118 F1
**Ripon Cl**
Cleveleys FY5 . . . . 175 E5
Great Eccleston PR3 . . . . 156 C5
Southport PR8 . . . . 35 F3
**Ripon Hall Ave** BL0 . . . . 50 B4
**Ripon Pl** LA3 . . . . 212 E6
**Ripon Rd**
Blackpool FY1 . . . . 130 D4
Lytham St Anne's FY8 . . . . 90 D5
Oswaldtwistle BB5 . . . . 103 C5
**Ripon St**
Blackburn BB1 . . . . 102 B4
Nelson BB9 . . . . 148 D7
Preston PR1 . . . . 117 E2
**Ripon Terr** PR1 . . . . 118 F1
**Risedale Dr** PR3 . . . . 140 B7
**Risedale Gr** BB2 . . . . 81 A7
**Rise The** LA5 . . . . 221 B6
**RISHTON** . . . . 124 C2
**Rishton Meth Prim Sch** BB1 . . . . 124 B1
**Rishton Rd**
Clayton-le-M BB5 . . . . 124 E3
Wilpshire BB1 . . . . 123 C5
**Rishton St** FY1 . . . . 130 C4
**Rishton Sta** BB1 . . . . 103 A8
**RISING BRIDGE** . . . . 85 A8
**Rising Bridge Rd** BB4, BB5 . . . . 85 A7
**Ritherham Ave** FY5 . . . . 175 D3
**River Bank Terr** BB5 . . . . 125 E6
**River Cl** L37 . . . . 12 B1
**River Dr** BB12 . . . . 126 D8
**River Hts** PR5 . . . . 77 C8
**River Lea Gdns** BB7 . . . . 166 F8
**Rivermead Ct** PR3 . . . . 204 C1
**Rivermead Dr** PR3 . . . . 181 C8
**Rivermeade** PR8 . . . . 35 D4
**River Par** PR1 . . . . 96 D6
**River Rd**
Thornton FY5 . . . . 176 D4
Thornton, Stanah FY5 . . . . 176 E3
**Riversedge Rd** PR25 . . . . 59 C8
**Rivers Edge The** OL12 . . . . 71 C1
**Riversgate** FY7 . . . . 198 F4
**Riverside**
Bamber Bridge PR5 . . . . 77 E7
Clitheroe BB7 . . . . 166 B8
Hightown L38 . . . . 2 F4
**Riverside** *continued*
Preston PR1 . . . . 96 E5
**Riverside Ave** PR26 . . . . 76 E4
**Riverside Bsns Ctr** BB9 . . . . 170 E1
**Riverside Chalet Pk** FY6 . . . . 154 D4
**Riverside Cl**
Halton LA2 . . . . 219 C6
Leyland PR26 . . . . 76 E4
**Riverside Cres** PR26 . . . . 58 A2
**Riverside Ct** OL12 . . . . 71 D4
**Riverside Cvn Site** PR9 . . . . 55 D3
**Riverside Dr**
Hambleton FY6 . . . . 177 B1
Ramsbottom BL0 . . . . 50 B2
**Riverside Fold** BB12 . . . . 169 E5
**Riverside Ind Est** BB5 . . . . 124 D2
**Riverside Ind Pk** PR3 . . . . 181 C2
**Riverside Lofts** LA1 . . . . 218 C1
**Riverside Mews**
Padiham BB12 . . . . 126 F6
Whitewell Bottom BB4 . . . . 86 F4
**Riverside Mill** 3 BB8 . . . . 171 B4
**Riverside Park Ind Est** LA1 . . . . 218 F4
**Riverside Pk** BB4 . . . . 86 F4
**Riverside Rd** PR1 . . . . 96 E5
**Riverside Terr** 4 BB18 . . . . 197 B1
**Riverside View** BB5 . . . . 124 E4
**Riverside Wlk** BB4 . . . . 68 A7
**Riversleigh Ave**
Blackpool FY1 . . . . 152 C1
Lytham St Anne's FY8 . . . . 90 E3
**Riversleigh Ct** FY8 . . . . 90 E3
**Rivers St** WN5 . . . . 10 E6
**River St**
Bacup OL13 . . . . 87 F1
Blackburn BB1 . . . . 101 F4
Colne BB8 . . . . 171 D4
Darwen BB3 . . . . 81 F2
Lancaster LA1 . . . . 218 C1
Preston PR1 . . . . 96 E7
Ramsbottom BL0 . . . . 50 C6
Trawden BB8 . . . . 172 C3
**Rivers View Fold** LA2 . . . . 226 A8
**Riversway**
Blackpool FY3 . . . . 130 F6
4 Lancaster LA1 . . . . 218 D2
Poulton-le-F FY6 . . . . 153 F5
Preston PR2, PR4 . . . . 95 D8
**Riversway Bsns Village** PR2 . . . . 96 A8
**Riversway Dr** BB3 . . . . 81 F6
**Riversway Enterprise Workshops** PR2 . . . . 95 E8
**Riversway Managed Workshops** 1 PR2 . . . . 95 F8
**Riversway Motor Pk** PR2 . . . . 95 D8
**River View**
Glasson LA2 . . . . 209 E5
Tarleton PR4 . . . . 57 A8
**Riverview Ct** LA4 . . . . 217 B3
**River Way** BB9 . . . . 170 D4
**Riverway Cl** PR5 . . . . 77 D8
**RIVINGTON** . . . . 44 F2
**Rivington Ave**
Adlington PR6 . . . . 31 B7
Blackpool FY2 . . . . 152 D5
**Rivington & Blackrod High Sch (Lower)** BL6 . . . . 32 B4
**Rivington & Blackrod High Sch (Upper)** BL6 . . . . 32 B6
**Rivington Cl**
Poulton-le-F FY6 . . . . 153 D3
Southport PR8 . . . . 35 A3
Tarleton PR4 . . . . 56 F8
Rivington Ctry Pk★ BL6 . . . . 32 A8
**Rivington Dr**
Burscough L40 . . . . 25 E3
Up Holland WN8 . . . . 10 C7
**Rivington Hall Cl** BL0 . . . . 50 C4
**Rivington La**
Adlington PR6 . . . . 31 D6
Horwich BL6 . . . . 32 A7
Rivington BL6 . . . . 44 F1
**Rivington Park Ind Sch** BL6 . . . . 32 B6
**Rivington Pl** PR7 . . . . 29 D6
**Rivington Prim Sch** BL6 . . . . 44 F1
**Rivington Rd**
Belmont BL6, BL7 . . . . 46 B4
Chorley PR6 . . . . 61 E1
**Rivington St**
Blackburn BB1 . . . . 102 B4
Blackrod BL6 . . . . 31 D2
Rochdale OL12 . . . . 52 E1
**Rivington View** PR6 . . . . 61 E1
**Rixton Gr** FY5 . . . . 176 B4
**ROACH BRIDGE** . . . . 98 F6
**Roach Bridge Cotts** PR5 . . . . 98 E6
**Roach Rd** PR5 . . . . 99 B4
**Roach St** BL9 . . . . 33 C1
**Road La** OL12 . . . . 52 D4
**Robbin's Bridge** L31 . . . . 5 E5
**Roberts Ct**
Leyland PR25 . . . . 59 F8
Warton LA5 . . . . 223 D6
**Robertson Ct** FY7 . . . . 198 F1
**Roberts St**
2 Chorley PR7 . . . . 43 C7
Nelson BB9 . . . . 148 F8
7 Rawtenstall BB4 . . . . 86 A3
**Robert St**
Accrington BB5 . . . . 104 C7
Barnoldswick BB18 . . . . 196 B2
Blackburn BB2 . . . . 101 E3
Colne BB8 . . . . 171 E5
15 Darwen BB3 . . . . 81 F2
Great Harwood BB6 . . . . 124 D6
43 Lancaster LA1 . . . . 214 F8
Newchurch BB4 . . . . 86 F2
Oswaldtwistle BB5 . . . . 103 D3
Ramsbottom BL0 . . . . 68 C1
**Robin Bank Rd** BB3 . . . . 82 A2
**Robin Cl** PR7 . . . . 42 D3
**Robin Cres** LA3 . . . . 212 F6
**Robin Croft** LA2 . . . . 241 A1
**Robin Hey** PR26 . . . . 76 B1
**Robin Hill Dr** WN6 . . . . 29 B2
**Robin Hill La** WN6 . . . . 29 C3
**ROBIN HOOD** . . . . 28 C4
**Robin Hood La** WN6 . . . . 28 C4
**Robin House La** BB10 . . . . 149 C4
**Robin La**
High Bentham LA2 . . . . 239 D8
Hill Dale WN8 . . . . 27 C5
Rimington BB7 . . . . 231 B1
**Robin Rd** BL0 . . . . 50 B2
**Robins Cl** FY6 . . . . 153 A4
**Robins La**
Blackpool FY6 . . . . 153 A4
Carleton FY6 . . . . 153 A6
**Robinson Ct** BB18 . . . . 196 A3
**Robinson Fold** BB18 . . . . 196 A3
**Robinson La** BB9, BB10, BB12 . . . . 148 A4
**Robinson St**
Blackburn BB1 . . . . 102 B7
Burnley BB10 . . . . 128 A8
Chatburn BB7 . . . . 190 E5
Colne BB8 . . . . 171 C5
Foulridge BB8 . . . . 194 D1
Fulwood PR2 . . . . 117 D3
15 Horwich BL6 . . . . 32 B4
**Robin St** PR1 . . . . 118 D1
**Robson St** BB9 . . . . 148 B6
**Robson Way** FY3 . . . . 153 A2
**ROBY MILL** . . . . 19 B3
**Roby Mill** WN8 . . . . 19 B3
**ROCHDALE** . . . . 52 C2
**Rochdale Girls Sch** OL12 . . . . 52 F1
**Rochdale Infmy** OL12 . . . . 52 F1
**Rochdale Old Rd** BL9 . . . . 33 D4
**Rochdale Rd**
Bacup OL13 . . . . 88 A1
Britannia OL13 . . . . 71 B8
Bury BL9 . . . . 33 B2
Edenfield BL0 . . . . 68 F2
Ramsbottom BL0 . . . . 51 B7
**Rochester Ave**
Cleveleys FY5 . . . . 175 F4
Morecambe LA4 . . . . 217 D3
**Rochester Cl** 3 OL13 . . . . 88 A7
**Rochester Dr** BB10 . . . . 148 C3
**Rochford Ave** FY5 . . . . 175 E1
**Rock Bridge Fold** BB4 . . . . 86 E5
**Rock Brow** PR3 . . . . 163 B7
**Rockburgh Cres** PR4 . . . . 75 A5
**Rockcliffe Ave** OL13 . . . . 87 E1
**Rockcliffe Dr** OL13 . . . . 87 E1
**Rockcliffe Rd** OL13 . . . . 87 F1
**Rockcliffe St** 5 BB4 . . . . 86 A3
**Rockcliffe Villas** OL13 . . . . 70 E8
**Rockfield Gdns** 2 L31 . . . . 5 C2
**Rockfield Rd** BB5 . . . . 104 D6
**Rockfield St** BB2 . . . . 101 E3
**Rock Fold** BL7 . . . . 47 F1
**Rock Gdns** PR5 . . . . 99 B3
**Rock Hall Rd** BB4 . . . . 85 B3
**Rockhaven Ave** BL6 . . . . 32 C4
**Rockingham Rd** FY2 . . . . 152 D3
**Rock La**
Burnley BB11 . . . . 128 B3
Tockholes BB3 . . . . 81 A3
Trawden BB8 . . . . 172 C3
**ROCKLIFFE** . . . . 88 A2
**Rockliffe La** OL13 . . . . 88 A1
**Rockliffe Rd** OL13 . . . . 87 F1
**Rockliffe St** BB2 . . . . 101 E2
**Rock m' Jock** LA2 . . . . 237 B3
**Rockmount** BB7 . . . . 189 F3
**Rock St**
Accrington BB5 . . . . 104 E2
Clitheroe BB7 . . . . 166 E8
18 Haslingden BB4 . . . . 85 B3
Horwich BL6 . . . . 32 B3
Shuttleworth BL0 . . . . 50 E7
Thornton FY5 . . . . 176 B4
**Rock Terr**
Bolton BL7 . . . . 47 F1
Pendleton BB7 . . . . 167 B4
13 Rawtenstall BB4 . . . . 86 A7
**Rock Villa Rd** PR6 . . . . 61 C8
**Rockville** BB9 . . . . 170 E5
**Rockville Ave** FY5 . . . . 152 F8
Rock Water (Bird Conservation Ctr)★ BB10 . . . . 129 C2
**Rockwood Cl** BB10 . . . . 148 E3
**Roddlesworth La** PR6 . . . . 63 E8
Roddlesworth Nature Trail★ BB3 . . . . 64 B8
Roddlesworth Visitor Ctr★ BB3 . . . . 64 B8
**Rodhill La** BB7 . . . . 230 B3
**Rodney Ave** FY8 . . . . 110 E1
**Rodney St**
Blackburn BB2 . . . . 101 C3
3 Preston PR1 . . . . 96 F8
**Rodwell Wlk** FY3 . . . . 130 F8
**Roebuck Cl** BB2 . . . . 101 D3
**Roebuck Prim Sch** PR2 . . . . 117 D2
**Roebuck St** PR2 . . . . 117 C2
**Roeburndale Cres** LA3 . . . . 213 A8
**Roeburndale Rd** LA2 . . . . 238 B1
**Roeburn Dr** LA3 . . . . 217 F2
**Roeburn Hall** PR1 . . . . 96 E8
**Roeburn Pl** LA1 . . . . 218 C2
**Roeburn Terr** LA2 . . . . 238 D6
**Roedean Ave** LA4 . . . . 217 F4
**Roedean Cl**
Maghull L31 . . . . 5 D2
Thornton FY5 . . . . 176 A2
**Roe Greave Rd** BB5 . . . . 103 D3
**Roehampton Cl** 11 FY5 . . . . 176 A2
**Roe Hey Dr** PR7 . . . . 42 F2
**Roe La** PR9 . . . . 35 E8
**ROE LEE** . . . . 122 E1
**Roe Lee Ind Est** BB1 . . . . 122 F1
**Roe Lee Park Prim Sch** BB1 . . . . 122 F2
**Roe Lee Pk** BB1 . . . . 122 F2
**Roe-Park Mews** PR9 . . . . 35 D8
**Roe St** OL12 . . . . 52 C1
**Rogerley Cl** FY8 . . . . 91 A4
**Rogersfield** BB6 . . . . 123 B8
**Rolleston Rd** BB2 . . . . 101 B4
**Roman Cres** LA2 . . . . 237 C3
Roman Mus★ PR3 . . . . 141 E3
**Roman Rd**
Blackburn BB1, BB2 . . . . 82 B8
Preston PR1 . . . . 97 B7
Whittlestone Head BB3 . . . . 66 A4
**Roman Way**
Cleveleys FY5 . . . . 175 F1
Clitheroe BB7 . . . . 167 A8
Kirkham PR4 . . . . 114 C4
Red Scar PR2 . . . . 119 C6
**Roman Way Ind Est** PR2 . . . . 119 C6
**Rome Ave** BB11 . . . . 127 C4
**Romford Rd** PR1 . . . . 118 C2
**Romford St** 2 BB12 . . . . 127 C7
**Romiley Dr** WN8 . . . . 17 F2
**Romney Ave**
Barrowford BB9 . . . . 170 D3
Blackpool FY4 . . . . 130 D1
Burnley BB11 . . . . 127 E3
Fleetwood FY7 . . . . 198 E3
**Romney St** BB9 . . . . 148 D7
**Romney Wlk** BB1 . . . . 102 C4
**Romsey Ave** L37 . . . . 12 B2
**Rona Ave** 4 FY4 . . . . 110 F6
**Ronald St**
Blackburn BB1 . . . . 102 C5
Burnley BB12 . . . . 127 A5
**Ronaldsway**
Nelson BB9 . . . . 171 B2
Preston PR1 . . . . 118 D3
**Ronaldsway Cl** OL13 . . . . 88 B1
**Ronbury Cl** 1 BB9 . . . . 170 C1
**Roney St** BB2 . . . . 101 C5
**Ronwood Cl** PR4 . . . . 155 F1
**Ronwood Ct** PR2 . . . . 96 B8
**Roocroft Sq** BL6 . . . . 31 C2
**Roods The** LA5 . . . . 223 E6
**Rookery Ave** WN6 . . . . 19 E8
**Rookery Cl**
Chorley PR7 . . . . 43 A6
Kingsfold PR1 . . . . 96 F2
**Rookery Ct** PR1 . . . . 96 F1
**Rookery Dr** PR1 . . . . 96 F2
**Rookery Rd**
Barnoldswick BB18 . . . . 196 C3
Southport PR9 . . . . 53 F1
**Rook St**
Barnoldswick BB18 . . . . 196 B2
Colne BB8 . . . . 171 D5
Nelson BB9 . . . . 170 E1
Preston PR1 . . . . 118 B1
3 Ramsbottom BL0 . . . . 50 C6
**Rookwood** PR7 . . . . 41 B6
**Rookwood Ave** PR7 . . . . 61 C2
**Rooley Moor Rd**
Bacup OL12, OL13 . . . . 70 C4
Rochdale OL12 . . . . 52 A3
Rochdale, Spotland Fold OL12 . . . . 52 C1
**Rooley St** OL11, OL12 . . . . 52 C1
**Rooley View** OL13 . . . . 87 E1
**Roosevelt Ave** LA1 . . . . 214 D7
**Roots La** PR4 . . . . 135 E2
**Ropefield Way** OL12 . . . . 52 E3
**Rope Wlk** PR3 . . . . 181 C7
**Rosary Ave** FY4 . . . . 130 E1
**Roscoe Ave** FY5 . . . . 176 D2
**Roscoe Lowe Brow** PR6 . . . . 31 D7
**ROSEACRE** . . . . 134 D6
**Roseacre** FY4 . . . . 110 C5
**Roseacre Cl** BB4 . . . . 86 F4
**Roseacre Dr** PR4 . . . . 156 A1
**Rose Acre La** LA5 . . . . 225 F2
**Roseacre Pl**
Lytham St Anne's FY8 . . . . 90 B8
5 Preston PR2 . . . . 116 E1
**Roseacre Prim Sch** FY4 . . . . 110 C5
**Roseacre Rd**
Roseacre PR4 . . . . 134 D6
Wharles PR4 . . . . 134 F4
**Rose Ave**
Blackpool FY1 . . . . 130 D2
Burnley BB11 . . . . 127 E4
Fulwood PR2 . . . . 117 C3
**Rosebank**
8 Blackpool FY5 . . . . 152 F8
Clayton-le-M BB5 . . . . 125 A3
Edenfield BL0 . . . . 68 D1
2 Preston PR2 . . . . 116 C1
**Rose Bank**
Lancaster LA1 . . . . 215 A5
Rawtenstall BB4 . . . . 86 A3
**Rosebank Ave** 3 FY4 . . . . 110 C5
**Rose Bank St** OL13 . . . . 87 F3
**Rosebay Ave** BB2 . . . . 80 D8
**Rosebay Cl** L37 . . . . 12 A3
**Roseberry Ave** PR4 . . . . 116 E5
**Roseberry Cl** BL0 . . . . 50 C3
**Rosebery Ave**
Blackpool FY4 . . . . 110 B6
Lancaster LA1 . . . . 215 A5
Lytham St Anne's FY8 . . . . 90 B4
Morecambe LA4 . . . . 217 C4
**Rosebery St**
Burnley BB10 . . . . 148 B2
Southport PR9 . . . . 36 A6
Todmorden OL14 . . . . 109 C1
**Rosebowl View** L40 . . . . 24 B4
**Rose Cl** PR25 . . . . 77 E2
**Rose Cotts**
Low Bentham LA2 . . . . 239 B8
Preesall FY6 . . . . 200 C3
**Rose Cres**
Skelmersdale WN8 . . . . 17 E1
Southport PR8 . . . . 21 C2
**Rosecroft Cl** L39 . . . . 15 E6
**Rose Ct**
Blackburn BB2 . . . . 101 B6
1 Fleetwood FY7 . . . . 198 F4
Haslingden BB4 . . . . 85 B5
**Rosedale Ave**
Blackpool FY4 . . . . 131 A2
Heysham LA3 . . . . 213 A8
**Rosedale St** BB4 . . . . 85 F5
**Rosedene** LA2 . . . . 218 D7
**Rosedene Cl** PR4 . . . . 116 E5
**Rosefinch Ct** FY3 . . . . 131 B2
**Rosefinch Way** FY3 . . . . 131 B3
**Rose Fold**
Middleforth Green PR1 . . . . 96 D4
Thornton FY5 . . . . 176 B4
**Rose Fold Cotts** PR1 . . . . 96 D4
**Rosegarth** LA2 . . . . 218 D7
**Rose Gdns** PR4 . . . . 73 E4
**Rose Gr** LA2 . . . . 210 F4
**ROSE GROVE** . . . . 127 B6
**Rosegrove Cvn Pk** FY6 . . . . 200 A6
**Rosegrove Inf Sch** BB12 . . . . 127 A6
**Rosegrove La** BB11 . . . . 127 B5
**Rose Grove Sta** BB11 . . . . 127 B5
**ROSEHILL** . . . . 65 C7
**ROSE HILL** . . . . 127 F3
**Rose Hill**
Euxton PR7 . . . . 60 C4
Ramsbottom BL0 . . . . 50 B6
Southport PR8, PR9 . . . . 35 D6
**Rosehill Ave**
Burnley BB11 . . . . 127 E4
12 Nelson BB9 . . . . 170 F1
**Rose Hill Ave** BB1 . . . . 102 A4
**Rosehill Bsns Pk** 1 PR9 . . . . 35 D6
**Rosehill Dr** L39 . . . . 15 C2
**Rosehill Mans** L39 . . . . 15 C2
**Rosehill Mt** BB11 . . . . 127 E4
**Rosehill Rd**
Burnley BB11 . . . . 127 F3
Nelson BB8 . . . . 171 A2
**Rose Hill Rd** BB2 . . . . 100 C1
**Rose Hill St**
Bacup OL13 . . . . 87 F2
Darwen BB3 . . . . 65 B8
Rawtenstall BB4 . . . . 106 A1
**Rose Hill Terr** 7 BB3 . . . . 65 B8
**Rose La** PR1 . . . . 118 C3
**Roseland Ave** BB9 . . . . 148 C6
**Roseland Cl** L31 . . . . 5 B4
**Rose Lea** PR2 . . . . 118 D6
**Roselea Dr** PR9 . . . . 54 C4
**Roselyn Ave** FY4 . . . . 110 C5
**Rosemary Ave**
Blackpool FY4 . . . . 110 C5
Cleveleys FY5 . . . . 175 F3
**Rosemary Ct**
Formby L37 . . . . 11 F3
1 Kingsfold PR1 . . . . 96 C2
**Rosemary La**
Formby L37 . . . . 11 F3
Haskayne L39 . . . . 14 B4
8 Lancaster LA1 . . . . 214 F8
Swillbrook PR4 . . . . 136 A1
**Rosemeade Ave** PR5 . . . . 77 B8
**Rosemede Ave** FY4 . . . . 130 F2
**Rosemount** OL13 . . . . 88 A4
**Rose Mount** BB4 . . . . 86 F1
**Rosemount Ave**
Barnoldswick BB18 . . . . 196 A3
Burnley BB11 . . . . 127 E4
Knott End-on-S FY6 . . . . 200 A5
**Rosendale Cl** 5 OL13 . . . . 88 B3
**Rosendale Cres** OL13 . . . . 88 B3
**Rose Path** L37 . . . . 12 A2
**Rose Pl**
Accrington BB5 . . . . 104 B4
Ormskirk L39 . . . . 15 D2
**Rose St**
Accrington BB5 . . . . 104 B4
Bacup OL13 . . . . 87 F2
6 Blackburn BB2 . . . . 101 E3
Darwen BB3 . . . . 82 B1

Rose St *continued*
Leyland PR25 . . . 77 B3
[10] Morecambe LA4 . . . 217 B6
Newchurch BB4 . . . 86 E2
[14] Preston PR1 . . . 97 A7
Rose Terr
Bacup OL13 . . . 70 F8
Preston PR2 . . . 117 B2
Rose Vale St BB4 . . . 86 B2
Roseway
Blackpool FY4 . . . 110 C5
Lytham St Anne's FY8 . . . 90 B6
Poulton-le-F FY6 . . . 153 C3
Preston PR2 . . . 117 A1
Rosewood PR4 . . . 116 E5
Rosewood Ave
Blackburn BB1 . . . 101 F8
Burnley BB11 . . . 127 E3
Haslingden BB4 . . . 85 C3
Higher Walton PR5 . . . 98 C3
Rosewood Cl
Chorley PR7 . . . 43 D6
Lytham St Anne's FY8 . . . 90 E4
[1] Thornton FY5 . . . 176 D1
Rosewood Ct PR5 . . . 98 B3
Rosewood Dr PR5 . . . 98 B3
Rosewood Pk BB1 . . . 101 F8
Rosewood Prim Sch
BB11 . . . 127 E3
Roshaw PR2 . . . 139 C1
Rosklyn Rd PR6 . . . 43 E7
Rosley St BB8 . . . 172 B5
ROSSALL BEACH . . . 175 D5
Rossall Cl
Coupe Green PR5 . . . 98 E3
Fleetwood FY7 . . . 175 D8
Padiham BB12 . . . 126 D6
Rossall Ct
Cleveleys FY5 . . . 175 C5
Fleetwood FY7 . . . 198 E3
Rossall Dr PR2 . . . 117 C4
Rossall Gate FY7 . . . 175 C8
Rossall Gdns FY5 . . . 175 D4
Rossall Grange La
FY7 . . . 198 D3
Rossall Hospl FY7 . . . 175 C8
Rossall La FY7 . . . 175 E7
Rossall Rd
Blackpool FY3 . . . 130 D7
Chorley PR6 . . . 61 E1
Cleveleys FY5 . . . 175 D3
Fulwood PR2 . . . 117 C4
Lancaster LA1 . . . 218 A2
Lytham St Anne's FY8 . . . 90 D4
Rossall Sch FY7 . . . 175 C6
Rossall St PR2 . . . 117 C1
Rossall Terr BB2 . . . 101 E1
Rossendale Ave
Burnley BB11 . . . 127 E2
Lancaster LA1 . . . 211 B8
Morecambe LA4 . . . 217 C6
Rossendale Ave N FY5 . . . 176 B2
Rossendale Ave S FY5 . . . 176 B1
Rossendale General Hospl
BB4 . . . 85 D2
Rossendale Mus★ BB4 . . . 85 E2
Rossendale Rd
Burnley BB11 . . . 127 C3
Lytham St Anne's FY8 . . . 90 A7
Rossendale Sch BL0 . . . 51 A7
Rosser Ct [18] BB9 . . . 148 E8
Rossett Ave FY4 . . . 131 C1
Rossetti Ave BB11 . . . 127 F3
Rossington Ave FY2 . . . 152 E5
Rosslyn Ave FY6 . . . 200 A6
Rosslyn Cres FY6 . . . 200 B5
Rosslyn Cres E FY6 . . . 200 B5
Rossmoyne Rd LA1 . . . 215 A4
Ross St
Brierfield BB9 . . . 148 B5
Darwen BB3 . . . 65 A6
Rostle Top Rd [6]
BB18 . . . 197 B1
Rostrevor Cl [4] PR26 . . . 76 B1
Rostron Cres L37 . . . 11 E1
Rostron Rd BL0 . . . 50 B6
Rostron's Bldgs BB4 . . . 86 D1
Rothay Ave FY7 . . . 198 D2
Rothbury Pl FY8 . . . 91 C4
Rotherhead Cl BL6 . . . 31 F2
Rotherwick Ave PR7 . . . 43 B7
Rothesay Cres LA3 . . . 212 D5
Rothesay Rd
Blackburn BB1 . . . 102 D3
Brierfield BB9 . . . 148 C6
Heysham LA3 . . . 212 D5
Rothley Ave PR8 . . . 21 A4
Rothsay Rd LA3 . . . 212 E5
Rothwell Ave BB5 . . . 104 C4
Rothwell Cl L39 . . . 15 D5
Rothwell Cres PR2 . . . 118 F4
Rothwell Ct PR25 . . . 77 A2
Rothwell Dr
Fleetwood FY7 . . . 198 D3
Ormskirk L39 . . . 15 B2
Southport PR8 . . . 21 A4
Rothwell Lo [5] PR2 . . . 118 F4
Rothwell Rd PR6 . . . 31 B7
Rothwell St BL0 . . . 50 B6
Rotten Row
Caton LA2 . . . 237 D3
Southport PR8 . . . 34 F6
Rough Hey Gate BB5 . . . 103 F2
Rough Hey Ind Est
PR2 . . . 119 B7
Rough Hey Pl PR2 . . . 119 B7
Rough Hey Rd PR2 . . . 119 B7
Rough Heys BB5 . . . 104 A2
Rough Heys La FY4 . . . 110 E7
Rough Hill La BL9 . . . 33 E4
Rough Lea Rd FY5 . . . 175 D2
ROUGHLEE . . . 170 B5
Roughlee CE Prim Sch
BB12 . . . 169 F4
Roughlee Gr BB10 . . . 128 D5
Roughlee Old Hall
BB9 . . . 170 A5
Rough Lee Rd BB5 . . . 104 C4
Roughlee St BB9 . . . 170 D2
Roughlee Terr BB11 . . . 106 B4
Roughwood Dr L33 . . . 1 A4
Round Acre
Bamber Bridge PR1 . . . 97 A1
Nab's Head PR5 . . . 99 E7
Round Barn BL7 . . . 66 B3
Roundell Rd BB18 . . . 196 C3
Roundel St BB10 . . . 148 B2
Roundhay FY4 . . . 110 F8
ROUNDHILL . . . 84 E6
Roundhill La BB4 . . . 85 A7
Round Hill Pl BB10 . . . 128 E1
Roundhill Rd BB4, BB5 . . . 84 E6
Roundhill View BB5 . . . 85 A8
Roundhouse The [44]
LA1 . . . 214 F8
Round Mdw PR26 . . . 76 C1
Round Meade The L31 . . . 5 C2
Roundway FY7 . . . 175 C8
Roundway Down PR2 . . . 117 C7
Roundway The L38 . . . 2 F3
Round Wood PR1 . . . 96 C7
Roundwood Ave BB10 . . . 148 A4
Rowan Ave
Fulwood PR2 . . . 119 A4
[2] Horwich BL6 . . . 32 E1
Oswaldtwistle BB5 . . . 103 D2
Rowan Bank LA2 . . . 219 C7
Rowan Cl
Blackburn BB1 . . . 123 B1
Bonds PR3 . . . 181 D6
Burscough Bridge L40 . . . 25 F6
Clifton PR4 . . . 115 D1
Higher Penwortham PR1 . . . 96 B3
Rochdale OL12 . . . 52 B3
Rowan Croft PR6 . . . 78 B1
Rowan Dr BL9 . . . 33 B3
Rowangate PR2 . . . 118 C7
Rowan Gr
Burnley BB10 . . . 128 C6
Chorley PR6 . . . 61 C3
Rowan Ho PR7 . . . 42 F6
Rowan La WN8 . . . 18 B4
Rowans The
[6] Adlington PR6 . . . 31 A8
Aughton L39 . . . 6 A7
Poulton-le-F FY6 . . . 153 A2
Rowan Tree Cl BB5 . . . 104 D7
Rowberrow Cl PR2 . . . 118 D6
Rowen Pk BB2 . . . 101 B8
Rowland Ave BB9 . . . 149 A8
Rowland Cl FY5 . . . 175 F2
Rowland La FY5 . . . 175 F2
ROWLANDS . . . 50 D2
Rowlands Rd BL9 . . . 50 D2
Rowland St BB5 . . . 104 A5
Rowley La BB10 . . . 128 D6
Rowley Trad Est FY8 . . . 89 D7
Rowntree Ave FY7 . . . 198 F3
Roworth Cl PR5 . . . 97 E3
Rowsley Rd FY8 . . . 89 D7
Row The
Garstang PR3 . . . 226 C2
Heapey PR6 . . . 62 D3
Silverdale LA5 . . . 224 E3
Rowton Heath PR2 . . . 117 C7
Roxburgh Rd FY4 . . . 111 A6
Roxton Cl BL6 . . . 32 B5
Royal Albert Cotts LA1 . . . 214 E4
Royal Ave
Blackpool FY3 . . . 130 F3
Fulwood PR2 . . . 117 E6
Kirkham PR4 . . . 114 B4
Leyland PR25 . . . 59 E7
Royal Bank Rd FY3 . . . 130 E3
Royal Beach Ct FY8 . . . 89 D7
Royal Birkdale Golf Links
PR8 . . . 34 D3
Royal Blackburn Hospl
BB1 . . . 102 B2
Royal Brook Ho [7]
PR1 . . . 118 A1
Royal Cl L37 . . . 12 A1
Royal Cres L37 . . . 12 A1
Royal Cross Prim Sch
PR2 . . . 116 E1
Royal Ct
Burnley BB10 . . . 148 F3
[11] Lancaster LA1 . . . 214 F7
Royal Dr PR2 . . . 117 D3
Royal Fold LA3 . . . 212 E8
Royal Gdns BL0 . . . 50 A3
Royal Lancaster Infmy
LA1 . . . 214 F7
Royal Lytham & St Anne's
Golf Course FY8 . . . 90 B5
ROYAL OAK . . . 6 F4
Royal Oak Ave BB1 . . . 122 E1
Royal Oak Bldgs [16]
FY4 . . . 130 B1
Royal Oak Cotts BB9 . . . 170 B4
Royal Oak Mdw LA2 . . . 238 B8
Royal Pk PR8 . . . 34 E4
Royal Pl FY8 . . . 90 C8
Royal Preston Hospl The
PR2 . . . 117 F6
Royal Rd LA4 . . . 217 C6
Royals The FY8 . . . 90 A6
Royal Terr PR8 . . . 35 A7
Royal Troon Ct PR4 . . . 114 A4
Royalty Ave PR4 . . . 96 A1
Royalty Gdns PR4 . . . 76 A8
Royalty La PR4 . . . 76 A8
Royalty Mall LA4 . . . 217 A5
Royal Umpire Cvn Pk
PR26 . . . 58 E3
Royds Ave
Accrington BB5 . . . 104 C3
Morecambe LA3 . . . 216 D2
Royds Gr LA3 . . . 216 D1
Royds Rd OL13 . . . 70 A7
Royds St
Accrington BB5 . . . 104 C4
Bury BL9 . . . 33 D4
Lytham St Anne's FY8 . . . 89 E5
Roylen Ave FY6 . . . 153 B5
Royle Rd
[4] Burnley BB12 . . . 127 F6
Burnley BB12 . . . 127 F7
Chorley PR7 . . . 43 C8
Royles Brook Cl [9]
FY5 . . . 176 B3
Royles Ct FY5 . . . 176 B2
Royle St [1] FY1 . . . 130 B1
Roynton Rd BL6 . . . 32 B7
Royshaw Ave BB1 . . . 101 E8
Royshaw Cl BB1 . . . 101 E8
Roy St OL14 . . . 109 A1
Royston Cl BL8 . . . 49 F1
Royston Rd FY6 . . . 153 F5
Royton Dr PR6 . . . 61 C5
Ruby St
Blackburn BB1 . . . 122 F2
Ramsbottom BL0, BL9 . . . 50 C3
Ruddington Rd PR8 . . . 35 E2
Rudd St BB4 . . . 85 A3
Rudman St OL12 . . . 52 E2
Rudyard Ave WN6 . . . 29 E2
Rudyard Dr BB3 . . . 65 D8
Rudyard Pl
Blackpool FY3 . . . 130 F7
Lytham St Anne's FY8 . . . 89 E8
Ruecroft Cl WN6 . . . 19 D8
Ruff La L39, L40 . . . 16 B4
RUFFORD . . . 39 C3
Rufford Ave L31 . . . 5 E3
Rufford CE Sch L40 . . . 39 B4
Rufford Cl PR7 . . . 43 B3
Rufford Cotts L40 . . . 38 C6
Rufford Dr PR9 . . . 54 F5
Rufford New Hall L40 . . . 39 B5
Rufford Old Hall★ L40 . . . 39 C5
Rufford Park La L40 . . . 39 A5
Rufford Rd
Bispham Green L40 . . . 39 F1
Lytham St Anne's FY8 . . . 90 D5
Southport PR9 . . . 54 C4
Rufford Sta L40 . . . 39 D4
Rufus St PR1 . . . 118 C2
Rugby Ave BB5 . . . 104 C7
Rugby Cl WN5 . . . 10 E5
Rugby Dr WN5 . . . 10 F8
Rugby St [9] FY4 . . . 130 D1
Rumley's Fold BB11 . . . 127 E2
Runcorn Ave FY2 . . . 152 F2
Rundle Rd PR2 . . . 117 D3
RUNNEL BROW . . . 26 B4
Runnel The L39 . . . 23 B1
Runnymede Ave FY5 . . . 175 D2
Runriggs The FY5 . . . 176 B1
Runshaw Ave WN6 . . . 19 E8
Runshaw Coll PR7 . . . 60 E4
Runshaw Hall PR7 . . . 60 A5
Runshaw Hall La PR7 . . . 60 A5
Runshaw La
Euxton PR7 . . . 60 B3
Runshaw Moor PR7 . . . 59 E3
RUNSHAW MOOR . . . 59 E4
Runshaw Sixth Form Coll
PR25 . . . 60 B6
Rupert St
Carnforth LA5 . . . 223 D3
Nelson BB9 . . . 148 C7
Rochdale OL12 . . . 52 C1
RUSH BED . . . 86 A6
Rushbed Cotts BB4 . . . 86 A6
Rushbed Dr BB4 . . . 86 A6
Rushden Rd L32 . . . 1 A1
Rushes Farm Cl BB5 . . . 103 C4
Rushey Cl BB4 . . . 86 A6
Rush Hey Bank BB11 . . . 107 D8
Rushley Dr LA2 . . . 220 D1
Rushley Mount LA2 . . . 220 D1
Rushmoor Cl BB4 . . . 106 A1
Rushton Ave BB18 . . . 197 B1
Rushton Cl BB9 . . . 171 B2
Rushton St
[5] Bacup OL13 . . . 70 E8
Barrowford BB9 . . . 170 D3
Great Harwood BB6 . . . 124 B4
Rushworth Bldgs OL13 . . . 70 C8
Rushworth St E [6]
BB10 . . . 148 B1
Rushworth St W [14]
BB10 . . . 148 B1
Rushy Field BB5 . . . 124 F5
Rushy Hey PR5 . . . 77 A7
Rushy Hill View [18]
OL12 . . . 52 C1
Ruskin Ave
[9] Blackpool FY1 . . . 130 B2
Colne BB8 . . . 171 D6
Leyland PR25 . . . 77 A1
Oswaldtwistle BB5 . . . 103 C5
Padiham BB12 . . . 126 E7
Ruskin Ave *continued*
Thornton FY5 . . . 176 A3
Ruskin Cl PR4 . . . 56 F6
Ruskin Dr LA4 . . . 217 E6
Ruskin Gr
Bolton-le-S LA5 . . . 221 A5
Hapton BB11 . . . 126 C4
Ruskin Ho LA1 . . . 218 C4
Ruskin Pl BB9 . . . 170 F2
Ruskin Rd
Freckleton PR4 . . . 93 B6
[2] Lancaster LA1 . . . 218 D3
Ruskin St
Burnley BB10 . . . 148 A2
Preston PR1 . . . 97 B6
Rusland Ave FY4 . . . 131 D1
Rusland Dr PR5 . . . 98 E4
Ruslands Gdns LA4 . . . 217 C4
Russell Ave
Blackpool FY5 . . . 152 D8
Colne BB8 . . . 171 E6
Leyland PR25 . . . 60 C8
Preston PR1 . . . 98 A8
Southport PR9 . . . 36 A7
Russell Ct
Burnley BB11 . . . 128 B4
Lytham St Anne's FY8 . . . 89 F6
Southport PR9 . . . 54 B4
Russell Dr LA4 . . . 218 A4
Russell Mews [40] LA1 . . . 214 F8
Russell Pl BB6 . . . 124 B5
Russell Rd
Carnforth LA5 . . . 223 E1
Southport PR9 . . . 36 A6
Russell Sq PR6 . . . 61 D1
Russell Sq W [6] PR6 . . . 61 D1
Russell St
Accrington BB5 . . . 104 C5
Bacup OL13 . . . 87 F4
Blackburn BB2 . . . 101 E3
[39] Lancaster LA1 . . . 214 F8
[6] Nelson BB9 . . . 148 D8
Russell Terr BB12 . . . 126 D7
Russia St BB5 . . . 103 F6
Rutherford Pl FY8 . . . 110 B4
Ruthin Cl BB1 . . . 101 E7
Ruthin Ct PR2 . . . 116 F3
Ruthin Dr FY5 . . . 176 D2
Ruth St
Edenfield BL0 . . . 68 D2
Whitworth OL12 . . . 71 D1
Rutland Ave
[1] Bamber Bridge PR5 . . . 97 D3
Blackburn BB1 . . . 102 E4
Burnley BB12 . . . 127 A6
Cleveleys FY5 . . . 175 E3
Fleetwood FY7 . . . 198 F3
Freckleton PR4 . . . 93 C7
Lancaster LA1 . . . 215 A5
Poulton-le-F FY6 . . . 153 C3
Rutland Cl
Clayton-le-M BB5 . . . 124 F3
Garstang PR3 . . . 181 B8
Rutland Cres L39 . . . 15 E7
Rutland Ct FY8 . . . 90 D5
Rutland Pl [8] BB12 . . . 126 D7
Rutland Rd
Lytham St Anne's FY8 . . . 90 D5
Southport PR8 . . . 35 D5
Rutland St
Accrington BB5 . . . 103 F5
Blackburn BB2 . . . 101 B3
Colne BB8 . . . 171 F5
[1] Nelson BB9 . . . 170 F1
Preston PR1 . . . 97 C8
Rutland Wlk BB4 . . . 68 A8
Ryan Cl PR25 . . . 76 E1
Ryburn Ave
Blackburn BB2 . . . 101 B6
Blackpool FY4 . . . 130 E1
Ryburn Rd L39 . . . 15 E4
Rycliffe St BB12 . . . 146 C1
Rydal Ave
Bamber Bridge PR5 . . . 97 D2
Blackpool FY1 . . . 130 C3
Darwen BB3 . . . 65 A8
Fleetwood FY7 . . . 198 E4
Formby L37 . . . 11 D3
Freckleton PR4 . . . 93 A6
Kingsfold PR1 . . . 96 C3
Orrell WN5 . . . 10 F7
Poulton-le-F FY6 . . . 153 D3
Thornton FY5 . . . 176 B1
Rydal Cl
[5] Accrington BB5 . . . 125 D1
Blackrod BL6 . . . 31 C3
Burnley BB10 . . . 148 C4
Fulwood PR2 . . . 118 C4
Padiham BB12 . . . 146 C1
Rydal Ct LA4 . . . 217 B5
Rydal Gr
Knott End-on-S FY6 . . . 199 F6
[1] Morecambe LA3 . . . 216 D2
Rydal Mount BB1 . . . 82 F6
Rydal Pl
Chatburn BB7 . . . 190 C3
Chorley PR7 . . . 43 C6
Colne BB8 . . . 172 A5
Rydal Rd
Blackburn BB1 . . . 102 A7
Hambleton FY6 . . . 177 C2
Haslingden BB4 . . . 68 C8
Hest Bank LA5 . . . 220 F4
Lancaster LA1 . . . 215 A8
Lytham St Anne's FY8 . . . 89 E8
Morecambe LA3 . . . 216 D2
Preston PR1 . . . 118 D2
Rydal St BB10 . . . 148 A2
Ryddingwood PR1 . . . 96 B6
Ryde Cl BB4 . . . 85 C1
Ryden Ave
Cleveleys FY5 . . . 175 D3
Leyland PR25 . . . 77 C1
Ryden Rd BB1 . . . 122 D6
Ryder Cl L39 . . . 15 C2
Ryder Cres
Ormskirk L39 . . . 15 C1
Southport PR8 . . . 21 E7
Ryding Cl PR26 . . . 76 E3
Rydinge The L37 . . . 12 A6
Ryding's La PR9 . . . 55 D8
Rydings The BB6 . . . 143 A1
Ryecroft PR6 . . . 62 A7
Ryecroft Ave FY6 . . . 177 C1
Ryecroft La BL7 . . . 46 C5
Ryecroft Pl FY6 . . . 177 C2
Ryefield PR6 . . . 62 A7
Ryefield Ave
Haslingden BB4 . . . 85 B2
Kingsfold PR1 . . . 96 D2
Ryefield Ave W BB4 . . . 85 A2
Ryefield Pl BB4 . . . 85 B2
Rye Gdns BB2 . . . 81 D6
Rye Gr [3] BB12 . . . 126 D7
Ryeground La L37 . . . 12 A5
Ryeheys Rd FY8 . . . 89 E8
RYELANDS . . . 218 C2
Ryelands Cres PR2 . . . 95 E8
Ryelands Prim Sch
LA1 . . . 218 B2
Ryelands Rd LA1 . . . 218 C2
Rye Moss La L37 . . . 4 B8
Rye St PR1 . . . 118 A1
Ryknild Way LA3 . . . 217 F3
Ryland Ave FY6 . . . 153 C3
Rylands Rd PR7 . . . 43 B7
Rylands St BB10 . . . 148 B1
Ryldon Pl FY4 . . . 131 A2
Rylstone Dr
Barnoldswick BB18 . . . 196 A2
Morecambe LA3 . . . 216 D1
Rymer Gr PR4 . . . 75 B8
Rymers Gn L37 . . . 11 E4
Ryscar Way FY2 . . . 152 F6
Rysdale Cres LA4 . . . 217 C4
Ryson Ave FY4 . . . 130 F1


## S


SABDEN . . . 145 F8
Sabden Brook Ct BB7 . . . 146 A8
Sabden Pl FY8 . . . 90 C7
Sabden Prim Sch BB7 . . . 145 F8
Sabden Rd
Higham BB12 . . . 146 F6
Padiham BB12 . . . 146 B4
Whalley BB7 . . . 145 A4
Saccary La BB1, BB2 . . . 122 A4
Sackville Gdns BB9 . . . 148 A5
Sackville St
Barnoldswick BB18 . . . 196 B1
Blackpool FY4 . . . 110 C6
Brierfield BB9 . . . 148 B5
[10] Burnley BB11 . . . 127 F5
Chorley PR6 . . . 43 E7
Nelson BB9 . . . 148 F7
Sacred Heart RC Prim Sch
Blackburn BB2 . . . 101 B6
Chorley PR6 . . . 43 E7
Church BB5 . . . 103 F6
Colne BB8 . . . 171 D7
Preston PR2 . . . 117 C1
Thornton FY5 . . . 176 B3
Saddle Lo [11] PR2 . . . 118 F4
Saddler Nook La LA6 . . . 241 C8
Saddlers Mews [5]
BB7 . . . 166 E8
Sadlers Row FY8 . . . 90 D7
Sadler St [3] BB5 . . . 103 E5
Saer Cl FY7 . . . 198 D3
Saffron Cl [4] BB9 . . . 170 C1
Sagar Dr PR4 . . . 93 A6
Sagar Fold
Colne BB8 . . . 171 F5
Ormskirk L39 . . . 6 D8
Sagar Holme Terr BB4 . . . 86 E5
Sagar La OL14 . . . 109 D3
Sagar St
Eccleston PR7 . . . 41 C6
Nelson BB9 . . . 148 E8
Sage Cl FY2 . . . 152 F3
Sage Ct PR1 . . . 96 C2
Sage La PR1 . . . 118 B3
Sahara Fold [1] BB1 . . . 102 A7
St Aidan's Ave
Blackburn BB2 . . . 101 D2
Darwen BB3 . . . 65 B8
St Aidan's CE Prim Sch
Bamber Bridge PR5 . . . 97 F1
Blackburn BB2 . . . 101 C2
St Aidan's CE Tech Coll
FY6 . . . 200 B3
St Aidan's Cl BB2 . . . 101 C1
St Aidans Pk [9] PR5 . . . 97 E2
St Aidan's Rd [8] PR5 . . . 97 E2
St Alban's Ct [2] BB1 . . . 101 F6
St Alban's Pl PR7 . . . 43 D5
St Alban's RC Prim Sch
BB1 . . . 101 F6
St Albans Rd
Morecambe LA4 . . . 217 F6
Rishton BB1 . . . 103 A8

St Alban's Rd
Blackpool FY1 130 D4
Darwen BB3 81 E4
Lytham St Anne's FY8 89 F7
St Ambrose Terr 5 PR25 77 B2
St Andrew's Ave
Cleveleys FY5 175 D2
Preston PR2 117 B2
St Andrew's CE Prim Sch
Oswaldtwistle BB5 103 D4
Preston PR2 117 B1
Ramsbottom BL0 50 B5
St Andrews Cl
3 Colne BB8 171 C3
Euxton PR7 60 D4
Lancaster LA1 215 C8
St Andrew's Cl
Leyland PR25 60 A7
Oswaldtwistle BB5 103 D4
Ramsbottom BL0 50 C4
St Andrews Ct
Lytham St Anne's FY8 89 E7
Southport PR8 35 B6
St Andrew's Ct FY5 175 D2
St Andrew's Ct 1 BB5 103 D3
St Andrews Gate FY8 89 D7
St Andrews Gr LA4 217 D6
St Andrew's Maghull CE Prim Sch L31 5 D1
St Andrew's Pl
Blackburn BB1 101 D6
Southport PR8 35 B6
St Andrews Rd BB6 143 C6
St Andrew's Rd PR1 118 A2
St Andrew's Rd N FY8 89 E7
St Andrew's Rd S FY8 89 F6
St Andrew's St
Blackburn BB1 101 D6
4 Burnley BB10 148 B1
St Andrews Way PR25 60 A8
St Anne & St Joseph's RC Prim Sch BB5 104 D5
St Anne's Ave LA4 217 F5
St Annes Cl
5 Blackburn BB1 101 F3
4 Church BB5 103 E5
St Anne's Cl
Caton LA2 237 D3
Formby L37 11 F6
St Anne's Coll & Jun Sch FY8 89 E5
St Anne's Cres BB4 86 F3
St Annes Ct FY4 130 C1
St Anne's Ct WN6 19 F5
St Anne's Dr BB12 147 D7
St Anne's on-the-sea Sta FY8 89 E7
St Anne's Path L37 11 F6
St Anne's Pl 18 LA1 214 F8
St Anne's RC Prim Sch
Blackburn BB2 101 D4
Leyland PR25 59 D8
Ormskirk L39 15 E4
St Annes Rd
Blackpool FY4 110 D7
4 Chorley PR6 43 E7
Great Eccleston PR3 156 C5
Horwich BL6 32 C4
Southport PR9 53 F4
St Anne's Rd
Formby L37 11 F6
Leyland PR25 77 C3
Ormskirk L39 15 D4
St Anne's Rd E FY8 89 F7
St Anne's Rd W FY8 89 E6
St Anne's St
Padiham BB12 126 C7
Preston PR1 118 A2
St Anne's Way BB12 147 D7
St Ann's Ct BB7 166 B8
St Ann's Sq BB7 166 C8
St Ann's St 4 BB2 101 E3
St Anthony's Cl PR2 117 C4
St Anthony's Cres PR2 117 C4
St Anthony's Dr PR2 117 C4
St Anthonys Pl PR4 114 A4
St Anthony's Pl 7 FY1 130 C7
St Anthony's RC Prim Sch PR2 117 C4
St Anthony's Rd PR1 118 A2
St Antony's RC Prim Sch BB1 102 C3
St Augustine of Canterbury RC Prim Sch BB12 127 B6
St Augustine's RC High Sch Billington BB7 144 A4
St Augustine's RC Prim Sch PR1 97 A7
St Austell Dr BL8 49 F2
St Austell Pl LA5 221 C8
St Austin's Pl PR1 97 A7
St Austin's Rd PR1 97 A7
St Barnabas' Pl PR1 118 A1
St Barnabas' & St Paul's CE Prim Sch BB2 101 D5
St Barnabas St
Blackburn BB2 101 C5
2 Darwen BB3 65 B6
St Bartholomewis CE Prim Sch OL12 52 C8
St Bartholomew's Parish CE Prim Sch BB6 124 C6
St Bede's Ave FY1 130 B1
St Bedes Cl L39 15 D3
St Bedes Pk BB3 81 E5
St Bede's RC High Sch
Blackburn BB2 81 A8
Lytham St Anne's FY8 91 C4
Ormskirk L39 15 D4
St Bee's Cl BB2 101 F1
St Benet's Cl PR5 97 D1
St Bernadettes RC Prim Sch LA1 215 B4
St Bernadette's RC Prim Sch FY2 152 D5
St Bernard Ave FY3 130 F7
St Bernard's RC Prim Sch PR2 116 C1
St Bernard's Rd FY6 199 E6
St Brides Cl BL6 32 A4
St Catherine Cl FY3 153 B1
St Catherine's CE Prim Sch BL6 32 A3
St Catherines Cl 4 PR25 77 C2
St Catherines Ct
Horwich BL6 32 B3
26 Lancaster LA1 214 F8
St Catherine's Dr PR2 117 C4
St Catherine's RC Prim Sch PR25 77 C2
St Catherines Way PR5 77 C7
St Cecilia's RC Tech Coll PR3 140 A6
St Cecilia St BB6 124 D5
St Celia's Way LA4 217 E6
St Chad's Ave BB7 190 D5
St Chad's CE Prim Sch FY6 153 D3
St Chads Cl FY6 153 D2
St Chad's Dr LA1 218 B3
St Chad's RC Prim Sch PR6 61 F6
St Chad's Rd
Blackpool FY1 130 B2
Preston PR1 118 C1
St Charles' RC Sch BB1 124 B1
St Charles' Rd BB1 124 B1
St Christines Ave PR25 77 C4
St Christopher's CE High Sch BB5 104 A7
St Christopher's Rd PR1 118 A2
St Christopher's Way LA4 217 D6
St Clair Dr PR9 54 A1
St Clair Rd BL8 49 F3
St Clares Ave PR2 118 A6
St Clare's RC Prim Sch PR2 117 F7
St Clemance Ct 19 BB9 170 D3
St Clements Ave PR25 77 C3
St Clement's Ave FY3 130 E5
St Clements Cl 3 BB1 102 B4
St Clements Ct BB9 170 C3
St Clement St BB1 102 B4
St Crispin Way BB4 85 A2
St Cuthbert's CE Prim Sch
Darwen BB3 81 E3
Halsall L39 23 B1
St Cuthberts Cl BB3 81 E3
St Cuthbert's Cl
1 Fulwood PR2 117 D3
1 Lytham St Anne's FY8 91 A3
Southport PR9 54 A2
St Cuthbert's Ct 6 FY8 91 A3
St Cuthbert's RC Prim Sch FY4 110 C8
St Cuthbert's Rd
Bamber Bridge PR5 97 A1
Preston PR1 118 A2
Southport PR9 54 A2
St Cuthbert St BB10 148 C2
St David's Ave
Blackburn BB2 80 E7
Cleveleys FY5 175 D2
St David's Gr FY8 89 D8
St David's Rd
Leyland PR25 77 C2
Preston PR1 118 A2
St David's Rd N FY8 89 D8
St David's Rd S FY8 89 F6
St David's Wood BB5 104 D7
St Deny's Croft 4 BB7 189 E1
St Edmund Hall Cl BL0 50 C4
St Edmund's RC Prim Sch WN8 17 F1
St Edmund's Rd FY4 130 E1
St Edmund's St BB6 124 D5
St Edward's RC Prim Sch BB3 81 E4
SS John Fisher & Thomas More RC High Sch BB8 171 B2
SS Peter & Paul RC Prim Sch L40 40 F2
St Frances Cl 4 BB1 101 F3
St Francis Cl PR2 118 A7
St Francis of Assisi RC Prim Sch WN8 9 D7
St Francis RC Prim Sch PR3 161 A2
St Francis' Rd BB2 101 A2
St Gabriel Cl WN8 19 C3
St Gabriel's Ave BB1 122 F3
St Gabriel's CE Prim Sch BB1 122 E2
St George Ct FY1 130 D6
St George's Ave
Blackburn BB2 101 B1
St George's Ave *continued*
Cleveleys FY5 175 D2
Lytham St Anne's FY8 89 E7
St George's CE High Sch FY4 111 A8
St George's CE Prim Sch PR7 43 E5
St Georges Cl BB8 171 C3
St George's Ct 10 PR7 43 D7
St George's La
Cleveleys FY5 175 D2
Lytham St Anne's FY8 89 E6
St Georges Pk PR4 113 E6
St George's Pl PR9 35 B7
St George's Quay LA1 218 C1
St Georges Rd BB9 148 F7
St George's Rd
Blackpool FY4 110 C6
Formby L37 11 E4
Hightown L38 2 F5
Lytham St Anne's FY8 89 E6
Preston PR1 118 A2
St George's Sh Ctr 8 PR1 96 F7
St George's Sq
Burnley BB10 148 C1
Lytham St Anne's FY8 89 D7
St George's St PR7 43 C7
St Georges Terr BB3 81 F1
St George's Terr BB4 70 A6
St Gerrard's Rd PR5 97 A1
St Giles St 7 BB12 146 C1
St Giles Terr 6 BB12 146 C1
St Gregory Rd PR1 118 B2
St Gregory's Pl PR7 43 C5
St Gregory's RC Prim Sch
Chorley PR7 43 C5
Maghull L31 5 C4
Preston PR1 118 B3
St Helens Cl BB5 103 F3
St Helen's Cl PR3 181 A2
St Helens Rd L39 16 A2
St Helen's Rd
Clayton Green PR6 78 C1
Overton LA3 209 E8
St Helens Well PR4 57 A5
St Helier Cl BB2 81 C8
St Helier's Pl PR3 137 A7
St Heliers Rd FY1 130 C1
St Hilda's Cl PR7 43 C4
St Hilda's Rd FY8 89 D8
St Hilda's Way PR7 43 C4
St Hubert's Rd BB6 124 C4
St Hubert's St BB6 124 D5
St Ignatius' Pl 6 PR1 97 A8
St Ignatius' RC Prim Sch PR1 97 A8
St Ignatius' Sq 5 PR1 97 A8
St Ives Ave
Blackpool FY1 130 E3
Freckleton PR4 93 A6
St Ives Cres PR2 117 A4
St Ives Rd BB1 102 D4
St James CE Prim Sch BB3 82 A7
St James' CE Prim Sch
Blackburn, Brookhouse BB1 101 E7
Darwen BB3 82 B2
St James Cl
Bamber Bridge PR5 77 B8
Church BB5 103 E7
3 Haslingden BB4 85 B3
Ormskirk L40 16 C3
St James' Cres BB3 82 B2
St James Ct
1 Bamber Bridge PR5 77 B8
Blackburn BB1 101 E7
Heysham LA3 212 E7
9 Lancaster LA1 214 E8
Standish WN6 29 D2
St James Ho BB5 104 B5
St Jamesi St BB4 69 E8
St James' Lanehead CE Prim Sch BB10 148 D2
St James Lo
Leyland PR26 59 B8
Lytham St Anne's FY8 90 A5
St James Mews BB5 103 E7
St James Pl
4 Padiham BB12 126 D8
Southport PR8 35 B5
St James' RC Prim Sch
Orrell WN5 10 D4
Skelmersdale WN8 18 B4
St James Rd
Blackpool FY4 110 C6
Church BB5 103 E7
Orrell WN5 10 D4
St James' Rd 10 BB18 196 B2
St James Row BB4 86 A3
St James's CE Prim Sch BB7 166 E7
St James's Dr LA6 240 B7
St James's Fold BB1, BB3 82 B7
St James's Gdns PR26 59 B8
St James's La 7 BB11 128 A6
St James's Pl
Blackburn BB1 101 E7
9 Chorley PR6 43 E7
St James Sq 15 OL13 87 F3
St James' Sq 11 BB18 196 B2
St James's Rd
Blackburn BB1 101 E7
Preston PR1 117 F2
St James's Row 13 BB11 127 F6
St James's St
Burnley BB11 127 F6
Burnley BB11 128 A6
8 Chorley PR6 43 E7
Clitheroe BB7 166 E7
St James St
Bacup OL13 87 F2
7 Brierfield BB9 148 B5
1 Rawtenstall BB4 86 A3
Southport PR8 35 B6
St James' St
Accrington BB5 104 B5
Blackburn BB2 101 C1
St Jame's Terr PR5 99 E7
St James-the-Less RC Prim Sch BB4 85 F3
St Jerome's RC Prim Sch L37 11 C3
St John Ave FY7 198 D2
St John Bosco RC Prim Sch L31 5 B2
St Johnís St BB4 69 F8
St John Rigby RC Sixth Form Coll WN5 19 F2
St Johns Ave
Kirkham PR4 113 F4
Smallwood Hey PR3 201 C5
St John's Ave
Darwen BB3 65 B8
Morecambe LA3 216 E2
Poulton-le-F FY6 153 E5
Silverdale LA5 224 C3
Thornton FY5 176 D1
St John's CE & Meth Prim Sch PR6 62 E7
St John's CE Prim Sch
Blackpool FY1 130 C5
Great Harwood BB6 124 C4
Higham BB12 147 A6
Nelson BB9 149 B8
Southport PR9 54 C5
St John's CE Prim Sch, Cliviger BB10 108 B6
St Johns Cl PR6 61 B7
St John's Cl
Accrington BB5 104 E2
6 Rawtenstall BB4 86 A7
Read BB12 145 D2
St Johns Ct
Fulwood PR3 137 F1
17 Ramsbottom BL0 50 C6
Southport PR8 21 D4
St John's Ct
5 Bacup OL13 87 F3
8 Blackpool FY1 130 C5
6 Burnley BB12 127 C6
6 Lytham St Anne's FY8 91 C3
St John's Gn PR25 76 E1
St John's Gr
Morecambe LA3 216 E2
Silverdale LA5 224 C3
St John Southworth RC Prim Sch BB9 148 D7
St John's Pl
Nelson BB9 149 A8
16 Preston PR1 97 A7
St John's RC Prim Sch
Burscough L40 25 E2
Poulton-le-F FY6 153 E4
Skelmersdale WN8 18 C1
St John's Rd
5 Burnley BB12 127 C6
Morecambe LA3 216 D2
Padiham BB12 126 C7
Southport PR8 34 F1
Walton-le-D PR5 97 D5
St John's Sh Ctr 18 PR1 97 A8
St John's St
Darwen BB3 65 B8
Great Harwood BB6 124 C4
Lytham St Anne's FY8 91 C3
St John's Stonefold CE Prim Sch BB5 85 A7
St John St
Bacup OL13 87 F3
Colne BB8 171 E5
Horwich BL6 32 B3
St John's Terr LA3 217 C2
St John Stone RC Prim Sch PR8 21 D2
St Johns Wood FY8 90 E3
St John The Baptist RC Prim Sch
Burnley BB10 148 C3
Padiham BB12 126 C7
St John Vianney's RC Prim Sch FY1 130 E2
St John with St Augustine CE Prim Sch BB5 104 C7
St John with St Michael CE Prim Sch OL12 71 E5
St Joseph & St Bede RC Prim Sch BL9 33 B4
St Josephs Cl FY3 130 E5
St Joseph's Con Ctr WN8 19 B2
St Josephs Convent Sch BB12 127 A8
St Josephs Pl PR6 61 D1
St Joseph's RC High Sch & Sports Coll BL6 32 E1
St Joseph's RC Prim Sch
Bacup OL13 70 D8
Barnoldswick BB18 196 B3
Chorley PR6 61 D2
Darwen BB3 65 A8
Gregson Lane PR5 98 E1
Hurst Green BB7 164 F1
St Joseph's RC Prim Sch *continued*
Kirkham PR4 113 F7
Lancaster LA1 218 D3
Preston PR1 118 C1
Ramsbottom BL0 50 B6
Shevington Moor WN6 29 A3
Withnell PR6 80 A1
St Joseph's Terr 1 PR1 118 C1
St Judes Ave PR25 77 C4
St Jude's Ave PR5 97 D1
St Katherines Dr BL6 31 C3
St Kentigern's RC Prim Sch FY3 130 D5
St Kitts Cl BB3 81 E6
St Laurence's CE Prim Sch PR7 61 C1
St Lawrence Ave BB2 101 B8
St Lawrence's Ave PR3 137 B8
St Lawrence St BB6 124 C5
St Leger Ct 11 BB5 104 C5
St Leonard Ct 6 LA1 218 E1
St Leonard's Ave BL6 32 F1
St Leonards CE Prim Sch BB2 121 A5
St Leonard's CE Prim Sch
Bamber Bridge PR5 97 C4
Langho BB6 143 E2
Padiham BB12 146 C1
St Leonard's Cl PR2 117 A3
St Leonard's Ct FY8 89 D8
St Leonard's Gate LA1 214 F8
St Leonard's Rd FY3 131 A3
St Leonard's Rd E FY8 89 E8
St Leonard's Rd W FY8 89 D8
St Leonard's St 8 BB12 146 C1
St Louis Ave FY3 130 F7
St Lucia Cl BB3 81 F6
St Luke & St Philip's CE Prim Sch BB2 101 D3
St Luke's Bldg 2 PR8 35 D6
St Luke's CE Prim Sch
Formby L37 11 D1
Lancaster LA1 218 D3
Slyne LA2 218 C8
St Luke's Church Rd L37, L38 2 C8
St Lukes Ct 2 LA1 214 E8
St Luke's Ct 1 FY4 110 C6
St Luke's Dr
Formby L37 11 C2
Orrell WN5 10 E4
St Luke's Gr PR9 35 E7
St Luke's Pl 9 PR1 118 C1
St Luke's Rd
Blackpool FY4 110 C6
Southport PR9 35 D7
St Margarets Cl PR2 117 A4
St Margaret's Ct
1 Blackburn BB1 102 B5
1 Fleetwood FY7 199 A4
St Margaret's Gdns BB11 126 C4
St Margaret's Rd
Bolton-le-S LA5 221 B6
1 Leyland PR25 77 C2
Morecambe LA4 217 D6
St Margarets Way BB1 102 B5
St Maria Goretti RC Prim Sch PR2 118 F5
St Marie's RC Prim Sch
Kirkby L33 1 A3
Standish WN6 29 E2
St Mark's CE Prim Sch L40 23 D8
St Mark's Pl
Blackburn BB2 101 B4
1 Blackpool FY3 130 E8
St Mark's Pl E 5 PR1 96 D8
St Mark's Pl W 4 PR1 96 D8
St Mark's Rd
Blackburn BB2 101 B4
Preston PR1 96 D8
St Marlow Ave 3 PR25 77 C3
St Martins Cl FY6 153 B5
St Martin's Ct FY5 175 F2
St Martin's Dr BB2 80 D8
St Martin's Rd
Blackpool FY4 110 C6
Lancaster LA1 215 A7
Preston PR1 118 A2
St Mary CE Prim Sch BB2 121 D2
St Mary Cl FY3 153 B1
St Mary Magdalene's RC Prim Sch BB12 127 D8
St Mary Magdalen's CE Prim Sch BB5 104 B7
St Mary Magdalen's RC Prim Sch PR1 96 E4
St Mary & St Andrew's RC Prim Sch PR3 137 A5
St Mary & St Michael RC Prim Sch PR3 181 C6
St Mary's Ave
Bamber Bridge PR5 97 D1
Barnoldswick BB18 196 D3
St Mary's CE Prim Sch
Eccleston PR7 41 C6
Hawkshaw BL8 49 B2
Spen Brook BB12 169 C3
St Marys Cl
Blackburn BB1 102 B5
Longridge PR3 140 A8
8 Preston PR1 97 C8

St Mary's Cl PR5 97 D1
St Mary's Coll BB1 101 E7
St Mary's Ct
Clayton-le-M BB5 124 F2
Mellor BB2 121 E2
Preston PR1 97 B8
Rawtenstall BB4 85 F2
St Mary's Dr BB6 143 D1
St Mary's Gate
Burnley BB11 128 B5
Euxton PR7 60 C3
St Mary's Gdns
Mellor BB2 121 E2
Southport PR8 21 F7
St Mary's Par LA1 214 E8
St Mary's Rawtenstall CE Prim Sch BB4 85 F3
St Mary's RC Coll FY3 130 F7
St Mary's RC High Sch PR5 97 F1
St Mary's RC Prim Sch
Accrington BB5 103 F4
Bacup OL13 88 B2
Burnley BB10 128 B6
Chipping PR3 185 E3
Chorley PR7 43 A7
Claughton PR3 182 D1
Clayton-le-M BB5 124 F3
Fleetwood FY7 199 A5
Great Eccleston PR3 156 B5
Haslingden BB4 85 C2
Horwich BL6 32 D2
Langho BB6 143 C1
Morecambe LA4 217 C6
Osbaldeston BB2 121 D4
Sabden BB7 145 F7
St Mary's RC Prim Sch Scarisbrick L40 24 A7
St Mary's Rd
Bamber Bridge PR5 97 E1
Great Eccleston PR3 156 B5
Heysham LA3 212 E8
St Mary's & St Benedicts RC Prim Sch PR5 97 E1
St Mary's & St Joseph's RC Prim Sch BB2 101 F3
St Mary's St N 7 PR1 97 B8
St Mary's St
6 Clitheroe BB7 189 E1
Nelson BB9 148 C8
Preston PR1 97 B8
St Mary's Terr 6 BB4 86 A2
St Mary's Way BB4 86 A2
St Marys Wharfe BB1 101 F3
St Mary's Wlk 16 PR7 43 C8
St Matthew's CE Prim Sch BB1 101 F4
St Matthew's CE Sch PR1 97 D8
St Matthew's Ct 9 BB11 127 E5
St Matthew St BB11 127 E5
St Michael & All Angels CE Prim Sch BB8 171 E8
St Michael Rd L39 5 F7
St Michael & St John's RC Prim Sch BB7 166 E8
St Michael's CE High Sch PR7 61 C1
St Michael's CE Prim Sch PR4 114 B5
St Michaels Cl
Fulwood PR2 117 D3
Normoss FY3 131 A8
St Michael's Cl
Blackburn BB2 80 E7
Bolton-le-S LA5 221 A4
Chorley PR7 61 B1
Southport PR9 53 F3
St Michael's Cres LA5 221 A4
St Michael's Ct
Barrowford BB9 170 C2
1 Blackburn BB1 101 F6
St Michael's Gr
Bolton-le-S LA5 221 A4
Morecambe LA4 217 C4
St Michael's La LA5 221 A4
ST MICHAEL'S ON WYRE 157 C7
St Michael's-on-Wyre CE Prim Sch PR3 157 C6
St Michaels Pk L39 6 A7
St Michael's Pl
Bolton-le-S LA5 221 A4
Newsham PR3 137 B5
St Michaels Rd
Blackpool FY2 152 D3
Kirkham PR4 114 C5
St Michael's Rd
Duncombe PR3 158 D4
4 Leyland PR25 77 C3
Preston PR1 118 A2
St Michael's St BB1 101 F7
St Michaels Terr PR26 58 B2
St Michael with St John CE Prim Sch BB1 101 E6
St Mildred's Way LA3 212 E6
St Monica's Way FY4 131 D1
St Nicholas Arcs 13 LA1 214 F8
St Nicholas' Ave BB7 145 F8
St Nicholas CE Prim Sch BB5 103 F7
St Nicholas' CE Prim Sch FY4 111 A4
St Nicholas Cres LA5 221 B6
St Nicholas Gr PR4 113 B4
St Nicholas La LA5 221 A6
St Nicholas Rd
Blackpool FY4 111 B5
Church BB5 103 F7
St Ogg's Rd LA4 217 C3
St Oswald Ho LA1 215 A6
St Oswald's Cl
Blackburn BB1 102 E4
Preston PR1 118 C2
St Oswalds Ct PR7 29 E8
St Oswald's RC Prim Sch
Accrington BB5 104 A3
Coppull PR7 29 D8
Longton PR4 75 B8
St Oswald's Rd BB1 102 E4
St Oswald St LA1 215 A6
St Patrick's Pl PR5 97 E4
St Patrick's RC Prim Sch
Heysham LA3 213 A8
Southport PR9 54 A2
Walton-le-D PR5 97 E4
St Patrick's Rd N FY8 89 E7
St Patrick's Rd S FY8 89 F6
St Patrick's Wlk LA3 212 E7
St Paul's Ave
Blackburn BB2 101 D5
Lytham St Anne's FY8 90 B4
Preston PR1 118 A1
St Paul's CE Prim Sch
Bury BL9 33 B4
Nelson BB9 148 D6
Oswaldtwistle BB5 103 E4
St Pauls Cl PR26 76 F7
St Paul's Cl
Adlington PR6 31 A8
Clitheroe BB7 166 C8
St Paul's Ct
5 Burnley BB11 127 F5
12 Oswaldtwistle BB5 103 E4
10 Preston PR1 97 A8
St Paul's Dr
Caton LA2 237 D3
Lancaster LA1 214 F5
St Pauls Mans 4 PR8 35 A6
St Paul's Pas PR8 35 A6
St Paul's RC Prim Sch BB2 80 D8
St Paul's Rd
Blackpool FY1 130 B8
Lancaster LA1 214 F5
Nelson BB9 148 E6
Preston PR1 118 A1
1 Rishton BB1 124 A1
St Paul's Sq
Preston PR1 97 A8
Southport PR8 35 A6
St Paul's St
Blackburn BB2 101 D5
Bury BL9 33 A3
Clitheroe BB7 166 C8
Oswaldtwistle BB5 103 E4
4 Ramsbottom BL0 50 C6
Southport PR8 35 A6
St Paul's Terr
Clitheroe BB7 166 C8
Hoddlesden BB3 82 E2
St Paul's Villas BL9 33 A3
St Paul's Wlk 4 FY8 90 C4
St Peter & St Paul's CE Prim Sch BB1 124 A2
St Peter's Ave
Formby L37 11 D4
Haslingden BB4 85 B2
St Peter's CE Prim Sch
Accrington BB5 104 A2
Burnley BB11 128 A6
Chorley PR6 61 E2
Fulwood PR2 117 F7
Heysham LA3 212 E7
St Peter's Cl
Darwen BB3 65 B8
Formby L37 11 D4
Salesbury BB1 122 D6
St Peter's Ctr 8 BB11 128 A6
St Peters Mews 16 LA1 215 A8
St Peter's Pl
Fleetwood FY7 199 B4
7 Haslingden BB4 85 B2
St Peter's RC Cath★ LA1 215 A8
St Peter's RC High Sch Visual Arts Coll WN5 10 F7
St Peter's RC Prim Sch
Blackburn BB2 101 B2
Lytham St Anne's FY8 91 C5
Newchurch BB4 86 E2
St Peter's Rd
Lancaster LA1 215 A8
Newchurch BB4 86 E2
Southport PR8 35 A3
St Peter's Sq 8 PR1 96 E8
St Peter's St
Chorley PR6 61 E1
1 Preston PR1 96 F8
St Peter St
Blackburn BB2 101 E4
2 Rishton BB1 124 A1
St Philip's CE Prim Sch
Nelson BB9 148 E8
Southport PR8 35 C5
St Philip's Ct BB2 101 C3
St Philip's Rd PR1 118 A2
St Philip's St
Blackburn BB2 101 B3
13 Nelson BB9 170 E1
St Philip St BB10 148 A1
St Pius X Prep Sch PR2 117 E4
St Richard's RC Prim Sch WN8 17 D1
St Saviour's Cl PR5 77 F7
St Saviours Ct OL13 87 F1
St Silas's CE Prim Sch BB2 101 B6
St Silas's Rd BB2 101 B6
St Stephenís Rd WN6 29 C1
St Stephen's Ave
8 Blackburn BB1 102 A7
Blackpool FY2 152 B2
St Stephen's CE Inf Sch BB1 102 B7
St Stephen's CE Jun Sch BB1 102 B7
St Stephen's CE Prim Sch BB11 128 B4
St Stephen's CE Sch PR1 96 E6
St Stephens Rd PR4 113 F4
St Stephen's Rd
9 Blackburn BB1 102 A7
Hightown L38 2 F4
Preston PR1 118 B2
St Stephen's St 2 BB11 128 B4
St Stephen's Tockholes CE Prim Sch BB3 81 A3
St Stephen's Way BB8 171 F6
St Teresa's Ave FY5 175 D1
St Teresa's RC Inf Sch PR8 35 A4
St Teresa's RC Prim Sch
Cleveleys FY5 175 D1
Preston PR1 118 E1
Up Holland WN8 19 B1
St Theodore's RC Sports Coll & Sixth Form BB10 128 B7
St Theresas Ct 2 PR4 114 B5
St Theresa's Dr PR2 117 C4
St Thomas CE Prim Sch
Blackburn BB1 102 B5
Maghull L31 5 D4
St Thomas' CE Prim Sch
Bury BL9 33 B1
Lytham St Anne's FY8 89 F6
St Thomas Cl
Blackpool FY3 153 B1
Haslingden BB4 68 A7
St Thomas Ct 4 BL9 33 A2
St Thomas More Wlk LA1 214 D8
St Thomas' Pl PR1 117 F1
St Thomas Rd PR4 114 A4
St Thomas' Rd
Lytham St Anne's FY8 89 F6
Preston PR1 118 A2
St Thomas's Ct WN8 10 C7
St Thomas's Rd
Chorley PR7 43 C8
Rawtenstall BB4 86 A7
St Thomas's Sq 4 PR7 43 C8
St Thomas St BB1 102 B4
St Thomas' St PR1 117 F1
St Thomas the Martyr CE Prim Sch WN8 10 B7
St Veronica's RC Prim Sch BB4 68 B7
St Vincent Ave FY1 130 E3
St Vincent RC Prim Sch OL12 52 A1
St Vincents Cl BB3 81 F6
St Vincents Rd PR2 117 F5
St Vincent's Way PR8 35 A4
St Walburga's Rd FY3 130 F7
St Walburge Ave PR2 96 E8
St Walburges Gdns 8 PR2 96 D8
St Wilfredís Dr OL12 52 D4
St Wilfrid's CE High Sch & Tech Coll BB2 101 D3
St Wilfrid's CE Prim Sch LA2 219 C7
St Wilfrid's Pk LA2 219 C7
St Wilfrid's Rd WN6 29 F1
St Wilfrid St 3 PR1 96 F7
St Wilfrid's Terr PR3 140 A7
St Wilfrid's Way WN6 29 E1
St Williams RC Prim Sch PR3 201 E4
St Wulstan's RC Prim Sch BB6 124 C5
St Wulstan's & St Edmund's RC Prim Sch FY7 198 E3
St Wyburn Ct PR8 34 F5
Salcombe Ave FY2 152 F2
Salcombe Dr PR9 54 A5
Salcombe Rd FY8 110 C1
Salem Mews LA3 212 E8
Salem St BB4 85 B3
Salerno St BB11 127 C4
SALESBURY 122 D6
Salesbury CE Prim Sch BB1 122 D7
Salesbury View BB1 122 F4
Sales's La BL9 51 B3
Salford BB1 101 E5
Salford Ct PR8 21 C5
Salford Rd
Galgate LA2 211 A3
Southport PR8 21 C5
Salford St BL9 33 A4
Salisbury Ave
5 Grimsargh PR2 139 D1
Knott End-on-S FY6 199 E5
Salisbury Cl 1 LA3 217 B2
Salisbury Ct
Knott End-on-S FY6 199 E5
Lancaster LA1 214 D8
Salisbury Rd
Blackpool FY1 130 D4
Brinscall PR6 62 F8
Darwen BB3 81 E3
Horwich BL6 32 F1
Lancaster LA1 214 D8
Preston PR1 96 D7
Salisbury St
3 Chorley PR7 43 D7
Colne BB8 171 E5
Great Harwood BB6 124 E6
15 Haslingden BB4 85 B3
5 Preston PR1 118 D1
Southport PR9 36 A6
Sallowfields WN5 10 D5
Sally Barn Cotts BB4 68 E8
Sally's La PR9 54 A2
Salmesbury Ave FY2 152 E2
Salmesbury Hall Cl BL0 50 B5
Salmons Leap PR4 113 E4
Salmon St PR1 97 C7
Salop Ave FY2 152 C4
Saltash Rd FY5 176 B5
Salt Ayre La
Lancaster LA1 218 B1
Morecambe LA1 217 F1
Saltburn St BB12 127 B6
SALTCOTES 91 D5
Saltcotes Pl FY8 91 D4
Saltcotes Rd FY8 91 D7
Salter Fell Rd LA1 218 B2
Salterford La BB10 129 A4
SALTERFORTH 194 D7
Salterforth La
Barnoldswick BB18 196 E2
Salterforth BB18 194 D7
Salterforth Prim Sch BB18 194 D8
Salterforth Rd BB18 197 A1
Salter St PR1 117 F1
Salthill Gdns BB7 189 F1
Salthill Ind Est BB7 190 A2
Salthill Rd BB7 189 F1
Salthill View BB7 189 F1
Salthouse Ave FY1 130 C3
Salt Marsh Cl FY6 177 B1
Salt Marsh La FY6 177 B1
Saltpit La L31 5 E1
Salt Pit La L40 40 F3
Salus St BB10 148 C1
SALWICK 115 E3
Salwick Ave FY2 152 D5
Salwick Cl PR9 53 F5
Salwick Pl
Lytham St Anne's FY8 90 A8
Preston PR2 116 E1
Salwick Rd PR4 135 B3
Salwick Sta PR4 115 C5
Sambourn Fold PR8 21 A5
SAMLESBURY 119 E1
Samlesbury Aerodrome BB2, PR5 120 F3
SAMLESBURY BOTTOMS 99 D6
Samlesbury CE Sch PR5 119 D1
Samlesbury Hall★ PR5 120 E2
Samuel's Ct LA1 215 A8
Samuel St
Bury BL9 33 A3
Preston PR1 97 D8
Sanctuary The 5 FY4 110 C5
Sandbank Gdns OL12 71 C2
Sandbeds La LA2 238 A8
Sand Beds La BL0, BB4 69 B5
Sandbridge Ct PR3 181 C8
Sandbrook Gdns WN5 10 D5
Sandbrook Rd
Orrell WN5 10 C5
Southport PR8 21 D4
Sandbrook Way PR8 21 C3
Sandcastle Waterpark★ FY4 110 A8
Sanderling Cl
6 Cleveleys FY5 152 F8
Lytham St Anne's FY8 90 E7
Sanderling Rd L33 1 A3
Sanders Gr LA4 217 A4
Sanderson La PR7 28 A8
Sanderson St 9 BL9 33 A3
Sandersons Way FY4 110 F8
Sandfield 4 FY5 176 A2
Sandfield Cotts L39 15 D2
Sandfield Ho 6 LA1 215 A3
Sandfield Pk L39 15 D2
Sandfield Rd OL13 88 A1
Sandfield St 11 PR25 77 B1
Sandford Dr L31 5 D2
Sandford Rd WN5 10 C5
Sandgate
Blackpool FY4 110 D5
Chorley PR7 43 D5
Lytham St Anne's FY8 89 C7
SANDHAM'S GREEN 111 C8
Sandham St 7 PR6 43 D8
Sandhams Way FY4 111 D8
Sandheys Dr PR9 53 F1
Sandhills L38 2 F3
Sandhills Ave FY4 110 B5
Sandhills Cl BB18 194 E8
Sandhill St BB3 65 B5
Sandholme La PR3 182 A4
Sandholme Villas BB18 197 A1
Sandhurst Ave
Blackpool FY2 152 C5
Lytham St Anne's FY8 89 E7
Sandhurst Cl
Formby L37 11 C1
9 Kirkham PR4 113 F5
Sandhurst Ct FY8 89 D6
Sandhurst Grange FY8 89 E7
Sandhurst St BB11 128 B6
Sandhurst Way L31 5 B5
Sandicroft Ave FY6 177 C1
Sandicroft Pl FY6 200 B4
Sandicroft Rd FY1 152 C1
Sandilands Gr L38 2 F3
Sandiway Ct PR9 35 E8
Sandiway Dr BB10 148 F3
Sandiways L31 5 E1
Sandiways Cl FY5 153 C8
Sand La LA5 223 C4
Sandon Pl FY4 110 C4
Sandon Rd PR8 34 F1
Sandon St
Blackburn BB2 101 C3
Darwen BB3 82 B2
Sandon Terr BB2 101 C3
Sandown Cl PR4 113 E5
Sandown Ct
31 Preston PR1 97 A7
10 Southport PR9 35 C8
Sandown Rd
Haslingden BB4 85 C2
Lancaster LA1 215 B3
Thornton FY5 176 B1
Sandpiper Cl
8 Blackburn BB1 101 F6
Normoss FY3 131 B6
Sandpiper Cres PR5 98 A2
Sandpiper Ct FY5 175 C2
Sandpiper Pl 7 FY5 175 F1
Sandpiper Sq 5 BB11 127 C5
Sandridge Ave PR7 43 B7
Sandridge Pl FY4 110 B4
Sandringham Ave
Leyland PR25 77 C1
Thornton FY5 176 B1
Sandringham Cl
Adlington PR7 30 E6
5 Barrowford BB9 170 C1
Blackburn BB1 122 E1
Tarleton PR4 57 A6
Whalley BB7 144 A7
Sandringham Ct
Lytham St Anne's FY8 90 D4
3 Morecambe LA4 217 A4
Southport PR9 35 B8
Sandringham Dr
Brinscall PR6 62 F8
Ramsbottom BL8 50 A1
Sandringham Gr 2 BB4 85 A1
Sandringham Lo 2 FY5 175 D2
Sandringham Park Dr PR4 76 A8
Sandringham Rd
Bamber Bridge PR5 97 D3
Chorley PR7 43 B8
Darwen BB3 81 E4
Eccleston PR7 41 C7
Formby L37 11 E1
Horwich BL6 32 E2
Lytham St Anne's FY8 90 A5
Morecambe LA4 217 A4
Southport, Ainsdale PR8 21 C5
Southport PR8 34 E3
Sandringham Way PR4 116 E6
Sands Cl BB1 124 B2
Sandsdale Ave PR2 118 C5
SAND SIDE 205 D2
Sandside Cvn & Camping Pk LA5 220 F5
Sandside Dr LA4 217 C3
Sands Rd BB1 124 B2
Sands The
Blackpool FY4 110 B4
Whalley BB7 144 C5
Sands Way FY1 130 C3
Sandwell Ave FY5 176 C2
Sandwell Brow PR3 204 E7
Sandwich Cl BB1 102 C4
Sandwick Cl PR2 117 E7
Sandy Bank Rd BL7 48 D5
Sandy Bank Terr BB4 69 D8
Sandybeds Cl BB5 104 D2
Sandybrook Cl PR2 118 E5
Sandy Brook Ho PR2 117 F7
Sandy Cl
Cleveleys FY5 175 C3
Newburgh WN8 27 A2
Sandycroft PR2 118 F2
Sandyfields PR4 116 E6
Sandyforth Ave FY5 176 B3
Sandyforth La PR4 117 A8
Sandygate BB11 127 F6
Sandy Gate La PR4 137 B2
Sandyhall La BB9 170 A2
Sandy La
Accrington BB5 104 E5
Adlington PR7 30 F6
Barrowford BB9 170 D2
Bispham Green L40 39 F2
Blackburn BB3 81 E6
Blackpool FY4 111 A4
Brindle PR5, PR6 79 C6

Sandy La *continued*
Brinscall PR6 62 E8
Clayton Green PR6 78 C3
Cottam PR4 116 D7
Fleetwood FY7 175 D7
Hambleton FY6 177 C1
Hightown L38 3 A3
Holmeswood L40 38 D5
Leyland PR25 60 A8
Maghull, Holt Green L39 6 B6
Maghull, Lydiate L31 5 C5
Mawdesley L40 40 A1
Newburgh WN8 26 F1
Ormskirk L40 16 D7
Orrell WN5 10 D4
Out Rawcliffe PR3 178 F1
Pleasington BB2 100 C2
Preesall FY6 200 B4
Skelmersdale WN8 17 D1
Sollom L40 39 A8
Thorpe Green PR6 78 E4
Sandy La Ctr WN8 17 D1
SANDYLANDS 216 E2
Sandylands Arc LA3 216 D3
Sandylands Com Prim Sch LA3 216 E3
Sandylands Prom LA3 216 D3
Sandy Pl 7 PR25 60 A8
Sandy Way L40 38 D4
Sanfield Cl L39 15 E6
Sangara Dr BB3 81 F7
Sangness Dr PR8 35 E3
Sanrava Ave FY4 111 F6
Sansbury Cres BB9 171 A2
Santon Cl PR4 114 A7
Sanvino Ave PR8 21 D5
Sapphire St BB1 122 F1
Sarah La PR26 57 F5
Sarahs Fold FY6 177 C7
Sarah St
Britannia OL13 71 C8
Darwen BB3 82 B1
Edenfield BL0 68 E3
Sark Gdns BB2 101 F1
Sarmatian Fold PR3 141 D3
Sarscow La PR26 58 E2
Saswick Ct PR4 134 B7
Saul's Dr LA5 224 A8
Saul St PR1 96 F8
Saunder Bank BB11 128 A5
Saunder Height La BB4 86 A8
Saunders Cl BB4 86 A7
Saunders' La
Hutton PR4 95 D2
New Longton PR4 95 E1
Saunders Mews PR7 43 C3
Saunders Rd BB2 101 C5
Saunders St PR9 53 C1
Savick Ave PR2 116 D1
Savick Cl PR5 77 F8
Savick Ct PR2 117 D4
Savick Rd PR2 117 D4
Savick Way PR2 116 E3
Saville Ave FY6 153 B6
Saville Rd
Blackpool FY1 130 C1
Maghull L31 5 C3
Saville St PR7 43 C5
Savon Hook L37 12 B1
Savoy Ave 1 LA3 217 C2
Savoy St
Accrington BB5 103 F5
4 Preston PR1 96 E7
Sawdon Ave PR8 35 E3
SAWLEY 230 C1
Sawley Abbey* BB7 230 C1
Sawley Ave
Accrington BB5 104 D7
Blackpool FY4 110 D5
Lytham St Anne's FY8 90 C6
Read BB12 145 D1
Sawley Cl BB3 65 C8
Sawley Cres PR2 118 F2
Sawley Dr BB6 124 E6
Sawley Rd
Chatburn BB7 190 E6
Grindleton BB7 190 C8
Sawley BB7 230 C1
Sawmills Ind Est FY1 130 D6
Sawrey Ct BB5 124 E2
Sawthorpe Wlk FY6 153 B3
Sawyer St 5 OL12 52 F1
Saxby Gr FY4 130 F1
Saxenholme PR8 34 F5
Saxifield St BB10 148 E3
Saxon Cl
Oswaldtwistle BB5 103 C5
Thornton FY5 153 C8
Saxon Hey PR2 117 C3
Saxon Hts LA3 212 F5
Saxon Lo
Southport PR8 34 F5
Southport PR8 35 A5
Saxon Rd PR8 34 F5
Saxon St BB10 128 A7
Scafell Ave LA4 217 D5
Scafell Cl BB12 127 C8
Scafell Rd
Lancaster LA1 218 E2
Lytham St Anne's FY8 111 A2
Scaffold La L38 3 D4
SCAITCLIFFE 104 B5
Scaitcliffe St BB5 104 B5
Scale Farm Rd LA1 218 A2
SCALE HALL 218 A2
Scale Hall La
Lancaster LA1 218 B2
Newton-w-S PR4 115 A2
Scarborough Rd
Blackburn BB2 102 A1
Lytham St Anne's FY8 111 A1
Scar End Cl OL13 88 A8
Scargill Rd LA5, LA6 221 F1
SCARISBRICK 23 E7
Scarisbrick Ave
Parbold WN8 27 C2
Southport PR8 35 A7
Scarisbrick Cl L31 5 E3
Scarisbrick Ct PR8 35 C6
Scarisbrick Ho 3 L39 15 F5
Scarisbrick New Rd PR8 35 D5
Scarisbrick Pk L40 24 A6
Scarisbrick St
Ormskirk L39 15 E6
Southport PR9 35 B7
Scarlet St PR6 43 E7
Scarlett Dr PR4 95 F2
Scarlett St BB11 127 E5
Scarr Dr OL12 52 F3
Scarr La BB2 101 A6
Scarr Terr OL12 71 D2
Scarsdale Ave FY4 110 C5
Scar St BB2 101 B3
SCARTH HILL 16 B1
Scarth Hill La L39 16 A2
Scarth Hill Mans L39 15 E2
Scarth La BB12 126 B5
Scarth Pk WN8 9 C7
Scawfell Rd PR7 43 B5
Sceptre Way PR5 78 B6
Schleswig St PR1 97 A8
Schleswig Way PR26 59 C7
Schofield Ave FY3 131 B7
Schofield Cl BB4 85 F2
Schofield Rd BB4 85 F2
Schofield St
Darwen BB3 81 F2
Haslingden BB4 68 A6
2 Rawtenstall BB4 69 E8
Schola Green La
Morecambe LA4 217 B5
Morecambe, West End LA4 217 B4
Scholars Ct FY8 89 E5
Scholars Gn PR2 116 C1
Scholars Way 14 BL9 33 A4
Scholefield Ave BB9 148 E5
Scholefield La BB9 148 F5
Scholes Bank BL6 32 A5
Scholes St BB3 81 F2
Scholey Head La BB10 108 A8
School Ave L37 11 F3
School Brow PR6 61 B7
School Cl
Ormskirk L39 15 C1
Southport PR8 35 B2
School Ct
Bolton BL7 47 E2
Edenfield BL0 68 D2
School Field PR5 78 B5
School Fields BB18 197 B3
Schoolfold PR4 73 E4
School Hillocks Cotts 4 PR5 77 A8
School Ho The BB10 148 D2
Schoolhouse Fold BB11 126 C3
School House Gn L39 15 F5
School House Gr L40 25 D5
Schoolhouse La LA2 219 D7
School House La BB5 104 B1
School House Mews 7 PR6 43 E7
School La
Bamber Bridge PR5 97 F2
Blackburn BB1 82 D8
Brinscall PR6 62 E8
Burnley BB11 128 A7
Burscough Bridge L40 25 F5
Catforth PR4 136 A4
Earby BB18 197 B2
Edgworth BL7 48 D8
Euxton PR7 60 D3
Farington PR5 76 F7
Formby L37 11 F3
Forton LA2, PR3 207 B3
Freckleton PR4 93 C7
Hammerton Mere BB7 235 E3
Haskayne L39 13 F4
Inskip PR4 157 D1
Kirkham PR4 114 B5
Laneshaw Bridge BB8 172 E6
Leyland, Moss Side PR26 59 A8
Leyland PR25 77 A1
Longton PR4 75 A8
Lytham St Anne's FY8 91 A3
Maghull L31 6 A1
Mawdesley L40 40 C1
Mereclough BB10 129 A1
Newton-w-S PR4 115 A2
Ollerton Fold PR6 79 F4
Out Rawcliffe PR3 178 F2
Over Kellet LA6 237 B8
Pilling PR3 201 C6
Preesall FY6 200 B3
Simonstone BB12 145 F1
Skelmersdale WN8 17 E1
Standish WN6 29 D1
Up Holland, Roby Mill WN8 19 B3
Up Holland WN5, WN8 10 C7
Westhead L40 16 E3
School La *continued*
Winmarleigh PR3 203 F6
Wray LA2 238 D6
SCHOOL LANE 97 F2
School Rd
Blackpool FY4 111 B5
Heysham LA3 212 E7
Hightown L38 2 F4
Thornton FY5 153 C8
School St
Accrington BB5 104 B6
Bacup OL13 70 B8
Bamber Bridge PR5 97 F2
Bury BL9 33 B1
Colne BB8 171 D4
Darwen BB3 82 A1
Great Harwood BB6 124 C4
Horwich BL6 32 C3
Kelbrook BB18 195 A6
Leyland PR25 77 B2
Nelson BB9 148 C8
Preston PR1 96 E7
Ramsbottom BL0 50 B5
Rawtenstall BB4 86 A8
Rishton BB1 124 B1
Walmer Bridge PR4 74 F5
Whitewell Bottom BB4 86 F4
School Terr
Salterforth BB18 194 D8
Whitworth OL12 71 C1
School View BL7 48 D8
School Villas LA2 211 B5
Schwartzman Dr PR9 55 A6
SCORTON 204 E6
Scorton Ave FY3 130 F7
Scorton CE Prim Sch PR3 204 E6
Scorton Hall Pk PR3 204 E6
Scorton Ho LA1 215 A2
Scotch Green La PR3 160 A6
SCOTFORTH 215 A3
Scotforth Ct 1 LA1 215 A3
Scotforth Rd
Lancaster LA1 215 A4
Preston PR1 97 C8
Scotforth St Paul's CE Prim Sch LA1 215 A4
Scotland Bank Terr BB2 81 C8
Scotland La BL9 33 D8
Scotland Pl 11 BL0 50 C6
Scotland Rd
Carnforth LA5 223 E3
15 Nelson BB9 170 D1
Scotshaw Brook Ind Est BB3 81 E7
Scotswood Ave FY4 110 D6
Scott Ave
Accrington BB5 104 E2
Morecambe LA4 216 F3
Simonstone BB12 145 E2
Scott Cl
Blackpool FY4 110 F8
Maghull L31 5 D1
Oswaldtwistle BB5 103 D5
Scott Dr L39 15 F7
Scott Gr LA4 217 A4
Scott Laithe La BB7 230 E3
Scott Mews FY4 110 F8
Scott Park Rd BB11 127 E4
Scott Rd LA3 216 F3
Scott St
Clayton-le-M BB5 124 F3
Nelson BB9 170 D1
Padiham BB12 126 F7
Southport PR9 36 A7
Scott's Wood PR2 117 D7
SCOUT 86 E2
Scout Bottom Ind Est BB4 86 F3
Scout Rd
Bolton BL7 47 A1
Edenfield BL0 69 A2
Newchurch BB4 86 F3
Scowcroft Dr LA4 217 E5
Scow Croft La PR6 62 D4
Scriffen La LA2 211 D3
SCRONKEY 201 E3
Scudamore Cres 6 FY4 130 D1
Seabank Rd
Fleetwood FY7 199 A5
Southport PR9 35 B8
Seaborn Dr LA4 217 E6
Seaborn Gr LA4 217 D6
Seaborn Rd LA4 217 D6
Seabourne Ave FY4 110 B7
Seabrook Dr FY5 152 E8
Seacole Cl BB1 102 B1
Seacrest Ave FY1 130 C8
Seacroft Cres PR9 54 B5
Seafield L37 12 A2
Seafield Rd
Blackpool FY1 130 B8
Lytham St Anne's FY8 90 F3
Southport PR8 21 C6
Seafore Cl L31 5 B4
Sealand Ave L37 11 E2
Sealand Cl L37 11 D2
Seascale Cl BB2 102 A1
Seasiders Way FY1 130 B3
Seathwaite Ave
Blackpool FY4 131 C1
Morecambe LA3 216 E2
Seathwaite Way BB5 104 E8
Seaton Ave FY5 175 E4
Seaton Cres FY8 89 C8
Seaton Pl WN8 17 E3
Seaton Way PR9 54 A5
Seattle Ave FY2 152 E2
Sea View
Lancaster LA1 215 A5
Longridge PR3 161 D2
Walmer Bridge PR4 74 F5
Sea View Cl LA2 218 B8
Sea View Dr LA2 218 B8
Seaview Way FY7 199 B3
Sea Wall FY7 198 C3
Seawell Ave LA3 216 D2
Second Ave
Blackpool FY4 110 C7
Bury BL9 33 D4
Church BB5 104 A8
Preesall Park FY6 200 D1
Second Terr LA3 209 B4
Sedbergh Ave FY4 130 F1
Sedbergh Cl 2 BB5 104 D5
Sedbergh Jun Sch LA2 239 B8
Sedberg St PR2 117 D3
Sedburgh St BB10 148 C2
Seddon Pl WN8 17 E3
Sedge Ct 8 LA3 217 B2
Sedgefield PR4 74 E8
Sedgeley Mews PR4 93 A6
Sedgfield Cl FY4 110 F6
Sedgley Ave PR4 93 A6
Sedgwick St PR1 118 A1
Sedum Gdns BB5 125 E2
Sedwell Cl FY8 90 F4
Seedall Ave BB7 166 D7
Seedhill Terr 13 BB9 170 D1
SEED LEE 78 C7
Seedlee Rd PR5 78 A6
Seed St
Blackpool FY1 130 C6
Preston PR1 96 F8
Sefton Ave
4 Burnley BB11 127 E5
Orrell WN5 10 D5
Poulton-le-F FY6 153 D1
Sefton Cl
Clayton-le-M BB5 125 A3
Darwen BB3 65 C6
Orrell WN5 10 D5
Sefton Ct FY8 89 D7
Sefton Dr
Bury BL9 33 A6
Lancaster LA1 218 B2
Sefton Gdns L39 6 D7
Sefton Ho L40 25 F3
Sefton La BL6 32 E1
Sefton Rd
Bamber Bridge PR5 97 D3
Formby L37 11 E2
Lytham St Anne's FY8 89 F7
Morecambe LA3 216 E3
Orrell WN5 10 D5
Sefton St
Brierfield BB9 148 B5
Colne BB8 171 F5
Southport PR8 35 C5
Sefton Terr 3 BB11 127 E5
Sefton View WN5 10 D5
Segar's La PR8, L39 22 B4
Segar St
19 Great Harwood BB6 124 C5
Kirkham PR4 113 F6
Selborne Mews BB2 101 B3
Selborne St
Blackburn BB2 101 B3
Preston PR1 97 B6
Selbourne Rd FY1 130 D6
Selbourne Terr BB18 197 C2
Selby Ave
Blackpool FY4 110 D5
Cleveleys FY5 175 F4
2 Lancaster LA1 218 D4
Selby Cl BB5 104 E3
Selby Dr L37 12 B2
Selby Pl WN8 17 D2
Selby Rd PR4 113 F5
Selby St
Colne BB8 171 C5
Nelson BB9 148 E7
Preston PR1 117 D1
Seldon St
11 Colne BB8 171 D4
15 Nelson BB9 170 E1
Selkirk Cl 6 BB1 102 A4
Selkirk Dr PR5 97 D2
Selkirk St BB11 127 D4
Sellers St PR1 118 C1
Selous Rd BB2 101 B3
Selside Dr LA4 217 B3
Selworthy Rd PR8 34 E3
Senior Ave FY4 130 F1
Seniors Dr FY5 175 F3
Senset Well La LA5 223 E5
Sephton Dr L39 15 F7
Sephton St 7 PR5 77 A8
Sergeant St 11 PR5 77 F8
Serpentine Rd BB11 127 F4
Serpentine The
3 Lytham St Anne's FY8 91 A3
Ormskirk L39 6 D8
Sett End Rd W BB1 102 C1
Sett End Road N BB1 102 D2
Settle La BB7 231 B7
Settle Pl FY8 90 C7
Settle Terr BB10 148 C2
Seven Acres PR5 78 C5
Seven Hos BB1 102 D4
Sevenoaks PR7 43 C4
Sevenoaks Ave PR8 21 B5
Sevenoaks Ct 2 FY5 152 F8
Sevenoaks Dr FY5 152 F8
Seven Sands PR4 95 A1
SEVEN STARS 59 D7
Seven Stars Prim Sch PR25 59 D7
Seven Stars Rd PR25 59 D7
Seventh Ave FY4 110 C6
Seven Trees Ave BB1 102 A8
Severn Ave FY7 175 D8
Severn Ct LA3 217 F2
Severn Dr PR5 97 D2
Severn Hill PR2 117 C8
Severn Ho 10 PR1 97 D8
Severn Rd FY4 110 B7
Severn St PR3 140 A7
Seville Ct FY8 90 D3
Seymour Ave LA3 212 F7
Seymour Ct PR1 117 D2
Seymour Dr L31 5 E3
Seymour Gr LA3 212 F7
Seymour Rd
Blackpool FY1 130 C2
Fulwood PR2 117 C3
Lytham St Anne's FY8 90 D4
Seymour St
Chorley PR6 43 E8
2 Fleetwood FY7 198 F4
5 Lancaster LA1 215 A8
Shacklady Rd L33 1 A4
Shackleton Rd PR4 114 B2
Shackleton St
Burnley BB10 128 B8
Todmorden OL14 109 C1
Shade La PR7 43 D1
Shade Row FY6 200 B3
SHADSWORTH 102 D3
Shadsworth Bsns Pk BB1 102 C1
Shadsworth Cl BB1 102 C4
Shadsworth Inf Sch BB1 102 D4
Shadsworth Jun Sch BB1 102 C2
Shadsworth Rd BB1 102 C3
Shady La
Clayton-le-W PR5, PR25 77 E3
Slyne LA2 218 C8
Shaftesbury Ave
Blackpool FY2 152 C2
Burnley BB11 127 F3
Cleveleys FY5 175 D5
Darwen BB3 81 E3
Great Harwood BB6 124 E6
Higher Penwortham PR1 96 B6
New Longton PR4 75 F8
Normoss FY3 131 B6
Southport PR8 22 A8
Shaftesbury Cl FY8 90 D5
Shaftesbury Ct FY2 152 C2
Shaftesbury Gr PR8 35 A1
Shaftesbury Pl
Chorley PR7 43 B8
Lancaster LA1 214 F4
Shaftesbury Rd PR8 35 A1
Shakeshaft St 11 BB1 102 A4
Shakespeare Ave BB6 124 B4
Shakespeare Ctr The PR8 35 B5
Shakespeare Prim Sch FY7 198 E4
Shakespeare Rd
Fleetwood FY7 198 E4
Lancaster LA1 218 C4
Preston PR1 118 D1
Shakespeare St
Padiham BB12 126 D7
Southport PR8 35 B5
Shakespeare Terr PR6 61 D2
Shakespeare Way BB2 101 C3
Shalbourn Rd FY8 90 A4
Shale St BB12 127 D6
Shalgrove Field PR2 117 C7
Shallow Valley Ct 9 BB5 103 E5
Shalom Lo FY8 89 F5
Shannon Sq BB10 148 C2
Shannon St FY1 130 B3
Shanter Cl OL12 71 E6
Shap Cl
Accrington BB5 104 E3
Barrowford BB9 170 D4
Shap Ct FY7 198 D1
Shap Gr BB10 148 A3
Shard La FY6 154 B8
Shard Rd FY6 154 B6
Shards Ct 17 LA1 218 D2
Sharley Fold PR3 140 B7
Sharman Ave FY8 110 F1
SHARNEYFORD 88 C5
Sharneyford Prim Sch OL13 88 C5
Sharoe Bay Ct PR2 117 F6
SHAROE GREEN 117 E6
Sharoe Green La PR2 117 F7
Sharoe Green Pk PR2 118 A5
Sharoe Mount Ave PR2 117 F7
Sharow Gr FY1 130 D3
Sharpe's Ave LA1 215 A5
Sharpes Mill LA1 214 F7
Sharples Ct PR3 140 A8
Sharples Gn BL7 48 D6
Sharples Mdw BL7 48 D6
Sharples St
Accrington BB5 103 F5
Blackburn BB2 101 D3

Sharp St
1 Barrowford BB9 ... 170 D3
Burnley BB10 ... 148 B1
Sharratts Path PR7 ... 42 F4
Sharrock St 7 PR8 ... 35 B7
Shawbridge Ct BB7 ... 166 F8
Shaw Bridge St 4
BB7 ... 166 F8
Shawbrook Cl
Euxton PR7 ... 60 C5
Hapton BB11 ... 126 C4
Shaw Brook Cl BB1 ... 103 A8
Shaw Brook Rd PR25 ... 59 E6
Shaw Brow PR6 ... 61 B7
Shawbury Cl BL6 ... 31 D1
Shaw Cl
Blackburn BB2 ... 101 D5
Shirdley Hill L39 ... 23 A6
Shawcliffe La BB6, BB7 ... 144 B2
SHAWCLOUGH ... 52 C2
Shawclough Cl OL12 ... 52 D3
Shawclough Com Prim Sch
OL12 ... 52 E3
Shawclough Dr OL12 ... 52 D3
Shawclough Mews BB4 ... 86 F3
Shawclough Rd OL12 ... 52 C3
Shaw Clough Rd BB4 ... 86 F3
Shaw Clough St BB4 ... 86 F3
Shawclough Way OL12 ... 52 D3
Shaw Cres L37 ... 12 B3
Shawes Dr PR6 ... 31 C7
SHAWFIELD ... 52 A2
Shawfield 4 BB4 ... 85 F1
Shawfield La OL12 ... 52 A2
SHAWFORTH ... 71 D6
SHAW GREEN ... 59 D2
Shaw Hall Cvn Site L40 ... 24 B4
Shawhead Cotts BB8 ... 195 E1
Shaw Hill PR6 ... 61 B7
Shaw Hill Dr PR6 ... 61 B6
Shaw Hill St PR7 ... 43 C7
Shaw La
Haskayne L39 ... 13 E6
Nether Kellet LA6 ... 221 F4
Todmorden OL14 ... 109 C3
Shaw Rd
Blackpool FY1 ... 130 B1
Horwich BL6 ... 32 B5
Shaw's Ave PR8 ... 35 A1
Shaws Garth L39 ... 23 A6
Shaw's La PR3 ... 201 A3
Shaw Sq 4 BB18 ... 197 B2
Shaw's Rd PR8 ... 35 A1
Shaw St
Blackburn BB2 ... 101 D5
Bury BL9 ... 33 B3
Colne BB8 ... 171 D4
Haslingden BB4 ... 85 B6
2 Lancaster LA1 ... 215 A8
2 Preston PR1 ... 118 A1
Shay La
Longridge PR3 ... 139 F6
Slaidburn BB7 ... 229 B7
Shay Lane Ind Est PR3 ... 139 F5
Shays Dr BB7 ... 167 A7
Shay The 10 FY5 ... 152 F7
Shear Bank Cl BB1 ... 101 D6
Shear Bank Gdns BB1 ... 101 D6
Shear Bank Rd BB1 ... 101 D6
Shear Brow BB1 ... 101 D7
Shearwater Dr BB1 ... 101 F6
Sheddon Gr BB10 ... 128 E5
Shed St
Colne BB8 ... 171 C4
Oswaldtwistle BB5 ... 103 D3
Whitworth OL12 ... 71 D1
Sheep Gap OL12 ... 52 B1
Sheep Gn BB4 ... 85 B3
Sheep Hill Brow PR6 ... 78 A3
Sheephill La PR4 ... 76 A7
Sheep Hill La
Clayton Green PR6 ... 78 B3
Clayton-le-W PR6, PR25 ... 77 F2
Sheep House La BL6 ... 45 A3
Sheffield Dr PR2 ... 116 D1
Sheldon Ave WN6 ... 29 E2
Sheldon Ct 1 PR1 ... 117 F1
Shelfield La BB10 ... 149 F7
Shelfield Rd BB9 ... 171 B1
Shelley Cl
Blackpool FY2 ... 152 F6
Bolton-le-S LA5 ... 221 A5
Coppull PR7 ... 29 F8
Shelley Dr
Accrington BB5 ... 104 E2
Eccleston PR7 ... 41 D5
Ormskirk L39 ... 15 D6
Shelley Gdns BB6 ... 124 B4
Shelley Gr
Blackpool FY5 ... 152 D8
Darwen BB3 ... 82 C1
Southport PR8 ... 35 F6
Shelley Mews PR2 ... 117 D1
Shelley Rd PR2 ... 117 C2
Shellfield Rd PR9 ... 54 A4
Shellingford Cl WN6 ... 19 D7
Shelton Dr PR8 ... 21 A4
Shenley Way PR9 ... 54 D5
Shenstone Rd FY3 ... 130 F7
Shepherd Rd FY8 ... 90 A7
Shepherd Rd N FY8 ... 90 A8
Shepherd's Ave PR3 ... 181 D4
Shepherds Cl
Blackrod BL6 ... 31 C3
Ramsbottom BL8 ... 49 F1
Shepherds Gn BB4 ... 87 A8
Shepherd's La L39 ... 14 E5
Shepherd St
Bacup OL13 ... 87 F3
Bury BL9 ... 33 A1
Darwen BB3 ... 65 A7
9 Lytham St Anne's FY8 ... 91 B3
Preston PR1 ... 97 A7
Shepherds Way PR6 ... 43 D8
Sheppard St FY1 ... 130 B4
Sheraton Pk PR2 ... 117 A6
Sherborne Lo 9 PR2 ... 118 F4
Sherbourne Cl FY6 ... 153 C5
Sherbourne Cres PR1 ... 118 B3
Sherbourne Ct FY6 ... 153 C5
Sherbourne Rd
Accrington BB5 ... 104 E3
Blackpool FY1 ... 130 C7
Hambleton FY6 ... 177 C2
Sherbourne St 5 PR6 ... 43 D7
Sherburne Ave 4 PR4 ... 113 F5
Sherburn Rd PR1 ... 96 E3
Sherburn Sch PR1 ... 118 A3
Sherdley Rd PR5 ... 77 B7
SHERFIN ... 85 B7
Sherfin Nook BB5 ... 85 B7
Sherfin Side BB5 ... 85 B7
Sheridan Rd BB8 ... 172 D6
Sheridan St
Burnley BB10 ... 148 E2
6 Nelson BB9 ... 170 F2
Sheriff St OL12 ... 52 E1
Sheringham Ave FY5 ... 152 D7
Sheringham Way FY6 ... 153 E3
Sherrat St WN8 ... 17 D1
Sherringham Rd PR8 ... 34 E2
Sherrington Ct PR8 ... 35 A3
SHERWOOD ... 118 A6
Sherwood Ave
Blackpool FY3 ... 130 E8
Ormskirk L39 ... 15 C2
Sherwood Ct BB10 ... 128 C5
Sherwood Dr WN8 ... 18 D3
Sherwood Ho PR8 ... 21 C5
Sherwood Lo PR8 ... 34 F5
Sherwood Pl
Chorley PR6 ... 43 D8
2 Cleveleys FY5 ... 175 F1
Sherwood Prim Sch
PR2 ... 118 A7
Sherwood Rd
Blackburn BB1 ... 102 B3
Lytham St Anne's FY8 ... 90 C6
Sherwood Way
Accrington BB5 ... 125 A1
Fulwood PR2 ... 118 A7
Shetland Cl
Blackburn BB1 ... 102 C3
Wilpshire BB1 ... 122 F7
Shetland Rd FY1 ... 130 C2
SHEVINGTON ... 19 F5
Shevington Com Prim Sch
WN6 ... 19 F6
Shevington Cswy PR26 ... 58 B2
Shevington La WN6 ... 29 B1
SHEVINGTON MOOR ... 29 B2
Shevington Moor WN6 ... 29 A2
Shevington's La L33 ... 1 A6
SHEVINGTON VALE ... 19 E7
Shevington Vale Prim Sch
WN6 ... 19 E8
Shilton St BL0 ... 50 B5
Shipley Cl FY3 ... 153 B1
Shipley Rd FY8 ... 90 B7
Shipper Bottom La BL0 ... 50 D5
Shirdley Cres PR8 ... 21 C3
SHIRDLEY HILL ... 22 F6
Shire Bank Cres PR2 ... 117 E5
Shireburn Ave BB7 ... 166 C7
Shireburn Cotts BB7 ... 164 E1
Shireburn Cvn Pk BB7 ... 189 B1
Shireburne Holiday Pk
BB7 ... 166 B8
Shireburn Rd L37 ... 11 D5
Shire La BB7 ... 142 D8
SHIRESHEAD ... 207 E3
Shireshead Cres LA1 ... 215 A2
Shires The BB2 ... 81 D6
Shirewell Rd WN5 ... 10 E5
Shirley Cres FY2 ... 152 D6
Shirley Gdns BB3 ... 80 F2
Shirley Hts FY6 ... 153 D4
Shirley La PR4 ... 95 A1
Shop La
Accrington BB5 ... 104 D5
Higher Walton PR5 ... 98 B4
Maghull L31 ... 5 C1
SHORE ... 109 C2
Shore Ave BB10 ... 148 F2
Shore Cl LA5 ... 224 B2
Shore Cotts LA5 ... 224 B3
Shorefield Mount BL7 ... 47 E1
Shore Fields 4 FY3 ... 131 A8
Shorefields Cvn Pk
LA3 ... 208 E7
Shore Gn
Cleveleys FY5 ... 175 F3
Silverdale LA5 ... 224 B2
Todmorden OL14 ... 109 C2
Shore New Rd OL14 ... 109 B1
Shore Rd
Blackpool FY5 ... 152 C8
Hesketh Bank PR4 ... 73 C4
Heysham LA3 ... 212 D6
Silverdale LA5 ... 224 B2
Southport PR8 ... 21 B6
Shoreside Prim Sch
PR8 ... 21 B4
Shore The LA5 ... 220 F5
SHOREY BANK ... 82 A2
Shorey Bank BB11 ... 128 A6
Shorrock La BB2 ... 101 B1
Shorrocks Ave PR3 ... 157 C8
Shorrock St BB3 ... 65 A8
Short Clough Cl BB4 ... 86 A6
Short Clough La BB4 ... 86 A6
Shorten Brook Dr BB5 ... 125 E6
Shorten Brook Way
BB5 ... 125 E6
Short La PR3 ... 137 F5
Shortlands Dr LA3 ... 212 E7
Shortlands The BB12 ... 146 C2
Shortridge Rd FY4 ... 110 F8
Short St
Bacup OL13 ... 70 B8
Colne BB8 ... 171 D4
Showfield BB10 ... 129 B6
Showley Brook Cl BB1 ... 122 F4
Showley Ct BB1 ... 122 E6
Showley Rd BB1 ... 122 A6
Shrewsbury Cl PR4 ... 114 C5
Shrewsbury Dr
Lancaster LA1 ... 215 B5
Thornton FY5 ... 176 A2
Shropshire Dr BB1 ... 122 F6
Shuttle Cl BB5 ... 104 A6
SHUTTLEWORTH ... 50 E8
Shuttleworth Coll
BB12 ... 127 A7
Shuttleworth Mead Bsns
Pk BB12 ... 126 B7
Shuttleworth Rd PR1 ... 117 F2
Shuttleworth St
Burnley BB10 ... 148 B2
Earby BB18 ... 197 B2
6 Padiham BB12 ... 126 C8
Rishton BB1 ... 124 B2
Shuttling Fields La PR5 ... 98 B2
Sibbering Brow Preston Rd
PR7 ... 42 C7
Siberia Mill BB10 ... 148 F3
Sibsey St LA1 ... 214 E7
Siddow's Ave BB7 ... 166 D7
Sidebeet La BB1 ... 102 E7
Sidegarth Gate LA2 ... 237 C7
Sidegarth La LA2 ... 237 D7
Side La BB7 ... 192 C7
Sidford Ct FY3 ... 130 F8
Sidgreaves La PR4 ... 116 B4
Siding La
Kirkby L33 ... 1 C7
Rainford WA11 ... 8 C1
Siding Rd FY7 ... 199 A3
Sidings Bsns Pk The
BB7 ... 144 C6
Sidings Rd LA3 ... 212 F2
Siding St OL13 ... 70 C8
Sidings The
Britannia OL13 ... 71 A8
5 Colne BB8 ... 171 C4
Darwen BB3 ... 65 B7
Low Bentham LA2 ... 239 C8
Whalley BB7 ... 144 C6
Sidmouth Ave BB4 ... 85 C2
Sidmouth Rd FY8 ... 110 C1
Sidney Ave
Becconsall PR4 ... 73 F3
Blackpool FY2 ... 152 E2
Sidney Rd PR9 ... 35 F8
Sidney Terr 4 LA1 ... 215 A8
Siemens St BL6 ... 32 C2
Signal Ho BB5 ... 103 F4
Silbury Cl BB2 ... 82 A8
Silcock's Cotts FY5 ... 176 F1
Silk Mill La PR3 ... 160 B3
Silloth Cl BB2 ... 101 F1
Silly La LA2 ... 239 D2
Silsden Ave PR2 ... 118 D5
Silsden Cl FY3 ... 153 B1
Silver Birch Way L31 ... 5 B5
Silverburn 4 FY8 ... 90 A8
SILVERDALE ... 224 C3
Silverdale
Becconsall PR4 ... 73 F3
Blackpool FY2 ... 152 E6
Southport PR8 ... 34 E4
Silverdale Ave
Fleetwood FY7 ... 198 D1
Heysham LA3 ... 212 F7
Silverdale Cl
Blackburn BB2 ... 81 F8
Burnley BB10 ... 148 B3
Clayton-le-M BB5 ... 124 E2
Coupe Green PR5 ... 98 E4
Leyland PR25 ... 60 B6
Silverdale Ct PR8 ... 35 E4
Silverdale Dr PR2 ... 118 E5
SILVERDALE GREEN ... 224 D3
Silverdale Moss Rd
LA5 ... 224 D7
Silverdale Rd
Arnside LA5 ... 224 C8
Chorley PR6 ... 43 E7
Lytham St Anne's FY8 ... 90 C7
Yealand Redmayne LA5 ... 225 E4
Silverdale St John's CE
Prim Sch LA5 ... 224 C3
Silverdale Sta LA5 ... 224 F3
Silvermere Cl 20 BL0 ... 50 B5
Silver Ridge Cvn Pk
LA7 ... 225 E8
Silversmiths Row FY8 ... 90 D7
Silver St
Clifton PR4 ... 115 D1
Hurst Green BB7 ... 164 E1
8 Preston PR1 ... 97 A6
Ramsbottom BL0 ... 50 C6
Silverstone Gr L31 ... 5 B4
Silverthorne Dr PR9 ... 53 F1
Silverwell St BL6 ... 32 B4
Silverwood Ave FY4 ... 110 D8
Silverwood Cl FY8 ... 90 E4
Silverwood Ct 1 FY4 ... 110 D8
Silvester Rd PR7 ... 43 C6
Silvia Way FY7 ... 198 E4
Simfield Cl WN6 ... 29 D1
Simmonds Way BB9 ... 148 B7
Simmons Ave PR5 ... 97 B3
Simmons' St BB2 ... 101 D5
Simmons Way BB5 ... 125 A3
Simms Cl BL0 ... 50 A5
SIMONSTONE ... 145 E1
Simonstone Bsns Pk
BB12 ... 125 F7
Simonstone La BB12 ... 125 E8
Simonstone Rd BB12,
BB7 ... 145 F6
Simonstone St Peter's CE
Prim Sch BB12 ... 145 F1
Simonswood Ind Pk L33 ... 1 B6
Simonswood La
Kirkby L33 ... 1 A2
Royal Oak L39 ... 6 F3
Simonswood Wlk L33 ... 1 A2
Simpson Cl BB18 ... 196 D3
Simpson Ct 26 PR1 ... 97 A7
Simpson St
Blackpool FY4 ... 110 B8
Hapton BB12 ... 126 C4
Oswaldtwistle BB5 ... 103 D3
9 Preston PR1 ... 96 F8
Simpson Street Ind Units
BB12 ... 126 C5
Sinclair Ct FY8 ... 90 B7
Sineacre La L33, L39 ... 1 E8
SINGLETON ... 154 E1
Singleton Ave
Horwich BL6 ... 32 C5
Lytham St Anne's FY8 ... 90 B8
Read BB12 ... 145 D2
Singleton CE Prim Sch
FY6 ... 154 E1
Singleton Cl PR2 ... 117 F7
Singleton Ct 4 FY1 ... 130 B4
Singleton Hall FY6 ... 154 E3
Singleton Rd
Weeton Camp PR4 ... 132 E6
Weeton PR4 ... 132 F4
Singleton Row 14 PR1 ... 96 F8
Singleton St 3 FY1 ... 130 B3
Singleton Way PR2 ... 117 F7
Sion Brook Ho PR2 ... 118 F4
Sion Cl PR2 ... 118 F4
Sion Hill PR2 ... 118 F4
Sir Frank Whittle Way
FY4 ... 110 D4
Sir John Thursby Com Coll
BB10 ... 148 D1
Sir Simon's Arc 27 LA1 ... 214 F8
Sir Tom Finney Way PR1,
PR2 ... 118 B3
Sir William Hartley Ct
BB8 ... 172 C6
Six Acre La PR4 ... 75 C6
Six Arches Cvn Pk
PR3 ... 204 D8
Sixfields 13 FY5 ... 152 F7
Sixpenny La L37 ... 21 D1
Sixth Ave
Blackpool FY4 ... 110 C7
Bury BL9 ... 33 D4
Sizehouse St 22 PR1 ... 96 F8
Size House Village 6
BB4 ... 85 B2
Sizergh Ct LA1 ... 214 D7
Sizergh Rd LA4 ... 217 E5
Sizer St PR1 ... 117 F1
Size St OL12 ... 71 D1
Skaithe The BB7 ... 229 C7
Skeffington Rd PR1 ... 118 C1
Skeleron La BB7 ... 192 B6
SKELMERSDALE ... 18 A1
Skelmersdale & Ormskirk
Colls (Westbank Campus)
WN8 ... 9 B8
Skelmersdale Rd L39,
WN8 ... 8 B7
Skelmersdale Sports Ctr
WN8 ... 9 C7
Skelshaw Cl BB1 ... 102 A3
Skelton St BB8 ... 171 E5
Skelwith Rd FY3 ... 131 B2
Skerryvore Res Pk
FY4 ... 110 D6
SKERTON ... 218 C4
Skerton 1 LA1 ... 218 D2
Skerton Com High Sch
LA1 ... 218 D2
Skerton Com Prim Sch
LA1 ... 218 D2
Skerton Ct LA1 ... 218 D2
Skerton Ho 6 LA1 ... 218 D2
Skiddaw Cl BB12 ... 147 C1
Skiddaw Rd
Blackpool FY4 ... 110 F8
Lancaster LA1 ... 218 E2
Skiddaw St BB1 ... 102 A5
Skip La PR4 ... 95 B3
SKIPPOOL ... 153 F6
Skippool Ave FY6 ... 153 E5
Skippool Rd FY5 ... 153 E7
Skipton Ave
Carleton FY6 ... 153 C5
Southport PR9 ... 54 C6
Skipton Cl
Bamber Bridge PR5 ... 97 F2
Skipton Cl *continued*
Blackpool FY4 ... 130 F1
Skipton Cres PR2 ... 118 E5
Skipton Gate LA6 ... 242 C2
Skipton Old Rd
Colne BB8 ... 172 C7
Foulridge BB8 ... 194 E2
Skipton Rd
Barnoldswick BB18 ... 196 D4
Colne BB8 ... 171 E6
Earby BB18 ... 197 B3
Foulridge BB8 ... 194 E2
Lytham St Anne's FY8 ... 90 B6
Trawden BB8 ... 172 B3
Skipton Road Bsns Ctr
BB18 ... 196 B3
Skipton St
2 Morecambe LA4 ... 217 A5
Nappa BB7 ... 231 D7
Ski Rossendale★ BB4 ... 85 E3
SKITHAM ... 179 B4
Skitham La PR3 ... 179 D4
Skull House La WN6 ... 19 D8
Skull House Mews
WN6 ... 19 C8
Skye Cl OL10 ... 33 F1
Skye Cres BB1 ... 102 C3
Slack BB12 ... 146 F6
Slack Booth BB8 ... 172 C1
Slackey La PR9 ... 54 C4
Slack Gate OL12 ... 52 F8
Slack La LA2 ... 209 C1
Slack's La PR6 ... 44 B2
Slackwood La LA5 ... 224 E2
Slade La BB12 ... 146 C1
Sladen St OL12 ... 52 F1
Slade St PR1 ... 96 E7
SLAIDBURN ... 229 C7
Slaidburn Ave
Burnley BB10 ... 128 D5
Rawtenstall BB4 ... 86 A4
Slaidburn Brennands Prim
Sch BB7 ... 229 C7
Slaidburn Cres PR9 ... 54 B5
Slaidburn Dr
Accrington BB5 ... 104 A4
Lancaster LA1 ... 215 A3
Slaidburn Heritage Ctr★
BB7 ... 229 C7
Slaidburn Ind Est PR9 ... 54 B5
Slaidburn Pl PR2 ... 119 A2
Slaidburn Rd
Fulwood PR2 ... 119 A2
Lowgill LA2 ... 239 E4
Waddington BB7 ... 189 A6
Waddington, Newton Fells
BB7 ... 229 C2
Slaidburn Wlk 5 FY3 ... 131 A8
Slape La LA6 ... 240 C8
Slate La WN8 ... 17 C2
Slater Ave
Colne BB8 ... 171 D6
Horwich BL6 ... 32 C4
Slater La
Leyland, Moss Side
PR26 ... 59 B8
Leyland, Seven Stars
PR25 ... 59 D8
Slater Rd FY5 ... 175 C2
Slater St BB2 ... 101 C1
Slinger Rd FY5 ... 175 C3
Slip Inn La 29 LA1 ... 214 F8
Slipper Lowe Brow BB3 ... 64 A5
Sliven Clod Rd BB4 ... 105 E2
Sluice La L40 ... 39 B3
SLYNE ... 218 D8
Slyne Cvn Pk LA2 ... 218 D8
Slyne Hall Hts LA2 ... 221 A1
Slyne Rd
Bolton-le-S LA2, LA5 ... 221 A2
Lancaster LA1 ... 218 D3
Morecambe LA4 ... 218 A5
Slynewoods LA2 ... 218 F7
Smalden La BB7 ... 230 A3
Smalley Croft PR1 ... 96 F3
Smalley St
Burnley BB11 ... 128 B4
Standish WN6 ... 29 E1
Smalley Thorn Brow
BB6 ... 123 F6
Smalley Way BB2 ... 101 E2
Small La
Bescar L40 ... 37 E1
Ormskirk, Clieves Hills
L39 ... 15 A3
Ormskirk L39 ... 15 F4
Small La N L39 ... 23 E2
Small La S L39 ... 14 D6
Smallshaw Ind Est
BB11 ... 127 C5
Smallshaw La BB11,
BB12 ... 127 B5
Smallshaw Rd OL12 ... 52 A4
SMALLWOOD HEY ... 201 B5
Smallwood Hey Rd
PR3 ... 201 C5
Smeaton St BL6 ... 32 C2
Smethurst Hall Pk WN5 ... 10 C2
Smethurst Hall Rd BL9 ... 33 F4
Smethurst Rd WN5 ... 10 C2
Smirthwaite St BB11 ... 127 D5
Smith Ave PR4 ... 73 F1
Smith Brow BL6 ... 31 C3
Smith Cl PR2 ... 139 C1
Smith Croft PR26 ... 59 B8

SMITH GREEN 211 C3
Smithills Cl PR6 61 E1
Smithills Hall Cl BL0 50 C5
Smith La BL7 47 F1
Smith Rd FY5 175 D2
Smith's La PR4 57 A1
Smith St
Adlington PR7 30 F6
13 Bamber Bridge PR5 77 F8
Barnoldswick BB18 196 A1
Burnley BB12 127 E6
Bury BL9 33 A3
Chorley PR7 43 D6
Colne BB8 171 C4
3 Kirkham PR4 113 F5
Nelson BB9 148 F8
Ramsbottom BL0 50 B5
Skelmersdale WN8 17 D1
Whittle-le-W PR6 61 C8
Worsthorne BB10 129 B5
Smithy Bridge St 9
BB5 103 D3
Smithy Brow
Abbeystead LA2 232 F1
Haslingden BB4 85 B4
Newburgh WN8 27 A1
Wrightington Bar WN6 28 C8
Smithy Brow Ct BB4 85 B4
Smithy Cl
Brindle PR6 78 F5
Formby L37 12 B4
Garstang PR3 181 C8
Stalmine FY6 177 C7
Smithy Ct PR4 74 E2
Smithy Cvn Pk PR3 204 A5
Smithyfield Ave BB10 128 F6
Smithy Fold
Rochdale OL12 52 C1
Wrea Green PR4 113 B4
Smithy Glen Dr WN5 10 E4
Smithy Gn L37 12 B4
Smithy La
Aughton L39 6 A6
Brindle PR6 78 F6
Claughton PR3 182 B2
Foulridge BB8 171 B8
Haskayne L39 14 A6
Heysham LA3 212 E6
Holmeswood L40 38 C6
Hurlston Green L40 24 B3
Lytham St Anne's FY8 90 C6
Mawdesley L40 40 C2
Much Hoole PR4 74 E2
Preesall FY6 200 B3
Staining FY3, FY6 131 E6
Stalmine FY6 177 C7
Westhouse LA6 242 E4
Smithy Lane Ends L40 24 D6
Smithy Mews 9 FY1 130 C7
Smithy Row BB7 164 E1
Smithy St
2 Bamber Bridge PR5 77 E8
9 Haslingden BB4 85 B3
7 Ramsbottom BL0 50 C6
Smithy Wlk L40 25 E5
Smythe Croft PR9 54 A2
Snaefell Rd BB2 101 E1
Snape Gn
Scarisbrick PR8 23 D8
Southport PR8 36 E1
SNAPE GREEN 36 E1
Snape La LA5 225 F1
Snape Rake La PR3 183 D4
Snape St BB3 81 F3
Snapewood La PR3 204 B3
Snell Gr BB8 171 F6
Sniddle Hill La BB3 64 E8
Snipe Cl
Cleveleys FY5 175 F5
Normoss FY3 131 B6
Snipewood PR7 41 B6
Snoballey L40 24 B4
Snodworth Rd BB6 123 D7
Snowden Ave LA3 216 D3
Snowden St 1 BB12 127 B6
Snowdon Ave BB1 101 E7
Snowdon Cl FY1 130 D3
Snowdon Dr BL6 32 C5
Snowdon Rd FY8 111 A2
Snowdrop Cl
Clayton-le-W PR25 77 E2
Haslingden BB4 67 F8
Snow Hill PR1 96 F8
Snowhill La PR3 204 F6
Snowshill Cres FY5 152 F7
Snow St BB1 101 F6
Sod Hall La PR4 76 A5
Sollam's Cl 4 PR5 97 F2
SOLLOM 57 B2
Sollom La PR4 57 B2
Solway Ave BB2 100 F1
Solway Cl
Blackpool FY2 152 C6
Middleforth Green PR1 96 E3
Somerby Rd LA4 217 C4
Somerford Cl BB12 127 D7
Somersby Cl PR5 97 E3
Somerset Ave
Blackpool FY1 130 D3
Chorley PR7 61 C1
Clitheroe BB7 189 F2
Darwen BB3 81 F3
Lancaster LA1 215 A6
Wilpshire BB1 122 F6
Somerset Cl BB5 103 F3
Somerset Ct FY1 130 D3
Somerset Dr PR8 21 C3
Somerset Gr
Church BB5 103 F7
6 Rochdale OL11 52 A1
Somerset Pk PR2 117 B7
Somerset Pl BB9 171 A1
Somerset Rd
Leyland PR25 77 B2
Preston PR1 118 A1
Rishton BB1 124 A1
Somerset St BB11 128 A4
Somerset Wlk BB4 68 B8
Somerton Cl WN6 29 D1
Sorrel Cl
Cleveleys FY5 175 F5
Knott End-on-S FY6 200 A6
Sorrel Ct 2 PR1 96 C2
Soudan St BB10 148 B2
SOUGH
Darwen 65 B7
Earby 195 A8
Sough La
Belthorn BB1 83 A7
Blackburn BB1, BB5 102 F2
Earby BB18 195 A7
Sough Rd BB3 65 B7
Soulby Cl 3 BB2 101 C1
South Ave
Barnoldswick BB18 196 B3
Chorley PR7 43 D6
Cleveleys FY5 175 C4
Morecambe LA4 217 C5
New Longton PR4 75 F8
Southbank Ave FY4 111 A7
Southbank Rd PR8 35 C5
Southbourne Ave FY6 153 C2
Southbourne Rd FY3 131 A2
Southbrook Rd PR25 76 F1
Southcliffe BB6 124 B6
Southcliffe Ave BB12 127 C7
South Cliff St 5 PR1 96 E6
South Clifton St FY8 91 B3
South Cross St BL9 33 A1
Southdene WN8 27 B2
Southdown Dr FY5 153 D8
Southdowns Rd PR7 43 D6
South Dr
Appley Bridge WN6 28 C2
Fulwood PR2 117 E7
Inskip PR4 135 C8
Lancaster LA1 211 B6
Padiham BB12 126 E8
South East Dr LA1 211 B7
South End PR1 96 E5
Southern Ave
Burnley BB12 127 C7
Preston PR1 97 C6
Southern Cl PR3 140 A6
Southern Ct BB12 127 C8
Southern Par PR1 97 B6
Southern Rd PR8 35 A6
Southey Cl PR2 117 F7
Southey St 2 BB11 127 E6
SOUTHFIELD 149 B6
Southfield PR4 74 E3
Southfield Cotts BB10 149 B6
Southfield Dr
New Longton PR4 75 F7
Poulton-le-F FY3 131 C8
West Bradford BB7 189 F5
Southfield Gdns PR4 74 E3
Southfield La BB8, BB10 149 C7
Southfield Rd BL0 50 A2
Southfield Sq BB9 148 F8
Southfield St BB9 148 F7
Southfield Terr BB8 172 E6
Southfleet Ave FY7 198 E1
Southfleet Pl FY7 198 E1
Southfold Pl FY8 91 A4
Southgate
Fleetwood FY7 175 D8
Fulwood PR2 117 D5
Morecambe LA3 217 E2
Preston PR1 117 F1
Whitworth OL12 52 C7
Southgates PR7 42 D3
South Gr
Barton PR3 137 B8
Fulwood PR2 117 E8
Morecambe LA4 217 C5
South Hey FY8 90 C6
South Holme FY8 91 B4
South King St FY1 130 C5
Southlands PR4 114 A4
Southlands Ave PR5 97 C1
Southlands Dr PR26 59 C8
South Lawn FY1 130 E2
South Meade L31 5 B1
South Meadow La PR1 96 E6
South Meadow St PR1 97 A8
South Moss Rd FY8 90 C7
South Par FY5 175 E1
South Park Dr FY3 130 F2
South Pk FY8 91 A4
SOUTHPORT 35 C3
Southport Barn Cotts
BB7 230 C1
Southport Botanic Gdns★
PR9 54 B2
Southport Coll PR9 35 C7
Southport Ent Ctr PR9 36 A6
Southport FC PR8 35 E5
Southport & Formby District General Hospl
PR8 35 E4
Southport General Infmy
PR8 35 D5
Southport Holiday Ctr
PR8 20 F6
Southport New Rd
Banks PR9 54 F5
Holmes PR4 56 D3
Mere Brow PR4, PR9 55 D3
Southport Old Rd L37 12 B7
Southport Rd
Chorley PR7 43 A8
Formby L37 12 A5
Haskayne L39 14 A6
Hurlston L40 24 A2
Maghull L31, L39 5 B5
Ormskirk L39, L40 15 D8
Scarisbrick L40, PR8 23 E7
Southport PR8 36 B2
Ulnes Walton PR26, PR7 59 B2
Southport Sta PR8 35 B7
Southport Terr PR6 43 E7
South Prom FY8 89 E5
South Rd
Bretherton PR26 57 F5
Coppull PR7 42 E1
Lancaster LA1 214 F7
Morecambe LA4 217 D5
Thornton FY5 176 D3
South Ribble Ind Est
PR5 97 C5
South Ribble Mus & Ex Ctr★ PR25 60 A8
South Ribble St 8 PR5 97 C6
SOUTH SHORE 110 C8
South Shore Hospl
FY4 110 C5
South Shore St
6 Church BB5 103 E5
Haslingden BB4 85 A3
Southside PR7 60 C3
South Sq
Blackpool FY3 130 D6
Cleveleys FY5 175 D5
South St
Accrington BB5 104 C5
Accrington, Hillock Vale
BB5 104 E8
Bacup OL13 88 A3
Burnley BB11 128 A6
16 Darwen BB3 82 A1
Great Eccleston PR3 156 B5
Haslingden BB4 85 C1
Lytham St Anne's FY8 91 D4
Newchurch BB4 86 E1
Ramsbottom BL0 50 D6
16 Rawtenstall BB4 86 A3
South Strand FY7 175 E7
South Terr
Abbey Village PR6 80 C2
Ormskirk L39 15 E4
Ramsbottom BL0 68 C2
South Valley Dr BB8 171 C3
South View
2 Bamber Bridge, Lostock Hall PR5 77 A7
Bamber Bridge PR5 77 B7
Belmont BL7 46 C5
Bretherton PR26 57 F6
Cumeragh Village PR3 138 F6
Dolphinholme LA2 226 A8
Fisher's Row PR3 201 F4
4 Great Harwood BB6 124 C5
20 Haslingden BB4 85 B3
Kirkham PR4 114 A4
Moss Side FY8 112 D1
Nelson BB9 148 D7
Read BB12 145 E3
South View St OL14 109 C1
South View Terr 1
PR25 60 A8
South Villas 17 OL13 70 C8
SOUTHWARD BOTTOM 108 A8
South Warton St FY8 91 C3
Southway
Fleetwood FY7 198 D1
Skelmersdale WN8 18 B1
South Westby St 2 FY8 91 B3
South West Dr LA1 211 A7
Southwood Ave FY7 198 F3
Southwood Cl FY8 90 E4
Southwood Dr BB5 104 E3
Southworth Ave FY4 110 E7
Southworth St BB2 101 D2
Southworth Way FY5 175 E5
Sovereign Ct FY5 175 D1
Sovereign Ct FY6 154 A3
Sovereign Gate FY4 110 F5
Sow Clough Rd OL13 87 D1
Sowerby Ave FY4 110 D8
Sowerby Rd PR3 157 E3
Sowerby St 4 BB12 126 C8
SOWER CARR 177 D4
Sower Carr La FY6 177 D4
Spa Ct LA4 217 E7
Spa Fold L40 17 A4
Spa Garth BB7 166 F8
Spa La L40, WN8 17 C4
Spalding Ave PR3 181 D6
Spa Rd PR1 96 D8
Spark La L40 39 B6
Sparrable Row BB10 149 B3
Sparrowhawk Dr FY6 200 B4
Sparrow Hill WN6, WN8 28 A2
Sparth Ave BB5 124 F3
Sparth Rd BB5 124 F3
Spa St
Burnley BB12 127 E7
Spa St *continued*
Padiham BB12 126 D8
3 Preston PR1 96 D8
Speakmans Dr WN6 19 C6
Speedie Cl BB2 81 D8
Speedwell Cl FY5 175 F5
Speedwell St BB2 101 B2
Speke St BB2 101 B2
SPEN BROOK 169 D2
Spen Brook Cotts
BB12 169 C2
Spenbrook Rd BB12 169 C3
Spen Brow LA2 239 B6
Spencer Ct FY1 130 C7
Spencer Fold BB12 169 F1
Spencer Gr BB6 124 B5
Spencers Dr PR4 57 A8
Spencers La WN8 9 B7
Spencer's La
Orrell WN5 10 D7
Southport L39 22 B3
Spencer St
Accrington BB5 104 D6
Burnley BB10 148 A1
Ramsbottom BL0 50 B5
14 Rawtenstall BB4 86 A7
Spen Cnr FY4 130 D1
Spendmore La PR7 42 E1
Spen Farm FY4 111 C8
Spen La PR4 114 E6
Spenleach La BL8 49 D3
Spen Pl FY4 110 F8
Spenser Cl BB10 129 C4
Spenser St BB12 126 D7
Spey Cl
Leyland PR25 59 E8
Standish WN6 29 D1
Speyside FY4 110 D7
Spindle Berry Ct 5
BB5 104 C4
Spindle Cl BB1 101 F7
Spinnakers The FY8 89 E5
Spinners Ct
Buckshaw Village PR7 60 E6
Lancaster LA1 214 F7
Spinners Gn OL12 52 F2
Spinners Sq PR5 77 E7
Spinney Apts WN8 19 C1
Spinney Brow PR2 118 D4
Spinney Cl
Lucas Green PR6 61 B6
New Longton PR4 75 F8
Ormskirk L39 15 D3
Spinney Croft PR3 140 A7
Spinney La LA5 224 C8
Spinneyside BB2 101 D3
Spinney The
Arnside LA5 224 C8
Blackburn BB2 101 A8
Burnley BB12 127 D8
Chapeltown BL7 48 C2
Chorley PR6 61 C3
Cleveleys FY5 152 F7
Formby L37 12 A5
Grindleton BB7 190 B7
Heysham LA3 213 A7
Lancaster LA1 215 B5
Poulton-le-F FY6 153 E4
Preston PR1 95 F3
Rochdale OL12 52 D3
Tarleton PR4 57 A7
Spinning Ave BB1 82 D8
Spinnings The BL0 50 C3
Spire Cl BB3 65 D8
Spiredale Brow WN6 29 F2
Spires Gr PR4 116 E5
Spodden Cotts OL12 71 D2
Spodden Fold OL12 52 C8
Spod Rd OL12 52 D1
SPOTLAND FOLD 52 C1
Spotland Tops OL12 52 B1
Spouthouse La BB5 125 F1
Spout Houses BB9 170 D8
Spout La LA2 241 F1
Spread Eagle St BB5 103 C5
Spring Ave BB6 124 C6
Springbank BB9 170 E5
Spring Bank
Appley Bridge WN6 19 C8
Garstang PR3 181 C6
11 Preston PR1 96 E7
Silverdale LA5 224 C3
Whitworth, Broadley
OL12 52 D4
Whitworth OL12 71 D1
Springbank Ave FY5 176 C2
Springbank Gdns BB4 105 F2
Spring Bank Terr BB2 101 C2
Springbrook Ave FY5 152 F8
Spring Brook Ho BB5 124 F2
Springburn Cl BL6 32 D1
Spring Cl
Kirkby L33 1 A5
Ramsbottom BL0 50 B6
Southport PR8 35 A5
Spring Cres PR6 61 E5
Springcroft 1 PR25 77 C3
Spring Ct 15 BB8 171 D5
Springdale Rd BB6 123 C8
Springfield
Blacko BB9 170 D8
High Bentham LA2 239 E8
Spring Field WA11 8 E2
Springfield Ave
Accrington BB5 103 F4
Bacup OL13 88 A3
Blackburn BB2 100 E1
Earby BB18 197 C1
Springfield Ave *continued*
Kirkham PR4 113 E5
Springfield Bank BB11 128 B5
Springfield Cl
Burscough L40 25 D2
Formby L37 11 C2
Whalley BB7 144 D6
Springfield Com Prim Sch
BB11 128 B4
Springfield Cres LA2 239 E8
Springfield Ct
19 Bacup OL13 88 A3
1 Blackpool FY3 130 E3
Springfield Dr
Newchurch BB4 86 E1
Thornton FY5 176 B4
Springfield Flats 8
BB3 65 A8
Springfield Gdns
Nether Kellet LA6 221 F5
Scorton PR3 204 E6
Springfield Ho 2 L37 12 A3
Springfield Ind Est 9
PR1 117 E1
Springfield Mews 2
BB5 103 D3
Springfield Rd
Adlington PR6 31 A8
Blackpool FY1 130 B6
Burnley, Burnley Wood
BB11 128 A4
Burnley, Fulledge BB11 128 B5
1 Chorley PR7 43 C8
Coppull PR7 29 E8
Great Harwood BB6 124 B4
Horwich BL6 32 E1
Leyland PR25 59 D7
Lytham St Anne's FY8 89 E6
Maghull L39 5 F6
Nelson BB9 148 E6
4 Ramsbottom BL0 50 A2
Rawtenstall BB4 86 B3
Springfield Rd N PR7 29 E8
Springfield St
Blackburn BB2 101 B3
Darwen BB3 65 A8
Lancaster LA1 214 F7
Morecambe LA4 216 F4
Oswaldtwistle BB5 103 D4
Preston PR1 117 E1
Springfield Terr
Blackburn BB2 101 A1
Fleetwood FY7 176 A6
Springfield View BB11 106 C5
SPRING GARDENS 87 B8
Spring Gardens Rd
BB8 171 D4
Spring Gardens St 4
BB4 69 F8
Spring Garden St 41
LA1 214 F8
Spring Gardens Terr 3
BB12 146 C1
Spring Gdns
8 Accrington BB5 104 C5
12 Bacup OL13 88 A3
12 Darwen BB3 65 A8
Freckleton PR4 93 B8
12 Horwich BL6 32 B4
Kingsfold PR1 96 F2
Leyland PR25 59 F8
Lytham St Anne's FY8 110 F1
Rawtenstall BB4 69 F6
8 Rawtenstall, Crawshawbooth BB4 86 A7
Spring Gr BB8 172 C6
Spring Hall BB5 124 F5
SPRING HILL 103 F5
Spring Hill
6 Blackburn BB1 101 E5
Freckleton PR4 93 D7
Springhill Ave OL13 70 D8
Spring Hill Com Prim Sch
BB5 104 A4
Spring Hill Com Prim Sch (Hannah St) BB5 104 B5
Spring Hill Rd
Accrington BB5 103 F4
Burnley BB11 127 F4
Springhill Villas OL13 70 D8
Spring La
Blackburn BB2 101 B3
10 Colne BB8 171 D5
Haslingden BB4 85 B4
Nab's Head PR5 99 C8
Spring Mdw
Clayton-le-W PR25 77 E1
3 Clitheroe BB7 189 E1
Mere Brow PR4 55 F2
Spring Mdws
Clayton-le-M BB5 125 A3
Darwen BB3 65 D7
Springmount BB18 197 C2
Springmount Dr WN8 27 C5
Spring Pl
Colne BB8 171 D5
Whitworth OL12 71 D3
Spring Rd WN5 10 F8
Spring Row BB8 172 C6
Springsands Cl PR2 118 E5
SPRING SIDE 86 B3
Spring Side
Rawtenstall BB4 69 F6
Whitworth OL12 71 D4
Spring Side Cotts BL7 47 A2
Springs Mews PR6 61 E6
Springs Rd
Chorley PR6 61 D2

**Springs Rd** *continued*
Longridge PR3 140 B8
**Spring St**
Accrington BB5 103 F4
Bacup OL13 87 F1
Bank Lane BL0 50 D7
Horwich BL6 32 B4
6 Leyland PR25 77 B1
Nelson BB9 148 C7
5 Oswaldtwistle BB5 103 E4
Ramsbottom BL0 50 B6
Rawtenstall BB4 86 A8
Rishton BB1 124 B2
Todmorden OL14 109 C1
**Spring Terr**
4 Bacup OL13 70 D8
Goodshaw Chapel BB4 105 F2
Langho BB6 143 D1
Oswaldtwistle BB5 103 D4
5 Rochdale OL11 52 A1
**Spring Terr S** 5 BB4 85 E2
**Springthorpe St** 5 BB3 65 B6
**Springvale** BB5 103 F4
**SPRING VALE** 65 C7
**Spring Vale** PR3 207 B3
**SPRING VALE** 85 A2
**Springvale Bsns Pk**
BB3 65 B6
**Spring Vale Garden Village**
BB3 65 C6
**Spring Vale Rd** BB3 65 B7
**Spring View**
Blackburn BB2 101 C5
Holme Chapel BB10 108 A8
**Spring Villas** 5 OL14 109 B1
**Springwater Ave** BL0 50 A3
**Springwood Cl** PR5 97 A3
**Springwood Dr**
Chorley PR7 43 E5
Rufford L40 39 A5
Spring Wood Nature Trail* BB7 144 E5
**Springwood Rd** BB10 128 E5
**Spring Wood St** BL0 50 B7
**Spring Yd** 5 BB8 171 D5
**Sprodley Dr** WN6 28 B2
**Spruce Ave**
Bury BL9 33 B2
Lancaster LA1 214 F4
**Spruce Cl** PR2 118 C7
**Spruce Ct** 1 BB5 104 E8
**Spruce St** BL0 50 B5
**Spruce Way** L37 11 C3
**Sprucewood Cl** BB5 104 D6
**Spurrier St** PR26 77 A4
**Spymers Croft** L37 12 A6
**Square House La** PR9 55 C6
**Square La**
Burscough L40 25 E3
Catforth PR4 135 F4
**Square St** BL0 50 C6
**Square The**
Bacup OL13 87 F2
Blackpool FY3 131 A2
Brinscall PR6 62 F7
Burton-in-K LA6 240 B7
Cleveleys FY5 175 D5
Cumeragh Village PR3 138 F5
Great Eccleston PR3 156 B5
Hurlston Green L40 24 B4
1 Leyland PR25 77 B2
Scorton PR3 204 E6
Waddington BB7 189 B4
Walton le-D PR5 97 F5
Whalley BB7 144 C5
Worsthorne BB10 129 B5
**Squire Rd** BB9 148 F8
**Squires Cl** PR5 98 E2
**Squires Ct**
7 Blackpool FY4 110 C5
10 Lytham St Anne's FY8 91 B3
**SQUIRES GATE** 110 B5
Squires Gate Ind Est
FY4 110 E4
**Squires Gate La** FY4 110 D5
**Squire's Gate Rd** PR2 117 C3
Squires Gate Sta FY8 110 B4
**Squires Rd** PR1 96 C6
**Squires Wood** PR2 118 D6
**Squirrel Fold** PR2 118 F2
**Squirrel Gn** L37 11 C5
**Squirrel La** BL6 32 A4
**Squirrels Chase** PR4 115 D1
**Squirrel's Chase** PR5 77 A7
**Squirrels Cl** BB5 104 E8
**Stable Cl**
Gisburn BB7 231 B3
Kirkham PR4 114 A6
**Stable La** PR6 62 A7
**Stables Cl** BB4 86 A6
**Stables The**
Leyland PR7 60 A5
Thornton FY5 176 B3
Whitworth OL12 71 C1
**Stable Yd** PR3 201 E5
**Stack Croft** PR6 78 A2
**Stackhouses The** 2
BB11 128 A6
**Stack La** OL13 71 B8
**STACKSTEADS** 70 B8
**Stadium Ave** FY4 110 E5
**Staffa Cres** BB1 102 D4
**Stafford Ave** FY6 153 D1
**Stafford Cl** PR4 156 A1
**Stafford Moreton Way**
L31 5 D1
**Stafford Rd**
11 Preston PR1 118 A1
**Stafford Rd** *continued*
Southport PR8 35 A1
**Stafford St**
Burnley BB10 128 A7
Darwen BB3 81 F4
Nelson BB9 149 A8
Skelmersdale WN8 17 D1
**STAGHILLS** 86 D1
**Staghills Rd** BB4 86 D1
**Stainburn Cl** WN6 19 E6
**Stainforth Ave** FY2 152 E5
**STAINING** 131 E5
**Staining Ave** PR2 95 F8
**Staining CE Prim Sch**
FY3 131 D5
**Staining Old Rd** FY3,
FY6 131 D7
**Staining Rd** FY3 131 C6
**Staining Rd W** FY3 131 D5
**Staining Rise** FY3 131 E5
**Stainton Dr** BB12 127 E8
**Stainton Gr** 1 LA4 217 E4
**STAKE POOL** 201 E4
**Stakepool Dr** PR3 201 E4
**Stakes Hall Pl** BB2 101 C2
**Stalls Rd** LA3 212 F2
**STALMINE** 177 C7
**Stalmine Ctry Pk** FY6 177 D5
**Stalmine Hall Pk** FY6 177 C8
**STALMINE MOSS**
SIDE 177 E7
**Stalmine Prim Sch**
FY6 177 D7
**Stamford Ave** FY4 110 D7
**Stamford Ct** FY8 89 D8
**Stamford Dr** PR6 61 C5
**Stamford Pl** 3 BB7 189 F1
**Stamford Rd**
Skelmersdale WN8 17 D2
Southport PR8 35 B2
**Stanagate** PR4 115 C1
**STANAH** 176 E2
**Stanah Gdns** FY5 176 E2
Stanah Prim Sch FY5 176 D1
**Stanah Rd** FY5 176 E2
**Stanalee La** PR3 160 B8
**Stanbury Cl**
Burnley BB10 148 E2
Bury BL9 33 D1
**Stanbury Dr** BB10 148 E2
**Stancliffe St** BB2 101 C3
**Standedge Cl** BL0 50 C4
**Standen Hall Cl** BB10 148 E3
**Standen Hall Dr** BB10 148 D3
**Standen Park Ho** LA1 215 C8
**Standen Rd** BB7 166 F7
**Standen Road Bglws**
BB7 166 F7
**Standhouse La** L39 15 C2
**Standing Stone La** BB8,
BB9 194 A2
**STANDISH** 29 F2
Standish Com High Sch
WN6 29 C2
Standish St Wilfrid's CE
Prim Sch WN6 29 F1
**Standish St**
Burnley BB11 128 A6
Chorley PR7 43 D7
**Standridge Clough La**
BB18 197 D1
**Standroyd Dr** BB8 172 A5
**Standroyd Rd** BB8 172 A5
**Standside Pk** WN8 8 D8
**Stanford Gdns** BB2 102 A1
**Stanford Hall Cres** BL0 50 B4
**Stangate** L31 5 B2
**Stang Top Rd** BB9 169 F6
**STANHILL** 103 B4
**Stanhill La** BB5 103 C4
**Stanhill Rd** BB1, BB5 102 F4
**Stanhill St** BB5 103 C3
**Stanhope Ave** LA3 217 E3
**Stanhope Ct** LA3 217 F3
**Stanhope Rd** 1 FY1 130 C7
**Stanhope St**
Burnley BB12 127 F7
Darwen BB3 82 A2
Preston PR1 117 E2
**Stanier Pl** BL6 32 C2
**Stanifield Cl** PR25 77 B3
**Stanifield La** PR5, PR25 77 C5
**Stankelt Ho** LA5 224 C2
**Stankelt Rd** LA5 224 C2
**Stanlawe Rd** L37 11 E6
**STANLEY** 17 E3
**Stanley Ave**
Cleveleys FY5 175 E2
Hutton PR4 95 D2
Leyland PR25 77 C4
Middleforth Green PR1 96 E5
Poulton-le-F FY6 153 D3
Southport PR8 34 F3
**Stanley Cl** PR3 140 B7
**Stanley Croft** PR4 137 B3
**Stanley Ct**
Accrington BB5 104 D7
Burscough Bridge L40 25 E5
Chipping PR3 185 E3
**Stanley Ct** BB6 124 E5
**Stanley Ct** PR4 114 B4
**Stanley Dr**
Darwen BB3 65 B5
Hornby LA2 238 B7
**Stanleyfield Cl** PR1 118 A1
**Stanleyfield Rd** PR1 118 A1
**Stanley Fold** PR5 76 F8
**STANLEY GATE** 7 E7
**Stanley Gate**
Fleetwood FY7 198 D3
Mellor BB2 121 E2
**Stanley Gr**
Higher Penwortham
PR1 96 A5
Horwich BL6 32 D1
Stanley High Sch Sports
Coll PR9 53 F4
**Stanley Ho** PR1 96 E7
**Stanley Mews** PR4 134 E7
**Stanley Mount** 6 OL13 87 F3
**Stanley Park Cl** FY3 130 F3
**Stanley Pl**
9 Chorley PR7 43 C8
Lancaster LA1 214 D8
Preston PR1 96 E7
Stanley Prim Sch FY3 131 B2
**Stanley Range** BB2 101 B1
**Stanley Rd**
Blackpool FY1 130 C4
Fleetwood FY7 198 F3
Formby L37 11 E6
Kirkham PR4 113 F7
Leyland PR25 77 C4
Lytham St Anne's FY8 90 D3
Morecambe LA3 216 E3
Up Holland WN8 10 B7
**Stanley St**
Accrington BB5 104 C6
Accrington BB5 104 D6
Bacup OL13 87 F4
Blackburn BB1 102 B6
Brierfield BB9 148 B6
6 Burnley BB11 127 F5
Carnforth LA5 223 D1
Colne BB8 171 D5
Kirkham PR4 114 B4
10 Leyland PR25 77 B1
Longridge PR3 140 A8
4 Morecambe LA4 217 B6
Nelson BB9 148 D8
Ormskirk L39 15 F5
Oswaldtwistle BB5 103 D3
Preston PR1 97 B8
Ramsbottom BL0 50 B5
Rochdale OL12 52 E1
Southport PR9 35 B8
**Stanley Terr** PR1 96 E7
**Stanley Villas** PR5 99 B4
**Stanley Way** WN8 17 E3
**Stanmere Ct** BL8 49 B3
**Stanmore Ave** FY4 110 F6
**Stanmore Dr** LA1 214 E5
**Stannanought Rd** WN8 18 E2
**Stanner Lo** FY8 110 F2
**Stanning Cl** PR25 59 E8
**Stanrose Cl** BL7 47 E1
**Stansfeld St** BB2 101 C3
**Stansfield Ave** L31 5 F1
**Stansfield Cl** 7 BB9 170 D4
**Stansfield Rd** BB4 69 E8
**Stansfield St**
2 Bacup OL13 70 C8
Blackpool FY1 130 C1
Burnley BB11 127 B5
7 Darwen BB3 65 A8
Nelson BB9 148 E8
**Stansfield Terr** 6
OL14 109 B1
**Stansford Ct** PR1 96 D4
**Stansted Rd** PR7 43 A7
**Stansy Ave** LA3 216 E1
**Stanthorpe Wlk** BB10 148 A1
**STANWORTH** 80 C4
**Stanworth Brow** PR6 80 A5
**Stanworth Rd** BB9 148 D8
**Stanworth St** BB10 129 B5
**Stanworth Terr** PR6 80 B4
**Stanzaker Hall Dr** PR3 158 D7
**Stapleton Rd** L37 11 D1
**Star Bank** OL13 70 D7
**Starbeck Ave** FY4 130 D1
**Starfield Cl** FY8 91 A4
**Starkie St**
Blackburn BB1 101 F5
Burnley BB11 127 E5
Darwen BB3 65 B8
12 Leyland PR25 77 B1
Preston PR1 96 F6
**Star La** BL6 31 F3
**Starr Gate** FY4 110 B4
**Starrgate Dr** PR2 116 E1
**Star St**
Accrington BB5 103 F5
Darwen BB3 82 B1
**Startifants La** PR3 184 F4
**Startifants Lane End**
PR3 185 A5
**Startley Nook** PR4 76 B6
**States Rd** FY8 90 B6
**Statham Rd** WN8 17 E3
**Statham Way** L39 15 E4
**Station App**
Burscough Bridge L40 25 E5
Ormskirk L39 15 F5
**Station Ave** WN5 10 D5
**Station Bldgs** LA5 223 D2
**Station Brow** PR25 77 B2
**Station Cl**
Rishton BB1 103 A8
Wilpshire BB1 122 F4
**Station Cotts** LA6 241 D2
**Station Ct**
Bacup OL13 88 A1
Hornby LA2 238 B7
**Station La**
Burton-in-K LA6 240 B7
**Station La** *continued*
Nateby PR3 203 B1
Newsham PR3 137 A5
Scorton PR3 204 D7
**Station Par** OL14 108 F1
**Station Rd**
Adlington PR7 31 A6
Bamber Bridge PR5 77 E8
Banks PR9 54 F5
Barnoldswick BB18 196 B2
Blackpool FY4 110 B8
Blackrod BL6 31 E1
Caton LA2 237 C3
Chapeltown BL7 48 C4
Clitheroe BB7 166 E8
Coppull PR7 42 F1
Croston PR26 58 B3
Fleetwood FY7 199 A4
Foulridge BB8 194 D1
Great Harwood BB6 124 D5
Haskayne L39 13 E7
Haslingden, Bridge End
BB4 68 A7
Haslingden, North Hag
BB4 85 B4
Hesketh Bank PR4 73 F3
Hest Bank LA2 220 D1
High Bentham LA2 239 D7
Hoghton PR5 99 B2
Holme Mills LA6 240 B8
Hornby LA2 238 B7
Huncoat BB5 125 E2
2 Kirkham PR4 113 F5
Lancaster LA1 214 E8
Lytham St Anne's FY8 91 B3
Maghull, Lydiate L31 5 A6
Morecambe LA4 217 B5
New Longton PR4 75 F8
Ormskirk L39 15 F6
Padiham BB12 126 C8
Parbold WN8 27 C2
Poulton-le-F FY6 153 E4
Ramsbottom BL8 49 F1
Rimington BB7 191 E8
Rishton BB1 124 A1
Rufford L40 39 D4
Salwick PR4 115 C4
Singleton FY6 132 C8
Southport PR8 21 C5
Thornton FY5 176 D1
Todmorden OL14 109 C1
Walmer Bridge PR4 74 D4
Whalley BB7 144 C5
Whitworth, Broadley
OL12 52 C5
Whitworth OL12 71 D3
Wrea Green PR4 113 B4
Station Road Ind Est
BB6 124 E5
**Station Sq** FY8 91 A3
**Station Terr**
Abbey Village PR6 80 C2
Blackpool FY4 110 B8
**Station View** BB6 143 D1
**Station Way**
Garstang PR3 181 C8
Hornby LA2 238 B7
**Station Yd** BB18 197 A2
**Staunton St** LA5 223 D3
**Staveley Ave** L40 25 E4
**Staveley Gr** FY7 198 D2
**Staveley Pl** PR2 116 E2
**Staveley Rd**
Skelmersdale WN8 17 E3
Southport PR8 21 D4
**STAYNALL** 177 A4
**Staynall La** FY6 177 B4
**Stead St** BL0 50 C6
**Sted Terr** BB1 101 E6
**Steeley La** PR6 43 D7
**Steeple View** PR2 96 D8
**Steer St** BB10 148 B1
**Steeton Rd** FY3 153 B1
**Stefano Rd** 1 PR1 97 C8
**Steiner's La** BB5 103 E7
**Steiner St** BB5 104 A6
**Stephenage Pk** PR1 97 A2
**Stephendale Ave** PR5 78 B8
**STEPHEN MOOR** 235 F1
**Stephens Gr** LA3 209 D8
**Stephenson Dr** BB12 127 C7
**Stephenson St**
2 Chorley PR6 43 E7
Horwich BL6 32 B2
**Stephenson Way** L37 12 C3
**Stephen St**
Blackburn BB2 101 B2
Lytham St Anne's FY8 89 E7
**Step Row** OL13 87 F5
**Sterling Pl** OL10 33 F1
**Sterndale Ave** WN6 29 E2
**Stevant Way** LA3 217 F2
**Stevenson Ave** 2 PR25 77 C3
**Stevenson St E** BB5 104 A5
**Stevenson St W** BB5 103 F5
**Steward Ave** LA1 215 B5
**Stewart Cl** LA5 224 B8
**Stewart Ct** 9 LA1 218 D2
**Stewart St**
Blackburn BB2 81 D8
Burnley BB11 128 B4
11 Preston PR1 96 D8
**Stiles Ave** PR4 95 C1
**Stiles The** L39 15 E5
**Stirling Cl**
Chorley PR6 43 E7
Clitheroe BB7 166 C6
1 Leyland PR25 77 C1
**Stirling Ct**
8 Blackpool FY1 130 D7
Lane Bottom BB10 149 B4
Southport PR9 54 A2
**Stirling Dr** BB1 101 F4
**Stirling Ind Est** BL6 32 C2
**Stirling Rd**
Blackpool FY3 130 D7
Lancaster LA1 215 A7
**Stirling St** BB2 101 B1
**STOCK** 231 F4
**Stockbridge Cotts**
BB7 164 E3
**Stockbridge Dr** BB12 126 E8
**Stockbridge Rd** BB12 126 D7
**Stock Cl** OL12 52 E2
**Stockclough La** BB2 80 D6
**Stockdale Cres** PR5 77 F8
**Stockdove Way** FY5 175 E3
**Stockdove Wood** FY5 175 E3
**Stockholm St** BB11 127 B5
**Stockley Cres** L39 7 E6
**Stockley Dr** WN6 19 E8
**Stockpit Rd** L33 1 D2
**Stocks Cl** PR6 79 B1
**Stocks Ct**
Heskin Green PR7 41 E3
5 Poulton-le-F FY6 153 D3
**Stocksgate** OL12 52 B2
**Stocks La**
Barnoldswick BB7 193 A7
Carleton FY6 153 A3
Heskin Green PR7 41 E3
**Stocks Lane End** PR3 181 D2
**Stocks Park Dr** BL6 32 C3
**Stocks Rd** PR2 117 C2
Stocks Resr & Gisburn
Forest Walks* BB7 235 E3
**Stocks St** 7 PR1 96 E8
**Stockwood Cl** BB2 101 A8
**Stockydale Rd** FY4 111 A6
**STODDAY** 214 C2
**Stoke Ave** FY1 130 D2
**Stokes Hall Ave** PR25 60 A8
**Stoneacre Dr** PR6 44 A1
**Stonebarn Dr** L31 5 C3
**Stonebridge Cl** 6 PR5 77 C8
**Stone Bridge La** BB5 103 E3
**Stonebridge Terr** PR3 140 A7
**Stonechat Cl** FY3 131 B6
**Stone Cl** BL0 50 A4
**Stonecroft** BB9 170 E6
**Stone Croft** PR1 96 D2
**Stonecroft Rd** PR25 59 D7
**Stonecrop** WN6 28 D1
**Stonecross Cl** BB5 103 E5
**Stone Cross Gdns** PR3 181 D2
**Stone Edge Rd** BB9 170 E6
**Stone Edge View** BB9 170 E6
**Stonefield**
Longton PR4 74 F8
Middleforth Green PR1 96 E4
**Stonefield Cotts** BB2 100 B2
**Stone Fold** BB5 85 B8
**Stonefold Ave** PR4 95 C1
**Stonegate Fold** PR6 44 B1
**Stone Hall La**
Skelmersdale WN8 18 F4
Up Holland WN8 19 A5
**Stonehill Cres** OL12 52 A3
**Stonehill Dr** OL12 52 B3
**Stone Hill Dr** BB1 123 A1
**Stone Hill La** OL12 52 A2
**Stonehill Rd** OL12 52 B3
Stoneholme Ind Est
BB4 86 A8
**Stoneholme Rd** BB4 86 A8
**Stone Holme Terr** BB4 86 A8
**Stonehouse Gn** PR6 78 B3
**Stoneleigh Cl** PR8 21 C4
**Stoneleigh Ct** LA5 224 C3
**Stonemasons Ct** FY3 130 E7
**Stone Mill Cotts** BL7 48 D4
**Stone Moor Bottom**
BB12 126 C6
**Stone Pits** BL0 68 E3
**Stone Row Head** LA1 215 C8
**Stoner Rd** PR7 30 F7
**Stones Bank Rd** BL7 47 B5
**Stones La** PR3 181 E3
**Stone St**
Haslingden BB4 84 F2
Rawtenstall BB4 69 F8
**Stone Trough Brow**
BB18 194 F4
**Stoneway Rd** FY5 175 E1
**Stonewell** 17 LA1 214 F8
**Stoney Bank Rd** BB18 197 C2
**Stoney Brow** WN8 19 B1
**Stoney Butts** PR2 95 D8
**Stoneycroft** BB10 129 A5
**Stoneycroft Ave** BL6 32 D4
**Stoneycroft Cl** BL6 32 D5
**Stoney Croft Dr** LA5 223 E6
**Stoney Ct** BB8 194 E1
**Stoneygate**
Cleveleys FY5 175 F1
17 Preston PR1 97 A7
**Stoneygate La** WN6 28 B2
**STONEYHOLME** 127 F8
Stoneyholme Com Prim
Sch BB12 127 F8
**Stoney Holt** PR25 77 E1
**Stoneyhurst Ave**
Burnley BB10 128 D5

Stoneyhurst Ave *continued*
Thornton FY5 153 D8
Stoneyhurst Ht BB9 148 D4
Stoney La
Adlington PR7 30 E4
Bamber Bridge PR5 77 C6
Foulridge BB8 194 E1
Freckleton PR4 93 B5
Galgate LA2 211 B3
Hambleton FY6 177 C2
Longridge PR3 161 C7
Parbold WN6, WN8 27 E4
Stoney Royd OL12 71 D1
Stoney St BB11 128 B4
Stony Bank PR6 79 A6
Stonybutts 9 BB1 101 E5
Stonycroft Ave FY4 110 C5
Stonycroft Pl 2 FY4 110 C5
Stony Fold Brow BB3 64 A5
Stonygate La PR3 141 D6
Stony Hill Ave FY4 110 C5
Stonyhurst PR7 43 C4
Stonyhurst Cl
Blackburn BB2 101 D4
Padiham BB12 126 E6
Stonyhurst Coll BB7 165 A3
Stonyhurst Coll Gdns* BB7 165 A2
Stonyhurst Rd BB2 101 D4
Stony La
Cockerham PR3 206 F2
Hollins Lane PR3 207 D3
Todmorden OL14 109 E2
Stoopes Hill BB18 197 C2
Stoops Fold BB2 121 E2
Stoops La BB7 191 F8
Stoop St BB11 127 C5
Stopes Brow BB1, BB3 82 A7
Stopford Ave FY2 152 E2
Stopford Ct 1 BB5 124 F3
Stopgate La L33 1 C7
Stopper La BB7 192 B7
STOPPER LANE 192 A8
Store St
Blackburn BB3 82 A7
17 Haslingden BB4 85 B3
Horwich BL6 32 C4
Storey Ave LA1 214 D8
Storey Hall LA1 214 E5
Storey Inst LA1 214 E8
Stork Cl FY5 175 F1
Stork St BB3 65 D8
Storrs La LA5 225 B4
Storwood Cl WN5 10 E5
Stott St
1 Nelson BB9 148 D8
Rochdale OL12 52 F1
Stour Lo PR2 117 C6
Stourton Rd PR8 21 C4
Stourton St BB1 124 A2
Stout St BB2 101 D4
Straight Up La PR9 36 D8
Strait La LA2 232 F1
Straits BB5 103 E4
Straits La BB12 145 D2
STRAITS THE 76 D1
Straits The PR5 99 B2
Strand Rd PR1 96 D7
Strand St W PR2 96 C8
Strands Farm Ct LA2 238 B7
Strand The
Blackpool FY1 130 B6
Fleetwood FY7 175 D8
Horwich BL6 32 D3
Strange St BB11 128 B4
Strang St 9 BL0 50 C6
Strang Stee 6 BB7 166 E8
Stransdale Cl 5 PR3 181 B7
Stratfield Pl 5 PR25 77 B1
Stratford Cl
Lancaster LA1 218 C3
Southport PR8 21 A6
Stratford Dr PR2 117 D4
Stratford Pl
Blackpool FY1 130 E2
2 Fleetwood FY7 198 E4
Stratford Rd
Chorley PR6 43 D8
Lytham St Anne's FY8 90 B7
Stratford Way
7 Accrington BB5 104 A7
Colne BB8 171 F5
Strathaven Pl 5 OL10 33 F1
Strathclyde Rd BB1 102 A4
Strathdale FY4 110 F7
Strathmore Cl BL0 50 C4
Strathmore Gr PR7 43 B7
Strathmore Rd PR2 117 E3
Strathyre Cl FY2 152 F5
Stratton Ct BB9 148 E6
Stratton Gr BL6 32 B5
Strawberry Bank 1 BB1 101 D5
Strawberry Fields PR7 61 B3
Strawberry Mews 1 LA3 212 F8
Streatly Wlk BB2 82 A8
STREET 226 A6
Street The PR6 44 E3
Strellas La LA5 221 C1
Stretton Ave FY4 110 E8
Stretton Dr PR9 35 F8
Stretton Rd BL0 50 A2
Strickens La PR3 182 C6
Strickland Dr LA4 217 E5
Stricklands La PR1 96 E4
Strickland's La FY6 177 D6
Strike La PR4 93 B8
Strine The L40, PR4 57 A1
Stromness Gr 3 OL10 33 F1
STRONGSTRY 68 C2
Strongstry Rd BL0 68 C2
Stronsay Pl FY2 152 F6
Stroyan St BB10 128 C5
Strutt St 2 PR1 118 B1
Stryands PR4 95 C1
Stuart Ave
Bacup OL13 70 D8
Morecambe LA4 217 D6
Stuart Cl
14 Darwen BB3 82 A1
Fulwood PR2 118 E3
Stuart Pl FY3 153 A1
Stuart Rd
Fulwood PR2 118 E3
Thornton FY5 176 C2
Stuart St
Accrington BB5 104 B7
5 Barnoldswick BB18 196 C2
STUBBINS
Catterall 181 F2
Ramsbottom 68 B1
Stubbins La
Catterall PR3 181 F2
Ramsbottom BL0 50 C8
Sabden BB7 146 A7
Stubbins St BL0 68 C1
Stubbins Vale Cvn Pk BB7 146 A7
Stubbins Vale Rd BL0 68 C1
Stubbins Vale Terr BL0 68 B1
Stubbylee La OL13 70 F8
Stubley Holme OL14 109 A1
Stubley La OL14 109 B1
Studfold PR7 61 B2
Studholme Ave PR1 96 E2
Studholme Cl 8 PR1 96 E2
Studholme Cres PR1 96 E2
Studley Ct PR9 53 D1
Stump Cross La BB7 230 F5
Stump Hall Rd BB12 146 F7
Stump La PR6 43 D8
Stunstead Cotts BB8 172 C2
Stunstead Rd BB8 172 C3
Sturgess Cl L39 15 F7
Sturminster Cl 5 PR1 96 E2
Styan St FY7 199 A4
STYDD 141 E4
Stydd La PR3 141 E4
Sudell Ave L31 5 F2
Sudell Cl BB3 82 C1
Sudell Cross 20 BB1 101 E5
Sudell La L31, L39 5 E6
Sudell Prim Sch BB3 82 B1
Sudell Rd BB3 82 B1
Sudellside St BB3 82 B1
Suffolk Ave BB12 127 A6
Suffolk Cl PR25 59 E6
Suffolk Rd
Blackpool FY3 131 A2
Preston PR1 118 A1
Southport PR8 22 A8
Suffolk St BB2 101 C2
Sugar Stubbs La PR9 55 C4
Sugham La LA3 212 F8
Sulby Cl PR8 34 F3
Sulby Dr
Fulwood PR2 118 F5
Lancaster LA1 214 F6
Sulby Gr
Fulwood PR2 119 A5
Morecambe LA4 217 E6
Sulby Rd BB2 101 E1
Sullivan Dr BB2 102 A1
Sullom Side La PR3 182 C5
Sullom View PR3 181 C6
Sultan St BB5 104 D7
Sulyard St LA1 214 F8
Summerdale Dr BL0 50 B2
Summerer Gr PR4 132 F6
Summerfield
Leyland PR25 76 F3
Thornton-in-C BD23 197 A5
Summerfield Cl PR5 97 B2
Summerfield Dr LA2 218 C7
Summerfields
Coppull PR7 29 F7
Lytham St Anne's FY8 89 C8
Summerhill LA2 239 D7
SUMMERSEAT 50 C2
Summerseat La BL0 50 A2
Summerseat Meth Prim Sch BL9 50 D2
Summerseat Sta* BL9 50 C2
Summersgill Rd LA1 218 B2
Summer St
Horwich BL6 32 B4
Nelson BB9 148 C7
Skelmersdale WN8 18 A4
Summerton Wlk BB3 82 A2
Summer Trees Ave PR2 116 D3
Summerville 4 FY4 110 C6
Summerville Ave FY3 131 E5
Summerville Wlk 4 BB2 101 D5
Summerwood Cl FY2 152 D1
Summerwood La L39 23 C1
Summit Cl BL9 33 F4
Summit Dr PR4 93 C6
Summit St BL9 33 F4
Summit The BD23 197 A5
Summit Works BB11 127 E2
Sumner Ave L39 13 F4
Sumner Rd L37 11 F3
Sumners Barn PR2 118 E6
Sumner's La PR26 40 A7
Sumner St
Blackburn BB2 101 E3
Leyland PR25 77 A1
Sumpter Croft PR1 96 E2
Sumpter Ct PR1 96 F2
Sunacre Ct 6 LA3 216 E3
Sunbank Cl OL12 52 D2
Sunbury Ave PR1 96 D3
Sunbury Dr PR8 21 B4
Suncliffe Rd BB9 148 D4
Suncourt PR8 34 F6
SUNDERLAND 209 B4
Sunderland Ave
Cleveleys FY5 175 F4
Hambleton FY6 177 D2
Sunderland Dr LA3 217 A2
Sunderland St BB12 127 B6
Sunfield Cl FY4 111 A7
Sunnindale Ave BB4 87 A1
Sunningdale PR4 137 B3
Sunningdale Ave
Blackpool FY4 131 A2
Fleetwood FY7 175 D7
Hest Bank LA2 220 D1
Sunningdale Cl PR4 114 A4
Sunningdale Cres LA2 220 D1
Sunningdale Ct FY8 90 A6
Sunningdale Dr
Buckshaw Village PR7 60 E6
Thornton FY5 153 D8
Sunningdale Gdns
Burnley BB10 148 D3
Formby L37 11 E3
Sunningdale Pl PR4 135 C8
Sunny Bank
Kirkham PR4 113 F5
Middleforth Green PR1 96 F3
Sunny Bank Ave
Blackpool FY2 152 C4
Newton-w-S PR4 115 A2
Sunny Bank Cl BB4 68 A6
Sunny Bank Cotts BB4 67 F5
Sunnybank Dr BB5 103 C2
Sunnybank Gdns BB2 101 E1
Sunny Bank Ind Est FY6 177 D1
Sunny Bank Mill PR4 113 F5
Sunny Bank Prep Sch BB11 127 E4
Sunnybank Rd LA5 221 A5
Sunny Bank Rd BB2 101 E1
Sunnybank St
Darwen BB3 82 A1
8 Haslingden BB4 85 A3
Sunny Bank Terr 11 OL14 109 B1
SUNNY BOWER 123 B1
Sunny Bower Cl BB1 123 B1
Sunny Bower Rd BB1 123 B1
Sunny Brow PR7 43 A2
Sunnycliff Ret Pk LA3 217 D1
Sunny Dr WN5 10 F6
Sunnyfield Ave
Holme Chapel BB10 108 A8
Morecambe LA4 217 E6
Sunnyfield La BB3 66 A8
Sunnyfields L39 16 A5
Sunnyhill PR2 118 C5
Sunnyhill Cl BB3 81 D2
SUNNYHURST 81 D2
Sunnyhurst BB3 81 D1
Sunnyhurst Ave FY4 110 D6
Sunnyhurst Cl BB3 81 D2
Sunnyhurst La BB3 81 D2
Sunnyhurst Rd BB2 101 D4
Sunnyhurst Res Pk FY4 110 D6
Sunnyhurst Wood Visitor Ctr* BB3 81 D2
Sunny Lea St BB4 85 F5
Sunnymede Dr L31 5 D3
Sunnymede Sch PR8 34 F6
Sunnymede Vale BL0 50 A3
Sunnymere Dr BB3 81 E2
Sunny Rd PR9 54 A2
Sunnyside
5 High Bentham LA2 239 D8
Ormskirk L39 6 C7
Southport PR8 34 F3
Sunnyside Ave
Billington BB7 144 B4
1 Blackburn BB2 80 E8
Ribchester PR3 141 D3
Warton PR4 92 E6
Wilpshire BB1 123 A7
Sunnyside Camp Site LA3 217 A2
Sunnyside Cl
Freckleton PR4 93 B7
Lancaster LA1 214 E7
Rawtenstall BB4 86 A6
Sunnyside Ct PR9 53 C1
Sunnyside Cvn Pk PR3 158 F5
Sunnyside La LA1 214 E7
Sunnyside Terr FY6 200 C3
Sunny View PR6 80 C2
Sunset Cl L33 1 A5
Sun St
Colne BB8 171 E5
Lancaster LA1 214 F8
Nelson BB9 148 C8
Oswaldtwistle BB5 103 E4
Ramsbottom BL0 50 B7
Sun Terr OL14 109 B1
Super St BB5 124 E4
Surgeon's Ct PR1 96 F7
Surrey Ave
Burnley BB12 127 B7
Darwen BB3 81 F3
Surrey Cl PR9 54 C5
Surrey Rd
Barrowford BB9 170 D2
Blackburn BB1 102 D5
Surrey St
Accrington BB5 104 D6
Preston PR1 97 C8
Sussex Ave BL9 33 E1
Sussex Cl
Church BB5 103 F7
Standish WN1 30 B1
Sussex Dr
Blackburn BB1 102 A4
Garstang PR3 181 B7
Haslingden BB4 68 B8
Sussex Rd
Blackpool FY3 130 E6
Rishton BB1 102 F8
Southport PR8, PR9 35 D6
Sussex St
25 Barnoldswick BB18 196 B2
Burnley BB11 128 B4
1 Nelson BB9 170 E1
Preston PR1 118 A1
Sussex Wlk 10 BB1 102 A4
Sutch La L40 26 B5
Sutcliffe St
Britannia OL13 71 C8
18 Burnley BB11 127 F6
Burnley, Harle Syke BB10 148 F3
7 Chorley PR7 43 D7
Sutcliffe Terr BB1 82 F6
Sutherland Cl BB1 123 A7
Sutherland Rd
Blackpool FY1 130 C8
Heywood OL10 33 F1
Sutherland St BB8 171 C4
Sutherland View 2 FY1 130 C7
Sutton Ave
Burnley BB10 148 D2
Tarleton PR4 57 A8
Sutton Cres BB5 125 F1
Sutton Dr PR2 95 D8
Sutton Fold PR6 44 A1
Sutton Gr PR6 61 F4
Sutton La
Adlington PR6 31 B8
Tarleton PR4 56 F5
Sutton Pl FY1 130 C4
Sutton Rd L37 11 E1
Sutton's La L37 12 E3
Sutton St
Blackburn BB2 80 D8
Weeton Camp PR4 132 E6
Swainbank St BB11 128 B5
Swaine St BB9 148 C8
Swainson St
11 Blackpool FY1 130 C6
Lytham St Anne's FY8 90 F3
Swain St 5 OL12 52 E1
Swainstead Raike BD24 236 E8
Swaledale LA2 211 B4
Swaledale Ave BB10 148 B4
Swalegate L31 5 C2
Swallow Ave 1 PR1 96 E4
Swallow Cl
Blackpool FY3 131 B2
Thornton FY5 176 A4
Swallow Ct
Clayton Green PR6 78 C1
Heysham LA3 212 F6
Swallow Dr
Blackburn BB1 101 E6
Bury BL9 33 B4
Swallow Field PR4 74 E3
Swallowfields
Blackburn BB1 101 E8
Cottam PR4 116 E5
Swallowfold 3 PR2 139 D1
Swallow Pk 6 BB11 127 C5
Swallow Wharf 8 LA1 218 E1
Swanage Ave FY4 110 B6
Swanage Rd BB10 148 C1
Swan Alley 2 L39 15 E5
Swan Cl L40 37 B2
Swan Delph L39 15 C2
Swan Dr FY5 175 F1
Swan Farm Cl BB3 81 F7
Swanfield Ct BB8 172 A5
Swanfield Terr BB8 172 A5
Swan La L39 5 F6
Swan Mdw BB7 189 D1
Swanpool La L39 15 C2
Swan Rd BL8 49 F2
Swansea St PR2 96 C8
Swansey La PR6 78 C1
Swan St
Blackburn BB2 101 E3
Darwen BB3 65 B6
Preston PR1 97 C8
Swan Yd 1 LA1 215 A7
Swarbrick Ave PR2 139 D1
Swarbrick Cl FY1 130 D7
Swarbrick Ct PR3 140 B7
Swarbrick St PR4 114 A4
Sweet Briar Cl
Clayton-le-M BB5 124 E4
Rochdale OL12 52 E2
Sweet Briar La OL12 52 E2
Sweetclough Dr BB12 126 F6
Swift Cl
Blackburn BB1 101 F5
Blackpool FY3 131 B3
Swift Gdns LA3 212 F5
Swiftis Fold WN8 8 D8
Swilkin La FY6 177 E6
SWILLBROOK 136 B2
Swill Brook La 1 PR1 97 C6
Swinburne Cl 2 BB5 104 E2
Swinburn Gr WN5 10 D1
Swinden Hall Rd BB9 170 E2
Swinden La BB8 171 A2
Swindon Ave 7 FY4 110 D8
Swindon St BB11 127 D5
Swinglehurst Cotts PR3 185 E3
Swinglehurst La PR3 185 E3
Swinless St BB10 128 B8
Swinshaw Cl BB4 106 A2
Swinside PR4 116 D4
SWISS CLOUGH 86 F1
Swiss St BB5 103 F6
Swithemby St BL6 32 A4
Sword Meanygate PR4 56 C6
Sycamore Ave
Blackpool FY4 110 F5
Burnley BB12 127 B7
Euxton PR7 60 D3
Garstang PR3 181 B8
Nelson BB9 149 A8
Sycamore Bglws BB7 231 C3
Sycamore Cl
Blackburn BB1 101 F8
Burnley BB12 127 C6
Elswick PR4 156 A1
Fulwood PR2 118 C6
Mawdesley L40 40 C2
Rishton BB1 103 B8
Sycamore Cres
Caton LA2 237 C3
Clayton-le-M BB5 125 A5
1 Rawtenstall BB4 85 F1
Sycamore Ct
Chorley PR7 43 B5
Thornton-in-C BD23 197 B5
Sycamore Dr
Kirkham PR4 113 D4
Middleforth Green PR1 96 E3
1 Skelmersdale WN8 17 E2
Sycamore Gdns
Foulridge BB8 194 D1
Heysham LA3 212 E6
Sycamore Gr
Accrington BB5 104 E3
Darwen BB3 82 B2
Formby L37 11 C1
Lancaster LA1 214 D8
Sycamore Ho PR7 42 F6
Sycamore Rd
Bilsborrow PR3 159 A5
Blackburn BB1 101 F8
Caton LA2 237 C3
Chorley PR6 61 D2
Fulwood PR2 118 E2
Sycamore Rise
Brierfield BB9 148 D5
Foulridge BB8 194 D1
Sycamore Trad Est FY4 110 F5
Sycamore Way BB18 196 A1
Sycamore Wlk 1 BL6 32 E1
Syd Brook La PR26, L40 40 E7
Sydenham Terr OL12 52 D3
Sydney Ave BB7 144 D5
Sydney St
Accrington BB5 104 C6
Accrington, Enfield BB5 125 A1
1 Burnley BB11 127 F6
Darwen BB3 65 B7
Hoddlesden BB3 82 F1
Lytham St Anne's FY8 89 F6
Sydney Terr BB8 172 C3
SYKE 52 F4
Sykefield BB9 148 A5
Syke Hill 13 PR1 97 A7
Syke House La PR3 160 E4
Syke La OL12 52 F4
Sykelands Ave LA2 219 D7
Sykelands Gr LA2 219 D7
Syke Rd OL12 52 F4
Sykes Cl BB18 194 E8
SYKE SIDE 85 B1
Syke Side Dr BB5 125 E6
Syke St PR1 97 A7
Sylvancroft PR2 117 A5
Sylvan Dr BB11 127 B4
Sylvan Gr PR5 98 A2
Sylvan Pl LA3 212 E6
Sylvester St LA1 214 E7
Symonds Rd PR2 117 E3

T

Tabby Nook PR4 55 F2
Tabby's Nook
Newburgh WN8 27 A1
Skelmersdale WN8 18 A8
Taberner Cl WN6 29 F1
Tabley La PR4 116 E7
Tabor St BB12 127 D6
Tadema Gr BB11 127 F2
Tadlow Cl L37 11 C1
Tag Croft PR2 116 F5
Tag Farm Ct PR2 116 F5
TAGG WOOD 50 A5
Tagg Wood View BL0 50 A5
Tag La PR2 117 A4

Talaton Cl PR9 54 A5
Talbot Ave 4 BB5 124 F2
Talbot Cl
Clitheroe BB7 166 F7
Rawtenstall BB4 68 E8
Talbot Ct
11 Blackpool FY4 130 B1
3 Lytham St Anne's FY8 90 A8
Talbot Dr
Burnley BB10 148 F2
Euxton PR7 60 D2
Southport PR8 35 B6
Talbot Gr BL9 33 A6
Talbot Ho PR7 61 C2
Talbot Rd
Accrington BB5 104 A8
Blackpool FY1, FY3 130 C6
Leyland PR25 76 E2
Lytham St Anne's FY8 91 C4
Middleforth Green PR1 96 E5
Preston PR1 96 D7
Talbot Row 2 PR7 60 D1
Talbot Sq FY1 130 B5
Talbot St
Burnley BB11 128 B6
Burnley, Harle Syke BB10 148 F2
Chipping PR3 185 E3
Chorley PR6 61 E1
Colne BB8 171 D6
Fulwood PR2 117 D4
Rishton BB1 124 C1
Southport PR8 35 A6
Talbot Terr 1 FY8 91 B3
Tall Trees LA1 218 D4
Tamar Cl PR25 60 B7
Tamar St PR1 97 E8
Tamneys The WN8 17 F1
Tancaster WN8 17 E1
Tanfield Nook WN8 27 C2
Tanfields WN8 17 F1
Tanglewood PR2 118 B5
Tan Hill Dr LA1 218 D3
TANHOUSE 9 D8
Tanhouse 6 LA2 211 A4
Tan House Cl WN8 27 C3
Tanhouse La PR6 61 F6
Tan House La WN8 27 C2
Tanhouse Rd WN8 9 E7
TANNERS 50 B7
Tanners Croft 5 BL0 50 B6
Tannersmith La L40 40 F5
Tanners St BL0 50 B6
Tanner St 15 BB11 127 F6
Tanners Way FY8 90 D7
Tan Pit Cotts WN8 19 C4
Tanpits La LA6 240 B7
Tanpits Rd BB5 103 F6
Tansley Ave PR7 42 D1
Tansley Cl BL6 32 C2
Tansy La PR3 206 F4
TANTERTON 117 A6
Tanterton Hall Rd PR2 117 A6
Tanyard Cl PR7 42 D1
Tan Yard La PR3 140 C8
Tan Yd PR3 140 C8
Taper St BL0 50 B6
Tape St 2 BL0 50 B6
Tapestry St BB2 101 D1
Tarbert Cres BB1 102 D4
Tarbet St LA1 215 A7
TARDY GATE 77 B8
Tardy Gate Trad Ctr PR5 77 A8
TARLETON 57 A7
Tarleton Ave BB11 128 B4
Tarleton Com Prim Sch PR4 56 F8
Tarleton High Sch PR4 57 A7
Tarleton Holy Trinity CE Prim Sch PR4 57 A5
Tarleton Lo FY8 89 F4
Tarleton Mere Brow CE Prim Sch PR4 55 F2
Tarleton Rd PR9 36 A8
Tarleton St BB11 128 B4
TARLSCOUGH 38 D1
Tarlscough La L40 38 D1
Tarlswood WN8 17 F1
Tarnacre Hall Bsns Pk PR3 180 D1
Tarnacre Hall Mews PR3 180 D1
Tarnacre La PR3 180 E2
Tarnacre View PR3 181 C6
Tarn Ave BB5 124 F4
Tarnbeck Dr L40 40 D2
Tarnbrick Ave PR4 93 C7
TARNBROOK 233 B2
Tarnbrook Cl
Crag Bank LA5 223 C1
Hest Bank LA5 220 F2
Tarn Brook Cl BB5 125 F1
Tarnbrook Cotts PR3 201 E5
Tarnbrook Dr FY3 131 A7
Tarnbrook Rd
5 Heysham LA3 212 F8
2 Lancaster LA1 218 B2
Tarn Brow L39 15 C3
Tarn Cl PR1 95 F4
Tarn Cotts LA5 221 C6
Tarn Ct FY7 198 D1
Tarn Hows Cl 1 PR7 43 B5
Tarn La LA6 240 B6
Tarn Rd
Formby L37 11 D3
Thornton FY5 153 D7
Tarnside FY4 131 B1
Tarnside Rd WN5 10 E6
Tarnsyke Rd LA1 218 B2
Tarnwater La LA2 210 E7
Tarnway Ave FY5 153 D8
Tarradale PR4 94 F1
Tarragon Dr FY2 152 F4
Tarry Barn La BB7 167 A3
Tarvin Cl
Burnley BB10 148 F3
Southport PR9 54 D5
Taskers Croft BB7 144 F8
Tasker St 13 BB5 104 C6
TATHAM 238 D8
Tatham Ct FY7 198 C1
Tatham Fells CE Prim Sch LA2 239 C4
Tattersall Sq BB4 86 F3
Tattersall St
5 Blackburn BB2 101 E4
Haslingden BB4 85 B6
Oswaldtwistle BB5 103 D4
2 Padiham BB12 126 D8
Tatton St BB8 171 B3
Tauheedul-Islam Girls' High Sch BB1 101 E6
Taunton Rd BB2 101 B5
Taunton St
8 Blackpool FY4 130 D1
Preston PR1 118 D1
Tavistock Dr PR8 21 B6
Tavistock St BB9 170 F1
TAWD BRIDGE 9 B7
Tawd Rd WN8 9 C8
TAWD VALLEY PARK 18 A2
Taybank Ave FY4 110 D7
Taydale Cotts BB10 148 E3
Taylor Ave
Blackburn BB2 81 C7
Newchurch BB4 86 F2
Ormskirk L39 16 A5
Taylor Cl BB2 101 C3
Taylor Ct 1 BB4 85 A3
Taylor Gr LA4 217 F6
Taylor Holme Ind Est OL13 70 B8
Taylor St W 4 BB5 104 B6
Taylor's Bldgs BB6 143 D1
Taylors Cl FY6 153 C5
Taylor's Ind Est PR3 201 E5
Taylor's La
Fisher's Row PR3 201 D6
Holmes PR4 56 D3
Taylor's Meanygate PR4 56 A7
Taylors Pl 18 OL12 52 F1
Taylor St
Barnoldswick BB18 196 A2
Blackburn BB2 101 D3
Brierfield BB9 148 B6
Burnley BB10 128 A8
Bury BL9 33 A3
Chorley PR7 43 B5
Clitheroe BB7 166 F8
Darwen BB3 65 A8
Haslingden BB4 85 B6
Horwich BL6 32 B3
Preston PR1 96 D6
6 Rawtenstall BB4 86 A3
Rochdale OL12 52 F1
Skelmersdale WN8 17 C1
Whitworth OL12 52 D8
Taymouth Rd 5 FY4 111 A6
Tay St
Burnley BB11 127 D5
3 Preston PR1 96 D6
Taywood Cl FY6 153 F4
Taywood Rd FY5 176 A4
Teak St BL9 33 B2
Teal Cl
Blackburn BB1 101 D8
Leyland PR25 59 D7
Ormskirk L39 15 C2
Thornton FY5 176 A4
Teal Ct FY3 131 B6
Teal La FY8 90 E7
Teanlowe Ctr FY6 153 D3
Tears La WN8 26 F1
Teasel Wlk 6 LA3 217 B2
Tebay Ave
Cleveleys FY5 175 D4
Kirkham PR4 114 C5
Tebay Cl L31 5 F2
Tebay Ct LA1 218 C4
Tedder Ave
Burnley BB12 127 B6
Southport PR9 36 A7
Teenadore Ave 1 FY4 110 E7
Tees Ct FY7 198 D2
Teesdale 8 LA2 211 A4
Teesdale Ave FY2 130 D8
Tees St PR1 118 C2
Teil Gn PR2 118 E6
Telford St
Burnley BB12 127 C7
Horwich BL6 32 D2
Telletholme Ind Est L40 25 B3
Temperance St 8 PR6 43 E8
Temple Cl 2 BB1 102 B4
Temple Ct
11 Preston PR1 96 F7
Yealand Redmayne LA5 225 D5
Temple Dr BB1 102 B4
Templegate Cl WN6 29 F2
Templemartin 2 WN8 17 F2
Temple St
10 Blackpool FY1 130 B5
Burnley BB11 128 B5
Colne BB8 171 E6
Temple St *continued*
Nelson BB9 148 F8
Templeton Cl BB3 82 A2
Temple Way PR6 61 D3
Tenby 2 WN8 17 E2
Tenby Cl BB1 101 E7
Tenby Gr 6 OL12 52 C1
Tenby Rd 7 PR1 97 A6
Tenby St OL12 52 C1
Tennis St BB10 128 A8
Tennyson Ave
Chorley PR7 43 C6
Lytham St Anne's FY8 91 D4
Oswaldtwistle BB5 103 C4
Padiham BB12 126 E7
Read BB12 145 D2
Thornton FY5 176 A3
Warton PR4 92 D6
Tennyson Cl LA5 221 A5
Tennyson Dr
Blackpool FY2 152 F6
Longshaw WN5 10 D1
Ormskirk L39 15 D6
Tennyson Mill Ct PR1 118 D1
Tennyson Pl
Bamber Bridge PR5 97 D2
Great Harwood BB6 124 B4
Tennyson Rd
Blackpool FY3 130 F7
Colne BB8 171 D5
Fleetwood FY7 199 A4
Preston PR1 118 D1
Tennyson St
Burnley BB11 127 D5
Burnley, Harle Syke BB10 148 F3
6 Hapton BB12 126 C4
Ten Row LA2 209 E5
Tensing Ave FY2 152 D5
Tensing Rd L31 5 D1
Tenterfield St
23 Preston PR1 96 F8
6 Rawtenstall BB4 69 F8
Tenterheads 8 BB4 69 F7
Terance Rd 2 FY4 110 E8
Tern Gr LA3 212 F5
Terrace Row BB7 144 C4
Terrace St PR1 118 C1
Terrace The 8 LA2 239 B8
Terra Cotta Bldgs BB4 107 A1
Terry St BB9 171 A2
Tetbury Cl 6 BB2 80 E8
Teven St 5 PR5 97 E1
Teversham WN8 17 F2
Teviot 5 WN8 17 E2
Teviot Ave FY7 198 D3
TEWITFIELD 240 A4
Tewkesbury 4 WN8 17 E2
Tewkesbury Ave FY4 110 D5
Tewkesbury Cl BB5 104 E3
Tewkesbury Dr FY8 91 D5
Tewkesbury St BB2 101 B1
Thames Ave BB10 148 C3
Thames Dr WN5 10 F7
Thames Ho 8 PR1 97 D8
Thames Prim Sch FY4 110 B7
Thames Rd FY4 110 B7
Thames St PR4 114 F2
Thane Row BB11 107 D7
Thanet WN8 17 F2
Thanet Lee Cl BB10 128 E1
Thealby Cl WN8 17 E2
Theatre St PR1 96 F7
THE GREAVES 214 F6
Thelma St BL0 50 B6
Thermdale Cl 3 PR3 181 B7
Thetis Rd LA1 214 C8
Thickrash Brow LA2 239 D7
Third Ave
Blackpool FY4 110 C7
Bury BL9 33 D4
Preesall Park FY6 200 C1
Thirlmere Ave
Burnley BB10 148 A2
Carleton FY6 153 C4
Colne BB8 171 F6
Fleetwood FY7 198 C1
Formby L37 12 A2
Haslingden BB4 68 C8
Horwich BL6 32 C2
1 Orrell WN5 10 F7
Padiham BB12 146 C2
Up Holland WN8 10 B7
Thirlmere Cl
2 Accrington BB5 125 D1
Adlington PR6 31 B8
6 Blackburn BB1 101 F6
Knott End-on-S FY6 199 F6
Longton PR4 75 B8
Maghull L31 5 E2
Thirlmere Ct LA1 218 F1
Thirlmere Dr
Darwen BB3 82 C2
Longridge PR3 139 F5
Morecambe LA4 217 A4
Southport PR8 21 B3
Withnell Fold PR6 79 D2
Thirlmere Gr LA4 217 B4
Thirlmere Rd
Blackpool FY4 110 C7
Blackrod BL6 31 C3
Burnley BB10 128 E5
Chorley PR7 43 B6
Hightown L38 3 A4
Lancaster LA1 218 F2
Preston PR1 118 F1
Thirlmere Way BB4 106 A1
Thirsk WN8 17 E2
Thirsk Ave FY8 90 B7
Thirsk Gr FY1 130 D2
Thirsk Rd LA1 215 B4
Thistle Break LA3 213 A7
Thistle Cl
Chorley PR6 43 E8
Cleveleys FY5 175 F5
Hesketh Bank PR4 73 E4
Thistlecroft PR2 117 A5
Thistle Ct L40 25 F6
Thistlemount Ave BB4 86 F1
Thistle St 15 OL13 87 F2
THISTLETON 133 D8
Thistleton Mews 3 PR9 35 C8
Thistleton Rd
Elswick PR4 155 C1
Preston PR2 95 E8
Thomas Gr LA4 217 B5
Thomason Fold BL7 48 D6
Thomas St
Blackburn BB2 101 D4
Brierfield BB9 148 A5
Burnley BB11 128 A5
Colne BB8 171 C4
7 Haslingden BB4 85 A3
6 Lytham St Anne's FY8 91 B3
Nelson BB9 148 E7
7 Oswaldtwistle BB5 103 D3
4 Preston PR1 97 B7
Todmorden OL14 109 C1
Whitworth OL12 71 D2
Thomas's Weind PR3 181 C7
Thompson Ave L39 16 B5
Thompson Dr BL9 33 C3
Thompson St
Blackburn BB2 101 C4
Darwen BB3 65 B7
Horwich BL6 32 A3
8 Kirkham PR4 113 F6
Padiham BB12 126 D7
Preston PR1 118 D1
Thompson Street Ind Est BB2 101 C4
Thonock Rd LA4 217 D3
Thorburn Dr OL12 52 B7
Thornbank FY3 131 B7
Thorn Bank OL13 88 A2
Thornbank Dr PR3 181 D2
Thornbeck Ave L38 2 F3
Thornber 1 WN8 17 F2
Thornber Ct BB10 148 C1
Thornber Gr FY1 130 D3
Thornber St BB2 101 C3
Thornbridge Ave L40 25 E3
Thornbury WN8 17 F2
Thornby 3 WN8 17 F2
Thorncliffe Dr BB3 65 D8
Thorn Cres 7 OL13 88 A2
Thorncross 7 FY5 152 F8
Thorndale 4 WN8 17 F2
Thorn Dr OL13 88 A2
Thorne St BB9 171 A2
Thorneybank Ind Est BB11 126 C2
Thorney Bank St 7 BB11 127 F5
Thorneycroft Cl FY6 153 B5
THORNEY HOLME 169 E5
Thorneyholme RC Prim Sch BB7 228 C5
Thorneyholme Rd BB5 104 C8
Thorneyholme Sq BB12 169 E5
Thorneylea
Blackburn BB2 81 D7
Whitworth OL12 71 D1
Thornfield
Bretherton PR26 57 F7
Lancaster LA1 214 F5
Much Hoole PR4 74 E3
Thornfield Ave
Fulwood PR2 118 F3
Longridge PR3 140 A8
Newchurch BB4 86 E1
8 Rawtenstall BB4 69 F8
Thornton FY5 153 D8
Thornfield Cvn Pk FY3 131 D5
Thorngate PR1 96 B4
Thorngate Cl PR1 96 B4
Thorn Gdns OL13 88 A2
Thorn Gr
Blackpool FY1 130 E2
Colne BB8 171 F6
Thornham Ct FY3 130 E5
Thornhill L39 6 B8
Thornhill Ave
Knott End-on-S FY6 200 A5
Rishton BB1 103 A8
Thornhill Cl
Blackpool FY4 110 F5
Ormskirk L39 6 B8
Thorn Hill Cl BB1 102 A5
Thornhill Rd
Chorley PR6 61 E2
Leyland PR25 59 D8
Ramsbottom BL0 50 A1
Thornhill St BB12 127 A6
Thorn La PR3 140 B2
Thornlea Dr OL12 52 B2
Thornleigh Cl 10 FY5 176 A2
Thornleigh Dr LA6 240 C7
Thornley Ave BB1 102 C6
Thornley Pl PR2 119 A3
Thornley Rd PR2 119 A3
Thornpark Dr 3 PR2 116 D1
Thorns Ave LA2 220 D1
Thorn St
Bacup OL13 88 A2
Burnley BB10 128 A8
Clitheroe BB7 166 D8
Great Harwood BB6 124 D6
Preston PR1 118 C1
Ramsbottom BL0 50 C3
Rawtenstall BB4 85 F5
Sabden BB7 146 A7
Thorns The L31 5 B2
Thornthwaite Rd PR4 116 D4
THORNTON 176 C3
Thornton WN8 17 F2
Thornton Ave
Fulwood PR2 117 B4
Lytham St Anne's FY8 90 B8
Morecambe LA4 217 C6
Thornton Cl
Accrington BB5 104 A8
Blackburn BB2 81 F8
Rufford L40 39 C4
Thornton Cleveleys Baines Endowed Prim Sch FY5 176 C1
Thornton Cleveleys Manor Beach Prim Sch FY5 175 D3
Thornton Cleveleys Red Marsh Sch FY5 176 B3
Thornton Cleveleys Royles Brook Prim Sch FY5 176 A2
Thornton Cres
Burnley BB10 128 E5
2 Morecambe LA4 217 C5
Thornton Ctr FY5 176 C1
Thornton Dr
Coupe Green PR5 98 D4
Leyland PR26 76 E4
Thornton Gate FY5 175 C4
Thornton Gr 1 LA4 217 C5
Thornton Hall Mews FY5 153 E7
Thornton Hts BD23 197 A5
THORNTON-IN-CRAVEN 197 A6
Thornton in Craven Com Prim Sch BD23 197 B6
THORNTON IN LONSDALE 242 F4
Thornton La
Ingleton LA6 242 F5
Morecambe LA4 217 C6
Thornton Manor Ct BD23 197 A5
Thornton Pl FY5 176 A4
Thornton Prim Sch FY5 176 B3
Thornton Rd
Burnley BB10 128 E5
Morecambe LA4 217 C6
Southport PR9 35 F7
Thorntrees Ave
Newsham PR3 137 B5
Preston PR2 116 D1
Thorn View BL9 33 C3
Thornway Ave FY5 153 D8
Thornwood WN8 17 F2
Thornwood Cl
5 Blackburn BB1 122 E1
Lytham St Anne's FY8 90 E4
Thoroughfare The LA5 223 D5
Thoroughgood Cl L40 25 D2
Thorough Way PR3 203 E7
Thorpe WN8 17 F2
Thorpe Ave LA4 217 F4
Thorpe Cl PR1 117 F1
THORPE GREEN 78 E4
Thorpe St BL0 50 B5
Thorvald Gdns LA4 217 F4
Thrang Brow La LA5 225 C6
Threagill La LA5 223 F5
Three Brooks Way BB5 103 D2
Threefields PR2 117 A5
Three Lane Ends PR6 62 C4
Three Nooks PR5 78 C5
Three Oaks Cl L40 26 B2
Three Point Bsns Pk BB4 85 A2
Three Pools PR9 54 C3
Three Rivers Pk BB7 189 D7
Three Tuns La L37 11 F3
Three Turns PR3 142 A8
Threlfall PR7 60 F2
Threlfall Rd FY1 130 D1
Threlfall's La PR9 53 F2
Threlfall St 1 PR2 117 C1
Threshers Ct PR3 207 C2
Threshfield Ave LA3 212 F8
Thrimby Ct LA4 217 B4
Thrimby Pl LA4 217 B4
Thropps La PR4 75 D6
Throstle Cl BB12 128 A7
Throstle Gr LA2 218 D8
Throstle Mill OL13 87 F2
Throstle Nest La PR3 203 C4
Throstle Nest Mill Bsns Ctr BB9 170 E1
Throstle St
Blackburn BB2 101 C4
7 Nelson BB9 170 E1
Throstle Way 8 FY5 175 F1
Throstle Wlk LA2 218 D8
Throup Pl BB9 170 E2
Thrum Fold OL12 52 D3

Thrum Hall La
Rochdale, Lower Healey OL12 52 E3
Rochdale OL12 52 D3
Thrush Dr BL9 33 B4
Thrushgill Dr LA2 219 D7
Thrush St OL12 52 C1
Thurcroft Dr WN8 17 E2
Thurland Ct 2 LA4 217 A3
Thurland Mill Cotts LA6 241 D3
Thurnham Glasson Christ Church CE Prim Sch LA2 209 E4
Thurnham Mews 7 LA1 214 F7
Thurnham Rd PR2 95 E8
Thurnham St LA1 214 F7
Thursby Ave FY4 110 D6
Thursby Cl PR8 21 B3
Thursby Pl 13 BB9 170 F2
Thursby Rd
Burnley BB10 148 C1
Nelson BB9 170 F2
Thursby Sq BB10 128 A8
THURSDEN 149 D2
Thursden Ave BB10 148 F3
Thursden Pl BB9 171 B1
Thursfield Ave FY4 110 E8
Thursfield Rd BB10 128 B5
Thursford Gr BL6 31 D1
Thursgill Ave 3 LA4 217 C3
Thurston WN8 17 E2
Thurston Rd PR25 77 A1
Thurston St BB11 128 B6
Thurtell Cotts LA2 237 B3
Thwaite Brow La LA5 221 B6
Thwaite La LA2 239 C5
Thwaites Ave BB2 121 E2
Thwaites Cl BB1 102 D2
Thwaites Rd BB5 103 C4
Thwaites St BB5 103 C3
Thyme Cl FY2 152 F3
Tiber Ave BB11 127 C4
Tiber St PR1 97 B7
Tibicar Dr E LA3 216 D1
Tibicar Dr W LA3 216 D1
Tib St 18 BL0 50 B5
Tiger The PR25 76 D2
Tilbury Gr WN6 19 D7
Tilcroft WN8 17 E2
Timber Brook PR7 61 A2
Timberhurst BL9 33 D2
Timber St
Accrington BB5 104 C5
Bacup OL13 87 F1
Brierfield BB9 148 B6
Timbrills Ave BB7 145 F8
Timms Cl L37 11 F5
Timms La L37 11 F5
Tincklers La PR7 41 A6
Tinedale View BB12 146 D1
Tinker Brook Cl BB5 103 D2
Tinkerfield PR2 117 E7
Tinker's La LA2 226 B7
Tinklers La BB7 229 E7
Tinline St BL9 33 A2
Tinniswood PR2 117 B1
Tinsley Ave PR8 35 E3
Tinsley's La PR8 36 A1
Tintagel WN8 17 E2
Tintagell Cl BB2 80 C7
Tintern Ave
Chorley PR7 43 D5
Rochdale OL12 52 E2
Tintern Cl
Accrington BB5 104 E2
Read BB12 145 D1
Tintern Cres BB1 102 B8
Tintern Dr L37 12 B2
Tippet Cl BB2 102 A1
Titan Way PR26 76 B2
Tithebarn Gate FY6 153 D4
Tithebarn Hill LA2 209 E5
Tithe Barn La
Knowley PR6 62 A4
Runshaw Moor PR25, PR7 59 F5
Scorton PR3 204 E5
Tithebarn Pl FY6 153 D4
Tithebarn Rd PR8 35 E7
Tithebarn St
Poulton-le-F FY6 153 D4
Preston PR1 97 A8
Up Holland WN8 10 B7
Tittrington Brow BB7 229 C2
Tiverton Ave WN8 17 E2
Tiverton Cl PR2 117 F8
Tiverton Dr
Blackburn BB2 81 C8
Burnley BB10 148 F3
TOCKHOLES 81 A2
Tockholes Rd
Darwen BB3 81 E2
Tockholes BB3 81 A3
Todber Cvn Pk BB7 231 C1
Todd Carr Rd BB4 86 F1
Todd Hall Rd BB4 84 F4
Todd La N PR5 97 C2
Todd La S PR5 77 C8
Todd's La PR9 55 A6
Tod Holes La BD23 236 E4
Todmorden Old Rd OL13 88 B5
Todmorden Rd
Bacup OL13 88 B4
Todmorden Rd *continued*
Burnley BB11 128 B3
Cockden BB10 149 B1
Lytham St Anne's FY8 89 C8
Toll Bar Bsns Pk 13 OL13 70 D8
Toll Bar Cres LA1 214 F3
Toll Bar Ct LA6 240 C7
Tollgate PR1 96 E4
Tollgate Cres L40 25 C2
Tollgate Rd L40 25 B3
Tolsey Dr PR4 95 D2
Tom Benson Way PR2, PR4 116 F4
Tom La BB4 86 F2
Tomlinson Rd
Heysham LA3 212 F6
Leyland PR25 76 F2
Preston PR2 117 C2
Tomlinson St BL6 32 B3
TONACLIFFE 52 C6
Tonacliffe Prim Sch OL12 52 C6
Tonacliffe Rd OL12 52 E6
Tonacliffe Terr OL12 52 C7
Tonacliffe Way OL12 52 C6
Tongbarn WN8 17 E2
TONG END 71 C2
Tong End OL12 71 C2
Tong La
Bacup OL13 88 B2
Britannia OL13 71 C8
Whitworth OL12 71 D1
Tongues La FY6 200 C6
TONTINE 10 D5
Tontine WN5 10 C5
Tontine Rd WN5, WN8 10 C6
Tontine St BB1 101 E5
Toogood La WN6 28 D6
Tootell St PR7 43 B6
Tootle La L40 39 A3
Tootle Rd PR3 140 B8
Top Acre PR4 95 C1
Top Acre Rd WN8 9 C7
Topaz St BB1 122 F2
Topaz Way PR6 43 E6
Top Barn La BB4 86 E1
Topiary Gdns PR3 181 D4
Top Locks L40 26 A4
Top of Fawna Rd PR3 163 D1
Top Of Heap OL10 33 F2
TOP OF RAMSGREAVE 122 C3
Top of Wallsuches BL6 32 F4
Top o' th' Croft BB2 81 D8
TOP O' TH' LANE 78 F3
TOPPING FOLD 33 D3
Topping Fold Rd BL9 33 C3
Topping St
Blackpool FY1 130 B5
Bury BL9 33 A3
Toppings The PR3 181 C6
Top Row BB7 145 F8
Tor Ave BL8 49 F2
Torcross Cl PR9 54 A5
Tor End Rd BB4 67 F6
Tor Hey Mews BL8 49 F2
Tormore Cl PR6 62 A3
Toronto Ave
Blackpool FY2 152 E3
Fleetwood FY7 198 E2
Toronto Rd BB2 101 C8
Torquay Ave
Blackpool FY3 131 A2
Burnley BB10 148 D2
Torra Barn Cl BL7 47 E3
Torrentum Ct FY5 176 C1
Torridon Cl BB2 100 F1
TORRISHOLME 218 A4
Torrisholme Com Prim Sch LA4 217 F5
Torrisholme Rd LA1 218 B3
Torrisholme Sq 8 LA4 217 F4
Torside Gr FY6 153 B3
Torsway Ave FY3 130 F6
Torver Cl BB12 127 B8
Tor View
Haslingden BB4 85 C1
Rawtenstall BB4 86 A1
Tor View Rd BB4 85 C1
Tor View Sch BB4 68 D8
TOSSIDE 236 C2
Totnes Cl FY6 153 C5
Totnes Dr PR9 54 A5
Tottenham Rd BB3 81 F6
Tottington Rd BL7, BL8 48 F2
Tottleworth BB6 124 C3
Tottleworth Rd BB1 124 C2
Toulmin Cl PR3 181 D2
Tourer Terr L40 24 B4
Towbreck Gdns FY6 131 E8
Tower Ave
Lancaster LA1 211 B7
Ramsbottom BL0 50 A5
Tower Bldgs 11 PR9 35 C8
Tower Cl FY5 176 A4
Tower Cotts 3 LA3 212 E7
Tower Ct
Chapeltown BL7 48 C4
Lancaster LA1 214 F7
Tower Dene Sch PR9 53 F2
Tower End L37 11 C5
Tower Gn PR2 117 F7
Tower Hill
Clitheroe BB7 189 F1
Ormskirk L39 16 A5
Tower Hill Rd WN8 10 B6
Tower La PR2 117 F7
Tower Nook WN8 10 A5
Tower Rd
Blackburn BB2 100 E2
Darwen BB3 65 B8
Towers Ave L31 5 C2
Towers Ct BB2 101 D3
Tower St
13 Bacup OL13 87 F2
Blackpool FY1 130 B5
Chapeltown BL7 48 C4
Oswaldtwistle BB5 103 C5
Todmorden OL14 109 A1
Tower View
Belthorn BB1 83 A5
Blackpool FY2 152 D2
Blackrod BL6 31 C3
Darwen BB3 82 C1
Higher Penwortham PR1 96 C7
TOWN BENT 103 D2
Town Brook Ho 5 PR1 117 E1
Town Brow PR25 77 F2
TOWN CENTRE 18 C1
Towneley Ave BB5 125 F2
Towneley Cl LA1 214 D7
Towneley Hall (Art Gall & Mus)* BB11 128 C2
Towneley High Sch BB11 128 C4
Towneley Ho PR3 140 A7
Towneley Par PR3 140 A7
Towneley Rd PR3 140 A7
Towneley Rd W PR3 140 A7
Towneley St BB10 148 B1
TOWN END 155 C8
Town End
Bolton-le-S LA5 221 A3
Kirkham PR4 114 A5
Slaidburn BB7 229 C7
3 Thornton FY5 176 A2
Town End Cl L39 15 D4
Town End Fold LA5 223 C5
Townfield Ave BB10 128 F6
Townfield Cl PR4 74 F7
Townfield La LA2 218 C7
Townfields 1 BB11 128 B5
Towngate
Eccleston PR7 41 B7
Foulridge BB8 194 D1
Leyland PR25 60 A8
Leyland PR25 77 A1
Leyland, Wade Hall PR25 59 F7
Town Gate BB6 124 C5
Towngate Works L40 40 E2
TOWN GREEN 6 D7
Town Green Ct L39 6 C8
Town Green Gdns L39 6 C8
Town Green La L39 6 C8
Town Green Sta L39 6 C8
Town Hall Sq 8 BB6 124 C5
Town Hall St
16 Blackburn BB2 101 E5
9 Great Harwood BB6 124 C5
TOWN HEAD 196 A1
Town Head BB18 196 A1
Town Hill Bank BB12 146 D1
Town House Rd BB9 149 B8
Town La
Coppull PR7 42 C1
Heskin Green PR7 41 C2
Much Hoole PR4 74 D1
Southport PR8 35 E3
Whittle-le-W PR6 61 D6
Town Lane (Kew) PR8 35 E3
Townlea Cl PR1 96 A3
Townley Ave FY4 110 E8
Townley La PR1 95 D4
Townley St
Brierfield BB9 148 B5
Burnley, Harle Syke BB10 148 F3
Chorley PR6 43 D7
Colne BB8 171 E6
Morecambe LA4 217 B6
Town Rd PR26 58 B2
TOWNSEND FOLD 68 E8
Townsend St
Haslingden BB4 85 A3
Rawtenstall BB4 69 F8
Townsfield LA5 224 C4
Townshill Wlk PR4 114 A6
Townside Gate PR3 156 B5
Townsley St BB9 148 E6
TOWN'S MOOR 101 E3
Townsmoor Ret Pk 7 BB2 101 E3
Townsway PR5 77 C8
Town View BB1 101 F4
Town Wlk BB1 101 F4
Towpath Wlk 2 LA5 223 D1
Tow Scar Rd LA6 242 F6
Toxhead Cl BL6 32 A3
Tracks La WN5 10 D3
Trafalgar Cl PR2 117 D3
Trafalgar Ct PR8 34 F3
Trafalgar Ho BB11 127 E6
Trafalgar Mall 3 BB9 148 E8
Trafalgar Rd
Blackpool FY1 130 B2
Lancaster LA1 215 A6
Southport PR8 34 E3
Trafalgar St
Burnley BB11 127 F5
Chorley PR6 61 C1
Lytham St Anne's FY8 89 F7
Trafford Gdns BB7 166 D1
Trafford St PR1 117 E2
Tramway La PR5 78 B6
Tranmere Ave LA3 216 D1
Tranmere Cres LA3 216 D1
Tranmere Rd FY4 130 E1
Tranmoor PR4 74 F6
Trans Brittania Enterprise Est BB11 127 B3
Trap Hill L37 11 C2
Trapp La BB12 145 F2
Trash La
Rimington BB7 231 B1
Tockholes BB3 81 B2
Travellers Ct BB7 231 C3
Travers Lo 8 PR2 118 F4
Travers Pl PR2 96 C8
Travers St BL6 32 D1
Travis St BB10 128 A8
TRAWDEN 172 C2
Trawden Cl BB5 104 C4
Trawden Cres PR2 118 E4
Trawden Forest Prim Sch BB8 172 C2
Trawden Rd BB8 172 B4
Traylen Way OL12 52 A1
TREALES 114 D6
Treales CE Prim Sch PR4 134 E2
Treales Rd PR4 115 B6
Trecastle Rd L33 1 A4
Tredgold St BL6 32 C2
Treen Cl PR9 54 B6
Treesdale Cl PR8 34 F4
Treetops Ave BL0 50 A3
Treetop Villas PR9 53 F4
Trefoil Cl FY5 176 A5
Tremellen St BB5 104 A6
Trengrove St 7 OL12 52 C1
Trent Ave L31 5 F2
Trent Cl
Burscough Bridge L40 25 F5
Morecambe LA3 217 F2
Trent Rd
Blackpool FY4 110 B7
Nelson BB9 149 A8
Trent St
Longridge PR3 139 F7
Lytham St Anne's FY8 91 D3
Tresco Cl BB2 101 B1
Tretower Way FY5 176 D2
Trevarrick Ct BL6 32 E2
Trevelyan Dr WN5 10 D1
Trevor Cl BB1 101 F7
Trevore Dr WN1 30 B1
Trevor Rd
Burscough L40 25 E4
Southport PR8 21 C4
Triangle The
Accrington, Hillock Vale BB5 104 E8
Fulwood PR2 117 E4
Trident Pk BB1 102 C8
Trident Way BB1 102 C8
Trigge Ho PR7 61 C2
Trigg La PR6 62 D5
Trillium Way BB3 82 A7
Trinity CE Sch WN8 17 F1
Trinity Cl
Brierfield BB9 148 C5
Freckleton PR4 93 B7
Padiham BB12 126 D6
Trinity Ct 3 BB1 101 F6
Trinity Fold 20 PR1 96 F8
Trinity Gdns
Southport PR8 35 A6
Thornton FY5 176 A3
Trinity Gn BL0 50 B2
Trinity Mews PR9 35 C7
Trinity Pl 24 PR1 96 F8
Trinity Rd PR7 43 B7
Trinity & St Michael's CE/ Meth Prim Sch PR26 58 C2
Trinity St Peter's CE Prim Sch L37 12 A5
Trinity St
15 Bacup OL13 70 C8
Blackburn BB1 101 F6
Oswaldtwistle BB5 103 D3
Trinity Student Village PR1 96 F8
Trinity Twrs 6 BB11 127 E6
Trinity Wlks PR4 57 A5
Trinket La LA2 238 E6
Tristan Ave PR4 75 A5
Troon Ave
Blackburn BB1 102 C3
Thornton FY5 153 D8
Troon Cl PR7 60 D4
Troon Ct PR1 96 A6
TROUGH GATE 71 D8
Trough of Bowland* BB7 227 F7
Trough Rd BB7 228 B5
Troughton Cres 1 FY4 110 E8
Trout Beck BB5 124 F4
Troutbeck Ave
Fleetwood FY7 198 D2
Forton PR3 207 B3
Maghull L31 5 E2
Troutbeck Cl
Burnley BB12 127 B8
Hawkshaw BL8 49 B2
Troutbeck Cres FY4 111 D8
Troutbeck Dr BL0 50 C7
Troutbeck Pl PR2 118 E5
Troutbeck Rd
Chorley PR7 43 B5
Lancaster LA1 218 E1
Troutbeck Rd *continued*
Lytham St Anne's FY8 110 D1
Trout St
8 Burnley BB10 128 A8
Preston PR1 97 C7
Trower St PR1 97 B6
Troy St BB1 101 F7
Trumacar Com Prim Sch LA3 212 E5
Trumacar La LA3 212 F5
Trumacar Terr LA3 212 E5
Truman Ave LA1 214 C7
Trumley Ct LA3 217 A2
Trundle Pie La L39 14 C6
TRUNNAH 176 B3
Trunnah Gdns FY5 176 B3
Trunnah Rd FY5 176 B3
Truro Ave PR9 54 B5
Truro Pl 8 PR1 118 D1
Truro St 7 FY4 130 D1
Truscott Rd L40 25 D4
Tucker Hill BB7 189 E1
Tucker's Hill Brow WN2 31 B1
Tudor Ave
Preston, Lea PR2 116 D1
Preston PR1 118 F1
Tudor Cl
Carleton FY6 153 A4
1 Cleveleys FY5 175 F1
Darwen BB3 82 A2
Langho BB6 143 D1
Preston PR2 116 D1
Tudor Croft PR5 77 C7
Tudor Ct
Lytham St Anne's FY8 89 D8
Ormskirk L39 15 F6
Tudor Dr PR4 114 B2
Tudor Gate FY8 90 B8
Tudor Gdns L38 2 F4
Tudor Gr 2 LA4 217 E6
Tudor Mans PR8 34 F6
Tudor Pl FY4 110 B6
Tudor Rd
Bamber Bridge PR1 97 A2
Lytham St Anne's FY8 89 D8
Southport PR8 21 B6
Tuer St PR25 76 F2
Tulip Gr OL12 52 E3
Tulketh Ave PR2 117 B1
Tulketh Brow PR2 117 C1
Tulketh Com Sports Coll PR2 117 B4
Tulketh Cres PR2 117 C1
Tulketh Rd PR2 117 B1
Tulketh St PR8 35 B7
Tunbridge Pl 7 PR1 118 D1
Tunbridge St 4 PR1 118 D1
Tunbrook Ave PR2 139 E1
Tunley Holme PR5 78 C5
Tunley La WN6 28 E5
Tunley Moss WN6 28 E4
Tunnel St
Burnley BB12 127 D6
5 Darwen BB3 65 C7
TUNSTALL 241 E4
Tunstall Dr BB5 125 B1
Tunstall Ho 10 LA1 215 A3
Tunstall St LA4 217 A5
Tunstead Ave BB12 125 E8
Tunstead Cres OL13 87 C1
Tunstead La BB4, OL13 87 B1
Tunstead Mill Terr 3 OL13 70 B8
Tunstead Rd OL13 70 C8
Tunstill Fold BB12 169 F1
Tunstill St BB10 148 B1
Turbary Rd LA6 242 E7
Turbary The PR2 117 C3
Turflands PR26 58 B1
Turf Mdw BB4 106 A2
Turf Moor Football Gd (Burnley FC) BB10 128 B6
Turf St BB11 128 B6
Turkey Red Ind Est BB5 84 F8
Turkey St
Accrington BB5 104 D7
Out Rawcliffe PR3 178 A1
Turks Head Yd 22 PR1 97 A7
TURN 69 A1
Turnacre L37 12 B6
Turnberry WN8 17 D2
Turnberry Ave FY5 153 D8
Turnberry Cl
Kirkham PR4 114 A4
Morecambe LA4 217 D6
Turnberry Way PR9 54 D5
Turnbridge Rd L31 5 C3
Turnbury Cl PR7 60 D4
Turncroft Rd BB3 65 B8
Turner Ave PR5 77 A7
Turner Fold BB12 145 D3
Turnerford Cl 4 BL7 47 E1
TURNER GREEN 120 C2
Turnerís Pl OL12 52 E3
Turner Rd BB9 148 B8
Turner St
3 Bacup OL13 70 C8
4 Barnoldswick BB18 196 C2
Clitheroe BB7 166 E7
3 Preston PR1 118 A1
Rochdale OL12 52 E1
Turney Crook Mews 9 BB8 171 D5
Turnfield PR2 116 F6
Turning La PR8 36 A1
Turn La BB3 64 F8
Turnpike BB4 86 F1
Turnpike Fold LA2 218 D5

Turnpike Gr BB5 103 C5
Turnpike Rd L39 15 A2
Turnpike The PR2 117 D6
Turn Rd BL0 50 E8
Turnstone FY3 131 B6
TURPIN GREEN 77 B1
Turpin Green La PR25 77 B1
Turton Belmont Com Prim Sch BL7 46 C5
TURTON BOTTOMS 48 D4
Turton Dr PR6 61 E1
Turton & Edgworth CE/ Meth Prim Sch BL7 48 D5
Turton Gr BB10 128 D6
Turton Hollow Rd BB4 86 A8
Turton Rd BL8 49 B1
Turton Twr* BL7 48 C3
Tuscan Ave BB11 127 C5
Tuscany Gr BB6 143 C6
Tuson Croft PR4 74 F8
Tuson Dr PR2 96 E8
Tuson Ho 2 PR1 96 E2
Tustin Ct PR1 96 C8
Tuxbury Dr FY5 153 D8
Tuxford Ct 1 FY8 90 D6
Tuxford Rd FY8 90 C6
Tweed St
  Blackburn BB2 81 D8
  4 High Bentham LA2 239 D8
  5 Lytham St Anne's FY8 89 E6
  Nelson BB9 149 A8
Tweed Street Ct 3 LA2 239 D8
Tweedys Ct PR3 185 C4
Twemlow Par
  Heysham LA3 212 F8
  Morecambe LA3 216 D1
Twenty Acre La PR4 75 B1
Twickenham Pl 4 FY8 90 D6
Twig La L31 5 E1
Twinegate OL12 52 E3
Twine Valley Ctry Pk* BL0 51 A8
Twine Wlk LA6 242 C3
Twin Lakes Ind Est PR26 58 A3
Twistfield Cl PR8 34 F5
Twist Moor La PR6 63 B8
TWISTON 192 A4
Twiston La BB7 191 D5
Twitter La BB7 189 A3
Two Acre La PR1 96 C1
Two Brooks La BL8 49 B2
Two Laws Rd BD22 174 C1
Two Saints Pl 8 L39 15 E5
Twyford Cl L31 5 E1
Twyn Ghyll Cvn Site BB7 231 B6
Tyldesley Rd FY1 130 B3
Tyne Ave 4 FY3 130 D4
Tyne Cl FY5 175 E5
Tynedale Pl FY3 153 A1
Tynedale Rd FY3 153 B1
Tyne St
  1 Bamber Bridge PR5 97 F1
  4 Preston PR1 96 D6
Tynwald Rd BB2 101 E1
Tyrer Rd L39 15 F7
Tyrer's Ave L31 5 B5
Tyrers Cl L37 11 F2
Tyrone Ave FY2 152 D2
Tyseley Gr BB18 197 A1
Tythebarn St BB3 82 B1

## U

Udale Pl 1 LA1 218 C2
Uggle La LA1 214 F3
Uldale Cl
  Nelson BB9 148 E6
  Southport PR8 21 B3
Ullswater Ave
  Accrington BB5 125 D1
  Fleetwood FY7 175 D8
  Morecambe LA4 217 D4
  Orrell WN5 10 F7
  Rochdale OL12 52 C1
  Thornton FY5 176 B1
Ullswater Cl
  Blackburn BB1 101 F6
  Hambleton FY6 177 C2
  3 Rishton BB1 124 A1
Ullswater Cres
  Carnforth LA5 221 E8
  Thornton FY5 176 B1
Ullswater Rd
  Blackpool FY4 110 C7
  Burnley BB10 128 F5
  Chorley PR7 43 B6
  Fulwood PR2 118 C4
  Lancaster LA1 215 A8
Ullswater Way BB4 106 A1
ULNES WALTON 59 A2
Ulnes Walton La PR26 59 A6
Ulpha Cl BB12 127 B8
Ulster Rd LA1 215 B5
Ulster St BB11 127 D5
Ulverston Cl
  Blackburn BB2 102 A1
  Maghull L31 5 E2
Ulverston Cres FY8 90 C7
Ulverston Dr BB1 124 A1
Underbank Cl 3 OL13 87 F3
Underbank Ho 1 OL13 87 F3
Underbank Rd
  Haslingden BB4 84 F3
  Rising Bridge BB5 85 A7
Underbank Rd *continued*
  Thornton FY5 176 F1
Underbank Way 2 BB4 85 A3
Under Billinge La BB2 100 F4
Underley St BB10 148 C3
Under Wood PR2 117 C3
Unicon Pk BB4 84 F3
Union Cl WN5 10 E5
Union Ct 18 OL13 70 C8
Union La PR3 178 C7
Union Pas 6 PR4 114 A5
Union Rd
  Oswaldtwistle BB5 103 D3
  Rawtenstall BB4 85 D2
Union St
  Accrington BB5 104 B6
  Bacup, Rockliffe OL13 87 F2
  Bacup, Stacksteads OL13 70 C8
  Blackburn BB2 101 E3
  6 Bolton BL7 47 D2
  Brierfield BB9 148 B5
  Chorley PR7 43 C8
  Clitheroe BB7 166 C8
  Colne BB8 171 E5
  Darwen BB3 82 A1
  Haslingden BB4 85 A3
  5 Morecambe LA4 217 A5
  10 Preston PR1 96 F8
  Ramsbottom BL0 50 C6
  Rawtenstall BB4 86 A3
  Southport PR9 35 C8
  Whittle-le-W PR6 61 C8
  Whitworth OL12 52 C8
Union Terr
  Clow Bridge BB4 106 A4
  Rawtenstall BB4 86 B2
Unit Rd PR8 21 D5
Unity St
  3 Barnoldswick BB18 196 C2
  Blackburn BB2 101 E2
  Kelbrook BB18 195 A6
Unity Trad Est BB2 101 D4
Unity Way BB4 85 F3
Univ of Central Lancashire PR1 96 E8
Univ of Central Lancashire Avenham Bldg PR1 97 A6
Univ of Cumbria LA1 215 B6
Univ of Lancaster LA1 211 B7
Unsworth Ave FY6 200 A4
Unsworth St OL13 70 D7
Up-Brooks BB7 190 A1
Up-Brooks Ind Est BB7 190 A1
UP HOLLAND 10 B6
Up Holland High Sch WN5 10 C4
Upholland Rd WN5 10 D2
Upholland Roby Mill CE Prim Sch WN8 19 B3
Upholland Sta WN8 9 F4
Uplands Chase PR2 117 B6
Uplands Dr BB12 147 D7
Upper Ashmount BB4 86 C1
Upper Aughton Rd PR8 35 B4
Upper Cliffe (Bersham Dr) BB6 124 C6
Upper George St 23 OL12 52 F1
Upper Hill Way BB18 194 B7
Upper Lune St FY7 199 B5
Upper Mead BL7 47 F1
UPPER THURNHAM 210 B2
Upper Westby St FY8 91 A3
Upphall La LA6 240 C4
Uppingham WN8 17 D1
Uppingham Dr BL0 50 B7
Upton Ave PR8 21 B6
Upton Barn L31 5 C2
Upwood Cl FY2 152 E5
Urban View PR6 62 F8
Ushers Mdw LA1 214 E7
Usk Ave FY5 176 D2

## V

VALE 109 C1
Vale Ave BL6 32 A3
Vale Cl WN6 19 E8
Vale Coppice
  Horwich BL6 32 A3
  Ramsbottom BL0 50 C3
Vale Cotts BL6 31 F2
Vale Cres PR8 21 C2
Vale Croft WN8 10 A6
Vale Ct BB5 125 F1
Vale Gr L32 1 A1
Vale Ho 9 BL7 47 D2
Vale House Cl BB7 144 C5
Vale La L40 17 F5
Vale Mill Ct BL0 68 D5
Valentia Rd FY2 152 D3
Valentines La PR2, PR4 116 E4
Valentines Mdw PR4 116 E4
Vale Rd LA1 218 C3
Vale Royal PR4 114 C5
Vale St
  Bacup OL13 88 A3
  Blackburn BB2 101 E2
  Darwen BB3 81 F2
  Haslingden BB4 85 B4
Vale Terr
  Calder Vale PR3 182 E8
  Newchurch BB4 86 F3
Vale The
  Appley Bridge WN6 19 D8
Vale The *continued*
  Bamber Bridge PR5 97 B2
  Fulwood PR2 117 F5
Valeway Ave FY5 152 D8
Valley Cl BB9 171 A1
Valley Ctr The 4 BB4 86 A2
Valley Dr
  Barnoldswick BB18 196 D4
  Padiham BB12 126 D8
Valley Forge Bsns Pk BB9 170 D2
Valley Gdns
  2 Earby BB18 197 B2
  Padiham BB11 126 F4
Valley Hts BB8 171 E5
Valley Mill Ct BB8 172 E6
Valley Mill La BL9 33 A1
Valley Rd
  Barnoldswick BB18 196 C2
  Earby BB18 197 B2
  Higher Penwortham PR1 96 D5
  Hoghton PR5 99 F3
  Longridge PR3 140 C7
  Wilpshire BB1 122 F5
Valley St BB11 127 B4
Valley Terr BB12 145 E1
Valley View
  Bamber Bridge PR5 97 A3
  Chorley PR6 43 E7
  Fulwood PR2 118 A4
  Whitworth OL12 71 D4
Valligates BB1 102 B7
Vance Rd FY1 130 B4
Vancouver Cres BB2 101 C8
Vandyck Ave BB11 127 E2
Vardon Rd BB2 101 B2
Varley St
  Colne BB8 171 F6
  2 Darwen BB3 82 A1
  Preston PR1 118 A2
Varlian Cl L40 16 C3
Vaughan Cl L37 11 D4
Vaughan Rd PR8 35 B4
Vaughan St BB9 148 F7
Vauxhall St BB2 101 B3
Vauze Ave BL6 31 D1
Vauze House Cl BL6 31 D2
Veevers St
  Brierfield BB9 148 A6
  7 Burnley BB11 127 F6
  Padiham BB12 126 D8
Velvet St BB2 81 D8
Venables Ave BB8 171 F6
Venice Ave BB11 127 C4
Venice St BB11 127 D5
Ventnor Pl PR2 117 A4
Ventnor Rd
  Blackpool FY4 110 B6
  1 Chorley PR7 43 B6
  Haslingden BB4 85 C1
Venture Ct BB5 125 D5
Venture Cvn Pk LA4 217 B3
Venture Rd FY7 176 A6
Venture St OL13 88 A3
Venture Works L33 1 C1
Verax St OL13 87 F1
Verbena Cl BB3 82 A7
Verbena Dr FY6 199 F6
Vermont Gr FY5 152 E8
Verna St 15 BL0 50 C6
Vernon Ave
  Blackpool FY3 130 E3
  Warton PR4 92 E6
Vernon Cres LA2 211 A3
Vernon Ct
  4 Galgate LA2 211 A4
  Southport PR8 35 D5
Vernon Lo FY8 89 F5
Vernon Pk 3 LA2 211 A4
Vernon Rd
  Laneshaw Bridge BB8 172 D6
  Lytham St Anne's FY8 110 E1
  Ramsbottom BL8 50 A1
  Southport PR9 36 A8
Vernon St
  Blackburn BB2 101 E4
  Darwen BB3 82 B1
  Nelson BB9 148 E7
  Preston PR1 117 F1
Verona Ave BB11 127 C5
Verona Ct 6 FY5 176 A2
Veronica St BB3 81 E4
Verulam Rd PR9 54 B3
Vesta St 6 BL0 50 B6
Vevey St PR25 77 A1
Viaduct Rd PR5 99 F2
Vicarage Ave
  5 Burnley BB12 126 B8
  Caton LA2 237 C3
  Cleveleys FY5 175 D3
Vicarage Cl
  Adlington PR6 31 A8
  Burton-in-K LA6 240 C7
  Euxton PR7 60 D3
  Formby L37 11 D4
  Fulwood PR2 117 F4
  Lytham St Anne's FY8 89 F7
  2 Morecambe LA3 217 C2
  Ormskirk L40 16 B3
  Wrea Green PR4 113 B4
Vicarage Ct BB3 82 A3
Vicarage Dr BB3 65 C8
Vicarage Fold BB7 144 F7
Vicarage Gdns L40 25 D4
Vicarage La
  Accrington BB5 104 E1
  Banks PR9 54 F7
  Blackpool FY4 130 E1
Vicarage La *continued*
  Burton-in-K LA6 240 C7
  Churchtown PR3 181 A2
  Fulwood PR2 117 F4
  Newton-w-S PR4 115 A3
  Ormskirk L40 16 C3
  Rawtenstall BB4 85 F2
  Samlesbury PR5 119 E1
  Wilpshire BB1 122 F6
Vicarage Rd
  Barnoldswick BB18 196 C3
  Blackrod BL6 31 D2
  Formby L37 11 D4
  Kelbrook BB18 195 A6
  Nelson BB9 148 D7
  Orrell WN5 10 D4
  Poulton-le-F FY6 153 E3
Vicarage Rd W BL6 31 C2
Vicarage St 3 PR6 61 D1
Vicarage Wlk L39 15 E5
Vicar La LA6 241 C2
Vicarsfields Rd PR25 60 A7
Vicar St
  Blackburn BB1 101 F5
  Great Harwood BB6 124 C4
Viceroy Ct 3 PR8 35 A6
Vickers Dr WN8 9 E8
Vickers Ind Est LA3 217 C2
Vickers Way LA3 217 E2
Victor Ave LA4 217 E6
Victoria Apartments 20 BB12 146 C1
Victoria Ave
  Accrington BB5 104 D2
  2 Blackburn BB2 80 E8
  Brierfield BB9 148 B6
  Chatburn BB7 190 E5
  Lancaster LA1 214 F5
Victoria Bldgs
  Darwen BB3 82 E3
  Formby L37 11 E5
  9 Low Bentham LA2 239 B8
  1 Preston PR1 96 F7
Victoria Bridge Rd PR8 35 C6
Victoria Bsns & Ind Ctr BB5 104 B4
Victoria Cl BB7 144 A7
Victoria Cross 4 BB1 101 E6
Victoria Ct
  7 Blackburn BB1 101 E5
  Broughton PR3 137 C2
  Chatburn BB7 190 D5
  Croston PR26 58 B3
  Fulwood PR2 117 E3
  Horwich BL6 32 C3
  Padiham BB12 126 E7
  Skelmersdale WN8 17 D1
  4 Southport PR8 34 F4
Victoria Dr BB4 85 B2
Victoria Gdns BB9 170 C2
Victoria Lo BB12 145 D2
Victoria Mans
  Blackpool FY3 131 A6
  Preston PR2 96 A7
Victoria Mews
  7 Clitheroe BB7 166 D7
  9 Earby BB18 197 B2
  Morecambe LA4 217 C6
  Southport PR9 35 D7
Victoria Mill BB18 197 B2
Victorian Lanterns BL9 50 C2
Victoria Par
  Morecambe LA4 217 C6
  Preston PR2 117 B1
  7 Rawtenstall BB4 69 E8
Victoria Park Ave
  Leyland PR25 59 D7
  Preston PR2 116 D1
Victoria Park Dr PR2 116 D1
Victoria Pk WN8 17 C1
Victoria Pl
  Halton LA2 219 C6
  6 Lancaster LA1 214 F7
Victoria Quay PR2 96 A7
Victoria Rd
  Barnoldswick BB18 196 C2
  Earby BB18 197 B2
  Formby L37 11 D5
  Fulwood PR2 118 A4
  Horwich BL6 32 C2
  Ince Blundell L38 3 E3
  Kirkham PR4 113 F5
  Lytham St Anne's FY8 89 F5
  Ormskirk L39 15 C2
  Padiham BB12 126 E7
  Pleasington BB2 100 C1
  Poulton-le-F FY6 153 E4
  Preston PR5 97 D5
Victoria Rd E FY5 176 B1
Victoria Rd W FY5 175 E2
Victoria Sq FY5 175 D2
Victoria St
  Accrington BB5 104 B5
  Bacup OL13 70 D8
  Bamber Bridge PR5 77 B8
  Barrowford BB9 170 D3
  25 Blackburn BB1 101 E5
  Blackpool FY1 130 B5
  Blackrod BL6 31 D2
  1 Burnley BB11 127 F5
  Burscough Bridge L40 25 E5
  Carnforth LA5 223 D1
  Chorley PR7 43 D7
  Church BB5 103 E6
  Clayton-le-M BB5 124 F2
  Clitheroe BB7 166 D7
  22 Darwen BB3 82 A1
  7 Earby BB18 197 B2
Victoria St *continued*
  Fleetwood FY7 199 B5
  Great Harwood BB6 124 D5
  Haslingden BB4 85 A3
  Longridge PR3 140 A7
  Lytham St Anne's FY8 91 C3
  Morecambe LA4 217 A5
  Nelson BB9 148 D8
  Oswaldtwistle BB5 103 D3
  Preston PR1 117 E1
  Ramsbottom BL0 50 B6
  Rawtenstall, Lower Cloughfold BB4 86 C1
  Rawtenstall, Waterfoot BB4 69 E8
  Rishton BB1 124 B1
  22 Rochdale OL12 52 F1
  Southport PR9 35 B8
  Todmorden OL14 109 C1
  Wheelton PR6 62 A7
  Whitworth OL12 52 C8
Victoria Terr
  Abbey Village PR6 80 B2
  12 Bamber Bridge PR5 77 A8
  Billington BB7 144 A4
  Calder Vale PR3 182 E8
  2 Chorley PR6 61 D1
  Glasson LA2 209 F5
  5 Leyland PR25 60 A8
  Mellor Brook BB2 121 C3
  Tockholes BB3 80 F2
  Wheelton PR6 62 A7
Victoria Way
  Formby L37 11 D5
  Rawtenstall BB4 86 C2
  Southport PR8 34 F7
Victoria Wharf LA1 218 C1
Victoria Works Ind Est BB11 127 B5
Victor St BB5 124 F3
Victory Ave PR9 36 A7
Victory Bvd FY8 91 D3
Victory Cl BB9 148 E8
Victory Ctr The 2 BB9 148 E8
Victory Rd FY1 130 C6
Victrex Rd FY5 176 D4
Viewfield Mews BB2 101 B5
View Rd BB3 81 E5
View St PR7 41 C7
Vihiers Cl BB7 144 C6
Viking Cl PR8 35 A4
Viking Way LA3 212 F5
Village Cl WN8 8 D8
Village Croft PR7 60 D3
Village Ct OL12 71 C1
Village Dr PR2 118 F2
Village Green La PR2 116 F6
Village Row PR8 21 C5
Village The FY6 154 E1
Village Way
  Blackpool FY2 152 D5
  Hightown L38 2 F4
  Skelmersdale WN8 8 D8
Villas Ct LA1 214 E7
Villas Rd L31 6 B2
Villas The PR4 116 E5
Villa Way PR3 181 C6
Villiers Ct PR1 117 E2
Villiers St
  Burnley BB11 127 C5
  Bury BL9 33 A3
  Padiham BB12 126 D7
  Preston, Maudlands PR1 117 D2
  Preston PR1 117 E2
Vincent Ct BB2 81 D8
Vincent Rd BB9 148 F8
Vincent St
  Blackburn BB2 81 D8
  Colne BB8 171 F6
  8 Lancaster LA1 215 A7
Vincit St BB10 128 C8
Vine Ct FY2 152 C1
Vinery The PR4 75 F8
Vine St
  6 Accrington BB5 104 A6
  Brierfield BB9 148 B5
  Chorley PR7 61 C1
  Lancaster LA1 214 F6
  Oswaldtwistle BB5 103 C3
  Preston PR1 96 D8
  Ramsbottom BL0 50 A4
Viola Cl WN6 29 D2
Violet Ct BB1 101 F6
Violet St BB10 148 A1
Virginia Ave L31 5 D3
Virginia Gr L31 5 C3
Virginia St PR8 35 C6
Viscount Ave BB3 82 A6
Viscount Dr LA1 214 E4
Vivary Way BB8 171 B5
Vivian Dr PR8 35 A2
Vulcan Rd PR4 114 B1
Vulcan St
  4 Nelson BB9 170 F1
  Southport PR9 35 C7

## W

Wackersall Rd 3 BB8 171 B3
WADDINGTON 189 C4
Waddington Ave BB10 128 D6
Waddington Ct FY8 90 C6

Waddington Hospl (Almshouses) BB7 189 B5
Waddington Rd
Accrington BB5 104 D6
Clitheroe BB7 189 E1
Fulwood PR2 119 A2
Lytham St Anne's FY8 90 C7
West Bradford BB7 189 D5
Waddington St
Earby BB18 197 B2
3 Padiham BB12 126 D8
Waddington & West Bradford CE Prim Sch BB7 189 C5
Waddow Gn BB7 166 C8
Waddow Gr BB7 189 C4
Waddow View BB7 189 B4
Wade Brook Rd PR26 58 F6
WADE HALL 59 E7
Wades Croft PR4 93 C6
Wades Ct FY3 152 F1
Wade St BB12 146 D1
Wadham Rd PR1 97 B6
Wagon Rd LA2, PR3 226 B8
Wagstaff Cl BB2 81 C8
Waidshouse Cl BB9 148 E6
Waidshouse Rd BB9 148 E6
Wain Ct BB2 101 B4
Waingap Cres OL12 52 D8
Waingap Rise OL12 52 F4
Waingap View OL12 52 D7
Waingate
Grimsargh PR2 139 C1
Rawtenstall BB4 86 B3
Waingate Cl BB4 86 B3
Waingate Ct PR2 139 C1
Waingate La BB4 86 B3
Waingate Rd BB4 86 B3
Waitholme La LA5 240 A7
Wakefield Ave LA4 217 D6
Wakefield Dr LA1 215 A4
Wakefield Rd FY2 152 E4
Walden Rd BB1 122 F4
Waldon St PR1 97 E8
Waldron WN8 8 D8
Walesby Pl FY8 90 D5
Wales Rd BB4 86 F1
Wales Terr BB4 86 F1
Walgarth Dr PR7 43 B7
Walkdale PR4 95 D2
Walkden Barn Cotts BB5 103 A1
Walkden Cotts L39 1 E8
Walker Ave 1 BB5 104 A4
Walker Cl L37 11 F2
WALKER FOLD 164 C8
Walker Gr LA3 212 F7
Walker La PR2 117 B6
Walker Office Pk BB1 82 C8
Walker Park Ind Est BB1 82 C7
Walker Pl PR1 97 B7
Walker Rd BB1 82 C7
Walkers Hill FY4 111 A7
WALKER'S HILL 111 A7
Walkers Ind Est LA3 212 F3
Walker St
Blackburn BB1 101 F4
Blackpool FY1 130 B6
Clitheroe BB7 166 F8
Preston PR1 96 F8
Walker Way FY5 176 B4
WALK MILL 107 F8
Walk Mill Pl BB10 128 E1
Walk The
Hesketh Bank PR4 73 C4
Southport PR8 35 A5
Wallace Hartley Mews 1 BB8 171 D5
Wallace La PR3 207 C4
WALLBANK 52 B7
Wallbank Dr OL12 52 C7
Wallbrook Ave WN5 10 D1
Wallcroft St WN8 8 E8
Walleach Farm Cvn Pk BL7 48 E6
Walled Garden The PR6 61 B6
Wallend Rd PR2 95 D7
Waller Ave FY2 152 C5
Waller Hill BB8 194 D1
Wallets Wood Ct PR7 43 A5
Walletts Rd PR7 43 B6
Walling's La LA5 224 B4
Wall La PR3 155 E5
Wall St
Blackpool FY1 130 C7
Newchurch BB4 86 E2
Wallstreams Ct BB10 129 B5
Wallstreams La BB10 129 B5
Wallsuches BL6 32 F4
WALMER BRIDGE 74 F5
Walmer Ct PR8 34 F4
Walmer Gn PR4 74 F5
Walmer Rd
Lytham St Anne's FY8 89 F8
Southport PR8 35 A3
Walmersley Old Rd BL9 50 F2
Walmersley Rd BL9 50 E2
Walmsgate BB18 196 B2
Walmsley Ave BB1 103 B8
Walmsley Bridge La
Bilsborrow PR3 159 E8
Claughton PR3 182 E1
Walmsley Brow BB7 144 B4
Walmsley CE Prim Sch BL7 47 E1
Walmsley Cl
Church BB5 103 E6
Garstang PR3 181 C7
Walmsley Ct BB5 124 F1
Walmsley St
Darwen BB3 82 B2
Fleetwood FY7 199 A4
18 Great Harwood BB6 124 C5
Rishton BB1 124 B1
Walney Cl 8 PR2 116 C1
Walney Gdns BB2 101 F1
Walney Pl FY3 131 A7
Walnut Ave
Bury BL9 33 C3
Haslingden BB4 85 C3
Walnut Cl PR1 96 B3
Walnut St
Bacup OL13 87 F3
3 Blackburn BB1 102 A7
Southport PR8 35 C4
Walpole Ave FY4 110 B5
Walpole St
Blackburn BB1 101 F4
9 Burnley BB10 148 B1
Walro Mews PR9 54 A3
Walsden Gr BB10 128 C6
Walshaw La BB10 148 D2
Walshaw St BB10 128 B8
Walsh Fold BL7 48 D2
Walsh St
Blackburn BB2 101 E2
Horwich BL6 32 B4
Walter Ave FY8 111 A2
Walter Pl FY8 111 A2
Walter Robinson Ct FY3 130 D6
Walter St
5 Accrington BB5 104 B6
Blackburn BB1 102 A4
Brierfield BB9 148 B5
Darwen BB3 65 B5
Huncoat BB5 125 E2
Oswaldtwistle BB5 103 D3
Walter Street Prim Sch BB9 148 B5
Waltham Ave FY4 110 D5
Waltham Cl BB5 104 E3
Waltham Ct LA2 219 C7
WALTHEW GREEN 19 C3
Waltho Ave L31 5 E1
Walton Ave
Higher Penwortham PR1 96 B3
Morecambe LA4 217 F5
Walton Cl OL13 88 A1
Walton Cottage Homes BB9 171 A1
Walton Cres BB2 102 A1
Walton Gn PR5 97 C4
Walton Gr LA4 217 F5
Walton Hts 18 BB8 171 D4
Walton La BB9 171 A1
WALTON-LE-DALE 97 D4
Walton-le-Dale Art Coll & High Sch PR5 97 F2
Walton-le-Dale Com Prim Sch PR5 97 D2
Walton's Par PR1 96 E7
Walton St
Accrington BB5 125 A1
Adlington PR7 31 A6
Barrowford BB9 170 E4
Colne BB8 171 D4
8 Nelson BB9 170 E1
Southport PR9 35 C8
WALTON SUMMIT 78 B7
Walton Summit Ctr PR5 78 A6
Walton Summit Rd PR5 78 A7
Walton View PR1 97 D8
Walverden Ave 4 FY4 110 D8
Walverden Cres 3 BB9 148 F8
Walverden Prim Sch BB9 148 F8
Walverden Rd
Brierfield BB9 148 D5
Lane Bottom BB10 149 B4
Walverden Terr BB9 148 F7
Wanes Blades Rd L40 26 E5
Wanishar La L39 14 A5
Wanless Villas BB18 194 D6
Wansbeck Ave FY7 198 D2
Wansbeck Ho FY7 198 D2
Wansfell Rd BB7 166 C7
Wanstead Cres FY4 130 E1
Wanstead St PR1 97 E8
WAPPING 196 A2
WARBRECK 152 D1
Warbreck Ct FY2 152 B1
Warbreck Dr FY2 152 B2
Warbreck Hill Rd FY2 152 D1
Warburton Bldgs 3 BB4 84 F1
Warburton St 1 BB4 84 F1
Warbury St PR1 118 E1
Warcock La OL13 88 B3
Ward Ave
Cleveleys FY5 175 D3
Formby L37 11 D2
Oswaldtwistle BB5 103 C3
Warde St 10 BB9 148 E8
Ward Green Cross PR3 141 A7
Ward Green La PR3 141 A7
Wardle Ct PR6 61 C6
Wardle Dr FY5 175 F3
Wardle St OL13 70 D8
Wardley's La FY6 177 A3
Ward's End PR1 97 A7
Ward St
Bamber Bridge PR5 77 B7
Belmont BL7 46 C5
5 Blackpool FY1 130 B1
Burnley BB11 127 E6
Chorley PR6 43 E7
Great Harwood BB6 124 C5
Kirkham PR4 114 A4
Wareham Cl BB5 125 B1
Wareham Rd FY3 152 F1
Wareham St BB1 102 A7
Warehouse La BB8 194 D1
Warehouse The 7 PR1 117 E1
Waring Dr FY5 176 A2
Warings The
Heskin Green PR7 41 E4
Nelson BB9 148 E6
Warkworth Terr 13 OL13 88 A3
Warley Ave LA3 217 E4
Warley Dr LA3 217 E4
Warley Rd FY1 130 C8
Warley Wise La BB8 195 F3
Warmden Ave BB5 104 E3
Warmden Gdns BB1 102 A7
Warne Pl LA1 218 B1
Warner Rd PR1 118 D1
Warner St
Accrington BB5 104 C5
Haslingden BB4 85 B3
Warpers Moss Cl L40 25 F5
Warpers Moss La L40 26 A5
Warren Ave N FY7 198 F4
Warren Ave S FY7 198 F4
Warren Cl LA2 218 C8
Warren Ct PR8 34 E5
Warren Dr
Barrowford BB9 170 C3
Blackpool FY5 152 E7
Britannia OL13 71 C8
Slyne LA2 218 C8
Warren Fold BB7 142 F8
Warren Gn L37 11 D3
Warren Gr
Blackpool FY5 152 E8
Heysham LA3 212 E5
Warrenhouse Rd L33 1 B4
Warrenhurst Ho 1 FY7 198 F3
Warrenhurst Rd FY7 199 A4
Warren Manor FY5 152 E8
Warren Rd
Heysham LA3 212 E5
Southport PR9 36 A8
Warrenside Cl BB1 123 A4
Warren St FY7 199 B4
Warren The
Blackburn BB2 101 A7
Fulwood PR2 118 E6
Warrington St BB1 102 A8
Warrington Terr BB6 144 D8
Warth La
Ingleton LA6 242 F2
Rawtenstall BB4 69 D8
WARTON
Carnforth 223 D5
Lytham St Anne's 92 D6
Warton Archbishop Hutton's Prim Sch LA5 223 D5
Warton Ave LA3 212 E6
WARTON BANK 92 C4
Warton Crag Nature Reserve* LA5 223 C6
Warton Old Rectory* LA5 223 D5
Warton Pl PR7 43 A8
Warton Rd LA5 223 D2
Warton St
Lytham St Anne's FY8 91 C3
2 Preston PR1 96 E6
Wartonwood View 1 LA5 223 D1
Warwick Ave
Accrington BB5 104 B7
Clayton-le-M BB5 124 F3
Cleveleys FY5 175 F4
Darwen BB3 81 E3
Lancaster LA1 215 A5
Morecambe LA4 217 F6
Warwick Cl
Church BB5 103 F7
Fulwood PR2 117 E4
Ramsbottom BL8 50 A1
Southport PR8 35 B4
Warwick Dr
Barnoldswick BB18 196 F1
Brierfield BB9 148 D5
Clitheroe BB7 189 F2
Padiham BB12 126 D7
Warwick Pl
Fleetwood FY7 199 A5
Normoss FY3 131 B8
Warwick Rd
Bamber Bridge PR5 97 D4
Blackpool FY3 130 D7
Eccleston PR7 41 C7
Leyland PR25 59 E7
Lytham St Anne's FY8 89 F6
Warwick St
Adlington PR7 30 F6
Church BB5 103 F7
Haslingden BB4 85 B3
Warwick St *continued*
Longridge PR3 140 A8
Nelson BB9 148 E7
Preston PR1 96 F8
Southport PR8 35 B4
Wasdale Ave
Blackburn BB1 102 C3
Maghull L31 5 F2
Wasdale Cl
Leyland PR25 60 B6
Padiham BB12 146 C1
Wasdale Gr PR3 139 F5
Wasdale Rd FY4 111 A8
Washbrook Cl BB7 166 D1
Washbrook Way L39 15 E4
Washburn Ct LA3 217 F2
Washington Ave
Blackpool FY2 152 E2
3 Morecambe LA4 217 B5
Washington Cl LA1 214 D7
Washington Ct FY2 152 E2
Washington Dr LA5 223 E6
Washington Hall Fire Brigade Training Ctr PR7 60 F2
Washington La PR7 60 F2
Washington St BB5 104 C6
Wash La BL9 33 B2
Waste La LA2 226 C7
Wastwater Dr 4 LA4 217 E4
Watchyard La L37 12 A4
WATER 87 A8
WATERBARN 70 A8
Waterbarn La OL13 70 B8
Waterbarn St BB10 148 B1
Waterdale FY2 152 E5
WATERFALL 101 C2
Waterfall Mills BB2 101 B2
Waterfall Terr BL7 46 C5
Waterfield Ave BB3 65 B6
Water Fold BB4 87 A8
Waterfold Bsns Pk BL9 33 B1
Waterfold La BL9 33 C1
WATERFOOT 69 E8
Waterfoot Ave
Blackpool FY3 130 E6
Southport PR8 21 B3
Waterfoot Bsns Ctr 6 BB4 86 F2
Waterfoot Prim Sch BB4 69 F8
Waterford Cl
Adlington PR6 44 A1
Fulwood PR2 118 C5
Waterford St BB9 170 F1
Waterfront 2 BB1 101 F3
Waterfront Marine & Ind Est FY8 91 E3
Water Head PR2 117 B3
Waterhead Cres FY5 152 C6
Waterhouse Gn PR6 61 B7
Waterhouse Nook BL6, PR7 31 A5
Watering Pool La PR5 97 B1
Water La
Edenfield BL0 68 D2
Preston PR2 117 D1
Southport PR9 54 D5
Waterleat Glade FY6 131 E8
WATERLOO 81 B8
Waterloo Cl BB2 81 B8
Waterloo Prim Sch FY4 130 D1
Waterloo Rd
Blackpool FY4 130 D1
Burnley, Burnley Wood BB11 128 B4
Burnley, Fulledge BB11 128 B5
Clitheroe BB7 166 F8
Kelbrook BB18 195 A6
Preston PR2 117 C1
Southport PR8 34 E2
Waterloo St
Accrington BB5 125 A1
Chorley PR7 61 C1
Waterloo Terr PR2 117 C1
Watermans Cl BL6 32 C4
Water Mdws BB2 81 D7
Watermede WN5 10 E3
Waters Edge
3 Blackburn BB1 101 F4
Whalley BB7 144 C4
Water's Edge PR2 116 F3
Waters Edge Gn PR3 181 C6
Waterside FY2 152 D2
WATERSIDE
Brierfield 147 F6
Colne 171 E4
Darwen 82 E3
Waterside LA1 218 D1
Waterside Cl PR3 181 B7
Waterside Ind Est BB8 171 E4
Waterside Mews BB12 126 D8
Waterside Pl LA4 217 B3
Waterside Rd
Colne BB8 171 D4
Haslingden BB4 85 A2
Ramsbottom BL0, BL8, BL9 50 C3
Waterside Terr
10 Bacup OL13 87 F3
Darwen BB3 82 E3
WATERSLACK 224 E6
Waterslack Rd LA5 224 E6
Waters Reach
Cleveleys FY5 175 C3
Lytham St Anne's FY8 90 D3
Water St
9 Accrington BB5 104 C6
Adlington PR7 31 A6
1 Bamber Bridge PR5 97 F2
4 Bolton, Egerton BL7 47 D2
Brindle PR6 78 F5
Chorley PR7 61 C1
Clayton-le-M BB5 124 F5
1 Colne BB8 171 E5
Earby BB18 197 B2
Great Harwood BB6 124 C5
Hapton BB12 126 C4
Lancaster LA1 218 D1
Nelson BB9 148 E8
8 Ramsbottom BL0 50 B5
Rawtenstall BB4 86 A8
Ribchester PR3 141 E3
Whitworth OL12 52 C8
Worsthorne BB10 129 B5
Waterworks Cotts L39 6 F4
Waterworks Rd L39 16 A6
Watery Gate La PR3, PR4 156 D3
Watery La
Darwen BB3 65 B6
Garstang PR3 204 E1
Lancaster LA1 218 B3
Preston, Fishwick PR1 97 E7
Preston PR2 96 B8
Watery Lane Ind Est BB3 65 B6
Watford St 5 BB1 101 E6
Watkin La PR5 77 B7
Watkin Rd PR6 61 B8
Watkins Cl BB9 148 C4
Watling Cl LA3 217 E3
Watling Gate BB6 143 C6
Watling St BL8 49 A1
Watling Street Rd
Fulwood, Brookfield PR2 118 E5
Fulwood PR2 118 B3
Watson Ct FY4 110 D7
Watson Gdns OL12 52 D2
Watson Mews FY4 110 D8
Watson Rd FY4 110 C7
Watson St
Blackburn BB2 101 B2
8 Oswaldtwistle BB5 103 E4
Watton Beck Cl L31 5 F2
Watts Cl L33 1 A4
Watts St BL6 32 C2
Watt St
Burnley BB12 127 C7
Sabden BB7 145 F7
Wavell Ave PR9 36 B7
Wavell Cl
Accrington BB5 104 F1
Southport PR9 36 B7
Wavell St BB12 127 C6
WAVERLEDGE 124 B4
Waverledge Bsns Pk BB6 124 B4
Waverledge Rd BB6 124 B4
Waverledge St BB6 124 C4
Waverley WN8 17 D1
Waverley Ave
Blackpool FY1 130 C8
Fleetwood FY7 198 D3
Waverley Cl
Brierfield BB9 148 D4
Read BB12 145 D1
Waverley Dr
New Longton PR4 75 F7
Tarleton PR4 57 A6
Waverley Gdns PR2 118 E2
Waverley Pl BB2 101 B5
Waverley Rd
Accrington BB5 104 E3
Blackburn BB1 102 F4
Preston PR1 118 D1
Wilpshire BB1 122 E4
Waverley St
1 Burnley BB11 127 E6
Southport PR8 35 A7
Waxy La PR4 93 C7
Wayfarers Arc PR8 35 B7
Way Gate FY5 175 D5
Wayman Rd FY3 130 D6
Wayoh Croft BL7 48 D6
Wayside FY6 199 D5
Way The LA3 217 F3
Weald The PR4 116 D5
Weasel La BB3 81 B2
Weatherhill Cres BB9 148 E5
Weaver Ave L40 25 F5
Weaver's Brow PR6 43 F5
Weavers Cl FY8 90 D7
Weaver's Croft BB7 144 A4
Weavers Ct
Blackburn BB2 101 C5
Buckshaw Village PR7 60 E6
Trawden BB8 172 B2
Weavers Mews BB3 81 F1
Weavers Triangle Ctr The* BB11 127 F5
Webber Ct BB11 127 A3
Webber Rd L33 1 C1
Webb St BL6 32 C3
Weber St BB4 86 D1
Webster Ave FY4 110 E7
Webster Gdns PR4 75 A4
Webster Gr LA4 218 A6
Webster St PR2 117 C1
Wedgewood Rd BB5 125 F1
Wedgwood Ct FY8 90 A7
WEETON 132 F2

Weeton Ave
Blackpool FY4 110 E5
Cleveleys FY5 175 D3
Lytham St Anne's FY8 90 A8
WEETON CAMP 132 D5
Weeton Pl 4 PR2 116 E1
Weeton Prim Sch PR4 132 E6
Weeton Rd
Great Plumpton PR4 112 F7
Kirkham PR4 113 C8
Weeton Camp FY6, PR4 132 E7
Weeton PR4 132 F2
Weeton St Michael's CE Prim Sch PR4 132 E1
Weets View BB18 196 C3
Weind The PR3 156 B5
WEIR 88 A7
Weir Bottom OL13 88 A7
Weirden Cl PR1 96 C1
Weir La OL13 88 A7
Weir St BB2 101 E4
Welbeck Ave
Blackburn BB1 102 B8
Blackpool FY4 130 E1
Fleetwood FY7 198 F3
Welbeck Cl 8 PR5 97 E1
Welbeck Gdns FY7 198 F3
Welbeck Ho 4 FY7 198 F4
Welbeck Rd PR8 35 A4
Welbeck Terr PR8 35 A4
Welbourne WN8 17 D1
Welburn Cl WN5 10 E5
Welburn Wlk FY5 176 D2
Welbury Cl 5 BB18 197 B2
Weldale 5 PR8 34 F4
Weld Ave PR7 43 C5
WELD BANK 43 C5
Weldbank La PR7 43 C5
Weldbank St PR7 43 C5
Weld Blundell Ave L31 5 B5
Weld Dr L37 11 D4
Weldon Dr L39 15 F4
Weldon St BB11 127 E5
Weld Par 2 PR8 34 F4
Weld Rd PR8 34 F5
Welland Cl FY2 152 E4
WELL BANK 85 A3
Wellbrow Dr PR3 140 B8
Wellbrow Terr OL12 52 D2
Wellcross Rd WN8 10 B6
Well Ct
Clitheroe BB7 189 F1
Standish WN6 29 E1
Wellesley St BB12 126 F6
Wellfield PR4 94 F1
Well Field BB5 125 A2
Wellfield Ave PR25 76 F1
Wellfield Bsns & Ent Coll PR25 76 F1
Wellfield Bsns Pk PR1 96 D8
Wellfield Dr BB12 127 D7
Wellfield La L40 16 C3
Wellfield Methodist & Anglican Church Sch BB12 127 D8
Wellfield Rd
Bamber Bridge PR5 77 A7
Blackburn BB2 101 C6
Preston PR1 96 D8
Wellfold BB7 166 F8
Wellgate BB7 166 F8
Wellhead BB8 172 B4
Well Head Rd BB12 169 A3
Wellhouse Rd BB18 196 B2
Wellhouse Sq 20 BB18 196 B2
Wellhouse St BB18 196 B2
Wellington Ave PR25 60 B8
Wellington Cl WN8 9 E8
Wellington Ct
7 Accrington BB5 104 C5
3 Burnley BB10 128 B5
Wellington Fold 3 BB3 82 A1
Wellington Mews BL7 48 D4
Wellington Pl PR5 97 D2
Wellington Rd
Blackburn BB2 101 C3
Blackpool FY1 130 B2
Chapeltown BL7 48 D4
Lancaster LA1 215 A5
Preston PR2 117 C1
Wellington St
Accrington BB5 104 C5
Barnoldswick BB18 196 B1
Chorley PR7 61 C1
Clayton-le-M BB5 124 F2
Great Harwood BB6 124 C4
Kirkham PR4 113 F5
Lytham St Anne's FY8 91 D3
16 Nelson BB9 170 D1
Preston PR1 96 D8
19 Rochdale OL12 52 F1
1 Southport PR8 35 A6
Wellington Street St Johns BB1 101 D6
Wellington Terr LA4 217 B5
Well La
Brinscall PR6 62 F7
Haskayne L39 13 E6
Little Eccleston PR3 155 D6
Warton LA5 223 E5
Yealand Redmayne LA5 225 E3
Wellogate Gdns FY4 110 D6
Well Orch PR5 78 B5
Wellow Pl FY8 90 C5
Well St N BL0 68 C2
Well St W 6 BL0 50 B5
Wells Cl
Morecambe LA3 217 B2
Wells Cl *continued*
Thornton FY5 176 A2
Wells Fold Cl PR6 78 C1
Well Springs 2 BB3 82 C1
Wells St
Haslingden BB4 85 B3
9 Preston PR1 118 D1
Well St
Burnley BB12 126 B8
Newchurch BB4 86 F3
Rishton BB1 124 B2
Well Terr 1 BB7 189 F1
Welsby Rd PR25 59 D8
Welwyn Ave PR8 21 E6
Welwyn Pl FY5 175 E1
Wembley Ave
Blackpool FY3 130 E8
Higher Penwortham PR1 96 B5
Poulton-le-F FY6 153 E3
Wembley Ct PR1 96 B5
Wembley Rd FY5 176 B4
Wemyss Cl 1 LA3 212 E7
Wendover Rd FY6 153 A6
Wenlock Cl BL6 32 C6
Wenning Ave
High Bentham LA2 239 D7
Maghull L31 5 E2
Wenning Ct LA3 217 F2
Wenning Pl LA1 218 C2
Wenning St BB9 148 F7
WENNINGTON 241 E1
Wennington Hall Sch LA2 241 E1
Wennington Rd
Southport PR9 35 F7
Wray LA2 238 D6
Wennington Sta LA2 238 E8
Wensley Ave FY7 198 E1
Wensley Bsns Pk BB2 101 B4
Wensley Cl BB11 127 E3
Wensleydale Ave FY3 131 A7
Wensleydale Cl
Maghull L31 5 B2
Thornton FY5 153 D8
Wensley Dr
Accrington BB5 104 D5
Lancaster LA1 218 D3
WENSLEY FOLD 101 C4
Wensley Fold CE Prim Sch BB2 101 B5
Wensley Pl PR2 118 D4
Wensley Rd BB2 101 B4
Wentcliffe Dr BB18 197 B1
Wentworth Ave
Fleetwood FY7 175 D7
Inskip PR4 135 C8
Wentworth Cl
Higher Penwortham PR1 96 A6
Southport PR8 21 C4
Wentworth Cres LA3 217 B2
Wentworth Ct PR4 114 B4
Wentworth Dr
Broughton PR3 137 C3
Euxton PR7 60 D4
Lancaster LA1 215 C7
Thornton FY5 153 D8
Wentworth Mews FY8 90 A6
Wentworth Pl PR3 137 C3
Werneth Cl PR1 96 F1
Wescoe Cl WN5 10 E5
WESHAM 114 A6
Wesham Cross PR4 113 F7
Wesham Hall Cl PR4 114 A6
Wesham Hall Rd PR4 114 A6
Wesham Park Hospl PR4 113 F7
Wesleyan Row BB7 166 E8
Wesley Cl LA2 239 D8
Wesley Ct
3 Fleetwood FY7 199 B5
16 Great Harwood BB6 124 C5
Wesley Dr LA3 212 F7
Wesley Gr 5 BB12 127 D7
Wesley Mews FY4 111 A7
Wesley Pl
Bacup OL13 87 E1
Higham BB12 146 F6
Wesley St
Bamber Bridge PR5 77 F8
Blackburn BB1 101 F7
Brierfield BB9 148 B6
Church BB5 103 F6
Oswaldtwistle BB5 103 E5
8 Padiham BB12 126 D8
Sabden BB7 145 F8
Southport PR8 35 B7
Wesley Terr 1 OL13 88 A7
Wesley Way LA2 239 D8
Wessex Cl
Accrington, Hillock Vale BB5 104 F8
Standish WN1 30 B1
West Ave
Barnoldswick BB18 196 B2
Fulwood PR2 117 A6
Lancaster LA1 211 A6
West Bank PR7 43 C8
Westbank Ave FY4 111 A7
West Bank Ave FY8 90 E3
West Beach FY8 91 A2
Westboro Cl LA3 216 D1
Westbourne BB4 68 A8
Westbourne Ave
Blackpool FY1 130 C1
Burnley BB11 127 D3
Wrea Green PR4 113 B3
Westbourne Ave S BB11 127 E3
Westbourne Ct FY6 199 D5
Westbourne Dr LA1 214 D7
Westbourne Gdns PR8 34 D4
Westbourne Pl LA1 214 D8
Westbourne Rd
Chorley PR7 43 B6
Cleveleys FY5 175 D5
Knott End-on-S FY6 199 D5
Lancaster LA1 214 D7
Middleton LA3 213 A2
Southport PR8 34 D4
Warton LA5 223 C4
WEST BRADFORD 189 F5
West Bradford Rd
Clitheroe BB7 189 F4
Grindleton BB7 190 A6
Waddington BB7 189 C5
West Bridge L31 5 C1
Westbrook Cres PR2 117 A3
Westbury Cl
Blackpool FY5 152 C7
Burnley BB10 148 E2
Westbury Gdns BB1 102 C4
WESTBY 112 E4
Westby Ave FY4 110 E5
Westby Cl FY4 111 D7
Westby Ct FY6 153 D2
Westby Gr FY7 199 B5
Westby Pl PR2 116 F1
Westby Rd
Lytham St Anne's FY8 89 E8
Westby PR4 112 E5
Westby St FY8 91 B3
Westby Way FY6 153 D2
West Cliff PR1 96 E6
Westcliffe BB6 124 B6
West Cliffe FY8 91 C3
Westcliffe Ct PR8 34 F5
Westcliffe Dr
Blackpool FY3 130 E8
Morecambe LA3 217 A2
Westcliffe Gr LA3 217 A2
Westcliffe Rd PR8 34 F5
Westcliffe Residential Cvn Pk LA3 217 A2
Westcliffe Wlk BB9 148 E7
Westcliff Prim Sch FY5 152 C6
West Cliff Terr PR1 96 E6
West Close Ave BB12 146 F5
West Close Rd BB18 196 B3
Westcote St 6 BB3 65 B6
West Craven Bsns Pk BB18 197 B3
West Craven Dr BB18 197 B3
West Craven High Tech Coll BB18 196 C1
West Cres
Accrington BB5 104 B8
Broughton PR3 137 C3
Westcroft PR4 74 E3
West Ct FY5 175 C5
Westdene PR9 53 D1
West Dene WN8 27 B2
West Dr
Clayton-le-W PR25 77 D3
Cleveleys FY5 175 E3
Inskip PR4 135 C8
Kirkham PR4 113 E7
Lancaster LA1 218 B2
Whalley BB7 144 A7
West Dr W FY5 175 D3
West End
Great Eccleston PR3 156 A5
Higher Penwortham PR1 96 B6
WEST END
Morecambe 217 B3
Oswaldtwistle 103 C5
Westend Ave PR7 29 D8
West End Bsns Pk BB5 103 B5
West End La PR4 92 B5
West End Prim Sch
Morecambe LA3 216 F4
Ormskirk L39 15 E7
Oswaldtwistle BB5 103 C5
West End Rd LA4 217 A4
Westend Residential Pk PR4 113 D5
West End Terr PR8 35 A7
Westerdale Dr PR9 55 B5
Westerlong PR2 116 D1
Western Ave
Burnley BB11 127 E4
Leyland PR7 60 D7
Western Ct OL13 70 B8
Western Dr PR25 76 D2
Western Rd OL13 70 C8
West Exchange St 7 BB8 171 D4
Westfield
Bamber Bridge PR5 77 A8
1 Nelson BB9 170 D1
Westfield Ave
Blackpool FY3 153 A1
Fleetwood FY7 198 E2
Normoss FY3 131 B7
Read BB12 145 D1
Westfield Cl BB7 144 A7
Westfield Ct FY5 176 B4
Westfield Dr
Bolton-le-S LA5 221 A6
Fulwood PR2 118 E4
Gregson Lane PR5 98 D1
Leyland PR25 76 E1
Warton PR4 92 F5
Westfield Dr *continued*
West Bradford BB7 189 E6
Westfield Gr LA4 217 A4
Westfield Hamlet LA5 221 C2
Westfield Rd FY1 130 D1
West Field Rd BB18 196 A4
Westfields PR26 58 A2
Westgate
Barnoldswick BB18 196 A1
Burnley BB11 127 E6
Fulwood PR2 117 D5
Leyland PR25 59 F8
Morecambe LA3, LA4 217 C3
Read BB12 145 C1
Skelmersdale WN8 8 D8
Whitworth OL12 52 B7
West Gate FY7 198 D4
Westgate Ave
Morecambe LA3 217 B2
Ramsbottom BL0 50 A2
Westgate Cl OL12 52 B7
Westgate Cvn Pk LA3 217 A2
Westgate Dr WN5 10 D5
Westgate La LA6 242 E5
Westgate Park Rd LA4 217 C3
Westgate Prim Sch LA4 217 B3
Westgate Rd FY8 110 C4
Westgate Trad Ctr 2 BB11 127 F6
West Gdns 1 OL13 70 B8
WEST GILLIBRANDS 8 E8
West Gillibrands Ind Est WN8 8 E8
West Hall La LA6 241 C7
Westham St LA1 215 A7
Westhaven PR9 35 D8
Westhaven Cres L39 15 C1
WESTHEAD 16 D4
Westhead Ave L33 1 A1
Westhead Cl L33 1 A1
Westhead Lathom St James' CE Prim Sch L40 16 E4
Westhead Rd PR26 58 B2
Westhead Wlk
1 Fleetwood FY7 198 F2
Kirkby L33 1 A1
West Hill BB9 170 D4
Westholme Ct PR9 53 C1
Westholme Sch (Boys) BB2 101 A6
Westholme Sch (Lower) BB2 101 A5
Westholme Sch (Middle) BB2 101 A6
Westholme Sch (Upper) BB2 100 E6
Westhoughton Rd PR6, PR7 30 F8
WESTHOUSE 242 E5
West Ing La BD23 231 D5
West La
Downham BB7 191 A4
Formby L37 11 F6
West Lancashire Light Rly* PR4 73 F2
Westland Ave BB3 64 F8
Westlands PR26 59 C7
Westlands Ct FY5 153 B8
West Lane Hill LA2 239 D6
Westleigh Rd PR2 116 F1
West Leigh Rd BB1 101 C8
West Lo FY6 177 C1
West Mdw PR2 116 E3
West Meade L31 5 B2
Westminster Ave LA4 216 F4
Westminster Cl
Accrington BB5 104 E3
Darwen BB3 81 E3
11 Morecambe LA3 217 B2
Read BB12 145 D1
Westminster Dr PR8 21 A4
Westminster Pl
Eccleston PR7 41 A8
Hutton PR4 95 D1
Westminster Rd
Blackpool FY1 130 C8
Chorley PR7 43 C7
Darwen BB3 81 E3
Morecambe LA3, LA4 216 E3
Westmoor Gr LA3 212 E5
Westmoreland Rd PR8 35 D5
Westmoreland St BB9 148 C8
Westmorland Ave
Blackpool FY1 130 D3
Cleveleys FY5 175 D4
Westmorland Cl
Darwen BB3 65 C6
Higher Penwortham PR1 96 B4
Leyland PR25 59 E7
Westmorland Sch PR7 43 C5
Westmorland St BB11 127 D5
West Moss La FY8 111 E1
West Mount WN5 10 F6
Weston Pl 4 FY1 130 D1
Weston St 9 PR2 96 D8
Westover Ave LA5 223 E5
Westover Cl L31 5 C1
Westover Gr LA5 223 E5
Westover Rd
Maghull L31 5 C1
Warton LA5 223 E5
Westover St LA4 217 B5
West Paddock PR25 59 E8
West Park Ave PR2 116 F2
West Park Cl WN8 8 D8
West Park Dr FY3 130 E4
West Park La PR2 117 A2
West Park Rd BB2 101 C6
West Pennine Bsns Pk OL13 87 F5
WEST PIMBO 9 D4
West Pimbo Ind Est WN8 9 D4
West Pk PR9 53 D1
West Rd
Fulwood PR2 117 F3
Lancaster LA1 214 E8
Thornton FY5 176 C3
Westside FY4 110 F8
West Sq PR4 75 A8
West St
9 Blackpool FY1 130 B5
Burnley BB10 128 C8
Chorley PR7 43 C7
Colne BB8 171 E4
Great Harwood BB6 124 C4
Lancaster LA1 214 F5
Morecambe LA3 216 E4
7 Nelson BB9 170 D1
Padiham BB12 126 B8
7 Ramsbottom BL0 50 B5
Rawtenstall BB4 69 E8
Southport PR8 35 A7
West Strand PR1 96 D8
West Street Com Prim Sch BB8 171 E4
West View
Bacup, Lane Head OL13 88 A4
Bacup, Waterbarn OL13 70 B8
Bamber Bridge PR5 77 E7
Blackburn BB2 101 B4
Blackpool FY1 130 C3
Carnforth LA5 223 D3
Clitheroe BB7 166 D7
Elswick PR4 155 F1
Garstang PR3 181 C7
Glasson LA2 209 E5
Grindleton BB7 190 B8
Haslingden, Bridge End BB4 68 A7
Haslingden, North Hag BB4 85 B4
Hollins Lane PR3 207 D2
Holme Chapel BB10 108 A8
Kirkham PR4 113 F7
Longton PR4 75 A8
4 Newchurch BB4 86 F1
1 Ormskirk L39 15 F5
Oswaldtwistle BB5 103 E4
Parbold WN8 27 C2
Preston PR1 118 C2
Ramsbottom BL0 68 C2
Waddington BB7 189 B4
Wheelton PR6 62 A7
West View Ave 8 FY1 130 B2
West View Pl BB2 101 B6
West View Rd
1 Morecambe LA4 217 A5
Whitewell Bottom BB4 86 F5
West View Terr
Billington BB7 144 A4
Padiham BB12 126 C7
1 Preston PR1 96 D8
Tockholes BB3 81 A2
Westway
Burnley BB11 127 D6
Freckleton PR4 93 A6
Fulwood PR2 118 A4
Hightown L38 2 F4
Maghull L31 5 C2
West Way
Chorley PR7 61 A2
Fleetwood FY7 175 D8
Westway Ct PR2 118 B4
Westwell Gr 2 FY1 130 C4
Westwell Rd 4 PR6 61 D1
Westwell St
Darwen BB3 81 E4
14 Great Harwood BB6 124 C5
West Wlk BL7 47 D2
Westwood Ave
Blackpool FY3 130 E4
2 Fleetwood FY7 198 E3
Poulton-le-F FY6 153 E3
Rishton BB1 124 A1
Westwood Cl PR8 35 E3
Westwood Ct BB1 102 A6
Westwood Mews FY8 91 A3
Westwood Prim Sch PR5 78 C4
Westwood Rd
Burnley BB12 127 C8
Clayton Brook PR5, PR6 78 C4
Leyland PR25 77 A2
Lytham St Anne's FY8 91 A3
Westwood St BB5 104 B7
Wetherall St PR2 117 D1
Wetherby Ave FY4 110 B5
Wetherby Ct BL6 32 A4
Wetherfield Cl LA1 218 E4
Weymouth Rd FY3 130 F3
Weythorne Dr BL9 33 F4
WHALLEY 144 B5
Whalley Abbey* BB7 144 B5
WHALLEY BANKS 144 D3
Whalley Banks BB2 101 D4
Whalley Banks Trad Est BB2 101 D4
Whalley CE Prim Sch BB7 144 C5

Whalley Cres
Darwen BB3 82 B1
Staining FY3 131 E5
Whalley Dr
Formby L37 12 A2
Ormskirk L39 6 D8
Rawtenstall BB4 86 A4
Whalley Gdns OL12 52 B1
Whalley Ind Pk BB7 144 D8
Whalley La FY4 111 A8
Whalley New Rd BB1 122 F1
Whalley Old Rd
Billington BB6, BB7 144 B3
Blackburn, Bank Hey BB1 123 B1
Blackburn, Cob Wall BB1 102 A7
Whalley Pl FY8 90 B6
Whalley Range BB1 101 F6
Whalley Range Bsns Pk 14 BB1 101 F6
Whalley Rd
Accrington BB5 104 B7
Bank Lane BL0 50 E7
Barrow BB7 166 D2
Billington BB6, BB7 143 F3
Burnley BB12 126 B8
Clayton-le-M BB5, BB6 124 F5
Clitheroe BB7 166 D5
Heskin Green PR7 41 D4
Hurst Green BB7 165 B1
Lancaster LA1 218 D4
Langho BB6 143 D1
Mellor Brook BB2 121 C3
Read BB12 145 C1
Rochdale OL12 52 B1
Sabden BB7 145 D6
Turner Green BB2, PR5 120 C2
Wilpshire BB1, BB6 123 B7
WHALLEYS 18 B5
Whalleys Rd WN8 18 B5
Whalley St
2 Bamber Bridge PR5 97 F2
Blackburn BB1 101 E6
Burnley BB10 148 A1
5 Chorley PR7 43 C7
5 Clitheroe BB7 166 D8
Whalley Sta BB7 144 B6
Whalley Terr BB3 81 B6
Wham Bottom La OL12 52 D4
Wham Brook Cl BB5 103 B5
Wham Hey PR4 76 A7
Wham La
New Longton PR4 76 A7
Walmer Bridge PR4 75 D4
Whams La LA2 207 D7
Wharfdale Ave BB10 148 B4
Wharfe Ct LA3 217 F3
Wharfedale
Blackpool FY4 110 F7
Galgate LA2 211 B4
Wharfedale Ave
Fulwood PR2 118 E5
Thornton FY5 176 B3
Wharfedale Cl
Blackburn BB2 80 D7
Leyland PR25 60 A7
Wharfedale Ct FY6 153 C3
Wharfedale Rd LA1 214 D8
Wharf Ho 8 BB2 101 B1
Wharf St
Blackburn BB1 101 F5
Lytham St Anne's FY8 91 C3
Rishton BB1 124 C1
WHARLES 134 F4
Wharton Ave FY5 176 D1
Whave's La PR6 79 D4
Wheatacre WN8 8 E8
Wheatcroft Ave BB12 147 D8
Wheatfield PR26 59 A8
Wheatfield Cl 1 FY5 152 F7
Wheatfield Ct 8 LA1 214 E8
Wheatfield St
Lancaster LA1 214 E8
Rishton BB1 124 B2
Wheathead La BB9 170 B8
Wheatholme St BB4 86 B2
Wheat La L40 26 A4
Wheatlands Cres FY3 131 C2
Wheatley Cl
3 Burnley BB12 127 D7
Fence BB12 147 D7
Wheatley Dr PR3 140 B8
Wheatley Gr BB9 170 C3
WHEATLEY LANE 169 F1
Wheatley Lane Methodist Prim Sch BB12 147 E8
Wheatley Lane Rd
Barrowford BB9 170 B2
Fence BB12 147 E8
Wheatsheaf Ave PR3 140 A7
Wheatsheaf Wlk
4 Ormskirk L39 15 E5
Standish WN6 29 D1
Wheat St
1 Accrington BB5 104 A6
Padiham BB12 126 D7
Wheel La PR3 201 A6
WHEELTON 62 A7
Wheelton La PR25 77 A3
Wheelwright Cl BB7 231 B3
Wheelwrights Wharf L40 23 F4
Whelan Cl BB2 81 D7
Whernside FY4 110 F7
Whernside Cl BB18 196 A2
Whernside Cres PR2 118 D5
Whernside Gr LA5 223 F2
Whernside Rd LA1 218 B3
Whernside Way PR25 77 C1
Whewell Row BB5 103 C5
Whimberry Cl 1 PR6 43 E8
Whimbrel Dr FY5 176 A4
Whin Ave LA5 221 B6
Whinberry Ave BB4 86 A1
Whinbrick Cotts PR4 113 B6
Whin Dr LA5 221 B6
Whinfell Dr LA1 215 A3
Whinfield Ave
7 Chorley PR6 61 D1
Fleetwood FY7 198 E2
Whinfield La PR2 96 A8
Whinfield Pl
Blackburn BB2 101 A6
Preston PR2 96 A8
Whinfield St 9 BB5 125 A1
Whin Gr LA5 221 B6
Whin La PR3 155 B8
WHIN LANE END 155 A8
Whinney Brow La PR3 207 C3
Whinneyfield La PR4 136 D2
Whinney Fold LA5 224 B2
Whinney Heys Rd FY3 131 A6
Whinney Hill Rd BB5 125 C1
Whinney La
Blackburn BB2 101 C8
Euxton PR7 60 E3
Langho BB6 143 D1
Mellor BB2 122 B2
Whinny Clough Ct 1 PR2 117 B1
WHINNY HEIGHTS 102 A2
Whinny La FY6 199 E4
Whinnysty La LA3 216 D1
Whinpark Ave FY3 131 A6
Whinsands Cl PR2 118 D5
Whins Ave BB7 145 E7
Whinsfell View LA4 217 B5
Whins La
Read BB12 145 E3
Wheelton PR6 62 A8
Whins The BB7 145 E7
Whipney La BL8 49 E1
Whipp Ave BB7 166 D7
Whitaker Gn 8 BB4 85 E2
Whitaker St BB5 104 B7
Whitbarrow Sq 8 LA1 215 A8
Whitburn WN8 17 D1
Whitburn Rd L33 1 A4
Whitby Ave
Fulwood PR2 116 F5
Southport PR9 54 D6
Whitby Dr BB2 102 A1
Whitby Pl PR2 116 F5
Whitby Rd
Lytham St Anne's FY8 111 A1
Morecambe LA4 217 C5
Whiteacre WN6 29 A2
Whiteacre La BB6 144 E8
White Acre Rd BB5 104 E2
Whiteacres Cl BB11 127 E4
White Ash Est BB5 103 D4
White Ash La BB5 103 D3
White Ash Sch BB5 103 C4
Whitebeam Cl
Cleveleys FY5 175 F5
Higher Penwortham PR1 96 B3
Whitebeck La LA6 240 B4
WHITEBIRK 102 C6
White Birk Cl BL8 49 F2
Whitebirk Dr BB1 102 C8
Whitebirk Ind Est BB1 102 B8
Whitebirk Rd BB1 102 D5
White Bull St 4 BB12 127 C6
White Carr La
Bury BL9 51 A1
Cleveleys FY5 153 A8
Hollins Lane PR3 207 E4
Treales PR4 134 C2
WHITECHAPEL 160 D7
Whitecoats Dr FY8 91 D4
Whitecrest Ave 3 FY5 175 F4
Whitecroft Ave 8 BB4 85 B2
Whitecroft Cl BB4 85 B2
Whitecroft La BB2 121 E2
Whitecroft Mdws BB4 85 B2
Whitecroft View BB5 104 E2
White Cross Ind Est LA1 214 F7
White Cross St LA1 214 F7
WHITEFIELD 148 C8
Whitefield Cl
Hightown L38 2 F2
Rufford L40 39 C3
Whitefield Inf Sch BB9 148 C8
Whitefield Mdw 5 PR5 97 F1
Whitefield Pl LA3 217 C2
Whitefield Prim Sch PR1 96 A4
Whitefield Rd PR1 96 A4
Whitefield Rd E PR1 96 B4
Whitefield Rd W PR1 96 A4
Whitefield St BB12 126 C4
Whitefield Terr BB11 128 B3
Whitefriar Cl PR2 117 A5
Whitegate LA3 217 D3
Whitegate Bsns Ctr LA3 217 D3
Whitegate Cl BB12 126 E7
Whitegate Dr FY3 130 E3
White Gate Fold PR7 42 E3
Whitegate Gdns BB12 126 E7
Whitegate Lo 5 FY1 130 E3
White Gates 5 BL7 47 E1
White Gr BB8 171 C6
Whitehalgh La BB6 143 C1
WHITEHALL 65 B5
Whitehall Ave WN6 19 E8
Whitehall Cl 3 FY8 89 E6
Whitehall La
Blackrod BL6 31 D3
Grindleton BB7 230 A1
Whitehall Rd
Blackburn BB2 101 B7
Darwen BB3 65 A5
Whitehall St
Darwen BB3 65 B5
Nelson BB9 170 F1
Rochdale OL12 52 F1
Whitehaven Cl
Blackburn BB2 102 A1
Southport PR8 21 B3
Whitehaven St 7 BB11 127 E5
Whitehead Cl FY3 131 D5
Whitehead Dr PR26 76 E3
Whitehead St
Blackburn BB2 101 C5
21 Rawtenstall BB4 86 A3
Whitehey WN8 8 E8
Whitehey Rd WN8 8 E8
White Hill Cl OL12 52 D4
Whitehill Rd FY4 111 E6
WHITEHOLME 152 E7
Whiteholme Dr FY6 153 B6
Whiteholme Pl 3 PR2 116 E1
Whiteholme Rd FY5 152 F7
White Horse Cl BL6 32 C5
White Horse La PR3 158 E1
Whitehough Outdoor Education Ctr BB12 169 E6
Whitehough Pl BB9 171 B1
Whitehouse Ave L37 12 A3
Whitehouse La L37 12 A3
White House La
Bescar L40 37 C1
Lane Heads PR3 156 E4
Whitehouse Residential Pk Homes PR3 204 C6
White Lea PR3 204 C1
Whiteledge Rd WN8 9 B6
White Lee Ave BB8 172 C2
White Lee La PR3 183 C2
Whitelees Way FY6 153 D3
Whitelens Ave 4 PR2 116 C1
Whiteley Ave BB2 101 A1
White Leys Cl BB18 196 F1
Whiteleys La L40 16 D2
Whiteley St BB4 85 C1
Whitelow Rd BL0 50 E5
WHITE LUND 217 D2
White Lund Ave LA3 217 C2
White Lund Rd LA3 217 C2
White Lund Trad Est LA3 217 D2
Whitely Gr L33 1 A6
White Mdw PR2 116 E3
Whitemoor Rd BB8 194 C2
Whitemoss OL12 52 B2
Whitemoss Ave FY3 131 B7
Whitemoss Bsns Pk WN8 8 F6
White Moss La FY6 177 E4
White Moss Rd WN8 8 C7
White Moss Rd S WN8 8 D7
Whitendale 8 LA1 218 A2
Whitendale Cres BB1 102 A3
Whitendale Dr
Bamber Bridge PR5 77 F8
Hest Bank LA5 220 F2
Whitendale Hall PR1 117 F1
Whitepits La LA2 239 D5
Whiterails Dr L39 15 D6
Whiterails Mews L39 15 D6
Whiteray Rd 9 LA1 218 B2
White Rd BB2 101 B6
Whiteside Fold OL12 52 A1
Whiteside St 7 FY1 130 C6
Whiteside Way FY5 175 E3
White St
2 Burnley BB12 127 B6
Colne BB8 171 B4
WHITE STAKE 76 B8
Whitestock WN8 8 E8
Whitethorn Cl PR6 78 A2
Whitethorne Mews FY5 153 C8
Whitethorn Mews FY8 111 A2
Whitethorn Sq 4 PR2 116 D1
White Walls Cl BB8 171 A3
Whitewalls Dr BB8 171 A4
Whitewalls Ind Est
Colne BB8 171 A3
Nelson BB9 170 F2
WHITEWELL 228 D2
WHITEWELL BOTTOM 86 F5
Whitewell Cl PR3 181 D3
Whitewell Dr BB7 166 C7
Whitewell Pl 11 BB1 101 F6
Whitewell Rd
Accrington BB5 104 D8
Dunsop Bridge BB7 228 C4
Whitewell Vale BB4 86 F2
Whitewood Cl FY8 90 E4
Whitley Ave
4 Blackpool FY3 130 D5
Cleveleys FY5 175 E5
Whitley Rd WN8 19 D3
Whitmoor Cl 7 LA4 217 B5
Whitmore Dr PR2 119 A2
Whitmore Gr PR2 119 A2
Whitmore Pl PR2 119 A2
Whitpark Gr BB12 127 D7
Whitstone Dr WN8 9 D7
Whittaker Ave FY3 130 E7
Whittaker Cl BB12 127 B8
Whittakers La BB7 189 F8
Whittaker St BB2 101 C5
Whittam Ave FY4 130 E1
Whittam Cres BB7 144 B6
Whittam Ct BB10 129 B6
Whittam Rd
Chorley PR7 43 B5
Whalley BB7 144 B6
Whittam St BB11 127 F5
Whitters La PR3 203 D2
Whittingham Dr BL0 50 C3
Whittingham La
Goosnargh PR3 138 C5
Grimsargh PR2 139 B2
Whittingham Rd PR3 139 F7
WHITTINGTON 241 D7
Whittle Cl BB7 189 F1
Whittle Ct BB12 127 E7
Whittle Dr L39 15 E7
WHITTLEFIELD 127 D7
Whittlefield Prim Sch BB12 127 D7
Whittle Gn PR4 136 E3
Whittle Hill
Bolton BL7 47 E3
Woodplumpton PR4 136 E3
WHITTLE HILLS 61 C8
Whittle La WN6, WN8 27 F4
WHITTLE-LE-WOODS 61 C7
Whittle-le-Woods CE Prim Sch PR6 61 B8
Whittle Pk PR6 78 B2
Whittles St OL13 71 B8
Whittle St
Haslingden BB4 85 A2
Rawtenstall BB4 86 A3
WHITTLESTONE HEAD 65 F4
Whitton Mews 5 BL6 32 B4
Whittycroft Ave BB9 170 E6
Whittycroft Dr BB9 170 E6
Whitwell Ave 4 FY4 110 C5
Whitwell Cl WN6 29 D2
Whitwell Gdns BL6 32 B5
WHITWORTH 71 D1
Whitworth Com High Sch OL12 52 C8
Whitworth Dr PR7 43 A7
Whitworth Heritage Mus★ OL12 71 C1
Whitworth Rake OL12 52 D8
Whitworth Rd OL12 52 F2
Whitworth Sq OL12 52 D8
Whitworth St
Horwich BL6 32 C2
Kirkham PR4 113 F6
Whitworth Water Ski Ctr★ OL12 71 C2
Whitworth Way BB18 196 C4
Wholesome La
Bescar PR9 37 E3
New Longton PR4 75 E5
Whytha Rd BB7 192 D6
Wickentree Holt OL12 52 A1
Wicken Tree Row BB12 145 F3
Wickliffe St 9 BB9 170 F1
Wicklow Ave FY8 91 E5
Wicks Cres L37 11 C4
Wicks Gdns L37 11 D3
Wicks Gn L37 11 C3
Wicks Green Cl L37 11 C3
Wicks La L37 11 D3
Wickworth St BB9 149 A7
Widford Wlk BL6 31 E1
Widgeon Cl FY5 175 F4
Widow Hill Ct BB10 148 D1
Widow Hill Rd BB10 148 D1
Wigan La
Adlington PR7, WN1 30 D7
Chorley PR7 43 E2
Wigan Rd
Bamber Bridge PR5 77 E7
Euxton PR7, PR25 60 C5
Ormskirk L39 16 A5
Skelmersdale WN8 8 F8
Westhead L40 16 E4
Wigeon Row FY8 90 E7
Wiggins La L40 38 B6
WIGGLESWORTH 236 F4
Wight Moss Way PR8 35 D3
Wignalls Mdw L38 2 F3
Wignall St 8 PR1 118 C1
Wigston Cl PR8 21 B4
Wigton Ave PR25 59 D7
Wilbraham St PR1 118 C1
Wilcove WN8 17 F1
WILDERSWOOD 32 D5
Wilderswood Ave BL6 32 C4
Wilderswood Cl PR6 78 C2
Wilderswood Ct BL6 32 C4
Wilding's La FY8 90 B8
Wild La FY4 111 D4
Wildman St
3 Blackpool FY3 130 D7
Preston PR1 117 E2
Wildoaks Dr FY5 153 D8
Wilds Pl BL0 50 B5
Wildwood Cl BL0 50 A4
Wild Wood Rise OL14 109 C1
Wilfield St BB11 127 E6
Wilford St FY3 130 E7
Wilfred Dr BL9 33 B4
Wilfred St BB5 104 C4
Wilfrid's Pl WN6 29 F1
Wilkie Ave BB11 127 E2
Wilkinson Ave FY3 130 E4
Wilkinson Mount 6 BB18 197 B2
Wilkinson St
Bamber Bridge PR5 77 D8
Barrowford BB9 170 C2
Clow Bridge BB11 106 B4
Haslingden BB4 85 B4
Higham BB12 146 F5
Nelson BB9 148 E7
Wilkinson Way
Blackburn BB1 102 C1
Knott End-on-S FY6 199 F5
Wilkin Sq 7 BB7 166 E8
Willacy La PR4 135 E3
WILLACY LANE END 135 E3
Willacy Par LA3 216 E2
Willard Ave WN5 10 D3
Willaston Ave BB9 170 E8
Willerby Way PR3 204 E3
Willey La LA2 206 D6
William Griffiths Ct BB2 101 B2
William Henry St 6 PR1 97 C8
William Herbert St 13 BB1 101 F6
William Hopwood St 8 BB1 102 A4
Williams Ave LA4 218 A6
Williams Dr BB2 102 A1
Williams La PR2 118 C7
Williamson Park Butterfly Ho★ LA1 215 B7
Williamson Rd LA1 215 A8
Williams Pl 2 BB9 148 F8
Williams Rd BB10 128 B8
William St
Accrington, Enfield BB5 125 A1
Accrington, Lower Fold BB5 104 C7
11 Bamber Bridge PR5 77 A8
Blackburn BB2 101 E2
3 Blackpool FY3 130 E7
Brierfield BB9 148 B6
Britannia OL13 71 C8
Carnforth LA5 223 D3
Colne BB8 171 E4
11 Darwen BB3 82 A1
5 Earby BB18 197 B1
Horwich BL6 32 A3
17 Nelson BB9 170 E1
Ramsbottom BL0 68 C1
Whitworth OL12 71 C1
William Thompson Rec Ctr BB11 128 A5
William Young Cl PR1 118 C2
Willis Rd BB2 101 A2
Willis St 6 BB11 127 E5
Willoughby Ave FY5 175 D2
Willoughby St 6 BB1 101 E6
Willow Ave BB4 86 A4
Willow Bank
Bilsborrow PR3 159 A5
Darwen BB3 65 A6
Willowbank Ave FY4 110 E6
Willowbank Cotts PR26 58 B2
Willowbank Ct FY6 153 B5
Willowbank Holiday Home & Touring Pk PR8 21 B2
Willow Bank La BB3 81 F1
Willow Brook
8 Accrington BB5 104 B6
Shirdley Hill L39 23 A6
Willow Chase PR4 113 D4
Willow Cl
Adlington PR6 31 B8
Bamber Bridge PR5 77 A8
Barrowford BB9 170 B1
Clayton-le-M BB5 124 E3
Forton PR3 207 B3
Gregson Lane PR5 98 E1
Higher Penwortham PR1 96 A4
Knott End-on-S FY6 200 A6
Thornton FY5 176 D1
Willow Coppice PR2 116 E3
Willow Cres
Burscough Bridge L40 25 F6
Clayton-le-W PR25 77 D3
Fulwood PR2 118 E2
Willowcroft Dr FY6 177 B1
Willow Ct
Poulton-le-F FY6 154 A3
Standish WN6 29 E2
5 Thornton FY5 176 D1
Willow-Dale FY5 176 D1
Willowdene FY5 175 E1
Willow Dr
Barrow BB6 144 D8
Charnock Richard PR7 42 D3
Freckleton PR4 93 A5
Garstang PR3 204 C1
Kirkham PR4 114 B7
Nelson BB9 149 A8
Poulton-le-F FY6 131 D8
Skelmersdale WN8 17 E1
Wrea Green PR4 113 C4
Willow End L40 25 F4
Willow Field PR6 78 C3
Willow Field Chase PR5 99 B2
Willowfield Rd LA3 213 A7
Willow Gn
5 Ormskirk L39 15 F5
Preston PR2 96 A8
Rufford L40 39 A3

Willow Gr
Blackpool FY3 . . . 153 A1
Formby L37 . . . 11 F4
Goosnargh PR3 . . . 138 D6
Hambleton FY6 . . . 177 B2
Lancaster LA1 . . . 215 B8
Morecambe LA4 . . . 217 F6
Southport PR9 . . . 35 E7
West Bradford BB7 . . . 189 D7
Willow Grove Cvn Pk PR3 . . . 156 A5
Willowgrove Pk FY6 . . . 200 B4
Willowhey PR9 . . . 53 F4
Willow Hey
8 Haslingden BB4 . . . 84 F1
Skelmersdale WN8 . . . 17 F1
Tarleton PR4 . . . 57 A7
Willow La LA1 . . . 214 C7
Willow Lane Com Prim Sch LA1 . . . 214 D8
Willow Lo FY8 . . . 90 C7
Willowmead Pk FY8 . . . 112 F2
Willowmead Way OL12 . . . 52 A2
Willow Mill LA2 . . . 237 C3
Willow Mount BB1 . . . 122 F3
Willow Pk
Oswaldtwistle BB5 . . . 103 C2
Southport PR8 . . . 35 A5
Willow Pl PR4 . . . 155 F1
Willow Rd
Chorley PR6 . . . 61 E2
Wymott PR26 . . . 58 F6
Willows Ave
Cleveleys FY5 . . . 175 E1
Lytham St Anne's FY8 . . . 90 E3
Willows La
Accrington BB5 . . . 104 A3
Kirkham PR4 . . . 113 F5
Willows Park La PR3 . . . 140 B8
Willows RC Prim Sch The PR4 . . . 113 F5
Willow St
Accrington BB5 . . . 104 B6
Blackburn BB1 . . . 102 A7
Burnley BB12 . . . 127 E6
Bury BL9 . . . 33 B2
Clayton-le-M BB5 . . . 124 E3
Darwen BB3 . . . 81 F1
Fleetwood FY7 . . . 199 A4
Great Harwood BB6 . . . 124 C4
Haslingden BB4 . . . 85 B3
Rawtenstall BB4 . . . 69 E8
Willows The
Chorley PR7 . . . 43 B4
Coppull PR7 . . . 29 E8
Kirkham PR4 . . . 113 E4
Lytham St Anne's FY8 . . . 90 E3
Mawdesley L40 . . . 40 C2
Mellor Brook BB2 . . . 121 C3
Southport PR8 . . . 34 F6
Whitworth OL12 . . . 52 C5
Willow Tree Ave
Broughton PR3 . . . 137 D3
Rawtenstall BB4 . . . 85 E2
Willow Tree Cres PR25 . . . 76 D1
Willow Tree Gdns 3 FY5 . . . 176 D1
Willow Trees Dr BB1 . . . 122 C1
Willow Way PR4 . . . 75 F7
Willow Wlk WN8 . . . 18 B4
Wills Ave L31 . . . 5 C2
Willshaw Rd FY2 . . . 152 B1
Wilmar Rd PR25 . . . 77 C2
Wilmcote Gr PR8 . . . 21 B4
Wilmore Cl BB8 . . . 171 C5
Wilmot Rd PR2 . . . 118 E3
WILPSHIRE . . . 122 E5
Wilpshire Banks BB1 . . . 122 F4
Wilpshire Rd BB1 . . . 123 E4
Wilsham Rd WN5 . . . 10 E5
Wilson Cl PR4 . . . 57 A7
Wilson Dr PR4 . . . 155 F1
Wilson Fold BB12 . . . 127 B6
Wilson Fold Ave BL6 . . . 32 F1
Wilson Gr LA3 . . . 212 E8
Wilson's Endowed CE Prim Sch LA6 . . . 237 B8
Wilson Sq FY5 . . . 152 D7
Wilson St
Blackburn BB2 . . . 101 D2
Bury BL9 . . . 33 A1
Clitheroe BB7 . . . 166 E7
Foulridge BB8 . . . 194 D1
Horwich BL6 . . . 32 A4
Wilton Cl
Blackburn BB2 . . . 100 F8
Lancaster LA1 . . . 218 E4
Wilton Ct BB2 . . . 100 F7
Wilton Gr PR1 . . . 96 A4
Wilton Par FY1 . . . 130 B7
Wilton Pl 3 PR25 . . . 77 B1
Wilton St
Barrowford BB9 . . . 170 D3
Brierfield BB9 . . . 148 B5
Burnley BB10 . . . 148 B1
Wiltshire Ave BB12 . . . 127 B7
Wiltshire Dr BB4 . . . 68 B8
Wiltshire Mews PR4 . . . 116 D5
Wilvere Ct FY5 . . . 152 C7
Wilvere Dr FY5 . . . 152 C8
Wilworth Cres BB1 . . . 122 E2
Wimberley Banks BB1 . . . 101 F7
Wimberley Gdns 7 BB1 . . . 101 E6
Wimberley Pl 8 BB1 . . . 101 E6
Wimberley St BB1 . . . 101 E7
Wimbledon Ave FY5 . . . 152 D7
Wimbledon Ct FY5 . . . 152 D6
Wimborne FY8 . . . 89 F5
Wimborne Cl BL6 . . . 32 F1
Wimbourne Pl FY4 . . . 110 B6
Wimbrick Cl L39 . . . 15 D4
Wimbrick Cres L39 . . . 15 D3
Winchcombe Rd FY5 . . . 152 E7
Winchester Ave
Accrington BB5 . . . 104 C7
5 Blackpool FY4 . . . 130 D1
Chorley PR7 . . . 43 E4
Lancaster LA1 . . . 215 B5
Morecambe LA4 . . . 217 D6
Winchester Cl
Morecambe LA3 . . . 217 B2
4 Orrell WN5 . . . 10 F7
Winchester Dr FY6 . . . 153 B6
Winchester Rd
Longshaw WN5 . . . 10 D2
Padiham BB12 . . . 126 D6
Winchester St BB1 . . . 102 A3
Winchester Way 2 PR3 . . . 181 B7
Winckley Ct 12 PR1 . . . 96 F7
Winckley Rd
Clayton-le-M BB5 . . . 124 F2
Preston PR1 . . . 96 E6
Winckley Sq PR1 . . . 96 F7
Winckley St 10 PR1 . . . 96 F7
Winder Garth LA6 . . . 240 B1
Winder La PR3 . . . 207 B2
Windermere Ave
Accrington BB5 . . . 125 D1
Burnley BB10 . . . 148 A2
Clitheroe BB7 . . . 166 C7
Colne BB8 . . . 171 F6
Fleetwood FY7 . . . 175 D8
Leyland PR25 . . . 77 A3
Morecambe LA4 . . . 217 D4
Windermere Cl 4 BB1 . . . 101 F6
Windermere Cres PR8 . . . 21 C3
Windermere Ct 4 LA4 . . . 217 D4
Windermere Dr
Adlington PR6 . . . 44 B1
Darwen BB3 . . . 82 C3
Maghull L31 . . . 5 E2
Rainford WA11 . . . 8 F2
Ramsbottom BL0 . . . 50 C7
Rishton BB1 . . . 124 A1
Windermere Ho PR1 . . . 96 B4
Windermere Rd
Bacup OL13 . . . 88 A3
Blackpool FY4 . . . 110 C8
Bolton-le-S LA5 . . . 221 A4
Carnforth LA5 . . . 221 E8
5 Chorley PR6 . . . 43 E7
Fulwood PR2 . . . 118 C4
Hightown L38 . . . 3 A4
Lancaster LA1 . . . 215 B8
Orrell WN5 . . . 10 F8
Padiham BB12 . . . 146 C2
Preston PR1 . . . 119 A1
Windermere Sq FY8 . . . 110 F2
Windermere St 4 OL12 . . . 52 F2
Windfield Cl L33 . . . 1 A6
Windflower Dr PR25 . . . 77 E3
Windgate
Much Hoole PR4 . . . 74 E2
Tarleton PR4 . . . 57 B5
Windgate Fold PR4 . . . 57 A5
Windham Pl LA1 . . . 218 A3
Windholme 6 LA1 . . . 218 A2
Windle Ash L31 . . . 5 C2
Windle Cl FY4 . . . 110 B4
Windmill Animal Farm* L40 . . . 38 B4
Windmill Ave
Kirkham PR4 . . . 114 C4
Ormskirk L39 . . . 15 F5
Windmill Cl FY3 . . . 131 E5
Windmill Cotts BB2 . . . 121 C1
Windmill Ct 9 LA1 . . . 215 A3
Windmill Cvn Site FY4 . . . 111 E8
Windmill Ho
1 Blackpool FY4 . . . 110 F6
Southport PR9 . . . 53 F2
Windmill Hts WN8 . . . 10 A8
Windmill La PR6 . . . 79 B7
Windmill Pl 3 FY4 . . . 110 F6
Windmill Rd WN8 . . . 9 F7
Windmill St LA1 . . . 214 D8
Windmill View PR4 . . . 114 A6
Windrows WN8 . . . 17 F1
Windrush Ave BL0 . . . 50 A2
Windrush The OL12 . . . 52 C4
Windsor Ave
Adlington PR7 . . . 30 F6
Blackpool FY4 . . . 110 B8
Church BB5 . . . 104 A8
Clitheroe BB7 . . . 166 C7
Fulwood PR2 . . . 117 B2
Haslingden BB4 . . . 85 A1
Lancaster LA1 . . . 215 B5
Longridge PR3 . . . 139 F7
Middleforth Green PR1 . . . 96 C3
Morecambe LA4 . . . 217 A3
Newchurch BB4 . . . 86 E1
New Longton PR4 . . . 96 A1
Thornton FY5 . . . 176 B2
Windsor Cl
Blackburn BB1 . . . 102 B3
Burscough L40 . . . 25 E3
Chorley PR7 . . . 43 B7
Leyland PR25 . . . 59 D7
Ramsbottom BL8 . . . 50 A1
Read BB12 . . . 145 D2
Windsor Ct
Poulton-le-F FY6 . . . 153 E3
Southport PR8 . . . 34 E4
Windsor Dr
Brinscall PR6 . . . 62 E8
Fulwood PR2 . . . 117 D6
Horwich BL6 . . . 32 E2
Windsor Gdns PR3 . . . 181 B7
Windsor Gr LA4 . . . 217 A4
Windsor Lo 3 FY8 . . . 90 D4
Windsor Pl
Barnoldswick BB18 . . . 196 D3
1 Fleetwood FY7 . . . 199 B5
Windsor Rd
Bamber Bridge PR5 . . . 97 D3
Blackburn BB2 . . . 101 B6
Blackburn, Knuzden Brook BB1 . . . 102 E4
Chorley PR7 . . . 43 B7
Darwen BB3 . . . 81 F3
Eccleston PR7 . . . 41 C7
Formby L37 . . . 11 F1
Garstang PR3 . . . 181 B7
Great Harwood BB6 . . . 124 D5
6 Kirkham PR4 . . . 113 F5
Lytham St Anne's, Ansdell FY8 . . . 90 D4
Lytham St Anne's FY8 . . . 90 A5
Morecambe LA3 . . . 216 F3
Normoss FY3 . . . 131 B7
Southport PR9 . . . 35 D7
Up Holland WN8 . . . 10 A8
Windsor St
Accrington BB5 . . . 104 C6
Burnley BB12 . . . 127 C6
Colne BB8 . . . 171 E5
Nelson BB9 . . . 149 A7
Windsor Terr FY7 . . . 199 B5
Windy Bank BB8 . . . 171 E5
Windy Harbour Holiday Ctr FY6 . . . 154 F5
Windy Harbour Rd
Singleton FY6 . . . 155 A4
Southport PR8 . . . 21 E7
Windyhill 36 LA1 . . . 214 F8
Windy Hill LA2 . . . 239 E8
Windy St PR3 . . . 185 E3
Winery La PR5 . . . 97 C5
WINEWALL . . . 172 C4
Winewall La BB8 . . . 172 C5
Winewall Rd BB8 . . . 172 B5
Wingate Ave
Blackpool FY5 . . . 152 D7
Morecambe LA4 . . . 217 C4
Wingate Pl FY5 . . . 152 D8
Wingates 2 PR1 . . . 96 C3
Wingate-Saul Rd LA1 . . . 214 E7
Wingrove Rd FY7 . . . 198 F2
Winifred Ave BL9 . . . 33 F4
Winifred La L39 . . . 6 B8
Winifred St
Blackpool FY1 . . . 130 B4
Ramsbottom BL0 . . . 50 B5
Rochdale OL12 . . . 52 B1
WINMARLEIGH . . . 203 E4
Winmarleigh CE Prim Sch PR3 . . . 203 E5
Winmarleigh Rd
Lancaster LA1 . . . 215 A2
Preston PR2 . . . 117 B1
Winmarleigh St 3 BB1 . . . 102 C5
Winmarleigh Wlk BB1 . . . 102 C4
Winmoss Dr L33 . . . 1 A5
Winnipeg Cl BB2 . . . 101 B8
Winnipeg Ct FY2 . . . 152 E3
Winnipeg Pl FY2 . . . 152 E3
Winscar Wlk FY6 . . . 153 B3
Winsford Cres FY5 . . . 152 C8
Winsford Wlk BB11 . . . 127 B5
Winslow Ave FY6 . . . 153 B5
Winslow Cl 7 PR1 . . . 96 E2
Winsor Ave PR25 . . . 60 B8
Winstanley Coll WN5 . . . 10 F3
Winstanley Gr 1 FY1 . . . 130 C5
Winstanley Rd
Orrell WN5 . . . 10 F3
Skelmersdale WN8 . . . 8 F8
Winster Cl PR5 . . . 98 E4
Winster Ct BB5 . . . 124 E2
Winster Pk LA1 . . . 218 A2
Winster Pl FY4 . . . 131 D1
Winsters The WN8 . . . 17 F1
Winster Wlk LA1 . . . 218 A2
Winston Ave
Cleveleys FY5 . . . 175 F2
Lytham St Anne's FY8 . . . 90 B6
Winston Cres PR8 . . . 35 E2
Winston Rd BB1 . . . 101 D7
Winterburn Rd BB2 . . . 81 C7
Winter Gardens Arc 12 LA4 . . . 217 A5
Winter Hey La BL6 . . . 32 B3
Winter Hill Cl PR2 . . . 119 C7
Winterley Dr BB5 . . . 125 E1
Winterton Rd BB3 . . . 82 A2
Winthorpe Ave LA4 . . . 217 D3
Winton Ave
Blackpool FY4 . . . 131 A1
Fulwood PR2 . . . 117 F6
Winton Gn BL6 . . . 32 F1
Winward Cl BB3 . . . 81 F6
Wiseman Cl LA4 . . . 217 C4
Wiseman St BB11 . . . 127 F6
Wisp Hill Gr LA2 . . . 219 D6
Wisteria Dr BB3 . . . 82 B7
WISWELL . . . 144 F7
Wiswell Cl
Burnley BB10 . . . 148 E2
Rawtenstall BB4 . . . 86 A4
Wiswell La BB7 . . . 144 D6
Wiswell Shay BB7 . . . 144 E7
Witham Cl WN6 . . . 29 D1
Witham Rd WN8 . . . 17 D1
Withens Rd L31 . . . 5 D3
Witherslack Cl 7 LA4 . . . 217 B3
Withers St BB1 . . . 101 F4
Withgill Piggery Cotts BB7 . . . 165 E6
Within Gr BB5 . . . 104 D8
WITHIN GROVE . . . 125 E1
Withington La PR7 . . . 41 E2
Within Lea PR5 . . . 77 E8
Withins Field L38 . . . 2 F3
Withins La L37 . . . 4 A7
WITHNELL . . . 80 B1
WITHNELL FOLD . . . 79 C3
Withnell Fold PR6 . . . 79 C2
Withnell Fold Old Rd PR6 . . . 79 E1
Withnell Fold Prim Sch PR6 . . . 79 C3
Withnell Gr PR6 . . . 61 E1
Withnell Rd FY4 . . . 110 B8
Withy Ct PR2 . . . 117 E3
Withy Grove Cl PR5 . . . 97 F1
Withy Grove Cres PR5 . . . 97 F1
Withy Grove Rd PR5 . . . 97 F1
Withy Par PR2 . . . 117 E4
Withy Trees Ave PR5 . . . 97 F1
Withy Trees Cl PR5 . . . 97 F1
Witney Ave BB2 . . . 80 E8
Wittlewood Dr BB5 . . . 125 B1
WITTON . . . 101 B3
Witton Ave FY7 . . . 198 E1
Witton Ctry Pk* BB2 . . . 100 F4
Witton Ctry Pk Visitor Ctr* BB2 . . . 100 F3
Witton Gr FY7 . . . 198 E1
Witton Par BB2 . . . 101 C3
Witton Park High Sch BB2 . . . 101 A4
Witton St PR1 . . . 97 B8
Woborrow Rd LA3 . . . 212 E8
Woburn Cl BB5 . . . 104 E3
Woburn Gn PR25 . . . 77 B2
Woburn Rd FY1 . . . 130 C7
Woburn Way PR3 . . . 181 D2
Wold The PR6 . . . 62 A3
Wolfenden Gn BB4 . . . 69 F8
Wollaton Dr PR8 . . . 35 F3
Wolseley Cl PR25 . . . 60 A8
Wolseley Pl 20 PR1 . . . 97 A7
Wolseley Rd PR1 . . . 96 E5
Wolseley St
Blackburn BB2 . . . 101 D1
Lancaster LA1 . . . 215 A8
Wolsey Cl FY5 . . . 175 E3
Wolsley Rd
Blackpool FY1 . . . 130 B1
Fleetwood FY7 . . . 198 F4
Wolverton WN8 . . . 8 F8
Wolverton Ave FY2 . . . 152 B2
Woodacre Rd PR2 . . . 119 A2
Woodale Laithe BB9 . . . 170 C3
Wood Bank
Haslingden BB4 . . . 67 F6
Kingsfold PR1 . . . 96 C3
Woodbank Ave BB3 . . . 81 E2
Woodbank Ct 3 FY5 . . . 152 F7
Woodbine Gdns BB12 . . . 127 C7
Woodbine Rd
Blackburn BB2 . . . 101 B6
Burnley BB12 . . . 127 C6
Woodbine Terr OL14 . . . 109 B1
Woodbridge Gdns OL12 . . . 52 C2
Woodburn Cl BB2 . . . 101 A8
Woodbury Ave
Blackburn BB2 . . . 101 D2
Fence BB12 . . . 147 D7
Woodchat Ct PR7 . . . 42 F5
Wood Cl BB9 . . . 170 A5
Wood Clough Platts BB9 . . . 148 A5
Woodcock Cl
Bamber Bridge PR5 . . . 98 A2
Thornton FY5 . . . 176 A5
Woodcock Est PR5 . . . 77 B6
Woodcock Fold PR7 . . . 41 C7
Woodcock Hill Rd BB2 . . . 100 B3
Woodcote Cl L33 . . . 1 A4
Woodcourt Ave BB11 . . . 127 D3
Woodcrest BB1 . . . 122 F5
Woodcroft
Appley Bridge WN6 . . . 19 E6
Skelmersdale WN8 . . . 8 F8
Woodcroft Ave BB4 . . . 85 F5
Woodcroft Cl PR1 . . . 96 C2
Woodcroft St BB4 . . . 85 F5
Wood End
Brierfield BB12 . . . 147 F3
Kingsfold PR1 . . . 96 C1
Wood End Rd PR6 . . . 78 B2
Woodfall PR7 . . . 61 B2
Woodfield PR5 . . . 78 C6
Woodfield Ave
Accrington BB5 . . . 104 D3
3 Blackpool FY1 . . . 130 B2
Rochdale OL12 . . . 52 E2
Woodfield Cl PR1 . . . 96 B4
Woodfield Ct FY5 . . . 176 B1
Woodfield Rd
Blackpool FY1 . . . 130 B2
Chorley PR7 . . . 61 C1
Ormskirk L39 . . . 15 D3
Woodfield Rd *continued*
Thornton FY5 . . . 176 D1
Woodfields
Hurst Green BB7 . . . 165 B3
Simonstone BB12 . . . 145 E3
Woodfield Terr BB9 . . . 148 C5
Woodfield View BB7 . . . 144 C5
Woodfold PR1 . . . 96 B3
Woodfold Cl BB2 . . . 121 C3
Woodfold Hall BB2 . . . 100 B7
Woodfold La PR3 . . . 204 C5
Woodfold Park Farm BB2 . . . 100 B8
Woodfold Pl BB2 . . . 101 B5
Woodford Copse PR7 . . . 43 A7
Woodgate LA3 . . . 217 F2
Woodgate Ave BL9 . . . 33 D4
WOODGATE HILL . . . 33 D4
Woodgate Hill Rd
Bury BL9 . . . 33 C3
Bury, Woodgate Hill BL9 . . . 33 D4
Woodgate Pk LA3 . . . 217 F2
Woodgates Rd BB2 . . . 100 F5
Wood Gn
Kirkham PR4 . . . 114 B7
Leyland PR25 . . . 76 E2
Wood Green Dr FY5 . . . 152 F8
Woodgrove Rd BB11 . . . 128 B3
Woodhall Cres PR5 . . . 98 E4
Woodhall Gdns FY6 . . . 177 C2
Woodhart La PR7 . . . 41 C5
Woodhead Cl
Ramsbottom BL0 . . . 50 C4
Rawtenstall BB4 . . . 87 A2
Woodhead Rd BB12 . . . 145 D2
WOODHEY . . . 50 B3
Wood Hey Gr OL12 . . . 52 F4
Woodhey High Sch BL0 . . . 50 A3
Woodhey Rd BL0 . . . 50 A3
Woodhill Ave LA4 . . . 217 A3
Woodhill Cl LA4 . . . 217 A3
Woodhill La LA4 . . . 217 A4
WOOD HOUSE . . . 229 B8
Wood House La BB7 . . . 229 A8
Woodhouse Rd FY5 . . . 153 E8
Woodhurst Dr WN6 . . . 29 D1
Wood La
Edenfield BL0 . . . 68 D2
Haskayne L37, L39 . . . 13 D1
Heskin Green PR7 . . . 41 E3
Hoscar L40 . . . 26 E5
Mawdesley L40 . . . 40 D5
Parbold WN8 . . . 27 D2
Wrightington Bar WN6, PR7 . . . 28 E8
Woodland Ave
Bacup OL13 . . . 87 F5
Bescar L40 . . . 23 F7
Thornton FY5 . . . 176 B2
Woodland Cl
Hambleton FY6 . . . 177 D1
Wrea Green PR4 . . . 113 B3
Woodland Cres FY6 . . . 200 A6
Woodland Ct BB3 . . . 82 D1
Woodland Dr
Clayton-le-M BB5 . . . 124 F5
Poulton-le-F FY6 . . . 153 E1
Standish WN6 . . . 29 E2
Woodland Gr
Blackpool FY3 . . . 130 E4
Bolton BL7 . . . 47 D2
Higher Penwortham PR1 . . . 96 B5
Woodland Pk BB7 . . . 144 C5
Woodland Pl BB3 . . . 81 F7
Woodland Rd OL12 . . . 52 C2
Woodlands Ave
Bamber Bridge PR5 . . . 98 A2
Blackburn BB2 . . . 100 E1
Fulwood PR2 . . . 118 E2
Kingsfold PR1 . . . 96 E2
8 Kirkham PR4 . . . 113 F5
Woodlands Cl
Blackburn BB1 . . . 102 B4
Formby L37 . . . 11 D2
Newton-w-S PR4 . . . 114 F3
Ormskirk L39 . . . 16 A4
Rawtenstall BB4 . . . 86 D1
Southport PR9 . . . 35 D8
Woodlands Cnr BB1 . . . 101 D6
Woodlands Com Prim Sch WN8 . . . 18 C2
Woodlands Cres PR3 . . . 137 B5
Woodlands Ct 5 FY8 . . . 90 D4
Woodlands Dr
Fulwood PR2 . . . 117 E8
Kirkham PR4 . . . 114 B7
Leyland PR25 . . . 76 F1
Morecambe LA3 . . . 216 E2
Shevington WN6 . . . 19 F4
Silverdale LA5 . . . 224 C4
Warton PR4 . . . 92 C5
West Bradford BB7 . . . 189 D7
Whalley BB7 . . . 144 C5
Woodlands Gr
Darwen BB3 . . . 81 D2
Grimsargh PR2 . . . 139 E1
Morecambe LA3 . . . 216 E2
Padiham BB12 . . . 146 B1
Woodlands Mdw PR7 . . . 43 C3
Woodlands Prim Sch L37 . . . 11 D3
Woodlands Rd
Edenfield BL0 . . . 68 D2
Formby L37 . . . 11 D3
Lancaster LA1 . . . 218 E4

Woodlands Rd *continued*
  Lytham St Anne's FY8 ... 90 D4
  Nelson BB9 ... 148 F8
Woodlands Sch FY3 ... 130 E4
Woodlands The
  Brockhall Village BB6 ... 143 C6
  Garstang PR3 ... 181 B8
  [6] Preston PR2 ... 116 E1
  Ring o'Bells L40 ... 26 A3
  Southport PR8 ... 21 C5
Woodlands View
  Lytham St Anne's FY8 ... 90 D5
  Over Kellet LA6 ... 237 B8
Woodlands Way
  Longton PR4 ... 74 F8
  Newsham PR3 ... 137 B5
Woodland Terr OL13 ... 87 F4
Woodland View
  Bacup OL13 ... 87 F4
  Brinscall PR6 ... 62 F7
  Great Harwood BB6 ... 124 C6
Wood Lark Dr PR7 ... 42 F5
Wood Lea Bank [9] BB4 ... 69 F8
Woodlea Chase BB3 ... 65 C3
Woodlea Cl PR9 ... 54 D5
Woodlea Gdns BB9 ... 148 D5
Woodlea Jun Sch PR25 ... 59 F8
Woodlea Rd
  Blackburn BB1 ... 102 B4
  Leyland PR25 ... 59 F8
Wood Lea Rd BB4 ... 69 F8
Woodlee Rd PR4 ... 73 F2
Woodleigh Cl L31 ... 5 B5
Woodley Ave
  Accrington BB5 ... 104 C4
  Thornton FY5 ... 176 D1
Woodley Park Rd WN8 ... 18 B4
Woodmancote PR7 ... 61 B2
Woodman La LA6 ... 241 F6
Woodmoss La PR8, L40 ... 36 E2
WOODNOOK ... 104 B4
Wood Nook [2] BB4 ... 86 A7
Woodnook Prim Sch
  BB5 ... 104 C4
Woodnook Rd WN6 ... 19 E8
Wood Park Rd FY1 ... 130 E1
Woodpecker Hill [3]
  BB11 ... 127 C5
WOODPLUMPTON ... 136 E2
Woodplumpton La
  PR3 ... 137 C2
Woodplumpton Rd
  Burnley BB11 ... 127 F1
  Fulwood PR2 ... 117 C3
  Woodplumpton, Moor Side
  PR4 ... 136 D4
  Woodplumpton PR4 ... 136 E2
Woodplumpton St Anne's
  CE Prim Sch PR4 ... 136 D2
Woodridge Ave FY5 ... 152 C8
WOOD ROAD ... 50 C1
Wood Road La BL8, BL9 ... 50 C1
Woodrow WN8 ... 8 E8
Woodrow Dr WN8 ... 27 A1
Woodroyd Dr BL9 ... 33 C3
Woodruff Cl FY5 ... 175 F5
Woodrush LA4 ... 217 F6
Woods Brow BB2 ... 120 D5
Wood's Brow PR3 ... 141 B6
Woods Cl L39 ... 14 A4
Woods End PR1 ... 97 B6
Woodsend Cl BB2 ... 82 A8
WOODSFOLD ... 135 E6
Woods Gn PR1 ... 96 E6
Woodside
  Blackpool FY4 ... 111 E7
  Chorley PR7 ... 43 E4
  Euxton PR7 ... 60 C3
  Haslingden BB4 ... 85 C1
  Leyland PR25 ... 77 C4
Woodside Ave
  Clayton Green PR6 ... 78 B1
  Fulwood, Cadley PR2 ... 117 E4
  Fulwood, Ribbleton PR2 ... 118 E3
  New Longton PR4 ... 75 F7
  Rishton BB1 ... 102 F8
  Southport PR8 ... 21 B3
Woodside Cl
  Huncoat BB5 ... 125 F1
  Up Holland WN8 ... 10 C8
Woodside Cres BB4 ... 86 D1
Woodside Dr
  Blackpool FY3 ... 131 A5
  Ramsbottom BL0 ... 50 A5
Woodside Gr BB2 ... 81 A8
Woodside Pk FY6 ... 200 D1
Woodside Pk Cvn Pk
  FY6 ... 200 D1
Woodside Rd
  Accrington, Hillock Vale
  BB5 ... 104 E8
  Huncoat BB5 ... 125 F1
  Simonstone BB12 ... 145 E2
Woodside Terr BB9 ... 148 C8
Woods La PR3, PR4 ... 135 E8
Wood's La PR3 ... 180 A6
Woodsley St BB12 ... 127 B5
Wood St
  Blackpool FY1 ... 130 B5
  Brierfield BB9 ... 148 B5
  Burnley BB10 ... 128 A8
  Church BB5 ... 103 E5
  Colne BB8 ... 171 E4
  Darwen BB3 ... 81 F1
  Fleetwood FY7 ... 175 E8
  Great Harwood BB6 ... 124 E5
  Hapton BB12 ... 126 C4
  Horwich BL6 ... 32 C3
  [1] Lancaster LA1 ... 214 F8
  Lytham St Anne's FY8 ... 89 E6
  Poulton-le-F FY6 ... 154 A3
  Ramsbottom BL0 ... 50 B5
Woodstock Ave FY5 ... 153 C8
Woodstock Cl [8] PR5 ... 77 C8
Woodstock Cres BB2 ... 80 E8
Woodstock Dr PR8 ... 21 F8
Woodstock Gdns FY4 ... 110 B7
Woodstock St [12] OL12 ... 52 C1
Wood Street Livesey Fold
  [9] BB3 ... 81 F2
Wood Terr
  Chatburn BB7 ... 190 E5
  Simonstone BB12 ... 145 F2
Woodtop [1] BB11 ... 127 D5
WOOD TOP ... 85 E1
WOODVALE ... 21 B2
Woodvale
  Darwen BB3 ... 81 F1
  Leyland PR26 ... 59 A8
Woodvale Ct PR9 ... 55 A5
Woodvale Rd
  Clayton Green PR6 ... 78 B3
  Southport PR8 ... 21 D2
Wood View
  Blackburn BB2 ... 100 F1
  Burton in L LA6 ... 242 C3
Wood View La FY6 ... 177 C7
Woodville Rd
  Adlington PR6 ... 43 F1
  Blackburn BB1 ... 102 A7
  Brierfield BB9 ... 148 C6
  [2] Chorley PR7 ... 43 C8
  Kingsfold PR1 ... 96 D2
Woodville Rd W [5] PR1 ... 96 C2
Woodville St
  Lancaster LA1 ... 215 A8
  Leyland PR25 ... 77 B2
Woodville Terr
  Darwen BB3 ... 65 B6
  Lytham St Anne's FY8 ... 90 F3
Woodward Rd L33 ... 1 D4
Woodway PR2 ... 117 C4
Woodwell La LA5 ... 224 C1
Wookey Cl PR2 ... 118 D6
Wooley La BB5 ... 104 F2
Woolman Rd FY1 ... 130 C4
Woolpack BB8 ... 171 E3
Woolwich St BB1 ... 102 B5
Woone La BB7 ... 166 D7
Worcester Ave
  [4] Accrington BB5 ... 104 A7
  Garstang PR3 ... 181 B8
  Lancaster LA1 ... 215 B5
  Leyland PR25 ... 60 B8
Worcester Gdns PR4 ... 116 D5
Worcester Pl PR7 ... 43 E3
Worcester Rd
  Blackburn BB1 ... 102 C5
  Blackpool FY3 ... 131 A3
Worden Brook Cl PR7 ... 60 E6
Worden Cl PR25 ... 59 F7
Worden La PR25 ... 60 A7
Worden Pk★ PR25 ... 59 F7
Worden Rd PR2 ... 117 D3
Worden Sp Coll PR25 ... 76 E1
Wordens The PR25 ... 60 B7
Wordsworth Ave
  Blackpool FY3 ... 131 B2
  Bolton-le-S LA5 ... 221 A5
  Longshaw WN5 ... 10 D1
  [5] Lytham St Anne's FY8 ... 91 D4
  Orrell WN5 ... 10 F6
  Padiham BB12 ... 126 E7
  Thornton FY5 ... 176 A2
  Warton PR4 ... 92 E6
Wordsworth Cl
  Ormskirk L39 ... 15 D6
  Oswaldtwistle BB5 ... 103 C4
Wordsworth Ct [1] FY8 ... 90 C4
Wordsworth Dr BB6 ... 124 B4
Wordsworth Gdns BB3 ... 82 B1
Wordsworth Ho LA1 ... 218 C4
Wordsworth Pl PR5 ... 97 D2
Wordsworth Rd
  Accrington BB5 ... 104 A4
  Colne BB8 ... 171 D5
Wordsworth St
  Burnley, Harle Syke
  BB10 ... 148 F2
  Burnley, Whittlefield
  BB12 ... 127 C6
  [5] Hapton BB12 ... 126 C4
Wordsworth Terr PR6 ... 61 D2
Workshop Rd LA3 ... 212 F2
Worrall St [1] OL12 ... 52 D2
Worsicks Cotts FY6 ... 154 E1
Worsley Ave FY4 ... 110 C7
Worsley Cl FY6 ... 199 E5
Worsley Ct [13] BB5 ... 103 E4
Worsley Rd FY8 ... 90 C5
Worsley St
  Accrington BB5 ... 104 D4
  Rising Bridge BB5 ... 85 A8
Worsten Ave BB2 ... 101 C1
WORSTHORNE ... 129 B5
Worsthorne Prim Sch
  BB10 ... 129 A6
WORSTON ... 190 D2
Worston Cl
  Accrington BB5 ... 103 F4
  Rawtenstall BB4 ... 86 A4
Worston La BB6 ... 124 F6
Worston Pl BB2 ... 101 C5
Worswick Cres [3] BB4 ... 86 A2
Worswick Gn BB4 ... 86 B2
Worthalls Rd BB12 ... 145 D1
Worthing Cl PR8 ... 34 F3
Worthing Rd PR2 ... 117 A4
Worthington Rd FY4 ... 111 B4
Worthy St PR6 ... 43 E7
Wove Ct PR1 ... 117 E2
Wraith St BB3 ... 65 A8
WRANGLING THE ... 101 D3
WRAY ... 238 D6
Wray Cres
  Wrea Green PR4 ... 113 C4
  Wymott PR26 ... 58 F6
Wray Ct LA1 ... 218 C4
Wray Gr FY5 ... 152 D8
WRAYTON ... 241 E3
Wray with Botton Endowed
  Prim Sch LA2 ... 238 D6
Wraywood Ct FY7 ... 198 C1
WREA GREEN ... 113 B3
Wren Ave PR1 ... 96 E5
Wren Cl
  Carleton FY6 ... 153 A4
  Thornton FY5 ... 153 D8
Wren Dr BL9 ... 33 B4
Wren Gr FY3 ... 130 E2
Wrennalls La PR7 ... 41 B5
Wren St
  Burnley BB12 ... 127 C6
  Nelson BB9 ... 148 F8
  Preston PR1 ... 118 B2
WRIGHTINGTON ... 28 D4
WRIGHTINGTON BAR ... 28 F7
Wrightington Hospl
  WN6 ... 28 D2
Wrightington Mossy Lea
  Prim Sch WN6 ... 28 F6
Wright St W [3] BL6 ... 32 B4
Wrights Fold PR25 ... 60 C8
Wright St
  Chorley PR6 ... 43 E8
  Horwich BL6 ... 32 B4
  [6] Kirkham PR4 ... 113 F6
  Southport PR9 ... 35 C7
  [9] Weir OL13 ... 88 A7
Wrights Terr PR8 ... 35 B3
Wrigleys Cl L37 ... 11 F5
Wrigleys La L37 ... 11 F5
Written Stone La PR3 ... 162 E1
Wroxham Cl BB10 ... 148 D2
Wroxton Cl FY5 ... 152 F7
Wycherley Rd OL12 ... 52 B2
Wychnor PR2 ... 117 B7
Wycollar Cl BB5 ... 104 C4
Wycollar Dr BB2 ... 101 A6
Wycollar Rd BB2 ... 101 B6
WYCOLLER ... 173 A3
Wycoller Ave BB10 ... 128 D5
Wycoller Ctry Pk★
  BB8 ... 173 B3
Wycombe Ave FY4 ... 110 B6
Wyfordby Ave BB2 ... 101 A7
Wyke Cop Rd PR8, PR9 ... 36 D2
Wykeham Gr OL12 ... 52 B1
Wykeham Rd PR8 ... 91 B4
Wyke La PR8, PR9 ... 36 E6
Wyke Wood La PR9 ... 36 F7
Wyllin Rd L33 ... 1 A2
WYMOTT ... 58 F6
Wymundsley PR7 ... 61 A2
Wyndene Cl PR3 ... 140 C8
Wyndene Gr PR4 ... 93 B6
Wyndham Gdns FY4 ... 110 D6
Wyndham Pl LA4 ... 217 F6
Wynfield PR5 ... 97 F2
Wynnstay Ave L31 ... 5 D3
Wynnwood Ave [1]
  FY1 ... 130 D8
Wynotham St BB10 ... 148 C1
Wyre Ave PR4 ... 114 B5
Wyre Bank PR3 ... 157 B6
Wyre Cl
  Great Eccleston PR3 ... 156 C5
  Morecambe LA3 ... 217 F2
Wyre Cres BB3 ... 81 D4
Wyre Ct
  Fleetwood FY7 ... 198 E3
  Poulton-le-F FY6 ... 154 A3
Wyredale Ct FY7 ... 198 F3
Wyredale Rd FY8 ... 89 C8
Wyre Estuary Ctry Pk★
  FY5 ... 176 E3
Wyrefields FY6 ... 154 A3
Wyre Gr FY1 ... 130 C3
Wyre Ho LA1 ... 214 F7
Wyre La PR3 ... 204 D1
Wyre Rd FY5 ... 153 F6
Wyresdale Ave
  Accrington BB5 ... 104 A8
  Blackpool FY2 ... 152 D4
  [3] Morecambe LA3 ... 216 E1
  Poulton-le-F FY6 ... 153 C3
  Southport PR8 ... 35 D4
Wyresdale Cres
  Fulwood PR2 ... 118 D4
  Glasson LA2 ... 209 E4
  Scorton PR3 ... 204 E7
Wyresdale Ct LA1 ... 215 B7
Wyresdale Dr PR25 ... 60 B6
Wyresdale Gdns LA1 ... 215 B7
WYRESDALE PARK ... 204 F7
Wyresdale Rd
  Knott End-on-S FY6 ... 199 D5
  Lancaster LA1 ... 215 B6
  Quernmore LA2 ... 232 A6
Wyreside PR3 ... 155 E8
Wyre Side Cl PR3 ... 181 C8
Wyreside Dr FY6 ... 177 B2
Wyreside Ecology & Visitor
  Ctr★ FY5 ... 176 E3
Wyreside Hall LA2 ... 226 B7
Wyre St
  Fleetwood FY7 ... 198 F3
  Kirkham PR4 ... 113 F6
  Lytham St Anne's FY8 ... 90 A7
  Padiham BB12 ... 126 D8
  Preston PR2 ... 117 C1
Wyre Vale Pk PR3 ... 204 B1
Wyre View
  [14] Fleetwood FY7 ... 199 B5
  Knott End-on-S FY6 ... 199 E5
Wytham St [6] BB12 ... 126 D7
Wythburn Ave BB2 ... 80 E8
Wythburn Cl BB12 ... 127 B8
Wythorpe Croft LA4 ... 217 B4
Wyvern Way FY6 ... 153 C5

## X

XL Bsns Pk WN8 ... 17 C3

## Y

Yale St BL7 ... 48 D4
Yardley Ctr L33 ... 1 C1
Yardley Rd L33 ... 1 C1
Yare St [7] BB4 ... 69 F8
Yarlside La BD23 ... 231 E4
Yarmouth Ave BB4 ... 85 C2
Yarm Pl BB11 ... 128 A6
Yarraville St BB4 ... 86 A2
Yarrow Ave L31 ... 5 F2
Yarrow Cl
  Croston PR26 ... 58 B2
  Withnell PR6 ... 80 A1
Yarrow Gate PR7 ... 43 E6
Yarrow Gr BL6 ... 32 B4
Yarrow Mill PR6 ... 43 E6
Yarrow Pl PR25 ... 59 D8
Yarrow Rd
  Chorley PR6 ... 43 E6
  Leyland PR25 ... 59 D8
Yarrow Valley Pk★ PR7 ... 43 A2
Yarrow Wlk [5] LA3 ... 217 B2
Yarwood St BL9 ... 33 A2
Yates Fold BB2 ... 101 F2
Yates St
  Blackpool FY1 ... 130 B6
  Chorley PR7 ... 43 B5
Yeadon WN8 ... 18 B1
Yeadon Gr PR7 ... 43 A7
Yeadon Way FY4 ... 110 D7
Yealand Ave LA3 ... 212 F6
Yealand CE Prim Sch
  LA5 ... 225 E3
YEALAND CONYERS ... 225 F1
Yealand Dr LA1 ... 215 A4
Yealand Gr LA5 ... 223 E2
Yealand Rd LA5 ... 225 E2
YEALAND
  REDMAYNE ... 225 E4
YEALAND STORRS ... 225 C5
Yeargate Ind Est BL9 ... 33 D2
Yellow Hall BB18 ... 195 A5
Yellow House La PR8 ... 35 B6
Yenham La LA3 ... 213 E1
Yerburgh Rd BB2 ... 121 E2
Yewbarrow Cl BB12 ... 147 C1
Yew Ct FY7 ... 198 C1
Yewdale WN8 ... 18 A1
Yewdale Ave LA3 ... 212 F6
Yew Gn PR4 ... 114 B7
Yewlands Ave
  [4] Bamber Bridge PR5 ... 97 F1
  Fulwood PR2 ... 117 E6
  Heskin Green PR7 ... 41 F3
  [3] Leyland PR25 ... 77 A1
Yewlands Cres PR2 ... 117 E6
Yewlands Dr
  Burnley BB10 ... 148 B3
  Fulwood PR2 ... 117 E6
Yewlands Dr *continued*
  Garstang PR3 ... 204 C1
  [2] Leyland PR25 ... 77 A1
Yew St
  [10] Blackburn BB1 ... 102 A7
  [2] Bury BL9 ... 33 C3
Yewtree Ave PR2 ... 119 A4
Yew Tree Ave
  Euxton PR7 ... 60 C4
  Grimsargh PR2 ... 139 C2
Yewtree Cl PR7 ... 43 C3
Yew Tree Cl
  Garstang PR3 ... 181 B8
  Newton-w-S PR4 ... 114 F3
  Wilpshire BB1 ... 122 E6
Yew Tree Dr
  Blackburn BB2 ... 122 B1
  Low Bentham LA2 ... 239 C8
  Oswaldtwistle BB5 ... 103 F3
Yew Tree Gdns
  Silverdale LA5 ... 224 C2
  Stalmine FY6 ... 177 C8
Yewtree Gr PR5 ... 77 A7
Yew Tree Gr BB4 ... 68 F8
Yew Tree Rd
  Blackpool FY3 ... 153 A1
  Ormskirk L39 ... 15 E7
YORK ... 123 D8
York Ave
  Cleveleys FY5 ... 175 D2
  Fleetwood FY7 ... 198 E3
  Fulwood PR2 ... 117 E4
  Haslingden BB4 ... 68 B8
  Southport PR8 ... 35 A5
York Cl
  [4] Bamber Bridge PR5 ... 97 D3
  Clayton-le-M BB5 ... 124 F3
  Formby L37 ... 11 F6
  Leyland PR25 ... 59 E7
York Cres BB1 ... 122 F3
York Dr
  Great Eccleston PR3 ... 156 C5
  Kirkham PR4 ... 114 B2
  Ramsbottom BL0 ... 50 A4
Yorke St [2] BB11 ... 127 F5
York Fields BB18 ... 196 B1
York Gdns PR8 ... 35 A5
York Gr PR3 ... 181 B7
York Ho LA1 ... 215 A5
York La BB6 ... 123 D8
York Manor PR8 ... 35 A5
York Pl
  Accrington BB5 ... 104 B7
  Adlington PR6 ... 31 A8
  Morecambe LA4 ... 217 C5
York Rd
  Blackpool FY2 ... 152 B4
  Formby L37 ... 12 A3
  Lancaster LA1 ... 215 A5
  Langho BB1, BB6 ... 123 D6
  Lytham St Anne's FY8 ... 89 F5
  Southport PR8 ... 34 F4
Yorkshire Cl PR7 ... 60 F6
Yorkshire St E LA4 ... 216 F4
Yorkshire St W LA3 ... 216 E4
Yorkshire St
  Accrington BB5 ... 104 C4
  [16] Bacup OL13 ... 87 F3
  Blackpool FY1 ... 130 B3
  Burnley BB11 ... 128 B6
  Huncoat BB5 ... 125 E2
  [16] Nelson BB9 ... 148 E8
York St
  Accrington BB5 ... 104 B7
  Bacup OL13 ... 87 F5
  Barnoldswick BB18 ... 196 B2
  Blackburn BB2 ... 101 E3
  Blackpool FY1 ... 130 B3
  Bury BL9 ... 33 A2
  Chorley PR7 ... 43 D7
  Church BB5 ... 103 E6
  Clitheroe BB7 ... 189 F1
  Colne BB8 ... 171 F5
  Great Harwood BB6 ... 124 D5
  Nelson BB9 ... 148 F8
  Oswaldtwistle BB5 ... 103 C3
  Rawtenstall BB4 ... 86 A7
  Rishton BB1 ... 124 A1
York Terr
  Blackburn BB2 ... 80 D8
  [4] Southport PR9 ... 35 C8
York View BB3 ... 81 B6
Young Ave PR25 ... 77 C1
Young St
  Blackburn BB2 ... 101 B2
  Ramsbottom BL0 ... 50 B6

## Z

Zama St [9] BL0 ... 50 A4
Zebudah St BB2 ... 101 C2
Zetland St
  Preston PR1 ... 97 C7
  Southport PR9 ... 35 D7
Zion Rd BB1 ... 102 A8
Zion St
  Bacup OL13 ... 88 A3
  Colne BB8 ... 171 D4